Introduction

The *Time Out Eating & Drinking Guide* is the most authoritative and comprehensive guide to good restaurants and cafés in the capital. This is not just because we have a great passion for food, and for finding the best places to eat and drink in London. What you have in your hands is the only London guide for which anonymous critics pay for their meal and drinks just like a regular customer. We do not tell the restaurants we are coming, nor do we reveal who we are after the meal. Restaurants can exert no pressure on us as to the content of their reviews, and do not pay to be included in the guide. Our editors select all the establishments featured on merit and interest alone.

We want our readers to know just what the experience of eating at each restaurant might be like for them, and take pains to ensure that our reviewers remain totally objective on your behalf. Our insistence on undercover reporting means that our experience is much more likely to reflect your experience. This can't be said of well-known newspaper restaurant columnists: they often receive preferential treatment from restaurant kitchens, that have their photographs pinned up to ensure the critics do not go unrecognised (and those critics are inclined to feel insulted or ill-treated if they are not recognised, adding further bias to their reviews).

Many of our reviewers have extraordinary expertise in specialist areas. Several are trained cooks or former chefs, others are well-established food and/or wine authors, and some are simply dedicated enthusiasts who have lived abroad and learned much about a particular region's cuisine. Our contributors include chefs who have worked in the grand hotels of India and in kaiseki restaurants of Japan, expert bakers and baristas, award-winning wine writers, and food lovers hailing from Iran, Russia and Malaysia.

For the weekly *Time Out London* magazine alone, our reviewers visit around 200 new places every year. Their better discoveries are then included in this guide. Reviewers also check other new openings as well as revisiting places included in previous editions. We also take in feedback and recommendations from users of the Time Out website (www.timeout.com/restaurants). Then we eliminate the also-rans to create the list of London's best eateries that this guide represents. We hope you find it useful, and that it helps you get more enjoyment from eating out in the capital.

Contents

timeout.com/restaurants

Features

Restaurants

Cheap Eats

Maps & Indexes

Drinking

Published by

Time Out Guides Limited
Universal House
251 Tottenham Court Road
London W1T 7AB
Tel +44 (0)20 7813 3000
Fax +44 (0)20 7813 6001
email guides@timeout.com
www.timeout.com

Editorial

Editors Sarah Guy, Cath Phillips
Deputy Editor Phil Harriss
Group Food & Drink Editor Guy Dimond
Listings Editors Olivia Rye, William Crow

Editorial Director Sarah Guy
Management Accountant Margaret Wright

Design

Senior Designer Kei Ishimaru
Designer Darryl Bell
Guides Commercial Senior Designer Jason Tansley

Picture Desk

Picture Editor Jael Marschner
Deputy Picture Editor Ben Rowe

Advertising

Sales Director St John Betteridge
Senior Account Manager Michelle Daburn
Account Managers Deborah Maclaren, Helen Debenham @ The Media Sales House

Marketing

Head of Circulation Dan Collins

Production

Production Editor Dave Faulkner
Production Controller Katie Mulhern-Bhudia

Time Out Group

Chairman & Founder Tony Elliott
Chief Executive Officer Tim Arthur
Chief Financial Officer Matt White
MD Magazine & Guides Greg Miall
UK Chief Commercial Officer David Pepper
Group IT Director Simon Chappell
Group Marketing Director Carolyn Sims

Sections in this guide were written by

African Ronnie Haydon; **The Americas** Tania Ballantine, Richard Ehrlich, Neil McQuillian; **Brasseries** Guy Dimond, Sarah Guy, Ellen Hardy, Lisa Harris, Jenni Muir, Cath Phillips, Celia Plender; **British** Guy Dimond, Euan Ferguson, Sarah Guy, Nick Rider; **Caribbean** Yolanda Zappaterra; **Chinese** Tania Ballantine, Jacob Benoit, Lee Chuk-Kwan, Phil Harriss, Jeffrey Ng, Sally Peck, Celia Plender, Christine Yeo; **East European** Silvija Davidson, Phil Harriss, Janet Zmroczek; **Fish** Silvija Davidson, Emma Howarth, Ruth Jarvis, Cath Phillips, Caroline Stacey; **French** Guy Dimond, Euan Ferguson, Casilda Grigg, Roopa Gulati, Nick Rider; **Gastropubs** Guy Dimond, Alexi Duggins, Claire Fogg, Will Fulford Jones, Sarah Guy, Cath Phillips; **Global** Guy Dimond, Ellen Hardy, Sally Peck; **Greek** Emma Howarth; **Hotels & Haute Cuisine** Silvija Davidson, Euan Ferguson, Roopa Gulati, Ruth Jarvis, Jenni Muir, Jeffrey Ng; **Indian** Euan Ferguson, Eddy Frankel, Roopa Gulati, Phil Harriss, Shalinee Singh, Caroline Stacey; **Italian** Silvija Davidson, Casilda Grigg, Rachel Halliburton, Ruth Jarvis, Jenni Muir, Jeffrey Ng, Yolanda Zappaterra; **Japanese** Kei Kikuchi, Celia Plender; **Jewish** Judy Jackson; **Korean** Celia Plender; **Malaysian, Indonesian & Singaporean** Jeffrey Ng; **Middle Eastern** Zena Alkayat, Ellen Hardy, Matthew Lee, Ros Sales; **Modern European** Guy Dimond, Richard Ehrlich, Claire Fogg, Casilda Grigg, Sarah Guy, Ruth Jarvis, Rob Orchard, Cath Phillips, Celia Plender, Nick Rider, Caroline Stacey; **North African** Caroline Stacey; **Pan-Asian & Fusion** Susan Low, Shalinee Singh; **Spanish & Portuguese** Eleanor Aldridge, Casilda Grigg, Lisa Harris, Caroline Hire, Susan Low, Nick Rider; **Steak & Chicken** Eleanor Aldridge, Jessica Cargill Thompson, Richard Ehrlich, Sarah Guy; **Thai** Celia Plender; **Turkish** Matthew Lee; **Vegetarian** Jan Fuscoe; **Vietnamese** Lewis Essen; **Budget** Alexi Duggins, Eddy Frankel, Olivia Rye; **Cafés** Jessica Cargill Thompson, Silvija Davidson, Sarah Guy, Lisa Harris, Jenni Muir, Emily Kerrigan, Shalinee Singh; **Coffee Bars** Richard Ehrlich; **Fish & Chips** Jessica Cargill Thompson, Silvija Davidson, Dave Faulkner, Neil McQuillian, Jenni Muir, Olivia Rye; **Ice-cream Parlours** Jael Marschner, Jenni Muir, Olivia Rye; **Pizzerias** Eleanor Aldridge, Silvija Davidson, Emily Kerrigan, Jael Marschner, Olivia Rye; **Bars** Euan Ferguson, Richard Ehrlich; **Eating & Entertainment** Olivia Rye, Heather Welsh; **Wine Bars** Silvija Davidson, Ruth Jarvis.

Additional reviews by Zena Alkayat, Nick Amato, Tania Ballantine, Jessica Cargill Thompson, Simon Coppock, Silvija Davidson, Guy Dimond, Alexi Duggins, Richard Ehrlich, Anne Faber, Euan Ferguson, Claire Fogg, Eddy Frankel, Sarah Guy, Ellen Hardy, Lisa Harris, Phil Harriss, Ronnie Haydon, Caroline Hire, Emma Howarth, Ruth Jarvis, Emily Kerrigan, Kei Kikuchi, Matthew Lee, Susan Low, Jael Marschner, Jenni Muir, Neil McQuillian, Jeffrey Ng, Anna Norman, Rob Orchard, Sally Peck, Cath Phillips, Celia Plender, Natasha Polyviou, Olivia Rye, Ros Sales, Veronica Simpson, Tom Smith, Christine Yeo, Yolanda Zappaterra, Janet Zmroczek.

The Editors would like to thank Annie Bishop, Guy Dimond, Rebecca Knott, Tom Smith, John Watson, Heather Welsh.

Maps JS Graphics (john@jsgraphics.co.uk). Maps 1-18 and 24 are based on material supplied by Alan Collinson and Julie Snook through Copyright Exchange. London Underground map supplied by Transport for London.

Back cover photography by Rob Greig, Ming Tang-Evans and Ed Marshall.

Photography pages 10 (top), 11, 23 (left), 24, 28, 65, 103, 189, 241, 243, 244, 249, 277, 316, 322 (left), 323 Ed Marshall; 10 (bottom), 255, 305 (left) Michelle Grant; 20, 21, 61, 63, 69, 94, 129 (left), 142, 231, 250, 252, 254, 266, 271, 275, 276, 279, 280, 293, 310, 315 Jessica Long; 21 (right), 22, 137, 139, 160, 199, 201, 205, 245, 256, 263, 264, 269, 270325 Britta Jaschinski; 23, 33, 34, 35 (left), 40, 47, 68 (top and middle left), 76 (right), 75, 77, 81, 83, 90, 99 (left), 104, 112 (bottom), 122 (right), 128, 141 (top), 164, 184 (left), 186, 219, 220, 223, 226, 228, 232, 234, 237, 239, 258, 267284 (left), 285, 288, 298 (left), 290, 300, 302 (right), 304, 306, 307, 317 (right), 318, 328 Rob Greig; 27 Yeshen Venema; 31, 107, 127, 210, 308 Olivia Rutherford; 35 (right), 53, 76, 80, 115 (right), 116, 117, 145, 176 (right), 178, 192 (left), 197, 256 (left), 257, 278 Jael Marschner; 43, 51, 58, 68 (middle right and bottom), 95 (middle), 89, 105, 112, 113, 119 (left), 123, 161 (middle), 166, 173, 181, 183, 194, 208, 209, 212, 230, 234 (middle), 259 (top), 292, 294 Ming Tang-Evans; 46, 129, 146, 147, 268, 322 (right) Jamie Lau; 48, 60 Yusuf Ozkizil; 55 Ben Carpenter; 64, 72, 73, 149 (middle), 152, 163, 181 (right), 182, 192, 233, 305 (right), 310 (right), 314 (top) Jonathan Perugia; 71, 102, 284, 286, 289, 291, 292 (left), 297 (middle) Tricia de Courcy Ling; 79 Cath Lowe; 82, 141 (bottom), 212 (left), 259 (top right) Jitka Hynkova; 98, 109, 148 (right), 151, 222, 225, 227 Helen Cathcart; 99, 108, 110, 132, 184, 185, 307 (left) Alys Tomlinson; 112 (top middle), 114, 213 Martin Daly; 119, 120, 124, 126, 204, 259 (bottom) Michael Franke; 121 Nerida Howard; 122 (left), 322 (right) Scott Wishart; 131, 148 (left), 149 Paul Winch-Furness; 158 Stephen Barber; 161 (left), 167 Heloise Bergman; page 171, 297 Louise Haywood-Schieffer; 176 (left), 177 David Axelbank; 211 Celia Topping; 235 Gareth Gardner; 266 Kate Swanson, 290 (bottom) Simon Leigh; 299 Zed Jameson; 317, 321 Tom Baker.

The following images were provided by the featured establishment: pages 25, 29, 35 (middle), 36, 39, 45, 48 (right), 52, 56, 61 (left), 62, 64 (middle), 66, 75 (bottom), 81 (left), 84, 85, 86, 87, 93, 95, 96, 100, 101, 106, 111, 115, 155, 161 (right), 168, 170, 172, 173 (middle), 174, 175, 179, 176 (middle), 190, 192, 198, 200, 202, 203, 214, 217, 218, 221, 242, 247, 271 (left), 272, 273, 283, 298, 301, 302, 303311, 312, 313, 314 (bottom).

Printed by Wyndeham Group
Time Out Group uses paper products that are environmentally friendly, from well-managed forests and mills that used certified (PEFC) Chain of Custody pulp in their production.

ISBN 978-1-90504-279-1

Distribution by Comag Specialists (01895 433 800). For further distribution details, see timeout.com.

{ DAAWAT }

An indian culinary feast

Try traditional Indian foods prepared and cooked by our head chef and his team who are all highly experienced in Indian cuisine.

All of our dishes are freshly prepared with natural ingredients, ranging from street food, to the more extravagant and unusual, we guarantee this will be a food experience not to be missed!

EXPERIENCE OUR THALI MENU FROM £7.95

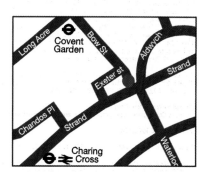

Daawat 2 Burleigh Street, London WC2R 0JJ
t: 020 7379 4737 | **e:** restaurants@strandpalacehotel.co.uk

www.strandpalacehotel.co.uk

About the guide

LISTED BY AREA
The restaurants in this guide are listed by cuisine type: British, Chinese, Indian, Middle Eastern, Modern European etc. Then, within each chapter, they are listed by geographical area: ten main areas (in this example, East), then by neighbourhood (Shoreditch). If you are not sure where to look for a restaurant, there are two indexes at the back of the guide to help: an A-Z Index (starting on p370) listing restaurants by name, and an Area Index (starting on p354), where you can see all the places we list in a specific neighbourhood.

STARS
A red star ★ means that a venue is, of its type, very good indeed. A green star ★ identifies budget-conscious eateries – expect to pay up to £25 per head for a three-course meal, or its equivalent (not including drinks and service).

NEW
The NEW symbol means new to this edition of the *Eating & Drinking Guide*. In most cases, these are brand-new venues.

TIME OUT HOT 50
The HOT 50 symbol means the venue is among what we consider to be London's top 50 iconic eating and drinking experiences. For details of the complete 50, *see p8*.

OPENING HOURS
Times given are for last orders rather than closing times (except in cafés and bars).

PRICES
We have listed the cheapest and most expensive main courses available in each restaurant. In the case of many oriental restaurants, prices may seem lower – but remember that you often need to order several such dishes to have a full meal.

COVER CHARGE
An old-fashioned fixed charge may be imposed by the restaurateur to cover the cost of rolls and butter, crudités, cleaning table linen and similar extras.

MAP REFERENCE
All restaurants that appear on our street maps (starting on p330) are given a reference to the map and grid square where they can be found.

SERVICES
These are listed below the review.

Babies and children We've tried to reflect the degree of welcome extended to babies and children in restaurants. If you find no mention of either, take it that the restaurant is unsuitable.

Disabled: toilet means the restaurant has a specially adapted toilet, which implies that customers with walking disabilities or wheelchairs can get into the restaurant. However, we recommend phoning to double-check.

Vegetarian menu Most restaurants claim to have a vegetarian dish on the menu. We've highlighted those that have made a more concerted effort to attract and cater for vegetarian (and vegan) diners.

East
Shoreditch

★ ★ Popup HOT 50
Near Old Street, EC1V 2XY (9876 4321). Old Street tube/rail. **Lunch served** 8am-noon, **dinner served** 7pm-midnight daily. **Main courses** £8-£15.50. **Set dinner** £12 2 courses, £18 3 courses. **Cover** £1. **Credit** AmEx, MC, V.
The team behind Pimped Shed and the Preener have another mover and shaker on their hands. The Popup, aka the 'Where Were You?', vanished in a haze of builder's rubble the night before you heard of it. The press launch – held amid a glittering array of steel joists and neo-Dagenham artworks – gave co-owner Dudley Foam the chance to explain to the assembled crowd what they had missed at the pre-pop-up pop-up (small plates of Luxembourg-Paraguayan comfort food, apparently). But what of the menu here? On-trend gourmet turkey twizzlers are blended with a playful side dish of heritage crabsticks by a crew of black-clad mixologists, glistening and hirsute behind their Black & Decker Workmates. Dessert – salted wine gum and Mint Imperial syllabub – comes warm from the centrifuge. The Popup is currently firming up its branding: expect pop-up waiting staff (holograms from another dimension), greeters (pre-pop-up pop-ups only) and out-there drinks lists (sediment-swirling natural wines with a soupçon of mortar dust). A post-pop-up pop-up, sited on the edgier outskirts of Hounslow, is already at pre-development stage.
Available for hire. Bookings not accepted. Tables outdoors (9, pavement). Takeaway service. Vegetarian menu. **Map 6 Q4.**

Anonymous, unbiased reviews

The reviews in the *Eating & Drinking Guide* are based on the experiences of Time Out restaurant reviewers. Venues are always visited anonymously, and Time Out pays the bill. No payment or PR invitation of any kind has secured or influenced a review. The editors select which places are listed in this guide, and are not influenced in any way by the wishes of the restaurants themselves. Restaurants cannot volunteer or pay to be listed; we list only those we consider to be worthy of inclusion. Advertising and sponsorship has no effect whatsoever on the editorial content of the *Eating & Drinking Guide*. An advertiser may receive a bad review, or no review at all.

Brilliant Restaurant

North Indian Cuisine with a Kenyan slant

The Brilliant family looks forward to welcoming you...

Brilliant Restaurant was voted as one of Gordon Ramsay's Best Indian Restaurants

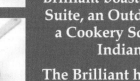

The Brilliant Restaurant and Banqueting Suite devotes itself to serving freshly prepared authentic food using only the finest and locally sourced ingredients.

Brilliant boasts an in-house Banqueting Suite, an Outdoor Catering Service and a Cookery School offering specialist Indian cookery courses.

The Brilliant has won many awards and accolades, including The British Curry Award as well as winning the title of Ramsay's Best Restaurant on the Channel 4 Series.

Brilliant success is due to creating tastes of the palette which have delighted generations from all over the world. We look forward to welcoming and delighting you too.

Brilliant Cookery Courses
By Brilliant Restaurant

Accredited by **UNIVERSITY OF WEST LONDON**
The Asian and Oriental Hospitality Academy

You can now learn to cook 'Brilliant' style with one of our specialist cookery courses suitable for everyone, especially curry lovers.

Become a 'Brilliant' chef within hours.

Courses are enjoyable and constructive, last 3 hours and candidates take away all the food they cook with them to enjoy at home.

Visit www.brilliantrestaurant.com for menus and calendar.

Time Out's Hot 50

We have picked 50 places, entirely subjectively, that we believe offer some of London's most interesting eating experiences. We're not saying these venues have the best food and drink in the capital, but we believe each adds something life-enhancing to our city. Here they are, in alphabetical order. Each review is marked with a HOT 50 symbol in the relevant chapter of the guide.

Amaya
Indian p131.
Sparkling and sophisticated modern Indian grill.

Ariana II
Global p114.
A multi-faceted Afghan menu, low prices, and a warm welcome await at this Kilburn diner.

Baltic
East European p79.
Classic East European dishes are given a contemporary spin at this still-glamorous restaurant and jazz bar.

Barrafina
Spanish p222.
A pint-sized space offering stylish, authentic tapas and a fine selection of sherries and Spanish wines.

Barshu
Chinese p68.
The fiery flavours of Sichuanese cooking, served in style.

Bentley's Oyster Bar & Grill
Fish p82.
Take a seat at the art nouveau bar for freshly shucked oysters and London's best fish pie.

Bistrotheque
French p94.
Bistro food and a modish bar make for an original combination at this east London hotspot.

Le Café Anglais
Modern European p198.
Rowley Leigh's attractive Bayswater brasserie, with a crowd-pleasing menu.

Cah Chi
Korean p178.
One of the best Korean restaurants in the UK, in SW20.

Caravan King's Cross
Brasseries p38.
A second branch of the restaurant, bar and coffee roastery, in a handsome new development behind King's Cross.

Chin Chin Laboratorists
Ice-cream Parlours p300.
Experimental and talented ice-creamists, in Camden Market.

Clarke's
Modern European p199.
Established in 1984, Sally Clarke's restaurant was a pioneer of Modern European cooking and continues to thrive (and expand).

Czechoslovak Restaurant
East European p80.
The city's only Czech restaurant and bar is a piece of living history.

Eagle
Gastropubs p100.
Still going strong, the original gastropub: staying true to its drinking roots while serving great food.

Franco Manca
Pizza & Pasta p305.
One of the first eateries to open in Brixton Market, serving probably the best pizzas in London.

La Fromagerie
Cafés p272.
Dine among the deli ingredients at this charming fine food store.

Gökyüzü
Turkish p253.
No fuss, no frills – just excellent Turkish food in London's main Turkish neighbourhood.

Gilbert Scott
British p50.
Exuberant Victorian architecture, matched with a best-of-British menu from Marcus Wareing.

Grill at the Dorchester
British p51.
Peerless British food, bonkers Scottish decor, in one of London's grandest hotels.

Hawksmoor
Steakhouses p235.
Will Beckett and Huw Gott's very British steakhouse and cocktail bar – now with several branches.

Hix
British p51.
Mark Hix's fun British restaurant with characterful downstairs bar.

J Sheekey
Fish p82.
A West End institution that oozes old fashioned glamour.

Koya
Japanese p166.
This udon specialist demonstrates the beauty of keeping it simple, in both food and decor.

Ledbury
Hotels & Haute Cuisine p127.
Thrill to the cooking of Aussie chef Brett Graham in Notting Hill.

Mandalay
Global p112.
Sample first-rate Burmese fare at this otherwise basic caff.

Meat Liquor
The Americas p24.
A cult no-bookings joint that's worth the queue for the Deep South cooking and the 'dead hippie' burger.

Modern Pantry
Pan-Asian & Fusion p214.
Some of the best fusion food in town, served in bright, white Clerkenwell premises.

Momo
North African p212.
A great Maghrebi soundtrack, cool Marrakech decor and some of the best Moroccan food in London.

Moro
Spanish p220.
Enduringly popular Exmouth Market restaurant with a menu that stretches from Spain right along the Mediterranean.

NOPI
Pan-Asian & Fusion p215.
Yotam Ottolenghi's newer and smarter big brother of the Ottolenghi cafés.

Petersham Nurseries Café
Modern European p211.
Inventive cooking in delightful bucolic surroundings.

Poppies
Fish & Chips p296.
Retro Spitalfields chippie with top-notch frying and more than a hint of *Happy Days* about the decor.

Quality Chop House
Wine Bars p322.
The place has had a chequered history, but these handsome premises now hold a laudable wine bar.

Rasa W1
Indian p131.
A rare opportunity to sample the authentic and surprisingly fiery fish cookery of Kerala.

River Café
Italian p157.
The wood-fired oven takes centre stage in this world-famous, yet surprisingly relaxed, Hammersmith classic.

Roka
Japanese p163.
Spectacularly designed restaurant based around a central grill, and great for Fitzrovia people-watching.

St John
British p49.
Fergus Henderson's uncompromising approach to food, and especially meat, has inspired a new generation of chefs both here and abroad.

Sakonis
Indian p145.
The original Indian vegetarian chat (snack) house, serving South Indian and Gujarati dishes.

Singapore Garden
Malaysian, Indonesian & Singaporean p183.
A beacon of excellent Straits cooking for many years.

Song Que
Vietnamese p262.
Authentic Vietnamese dishes at affordable prices.

Spuntino
The Americas p26.
A slice of New York's Lower East Side in the heart of Soho.

Sweetings
Fish p81.
Old-world bonhomie and classic British fish dishes since 1889.

10 Greek Street
Modern European p197.
A small, unshowy Soho bistro that's made a name for itself with a menu that's always interesting but never gimmicky.

Terroirs
Wine Bars p325.
Natural wines and small plates pioneer that's inspired a vat of imitators.

Towpath
Cafés p282.
Quirky canalside café in N1.

Les Trois Garçons
French p95.
Home to hippo heads, stuffed bulldogs and vintage handbags, as well as terrific French food.

Viajante
Hotels & Haute Cuisine p128.
Nuno Mendes' Bethnal Green outpost of cutting-edge cuisine.

Vinoteca
Wine Bars p325.
A model wine bar with well-priced, well-rendered cooking, and all wines to take home at retail price.

Wolseley
Brasseries p38.
A decade on, and this former car showroom still feels like one of London's most exciting destinations, day or night.

Yauatcha
Chinese p69.
Still a hot destination for first-rate dim sum, served all day.

Delicious freshly prepared cuisines from around the world.

A hub for food lovers at The Great Eastern Market, Westfield Stratford City

One of the unique highlights of Westfield Stratford City is the gastronomic hub Great Eastern Market, where hungry shoppers can enjoy a variety of flavours from around the world. From Asian to Mediterranean to Russian, right down to traditional British fare, there's something to suit everyone's tastes.

Located at the entrance to the 32,000 sq ft Waitrose food store, the area takes inspiration from some of the world's famous international food markets – as well as paying homage to the original Great Eastern Market, which stood in Stratford a century ago.

The Market is made up of over 14 mostly independent retailers, each of whom are connoisseurs of their particular cuisine, and serving food made from high-quality produce and freshly prepared on site.

Why not sate your appetite with a bowl of Pasta Remoli's handmade pasta, topped with one of their many delicious Italian ragu sauces? Or, if you have a sweet tooth, you might want to try one of the delicious French macaroons from boutique patisserie l'Orchidee.

And coffee lovers looking for freshly roasted and unusual blends, served with a slice of mouth-watering cake, are sure to find both at the specialist Grind Coffee Bar.

For something a little stronger, Tap East boasts a carefully curated selection of more than 150 beers, many of which are brewed on site while customers watch from the bar area.

The Great Eastern Market is located in Europe's largest urban shopping centre. Westfield Stratford City offers an impressive wealth of outlets and leisure facilities – 250 shops, 70 bars and restaurants, a 17-screen Vue Cinema, an All Star Lanes bowling alley and the UK's largest casino.

Westfield STRATFORD CITY

For further information visit **uk.westfield.com/stratfordcity**

Currently trending

Guy Dimond, Time Out London*'s Food & Drink Editor, works out what's here to stay.*

'What are the latest restaurant trends?' is a question we're asked all the time. Because, after all, we should know. Time Out's reviewers not only live in one of the most vibrant culinary cities in the world, we also eat out a lot, in the very newest and best places: more than a thousand times a year, just in the research involved in updating this guide. While it's tempting to give a glib answer – 'next year we'll all be eating Korean-Uzbek fusion food,' for example – predicting the future has always been a mug's game. However, we don't mind making a few guesses, extrapolating from the strongest currents (out of many) of the past two years. Here are the trends we think are likely to continue for some time to come.

Pop-ups

The very term became meaningless the moment it was coined, as it was immediately seized on by marketeers as a 'trendy' way to run a business. Of course, a pop-up can mean anything that isn't going to last forever. But which restaurant does? Early in 2013, Jamie Oliver was widely derided for branding Jamie Oliver's Diner near Piccadilly Circus a 'pop-up', despite the fact it has a three-year lease – longer than the life cycle of many 'permanent' restaurants. In the sense most commonly used, a restaurant pop-up exists for a much shorter time: days or weeks, not usually months. Often, they're diminutive operations, catering for small numbers of diners during their limited run.

So what are pop-ups for? Many are run by would-be restaurateurs who don't have the capital to open a full-blown restaurant, and are a way to test-drive a dining concept and generate pre-opening interest. Frequently, such pop-ups are no cheaper than a 'normal' restaurant, and can be considerably less well organised. Long waits for courses, and dishes that can be as much hit as miss, are all part of the experience. Yet whenever a pop-up, er, pops up, you can be sure that restaurant novelty-chasers and the social-media savvy will be there, blogging and tweeting – whether or not it's actually worth all the attention. Some pop-ups simply disappear, others do go on to be successful small restaurants in proper premises.

Over the past couple of years, big-name chefs and capital-rich restaurant groups have noticed the cachet attached to running a pop-up. This has resulted in a spate of me-too organisations trying to look like they're part of the gang. Partly for this reason, pop-ups seem likely to be with us for some time to come. And in May 2013, Communities Secretary Eric

Pickles announced the relaxation of planning regulations, making it easier to agree change of use for premises, to encourage urban and high-street regeneration. More pop-ups seem likely.

Underground restaurants

Also sometimes known as dining clubs, these are essentially dinner parties where guests pay for their meals. Many such venues start out in very ad hoc ways – a friend of a friend is cooking Latvian food, say, and you're invited in exchange for a contribution towards the meal. More established and commercial supper clubs cook regularly, have unregulated premises (and therefore operate illegally as restaurants, hence the term 'underground'), and so of necessity promote themselves via Facebook or other social media. A few supper clubs become significant earners for the people who run them – partly because they keep costs low by being untroubled by declaration of earnings to HM Revenue & Customs, do not have to pass food hygiene and safety inspections, and are effectively shebeens if they also sell alcohol. Some supper clubs can also be immense fun, and are a very different and more sociable form of eating out than going to a restaurant. But – caveat emptor – do not expect restaurant standards of cooking or service, or lower prices commensurate with the lack of professionalism of the event. There is, of course, some blurring of the boundaries between legal pop-ups and (illegal) underground restaurants.

Dude food

A refreshing alternative to fine dining: no tablecloths, no airs and graces, and sometimes no cutlery – all that's missing is the Confederate flag and waitresses in Daisy Duke shorts. On the menu you might expect to find the constituents of US food: hot dogs, barbecued meats, deep-fried everything, big portions and little regard for fat content or your five-a-day. It's tasty, it's from the southern USA, and it seems it's here to stay.

Burger joints

You might be forgiven for thinking this is part of the 'dude food' trend, something that will blow over in a year or two. We don't think so. Gourmet burger joints have been blossoming across London for a decade (Gourmet Burger Kitchen, Byron and many others), unabated by setbacks such as early 2013's horsemeat scandal. Pop-ups in pubs, dedicated 'Honest' and 'Dirty' burger joints, even international chains from the US have been muscling in on the scene. Are we saturated yet? With salt, fat and calories, maybe – but it seems our appetite for the burger is still not sated.

No-bookings restaurants

We've always had them – from McDonald's to Wagamama, there will always be a place for spontaneity. But in recent years, no-booking restaurants have really upped their game, away from fast-food joints or casual dining. In a recent Tuesday night foray into Soho, at 7pm we were told there was a two-hour wait for a table at 10 Greek Street, and a two-and-a-half-hour wait for a table at Polpo (neither takes reservations for dinner). No bookings may be great as a business model for restaurants, which will rarely or never have an empty seat – but is this progress, from the diner's point of view? We're not so sure.

Craft beers

'Craft beer' is used to describe good-quality beers from small artisanal makers, which don't fit into the usual 'real ale' category. Real ales are English-style beers that are unpasteurised, cask-conditioned and 'live', usually with fuller and more complex flavours than their more insipid nitrokeg-stored and -dispensed cousins. In contrast, craft beers often use the bolder flavours of North American hops, and may have been pasteurised, bottled or even sold in pressurised kegs filled with inert nitrogen gas (a method of storing and dispensing beer that, traditionally, was anathema to real ale enthusiasts). Craft beers tend to be very well made, but bend the old rules that define a 'real ale'. They've been shaking up the London pub scene to such an extent that even huge pub companies such as Young's are now stocking craft beers (in Young's case, in collaboration with the Meantime Brewery). We'll raise a glass to this handsome marriage.

Chicken

The stats show there's money to be made, by the lucky, in the catering profession; further research shows that by keeping a formula ultra-simple, by producing something that almost everyone likes (or at least doesn't dislike), is affordable and is easy to replicate – you just might be on to a winner. In the past few years, business wizards have seized on soup bars, frozen yoghurt outlets and, most recently, chicken restaurants as being the best way to make an easy killing. Only time will tell what's here to stay and what's just another flash in the pan.

Where to...

Got the hunger, the people, the occasion, but not the venue? These suggestions will help you find the perfect spot to eat, drink and be merry.

Kipferl

GO FOR BREAKFAST
Breakfast is offered every day unless stated otherwise. *See also* **Brasseries**, **Cafés** and **Budget**.

Abbeville Kitchen (Sat, Sun) Modern European p203
Adam's Café (Mon-Sat) North African p212
Albion British p57
Berners Tavern Modern European p194
Bistrot Bruno Loubet French p86
Boulestin French p90
Brasserie Zédel (Café) French p91

Butcher & Grill Steak & Chicken p236
Café Chula The Americas p34
Carluccio's Caffè Italian p151
Canteen British p59
Cecconi's Italian p153
Cinnamon Club (Mon-Fri) Indian p136
Comptoir Libanais Middle Eastern p189
Le Coq d'Argent (Mon-Fri) French p85
Dean Street Townhouse British p51
Dishoom Indian p129
Fifth Floor (Café, Mon-Sat) Modern European p195
Goring Hotel British p53
Grill at the Dorchester British p51
Hampshire Hog Gastropubs p101
Hawksmoor (Mon-Fri) Steak & Chicken p235
Honey & Co Middle Eastern p184
Indian YMCA Indian p130
Kipferl Global (Tue-Sun) p114
Kopapa (Mon-Fri) Pan-Asian & Fusion p214
Lutyens (Mon-Fri) French p86
Mamuska! East European p79
Modern Pantry (Mon-Fri) Pan-Asian & Fusion p214
New Asian Tandoori Centre (Roxy) Indian p144
NOPI (Mon-Fri) Pan-Asian & Fusion p215
Orange Public House & Hotel Gastropubs p100
Paramount (Mon-Fri) Modern European p192
Plum & Spilt Milk British p50
The Providores & Tapa Room Pan-Asian & Fusion p215
Roast (Mon-Sat) British p57
Rochelle Canteen (Mon-Fri) British p58
St John Bread & Wine British p59
Sakonis (Sat, Sun) Indian p145

Oxo Tower Restaurant, Bar & Brasserie

San Carlo Cicchetti Italian p154
Simpson's-in-the-Strand (Mon-Fri) British p53
Smiths of Smithfield Modern European p193
Sotheby's Café (Mon-Fri) Modern European p195
Whyte & Brown Steak & Chicken p237
York & Albany Modern European p210

EAT/DRINK BY THE WATERSIDE
See also the Southbank Centre branches of **Giraffe** and **Wagamama**.

Blue Elephant Thai p245
Blueprint Café Modern European p207
Dock Kitchen Modern European p200
Lido Café Cafés p278
Camino (Docklands branch) Spanish p221
Gaucho (Tower Bridge and Richmond branches) The Americas p29
Gun Gastropubs p106
Narrow Gastropubs p106
Pavilion Café Cafés p282
Le Pont de la Tour Modern European p207
Royal China (Docklands branch) Chinese p72
Skylon Modern European p204
Stein's Global p114
Towpath Cafés p282
Waterhouse Brasseries p44

ENJOY THE VIEW
Barbecoa The Americas p23
Blueprint Café Modern European p207
Le Coq d'Argent French p85
Duck & Waffle Brasseries p36
Galvin at Windows Hotels & Haute Cuisine p123
Hutong Chinese p73

Pavilion Café

Tramshed

WHERE TO...

Oxo Tower Restaurant, Bar & Brasserie
Modern European p204
Min Jiang Chinese p73
Nipa Thai p244
Oblix The Americas p27
Paramount Modern European p192
Plateau Modern European p207
Roast British p57
Rooftop Café Brasseries p42
Skylon Modern European p204
Smiths of Smithfield (Top Floor)
Modern European p193
Sushisamba The Americas p29

SHARE DISHES
See also **Indian**, **Middle Eastern** and **Spanish & Portuguese**.

Begging Bowl Thai p247
Bocca di Lupo Italian p154
Caravan King's Cross Brasseries p38
Dinings Japanese p164
E&O Pan-Asian & Fusion p217
Kopapa Pan-Asian & Fusion p214
Lalibela African p22
Lardo Italian p159
NOPI Pan-Asian & Fusion p215
Norfolk Arms Gastropubs p99
Ottolenghi Brasseries p47
Terroirs Wine Bars p325
Wahaca The Americas p30

TAKE AFTERNOON TEA
See also **Cafés** and **Brasseries**.

Bar Boulud French p88
Brasserie Zédel French p91
Dean Street Townhouse British p51
Les Deux Salons French p87
Kipferl Global p114
Modern Pantry Pan-Asian & Fusion p214
Momo North African p212
National Dining Rooms (Bakery)
British p53
Paramount Modern European p192
Restaurant at St Paul's British p49
Sotheby's Café Modern European p195

TAKE THE KIDS
See also **Cafés** and **Ice-cream Parlours**.

Avalon Gastropubs p104
Bill's Brasseries p37
Bistro Union Brasseries p41
Blue Elephant Thai p245
Breakfast Club Brasseries p44
Byron Steak & Chicken p240
Carluccio's Caffè Italian p151
Chapters All Day Dining Brasseries p42
Depot Brasseries p40
Duke of Cambridge Gastropubs p108
E&O Pan-Asian & Fusion p217
La Famiglia Italian p157
Gallery Mess Brasseries p41
Georgina's Brasseries p40
Giraffe Brasseries p46
Gourmet Burger Kitchen
Steak & Chicken p240
Greenberry Café Brasseries p47
Imli Street Indian p135
Jamie's Italian Italian p160
Jamie Oliver's Diner The Americas p25
Junction Tavern Gastropubs p110
Kentish Canteen Brasseries p47
Made in Camden Brasseries p47
Masala Zone Indian p129
Nando's Steak & Chicken p242
Perkin Reveller Brasseries p36
Saravana Bhavan Indian p143
Stein's Global p114
Tramshed Steak & Chicken p239
Wagamama Pan-Asian & Fusion p216

PEOPLE-WATCH
Albion British p57
Balthazar Brasseries p37
Bar Boulud French p88
Berners Tavern Modern European p194
Brasserie Zédel French p91
Le Café Anglais Modern European p198
Le Caprice Modern European p196
Colbert Brasseries p35
Dean Street Townhouse British p51
Delaunay Brasseries p37
Dock Kitchen Modern European p200

Henry Root Modern European p202
Hix British p51
The Ivy Modern European p194
Lemonia Greek p118
Meat Liquor The Americas p24
Quo Vadis British p52
Riding House Café Brasseries p37
Scott's Fish p82
Sketch: Lecture Room & Library
Hotels & Haute Cuisine p125
Wolseley Brasseries p38
Tramshed Steak & Chicken p239
Yauatcha Chinese p69
Zuma Japanese p164

TRY UNUSUAL DISHES
Adulis African p21
Ariana II Global p114
Asadal Korean p177
Baozi Inn Chinese p70
Barshu Chinese p68
Cah Chi Korean p178
Caravan King's Cross Brasseries p38
Champor-Champor Pan-Asian & Fusion p218
Clove Club British p57
Dabbous Hotels & Haute Cuisine p120
Dinner by Heston Blumenthal
Hotels & Haute Cuisine p121
Dock Seafood Restaurant Fish p83
Duck & Waffle Brasseries p36
Esarn Kheaw Thai p245
Faanoos II Middle Eastern p187
Hélène Darroze at the Connaught
Hotels & Haute Cuisine p124
Hereford Road British p55
Hibiscus Hotels & Haute Cuisine p125
Hunan Chinese p64
KaoSarn Thai p247
Kopapa Pan-Asian & Fusion p214
Lima London The Americas p30
Lola Rojo Spanish p226
Mandalay Global p112
Masa Global p114
Modern Pantry Pan-Asian & Fusion p214
The Providores & Tapa Room
Pan-Asian & Fusion p215
Sake No Hana Japanese p165

Asadal

naamyaa

BANGKOK CAFE

created by the Busaba Eathai Group

Serving an eclectic menu of dishes from East and West

Monday - Friday
12pm - 11pm

Saturday
Brunch: 9am-5pm
Dinner: 5pm-11.30pm

Sunday
Brunch: 10am - 5pm
Dinner: 5pm-10.30pm

407 St. John Street
Isilington
EC1V 4AB
London

For reservations
020 3122 0988

View our menu at
www.naamyaa.com

Fields Bar & Kitchen

Yalla Yalla

Eyre Brothers

fat free frozen yogurt

udderly scrumptious
fat free frozen yogurt

Harrods
4th Floor Way-In
Harrods Ltd
Knightsbridge
London SW3 1QE
tel: +44 207 730 1234

Finchley Road
O2 Shopping Centre
Ground Floor
255 Finchley Road
London NW3 6LU
tel: +44 207 433 8168

Canary Wharf
Canary Wharf shopping centre
Canada Square
(near Waitrose Food & Home)
London E14 5LQ
tel: +44 207 516 0171

Stratford
Westfield Stratford
Centre Mall
(next to Superdry)
London E20 1EJ
tel: +44 2085 348 667

Stansted
Stansted Airport
Airside
(flights out, after
security control)
tel: +44 1279 681 900

Milton Keynes
MK1 shopping centre
Silbury Arcade
(outside Boots)
Milton Keynes MK9 3ES
tel: +44 1908 691 591

Bromley
The Glades Shopping Centre
Bromley
Kent BR1 1DD
tel: +44 208 313 1340

Bluewater
Bluewater Centre
Thames Walk Mall
Greenhithe
Kent DA9 9SL
tel: +44 132 238 4909

Derby
Westfield shopping centre
(ground floor near WHSmith)
Derby DE1 2PQ
tel: +44 133 220 8267

Cardiff
St. David's shopping centre
Lower Grand Arcade
St. David's Dewi Sant
CF10 2ER
tel: +44 2920 344 616

Leeds
White Rose shopping centre
Ground Floor Central Arcade
Dewsbury Road
Leeds LS11 8LU

visit us at **www.yoomoo.com** find us on facebook.com/yoomooyogurt & @yoomoo on twitter

Morito

WHERE TO...

Gökyüzü

Berners Tavern

Restaurants

African

This section should perhaps be re-titled 'The Former Abyssinia', since the only restaurants we can currently recommend wholeheartedly are from that northern section of the Horn of Africa, with a bit of Hammersmith Somalia added on for good measure. It's interesting that London is home to such a disproportionately large number of good Ethiopian and Eritrean restaurants, when the city has so many sizeable African communities hailing from Sudan, Kenya, Uganda and Ghana, to name but four, but whose members have remained relatively resistant to the restaurant business. Sure, there are a few suya (meat kebab) spots and Nigerian kitchens in Peckham and Lewisham, and the successful Spinach & Agushi (spinachandagushi.co.uk), with its stalls in Portobello Road, Exmouth and Broadway markets, has made Ghanaian street food a force to reckon with, but it's Abyssinian cuisine you'll be dining on if you want a full restaurant experience.

Perhaps the reason for the cuisine's popularity is the sense of occasion – food as friendship – that it embraces. Eating Ethiopian or Eritrean meals raises communal dining to exotic levels. Diners sit around a grand platter lined with injera (pancake-like bread made from teff flour). No knives or forks are employed; you tear off little bits of bread to scoop up the hearty stews and bakes. You're also encouraged to feed each other in order to cement love and commitment.

Then there is the coffee ceremony. Ethiopia is the birthplace of coffee, and much is made of the serving of the freshly roasted and ground beans, steeped with spices, wreathed in incense fumes and served with a bowl of warm popcorn. Our token Somali choice, **The Village**, favours tea over coffee, a lovely spicy/sweet beverage to accompany the equally sweet puddings, which its Ethiopian neighbours don't much bother with. For restaurants specialising in the cuisines of North Africa, *see p212*.

West
Hammersmith

★ The Village
95 Fulham Palace Road, W6 8JA (8741 7453, www.somalirestaurant.co.uk). Hammersmith tube. **Meals served** 11.30am-11.30pm daily. **Main courses** £6-£12. **Unlicensed** no alcohol allowed. **Credit** MC, V. Somali
There's something of the community centre about this basement restaurant – it's a little shabby, with workaday furniture, sauces served in polystyrene cups and an easy-clean tiled floor – but service is sweet and the food gratifyingly handmade and tasty. And it certainly seems to be a meeting and eating place for the Somali community. Much of the menu reflects Somalia's inclusion in Italian East Africa until 1960, so pasta dishes sit alongside soft Somali bread, stews and spices. In fact, there's not much to scare the timid newcomer to African food. Dish names may seem difficult, but translate thus: spiced fried chicken with salad leaves and chilli dressing; goat's cheese salad and sweet chilli; chicken and falafel. They're as delicious as they sound. Prawns on a bed of salad were spicy and juicy, the chicken was tender and the Somali pancake (anjeero – similar to Ethiopian injera) wrapped around an orange-sauced vegetable medley was comfortingly doughy. We couldn't resist the maize meal mash (similar to white polenta but much more flavourful) served with a sort of vegetable broth. Date cake with ice-cream and a caramel-flavoured sauce made a satisfyingly sweet conclusion. The Village is alcohol-free, but there are good fruit smoothies and the Somali spiced coffee and tea are wonderful.
Available for hire. Babies and children admitted. Takeaway service. **Map 20 C5**.

Westbourne Park

★ Mosob
339 Harrow Road, W9 3RB (7266 2012, www.mosob.co.uk). Westbourne Park tube. **Dinner served** 6-11.30pm Mon-Fri. **Meals served** 3pm-midnight Sat; 3-11.30pm Sun. **Main courses** £8.30-£13.95. **Set meal** £12.95-£19.95 per person (minimum 2). **Credit** MC, V. Eritrean
A mosob is a handwoven table around which people gather to eat. This is one of the many facts about Eritrean cuisine we learned at this welcoming restaurant. In fact, instruction on Eritrean life and culture goes well beyond food, because the people who run Mosob are on a mission to promote their homeland. A very good job they do too: in the gaps between courses, our beaming waiter produced a well-thumbed book about the buildings of Asmara, and we also learned about the Italian occupation – at which point the pudding list (tartufo classico, tiramisu) became clear. But the main event is the cooking, especially the gloriously diverse vegetarian choices; these include beautifully spiced lentils (timtimo), pounded and stewed chickpeas (shiro) and spinach (hamli), and often involve cottage cheese. Meat eaters also fare well, thanks to the likes of the Mosob special (marinated lamb chops with spinach and lentils) and the muscular

combination of hamli mis siga (tender stewed beef with spinach and garlic). Everything is served on spongy, yeasty injera, which is also used to scoop up the food. After such a feast, plus a few Serengeti lagers and the warm popcorn served as part of the final coffee ceremony, we didn't need feeding again for 24 hours.

Babies and children welcome: high chairs. Booking advisable Fri, Sat. Separate room for parties, seats 20. Takeaway service. Vegan dishes. Vegetarian menu. **Map 1 A4.**

South

Brixton

★ Asmara

386 Coldharbour Lane, SW9 8LF (7737 4144). Brixton tube/rail. **Dinner served** 5.30pm-midnight daily. **Main courses** £7.20-£9.80. **Set meal** £30 (2 people) vegetarian, £32 (2 people) meat. **Credit** MC, V. Eritrean

In common with London's other Eritrean restaurants, this low-key Brixton café named after the capital of Eritrea and decorated with a few East African touches, trades on its novelty value. Staff are efficient and well-versed in the 'have you eaten Eritrean food before?' schtick. The chicken dishes are particularly popular – well-seasoned ghee sauce

seems to complement the meek white meat with aplomb. But we opted for the vegetarian mosob meal for two, consisting of red and green lentil stews, spinach, fried and sauced mixed vegetables and a smooth, spicy dish of ground chickpeas. The injera was plentiful, and also lighter and less spongy than others we have sampled. True to tradition, it serves as both plate and fork (scoop up the stews with torn-off pieces of bread, but try not to lick your fingers in the process – this is food to be shared). The set menus include the much-vaunted coffee ceremony, with its attendant waftings and frankincense burning. The coffee is excellent: roasted (under your nose) to perfect richness and tinged carefully with cardamom and cloves. A big bowl of fresh, warm, salty popcorn ensures that no one feels cheated by the absence of puds.

Babies and children welcome: high chairs. Booking advisable Fri, Sat. Separate room for parties, seats 35. Takeaway service. Vegan dishes. Vegetarian menu. **Map 22 E2.**

Kennington

Adulis

44-46 Brixton Road, SW9 6BT (7587 0055, www.adulis.co.uk). Oval tube. **Dinner served** 5pm-midnight Mon-Fri. **Meals served** noon-1am Sat, Sun. **Main courses** £10.95-£13.95. **Credit** MC, V. Eritrean

Named after a port on the Red Sea, this coffee- and spice-scented restaurant provides a large and lovely Eritrean feast (though note that the lunchtime opening hours can be rather erratic – phone to check). It's an interesting-looking venue: lots of dark furniture, a bar-front studded with seaside rocks, and walls punctuated with little alcoves containing random finds (from Aladdin lamps to model ships to old-fashioned dial phones). The menu has some intriguing additions too, though, sadly, the linseed stew wasn't available on our visit. We settled for a chilli-scattered dish of crushed fava beans, stewed long in olive oil and onions and served with piles of toasted pitta. There are also fish dishes, as well as tender, fragrant ground-beef kitfo and other spicy stews. The sharing platters showcase the star turns on both meat and vegetarian fronts: little dollops of chicken or lamb stew (fried tripe, also available, doesn't figure on these platters), spicy chickpeas or lentils, fried greens and spinach with cottage cheese. Big-flavoured dishes like this call for a long cold drink, such as Savanna cider (from South Africa) and Tusker beer (Kenya), or there's sweet, delicately spiced Eritrean honey wine.

Babies and children welcome: high chairs. Booking advisable weekends. Separate room for parties, seats 100. Takeaway service. Vegetarian menu. **Map 16 M13. For branch see index.**

Mosob

Kitfo House

Menu

Accra or **akara**: bean fritters.
Aloco: fried plantain with hot tomato sauce.
Asaro: yam and sweet potato porridge.
Ayeb or **iab**: fresh yoghurt cheese made from strained yoghurt.
Berbere: an Ethiopian spice mix made with many hot and aromatic spices.
Cassava, **manioc** or **yuca**: a family of coarse roots that are boiled and pounded to make bread and various other farinaceous dishes. There are bitter and sweet varieties (the bitter variety is poisonous until cooked).
Ground rice: a kind of stiff rice pudding served to accompany soup.
Injera, **enjera** or **enjerra**: a soft, spongy Ethiopian and Eritrean flatbread made with teff/tef (a grain originally from Ethiopia), wheat, barley, oats or cornmeal. Fermented with yeast, it should have a distinct sour tang.
Pepper soup: a light, peppery soup made with either fish or meat.
Wot or **we'ts**: a thick, dark sauce made from slowly cooked onions, garlic, butter and spices – an essential component in the aromatic stews of East Africa. **Doro wot**, a stew containing chicken and hard-boiled eggs, is a particularly common dish.

Vauxhall

★ Kitfo House

49 South Lambeth Road, SW8 1RH (7735 8915). Vauxhall tube/rail. **Meals served** 8.30am-11pm Mon-Fri; 10.30am-11pm Sat, Sun. **Main courses** £5.50-£7.95. **Credit** MC, V. Eritrean

Oriental fire meets the subtler seasonings typical of the Horn of Africa – by way of standard breakfast fry-ups – in this multifunctional Vauxhall café. The split personality is down to the fact that Kitfo House is an Eritrean restaurant that likes to make the most of its Thai chef at lunchtime. The Thai options are cheaper than the African ones: powerfully flavoured kaeng pa (jungle curry), served with a mound of rice, costs just £5.50. The Eritrean version of scrambled eggs, jumbled with green chillies and chopped tomatoes, is a gloriously tasty dish. It can be served with pitta, or, like the rest of the Eritrean specials, with a whole basket of rolled-up injera (spongy and slightly sour: the national bread) that you use as a scoop or plate. Vegetarians can choose delicious messes of spinach, lentils and cottage cheese, while meat eaters are wowed by tender beef stewed in spices – the restaurant's namesake dish. As a grand finale, treat yourself to the Eritrean coffee ceremony: it's a heady and stimulating experience, with incense and popcorn as the trimmings.
Available for hire. Babies and children admitted. Disabled: toilet. Separate room for parties, seats 20. Takeaway service. Vegetarian menu. **Map 16 L13**.

North
Kentish Town

Muya

13 Brecknock Road, N7 0BL (3609 0702, www.muyarestaurant.co.uk). Kentish Town tube/rail or Camden Road rail. **Lunch served** 11am-5pm Mon-Fri; noon-5pm Sat. **Dinner served** 6-11pm Mon-Sat; 6-10pm Sun. **Main courses** £8.95-£16.50. **Credit** MC, V. Ethiopian

Muya's look could be described as Rift Valley safari chic, with animal skins adorning chairs and bar, and cool jazz on the sound system. The coolness extends to a degree of insouciance on the part of the waiting staff, who were wont to disappear for stretches. When present, however, they were charming and keen to explain the niceties of eating Ethiopian. The menu, unlike the decor, is authentic, down to the all-important coffee, imported in small amounts directly from Addis. Meat eaters love key wot, a fabulously rich beef stew that uses Berbere spices (cumin, turmeric, fenugreek, paprika, ginger and nutmeg), while kibe – a lip-smacking concoction of spice in ghee that's used in a number of the stews – lends a fabulous richness to lamb and chicken. But vegetarians and vegans do uncommonly well in Ethiopian restaurants, as proved by our huge tray of two types of spiced lentil, yellow split peas, collard greens, spinach and more injera than we knew what to do with. This is partly due to the numerous fasting days prescribed by the Ethiopian Orthodox Church, when meat and dairy products are forbidden. With a cold Castel beer and a coffee ceremony to close the meal, we left happy.
Babies and children welcome: high chairs. Separate room for parties, seats 20. Takeaway service. Vegan dishes. Vegetarian menu. **Map 26 C5**.

Queen of Sheba

12 Fortess Road, NW5 2EU (7284 3947, www.thequeenofsheba.co.uk). Kentish Town tube/rail. **Lunch served** noon-3pm, **dinner served** 6-11pm Mon-Sat. **Meals served** noon-10pm Sun. **Main courses** £7-£13.50. **Set meal** £30-£40 (2-3 people). **Credit** MC, V. Ethiopian

This tiny restaurant is the perfect destination for those unacquainted with the joys of Ethiopian cuisine; the smiley, chatty staff will happily talk you through the menu and, if necessary, offer tactical advice on eating with injera, the sour, spongy pancake that comes with every meal. And you won't be disappointed if you do know your kitfo (raw beef marinated in spices; available in two varieties here) from your doro wat (chicken and egg stew): the food isn't dumbed down, although the heat setting is dropped for local palates. We loved the gomen injera (spinach and crumbly cottage cheese rolled in injera), while zilbo stew combined collard greens with tender strips of lamb and a heady mix of ginger and garlic. The lentil and cabbage stews in the vegetarian platter were slightly underwhelming – we'd have liked more of a kick – but the well-balanced use of turmeric and ginger enlivened the platter's third component, a yellow split-pea dal. Ethiopian trinkets, furniture and art make this an atmospheric place for a leisurely meal, and it's great to see St George – Addis Ababa's favourite beer – on the menu. The coffee is served authentically: slowly, ceremonially and very, very strong.
Available for hire. Babies and children welcome: high chairs. Booking advisable Fri, Sat. Takeaway service. Vegan dishes. Vegetarian menu. **Map 26 B4**.

Tufnell Park

Lalibela

137 Fortess Road, NW5 2HR (7284 0600, www.lalibelarestaurant.co.uk). Tufnell Park tube or bus 134, 214, C2. **Dinner served** 6-10pm Mon-Sat; 6-9.30pm Sun. **Main courses** £10-£11.99. **Credit** MC, V. Ethiopian

Lalibela charms from the moment you cross the threshold and smell the coffee beans roasting by the bar. It resembles the home of an eccentric africophile uncle: full of carvings, figurines, textiles, instruments and portraits of elegant Ethiopian luminaries. The smiling and attentive manager is keen to recommend dishes and explain how they can be served (on a very fine circle of injera). Unlike most Ethiopian/Eritrean restaurants, Lalibela doesn't offer sharing platters, but the menu is long and there are plenty of adventurous house specials. To start, Lalibela salad – beetroot and potato served warm – was tangy and sweet, and spiced chicken salad packed a punch. For mains, we tried fried lamb with spinach and spring greens, as well as a little separate pot of spiced couscous, just in case we developed injera fatigue. Tofu-spinach tibs (tibs are sautéed dishes) was deliciously savoury, if very oily. Fried-fish tibs, with tomatoes and peppers, was delicately flavoured with rosemary and lemon juice and went well with shiro (peas, shallots and hot spices). It was a hot and steamy night, so we eschewed the coffee ceremony in favour of a couple of cold St George beers (from Ethiopia).
Babies and children welcome: high chairs. Booking advisable Thur-Sat. Takeaway service. Vegetarian menu. **Map 26 B3**.

The Americas

NORTH AMERICAN

It's the mood of the moment – creating new or improved versions of classic dishes that have become clichés. Though much of the North American culinary repertoire reaching these shores has been turned into fast-food fodder, there are pockets of excellence. Gourmet burgers are an obvious manifestation, and some of the best of these venues can be found on p240; **Meat Liquor**'s Dead Hippie burger deserves special mention. The re-creation of the US diner is also part of this zeitgeist – west London's **Lucky 7** and **Electric Diner** really impressed, but too many places believe it suffices to 'talk the talk' without getting the details right. Still, London's US dining scene remains exciting and dynamic, with plenty of new venues opening in the past year – including **Jamie Oliver's Diner**, and **Oblix** halfway up the Shard. The smokehouse trend also continues apace, with **Beard to Tail** the best of the new crop.

Central
City

Barbecoa
20 New Change Passage, EC4M 9AG (3005 8555, www.barbecoa.com). St Paul's tube. **Meals served** 11.45am-11pm Mon-Fri; 10.30am-11pm Sat; 10.30am-10.30pm Sun. **Main courses** £16-£65. **Credit** AmEx, MC, V.
The view here, of the looming dome of St Paul's, must be among the most imposing in London. We hope it's appreciated by the City dudes at whom Barbecoa – a joint venture between Jamie Oliver and American barbecue maestro Adam Perry Lang – is clearly aimed. This is meat territory: steaks, roasts, pit barbecue. The brunch menu, available at weekends and bank holidays, gives a full flavour of the restaurant's considerable abilities. Tender shredded short-ribs came in a massive portion with heavenly chipotle salsa. A porchetta BLT cut the salty richness of the pork with fine acidity from cranberry salsa. Baked beans were superbly seasoned and carefully cooked. The big complaint is that some food is unnecessarily (verging on unpleasantly) greasy. That BLT, already rich from fatty porchetta, came on sourdough bread that had been oiled before grilling. The ribs sat on a naan so greasy from the meat we couldn't contemplate eating it. These are solvable problems, but the

kitchen had better solve them. Service was polished and friendly. The well-chosen wine list is for rich people (little below £35). The cocktails are unusual, and ours was well executed. Try to avoid the excessive richness, and you'll have a great time. *Available for hire. Babies and children welcome: high chairs; nappy-changing facilities. Booking advisable. Disabled: lift; toilet. Separate room for parties, seats 40. Tables outdoors (5, terrace).* **Map 11 P6.**

Covent Garden

Christopher's
18 Wellington Street, WC2E 7DD (7240 4222, www.christophersgrill.com). Covent Garden tube.
Bar **Open/meals served** 11.30am-midnight Mon-Wed; 11.30am-1.30am Sat; 11.30am-10.30pm Sun.
Restaurant **Lunch served** noon-3pm Mon-Fri. **Brunch served** 11.30am-3.30pm Sat, Sun. **Dinner served** 5-11.30pm Mon-Sat; 5-10.30pm Sun.
Both **Main courses** £17.95-£68. **Set meal** (5-6.15pm Mon-Sat) £16 2 courses, £22 3 courses. **Credit** AmEx, MC, V.
This Covent Garden fixture reopened in spring 2013 after a major refurbishment of its grand premises (Grade II-listed and formerly a casino). Everything we ate during our weekday lunch was excellent: two starters from the carte and a couple of dishes

from the set lunch. Two clichés of London's American restaurant scene, caesar salad and crab cakes, were flawlessly executed. From the set lunch, beef carpaccio was top-notch yet almost overshadowed by a main of blackened salmon with 'jambalaya risotto'. The flavourful rice showed real understanding of cajun seasoning – rare in London – and the flavourful fish was properly blackened while remaining juicy within. You can pay serious money for steak or Maine lobster, but the Martini Bar serves relatively inexpensive meals. The pre- and post-theatre set menu is a bargain, and brunch offers everything from granola to ribeye steak. Service is confident and competent, and the wine list is a welcome rarity for places of this kind: ignoring expensive trophy bottles, sharply focused on offering quality at every price range, starting from around £20. Many US-style restaurants have popped up since this venue opened in 1991. They still have much to learn from Christopher's. *Babies and children welcome: children's menu; high chairs. Booking advisable. Separate room for parties, seats 40.* **Map 18 F4.**

Joe Allen
13 Exeter Street, WC2E 7DT (7836 0651, www.joeallen.co.uk). Covent Garden tube. **Meals served** noon-midnight Mon-Thur; noon-12.45am Fri; 10am-12.45am Sat; 10am-11.30pm Sun. **Brunch served** 10am-4pm Sat, Sun. **Main courses** £10.95-£25.95. **Set meal** (Mon, Sun;

Jamie Oliver's Diner

noon-7pm Tue-Sat) £16.50 2 courses, £19.50 3 courses incl glass of wine. **Credit** AmEx, MC, V. New ownership since late 2012 has given this Theatreland old-timer a shot in the arm. Not much has changed in terms of decor; the slightly scuffed basement room still has the same happy mix of show posters and photos on bare brick walls, and a pianist still tinkles away in the evenings. The biggest change is in the much-improved kitchen, which is now producing decent-to-good versions of American brasserie standards. You'll find big salads (including a punchy but balanced bowlful of avocado, pecan, bacon and blue cheese dressing), fish dishes (yellowfin tuna with avocado and coriander salsa was a good piece of fish exactly grilled, though the salsa contained little coriander), egg dishes, chilli con carne and steaks (a small sirloin steak was cooked as requested, and came with plentiful golden fries). Old favourites – the tasty black bean soup, for example – remain. A membrillo-like strawberry jelly with roasted peanut ice-cream was, like the rest of the dishes we tried, good without being memorable. As for drinks, all bases are covered by a choice of reasonably priced cocktails, a range of US beers, a global wine list and properly made coffee. The other major difference is in the service: it's now efficient and comes with a smile.
Babies and children welcome: booster seats; high chairs. Booking advisable. Entertainment: pianist 7-11pm Mon-Thur, 8pm-midnight Fri, Sat, noon-4pm Sun. Separate room for parties, seats 50. **Map 18 E4.**

★ Mishkin's

25 Catherine Street, WC2B 5JS (7240 2078, www.mishkins.co.uk). Covent Garden tube. **Meals served** 11am-11.30pm Mon-Sat; noon-10.30pm Sun. **Main courses** £6-£13. **Credit** AmEx, MC, V.

Mishkin's calls itself 'a kind-of Jewish deli with cocktails', which is a pretty good description, though it omits the knowingness of the place and the fact that the menu is much too short for a real Jewish deli. Still, what's listed is generally pretty good. We're partial to the reuben (pastrami, sauerkraut, swiss cheese and russian dressing on toasted rye bread), though it's no bargain at £11. Sides such as chips, fried onion rings and coleslaw (most recently cauliflower and caraway) are hard to resist too, especially if you've plumped for the burger. But some dishes are a bit so-what – 'house' fish cakes with beets and horseradish, for example, managed to be bland. It's an attractive selection, though, mixing tradition (chicken matzo ball soup) and innovation (cod cheek popcorn), sometimes in the same dish (smoked mackerel latkes), and prices are just about reasonable given the location. The small, shabby-chic, NYC-style interior is low-lit, which means diners can't always appreciate the mass of decorative touches (including a cabin-like table at the back). Staff are young, friendly and attentive, and can mix a mean cocktail. Mishkin's belongs to Russell Norman and Richard Beatty's stable of restaurants, along with Spuntino and the three branches of Polpo.
Available for hire. Babies and children admitted. Booking advisable, essential weekends. **Map 18 E4.**

King's Cross

Shrimpy's

King's Cross Filling Station, Goods Way, N1C 4UR (8880 6111, www.shrimpys.co.uk). King's Cross St Pancras tube/rail. **Meals served** 11am-10.30pm daily. **Main courses** £15-£20. **Credit** (cash not accepted) AmEx, MC, V.
This unusually located place (in a disused filling station just north of King's Cross) was a sensation

when it opened in 2012. Word of mouth left novelty-seekers gasping for one of the trademark soft-shell crab burgers – and unable to get a table. A year on, bagging a table was dead easy at lunchtime. And our meal made us wonder what all the fuss had been about. There was some pleasing cooking: a bracingly acidic chicory slaw with pomegranate, and a boldly spiced hash made with shin of beef. But some food was simply inert. Prawn fritters had a woollen texture within, no crunch without, and vanishingly small prawn content. The real shock came with that famous crab burger: ours was simply crunchy batter with a vaguely marine taste, given most of its character by chilli sauce and dwarfed by a pillow-sized (and tasteless) soft roll. Shrimpy's is due to shuffle off in 2014, when the site is redeveloped. It's a shame we'll be deprived of such a nice-looking venue, but the gastronomic loss is nothing to lose sleep over.
Babies and children admitted. Booking advisable weekends. Tables outdoors (6, terrace). **Map 4 L2.**

Marylebone

★ Meat Liquor HOT 50

74 Welbeck Street, W1G 0BA (7224 4239, www.meatliquor.com). Bond Street tube. **Meals served** noon-11pm Mon-Thur; noon-1am Fri, Sat; noon-10.30pm Sun. **Main courses** £3-£10. **Credit** MC, V.
Just getting into this cult destination can feel like cause for celebration. Not only is the queue epic, but Meat Liquor employs 'good cop, bad cop' strategies to manage it. On our visit, Bad Cop was played by a giant bouncer who prowled along the line ink-stamping hands: a ploy that stops late-comers from joining their friends mid-queue. Good Cop, meanwhile, was a doe-eyed girl with a tray of the famed deep-fried pickles to quell munchies. Inside,

it's dark and violently loud: more hell-raising nightclub than restaurant. Signs point out the rules ('No suits', 'No ballet pumps'). The graffiti murals are occult-themed, and the staff heavily tattooed. The Deep South cooking is gutsy stuff, with the likes of crunchy-coated 'bingo wings' served not only with a terrific Louisiana-style hot sauce but an authentic blue cheese dip. There are cheese steaks and dogs, though the real show-stoppers are the burgers, with their firm, bouncy buns and juicy, pink-middled patties. The excellent 'dead hippie', made with a double layer of patties, has finely diced raw onion, molten cheese, shredded lettuce and thick slices of gherkin – not forgetting the mellow and tangy 'secret' burger sauce. Sides are no side attraction, from perfect skinny fries to pillowy onion rings, and staff make a mean cocktail too.
Bookings not accepted. Children admitted before 6pm. Disabled: toilet. **Map 9 H6.**

Mayfair

Burger & Lobster
29 Clarges Street, W1J 7EF (7409 1699, www. burgerandlobster.com). Green Park tube. **Meals served** noon-10.30pm Mon-Sat; noon-5.30pm Sun. **Main courses** £20. **Credit** AmEx, MC, V.
Don't be put off by the gimmicky concept or swanky addresses of the four branches of this Russian-owned chain; this sleek eaterie offers remarkably good value … if you order the lobster. As you walk through the door in the Mayfair branch (an attractively converted pub), a blackboard tells you all you need to know about the menu: you may order a lobster (boiled, grilled or in a brioche roll with mayonnaise), or you may have a burger, all served with a substantial and tasty salad and french fries, for £20. The simplicity of the pricing – while absurd for what is a fairly average burger – cuts neatly past the usual 'market price' for lobster, which can work out to over £30 elsewhere in town. The grilled version got top marks on our visit: the lobster was a fresh, quality specimen, perfectly cooked – and tasted divine dipped in drawn butter. For dessert, there's either an entirely average chocolate brownie or a delicious lime mousse that offers a tart finishing touch to a satisfying meal. If you'd like to make an evening of it, do: the bar has a range of fine cocktails and a decent selection of beers on tap.
Babies and children admitted. Bookings not accepted. **Map 9 H8.**
For branches see index.

Soho

Jamie Oliver's Diner NEW
23A Shaftesbury Avenue, W1D 7EF (3697 4117, www.jamieoliversdiner.com). Piccadilly Circus tube. **Meals served** noon-midnight daily. **Main courses** £5-£16.50. **Credit** MC, V.
Jamie Oliver has become the latest restaurateur to join the bandwagon – sorry, dining trend – that is US 'dude food'. But before you stick the knife in, remember that this is a natural progression for the slayer of the turkey twizzler. He's spent a huge amount of time Stateside and co-owns US-style grill Barbecoa with barbecue maestro Adam Perry Lang. Running on a three-year lease, this no-bookings newcomer stretches the definition of pop-up. But it's on-brand Oliver: free-range meat ('because happy pigs mean better flavour') and a zero-landfill promise, meaning that leftovers are composted, recycled or upcycled. The interior mixes reclaimed and recycled furnishings, finishing the wholesome

vibe with a U-rated 1950s soundtrack and dinosaur theme (complete with full-scale models). It's squarely pitched at out-of-towners and families, yet has resisted the urge to cut corners in the kitchen. Burgers came with a proper patty (thick, nicely charred outer, lipstick-pink middle), toasted sesame bun and old-school trimmings (a light burger sauce and shredded lettuce); dirty barbecue ribs combined fall-off-the-bone meat and a tangy mustard marinade. This is a cheery, people-pleasing place brought to you by a cheery, people-pleasing chap.
Babies and children welcome: children's menu; high chairs; nappy-changing facilities. Bookings not accepted. Disabled: toilet. Takeaway service. **Map 17 B5.**

Pitt Cue Co
1 Newburgh Street, W1F 7RB (no phone, www.pittcue.co.uk). Oxford Circus tube. **Lunch served** noon-3pm Mon-Sat; noon-4pm Sun. **Dinner served** 6-10.30pm Mon-Sat. **Main courses** £9.50-£16. **Credit** MC, V.
Come to this trailblazing rib joint on a Friday or Saturday night and there's one certainty: a painfully long queue. Not only do you have to shuffle along patiently, but once inside, you still might have to wait a little longer (though at least you can order drinks). Even if you play smart and come one quiet weekday lunchtime, you may still endure a brief pause, but for rib-lovers, it'll be worth it. The Pitt Cue-ers honed their craft under a bridge on the South Bank, selling to a demanding, social media-savvy, twentysomething audience – and their cooking rarely misses a beat. On our visit, the gargantuan signature ribs arrived with blistered, blackened skin, revealing ruby fall-off-the bone meat that was both smoky and dangerously rich. To cut through it, there was a finely shredded slaw, with two kinds of cabbage, coriander seeds and a zingy vinaigrette. We also enjoyed chunky pieces of pork melting into a heap of wholesome beans, and hunks of chargrilled bread – this is proper cowboy food. Low lighting, sparse decor and a joyfully kooky soundtrack set the tone in the intimate basement room; if you opt for perching along the wall in the ground-floor bar, prepare to be jostled.
Babies and children admitted. Bookings not accepted. Takeaway service. **Map 17 A3.**

Electric Diner. See p26.

Soho Diner `NEW`

19-21 Old Compton Street, W1D 5JJ (7734 5656, www.sohodiner.com). Leicester Square tube. **Meals served** 11.30am-midnight Mon-Wed; 11.30am-2am Thur-Sat; 11am-11pm Sun. **Main courses** £7-£16. **Credit** AmEx, MC, V.
The Soho House group has rebranded the runt of its litter, Boheme Bar & Kitchen, as the new 'younger sister' to Notting Hill's hugely successful Electric Diner, introducing a new menu. But, as we feared, Soho Diner is as pedestrian as before, only this time with cooking straight off the US food bandwagon. A shrimp cocktail starter, served unappealingly on a side plate, lacked oomph. Honey-glazed chicken wings were too dry. A philly cheese steak sandwich had an arid bun. But kids will dig the enormous banana-split dessert, served with scoops of strawberry, vanilla and chocolate ice-cream. Hen parties will love the 'on-tap' cocktails: a bit sweet and synthetic (the cosmo is better than the mojito), but a steal at £6. And, to be fair, the burgers aren't bad. Choose a 'single' to get two patties, or a 'double' to get three. Juicy and served in a soft bun, they're improved by a slice of the thick, smoky off-menu bacon. So why go? Well, the people-watching from the window seats is second-to-none, with more bequiffed poseurs holding tiny dogs in man-bags than at London Fashion Week. Staff are lovely too. Two out of three ain't bad.
Babies and children welcome: high chairs. Bookings not accepted. Tables outdoors (4, pavement). **Map 17 C4.**

Spuntino `HOT 50`

61 Rupert Street, W1D 7PW (no phone, www.spuntino.co.uk). Piccadilly Circus tube. **Meals served** noon-12.45am Mon-Sat; noon-11pm Sun. **Main courses** £5-£10. **Credit** AmEx, MC, V.
For a lesson in how to make a silk purse out of a sow's ear, head to Spuntino. A challenge to find (look for 'number 61'), the venue is laid out as a bar – and a tiny one at that, with a smattering of fixed, backless seats allowing diners to perch along the counter. This is no wholesome 1950s-style diner, but a dark, grungy space where dim lights dangle in cages, the walls are cracked and battered, and the staff sport daring tattoos under flimsy vests (and that's just the girls). The anti-establishment vibe trickles into the menu, which is Italian-American with plenty of 'additude'. Served mostly on all-the-rage enamelled tin dishes, food features big bold flavours packed into tiny portions: from our dinky slider (mini-burger), filled with moist pulled pork and pickled apple, to a black-edged pizzetta (mini-pizza) topped with long stems of pleasantly bitter cicoria (Italian dandelion), thin salami slices and a hit of chilli. The salads are equally innovative, as seen in a tumble of kohlrabi and apple with crumbly feta, hazelnuts and black sesame seeds. Only dessert proved a let-down; our chocolate, pecan and bourbon cake had plenty of nuts but no discernible liquor.
Available for hire. Babies and children admitted. Bookings not accepted. **Map 17 B4.**

West
Ladbroke Grove

Electric Diner

191 Portobello Road, W11 2ED (7908 9696, www.electricdiner.com). Ladbroke Grove tube. **Breakfast served** 8am-noon daily. **Meals served** noon-11pm Mon-Wed; noon-midnight Thur-Sat; noon-10pm Sun. **Main courses** £5-£19. **Credit** AmEx, MC.
The Electric Diner, the latest restaurant on this site from Soho House, has outclassed its previous incarnations with style and ease. With its unfinished brick and concrete walls, low lighting, french grey-painted plank ceiling, red leather banquettes and lively open kitchen down one side, evoking a sort of chic US railway car diner, the spot easily delivers on atmosphere. The hip vibe extends to the menu, which features artery-unfriendly American classics: cheeseburgers (which arrive in a pretentious presentation on a small plate with a sharp knife sticking out of it like a sinister birthday candle); hot dogs; milkshakes (pleasantly creamy, sensibly sized). But each classic dish is well-thought-out and composed of good ingredients: French fries are thin and crispy, but made of flavourful potatoes; even a simple bibb lettuce and avocado salad was enlivened with finely chopped chives and tarragon, so it actually tasted of something. Accompany these with a vast range of cocktails or wine. The Diner gets extra points for having a children's menu with healthy, tasty food: salmon and broccoli was a great relief to a refined diner of modest age who tires easily of the frozen fish fingers foisted upon her elsewhere. Desserts are a must-have: a slice of classic lemon meringue pie was as big as Texas, and as bold. The speakers by every red leather booth seem an excessive distribution of club music, adding to an already noisy room, filled with sounds of shouted orders, gossiping young hipsters and sizzling grills. Sister restaurant Soho Diner opened in summer 2013.

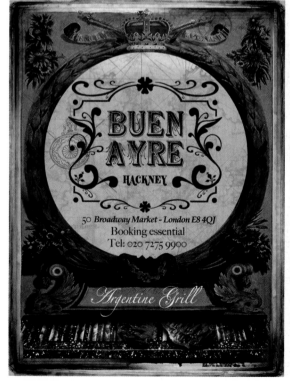

Beard to Tail

Babies and children welcome: high chairs; nappy-changing facilities; children's menu. Bookings not accepted. Tables outdoors (3, pavement). **Map 19 B3**.

Westbourne Park

★ Lucky 7

127 Westbourne Park Road, W2 5QL (7727 6771, www.lucky7london.co.uk). Royal Oak or Westbourne Park tube. **Meals served** noon-10.30pm Mon; 10am-10.30pm Tue-Thur; 9am-11pm Fri, Sat; 9am-10.30pm Sun. **Main courses** £6.95-£12.95. **Credit** MC, V.

Most London restaurants calling themselves diners aren't really diners at all: diners have a long, diverse menu. That complaint is pretty much the only one we can make about this tiny outpost of Tom Conran's empire. The American-retro decor is a smile from floor to ceiling, with outsized, wildly kitsch figurines stealing the show. The menu is 90% breakfast, burgers and outlandishly rich desserts, plus drinks including craft beers, some cocktails and many shakes. We had one of the few salads – a cobb with grilled chicken – and it was excellent: a variety of ingredients; tender, tasty chicken; exceptionally generous in portion. A cheeseburger was equally successful: flavourful beef cooked as requested, and with appetising garnishes. Fries were good, coleslaw thinly shredded and creamy. The menu also includes a few other sandwiches, hot dogs and eggy breakfast options (huevos rancheros alongside the traditional choices). The drawback is size – seating capacity is just a couple of dozen – and the no-bookings policy. So you'll often have to queue. But with quality this high, a queue is a small sacrifice. Tom Conran understands that when you work with food this simple, you need to get 100% out of every single detail. And he succeeds.
Babies and children welcome: children's menu. Bookings not accepted. Takeaway service. **Map 7 A5**.

South East

London Bridge & Borough

Oblix NEW

Level 32, The Shard, 31 St Thomas Street, SE1 9SY (7268 6700, www.oblixrestaurant.com). London Bridge tube/rail. **Lunch served** noon-

2.45pm Mon-Fri; noon-3.15pm Sat, Sun. **Dinner served** 6-11.45pm daily. **Main courses** £16-£54. **Credit** AmEx, MC, V.

This showy restaurant set nearly halfway up the Shard, western Europe's tallest building, is the latest venture from Rainer Becker, who's best known for his outstanding modern Japanese restaurants, Zuma (*see p164*) and Roka (*see p163*). Oblix is more West than East, though, and feels more awkward than its blingtastic siblings, with a Dubai-style blandness. The temptation, when you enter a room that's 32 floors up, is to rush to the windows, press your nose to the glass and take in the view. Most other bar-restaurants that find themselves similarly blessed allow you to do this freely, but the Oblix bar has bookable tables and chairs blocking this sought-after periphery, forcing you to invade someone else's space (do it anyway). A starter of tataki-style beef provided a few tasty morsels, while a main course of halibut was perfectly cooked, though came, rather oddly, with something resembling a dollop of lemon curd. Pork belly was perhaps the best dish: the meat pink and tender, the skin nicely crisped, and served with a piquant apple chutney. Desserts consisted mainly of ice-cream combinations, though the New York cheesecake was exemplary. Prices are as high as the setting, of course.
Babies and children welcome: high chairs. Booking essential. Disabled: lift; toilet. Dress: smart casual. **Map 12 Q8**.

East

Shoreditch

Beard to Tail NEW

77 Curtain Road, EC2A 3BS (7729 2966, www.beardtotail.co.uk). Old Street tube/rail or Shoreditch High Street rail.
Bar **Open** noon-11pm Mon-Sat; noon-9pm Sun.
Restaurant **Lunch served** noon-4pm, **dinner served** 6-10pm Mon-Sat. **Meals served** noon-8pm Sun. **Main courses** £10-£21.50.
Both **Credit** AmEx, MC, V.

The name's from a theory on the French origins of the word 'barbecue': both the connotations of smoke and fire, and 'eat every part of the beast' are apt. B2T is unashamedly focused on the pleasures of the flesh, with not much choice for vegetarians. But the meat-loving masses who flock here are

spoilt – it was one of the first places in London to embrace the US smokehouse trend, albeit with a British, cheffy twist, and it's still one of the best places to get your teeth into it. The menu ranges from the straightforward (ribs, sliders, steaks and burgers, all authentically hearty) to the more complex, with the likes of tender pork cheeks braised in honey and cloves, or trotter with sage and apricot. Equally as noteworthy are the fine cocktails, and rare American whiskeys and ryes – you can drink at the bar or head to the lively, embellished-industrial dining room at the back. Staff are exceptionally friendly and accommodating, even on busy nights when service can appear stretched. Beard to Tail is an ultra of-the-moment restaurant, but with enough substance to keep it current long after the barbecue bandwagon has rolled out of town.
Babies and children welcome: high chairs; nappy-changing facilities. Booking advisable. Disabled: toilet. Takeaway service. **Map 6 R4**.

North East

Haggerston

Duke's Brew & Que

33 Downham Road, N1 5AA (3006 0795, www.dukesjoint.com). Haggerston rail. **Open** 4pm-midnight Mon-Fri; 10am-midnight Sat; 10am-11pm Sun. **Brunch served** 11am-3pm Sat, Sun. **Dinner served** 6-10pm Mon-Thur; 5-10.30pm Fri, Sat; 5-9.30pm Sun. **Main courses** £10-£23.50. **Credit** AmEx, MC, V.

This converted boozer, on a corner site in De Beauvoir Town, has made a name for itself since opening in 2012. The offering: no-frills meat dishes, mainly smoked and barbecued; and a fabulous selection of beers, both own-brewed and from top domestic and foreign producers. The Duke's beef ribs were named one of *Time Out*'s 100 best dishes in London in 2012 – a high achievement for a newcomer. On the evidence of our most recent visit, however, the staff seemed to have taken their eye off the ball. The spare ribs were fine, but a trio of pulled pork sliders was dull and dry. The famous beef ribs were by far the best part of our meal, but, again, were dry and chewy where they should have been juicy and succulent. Baked beans and chips were good, though mac 'n' cheese was tough and leathery on top. Service seemed a bit clueless: our waiter

John Salt

confidently assured us the beer we asked for wasn't stocked and looked nonplussed when we pointed it out on the list. We hope this was just an off night. It doesn't take long to build a reputation for good food, but it also doesn't take long to lose it.

Babies and children admitted until 7pm. Booking advisable, essential weekends. Disabled: toilet. Tables outdoors (5, pavement). **Map 6 R1.**

North

Camden Town & Chalk Farm

The Diner

2 Jamestown Road, NW1 7BY (7485 5223, www.goodlifediner.com). Camden Town tube. **Meals served** 10am-11pm Mon-Thur; 10am-midnight Fri; 9am-midnight Sat; 9am-11pm Sun. **Main courses** £5.20-£9. **Credit** AmEx, MC, V.

The Camden branch of this popular chain was packed when we went for lunch, and the loud soundtrack (Johnny Cash, the Stones) made conversation difficult. Even more difficult was figuring out the appeal of the place, with its dark walls distinctly un-diner-like and its menu that reads like nothing you'll see in US diners. This chain is basically about burgers, breakfast and booze – with a section of hot dogs and a few sandwiches and salads thrown in. We could live without the authenticity if the Diner's food were better. In our two sandwiches – grilled cajun chicken breast and the 'Diner Po Boy', made with soft-shell crab – execution was woeful: stiffly breaded crabs had little taste of their own; and the fillings of swiss cheese (leathery), dill pickles and 'heirloom' tomatoes (both wilted) didn't make much impact. The chicken sandwich was marginally better, but again the filling was lacklustre. Coleslaw was way too sweet. Fries were the high point, crisp and hot, and service is sweet and smiling. Perhaps the burgers and dogs

are better, but in all it's hard to see how someone who had eaten in a good American diner would want to eat at this Diner.

Babies and children welcome: children's menu; high chairs; nappy-changing facilitites. Booking advisable. Disabled: toilet. Separate room for parties. Tables outdoors (8, pavement; 16, terrace). Takeaway service.
For branches see index.

Islington

John Salt NEW

131 Upper Street, N1 1QP (7704 8955, www.john-salt.com). Highbury & Islington tube/rail. **Lunch served** noon-3pm, **dinner served** 6-10pm Mon-Fri. **Meals served** noon-10pm Sat, Sun. **Dishes** £3.50-£12. **Credit** AmEx, MC, V.

On Upper Street, mostly a strip of uninspiring chains and unashamed party pubs, John Salt stands out. Its second chef (of three in one year) was Neil Rankin, one of the architects of London's US diner food takeover. He's no longer there, but the menu still makes full use of the smoker, the fryer and the grill: there's barbecued sardines with harissa; smoked short-rib cheeseburger; 'chicken fried' whitebait; coal-baked onions with yogurt. Even some of the ingredients have the whiff of fossil fuel about them: charcoal butter appears with potatoes and sorrel. It's all served on small plates, of course, which doesn't always work – timings were off on our visit, and the table wasn't big enough to comfortably accommodate the five dishes we ordered. The cooking is competent, if not exciting, and the drinks list thoughtful; a few craft beers feature, and cocktails are grown-up and fortifying. What stops John Salt scoring higher is the fact that the ground-floor bar gets massively busy – this is Upper Street, as discussed – leaving the upstairs restaurant to contend with the distant sounds of repetitive beats and an ever-increasing hubbub. A good place to kick off a night out in

Islington, perhaps, but not committed enough to warrant a special visit.

Babies and children welcome: high chairs; nappy-changing facilities. Booking advisable. Disabled: toilet. Tables outdoors (3, pavement; 2, terrace). **Map 5 O1.**

North Pole

188 New North Road, N1 7BJ (7354 5400, www.thenorthpolepub.co.uk). Essex Road or Haggerston rail. **Open** 11am-11pm Mon-Thur; 11am-midnight Fri, Sat; 11am-10.30pm Sun. **Meals served** noon-10pm Mon-Sat; noon-9.30pm Sun. **Main courses** £9-£17.50. **Credit** AmEx, MC, V.

This capacious, charmingly un-refurbished local has made a well-deserved name for itself as a purveyor of real ale and craft beers. There's a large choice of both, the casks well looked after, and the beers wide-ranging in country of origin. They help make the North Pole highly popular, and its attractions are obvious. So we were extremely disappointed to have a lacklustre lunch on our Saturday visit. Maybe the kitchen hadn't yet got into gear (we arrived just after noon), but there was something underpowered about the meal. A mushroom soup of the day was simply dull. A modish pulled pork sandwich was dry, and the meat lacked flavour. Ribs were cooked well but their barbecue sauce seemed generic. 'Sweetcorn fritter with basil dressing' was actually a sweetcorn pancake, and clumsy frying rendered it too oily. Elsewhere on the menu lie more sandwiches, pizzas, some substantial main courses and several snacks and starters. Selecting from that list, with a beautiful brew alongside, might be the best way to go. Final down-notes: service was inattentive and lacked genuine friendliness, and we detected a faint but unmistakable musty smell about the place. Never nice when you're eating.

Babies and children welcome: children's menu; high chairs. Tables outdoors (8, garden). Takeaway service. **Map 5 P1.**

LATIN AMERICAN

Latin American dining is enjoying its spot in the limelight too, and Peruvian restaurants in particular are flourishing, from the lowly yet highly authentic **Emanuel** in Elephant & Castle to the trendy yet excellent **Ceviche** in the West End. Three more Central and South American countries provided inspiration for new openings, with **Casa Negra**, a shabby-chic Mexican offshoot of **La Bodega Negra**, setting up shop in Shoreditch, and Brazilian **Galeto** getting into its samba rhythm in Soho. Top honours for the newbies this year, though, go to **Zoilo** for bringing sublime Argentinean small-plates cooking to Marylebone.

Central

City

Moo!
40-42 Middlesex Street, E1 7EX (7650 7948, www.moogrill.co.uk). Aldgate or Aldgate East tube or Liverpool Street tube/rail. **Meals served** 11am-11pm Mon-11pm Fri; 6-11pm Sat; noon-9pm Sun. **Main courses** £6.75-£19. **Credit** AmEx, MC, V. Argentinian

The orginal Cobb Street branch is tiny, so it's not surprising that Moo! opened a second venue, in late 2012. Also located among the dog-eared backstreets of the Square Mile, it has 65 covers – hardly huge, but our experience suggests it's about right for now. The service was concerning – staff were seriously friendly but short on English. Our food was excellent, however. An appetiser of chorizo on ciabatta was taken to another level by a fabulous version of chimichurri sauce: buzzing with herbs, it was as silky and red as the inside of a steak. An empanada filled with chunks of beef, egg and olive was a bargain at just over £2. The highlight was a fabulous portion of sweetbreads, tasting like slivers of tender chicken thigh and practically fizzing with lime. A ribeye was good though not mind-blowing, while a napolitana came as cheese-smothered breaded steak topped with a pleasingly tacky slice of tomato. Lomitos (sandwiches) with mainly meaty fillings, and steaks priced by the 100g, are also available. Menu graphics are chain-like, furniture looks a little cheap and they offer mayo and ketchup – this is fun, Argentinian dining without the wallet-busting steak worship.
Babies and children welcome. Booking advisable. Disabled: toilet. Takeaway service. **Map 12 R6.** **For branch see index.**

Sushisamba
Floors 38 & 39, Heron Tower, 110 Bishopsgate, EC2N 4AY (3640 7330, www.sushisamba.com). Liverpool Street tube/rail. **Lunch served** 11.30am-2.30pm, **dinner served** 5.30-11pm daily. **Main courses** £8-£42. **Credit** AmEx, MC, V. Brazilian/Peruvian/Japanese

Japan, Brazil and Peru come together here. That's not an eye-opener these days, but the entrance to this expensive New York import is. Take the glass elevator that clings to the side of Heron Tower, shoot up 38 floors in a few stomach-flipping seconds, then walk into a bar from which you can practically browse workers' emails in the Gherkin. Go on through to the double-height glasshouse of a restaurant, with its magnificent bamboo-lattice ceiling, and your table will likely face north across Spitalfields towards Alexandra Palace or east over Stepney and out to Essex. Allow time to drink in your surroundings, and maybe a cocktail or seasonal saké, while perusing a menu that will need deciphering by your well-drilled waiter, peppered as it is with terms such as 'tiradito', 'taquito', 'moqueca' and 'chicharrons'. It's all tough visual competition for a plate of food, but the sushi does its damnedest to catch the eye with cloaks of red or green yuba (soybean curd skin). Rather than leave all the fillings to battle it out in one big, bursting-at-the-seams futomaki, the Samba London roll makes a starlet of each one (crab, tuna, salmon, yellowtail, prawn, scallop, beef, avocado) by placing it on a rice-slice pedestal. With that view – impressive in daylight, awesome by night – this is a special-occasion destination; they get a lot of birthday bookings.
Available for hire. Babies and children welcome: high chairs. Booking essential. Disabled: lift; toilet. Dress: smart casual. **Map 12 R6.**

Clerkenwell & Farringdon

Gaucho Smithfield
93A Charterhouse Street, EC1M 6HL (7490 1676, www.gauchorestaurants.co.uk). Barbican tube or Farringdon tube/rail. **Meals served** noon-11pm Mon-Sat. **Main courses** £15.50-£96.60. **Credit** AmEx, MC, V. Argentinian

With its cowhide-and-bling interiors, sleek service, expense-account pricing and reputation for out-of-this-world meat, there was a touch of shock and awe about the Gaucho chain's rapid expansion across the capital. But with the acclaimed Goodman and Hawksmoor steakhouses more recently championing US and UK cattle, Londoners no longer buy quite so readily into the Argie steak legend. Certainly, our most recent visit had shortcomings. That we ordered bife de chorizo (sirloin) medium rare and it arrived with barely a trace of pink was only one failing: it simply didn't have the expected depths of flavour. Argentinian classics such as chorizo sausage and grilled provolone cheese feature among the starters, but there's plenty of ceviche too. A smart move: the citrus-cooked fish (more associated with Peru or Ecudaor) offers a light foil to the beef-heavy mains section. A shrimp causita was fresh and zingy, but lacked the kick our waiter said the leche de tigre ('tiger's milk' – ceviche marinade) would bring.

Sushisamba

Chips were adequate, but a mixed salad was oversalted, with under-ripe tomatoes and none of the promised olives. The exclusively Argentinian wine list includes a 'fine and rare' section, but even the regular list will make you gasp at the prices – the cheapest bottles nudge £30. Gaucho needs to woo us all over again.

Babies and children welcome: high chairs. Booking advisable. Disabled: toilet. Separate room for parties, seats 18. Takeaway service. **Map 5 O5.**
For branches see index.

Fitzrovia

Lima London

31 Rathbone Place, W1T 1JH (3002 2640, www.limalondon.com). Tottenham Court Road tube. **Lunch served** noon- 2.30pm, **dinner served** 5.30-10.30pm Mon-Sat. **Main courses** £16-£26. **Set lunch** (Mon-Fri) £20 3 courses. **Credit** AmEx, MC, V. Peruvian

Part of the 'Peruvian wave' of restaurants to hit the capital in 2012, Lima London pitched itself squarely at the high end. The modish rear dining room mixes the hum of low-level beats with polite chatter; only the occasional Inca-patterned cushion adds colour. Well-drilled staff bring out a medley of carefully crafted small plates. Our sea bream ceviche saw chunks of fish in 'tiger's milk' (the ceviche marinade) flecked with shards of hot aji limo chilli, and pieces of roasted corn (added at the table so as not to lose their crunch). Later, we enjoyed thick wedges of suckling pig – part dense meat, part salty, crispy crackling – nicely matched by a rough corn mash spiked with two kinds of peppers (piquillo and green rocoto). Only pudding went too far, with a perfectly adequate scoop of sweet dulce de leche ice-cream subjected to a barrage of unnecessary frills: from crumbs of Andean maca root (a radish-like indigenous plant reputed to enhance the libido) to a splodge of beetroot emulsion. The experience is prefaced by 'complimentary' breads and amuse bouches, but you'll pay for it in the end, with a bill that's as high as the Lost City.

Available for hire. Babies and children welcome: high chairs. Booking advisable. Tables outdoors (4, pavement). Vegan dishes. **Map 17 B2.**

Wahaca

19-23 Charlotte Street, W1T 1RL (7323 2342, www.wahaca.co.uk). Goodge Street or Tottenham Court Road tube. **Breakfast served** 8.30-11.30am Mon-Fri; 9am-2pm Sat, Sun. **Meals served** noon-11pm Mon-Fri; 11.30am-11pm Sat; noon-10pm Sun. **Dishes** £3.60-£4.85. **Main courses** £6.95-£9.95. **Credit** AmEx, MC, V. Mexican

Thomasina Miers's Mexican 'market food' concept is now an eight-strong chain (plus two street-food vans). The restaurants all share a cheery vibe, with young, efficient staff buzzing round bright interiors, as well as a commitment to sustainability and animal welfare. The large Charlotte Street branch has a takeaway hatch (which sells a few ingredients such as salsas, chillies and fresh corn tortillas, as well as lunches) and a mezcal bar on the first floor, in addition to the ground-floor restaurant. Tortillas loom large – in soft, crisp, toasted and chip variations, and in flour and corn versions – though there are also a few grills (fish, steak or chicken served with green rice). But no one is complaining – it's tasty, addictive stuff, with recent meals only revealing one dud – the mushroom quesadillas.

Favourites include the steak burrito (which comes with a zingy chipotle salsa); the little black bean tostadas (refried beans with avocado salsa, crema, cheese and fresh tomato salsa); the spicy slaw; and the guacamole (served with either tortilla chips or fennel pork scratchings). Puddings include a version of churros y chocolate. Breakfast is served here too: indulge in huevos rancheros, a burrito filled with Brindisa chorizo, or a dulce de leche doughnut. Drinks run from mocktails to tequila.

Babies and children welcome: high chairs; nappy-changing facilities. Bookings not accepted. Disabled: toilet. Tables outdoors (4, pavement). Vegan dishes. **Map 17 B1.**
For branches see index.

Holborn

Bull Steak Expert

54 Red Lion Street, WC1R 4PD (7242 0708, www.thebullsteakexpert.com). Holborn tube. **Lunch served** noon-3pm Mon-Fri. **Dinner served** 5.30-10pm Mon-Fri; 5.30-10.30pm Sat. **Main courses** £14.50-£38. **Credit** AmEx, MC, V. Argentinian

With two Inns of Court close by, this area isn't short on wise guys. But for know-how in his chosen field, executive chef Daniel Veron surely matches his barrister neighbours. Their prices can't be too different, either – starters here run from £7 for marinated aubergines and bread to around £15 for grilled king prawns or a sausage platter. You'll pay £8 just for a couple of empanadas. But this is a man (a former consultant to Gaucho) who has his own signature steak cuts. The sense of an old master playing by his own rules is evident also in his left-field parrillada, which brings lamb to the steak-chorizo-morcilla party, plus corn on the cob, humitas and salad. It costs £56 for two, but at least you shouldn't need sides. Medallón de lomo may have looked pale and uninteresting, bereft of any deep brown caramelising, yet this steak gave near-giddying flavour. The restaurant doesn't take itself too seriously, either, despite that 'expert' tag. 'You sat by the window last time, didn't you?' asked a waitress of one couple. There's expertise in that kind of service too.

Available for hire. Babies and children admitted. Booking advisable. Separate room for parties, seats 22-28. **Map 10 M5.**

Marble Arch

Casa Malevo

23 Connaught Street, W2 2AY (7402 1988, www.casamalevo.com). Marble Arch tube. **Lunch served** noon-2.30pm Mon-Fri; noon-3.30pm Sat, Sun. **Dinner served** 6-10.30pm Mon-Sat; 6-10pm Sun. **Main courses** £9.95-£26.95. **Credit** AmEx, MC, V. Argentinian

The neighbourhood has a wealthy and exclusive vibe, but Casa Malevo is a little hub of welcoming homeliness. That's partly thanks to the small, domestic-feeling interior, with its old-fashioned dresser and a back conservatory that overlooks gardens and a children's play area. Decor includes framed photographs of appropriate images such as steaks or a gaucho's spur. The bare brick walls (Argentinian steak restaurant standard issue, it seems) are even rougher than most. Happily, flavours followed this intense pattern. Starters came in simple blue and white enamel dishes, but there was nothing basic about the cooking. Sweetbreads were superb, as at sister restaurant

Zoilo, their thin, sweet crust giving way to a creamy, quivering interior. A delicate salad of beetroot, goat's cheese and rocket showed that these grill-masters are sensitive souls really. The salty caramelising on our steaks was just as finely achieved, a sharp hit before the full-flavoured flesh within. Both sirloin and ribeye were first rate. Service was cheery and pally – the staff seemed as happy to be there as we were.

Available for hire. Babies and children welcome: high chairs. Booking advisable. Separate room for parties, seats 12. Tables outdoors (3, pavement). **Map 8 F6.**

Marylebone

★ Zoilo

9 Duke Street, W1U 3EG (7486 9699, www.zoilo.co.uk). Bond Street tube. **Lunch served** noon-3pm, **dinner served** 5.30-10.30pm Mon-Sat. **Meals served** noon-9.30pm Sun. **Dishes** £3.50-£31.95. **Credit** AmEx, MC, V. Argentinian

There were no tables when we called to book. 'But we're a very counter-focused restaurant,' they told us. This sounded like maître d' spin, but on arrival all became clear, because this place is pretty much all counters: ground floor hugging the bar; downstairs around the kitchen. The few diners sat at actual tables looked a little left out by comparison. Watch us work, look how good we are, it seems to say. Rightly so. This is deconstructed, small-plates Argentinian cooking, and it works – with flavours as good as these, you want as many different mouthfuls as you can get. An empanada's pastry was expert, as enjoyable as its creamy spinach and raisin filling. Fried chunks of queso de chancho ('head cheese') were like a seriously adult version of chicken nuggets. A miniature steak (softened up with the sous vide treatment then blasted on the grill) was flawless, the flavour like undiluted beef cordial. But the full choirs came out for the sous vide-cooked octopus (with 'tuna mayo', no less) and again for some sweetbreads, which were so delicate it seemed cruel to bite into them. But we did, and how gently they submitted. Desserts run from a traditional, ultra-sweet 'tres leches' milk cake to a tart passionfruit sorbet, and most of the all-Argentinian wine list is available by the glass or small carafe. Chef Diego Jacquet has also teamed with restaurateur Alberto Abbate to open sister restaurant Casa Malevo.

Booking advisable. Disabled: toilet. Tables outdoors (2, pavement). **Map 9 G6.**

Pimlico

★ Rodizio Preto

72 Wilton Road, SW1V 1DE (7233 8668, www.rodiziopreto.co.uk). Victoria tube/rail. **Meals served** noon-10.30pm Mon-Thur; noon-11pm Fri, Sat; noon-10pm Sun. **Buffet** £19.95 (£14.95 vegetarian). **Credit** AmEx, MC, V. Brazilian

Don't let those images of toned Brazilians deceive you – the boys and girls from Ipanema are partial to a bit of all-you-can-eat too. It's done with more style here than your usual pile-it-high joint, although the decor – grey colour scheme, cheap-looking fixtures and fittings, plastic plants, double-glazed patio doors to the outdoor terrace – isn't that appealing. Following the rodizio formula, servers (known as passadors) bring out skewers of various meats that they slice on to your plate until you've had enough, indicated by flipping a card over on its

side from green to red. Everything was fairly mediocre, from a toothless caipirinha onwards. Meats were flavoursome mostly in a salt-heavy way, while chicken hearts were old-boots tough. The most interesting cut was the cupim (traditionally the hump of zebu cattle), which tasted like a very English piece of boiled silverside. Quality was patchy at the generous buffet and salad displays, although there were certainly moreish items, including pao de queijo, farofa for sprinkling, and some claggy croquette-like morsels such as bolinhos and coxinhas. You'll pay £14.95 for the buffet alone, and an extra fiver for all that meat, but the interest lies primarily in quantity and novelty. *Babies and children welcome: children's menu; high chairs; nappy-changing facilities. Booking advisable weekends. Vegetarian menu.* **Map 15 J10.**
For branches see index.

Soho

La Bodega Negra
16 Moor Street, W1D 5NH (7758 4100, www.labodeganegra.com). Leicester Square tube.
Café **Open** noon-1am Mon-Sat; noon-11.30pm Sun. **Meals served** noon-midnight Mon-Sat; noon-11pm Sun. **Main courses** £8-£12.
Restaurant **Open** 6pm-1am Mon-Sat; 6-11.30pm Sun. **Meals served** 6pm-midnight Mon-Sat; 6-10.30pm Sun. **Main courses** £11.50-£27.50.
Both **Credit** AmEx, MC, V. Mexican
The neon sign outside reads 'sex shop'; the mannequin in the entrance wears a PVC gimp suit. But the real excitement begins when you descend the stairs into the bowels of this nightclub-like restaurant. It's so dark and loud you'll need a moment to adjust (the light bulbs have been blacked out). Unfortunately, the cooking is the least thrilling aspect, though effort is put into presentation. On our visit, soft flour tacos with a tender beef filling arrived beautifully arranged on a specially designed wooden board; a crunchy cheese and roasted tomato quesadilla was served 'open'; pinto beans with a spicy chorizo kick came in a dinky glazed bowl. The highlight was the dish least concerned with its own looks: a rich lamb shank in intensely dark juices. Seafood cazuela (a one-pot dish like a wet paella), containing clams, squid, prawns and mussels, was creamy, tangy and perfectly fine, but not especially memorable. Factor in the small portions and two-hour table limits (though you can decamp to the bar), and you might wonder what the fuss is all about. But that would be missing the point. You come here to see and be seen, and for a thrilling atmosphere and exceptionally friendly service. A must-try.
Bookings not accepted dinner (café); bookings essential (restaurant). Children admitted (café). Disabled: toilet (café). Separate rooms for parties (restaurant), seats 25. **Map 17 C3.**

★ Ceviche
17 Frith Street, W1D 4RG (7292 2040, www.cevicheuk.com). Leicester Square tube.
Tapas served noon-11.30pm Mon-Sat; noon-10.30pm Sun. **Tapas** £3-£13. **Credit** AmEx, MC, V. Peruvian
According to the PR hype, 2012 was to have been the year of Peruvian cuisine. In the end, only a handful of restaurants made any lasting impression on the capital's dining scene, but of those, Ceviche shone the brightest. Wisely, it chose not to showcase Peru's appetite for guinea pig or

its fondness for grains and starches (the potato in particular), but its most sexy and metropolitan export: ceviche. Here, citrus-cured fish is available in half a dozen different forms. We were wowed by the Don Ceviche, which saw large chunks of meaty sea bass with a still-raw centre surrounded by amarillo chilli 'tiger's milk' (the ceviche marinade) and scattered with slivers of chilli, raw red onion and fresh coriander, with soft, diced sweet potato providing textural contrast. But there's more to Ceviche than ceviche, with a menu that ranges from terrific chargrilled meat and fish skewers (anticuchos) to a simple but perfectly executed corn cake, with a creamy middle and dry crumbly edge. Factor in the please-all seating options (trendy at the steel counter-bar, more comfortable in the rear dining area), the charismatic, attentive staff and the party atmosphere, and it's no wonder this place has been such a huge hit.
Babies and children admitted. Booking advisable. Vegan dishes. Vegetarian menu. **Map 17 C3.**

Galeto NEW
33 Dean Street, W1D 4PW (7434 1409, www.galeto.co.uk). Tottenham Court Road tube.
Meals served noon-11.30pm Mon-Thur; noon-midnight Fri, Sat; noon-10.30pm Sun. **Main courses** £6.95-£11.75. **Credit** AmEx, MC, V. Brazilian
This Soho corner site opened as a Brazilian café-bar-restaurant in summer 2013. The vibe is casual, the decor bright, the beats samba and bossa nova, the staff Brazilian. A short menu serves simple snack food and main dishes, very much in the Brazilian way: nothing too fancy, quite a lot of starch, and hunks of meat that could do with a bit more in the way of seasoning and flavour. Galeto – which means 'small chicken' – makes a big cluck about its half-chicken dish being marinated for 24

hours, then 'grilled to perfection', but the piece we tried was oddly insipid, if generously portioned; Nando's does a better version. A burger also had oddly bland-tasting beef. Much better were the starters and side dishes. The coxinhas (pear-shaped stuffed snacks) transported us back to Rio, as did the little bolinhos de bacalhau (salt cod fish cakes). And the fried manioc chips were well worth their £3.70 price tag, crisp and intriguingly textured. But Galeto seems to be primarily a place to pop into for a caipirinha or Brahma beer while en route somewhere else.
Available for hire. Babies and children admitted. Bookings not accepted. Tables outdoors (2, pavement). Takeaway service. **Map 17 B3.**

West
Westbourne Grove

★ Taqueria
139-143 Westbourne Grove, W11 2RS (7229 4734, www.taqueria.co.uk). Notting Hill Gate tube. **Meals served** noon-11pm Mon-Thur; noon-11.30pm Fri, Sat; noon-10.30pm Sun. **Main courses** £3.90-£8.75. **Set lunch** (noon-4pm Mon-Fri) £6.50 1 course. **Credit** MC, V. Mexican
The word 'taqueria' is traditionally associated with street stands churning out endless tacos. They do that here too, but in rather more salubrious surroundings and with a clipboard-toting greeter thrown in for good measure. It's a charming, independent-feeling little place of two rooms, with dark wood floors and pristine white walls decorated with a few Mexican film posters. The food is equally unfussy: a dozen or so tacos (using corn tortillas made in-house daily), a handful of tostadas and a

Lima London

few monthly changing specials. One taco of 'house-made chorizo' came topped with flavoursome mince; a slow-cooked pork version contained meat as soft as cotton wool; another of steak was just the right side of chewy. A ceviche tostada had great texture – silky yet chunky pollack – but didn't taste like the freshest of catches. Service was swift if somewhat harried. To drink, there's Mexican beer, aguas frescas, an extensive selection of mezcales and tequilas, and some fine cocktails. The delicious habanero hot sauce is made by sister operation Cool Chile, and available to buy. The acoustics were our only real cause for complaint – something about the main dining room amplified our fellow diners' chatter to wince-making levels.
Available for hire. Babies and children welcome: high chairs. Bookings not accepted Fri-Sun. Takeaway service. **Map 7 A6.**

South

Battersea

Santa Maria del Sur
129 Queenstown Road, SW8 3RH (7622 2088, www.santamariadelsur.co.uk). Queenstown Road rail. **Lunch served** noon-3pm, **dinner served** 6-10pm daily. **Main courses** £19-£25. **Credit** MC, V. Argentinian
Santa Maria is all about the steak – Argentinian, of course. Which sounds good for a place that prides itself on its parrilla skills, but not when almost everything except the beef was a disappointment. A starter of sweetbreads had the vinegary taste of jarred garlic and a damp, crumbly texture, while

sardines on toast was no more than the sum of its parts. Except for some decent, volcanically hot chips, the sides and accompaniments also missed the mark: a green salad was wilting and undressed; chimichurri was a clot of dried herbs suspended in oil and vinegar; bread rolls were boring. And yet our steaks were flavour bombs just waiting to go off. The house red (a 2010 malbec, the dominant grape on the list) was a good match. The combination of raw brick and warm-toned wood gives the place a stylishly robust look, and it's roomy too – a good thing, because it's often full. The first-class steaks are no doubt what draws the punters, but co-owner Alberto Abbate can't plead ignorance of matters non-beef – he has also had a hand in Argentinian joints Zoilo and Casa Malevo, where they really know how to make the whole menu work.
Babies and children welcome: high chairs; nappy-changing facilities. Booking advisable weekends. Entertainment: musicians, tango 8.30pm Mon. Tables outdoors (4, pavement).

Brixton

★ Casa Morita
9 Market Row, Brixton Market, SW9 8LB (8127 5107, www.casamorita.com). Brixton tube/rail. **Meals served** noon-10.30pm Tue-Fri; 10am-10.30pm Sat; 10am-10pm Sun. **Main courses** £7-£10. **Credit** AmEx, MC, V. Mexican
It's a good thing Casa Morita's menu is so brief – the potent cocktails don't do much for your reading comprehension. Like the food, they're tasty and remarkably cheap (just £5 for a smoky mezcal margarita). The bargain prices suit the setting, even if this is no longer any old indoor market thanks to

the arrival of a plethora of interesting eateries over the past few years. Taco appetisers used good, chewy corn tortillas; the version with chicken mole was a little dry, but it packed a decent chocolate hit. Cochinita pibil, a Yucatán peninsula speciality of pulled pork, gave subtle notes of orange juice and achiote, and was painter's-palette colourful, with pink marinated onions, sweetcorn-studded rice and adobe brown refried beans. Enchiladas suizas were, thankfully, not too creamy, and enlivened by a slop of tangy green tomatillo salsa. Service can be market-trader curt, and there aren't any toilets attached to the restaurant (though there are some in the market). Do finish with the chocolate cake: laced with morita and árbol chillis, it's a zingy dream for just £3.75.
Available for hire. Babies and children welcome: high chairs. Booking advisable. Tables outdoors (4, market). Takeaway service. **Map 22 E2.**

South East

Bermondsey

Constancia
52 Tanner Street, SE1 3PH (7234 0676, www.constancia.co.uk). Bermondsey tube or London Bridge tube/rail. **Dinner served** 6-10.30pm Mon-Sat. **Meals served** 1.30-9.30pm Sun. **Main courses** £9.75-£25. **Credit** AmEx, MC, V. Argentinian
It's all set up so nicely for a steak joint, in theory. There's the Tanner Street location, with its bovine connotations, while the 'olde London' Southwark atmosphere seems just right for meats grilled on an

THE AMERICAS

Zoilo. See p30.

ancient-looking parrilla grill. Yet Constancia's bland exterior, wedged beneath a modern residential block, accurately set the tone for our evening. Decor is as you'd expect from a homely Argentine restaurant: wood, raw brick, a few gaucho allusions (mounted horse head, lasso) and that hefty grill. With its chains, encrusted bars and blackened brick surround in plain view, the grill promises big flavours. Yet while a couple of chorizo criollos were fine (it's hard to go wrong with sausage), an ojo de bife (ribeye) was stringy and light on flavour. Coming after appetisers of dry, shreddable serrano ham, and a basket of poor-quality sliced baguette, it was a deal breaker. Constancia charges less than many of its competitors, but that hardly makes it cheap – it would be worth raising prices by a few quid if the result was meat with that true Argentinian magic.
Babies and children welcome: high chairs. Booking advisable Fri, Sat. Disabled: toilet. **Map 12 R9.**

Blackheath

Buenos Aires Café
17 Royal Parade, SE3 0TL (8318 5333, www.buenosairesltd.com). Blackheath rail. **Lunch served** noon-2.30pm Mon-Fri; noon-4pm Sat, Sun. **Dinner served** 6-10pm daily. **Main courses** £9-£31. **Credit** MC, V.
Argentinian
Is there a better spot in London for an Argentinian steak joint than this, right on the edge of Blackheath? Gazing through the big windows, that could be the pampas out there, where those famously flavoursome cattle are raised. The interior is promising too: small, intimate, a little higgledy-piggledy. With all the framed images on the walls, from photos of celebrities (the Queen, Rod Stewart) to a pencil sketch of Lionel Messi, it's pleasingly unpretentious too, like a restaurant in La Boca. This down-to-earth vibe was reinforced by the presence

of pizza and pasta on the menu, alongside the classics, and the chalked-up soup of the day: 'mixed vegetables' is all it said. No shame in that. There was shame, however, in a starter of sweetbreads that were caked in charcoal. Our polite complaint was met with what seemed like suppressed annoyance. A steak also went unfinished – we had wanted medium (not maximum) rare. A pizza genovese would have been fine if it wasn't so soggy underneath, and for £14.70 too. The best part was the bread, a robust French-style loaf – the heath was looking very bleak as we left – the pampas it ain't.
Babies and children welcome: booster seats. Booking essential. Tables outdoors (3, pavement). Vegetarian menu.
For branch see index.

Elephant & Castle

★ Emanuel
18 Amelia Street, SE17 3PY (3556 0670). Elephant & Castle tube/rail. **Lunch served** noon-5pm Mon-Thur; noon-3pm Sun. **Meals served** noon-10pm Fri, Sat. **Main courses** £9.95-£13.95. **Set lunch** (noon-4pm Mon-Fri) £7 2 courses incl soft drink. **Credit** AmEx, MC, V. Peruvian
Beneath a budget hotel off Walworth Road, Emanuel celebrates Peru with vim and vigour. Folk or salsa music increases in volume as you descend the staircase to the brightly lit basement. Here, the red and white of the Peruvian flag dominate: white walls and floor tiles, white paper on red tablecloths. Videos of treasured vocalists play on the TV. Such concentrated nostalgia finds favour with the Peruvian clientele, some of whom sing along. We've yet to find better renditions of Peruvian cooking in London. All the classics are here, which makes picking starters especially difficult. Ceviche is the obvious choice, but what about the chupe de camarones (shrimp chowder) from the astoundingly cheap set lunch that our neighbours were relishing? Papa a la huancaína won out, and the entirely authentic, dense yellow boiled potatoes covered in spicy, creamy, cheesy sauce didn't disappoint. Main courses are mostly plain (meat and rice assemblies, or fried fish), excepting the superb arroz de mariscos: squid, red pepper and plump prawns in a mound of turmeric-coloured rice, with a scallop shell full of 'tiger's milk' (the salty, lime-juice ceviche marinade) with raw red onions. Topped by two giant prawns, and flanked by two mussels, the dish looked as good as it tasted. Drink Cusqueña negra beer or Inca Kola, round off with intensely sweet dulce de leche, and leave with a dance to your step.
Available for hire. Babies and children welcome: high chairs. Booking advisable. Takeaway service.

East
Shoreditch

Casa Negra NEW
54-56 Great Eastern Street, EC2A 3QR (7033 7360, www.casanegra.co.uk). Shoreditch High Street rail. **Meals served** noon-midnight Mon-Sat. **Dinner served** 6-10.30pm Sun. **Main courses** £14-£20. **Set lunch** (noon-3pm Mon-Fri) £9.50 2 courses, £12.50 3 courses. **Credit** AmEx, MC, V. Mexican
The people behind Soho's La Bodega Negra have opened a relatively understated branch of their speakeasy-style Mexican bar-restaurant in

Shoreditch. What was once the elegant Great Eastern Dining Rooms now resembles a Peckham squat circa 1985. Tat art on black walls, coloured light bulbs dangling from wires, folding metal chairs and dark patterned rugs add to the contrived-shabby look. The main feature is a counter styled like a bar shack in a colonia (shanty town), complete with corrugated roof and advertising hoardings. A frozen margarita hit the spot, with quality tequilas and fruit juices used. The tacos were the weak link: pork pibil lacked the expected citrus tang, while fish tacos tasted overwhelmingly of vinegar from pickled jalapeños. A main course of beef short-rib was the best dish: a big piece of meat slow-cooked until virtually falling from the bone, its smoky chipotle chilli heat beautifully pepped up with sharp-sweet pineapple salsa. People come here looking for a Shoreditch scene, and as the music cranks up, maybe they'll find it. Service was cheerful and attentive on our visit – though waitresses wearing stone-washed jeans is perhaps a shade of irony too far.
Babies and children welcome: high chairs. Booking essential Fri, Sat. Disabled: toilet. Separate room for parties, seats 20. **Map 6 R4.**

Spitalfields

Boho Mexica
151-153 Commercial Street, E1 6BJ (7377 8418, www.bohomexica.co.uk). Liverpool Street tube/rail. **Lunch served** noon-2.30pm Wed-Fri. **Brunch served** 12.30-4.30pm Sat, Sun. **Dinner served** 5.30-10pm Mon, Tue; 5.30-11pm Wed, Thur; 5-11.30pm Fri, Sat; 5-10.30pm Sun. **Main courses** £10.50-£15.95. **Credit** AmEx, MC, V. Mexican
Boho Mexica's claims to authenticity rely on its domestic labour-of-love approach – chef Tia Patty, the owner's aunt, uses recipes learnt from her mother. While a starter of bland guacamole disappointed, painstaking care showed through in another of slow-cooked beef brisket, while crispy tostadas of green plantain topped with prawns and roasted habanero peppers were only happily glugging back our cocktails. The long, slim interior feels fresh and lively, with a bar that snakes through the whole restaurant. Cartoons of cocktail party guests on the walls reinforces the vibe of bonhomie; elsewhere, it's all mock adobe and colourful Mexican posters. The seating plan is casual, with places at the bar and even a tiny corner table for one – you could come in for tacos and a beer without feeling uncomfortable – plus a few tables set away from the chatter-filled hustle and bustle. Mains of pulled pork enchiladas with salsa roja, and puerco enchilanchado (chilli-marinated pork with plentiful side dishes) combined belly-filling substance with vibrant flavours, but pulpos encebollados (squid and baby octopus spiked with chilli, onion and lime) was far too tart.
Available for hire. Babies and children admitted. Booking advisable. Disabled: toilet. **Map 6 R5.**

North East
Hackney

Buen Ayre
50 Broadway Market, E8 4QJ (7275 9900, www.buenayre.co.uk). London Fields rail or bus 26, 48, 55. **Lunch served** noon-3pm Mon-Fri;

noon-3.30pm Sat, Sun. **Dinner served** 6-10.30pm daily. **Main courses** £13-£25.50. **Set meal** (Mon-Fri) £12 3 courses. **Credit** MC, V. Argentinian

Broadway Market's atmosphere of laid-back revelry should make it the perfect spot for Buen Ayre, chef-proprietor John Patrick Rattagan's attempt to bring casual Argentinian meat feasting to London. The layout is right – one small room, simply furnished, with the asado grill the focus at its centre. The beef on our 'deluxe' mixed grill (£53 for two, plus £4.50 for a side of above-average chips) certainly looked every charred, sticky inch the parrilla victim. Yet it didn't elicit the gushing response that other steak specialists in the capital can. What felt more appropriate to the no-frills set-up (and service, it must be said) was breaking into the crumbly black pudding, scooping up the oregano-sprinkled provolone and pricking the excellent sausages. Cheaper steaks are available, and one of those, the sweetbreads or a couple of chorizo would have suited our overall sense of the place better than that expensive parrilla. Wines are exclusively Argentinian, and desserts are the usual super-sweet selection, including assorted ice-creams, pancake with dulce de leche, and flan (crème caramel).
Babies and children welcome: high chairs. Booking advisable. Disabled: toilet. Tables outdoors (8, garden).

North
Camden & Chalk Farm

★ Café Chula
75 West Yard, Camden Lock Place, NW1 8AF (7284 1890, www.cafechula.co.uk). Camden Town tube. **Meals served** 8am-5pm Mon-Wed; 8am-10pm Thur; 8am-midnight Fri; 9am-1am Sat; 9am-5pm Sun. **Main courses** £5.50-£9. **Credit** MC, V. Mexican

Café Chula was riffing on a festival vibe the night we visited, with a two-piece band playing Latin-flavoured Bob Marley and Oasis covers. Decor is atmospherically distressed (scuffed paint, flaking mirrors, adobe-effect walls) and there are good

views of the canal, but the loud music sent us scarpering to the outdoor seating. A jug of weak margarita was out of step with the party atmosphere; more disappointing was that the most unusual taco topping – lengua, described as cow tongue – had run out. Once it's gone, it's gone, we supposed, with such a specialist ingredient; it was less understandable that mushrooms were off the menu too. We plumped for braised pork tacos instead, and the meat was delicious if lacking the described crispness. A generously sized main of enchiladas suizas (chicken with salsa verde and cheese) was a little bland, and there were no bottles of sauce on the table to spark it into life. A plate of camarones borrachas ('drunken prawns', enlivened with chilli and tequila), went the other way: flavoursome but too salty. One last unhappy festival parallel – the single unisex toilet really didn't smell so good.
Available for hire. Babies and children admitted. Tables outdoors (7, balcony). Vegetarian menu. **Map 27 C2.**

Highbury

Garufa
104 Highbury Park, N5 2XE (7226 0070, http://garufa.co.uk). Arsenal tube. **Meals served** 11am-10.30pm daily. **Main courses** £10.50-£40. **Set lunch** £10 1 course incl glass of wine, beer or soft drink. **Credit** MC, V. Argentinian

With leafy Highbury Park just down the road, and warm, unfussy decor – plain wood furniture and floor, rugged brick – the stage is set for simple, fruits-of-the-pampas pleasures. Which was what we got. The kitchen is separated from the dining room by a theatre-style red velvet curtain, and the food did its best to put on a show. Some non-Argentinian starters were available for a while – a quinoa salad, for instance, and tamales de pollo – but lack of interest saw them removed. It's hard to imagine them competing with the sweetbreads in any case: these little chunks, served with a tiny morcilla croquette and dressed rocket, were excellent. The parrillada mixta was, well, mixed. The flavour of two steaks – one a lean rump, the other a more tangled, sinewy ribeye – was just

about up to Argentinian standards. But a piece of pork, although tasty, looked terrible – curled at the edge like something you'd get with two veg at a greasy spoon. It sounds like damning with faint praise, but the chips were the stars here: they seemed to have been subjected to multiple fries, and were all the better for it.
Babies and children welcome: children's menu; high chairs; nappy-changing facilities. Booking advisable Fri, Sat. Takeaway service.

Islington

★ Tierra Peru
164 Essex Road, N1 8LY (7354 5586, www.tierraperu.co.uk). Angel tube or Essex Road rail or bus 38, 73. **Meals served** noon-11pm daily. **Main courses** £9-£19. **Set lunch** (noon-3pm) £12 2 courses, £15 3 courses. **Credit** AmEx, MC, V. Peruvian

From the Andes to the Pacific, the highs and lows of Peruvian terrain help to explain its varied cuisine. But what was going on behind the scenes at this small Essex Road eatery to account for our visit's ups and downs we could only guess at. Things began badly after our booked table was given away – though a couple of complimentary pisco sours helped keep us sweet. The starters were a success. Grilled baby octopus appeared smothered by black Peruvian botija olive cream, yet the sauce was light as sea foam and the olive flavour vibrant. A ceviche was fantastic, the fish barely coaxed out of rawness. At this stage, the owners' decision to move on from their original Camden market stall seemed justified, so it was a shame that one main – lightly battered fish and cassava – arrived unacceptably lukewarm. And the seafood in a creamy picante de mariscos stew seemed too subdued and insubstantial. The lengthy menu, trying to cover all their nation's culinary bases, probably doesn't help. Decor is simple – polished dark-wood tables, long brown banquette, white walls adorned with colour photos – and the drinks list includes Peruvian beer, wines and Inca Kola.
Available for hire. Babies and children welcome: high chairs. Disabled: toilet. Takeaway service. **Map 5 P1.**

Casa Negra. See p33.

Brasseries

To have a brasserie open in the neighbourhood says something about a district. It's a mark of urbanity, a place where deliciously naughty breaks can be taken, mid-afternoon, to indulge in meals that are out of kilter with the breakfast-lunch-dinner norm. You'd have searched in vain for a brasserie in Dalston 20 years ago, but now **Jones & Sons** and **Floyd's** have both appeared in the past year, with **Mr Buckley's** and **Rawduck** also opening close by in Hackney. And café society in Peckham – which once meant Bert's pie and mash shop – now includes the hip Barcelona-style venue **Peckham Refreshment Rooms**.

In central London, brasseries fulfil a function other than that of the neighbourhood hangout, being great for tourists, shoppers and theatregoers who might not be able or willing to fit in with traditional meal times. Our favourites continue to be the grand destination venues: the **Wolseley** on Piccadilly and (especially) its sibling the **Delaunay** on Aldwych, with **Caravan** in King's Cross also taking some beating. But this year's big noise has been the opening of **Balthazar** (just around the corner from the Delaunay): a handsome Parisian-by-way-of-Manhattan brasserie with nostalgic transatlantic dishes.

Central

Belgravia

Colbert
51 Sloane Square, SW1W 8AX (7730 2804, www.colbertchelsea.com). Sloane Square tube. **Meals served** 8am-11pm Mon-Thur; 8am-11.30pm Fri, Sat; 8am-10.30pm Sun. **Main courses** £6.95-£30. **Credit** AmEx, MC, V.
This Sloane Square brasserie (from the group behind the Wolseley, the Delaunay and Brasserie Zédel) pays homage to grand Continental tradition with marble, linen napkins and mirrors aplenty, plus a classic French and middle-European menu. Colbert feels more casual and local than its siblings, and the posters in the booth-lined bar area advertising performances by Laurence Olivier and Vivien Leigh next door at the Royal Court Theatre lend a sense of history to the new arrival. It also trumps the others with pavement tables, providing a front-row seat from which to admire the beautiful people of SW3. Mains such as wiener schnitzel are well executed, but you need to order side dishes to compose a rounded meal, and this is where it makes its money: £3.50 for a side salad consisting of five leaves of Boston lettuce and a few slices of spring onion is a bit cheeky. Still, for the most part, the food is very tasty: a salty smoked haddock florentine – served on a bed of spinach, under a perfectly poached egg, all in a buttery cream sauce – was deliciously decadent. The menu is strong on breakfast and snack dishes too – croque grand'mère is a perfectly fried brioche filled with melted comté cheese, bayonne ham and béchamel sauce, topped with a fried egg. For our money, Colbert serves the best lunch in the area.
Babies and children welcome: high chairs. Booking advisable. Disabled: toilet. Tables outdoors (10, pavement). **Map 15 G11**.

Bloomsbury

Gail's Kitchen NEW
11-13 Bayley Street, WC1B 3HD (7323 9694, www.gailskitchen.co.uk). Tottenham Court Road tube. **Breakfast served** 7-11am Mon-Sat; 8am-noon Sun. **Lunch served** noon-3pm Mon-Sat; noon-4pm Sun. **Dinner served** 5.30-10.30pm Mon-Sat. **Main courses** £7-£9.50. **Credit** MC, V.
Pastries, cakes, sweetmeats and dinky sandwiches – this is the stuff for which upmarket bakery chain Gail's is known. But this site, inside the long-established Myhotel, is a little different to the rest, as it's the company's first foray into the restaurant business. Ginger banquettes line one wall; salvaged-wood tables and white wire-frame chairs punctuate the room. As you'd expect, bread plays a central role on the menu of small plates, with dishes such as mackerel rillettes with toasted rye. Smoked shell-on prawns, served with a charred slice of caramelised garlic-pocked bread, came in an appealing pile, ready to be dunked into a pot of aïoli. Fresh from the pizza oven on display in the open kitchen, a 'white' pizza took the form of an oblong of pillowy baked dough drizzled with olive oil and topped with rich burrata cheese, violet artichoke wedges, parma ham and bread croûtons for added bite. But the chefs aren't just here to showcase their baking skills, as a well-executed dish of braised shin of beef with al dente pearl barley proved. Although the small plates are a little on the pricey side, friendly service and an appealing menu add up to a winning formula.
Available for hire. Babies and children welcome: high chairs. Booking advisable breakfast; Fri, Sat. Disabled: toilet. Tables outdoors (5, terrace). Takeaway service. **Map 17 C1**.

City

Bread Street Kitchen
One New Change, 10 Bread Street, EC4M 9AB (3030 4050, www.breadstreetkitchen.com). St Paul's tube. **Breakfast served** 7-10.45am Mon-Fri. **Meals served** 10.45am-11pm Mon-Fri; 11.30am-11pm Sat; 11am-8pm Sun. **Main courses** £12.50-£31. **Credit** AmEx, MC, V.
Part of the Gordon Ramsay Holdings stable, Bread Street Kitchen is set in the glitzy One New Change shopping centre (next to Jamie Oliver's Barbecoa) and on the doorstep of St Paul's Cathedral, so its customers are nicely diverse: City suits, tourists, shoppers, families. The space is vast – you can

barely see from one end to the other – with floor-to-ceiling windows on one side, and a long open kitchen on the other. The wow-factor design (courtesy of Russell Sage, responsible for many of London's best-looking restaurants) takes industrial-cum-brasserie chic to a new level, using curved banquettes in gold and green to break up the space, and throwing in plenty of exposed ductwork, white tiles and metal grilles. The menu is pretty huge too, with influences from Britain, Italy, the States and beyond; there's lots of fish, but also pork chops and ribeye (courtesy of the Josper grill), and the likes of oriental duck salad. It's a fun place to eat, with friendly and focused staff, and mostly excellent cooking. Roasted cod with capers, artichoke and a red wine sauce was hearty and rich, but a salad of couscous, cranberries, radish and mint was too much like a M&S takeaway pot. Sides include macaroni cheese and classy chips – fluffy interior, crunchy golden exterior. BSK also offers breakfast and weekend brunch, and there's a bar downstairs, at street level.

Babies and children welcome: children's menu; crayons; high chairs. Booking advisable. Disabled: lift; toilet. **Map 11 P6**.

Duck & Waffle

40th Floor, Heron Tower, 110 Bishopsgate, EC2N 4AY (3640 7310, www.duckandwaffle. com). Liverpool Street tube/rail. **Breakfast served** 6-10.30am, **lunch served** 11.30am-3.30pm Mon-Fri. **Brunch served** 9am-3.30pm Sat, Sun. **Dinner served** 5.30pm-11pm, **reduced menu served** midnight-6am daily. **Dishes** £17-£38. **Credit** AmEx, MC, V.

There's a dedicated entrance for the restaurants in Heron Tower, from where a glass lift will whizz you in seconds up to Duck & Waffle on the 40th floor, or its glitzier sibling Sushisamba (*see p29*) two floors below. The views are, as you might expect, stunning – if you're pointed in the right direction and, preferably, sitting at a window table (many of which are for two diners only). Alternatively, linger in the entrance bar, where you can press your nose against the glass and gawp unhindered. Food is an on-trend mix of small plates, raw offerings (oysters, ceviche) and a few main courses (including roast chicken and the namesake duck confit and waffle). Our dishes ranged widely, from the spot-on (three dense pollock balls in creamy lobster sauce) to bonkers (who thought it a good idea to combine beetroot chunks with watery goat's curd and sticky knobs of honeycomb crisp?). Prices are as sky-high as the setting: it cost £8 for a harissa-tinged herdwick mutton slider that was undoubtedly tasty, but came unadorned and vanished in a mouthful. Desserts of cold rice pudding, and chocolate brownie sundae, were better (and bigger). Service wavered between keen and offhand. Another downer: all that glass, plus marble and wood tables and a low ceiling (with yellow 'waffle' design), means the acoustics are terrible. Duck &Waffle is open 24/7, so breakfast or late-night snacks are further possibilities.

Available for hire. Babies and children welcome: high chairs. Booking essential. Disabled: lift; toilet. Separate room for parties, seats 18. **Map 12 R6**.

Perkin Reveller NEW

The Wharf at the Tower of London, EC3N 4AB (3166 6949, www.perkinreveller.co.uk). Tower Hill tube or Tower Gateway tube/DLR. **Breakfast served** 9-11.30am, **lunch served**

Bird of Smithfield

11.30am-3.30pm, **tea served** 3.30-5.30pm daily. **Dinner served** 5.30-10.30pm Mon-Sat. **Main courses** £12.50-£28. **Set lunch** (Mon-Sat) £16 2 courses, £19 3 courses. **Credit** AmEx, MC, V.

This dining room of sparse glass and white walls is named after the cook's apprentice in Chaucer's *Canterbury Tales*, who was more partial to revelry than hard work. The reason for the choice of name only becomes clear when you realise that the location, on Tower Wharf, had its initial construction overseen by Chaucer. Luckily, the Reveller's executive chef, Andrew Donovan, takes his cooking more seriously than did the apprentice Perkin. Food is a seasonal mix of classic British and Modern European dishes, with a few steaks for good measure. A clever starter of venison 'cottage pie' – tender chunks of juniper-scented venison topped with a creamy potato purée foam scattered with crisp ham pieces – was served in a glass teacup. Equally well presented and flavoured was the rich cornish fish stew. It had been infused with saffron, and filled with a mix of white fish, shellfish and baby vegetables; the overall effect was similar to a bouillabaisse. To finish, a vanilla cheesecake made with Rosary goat's cheese had bold flavour and light texture, balanced well by a berry sorbet. The Perkin Reveller may not be able to compete with the conviviality of the 14th-century taverns of Chaucer's time, but it's worth a pilgrimage if you're looking for quality cooking among the tourist traps near the Tower.

Available for hire. Babies and children welcome: children's menu; high chairs; nappy-changing facilities. Booking advisable. Disabled: toilet. Tables outdoors (5, terrace). **Map 12 R8**.

Clerkenwell & Farringdon

Bird of Smithfield NEW

26 Smithfield Street, EC1A 9LB (7559 5100, www.birdofsmithfield.com). Farringdon tube/rail. **Bar Open/snacks served** 8am-10pm Mon-Sat. **Snacks** £2-£15.

Restaurant **Lunch served** noon-2.45pm, **dinner served** 6-10pm Mon-Sat. **Main courses** £12-£27.

Both **Credit** AmEx, MC, V.

Do you ever tire of queuing for pop-up diners that serve dog's dinners? Then join this club, which requires no membership and where the staff greet you with smiles, a comfy seat and your favourite drink. Bird's five narrow floors cover the gamut: rooftop bar, smart dining room, lounge bar, private dining room and basement cocktail bar. It's open from breakfast to dinner, then late into the night. Yet it still feels like a smart, if slightly *rus in urbe*, members' club with its well-drilled service, laid-back vibe and *Country Living* decor. Chef-proprietor Alan Bird has headed the kitchen at the Ivy and was executive chef at the Soho House Group, so it's little wonder the menu also reflects a particular kind of modern Britishness. A starter of lightly soused baby vegetables had an intense, earthy flavour of carrot and radish – the very essence of a springtime garden. A buttery sole was topped with savoury brown shrimps and the slightly bitter leaves of foraged sea beet and sea purslane. Calf's liver was trimmed into tidy tiles, then pan-fried and topped with sage butter, crisped bacon and slow-cooked onions. Puddings included the irresistible pun of Bird's custard with rhubarb.

Babies and children admitted until 4pm. Booking advisable. Disabled: toilet. Separate room for parties, seats 26. Tables outdoors (6, terrace). **Map 11 O5**.

Potato Merchant

55 Exmouth Market, EC1R 4QL (7837 0009, www.thepotatomerchant.com). Angel tube or bus 19, 38, 341. **Breakfast served** 9.30am-noon Mon-Fri. **Brunch served** 10am-5pm Sat; 11am-4pm Sun. **Meals served** noon-10.30pm Mon-Sat. **Dishes** £2.50-£14. **Credit** AmEx, MC, V.

This small-plates restaurant uses the world's favourite tuber as its marketing shtick. There are some 200 varieties of spud in the UK, and Potato Merchant exists to celebrate them. Yet the kitchen only cooks with a limited selection of common-or-garden types – just a dozen varieties on our visit. The potatoes are given various northern European treatments. Tartiflette should have been a highlight – reblochon cheese, lardons and onions give the dish a fatty attraction – but served in a tiny, paper-lined punnet, the portion was a little too meagre, and too dry. Fat chips, fried in beef dripping, were crisp on the outside, but disappointingly floury on the inside. Salt-cod fritters were served with a good mayo, though the salt cod within needed more texture, less goo. The best dish had pink fir apples as a mere accompaniment to the centrepiece – smoked herring that was firm, oily and of Scandinavian perfection. But the shortcomings need to be set against PM's usefulness as a casual, drop-in sort of bar for the post-Atkins diet era; the own-made crisps are flavoursome, salty and go well with a beer or glass of wine.

Available for hire. Babies and children welcome: high chairs. Booking advisable. Disabled: toilet. Tables outdoors (8, pavement). Map 5 N4.

Covent Garden

Balthazar NEW

4-6 Russell Street, WC2E 7BN (3301 1155, www.balthazarlondon.com). Covent Garden tube. **Breakfast served** 7.30-11am, **lunch served** noon-3.15pm Mon-Fri. **Brunch served** 10am-3.30pm Sat, Sun. **Afternoon tea served** 3-5.30pm daily. **Dinner served** 5.30-11pm Mon-Thur; 5.30-11.45pm Fri, Sat; 5.30-10.30pm Sun. **Main courses** £13-£37. **Credit** AmEx, MC, V.
In early 2013, Keith McNally's much-anticipated NYC import Balthazar finally opened, and London got to see what this Manhattan interpretation of a French brasserie was actually like. The response was positive, and for weeks afterwards it was hard to get a table. Chef Robert Reid has tinkered little with the nostalgic transatlantic menu, and we loved signature dishes such as the onion soup (grilled gruyère lid on thick country bread, immersed in a rich and sweet chicken stock); duck shepherd's pie was another powerfully flavoured treat. More recently, some of the gloss seems to have worn off (though service remains prompt and friendly). The cheeseburger, no bargain at £17, was a chunky patty but had little flavour, and needed more than the limited, bland trimmings to give it an oomph that might have justified the price tag. A pleasant gruyère and herb omelette tasted as though it had lingered a little too long at the pass. Best was pavlova (one of several delightfully retro desserts) – it may not have looked like a classic version (the meringue sat on the fruit, rather than the other way round), but it tasted good. Bread, from master baker Jon Rolfe, is a must-try. Balthazar London mimics the New York original perfectly, with red awnings, red leather banquettes, giant antiqued mirrored walls and mosaic floors, but to English eyes, the decor can look a little too close to any old chain brasserie. On current showing, the Delaunay (a few streets away) offers more bang for your buck.
Babies and children welcome: high chairs; nappy-changing facilities. Disabled: lift; toilet. Map 18 E4.

Bill's

13 Slingsby Place, St Martin's Courtyard, WC2E 9AB (7240 8183, www.bills-website.co.uk). Covent Garden tube. **Meals served** 8am-11pm Mon-Fri; 9am-11pm Sat; 9am-10.30pm Sun. **Main courses** £8.95-£15.95. **Credit** AmEx, MC, V.

Growing like topsy, Bill's now stretches from its East Sussex home right across the south of England and into Wales. This St Martin's Courtyard branch was the first in the capital and now one of two in Covent Garden alone. The formula is clearly working. Grocery-lined shelves add plenty of colour, if not turnover. Cutlery is piled in old McCann's oatmeal tins. Blackboards are 'chalked' with recipes, chirpy ideas for increasing your spend, and invitations to become friends on Facebook. The broad menu and relaxed style suits many an occasion, from breakfast to post-theatre cocktails. Several tables were indulging in traditional afternoon tea on our visit (at under a tenner, it's a wallet-friendly alternative to nearby hotels), but we opted for the 'lighter mains' section of the menu. Grilled sea bream wasn't London's most sparkling, and paired with a 'cous cous' of grated raw cauliflower, watercress and lemon, the predominant flavour was bitterness. Warm pecan pie arrived a mix of searingly hot and lukewarm in temperature, though the flavour was fine and the malted banana ice-cream that accompanied it was delicious. Service was well meaning if a tad slow and scatty. In all, Bill's is good to know.
Babies and children welcome: children's menu; high chairs; nappy-changing facilities. Disabled: toilet. Tables outdoors (6, courtyard). Takeaway service. Vegan dishes. Vegetarian menu. Map 18 D4.
For branches see index.

★ Delaunay

55 Aldwych, WC2B 4BB (7499 8558, www.the delaunay.com). Covent Garden or Temple tube, or Charing Cross tube/rail. **Breakfast served** 7-11.30am Mon-Fri; 8-11am Sat, Sun. **Brunch served** 11am-5pm Sat, Sun. **Tea served** 3-6.30pm daily. **Meals served** 11.30am-midnight Mon-Sat; 11.30am-11pm Sun. **Main courses** £6-£27. **Cover** (lunch, dinner) £2. **Credit** AmEx, MC, V.
The Delaunay was Chris Corbin and Jeremy King's 2012 follow-up to the Wolseley and, like that handsome behemoth, it looks like it's been here for decades. Grand European cafés provide the inspiration, and the interior is a treat – a David Collins-designed mix of green leather banquette seating, dark wood, brass rails, antique mirrors and a black and white marble floor. The café and bar area leads through to the main dining room; next door is the Counter (a café serving savouries, cakes and coffee, with takeaway available). The menu runs from breakfast to dinner, taking in afternoon tea (a not-to-be-missed opportunity to try the Austrian-biased cakes, all made in-house). There's a dish of the day (goulash, say, or chicken curry), soups, salads and egg dishes, plus savouries (welsh and buck rarebits) and crustacea. The sandwich selection runs from croque monsieur to a brioche burger with french fries. Starters include steak tartare and smoked salmon plates; mains take in kedgeree and choucroute à l'Alsacienne. There's also a good choice of sausages, served with potato salad, sauerkraut and caramelised onions: try the käsekrainer (an Austrian meat and cheese version). In short, there's something for everyone, at prices that aren't greedy given the setting, the quality of the service and the assuredness of the menu.
Babies and children welcome: crayons; high chairs; nappy-changing facilities. Booking advisable. Disabled: toilet. Separate rooms for parties, seating 8, 12 and 24. Vegetarian menu. Map 18 F4.

Fitzrovia

Riding House Café

43-51 Great Titchfield Street, W1W 7PQ (7927 0840, www.ridinghousecafe.co.uk). Oxford Circus tube. **Breakfast served** 7.30am-noon Mon-Fri; 9-11.30am Sat, Sun. **Lunch served** noon-3.30pm Mon-Fri; noon-4pm Sat, Sun. **Dinner served** 6-10pm Mon-Sat; 6-9.30pm Sun. **Main courses** £11-£25. **Credit** AmEx, MC, V.
Riding House Café really does have a bit of everything. You can sit at individual settings, or at the grand candelabra-lit communal dining table; in the more secluded dining room, or on low chairs in the lounge – or soak up the action at the buzzing bar. There are antiques, curios (wall lamps made from stuffed squirrels, for instance) and architectural salvage from around the globe. You can roll up in a work suit, or shorts and flip flops. Bring your agent or your kids. You could drink a coffee, a pre-dinner cocktail, a Riding House mocktail, something from the wide-ranging wine list, or a beer. You might eat full-sized brasserie dinners, tapas-like sharing plates, or bar snacks. Come for breakfast, lunch, dinner, weekend brunch, Sunday roast, or anything in between. It's whatever eating experience you want it to be, though there's little choice in your co-diners – an almost uniformly media crowd. The food, though nice enough, didn't blow our minds. The Moorish lamb was succulent and tender, the soft-shell crabs crunchy, the cheeseburger juicy and the chips tasty, yet there was nothing we'll remember in three days' time. The cocktails, on the other hand, are creative concoctions topped with mini salad sculptures. With attentive service and a lively atmosphere, this is a great place to watch Fitzrovia go by.
Babies and children welcome: children's menu; high chairs; nappy-changing facilities. Booking advisable. Disabled: toilet. Separate room for parties, seats 14. Map 9 J5.

Villandry

170 Great Portland Street, W1W 5QB (7631 3131, www.villandry.com). Great Portland Street tube.
Café/bar **Open** 7.30am-10.30pm Mon-Fri; 8am-10.30pm Sat; 9am-6pm Sun. **Main courses** £11.50-£15.
Restaurant **Lunch served** noon-3pm, **dinner served** 6-10.30pm Mon-Fri. **Meals served** 8am-10.30pm Sat; 9am-6pm Sun. **Main courses** £11.50-£22.50. **Set meal** £30 3 courses incl coffee, £40 4 courses incl coffee.
Both **Credit** AmEx, MC, V.
Villandry's marbled pâtisserie counter – crammed with temptations such as salted caramel and walnut tarts, blackberry éclairs and chocolate mousses – deservedly takes centre stage at this self-proclaimed 'grand café'. The venue has several distinct areas. The café overlooking Great Portland Street is the buzziest, even on a Saturday evening. Behind it, the refurbished central bar strikes a rather imposing note, thanks to a formidable shade of red, while the more formal dining room on the Bolsover Street side is, by contrast, a model of understatement. It's not often you find a restaurant where diners are happy to eat alone, but this is one such place, owing to the unshowy, affordable menu and the chance to sit unhurried and unjudged by easygoing staff. The menu covers all bases: burgers, salads, steaks, plenty of fish and seafood, and weekend brunch. Duck confit was tender and moist, and plum

crumble a deliciously fruity concoction topped with chantilly cream. Villandry seems genuinely happy to accommodate your whims, whether that's a simple quiche in the restaurant or takeaway chocolates from the compact grocery area. It seems the owners have thought of everything: come summer, there's a juice bar and a counter serving frozen yoghurt and ice-cream.

Available for hire. Babies and children welcome: children's menu; high chairs; nappy-changing facilities. Booking advisable. Tables outdoors (13, pavement). Takeaway service. **Map 3 H5**.
For branch see index.

Holborn

Fields Bar & Kitchen NEW

Lincoln's Inn Fields, WC2A 3LH (7242 5351, www.fieldsbarandkitchen.com). Holborn tube.
Breakfast served *Summer* 8-11.30am daily. *Winter* 9-11.30am daily. **Meals served** *Summer* noon-9pm daily. *Winter* noon-4.30pm daily. **Main courses** £8.95-£14.50. **Credit** AmEx, MC, V.
Benugo has a thing for ancient spots. Operating from venerable institutions such as the British Museum and Westminster Abbey, the chain has taken its catering to a fair few now. This latest venue is no less invested with history, as Lincoln's Inn Fields was laid out in the 17th century by Inigo Jones. Situated slap-bang in the centre of the park, next to the tennis courts, Fields is anything but fusty and old-fashioned. The long space was formerly home to the Terrace in the Fields, and has changed little since then. In appearance, it's somewhere between a sailing boat and a Scandinavian summerhouse, with chunky blond-wood beams and wall-to-ceiling windows. The food is unlikely to offend, or get pulses racing. As well as familiar grab-and-go Benugo all-day café items – muffins, sandwiches and the like – there's an Italianate restaurant menu featuring pizzas, salads and a handful of meat dishes. A crisp-edged margherita was decent enough, scattered with rocket and served fresh from the wood-fired oven. Cornish lamb cutlets were tender and juicy, yet the accompanying caponata seemed rather closer to a finely chopped ratatouille. Fields was busy with local lawyers and business people on our visit: understandably so, given the attractive setting. The outdoor tables also look appealing.
Available for hire. Babies and children welcome: high chairs; nappy-changing facilities. Booking advisable. Disabled: toilet. Tables outdoors (16, terrace). Takeaway service. **Map 10 M6**.

King's Cross

★ Caravan King's Cross HOT 50

Granary Building, 1 Granary Square, N1C 4AA (7101 7661, www.caravankingscross.co.uk). King's Cross St Pancras tube/rail. **Breakfast served** 8-11.30am Mon-Fri. **Brunch served** 10am-4pm Sat, Sun. **Meals served** noon-10.30pm Mon-Fri; 5-10.30pm Sat. **Main courses** £13-£17. **Credit** AmEx, MC, V.
Whereas the original Caravan (on Exmouth Market) is a small space, with a neighbourhood vibe, this offshoot is an altogether bigger, more urbane operation. The large, industrial-looking room lacks intimacy, but has a laid-back buzz and great people-watching opportunities. The ethos is the same in both branches: welcoming, efficient staff and a menu of what they call 'well travelled food'. Most are small plates – deep-fried duck egg with baba

ganoush, chorizo oil and crispy shallots, say, or grits, collard greens and brown shrimp butter – plus a few large plates and (at King's Cross only) a handful of first-class pizzas. The results are always interesting: recent favourites include a richly flavoured celeriac gratin with parsley, walnut and a brandy apple topping, and naughty-but-nice crispy fried chicken (in cubes) with jerk mayo and pawpaw salsa (both King's Cross); and meaty, comforting ham hock croquettes and zingy burmese chicken salad (Exmouth Market). Jalapeño cornbread with chipotle butter is hard to resist from either menu, and it's always worth ordering a pudding. Breakfast and brunch menus apply the same pick-and-mix attitude as the all-day one. Drinks are equally good, from the global wine list to the own-roast coffee. The fruity Caravan blend is perfectly brewed, whether as a textbook espresso or an expertly feathered flat white. The setting, next door to the Grain Store (*see p195*) and overlooking the fountains of the piazza-like Granary Square, is a further plus. One caveat – we're not convinced by the unisex loos.
Available for hire. Babies and children welcome: high chairs; nappy-changing facilities. Booking advisable; not accepted brunch. Disabled: toilet. Tables outdoors (15, courtyard). **Map 4 L2**.
For branch see index.

Karpo

23-27 Euston Road, NW1 2SD (7843 2221, www.karpo.co.uk). King's Cross St Pancras tube/rail. **Breakfast served** 7-11.30am Mon-Fri; 8-11.30am Sat, Sun. **Lunch served** noon-3pm Mon-Fri; 12.30-4pm Sat, Sun. **Reduced menu served** 3-5pm Mon-Fri; 4-5pm Sat, Sun. **Dinner served** 5.30-10.30pm Mon-Sat; 5.30-9pm Sun. **Main courses** £9-£19. **Credit** AmEx, MC, V.
A hypercoloured graffiti mural covering the top four floors of the building sounds warning bells. Is Karpo going to be a style-over-content kind of joint? Thankfully, no – the food delivers innovative flavours, the staff are friendly, and the location is ideal for an easygoing dinner date or catching up with friends near King's Cross. A small entrance opens up to the main restaurant, giving a wide view on to chefs working in the kitchen. Dark decor and a quirky wall covered in plants keep the bohemian look going inside, but the focus is on the food. We started with cocktails in the railway-inspired basement bar, where you can also order nibbles such as soft-centered ham croquettes from the upstairs menu. From a seasonally changing menu, mains are playful: roast venison came with an on-trend side serving of tender salt-baked celeriac, but it tried too hard with an overly sweet chocolate garnish to the meat. Mac 'n' cheese went retro, arriving in a hot cast-iron pan, and the mixed leaf salad had a tangy red wine vinegar dressing. To finish, rhubarb fool was a tasty riff on traditional trifle, coming with a rich custardy cream served between layers of stewed rhubarb, pistachio nibs and a fine shortbread crumb.
Available for hire. Babies and children welcome: high chairs. Booking advisable. Separate room for parties, seats 30. Takeaway service. **Map 4 L3**.

Piccadilly

★ Wolseley HOT 50

160 Piccadilly, W1J 9EB (7499 6996, www.thewolseley.com). Green Park tube.
Breakfast served 7-11.30am Mon-Fri; 8-11.30am Sat, Sun. **Lunch served** noon-3pm

Mon-Fri; noon-3.30pm Sat, Sun. **Tea served** 3-6.30pm Mon-Fri; 3.30-5.30pm Sat; 3.30-6.30pm Sun. **Dinner served** 5.30pm-midnight Mon-Sat; 5.30-11pm Sun. **All-day menu served** 11.30am-midnight Mon-Sat; 11.30am-11pm Sun. **Main courses** £12-£29.75. **Set tea** £9.75-£22.50; £32.50 incl glass of champagne. **Cover** £2. **Credit** AmEx, DC, MC, V.
A self-proclaimed 'café-restaurant in the grand European tradition', the Wolseley combines London heritage and Viennese grandeur. Its black, gold and cream colour scheme suggests prestige, and you might easily imagine the buzz of conversation and the chink of crockery to have reverberated around the high ceilings since the 1920s. Yet the venue is only a decade old. Nevertheless, it's now firmly on many a London visitor's checklist, alongside nearby bastion of tradition Fortnum & Mason. The kitchen is much-celebrated for its breakfasts, and the scope of the main menu is admirable. From oysters, steak tartare or soufflé suisse, via wiener schnitzel or grilled halibut with wilted spinach and béarnaise, to tarte au citron or apple strudel, there's something for everyone. On the Sunday afternoon of our visit, however, three-tiered afternoon tea stands were in abundance, enjoyed by a diverse mix of patrons: from Japanese businessmen to groups of female friends. Mini cakes and scones on the top tier are as English as the jam that accompanies them, while crustless finger sandwiches at the bottom are replenished by formal staff from a huge service team. Our waiter appeared a touch jaded, but he was certainly efficient, and dealt with complaints about the next table about weak coffee with grace.
Babies and children welcome: high chairs; nappy-changing facilities. Booking advisable. Disabled: toilet. Separate room for parties, seats 12. **Map 9 J7**.

Soho

Kettner's

29 Romilly Street, W1D 5HP (7734 6112, www.kettners.com). Leicester Square or Piccadilly Circus tube. **Meals served** noon-10.45pm Mon-Wed; noon-11.15pm Thur-Sat; noon-9.15pm Sun.
Main courses £9.95-£29.95. **Set meal** (5-6.30pm) £16.50 2 courses, £19.50 3 courses. **Credit** AmEx, MC, V.
A Georgian-chic champagne bar with a restaurant next door that's buzzing every night of the week, Kettner's is a safe bet in Soho. The cocktail bar has lavish velvet curtains, plush seating and low-lit alcoves filled with the tinkle of laughter and champagne flutes, while the restaurant suits groups who want a bit of glamour and history (Oscar Wilde dined here), but don't necessarily crave too many surprises on the menu. Large windows and distressed white woodwork create a relaxed and upmarket feel, but the tables are close together and soft electro music keeps a modern edge. You get what you expect from a quality brasserie: steak cooked perfectly, chips triple fried, service a little flirty, and there's always crème brûlée on the menu. A buffalo mozzarella starter came with a dense confit of tomatoes and deliciously sharp basil dressing, and this lightness was carried through to the salmon and prawn fish cakes served with buttery poached egg for mains. Potato gratin was a little dry, but you could forgive the kitchen once you tasted the rich and cheddary cauliflower cheese. Mango and passionfruit pavlova was, much like the rest of the meal, very well executed if a little predictable.

Babies and children welcome: children's menu; high chairs; nappy-changing facilities. Booking advisable Thur-Sat. Disabled: toilet. Entertainment: pianist 6.30-9.30pm Tue-Sat. Separate rooms for parties, seating 12-85. Map 17 C4.

Princi

135 Wardour Street, W1F 0UT (7478 8888, www.princi.co.uk). Leicester Square or Tottenham Court Road tube. **Breakfast served** 8-11.30am Mon-Fri; 8-11am Sat; 8.30-11am Sun. **Meals served** noon-11.30pm Mon-Fri. **Brunch served** 11am-4.30pm Sat, Sun. **Dinner served** 4.30-11.30pm Sat; 4.30-10pm Sun. **Main courses** £7.50-£11.50. **Credit** AmEx, MC, V.

Introduced to London by Alan Yau in 2008, this smart outpost of a Milanese bakery chain remains a popular all-day option. It's an airy, good-looking room, with a sandstone interior, long black marble counters and a (slightly odd) water feature that runs the length of one wall. The food is varied enough to keep diners coming back for more: as well as cakes, pastries and breads, there's a choice of filled focaccia (parma ham, say, or mortadella), hot dishes (lasagne, aubergine parmigiana), slices of pizza and lots of attractive salads (chicken and avocado, mozzarella and tomato). Prices are higher than average, but it's all quality, seasonal stuff – a sweet blood orange juice being one glorious example. Not everything works – gem lettuce, caper and grilled pepper salad was super-salty; a quattro formaggi pizza slice tasted great but was barely warm – but most things do. The only real deterrent is the self-service set-up, which is slightly chaotic, despite the best efforts of the charming staff, and you have to rejoin the queue for cake or (excellent) coffee. Finding a seat at the communal counters can also be something of a trial. Opt out by dining in the pizzeria (to the left as you enter), which offers table service and a marginally calmer atmosphere in which to enjoy a short but classy range of pizzas. *Babies and children admitted. Bookings not accepted. Disabled: toilet.* Map 17 B4.

Strand

Tom's Kitchen

Somerset House, Strand, WC2R 1LA (7845 4646, www.tomskitchen.co.uk). Temple tube. **Brunch served** 10am-4pm Sat, Sun. **Lunch served** noon-3pm Mon-Fri. **Dinner served** 6-10pm Mon-Sat. **Main courses** £12.50-£29.50. **Credit** AmEx, DC, MC, V.

Occupying part of historic Somerset House near the river, Tom's Kitchen is made up of a bar room, and three interlinking dining rooms, all pleasant, high-ceilinged spaces with little personality. Large modern canvases hang on white walls; seating is a mix of banquettes, booths and chairs at modern wooden tables. Tom Aikens runs the place in conjunction with the Compass Group, and there is a slight air of the corporate about the place, dispelled on our evening visit by charming, solicitous service. The menu is divided into 'classics' (grilled open steak sandwich, nicely garlicky, and served with watercress, tomato, shallot rings and excellent, triple-cooked chips) and seasonal dishes (rich venison casserole with root vegetable mash and a slightly-too-sweet gravy). There are also daily specials (smooth butternut squash soup, very tomatoey risotto), and a short list of puds. Maple syrup and cinnamon-stick crème brûlée did the job, but the baked alaska (only

Fields Bar & Kitchen

available to share) may have offered more excitement. Weekend brunch adds eggy dishes and hefty salads to the mix. All decent enough, but with few fireworks, and one big drawback – the prices are simply too high for the quality on offer. Also on the premises are Tom's Deli (a daytime café) and Tom's Terrace (on the terrace facing the Thames, open spring and summer only). *Babies and children welcome: high chairs; nappy-changing facilities. Booking advisable. Disabled: toilet.* Map 18 F5.

For branches see index.

West
Chiswick

High Road Brasserie

162-166 Chiswick High Road, W4 1PR (8742 7474, www.highroadhouse.co.uk). Turnham Green tube. **Meals served** 7am-11pm Mon-Thur; 7am-midnight Fri; 8am-midnight Sat; 8am-10pm Sun. **Main courses** £11-£16. **Credit** AmEx, MC, V.

Perennially packed, noisy with chatter and with tables spilling on to the broad pavements of Chiswick High Road, this venture (from the Soho House group) continues to strike a chord with the dapper denizens of W4. Pitched between a grand café and an art deco bar, it has cleverly nailed a look that transcends generations; parents and teenagers can dine together at a venue that offends neither's sensibilities. The all-day menu is accessible, featuring fail-safe favourites such as full english breakfast, buttermilk pancakes, croque monsieur, steaks from the grill and simple mains such as plaice goujons with fries. Vitamin smoothies are an antidote to the comfort food, but given that our waitress visibly wrinkled her nose when describing their hyper-nutritious contents, we're not sure how often they're ordered. Mostly, customers are here for hangover-friendly dining. A fish pie was packed with succulent chunks of salmon and haddock, while avocado on toast came with a perfectly poached egg. Desserts are knowingly retro: black forest gateau or crêpes suzette, for instance. Prices are a little high, given that portions are on the modest side, but no one here gives a hoot. *Babies and children welcome: children's menu; crayons; high chairs; nappy-changing facilities. Booking advisable, essential dinner and weekends. Disabled: toilet. Tables outdoors (14, pavement).*

Westbourne Grove

Daylesford Organic

208-212 Westbourne Grove, W11 2RH (7313 8050, www.daylesfordorganic.com). Ladbroke Grove or Notting Hill Gate tube. **Meals served** 8am-6pm Mon-Sat; 10am-3pm Sun. **Main courses** £9.95-£14.95. **Credit** AmEx, MC, V.
There's much to like about Daylesford Organic's field-to-fork ethos, providing Notting Hill with fresh, organic food direct from the farm. The ground-floor grocery, deli and bakery are the stuff of foodie fantasy. Upstairs, the open café kitchen puts this same beautiful produce to good use. Brunch is a straightforward but splendidly executed affair of scrambled eggs with smoked salmon and the like; come for portobello mushrooms on sourdough with Portobello's moneyed residents and choose to detox (bircher muesli and wheat-free toast) or retox (bloody marys). But the place really comes into its own for lunch. Seasonal salads of, say, marinated courgette pasta, or raw slaw with cashews and a sticky soy and ginger dressing are substantial meals in their own right, bursting with health and spanking fresh ingredients. Our burger was also a belter – but at £13, it should have been. We understand that top-tier produce doesn't come cheap, but paying £4 for a small freshly squeezed juice or a tenner for smoked salmon on pumpernickel seems overkill, especially when you factor in a long wait for a communal table and over-worked staff who rush around like headless chickens. Organic, free-range ones, of course.
Babies and children welcome: crayons; high chairs; nappy-changing facilities. Bookings not accepted. Disabled: toilet. Tables outdoors (6, pavement). Takeaway service. Vegan dishes. **Map 7 A6.**
For branch see index.

Granger & Co

175 Westbourne Grove, W11 2SB (7229 9111, www.grangerandco.com). Notting Hill Gate tube. **Breakfast served** 7am-noon Mon-Sat; 8am-noon Sun. **Lunch served** noon-5pm daily. **Dinner served** 5-10.30pm Mon-Sat; 5-10pm Sun. **Main courses** £13.50-£22.80. **No credit cards**.
At the time of writing, this is the only UK outlet from Australian Bill Granger – restaurateur and author of a number of cookery books – though another is planned (in Clerkenwell). Notting Hill has taken to this simply decorated, no-bookings eaterie with a passion – queues form at weekends for brunch, and even early in the week the tightly packed tables and stools along the bar are fully occupied. It's no wonder: the room is appealing and light-filled, the global menu inventive without being alarming, and the cooking assured. There are snacks (crispy salt and pepper squid with lime aïoli), starters (ceviche salmon with grapefruit, avocado and sesame), pasta dishes, a steak and a burger, plus a range of globe-trotting dishes; lunch sees more soups, sandwiches and salads. At dinner, both the beef burger (which came with tomato relish and pickled courgette, and had a proper meaty taste) and fried brown rice packed with crab, chorizo and kimchee (punchy in all the right ways) passed with flying colours; the next table enthused about tumeric-spiced chicken with slaw, and lime and coconut dressing. Prices are on the high side, but portions are generous – especially the puddings. A heap of banana fritters was perfectly matched

Caravan King's Cross. See p38.

with caramel and honey ice-cream, and a bowl-like white chocolate and pistachio pavlova groaned under a mass of strawberries and rosewater cream. Excellent, attentive service saw a late-arriving item instantly whisked off the bill.
Babies and children welcome: high chairs. Bookings not accepted. Disabled: toilet. Tables outdoors (3, pavement). Takeaway service. **Map 19 C3.**

South West

Barnes

Depot

Tideway Yard, 125 Mortlake High Street, SW14 8SN (8878 9462, www.depotbrasserie.co.uk). Barnes Bridge or Mortlake rail, or bus 209. **Lunch served** noon-3pm Mon-Fri; 11am-3.30pm Sat; noon-5pm Sun. **Dinner served** 6-11pm daily. **Main courses** £10.95-£21.95. **Set lunch** (Mon-Fri) £12.95 2 courses, £15.95 3 courses. **Credit** AmEx, DC, MC, V.
'If it ain't broke, don't fix it' could be the motto of this riverside restaurant, which continues serenely through its third decade. Originally part of the stables and coach house for Barnes Council's refuse depot (hence the name), it's a handsome spot, all gleaming wood, bare brick and striped banquettes, with a separate bar at one end. A skeleton boat hangs from the ceiling, and the window tables are much sought after (inevitably, the place is packed for the Boat Race). It caters for all kinds of diners, from loved-up couples to multi-generational family groups. The menu majors in comforting brasserie staples done well – bavette with chips and béarnaise, smoked-chicken caesar salad, an exemplary fish cake – with the occasional inventive twist (goat's cheese soufflé with saffron-poached pears) or seasonal ingredient (wild garlic). Desserts have always been a strong point: tangy lemon posset with blackberries and crumbly shortbread was a treat, but it's the sticky, creamy, indulgent

eton mess that always wins us over. Sunday roast lunch is something of a local tradition. Drinks run from cocktails to a fairly priced wine list, and there's always some kind of set menu or special deal. Staff are friendly, but can get overwhelmed when the place is full.
Available for hire. Babies and children welcome: children's menu; crayons; high chairs; nappy-changing facilities. Booking advisable. Tables outdoors (11, courtyard).

Georgina's

56 Barnes High Street, SW13 9LF (8166 5559, www.georginasrestaurants.com). Barnes Bridge rail or bus 209, 283. **Breakfast served** 10am-4pm daily. **Lunch served** 11am-4pm daily. **Dinner served** 6-9pm Wed-Sat. **Main courses** £10-£14. **Credit** AmEx, MC, V.
This low-key café/brasserie has found its niche, targeting the affluent daytime population of Barnes – many of them women and several toting baby buggies alongside their designer handbags. White walls and furniture and a large skylight make the wedge-shaped space bright and appealing. Takeaway coffees and fresh pastries are dispensed from the display counter by the door; at the back is a small enclosed courtyard. Breakfast, lunch and brunch are the mainstays, with dinner available at the end of the week – and then only until 9pm. Start the day with a fruit platter, an excellent cheese omelette or build your own breakfast. Avocado and tomato on toast was just that: unadorned (and under-ripe) slices. Tastier and better value are the toasties, including a rich and moreish version with aubergine, onion relish and blue cheese. You'll also find half a dozen Mediterranean-style salads and uncomplicated main courses (beef and lamb burgers with chips, grilled prawns with stir-fry vegetables). Children get a wider-than-usual choice, from pancakes with banana to salmon with veg. Drinks encompass cocktails, decent coffees, freshly made smoothies and juices (the zingy carrot, apple and ginger is recommended). Young staff are well-meaning, but service tends to falter at busy times.

Available for hire. Babies and children welcome: children's menu; high chairs. Booking advisable; not accepted lunch Sat, Sun. Disabled: toilet. Tables outdoors (3, garden). Takeaway service.

Chelsea

Gallery Mess

Saatchi Gallery, Duke of York's HQ, King's Road, SW3 4LY (7730 8135, www.saatchi-gallery.co.uk). Sloane Square tube.
Bar **Open/snacks served** 10am-9.30pm Mon-Sat; 11.30am-6.30pm Sun. **Snacks** £3.50-£14.
Restaurant **Breakfast served** 10am-1pm Sat, Sun. **Meals served** 11.30am-9.30pm Mon-Sat; 11.30am-6.30pm Sun. **Main courses** £12.50-£22. **Set tea** (2.30-6pm) £9.50-£11.50 (£22.50 incl champagne).
Both **Credit** AmEx, MC, V.
As befits its Chelsea location, this welcoming brasserie at the Saatchi art gallery is smarter than most. The white linen tablecloths, exposed brickwork and impressive bar are all somewhat in thrall to the vaulted ceiling and expansive curtain of floor-to-ceiling arched windows running the length of the listed interior. There's also a large outdoor terrace. Naturally, the art addict touches are present and correct – a giant shoe sculpture here, a neon picture there – but the menu itself is a lesson in conservative precision. Service is disarmingly friendly, the wine list modest (but with plenty of choice by the glass) and mains offer comforting flavours and proportions. So you'll find cod and chips, steak sandwich, charcuterie and smoked fish platters, caesar salad and afternoon tea. Chicken breast fricassée was delicately presented with a drizzle of foamy cep sauce, but served with slightly rubbery gnocchi. Smoked haddock came with a rich hollandaise and a perfectly poached egg. As for dessert, they don't come much more old-school than steamed rhubarb pudding or knickerbocker glory.
Available for hire. Babies and children welcome: children's menu; high chairs; nappy-changing facilities. Booking advisable lunch, dinner. Disabled: toilet. Separate room for parties, seats 60. Tables outdoors until 5.30pm Nov-Apr; until 9.30pm May-Oct (24, terrace). **Map 14 F11**.

South
Balham

Harrison's

15-19 Bedford Hill, SW12 9EX (8675 6900, www.harrisonsbalham.co.uk). Balham tube/rail. **Breakfast served** 9am-noon, **brunch served** noon-4pm Sat, Sun. **Lunch served** noon-4pm Mon-Fri. **Snacks served** 4-6pm daily. **Dinner served** 6-10.30pm Mon-Sat; 6-10pm Sun. **Main courses** £13-£20. **Set meal** (lunch Mon-Thur; dinner Mon-Thur, Sun) £13.50 2 courses, £16.50 3 courses. **Credit** AmEx, MC, V.
Harrison's started out in 2007 as the most ambitious bar-brasserie in Balham, expensively furnished and clearly aimed at the new money flooding into the area. But within a few years the menu had been dumbed down, and it was no longer the hot ticket for SW12 residents. It coasted along until the end of 2012, when the ground-floor dining area was given a mini makeover, the basement function room turned into a glam cocktail bar, and a new chef and

menu deployed. Anyone expecting the fervour of its heyday may be disappointed, though, as the menu has lost focus, and now tries to please all-comers: steaks, curries, nods to Asia, Italian nibbles – all are there. There's nothing wrong with simple dishes done well, however, and we were pleased with chicken schnitzel served with caper butter on creamed sweetcorn, and a shepherd's pie that was so artfully piped with potato mash even Fanny Cradock would have approved. A few dishes are bang on trend – a starter of 'chilled crab trifle' was layered with avocado and prettily served in a glass preserving jar. Prices are hardly recession-busting (cheeseburger and chips, £12), though the set menus are better value. Harrison's has a friendly, laid-back vibe – but if you're after a food-led venue, look elsewhere.
Available for hire. Babies and children welcome: children's menu; crayons; high chairs; nappy-changing facilities. Booking advisable Fri-Sun. Disabled: toilet. Separate rooms for parties, seating 14. Tables outdoors (6, terrace).
For branch (Sam's Brasserie & Bar) see index.

Clapham

Bistro Union

40 Abbeville Road, SW4 9NG (7042 6400, www.bistrounion.co.uk). Clapham Common or Clapham South tube. **Lunch served** noon-3pm Mon-Fri. **Brunch served** 11am-3pm Sat; 11am-4pm Sun. **Dinner served** 6-10pm Mon-Sat. **Main courses** £10-£24. **Credit** AmEx, MC, V.
This self-styled 'quintessentially British bistro' succeeds on so many levels: the staff are chummy and welcoming; the room looks rustic and quirky, with stripped floorboards, an appealing grey, white and yellow colour scheme and cutlery kept in drawers under the tables; and there's a very enticing selection of bar nibbles, own-made preserves and fruit gins on display that sets the tone for the slightly homespun approach of the kitchen. Snacks (available all day) include cheese and Marmite straws, anchovy toasts, pickled sardines, and smoked pig's cheek with cornichons – slightly bitter and umami flavours are a recurring theme through these. The main courses lean more towards Anglo-American-French comfort food: salt beef hash with fried egg and pickles (part of the Sunday brunch offering), Middlewhite pork faggots with 'bashed neeps', and a mac 'n' cheese that contained soft shards of leek and was crisply gratinéed. The puds are more firmly on British soil: rhubarb trifle, say, or apple crumble. Note that the tall wooden stools at the bar can't be booked – and these offer the best spectator seats. Deservedly popular locally, Bistro Union is the second Clapham venture from Adam Byatt, who runs smart restaurant Trinity (*see p203*) in Clapham Old Town.
Babies and children welcome: children's menu; high chairs. Booking advisable Sat, Sun. Tables outdoors (2, terrace). **Map 22 A3**.

Vauxhall

Brunswick House Café

30 Wandsworth Road, Vauxhall Cross, SW8 2LG (7720 2926, www.brunswickhouse.co). Vauxhall tube/rail. **Lunch served** noon-3pm Mon-Sat; noon-4pm Sun. **Dinner served** 6-10.30pm Mon-Sat. **Main courses** £13-£17. **Credit** MC, V.

This Georgian mansion, a tiny beacon of classic calm amid the high-rise apartments and noisy chaos of Vauxhall Cross, has no trouble packing in a young, high-spending, professional clientele. Some are simply stopping by for a cocktail while perusing the desirable bric-a-brac on offer from architectural salvage company Lassco, but most are here to meet, drink, eat and generally enjoy the place's markedly non-corporate hospitality. It's an appealing combination of boho-chic comfort, fluctuating lighting (of an evening) and minimalist menu presentation, along with a brilliantly tended bar and extensive lounge. Cocktails are prepared with panache and are good value; the food perhaps less so – following a punchy Pimm's, an appealing-sounding summery starter of 'asparagus, peas and berkswell' disappointed by occasioning a needle-in-a-haystack search beneath a mound of rocket. A main course of grey mullet would have worked better as a starter: both the potato accompaniment and sea greens turned out to be cold salads, and explained why the waitress pressed us to order vegetable side dishes (at extra charge). Bread – chunky and pleasing sourdough – also costs extra after the first slice. Puddings proved a curate's egg: excellent, crunchy brown bread ice-cream and strawberry 'tart' with thin, soft pastry and a slippery cheesecake filling.
Babies and children welcome: nappy-changing facilities. Booking advisable. Separate rooms for parties, seating 10-120. **Map 16 L12**.

South East
Bankside

The Table

83 Southwark Street, SE1 0HX (7401 2760, www.thetablecafe.com). Southwark tube or London Bridge tube/rail. **Breakfast served** 7.30-11am, **lunch served** noon-3pm Mon-Fri. **Brunch served** 8.30am-4.30pm Sat, Sun. **Dinner served** 6-10.30pm Mon-Sat. **Main courses** £12-£15. **Credit** AmEx, MC, V.
The Shard is casting its shadow over Southwark Street in more ways than one. Upmarket hotels are mushrooming around the Table, and nearby pubs are crowded with office workers, but on our arrival this large modern dining room with communal bench seating was empty. It's a different story during the day, when large groups come here to tuck into breakfasts (or weekend brunches) of bircher muesli, hot waffles with maple syrup, and 'the Borough full english'. Lunch is also popular: for a meze-like Mediterranean platter, say, or caesar salad. The staff are lovely, moving tables out into the courtyard as requested, and giving diners just the right degree of attention. Sadly, our meal didn't measure up to such service, its high-point starter of a flavoursome St Mungo's allotment salad quickly sliding into mediocrity. A flavoursome onglet steak was nicely set off by duck-fat roasted potatoes, but confit of duck was salty, dry, and dumped amid a huge mustard-mash cowpat. A tough, stale meringue with custard and fruit felt like a woeful *Come Dine With Me* dessert. Hints of high-quality ingredients and snappy ideas are generally undone by inelegant presentation. The Table needs to rediscover its polish.
Babies and children welcome: high chairs. Disabled: toilet. Entertainment: DJ 5.30-11pm Fri. Tables outdoors (15, terrace). Takeaway service. **Map 11 O8**.

Blackheath

Chapters All Day Dining

43-45 Montpelier Vale, SE3 0TJ (8333 2666, www.chaptersrestaurants.com). Blackheath rail. **Breakfast served** 8-11.30am, **lunch served** noon-3pm Mon-Fri. **Brunch served** 8am-3pm Sat; 9am-4pm Sun. **Tea served** 3-6pm Mon-Sat; 4-6pm Sun. **Dinner served** 6-11pm Mon-Sat; 6-9pm Sun. **Main courses** £9.45-£30.50. **Set lunch** (Mon-Thur) £12.95 2 courses, £14.95 3 courses. **Set dinner** (Mon-Thur) £14.95 2 courses, £17.95 3 courses. **Credit** AmEx, MC, V.

Very much a local favourite for everything from casual suppers to birthday celebrations, Chapters suits a wide range of diners: couples on a date night, groups of chums, and families with small children. No mean feat, and staff work hard to keep things moving smoothly. There are breakfast, bar and brunch menus alongside the all-day list; service comes with a smile; and prices are pretty keen (the set meal deals and children's menus are particularly good value). Quality can fluctuate a bit, but beer-battered fish and chips with tartare sauce, and most things from the Josper grill (burger with all the trimmings and chips; spatchcock chicken with lemon and thyme; ribeye and fillet steaks) are safe bets. Most recently, asparagus with a 'crispy' poached egg and apple and walnut salad was a stellar starter, but omelette arnold bennett overfaced us – richly savoury, yet a relentlessly big portion with little in the way of contrasting accompaniment. A global wine list has plenty of options by the glass and 500ml pichet. The modern decor plays it safe, with the light-filled ground floor being preferable to the basement, and pavement tables available for drinks.
Available for hire. Babies and children welcome: children's menu; high chairs; nappy-changing facilities. Booking advisable. Disabled: toilet. Separate room for parties, seats 50. Tables outdoors (4, pavement).

Brockley

Gantry NEW

188 Brockley Road, SE4 2RL (8469 0043, www.thegantry.co.uk). Brockley rail. **Breakfast served** 10am-2pm Tue-Sat; 10am-1pm Sun. **Lunch served** noon-4pm Tue-Sun. **Meals served** 5-10pm Mon; 11.30am-10pm Tue-Fri; 10am-10pm Sat; 10am-9pm Sun. **Main courses** £5.50-£25. **Credit** MC, V.

Stumbling across the Gantry is something of an *Alice in Wonderland* experience. First, you discover what appears to be a tiny scruffy bar serving interesting beers, ciders, cocktails and good coffees. Walk down the narrow staircase, and you'll come to an elegant panelled dining room, painted a tasteful shade of National Trust sludge, with patterned ceramic tiles on the floor and flower-filled glass jugs. Then, further down the quaintly furnished corridor, you enter yet another world: a charming and rustic conservatory, overlooking a hidden garden. But there's nothing Mad Hatter's tea party about the food. It's good, seasonal modern British food cooked and served by a very proficient crew who seem like they might have drifted here from somewhere much smarter. A tiny, pastry-wrapped parcel of deep-fried goat's cheese was just about perfect, as was the 'sharing antipasti' meat platter of artfully piled slivers of fine hams and salamis. Excellently al dente seafood risotto was dense with shellfish, but mushroom, beetroot and quinoa crumble was bland. Puddings were also variable: chocolate mousse with berries vanished in seconds, but banoffi cheesecake was too sickly to finish. Gantry does a brisk trade at lunchtime too, when the likes of merguez sausage wrap and eggs benedict are also served.
Babies and children welcome: high chairs; nappy-changing facilities. Booking advisable. Separate rooms for parties, seating 14, 16 and 24. Tables outdoors (11, garden; 5, terrace). Takeaway service.

Camberwell

No 67

South London Gallery, 67 Peckham Road, SE5 8UH (7252 7649, www.southlondongallery.org). Bus 12, 36 or 171. **Breakfast served** 9am-11.30pm, **lunch served** noon-3.30pm Tue-Fri. **Brunch served** 10am-3.30pm Sat, Sun. **Dinner served** 6.30-10pm Mon-Sat. **Main courses** £11.80-£14.60. **Set dinner** (Wed, Thur) £20 3 courses. **Credit** AmEx, MC, V.

As you'd expect of a gallery eaterie, No 67 is a bright, soaring space, with huge windows for natural light and a curvy, billowing garden flanked by more seating. Even more gratifyingly, the place doesn't just trade on its looks. The food is lovely, and pretty good value, especially the three-course dinner for £20 on Wednesday and Thursday. With seasonal treats on the set menu, such as a golden-crumbed asparagus with hollandaise, or courgette, pea and artichoke risotto – and lemon posset, chocolate and Calvados mousse or a cheeseboard for pudding – this is pretty much the perfect treat for a summer's evening. On the lunch menu, a seasonal soup is always on offer (we enjoyed spinach and potato), then there's the locally famous date and walnut welsh rarebit with pickles and salad. The meze is a vivid palette of rubious, slightly bitter, nutmeggy beetroot purée, emerald-flecked tsatsiki, golden hazelnut bulgar with ribbons of red pepper, and glossy black and green olives; they were artfully arranged on a white plate, and framed by several slices of griddled bread streaked with olive oil. The cake selection included a beetroot number and a gluten-free brownie, but we were glad to sample the almond and strawberry tart – the pastry was a crisp, buttery revelation. Impressive on all fronts.
Babies and children welcome: high chairs; nappy-changing facilities. Disabled: toilet. Separate room for parties, seats 26. Tables outdoors (5, pavement; 4, garden). Takeaway service. Map 23 B2.

Crystal Palace

Joanna's

56 Westow Hill, SE19 1RX (8670 4052, www.joannas.uk.com). Crystal Palace or Gipsy Hill rail. **Breakfast served** 10-11.45am daily. **Meals served** noon-11pm Mon-Sat; noon-10.30pm Sun. **Main courses** £11.75-£32.50. **Set meal** (lunch Mon-Sat; dinner Mon-Wed) £13 2 courses, £17 3 courses. **Credit** AmEx, MC, V.

Joanna's is a Crystal Palace stalwart, known to locals as the place to go if you want a bit of West End glam without the journey. Wood panelling, whitewashed brick walls and a well-stocked wooden bar bring to mind an old-school New York vibe. Waiting staff are smartly turned out in black and white and there are linen tablecloths, starched napkins and polished cutlery, but the ambience is far from stuffy. Brasserie classics such as steak frites and smoked haddock with poached egg are interspersed with favourites from further afield, including king prawn tempura, thai fish cakes and crispy duck salad. Although the menu does feel a little disparate, dishes are executed with aplomb. Baked cod with olive oil mash was cooked to perfection and beautifully complemented by a sweet red pepper compote. Onglet steak with fries and garlic butter was simple and satisfying. Sticky toffee pudding also delivered, with a light sponge and finger-licking toffee sauce. Don't expect to be blown away by innovation – Joanna's popularity is down to excellent service and good-quality food in stylish surroundings.
Babies and children welcome until 6pm: booster seats; children's menu; high chairs. Booking advisable, essential weekends. Tables outdoors (3, pavement).

London Bridge & Borough

Elliot's

12 Stoney Street, SE1 9AD (7403 7436, www.elliotscafe.com). London Bridge tube/rail. **Breakfast served** 8-11am Mon-Sat. **Lunch served** noon-3pm Mon-Fri; noon-4pm Sat. **Dinner served** 6-10pm Mon-Sat. **Main courses** £12-£23. **Credit** AmEx, MC, V.

Light and airy, with stripped brick walls and a contemporary feel, Elliot's is a busy little spot full of tourists, dates and business people; in the evenings it can get noisy. Sit out front and watch the world go by, perch at the bar or take a seat in the bright back area with a glass roof above your head. The seasonal, ever-changing menu is small but innovative, and carefully sourced (they deal directly with growers and producers); bread is excellent. Smaller plates such as crab on toast or buffalo mozzarella and polenta are listed alongside larger plates, which include the ever-popular (but weekday lunchtime only) burger. Served in a toasted sesame-seed bun, with fried maris potatoes, a pile of pickles, ketchup and mustard, the burger was too juicy to pick up, and oozed with cheese and fried onions. The meat was tender, delicious and still a little pink in the middle. At dinner, lemon sole, wild garlic and fino (a large plate) was good, but there were no more than a few slivers of wild garlic in the sherry-based sauce, making a side dish a must. Jersey Royals with bacon and shallots went nicely with both this and a (small) plate of three scallops with herb butter. Well-mannered, very engaged service is on the evangelical side when it comes to the natural wines (orange wines are listed alongside the expected white, red and rosé).
Booking advisable. **Map 11 P8.**

Rooftop Café NEW

The Exchange, 28 London Bridge Street, SE1 9SG (3102 3770, www.theexchange.so/rooftop). London Bridge tube/rail. **Brunch served** 8am-3pm Mon-Fri. **Dinner served** 6-10.30pm Thur, Fri. **Meals served** 10am-10.30pm Sat. **Main courses** £10-£14. **No credit cards.**

Admittedly, just getting here is half the fun – there's a sense of achievement once you've successfully navigated entry-phone, lift and winding stairs and corridors. But what you find at the end of the journey is also pretty special. The café of a co-working enterprise that happens to be open to the

public, the Rooftop has exceptional views over the City, along with a neck-cricking, vertiginous proximity to the Shard next door. In summer, the enormous deck terrace planted with herbs and vegetables is a wonderful treat, while the small inner café with its wooden floor and colourful furniture is a pretty eyrie on cooler days. We relished the breakfast – excellent, generous bread and scrambled eggs with thick-cut smoked salmon or luscious bacon, flanked by sparky bloody marys – but the kitchen also runs to lunch and tea during the week, and dinner Thursday to Saturday, when a cut-above menu features the likes of 'rabbit, prosciutto, mango, almond, watercress' or 'flourless chocolate cake, blackberries'; a winter's day was brightened by crunchy potato cake topped with a portobello mushroom and poached duck egg. Wines, from the same suppliers used by Brawn and Terroirs, are well chosen and sensibly priced; bread is from the excellent Paul Rhodes Bakery.
Available for hire. Babies and children admitted. Booking advisable. Separate room for parties, seats 14. Tables outdoors (10, terrace). **Map 12 Q8.**

Peckham

Peckham Refreshment Rooms NEW
12-16 Blenheim Grove, SE15 4QL (7639 1106, www.peckhamrefreshment.com). Peckham Rye rail. **Lunch served** 11am-3pm Mon-Fri.

Brunch served 10am-3pm Sat. **Dinner served** 6-10.30pm Mon-Sat. **Dishes** £5-£10. **Credit** MC, V.
A little slice of Barcelona has landed in Peckham: a slick, pared-down, friendly little tapas bar where you might swig a quick beer or down a carafe of wine and grab some tasty snacks before (or after) a big night out. The cheap and cheerful vibe – raw plaster walls, a scruffy poured-concrete floor and a big slab of glossy burgundy MDF for a bar – belies the speed at which you can rattle through £50 on the small platters of pan-European nibbles. The basic menu consists of Spanish cheeses, meats and snacks, with a few interesting southern European dishes. More enticing are the daily-changing seasonal specials, such as an exquisite dandelion, broad bean and goat's cheese salad; spears of lemon- and butter-drenched asparagus with a heavenly curd dip; some tasty (though marginally overcooked) king prawns with garlic and tangy chorizo; and a skewer of monkfish served with saffron potatoes and a sprinkling of shrimps and clams. Puddings – a dense, delicious pot au chocolat, and a dreamy lemon posset served with a crumbling disc of shortbread – were a resounding success, as was the friendly and attentive service. The hipness quotient really cranks up in the evening, attracting Peckham's art-scene crowd.
Available for hire. Babies and children admitted. Bookings not accepted. Disabled: toilet. **Map 23 C3.**

East
Shoreditch

Mr Buckley's NEW
277 Hackney Road, E2 8NA (3664 0033, www.mrbuckleys.com). Hoxton rail. **Open** noon-midnight Mon-Thur; noon-2am Fri; 10am-2am Sat; 10am-midnight Sun. **Meals served** noon-11pm Mon-Fri; 10am-11pm Sat, Sun. **Dishes** £4-£7.50. **Credit** AmEx, MC, V.
It's just a bit too cool for school, the Hackney Road, where grotty pubs and pound shops shoulder up against wine boutiques and studios with blokes selling hand-whittled wooden spoons for six quid a throw. And then there's Mr Buckley's, a coolly understated two-level space serving high-concept, internationally influenced 'small plates' to the sort of well-dressed people who want to eat that sort of thing in east London. There's nothing really wrong with any of this, but the food is hit and miss, the flavours so intensely concentrated that your taste buds can give up in confusion. We had the recommended three dishes per person. Only one dish – sweet and sticky jerk steak with smoked paprika and mango butter and sweet potato crisps – really delivered. Lobster mac and cheese, in theory a fun idea, just tasted odd and jarred with everything else – items such as ragstone goat's cheese or asparagus and quails' eggs, which by

Peckham Refreshment Rooms

BRASSERIES

themselves might have been more pleasant to eat. Desserts were better for being one per person: notably, a moreish banana cake with peanut butter. Order carefully, or perhaps stick to the basement cocktail bar to get some of the hip local vibe. *Available for hire. Babies and children admitted. Booking advisable Thur-Sun. Tables outdoors (2, pavement).* **Map 6 S3**.

Salvation Jane

1 Oliver's Yard, 55 City Road, EC1Y 1HQ (7253 5273, www.salvationjanecafe.co.uk). Old Street tube/rail. **Breakfast served** 7.30-11.30am, **lunch served** noon-3pm daily. **Brunch served** 9am-3.30pm Sat, Sun. **Dinner served** 6-9pm Tue-Fri. **Main courses** £6.50-£12. **Credit** MC, V.

The eastern outpost of Fitzrovia's Lantana (*see p271*) is roomier and serves an evening menu as well as the lunch and breakfast dishes Lantana is known for. The stack of corn fritters with crispy bacon, spinach and roast tomato, with avocado-chilli-lime salsa and crème fraîche, is a must-try in both locations. More sizeable mains such as a moreish Asian sticky chicken salad with nuoc cham dressing generally hit the spot too. Good, own-made cakes are baked daily, and often reflect the café's Antipodean heritage – you might see friands arrayed on the counter. Weekend brunch is popular, for the easygoing atmosphere as much as the near-perfect comfort food. Such dishes include delicious french toast (a dreamy toasted coconut version with ricotta, lime syrup and pistachio), inventive eggy combos, and specials such as grilled asparagus with black pudding, roast tomato, poached egg and hollandaise on sourdough. Add a generous bloody mary and you're set up for the day. Noise reverberates around the industrial space (all exposed pipework and bare walls), but, visually at least, Salvation Jane is softened by a charming collection of mid-century modern bits and pieces. Staff are kept busy, working both the room and the outdoor terrace, but efficiency can tail off at night. *Available for hire. Babies and children admitted. Disabled: toilet. Tables outdoors (8, courtyard). Takeaway service. Vegan dishes.* **Map 6 Q4**.

Waterhouse

10 Orsman Road, N1 5QJ (7033 0123, www.waterhouserestaurant.co.uk). Haggerston rail or bus 67, 242. **Lunch served** noon-3pm, **dinner served** 6-10pm Tue-Sat. **Main courses** £8-£13.50. **Set lunch** £10 2 courses. **Set dinner** £16 2 courses. **Credit** MC, V.

Surrounded by industrial units just off the Kingsland Road, Waterhouse has an improbable location. Recently refurbished, the space is modern and bright, thanks to floor-to-ceiling windows overlooking the Regent's Canal. The outdoor tables are prime spots for people- (and duck-) watching, as Haggerston's cyclists and dog-walkers parade along the opposite side of the waterway. The restaurant is part of a scheme to train underprivileged locals in the catering trade via the charity Shoreditch Trust, so don't be surprised to hear the head chef putting apprentices through their paces in the open kitchen. It's all part of the atmosphere, and results in excellent value, with most daytime mains costing £6 (prices are higher for dinner). The grill was put to good use in a verdant appetiser of chargrilled courgette, asparagus and peas, and imparted a Mediterranean flavour to a main course of bream. Spiced lamb lasagne was a hearty rendition of a classic, and all

the dishes were enticingly presented. To drink, there's a brief wine list and beers from east London breweries. Far from being worthy, Waterhouse offers an object lesson in making sustainability and social enterprise in the food world seem dynamic and forward-looking. *Available for hire. Babies and children welcome: high chairs; nappy-changing facilities. Disabled: toilet. Separate room for parties, seats 30. Tables outdoors (10, towpath). Takeaway service.* **Map 6 R2**.

Spitalfields

Breakfast Club

12-16 Artillery Lane, E1 7LS (7078 9633, www.thebreakfastclubcafes.com). Liverpool Street tube/rail or Shoreditch High Street rail. **Meals served** 7.30am-10pm Mon-Fri; 9am-10.30pm Sat; 9am-9pm Sun. **Main courses** £3.50-£11. **Credit** AmEx, MC, V.

Hey, kids! With the aura of a chipper kids' TV presenter, the Breakfast Club invites punters to wallow in an ersatz homage to 1980s youth, with Roland Rat posters and the soundtrack of a '90s adolescence. Given that many of these now thirty-somethings have children of their own in tow, it seems odd to make them struggle by not providing a single high chair to cater to what must be a good chunk of the venue's target demographic. Whatever, folks are willing to queue for the comfort food at weekends. A long list of brunch options runs from sweet – a moreish stack of french toast with cinnamon apples – to savoury, with a chorizo hash that makes you mop up every drop of paprika-inflected lard with your home fries. Burgers, burritos and baked potatoes round out the menu. It's hearty and at times heart-stopping, though smoothies with waggish names such as the 'Pommy Granny' (pomegranate and berries) add a healthful note. The beaten-up decor crosses the line into needing some plasterwork in corners, and service was merely functional, but it's a hit formula nonetheless for this mini chain. *Available for hire. Babies and children welcome: nappy-changing facilities. Bookings not accepted before 5pm weekends. Disabled: toilet. Takeaway service.* **Map 12 R5**. **For branches see index.**

North East

Dalston

Floyd's NEW

89 Shacklewell Lane, E8 2EB (7923 7714). Dalston Kingsland rail. **Meals served** 11am-11pm daily. **Main courses** £10-£12.80. **No credit cards.**

A contemporary brasserie run by a former fashion model in the rundown but trendy environs of Dalston, Floyd's should be enormously irritating. But with a certain charm and some serious know-how in the kitchen, Konrad Lindholm and his team are pulling it off. A pretty, pale blue-painted space with shelves of books here, Middle Eastern tiles there and flowers on every wooden table sets the scene. The staff are easygoing and the menu competently covers the bases, from breakfast through mains to snacks and puddings – the combination successfully pulls in the regulars. We stopped by for a late lunch and had a chilled cucumber and yoghurt soup, which is easy to get

wrong but here was spot-on: tart and sweet, heady with garlic and a hint of dill, scattered with chives and slicked with olive oil. The soup could have done with some accompanying bread, but this minor blip was forgiven with the arrival of a towering plate of ingenious courgette linguine with almond and parsley pesto, nutty wild mushrooms, rocket and parmesan – a juicy plateful of deep flavours offering all the pleasures of pasta with none of the carb coma. A definite winner. *Available for hire. Babies and children admitted. Takeaway service.* **Map 25 C4**.

Jones & Sons NEW

23-27 Arcola Street, E8 2DJ (7241 1211, www.jonesandsonsdalston.com). Dalston Kingsland rail. **Lunch/brunch served** 9am-3pm Mon-Fri; 11am-4pm Sat, Sun. **Dinner served** 6.30-10.30pm daily. **Main courses** £12-£20. **Credit** (over £5) MC, V.

This spot on Arcola Street used to be home to the theatre of the same name until that had to leave in 2011. Two years on, a not-for-profit arts promotion organisation (called Cell Project Spaces) has taken on the building, and the theatre area is open to the public again as this 50-cover restaurant. Much thought has gone into the look. It's undoubtedly on trend – as are the well-coiffed staff and diners – but it's also understated. Set back where the stage used to be, the open-plan, bright white kitchen is built into what looks like a house-shaped theatre set. Industrial ship lamps hang from the ceiling, brickwork is exposed, and mismatched chairs have Scandinavian charm. The Modern European menu is well considered and well priced. Beef carpaccio was subtly perfumed with white truffle; seared scallops were dressed with samphire and light lemon zest purée; steaks were chargrilled. Each dish was attractively presented, but much of what we ate was under-seasoned. We've no complaints about the drinks list, though. Craft beers from London breweries – including Kernel and Meantime – are available, coffee is from Monmouth, the wines are reasonably priced, and the bar staff can mix a mean dirty martini. It wouldn't take much for this Dalston brasserie to go from decent to a real destination. Supplying salt shakers would be a start. *Available for hire. Babies and children welcome: high chairs. Disabled: toilet. Takeaway service.* **Map 25 C4**.

A Little of What You Fancy

464 Kingsland Road, E8 4AE (7275 0060, www.alittleofwhatyoufancy.info). Dalston Junction rail or bus 67, 242. **Meals served** 11am-10pm Tue, Wed; 9am-10pm Thur, Fri; 10am-10pm Sat; 11am-5pm Sun. **Main courses** £12-£16. **Credit** MC, V.

A little blast of shabby chic on a very urban stretch of road. Diners sit on old school chairs at wooden tables, each with a little flowering pot plant; boxes of veg are piled at the end of the open kitchen; and a sign advertises eggs for sale. At weekends, it's lively all day long. Brunch centres on eggs served lots of ways, including scrambled with chorizo and roasted tomatoes. The regularly changing lunch menu features some lighter dishes such as good serrano ham with guindilla peppers and sourdough toast, as well as the likes of moules marinière. The kitchen shifts up a gear for dinner, with robust combinations such as pan-fried cod fillet with chorizo, fino and fennel broth with fried potatoes; or braised rabbit leg – which came with a white

Jones & Sons

wine cream sauce that had a deftly light lemony touch that didn't dominate the distinctive taste of the meat. Smooth, buttery mash completed the picture. Pomegranate and pistachio mess was glorious: light, not too sweet and – best of all – with nicely sticky meringue. Service is informal (and occasionally offhand), but in general this place scores well for feel-good factor. You can also catch the ALOWYF team serving lunch at the French House pub in Soho (49 Dean Street, W1D 5BE, 7437 2477; noon-4pm Mon-Fri).
Available for hire. Babies and children welcome until 7pm: high chairs. Booking advisable Thur-Sat. Disabled: toilet. Takeaway service.

Hackney

Hackney Picturehouse Bar & Kitchen
Hackney Picturehouse, 270 Mare Street, E8 1HE (0871 902 5734, www.picturehouses.co.uk). Hackney Central rail. **Meals served** noon-10pm Mon-Fri; 11am-10pm Sat, Sun. **Main courses** £5-£12.50. **Credit** MC, V.
Why would anyone choose to eat in a cinema? Because, despite Hackney's food renaissance, there's a pocket of epicurean resistance centred firmly around the Picturehouse, something the mini chain set out to exploit when it opened here in 2011. The large, light-filled foyer contains an assortment of shared tables with bench seating and some smaller tables, offering lots of space even at the busy intersections of movies ending and starting. The menu is a clever mix of snacks (such as mini pizzas and fat chips) through to burgers, daily specials and that often dismal offering, the sharing platter. This one is better than most, but not much, its selection of unimaginative antipasto staples doing little to excite. Much better are the small plates – the hot dogs and pimientos de padrón are particularly popular, and deservedly so, with the former a perfect marriage of sausage, bun and sauerkraut, and the latter as good as anything you'll get in Galicia. Specials of pastas, savoury tarts and salads are acceptable, but this is a place for a light

bite, rather than a full meal. The impressive range of locally brewed beers includes tipples from Beavertown alongside the more obvious selection from London Fields Brewery.
Babies and children welcome: high chairs; nappy-changing facilities. Bookings not accepted. Disabled: toilet. Separate room for parties, seats 60. Tables outdoors (3, pavement). Vegan dishes.

Market Café
2 Broadway Market, E8 4QG (7249 9070, http://market-cafe.co.uk). London Fields rail or bus 26, 48, 55.
Bar **Open** noon-11pm Mon-Thur; noon-midnight Fri; 10am-midnight Sat; 10am-10pm Sun.
Restaurant **Brunch served** 10am-5pm Sat, Sun. **Meals served** noon-10pm Mon-Thur; noon-10.30pm Fri; 6-10.30pm Sat; 6-10pm Sun. **Main courses** £9.50-£18.50.
Both **Credit** MC, V.
Thanks to its prime position overlooking the canal at the bottom end of Broadway Market, this place attracts, as you might expect, plenty of Hackney hipsters. Much about the venue is fun – the studiedly casual decor with vintage wallpaper and Formica tables, the relaxed bar area and the prosecco on tap – but compared to other restaurants in the area, the kitchen (run by Hugo Warner, formerly of Benugo) doesn't quite manage to distinguish itself. The menu is concise, with strong Italian touches including hand-cut pasta. A starter of potted duck with piccalilli made up in generosity what it lacked in real moreishness; arancini with a good, deep-flavoured romesco sauce were rather sedate versions of what should be unctuous treats. The risotto of the day – nero with prawns – was perfectly unmemorable. Veal escalope was the only truly standout dish: dark, oily and crunchy. The bill for all this was on the high side, although there are several very well-priced wines by the bottle. For people-watching and some decent dishes, the Market Café is fine – just don't expect fireworks.

Available for hire. Babies and children welcome: high chairs. Booking advisable. Tables outdoors (5, terrace).

Railroad
120-122 Morning Lane, E9 6LH (8985 2858, www.railroadhackney.co.uk). Hackney Central rail. **Breakfast served** 10am-3.30pm, **lunch served** noon-3.30pm Wed-Sun. **Dinner served** 7-9.30pm Wed-Sat. **Main courses** £10-£15. **Set dinner** (7-9.30pm Wed, Thur) £16 2 courses, £19.50 3 courses. **Credit** MC, V.
Initially winning acclaim for its brunch, this cosy spot on Homerton's fast-gentrifying Morning Lane is now a local fave for lunch and dinner too. Gone are the open-mic nights, and in has come a sharpened focus on Railroad's eclectic, homely dishes, which run the gamut from moroccan eggs to ajo blanco. The seating options are also diverse, with diner-style tables arranged next to battered school chairs. Although the space leaves you in no doubt you're in Hackney – an arty black and white photo of an obscure indie singer graces the wall, and craft beers line the shelves – the atmosphere is easy-going. Beetroot borani made a lip-smacking start. This yoghurt, beetroot and garlic purée (popularised by Moro) was taken to new heights with the addition of orange blossom. Mains were also good. Line-caught mackerel came with a (slightly too moist) bulgar wheat, dill and yoghurt salad; and birria – a Mexican stew of pork shoulder, chipotle chillies and sweet potato – was rich and hearty. After a break to peruse the books for sale (cookery books sit beside literary classics), we enjoyed a sensationally light yet rich Cru Virunga chocolate cake and a Square Mile espresso – the perfect end to a civilised evening.
Babies and children welcome: high chair. Booking advisable dinner; not accepted lunch. Separate room for parties, seats 20.

Rawduck **NEW**
5 Amhurst Road, E8 1JB (8986 6534, www.rawduckhackney.co.uk). Hackney Central rail. **Meals served** 8am-10pm Mon-Fri; 10am-10pm Sat; 10.30am-5.30pm Sun. **Main courses** £6-£7. **Credit** MC, V.
The people behind Ducksoup in Soho have moved upstream to Hackney to open their second venture. Echoing the venue's name, the look here is raw, though this is no ugly duckling. The thin strip of a space is flanked on one side by a poured concrete counter, and on the other by matching concrete tables meant for sharing. Friendly staff and old vinyl spinning at the back give the place a casual feel. As with Ducksoup, the emphasis is on quality ingredients, assembled simply. By day, Rawduck has a trendy café vibe with buttery breakfast buns from nearby Violet Cakes, sandwiches on E5 Bakehouse breads, and coffee from Caravan. By night it transforms into a wine bar with natural and biodynamic wines, mostly French and Italian. Don't be put off by the prices on the board: the bottles hanging in front of it are generally cheaper, as are the carafes. A scoop of soft rillettes speckled with black pepper made a pleasing accompaniment to a punchy Apulian red. Spatchcocked quail looked like it had slipped under a cartoon steamroller, but the meat was surprisingly tender. Rawduck's proximity to Hackney Central station should make it a popular stop-off.
Available for hire. Babies and children admitted. Bookings not accepted. Disabled: toilet. Tables outdoors (2, pavement).
For branch (Ducksoup) see index.

Hackney Wick

Hackney Pearl

11 Prince Edward Road, E9 5LX (8510 3605, www.thehackneypearl.com). Hackney Wick rail.
Open 8am-11pm Mon-Fri; 10am-11pm Sat, Sun.
Lunch served noon-4pm, **dinner served** 6-10pm daily. **Brunch served** 10am-4pm Mon-Fri; 10am-1pm Sat, Sun. **Main courses** £11.50-£14.70. **Credit** MC, V.

Hackney Wick draws the young and arty in ever-increasing numbers, but it's still an uninviting prospect as you thread your way through the concrete landscape created by the mix of estates, industrial sprawl and dual carriageway overhead. So the little enclave that includes the Pearl, an enterprising Argos-style vinyl shop, a bike shop and an architectural salvage store provides a welcome oasis, especially if it's sunny and you can sit out on the street. The interior is equally delightful, a homely space that's nailed the shabby-chic aesthetic to perfection. Would that the food were so spot-on. A celeriac remoulade was richly perfect, a meze selection tangy and spicy, but the more substantial dishes were disappointing. Onglet with baked chips featured overcooked, flavourless meat, and the (gigantic) meatloaf that our friendly waitress assured us was the best she'd ever tasted turned out to be bland and under-seasoned, its accompanying tomato sauce little more than, well, tomato sauce. At £12.50, we'd hoped for something a bit special. Still, the huge wedges of cake are delicious, and the coffee is good, making it a fine place to stop if you happen to be buying a bike, a piece of architectural salvage or a record.
Available for hire. Babies and children welcome: high chairs; nappy-changing facilities. Booking advisable. Disabled: toilet. Tables outdoors (7, terrace; 6, pavement). Takeaway service.

Stoke Newington

Homa

71-73 Stoke Newington Church Street, N16 0AS (7254 2072, www.homalondon.co.uk). Stoke Newington rail or bus 73, 393, 476. **Open** 9am-10.30pm Mon-Sat; 10am-10pm Sun. **Brunch served** 10am-3pm Mon-Fri; 10am-4pm Sat, Sun. **Lunch served** noon-3pm Mon-Fri; noon-4pm Sat; noon-5pm Sun. **Dinner served** 6-10.30pm Mon-Fri; 6.30-10.30pm Sat; 6-10pm Sun. **Main courses** £6.50-£18. **Credit** MC, V.

Although Homa's decorative floor tiles make for a pleasing entrance, its new wooden tables and neutral walls are a bit uninspiring, and cleanliness isn't always up to scratch – we arrived to crumbs on a seat, as well as a bin in the ladies that was crying out to be emptied. A basket of focaccia, delivered by a friendly waiter, was also on the stale side. Things improved with a lovely starter of burrata with a delicately sweet caponata – a perfect match. Mains, from a list of hearty Mediterranean classics, brought the overall standard firmly back down to average, however. A plate of tender ox cheeks served with a rich gravy was quite small for the price, and served lukewarm; a funghi pizza had a perfect base but a very sparse tomato sauce topping and less-than-generous helping of mushrooms. Own-made ice-cream helped to lift our spirits – which were, however, dampened again when we were presented with the wrong (much more expensive) bill. Twice. Still, Homa's Church Street terrace appears to be as popular as ever on fine days, and if you're looking for a pleasant enough spot to have brunch or sip wine (from an extensive list), you could do far worse.
Babies and children welcome: high chairs; nappy-changing facilities. Booking advisable. Disabled: toilet. Separate room for parties, seats 40. Tables outdoors (14, terrace). Takeaway service. **Map 25 B1.**

North

Belsize Park

Giraffe

196-198 Haverstock Hill, NW3 2AG (7431 3812, www.giraffe.net). Belsize Park tube. **Meals served** 8am-11pm Mon-Fri; 9am-11pm Sat; 9am-10.30pm Sun. **Main courses** £6.95-£15.95. **Credit** AmEx, MC, V.

This hit chain's purchase by Tesco ruffled a few fans' feathers, but so far Giraffe does not seem to have changed its spots. Quality bangers and burgers, check. Esteemed coffee supplier, check. Global grab-bag of ingredients, check. The firm is renowned for its zippy service and happy accommodation of children, so we were surprised to find these qualities somewhat lacking; the waitress confessed she had a hangover. Our food was true to form, however. The winning dish was a menu staple: hot Thai-style duck stir-fry, which showcases the moreish combination of chilli jam, basil and mint. Giraffe's burritos and waist-conscious salads are also reliable, as are the skin-on fries. The kids' menu has options that appeal equally to parents and their offspring, including grilled salmon, a couple of chicken dishes and pasta pomodoro. Ice-cream comes from the admired producer Jude's, but otherwise desserts tend to disappoint – apple and cherry crumble was predictably over-sweet. If you want something yummy, mummies, browse the list of cocktails instead. Giraffe's menu changes according to the time of day; various (sometimes confusing) deals are offered at certain times, so hit the right moment and you can eat and drink cheaply indeed.
Babies and children welcome: children's menu; crayons; high chairs; nappy-changing facilities. Booking advisable. Disabled: toilet. Tables outdoors (16, terrace). Takeaway service.
Map 28 C3.
For branches see index.

Rawduck. See p45.

Greenberry Café

Camden & Chalk Farm

Greenberry Café NEW
*101 Regents Park Road, NW1 8UR (7483 3765,
www.greenberrycafe.co.uk). Chalk Farm tube.*
Breakfast served 9am-3pm daily. **Lunch
served** noon-3pm Mon-Sat; noon-4pm Sun.
Dinner served 6-11pm Mon-Sat. **Main
courses** £9.50-£19.75. **Set meal** (noon-3pm,
6-11pm Mon-Fri) £11 2 courses, £13.50 3 courses.
Credit MC, V.
When Greenberry Café opened in late 2012, we
praised the adventurous cooking and welcoming
atmosphere. Returning a few months later, we
found that the vibe remains the same, but the
kitchen radiance has dimmed and the global reach
had been curtailed. Greenberry's simple breakfast
menu is served until 3pm; at noon it segues into a
traiteur list (salads or simple plates such as Stoke
Newington smoked salmon with soda bread). A
more substantial menu is also served at lunch and
dinner. From this, neither a bland yellowfin tuna
carpaccio nor a slightly woolly heritage tomato and
parmesan salad hit the spot. But roast sea bream
with new potatoes, peas and broad beans worked
a treat – cooked just-so (tender fish, crisp and salty
skin) and full of summer flavour. Pulled pork bun
with a smear of apple purée and red cabbage
coleslaw was more workaday. Owner Morfudd
Richards' own-made ice-creams are available for
dessert, alongside the likes of salted chocolate tart.
The short but sweet wine list has excellent tasting
notes. During the day, Greenberry may be a little
too family-friendly for some; in the evening,
everyone from dog-walkers (and their pooches) to
groups of friends pile in to the unfussily decorated
room. It's a great haunt for locals, but unless the
kitchen dials it up a notch or two, not worth
crossing town for.
*Available for hire. Babies and children welcome:
children's menu; high chairs. Booking advisable
breakast Sat, Sun. Tables outdoors (4, pavement).
Takeaway service.* **Map 27 A1.**

Made in Camden
*Roundhouse, Chalk Farm Road, NW1 8EH
(7424 8495, www.madeincamden.com). Chalk
Farm tube.* **Lunch served** noon-2.30pm Tue-
Fri. **Brunch served** 10.30am-3pm Sat, Sun.
Dinner served 6-10.30pm Mon-Sat. **Main
courses** £7.95-£16. **Set lunch** £7 1 course,
£8.95 2 courses, £11.95 3 courses. **Credit**
AmEx, MC, V.
This bar and restaurant in the Roundhouse concert
venue has won much applause, but there has been
a recent change of cast in the kitchen and our dinner
was a mix of hits and flops. A cold, rubbery soft-
poached egg took centre stage in a dish purportedly
starring asparagus and miso butter. Yet the kitchen
is capable of excellent fusion cooking, as shown in
a memorable plate of fennel with feta, pistachios,
salted caramel, lemon zest and dill. Lush smoky
baba ganoush sparkling with pomegranate seeds
led the meze board; beetroot purée with nigella
tasted great but was too watery. Beautifully crisp
calamares had been winningly sprinkled over yuzu
aïoli and chilli jam; in contrast, desserts, including
a tropical twist on tiramisu, lacked finesse. The
intelligent wine list starts at £18 per bottle and is
brief but diverse, including 15 by-the-glass options.
Alternatively, there are Camden Town ales on
draught, a wide choice of bottled beers and an
appealing cocktail list. Once the concert-goers have
taken their seats, noise diminishes and the red and
wood-toned room transforms into a fabulously
chilled spot well worth considering as an alternative
to standalone restaurants.
*Babies and children welcome: high chairs; nappy-
changing facilities. Booking advisable. Disabled:
toilet.* **Map 27 B1.**

Islington

★ Ottolenghi
*287 Upper Street, N1 2TZ (7288 1454,
www.ottolenghi.co.uk). Angel tube or Highbury
& Islington tube/rail.* **Meals served** 8am-10pm
Mon-Wed; 8am-10.30pm Thur-Sat; 9am-7pm Sun.
Main courses £11-£17. **Credit** AmEx, MC, V.
Hit cookbooks have made this flagship branch of
the burgeoning Ottolenghi empire a point of
pilgrimage for foodies the world over. Those
Americans brunching nearby are as likely to be
tourists as local émigrés from the banking sector,
and back in the US they'll rarely have seen french
toast as fat and fluffy as found here. Made from
brioche and served with crème fraîche and a thin
berry and muscat compote, it makes a heady start
to the day and, regrettably, tends to prevent further
indulgence in tempting muffins and pastries. If
you're not seeking a sugar-high, alternatives
include welsh rarebit, scrambled eggs with smoked
salmon or a lively chorizo-spiked take on baked
beans served with sourdough, fried egg and black
pudding. The queue at the front contains much
takeaway custom for the lavish spread of taste-
tingling salads, cakes and nibbles such as flaky
cheese straws. In the evening (when bookings are
taken), the cool white interior works a double shift
as a smart and comparatively pricey restaurant
serving elegant fusion dishes for sharing. Expect
the likes of grilled quail with smoked chilli
chocolate sauce, potato, pak choi and sesame – and
expect to have trouble snaring a table. The three
other branches are smaller, operating as deli-shops
rather than restaurants.
*Babies and children welcome: high chairs. Booking
advisable dinner; not accepted lunch. Takeaway
service.* **Map 5 O1.**
For branches see index.

Kentish Town

Kentish Canteen
*300 Kentish Town Road, NW5 2TG (7485 7331,
www.kentishcanteen.co.uk). Kentish Town tube.*
Meals served 10am-10.30pm Mon-Fri; 9am-
10.30pm Sat, Sun. **Main courses** £5-£17. **Set
meal** (noon-7pm Mon-Fri) £11 1 course incl glass
of wine or beer. **Credit** AmEx, MC, V.
A spacious spot, the Canteen has big picture
windows, a Kentish Town-themed mural on one wall
and brasserie-style seating covered in faux-leather.
The menu leaps around a bit, from dips and fish and
chips to ambitious-sounding mains (braised beef
cheeks with polenta and thyme jus), to pub-grub
fare such as spicy buffalo chicken wings with blue
cheese dip. To start, 'salt 'n' pepper squid' had a
softly spicy coating, and chilli jam added a pleasant
edge; pumpkin ravioli was smooth and well cooked.
But a main of poached bream and saffron bisque
was a serious misfire: everything was almost taste-
free – the lacklustre fish sat in a heavy, bland bisque
(despite chilli flakes) with mushy prawns and
mussels; it was served with 'croûtons' that were
actually slices of fried baguette. A less ambitious
dish, steak frites, was OK. Brunch might be a safer
bet, when burgers, egg dishes and baked goods are
joined by the likes of chorizo salad. In its favour, we
liked the fact that the Canteen attracts a mixed bag
of diners (families, couples, work groups) for
everything from drinks to a full meal. A useful place
if you live locally, with friendly staff adding to the
appeal. The basement is home to Shebeen bar.
*Available for hire. Babies and children welcome:
children's menu; high chairs; nappy-changing
facilities. Booking advisable Sat, Sun. Disabled:
toilet. Separate room for parties, seats 45.
Tables outdoors (9, terrace).* **Map 26 B4.**

British

'What does it mean to be British?' is a question oft-asked, with answers regularly reinterpreted. Likewise, 'What is meant by British cuisine?' To define the cooking style of 'British' restaurants in 2014 is to get to the heart of the revolution that has transformed the London dining scene over the past quarter-century. A rediscovery of lost recipes from Britain's culinary heritage has certainly played its part in forging the current repertoire, though the best of today's restaurants are no nostalgic throwbacks. Fergus Henderson is rightly renowned as a pioneer, yet many of the dishes served at his **St John** follow in traditions other than his own. It is the reinvention of domestic cookery, Britain's indigenous peasant cuisine that used the cheapest cuts of meat and offal, for which Henderson should be lauded. A culinary movement has duly been inspired, giving us restaurants such as the excellent **Hereford Road**, run by St John alumni, as well as a raft of other establishments – the first-rate **Brawn** among them – dedicated to 'nose to tail eating'. Yet there are other strands to the cuisine, including that developed by haute cuisine practitioners such as Richard Corrigan (**Corrigan's Mayfair**) and Jason Atherton (**Social Eating House**). Vitality suffuses this chapter, with great new restaurants such as the **Clove Club** opening in the past year, to contrast with centuries-old classics like **Wiltons** and **Simpson's-in-the-Strand**.

Central
City

Boisdale of Bishopsgate
Swedeland Court, 202 Bishopsgate, EC2M 4NR (7283 1763, www.boisdale.co.uk). Liverpool Street tube/rail.
Bar **Open** 11am-9.30pm Mon-Fri.
Restaurant **Lunch served** noon-3pm, **dinner served** 6-9.30pm Mon-Fri. **Main courses** £16.50-£32.50. **Set meal** £12.50, £19.75 2 courses.
Both **Credit** AmEx, MC, V.
Make your way down a Dickensian London court to enter a Hollywood-esque version of auld Edinburgh, with tartan seats, dark red and green walls, aged-looking woodwork and waitresses in wee tartan skirts. There's a smart bar at ground level, and a cavern-like basement housing the main dining room. For all the shortbread-tin heritage vibe, this branch of Boisdale is a comfortable and well-run spot, where you immediately feel well looked after. The 'Jacobite' set menu – a City bargain at £19.75 – included what may be the world's finest scotch egg, made with smooth, savoury haggis offset by hot mustard relish. To follow, a chicken and mushroom pie in perfectly

crisp pastry was a similarly enjoyable mix of comfort food and sophistication. Prices shoot up for the carte, which includes an imposing choice of Aberdeen Angus steaks, as well as oysters and other Scottish options. All three Boisdales host very respectable music programmes, with leading performers in jazz and other styles. They also share similarly impressive – but not overpriced – wine lists, and, naturally, a magnificent choice of whiskies. Havana cigars are a speciality too, but nowadays aficionados are advised to head for the Belgravia branch and its heated cigar terrace.
Available for hire. Babies and children admitted. Booking essential dinner. Dress: smart casual. Separate room for parties, seats 44. **Map 12 R5**.
For branches see index.

Paternoster Chop House
Warwick Court, Paternoster Square, EC4M 7DX (7029 9400, www.paternosterchophouse.co.uk). St Paul's tube. **Lunch served** noon-3.30pm Mon-Fri; noon-4pm Sun. **Dinner served** 5.30-10.30pm Mon-Fri. **Main courses** £15-£25. **Set meal** £19.50 2 courses, £23 3 courses.
Credit AmEx, MC, V.
A no-nonsense name for this D&D London restaurant just across Paternoster Square from the London Stock Exchange. Traders pack in at lunchtime or after close-of-markets for steaks, chops, mixed grills and other manly main courses – although the atmosphere is casual. You don't have to work in the Square Mile to feel welcome, and plenty of families of tourists stop in post-St Paul's sightseeing. It's a modern, open and clean-lined space, with big windows looking on to the cathedral. Meat is butchered on site and is top quality; a 'Beast of the Day' comes with a biography, and fish makes much of its sustainable sourcing. To keep prices down, go for the 'Best of British' menu. At £19.50 for two courses, it's not bad value, though its options don't include the more expensive cuts of meat. Instead, you'll find solid renditions of fish and chips, kipper pâté or cottage pie – rich and full-flavoured, with Longhorn beef mince. Puddings are of the sweet and filling sort (apple and blackberry bakewell tart, lemon curd sponge) and there are Neal's Yard Dairy cheeses. D&D's typically polished and warm service operates throughout.
Available for hire. Babies and children welcome: high chairs; nappy-changing facilities. Booking advisable; essential lunch. Disabled: toilet. Separate room for parties, seats 13. Tables outdoors (15, courtyard). **Map 11 O6**.
For branch (Butlers Wharf Chop House) see index.

Restaurant at St Paul's

St Paul's Cathedral, St Paul's Churchyard, EC4M 8AD (7248 2469, www.restaurantat stpauls.co.uk). St Paul's tube.
Café **Open/meals served** 9am-5pm Mon-Sat; 10am-4pm Sun.
Restaurant **Lunch served** noon-3pm daily.
Tea served 2.30-4.30pm Mon-Sat. **Set lunch** £21.50 2 courses, £25.95 3 courses. **Set tea** £15.95-£21.25.
Both **Credit** MC, V.
In the giant crypt beneath St Paul's, not far from the self-service café, souvenir shop and monuments to Nelsonian sea captains, an area has been imaginatively set aside to form the Restaurant. Windows let in natural light (unlike in the main crypt), and plain and mellow-green woodwork, white walls and a teapot-lined dresser create a charming, airy, slightly rustic look. Any restaurant in a tourist attraction might be expected to be routine, but the kitchen here is admirably enterprising. Monthly changing lunch menus highlight fine-quality seasonal British produce. On our visit, carrot and spring onion terrine made a lovely refreshing starter, served with a delicate curry mayonnaise. To follow, crispy duck leg was cooked just right, and served with rich, satisfying black pudding. Now that blood sausage is fashionable, much of it is of variable quality, but this was first-rate. Service was bright and helpful, and there's a short but well-priced wine list. Overall, the 'City Lunch' is a classy bargain for the Square Mile. A larger roast menu is provided on Sundays, and after lunch (except on Sundays) very proper afternoon tea is served, with flowery plates, scones, jam and three-decker cake stands – as the Almighty ordained.
Babies and children welcome: high chairs; nappy-changing facilities. Booking advisable. Disabled: lift; toilet. **Map 11 O6.**

Clerkenwell & Farringdon

Medcalf

40 Exmouth Market, EC1R 4QE (7833 3533, www.medcalfbar.co.uk). Farringdon tube/rail or bus 19, 38, 341. **Lunch served** noon-3pm Mon-Sat; noon-3.30pm Sun. **Dinner served** 6-10pm Mon-Thur, Sat; 6-10.30pm Fri. **Main courses** £12.50-£22. **Credit** MC, V.
With its twinkling overhead lighting in the evening and pavement seating on warm days, Exmouth Market is a fine place to stroll along and choose a place to eat or drink. You could do a lot worse than Medcalf, one of the original catalysts in the rejuvenation of this Clerkenwell street. There's a bar room to one side where drinkers can enjoy London beers and spirits, or good-value wines by the glass and carafe; the cute little garden at the back is a boon. The dining room is wood-lined and treads a pleasing path between boho and smart, although the brown-paper menus and dressed-down waiters swing things right back to casual. Too casual sometimes – staff can be distracted and a bit ineffective, and on our last visit we witnessed several frustrated punters waving for service. Food is uncomplicated and resolutely British, with a roster of classics – Mersea oysters, chicken and mushroom pie, steak and chips, pork chop with turnips and cider sauce, sticky toffee pudding. Ingredients are seasonal, quality is high, and the cooking is competent enough to make Medcalf a very agreeable spot for lunch or dinner.

Babies and children welcome (until 7.30pm): high chairs. Booking advisable dinner. Disabled: toilet. Separate room for parties, seats 18. Tables outdoors (7, pavement; 5, garden). **Map 5 N4.**

★ St John `HOT 50`

26 St John Street, EC1M 4AY (7251 0848, www.stjohngroup.uk.com). Barbican tube or Farringdon tube/rail. **Lunch served** noon-2.45pm Mon-Fri; 1-2.30pm Sun. **Dinner served** 6-10.45pm Mon-Sat. **Main courses** £13.50-£23.80. **Credit** AmEx, MC, V.
Fergus Henderson and Trevor Gulliver's restaurant – now the heart of a mini-empire with branch, bakery and wine dealership – has been praised to the skies for reacquainting the British with the full possibilities of native produce, and especially anything gutsy and offal-ish. Perhaps as influential, however, has been its almost defiantly casual style: a Michelin-starred restaurant for people who run from the very idea. The mezzanine dining room in the former Smithfield smokehouse has bare white walls, battered floorboards and tables lined up canteen-style; the downstairs bar, with superb snacks, is equally basic. Exceptional staff are able to chat without allowing anything to go off-track. St John's cooking is famously full-on, but also sophisticated, concocting flavours that are delicate as well as rich. Black cuttlefish and onions was extraordinary, arriving in a supremely deep-flavoured ink-based sauce with a hint of mint; ox tongue was perfectly cooked to bring out every taste and texture, and served with fantastic horseradish. This is powerful cooking, so if you go for a full dinner, including the great neo-traditional puds, leave time for digestion. Wines – all French, many under St John's own label, and quite generously priced – are of a quality to match.
Babies and children welcome: high chairs. Booking advisable dinner and weekends. Disabled: toilet (bar). Separate room for parties, seats 18. **Map 5 O5.**

Covent Garden

Rules

35 Maiden Lane, WC2E 7LB (7836 5314, www.rules.co.uk). Covent Garden tube. **Meals served** noon-11.30pm Mon-Sat; noon-10.30pm Sun. **Main courses** £17.95-£34.50. **Credit** AmEx, MC, V.
Rules may look as though nothing has changed for 50 years (or more – the restaurant was established in 1798), but this old-stager hasn't made it this far without adapting to the times. Together with the dark wood and red colour scheme, patterned carpet, caricatures and old paintings are modern touches. Witness the Kate Middleton cocktail (Sipsmith gin, Pinky vodka, Lillet aperitif wine and crystallised violets and rose petals). A menu of classics, with an emphasis on game, runs from potted shrimps to saddle of rabbit. Everything is cooked plainly, but with care and using decent ingredients; for example, the sirloin steak with béarnaise and chips was pretty much perfect – golden chips, crunchy on the outside, hot and yielding on the inside; tender meat, grilled just-so and with real flavour. Guinea fowl caesar salad was an average salad lifted by top-notch bird; grilled plaice topped with artichokes and capers, served with a side of braised red peppers (from the specials list), scored for looks and flavour. Kir royal jelly with blackcurrant sorbet and summer fruits 'salad' made a good summer alternative to the wintery delights of golden syrup

sponge pudding with custard. Service is polite and attentive, characteristics much admired by the mainly middle-aged-and-over clientele. Like the menu, the Rhône Valley-oriented wine list holds no bargains, but is carefully constructed.
Babies and children welcome: high chairs. Booking advisable. Dress: smart casual; no shorts. Separate rooms for parties, seating 8-18. **Map 18 E5.**

Union Jacks

4 Central St Giles Piazza, WC2H 8AB (3597 7888, www.unionjacksrestaurants.com). Tottenham Court Road tube. **Open** noon-11pm Mon-Sat; noon-10pm Sun. **Main courses** £8-£13.50. **Credit** AmEx, MC, V.
One successful restaurant chain was never going to be enough for Jamie Oliver. With his 'Italian' brand spread across Britain, he opened the first Union Jacks in the fairly new Central Saint Giles development in late 2011; it was clear this was a blueprint rather than a one-off. The look is playground-punk (the titular flags, school chairs, just-so graffiti) with a huge dollop of GB nostalgia (teapots come with cosies on, for instance, and the soundtrack is pure 1990s Britpop). But behind all this, the menu is slightly baffling. 'British sharing plates' and 'British classics' include the likes of prawn cocktail, 'beans on toast' and 'empire chicken' – they're very fresh and generally successful, but not always easy dishes to share. Puds include such '70s faves as arctic roll and black forest gateau. The main concept, though, is 'flatbread pizzas', which essentially means sourdough bases topped with British versions of the classics. So a Margaret features lincolnshire poacher cheese, tomatoes and marjoram; a Woodman comes with wild mushrooms, cheddar and herbs. Despite the flames licking away in the wood-fired oven, the results aren't really good enough to explain why the pizza needed reinvention. But this is a fun place to eat: everything is suffused with Jamie's tongue-in-cheek humour, and staff are as enthusiastic as you'd hope.
Available for hire. Babies and children welcome: high chairs; nappy-changing facilities. Disabled: lift; toilet. Tables outdoors (25, courtyard). Takeaway service. **Map 18 D2.**
For branches see index.

Fitzrovia

Newman Street Tavern `NEW`

48 Newman Street, W1T 1QQ (3667 1445, www.newmanstreettavern.co.uk). Goodge Street tube. **Open** noon-11pm Mon-Sat; 10.30am-5pm Sun. **Lunch served** noon-3pm Mon-Fri. **Brunch served** 10.30am-4.30pm Sat, Sun. **Dinner served** 5.30-10.30pm Mon-Fri; 5.30-11pm Sat. **Main courses** £12-£23. **Credit** AmEx, MC, V.
There's a lot going on beind the scenes at this handsome but unassuming corner site. From bread-making to meat ageing, staff are very hands-on, and properly interested in provenance and seasonality. A tempting menu runs from bar snacks (cobnut saucisson, cornichons and onions) and seafood (oysters, brown crab on toast) to hefty mains such as grilled Galloway rib with horseradish. Fish and chips is a menu constant, though the fish regularly changes (pouting on our visit). Execution can falter: a starter of cured char with new potatoes and dill sounded alluring but could have done with more of the herb, while a main of grilled abalone tuna was a fine piece of fish clumsily cooked (frazzled at the

edge, almost raw at the middle). Spit-roast Middle White pork with creamy 'beer onions' was better – tasty and with good crackling, and we wolfed down a delicate elderflower jelly with strawberry sauce. An interesting selection of drinks includes cocktails (the Spritzrovia features rhubarb purée, Aperol and prosecco), sherries by the glass and Crate Brewery bitter on draught alongside a well-organised wine list. Staff are charming and on-the-ball. All in all, an ideal local (they even offer brunch at the weekend), surprisingly located in W1.

Available for hire. Babies and children welcome: high chairs; nappy-changing facilities. Booking advisable. Disabled: toilet. Tables outdoors (3, pavement). **Map 17 A1.**

Gloucester Road

Launceston Place

1A Launceston Place, W8 5RL (7937 6912, www.launcestonplace-restaurant.co.uk). Gloucester Road tube. **Lunch served** noon-2.30pm Tue-Sat; noon-3pm Sun. **Dinner served** 6-10.30pm Mon-Sat; 6.30-9.30pm Sun. **Set lunch** (Tue-Sat) £25 3 courses. **Set dinner** £48 3 courses, £65 tasting menu. **Credit** AmEx, MC, V.

Not original, naming a restaurant after its street – there are loads like that in London. But when it's as nice as this… Well, why not? LP's villagey part of Kensington is festooned with flowers in summer, and its rows of mansions are immaculate: this poshest outpost of the D&D London restaurant group fits in. It has the quirks and tics that the Michelin inspectors look for (it was awarded a star in 2013), but our recent visit showed irregularities. The carpets were a bit scuffed, for instance, and the men's toilets are tiny. Towards the end of a late lunch booking, we experienced rushed service. The peculiarly shaped series of rooms works better after dark, when the charcoal walls and spectral artworks lend gravitas. Standards of food are generally high; cooking is an accessible and inventive French/British marriage. A starter of salmon with mooli and sweet little cubes of pressed apple was made special by a sorbet-like scoop of iced horseradish, although hake with peas, broad beans and lettuce tasted too vegetal and 'green'. Launceston Place is a restaurant that makes living in Launceston Place even nicer than it undoubtedly already is, but a visit from further afield isn't always rewarded.

Available for hire. Babies and children welcome: high chairs. Booking advisable. Disabled: toilet. Separate room for parties, seats 10. **Map 7 C9.**

Holborn

Great Queen Street

32 Great Queen Street, WC2B 5AA (7242 0622). Covent Garden or Holborn tube. Bar **Open** 5-11.30pm Tue-Sat. *Restaurant* **Lunch served** noon-2.30pm Mon-Sat; noon-3pm Sun. **Dinner served** 6-10.30pm Mon-Sat. **Main courses** £10.80-£22. *Both* **Credit** MC, V.

A product of the noughties gastropub boom, Great Queen Street still turns out dishes in the tradition of its antecedents, and of the year it was founded (2007). Yet despite the casual feel, pub-like look and cacophony of voices, this is no pub – it's a sit-down restaurant where bookings are almost essential. The excellent location, mere steps away from central Covent Garden, ensures its perennial

popularity. The prized outdoor tables are almost never vacant, but walk-ins may find space at the bar stools towards the back, where the full menu is also served. The menu changes daily, is produce-led and is predominantly British. There's minimal fussing with ingredients; for example, a plump piece of bone-in smoked mackerel was served with a dollop each of cooked gooseberries and horseradish. Pork had been slow-cooked before having a generous quantity of cockles added to the stew. Vegetarian dishes are sometimes less imaginative, such as a simple tart of roast pepper, tomato and new-season garlic. Puddings might include a semifreddo, or an apricot and almond tart. The dozen or so wines by the glass are relatively affordable rather than covetable, a clue to Great Queen Street's priorities.

Babies and children welcome: high chair. Booking advisable Fri, Sat. Disabled: toilet. Tables outdoors (4, pavement). **Map 18 E3.**

King's Cross

Gilbert Scott `HOT 50`

St Pancras Renaissance London Hotel, Euston Road, NW1 2AR (7278 3888, www.thegilbert scott.co.uk). King's Cross St Pancras tube/rail. **Brunch served** 10am-2pm Sat, Sun. **Lunch served** noon-3pm, **dinner served** 5.30-11pm Mon-Fri. **Meals served** noon-11pm Sat; noon-10pm Sun. **Main courses** £14-£32. **Set meal** (noon-3pm, 5.30-6.30pm, 10-11pm Mon-Fri) £21 2 courses, £25 3 courses. **Credit** AmEx, MC, V.

The 2011 reopening of architect George Gilbert Scott's former Midland Grand Hotel has resurrected one of the most visually arresting edifices in London; its former Coffee Room is now home to this relatively casual venture from chef Marcus Wareing. His mark is evident in the well-drilled, personable service and flawless cooking. As with the rest of the hotel, the space is nothing short of spectacular – this is Victorian embellishment at its most exuberant, with pillars, gilt, cornicing and huge windows. But, thankfully, it's no temple to fine dining: the please-all, best-of-British menu shows off the dedication and imagination of the kitchen with dishes such as crispy pig's head with pickled cockles and sea herbs, or curried parsnip soup with onion bhajis. More traditional diners will be impressed by the sterling renditions of battered cod and chips, or beefburger with braised oxtail. Desserts continue the homeland theme: eccles cake with cheddar ice-cream, 'Mrs Beeton's snow egg', Irish cheese with honeycomb. The weekend brings roasts and a popular brunch, complete with pianist. The equally handsome bar at the entrance is good to know about in an area short of quality drinking options. Situated next to the Eurostar terminus, where continental Europeans disembark, this is a restaurant of which we can all be proud. Don't wait for a train journey to book a table.

Babies and children welcome: high-chairs. Booking advisable. Disabled: lift; toilet. Dress: smart casual. Separate room for parties, seats 18. **Map 4 L3.**

Plum & Spilt Milk `NEW`

Great Northern Hotel, King's Cross St Pancras Station, Pancras Road, N1C 4TB (3388 0818, www.plumandspiltmilk.com). King's Cross St Pancras tube/rail. **Breakfast served** 7-10am Mon-Fri; 8-11am Sat, Sun. **Lunch served** 11.30am-3.30pm Mon-Sat. **Brunch served** 11.30am-3pm Sun. **Dinner served** 5.30-11pm

daily. **Main courses** £8.50-£39.50. **Set lunch** (Mon-Fri) £19.50 2 courses, £23.50 3 courses. **Credit** AmEx, MC, V.

The Great Northern Hotel takes its signals from the King's Cross railway station that surrounds it. The livery looks swanky; the prices are high. The GNH even hired an ex-Ramsay celebrity chef to run its restaurant, but though Mark Sargeant didn't take up his post until some months after Plum & Spilt Milk opened, 'Sarge' is now in charge. Many dishes here are assembled, rather than cooked, though minimal intervention is commendable when the ingredients are first-rate, as in our starter plate of charcuterie. The accompanying celeriac remoulade was a nice touch, although the titular plum garnishing the plate made it resemble a ploughman's lunch. Toast topped with broad bean paste, pea shoots and crumbled caerphilly cheese was an equally simple but much more successful combination. The menu is British, in the broadest sense. So British it includes monkfish curry, juicy and well spiced, but served with slightly overcooked and over-salted rice, not the pilaf described on the menu. A vegetarian main course of potato dumplings – gnocchi, as Italians would call them – were oversized and pan-fried. The cocktails and wine service were, however, excellent; there are also two bars attached to the restaurant. Save the Great Northern Hotel for drinks or business meals when travelling, because flawed or not, it's still the best place to eat at King's Cross station.

Available for hire. Babies and children welcome: high chairs. Booking essential dinner. Disabled: toilet. Separate room for parties, seats 14. **Map 4 L3.**

Mayfair

★ Corrigan's Mayfair

28 Upper Grosvenor Street, W1K 7EH (7499 9943, www.corrigansmayfair.com). Marble Arch tube. **Lunch served** noon-2.30pm Mon-Fri; noon-3.45pm Sun. **Dinner served** 6-10.30pm Mon-Sat; 6-9.15pm Sun. **Main courses** £21-£38. **Set lunch** (Mon-Fri) £25 2 courses. **Set meal** (Mon-Fri, dinner Sat, Sun) £75 tasting menu; (Sun) £27 3 courses. **Cover** £2. **Credit** AmEx, MC, V.

As your coats are taken and reservations checked, a pianist tinkles away on a baby grand by the entrance of Richard Corrigan's Mayfair restaurant. If stopping for a drink, you're led to a long marble bar topped with individual railway-style lamps; those eating continue to the dusky, romantically lit dining room, which has any solemnity removed by humorous feathered lampshades and metal bird sculptures. Pure luxury seeps from the copper-panelled walls in Corrigan's, where, for a price, a near-perfect experience awaits. All menus – the daily 'market lunch', bar, à la carte, tasting – are heavy on meat and fish (though there's a separate vegetarian menu), and cooking is absolutely top class. A starter of battered and fried oysters on the half shell came with slices of smooth suckling pig sausage and ribbons of lightly pickled vegetables: impeccable mouthfuls each. The tasting menu at £75 shows off the adroitness of the chefs, but there's still room for a down-to-earth side dish of chips. After such a sumptuous display of hospitality, the £2 'cover charge' seems mean-spirited when the bill is more or less guaranteed to hit £50 a head – although most here won't notice it. There's plenty of scope for indulgence on the wine list too.

Plum & Spilt Milk

Babies and children welcome: high chairs. Booking advisable. Disabled: toilet. Separate rooms for parties, seating 4-25. Vegetarian menu. **Map 9 G7.**

The Grill at the Dorchester `HOT 50`

The Dorchester, 53 Park Lane, W1K 1QA (7629 8888, www.thedorchester.com). Hyde Park Corner tube. **Breakfast served** 7-10.30am Mon-Fri; 8-11am Sat, Sun. **Lunch served** noon-2.30pm Mon-Fri; 12.30-3pm Sat; 12.30-3.30pm Sun. **Dinner served** 6.30-10.30pm Mon-Fri; 6.30-11pm Sat; 7-10.30pm Sun. **Main courses** £19-£46. **Set lunch** (Mon-Sat) £27 3 courses. **Set dinner** £35 3 courses. **Set meal** £70 tasting menu (£95 incl wine). **Credit** AmEx, MC, V.

Huge paintings of bonnie Hielan' laddies and lasses prance exuberantly round the gilded walls of the Dorchester Grill. The grand room is a nostalgic Caledonia of tartan cushions and plaster thistles, though it's tempered by a huge display of English roses in the centre. There can be few more opulent rooms in which to eat in London. All the formalities of fine dining are observed here, from elaborate napkin rituals to the multitude of waiters who remember your name and pull your chair out for you. And in this iconic Park Lane hotel, the food is as much of a draw as the flawless service. Bread arrives with three types of butter, including a 'smoked charcoal' flavour. The grills themselves always include the likes of Angus beef and day-boat fish; you might also see suckling pig three ways with aubergine purée, or venison with berries. House smoked salmon is carved with great ceremony tableside. It's perhaps just a shame that most Londoners will feel restricted by the invisible barrier that exists outside such luxury hotels – ignore it and you're in for a memorable meal that will make special occasions extra special.
Babies and children welcome: children's menu; high chairs. Booking advisable, essential weekends. Disabled: toilet. Dress: smart casual. **Map 9 G7.**

St James's

Wiltons

55 Jermyn Street, SW1Y 6LX (7629 9955, www.wiltons.co.uk). Green Park or Piccadilly Circus tube. **Lunch served** noon-2.30pm, **dinner served** 5.30-10.30pm Mon-Fri. **Main courses** £17.50-£60. **Set lunch** £38 3 courses. **Set dinner** (5.30-6.30pm) £26 2 courses, £30 3 courses. **Credit** AmEx, MC, V.

Conversations overheard at Wiltons, which was established in 1742, are always a cut above. On our last visit, an elderly gent recounted where he sat at the Coronation to his grandson (who later pronounced 'grouse shooting is just the best' when describing his summer plans). It's no private club, though, as anyone with sufficient funds can enjoy the seductive comfort of the dining room (bustling but cosy) and the supremely attentive, courteous service – from men in regulation black-and-white and ladies in prim green dresses with a distinct look of school matron. The kitchen doesn't do experimental, but renders its chosen repertoire very well. Prices have even dropped slightly for the three-course set lunch, from which we tried a lovely, smooth warm vichyssoise with crisp-fried egg and truffle. Also included was the day's roast, beautifully pink lamb cooked to perfection, and an apple and blackberry crumble that was also spot on. Transfer to the carte and you can enjoy other British classics – hefty grilled meats, more roasts, Wiltons' famed fish, oysters and other seafood. The wine range is predictably grand, and details (breads, fresh petits fours) are exquisite. Nice to see standards being maintained, even if one can't often afford it.
Booking advisable. Dress: smart; long-sleeved shirt required; no sportswear. Vegetarian menu. **Map 17 B5.**

Soho

Dean Street Townhouse

69-71 Dean Street, W1D 3SE (7434 1775, www.deanstreettownhouse.com). Piccadilly Circus or Tottenham Court Road tube.

Breakfast served 7am-noon Mon-Fri; 8am-noon Sat, Sun. **Brunch served** noon-5pm Sat, Sun. **Tea served** 3-5pm daily. **Meals served** noon-midnight Mon-Sat; noon-10.30pm Sun. **Main courses** £13.50-£34. **Set dinner** (5-6.30pm, 10.15pm-midnight) £16.50 2 courses, £19.50 3 courses. **Credit** AmEx, MC, V.

All things to all people at all hours – whatever the Soho occasion, chances are Dean Street Townhouse fits the bill. A leisurely breakfast, elevenses with the morning papers, a brisk business lunch, afternoon tea, pre-theatre quickie, romantic dinner for two… and if that dinner gets uncontrollably romantic, there are rooms upstairs. As a result of this catch-all appeal, DST is buzzing from open until close, and efficient but sometimes distant staff keep things moving along briskly. The all-inclusiveness extends to the menu, which rarely startles, but cossets and comforts with classic British dishes (there's a great fish and chips with mushy peas, as well as cauliflower and Keen's cheddar soup, and liver with bacon and onions). Special note must be given to the other Scottish national dish perpetually on the carte: mince and tatties. Granpaw Broon might splutter into his tea cup at the £13.50 price tag, but it's as good a version as anyone south of Gretna has ever made. DST is spread across a series of Georgian-era rooms, which exude a sense of history while wearing lightly their classical upgrade: the only irritation being the too-low chairs in the side room, which force diners into sitting uncomfortably.
Babies and children welcome: high chairs. Booking advisable. Disabled: toilet. Tables outdoors (7, terrace). **Map 17 B3.**

Hix `HOT 50`

66-70 Brewer Street, W1F 9UP (7292 3518, www.hixsoho.co.uk). Piccadilly Circus tube. **Meals served** noon-11.30pm daily. **Main courses** £17.75-£36.50. **Set meal** (noon-6.30pm daily; 10.30-11.30pm Mon-Sat; 9.30-10.30pm Sun) £17.50 2 courses, £22.50 3 courses. **Credit** AmEx, MC, V.

BRITISH

Shed. See p55.

Mark Hix, who for years worked for Caprice Holdings, now has an empire of his own, with outlets in Selfridges and Brown's Hotel, standalone restaurants Hix Oyster & Chop House and Tramshed (*see p239*), plus the Hix Oyster & Fish House in Lyme Regis. But this Soho venture feels like the essential Hix, dotted with YBA artworks, nicely buzzy, and with an air of having been here for years (though it only opened in 2009). Mark's Bar in the basement is a further lure, with its speakeasy vibe and trad cocktails. Hotel majors in British meat (with steak to the fore) and fish; we relished chargrilled Launceston lamb cutlets with cucumber and mint. It's no bargain; the cutlets cost £22.50 and a side of spring veg was tiny at £4.25. The set meal is good value, though a slightly undercooked sausage (served with a sprightly heritage potato and green onion salad) was a disappointment after a scrape-the-plate-clean starter of whipped beetroot with sheep's curd and hazelnuts served with moreish, lightly grilled flatbread. Classic pudding fans should order the cox's apple pie, with custard poured at the table. Charming service adds to the general feeling of well-being.
Available for hire. Babies and children welcome: children's menu; high chairs; nappy-changing facilities. Booking advisable. Disabled: toilet. Separate room for parties, seats 10. Vegan dishes. Vegetarian menu. **Map 17 A4**.
For branches see index.

Quo Vadis
26-29 Dean Street, W1D 3LL (7437 9585, www.quovadissoho.co.uk). Leicester Square, Piccadilly Circus or Tottenham Court Road tube. **Breakfast served** 8-11am Mon-Fri. **Lunch served** noon-2.45pm, **dinner served** 5.30-11pm Mon-Sat. **Main courses** £14-£18.50. **Set meal** £17.50 2 courses, £20 3 courses. **Credit** AmEx, MC, V.
This West End institution has changed hands many times since Pepino Leoni opened it in 1926. It's now under the care of Sam and Eddie Hart, of Spanish restaurants Fino (*see p221*) and Barrafina (*see*

p222), with Jeremy Lee in charge of the kitchen – an arrangement that deserves to see Quo Vadis up to its centenary. It's one of those restaurants that keeps Soho a special place for dining out; you might imagine being a rare-book dealer or a theatrical agent entertaining an actor, and settle in among the leather banquettes and frosted mirrors for a long luxurious lunch, watching Dean Street life speed by through the stained-glass windows. As well as appealing menu regulars – smoked haddock fish cakes with aïoli, or crab and mayonnaise, say – there's a daily changing menu full of simple-sounding dishes that make stars of one or two great ingredients. Vegetables and fish feature profusely, with the likes of a winter salad of bitter leaves, beetroot, boiled egg and parmesan, or a whole grilled mackerel with pickled rhubarb. The theatre menu is good value and, unusually, available all day. The wine list focuses on France, Spain and Italy. Service is professional and slick, although falls short of personable; still, this is a legendarily agreeable spot for breakfast, lunch or dinner.
Babies and children welcome: high chairs. Booking advisable. Separate rooms for parties, seating 12 and 32. Tables outdoors (7, terrace). Vegetarian menu. **Map 17 B3**.

★ Social Eating House NEW
58-59 Poland Street, W1F 7NR (7920 7600, www.socialeatinghouse.com). Oxford Circus or Tottenham Court Road tube. **Lunch served** noon-2.30pm, **dinner served** 5.30-10.30pm Mon-Sat. **Main courses** £12-£23.50. **Set lunch** £18 2 courses, £21 3 courses. **Credit** AmEx, MC, V.
It's not easy to open a spate of brand-new restaurants and maintain high standards, but chef Jason Atherton has clearly moved on from being the sorcerer's apprentice (under Gordon Ramsay) to being the sorcerer himself. His Little Social deluxe French bistro (*see p89*) opened in March 2013, right opposite his fine-dining Pollen Street Social (*see p125*) in Mayfair. He followed that weeks later with this even more ambitious Soho restaurant, delegating the cooking to his long-time head chef at PSS, Paul Hood. Smoked duck 'ham',

egg and chips is a dish typical of Pollen Street Social's playfulness. The duck breast, cured and smoked on the premises, was accompanied by a breadcrumbed duck egg: molten in the middle and with an aroma of truffle oil. Umami was also plentiful in a roast cod main course that used powdered Japanese kombu seaweed in a glaze, served with a creamy sauce of roasted cockles and seasonal st george's mushrooms. Desserts too showed imagination and attention to detail; honey almond sponge was nicely paired with a scoop of goat's curd ice-cream. If you visit the basement (where the loos are housed), you can glimpse the kitchen, where Hood and his team work their magic with a spell-like calm.
Babies and children welcome until 8pm: high chairs. Booking advisable Thur-Sat. Disabled: toilet. Separate room for parties, seats 8. **Map 17 A3**.

Strand

Savoy Grill
Savoy Hotel, Strand, WC2R 0EU (7592 1600, www.gordonramsay.com/thesavoygrill). Embankment tube or Charing Cross tube/rail. **Lunch served** noon-3pm Mon-Sat; noon-4pm Sun. **Dinner served** 5.30-10.45pm Mon-Sat; 6-10.45pm Sun. **Main courses** £18-£38. **Set lunch** £26 3 courses. **Set dinner** (5.30-6.45pm Mon-Fri) £22 2 courses, £26 3 courses. **Credit** AmEx, MC, V.
It's a well trodden path to the Grill from the Savoy Theatre, across the concourse of the world-famous hotel. Many diners seem to combine a meal and a show for a quintessential London night out. As such, the vibe can be quite touristy, but that in no way detracts from the quality of the experience. Following the Savoy's epic £220 million refurbishment, completed in 2010, the restaurant looks as spectacular as it did in its heyday: a dark and glamorous room of polished wood, burnished mirrors and statement pendant lights. It's now run by Gordon Ramsay Holdings, who largely keeps things classic on the extensive French/British

menu. All the old favourites are here – snails in red wine, french onion soup, oysters, lobster thermidor, dover sole – and the grill itself sears a selection of steaks, chops and cutlets, from prime British breeds. At lunch, a trolley trundles around the tables dispensing a roast of the day with trimmings. Nothing is particularly cheap, of course, but the popular pre-theatre menu consists of simpler dishes and offers a more accessible route into this historic and celebrated dining room.
Available for hire. Babies and children welcome: high chairs; nappy-changing facilities. Booking advisable. Disabled: toilet. Dress: smart casual. Separate room for parties, seats 40. Vegetarian menu. **Map 18 E5.**

Simpson's-in-the-Strand
100 Strand, WC2R 0EW (7836 9112, www.simpsonsinthestrand.co.uk). Embankment tube or Charing Cross tube/rail. **Breakfast served** 7.15-10.30am Mon-Fri. **Lunch served** 12.15-2.45pm Mon-Sat. **Dinner served** 5.45-10.45pm Mon-Fri; 5-10.45pm Sat. **Meals served** 12.15-9pm Sun. **Main courses** £16.50-£33.50. **Set meal** (lunch, 5.45-7pm) £25.75 2 courses, £31 3 courses. **Credit** AmEx, MC, V.
This renowned London institution is technically part of the Savoy next door, but it seems untouched by the £220 million refurbishment the famous hotel received in 2010. It's like a public school refectory on a grand scale, with rows of tables (some looking rather scruffy around the legs), heavily varnished wall panels and huge chandeliers. An old-fashioned sense of British formality pervades – which is a major reason diners come here. You'll see plenty of retired colonel types, although Simpson's is also popular with tourists looking for an apparently unadulterated experience of bygone London. The signature dish is roast beef, and great haunches of it are wheeled around on trolleys to be carved at table. However, we feel this 185-year-old stalwart is resting on its laurels. Beyond the beef (with all the trimmings), there's not much on the menu to excite. At a recent breakfast, the classic dishes (eggs royale, muffins with bacon and eggs) were no more than OK. The pricing is cynical – £7.50 for a pot with two Twinings teabags and some boiling water. At least use loose leaf. For a sense of tradition, Simpson's is hard to beat, but some traditions aren't always worth upholding.
Babies and children welcome: high chairs; nappy-changing facilities. Booking advisable Fri-Sun. Disabled: toilet. Dress: smart casual; no shorts or trainers. Separate rooms for parties, seating 25 and 150. **Map 18 E5.**

Trafalgar Square

National Dining Rooms
Sainsbury Wing, National Gallery, Trafalgar Square, WC2N 5DN (7747 2525, www.peyton andbyrne.co.uk/the-national-dining-rooms). Charing Cross tube/rail.
Bakery **Meals served** 10am-5.30pm Mon-Thur, Sat, Sun; 10am-8.30pm Fri. **Main courses** £6-£10.
Restaurant **Lunch served** noon-3.30pm daily. **Dinner served** 5-7.30pm Fri. **Main courses** £18-£20. **Set meal** £27.50 2 courses incl glass of wine, £30.50 3 courses incl glass of wine.
Both **Credit** MC, V.
Skip past the droves of tourists congregating around Trafalgar Square, and congratulate yourself for knowing about this haven among the endless horror-show chain restaurants in the area. Ascend the stairs to Oliver Peyton's first-floor dining room – in the quieter Sainsbury Wing of the National Gallery – and enter a professionally run and peaceful place, where the views (over the Square in one direction, of a vast Paula Rego mural in the other) are matched by the superb food. It's formal and slick enough for a special occasion, yet would also do splendidly as a stop-off during a day's sightseeing. Prices are on the high side, but there's a set lunch including a glass of wine, which is well worth taking time over. Dishes are light, artfully presented and with clever additions. They also make the most of slap-bang-in-season ingredients: an early spring vegetable salad featured delicately braised chunks of squash, golden beetroot and carrot, a line of vivid beetroot 'dust' and horseradish popcorn. Poached chicken is enlivened with 'Marmite and bacon' toast; venison haunch may come with damsons and liquorice. Service on our visit was notably keen and accommodating. There are also set menus for Sunday lunch and afternoon tea. Note that dinner is available only on Fridays.
Babies and children welcome: children's menu; high chairs. Booking advisable. Disabled: toilet. **Map 17 C5.**
For branch (National Café) see index.

Victoria

Goring Hotel
Beeston Place, Grosvenor Gardens, SW1W 0JW (7396 9000, www.thegoring.com). Victoria tube/rail. **Breakfast served** 7-10am Mon-Fri; 7-10.30am Sat; 7.30-10.30am Sun. **Lunch served** 12.30-2.30pm Mon-Fri, Sun. **Dinner served** 6-10pm daily. **Set lunch** (Mon-Fri) £38 3 courses; (Sun) £39.50 3 courses. **Set dinner** (pre-theatre) £33 2 courses; £49.50 3 courses. **Credit** AmEx, MC, V.
Gaze around the plush dining room at this exquisite, family-owned hotel as bow-tied waiters glide serenely by, and only the branch-like Swarovski chandeliers remind you we left the Edwardian era a long time ago. Carpets and drapes are thick, colours muted, mobile phones most unwelcome. A refurbishment by Viscount Linley's design company gently updated the decor while preserving the refinement and understated luxury of the 103-year-old restaurant. Food is anything but stuffy, with sophisticated interpretations of British classics to the fore. Much is made of the 'only the best' ingredient-sourcing policy, and the quality is clear. A light hand in the kitchen is evident in the likes of a flavour-packed ham-knuckle terrine with a zingy cider apple foam, or a generous slice of poached salmon surrounded by painstakingly sliced slivers of crunchy spring vegetables. Those were both from the pre-theatre menu, which, though not exactly cheap at £33 for two courses, is more affordable than £49.50 for three. Puddings and cheeses are served from a trolley, as is beef wellington, in a wonderfully traditional manner. An indulgent experience: old-world English glamour with a modern touch.
Available for hire. Babies and children welcome: high chairs; nappy-changing facilities. Booking essential. Disabled: toilet (hotel). Dress: smart casual. Separate rooms for parties, seating 8-44. Tables outdoors (10, terrace). **Map 15 H9.**

Dairy. See p56.

West

Bayswater

★ Hereford Road

*3 Hereford Road, W2 4AB (7727 1144,
www.herefordroad.org). Bayswater tube.*
Lunch served noon-3pm Mon-Sat; noon-
4pm Sun. **Dinner served** 6-10.30pm Mon-
Sat; 6-10pm Sun. **Main courses** £10-£16.50.
Set lunch (Mon-Fri) £13 2 courses, £15.50
3 courses. **Credit** AmEx, MC, V.
St John in Farringdon has become something of a
culinary academy, sending its graduates out across
the city to spread the word. Hereford Road is run
by one of those nose-to-tail champions – head chef
Tom Pemberton has taken his use-every-cut
training to this moneyed part of west London. His
restaurant makes its intentions clear: the first thing
you see upon entering the long, narrow space is the
kitchen; if it were any more open you'd be eating
off the chefs' laps. Food takes centre stage here –
and what food it is. Sit and wonder how the
restaurant can manage to serve two courses for £13
at lunch as you tuck into hearty dishes such as
devilled duck livers with shallots, brill with roasted
cauliflower, or onglet and chips. The slightly fancier
à la carte menu includes the likes of kid's offal and
mash, or lamb rump with purple sprouting broccoli;
the most expensive main is still usually less than
£17. Down a small flight of stairs is a no-frills
dining room, with rather austere wooden furniture
(try to bag a booth) and only a large woven mural
as ornamentation. Service suits the environment –
it's quietly confident and refreshingly laid-back. A
wonderful place.
*Babies and children welcome: high chairs.
Booking advisable. Disabled: toilet. Tables
outdoors (3, pavement).* **Map 7 B6.**

Notting Hill

★ Shed NEW

*122 Palace Gardens Terrace, W8 4RT (7229
4024, www.theshed-restaurant.com). Notting
Hill Gate tube.* **Lunch served** noon-3pm
Tue-Fri, noon-4pm Sat. **Dinner served**
6-11pm Tue-Sat. **Dishes** £7.50-£9.50.
Credit MC, V.
From a distance, with its white wooden cladding
and high pitched roof, this restaurant does look
suspiciously like a shed. Home for years to the old
Ark restaurant, under brothers Oliver and Richard
Gladwin it's had a playful makeover that's as much
barnyard as back-garden, with piggy portraits, bits
of tractor, and charming staff in check shirts. It's
a fitting setting for the food, which goes beyond the
usual hackneyed take on British. Plates are small,
meant for sharing, and divided into sections such
as 'mouthfuls', 'fast cooking' and 'slow cooking'.
The menu changes regularly; many ingredients are
sourced from in or around the family farm in
Nutbourne, West Sussex (including wine from
Nutbourne Vineyards). From fresh-tasting carrot
houmous with sourdough breadsticks, to the meaty
goodness of the Nutbourne banger with own-made
mustard, it was all delicious, and inventive without
being tricksy. Hake with samphire, capers and a
slick of red pepper sauce was possibly our
favourite plate, though spatchcock quail with
cucumber, poppy seed and a delicate barbecue
sauce ran it close. Only a slightly too salty, overly
fatty veal blade with haricot beans and black

Rookery. See p56.

cabbage disappointed. Puddings are wickedly
good – the 'Magnum vienetta parfait' is a
reinvention of the old standard (with added salted
caramel and dark, dark chocolate) that has to be
tried. We'll be back – especially as prices are so very
reasonable for the area and the quality.
*Available for hire. Babies and children admitted.
Booking advisable. Tables outdoors (5, terrace).*
Map 7 B7.

South

Balham

★ Lamberts

*2 Station Parade, Balham High Road, SW12
9AZ (8675 2233, www.lambertsrestaurant.com).
Balham tube/rail.* **Lunch served** 12.30-2.30pm,
dinner served 6-10.30pm Tue-Sat. **Meals
served** noon-5pm Sun. **Main courses** £12-
£22. **Set dinner** (Tue-Thur) £17 2 courses,
£20 3 courses. **Set meal** (Sun) £20 2 courses,
£24 3 courses. **Credit** MC, V.
The words 'local' and 'seasonal' are bandied around
a great deal these days, but Lamberts puts its menu
where its mouth is. This swish Balham restaurant
changes its line-up every month, showcasing the
best regional British produce at that precise
moment. Even the aperitifs are local; on our visit, a
wickedly strong 'Tooting Stinger' was being made
with nettle cordial from just down the road, and gin
from west London distillery Sipsmith. Our
ingredient-led meal kicked off with a light and airy
cheese puff (gougère), made with goat's cheese from
a small Somerset producer, to accompany a soup of
short-season wild garlic and goat's milk foam.
Equally memorable was the wood-pigeon
wellington (eating from the wild is a big deal here),
which saw an unapologetically gamey and full-
flavoured slice of meat wrapped in a sublime
buttery pastry and served with a rich purée of
burnt onion. Ales and ciders are British too – only
the excellent and sensibly priced wine list (kicking
off with English sparkling wine) roams further
afield. Staff are refreshingly gregarious, while

owner Joe Lambert is on first-name terms with
many of the regulars. Bargain-hunters take note:
the midweek set dinner is an absolute steal.
*Available for hire. Babies and children welcome:
children's menu (lunch); high chairs. Booking
advisable, essential weekends. Tables outdoors
(3, pavement).*

Brixton

Salon NEW

*Cannon & Cannon, 18 Market Row, SW9
8LD (7501 9152, www.cannonandcannon.com).
Brixton tube/rail.* **Lunch served** noon-3pm Fri,
Sat. **Dinner served** 6-10pm Thur-Sat. **Main
courses** £9.50-£15. **Set lunch** £12.95 2
courses, £15.95 3 courses. **Set dinner** £29
4 courses. **Credit** AmEx, MC, V.
This shabby-chic eaterie sits above British deli
Cannon & Cannon in one of Brixton Market's
revamped shopping arcades. The ultra-casual
setting – scuffed paintwork, battered metal
furniture, a cramped kitchen – means Salon is a
take-it-as-it-comes operation, but that seems to suit
the clientele of locals and market tourists. Wine is
served in tumblers, and the chefs sometimes pop
out to deliver plates to tables themselves. Dishes
tend to be simple, with an emphasis on fresh, very
seasonal produce. At lunch, there's a deli menu of
small plates (including top-notch British charcuterie
and cheese) sourced from downstairs, as well as a
very good-value set menu. Highlights included
super-fresh fish cakes that combined smoked
mackerel, fluffy potato and dill to winning effect;
tender confit of mallard leg atop a substantial
helping of puy lentils and pancetta; and a gooey
dark chocolate tart incorporating a layer of tangy,
nicely bitter orange marmalade. Prosecco and
spring rhubarb juice made a zingy, refreshing
aperitif. Come dinner, there's a no-choice set menu
of five courses (with matching wines, if wanted) –
simpler for the kitchen, but a riskier proposition for
the diner.
*Available for hire (Sun only). Babies and children
welcome: high chairs. Booking essential. Tables
outdoors (2, market).* **Map 22 E2.**

BRITISH

BRITISH

Clapham

Dairy NEW

15 The Pavement, SW4 0HY (7622 4165, www.the-dairy.co.uk). Clapham Common tube. **Lunch served** noon-2.30pm Wed-Fri; noon-3pm Sat; noon-4pm Sun. **Dinner served** 6-9.45pm Tue-Sat. **Dishes** £5-£12. **Set dinner** £40 tasting menu (£68 incl wine). **Credit** MC, V.

Recycled furniture, workshop light fittings, a bar serving craft beers: it might look like another beer and burger joint, but the Dairy doesn't churn out a formula. Seasonal British ingredients are treated with a level of finesse that would be the envy of many Japanese restaurants. A robata grill is used not just for grilling meats, but for smoking butter (using apple-wood chips). A pat of this butter is served on a big beach pebble, with wholesome own-made bread. Such attention to detail permeates the menu. A fillet of mackerel is charred on the grill then placed on fennel. Beef short rib is slow-cooked for 24 hours before being served with grilled spring onions and bone marrow. Chef Robin Gill and his wife Sarah, who both used to work at Le Manoir aux Quat'Saisons, have created a food-led, but approachable bar and bistro – you could pop in for a morning coffee (an Allpress roast), bar snacks, a cocktail or a glass of biodynamic wine. Located just off Clapham's heaving high street, the Dairy could milk enough business from its late licence alone. But this is Clapham uncommon: a real, much more affordable alternative to high-end local restaurants such as Trinity.
Babies and children admitted. Booking essential dinner Fri, Sat. Tables outdoors (2, pavement). **Map 22 A2**.

Rookery

69 Clapham Common Southside, SW4 9DA (8673 9162, www.therookeryclapham.co.uk). Clapham Common or Clapham South tube. Bar **Open** 5.30-11pm Mon-Thur; 12.30pm-midnight Fri, Sat; 12.30-11pm Sun. *Restaurant* **Lunch served** noon-4pm Fri, Sat. **Dinner served** 6.30-10pm Mon-Sat. **Meals served** 12.30-8pm Sun. **Main courses** £12-£16. *Both* **Credit** MC, V.

The busy A24 runs along the western edge of Clapham Common. A few alfresco bars and a growing number of shisha joints cluster at the southern end, but the Rookery sits in the middle – and is a class apart. Inside, it's decorated in the current metropolitan look of bare brick with artsy industrial details. But this is more than somewhere to sip a flat white, savour a glass of Meantime Pale Ale or nurse a cocktail glass; it's also great for dining. A starter of coronation chicken was coarsely textured and coated in a sweetly spicy mayonnaise dressing, foiled by some baby naan breads. A fillet of salmon-like sea trout was pan-fried and served on a tangle of mussel shells, chopped leek, brown shrimp and a creamy cider sauce, evocative of seaside holidays. Some dishes could do with slight improvement. Smoked haddock fish cakes needed more meaty fish as they tasted mainly of deep-fried breadcrumbs, and a parmesan risotto hadn't quite melded with its wild mushrooms. But over many visits we've had more hits than misses. The Rookery is an ideal local perch for people who like a grown-up bar, a casual vibe and a menu that's smarter than it needs to be.

Beagle

Babies and children welcome: high chairs. Booking advisable. Separate room for parties, seats 25. Tables outdoors (12, terrace). **Map 22 A3**.

South East
East Dulwich

Franklins

157 Lordship Lane, SE22 8HX (8299 9598, www.franklinsrestaurant.com). East Dulwich rail. **Meals served** noon-10.30pm Mon-Sat; noon-10pm Sun. **Main courses** £13-£21. **Set lunch** (noon-5pm Mon-Fri) £13.95 2 courses, £16.95 3 courses. **Credit** MC, V.

An asset locally, and one that has stood the test of time – it's been in East Dulwich since 1999 (and previously the owners ran the Secret Garden restaurant at Franklins antiques shop in Camberwell). There's a commitment to careful sourcing (local where possible and at the very least from the UK, from dedicated producers), and a more adventurous menu than many neighbourhood restaurants. Try an oyster or two while perusing a menu that might include confit quail and celeriac remoulade or potted shrimps to start, followed by ox tongue with black pudding and chicory or whole rainbow trout with fennel, cucumber and dill. Cauliflower and rocket soup was a smooth opener, nicely matched with chunky own-made bread, but tender haunch of venison, served rare with sweetish red cabbage and quince, made more of an impression – though wasn't particularly gamey; a side of sprightly greens cut through the richness. Finish with cheese, savouries or a trad pudding such as butterscotch tart. There's a roast on Sundays too. Drinks run from a Sussex sparkling wine to fresh mint tea. The light back-room restaurant is given focus by the open kitchen and is patrolled by friendly staff; at the front is a livelier bar, plus outdoor seating. Franklins Farm Shop operates on the next corner.
Available for hire. Babies and children welcome: high chairs; nappy-changing facilities. Booking advisable. Disabled: toilet. Separate room for parties, seats 34. Tables outdoors (8, pavement). **Map 23 C4**.

London Bridge & Borough

Roast

The Floral Hall, Borough Market, Stoney Street, SE1 1TL (3641 7958, www.roast-restaurant.com). London Bridge tube/rail. **Breakfast served** 7-10.45am Mon-Fri; 8-11.30am Sat. **Lunch served** noon-3.45pm Mon-Sat; 11.30am-6.30pm Sun. **Dinner served** 5.30-10.30pm Mon-Fri; 6-10.30pm Sat. **Main courses** £16.50-£35. **Set lunch** (Mon-Sat) £35 3 courses. **Set meal** (5.30-6.30pm, 9.30-10.30pm Mon-Fri; 6-6.30pm, 9.30-10.30pm Sat) £30 3 courses. (Sun) £35 3 courses. **Credit** AmEx, MC, V.

As the hordes of Borough Marketeers stuff their faces while standing up, above them in the elegant mezzanine Floral Hall is the more refined eating option – the staunchly British Roast, which feels like the perfect restaurant to have at the heart of London's larder. The formal operation (grand pianist, precise service, gleaming tableware on white cloths) contrasts with the generally jolly crowd, who rock up for special occasions and family get-togethers in often casual clobber. It's a very pleasant place for a long lunch or luxurious breakfast. You'd be disappointed if the roasts themselves weren't up to scratch – but they're among the city's best. Free-range pork belly with apple sauce, Goosnargh chicken with bread sauce, or Blackface lamb with mint relish all appear. These are bracketed by sophisticated starters (we had grilled sardines with pickled beetroot and blood orange) and grown-up versions of British puds. Visit on a Sunday, as many do, and the menu is restricted to £35 for three courses, which although very filling seems rather steep – indeed, prices across the board aren't especially economical. Still, Roast is right at home amid the food-focused throng of Borough Market.

Available for hire. Babies and children welcome: children's menu; high chairs; nappy-changing facilities. Booking advisable. Disabled: lift; toilet. Dress: smart casual. **Map 11 P8**.

East

Shoreditch

Albion

2-4 Boundary Street, E2 7DD (7729 1051, www.albioncaff.co.uk). Shoreditch High Street rail. **Breakfast served** 8am-noon Mon-Fri; 8am-12.30pm Sat, Sun. **Meals served** 8am-11pm daily. **Main courses** £8-£14. **Credit** AmEx, MC, V.

Albion describes itself somewhat self-consciously as a 'caff', but no greasy spoon in London was ever designed and owned by Terence Conran, and certainly none has its own maître d'. But in spirit, at least, it is something approaching a café for 21st-century Shoreditch – a place where locals can drop in for a casual breakfast, lunch or dinner, or just a cup of tea and a slice of cake. The numerous tables set up for solo diners in the long, narrow, bright room seem to back that up. Menu descriptions suggest dishes wouldn't seem out of place in your average caff too – ham and mustard sandwich, devilled kidneys, sausage and mash, fish and chips, bacon and eggs on toast. They're all prepared with top-quality ingredients, great care and an eye for presentation. Mackerel salad contained generous chunks of smoked fish, interestingly bitter salad leaves and a blob of fiery horseradish cream. There's an equally posh 'corner shop' at the entrance, selling fruit, veg, groceries and baked goods – you can watch the tempting loaves being hauled out of the ovens in the open kitchen. The Albion formula is obviously a hit – as evidenced by a new branch (opened in summer 2013) just behind Tate Modern.

Babies and children welcome: high chairs; nappy-changing facilities. Bookings not accepted for fewer than 7 people. Disabled: toilet. Tables outdoors (11, pavement). Takeaway service. **Map 6 R4**. *For branch see index.*

Beagle NEW

397-400 Geffrye Street, E2 8HZ (7613 2967, www.beaglelondon.co.uk). Hoxton rail. *Bar* **Open** 4pm-midnight Mon, Tue; noon-midnight Thur-Sun. *Restaurant* **Lunch served** noon-3pm Thur-Sat; noon-5pm Sun. **Dinner served** 6-10.30pm Mon-Sat. **Main courses** £12.50-£20. *Both* **Credit** AmEx, MC, V.

Beagle is a smart café, bar and restaurant in the railway arches below Hoxton station. Setting it in such a dissonant location is clearly an act of faith for its owners, who have pursued this project with hound-like doggedness. Stylish outdoor seating marks it out from the usual car spares depots, and plate-glass windows reveal beautifully restored arches. A tiny coffee takeaway counter is by the left-hand entrance; the right-hand entrance opens into the capacious bar. Sophisticated cocktails concocted by acclaimed barman Myles Davies set the scene – a rhubarb bellini with vanilla hits the spot. Pass from the bar arch to the next room and you move into the dining area with its open kitchen. James Ferguson was head chef at the excellent Rochelle Canteen for four years, and the same back-to-basics British ethos is evident here. Grilled cuttlefish – scored and served like oriental squid – came with new potatoes and a salsa-like coriander pesto. Pigeon terrine was expertly made in-house, well textured and with a slightly gamey flavour. The solitary vegetarian main course was aubergine, grilled and smoked on the kitchen's wood grill. Beagle deserves success for making E2 a culinary destination beyond the area's famous budget Vietnamese cafés.

Available for hire. Babies and children welcome: high chairs. Booking advisable Thur-Sat. Disabled: toilet. Tables outdoors (8, terrace). **Map 6 R3**.

Clove Club NEW

Shoreditch Town Hall, 380 Old Street, EC1V 9LT (7729 6496, www.thecloveclub.com). Old Street tube/rail or Shoreditch High Street rail. *Bar* **Lunch served** noon-2.30pm Tue-Sat. **Dinner served** 6-11pm Mon-Sat. **Dishes** £4.50-£21. *Restaurant* **Lunch served** noon-2.30pm Tue-Sat. **Dinner served** 6-9.30pm Mon-Sat. **Set lunch** £35 3 courses. **Set dinner** £47 tasting menu. *Both* **Credit** MC, V.

It can sometimes be hard to know if a restaurant is trying to make food that you will savour, or is simply creating dishes to feed the Instagram craze. Taking no chances, Shoreditch's Clove Club is doing both. The menu is a masterpiece of contemporary aspirations – with a no-choice list of nine courses, there's no possibility of a fashion faux pas when ordering. It describes a succession of small, seasonal plates that champion British produce, yet are oddly esoteric. 'Radishes, sesame and gochuchang' only contained gochuchang – a Korean chilli paste – as a slight pink tinge to a mayonnaise dip. Leeks were poached and slit, then smoked mussels were inserted like peas in a split pod. The best dishes were those that didn't try so hard to impress. A dish of Red Ruby beef, ramson (wild garlic) and potato featured a generous piece of slow-cooked beef, very tender and moist. Clove Club's cooking is intentionally avant-garde. Everything screams 'look at me': the location in the former Shoreditch Town Hall, the austerity of the decor, the open kitchen and the other diners, many of them scenesters. Yet the restaurant is above parody, mainly because what it does, it does exceedingly well.

Available for hire. Babies and children welcome: high chairs. Booking essential Thur-Sat. Disabled: toilet. Vegetarian menu. **Map 6 R4**.

Fifteen

15 Westland Place, N1 7LP (3375 1515, www.fifteen.net). Old Street tube/rail. **Lunch served** noon-3pm, **dinner served** 6-10pm daily. **Main courses** £17.50-£23. **Set lunch** (Mon-Fri) £19 2 courses, £24 3 courses. **Credit** AmEx, MC, V.

Jamie Oliver's original Fifteen has rebranded itself as British under St John-alumnus chef Jon Rotherham, though its not-for-profit ethos – training disadvantaged apprentices in the culinary arts – remains constant. There's no longer a restaurant/trattoria divide over the two floors (street level and basement) and the menu is now mainly small plates, with a few mains. What hasn't changed is the approach: fine ingredients, treated without fuss, to be enjoyed. On a recent visit, good stuff started with breads (carrying a £4 price tag), served with 'farmhouse butter' and 'chicken butter', the latter a rustic, meaty melding of chicken fat and chicken morsels into the butter. Spare presentation and a retro feel came with devilled egg and smoked anchovy: lovely brown, salty mayonnaise piped into the halved hard-boiled eggs, joined by halved radishes (leaves and all). A summer salad, with many unusual leaves, had a rather salty dressing, while cuttlefish, courgette and herb vinaigrette was a perfect combination. A faultless main course followed: grilled salmon with baby beets and crème fraîche. Fellow diners were tucking into the hallmark roast chicken for two with gusto. To finish, lemon meringue pie packed a vibrantly lemony punch. Great food. Our only criticism? It was impossible to enter the disabled toilet without one of our party rising from the table.

Available for hire. Babies and children welcome: high chairs; nappy-changing facilities. Booking essential. Disabled: toilet. Dress: smart casual. **Map 6 Q3**.

Master & Servant NEW

8-9 Hoxton Square, N1 6NU (7729 4626, www.masterandservant.co.uk). Old Street tube/rail or Hoxton rail. **Brunch served** 10am-1pm Sat, Sun. **Lunch served** noon-3pm Mon-Sat; noon-3.30pm Sun. **Dinner served** 6-11pm Mon-Sat. **Main courses** £13.80-£29. **Set lunch** £15 2 courses, £18 3 courses. **Credit** AmEx, MC, V.

Clove Club. See p57.

Fergus Henderson's St John has spawned an entire genre of British restaurants in London. The oddly named Master & Servant is the latest, set up by ex-St John chefs. The room is bare-brick and low-lit: simple but appealing, less austere than St John but equally purposeful. A seasonal menu of high-quality British produce reflects the culinary heritage. Smoked cod roe with toasted sourdough was a taramasalata-like spread, well textured if a little pricey at £6.80 for a starter – and the toast was burnt at the edges. Duck hearts were more carefully prepared, the meat dark pink and surprisingly tender; they arrived devilled on the outside with a light spice coating, served with seasonal salad leaves. Ox cheek was beautifully slow-cooked and unctuous, with a tangle of remoulade-like celeriac gratings and a little fresh horseradish on top. It was the best dish, with a good wallop of roast meat flavours. Desserts from the daily changing menu might include rhubarb posset, pistachio doughnuts and honey syrup, or even chocolate éclair. Prices seem high for a restaurant that's not proper gentry, though a major consolation is that cocktails are provided by Happiness Forgets, the esteemed cocktail bar in the basement.
Available for hire. Babies and children welcome (lunch): high chairs. Booking essential Fri, Sat. Separate room for parties, seats 10. Tables outdoors (4, terrace). **Map 6 R3.**

Monikers NEW

16 Hoxton Square, N1 6NT (7739 6022). Old Street tube/rail or Shoreditch High Street rail. **Meals served** noon-10.30pm Tue-Sat; noon-9pm Sun. **Main courses** £10.50-£23.50. **Credit** AmEx, MC, V.
This new bar and restaurant has taken over the site recently vacated by the Hoxton Apprentice, a charitable restaurant that (long before Jamie Oliver's Fifteen) was set up to train young folk in

catering skills. Monikers is also a seat of learning, in a way. It occupies the shell of a former primary school, and so an education theme is drilled home through the decor. There's a periodic table on the wall and a huge revolving blackboard. Water is served in laboratory beakers. and toilets are divided into 'boys' and 'girls'. The very cool mezzanine is decked out like the upstairs of an old London bus, complete with vinyl seats. Food is A-grade: no spotted dick with lumpy custard here. Diners are encouraged to freestyle their way through the small plates menu and share dishes such as arbroath smokie salad, soused mackerel with fennel, and mini chorizos. The drinks menu is excellent too, containing a few London beers (Meantime, Camden, Kernel) and a list of grown-up cocktails – and you're not required to order any food. Going back to school never seemed so appealing.
Available for hire. Babies and children admitted. Booking advisable Thur-Sat. Disabled: toilet. Separate room for parties, seats 30. Tables outdoors (5, terrace). **Map 6 R3.**

Rivington Grill

28-30 Rivington Street, EC2A 3DZ (7729 7053, www.rivingtongrill.co.uk). Old Street tube/rail. *Bar* **Open/snacks served** 11am-1.30am Mon-Sat; 11am-11.30pm Sun.
Restaurant **Brunch served** 8-11am Mon-Fri. **Meals served** 11am-11.30pm Mon-Sat; 11am-10pm Sun. **Main courses** £10-£33.50. **Set lunch** (11am-4pm Sun) £22.50. **Set meal** £32.50-£38.50 3 courses.
Both **Credit** AmEx, MC, V.
The two London Rivingtons could be called the mid-market arm of the very smart Caprice Holdings group (Le Caprice, The Ivy, J Sheekey), although prices still aren't cheap. The dining space at the original is calm and white, with crisp linen and enough of both formality and trendiness to

gratify different audiences. Contemporary art, such as a Tracey Emin light sculpture, adds a splash of Shoreditch cool. Menus follow the distinctively British style set by Mark Hix (chef-supremo of Caprice group when the Rivington opened), using fresh, seasonal British ingredients from sustainable sources. The wine list offers an excellent choice by the glass or carafe. Which is all to the good, but the cooking for our Sunday lunch was pleasant without offering any kind of zip. Queenie scallops with garlic butter had mellow flavour, but hadn't been cleaned properly; strathdon blue cheese and chicory salad, and Sunday roast rib of beef and yorkshire pud were decent yet anonymous. Fish and chips was somewhat better than you get in most gastropubs, though at twice the price. Since the Rivington opens early, there's also a big choice of breakfast and brunch-style dishes. Perhaps these are what to go for.
Available for hire. Babies and children welcome: high chairs. Booking advisable. Separate room for parties, seats 34. Takeaway service. Vegetarian menu. **Map 6 Q4.**
For branch see index.

Rochelle Canteen

Rochelle School, Arnold Circus, E2 7ES (7729 5677, www.arnoldandhenderson.com). Shoreditch High Street rail. **Breakfast served** 9-11.30am, **lunch served** noon-3pm, **tea served** 3-4.30pm Mon-Fri. **Main courses** £12-£16. **Unlicensed. Corkage** £5. **Credit** MC, V.
Eating at Melanie Arnold and Margot Henderson's daytime-only spot remains a distinctive treat: entry is via a buzzer on a tiny door in the wall of an old Victorian school on Arnold Circus, now a hub of creative studios. Inside, a handful of outdoor tables and a former bike shed converted into an airy, modern space act as the canteen for the creatives

working here, and those lucky outsiders in the know. Once you're one of them, you'll find a short but enticing menu that, on our visit, included a pea soup with bantam egg and mint; grilled quails and green sauce; rabbit rillettes; and a pork chop with mustard and chard. The latter was perfect – the meat slightly charred on the outside, with a hint of pink in the middle and, best of all, a broad ribbon of melting fat and crispy skin running along one side. A colourful platter of herb gnocchi with courgettes and peppers tasted as lovely as it looked, and a dessert of chocolate pots was to die for, in just the way an indulgent, luscious chocolate dessert should be. Newcomers to the Shoreditch dining scene can come and go; Rochelle Canteen stands firm, and stands out.

Babies and children welcome: high chairs; nappy-changing facilities. Booking advisable Thur, Fri. Tables outdoors (12, courtyard). **Map 6 S4**.

Spitalfields

Canteen

2 Crispin Place, off Brushfield Street, E1 6DW (0845 686 1122, www.canteen.co.uk). Liverpool Street tube/rail. **Meals served** 8am-11pm Mon-Fri; 9am-11pm Sat; 9am-10pm Sun. **Main courses** £8-£14.50. **Set meal** (3-7pm Mon-Sat) £12.50 2 courses. **Credit** AmEx, MC, V.

In some ways, it's a surprise that Canteen's bold-and-British mini-chain has only expanded to four outlets since this original opened in 2006. Its locations are perfect for day-trippers or lunching office workers (the others are at the South Bank, Canary Wharf and Baker Street), the cooking is reliable, and the venues themselves are accessibly minimalist and stylish. The open kitchen sends out a Land's End to John O'Groats selection of classic dishes – arbroath smokie with poached egg, welsh rarebit, lancashire cheese tart with chicory, pie and mash. Canteen was one of the first places to trumpet locality and sustainability on its menus, a commendable stance that continues today: eggs and chicken are free-range, fish is from non-endangered species, farms and breeds are name-checked. And – perhaps due to the chain's limited size – results are dependably good. The pie fillings change every day and come with a scoop of perfectly creamy mash and flavourful gravy; daily roasts are as good as you'll find in the best gastropubs. There's also afternoon tea, plus a small list of trad bar snacks (scotch eggs, fish finger sandwiches) to go with the democratic wines, simple cocktails and British beers.

Babies and children welcome: high chairs; nappy-changing facilities. Booking advisable; bookings not accepted Sun. Disabled: toilet. Tables outdoors (10, plaza). Takeaway service. **Map 12 R5**. **For branches see index**.

St John Bread & Wine

94-96 Commercial Street, E1 6LZ (7251 0848, www.stjohngroup.uk.com). Liverpool Street tube/rail. **Breakfast served** 9-11am, **tea served** noon-4pm daily. **Lunch served** noon-6pm Mon-Fri; noon-4pm Sat, Sun. **Dinner served** 6-11pm Mon-Sat; 6-9pm Sun. **Dishes** £7.10-£17.10. **Credit** AmEx, MC, V.

St John's smaller offshoot has the same workaday style as its Smithfield parent: a bright, white, canteen-like space, no-frills furniture, walls lined with coat hooks, and a utilitarian bakery counter in one corner. Exceptionally well-informed staff in

Master & Servant. See p57.

whites give the impression they could be chefs bringing you each dish as soon as they've cooked it (which may sometimes be the case). The main difference is in menus: there are no real 'courses' for lunch or dinner (except a salad and soups that could pass as 'starters'), but medium-sized dishes that you can have in any order. The essential culinary approach is unchanged – an exploration of every under-appreciated British ingredient (especially gutsy meats), skill, imagination and second-to-none freshness – and it seems to work even better in small doses. Goat's curd and grilled spring onions on a slice of superb own-baked bread was made exhilarating by dashes of fabulously fresh mint; lamb onglet with chicory and anchovy didn't recall any old English recipe to mind, but was a wonderfully rich, perfectly balanced mix.

Monikers. See p58.

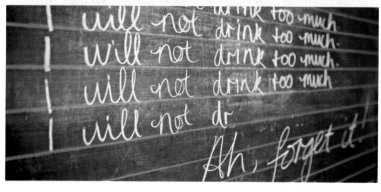

Generously sized puds are as big as mains, and wines are impressive. A hit for breakfast, with a renowned bacon sandwich, Bread & Wine now also offers afternoon tea.
Available for hire. Babies and children welcome: high chairs. Booking advisable. Takeaway service.
Map 12 S5.

North East
Clapton

Shane's on Chatsworth
62 Chatsworth Road, E5 0LS (8985 3755, www.shanesonchatsworth.com). Homerton rail.
Meals/dishes served 5-11pm Tue-Fri; 11am-

10.30pm Sat; 11am-9pm Sun. **Dishes** £2-£6.
'Shane' is Kiwi chef Shane Harrison, who set up this very local restaurant in early 2012 on Chatsworth Road, an up-and-coming high street in up-and-coming Clapton. It's a lo-fi-looking operation, with lampshades made of pegs, quirky animal sketches on the walls and packed-in tables. These are filled with gentrifying Hackneyites who were sure somewhere like this was going to open soon. Much is made on the website of the all-British sourcing policy, which could include herbs from Hackney Marshes just up the road. Dishes make the most of seasonal game and seafood: venison carpaccio with pickled carrots; rabbit and wood-pigeon pâté; hake with sea beet, chorizo and clams. More simple options include a perfectly cooked onglet steak with béarnaise, or mussels with nettles (again, picked nearby). The skill in the kitchen is evident, although prices can be steep – £2 for a slice of bread and butter is mean, even if the loaf is own-made. The wine list isn't great value either. Our only other grumble is that service failed to cope when the room was full; but overall, this cute little place is a sign that Clapton's early adopters were on to something.
Available for hire. Babies and children welcome: children's menu. Booking advisable dinner. Tables outdoors (4, pavement).

North
Camden Town & Chalk Farm

Market
43 Parkway, NW1 7PN (7267 9700, www.marketrestaurant.co.uk). Camden Town tube. **Brunch served** 11am-3pm Sun. **Lunch served** noon-2.30pm, **dinner served** 6-10.30pm Mon-Sat. **Main courses** £13-£17. **Set lunch** £10 2 courses. **Set dinner** (6-7pm) £17.50 2 courses. **Credit** AmEx, MC, V.
Camden Market doesn't provide much culinary incentive for Londoners to visit NW1, but Market in Camden is one of the best venues to eat in the area. 'Simple things, done well' is a phrase that could apply to the whole operation. The narrow space has been denuded back to its structural brick, adorned only with a few wall lights and prints. Chairs are salvaged from a school by the looks of things; specials are chalked on a blackboard. The proudly British and mainly meaty food is straightforward and effective too. A spring starter of golden and mauve beetroot was adorned simply with goat's cheese and pickled walnuts: more an assembly than a display of cheffy talent, but perfect nonetheless. You might move on to a signature pie – chicken and leek, say – or the 'modern British' modish standard of onglet and chips. Those chips were perfectly fat, crispy and seasoned, and also arrived with a grilled bream flavoured with lemon and rosemary. Service felt a bit 'by rote' on a quiet early evening visit, but got the job done. It seems Market has reined in its ambition slightly since opening, but when the place runs so comfortably in its groove, that's no bad thing.
Babies and children welcome: high chairs. Booking advisable. Separate room for parties, seats 12. Tables outdoors (2, pavement).
Map 3 H1.

Caribbean

Not so long ago, Caribbean cuisine in London consisted largely of Jamaican takeaway joints, but the raging popularity of street food and tiny down-home restaurants has brought a welcome extension to the variety of food offered. Yes, the caff-like **Jerk City** in Soho and **Etta's Seafood Kitchen** in Brixton Market still do a mean jerk chicken, but round the corner from Etta's at **Fish, Wings & Tings**, the focus is firmly on Trinidadian cooking. At the other end of the spectrum, Camden's **Mango Room** and Exmouth Market's **Cottons** continue to finesse traditional dishes, producing upmarket, refined takes on staples such as curried goat, oxtail stew and 'ground provisions' (vegetable side dishes). It's not easy to spin fried plantain, dumplings, and saltfish and ackee into modern, delicate recipes that retain their robust heart and heat, but these chefs are doing it with panache. The future? Does Ladbroke Grove's **Rum Kitchen** flag up a sea change with its fusion of Caribbean flavours and British dishes? Watch this space.

Central
Clerkenwell & Farringdon

Cottons
70 Exmouth Market, EC1R 4QP (7833 3332, www.cottons-restaurant.co.uk). Farringdon tube/rail or bus 19, 38, 341. **Meals served** noon-11pm daily. **Main courses** £13.50-£15. **Set meal** £19.50 2 courses, £22.50 3 courses. **Credit** MC, V.
Stepping into Cottons is like entering a colonial-era Caribbean dining room: all crisp white tablecloths and heavy furniture, warmly lit by dappled red and blue from the stained glass in the big windows. It's a perfect spot for romantic dining, and all around us couples looked lovingly into each other's eyes – probably to avoid accidentally looking into their neighbours' eyes, so tightly packed are the tables. The kitchen deserves praise for trying to add a touch of panache to down-home Caribbean cooking, but the results are too poor to merit more than a limp clap. A generously sized platter of jerk chicken wings, jerk pork ribs, fried plantain and deep-fried salt-cod fritters had deep, layered flavours, yet was smothered in a bland barbecue sauce. The same sauce returned for an unwelcome encore smothering spatchcocked slow-roasted jerk chicken – a dry, flavourless piece of meat. Oxtail stew with butter beans, a Jamaican classic, was better: rich with a full, satisfying flavour. Seeing our neighbours send back a chocolate fondant so overcooked as to be a dry, solid block, we decided to skip pudding. At these prices, the food should be much better.
Available for hire. Entertainment: DJs 9.30pm-2am Fri, Sat. Separate room for parties, seats 65. Takeaway service. **Map 5 N4**.
For branch see index.

Soho

★ Jerk City
189 Wardour Street, W1F 8ZD (7287 2878, www.jerkcity.co.uk). Tottenham Court Road tube. **Meals served** noon-10pm Mon-Wed; noon-11pm Thur-Sat; noon-8pm Sun. **Main courses** £6.50-£9.50. **No credit cards**.
Jerk City takes the idea of not changing a winning formula maybe a little too far. We'd say the menu hasn't changed in years, but it's more likely that it hasn't changed since the place opened. The decor and furnishings still feel like the student-flat section of an Ikea showroom. And the prices would still appeal to most students, though on a busy weekday lunchtime – the best time to come – the clientele is less uni, more workers after a taste of home-cooking. And they get it: this is proper Caribbean food from a menu that's short yet delivers. Choose from chicken (jerk, barbecue, brown stew or curry), curried mutton, oxtail, peppered steak, ackee and saltfish, stewed fish, roti (chicken, mutton, prawn or veg), or rice and peas. Jerk chicken comes, unusually, with a sauce rather than barbecued, but was extremely tasty, while mutton curry had the requisite richness and deep flavour produced by a well-sourced curry powder (the base of a West Indian curry, rather than the separate spice flavours you'd expect of an Indian curry). When everything around Wardour Street is changing so fast, there's something reassuring about Jerk City's refusal to move with the times.
Takeaway service. **Map 17 B3**.

West
Ladbroke Grove

Rum Kitchen `NEW`
6-8 All Saints Road, W11 1HH (7920 6479, http://therumkitchen.com). Ladbroke Grove or Westbourne Park tube. **Dinner served** 6-10.30pm Mon-Sat. **Brunch served** noon-4pm Sat, Sun. **Main courses** £10-£17. **Credit** AmEx, MC, V.
With its artfully sun-faded painted wooden slats cladding the walls, and corrugated iron over the bar, Rum Kitchen's decor is designed to invoke visions of liming on the beach. It succeeds nicely, making a welcome change from the downmarket café aesthetic that characterises so many Caribbean venues in London. Drink is also a draw, with the west London party crowd piling in to sample the 100 or so rums and cocktails. Menu-wise, the restaurant offers traditional Caribbean food next to more unusual dishes such as jerk lamb cutlets, pan-fried sea bass with butternut sofrito, or spicy fries

Rum Kitchen. See p61.

that it was tempting to linger over the outstanding own-made sorrel juice and gutsy ginger beer – but by then, a long queue was forming outside. *Available for hire. Babies and children welcome: high chairs; nappy-changing facilities. Booking advisable. Tables outdoors (6, pavement). Takeaway service. Vegetarian menu.* **Map 22 E2**.

★ Fish, Wings & Tings
3 Brixton Village Market, Coldharbour Lane, SW9 8PS (no phone). Brixton tube/rail. **Dinner served** 4-10pm Tue. **Meals served** 10am-11pm Wed-Sat; 10am-7pm Sun. **Main courses** £7.50-£9. **No credit cards**.
Situated on a corner spot in Brixton Village Market, Fish, Wings & Tings is a great place to check out some lesser-known Caribbean treats, beyond the Jamaican norm. Despite its short, to-the-point menu, this laid-back café does a good job of persuading you to be a little more adventurous. Trinidadian chef Brian Danclair might suggest changing your beer order from Red Stripe (Jamaican) to Carib (Trini), for instance. Likewise, the light, crumbly roti breads that come packed with a mix of potato, chickpea, pumpkin and prawn, or goat curry stew, might convince you that jerk chicken is not always the answer. Try, instead, shark and bake: small fillets of shark in a fried dough roll with spicy own-made condiments. Starters include deliciously crisp cod-fish fritters and king prawns in a Red Stripe tempura with own-made sauces. Yes, there's also jerk chicken, and it's tender and moist, served in a sweet-sour tamarind sauce with rice and coleslaw, but it's the Trini specialities that will keep us coming back – especially as a new menu is promised following a recent refurbishment.
Tables outdoors (6, pavement). Takeaway service. **Map 22 E2**.

North East
Hackney

★ Café Heath NEW
67 Mare Street, E8 4RG (3730 9952). London Fields rail or 26, 48, 55, 388, D6 bus. **Meals served** 6am-6pm Mon-Thur; 6am-8pm Fri; 8am-8pm Sat. **Main courses** £4-£6.50. **Set lunch** (noon-2pm Mon-Fri) £4 1 course. **Credit** AmEx, MC, V.
Bigger money might lie in Caribbean fine dining, but the soul of this cuisine lies in ventures like Café Heath. Opened in summer 2013 on the resolutely downmarket stretch of Mare Street opposite St Joseph's Hospice, this tiny space is kitted out with the kind of minimalist fittings that are not so much Hackney hipster, more the result of its previous incarnation as a Chinese takeaway. The menu is equally no-nonsense, with a range of daily lunch specials – jerk or stewed chicken, curry goat, oxtail and butter beans, escovitch fish and a range of sumptuous-sounding soups – alongside everyday items such as curried chickpea roti with tamarind sauce. A generous serving of oxtail came in a deep, rich sauce and was a fine example of this classic stew, served with rice and peas, and fried plantain. Stewed chicken had been caramelised and coated in a punchy sauce that stopped just short of overpowering the meat's flavours. Do try a (generous) slice of one of the homemade cakes – potato cake and carrot cake, on our visit – washed

and chilli jam. The kitchen does the staples well: ackee and saltfish with fried plantain and dumplings was fresh and light, if a little stingy on the saltfish. But jerk chicken caesar salad was an in-betweener: lacking the bigness of Vegas on the one hand and the lip-smacking heat and rich flavours of the Caribbean on the other. Our very friendly waitress told us that the menu was soon going to be 'authenticised' with some more Jamaican dishes and flavours. What the 21st-century local will make of that is anyone's guess. *Babies and children admitted. Booking advisable Thur-Sat. Disabled: toilet. Vegetarian menu.* **Map 19 B2**.

South
Brixton

★ Etta's Seafood Kitchen
85-86 Brixton Village Market, Coldharbour Lane, SW9 8PS (7737 1673, www.ettasseafood kitchen.com). Brixton tube/rail. **Meals served**
10am-7pm Tue, Wed, Sun; 10am-11pm Thur-Sat. **Main courses** £7.50-£14.50. **Credit** MC, V.
Brixton Village Market (formerly Granville Arcade) has become a prime dining destination thanks to the many cafés and restaurants that have opened among the fruit and veg, household goods and bric-a-brac stalls. It takes time to get going, though. At 7pm on a Saturday evening, Etta's was deserted, except for Etta herself and two cheerful helpers in the tiny kitchen. Decor is simple: white walls, plain wooden tables and more tables 'outside' in the covered market. The short but appealing menu of fish and shellfish dishes runs from cod and chips to lobster, and includes succulent, fresh-grilled shell-on prawns, and crispy, deep-fried whitebait. There's a couple of vegetarian dishes too. The flavours of steamed sea bass harmonised beautifully with the just-right piquancy of scotch bonnet peppers, while seafood curry featured assorted fish and a quarter-crab in a spicy stock. A nutcracker and metal skewer were provided for the crab: a hands-on affair not for the faint-hearted, but staff were brisk and efficient with their delivery of napkins and water bowls. So welcoming were they

down with the homemade pineapple or Guinness punch. From the space to the staff to the food, it is guileless but artful… properly Caribbean.
Babies and children admitted. Takeaway service.

North
Camden Town & Chalk Farm

Mango Room
10-12 Kentish Town Road, NW1 8NH (7482 5065, www.mangoroom.co.uk). Camden Town tube. **Lunch served** noon-4pm daily, **dinner served** 5-11pm daily. **Main courses** £7.50-£15.90. **Credit** AmEx, MC, V.
On a busy Camden Market Saturday, the Mango Room was not a happy place, with two large tables of disgruntled tourists and a bemused-looking Asian couple all wondering where their orders were. This was because the coolly stylish room (pink and bare-brick walls, colourful paintings, white tablecloths) was being tended by a lone waitress. She was making all the drinks too, which, given the popularity of the cocktails here, could mean a long wait – though she was coping bravely. Food, when it arrived, looked heavenly. Salt-cod fritters were light and airy, the fresh garnish and mango sauce creating a Caribbean scene in miniature. Their presentation was bettered only by the gorgeous palette of colours of Creole snapper fillet, a well-balanced dish in which the flavours of the fish were enhanced by a tangy green peppercorn sauce. Goat curry was rich yet delicate, the meat tender and, unusually, bone-free. A side of roti (the flaky Trinidadian version of the Indian flatbread), for mopping up the juices, was near-perfect. Such attention to detail comes at a cost, but it's worth it… Even the disgruntled tourists were smiling by the end of the meal.
Babies and children welcome: high chairs. Booking advisable weekends. Separate room for parties, seats 20. Takeaway service.
Map 27 D2.

Etta's Seafood Kitchen

Menu

Ackee: a red-skinned fruit with yellow flesh that looks like scrambled eggs when cooked; traditionally served in a Jamaican dish of salt cod, onion and peppers.
Bammy or **bammie:** pancake-shaped, deep-fried cassava bread, often served with fried fish.
Breadfruit: this football-sized fruit has sweet creamy flesh that's a cross between sweet potato and chestnut. Eaten as a vegetable.
Bush tea: herbal tea made from cerese (a Jamaican vine plant), mint or fennel.
Callaloo: the spinach-like leaves of either taro or malanga, often used as a base for a thick soup flavoured with pork or crab meat.
Coo-coo: a polenta-like cake of cornmeal and okra.
Cow foot: a stew made from the hoof of the cow, boiled with vegetables. The cartilage gives the stew a gummy or gelatinous texture.
Curried goat: usually lamb in London; the meat is marinated and slow-cooked until tender.
Dasheen: a root vegetable with a texture similar to yam (qv).
Escoveitched (or **escovitch**) **fish:** fish fried or grilled, then pickled in a tangy sauce with onions, sweet peppers and vinegar; similar to escabèche.
Festival: deep-fried, slightly sweet dumpling often served with fried fish.
Foo-foo: a Barbadian dish of pounded plantains, which are seasoned, rolled into balls and served hot.
Jerk: chicken or pork marinated in chilli spices, slowly roasted or barbecued.
Patty or **pattie:** a savoury pastry snack, made with turmeric-coloured shortcrust pastry, usually filled with beef, saltfish or vegetables.
Peas or **beans:** black-eyed beans, black beans, green peas and red kidney beans.
Pepperpot: traditionally a stew of meat and cassereep, a juice obtained from cassava.
Phoulorie: a Trinidadian snack of fried doughballs often eaten with a sweet tamarind sauce.
Plantain or **plantin:** a savoury variety of banana that is cooked like potato.
Rice and peas: rice cooked with kidney or gungo beans, pepper seasoning and coconut milk.
Saltfish: salt cod, classically mixed with ackee (qv) or callaloo (qv).
Sorrel: not the herb, but a type of hibiscus with a sour-sweet flavour.
Soursop: a dark green, slightly spiny fruit; the pulp, blended with milk and sugar, is a refreshing drink.
Yam: a large tuber, with a yellow or white flesh and slightly nutty flavour.

Chinese

Chinese is not a cuisine, it's a family of cuisines. On the mainland, the Han Chinese have established several distinctive regional styles of cooking. The main ones we encounter in the West are delicate Cantonese or, sometimes, spicy Sichuanese; but there are other major cuisines too centred around Shanghai, Hunan, and Beijing. Plus there are the street food dishes of Taiwan, and the culinary fusion of Chinese Singaporean cooking. The London scene has been transformed in the past decade. Alan Yau first made Chinese cuisine hip with the opening of **Hakkasan** in 2001. Dim sum specialist **Yauatcha** followed in 2004, with the Royal China group responding with **Royal China Club** in 2006. All these establishments serve predominantly Cantonese cuisine – offering stir-fries, plenty of fresh seafood, and dim sum, as do most of the Chinatown old-stagers – evidence of the historical links between Britain and Hong Kong. *See p70* **Chinatown on the cheap** for some of the best-value venues. More recently, though, it has been Sichuanese and Hunanese restaurants, serving the fiercely spicy, tongue-numbing food of western China, that have made the running, most notably the quartet that share the same ownership: **Barshu**, **Ba Shan**, **Baozi Inn** and the recently opened **Baiwei**. The spectacularly located newcomer **Hutong** also dishes up Sichuanese, as well as northern Chinese food, from its location halfway up the Shard. Otherwise, there still aren't many London representatives of northern and eastern Chinese food, though **Manchurian Legends** serves some of the lamb dishes popular in the north, and new arrival **A Wong** produces food from across the Chinese regions. This year's story, though, has been the Cantonese fight-back, with the opening of the Hakkasan Group's latest contender, **HKK**.

Central

Belgravia

★ Hunan

51 Pimlico Road, SW1W 8NE (7730 5712, www.hunanlondon.com). Sloane Square tube. **Lunch served** 12.30-2pm, **dinner served** 6.30-11pm Mon-Sat. **Set lunch** £30.80 per person (minimum 2). **Set dinner** £46.80 per person (minimum 2). **Credit** AmEx, MC, V.
Hunan is a rare beast: a restaurant held in high esteem, yet under the fashion radar. Perhaps it's because the setting is fairly run-of-the-mill, with its awkward layout ('front' and 'rear' sections divided by the service bar) and sparse decor (oriental prints, the odd Buddha). The cooking, however, is anything but ordinary. You'll be asked if there's anything you can't (or won't) eat, what level of spice you like and how hungry you are – and the kitchen will do the rest. Arriving in waves, the plates start small (a delectable nibble here, a mouthful there) and get progressively larger. The cooking is not exclusively Hunanese (a style like Sichuanese, yet more 'fiery

hot' than 'numbing hot'), but borrows from across China. We enjoyed the sour, peppery notes of a Sichuanese cucumber salad; the fragrant broth of our Shanghainese 'soup dumpling' (xiao long bau), and the chilli-laden unctuous sauce of a Hunanese dish of tender beef. After a dozen or so grazing dishes, out came the big guns: classic showpieces of crispy peking duck ahead of silky steamed sea bass with ginger and spring onions; then chewy hand-pulled noodles. Only if you exceed 18 dishes (nigh-on impossible) is there a surcharge. It's not cheap, and neither is the serious old-world wine list, but you'll feast like an emperor.
Babies and children admitted lunch. Booking essential. Vegetarian menu. **Map 15 G11**.

Chinatown

Baiwei NEW

8 Little Newport Street, WC2H 7JJ (7494 3605). Leiester Square tube. **Open** noon-11pm daily. **Main courses** £8.90-£12.90. **No credit cards**.
'One dish, one style; a hundred dishes, a hundred tastes.' Baiwei ('a hundred flavours' in Chinese) exemplifies this Sichuanese culinary adage. Despite

its Mao-era decor, it's a cosy place with a lengthy selection of authentic, home-style Sichuanese, Hunanese and northern dishes served by uncommonly friendly staff. True to another Chinese saying – 'China is the place for food, but Sichuan is the place for flavour' – the dishes from the south-western province feature abundant dried chillies, sichuan pepper and fragrant garlic. The slithery, rubbery bite of cold pig's ear, tongue and tripe tossed in tangy black vinegar made an appetising starter. Gong bao tofu (an interesting variation on the better-known gong bao chicken) consisted of silky pieces of pan-fried egg tofu coated in lustrous sweet and sour sauce, then lavished with crunchy peanuts and dried chillies. Long beans are an excellent choice of vegetable for pickling, as the bean cavities trap the sour brine. Here, they're mixed with lightly marinated minced pork that has been fried: a pleasing contrast of flavours. Only the dan dan noodles didn't live up to expectations; the ground beef was satisfyingly chewy and the sauce aromatic, but the alkaline noodles were limp and waterlogged. Baiwei is the newest addition to the Barshu, Ba Shan and Baozi Inn restaurant group. *Booking advisable. Takeaway service.* **Map 17 C4**.

Imperial China

White Bear Yard, 25A Lisle Street, WC2H 7BA (7734 3388, www.imperial-china.co.uk). Leicester Square or Piccadilly Circus tube. **Meals served** noon-11.30pm Mon-Sat; 11.30am-10.30pm Sun. **Dim sum served** noon-5pm daily. **Main courses** £8.50-£32.50. **Dim sum** £3.20-£4.50. **Set meal** £19.50-£45.50 per person (minimum 2). **Minimum** £10. **Credit** AmEx, MC, V.

A small wooden bridge spanning an ornamental fish pond, warm wood panelling, kind lighting and a second floor offering a view of the dining room below set this Cantonese stalwart apart from all others in Chinatown. Yet in every other respect, it's indistinguishable. Service is efficiently brusque to maximise customer turnover. We've often had to wait for a table, whether we had booked in advance or not – as if an empty seat, even for a minute, is seen as a threat to profits. No surprise, then, that dishes are delivered quickly. During a weekend dim sum lunch, about a dozen baskets arrived simultaneously, minutes after ordering. There were no standouts among the parade of dishes we tried, but we had no complaints either. The food is reliable, authentic and of decent quality. Portions can be rather miserly, however, especially given the high prices compared to rivals in the neighbourhood. Then again, Imperial China appears to get away with it. The relatively handsome and comfortable decor, accessible location and clean toilets seem to keep the venue consistently popular among both Chinese and Western diners.
Babies and children welcome: high chairs. Booking advisable. Disabled: toilet. Separate rooms for parties, seating 10-70. Tables outdoors (5, courtyard). Vegetarian menu.
Map 17 C4.

Joy King Lau

3 Leicester Street, WC2H 7BL (7437 1132, www.joykinglau.com). Leicester Square or Piccadilly Circus tube. **Meals served** noon-11.30pm Mon-Sat; 11am-10.30pm Sun. **Dim sum served** noon-5pm Mon-Sat; 11am-5pm Sun. **Main courses** £7.50-£18. **Dim sum** £2.60-£4.50. **Set meal** £12-£35 per person (minimum 2). **Credit** AmEx, MC, V.

The sign outside the restaurant translates as 'drunken men's tower' – yet while some Chinatown eateries get rowdy late at night, this seems unlikely at JKL, despite its proximity to Leicester Square. The decor is nicer than it appears from the outside, best described as being on the posh side of nondescript, over all three floors. The clientele is overwhelmingly and reassuringly Chinese, many of whom come for the long-renowned lunchtime dim sum. A robust air-conditioning and ventilation system (switched to US levels of chill on our visit) repels the summer heat and keeps the smell of grease in the kitchen. If you're not in a hurry (and not wearing anything white or that needs dry-cleaning), it's worth ordering a messy dish such as crab in pungent, fragrant black bean sauce, to see the kitchen excel and to exercise your shell-cracking skills. Other winners include crystal prawns with a perfectly juicy texture and the taste of the sea. Lowlights of our meal were what might be Chinatown's saltiest roast duck, and an aubergine dish that hadn't been stewed long enough to get rid of the skins' bitterness.
Babies and children welcome: high chairs. Booking advisable weekends. Takeaway service.
Map 17 C5.

Baiwei

City

HKK NEW

*88 Worship Street, EC2A 2BB (3535 1888,
www.hkklondon.com). Liverpool Street tube/rail
or Old Street tube/rail.* **Lunch served** noon-
2.30pm Mon-Fri. **Dinner served** 6-9.45pm
Mon-Sat. **Main courses** £16-£38. **Set lunch**
£28-£95. **Set dinner** £48-£95. **Credit** AmEx,
MC, V.

Cantonese cooking, one of the great cuisines of
China, isn't always presented at its best in London,
where many Cantonese restaurants tend to have
garish decor, abrupt service and slapped-together
dishes. But HKK (the latest venture from the
Hakkasan Group) reinvents the entire experience.
The eight-course tasting menu offered at lunch
(£48) demonstrates how sophisticated Cantonese
food can be. The tone is set the moment you enter
the elegant dining room, furnished on the
comfortable side of austere. And it's sealed the
moment you bite into the first starter, a delicate
mouthful of fried silken tofu, pickled water
chestnut, and shimeji mushroom tied with a
translucent strip of ibérico ham. The next course,
a trio of dim sum, was among the best we've had.
As was the peking duck, ceremoniously carved in
front of diners; the perfectly crisped skin is served
with both hoisin sauce and a pinch of sugar, just as
in Beijing's top roast-duck restaurants. Each
subsequent dish was equally flawless, but few
elicited the 'wow' we were anticipating. Despite the
innovative use of ingredients, the flavours were
resolutely familiar – though that is hardly a fault if
you're after authenticity. For the uninitiated, HKK
is a revelation. Just don't go with an empty stomach
or wallet: the portions are tiny, the bill is not.
*Babies and children admitted. Booking advisable.
Separate room for parties, seats 12.* **Map 6 R5**.

Fitzrovia

Hakkasan

*8 Hanway Place, W1T 1HD (7927 7000,
www.hakkasan.com). Tottenham Court
Road tube.*
Bar **Open** noon-12.30am Mon-Wed; noon-
1.30am Thur-Sat; noon-midnight Sun.
Restaurant **Lunch/dim sum served** noon-
3pm Mon-Fri; noon-4pm Sat, Sun. **Dinner
served** 6-11pm Mon-Wed, Sun; 5.30pm-
midnight Thur-Sat. **Main courses** £17-£61.
Dim sum £3-£20. **Set lunch** £28 2 courses.
Credit AmEx, MC, V.

More than a decade after it started wowing
London's big spenders with its classy Cantonese
cooking, this Michelin-starred trendsetter remains
a benchmark against which all high-end Chinese
restaurants should be judged. The basement's
stylish interior (all dark wood lattice screens and
moody lighting) still attracts the kind of beautiful
people who might suppress their appetites –
though there was little evidence of restraint on our
midweek night visit. Plate after plate landed on
tables around us, including signature dishes such
as silver cod roasted in champagne, and jasmine
tea-smoked organic pork ribs. We started with the
dim sum platter, a basket of superbly crafted
dumplings. The pastry was perfect in give and
texture, just elastic enough to encase generous
bites of flavour-packed meat and seafood. Sweet
and sour Duke of Berkshire pork served with
pomegranate was equally good, the melting
tenderness of top-quality meat turning the clichéd
staple into a luxury – Chinese takeaways should
weep with shame. Drinks run from cocktails via
high-priced wines to specialist teas. The original
Hakkasan that spawned a global empire (including
a newer branch in Mayfair) retains all its appeal:
cool enough to be seen in, yet authentic enough to
dash pretension.
*Available for hire. Babies and children admitted.
Booking essential, 3 mths in advance. Disabled:
lift; toilet. Entertainment: DJs 10.30pm Thur-
Sat.* **Map 17 C2**.
For branch see index.

HKK

Marylebone

Phoenix Palace

5 Glentworth Street, NW1 5PG (7486 3515, www.phoenixpalace.co.uk). Baker Street tube. **Meals served** noon-11.30pm Mon-Sat; 11am-10.30pm Sun. **Dim sum served** noon-4.45pm Mon-Sat; 11am-4.45pm Sun. **Main courses** £6.50-£48.80. **Dim sum** £3.80-£17.80. **Set meal** £23.80-£39.80 per person (minimum 2). **Credit** AmEx, MC, V.

The rule of thumb in Chinese restaurants is to look around for diners of Chinese extraction and be sceptical when you don't see them. That said, Phoenix Palace's dinnertime abundance of well-fed, tie-wearing western and south Asian men in late middle-age is an endorsement; they're the international businessmen used to the Cantonese food served in the upmarket Beijing, Shanghai and Hong Kong spots that this large restaurant most resembles. Expensive, heavy Asian wood decor, and Molton Brown hand cream in the women's toilets emphasise the similarities. The arena-like layout of raised tables on the edge of the central dining area is good for people-watching, and spying to see which tables are being the most bold with the expansive menu. The crispy duck pancakes here aren't London's best, but they didn't disappoint. Scallops in crispy green fried 'bird's nest' were tasty, though we suspect the MSG kick had been diminished for western palates. Service can let things down, with the occasional lengthy wait between courses, but the excellent har gau (shrimp dumplings) are a reminder of why reservations are a must for weekend dim sum – unless you want to queue for more than an hour.
Babies and children welcome: high chairs. Booking advisable. Separate rooms for parties, seating 12-30. Takeaway service; delivery service (over £10 within 1-mile radius). **Map 2 F4**.

★ Royal China Club

40-42 Baker Street, W1U 7AJ (7486 3898, www.royalchinagroup.co.uk). Baker Street or Marble Arch tube. **Meals served** noon-11pm Mon-Thur; noon-11.30pm Fri, Sat; noon-10.30pm Sun. **Dim sum served** noon-4.45pm daily. **Main courses** £9.50-£120. **Dim sum** £3.80-£7. **Set meal** £40-£90 per person (minimum 2). **Credit** AmEx, MC, V.

The 'club' in the name makes RCC sound like a members-only section of the Royal China Group, which isn't far from the truth. This, the premier link in the chain, has an air of quiet elegance found in five-star hotels, right down to the faint tinkling of a piano. The kitchen turns out consummate Cantonese cooking, using prized ingredients (abalone, lobster, veal) at every opportunity. At lunchtime, dim sum includes the signature cheung fun, which here comes filled with velvety dover sole and smooth pieces of scallop – all sitting in a puddle of sweet, smoky sauce. A quartet of siu mai (steamed pork dumplings) are topped not with a dice of carrot (as they would be in Chinatown), but with pearls of salmon roe, as you'd expect at the banqueting table. Even simple noodle dishes are elevated to premium status: our steak ho fun noodles were smothered in a dark, soy-laced sauce full of umami savouriness, heaped with expertly judged slices of medium-rare sirloin, and sprinkled with sesame seeds. Wherever possible, the polished, softly spoken staff employ silver-service methods, making everyone feel like a visiting dignitary.

Babies and children admitted. Booking advisable Sat, Sun. Separate room for parties, seats 24. Takeaway service. **Map 9 G5**.

Mayfair

China Tang

The Dorchester, 53 Park Lane, W1K 1QA (7629 9988, www.thedorchester.com). Hyde Park Corner tube. **Meals/dim sum served** noon-11.45pm daily. **Main courses** £12-£60. **Dim sum** £5-£22. **Set lunch** £27.50. **Credit** AmEx, MC, V.

David Tang's slinky dining room in the Dorchester's basement successfully manages to banish all thoughts of hotel restaurants from diners' minds. The separate Park Lane entrance helps, as do art deco furnishings evoking 1930s Shanghai. Only the moneyed, multinational clientele remind you of the locality. China Tang has formidable kitchen resources, so it would be a shame to stick to the western-oriented set meals (where cheung fun is renamed cannelloni) – though à la carte prices can intimidate. Despite the setting, Shanghainese cuisine is little in evidence, with Cantonese dominating. Hence, dim sum is a good choice, with most dishes costing around a fiver. Mango spring rolls with gai lan is among several vegetarian choices, and glutinous rice comes packed with seductive titbits for meat-eaters. Main course red-cooked lamb in clay pot is a marvellously savoury northern Chinese dish, the meat tender, the gravy profoundly flavoured, the texture enhanced by strips of resilient bean curd skin. Service was proper and polite, yet we noted some frayed edges: no one stationed at the ground-floor 'greeter's counter'; shouting in the kitchen drowning out diners' conversation; and Hugh Grant reading Shakespeare's Sonnet 18 stuck on a loop in the toilets. Enough 'darling buds', Hugh.
Babies and children welcome: high chairs. Booking advisable, essential weekends. Disabled: lift; toilet. Separate rooms for parties seating 8-80. **Map 9 G7**.

Kai Mayfair

65 South Audley Street, W1K 2QU (7493 8988, www.kaimayfair.co.uk). Bond Street or Marble Arch tube. **Lunch served** noon-2pm Mon-Fri; 12.30-2.30pm Sat, Sun. **Dinner served** 6.30-10.30pm Mon-Sat; 6.30-10pm Sun. **Main courses** £16-£53. **Set lunch** £27 3 courses (£39 incl wine). **Credit** AmEx, MC, V.

Kai feels like a labour of love by an Asian billionaire homesick for venues appropriate for special occasions with business partners. Unlike the boisterous 'Shanghai speakeasy' vibe found at China Tang, the atmosphere at Kai is more like a date at a museum with subdued patrons. Service is impeccable (it's possibly London's most over-staffed restaurant), the sofa seating is plush and the rotating collection of contemporary Chinese art is worthy of a Phillips auction (most notably, Zhang Xiangming's cartoonish *Beijing Girl* dominates one of the back walls). The food is generally delicious and oil-free, especially the 'chai' tofu parcels and a delicate sea bass served in broth, though hungrier diners may resent the minimalist portion sizes. The £27 set lunch is a steal, especially if you shell out another £12 for matching wines that include interesting Tokaji and Banyuls. It's the only cheap moment – hopefully, you'll have a sugar daddy (or mummy) to pay for the likes of lobster-poached noodles and peking duck. Kai is also that rare thing:

a Chinese restaurant that names the (non-Chinese) pastry chef responsible for its decadent chocolate desserts. Both '6 shades of chocolate and peanuts' and a palate-cleansing course featured the whimsical touch of popping candy.
Babies and children welcome: high chairs. Booking advisable lunch, essential dinner. Separate rooms for parties, seating 6-12. Vegetarian menu. **Map 9 G7**.

Princess Garden

8-10 North Audley Street, W1K 6ZD (7493 3223, www.princessgardenofmayfair.com). Bond Street tube. **Dim sum served** noon-4pm daily. **Lunch served** noon-4pm Mon-Fri; noon-4.30pm Sat, Sun. **Dinner served** 6.30-11pm Mon-Sat; 6.30-10.20pm Sun. **Main courses** £9.50-£42. **Dim sum** £2.80-£3.50. **Credit** AmEx, MC, V.

Once upon a time, it was fit for a princess, but this Mayfair restaurant is no longer Cantonese royalty. That's not to say Princess Garden is without fans. On our visit, the room was full of ostentatiously wealthy foreign families (although, tellingly, none of Chinese origin) and a smattering of business-lunch parties. The venue resembles a luxury hotel lobby, with an expensively tiled floor, minimalist furnishings, inoffensive muzak and well-spoken staff. It's a pity, however, that the staff's manner isn't as pleasant as their uniforms; on our visit, they treated us as an inconvenience, and rushed us through our meal. This might have been tolerable if the cooking were outstanding, but standards are extremely variable. A plate of beef ho fun was unpleasantly greasy, as were the yam croquettes, which had been deep-fried a touch too long. By contrast, our steamed dim sum were excellent: from the soft doughy char siu buns with sweet and sticky roasted pork, to a seafood take on siu mai made with sweet chunks of prawns, a slice of scallop and a sliver of gai lan (chinese broccoli). Nevertheless, these bright points weren't enough to rescue the overall experience.
Babies and children welcome: high chairs. Booking advisable. Separate rooms for parties, seating 6-50. Takeaway service. **Map 9 G6**.

Paddington

Pearl Liang

8 Sheldon Square, W2 6EZ (7289 7000, www.pearlliang.co.uk). Paddington tube/rail. **Meals served** noon-11pm, **dim sum served** noon-4.45pm daily. **Main courses** £8.80-£60. **Dim sum** £3-£5. **Set meal** £25 per person (minimum 2); £38 per person (minimum 4). **Credit** AmEx, MC, V.

Don't let the Crossrail construction works around Paddington station or the less-than-lovely glass and concrete tower blocks put you off coming here. The spacious room is a real looker – sexy enough to get even a panda in the mood for love – with its dark slate flooring, mauve chair covers, and flower blossom designs that appear on lampshades and a long wall mural. There's a moodily lit cocktail bar too. Pearl Liang remains very popular – the place was already heaving when we arrived. The extensive menu focuses on Cantonese fare, but also strays into south-east Asia with the likes of pad thai and kway teow. Luxury ingredients such as abalone and shark's fin appear in various guises. We've yet to be disappointed with the dim sum (visit during the day for the full selection). Steamed dumplings take pride of place, including prawn laced with a smear of wasabi. The inventive streak

Royal China Club. See p67.

continued with heavenly morsels filled with prawn, courgette and celery, while prawn and barbecued pork versions of cheung fun provided a medley of umami flavours. Diced water chestnuts gave a lovely bounce to fried octopus cake, with a hint of coriander adding a final exotic touch. A dish of lobster noodles was slightly overcooked. Service was fast, but not, thankfully, furious.
Babies and children welcome: high chairs. Booking advisable. Disabled: toilet. Separate room for parties, seats 40. Takeaway service. **Map 8 D5**.

Pimlico

A Wong NEW

70 Wilton Road, SW1V 1DE (7828 8931, www.awong.co.uk). Victoria tube/rail. **Lunch served** noon-2.30pm Tue-Sat. **Dinner served** 5.30-10pm Mon-Sat. **Main courses** £7-£12.95. **Set meal** £12.95 2 courses, £38.88 8 courses. **Credit** AmEx, MC, V.
Andrew Wong's pared-back venture beautifully reinterprets Chinese cooking using the finest ingredients. Unlike his contemporaries (the likes of Hakkasan), however, Wong elevates the cuisine without hiking the prices. Dim sum and snacks inspired by street food can be ordered individually, inviting anyone to pop in for daikon cake with wind-dried sausage and shrimp. The tasting menu is a relative bargain at £38.88 for eight auspicious courses (eight being a lucky number for the Chinese), showcasing Wong's passion for China's diverse regional fare. Poached razor clam with sea cucumber, pickled cucumber, vinegar tapioca and wind-dried sausage produced a gorgeous mouthful of contrasting textures and flavours. Chilli barbecued pineapple with a light, tangy Beijing-style yoghurt was a revelation – proof that dairy and dessert can successfully feature in a Chinese meal. Gung bao chicken was less enjoyable; cutting back on the cornflour resulted in a watery sauce that failed to cling to the generous chunks of corn-fed chicken breast. The pace of the courteous service was also disappointing; it took up to 20 minutes for courses to arrive. In this café-like space with bare tables and hard-backed seats, that makes for an uncomfortable wait, one that marred an otherwise enjoyable meal.
Available for hire. Babies and children welcome: high chairs. Booking advisable. Separate room for parties, seats 30. Tables outdoors (3, patio). Takeaway service. **Map 15 J10**.

Soho

Barshu HOT 50

28 Frith Street, W1D 5LF (7287 6688, www.bar-shu.co.uk). Leicester Square or Tottenham Court Road tube. **Meals served** noon-11pm Mon-Thur, Sun; noon-11.30pm Fri, Sat. **Main courses** £9.90-£30.90. **Credit** AmEx, MC, V.
The distance north of Shaftesbury Avenue, though only 20 metres, is significant. Barshu (the original of a quartet along with Ba Shan, Baozi Inn and newcomer Baiwei) is distinct from Chinatown's mostly Cantonese restaurants in looks and pricing, as well as cuisine (Sichuanese). The dark wooden ground floor is brightened by red lanterns and partitioned by a beautifully carved screen; upstairs is similarly woody. Despite such rusticity, you could spend extravagantly here – though there are ways to lessen the bill. Order tea (£2 per person) rather than wine (the cheapest bottle is £21.90). You'll need

to slake your thirst to counteract the fiery, numbing and sour flavours that characterise western Chinese cookery. The menu holds much interest, listing the likes of pea jelly, prairie tripe, and stir-fried chicken gizzards with pickled chilli – each dish is depicted. To start, order from the 'Chengdu street snacks' section, rather than the pricey appetisers; sweet-potato noodles in hot and sour sauce was a filling bowlful of noodle soup, chilli oil and numbing peppercorns, for just £4. Main courses of fish-fragrant pork slivers (a pleasing textural mix including wood-ear fungus and crunchy bamboo shoot) and stir-fried long beans, chopped small and well-paired with minced pork, also hold delight. Drawbacks? Many dishes are hot and oily, so order steamed rice and (expensive) plain vegetables for balance. Service could be sharper too, but Barshu nevertheless remains London's prime exponent of this alluring cuisine.

Babies and children welcome: high chairs. Booking advisable Fri, Sat. Disabled: toilet. Separate room for parties, seats 24. **Map 17 C4**.

Ba Shan

24 Romilly Street, W1D 5AH (7287 3266, www.bashanlondon.com). Leicester Square tube. **Meals served** noon-11pm Mon-Thur, Sun; noon-11.30pm Fri, Sat. **Main courses** £8.90-£16.90. **Credit** AmEx, MC, V.

The warren of distressed hutong rooms and twanging music might make patrons of this Hunanese eaterie feel like extras in *Kill Bill*. Posters celebrate Mao's paeans to chilli-fuelled revolution – ironic, we hope, but it's hard to tell when the service tends to the authentically brusque. Unfortunately, the kitchen seems to have been resting on its laurels of late, and prices have crept higher. The once-famously fiery dishes seem to have been toned down for non-Chinese (who account for a decided minority of diners), so it's worth a word with staff if you're after genuine south-western Chinese heat. Otherwise, stick to dishes displaying the double chilli icon. The most fun and expensive choice on the menu is the whole sea bass in red chilli, de-boned at your table should you wish and served in a big bowl of broth – ideally soaked up by a second serving of noodles. Pork dumplings were tasty if unremarkable; green chilli-stuffed shrimp looked great but lacked pungency. Bean curd puffs were crunchy-sticky goodness. The kitchen also produces a serviceable General Tso's chicken, for more mainstream tastes. Ba Shan is much more enjoyable and civilised than many local competitors; it's still popular too, so reservations are recommended.

Babies and children welcome: high chairs. Booking advisable. Disabled: toilet. Separate room for parties, seats 12. **Map 17 C4**.

★ Yauatcha [HOT 50]

15 Broadwick Street, W1F 0DL (7494 8888, www.yauatcha.com). Leicester Square or Tottenham Court Road tube. **Dim sum served** noon-11.45pm Mon-Sat; noon-10.30pm Sun. **Dim sum** £4-£15. **Set meal** (3-6pm Mon-Fri) £14.44 per person (minimum 2). **Credit** AmEx, MC, V.

Such acutely stylish venues rarely last, but after a decade Yauatcha can add longevity to its enviable list of attributes. So why do people still glide down the stairs of this self-styled Taipei tea house into its sensual basement? The design helps: the long bar, spotlit black tables and illuminated fish tank still have allure, and the nightclub vibe is boosted by beautiful staff and bass-heavy beats. Even being shunted away to seats behind the staircase has benefits (privacy). And there's substance behind the style. Day-and-night dim sum was a Yauatcha innovation, and a special of scallop and edamame crystal dumplings produced three delicate, pendulous sacs filled with a textural mix of resilient beans, crunchy carrot morsels, flavourful fragments of scallop and juicy sweetcorn. Gai lan came with just enough salted fish sauce to pique the palate, and fragrant lotus leaf rice held moist treats of egg, chicken and dried shrimps. Exotic teas and East-West fusion desserts (yuzu brûlée tart) are highlights too (sample them in the ground-floor tea room), and main courses hold interest (sea bass with shiitake and wolfberry, say), but grazing on exquisite snacks is the primary culinary draw – though prices might make you wince.

Available for hire. Babies and children admitted. Booking advisable. Disabled: lift; toilet. **Map 17 B3**.

A Wong

Chinatown on the cheap

★ Baozi Inn

25 Newport Court, WC2H 7JS (7287 6877, www.baoziinnlondon.com). Leicester Square tube. **Meals served** noon-10pm daily. **Main courses** £4.50-£7.50. **No credit cards.**

The decor, inspired by Beijing's hutongs circa 1952, signals Communist Revolution kitsch. The scale of the interior is also authentically mid-20th-century Chinese – the wooden seats and tables are best suited to diners of smaller stature. Yet Baozi Inn is a great drop-in spot for Beijing- and Chengdu-style street snacks. True to Sichuanese form, red is present in most dishes – if not as a slick of potent chilli oil, then in lashings of sliced or whole chillies. This is a good place to try a big bowl of dan dan noodles, with their mild heat and the slightly numbing effect of the sichuan pepper in the ground pork sauce (though on our most recent visit, the dish was over-salted). Dumplings in soup are also a good choice, while the eponymous baozi – steamed bread bun filled with pork or vegetables, a dish typical of northern China – can also be bought takeaway at the small shop next door, where a huge pot of chillies and sichuan pepper boils like a witches' cauldron, and is used as the hotpot for a choice of skewers. Lamb, cuttlefish ball, shiitake mushroom, dried bean curd, 'prawn balls' that are hollow like macaroni – they're all destined for the pot, cook in a couple of minutes and cost a mere £1-£1.20 per skewer.

Bookings not accepted. Children admitted. Takeaway service. **Map 17 C4.**

★ Café TPT

21 Wardour Street, W1D 6PN (7734 7980). Leicester Square or Piccadilly Circus tube. **Meals served** noon-1am daily. **Main courses** £6.50-£22. **Set meal** £11.50-£12 per person (minimum 2). **Credit** AmEx, MC, V.

The menu in the window of Café TPT looks longer than the complete musings of Confucius. It's not unusual to see a big menu in Chinatown, but such a vast repertoire seems impossible from a kitchen galley the size of an origami junk. Not so, because dishes from Hong Kong, mainland China and the diaspora are all produced competently, and some of them with commendable aplomb. The Cantonese dishes tend to be better than the Malaysian ones: roast duck on rice was succulent, and a generous helping. A sizzling dish of stuffed tofu, served in a hot stone bowl, was a highlight. Seafood is also a strength, with around 50 dishes to choose from; our squid, part of a noodle dish, was fresh and pert. Many customers were moved to speechlessness by their bubble teas – this is a good place to try these Taiwan-style drinks. TPT isn't the cheapest of the budget Chinatown cafés, but both cooking and service are better than you might expect.

Available for hire. Babies and children welcome: high chairs. Takeaway service. Vegetarian menu. **Map 17 B5.**

★ Canton

11 Newport Place, WC2H 7JR (7437 6220). Leicester Square tube. **Meals served** noon-11.30pm daily. **Main courses** £5.50-£10. **Set meal** £14.50-£23.50. **Credit** MC, V.

A longstanding feature of Chinatown, this unassuming café changed hands in 2012, losing it a few of its more ardent fans. The dishes we sampled a few months later suggested why. The best came first: a great-value 'starter' portion of wun tun soup, which translated to a large bowl of broth containing five juicy pork dumplings (costing a mere £3.50). We also enjoyed a plate of barbecued duck, warmed and removed from the bone, but were disappointed by the accompanying sauce, which was swimming in oil. A plate of salt and chilli squid delivered on texture, but the dish was marred by an excess of sodium. Our advice? Stick to the one-bowl, rice-with-meat dishes, which are served the traditional way (with the rice warm and the roast meat cold), and at £5.50 remain an eminently wallet-friendly meal. Service was pleasant, and the space unusually calm by Chinatown standards, helped by the easy-listening Cantonese soundtrack playing in the background. The setting is simple: just a single room, decked out in neutral tones and wood-veneer furniture.

Babies and children welcome: high chairs. Separate room for parties, seats 30. Takeaway service. **Map 17 C4.**

★ Four Seasons

23 Wardour Street, W1D 6PW (7287 9995, www.fs-restaurants.co.uk). Leicester Square or Piccadilly Circus tube. **Meals served** noon-11.30pm Mon-Thur, Sun; noon-midnight Fri, Sat. **Main courses** £8-£30. **Set meal** £16.50-£23 (minimum 2). **Credit** MC, V.

Famed for its Cantonese-style roast duck, this modest restaurant displays barbecued meats – pork ribs, pork belly and whole ducks – in the window facing busy Wardour Street. Curious passers-by stop and stare; drooling is acceptable. Of the two Four Seasons in Chinatown, this branch has the friendlier service. On our most recent visit (one of many), the roast duck was slightly disappointing. Our duck happened to be a greedy one with too thick a layer of fat, and the skin was almost chewy as a result of being drenched in the accompanying sauce. Better was the crispy pork belly: a tri-layer of perfectly crisp skin, melt-in-your-mouth fatty middle and juicy lean meat. Fujian fried rice was fragrant, with a generous topping of savoury seafood and meaty titbits, but like the beef ho fun, it was a little heavy-handed on the seasoning. If you're overwhelmed by the vast choice of dishes – hundreds on the regular menu, dozens more on the 'chef's special' menu with non-Cantonese dishes – choose one of the simple yet good-value set meals. Open until late, Four Seasons is a decent choice for a late-night meal in central London that won't burn a hole in your pocket.

Babies and children welcome: high chairs. Booking advisable. Takeaway service. **Map 17 B5.** **For branches see index.**

★ HK Diner

22 Wardour Street, W1D 6QQ (7434 9544, www.hkdiner.com). Leicester Square or Piccadilly Circus tube. **Meals served** 11am-4am daily. **Main courses** £5-£25. **Set meal** £11-£32 per person (minimum 2). **Minimum** £6. **Credit** MC, V.

Pay attention as you walk along Wardour Street, adjacent to Leicester Square – it's easy to miss HK Diner's narrow frontage. The interior is bigger than you might expect, and staff will hasten you towards any unoccupied booth seating. The menu covers Chinese standards, such as roast duck (impessively succulent) and various Chinese greens stir-fried with your choice of sauce, but on our last visit we were most struck by the generosity of the seafood (scallops, carved squid) in a noodle dish. Everything was perfectly cooked and the service was gracious, which is reflected in the prices being a little higher than the Wardour Street norm. The bubble teas (a long list, from mango to iced red bean with coconut milk) are excellent, and, usefully for night owls, the place is open until 4am. Note there's a minimum £6 a head charge.

Available for hire. Babies and children welcome: high chairs. Takeaway service. Vegetarian menu. **Map 17 C4.**

★ Leong's Legends

4 Macclesfield Street, W1D 6AX (7287 0288, www.leongslegends.co.uk). Leicester Square or Piccadilly Circus tube. **Meals served** noon-11pm Mon-Thur, Sun; noon-11.30pm Fri, Sat. **Dim sum served** noon-5pm daily. **Main courses** £4.50-£18.50. **Dim sum** £1.90-£6.50. **Credit** (over £12) MC, V.

If there's one thing the Restaurant Privilege group enjoy, it's change. Not content with running over a dozen restaurants (mostly in Chinatown, but also in Hampstead, Bayswater and the City) and dealing in various oriental cuisines, they also swap sites faster than tiles in a game of mah-jong. For the time being, you'll find the first of the Leong's Legends duo at this plum Chinatown address, just around the corner from Leong's Legends II. They offer a single concept: 'Taiwanese' cooking in tea house surrounds. In truth, the menus are dominated by Cantonese dishes, with just a sprinkling of Taiwanese options, but the decor delivers – doing away with white tablecloths and round tables in favour of dark woods and carved latticework. The cooking isn't always as successful, with dim sum particularly unreliable: on our visit, not only was the pastry of steamed siu mai (usually a dense pork dumpling, this was a minced prawn version) on the dry side and the filling lacklustre, but it wasn't even garnished properly. However, the full-flavoured one-bowl dishes (such as dark, sticky pork belly on a huge mound of steamed rice) are terrific value, and alone are reason to visit. *Babies and children admitted. Bookings not accepted. Tables outdoors (2, pavement). Takeaway service.* **Map 17 C4**. **For branch see index.**

★ Longji

47-49 Charing Cross Road, WC2H 0AN (7534 9898). Leicester Square tube. **Meals served** 11.30am-11pm Mon-Sat; 11am-10.30pm Sun. **Main courses** £5.50-£9.20. **Credit** (over £10) MC, V.
If you've ever wondered what a fast-food joint in Hong Kong looks like, Longji (formerly Café de Hong Kong) is it. A brightly lit, functional space of tiled floors and wood-veneer booths, it's spread over several floors, each with HK-pop piped overhead. It's deservedly popular with Chinese students – and, in fact, anyone with an eye for good value. Typical dishes such as soup with just-added instant noodles, or HK tea (black tea brewed with condensed milk) are here for the nostalgic, but the vast menu offers plenty more besides. A generous portion of sticky steamed rice came topped with two kinds of barbecued meat: slices of sweet roast pork and chunks of gamey, fatty roast duck. Equally excellent – and equally ample – was a bowl of soup noodles: slippery ho fun in a delicate garlicky broth, topped with bouncy, hawker-style fish balls and a couple of juicy pork and prawn wun tuns. The lengthy drinks list runs from exotic juices (honey melon, red bean) to on-trend bubble teas (papaya milk, taro), and traditional Chinese teas – though our chrysanthemum tea, served pre-brewed in a tall glass, was on the strong side.

Service is fast, and by London Chinatown standards, fairly friendly.
Booking advisable. Disabled: toilet. Takeaway service. **Map 17 C4**.

★ Manchurian Legends

16 Lisle Street, WC2H 7BE (7287 6606, www.manchurianlegends.com). Leicester Square or Piccadilly Circus tube. **Meals served** 11am-11pm Mon-Wed, Sun; 11am-11.30pm Thur-Sat. **Main courses** £6.50-£19.80. **Set lunch** £5.50-£11 2 courses. **Set dinner** (minimum 2) £18.80-£23.50 2 courses. **Credit** MC, V.
The hearty cuisine of north-eastern China is rare in London, but Manchurian Legends – which since summer 2012 has been ensconced in these folksy little premises – specialises in Dongbei dishes. The menu, brought by young smiling waitresses, is long and enticing, with robust meat and offal dishes dominating. Lamb, wheat (rather than rice) and hotpots characterise the cookery, so succulent, fatty lamb skewers with chilli and sesame-seed topping make an apt starter. Or try beef tendon and tripe in spicy sauce: tender meat and a welter of wobbly honeycomb tripe, doused in chilli oil and topped with peanuts, the vast portion was enough for three to share. Alternatively, there's a fine choice of fried dumplings. Next could come Manchurian hotpot (a DIY feast where diners dunk raw titbits into boiling stock), or a warming beef brisket stew with white carrot (the cinnamon-flavoured gravy permeated the turnip-like carrot, but the beef needed more cooking). Equally rich was a lusciously slithery but too oily aubergine and minced pork dish (the advertised broad bean sauce seemingly absent). Noodles are thick and appealing, but it would be nice to see some Xinjiang bread – and more vegetable dishes to counterbalance all the meaty richness.
Babies and children welcome: high chairs; nappy-changing facilities. Booking advisable. Takeaway service. **Map 17 C4**.

★ New Fook Lam Moon

10 Gerrard Street, W1D 5PW (7734 7615). Leicester Square or Piccadilly Circus tube. **Meals served** noon-11pm Mon-Sat; noon-10pm Sun. **Main courses** £11.50-£27. **Credit** MC, V.
This Hong Kong-style café offers an extensive menu of Cantonese classics, such as baked salted chicken, stewed eel with black bean sauce, and stuffed bean curd with aubergine and green pepper. The roast meats (duck, pork, chicken) are popular too, and, unusually, there are also a few (hard-to-spot) Malaysian dishes. Our fried ho fun arrived with mixed seafood and pork (char kway teow – stir-fried flat noodles, in another guise), and packed real punch. The taste of garlic and belachan (pungent shrimp paste) lingered on delightfully. Less thrilling was a dry, bland Hainanese chicken rice. We were lucky to have grabbed the last table on the packed ground floor, which is smart in brown (walls and floor tiles are uniformly bronzed), with mirrors down one side to brighten up the place. The basement is a bit soulless. Staff are friendly, but of limited help if you need menu advice.
Babies and children welcome: high chairs. Booking advisable. Takeaway service. **Map 17 C4**.

★ Wong Kei

41-43 Wardour Street, W1D 6PY (7437 8408, www.wongkeilondon.com). Leicester Square or Piccadilly Circus tube. **Meals served** noon-11.30pm Mon-Sat; noon-10.30pm Sun. **Main courses** £4.40-£10. **Set meal** £9.50-£14.50 per person (minimum 2). **No credit cards.**
Wong Kei conforms to what is now an outmoded stereotype of a Chinatown restaurant: brusque service, budget prices, indifferent food. From the grimy carpets to the snappy service, first impressions do little to raise expectations and, despite empty tables, our waiter made us share with two French backpackers. The menu remains almost biblical in length, with dozens of stir-fries covering everything from pork to seafood. The rice can often be overcooked, but you do get free tea and huge portions for low prices. Best was a dish of stuffed bean curd, green pepper and aubergine 'with meat' in black bean sauce: it was succulent and well made, if variable in temperature from tepid to warm. Less impressive was a mound of rice topped with braised pork belly; the promised preserved vegetables took some detective work to discover. And hotpot rice was a low point, with a meagre (if tasty) sausage topping. In fact, both these dishes were inferior to what you'd get from many a high-street Chinese takeaway. In Wong Kei's favour, the bill (written in Chinese script) doesn't contain a hidden service charge, as can still happen in too many restaurants in Chinatown.
Babies and children admitted. Takeaway service. Vegetarian menu. **Map 17 B4**.

Manchurian Legends

Red Pocket

West
Bayswater

Gold Mine
102 Queensway, W2 3RR (7792 8331).
Bayswater or Queensway tube. **Meals served**
noon-11pm daily. **Main courses** £6-£35.
Set meal £15.50 per person (minimum 2).
Credit MC, V.
Gold Mine is so renowned for its roast meats –
which can be seen hanging in the open kitchen by
the front window – that diners from near and far
can be seen tucking in here, both local students and
visitors from Hong Kong. The dining room seems
to have been decorated on a tight budget and, as
with many Chinese cafés, red (symbolising good
fortune) is a popular colour, appearing on carpets
and chairs. Large gold-framed pictures of vintage
Chinese scenes add a cheery note. Unsurprisingly,
top marks go to the Cantonese roast meats,
especially the duck and char sui (barbecued pork).
Flavours are big, and dishes can be oily. Thick-cut
pieces of deep-fried squid arrived with a whopping
amount of garlic and chilli. Equally hearty was the
'house special bean curd', which turned out to be
pei pa tofu served with shiitake and baby pak choi
in a dark soy sauce. Staff tend to be chirpy and
attentive. If you're in the area and after no-frills
Cantonese food, this is a little gem – though its next-
door neighbour Magic Wok is better.
Available for hire. Babies and children
admitted. Booking advisable. Takeaway
service. **Map 7 C6.**

Magic Wok
100 Queensway, W2 3RR (7792 9767).
Bayswater or Queensway tube. **Meals served**
noon-11pm daily. **Main courses** £6.50-£18.
Set meal £14-£20 per person (minimum 2).
Credit AmEx, MC, V.
This bustling restaurant has been serving no-
nonsense Cantonese food since the late 1980s, and
attracts a large, loyal band of regulars (including
visitors from overseas). They definitely don't visit
for the basic dining room with its well-worn
carpets, scruffy red chairs and plain walls adorned
with paintings of bucolic Chinese scenes. The rear
ground-floor section is the brighter and quieter part
of the restaurant, and preferable to elsewhere. Our
waitress seemed to have got out of the wrong side
of bed, although Albert Chan, the manager, a
veteran of Queensway, always makes us smile.
Many diners order the same dishes every time they
visit, and nostalgia can pay dividends. Tasty pork
ribs soup with lotus root and groundnut set us up
nicely for a homely, satisfying dish of minced pork
with salted fish. The kitchen can turn the flavour
dial to delicate too; the silky fleshiness of steamed
sea bass matched well with ginger and spring
onion. A meaty dish of braised duck, locked into a
layer of deep-fried yam and vamped up by a sweet
and sour sauce, was slightly marred by pieces of
dry poultry. Fortune cookies at the end of meal are
a nod to a bygone age, and all part of Magic Wok's
enduring appeal.
Babies and children welcome: high chairs.
Booking advisable dinner. Separate room for
parties, seats 30. Takeaway service. Vegetarian
menu. **Map 7 C6.**

Royal China
13 Queensway, W2 4QJ (7221 2535,
www2.royalchinagroup.biz). Bayswater
or Queensway tube. **Meals served** noon-
11pm Mon-Thur; noon-11.30pm Fri, Sat;
11am-10pm Sun. **Dim sum served** noon-
4.45pm Mon-Sat; 11am-4.45pm Sun. **Main**
courses £9-£60. **Dim sum** £3.20-£5.
Set meal £30-£38 per person (minimum 2).
Credit AmEx, MC, V.
This stalwart of London's dim sum parlours is
always a pleasure to visit. Its perennial popularity
ensures a lively atmosphere, and its authentic,
perfectly prepared little dishes are head and
shoulders above most of Chinatown's lazy
offerings. The long dining room at this original
Queensway branch is lined in mirrors and black
lacquered walls, with depictions of curling waves
and geese soaring above. Some of the capital's best
little packages of Cantonese treats are served here.
Beef balls feature wonderfully light ground beef
enlivened with strong accents of ginger and water
chestnut. Delicious wun tun soup has light
dumplings floating in a rich broth with an
undertone of five-spice, adding a depth rarely
found in this classic soup. Peruse the special dim
sum menu for more innovative dishes: crab and
spinach steamed dumplings, and prawn and chive
packages in batter were both a delight. We could
happily eat solely from the dim sum list, but the
main menu offers fantastic Cantonese and regional
Chinese dishes. The shaolin monk vegetarian clay
pot contained an outstandingly fresh assortment
of Chinese vegetables: bamboo, lotus root, mini pak
choi and tofu, all on cellophane noodles.

waxy texture, and were kicked into life by a vinegar dip. Golden-brown deep-fried yam croquettes with seafood were light and tasty. Finish with flaky egg custard tarts – reassuring proof, if any were needed, that the cooking is not overshadowed by the view. *Babies and children welcome: high chairs; nappy-changing facilities. Booking advisable, essential Thur-Sun. Disabled: lift; toilet. Separate room for parties, seats 20.* **Map 7 B8**.

Shepherd's Bush

Tian Fu NEW
37-39 Bulwer Street, W12 8AR (8740 4546). Shepherd's Bush tube/rail. **Meals served** 11am-11pm daily. **Main courses** £7.80-£26.80. **Dim sum** £3.50-£11. **Set menu** £18.80 per person (minimum 2). **Credit** MC, V.
There's no shortage of budget chop suey joints in Shepherd's Bush, but to find a proper Chinese restaurant serving more than the usual takeaway food is a challenge. Hidden around a corner off Uxbridge Road, a short walk from Shepherd's Bush Market tube station, this unassuming Sichuanese venue is easy to miss. Crowds, mostly of mainland Chinese diners, fill its spacious interior in the evening, when a cosy atmosphere is produced by dark wooden furniture and the fragrance of sichuan peppercorns. The signature dish (which most diners choose) is the classic Sichuanese tongue-numbing mala hotpot buffet. There's also a lengthy à la carte menu, mainly of south-western Chinese dishes, with a small dim sum selection. Prices are reasonable, and portions generous and uncompromising on chilli heat. Our 'water-boiled' fish came in a pot of fiery broth, topped with a layer of sizzling hot chilli oil and dried chillies. Equally appetising but non-spicy dishes include Hunan-style red braised pork belly and stir-fried green beans. The availability of uncommon ingredients such as frogs' legs, sea snails and loofah make Tian Fu quite different to anything else in the area. Singular too is the odd combination of a stained-glass window depicting Paris, and Taylor Swift playing on the sound system.
Babies and children welcome: high chairs. Booking advisable. Takeaway service. **Map 20 C2**.
For branch see index.

South
Battersea

Red Pocket NEW
Hotel Verta, Bridges Wharf, SW11 3RP (7801 3535, www.redpocketrestaurant.com). Clapham Junction tube/rail. **Meals/dim sum served** noon-10.30pm daily. **Main courses** £17-£59. **Dim sum** £4-£13. **Set meal** £30 per person 3 courses (minimum 2); £48-£108 per person 4 courses (minimum 2) . **Credit** AmEx, MC, V.
Battersea's riverside Hotel Verta describes itself as a 'hidden gem'. That's quite a stretch for a sterile business hotel next to the London Heliport, but apt for its new contemporary Chinese restaurant. Located at least 15 minutes' walk through industrial estates from the nearest rail station, Red Pocket is not easily accessible. But executive chef Weng Kong Wong, who last worked at Hakkasan, tries hard to make it worth the special journey. The £30 tasting menu of three courses, a vegetable side dish and rice is good value, offering first-rate food with even one order plentiful enough for two. A basket

of xiao long bao set the tone, with seven plump dumplings encased in pastel-hued pastry. A main course of wok-fried beef fillet tumbled from a cage of deep-fried vermicelli, the exquisitely tender meat glistening with a red wine and black pepper sauce. Hand-pulled noodles with shimeji mushrooms also exhibited meticulous handiwork – right down to the painstaking removal of the root ends from every single beansprout. Despite the red, gold and black decor, the dining room struggles to shake off its hotel lobby location. Not a place to see and be seen, but rather to taste and savour.
Available for hire. Babies and children welcome: high chairs; nappy-changing facilities. Booking advisable. Disabled: toilet. Tables outdoors (4, patio). **Map 21 B3**.

Clapham

Mongolian Grill
29 North Street, SW4 0HJ (7498 4448, www.mongolian-grill.co.uk). Clapham Common tube or Wandsworth Road rail. **Dinner served** 5-10pm Mon-Fri. **Meals served** 4.30-10.30pm Sat; 3-10.30pm Sun. **Main courses** £3.50-£10. **Set meal** £13.50 all-you-can-eat. **Credit** MC, V.
For the uninitiated, this backstreet restaurant in Clapham's Old Town may set alarm bells ringing. First, there's the 'red light district' glow (caused by a host of Chinese lanterns), but more unnervingly, the kitchen specialises in hotpot (sometimes known as 'Chinese fondue', a dish with its roots in Mongolia) and Korean barbecue (where food is cooked at an on-table grill). There's an enormous help-yourself buffet of fish, meat and vegetables – all raw. However, food hygiene is scrupulously maintained, with the steel containers frequently replenished by fresh items, and individual tongs used. To cook your ingredients, we recommend choosing a half-and-half hotpot. One side of our pot contained a subtle broth infused with juniper berries and dried plums – ideal for cooking delicately flavoured ingredients (from prawns and squid to broccoli and spinach). On the other was the popular spicy stock, laced with dried chillies, sichuan peppers and chinese peppercorns the size of garden peas: perfect for the more robust raw chicken wings and slivers of pork belly. The cheery female manager is on hand to explain how to make the best DIY dipping sauce; the remaining staff work silently but efficiently. More Soho than south London, Mongolian Grill is certainly not boring.
Babies and children welcome: high chairs. Booking advisable Sat, Sun. **Map 22 A1**.

South East
London Bridge & Borough

Hutong NEW
Level 33, The Shard, 31 St Thomas Street, SE1 9RY (7478 0540, www.hutong.co.uk). London Bridge tube/rail. **Lunch served** noon-2.45pm, **dinner served** 6-10.45pm daily. **Main courses** £8-£48. **Dim sum** £5.50-£6. **Set meal** £55 per person (minimum 2). **Credit** AmEx, MC, V.
The original Hutong in Hong Kong is a glitzy Chinese restaurant with magnificent views, mainly patronised by expats and tourists. And this London branch, halfway up the Shard, is exactly the same. The same Sichuanese and northern Chinese menu, the same mix of plate glass and ersatz Old Beijing decor, the same hard chairs – even some staff are the

Babies and children welcome: high chairs; nappy-changing facilities. Booking advisable; bookings not accepted lunch Sat, Sun. Separate rooms for parties, seating 20-40. Takeaway service. Vegetarian menu. **Map 7 C7**.
For branches see index.

Kensington

Min Jiang
10th floor, Royal Garden Hotel, 2-24 Kensington High Street, W8 4PT (7361 1988, www.min jiang.co.uk). High Street Kensington tube. **Lunch/dim sum served** noon-3pm, **dinner served** 6-10.30pm daily. **Main courses** £10-£65. **Dim sum** £4.60-£6.80. **Set dinner** £60-£80 per person (minimum 4). **Credit** AmEx, MC, V.
We're very fond of Min Jiang, not least for the superlative daytime views of Kensington Gardens from the tenth floor of the Royal Garden Hotel. There are many notable Chinese restaurants in London, but none with such a picture-perfect vista. The glassy main room is a serene space in which to dine, but also warm and welcoming, helped along by the emollient nature of the staff. The restaurant does a roaring trade with its own version of beijing duck – a dish not to be missed by a first-time visitor. The menu also features Sichuanese classics such as double-cooked pork with celery, and spicy clay pot venison, as well as luxury ingredients like lobster and abalone. Although the main dim sum chef has departed, standards have not been greatly affected. Poached beijing dumplings filled with chicken, prawn, chives and dried shiitake had a marvellous

Dim sum

The Cantonese term 'dim sum' can be translated as 'touch the heart'. It is used to refer to the vast array of dumplings and other titbits that southern Chinese people like to eat with their tea for breakfast or at lunchtime. This eating ritual is simply known as 'yum cha', or 'drinking tea' in Hong Kong. Many of London's Chinese restaurants have a lunchtime dim sum menu, and at weekends you'll find them packed with Cantonese families. A dim sum feast is one of London's most extraordinary gastronomic bargains: how else can you lunch lavishly in one of the capital's premier restaurants for as little as £15 a head?

Restaurants used to cease serving dim sum at 4pm or 5pm, when the rice-based evening menus took over. These days, however, since dim sum became fashionable outside the Chinese community, several establishments serve it all day and into the night. Dim sum lunches at the weekend tend to be boisterous occasions, so they are great for children.

In a few places, dim sum is served in traditional Hong Kong-style, from circulating trollies. Some of the snacks are wheeled out from the kitchen after being cooked; others gently steam as they go or are finished on the trolley to order. The trolley system has the great advantage that you see exactly what's offered, but on a quiet lunchtime some of the food may be a little tired by the time it reaches you. Other places offer snacks à la carte, so everything will be freshly cooked.

Dim sum menus are roughly divided into steamed dumplings, deep-fried dumplings, sweet dishes and so on. Try to order a selection of different types of food, with plenty of light steamed dumplings to counterbalance the heavier deep-fried snacks. If you are eating with a large group, make sure you order multiples of everything, as most portions consist of about three items. Tea is the traditional accompaniment. Musty bo lay (pu'er in Mandarin), grassy Dragon Well (long jing) or fragrant Iron Buddha (tie guan yin) are alternatives to the jasmine blossom that is usually served by default to non-Chinese guests. Waiters should leave the teapots filled throughout the meal; leave the teapot lid tilted at an angle or upside down to signal that you want a top-up.

Char siu bao: steamed bun stuffed with barbecued pork in a sweet-savoury sauce.
Char siu puff pastry or **roast pork puff:** triangular puff-pastry snack, filled with barbecued pork, scattered with sesame seeds and oven-baked.
Cheung fun: sheets of steamed rice pasta wrapped around fresh prawns, barbecued pork, deep-fried dough sticks, or other fillings, with a sweet soy-based sauce.
Chiu chow fun gwor: soft steamed dumpling with a wheat-starch wrapper, filled with pork, vegetables and peanuts.
Chive dumpling: steamed prawn meat and Chinese chives in a translucent wrapper.
Har gau: steamed minced prawn dumpling with a translucent wheat-starch wrapper.
Nor mai gai or **steamed glutinous rice in lotus leaf:** lotus-leaf parcel enclosing moist sticky rice with chicken, mushrooms, salty duck-egg yolks and other bits and pieces, infused with the herby fragrance of the leaf.
Paper-wrapped prawns: tissue-thin rice paper enclosing prawn meat, sometimes scattered with sesame seeds, deep-fried.
Sago cream with yam: cool, sweet soup of coconut milk with sago pearls and taro.
Scallop dumpling: delicate steamed dumpling filled with scallop (sometimes prawn) and vegetables.
Shark's fin dumpling: small steamed dumpling with a wheaten wrapper pinched into a frilly cockscomb shape on top, stuffed with a mix of pork, prawn and slippery strands of shark's fin.
Siu loon bao or **xiao long bao:** Shanghai-style round dumpling with a whirled pattern on top and a minced pork and soup filling.
Siu mai: little dumpling with an open top, a wheat-flour wrapper and a minced pork filling. Traditionally topped with crab coral, although minced carrot and other substitutes are common.
Taro croquette or **yam croquette:** egg-shaped, deep-fried dumpling with a frizzy, melt-in-your-mouth outer layer of mashed taro, and a savoury minced pork filling.
Turnip paste: a heavy slab of creamy paste made from glutinous rice flour and white oriental radishes, studded with wind-dried pork, sausage and dried shrimps, and fried.

same, brought over to help clone the successful original. What's different is the spicing: three dishes we tried in London were much less fiery, though not meek. A 'red lantern' of soft-shell crabs came in a huge bowl of decorative deep-fried chillies, yet the crisply cooked crabs were only agreeably spicy. Dan dan noodles had the recognisable ma-la ('numbing, spicy-hot') combination of this Sichuanese dish, but was slightly overcooked and heavy on the peanut sauce. From northern China, pleasingly fatty de-boned lamb was very tender, having been marinated, braised and then deep-fried. Lunchtime visitors who want to avoid spice can stick to the more delicate flavours of dim sum (the xiao long bao – shanghaiese soup dumplings – were well made). Service was good, the prices high: but then this is the Shard, not Chinatown. A great place to impress a date.
Babies and children admitted. Booking essential. Dress: smart; no sportswear. Separate rooms for parties, seating 8 and 12. **Map 12 Q8.**

East
Docklands

Yi-Ban
London Regatta Centre, Dockside Road, E16 2QT (7473 6699, www.yi-ban.co.uk). Royal Albert DLR. **Meals served** noon-10.30pm Mon-Sat; 11am-10pm Sun. **Dim sum served** noon-5pm daily. **Main courses** £4-£30. **Dim sum** £2.20-£4. **Set meal** £22-£38 per person (minimum 2). **Credit** AmEx, MC, V.
Visiting Yi-Ban by public transport can be a disconcerting experience, involving a trip on the DLR to Royal Albert station, then a walk along a deserted road and across a large car park to the first floor of the grey concrete box that is the London Regatta Centre. Once inside, you're greeted by a spacious room lined with floor-to-ceiling windows offering striking views across the dock of planes taking off and landing at City Airport. White tablecloths, cream leather chairs and pale wood floors are offset by an ornamental red wall at the far end. There's an outdoor deck for good weather. The menu is extensive, with Vietnamese as well as Chinese dishes, a particularly good selection of seafood (including luxe ingredients such as lobster and abalone) and a dozen hotpots including sea cucumber and 'duck's web' (the foot). The dim sum here is well regarded – a beef and bamboo shoot dumpling was light and tasty – and the lengthy menu includes photos, which is useful for novices. But standards can dip: sliced whelks in a mild curry sauce were rubbery, and we were disappointed by the roast duck (from the carte), which was drenched in a sticky orange sauce. Staff are informed and helpful. Note the restaurant gets very busy at weekends, so it's wise to book.
Available for hire. Babies and children welcome: high chairs; nappy-changing facilities. Booking advisable. Disabled: toilet. Separate room for parties, seats 30. Takeaway service.

North East
Dalston

Shanghai Dalston
41 Kingsland High Street, E8 2JS (7254 2878, www.shanghaidalston.co.uk). Dalston Kingsland rail or bus 38, 67, 76, 149. **Meals/dim sum**

served noon-11pm daily. **Main courses** £5.50-£7.80. **Dim sum** £2.80-£4.50. **Set meal** £20 per person (minimum 2). **Credit** MC, V.

Of all London's Chinese restaurants, Shanghai Dalston comes closest to creating a vibe of ironic retro chic. Roast ducks and pork hanging in the window obscure views of the beautiful former pie and mash shop interior, with green tiles featuring slithering eels in the front dining room. Sadly, the nominally eastern Chinese menu has more in common with the grim second dining room in the windowless back of the restaurant; the food has little to distinguish it from Anglo-Chinese restaurants across the country. Starters of 'Shanghai dumplings in chilli oil', wun tun soup, and grilled dumplings were universally bland. A dish described as 'clay pot-cooked slow-braised pork with tofu knots' in fact contained deep-fried tofu, leaving the stew uniform in texture. The enticingly named 'Shanghai devil lamb' promised a bold marinade of spices and chilli, wok-fried and served with dried seaweed, but arrived as a pile of lamb slices with onions, all bearing a vaguely aniseed flavour but lacking both complexity and seaweed. In such a lively neighbourhood, and in such a promising setting, the kitchen here should take more risks to elevate its food above the Chinese-takeaway norm.

Babies and children welcome: high chairs; nappy-changing facilities. Booking advisable. Disabled: toilet. Separate rooms for parties, both seating 45. Takeaway service. **Map 25 B5**.

North
Islington

Yipin China
70-72 Liverpool Road, N1 0QD (7354 3388, www.yipinchina.co.uk). Angel tube. **Meals served** noon-10.30pm daily. **Main courses** £6.90-£14.90. **Credit** MC, V.

For fans of the spicy, earthy flavours of China's Hunan province, there's little not to like at Yipin. The overwhelmingly vast menu also offers dishes in the southern Cantonese style – sweet, subtle and more familiar in the West – but stick to the kitchen's specialities, which hail from Hunan and the neighbouring Sichuan province, and feature bold, fiery food. Highlights include pickled runner beans with minced pork (a wonderfully sour medley of vegetables and meat), mouth-watering Sichuan chicken (tiny morsels of on-the-bone fried chicken hidden in a mountain of dried chillies), and dry-wok bean curd, which consists of large pieces of tofu in a ginger and chilli-heavy sauce. Twice-cooked pork, a Sichuanese classic, is delicious here; the thin slices of belly pork are delectably fatty, salty and dry, rather than greasy. While the peasant-style dishes are a little at odds with the hefty central Islington house prices, the humble double-fronted red and white dining room matches the food well, looking as if a trattoria once operated here. It suggests that the focus is on food, not aesthetics.

Babies and children welcome: high chairs. Booking advisable. Separate room for parties, seats 20. Takeaway service. Vegetarian menu. **Map 5 N1**.

Hutong. See p73.

East European

It's a trend we've noticed elsewhere: communities new to London from overseas generally take a while to settle before opening restaurants. And so it is with migrants from eastern Europe. Although many people from that region have visited these shores in the past decade, often to stay and work, there hasn't yet been a corresponding growth in restaurants specialising in the cuisine of their homelands. It seems the vanguard that form these communities in London are more likely to cook at home than eat out – hence the growth in eastern European food stores across the city. That's not to say the restaurant scene has been moribund. Georgian establishments have seen a notable increase in their number in the past few years, attracting expats but also other Londoners who've discovered this curious cuisine – a hybrid where hearty dumplings might share a menu with Persian-style stews – and its accompanying flavour-packed wines. Other news is the renaissance of that well-loved Polish institution **Daquise**, which was bought by its staff and former owners from a company that was planning to close it. Along with the equally characterful **Gay Hussar** (Hungarian) and **Czechoslovak Restaurant**, Daquise was part of the first wave of eastern European restaurants in London, established soon after World War II to cater for exiles from Communism. So, you'll find old-fashioned character aplenty here, but also glitz and glamour, provided by eternally fashionable **Baltic** (Polish) and Russian oligarch-magnet **Mari Vanna**. And what about good Lithuanian, Romanian and Bulgarian restaurants? Watch this space.

Central

Knightsbridge

★ Mari Vanna
116 Knightsbridge, Wellington Court, SW1X 7PJ (7225 3122, www.marivanna.co.uk).
Knightsbridge tube. **Lunch served** noon-3.30pm, **tea served** 3.30-5pm daily. **Dinner served** 7-11.30pm Mon-Sat; 7-10.30pm Sun. **Main courses** £14-£24. **Set lunch** (noon-3pm Mon-Fri) £18 2 courses, £25 3 courses. **Credit** AmEx, MC, V. Russian
Judging by the guest list on Mari Vanna's UK website, the London outpost of this extraordinary Russian restaurant 'chain' is as much a destination as the branches in New York, LA and Washington, DC (St Petersburg and Moscow boast the Russian originals). A trip here is certainly memorable. It's impossible not to gasp at the mirrors and chandeliers; the shelves overflowing with dolls, porcelain, books and knick-knacks; and the tapestries, both hanging and adorning the tables. During our lunchtime meal, the place was chock-a-block with Russian-speaking diners. The booking procedure may seem Soviet-strict, but the welcome is warm, and service – by beautiful Russian staff –

polite and attentive. It's the food, however, that might hasten a second visit. You can dine like a peasant or a tsar, but the simplest, relatively affordable options are a delight. From the breads, including coriander-scented rye, via traditional thirst-quenchers such as kvass (like a rye-bread root beer) or birch juice, to pirozhki – don't miss the sea bass version – and lactic-fermented pickles, there wasn't a discordant note. Tender beef stroganoff had just the right degree of paprika warmth, and sweet cherry dumplings paired with a shot of cherry-infused vodka proved an ideal end to a memorable meal.
Available for hire. Babies and children welcome: high chairs. Booking advisable. **Map 8 F8**.

Soho

Gay Hussar
2 Greek Street, W1D 4NB (7437 0973, www.gayhussar.co.uk). Tottenham Court Road tube. **Lunch served** 12.15-2.30pm, **dinner served** 5.30-10.45pm Mon-Sat. **Main courses** £12.75-£17.75. **Set lunch** £20.50 2 courses, £24.50 3 courses. **Credit** AmEx, MC, V. Hungarian
Mercifully for its devotees, the modern 'GH Soho' sign outside the time-honoured red frontage doesn't signal a flashy rebranding. Inside, all is as it should

be at the Gay Hussar: dark wooden panelling bedecked with political portraits or Martin Rowson caricatures; nicotine-brown ceiling; polite, prompt Hungarian staff; and shelves of political biographies. Gladstone stared bleakly down at our wooden settle, having perhaps eaten one too many dumplings. Since the restaurant's 1953 inception, the powerbrokers of the political left have dined here. Despite the odd tourist party, they were still in evidence during our good-value lunch. More than a dozen traditional Hungarian dishes are offered for starters and mains. On a sweltering July afternoon we should have ordered the chilled wild cherry soup, or even the fish terrine with beetroot sauce and cucumber. Nevertheless, bean soup, a hearty, salty, wintery 'soup of the day', was lifted by slices of intensely smoky sausage. Intense flavours also characterised a main course of paprika-rich venison goulash, served with splayed out gherkin, tangy red cabbage and couscous-like tarhonya. A glass of Bull's Blood (just £4.50) made a satisfying match. For afters? The fruity, jelly-like mixed berry pudding provides needed refreshment; were he still active during the Gay Hussar's 60-year lifetime, it might even have cheered up Gladstone.
Babies and children welcome: high chairs. Booking advisable dinner. Separate rooms for parties, seating 12 and 24. **Map 17 C3**.

South Kensington

Daquise

20 Thurloe Street, SW7 2LT (7589 6117,
http://daquise.co.uk). South Kensington tube.
Meals served noon-11pm daily. **Main**
courses £15-£22. **Set lunch** (noon-4pm
Mon-Fri) £9 2 courses. **Credit** MC, V. Polish
In May 2013, regulars were distressed at news that
this much-loved grande dame of London Polish
restaurants (established 1947) was to close.
However, the staff and the restaurant's previous
owners have rallied round to save the venerable
institution. The premises were given a makeover in
2009 by the Polish Gessler restaurant dynasty,
producing a shabby-chic, light and airy look: walls
stripped back to uneven plaster, plain wooden
tables and fresh flowers. The new regime sees
robust, flavourful, no-nonsense traditional dishes
served with great charm by the maître d' Tadeusz
Dembiński and his friendly team. Classic cold
starters of meltingly tender herring with cream,
apple, onion and flax oil, or beetroot with subtly
warming horseradish, are ladled directly from
capacious earthenware bowls. All the Polish
favourites such as zurek, barszcz and pierogi can
be relied upon here. Mains are assembled directly
at the table from well-worn saucepans, borne by the
chefs who lovingly prepared the dishes. Succulent
chicken poached in light broth with tender
vegetables and silky own-made pasta is comfort-
food extraordinaire. Home from Polish home, but
with a witty and stylish twist.
Available for hire. Babies and children admitted.
Booking advisable. **Map 14 D10.**

West
Bayswater

Colchis

39 Chepstow Place, W2 4TS (7221 7620,
www.colchisrestaurant.co.uk). Bayswater or
Notting Hill Gate tube.
Bar **Open/meals served** 6pm-midnight Tue-
Fri; noon-midnight Sat, Sun. **Main courses**
£3.50-£8.
Restaurant **Dinner served** 6-11pm Tue-Fri.
Meals served noon-11pm Sat; noon-10pm
Sun. **Main courses** £6-£16.
Both **Credit** AmEx, MC, V. Georgian
Notting Hill suavity versus hearty peasant cooking:
who wins? Notting Hill, of course, and Colchis –
serene in its stuccoed townhouse – presents a smartly
turned-out form of Georgian cuisine, with the rough
edges smoothed out. An eager-to-help, proudly
Georgian waiter got the meal off to a dashing start,
and the varied list of traditional starters increased
the appeal. Khinkali dumplings being unavailable on
our trip, chicken bazhe filled the slot well: chunks of
straight-from-the-grill chicken breast in a walnut
sauce that – like Middle Eastern fesenjan – expertly
balanced creaminess and tang, a wedge of polenta-
like gomi providing ballast. Khachapuri cheese bread
comes in three varieties (including boat-shaped with
an egg yolk), but main courses are limited to four
types of mtsvadi (shashlik) skewers, presented on a
wooden board with pristine rocket and tomato salad;
salmon arrived nicely seared and succulent, with a
little pot of salsa. To 'Georgianise' the dish, we asked
for the optional pomegranate nectar, which added
fruity zestiness just as the big helping of fish started

to pall. Honey cake (two warm chocolate and nut
sandwich fingers) was a highlight, as was the glass
of intense, dry Georgian Mukuzani wine. With a
polished wooden floor, jazz soundtrack and
sensitively lit front bar, Colchis dovetails perfectly
into the neighbourhood.
Available for hire. Babies and children admitted.
Booking advisable weekends. Tables outdoors
(3, terrace). **Map 7 B6.**

Kensington

Mimino

197C Kensington High Street, W8 6BA (7937
1551, www.mimino.co.uk). Kensington High
Street tube. **Dinner served** 6-11pm Tue-Thur;
6pm-midnight Fri, Sat. **Main courses** £10-£16.
Credit MC, V. Georgian
With its entrance down a dingy staircase off Allen
Street, Mimino hasn't the most delightful location.
Still, there's a relaxed vibe once you're ensconced in
the dimly lit basement, helped by friendly staff,
regulars chatting in Georgian (while contemplating
dumplings the size of small teepees), and a room in
a farrago of styles. An impressive rough-hewn round
wooden table with ten high-backed chairs stands at
the centre, its impact heightened on our visit by the
theme from *The Godfather* playing. Musicians and
dancers sometimes perform, and a partially mirrored
ceiling, plastic foliage and brick, cream or pine-clad
walls add to the mix. Food is characterised more by
volume than delicacy. A mixed meze featured
various vegetarian dips, including pkhali (spinach
and leeks mashed with walnut and spices) and lobio
(red beans with walnuts) with freshly made
khachapuri cheese bread; flavours were rather
similar and lacking in zest. Main courses consist of
stews, dumplings or kebabs. Chanakhi resembled a
hearty bowlful of irish stew, with tender lamb and
chunks of potato bulked out by onion and an
immense tomato. The Georgian wine list is well

Mari Vanna

worth exploring. So, a convivial venue with honest
food rather than exhilarating cooking.
Available for hire. Babies and children welcome:
high chairs. Booking advisable weekends.
Takeaway service. **Map 7 A9.**

Shepherd's Bush

Tatra

24 Goldhawk Road, W12 8DH (8749 8193,
www.tatrarestaurant.co.uk). Goldhawk Road tube.
Dinner served 6-10pm Mon-Thur; 6-11pm Fri.
Meals served noon-11pm Sat; noon-10pm Sun.
Main courses £9.70-£15.90. **Credit** AmEx,
MC, V. Polish
With its candlelit interior – smart in a retro 1980s
way – and its marvellous flavoured vodkas, Tatra
has proven a popular bolt-hole for Polish expats and
west London locals. However, good service and
consistency in the kitchen are key for neighbourhood
restaurants, and recent reports have been critical of
both. Service on our last visit verged on the chaotic.
A lone waitress seemed rushed off her feet while an
éminence grise fussed around the bar, ignoring
diners. After an hour, the waitress admitted our
order was lost. Apparently, there was no manager
to deal with complaints; we'd better just start all over
again: a cursory apology and no offer even of a
compensatory drink. Quick-to-prepare starters
seemed the best option: yeasty, pleasantly puffy
blinis with smoked salmon, vibrant roasted beetroot,
mushroom caviar and a slightly over-pickled
herring. A dull side salad (no better than one from
a supermarket packet) was unreasonably small. No
complaints, though, about gently fried mushroom
and sauerkraut-stuffed pierogis, with just the right
combination of caramelised crunchiness and silky-
soft pasta-like dough. Eventually, a manager
showed up to apologise with a complimentary
dessert and delicious frozen pear vodka, but it was
too little, too late.

Available for hire. Babies and children welcome: high chairs. Booking advisable weekends. Disabled: toilet. **Map 20 B2**.

South
Waterloo

★ Baltic `HOT 50`
74 Blackfriars Road, SE1 8HA (7928 1111, www.balticrestaurant.co.uk). Southwark tube. **Lunch served** noon-3pm Mon-Fri; noon-4.30pm Sat, Sun. **Dinner served** 5.30-11.15pm Mon-Sat; 5.30-10pm Sun. **Main courses** £12.50-£19. **Set meal** (noon-3pm, 5.30-7pm Mon-Fri; noon-3pm, 10-11pm Sat, Sun) £16.50 2 courses, £19.50 3 courses. **Credit** AmEx, MC, V. Eastern European

While Jan Woroniecki's other London restaurants, Wódka and Chez Kristof, have come and gone, Baltic shines on. It seems pretty recession-proof, regularly heaving with a mixed crowd attracted by the understated glamour of the pared-down monochrome decor punctuated by a supersized chandelier dripping shards of golden amber. For an intimate date, tables can seem a little too close and noise levels can be distracting, but you'll struggle to find elsewhere such enjoyable buckwheat blinis topped with smoked salmon, tender herring or juicy mushroom caviar. Alternatively, try a more earthy kaszanka – a haggis-like black sausage on crunchy potato pancake with tart apple. Home-style pleasures abound, such as rabbit braised in a fragrant broth flavoured with sweet prune and smoky bacon, served with little knobbly spaetzle dumplings. A more refined, perfectly moist roast cod on a bed of nutty kasza risotto with mushrooms and spinach is typical of Woroniecki's modern take on Polish/central European classics. Wine is quite pricey, so allow yourself to be enticed by the extensive vodka list – all are carefully described. Start with a classy clear vodka like Zytnia (rye), then move on to one of Baltic's own tasty ginger or spicy orange varieties: heaven in a shot glass.
Available for hire. Babies and children welcome; high chairs. Booking advisable. Disabled: toilet. Separate room for parties, seats 30. Tables outdoors (4, terrace). **Map 11 N8**.

South East
Elephant & Castle

★ Mamuska!
1st floor, Elephant & Castle Shopping Centre, SE1 6TE (3602 1898, www.mamuska.net). Elephant & Castle tube/rail. **Meals served** 9am-midnight Mon-Wed, Sun; 7am-12.30am Thur-Sat. **Main courses** £6. **No credit cards**. Polish

A Polish 'milk' bar ('bar mleczny') seems ideally suited to the Elephant & Castle shopping centre. More transport caff than a haven of Polish home cooking, Mamuska! offers filling fare, fast and at bargain prices. Spacious, clean and family-friendly, it's unsurprisingly popular with an eclectic clientele. Sadly, the food isn't exactly homely. We weren't looking for frills, and happily accepted the dense dough of the pierogi, and the simple garnish of long-cooked bacon lardons, as 'filling a gap'. If the pork filling of the meat dumplings was super-minced, and tasted recooked – well, that's the way you economise and fill an empty stomach. Decent bottled beer

Colchis. See p77.

(Zywiec, Zubr and the like) accompanied the starters nicely. Mains might have been more welcome were we still ravenous; as it was, kielbasa and goulash continued to fill without exciting. Potato dishes (mash, salad and pancakes) seemed stolid, and the 'dish of the day', a 'tenderised pork' escalope, proved so dry and chewy it defeated our best efforts. A mushroom sauce had little fungi flavour, and we wondered if a packet mix had come into play; chocolate cheesecake caused similar musings. Still, there's no arguing with the friendliness, humour, cleanliness and wallet-friendly pricing.
Babies and children welcome: high chairs; nappy-changing facilities. Booking advisable. Disabled toilet (shopping centre). Takeaway service.

North
Highbury

Tbilisi
91 Holloway Road, N7 8LT (7607 2536). Highbury & Islington tube/rail. **Dinner served** 6-11pm daily. **Main courses** £8-£11. **Credit** AmEx, MC, V. Georgian

Tbilisi is one of London's oldest Georgian restaurants and, to our minds, one of the best. Behind a nondescript frontage, the Holloway Road howling outside, it's a relaxing spot with mustard or dark red walls, wooden flooring and comfortable leather chairs. Knick-knacks are minimal: the odd tourist poster and a stylish display of Georgian wines (try the concentrated red Napareuli). Starters consist of three soups and a choice of meze dips. The quiet, congenial waiter should perhaps have clarified that each 'combination' of a bread and two dips was meant for two diners (we ordered two, which would have made an ample entire meal), but each dish was a delight: lovely doughy flatbread filled with feta-like cheese (khachapuri) or mashed beans (lobiani); a spicy liver stew with pomegranate seeds; russian salad sprinkled with fresh dill; ratatouille-like ajabsabdali; and ispanakhi, a light spinach and walnut blend. Main-course stews of chashushuli (tender beef in a tomato-based sauce)

and harcho (chicken with a ground walnut sauce, rather like Persian fesenjan, served with gomi, a polenta-like rice and cornmeal mix) were also appealing. Finish, if you're able, with tangy baked apple stuffed with ground walnuts and raisins, and waddle off, contented, into the night.
Available for hire. Babies and children welcome: high chairs. Booking advisable Fri, Sat. Separate room for parties, seats 40. Takeaway service.

Islington

Little Georgia
14 Barnsbury Road, N1 0HB (7278 6100, www.littlegeorgia.co.uk). Angel tube. **Dinner served** 7-11pm Tue-Fri. **Meals served** noon-11pm Sat, Sun. **Main courses** £8-£12. **Credit** MC, V. Georgian

While lacking the intimacy of the Hackney original, Islington's Little Georgia still stimulates interest in the under-documented culture of Georgia, with old telephones, traditional drinking horns and graphics-heavy political posters bringing originality to the jade-green and cream interior. Our likeable waiter – a Georgian version of the Cure's Robert Smith – lent additional flair. The menu is identical in both restaurants (owner Tiko Tuskadze cooks for both branches in this venue's kitchen). It's an ode to the country's comforting cuisine, which has influences from Europe and Asia. Cold starters include russian salad, a filling mix of potato, carrots, spring onion, peas, egg, dill and mayonnaise. Baked-to-order khachapuri (a moreish cheese-filled bread that's a national staple) is a don't-miss from the hot starters. In fact, the most intriguing dishes are starters, so a selection of these is ideal if you're keen to try new flavours. Homely mains – including chashushuli, a highly seasoned beef stew; a bean dish called kotnis lobio; and pan-fried poussin – are good too, especially on a cold winter's night. Unlike the BYO Hackney branch, this place is licensed, with an extensive wine list. Georgian wine is very good, but there are also Russian lagers such as Baltika.
Babies and children welcome: high chairs. Takeaway service; delivery service.
For branch see index.

Menu

Dishes followed by (Cz) indicate a Czech dish; (G) Georgian; (H) Hungarian; (P) Polish; (R) Russian. Others have no particular affiliation.

Bigos (P): classic hunter's stew made with sauerkraut, various meats and sausage, mushrooms and juniper.

Borscht: beetroot soup. There are many varieties: Ukrainian borscht is thick with vegetables; the Polish version (barszcz) is clear. There are also white and green types. Often garnished with sour cream, boiled egg or mini dumplings.

Caviar: fish roe. Most highly prized is that of the sturgeon (beluga, oscietra and sevruga, in descending order of expense), though keta or salmon caviar is underrated.

Chlodnik (P): cold beetroot soup, bright pink in colour, served with sour cream.

Galabki, golabki or **golubtsy:** cabbage parcels, usually stuffed with rice or kasha (qv) and sometimes meat.

Golonka (P): pork knuckle, often cooked in beer.

Goulash or **gulasz (H):** rich beef soup.

Kasha or **kasza:** buckwheat, delicious roasted: fluffy, with a nutty flavour.

Kaszanka (P): type of blood sausage that's made with buckwheat.

Khachapuri (G): flatbread; sometimes called Georgian pizza.

Kielbasa (P): sausage. Poland has dozens of widely differing styles.

Knedliky (Cz): bread dumplings.

Kolduny (P): small meat-filled dumplings (scaled-down pierogi, qv) often served in beetroot soup.

Koulebiaka, kulebiak or **coulebiac (R):** type of pie made with layered salmon or sturgeon, with eggs, dill, rice and mushrooms.

Krupnik (P): barley soup, and the name of a honey vodka (because of the golden colour of barley).

Latke: grated potato pancakes, fried.

Makowiec or **makietki (P):** poppy seed cake.

Mizeria (P): cucumber salad; very thinly sliced and dressed with sour cream.

Nalesniki (P): cream cheese pancakes.

Paczki (P): doughnuts, often filled with plum jam.

Pierogi (P): ravioli-style dumplings. Typical fillings are sauerkraut and mushroom, curd cheese or fruit (cherries, apples).

Pirogi (large) or **pirozhki** (small) **(R):** filled pies made with yeasty dough.

Placki (P): potato pancakes.

Shashlik: Caucasian spit-roasted meat.

Uszka or **ushka:** small ear-shaped dumplings served in soup.

Zakuski (R) or **zakaski (P):** starters, traditionally covering a whole table. The many dishes can include pickles, marinated vegetables and fish, herring, smoked eel, aspic, mushrooms, radishes with butter, salads and caviar.

Zrazy (P): beef rolls stuffed with bacon, pickled cucumber and mustard.

Zurek (P): sour rye soup.

North West
St John's Wood

Tamada

122 Boundary Road, NW8 0RH (7372 2882, www.tamada.co.uk). St John's Wood tube. **Lunch served** 1-4pm Sat, Sun. **Dinner served** 6-11pm Tue-Sun. **Main courses** £9-£17. **Credit** AmEx, MC, V. Georgian

Sit back on a beige banquette, sip a glass of rich dry saperavi red and contemplate the seemly surroundings at Tamada. Plate-glass windows look on to quiet, select Boundary Road, and upholstered chairs are tucked into plain wooden tables. True, the pastel-hued walls have large photos of Georgia to bring colour, and some appallingly fine Georgian crooners display their vibratos on the soundtrack, but tourist knick-knacks are kept in check. There's a small basement for overspill. A kind young waiter provides the Wi-Fi code without being asked – not that you'd need electronic diversions once the food arrives. Starters are divided into hot and cold lists. The mixed meze looks an enticing choice for two; alternatively, explore the wilder reaches with piping-hot kuchmachi: tender cubes of pork heart, liver and lung in a rich, mildly spicy gravy spiked with tangy pomegranate seeds. Next, plates of dumplings of impressive dimension are worth considering, though lobio is equally hearty: a red bean vegetarian stew the consistency of porridge, boosted by coriander, and served with pickled green tomatoes and gherkins. The famed khachapuri flatbread arrived straight from the oven, oozing mildly flavoured cheese (pricey at £7 for a naan-sized portion). A fruity, wobbly Georgian pudding, a zesty opaque jelly covered in ground walnuts, made a mercifully light conclusion to a highly satisfying meal.
Available for hire. Babies and children welcome: high chair. Booking advisable Fri, Sat. Separate room for parties, seats 28-35. Tables outdoors (4, pavement). Takeaway service. **Map 1 C1.**

West Hampstead

★ Czechoslovak Restaurant `HOT 50`

74 West End Lane, NW6 2LX (7372 1193, www.czechoslovak-restaurant.co.uk). West Hampstead tube. **Dinner served** 5-10pm Tue-Fri. **Meals served** noon-10pm Sat, Sun. **Main courses** £4-£12. **Credit** MC, V. Czech

Does the Czech Club realise its retro appeal? Frank Sinatra on a loop in its fabulous dining room – like a 1950s guesthouse, complete with chandelier, Axminster carpet and portrait of a shiny new Elizabeth II over the mantelpiece – and a wartime RAF advert on its menu might suggest so. But retro-hungry trendsters don't figure strongly among the clientele. Instead, you'll find plenty of eastern European accents, along with locals chewing a sausage and sipping Pilsner Urquells in the almost equally antediluvian bar or, in summer, the domestic-style back garden. Food is inexpensive and geared towards brawny workers taking on weight for the bitter eastern winters – schnitzels, dumplings and roasts, smothered in thick sauces. Cream, cheese and pork dominate, sometimes all together, as in a main course of tender wild boar roast with creamy, cheesy sauce and dumplings (actually doughy slices of white bread), which came with cranberry sauce balanced on a lemon slice, and, bizarrely, a segment of roast grapefruit. This immensity was a 'small' portion; a defibrillator should be on hand for anyone ordering 'large'. Tangy cabbage and sour cream soup began the meal; a thick pancake encasing well-stewed strawberries surrounded by a welter of whipped cream brought it to a solid conclusion. Service was polite yet geologically slow. The food? Filling. The experience? Unmissable.
Available for hire. Babies and children welcome: high chairs; nappy-changing facilities. Booking advisable weekends. Disabled: toilet. Tables outdoors (4, garden). Vegetarian menu. **Map 28 A3.**

Little Georgia. See p79.

Fish

Relative to seafood hotspots such as Madrid or Paris, London has easy access to the sea, and yet there are comparatively few restaurants here specialising in marine life. You'll usually have no trouble finding a chippie, of course – the best of which are listed in Fish & Chips, starting on p292 – but even though London's 1,000-year-old fish market, Billingsgate, has an important place in our city's history, its produce is given star billing at a surprisingly small number of establishments. Quality, however, can surpass the quantity. Among these disparate dining venues are some of the capital's most distinctive establishments: from celeb magnets such as **J Sheekey** and **Scott's** to that cherished cubby-hole of old London, **Sweetings**. Innovation as well as tradition can be found in this chapter. Although **Bentley's**, one of our favourite restaurants, will celebrate its centenary in 2016, under the guidance of top chef Richard Corrigan, its menu is anything but staid. New entry **Dock Seafood Restaurant** is right at the cutting edge of contemporary cuisine; and another recent opening, **Fish & Chip Shop**, gives a fashionably retro spin to the classic pairing. Special mention, though, goes to **Bonnie Gull**, whose fresh seaside flavours have already placed it in the top flight of London's purveyors of piscine treats.

Over-fishing is a perennial problem, so if you want to do your bit and order only species that are certified as sustainable, the Marine Stewardship Council's website, www.msc.org, is a good place to start.

Central
Belgravia

Olivomare
10 Lower Belgrave Street, SW1W 0LJ (7730 9022, http://olivorestaurants.com). Victoria tube/rail. **Lunch served** noon-2.30pm Mon-Fri; noon-3pm Sat, Sun. **Dinner served** 7-11pm Mon-Sat; 7-10.30pm Sun. **Main courses** £15-£22. **Credit** AmEx, MC, V.
It's a bold interior designer who decorates a Sardinian seafood restaurant in stark white with nary a drop of Mediterranean blue, but then Olivomare is a bold venture, serving modern fish dishes that are adventurous in their presentation but old-school in quality of produce and flavours – a winning combination. Sadly, the space itself, and the service, are less successful: it's hot and noisy, tables are far too close to one other, and initial unfriendly service created a sour note that could only be sweetened with good food. Luckily, it was. A grilled squid starter seemed pricey at £12, but was deliciously sweet, perfectly charred, and big enough for two to share. Spaghetti with half a lobster was equally well executed, the pasta perfectly al dente and continuing to soak up the rich tomato, garlic and lobster juices on the plate. Handmade lorighittas pasta with vongole and grey mullet roe missed the mark, though – the roe added an unwelcome breadcrumb texture to the pasta, and an overpowering flavour that killed the delicacy of the shellfish (a meagre portion). At the kinds of prices Olivomare charges to its clearly well-heeled clientele, a handful more clams would have gone a long way in tempting us to return.
Babies and children admitted. Booking advisable. Disabled: toilet. Tables outdoors (4, terrace).
Map 15 H10.
For branch (Olivetto) see index.

City

Sweetings [HOT 50]
39 Queen Victoria Street, EC4N 4SF (7248 3062, www.sweetingsrestaurant.com). Mansion House tube. **Lunch served** 11.30am-3pm Mon-Fri. **Main courses** £15-£33. **Credit** AmEx, MC, V.
Things don't change much at this enduring City classic, and that's the way everyone likes it. Rumour has it you're now allowed to use mobile phones, but the bill is still handwritten on a form that includes 'cigars' as the last category, the walls remain covered with photos of old sports teams, and many of the staff have been here for years. They serve regulars from behind counters fronted by stools, proffering sliced bread and butter and lemon wedges, filling glasses with the sauvignon blancs and chardonnays (mainly Burgundian) and Chablis that dominate the wine list. The main menu shows similar conservatism, with lobster and crab bisques prefacing a choice of fish and seafood dishes that read and taste like upmarket versions of a pub-side stall – smoked fish, whitebait, smoked trout and so forth. Top-quality fish are then served fried, grilled or poached to order, with a short side vegetable list (topped by peas). The handful of slightly more elaborate dishes includes a fish pie that bears witness to its well-practised makers in every light, succulent forkful. You can also get good crab and smoked fish rolls, fancier specials and old-school puddings. The relaxed, shirtsleeved City crowd is welcoming of incomers, as is the very able maître d'.
Available for hire (evening only). Babies and children admitted. Bookings not accepted. Takeaway service. **Map 11 P6.**

Fitzrovia

★ Bonnie Gull
21A Foley Street, W1W 6DS (7436 0921, www.bonniegull.com). Goodge Street, Oxford Circus or Tottenham Court Road tube.

Sweetings. See p81.

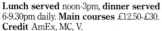

FISH

Lunch served noon-3pm, **dinner served** 6-9.30pm daily. **Main courses** £12.50-£30. **Credit** AmEx, MC, V.

After starting as a pop-up in Hackney in 2011, Bonnie Gull landed in Fitzrovia in 2012. The premises do a good job of evoking a seaside shack, with simple tables and chairs, a lot of blue and white (notably the jaunty awning), and ropework on the wall. Staff are engaged and welcoming, and the menu is something special. It changes daily, but super-fresh crab, simply served on a wooden platter, with the brown meat mixed with mayo in the shell and the white meat ready to be cracked out, is often featured and always worth ordering. Another menu staple is fish and chips, featuring haddock, chips cooked in beef dripping, mushy peas and the house ketchup. More complex dishes are beautifully presented, and equally good. Cornish hake with courgette purée, beer-battered courgette flower and courgette ribbons was an assured plateful, full of contrasting tastes, textures and colours – we savoured every mouthful. Puddings are a treat too: lemon curd tart with raspberry sorbet was zingy and indulgent, with delicate pastry. There are a couple of meat and vegetarian dishes, but you'd be mad to miss out on the carefully sourced British fish and seafood. Prices are very fair for central London. There's a short wine list, biased towards white, but with a few reds, included a couple of chilled options. In short – we like the cut of their jib.
Available for hire. Babies and children welcome: high chairs. Booking advisable. Tables outdoors (10, pavement). **Map 9 J5.**

Leicester Square

★ J Sheekey [HOT 50]
28-32 St Martin's Court, WC2N 4AL (7240 2565, www.j-sheekey.co.uk). Leicester Square tube.
Lunch served noon-3pm Mon-Sat; noon-3.30pm Sun. **Dinner served** 5.30pm-midnight Mon-Sat; 6-11pm Sun. **Main courses** £13.50-£39.50. **Set lunch** (Sat, Sun) £26.50 3 courses. **Cover** £2. **Credit** AmEx, MC, V.

After well over a century of service, Sheekey's status as a West End institution is assured. With its monochrome photos of stars of stage and screen, wooden panelling and cream crackle walls, and array of silver dishes atop thick white tablecloths, it oozes old-fashioned glamour. The separate booths and secluded tables cry out for romantic trysts – even a simple lunch has the thrill of a secret assignation. The white-aproned, black-waistcoated staff are charm incarnate, if alarmingly numerous – half a dozen greeted us between door and table. The menu, an ode to the bounty of the sea, runs from super-fresh oysters and shellfish via old-fashioned snacks (herring roe on toast) to upmarket classics (dover sole, lobster thermidor). The fish pie – a rich, comforting treat – is deservedly acclaimed, but we feel the shrimp and scallop burger merits similar status. Densely textured and full-flavoured, it came in a lightly toasted sesame seed bun with all the trimmings, including a little silver jug of spicy mayonnaise. Puds include eton mess, seasonal sorbets and ice-creams (elderflower and gooseberry ripple, on our visit). Amalfi lemon semifreddo with blackcurrants was a winner, each sugar-coated fruit a bomblet of zingy intensity. You can feast on crustacea (and some dishes from Sheekey's main menu) at the Oyster Bar next door – it's also easier to book.
Babies and children welcome: colouring books; high chairs. Booking essential. Disabled: toilet. Vegan dishes. Vegetarian menu. **Map 18 D5.**

Mayfair

Scott's
20 Mount Street, W1K 2HE (7495 7309, www.scotts-restaurant.com). Bond Street or Green Park tube. **Meals served** noon-10.30pm Mon-Sat; noon-10pm Sun. **Main courses** £8.75-£48. **Credit** AmEx, MC, V.

Now inevitably linked with Charles Saatchi and Nigella Lawson, Scott's had for the previous 162 years been best known for its fish. And with good reason: the seafood here is first class. The centrepiece

of the restaurant is a grand oyster bar where Mayfair types sip flutes of Gaston Chiquet and feast on fines de claires by the dozen. In the club-like seating area, diners get stuck in to Cornish sardines laced with parsley, sautéed monkfish cheeks with bordelaise sauce, and scampi provençale. We rhapsodised over the bass ceviche, a cheeky number bolstered by chunks of avocado, pepped up with a decent dose of jalapeño. We were also impressed with a tender halibut fillet and a meaty seared sea bass, swirled with lemon and herb butter and served with a heart-stopping mash. The only slight disappointment was a side salad made with lacklustre tomatoes, but any doubts were assuaged by the magnificent desserts (don't miss the bakewell pudding). Prices are steep bordering on vertical, but for an occasional treat and a touch of sleb-spotting, Scott's is worth the expense.
Babies and children welcome: high chairs. Booking essential dinner. Disabled: toilet. Separate room for parties, seats 40. Tables outdoors (7, pavement). Vegetarian menu. **Map 9 G7.**

Piccadilly

★ Bentley's Oyster Bar & Grill [HOT 50]
11-15 Swallow Street, W1B 4DG (7734 4756, www.bentleys.org). Piccadilly Circus tube.
Oyster Bar **Meals served** noon-midnight Mon-Sat; noon-10.30pm Sun. **Main courses** £8.50-£50.
Restaurant **Lunch served** noon-2.45pm Mon-Fri. **Dinner served** 5.30-10.45pm Mon-Sat. **Main courses** £19-£38. **Set dinner** (5.30-6.45pm Mon-Fri) £26 2 courses, £29 3 courses. **Cover** £2.
Both **Credit** AmEx, MC, V.

It's hard to believe that nine years have passed since Richard Corrigan first overhauled this grande dame of the capital's restaurant scene (established 1916). The interior remains as polished as ever, with art deco windows, the original marble oyster bar and wood panelling. Weeknights in the more formal first-floor Grill restaurant have a restrained business-dinner vibe, but the downstairs oyster bar is pleasingly laid-back. Theatrics at the gleaming marble counter (part staff speedily shucking, part competitive knocking 'em back) provide entertaining distraction as you decide between menu classics and imaginative daily specials. Our oysters (Dorset rock, Mersea natives) were exquisitely fresh, while mains of perfectly grilled langoustines, and scallops served with broad beans, crispy pork, parma ham, toasted cashew nuts and blood orange were faultless in flavour and presentation. Despite its proximity to touristy Piccadilly, Bentley's retains a distinctly London buzz. We sat among gregarious City boys, Notting Hill couples on third dates and Regent Street shoppers – the bar's tightly packed tables mean eavesdropping is inevitable. Even comically haphazard service – after the third omission, our smiling waiter took to periodically appearing at our table to check if he'd forgotten anything – failed to dampen our experience.
Available for hire. Babies and children welcome. Disabled: toilet. Dress: smart casual; no shorts. Separate rooms for parties, seating 14 and 60. Tables outdoors (10, terrace). **Map 17 A5.**

Soho

Wright Brothers Soho
13 Kingly Street, Kingly Court, W1B 5PW (7434 3611, www.thewrightbrothers.co.uk). Oxford Circus or Piccadilly Circus tube. **Meals served**

noon-10.45pm Mon-Sat; noon-5pm Sun. **Main courses** £11-£32. **Credit** AmEx, MC, V.
Wright Brothers' second branch is spread over three levels, including an enclosed shared courtyard at the rear. It attempts a similar aesthetic to the Borough Market original, with stripped floorboards, plain wooden tables, white tiling and exposed-filament light bulbs. Yet despite the venue's evident popularity, it doesn't convince. Maybe it's the larger space or the too-small tables or the West End mix of tourists and office workers, but this outlet lacks the genuine bonhomie and vivacity of the original. The most atmospheric seats are at the basement bar, where you can watch the chefs at work. Oysters are still the speciality, with top-quality bivalves coming from Wright Brothers' own beds on Cornwall's Helford River, and elsewhere depending on the season. Eat them unadorned or dressed (with ginger, chilli and soy, or caviar, or crème fraîche); alternatively, mix them with your choice of shellfish. The menu otherwise majors in crowd-pleasers – deep-fried whitebait or fish soup to start, moules marinière or salmon and smoked haddock fish pie for mains – that are decently turned out, but nothing special. Afters include the likes of mulled wine pear tart, chocolate mousse and British cheeses. The black-garbed staff are young and willing, if sometimes inexperienced.
Available for hire. Babies and children welcome; high chairs; nappy-changing facilities. Booking advisable. Disabled: toilet. Tables outdoors (9, courtyard). **Map 17 A4.**
For branches see index.

South West
Chelsea

Geales
1 Cale Street, SW3 3QT (7965 0555, www.geales.com). Sloane Square or South Kensington tube. **Lunch served** noon-2.30pm Tue-Fri. **Dinner served** 6-10.30pm Mon-Fri. **Meals served** noon-10.30pm Sat; noon-9.30pm Sun. **Main courses** £10.95-£22.50. **Set meal** (Tue-Fri) £9.95 2 courses. **Credit** AmEx, MC, V.
In business in Notting Hill since 1939, Geales opened this second branch, in Chelsea Green, only a few years ago. The menu is comfortingly old-fashioned – a list of dishes from the 1970s is displayed on the wall and, apart from the current absence of Bajan flying fish, little seems to have changed. Prawn cocktail and sticky toffee pudding have timeless appeal (especially in Chelsea, it seems). Atlantic prawns, served shell-on with aïoli, had a proper snap to them, but a dozen maldon rock oysters weren't the best specimens we've had. Mains include Scottish mussels, a lobster and shellfish platter to share, fish pie, and lobster tagliatelle – the last featured a rather cloying tomatoey sauce and lobster chunks that, although chunky, didn't taste of much. Most people are here for the posh fish and chips, and rightly so: a large hunk of cod, falling into fat white flakes, came encased in feather-light crispy batter. Chips cost extra, but were fine examples: firm, fluffy and golden. Looks aren't up to much: white tablecloths and black leather chairs in a nondescript room. To drink, there's a shortish wine list and a trio of Meantime bottled beers, but this is SW3, so surely it's got to be champers – top-quality bubbles from Ridgeview in Sussex, in fact.

Available for hire. Babies and children welcome: high chairs; nappy-changing facilities. Booking advisable. Disabled: toilet. Separate room for parties, seats 40. Tables outdoors (2, pavement). **Map 14 E11.**
For branch see index.

South East
London Bridge & Borough

Applebee's Café
5 Stoney Street, SE1 9AA (7407 5777, www.applebeesfish.com). London Bridge tube/rail. **Meals served** noon-9.45pm Mon-Thur. **Lunch served** 11.30am-4pm, **dinner served** 6-10pm Fri, Sat. **Main courses** £14.50-£23. **Set meal** (noon-6.30pm Mon-Thur) £16.95 2 courses, £19.95 3 courses. **Credit** MC, V.
This Borough Market stalwart, with a wet-fish counter at the front and a long, narrow dining space behind, is a lively and convivial spot for some reliable fishy fare. On a Thursday night, the place was humming with regulars, tourists, couples, families, young and old – all squeezed in, sitting at the tightly packed tables or on high stools along the bar watching the cooks at work. Plain wooden furniture and brick walls (bare or painted white) provide an unassuming backdrop. Staff are no-nonsense yet friendly. Main-course prices are quite high (starting at £14.50 for battered pollock and chips), but portions are generous and the fishmonger side of the business means you're guaranteed spanking-fresh ingredients. Hake with saffron potatoes, and sea bass with crispy leeks, were textbook examples of succulent, full-flavoured, deftly cooked fish. A starter of piri piri prawns had a proper chilli kick, and courgette fritti were light, crisp and obviously straight from the fryer. Fish soup, lobster risotto, salmon with

oriental vegetables: there's plenty of variety, but nothing for non-pescetarians. A bottle of Chilean riesling made a fine accompaniment. Only a dull mixed salad disappointed – apart, that is, from the toilet facilities, which are inadequate, rundown and really need sorting out.
Available for hire. Babies and children admitted. Disabled: toilet. Tables outdoors (4, pavement). Takeaway service. **Map 11 P8.**

East
Docklands

Dock Seafood Restaurant
2 Mastmaker Road, E14 9AW (7515 4334, www.thedockseafoodrestaurant.com). South Quay DLR. **Meals served** noon-10.30pm Mon-Sat. **Main courses** £10-£24. **Set lunch** (noon-3pm) £10 1 course, £15 2 courses. **Credit** AmEx, MC, V.
Martyn Meid may be reticent, his name not blazoned on menus or websites, but his modernist Nordic influenced-cooking is anything but. This little restaurant is Scandi-cool in white, glass and steel, carefully lit in the evening via arty light fittings and flickering candles, and looking out over the neon-lit South Quays development. Downstairs is a tiny takeaway serving the fish and chips that may yet prove a mainstay. The main menu has just occasional mentions of foams, powders and textures; on our visit, the waitress felt bound to warn us about the more 'deconstructed' dishes. Own-cured gravadlax came with squid ink aïoli, mint jelly, and so on, and was a great composition. Fish and chips – we tried cod and rock – proved gratifyingly traditional, and good as can be. Rather different treatments were at play with home-salted cod – its tomato powders and pastes provided a plateful of umami – and the simply named but

FISH

Bonnie Gull. See p81.

startlingly executed lemon sole with truffled celeriac. The most pungent of purées proved no match for a soft, almost-rotten fleshed fish hovering between the textures and tastes of Scandinavian specialities lutefisk and surströmming, a shock to the uninitiated and unforewarned. We needed our wines (a great selection, with umpteen by the glass) to wash away a truffle powder that tasted merely bitter. White chocolate powder (in deconstructed cheesecake) proved rather more palatable. There's currently an uneasy tension here between the traditional and the experimental; if you're after a straightforward experience, it's best to enquire very carefully before ordering.

Available for hire. Babies and children welcome: children's menu. Booking advisable Thur, Fri. Disabled: toilet. Tables outdoors (2, pavement). Takeaway service. **Map 24 B3**.

North East
South Woodford

Ark Fish Restaurant
142 Hermon Hill, E18 1QH (8989 5345, www.arkfishrestaurant.com). South Woodford tube. **Lunch served** noon-2.15pm Tue-Sat. **Dinner served** 5.30-9.45pm Tue-Thur; 5.30-10.15pm Fri, Sat. **Meals served** noon-8.45pm Sun. **Main courses** £12.25-£21.70. **Set lunch** (Tue-Fri) £16.95 2 courses, £19.25 3 courses. **Credit** MC, V.

Running the gamut from jellied eels to dover sole, the menu of the Ark, out in prosperous and pleasant South Woodford, sums up the East End diaspora towards Essex. It's hugely popular locally, particularly appreciated by a mature clientele, but has something for everyone (including tomato soup and fillet steak for fish-phobes). From welcome appetisers such as whelks, winkles and cockles through classic starters such as dressed crab and prawn cocktail, the seafood is sparklingly fresh. Look for swanky treats such as turbot on the specials board. Whatever the fish, the cooking is kept simple. Stonking portions of faves (cod, haddock) are juicily sealed in a coat of crisp batter,

grilled or poached, but for the more adventurous there's a hugely generous portion of plump seared scallops in garlic butter on perky mixed salad leaves. Chips are absolutely not McCain's, but fat, hand-cut and just a little leathery. Only the trifle, more Epping than Black Forest in its ordinariness, was a slight disappointment: great custard but dry sponge and few cherries. Bookings aren't taken for the conservatory-like dining room, though there's space to wait at the bar. Very friendly, alert staff manage everything exceptionally well; note that no service charge is added to the bill.

Babies and children welcome: children's menu; high chairs. Bookings not accepted.

North
Islington

Fish & Chip Shop NEW
189 Upper Street, N1 1RQ (3227 0979, www.the fishandchipshop.uk.com). Highbury & Islington tube/rail. **Meals served** noon-11pm Mon-Sat; noon-10pm Sun. **Main courses** £7-£32.50. **Set dinner** (5-6.30pm, 10-11pm Mon-Fri) £12 2 courses, £15 3 courses. **Credit** AmEx, MC, V.

There are restaurants you go to for the food, and restaurants you go to for a good time. Fish & Chip Shop is one of the latter. It's the solo venture of Des McDonald, once head chef at the Ivy before rising through the ranks to become CEO of Caprice Holdings (J Sheekey, Scott's, and so on). Suffice to say, he knows a thing or two about fish. So it's a little surprising the food here didn't make a bigger splash. It started well. Plump and sweet, the prawns in the 'cocktail' lounged on a pile of posh greens (pea shoots and the like) with a light, tangy marie rose sauce. Dessert shone too, a raspberry knickerbocker glory achieving that harmonious balance of sweet, tart and texture. In between, though, the boat rocked. Haddock, battered in Beavertown ale, was beautifully moist but under-seasoned. Even the chips were unexceptional. But if it's buzz you're after, you're in the right place. The restaurant combines buffed vintage styling with loud music and casual affectations (T-shirted staff,

wine in tumblers). It's for a good-looking, high-living crowd, all having a helluva time.

Available for hire. Babies and children welcome; high chairs. Booking advisable. Takeaway service. **Map 5 O1**.

Outer London
Richmond, Surrey

FishWorks
13-19 The Square, Richmond, Surrey TW9 1EA (8948 5965, www.fishworks.co.uk). Richmond tube/rail. **Meals served** noon-10.30pm daily. **Main courses** £13.95-£26.95. **Set meal** (noon-7pm Mon-Fri) £10.95 2 courses. **Credit** AmEx, MC, V.

FishWorks has a trio of branches in smarter parts of town; the Richmond outpost (the others are in Marylebone and Mayfair) is the most homely, and also has a cookery school upstairs. Set in a former market building with a high-pitched, skylit roof, it's airy and bright, painted in blue and white with cheery faux-naif seaside pictures. Freshness is key to the food, with daily deliveries from the south coast – check the blackboard for the catch of the day. Taramasalata and quality bread is a good opener, and we've always enjoyed the hearty, saffron-tinged fish stew. Shellfish fans get plenty of choice: oysters (available individually – a nice touch), whole crab and lobster, and platters of fruits de mer, served cold or roasted in a white wine and parsley broth. Our mains – sea bass and sea bream – were fine specimens, squeakily fresh and cooked just-so. But scallops served in the shell, although plump, were clumsily breadcrumbed and overcooked; and a lemon tart was no better than a posh supermarket version. The informal vibe and good-natured service suits all-comers, and it's ideal for family gatherings – though the kids' menu serves chips with almost everything.

Available for hire. Babies and children welcome: high chairs; nappy-changing facilities. Booking advisable. Disabled: toilet. Tables outdoors (3, pavement).

For branches see index.

Fish & Chip Shop

French

It has taken an age for Britain to overcome its inferiority complex with France over matters gastronomic. Time was when every self-respecting English aristocrat employed a French chef – Britain's native cooking being considered infra dig. Much of that has changed, of course, with London's restaurant revolution of the past 25 years. Yet as with all revolutions, the new guard needed to kick against the old. To emphasise that Modern British cuisine now led the avant-garde, we wanted our Gallic restaurants to be stereotypical *hor-hi-hor* bistros or ossified fine-dining temples. Hip? No, that was us – not them.

But things are starting to change. Having plundered Britain's culinary past, London restaurateurs are now taking renewed interest in the wealth of gastronomic treasures (ancient, modern and more especially regional) to be found across the Channel – treasures that in some cases are in danger of disappearing in their homeland. And these new venues aren't taking up residence in the affluent, staid suburbs, but in altogether edgier environs. So welcome, **Oui Madame**, to Stoke Newington; hello to Hackney's **Bouchon Fourchette**; greetings to **Chez Elles** in Brick Lane; and *bienvenue* to Bermondsey's **Casse-Croûte**.

Not that the (slightly) older guard aren't worth considering: London has some sublime French restaurants, and this year we give our garlands to Bayswater's highly creative **Angelus**, the luxe Knightsbridge brasserie **Bar Boulud**, the South-western expert **Club Gascon** in Farringdon, Wimbledon's modern classic, **Lawn Bistro**, and **Provender**, which continues to wow Wanstead. You can also find top French dining venues in our Brasseries (*see p35*) and Haute Cuisine (*p119*) chapters.

Central
Barbican

Morgan M
50 Long Lane, EC1A 9EJ (7609 3560, www.morganm.com). Barbican tube. **Lunch served** noon-2.30pm Mon-Fri. **Dinner served** 6-10.30pm Mon-Sat. **Main courses** £22.50-£26.50. **Set meal** (lunch Mon-Fri; 6-7pm Mon-Sat) £23.50 2 courses, £25.50 3 courses; £48-£52 tasting menu (£75.50-£82 incl wine). **Credit** AmEx, MC, V.
The restaurant doesn't give much away with its bland beige colour scheme and narrow dining area – Morgan Meunier prefers to let his resolutely French cooking do the talking. On our lunchtime visit, only a few tables were occupied, most by suited businessmen. Conversation was hushed, the service starched, and the atmosphere just a tad forbidding. The reasonably priced set menu was OK, good in parts, and occasionally outstanding. Top marks to plump ravioli cushions filled with flavoursome wine-cooked snails and crowned with a cloud of garlicky froth. A main course of crisp-skinned cod fillet was perfectly cooked and worked well with buttery parsley-purée risotto and caramelised parsnip – a triumph of contrasting flavours. Sadly, though, desserts didn't deliver. Hot pineapple soufflé was too sweet and marred by a grainy pina colada sorbet accompaniment. Woes continued with an unyielding genoa bread disc, sandwiched between fruity rhubarb compote and lacklustre Jurançon wine ice-cream. The hefty wine list features some serious French players, as well as lesser-known bottles. Perhaps we were unlucky with the lunchtime set menu, as dining from the pricey à la carte and tasting menus is of a higher order, and the vegetarian tasting selection is well received.
Available for hire. Babies and children admitted. Booking advisable weekends. Dress: smart casual. Vegetarian menu. **Map 11 O5**.

City

Coq d'Argent
No.1 Poultry, EC2R 8EJ (7395 5000, www.coqdargent.co.uk). Bank tube/DLR. *Brasserie* **Lunch served** 11.30am-3pm Mon-Fri. **Main courses** £15-£26. *Restaurant* **Breakfast served** 7.30-10am Mon-Fri. **Lunch served** 11.30am-3pm Mon-Fri; noon-3pm Sun. **Brunch served** noon-5.30pm Sat. **Dinner served** 5.30-10pm Mon-Sat. **Main courses** £19-£37.50. **Set lunch** (Sun) £25 2 courses, £28 3 courses. **Set meal** (lunch Mon-Fri; dinner) £26 2 courses, £29 3 courses. *Both* **Credit** AmEx, MC, V.
Coq d'Argent is accessed via a private lift, which speedily delivers City suits to a verdant rooftop garden, complete with its own lawn, trailing vines and ringed walkway. In summer, it's a great choice for alfresco dining, and the location offers striking skyline views across London. Indoor attractions include a circular bar, brasserie and corporate-styled restaurant. Expect regional French cooking, occasionally inspired by forays further afield. A first course of flavoursome beef carpaccio, topped with lightly pickled wild mushrooms and crunchy garden vegetables, benefited from an umami boost of dried pounded black olives. Crisp-skinned sea bass fillet, jauntily perched over softened, sliced fennel and courgettes, and sauced with a rich saffron-tomato velouté, also worked well as a main. Sadly, though, braised chicken cooked with mushrooms and baby onions was not a success.

Pale, flaccid-skinned chicken, dense mash and an unforgivably oily bread croûte delivered nothing of note. Desserts – tiramisu and roast plums – were OK, but no more. Well-meaning service wasn't as on-the-ball as expected, but despite misgivings, it's a buzzy destination of choice for bankers and their clients. And the cooking is decent enough – in parts. *Available for hire. Babies and children welcome: high chairs. Booking advisable. Disabled: lift; toilet. Dress: smart casual. Tables outdoors (34, terrace). Vegetarian menu.* **Map 11 P6**.

Lutyens

85 Fleet Street, EC4Y 1AE (7583 8385, www.lutyens-restaurant.co.uk). Blackfriars tube/rail or City Thameslink rail or bus 4, 11, 15, 23, 26.
Bar **Open** 7.30am-midnight, **breakfast served** 9.45-10.30am, **meals served** noon-9pm Mon-Fri. **Main courses** £12.50-£18.
Restaurant **Breakfast served** 7.30-9.45am, **lunch served** noon-2.45pm, **dinner served** 6-9.45pm Mon-Fri. **Main courses** £12.50-£37. **Set meal** £22 2 courses, £26 3 courses.
Both **Credit** AmEx, MC, V.
Lutyens, opened in 2009 by Terence Conran and Peter Prescott, is a City restaurant for all occasions. It consists of the restaurant proper, wine bar with bistro menu, cocktail bar, outdoor terrace, members' club and numerous private rooms for meetings and discreet splurges. Service is formal and tactful. Most of your fellow diners will be of the pinstriped type, and it's safe to say a great proportion of the spending is done on expenses. But there's still plenty here for everyone else: first, the site itself, in the former Reuters building designed by Sir Edwin Lutyens, is a corker. The façade displays that invincible Fleet Street pomp; inside, Conran has remodelled the space, adding a muted colour scheme with signature flourishes such as statement lighting and an open kitchen. The cold part of that sends out a lot of seafood – oysters, smoked salmon, ceviche – while the chefs manning the ovens and grills concentrate on French-slanted dishes of impeccable execution. The prix fixe menu might bring salmon tartare with perfect cubes of cucumber, say, or a simple plateful of cod with mussels and spring vegetables – it's good value, though sides at £4 and drinks will bump things up, of course. A reliably flawless experience.
Available for hire. Babies and children welcome: high chairs; nappy-changing facilities. Booking essential. Disabled: lift; toilet. Dress: smart casual. Separate rooms for parties, seating 6-28. Vegetarian menu. **Map 11 N6**.

Sauterelle

Royal Exchange, EC3V 3LR (7618 2483, www.sauterelle-restaurant.co.uk). Bank tube/ DLR. **Lunch served** noon-2.30pm, **dinner served** 6-9.30pm Mon-Fri. **Main courses** £17.50-£31. **Set meal** £20 2 courses, £23.50 3 courses, £45 tasting menu (£80 incl wine). **Credit** AmEx, MC, V.
Probably the best (only?) restaurant in London to be named after an insect, this D&D spot in the Royal Exchange takes its name from the French word for the golden grasshopper (on the roof) – a symbol of wealth and prosperity since Roman times. And as you sit in the comfortably appointed mezzanine above the expensive shops and grand café below, it's impossible to forget you're surrounded by the rich and powerful. However, Sauterelle is far more than an expense-account client-impresser of a place

– instead, there's a calm and understated elegance about it, which makes it worth a visit from outside the Square Mile. The set menu is good value at £20 for two courses, and offers many of the luxury ingredients of the more expensive menus (ham hock terrine with poached foie gras and pear and raisin chutney, for example, or aged beef with summer vegetables and red wine). Step up a level to the carte or 'market menu' to make the most of the modern yet circumspect French cooking. Service is polite and steady; the wine list is assembled to wow, but prices stay below the stratosphere. *Babies and children welcome: high chairs. Booking advisable. Disabled: lift; toilet. Dress: smart casual; no trainers. Separate room for parties, seats 26. Vegetarian menu.* **Map 12 Q6**.

Clerkenwell & Farringdon

Bistrot Bruno Loubet

86-88 Clerkenwell Road, EC1M 5RJ (7324 4455, www.bistrotbrunoloubet.com). Barbican tube or Farringdon tube/rail. **Breakfast served** 7-10.30am Mon-Fri; 7.30-11am Sat, Sun. **Lunch served** noon-2.30pm Mon-Fri. **Brunch served** noon-3pm Sat, Sun. **Dinner served** 6-10.30pm Mon-Sat; 6-10pm Sun. **Main courses** £13.50-£21.50. **Credit** AmEx, MC, V.
Chef Bruno Loubet has a lofty reputation, but his restaurant seemed to be coasting on our last visit – perhaps the launch of Grain Store (*see p195*) was having an effect? A signature dish, beetroot ravioli with rocket and parmesan, was lovely, finely blending sweet, savoury and subtle acidity; but 'duck pastrami' – really just cured duck – with coleslaw was pleasant and no more. Menus stray far from French tradition into global territory, often with radical flavour contrasts, as in another regular: braised beef indochine in an ultra-rich spicy sauce

offset by a mango fruit salad. It's certainly original, but this one lacked finesse. A summer seafood cassoulet featured salmon, cod and a seafood 'sausage' that had been very intricately put together, but also lacked any wow factor. Another sharp contrast appeared in a dessert, a fairly conventional chocolate and praline mousse topped by a very strong bitter-coffee jelly, a mix that divided opinion. The ground-floor space, in the chic Zetter hotel, is bright, airy and slightly functional; service is charming but rather slow. The wine list seems almost deliberately expensive – should you want a bottle rather than only a glass – with very little under £25.
Babies and children welcome: high chairs. Booking advisable. Disabled: toilet. Separate rooms for parties, seating 40-50. Tables outdoors (8, terrace). **Map 5 O4**.

★ Club Gascon

57 West Smithfield, EC1A 9DS (7796 0600, www.clubgascon.com). Barbican tube or Farringdon tube/rail. **Lunch served** noon-2pm Mon-Fri. **Dinner served** 6.30-10pm Mon-Thur; 6.30-10.30pm Fri, Sat. **Dishes** £12-£26. **Set lunch** £25 2 courses incl coffee or 3 courses. **Set dinner** £28 3 courses. **Set meal** £60 5 courses (£90 incl wine). **Credit** AmEx, MC, V.
The presence of the three-strong Gascon group (as well as Comptoir Gascon, there's wine bar Cellar Gascon) ensures that a small area of east-central London has a flavour of south-west France. This is the most expensive of the trio, a Michelin-starred sanctuary of haute cuisine. Heavy wooden screens shut out the world; inside is a serene and urbane room of greys and golds with marble panels. Head chef Pascal Aussignac is from Toulouse, and the hallmarks of the area's cuisine shine through in his food, although it's given the fancifications this level

Morgan M. See p85.

Bistrot Bruno Loubet

of restaurant requires. A playful approach means many dishes come with descriptions in inverted commas (garden pea 'risotto') or feature unusually prepared ingredients: a watercress velouté, for example, was soaked up by a pumpkin 'sponge'. Flavour combinations are bold – venison carpaccio with winkles, say, or 'nasturtium haddock, sorrel pulp and oyster leaf'. This adds to the sense of occasion, and the technique is flawless; perhaps less so the tendency to unorthodox plating. Glazed cod with verjuice and 'crunchy grapes' arrived on a 'burned pebble': not easy to eat off, and a lap-napkin was essential. However, everything else – from the ossau-iraty (sheep's milk cheese) 'breadsticks' to the spoon of popping-candy foam offered at the end – was note-perfect.
Available for hire. Booking essential Fri, Sat. Dress: smart casual; no trainers. Vegetarian menu. **Map 11 O5.**
For branch (Le Cercle) see index.

Comptoir Gascon
68 Charterhouse Street, EC1M 6HJ (7608 0851, www.comptoirgascon.com). Barbican tube or Farringdon tube/rail. **Lunch served** noon-2.30pm, **dinner served** 6.30-10pm Tue-Sat. **Main courses** £8-£14.50. **Credit** AmEx, MC, V.
The south-west of France, it would seem from Comptoir Gascon's menu, is not a good place to be a pig or a duck – or a vegetarian, for that matter. This bistro/deli, like its haute-cuisine big brother Club Gascon round the corner, specialises in the cuisine of Gascony: richer than Depardieu and earthier than Gainsbourg. The aforementioned porkers and quackers appear in various dishes – grilled duck hearts, crackling with duck egg, duck confit – while starters include the must-order 'piggy treats', a charcuterie board with saucisson, pâté, rillettes and slivers of cured tongue. Mains don't let up on the meat: there are several preparations of foie gras, rabbit and veal kidney (although cod with lavender-scented tomato compote was light and aromatic). Rustic, yes, but sophisticated too, and every dish comes with a bold whack of flavour. The wine list is exclusively focused on south-west

France, meaning this is a great place to explore the area's native lesser-seen grapes, such as courbu or manseng. The oddly shaped space is stripped back to brick in that typical Farringdon way, but manages to be cosy and welcoming, especially in the evening when twinkling candles add a touch of romance.
Available for hire. Babies and children welcome: high chairs. Booking advisable. Tables outdoors (4, pavement). **Map 11 O5.**

Covent Garden

Clos Maggiore
33 King Street, WC2E 8JD (7379 9696, www.closmaggiore.com). Covent Garden or Leicester Square tube. **Lunch served** noon-2.15pm daily. **Dinner served** 5-11pm Mon-Sat; 5-10pm Sun. **Main courses** £17-£29. **Set meal** (lunch Mon-Fri; 5-6pm, 10-11pm Mon-Thur) £15.50 2 courses (£19.50 incl half bottle of wine), £19.50 3 courses (£23.50 incl half bottle of wine); (lunch Sat; lunch, 5-9.30pm Sun) £22.50 3 courses (£26.50 incl half bottle of wine). **Set dinner** (5-6pm Fri, Sat) £22.50 2 courses. **Tasting menu** (lunch Mon-Fri; 5-10pm Mon-Sat; 5-9pm Sun) £49 (£81 incl wine); (lunch Sat, Sun) £39 (£64 incl wine). **Credit** AmEx, MC, V.
Romantic settings don't get more splendidly over-the-top than this. Take your pick from the wood-panelled restaurant or the atmospheric conservatory, bedecked in a forest of fake white blossoms that seem to extend into eternity as they bounce off the restaurant's mirrors. Fairy lights, candles and a fireplace add to the soft focus vibe. On our early evening visit, tables were filled with mature couples and curious tourists. It's a provençal-inspired menu, and although à la carte choices are pegged at the sharp end, the pre-theatre menu offering is a bargain. A cavernous bowl of gazpacho topped with crunchy croûtons and diced cucumber blew our socks off (in a good way) with its unashamedly pungent garlicky kick. Satisfyingly filling, a trio of meaty bites – foie gras terrine, herby pork shoulder confit and a tasty kofta – made for a carnivore's delight. Less

memorable, chunky roasted pollock fillet was tender and juicy, but overshadowed by a rich moat of vermouth cream, buttery crushed potatoes and softened leeks (more butter) – not one for the faint-hearted. Service is polished, if a tad austere, and the wine selection seriously impressive.
Babies and children welcome: high chairs. Booking essential weekends; 2 months in advance for conservatory. Dress: smart; no jeans or trainers. Vegetarian menu. **Map 18 D4.**

Les Deux Salons
40-42 William IV Street, WC2N 4DD (7420 2050, www.lesdeuxsalons.co.uk). Charing Cross tube/rail or Leicester Square tube. **Meals served** 1-11pm Mon-Sat; 11am-6pm Sun. **Main courses** £8.50-£30. **Set dinner** £9.95 2 courses, £19.75 3 courses. **Credit** AmEx, MC, V.
One of the trio of restaurants from powerhouse pairing Anthony Demetre and Will Smith (the others are Arbutus and Wild Honey), French brasserie Les Deux Salons comes with certain expectations. It certainly looks the part, the building rescued from its former incarnation as a Pitcher & Piano and turned into two sumptuous floors of gleaming black and white parquet, dark wood and deep leather banquettes. The menu isn't afraid to stray beyond the traditional brasserie remit, with items such as Cornish crab cakes and a house hot dog, and lets you splash out on oysters and veal or dip in with some very reasonable set menus. A shame, then, that the cooking on our last visit left us heaving a rather Gallic shrug – there was no zing, no ooh. We had a plain salad of cherry tomatoes with diced onion, and good fish soup with aïoli, followed by workmanlike salmon with butter beans and a tender but unexceptional iron pot of baby chicken with garlic and lemon, then shared a cone of velvety chocolate ice-cream. Service was unmemorable and presentation basic – a decent experience then, but one that failed to live up to the decor, reputation or prices.
Babies and children welcome: high chairs; nappy-changing facilities. Booking advisable. Separate rooms for parties, seating 10 and 24. Vegetarian menu. **Map 18 D5.**

Mon Plaisir

19-21 Monmouth Street, WC2H 9DD (7836 7243, www.monplaisir.co.uk). Covent Garden tube. **Meals served** noon-11.15pm Mon-Fri. **Lunch served** noon-3pm, **dinner served** 5.45-11.15pm Sat. **Main courses** £16.95-£23.95. **Set lunch** £12.95 2 courses, £15.95 3 courses. **Set meal** (5.45-7pm, after 10pm Mon-Sat) £12.95 2 courses, £14.95 3 courses incl coffee. **Credit** AmEx, MC, V.

Delightfully retro, Mon Plaisir is a longstanding Covent Garden fixture popular with theatregoers, tourists and, for some reason, studenty types out with their parents. Knick-knacks (framed prints, copper pans) abound in the four interconnecting dining areas, and there are even red-and-white checked tablecloths. Cooking focuses on bistro classics of the coq au vin, pork rillettes and steak-frites variety. A first course of onion tarte tatin was faultless – we appreciated the thyme-infused roast red onion half on a crisp puff pastry base, crowned with tangy goat's cheese and finished with peppery caramel syrup. Good news continued with a light yet intensely flavoured dish of seared scallops and steamed clams accompanied by reduced stock, cream and cooking juices from the clams. Desserts weren't in the same league – a chocolate profiterole filled with fresh mint ice-cream was overshadowed by an avalanche of stodgy chocolate sauce. Equally dispiriting, dark and milk chocolate mousse, served in a glass, was fridge-cold and leaden in texture. Service can be brusque when the tables get busy. If you're after a bargain, check out the great value pre-theatre and set lunch deals.

Babies and children welcome: high chairs. Booking advisable. Separate room for parties, seats 25. Vegetarian menu. **Map 18 D3**.

Holborn

Cigalon

115 Chancery Lane, WC2A 1PP (7242 8373, www.cigalon.co.uk). Chancery Lane or Temple tube. **Lunch served** noon-2.30pm, **dinner served** 6-9.45pm Mon-Fri. **Main courses** £12.50-£21. **Set meal** £19.50 2 courses, £24.50 3 courses. **Credit** AmEx, MC, V.

There's something anomalous about this attractive, lavender-hued Provençal specialist tucked in among lawyers' offices. Under the skylight and the potted olive trees, the discreet curved banquettes offer the impression of sitting in a Mediterranean courtyard – a welcome respite for legal eagles. Incongruity sometimes extends to the food as well. There's no doubting the culinary skills or authenticity of ingredients, but occasionally what should have been delightful is instead intriguing but frustratingly just wide of the mark. Perhaps that's the problem with novelty-seeking contemporary French cooking, and certainly all the olives and basil you could wish for are here. After a terrific tapenade, black olives appeared in bread, in a so-called confit of salmon (floating damply in a soupy lettuce velouté), and again with lambs' tongues, tiny potatoes and watercress. Beautifully cooked guineafowl was served with a drab-looking peach salsa and panisse (hefty chickpea chips), while the thrill of finding lamb's tongues was mitigated by the delicate flavour being swamped by dressing. Sea bass with perfectly crisp skin matched with tomatoes in different stages of cooked – from raw to confit – was more like it. Sadly, puddings rather misfired again. Tea and blood peach pot was a beige cream with pink purée

on top; blackberry île flottante was a spongey meringue speckled with the out-of-season fruit on an admittedly lovely custard.

Available for hire. Babies and children admitted. Booking advisable lunch. Vegetarian menu. **Map 11 N6**.

Knightsbridge

★ Bar Boulud

Mandarin Oriental Hyde Park, 66 Knightsbridge, SW1X 7LA (7201 3899, www.barboulud.com). Knightsbridge tube. **Lunch served** noon-3pm, **tea served** 3.30-5pm daily. **Dinner served** 5-11pm Mon-Sat; 5-10pm Sun. **Main courses** £11.75-£29. **Credit** AmEx, MC, V.

An outpost of the New York flagship, Bar Boulud is located in the basement of the majestic Mandarin Oriental and attracts a diverse mix of families, hotel guests, business people and romancing couples. Overseen by renowned chef Daniel Boulud, the restaurant has an eye-catching view of the open-plan kitchen where chefs work in zen-like calm. Charcuterie from Gilles Verot is a big draw, as are the elegant French brasserie options and finger-licking American staples. We've had burgers here and loved every bite – try a beef patty topped with pulled pork and green chilli mayonnaise or a French-US collaboration of beefy burger piled high with pork confit and morbier cheese. On our latest visit, we enjoyed such culinary gems as a robust french onion soup, resplendent with caramelised onions and topped with molten gruyère. A veritable mountain of steamed plump mussels cloaked in garlicky red chilli tomato sauce was another winner – every last saucy drop mopped up with chargrilled bread. The only downer was a lacklustre chocolate sponge layered with chilled coffee buttercream, although its accompanying scoop of coffee ice-cream saved the day. A class performance topped off by seamless service.

Babies and children welcome: high chairs; nappy-changing facilities. Booking advisable. Disabled: toilet. Dress: smart casual. Separate room for parties, seats 20. **Map 8 F9**.

Chabrot Bistrot d'Amis

9 Knightsbridge Green, SW1X 7QL (7225 2238, www.chabrot.co.uk). Knightsbridge tube. **Meals served** noon-11pm Mon-Sat; noon-10pm Sun. **Main courses** £12-£27.50. **Set meal** £14.50 2 courses, £19.50 3 courses. **Credit** AmEx, MC, V.

This diminutive bistro, located on a quiet side street, is dwarfed by neighbours Harrods and the Mandarin Oriental. It's a cosy, slightly cramped set-up and the decor plays up to the unmistakably French theme with a velvet curtain by the entrance, mirrors, wood panelling, and tea towel-like table linen. Prices are easy on the pocket for this part of town and the restaurant attracts plenty of office workers at lunchtime. Cooking has a southern slant, and the seafood and fish specialities are stellar choices. A starter of escabeche of lightly seared red mullet fillets tastefully perched over sliced softened onions delivered a tangy, vinegary flavour infused with warming auburn-hued saffron. Main courses weren't as memorable – chargrilled veal escalope needed an extra hit of strident sage to lift it from blandness. Happily, the accompanying frites were crisp and piping hot, and crushed pink peppercorns strewn over the green salad provided explosive hits of pungency. Desserts were acceptable – a sweet pastry tart filled with custardy crème pâtissière worked well with the astringency of fruity

blackcurrant jam and a pot of boozy cherries. Service doesn't miss a beat. A second branch in Smithfield, Bistrot des Halles, opened in 2013.

Available for hire. Babies and children admitted. Booking advisable. Separate room for parties, seats 30. **Map 8 F9**. **For branch see index**.

Racine

239 Brompton Road, SW3 2EP (7584 4477, www.racine-restaurant.com). Knightsbridge or South Kensington tube. **Lunch served** noon-3pm, **dinner served** 6-10.30pm Mon-Fri. **Meals served** noon-10.30pm Sat; noon-10pm Sun. **Main courses** £16.50-£28.50. **Set meal** (lunch, 6-7.30pm Mon-Sat) £15.50 2 courses, £17.75 3 courses; (lunch, 6-7.30pm Sun) £18 2 courses, £20 3 courses. **Credit** AmEx, MC, V.

Deep-red velvet curtains around the entrance, a dark interior of mirrors, wood and leather banquettes, and waiters in white shirts and black waistcoats combine at Racine to evoke a very proper Parisian brasserie. It's a style appreciated by the business lunchers, wealthy locals and tourists who form the core clientele. Chef-owner Henry Harris is British, but has absorbed all the classic French culinary arts, combining them with attentively sourced, mostly British ingredients. From the prix fixe menu, an onion velouté soup was deliciously sweet, smooth and delicately seasoned, and rabbit terrine had a great depth of punchy flavour. Out of the choice of just two mains, grey mullet with sage, capers and soubise sauce was another winner, full of subtle flavours; but in braised lamb with haricot beans and roast garlic, both meat and garlic were overpowered by an odd excess of mustardy spice. The set menu is good value, but go beyond a glass of wine and prices shoot up, as the list has scarcely any bottles under £25. Staff are very French, very professional and charming – as they need to be with a service charge at 14.5%.

Available for hire. Babies and children welcome: high chairs. Booking essential. Separate room for parties, seats 22. **Map 14 E10**.

Marylebone

Galvin Bistrot de Luxe

66 Baker Street, W1U 7DJ (7935 4007, www.galvinrestaurants.com). Baker Street tube. **Lunch served** noon-2.30pm Mon-Sat; noon-3pm Sun. **Dinner served** 6-10.30pm Mon-Wed; 6-10.45pm Thur-Sat; 6-9.30pm Sun. **Main courses** £16-£21.50. **Set lunch** £19.50 3 courses. **Set dinner** (6-7pm) £21.50 3 courses. **Credit** AmEx, MC, V.

The first of the Galvin brothers' restaurant empire, this polished, much-loved Marylebone bistro is classically French (veloutés, soufflés, purées) with the occasional nod to Italy (risotto, lasagna, panna cotta). The dining room is an inviting place, with its dark chocolate wood panelling, globe lighting and big bunches of scarlet gladioli. Lunch, ordered from the à la carte and £19.50 prix-fixe menus, was high on comfort and mostly tip-top. A smooth, nicely fatty pork and duck rillette was presented on a rustic slab of wood with super-fresh leaves and toasted sourdough. A main course of calf's liver came draped in bacon on a pool of gravy, accompanied by meltingly good potato purée. Salt-cod brandade was laced with olive oil and wonderfully creamy, though we were caught off-guard by the inclusion of a runny egg. Dessert didn't quite deliver. A Valrhona chocolate 'délice', served on a rectangular white plate, arrived fridge-cold with a lump of rock-hard honeycomb. It looked snazzy with its painterly streaks of chocolate, but was nothing like as good as a simple chocolate fondant. Service can be a little relaxed at times, and our table at the back felt cramped, but the excellent coffee ended things on a high.

Babies and children welcome: high chairs; nappy-changing facilities. Booking advisable. Disabled: toilet. Separate room for parties, seats 22. Tables outdoors (7, pavement). **Map 9 G5**.
For branch (Galvin La Chapelle) see index.

Mayfair

Brasserie Chavot

41 Conduit Street, W1S 2YF (7183 6425, http://brasseriechavot.com). Oxford Circus or Piccadilly Circus tube. **Lunch served** noon-2.30pm Mon-Fri; 12.30-2.30pm Sat. **Dinner served** 6-10.30pm Mon-Sat. **Meals served** 12.30-9pm Sun. **Main courses** £16-£24. **Credit** AmEx, MC, V.

Larousse Gastronomique states that 'the distinction of all brasseries is that they serve a limited menu at any time of the day.' Which Brasserie Chavot doesn't. But we'll forgive chef Eric Chavot the misleading moniker, as the intention is clearly to convey informality when compared to his previous haute cuisine restaurants. Yet Brasserie Chavot is still no casual, shuffle-in-late-wearing-your-onesie sort of place. The dining room is almost sepulchral in its formality, with smiling but no-nonsense service. A towering daube of beef had a wonderful depth of flavour. Slightly fancier was the duckling à l'orange, rescued from what could have been a 1970s sickly-sweet orange sauce by savoury pink meat and the slightly bitter contrast of caramelised endives. Not every dish wowed, though. A Mont Blanc dessert resembled a trifle-like sludge in its glass bowl, and the snails bourguignon were not improved by the addition of a fashionable espuma (foam) of potato. Brasserie Chavot is a smart, special-occasion French restaurant with appealing dishes by a great chef. But it needs to unbutton its collar just a little bit – or maybe lose that 'B' word.

Babies and children welcome: high chairs; nappy-changing facilities. Booking advisable. Disabled: toilet. **Map 9 J7**.

Little Social

5 Pollen Street, W1S 1NE (7870 3730, www.littlesocial.co.uk). Oxford Circus tube. **Lunch served** noon-2.30pm, **dinner served** 6-10.30pm Mon-Sat. **Main courses** £15-£23.50. **Set lunch** £21 2 courses, £25 3 courses. **Credit** AmEx, MC, V.

There was a hiatus of several years when French gastronomy seemed to be receding in London – little wonder, in a time of recession. But proper French cooking is too good to ever go away and now the bistro and brasserie are back, with luminary venues such as Balthazar and Brasserie Chavot joined by Jason Atherton's Little Social, opposite his flagship Pollen Street Social (*see p125*). Instead of replicating PSS's success, he's created a super-bistro, a luxe homage to Paris but with a slightly Manhattan accent. There's a cocktail bar that dominates the entrance: the drinks aren't cheap but they're expertly made, and you can eat at the bar if you wish. Beyond this are red leather booths; the further you venture, the more discreet the tables

Brasserie Chavot

Little Social. See p89.

become. Atherton's rule appears to be 'more is more', so a parmesan and squash soup also contained a poached egg, roasted mushrooms and croûtons; although busy, the dish was a riot of flavour. More single-note but equally excellent was braised ox cheek, served on a dollop of horseradish mash, propped up by a roasted ox bone complete with a tiny spoon for scooping out the marrow. The French staff are charming, the atmosphere intimate, the cooking first-rate, the wines by the glass desirable – and, with a good-value set lunch, a meal here needn't be rapaciously priced. The bistro is back with a bang.
Available for hire. Babies and children welcome: high chairs. Booking essential. Disabled: toilet. **Map 9 J6**.

La Petite Maison

54 Brooks Mews, W1K 4EG (7495 4774, www.lpmlondon.co.uk). Bond Street tube. **Lunch served** noon-2.30pm Mon-Fri; 12.30-2.45pm Sat, Sun. **Dinner served** 6-10.30pm Mon-Sat; 6.30-9pm Sun. **Main courses** £15-£70. **Credit** AmEx, MC, V.

On a sunny day, La Petite Maison gives a decent impression of somewhere on the Côte d'Azur, with its cream pillars, spacious dining room and light flooding in through big windows. It's a franchise of a renowned establishment in Nice, but unlike nearly all restaurants in France, it doesn't offer set menus to soften its prices (not shown on the otherwise-jaunty website, so they can come as a shock). If you're bothered about cost, however, it's fair to say you're not at one with the chatty, multinational, Mayfair clientele. Like its Gallic parent, LPM showcases French-Mediterranean cuisine and ingredients, in both sharing-friendly 'hors d'oeuvres' and main courses. The produce certainly delivered – gloriously juicy tomatoes – but on our visit the cooking was disappointingly short on flair. A provençal classic of salt-cod and potato brandade, in croquettes, was too salty (surely a basic with salt cod is washing the salt off properly) and lacked the smoothness of a really good brandade. In pasta with squid, prawns and chorizo, central flavours were masked by crude (and un-French) hot spice. Abundant staff ensure no one feels neglected, although the kitchen is a little slow. A properly grand wine list again focuses on southern France, with probably London's best choice of quality rosés.
Babies and children welcome: high chairs. Booking essential. Dress: smart casual. Tables outdoors (10, terrace). Vegetarian menu. **Map 9 H6**.

St James's

Boulestin NEW

5 St James's Street, SW1A 1EF (7930 2030, www.boulestin.com). Green Park tube.
Café Marcel **Open** 7am-11pm Mon-Wed; 7am-midnight Thur, Fri; 8am-midnight Sat; 8am-11pm Sun.
Restaurant **Lunch served** noon-2.45pm Mon-Fri; noon-3pm Sat. **Brunch served** 11am-4pm Sun. **Dinner served** 5.30-11pm Mon-Wed, Sun; 5.30pm-midnight Thur-Sat. **Main courses** £12.50-£37. **Set dinner** (5.30-6.45pm) £19.50 2 courses; £24.50 3 courses.
Both **Credit** AmEx, MC, V.
Marcel Boulestin opened a restaurant (now long-closed) near Leicester Square in 1925. This brand-

new Boulestin in SW1 is no relation, though it does pay homage to the era of the great chef. The menu lists oeufs en gelée – a dish that, much like old-school St James's, is preserved in aspic. Classic French cooking at its best shines in dishes such as daube of beef, which was slow-cooked and wonderfully tender. A boudin noir was moist and earthy in flavour, the black pudding succulent with cooked blood. Fish choices include dover sole meunière, and game – wild pigeon with girolles, lardons and kale, for example – is well represented too. A few dishes seem almost daringly modern with their rocket and preserved lemons, but, for the most part, this menu is as classic, French and retro as the grand setting. Rather than trying to impersonate an old master, this Boulestin is a sensitively updated reproduction. It aims to be as classic as a carefully poured glass of old Bordeaux, and is priced accordingly. At the front of the premises is Café Marcel, a more relaxed all-day operation, serving some of the same dishes, plus snacks such as croque monsieur. Service in both is as correct as the setting.
Available for hire. Babies and children welcome: high chairs. Booking advisable dinner Fri, Sat. Separate room for parties, seats 40. Tables outdoors (12, terrace). **Map 9 J8.**

Soho

Brasserie Zédel
20 Sherwood Street, W1F 7ED (7734 4888, www.brasseriezedel.com). Piccadilly Circus tube. **Bar Open** 4.30pm-midnight daily.
Café **Open** 8am-midnight Mon-Sat; 11.30am-midnight Sun.
Brasserie **Meals served** noon-11.45pm daily. **Main courses** £8-£17. **Set meal** £8.75 2 courses, £11.75 3 courses. **Credit** AmEx, MC, V.
Restaurateurs Chris Corbin and Jeremy King, creators of the Wolseley (*see p38*) and the Delaunay (*see p37*), have struck gold with this grand art deco basement brasserie. It's a huge set-up and attracts a mix of tourists, office types and couples. Affordable French staples are the big draw and set menus start at under a tenner for two courses. In the months after it opened, we'd been impressed by the quality of cooking and on-the-ball service, but recently we've detected a dip in standards. In a meal of hits and misses, highlights included a generous main course of beef bourguignon – meaty chunks simmered in a robust red wine, onion and garlic sauce, accompanied by buttery mash. The haché steak was less impressive, though; instead of chopped meat being shaped and loosely held together, we were presented with a salty, overcooked burger patty. Chocolate profiteroles helped to restore faith – the perfectly baked crisp globes of choux pastry, crammed with splendid whipped vanilla cream, went down a treat with an indulgent chocolate sauce. The house wine, priced at bargain basement rates, is great value. Let's hope the kitchen brigade is back on track soon, and service staff numbers are increased at busy times.
Available for hire. Babies and children welcome: high chairs; nappy-changing facilities. Booking advisable. Disabled: lift; toilet. Entertainment: cabaret evenings, call for details. Vegetarian menu. **Map 17 B5.**

Gauthier Soho
21 Romilly Street, W1D 5AF (7494 3111, www.gauthiersoho.co.uk). Leicester Square or Piccadilly Circus tube. **Lunch served** noon-

2.30pm Tue-Sat. **Dinner served** 6.30-10.30pm Mon-Sat. **Set meal** £40 3 courses, £50 4 courses, £60 5 courses; £70 tasting menu (£100-£130 incl wine); £60 vegetarian tasting menu (£90-£120 incl wine); (lunch, 5.30-7pm) £18 2 courses (£26 with half bottle of wine), £25 3 courses (£33 with half bottle of wine). **Credit** AmEx, MC, V.
Gauthier Soho is gracious to the point of being rarefied – there's even a bell on the front door to announce arrivals at the sumptuous Georgian townhouse. The dining areas, spread over two floors, are furnished in shades of cream, and the atmosphere is as hushed as the genteel conversation of the mainly mature clientele. Alexis Gauthier has made his name turning out cutting-edge French dishes, which often involve putting seasonal vegetables centre stage – perhaps buttery, slow-cooked fennel, baby turnips teamed with salmon, or beetroot purée partnered with scallops. As well as the carte, options include extravagant tasting menus. Top marks go to an intensely aromatic smoked seafood broth, studded with prawns and sea urchin and spiked with citrusy curd made from yuzu. Main courses were decent rather than exceptional. Flavoursome and tender (pink-cooked) lamb cutlets, roast sliced loin and confit of slow-cooked shoulder worked well with a meaty jus enriched with roasted garlic. Desserts were a disappointment: strawberry millefeuille, topped with a whirl of retro whipped cream, was let down by a flat-tasting mismatch of yoghurt and lime sorbet. Service is attentive – at times overly so. Gripes aside, Gauthier Soho remains a worthwhile special occasion indulgence.
Available for hire. Babies and children welcome: high chairs. Booking advisable. Dress: smart casual. Separate rooms for parties, seating 4-40. Vegetarian menu. **Map 17 C4.**

West
Bayswater

Angelus
4 Bathurst Street, W2 2SD (7402 0083, www.angelusrestaurant.co.uk). Lancaster Gate tube. **Meals served** 10am-11pm Mon-Sat; 10am-10pm Sun. **Main courses** £20-£32. **Set meal** (noon-6pm) £20 2 courses, £25 3 courses. **Credit** AmEx, MC, V.
On a sunny day, after a walk in Hyde Park, there are few better places to put the world to rights than an outdoor table at Angelus (the refurbished pub's interior isn't quite as inviting, with red banquettes, dark-wood panelling and a boudoir-like cocktail bar lending a slightly dated vibe). There's nothing retro about Thierry Tomasin's creative dishes. Simple yet sublime, a clear cucumber gazpacho was notable for its delicate flavour underpinned by a vinegary tang. More complex in flavour, we loved the juicy texture of poached salmon partnered with creamy beetroot purée. Mains showed star quality. A crisp-skinned seared sea bream fillet, surrounded by light lemongrass broth, was crowned with crisp-fried rice noodle rösti – a tasty play on South-east Asian flavours. Pineapple millefeuille teamed with passionfruit jelly and star anise ice-cream provided a fitting finale. Prices are eye-wateringly high, even for the all-day brasserie choices; however, the set menu (available until 6pm) is excellent value and decent carafes of wine that won't break the bank are available. Service is as smooth as silk.

Babies and children welcome: high chairs. Booking advisable. Disabled: lift; toilet. Separate room for parties, seats 22. Tables outdoors (5, terrace). **Map 8 D6.**

Chiswick

La Trompette
5-7 Devonshire Road, W4 2EU (8747 1836, www.latrompette.co.uk). Turnham Green tube. **Lunch served** noon-2.30pm Mon-Sat; 12.30-3pm Sun. **Dinner served** 6.30-10.30pm Mon-Sat; 7-9.30pm Sun. **Set lunch** (Mon-Sat) £27.50 3 courses; (Sun) £32.50 3 courses. **Set dinner** £45 3 courses. **Credit** AmEx, MC, V.
This long-established restaurant has had a makeover. The front terrace with fold-back doors and grey awning remains, but the restaurant itself is bigger – it has expanded next door, creating a private dining room. The new look of muted colours, gold banquettes, dark wood floors and discreet lighting provides an air of understated glamour, though some of the previous intimacy has been lost. There's also been a change in the kitchen – Rob Weston, head chef at the Square for 15 years, took over in early 2013. Otherwise, tables are still decked with starched white tablecloths and gleaming glassware; service throughout, from the maître d' to the sommelier (the wine list is one of the best in London), remains impeccable; and diners tend to be plummy-voiced locals with cash to splash. Heritage tomato, aubergine and goat's curd salad was a refreshing (if slightly watery) starter; Dorset lamb (glazed shoulder and roasted rump) was supremely succulent; pearly fat flakes of cod matched perfectly with fresh almond pesto – our dinner was beautifully cooked and presented, but lacked the kind of culinary fireworks we've experienced here in the past. Apricot soufflé was the most dramatic dish: a scoop of almond and bay leaf ice-cream was dropped through the crust, followed by apricot sauce, but the flavours were too faint – though we'd have happily guzzled more of the ice-cream.
For more classy cooking in the south-west suburbs, try sister restaurants Chez Bruce in Wandsworth (also French) and the Glasshouse (Modern European; *see p211*) in Kew.
Babies and children welcome: high chairs. Booking advisable. Disabled: toilet. Separate room for parties, seats 10. Tables outdoors (5, terrace).

Le Vacherin
76-77 South Parade, W4 5LF (8742 2121, www.levacherin.com). Chiswick Park tube/rail. **Lunch served** noon-3pm Tue-Sat, noon-4pm Sun. **Dinner served** 6-10.30pm Mon-Thur; 6-11pm Fri, Sat; 6-10pm Sun. **Main courses** £15-£26. **Set lunch** (Mon-Sat) £18.50 2 courses, £25 3 courses; (Sun) £25 3 courses. **Credit** AmEx, MC, V.
On a midweek evening, this popular neighbourhood bistro, with its retro prints and mirrors, was thrumming with Chiswick's spruce and moneyed *troisième âge* and a sprinkling of younger folk. It's the sort of place where a man might dine alone, linen napkin tucked into his shirt. The menu is classically French (snails, soufflé, duck à l'orange) but with Italian elements (tortellini, ravioli, risotto) and appealing British ingredients (Maldon oysters, Suffolk asparagus, dover sole). The largely French wine list is a lovingly assembled affair. Things began well – excellent bread and anchovy butter, a

smooth courgette velouté amuse-bouche, the comforting sight of waiters plating up cheese – but the momentum was quickly lost. A long delay in taking our order was followed by a stomach-rumbling wait for our mains, which we put down to the champagne-themed dinner for 30 taking place alongside us. Lamb with borlotti beans was more gastropub than fine dining – it didn't merit its hefty (£23) price tag. A 'rare' rump steak (part of an admirable £11.95 steak frites deal that included a glass of wine) was tough and underdone, the chips lacklustre. Tarte tatin featuring plump, jammy-sweet apples was let down by soggy pastry. A blip? We hope so.

Available for hire. Babies and children admitted. Booking advisable. Separate room for parties, seats 30.

For branch (Brasserie Vacherin) see index.

Earl's Court

Garnier

314 Earl's Court Road, SW5 9BQ (3641 8323, www.garnier-restaurant-london.co.uk). Earl's Court tube or West Brompton tube/rail. **Lunch served** noon-3pm Mon-Sat; noon-3.30pm Sun. **Dinner served** 6-10.30pm Mon-Sat; 6-10pm Sun. **Main courses** £16.50-£49. **Set lunch** (Mon-Sat) £18.50 3 courses; (Sun) £21.50 2 courses. **Credit** AmEx, MC, V.

What makes the perfect French bistro? A menu of timeless dishes? Discreet, flawless service? Red banquettes? Loads of big gold-framed mirrors? Or is it something indefinable, a sense of élan that comes only with the Gallic commitment to hospitality? Garnier has all these to spare. Although the restaurant opened only in 2012, it looks like it's been there forever; it's certainly not at the cutting edge of anything – but that's not the point. What diners get is a display of serious adroitness in the kitchen, with chefs clearly possessing deep knowledge of the principles that made French cooking a benchmark in the first place. There's soupe de poisson. Assiette de crudités. Snails, foie gras terrine, steak tartare. The menu is split traditionally, with 'Les Poissons' featuring scallops with cauliflower, and sole with parsley butter. From 'Les Viandes' came a beautifully tender shin of Scotch beef served with puréed vegetables. Bread and butter, and side dishes of potatoes and beans, are complimentary and excellent. Desserts include crêpes suzette and crème brûlée. The all-French wine list isn't greedily priced and offers value at the lower end too. Eric and Didier Garnier, the brothers behind this venture, are no strangers to the restaurant scene, and it shows.

Available for hire. Babies and children admitted. Booking advisable. Vegetarian menu. **Map 13 B11.**

Hammersmith

La Petite Bretagne [NEW]

5-7 Beadon Road, W6 0EA (8127 5530, www.la petitebretagne.co.uk). Hammersmith tube. **Meals served** 8am-10pm Mon-Fri; 10am-10pm Sat, Sun. **Main courses** £6.90-£8.90. **Credit** MC, V.

Mon dieu, a small patch of Brittany has popped up in the middle of Hammersmith. La Petite Bretagne prepares savoury galettes – made with gluten-free buckwheat flour – and sweet crêpes fresh to order. Classic savoury combinations include ham and cheese as well as spinach, egg and cheese, while sweet crêpes range from sugar and lemon juice to

nutella and banana. A chestnut crêpe was exemplary: the layer of crème de marrons generous, but thin enough for the pancake's subtle flavour to shine through. While galettes and crêpes are no longer a novelty in London, the kouign amann (a buttery Breton pastry) is sure to kindle a few puzzled looks, if only at how to correctly pronounce this regional speciality. Food can be ordered to take away, but it would be a shame not to linger in the stylish surroundings. Wooden tables are screen printed with a red gingham pattern, quirky lampshades dangle, and shelves contain salted caramel jars, colourful tins of sardines and Breton biscuits (all for sale). With cider brut on the menu and opening hours that extend from breakfast through to the evening, the café's casual atmosphere might be just what you need to spend *une agréable soirée* in Hammersmith.

Available for hire. Babies and children admitted. Booking advisable. Takeaway service. **Map 20 B4.**

South West

Wandsworth

Chez Bruce

2 Bellevue Road, SW17 7EG (8672 0114, www.chezbruce.co.uk). Wandsworth Common rail. **Lunch served** noon-2pm Mon-Fri; noon-2.30pm Sat, Sun. **Dinner served** 6.30-9.45pm Mon-Thur; 6.30-10pm Fri, Sat; 7-9pm Sun. **Set lunch** (Mon-Fri) £27.50 3 courses; (Sat, Sun) £35 3 courses. **Set dinner** £45 3 courses. **Credit** AmEx, MC, V.

Like a well-cut blazer, Chez Bruce may not be especially original, but it is largely reliable. In 2010 the restaurant expanded into the neighbouring site, but little changed (apart from the increased seating), and not much has altered since. With a pale colour scheme, tasteful framed art on the walls, proper glassware and staff in crisp shirts and ties, the look is a study in classic (if slightly dated) restaurant decor. The cooking is equally timeless, led decisively by the French school (foie gras, côte de boeuf), without much deference to culinary fads. Rillettes of wild sea trout, dill and crème fraîche were accompanied by a mouthful of smoked eel and a wide array of edible garnishes – from Lilliputian dices of apple to sprigs of watercress – to produce a plate of food that looked as good as it tasted. Tender, slow-cooked calf's cheek served with golden braised sweetbreads and perfectly al dente baby vegetables was no less impressive. Only a dessert of cloyingly sweet caramel topped with two mousses (milk chocolate, salted caramel) and pieces of honeycomb was uncharacteristically misjudged. The formal service was also a touch over-attentive. Our advice? Immerse yourself in the wine list – one of the finest (and best value) in the capital – and any minor slip-ups will quickly be forgotten.

Available for hire. Babies and children welcome lunch: high chairs. Booking essential. Disabled: toilet. Separate room for parties, seats 16.

Wimbledon

★ Lawn Bistro

67 High Street, SW19 5EE (8947 8278, www.thelawnbistro.co.uk). Wimbledon tube/rail. **Lunch served** noon-2.30pm Mon-Sat; noon-3pm Sun. **Dinner served** 6.30-10.30pm Mon-Sat. **Set lunch** (Mon-Sat) £14.95, £19.50 2

courses; £18.95, £22.50 3 courses; (Sun) £29.50 3 courses. **Set dinner** £32.50 2 courses, £37.50 3 courses; (6.30-7.15pm Mon-Thur) £27.95 3 courses incl glass of wine. **Credit** AmEx, MC, V.

More refined than you'd infer from its name alone, the Lawn Bistro is a classic French dining room that has added a strong independent voice to the chain restaurants and cafés of Wimbledon. Open since 2011, it offers accomplished French cuisine via two- or three-course prix fixe menus and a drinks list notable for French ciders, and beer from Wimbledon's By the Horns brewery. There's also a good range of global wine, with plenty by the glass. Ollie Couillaud, formerly head chef at La Trompette, does stray geographically, though, so don't be too surprised to find the likes of lamb with yorkshire pudding and mint sauce alongside dauphinois potatoes. Elegantly presented pan-fried sea bream synched well with pomegranate vinaigrette and artichoke purée, while guinea fowl leg with puy lentils benefited from smoky bacon lardons and a peppy salsa verde. Sweet seduction comes in the form of a baked alaska, torched at your table, for two to share, but the cheeseboard is also a temptation. The space itself is smart, grey and unremarkable, and service pleasantly attentive. Ring for details of 'wine dinners', when a specially conceived menu is designed around wines of a particular grape variety or region.

Available for hire. Babies and children welcome: high chairs. Booking advisable. Disabled: toilet. Separate room for parties, seats 20.

South

Battersea

Entrée

2 Battersea Rise, SW11 1ED (7223 5147, www.entreebattersea.co.uk). Clapham Junction rail. **Lunch served** noon-3.30pm Sat, Sun. **Dinner served** 6-10.30pm Tue-Sun. **Main courses** £14-£21. **Set meal** £20 2 courses, £24 3 courses. **Credit** MC, V.

Entrée, a Modern British, French-influenced bar and restaurant with Antipodean leanings, has proved a winning formula within the Clapham Junction/Battersea Rise nexus of bars and diners. The food has flair and the list of wines available by glass and carafe is remarkably extensive; yet both sit in the shadow of the carefully crafted atmosphere. The focus of activity, and source of considerable volume, is the speakeasy piano bar downstairs. Thus the evening clientele is youthful, or at the very least young enough at heart to feel at home among bare boards, half-naked walls, casual and decidedly hip waiting staff, and bouncing noise. Cocktails are almost de rigueur – we were asked half a dozen times, while perusing the menu, whether we would like 'water or something else' to start. Having resisted, we were nonetheless treated to an amuse-bouche – a well-crafted soup and herb-scented roll. Among an adventurous set of 'entrées', tunnel-boned quail turned out to be a brightly flavoured spatchcock; by contrast, a main course of 35-day aged rump of Cumbrian shorthorn, while markedly tender, was oddly light on flavour (though thrice-cooked crunchy chips and a wonderfully zesty béarnaise soothed any disappointment). For dessert, a chocolate fondant was just as it should be after the statutory 12-minute wait. Such elegance of presentation and taste means that even the not-so-young will leave without feeling short-changed.

La Petite Bretagne

Babies and children admitted weekends. Booking essential Fri, Sat. Dress: smart casual. Separate room for parties, seats 16. **Map 21 C4**.

Waterloo

RSJ

33 Coin Street, SE1 9NR (7928 4554, www.rsj.uk.com). Waterloo tube/rail. **Lunch served** noon-2.30pm Mon-Fri. **Dinner served** 5.30-11pm Mon-Sat. **Main courses** £12-£19. **Set meal** £16.95 2 courses, £19.95 3 courses. **Credit** AmEx, MC, V.

RSJ can appear to occupy a world of its own beside the artsy agglomeration and traffic of the South Bank. Its mellow cosiness seems more akin to somewhere much further upriver: Chiswick, say, or even Henley-on-Thames. The style and softly coloured decor haven't changed for a while, but this is probably how regulars (who rely on the restaurant for relaxed lunches and pre- or post-theatre dinners) like it. Food consistently displays high levels of skill and refinement in preparation and the sourcing of seasonal ingredients. From the excellent-value all-day set menu, a ham hock terrine with piccalilli was lovely, earthily textured and subtly flavoured without a hint of excess acidity; pan-roasted chicken suprême with olive oil mash was not so outstanding, yet still very pleasant. Splash out a bit more on the carte and you'll really see what the kitchen can do, in dishes such as the fresh fish of the day, or a distinguished côte de boeuf. Another special feature is the unique, fabulous wine list, one truly worth exploring. Drawn almost entirely from the Loire Valley, much of it sourced directly from producers, it has been assembled with expert discrimination; prices, by current standards, are a gift.
Available for hire. Babies and children admitted. Booking advisable. **Map 11 N8**.

South East
London Bridge & Borough

Casse-Croûte NEW

109 Bermondsey Street, SE1 3XB (7407 2140, www.cassecroute.co.uk). London Bridge tube/rail. **Meals served** 9am-10pm Mon-Sat; 9am-4pm Sun. **Main courses** £11.50-£14.50. **Credit** MC, V.

With José (*see p228*), Pizarro (*see p229*) and now Casse-Croûte, nifty eateries are blooming along Bermondsey Street like edible flowers. They're a tight-knit family, as the owner here, Hervé Durochat, is also a partner in José and Pizarro. Unlike those establishments, however, Casse-Croûte isn't Spanish, but a shot of warm, villagey France. There are just 20 covers in a room furnished in dark wood and embossed wallpaper, suggesting a patina of age. The place feels genuinely familial – in the opening week, Hervé was greeting customers with the Parisian double kiss. The menu of boldly chosen, smartly executed French classics really delivers. Delicate shavings of calf's head were given zip by a tangy sauce ravigote, while creamy mackerel rillettes were pepped up with mustard ice-cream. To follow, pollock on artichokes was heady with parsley and dill; and guinea fowl two ways – roast breast and slow-cooked dark meat – provided an earthy hit of good-quality game. The desserts were more workmanlike but admirable: punchy peach melba

FRENCH

and intense chocolate gâteau with powerfully minty ice-cream. With the sensible pricing, and a cheese and charcuterie selection planned, *nous reviendrons. Babies and children admitted. Booking essential.* **Map 12 Q9.**

East

Bethnal Green

Bistrotheque [HOT 50]

23-27 Wadeson Street, E2 9DR (8983 7900, www.bistrotheque.com). Bethnal Green tube/ rail or Cambridge Heath rail.
Bar **Open** 5.30pm-midnight Mon-Fri; 11am-midnight Sat; 11am-11pm Sun.
Restaurant **Brunch served** 11am-3.45pm Sat, Sun. **Dinner served** 6.30-10.15pm Mon-Thur, Sun; 6.30-10.45pm Fri, Sat. **Main courses** £13.50-£17.50. **Set dinner** (6.30-7.15pm, 9.45-close) 3 courses.
Both **Credit** AmEx, MC, V.
Head to the first floor of this East End trendsetter for the light, white restaurant and big oval bar (the Manchichi, where walk-ins can eat and good cocktails are mixed). Although the hipster count is high, the welcome and service are friendly, and there's a level of professionalism here that's missing from many local restaurants. The kitchen is capable of highs – duck confit with puy lentils

and mushrooms was a stellar version – but a steady B-plus is more usual. Pricing is variable too – the generous prix fixe is £17.50 for three good-sized courses, while a tiny portion of cured salmon salad with beetroot and horseradish remoulade was £14 (we can't imagine what the £8 size looks like). The menu (and short wine list) is more French-leaning than truly Gallic: a cheeseburger with pancetta and caramelised onions sits alongside onglet with chips and béarnaise sauce, and treacle tart with clotted cream next to crème brûlée. A popular weekend brunch adds the likes of (US-style) pancakes with bacon and maple syrup to the mix. Less welcome at brunch are the 90-minute dining slots, and the tables set uncomfortably close to the piano. Overall, a reliable but fun restaurant that hasn't become complacent.
Babies and children welcome: high chairs. Booking essential Thur-Sun. Entertainment: pianist 11am-4pm Sat, Sun. Separate rooms for parties, seating 20-96.

Brick Lane

★ Chez Elles [NEW]

45 Brick Lane, E1 6PU (7247 9699, www.chezellesbistroquet.co.uk). Aldgate East tube or Shoreditch High Street rail. **Lunch served** noon-3pm Wed-Sat. **Dinner served** 6-10.30pm Tue-Sat. **Brunch served** 11am-5pm

Sun. **Main courses** £11.50-£16.50. **Credit** AmEx, MC, V.
Chez Elles just narrowly misses being a naff parody of itself, saved by fantastic cooking and an unexpected location – somehow, the cutesy Parisian hipster vibe and chanson playlist grates far less on Brick Lane than it would in South Ken or Highgate. Maybe it's because there's no attempt at irony. From the Robert Doisneau prints to the white-painted iron love seat, from the crushed velvet banquettes to the impossibly good-looking staff and the 'is it classic, is it cliché?' menu – they really mean it. There's brunch and daily specials, and coffee and own-made cakes at a counter propping up (French) regulars, and a disarming, heavily accented welcome (the founding members met while working on the Eurostar). The wine list is a map on the wall with arrows to the grape-growing regions, and the main menu is beyond reproach. There was smoky, spicy, peppery charcuterie with lots of bread and salt. There was a circle of plump, soft, nutty snails swimming in garlic butter, better than many you'll get in Paris. There was a straightforwardly delicious onion tart with goat's cheese, and a seriously good, tearingly tender bavette steak with triple-fried chips. Your arteries might recoil, but you'll leave full of joie de vivre.
Available for hire. Babies and children welcome: high chairs. Booking advisable dinner. Vegan dishes. **Map 12 S5.**

Casse-Croûte. See p93.

Shoreditch

Boundary

2-4 Boundary Street, entrance at 9 Redchurch Street, E2 7DD (7729 1051, www.theboundary. co.uk). Shoreditch High Street rail. **Lunch served** noon-3.30pm Sun. **Dinner served** 6.30-10.30pm Mon-Sat. **Main courses** £20-£25. **Set meal** (lunch Sun) £19.50 2 courses, £24.50 3 courses; (dinner) £21.50 2 courses, £25.50 3 courses; £65 tasting menu. **Credit** AmEx, MC, V.

Beneath a Shoreditch street, down a muralled stairwell, are the vaults where restaurant mastermind Sir Terence Conran presents his vision of dining. It's a magnificent space with soaring, bare brick pillars, clever lighting and decor that mixes funky and luxury. Service is unrushed, and cooking – in a trademark open kitchen – is impeccably French. No tricks, no surprises, just superbly done. For a price, mind, and the prix fixe menu wasn't offered unprompted. From this, don't miss the charcuterie trolley with its rillettes, terrine and saucisson, giving as good as the carte. Monkfish with artichokes and broad beans, and duck confit with a sticky reduction, tiny fungi and the smoothest of mashed potatoes, were subtly excellent, as was an amuse-bouche of radishes with goat's butter. The seven-course tasting menu includes greatest hits such as the charcuterie, fish with seasonal veg, and beef fillet with ravioli and wild mushrooms. Though crème brûlée was terrific, more out-there desserts such as peach tarte tatin with thyme ice-cream or mandarin soufflé with roast almond ice-cream provide a sniff of innovation. Otherwise, the Chris Martin and Cara Delevingne lookalikes and expense account holders don't seek out this well-concealed location for experimentation. Or to eavesdrop – tables are very well spaced. The sommelier can help with an awesome list arranged by region; for stronger drinks, there's an over-furnished 1950s-style bar. Six floors up, the Boundary rooftop bar and grill are completely different.

Babies and children welcome: high chairs. Booking advisable dinner. Disabled: lift; toilet. Separate room for parties, seats 18. **Map 6 R4.**

Les Trois Garçons `HOT 50`

1 Club Row, E1 6JX (7613 1924, www.lestrois garcons.com). Shoreditch High Street rail. **Lunch served** noon-2.30pm Thur, Fri. **Dinner served** 6-9.30pm Mon-Thur; 6-10.30pm Fri, Sat. **Main courses** £15-£32.50. **Set lunch** £17.50 2 courses, £22 3 courses. **Set dinner** £66 tasting menu (£100 incl wine), £75 tasting menu (£105 incl wine). **Credit** AmEx, MC, V.

London's most extravagant restaurant interior gives the eye no idea where to settle. Inside this former pub is an entire zoo of stuffed, ceramic and other animals (a lion, a swordfish, an antelope with a tiara…), cascading glass, dangling handbags, giant, unearthly purple flowers and more – all to sustain the mood of ironic, decadent opulence. As a restaurant, Les Trois Garçons has two sides. It buzzes at night, when hip crowds come to enjoy inventive modern French cuisine at lofty prices. But, it also offers a set lunch menu, with similarly refined cooking at far lower cost – an exceptional deal, though one that attracts far fewer people (so much so that the management may drop it, so catch it while you can). A neat amuse bouche (not common in set menus) of horseradish cream on a beetroot

Androuet. See p96.

Oui Madame

chip was followed by a deliciously herby truffle and salt-cod brandade. Succulent beef rump in red wine jus on amaranthus leaves kept up the standard, and the trio of sorbets to finish – champagne, melon, lemon – was chilly perfection. Wines are suitably sophisticated, and service professional and charming. The 3G mini-empire also includes the equally louche Loungelover Bar next door and, most recently, Maison Trois Garçons 'lifestyle café' in nearby Redchurch Street.

Available for hire. Booking essential. Children admitted over 12yrs. Separate room for parties, seats 10. Map 6 S4.

Spitalfields

Androuet

107B Commercial Street, E1 6BG (7375 3168, www.androuet.co.uk). Liverpool Street tube/rail or Shoreditch High Street rail. **Lunch served** noon-2.50pm, **dinner served** 5-10pm Tue, Wed. **Meals served** noon-10pm Thur; noon-10.30pm Fri, Sat; noon-9.30pm Sun. **Main courses** £13.70-£19.50. **Credit** AmEx, MC, V.
Cheese is a pillar of civilisation, as many French gourmets must have said. And Parisian cheese merchant Androuet, in business since 1909, has added to its civilising mission with this London branch, showcasing fine cheeses – British, Italian and others, as well as French – with a likeable joie de vivre. Alongside the shop and its stunning cheese and fine-wine displays, the restaurant/wine bar combines a laid-back terrace on Spitalfields Market and a smaller interior, with a little belle époque grandeur provided by a glittering chandelier. Cheesy specialities are naturally highlights – two kinds of fondue, raclette and a

wonderful tartiflette (potatoes, bacon, onions and herbs baked in reblochon) with every texture and flavour just right, making it superb comfort food. Alternatively, you can try the impressive Androuet cheeseburger, or dally over constructing your own cheese-and-charcuterie board. Not everything is so cheesy – there's also a changing range of mains, salads, sandwiches and starters, such as a delightfully delicate chilled summer pea soup with (OK, slightly cheesy) goat's milk yoghurt. The wine list is almost as impressive as the cheese, and for once in London is very decently priced; charming, helpful service is in tone with the whole enterprise. The only problem could be that Androuet outgrows its small space.

Babies and children welcome: high chairs. Booking essential. Separate room for parties, seats 17. Tables outdoors (10, terrace). Map 12 R5.

North East
Hackney

Bouchon Fourchette [NEW]

171 Mare Street, E8 3RH (8986 2702, www.bouchonfourchette.co.uk). Hackney Central or London Fields rail. **Meals served** 5-10pm Mon; 9am-10pm Tue-Thur, Sun; 9am-11pm Fri, Sat. **Main courses** £8-£12. **Credit** AmEx, MC, V.
Sourdough pizza places, craft beer pubs and organic cafés are ten a penny in Hackney these days, but French-style bistro-cum-cafés? Nope. Here you'll find baskets filled with crusty baguettes and a sprinkling of other elements befitting a French

eaterie, but the overall vibe is decidedly East End thanks to exposed brickwork and second-hand tables. By day, there's a handful of simple café dishes to choose from: omelettes, croque monsieurs, gratins. By night, a roll-call of keenly priced classics takes over, such as snails steeped in garlic butter, coq au vin or a generous heap of rillettes with cornichons and sourdough toast. When it comes to that other mainstay of the inexpensive French restaurant, steak-frites, there's a huge difference between a good rendition and a bad one, and here it was underwhelming. Chunky chips were no better than the quality of bought-in versions, while the steak, though cooked à point, was underseasoned. Never mind: a rich crème caramel with just the right balance in the bitter and sweet sauce put things back on track.

Available for hire. Babies and children welcome: high chairs. Booking advisable Fri, Sat. Disabled: toilet. Tables outdoors (2, pavement). Takeaway service.

Stoke Newington

Oui Madame [NEW]

182 Stoke Newington Road, N16 7UY (07739 798566, http://oui-madame.joopp.com). Dalston Junction, Dalston Kingsland or Stoke Newington rail. **Dinner served** 6pm-midnight Mon-Wed; 6pm-1am Thur; 6pm-2am Fri, Sat. **Meals served** noon-10pm Sun. **Main courses** £6.50-£15. **Set dinner** £23 3 courses. **Credit** MC, V.
There's a French revolution sweeping our restaurant scene – grand Paris-style brasseries seem to be the flavour of the season in London's West End. But this little place on Stoke Newington Road is anything but grand; it's like one of those

casually hip places you might find in a less touristy bit of Paris where you sit drinking tumblers of house wine until it closes at an indeterminate hour. There's a £23 three-course set menu, limited in choice, enticing in description and restricted entirely to a single blackboard propped up helpfully next to your table. On it is listed the likes of pork confit terrine or salad with leaves foraged from Hackney Marshes. A further menu of small plates lets you pick and choose – maybe ginger-marinated salmon, a superior charcuterie plate or fennel and courgette 'carpaccio' with parmesan. They're all delightful, as no doubt are the many absinthes, which are best saved for a late-night visit (last orders are at midnight). In keeping with the Parisian feel, downstairs is a dim little cabaret space, where at weekends slightly rude acts perform in various states of dress. There's nothing else like this in Stoke Newington, and not much else like it in London – we say 'oui'.
Available for hire. Babies and children welcome. Separate room for parties, seats 40. Tables outdoors (8, terrace). **Map 25 C3.**

Wanstead

★ Provender
17 High Street, E11 2AA (8530 3050, www.provenderlondon.co.uk). Snaresbrook tube. **Breakfast served** 9.30-11.45am Sat, Sun. **Meals served** noon-9.30pm Mon-Thur; noon-10pm Fri, Sat; noon-5pm Sun. **Main courses** £9-£20. **Set meal** (Mon-Thur; noon-5.45pm Fri, Sat) £10.75 2 courses, £14.75 3 courses. **Credit** AmEx, MC, V.
When a brisk 'have you booked?' on a midweek night causes minor panic, a restaurant is getting it right. This modish bistro in a leafy suburb is packing 'em in with its take on the Gallic greats served brasserie hours. From breakfast to lunch deals and set menus, the carte encompasses everything from croque monsieur to charcuterie and rillettes, oysters and cassoulet, salads and grills presented in handsome 1930s style. For a selection of great starters, mix keenly priced casse-croûtes such as grass-green tapenade, radishes and aïoli with pricier entrées like stuffed mussels. If they took a while to arrive, it's because celeriac was being freshly grated into an elegant tangle for the remoulade, and slices of skinny baguette were being toasted to accompany spiced aubergine paired with a perky red pepper relish in imam biyaldi. From the linen tea-towel napkins to the potato and rosemary bun with the burger, the ordinary is improved on, and conviction shines through in the best of British and French ingredients: Blythburgh pork and ham, Welsh mussels, Boulogne herrings, Normandy butter. Mains came with a warning about hot plates. Steak-frites may be a speciality, but vegetarians shouldn't feel hard done by. Griddled asparagus, mushroom duxelles in puff pastry with hollandaise and a perfectly boiled egg with dazzlingly golden yolk was a gloriously rewarding dish. Meringue with passionfruit and coconut ice-cream made a triumphant ending. The all-French wine list kicks off with aperitifs and ends with Monbazillac. Don't leave it to chance. Book.
Available for hire. Babies and children welcome: children's menu; crayons; high chairs; nappy-changing facilities. Booking essential weekends. Disabled: toilet. Separate room for parties, seats 30. Tables outdoors (8, pavement).

North
Camden Town & Chalk Farm

L'Absinthe
40 Chalcot Road, NW1 8LS (7483 4848, www.labsinthe.co.uk). Chalk Farm tube. **Lunch served** noon-3pm Mon-Fri; noon-4pm Sat, Sun. **Dinner served** 6-10.30pm Mon-Sat; 6-9.30pm Sun. **Main courses** £9.95-£18. **Credit** AmEx, MC, V.
There's no piped music at L'Absinthe, but no need, as jaunty Gallic accordion tunes may start floating round your head anyway. In a placid part of Primrose Hill, it reproduces the feel of a classic French corner bistro as unerringly as a scene from *Amélie*: from the signs on windows to the snug tables and unfussily retro decor. Service is smiley and full of charm, and the cosily welcoming ambience draws in tablefuls of appreciative regulars. Menus feature suitably classic French comfort food – salade niçoise, fish soup, hachis parmentier, steaks, croque monsieur for lunch – in generous portions at generous prices. Dishes are reliably appealing, if sometimes over-rich. Pea soup and a lyonnaise salad with plenty of bacon lardons hit all the right notes as starters, and suprême of chicken with creamy tarragon sauce was very pleasant. So too was a properly traditional – if slightly heavy – duck confit with powerfully rich thyme jus. Desserts included a very smooth and large crème brûlée. Lunch menus are especially good value, and the attached wine shop provides an excellent list including a house red – Petit Mas – that's a robust snip at under £17.
Babies and children welcome: high chairs. Booking advisable weekends. Separate room for parties, seats 24. Tables outdoors (5, pavement). **Map 27 B2.**

Highgate

Côte
2 Highgate High Street, N6 5JL (8348 9107, www.cote-restaurants.co.uk). Archway tube. **Meals served** 8am-11pm Mon-Fri; 9am-11pm Sat; 9am-10.30pm Sun. **Main courses** £8.95-£17.95. **Set meal** (noon-7pm Mon-Fri) £9.95 2 courses, £11.95 3 courses. **Credit** AmEx, MC, V.
Restaurant chains find it notoriously hard to sustain standards as they grow. Plenty have begun well but become routine and listless, which makes the consistency that has won Côte its popularity all the more admirable. Their carefully chosen locales are airy and spacious, with decor that evokes a Parisian bistro look without fussy knick-knackery. Generalising about service in chains is especially rocky, but at every Côte we've visited staff have been attentive and concerned, belying any preconceptions about chain-anonymity. While family-friendly they also have the feel of a 'proper restaurant', and menus cover a canny range of options for varied publics: from light lunches and kid-friendly choices to more substantial, leisurely meals. There's nothing adventurous here, but reliably enjoyable French-based cooking, such as chargrilled breton chicken, or a special of the day, boudin noir with poached egg and caramelised apples. A meal is also very good value – despite some cheeky extra charges, such as £1.10 for a pat of garlic butter – and even more so if you opt for the lunch and pre-7pm set

menu, in Highgate a big hit with pensioners. Wines, similarly, include a choice of decent bottles for under £20: exceptional, nowadays.
Babies and children welcome: children's menu; high chairs; nappy-changing facilities. Booking advisable. Disabled: toilet. Tables outdoors (15, terrace).
For branches see index.

Islington

Almeida
30 Almeida Street, N1 1AD (7354 4777, www.almeida-restaurant.co.uk). Angel tube or Highbury & Islington tube/rail. **Lunch served** noon-2.15pm Tue-Sun. **Dinner served** 5.30-10.15pm Mon-Sat. **Main courses** £18-£22. **Set meal** (lunch Tue-Sun; 5.30-6.30pm, 9.30-10.30pm Mon-Sat) £17 2 courses, £20 3 courses. **Credit** AmEx, MC, V.
The route between the Almeida theatre over the road and this D&D London restaurant is a well-trodden one: visit of an evening and there's an exodus before curtain-up. The pre-theatre menu here, then, is often just that – and is excellent value at £17 for two courses, £20 for three. Those without a show to rush to can take more time over the sophisticated cooking, which is broadly modern French with a few excursions around Europe and Britain. On our last visit, Cornish pollock was paired with golden sultana and cauliflower couscous, and a risotto was rich with wild mushrooms and parmesan; both were from the set menu and served beautifully in glazed pottery dishes. Such thoughtful touches set the standard high – crisp water biscuits with the cheese were seeded and clearly own-made; the charcuterie board is a rustic plank of rillettes, terrines and scotch eggs, all produced in-house. The open kitchen looks on to a discreetly elegant, modern room enlivened by a vast, colourful mural and broadsided by a small bar with its own food menu. As a special-occasion alternative to the many restaurants in Islington, Almeida is a star.
Babies and children welcome: children's menu; high chairs; nappy-changing facilities. Booking advisable. Disabled: toilet. Separate rooms for parties, seating 10 and 18. Tables outdoors (8, pavement). Vegetarian menu. **Map 5 O1.**

North West
St John's Wood

L'Aventure
3 Blenheim Terrace, NW8 0EH (7624 6232, www.laventure.co.uk). St John's Wood tube or bus 139, 189. **Lunch served** 12.30-2.30pm Mon-Fri. **Dinner served** 7-11pm Mon-Sat. **Set lunch** £18.50 2 courses, £21.50 3 courses. **Set dinner** £31 2 courses, £39.50 3 courses. **Credit** AmEx, MC, V.
Everything about this elegant neighbourhood restaurant, from the classic handwritten menu to the Gallic service team and doorstopper of a wine list, flies the flag for all things French. There's a leafy terrace outside to recreate memories of holidays past; while indoors, tapestries, wood panelling and crisp white napery make for a smarter look. Reassuringly, bonhomie between staff and customers warms up the atmosphere. Cooking isn't always first-class; highlights included a first course of sliced scallops and plump mussels

cooked to perfection and sauced with a splendid saffron cream. Less dramatic, but just as tasty, pastel-hued hot pea soup delivered plenty of garden-fresh summery notes. Main courses were disappointing, though – pot-roasted chicken breast was too dry and the sautéed mushroom accompaniment uninspired. Similarly, roast duck breast was overcooked and the broad bean garnish and herby new potatoes couldn't rescue it from mediocrity. It took a jiffy to polish off the creamy crème anglaise from the île flottante, but the poached meringue had a discordantly salty flavour. Despite these occasional culinary misgivings, L'Aventure makes for a scenic setting and the service is spot-on.

Provender. See p97.

Available for hire. Babies and children admitted: high chairs. Booking advisable dinner. Tables outdoors (6, terrace). **Map 1 C2**.

Outer London
Richmond, Surrey

Chez Lindsay
11 Hill Rise, Richmond, Surrey, TW10 6UQ (8948 7473, www.chezlindsay.co.uk). Richmond tube/rail.
Crêperie Meals served 11am-10.45pm Mon-Sat; noon-10pm Sun. **Main courses** £3.95-£11.50.

Restaurant **Meals served** noon-10.45pm Mon-Sat; noon-10pm Sun. **Main courses** £10.75-£25. **Set meal** (noon-7pm Mon-Fri) £12.75 2 courses, £15.75 3 courses; (noon-7pm Sat, Sun) £23.75 2 courses, £27.75 3 courses.
Both **Credit** AmEx, MC, V.
The enduring appeal of this outpost of Brittany is easy to understand: an endearingly chaotic informality; a spacious yet homely wood- and wicker-clad dining area populated by couples, families and parties of friends; authentic regional cuisine served with Gallic charm; a flexible menu and cider/wine list. And a terrific riverside view at the back. On our last visit, we were greeted with an apologetic explanation of a menu substitution; walnuts were missing from the baked goat's cheese salad; and the menus were falling apart despite their duct tape plasters. But it somehow didn't matter a jot. Better-than-competent execution of both Breton and classic bistro dishes was punctuated with friendly chat about the exact composition of the Yermatt cocktail and the 'real' way of drinking Breton cider (from earthenware pichets, served in rustic bowls). The precision of the saucing (cider beurre blanc, tarragon-scented béarnaise, sweet caramel) and of the puff pastry and galettes justifies the prices – which can mount up. Finish with an apple and caramel crêpe, complete with calvados flambé.
Babies and children welcome: high chairs. Booking advisable weekends. Separate room for parties, seats 25.

Twickenham, Middlesex

Brula
43 Crown Road, Twickenham, Middlesex, TW1 3EJ (8892 0602, www.brula.co.uk). St Margarets rail. **Lunch served** noon-3pm Tue-Sun. **Dinner served** 6-10.30pm Tue-Sat. **Main courses** £16.50-£25.50. **Set lunch** £18 2 courses, £21.50 3 courses. **Set dinner** £27.50 3 courses. **Credit** AmEx, MC, V.
Conscious perhaps that even much loved establishments need to refresh a well-worn image, Brula was in the middle of an update on our visit: nothing so drastic as to lessen the Parisian brasserie feel of stained glass and frosted lace-effect windows, bentwood chairs and crisp napery; rather, a little lightening and brightening. A summery salad of heirloom tomatoes punctuated by crunchy white grelot onions and flecks of goat's cheese seemed all the more apt in the cheerier setting. More evidence of careful sourcing came in two dishes featuring Berkshire lamb: a deeply flavourful shoulder roast and crunchy breast confit melded French flavours with British produce to sound effect. Vegetables too are given their due – just-so charred gem lettuce, creamy dauphinoise, resonant artichoke purée – and there's even a vegetarian menu. A slight busy-ness muddies the effect at times: both artichoke chips and roast hazelnuts seemed an unnecessary intrusion in the lamb breast salad. A faultless, unadorned crème brûlée restored faith. As part of the revamp, a brasserie-style menu is available (9am-5pm Tue-Sat) alongside the main menu, offering pastries and savoury bites (quiche, charcuterie, salads). The extensive wine list with its collection of gems from south-west France deserves mention, as does the evident enthusiasm of the owner.
Available for hire. Babies and children welcome: high chairs. Booking advisable. Separate room for parties, seats 26. Vegetarian menu.

Gastropubs

'Is any pub in the capital not a gastropub?' you might ask. Such has been the transformation of the London boozer over the past 20 years, you're now dangerously likely to have to navigate waiting staff with platefuls of pork belly as you head to the bar for a pint of wallop – anywhere from Walthamstow to Wimbledon. The revolution has mirrored that of the London restaurant scene in general, with gastropubs being at the forefront of some food fashions. In the 1990s, fusion cooking took hold in many hostelries, with (sometimes wild) experiments being conducted on unsuspecting diners; and 'Thai-in-a-pub' still remains a notable sub-section of the genre (the basement karaoke room of the Heron, off Edgware Road, *see p243*, holds one of our favourite Thai venues).

The gastropub formula still has great pulling power. Top-flight chefs have got in on the act: Gordon Ramsay with the **Narrow**; the Ledbury's Brett Graham with his Michelin-starred **Harwood Arms**; and Claude Bosi (of haute-cuisine Hibiscus fame) has recently opened a second gastropub, the **Malt House** in Fulham. Other newcomers bringing new angles continue to arrive, such as barbecue specialist the **Smokehouse** in Islington. Some of the most successful operations have tried to replicate themselves by converting other pubs – giving rise to mini and not-so-mini chains such as the ETM Group (*see p106*).

To our minds, though, the best gastropubs haven't forgotten their origins, and two of our top choices this time remain great places for drinking, as well as eating: the **Anchor & Hope** in Waterloo and its sibling, the **Canton Arms** in Stockwell.

Central
Bloomsbury

Lady Ottoline
11A Northington Street, WC1N 2JF (7831 0008, www.theladyottoline.com). Chancery Lane or Russell Square tube. **Open** noon-11.30pm Mon-Sat; noon-10pm Sun. **Lunch served** noon-3pm Mon-Fri; noon-4pm Sat. **Dinner served** 6.30-10.30pm Mon-Sat. **Meals served** noon-8pm Sun. **Main courses** £10.95-£24. **Credit** MC, V.

This upmarket gastropub is part of the small Noble Inns stable, which includes the Princess of Shoreditch and the Pig & Butcher in Islington. All have a commitment to drink as well as food, with space given over to drinkers and a selection that runs from cocktails and real ales (four on rotation at any one time) to a thoughtful wine list. Food is served in the ground-floor bar at the Lady Ottoline, but for a more sedate meal, it's best to dine in the pleasant first-floor room. The menu is a bit more adventurous than most gastropubs – witness a starter of braised lamb's tongue, sweetbreads and sheep's curd – and ingredients are carefully sourced. Grilled sardines (a special) were fabulously fresh; also excellent was a creamy rabbit pie with toothsome pastry, and a robust starter of ham hock ballotine. A side of chicory and pomegranate salad was worth every penny of its £3.50 price tag. Less compelling was fish cake with poached egg, béarnaise and fennel salad. The kitchen can turn out quality puddings too, in this case marinated blood orange with white chocolate, and vanilla panna cotta with mulled figs. The latest addition to the group is barbecue specialist the Smokehouse in Islington.
Babies and children welcome until 6pm: high chairs. Booking advisable lunch; dinner Thur, Fri. Separate rooms for parties, seating 16 and 60. Tables outdoors (3, pavement).
Map 4 M4.
For branches (Pig & Butcher, Princess of Shoreditch) see index.

Norfolk Arms
28 Leigh Street, WC1H 9EP (7388 3937, www.norfolkarms.co.uk). Euston tube/rail. **Open** 11am-11pm Mon-Sat; noon-10.30pm Sun. **Lunch served** noon-3pm Mon-Fri; noon-4pm Sat. **Dinner served** 6-10.15pm Mon-Sat. **Meals served** noon-10.15pm Sun. **Tapas served** noon-10.15pm daily. **Main courses** £9.50-£13. **Tapas** £2-£12. **Credit** AmEx, MC, V.

'This is the most exciting opening in the vicinity in recent times.' You wouldn't know it as no date is given, but the 2006 *Time Out* quote adorning the front page of the Norfolk Arms website celebrated its seventh birthday in 2013. From E1 to W1, London is full of bars and restaurants that have been coasting for ages on the back of a good review received years earlier. Happily, the Norfolk Arms isn't one of them; although 2006 no longer qualifies as 'recent times', this smaller-than-it-looks corner pub retains its place among the best in the area. Unusually, the speciality is tapas – and pretty authentic tapas at that. The menu is worryingly long, but the kitchen seems to be on top of things. Highlights – all served in very generous portions given the reasonable prices (few of the standard tapas cost more than £5.50) – included a casually creamy tortilla; fennel and blood orange salad with flaked almonds; and deliciously light salt cod and potato croquettes. Only a slightly faded serving of pork belly with paprika struck a bum note in what was otherwise an impressive, enjoyable meal. Staff seem to give priority to diners over drinkers, and few people seem to come here for libations (draught Sagres, Theakston's XB) alone.

Available for hire. Babies and children admitted: high chairs. Booking advisable. Separate rooms for parties, seating 10 and 20. Tables outdoors (9, pavement). Map 4 L3.
For branches (Fat of the Land, Queen's Head & Artichoke) see index.

Clerkenwell & Farringdon

★ **Eagle** [HOT 50]
159 Farringdon Road, EC1R 3AL (7837 1353). Farringdon tube/rail. **Open** noon-11pm Mon-Sat; noon-5pm Sun. **Lunch served** 12.30-3pm Mon-Fri; 12.30-3.30pm Sat; 12.30-4pm Sun. **Dinner served** 6.30-10.30pm Mon-Sat. **Main courses** £5.10-£15. **Credit** MC, V.
Widely credited with launching the food-in-pubs revolution when it opened in its current form in 1991, the Eagle has long since passed into both legend and middle age. Still, if some of the kids it inadvertently spawned put half as much effort into their food as the Eagle, 'gastropub' might not have become such a dirty word – this high-ceilinged corner room remains a cut above the competition. Nothing's changed since last you were here: the globetrotting mains are still chalked twice daily above the bar/open kitchen; the service is still peerless (especially during lunch, when the place is humming); and the tables remain slightly too close together. You can just drink but few do, aware they're missing the big-flavoured likes of moreish tomato and bread soup; daisy-fresh scallops, panfried and served on toast with chorizo; and succulent leg of lamb with jansson's temptation (a potato gratin-style Swedish dish). The weakness remains the beers: if you don't get lucky with a guest (we did, with Hackney Brewery's creditable American Pale Ale), you'll be stuck with some familiar lagers and Charles Wells' perennially disappointing ales. Otherwise, perfect.
Babies and children admitted. Bookings not accepted. Tables outdoors (4, pavement). Map 5 N4.

Pimlico

Orange Public House & Hotel
37 Pimlico Road, SW1W 8NE (7881 9844, www.theorange.co.uk). Sloane Square tube. **Open** 8am-11.30pm Mon-Thur; 8am-midnight Fri, Sat; 8am-10.30pm Sun. **Breakfast served** 8am-11.30am daily. **Meals served** noon-10pm Mon-Sat; noon-9.30pm Sun. **Main courses** £12.50-£16.50. **Credit** AmEx, MC, V.
This smart gastropub with rooms is a perfect match for this exclusive corner of Pimlico, and attracts a well-heeled crowd. If the ground-floor bar and dining room is packed out, make your way to the quieter first floor. The decor has a deliberately weathered look (think distressed walls, 'aged' wooden tables and flooring, vintage French travel posters) – the effect is appealing, if a little forced. British ingredients have pride of place on the menu, so you'll find Bath Pig chorizo, Anglesey farmed sea bass and Cornish new potatoes. Yellow, red and pink heritage beetroots with salsify and a dollop of goat's curd resembled a summer garden on a plate. Wood-fired pizza with creative toppings are a speciality; Laverstoke buffalo mozzarella was used to good effect alongside confit yellowfin tuna, prawns, capers and tomato. Translucent (line-caught) cod atop chewy puy lentils and creamy mash was stirred into life by a velvety Madeira jus. Desserts (the likes of coffee panna cotta and sticky toffee pud) all cost £7. To drink, there are cocktails, fresh fruit juices, more than a dozen wines by the glass, and Adnams and Meantime beers on tap. Service is breezy.
The Orange is part of the Cubitt House Group of upmarket gastropubs in swanky parts of town: not far away, in Belgravia, are the Pantechnicon and the Thomas Cubitt; and there's also the Grazing Goat (also a hotel) in Marylebone.
Available for hire. Babies and children welcome: high chairs; nappy-changing facilities. Booking advisable. Disabled: toilet. Separate rooms for parties, seating up to 75. Tables outdoors (5, pavement). Map 15 G11.
For branches (Grazing Goat, Thomas Cubitt, Pantechnicon) see index.

West

Chiswick

Duke of Sussex
75 South Parade, W4 5LF (8742 8801, www.thedukeofsussex.co.uk). Chiswick Park tube. **Open** noon-11pm Mon-Thur, Sun; noon-11.30pm Fri, Sat. **Meals served** noon-10.30pm Mon-Sat; noon-9.30pm Sun. **Main courses** £11-£17.50. **Credit** AmEx, MC, V.
Overlooking Acton Green and with a substantial beer garden at the rear, the Duke of Sussex is a handsome 1890s Victorian boozer that was given a thorough gastrofication in 2007. Now owned by its then operators, Real Pubs, it has lasted well. The pub side is lively and serves good beer (including Dark Star's smokily sweet-bitter Art of Darkness and Triple fff's Rock Lobster), but it's the beautiful restaurant room that really stands out, almost the whole ceiling forming a giant 'skylight' – with cherubs to acknowledge its loftiness. The menu majors in Spanish cuisine, with a good range of tapas and more substantial dishes, usually with twists on the familiar – such as the quince aïoli that accompanied a pork chop, which had a properly unctuous thick fat layer and came with garlicky sliced potatoes 'a lo pobre'. Other highlights were the cheeseboard (manchego, sure, but also a smoky Basque idiazabal and picos de europa blue), coming with a Kilner jar of crackers and membrillo. The menu also has some non-Spanish pub favourites –

Orange Public House & Hotel

rib of beef and chips, pies, black pudding hash cake under an egg – but there seems little point in wandering far from the Iberian peninsula. *Babies and children welcome until 5pm: high chairs; nappy-changing facilities. Booking advisable dinner. Disabled: toilet. Tables outdoors (37, back garden; 3, front garden).* **For branches (Real Pubs) see index.**

Hammersmith

Hampshire Hog
227 King Street, W6 9JT (8748 3391, www.thehampshirehog.com). Ravenscourt Park or Hammersmith tube. **Open** 8am-11pm Mon-Fri; 9am-11pm Sat, Sun. **Breakfast served** 8am-noon Mon-Fri; 9am-noon Sat, Sun. **Lunch served** noon-4pm Mon-Fri; 12.30-4pm Sat, Sun. **Dinner served** 6-10.30pm Mon-Sat; 6-10pm Sun. **Main courses** £12-£22. **Credit** MC, V.
The Hampshire Hog in Hammersmith sounds like the start of a tortuous tongue-twister, but it's actually a 'pub and pantry', run by the team who put the Engineer gastropub in Primrose Hill on the map. Spacious and bright, with white walls, fancy mirrors and distressed furniture, it's an attractive place. Drinkers congregate at the front, diners at the back, next to the best feature: a large, partially shaded terrace and garden (though the rows of outdoor tables suggest it must get uncomfortably packed in good weather). The menu is more restaurant than pub, with Asian and Middle Eastern touches as well as standard gastro fare (gnocchi, ribeye and chips). Generous portions and plentiful (good) bread mean you won't go hungry. However, all our dishes were lacklustre, from the vegetarian sharing board with its limp tempura tofu and dried-out crudités to a special of overcooked stuffed chicken breast. Pork neck stuffed with apricot and tarragon was tender but lacked flavour, and dull vegetable purées popped up everywhere. The wine list offers plenty of choice by the glass, carafe and bottle, but beer drinkers won't be impressed. Service was well meaning if gauche. *Available for hire. Babies and children welcome: high chairs; nappy-changing facilities. Booking advisable. Disabled: toilet. Separate room for parties, seats 25. Tables outdoors (32, garden).* **Map 20 A4.**

Maida Vale

Truscott Arms NEW
55 Shirland Road, W9 2JD (7266 9198, www.thetruscottarms.com). Warwick Avenue tube.
Bar **Open** 10am-11pm Mon-Thur; 10am-midnight Fri, Sat; 10am-10.30pm Sun. **Meals served** noon-9pm Mon-Thur; noon-9.30pm Fri, Sat; noon-8.30pm Sun. **Main courses** £10-£12. *Restaurant* **Lunch served** noon-4pm, **dinner served** 6-9.30pm Tue-Fri. **Brunch served** 10am-1pm Sat, Sun. **Meals served** noon-9.30pm Sat; noon-8.30pm Sun. **Main courses** £14-£25. *Both* **Credit** MC, V.
Here's a handsome old devil who's scrubbed up well. A Victorian pub with high ceilings and big windows, the former Idlewild bar has recently been stripped back to a more spartan look with plenty of natural light, and has reverted to its original name. The ground-floor bar holds some commendable local draught and bottled ales: Redemption's Pale Ale, for example, or Camden Brewery beers. The first-floor dining room looks

Truscott Arms

smart and spacious, and the service was professional and smiling. Yet the menu sends mixed messages. A wagyu burger in brioche bun was merely adequate, the chunky chips crisp; but we're not convinced it was worth the extra fiver to have a few slivers of bone marrow added – £19 is a lot for a burger. Braised lamb belly was rather tough and fatty. The best main course was the simplest: cod grilled on a hotplate, with cockles, baby artichokes and cauliflower purée. Desserts were also patchy; a panna cotta was set too hard. The Truscott is a fine pub with a good attitude, but the dining room is pricey for this standard of cooking. In its favour, it still seems relatively undiscovered, and serves great coffee and bar snacks all day. *Available for hire. Babies and children welcome: children's menu; high chairs; nappy-changing facilities. Booking advisable. Separate room for parties, seats 60. Tables outdoors (13, garden).* **Map 1 C4.**

Shepherd's Bush

Princess Victoria
217 Uxbridge Road, W12 9DH (8749 5886, www.princessvictoria.co.uk). Shepherd's Bush tube. **Open** 11.30am-11pm Mon-Thur; 11.30am-midnight Fri, Sat; 11.30am-10.30pm Sun. **Lunch served** noon-3pm Mon-Sat; noon-4.30pm Sun. **Dinner served** 6.30-10.30pm Mon-Sat; 6.30-

9.30pm Sun. **Main courses** £10.50-£16.50. **Set lunch** (Mon-Fri) £12.50 2 courses, £15 3 courses. **Credit** MC, V.
We'll return to the Vicky time and again for its scotch eggs. Rolled from seasoned Middle White mince, they arrive crisp-shelled from the fryer and sliced in half to reveal a perfectly runny yolk. You could happily spend an evening knocking these back at the curving bar, along with the occasional helping of beef scrumpet and fine pints of bitter, but it would be a shame to miss out on the old-school dining room at the back. Lit by candelabra and ornately decorated skylights, it is equipped with heavy wooden furniture, gilt-edged portraits and gleaming mirrors: a reassuringly 19th-century combination that puts you in the mood for comfort eating. We enjoyed a stack of pan-fried polenta with a puck of goat's cheese and some sweet roasted peppers. Steak and kidney pie came with fluffy mashed potatoes, while slivers of exquisite rare roast beef (a Sunday special) were matched with buttered carrots and a towering yorkshire pud. The atmosphere round the bar was so pleasant that we stopped for one last drink before leaving. And, a couple of hours later, it felt rude not to give the scotch eggs a final whirl…
Babies and children welcome: high chairs. Booking advisable. Separate room for parties, seats 60. Tables outdoors (10, garden). **Map 20 A2.**

Harwood Arms

Westbourne Park

Cow

89 Westbourne Park Road, W2 5QH (7221 0021, www.thecowlondon.co.uk). Royal Oak or Westbourne Park tube. **Open** noon-11pm Mon-Sat; noon-10.30pm Sun. **Lunch served** noon-3.30pm, **dinner served** 6-10.30pm Mon-Fri. **Meals served** noon-10.30pm Sat; noon-10pm Sun. **Main courses** £10-£22. **Set lunch** (Sun) £22 2 courses, £26 3 courses. **Credit** MC, V.

Owner Tom Conran was a gastropub pioneer, and the Cow continues to serve fine, pricey, fish-oriented food in its upstairs restaurant. Eating in the smallish downstairs bar is a different proposition: seating is pub-style (small round tables, banquettes and stools); the short menu is chalked on a blackboard; and no reservations are taken. It's unpretentious, down to the anti-decor red lino and the yellowing ceiling, with drinkers at the front putting away well-poured Guinness and a good selection of Belgian and other beers, while diners at the back enjoy some fine food and a boho west London vibe. Again, seafood takes centre stage, with oysters, whelks and winkles, and prawns by the pint. Tiger prawns, for a starter, were big and juicy, served in an unashamedly rich sauce. But the star attraction was fish stew with rouille and croûtons: mussels, salmon, little bits of fish in batter, all packed into a heavily flavoured, dark, dense and soupy sauce, dotted with little flakes of chilli (the rouille also packed some chilli heat) – a sumptuous version of a classic. Tagliolini with crab, tomato and chilli was also a winner: a generous amount of crabmeat, subtly warm with chilli, served with pasta cooked precisely al dente. The likes of steak and sausages round out the bar menu. Staff were charming.

Available for hire. Babies and children admitted bar (until 4pm); restaurant. Tables outdoors (2, pavement). **Map 7 A5.**

South West

Barnes

Brown Dog

28 Cross Street, SW13 0AP (8392 2200, www.thebrowndog.co.uk). Barnes Bridge rail. **Open** noon-11pm daily. **Lunch served** noon-3pm Mon-Fri; noon-4pm Sat, Sun. **Dinner served** 7-10pm Mon-Sat; 6-9pm Sun. **Main courses** £13.95-£18. **Credit** AmEx, MC, V.

Little changes at this gastropub in the backstreets of Barnes, from the cordial welcome to the pleasing decor to the well-judged menu. Chunky wooden tables and green leather banquette seating, stripped floorboards and cream panelling provide an upmarket yet friendly look; big windows make it bright by day, while copper globe lights and a polished red ceiling give a cosy glow at night. At the back is a sunny courtyard. There are two real ales and a decent wine list, but most customers are here to dine. Simplicity is key to the shortish menu, which makes a virtue out of unfussy seasonal dishes that require minimal preparation and have wide appeal. So you'll find oysters, a half pint of prawns, dressed crab, steaks and straightforward fish dishes, with plenty of salads and chips. A succulent burger with fluffy chips, and leek and mushroom pie with smooth mash and crisp french beans – both hit the spot. Puds combine comfort and richness to pleasing effect, encompassing chocolate, seasonal fruit and top-notch ice-creams.

If you're in the West End, consider sister pub the Duke of Wellington in Marylebone. Design and vibe are similar to the Brown Dog's, but turned up a notch, so the upstairs restaurant sports white tablecloths and a fancier menu.

Babies and children welcome: high chairs; nappy-changing facilities. Booking advisable. Tables outdoors (12, garden). Vegetarian menu.

For branch (Duke of Wellington) see index.

Chelsea

Pig's Ear

35 Old Church Street, SW3 5BS (7352 2908, www.thepigsear.info). Sloane Square tube then bus 19, 22 or 319. **Open** noon-11pm Mon-Sat; noon-10.30pm Sun. **Lunch served** 12.30-3pm, **dinner served** 6-10pm Mon-Fri. **Meals served** noon-10pm Sat; noon-9pm Sun. **Main courses** £10-£22. **Credit** AmEx, MC, V.

Another year passes, and this Chelsea gastropub's decor equivalent of a mid-life crisis seemingly continues. Range Rovers line the quiet street it occupies off the King's Road, their blazer-clad owners propping up the bar. But the walls are bedecked with a scattering of retro bloke-ish furnishings, including a framed can of bitter, an *Evening Standard* billboard announcing George Best's death and posters harking back to the area's 1970s punk heyday, including a massive promo cartoon for the Sex Pistols' 'Holidays in the Sun'. Our Sunday afternoon visit saw a clientele of well-heeled twentysomethings, middle-aged couples and yummy mummies with squealing infants, all tucking into hearty if variable pub fare. Smoked salmon cannelloni on carrot purée was a thick finger of fish sitting atop an alarmingly yellow paste, but pork roast loin was far more successful – two thick slices of pork with light, delicate crackling and generously crusted roast potatoes. Real ales (from Sambrook's of Battersea, plus guest appearances from the likes of Cardiff's Brains) and Symonds cider are lapped up by the Chelsea crowd, who also enjoy indulging in the pub's selection of battered board games. It looks like this haven for middle-aged pursuits isn't at risk of running out of fans any time soon.

Babies and children admitted. Booking advisable dining room. Separate room for parties, seats 40. **Map 14 E12.**

Fulham

Harwood Arms

Corner of Walham Grove and Farm Lane, SW6 1QP (7386 1847, www.harwoodarms. com). Fulham Broadway tube. **Open/snacks served** 5-11pm Mon; noon-11pm Tue-Fri; noon-midnight Sat; noon-10pm Sun. **Lunch served** 12.30-3pm Tue-Fri; 12.30-4pm Sat, Sun. **Dinner served** 6.30-9.30pm Mon-Sat; 7-9pm Sun. **Main courses** £19-£22. **Set lunch** (Tue-Fri) £20 2 courses, £25 3 courses. **Credit** AmEx, MC, V.

The Harwood Arms looks like a pub (albeit an upmarket one) with its large windows, cream walls, green panelling, widely spaced scrubbed tables and bar counter offering a couple of real ales on tap – but, really, it's a restaurant. And a much sought-after one at that, so expect to book, provide credit card details and be given a two-hour time slot. Prime British produce is key, with a mounted deer's head reminding diners that game is a speciality (vegetarians take note: there's nothing for you here). A main course of grilled haunch of Berkshire roe deer was indeed special: deep-flavoured, tender, pinkish meat, accompanied by beetroot, slivers of roast onion, pickled mushrooms and a rich jus. Halibut (from the specials board) was also masterfully cooked, but in size smacked of fine dining rather than pub, with a mere smear of brown shrimp sauce and a few strands of samphire: not enough to make a complete dish. A starter of Cornish sardine 'tart' with heritage tomatoes failed to elevate the humble fish, but fig leaf and honey pudding with blood nectarine (fresh, and as ice-cream) was a fabulous mix of subtle, summery flavours. Our waiter (in a dressed-down uniform of pale blue shirts, skinny jeans and Converse trainers) provided gauche but efficient service. The brown-paper wine list is a serious affair, worth splashing out on.

Available for hire. Babies and children welcome: children's menu; high chairs. Booking essential. Vegetarian menu. **Map 13 A12.**

Malt House NEW

17 Vanston Place, SW6 1AY (7084 6888, www.malthousefulham.co.uk). Fulham Broadway tube. **Open** 11am-11pm Mon-Thur; 11am-midnight Fri, Sat; noon-10.30pm Sun. **Lunch served** noon-3pm, **dinner served** 6.30-10pm Mon-Sat. **Meals served** noon-8.30pm Sun. **Main courses** £12.50-£27. **Set lunch** £16.50 2 courses, £18.50 3 courses. **Credit** AmEx, MC, V.

Much like its award-winning neighbour the Harwood Arms, this Fulham dining room has a high-profile founder (Claude Bosi, of Mayfair's multi-starred Hibiscus, *see p125*), is also in a spruced-up, handsome old pub, and serves modern British cooking of the highest quality. Our visit kicked off with own-made pork scratchings: rich, dense and with the faintest hint of malt vinegar. Then came a hotpot of mutton and apricot, served in a Lilliputian cast-iron casserole, with a fan of wafer-thin potatoes revealing a mellow, yielding and full-flavoured stew. Triple-cooked chips were no less memorable: crispy on the outside and fluffy on the inside, just as a designer chip should be. Finally, pitched perfectly at the ladies who lunch, a light-as-air malted 'ice-cream' fashioned from soya milk, sprinkled with crumbled biscuit and given a moreish slick of buttery salted caramel. The cooking is the most creative and innovative aspect of the operation. Wines (a dozen of which are available by the glass or carafe), hail largely from France, with only a sprinkling from the New World; beers are a standard selection. Interiors leap straight from the pages of *Period Living* (all tongue-and-groove, soft wood tones and Farrow & Ball paint). Staff are polite and attentive. Bosi's other gastropub, the Fox & Grapes in Wimbledon, is an equally good bet.

Available for hire. Babies and children welcome: high chairs; nappy-changing facilities. Booking advisable Thur-Sat. Disabled: toilet. Tables outdoors (5, garden). **Map 13 A13.**
For branch (Fox & Grapes) see index.

Wimbledon

Earl Spencer

260-262 Merton Road, SW18 5JL (8870 9244, www.theearlspencer.co.uk). Southfields tube. **Open** 4-11pm Mon-Thur; 11am-midnight Fri, Sat; noon-10.30pm Sun. **Lunch served** 12.30-3pm Sat; 12.30-3.30pm Sun. **Dinner served** 7-10pm Mon-Sat; 7-9.30pm Sun. **Main courses** £10-£16. **Credit** AmEx, MC, V.

This much-loved neighbourhood pub consistently manages to conjure up the kind of seriously good seasonal dishes that do justice to its stature as a grand Edwardian boozer. The menu changes daily and is always posted online, an indication that people are lured here as much by the food as by the four cask-conditioned ales, among them Sambrook's

Malt House

GASTROPUBS

Wandle (a natural choice given the location). This is no more apparent than at Sunday lunchtime, when the fine selection of roasts, piled high with all the trimmings, are a huge draw for local families. During the evening it's a buzzier affair, with a healthy balance of diners and drinkers. Warm, own-baked bread arrived on the house – a simple yet thoughtful touch – and a starter of globe artichoke with vinaigrette was bang on season. Sea bass fillets proved a generous portion, bolstered by remarkably good chips, aïoli and watercress. Lamb shoulder had been gently slow-roasted to create a beautifully tender main, well balanced by nutty kale, smooth mash and minted gravy. Service is unfailingly friendly and staff seem well drilled. All in all, a proper pub with proper grub.

Babies and children welcome: high chairs. Separate room for parties, seats 70. Tables outdoors (10, patio).

South

Balham

Avalon

16 Balham Hill, SW12 9EB (8675 8613, www.theavalonlondon.com). Clapham South tube. **Open** noon-11pm Mon-Wed; noon-midnight Thur; noon-1am Fri; 11am-1am Sat; noon-10.30pm Sun. **Lunch served** noon-3.30pm Mon-Fri. **Brunch served** 11am-4pm Sat. **Dinner served** 6-10.30pm Mon-Sat. **Meals served** 11am-9pm Sun. **Main courses** £9.50-£21. **Credit** AmEx, MC, V.
The Avalon gastropub opened in 2008, aimed squarely at the young, affluent couples swarming into the Balham area. It remains one of the key hangouts for thirtysomething professionals seeking

Canton Arms

a decent real ale (such as Sambrook's Wandle or Timothy Taylor Landlord) to go with footie on the telly, or a decent glass of wine on one of the deep leather sofas. Away from the occasionally raucous front bar, there are three outdoor areas, ranging from a smokers' front terrace to an elaborately decked rear garden, complete with its own bar. The lavishly decorated dining room, with its steampunk-style chain-link chandeliers and Victoriana theme, has a menu that started out fairly ambitious, but over the years has increasingly resorted to fail-safe pub grub such as fish and chips, burgers and steaks. Roast pork belly – one of the more interesting choices – was nicely tender with a crisp skin, and came with well-flavoured braised red cabbage and apple sauce. A lemon posset was set firm like a panna cotta, and sticky toffee pudding resembled a brownie in appearance, but both were well received. Service is slow, and prices are on the high side for pub food, but this is Balham's poshest gastropub, where black labradors and country wellies are accessories everyone seems to aspire to.

Babies and children welcome: children's menu; crayons; high chairs; nappy-changing facilities. Booking advisable weekends. Disabled: toilet. Entertainment: DJ 9pm Fri, Sat. Separate room for parties, seats 20. Tables outdoors (22, garden; 10, pavement; 10, courtyard).
For branch (Rosendale) see index.

Clapham

Bobbin

1-3 Lilleshall Road, SW4 0LN (7738 8953, www.thebobbinclapham.com). Clapham Common tube. **Open** 5-11pm Mon-Thur; noon-midnight Fri, Sat; noon-10.30pm Sun. **Lunch served** noon-4pm Fri-Sun. **Dinner served** 6-10pm daily. **Main courses** £8-£17. **Credit** AmEx, MC, V.
In a quiet residential street not far from Clapham Common, Bobbin is an attractive neighbourhood gastropub. There's a handsome yet cosy front room with blue painted walls, tartan-backed banquettes, gold-framed mirrors, and globe lights above the bar; an airy conservatory at the rear and a pretty little walled garden. It offers a changing rota of proper ales (perhaps St Austell Tribute or something from Sambrook's) and good wines by the glass. Fresh flowers decorate the bar, there are a couple of real fires, and service is sunny. You can come here just for a pint or a coffee, but the food is the main focus, with typical gastropub dishes done well. A ribeye steak was well hung, tender and grilled rare, as requested; chips were of the chunky, skin-on type; salsa verde added kick. The vegetarian options are unusually well considered, including beetroot risotto in small or main-course sizes, and potato gnocchi doused in a rich gorgonzola sauce and liberally garnished with pine nuts and parmesan. Tempting desserts include sticky toffee pudding with ginger ice-cream.

Babies and children welcome: high chairs. Booking advisable, essential Sun. Separate room for parties, seats 30. Tables outdoors (11, garden). **Map 22 A1.**

Stockwell

★ Canton Arms

177 South Lambeth Road, SW8 1XP (7582 8710, www.cantonarms.com). Stockwell tube. **Open** 5-11pm Mon; 11am-11pm Tue-Sat; noon-

10.30pm Sun. **Lunch served** noon-2.30pm Tue-Sat; noon-4pm Sun. **Dinner served** 6-10pm Mon-Sat. **Main courses** £12-£15. **Credit** MC, V.
If this southern brother of Covent Garden's Great Queen Street and Waterloo's Anchor & Hope feels more like a pub than its siblings, there's good reason: although a few sausage roll-type snacks are available in the front room, this main bar is dedicated to drinkers, and they make the most of it. The open-plan layout and absence of soft furnishings amplifies any boisterousness for diners in the back; not to an off-putting degree, perhaps, but you'll notice it. Still, the kitchen remains on form, serving seasonal modern British cooking with a few continental influences. The menu is short: about five starters and five mains, plus two or three specials on a blackboard. Meat plays a big part, and rightly so: from roast venison tagliata via deep-fried lamb sweetbreads (a highlight) to crisped pork smothered in a slightly spicy rub and then barbecued over woodchips in the garden, they know how to bring the best out of savvily sourced ingredients. We had quibbles with some of the accompaniments (the salad with the tagliata was indifferent), but the kitchen, like the front-of-house staff, still gets much more right than it gets wrong. There are usually four ales on tap (Skinner's Betty Stogs, perhaps, or Timothy Taylor Golden Best); the wine list offers variety and quality.
Babies and children welcome until 9pm: high chairs; nappy-changing facilities. Bookings not accepted. Tables outdoors (8, pavement).

Tooting

Antelope
76 Mitcham Road, SW17 9NG (8672 3888, www.theantelopepub.com). Tooting Broadway tube.
Bar **Open** 4-11pm Mon-Wed; 4pm-midnight Thur; 4pm-1am Fri; noon-1am Sat; noon-11pm Sun. **Meals served** 5.30-10pm Mon-Fri.
Dishes £4-£6.
Restaurant **Dinner served** 6-10pm Mon-Thur; 6.30-10.30pm Fri, Sat. **Lunch served** noon-4pm Sat; noon-5pm Sun. **Main courses** £10.50-£15.
Both **Credit** MC, V.
A few years into its refurbished reincarnation as a gastropub, this spacious Tooting boozer (part of the Antic group, which has 30-plus pubs in south London) may have lost a little of its initial sparkle. But it's still undoubtedly one of the area's best pubs, with a fine real ale choice (Purity's Ubu, Adnams' Lighthouse and four regularly changing guest beers). Decor sits somewhere between public school assembly hall and junkyard, with dark wooden panelling and a black and white school photo overlooking an eclectic mix of German language cassettes, floral china teacups, and diners stabbing mismatched cutlery into solidly cooked modern European fare. A seafood stew's coarse, rich bisque was stuffed with a generous helping of prawns, mussels and squid, while a portion of fluffy ox tongue croquettes were dense with meat and topped with aromatic pickle. Expect to be upsold on the wine choice, though: despite service so thoroughly deferential that we were greeted with a salutation of 'menu for you, modarm?', an attempt to talk us into splashing out on vino descended into borderline farce. 'Just don't get the house wine,' pleaded the waiter. 'It's horrible!'
Babies and children welcome: high chairs. Booking advisable. Disabled: toilet. Separate room for parties, seats 90. Tables outdoors (10, terrace; 20, garden).

Waterloo

★ Anchor & Hope
36 The Cut, SE1 8LP (7928 9898). Southwark tube or Waterloo tube/rail. **Open** 5-11pm Mon; 11am-11pm Tue-Sat; 12.30-5pm Sun. **Lunch served** noon-2.30pm Tue-Sat; 2pm sitting Sun. **Dinner served** 6-10.30pm Mon-Sat. **Main courses** (Mon-Sat) £12-£20. **Set lunch** (Sun) £30-£35 min 3 courses. **Credit** MC, V.
Once there was just St John (*see p49*), then former St John chefs started to create their own restaurants using the same template – head-to-tail ingredients in simple but artful combinations, served in a relaxed setting. The Anchor & Hope, which opened more than a decade ago, is still showing how it's done. Handy for both the Young and Old Vics, it consists of a straightforward pub divided by a heavy central curtain from a dining room. Bookings aren't taken, so most evenings you join the waiting list for a table (45 minutes midweek is typical) and hover at the crammed bar enjoying a glass of wine or a pint (a couple from Wells plus a guest on handpump). Unlike some gussied-up gastros, the dining area retains the atmosphere of a pub, in a low-lit, art-festooned room, and the food is terrific: beautifully textured venison kofte were served on perkily dressed little gem lettuce leaves; cleaver-hacked rabbit came savagely red, with salty jus, fat chips and a big pot of béarnaise; and earthy beetroot and goat's curd salad was lightened by a gentle touch of mint. Puddings tend towards the classic: bakewell tart with heavy-duty clotted cream, say.
Babies and children welcome: high chairs. Bookings not accepted Mon-Sat; advisable Sun. Tables outdoors (5, pavement). **Map 11 N8.**

South East
East Dulwich

Palmerston
91 Lordship Lane, SE22 8EP (8693 1629, www.thepalmerston.net). East Dulwich rail or bus 176, 185, P13. **Open** noon-11pm Mon-Thur; noon-midnight Fri, Sat; noon-10.30pm Sun. **Lunch served** noon-2.30pm Mon-Fri; noon-3pm Sat, Sun. **Dinner served** 7-9.30pm Mon-Thur, Sun; 7-10pm Fri, Sat. **Main courses** £14-£19.50. **Set lunch** (Mon-Fri) £13.75 2 courses, £16.75 3 courses. **Credit** MC, V.
This East Dulwich stalwart's small dining room is so quiet and dimly lit of an evening you'd barely know it was part of a pub. Retro lampshades filter an orange glow on to a room decked out with dark wood panelling and a floor of ornate mosaic tiles. Despite an open doorway separating the dining area from the green leather banquette seating and open fire of the main bar, the only sounds are the quiet clink of staff polishing cutlery and the gentle murmur of middle-aged chatter from the couples populating the few well-spaced tables. A pricey menu (two courses and two pints of lager came in at around £70 for two) proved hit-and-miss, with meltingly soft scallops sharing a plate with chewy black pudding, and a portion of refreshing pickled girolles atop not-quite-tart-enough goat's cheese. This was once the leading light of the East Dulwich gastro revolution, but with dishes that fail to live up to their billing (or pricing), and the current glut of artisanal produce in SE22, it's hard not to feel that the Palmerston needs to change gear if it's to keep

Narrow. See p106.

ETM Group

Some of the best gastropubs in London are run by brothers Ed and Tom Martin. They're all upmarket, food-focused places – indeed, two of their venues (the **Botanist** and the **Chiswell Street Dining Rooms**) are restaurants – but each one has retained its own character while clearly having the ETM stamp (an idealised and handsome take on old drinking haunts, in which taxidermy and beer casks often feature). If you favour idiosyncracy over reliability, then they may not be for you, and prices are on the high side, but then so are standards. The **Angel & Crown** is the most centrally located; the **Hat & Tun**, the **Well** and the **White Swan** have the City fringes covered, and the **Cadogan Arms** fits perfectly into Chelsea. Our favourites include the tiny **Prince Arthur** (doing a very decent job as a new-style Hackney local), the **Jugged Hare** (a welcome addition to the Barbican's dining options) and, best of all, the brilliantly located **Gun** (*see below*). Their most ambitious project yet, **One Canada Square**, opens in autumn 2013 – it's very much not a gastropub, but a smart all-day bar and restaurant.

For address details of all the pubs, see the index.

Jugged Hare

pace with the competition. There are decent real ales and a sound selection of wines by the glass, but sluggish service certainly doesn't help – it took 45 minutes from ordering for our starters to appear. *Babies and children welcome: high chairs; nappy-changing facilities. Booking advisable dinner and weekends. Tables outdoors (8, pavement).* **Map 23 C4.**

New Cross

New Cross House
316 New Cross Road, SE14 6AF (8691 8875, www.thenewcrosshouse.com). New Cross or New Cross Gate rail. **Open** noon-midnight Mon-Thur, Sun; noon-1am Fri, Sat. **Meals served** noon-10pm Mon-Sat; noon-9.30pm Sun. **Main courses** £7-£11. **Credit** AmEx, MC, V.
The days when this was a sticky-floored, studenty gig den are now a distant memory. Funky young professionals now dominate, wine isn't available for less than £20 a bottle, and on a Friday night locals without reservations hover at the bar, fervently scanning tables for the first sign of movement. In the rear dining area, vast skylights pour light on to green and white tiled walls, smartly upholstered red leather booths and a big wood-fired pizza oven. A menu that leans towards American fast food has burgers, pizzas and foot-long hot dogs as mainstays, alongside a more European range of starters. We enjoyed tart, creamy cauliflower cheese dip served with squidgy, inch-thick breadcrumbed halloumi sticks, but a dry lamb burger and watery dill-based tsatsiki were less successful. Service can be rushed, but don't let that deter you from sticking around for dessert. The range of curious-sounding sweet takes on Italian cuisine are excellent, particularly a gooey chocolate, banana and marshmallow calzone. Be warned, though: it's not advisable to tackle it solo. The pub is part of the

Capital Pub Company, with numerous siblings, including the Florence microbrewery in Herne Hill and the Actress in East Dulwich, so there are house beers such as Weasel and Bonobo on tap.
Available for hire. Babies and children welcome: high chairs; nappy-changing facilities. Booking advisable Fri-Sun. Disabled: toilet. Tables outdoors (30, garden).

East

Docklands

Gun
27 Coldharbour, E14 9NS (7515 5222, www.thegundocklands.com). Canary Wharf tube or Blackwall DLR. **Open** 11am-midnight Mon-Sat; 11am-11pm Sun. **Lunch served** noon-3pm Mon-Fri; noon-4pm Sat, Sun. **Dinner served** 6-10.30pm Mon-Sat; 6.30-9.30pm Sun. **Main courses** £12.50-£28. **Credit** AmEx, MC, V.
Typical of the ETM chain, the Gun is an attractively spruced-up pub, with attentive staff and stiff prices. The focus is on making both diners and drinkers feel at home. The restaurant menu is available throughout – not just in the smartly dressed dining space – and there's a standalone bar menu too. The handsome bar counter is lined with real ales (Adnams bitter is a regular, and there's always a guest ale), but the Gun also offers cocktails and a global wine list. Cooking is assured, if not quite good enough to justify the prices: slow-cooked Middle White pork belly with battered skate knobs, carrot purée, sprout tops and ginger and port jus cost £19 for a small portion – making sides such as chips or dauphinoise potatoes a neccessity. Also, £9 seemed a lot for a (not very) devilled chicken liver starter. Better value is to be found on the bar menu, where £7.50 buys a substantial 'fish finger

sandwich' (more like goujons in toast) served with plenty of tartare sauce, and a decent steak sandwich with caramelised onions and horseradish cream is £9.50. Lightly themed (prints and a few antique pistols), with wooden floors, white walls and an open fire, the Gun is a fine spot in any weather, but its USP is the terrace. Refurbished in spring 2013 with fold-back glass panels, this is right on the river, looking out over the O2. Neophytes, beware – the pub can be tricky to find the first time around. For more ETM pubs, *see left*.
Available for hire. Babies and children welcome: high chairs; nappy-changing facilities. Booking advisable. Disabled: toilet. Separate rooms for parties, seating 16 and 22. Tables outdoors (10, terrace). **Map 24 C2.**
For branches (Angel & Crown, Botanist, Cadogan Arms, Chiswell Street Dining Rooms, Hat & Tun, Jugged Hare, Prince Arthur, Well, White Swan Pub & Dining Room) see index.

Limehouse

Narrow
44 Narrow Street, E14 8DP (7592 7950, www.gordonramsay.com/thenarrow). Limehouse DLR. **Open** noon-11pm Mon-Sat; noon-10.30pm Sun. **Lunch served** noon-3.30pm Mon-Sat; noon-4pm Sun. **Dinner served** 6-10.30pm Mon-Sat; 6-10pm Sun. **Main courses** £13-£29. **Set meal** (lunch Mon-Sat; 6-10pm Mon-Thur, Sun; 6-7pm Fri, Sat) £19 2 courses, £24 3 courses. **Credit** AmEx, MC, V.
It's difficult to pinpoint the moment at which the two-word phrase 'Gordon Ramsay' became associated less with stellar cooking and more with the unpleasant, pantomimic version of himself he plays on TV. At any rate, walking into a Ramsay restaurant today inspires mixed feelings; you're as likely to find yourself musing on his various misjudgments and tabloid run-ins as you are discussing the food. The ambience at this sprawling waterside gastropub – river views if you're lucky, white walls and poor acoustics if you're not – is inspired more by the Canary Wharf trading floor than the London local, with saloon-bar informality replaced by something more corporate. Although some people must treat it as their neighbourhood taproom, it doesn't feel like one. Still, the kitchen has its eye on the ball. The cooking isn't complex, but it's at its best when required to do something other than simply present the ingredients: flavourful chicken stew with garlic mash, broad beans and mushrooms, say, or lamb sweetbreads on toast. The burgers might have cut the mustard five years ago, but the underseasoned version we were served failed to stand comparison with rivals around town. Service is charm-free but alpha-dog efficient, delivered with a rictus grin.
Babies and children welcome: high chairs; nappy-changing facilities. Booking essential weekends. Disabled: toilet. Separate room for parties, seats 18. Tables outdoors (36, riverside terrace).

Shoreditch

Three Crowns [NEW]
8 East Road, N1 6AD (7842 8516, www.the 3crowns.co.uk). Old Street tube/rail. **Open** 7.30am-11.30pm Mon-Fri; 11am-11.30pm Sat; noon-5pm Sun. **Breakfast served** 8-11am Mon-Fri. **Lunch served** noon-3pm Mon-Fri; noon-4pm Sun. **Brunch served** 10am-3pm Sat.

Dinner served 6-10.30pm Mon-Sat. **Main courses** £10-£17. **Credit** AmEx, MC, V.

The new owners of this Old Street corner pub (which reopened in spring 2013) have their priorities right: a big bar at the front; a good selection of craft beers; lots of appealing bar snacks; and quieter tables further back at the 'smart end' if you want a full meal. Beers rotate but Meantime brews are a constant, including its Yakima Red, an amber ale. On our visit, 'guests' included Hackney Brewery Best, and Wells Eagle IPA. The bar was rammed with edge-of-City entrepreneurs, well groomed and studiedly cool, in contrast to the diverse hairstyles and body art of the chefs working in the open kitchen. Salted duck was cut into clean slivers, the sharply pickled endive and watercress cutting the fat. Cod had been crisped on the skin side, but once sat on a watery stock of artichoke hearts and potato, the fish quickly went soggy; the garlic in a well-made aïoli rescued the dish. Blood oranges topping a meringue had been cooked down, so that what remained was mostly white pith. Much better was a pistachio tart, topped with a dollop of stewed rhubarb and Jersey cream. The cooking may not have been perfect, but the fair pricing, decent beer and good attitude go a long way.

Available for hire. Babies and children welcome: high chairs. Disabled: toilet. **Map 6 Q3.**

North East
Dalston

Scolt Head
107A Culford Road, N1 4HT (7254 3965, www.thescolthead.co.uk). Haggerston rail. **Open** noon-11pm Mon-Thur, Sun; noon-midnight Fri,

Three Crowns

Sat. **Lunch served** 12.30-3.30pm Mon-Fri; 12.30-4pm Sat, Sun. **Dinner served** 6.30-10pm Mon-Sat; 6.30-9pm Sun. **Main courses** £10-£18.50. **Credit** MC, V.

A wholly unscientific survey suggests that more than half the pubs in De Beauvoir Town and nearby London Fields now have ambitions and/or pretensions towards gastropub status; even the boozy Prince George, a holdout for years, has succumbed and installed a kitchen. Demand in the area doesn't always meet supply, especially during the week. However, this cheery, capacious and altogether likeable corner pub was thriving on the Sunday lunchtime we visited. The kitchen understands its limits: four starters and four mains constituted a reassuringly short menu, even if not everything excelled. The lively flavours in a spiced carrot soup outshone the rather thin texture, and a small starter of barbecue ribs was too dry for comfort. Still, a Sunday roast anchored by tender lamb shoulder was very decent, while a pumpkin and mixed cheese strudel was, as they say, a good bake. On Sundays, bloody marys made with peppery Bloodshot vodka join an otherwise straightforward drinks list. The prices suggest that the management knows they're in a crowded market: £3.10 for a pint of ale is as cheap as you'll find outside a Wetherspoon's.

Available for hire. Babies and children welcome: high chairs; nappy-changing facilities. Booking advisable. Disabled: toilet. Tables outdoors (9, garden). **Map 6 R1.**

North
Archway

St John's
91 Junction Road, N19 5QU (7272 1587, www.stjohnstavern.com). Archway tube.
Bar **Open/meals served** 5-11pm Mon-Thur; noon-11pm Fri, Sat; noon-10.30pm Sun. **Main courses** £2.75-£12.50.
Restaurant **Lunch served** noon-3.30pm Fri; noon-4pm Sat, Sun. **Dinner served** 6.30-11pm Mon-Sat; 6.30-9.30pm Sun. **Main courses** £11.50-£19.
Both **Credit** AmEx, MC, V.

There's no denying St John's Tavern is a slick operation. The charmingly refurbished saloon bar is light and cheerful, while the huge adjacent dining hall works well as both informal gastroboozer and special-occasion restaurant. Staff strut the wide aisles between tables and booths with an air of authority backed by an open kitchen that serves well-crafted food of estimable provenance. Dishes tend to be modern British with Mediterranean influences – a big plate of Dorset snails with spinach tagliatelle, for instance, or roast leg of lamb with runner beans, Jersey Royals and salsa verde. They're not afraid to offer pub staples, but if creativity is more to your liking (gooseberry tapenade, anyone?) there's sure to be something tempting. Offal makes frequent appearances: jellied pig's head, say, with pickled green apple and beetroot purée, or lambs' kidneys with lentil, purslane and sweetcorn salad. The list of puddings and cheeses is dreamy, so do save room. Real ales are respected (there are handpumps in restaurant and bar) and the genial European wine list starts at £16 a bottle. If you can't get (or don't want) a table in the dining room, the appealing choice of bar nibbles includes cockles and whelks, montgomery's cheddar and patatas bravas.

Available for hire. Babies and children welcome: high chairs. Booking essential weekends. Tables outdoors (10, patio). **Map 26 B1**.

Camden & Chalk Farm

Prince Albert

163 Royal College Street, NW1 0SG (7485 0270, www.princealbertcamden.com). Camden Town tube or Camden Road rail. **Open** noon-11pm Mon-Thur; noon-midnight Fri; noon-1am Sat; noon-10.30pm Sun. **Lunch served** noon-3pm Mon-Fri; noon-5pm Sat, Sun. **Dinner served** 6-10pm Mon-Sat; 6-8pm Sun. **Main courses** £9.50-£16.95. **Set lunch** (Mon-Fri) £9.95 2 courses, £11.95 3 courses. **Credit** AmEx, MC, V.

Sitting on a stretch of Royal College Street without much to recommend it save for access to the Regent's Canal, the Prince Albert can't get a huge amount of passing trade. Still, even though the upstairs room (nominally a restaurant) was closed, a midweek evening in June saw it doing a decent trade in the airy, bright, street-level pub space. It still feels like a pub too – there were at least as many drinkers as diners when we visited, and the clientele covered an attractive mix of ages and genders. The menu is heavy on comfort cooking: appealing-looking and clearly popular burgers, served 2013-style on wooden boards with fattish chips; haddock and chips; scotch egg; sausage, mash and onion gravy. However, the rewards may lie in the 'seasonal specials' section, which on our visit included crab claws with garlic butter and sourdough toast; a chunky, perfectly pink lamb chop with vaguely minty yoghurt and 'aubergine caviar' (in layman's terms, baba ganoush); and some lovely braised beef short ribs, shredded and served in a little tower with mash and mushrooms. Beers include four ales and Meantime's London Lager. Service was polite but the place was plainly short-staffed: try as they might, a single bartender and a lone waiter/busboy couldn't quite keep up.

Babies and children welcome: children's menu; high chairs; toys. Disabled: toilet. Separate room for parties, seats 60. Tables outdoors (12, garden). **Map 27 E2**.

For branch (Adam & Eve) see index.

Crouch End

Queens Pub & Dining Room

26 Broadway Parade, N8 9DE (8340 2031, www.foodandfuel.co.uk). Finsbury Park tube/ rail then bus W7, or Crouch Hill rail. **Open** noon-11pm Mon-Thur, Sun; noon-midnight Fri, Sat. **Lunch served** noon-3pm, **dinner served** 6-10pm Mon-Thur. **Meals served** noon-10pm Fri, Sat; noon-9pm Sun. **Main courses** £9-£17.50. **Set lunch** (noon-3pm Mon-Thur; noon-6pm Fri) £5 1 course. **Credit** AmEx, MC, V.

An affable and reliable member of the Food & Fuel group, the Victorian-era Queens has all the capaciousness of that monarch in her later years. There's a large bar with central servery at the front, a separate sizeable dining room with open kitchen, and a decent garden area. The intricacy of the plasterwork ceilings and friezes, the dark wood panelling, decorative tilework and art nouveau stained glass remain a joy, thanks to sensitive refurbishment a decade ago. Delicious summer cup made with Sipsmith gin plus cucumber, earl grey tea, lemon verbena and fresh fruit typifies the effort put into the drinks side: there's an appealing range of real ales, carafes of house wine and, er, slushies too. The food is decent and good value if you stick with basics such as burgers and pasta – on our visit, a plate of juicy tiger prawns with garlic, herbs and linguine. A meze plate of houmous, olives, feta and pitta was indistinguishable from supermarket offerings, but sticky toffee pudding and accompanying Jude's ice-cream was as delightfully good as we remembered. Service, while a touch haphazard, was friendly and easy-going. With £5 weekday lunch deals and Wi-Fi available, there's no point waiting for the weekend to visit.

Available for hire. Babies and children welcome: high chairs; nappy-changing facilities. Disabled: toilet. Separate room for parties, seats 30. Tables outdoors (13, garden).

For branches (Food & Fuel) see index.

Islington

Drapers Arms

44 Barnsbury Street, N1 1ER (7619 0348, www.thedrapersarms.com). Highbury & Islington tube/rail. **Open** noon-11pm daily. **Lunch served** noon-3pm, **dinner served** 6-10.30pm Mon-Sat. **Meals served** noon-8.30pm Sun. **Credit** MC, V.

The flurry of publicity garnered by this large, airy pub upon its 2009 reopening was at least partly down to the media's love of its own – one of its owners at the time was Ben Maschler, son of veteran *Evening Standard* restaurant critic Fay. However, such connections can only take a place so far, and the Drapers Arms has thrived because it understands its clientele (well-to-do Islingtonians glad to be away from the Upper Street fray) and delivers what they've come to expect from an above-snuff local: namely, pricey wines, varied beers (Harveys Sussex Best, Sambrook's Wandle, Truman's Runner), neutral decor and thoughtfully seasonal cooking. The first three were very much present and correct when we visited, but the food was a little more hit-and-miss. Things certainly started well: smoked sprats were a perfect match for a mild horseradish and some pickled red cabbage, while a bowl of devilled sand eels came with an appealingly piquant tang. The mains, though, were less successful: lamb's leg steak arrived in an ocean of butter, while the kitchen's idea to serve caesar salad with quail worked about as well as one might have feared. We'll put it down to a sloppy night; take care when you order, and you should come away happier than we did.

Babies and children welcome: high chairs; nappy-changing facilities. Booking advisable weekends. Separate room for parties, seats 60. Tables outdoors (8, garden). **Map 5 N1**.

Duke of Cambridge

30 St Peter's Street, N1 8JT (7359 3066, www.dukeorganic.co.uk). Angel tube. **Open** noon-11pm Mon-Sat; noon-10.30pm Sun. **Lunch served** 12.30-5pm daily. **Dinner served** 6.30-10.30pm Mon-Sat; 6.30-10pm Sun. **Main courses** £13-£21. **Credit** MC, V.

Hundred Crows Rising

GASTROPUBS

Smokehouse

This well-established gastropub has a USP as 'Britain's first and only certified organic pub'. Its care for ingredients stretches to a strict fish policy, ensuring only UK fish caught through sustainable fishing with minimal discards are used; we just wish the end product wasn't so often lacklustre. A big, often buzzing outer room for drinkers leads to a welcoming, bare-bricked dining room, lit by a large skylight. The blackboard menu features dishes that encompass both gastropub staples, such as moules frites, and more creative dishes – perhaps pan-fried scallops with cauliflower purée and wild garlic. Among the mains, chickpea curry with basmati rice and yoghurt was fine, if rather lacking in depth of flavour. Better was a robust pork shoulder, chorizo and white bean cassoulet: tender pork, pieces of chewy chorizo and beans nicely squelchy in a thick, comforting sauce. Staff are generous with their attention and add to the warm vibe of the place: unsure about our second beer choice (the brews on offer are also organic, from the likes of Freedom and Pitfield), the waitress provided some samples and didn't seem annoyed when we ended up ordering our first one again.
Available for hire. Babies and children welcome: high chairs; nappy-changing facilities. Booking advisable. Separate room for parties, seats 50-60. Tables outdoors (4, pavement). Vegetarian menu. **Map 5 O2.**

Hundred Crows Rising
58 Penton Street, N1 9PZ (7837 3891, www.hundredcrowsrising.co.uk). **Open** 9am-11pm, **meals served** 9am-10.45pm daily.
Main courses £10-£19. **Credit** MC, V.
In its imperial period, this grand old pub garnered a mix of renown and notoriety for its DJ nights. However, the new owners of what was once the Salmon & Compasses have put the Technics out to pasture and are instead attempting to give Chapel Market its first worthwhile gastropub. Architecturally, it couldn't be more different from its sister pub, the Elk in the Woods: whereas the Elk is small, even cosy, Hundred Crows Rising is a classic corner pub with an open kitchen set theatrically on view. However, the menus share a similar comfort-cooking character, British dishes rubbing shoulders with global fare. The food is fine

enough, though often falls short of its menu billing: 'super hot scotch bonnet corned beef hash' seemed to be missing its pepper, while an otherwise decent burger advertised as 'spicy' was anything but. Skip the skimpy pint of chips and jump down to the kale, chorizo and potato hash for your side order. The beers (including four cask lines dedicated to the Old Dairy Brewery and a couple of keg beers from Chapel Down's Curious range) would benefit from savvier staff: when asked for a recommendation, the bartender freely admitted that she didn't know anything about beer.
Babies and children admitted. Booking advisable dinner. Disabled: lift; toilet. Separate room for parties, seats 50. Tables outdoors (6, pavement). **Map 5 N2.**

Smokehouse NEW
63-69 Canonbury Road, N1 2DG (7354 1144, www.smokehouseislington.co.uk). Highbury & Islington tube/rail. **Open** 4-11pm Mon-Fri; 11am-midnight Sat, Sun. **Dinner served** 6-10pm Mon-Fri. **Meals served** 11am-10pm Sat; 12.30-9pm Sun. **Main courses** £10-£21. **Credit** MC, V.
In the Big Smoke, chef Neil Rankin has become a high priest of barbecue. His latest kitchen is in this new gastropub, run by the small chain behind the excellent Princess of Shoreditch, Lady Ottoline and Pig & Butcher. Trendy though the menu seems – it includes French bistro dishes, carefully sourced British produce and even Korean flavours – the mutton chops come from the grill, not the barman's cheeks. Fatty and full-flavoured, they were best enjoyed using fingers rather than cutlery. Mullet is smoked, cut into translucent slivers and served with slices of white pickled clams, radishes and sea purslane. We can also vouch for the excellent stovies, a simple Scottish dish of leftovers similar to bubble and squeak. Here, a very superior version uses flavoursome lamb. Pit-roasted corn on the cob, slathered with buttery smoked béarnaise sauce, shows that a real barbecue expert doesn't just cook raw flesh. Rankin's on-trend, interesting dishes might be reason enough to visit Smokehouse, but there's more. Service is engaging and friendly, the country-modern look simple and attractive (especially if you like antlers) and the drinks list celebrates the diversity of craft beers – a score of

them on tap, many more by the bottle, none cheap but all worth savouring. There are also appealing wines by the glass, and an extensive range of real ciders. A breath of fresh air.
Babies and children welcome: high chairs; nappy-changing facilities. Booking advisable. Disabled: toilet.

Kentish Town

★ Bull & Last
168 Highgate Road, NW5 1QS (7267 3641, www.thebullandlast.co.uk). Kentish Town tube/rail then bus 214, C2, or Gospel Oak rail then bus C11. **Open** noon-11pm Mon-Thur; 9am-midnight Fri, Sat; 9am-10.30pm Sun. **Breakfast served** 9-11am Fri-Sun. **Lunch served** noon-3pm Mon-Fri; 12.30-4pm Sat, Sun. **Dinner served** 6.30-10pm Mon-Sat; 6.30-9pm Sun.
Main courses £14-£34. **Credit** AmEx, MC, V.
For a place with such a good reputation for its food, the Bull & Last is refreshingly pubby: heavy wooden furniture, velvet drapes, stuffed animals and old prints decorate both the bar and the upstairs dining room. The latter is a calmer and cooler place to eat than the ground-floor bar, and allows diners to focus on dishes such as king scallop carpaccio with pink grapefruit, crème fraîche, coriander and vinaigrette, or pig's cheek with watermelon pickle, basil and sesame – both fabulous ways to start a meal. Pea salad with pea fritters, ratte potatoes, shallots, pea shoots and cow's curd (available in starter and main course sizes) was light, fresh and packed with flavour. By contrast, truffoli pasta with fresh tomato sauce and mozzarella wasn't bad, but was more workaday (and overpriced at £14.50). Order was restored by peanut butter parfait with peanut brittle and caramelised rum banana (the perfect pudding for the sweet-toothed), and the ice-creams are good too – we particularly liked the Kernal stout one. There are (big) roasts at weekends. There's a changing selection of beers and ciders from small breweries (Redemption, Hackney Brewery, Cornish Crown) and a decent wine list, and service is lovely – unfussy but adept. As well as a cross-section of locals, the dog-friendly pub also attracts walkers (it's on the edge of the Heath).

GASTROPUBS

Bull & Last. See p109.

Babies and children welcome: high chairs; nappy-changing facilities. Booking advisable. Separate room for parties, seats 70. Tables outdoors (5, pavement). **Map 26 A3.**

Junction Tavern

101 Fortess Road, NW5 1AG (7485 9400, www.junctiontavern.co.uk). Tufnell Park tube or Kentish Town tube/rail. **Open** 5-11pm Mon-Thur; noon-midnight Fri, Sat; noon-11pm Sun. **Lunch served** noon-3pm Fri; noon-4pm Sat; noon-5pm Sun. **Dinner served** 6.30-10.30pm Mon-Sat; 6.30-9.30pm Sun. **Main courses** £11.50-£19.50. **Credit** MC, V.

Local favourite the Junction was sold in early 2013 to Camden Bars, but little has changed from its decade under the previous owners. The pub is still divided in two, with the dark red restaurant and open kitchen on the Fortess Road side, and a bar room on the other (where the counter is amply decorated with handpulls, including a couple of Wandles, Hopback TEA and Black Sheep Ale). This leads into an ample rear conservatory, which is nicely lit after dark. Vintage Bob Dylan on the stereo lends a pleasantly lived-in feel to the bar, while the eating area tends to fill rapidly at around 8pm with a mix of couples, families and groups of friends. The menu has a mid-European twang – salmon and cucumber here, a strudel there – but is rather unambitious. Parsnip soup with pear turned out to be a bit thin, with the pear just a blob of purée

dropped in. But mushroom risotto, and pork and mash with green beans and apple were decent enough, even if the meat was a tad dry and the crackling rather chewy. The standout dish, though, was the very red smoked salmon, with a nice bite to its horseradish cream. A fine pub, but no longer a pacesetter.

Babies and children welcome until 7pm: booster seats. Booking advisable. Separate room for parties, seats 35. Tables outdoors (16, garden). **Map 26 B4.**

Tufnell Park

Lord Palmerston

33 Dartmouth Park Road, NW5 1HU (7485 1578, www.geronimo-inns.co.uk). Tufnell Park tube. **Open/snacks served** noon-11.30pm Mon-Sat; noon-11pm Sun. **Lunch served** noon-3pm, **dinner served** 6.30-10pm Mon-Fri. **Meals served** noon-10pm Sat; noon-9pm Sun. **Main courses** £10.50-£18. **Set meal** (lunch Mon-Fri, dinner Mon) £14 2 courses, £18 3 courses. **Credit** AmEx, MC, V.

The Geronimo Inns chain (part of Young's) recently spruced up this Dartmouth Hill fixture, with pre-publicity offering a bewildering array of attractions, from cinema room to barber, in-pub deli to bread-making classes. First impressions banish any misgivings: this is still a very likeable pub, busy but well marshalled by smiley, sharp-witted

staff. There's a good range of ales (an excellently hoppy Redemption Big Chief being the pick), a solid wine list and decor that combines modern retro whimsy (top-hat Victorians and fighter planes, deer skull, Union Jack) with traditional pub comfort (chandeliers, fireplaces). From the blackboard menu, 'smoked potato terrine, poached duck egg' was a real hit: a peppery millefeuille of potato with perfectly runny egg and watercress – direct, handsomely presented and full of flavour. Gnocchi with roast squash and lemon butter was also good, if light on the chilli. After that, though, things went astray: fridge-cold beetroot with goat's curd and watercress was complicated by an over-sweet walnut praline; warm pigeon breast salad suffered from too few of the 'bitter leaves' and flavourless crackling. Still, this is a pub focused on returning to the heart of its community – and when the sun shines, the beer garden will help too.

Babies and children admitted. Booking advisable. Separate room for parties, seats 32. Tables outdoors (7, pavement; 12, garden). **Map 26 B3.**

North West
Hampstead

Horseshoe

28 Heath Street, NW3 6TE (7431 7206). Hampstead tube. **Open** 11am-11pm Mon-Thur; 11am-midnight Fri; 10am-midnight Sat; noon-10.30pm Sun. **Lunch served** noon-3.30pm Mon-Fri. **Brunch served** 11am-4pm Sat. **Dinner served** 6-10pm Mon-Thur; 6-11pm Fri, Sat. **Meals served** noon-9pm Sun. **Main courses** £8-£26. **Credit** AmEx, MC, V.

'Home of the Camden Town Brewery' reads the menu. But yes, this is the heart of Hampstead – presumably Jasper Cuppaidge, the thirtysomething Australian who runs both this cheery pub and the brewery (which has moved from the pub's basement to close-but-no-cigar Kentish Town), thought naming a beer label after one of London's poshest neighbourhoods might alienate more drinkers than it would attract. You'll find the full range of Camden keg beers here (Ink, a moreish stout, is comfortably the best), alongside cask ales, bottled offerings and an above-average wine list, but the food's no afterthought. On weeknights, a pretty standard gastropub menu takes hold. But the place really hums at weekends, when you'll need to dodge buggies, children and the occasional dog if you want to enjoy comfort cooking that sits on the fence separating brunch from lunch: on Saturdays, creamy macaroni cheese, eggs benedict, gigantic burgers best ordered medium rare; on Sundays, roasts galore. You won't find many surprises, but everything's done very well. We've heard grumblings about slow service in the past, but we had no complaints.

Available for hire. Babies and children welcome: high chairs; nappy-changing facilities. Booking advisable. Tables outdoors (2, pavement). **Map 28 B2.**

Old White Bear

1 Well Road, NW3 1LJ (7794 7719, www.theoldwhitebear.co.uk). Hampstead tube. **Open/tapas served** 5.30-11pm Mon; noon-11pm Tue-Thur; noon-11.30pm Fri, Sat; noon-10.30pm Sun. **Lunch served** noon-3pm Tue-Fri; noon-3.30pm Sat, Sun. **Dinner served**

6.30-10.30pm Mon-Sat; 5.30-10pm Sun. **Main courses** £12.50-£20.50. **Tapas** £3-£12. **Credit** AmEx, MC, V.

The renovation several years ago of this former Hampstead favourite left locals grumbling that a charismatic old boozer had been sacrificed on the altar of the gastropub gods. Certainly, first impressions for return visitors aren't good. Everything that hasn't been sanded has been Farrow & Balled, lending most surfaces a washed-out patina that found weary echoes in the soundtrack (Jamie Cullum singing Jimi Hendrix). Despite a menu that promises plenty (at these prices, so it should), the blandness extends to the cooking, which on our visit prioritised texture over taste to mixed effect. The best dish by far was a starter of omelette arnold bennett, as casually elegant as the classic recipe demands. However, chorizo-stuffed squid croquettes and tomato salsa were a mess, and the two mains lacked life: roast cod with spinach and olive oil mash relied heavily on the accompanying tapenade for its flavour, while calf's tongue served over butterbeans was a beige letdown. A decent-sized area at the front has been given over to drinkers, but the focus is on the food. It needs to be better to justify the spotlight.
Babies and children welcome: high chairs; nappy-changing facilities. Booking advisable. Disabled: toilet. Separate room for parties, seats 10-14. Tables outdoors (5, pavement).
Map 28 C2.

Spaniards Inn

Spaniards Road, NW3 7JJ (8731 8406, www.thespaniardshampstead.co.uk). Hampstead tube then bus 603. **Open** noon-11pm Mon-Sat;

noon-10.30pm Sun. **Meals served** noon-10pm Mon-Sat; noon-9pm Sun. **Main courses** £11.50-£22. **Credit** AmEx, MC, V.

Most Londoners know the Spaniards Inn – it's been a feature of Hampstead Heath since 1585, with Keats and Dickens both former quaffers. Now run by booze behemoth Mitchells & Butlers, it relaunched in 2013 but remains as atmospheric as you'd hope, with dark panels and low beams stretching through the bar and restaurant rooms. The real change is in the menu, which now aims for gastro heights with smart beer pairings for every dish (Czech black lager from Bernard Dark was a great match, as you'd hope at £4.94 a pint). But, all in all, it's pretty conservative – and priced a couple of notches above the norm. A beautifully tender gigot was among the more exciting options, but its bed of chickpeas (tingly with harissa), parsley, super-sweet tomatoes, black olives and chunks of merguez should have been warmed through. Fish and chips was good – the fish tightly sleeved in batter, the thin chips served in a modish paper-lined cup – but came with over-minted mushy peas and a too gentle tartare. Even bakewell tart was overshadowed by its sumptuous white chocolate and amaretti biscuit ice-cream. The big garden (with twinkling fairy lights at night and a doggie wash) backs right on to the Heath.
Booking advisable.

★ Wells

30 Well Walk, NW3 1BX (7794 3785, www.thewellshampstead.co.uk). Hampstead tube or Hampstead Heath rail. **Open** noon-11pm Mon-Sat; noon-10.30pm Sun. **Lunch served** noon-3pm Mon-Fri; noon-4pm Sat, Sun.

Dinner served 6-10pm Mon-Fri; 7-10pm Sat, Sun. **Main courses** £9.95-£18.95. **Credit** AmEx, MC, V.

The dining rooms above this very soigné Georgian pub are a useful addition to Hampstead's relatively limited restaurant scene. Three handsome spaces, each with good acoustics and their own colour scheme and fireplace, make the Wells perfect for family occasions – accordingly, Sunday lunch is a hot ticket. The menu is appealing without being faddish or daring; there's a section devoted to steaks. Watermelon, feta and mint soup topped with toasted pumpkin seeds was a refreshing twist on gazpacho. Perfectly grilled scallops came with crisp bacon, samphire and two fashionable puréed: shallot and rocket. Piping-hot mains prepared with skill and exuberance followed swiftly: beautifully crisp-skinned sea bass on tender fennel, courgette, chorizo, green beans and red pepper, with a precision-chopped provençal salsa; and swordfish on a terrific salad base of avocado, watercress, green beans, rocket, frisée and endive. Both dishes were generous and full of colour, vigour and flavour. A standout pavlova with marshmallowy meringue studded with upright strawberries looked almost heraldic; a crème brûlée was peerless. Add solicitous service and well-chosen wines at friendly prices and the Wells is a winner. Downstairs has a posh neighbourhood-pub vibe with leather sofas, backgammon boards and as much emphasis on wines as beers.
Babies and children welcome: children's menu; colouring books; high chairs; nappy-changing facilities. Disabled: toilet. Separate rooms for parties, seating 12 and 35. Tables outdoors (8, patio). **Map 28 C2.**

Lord Palmerston

Global

One of the joys of London – something that this multifarious city does better than anywhere else – is its unexpected enclaves of communities from all parts of the world. Often these communities might only inhabit a few houses in a few streets of a neighbourhood; sometimes they have a communal shop selling the comestibles of their homeland; occasionally, when sufficiently established, they give birth to a restaurant devoted to their national cuisine. Here we gather together the rarities: those dining establishments producing a cooking style scarcely represented in Britain. Students of gastronomy might find some missing pieces of the culinary jigsaw within these menus. Take Afghan cuisine, which has three disparately located yet worthy representatives in **Afghan Kitchen**, **Masa** and **Ariana II**, where you'll discover food that bridges the divide between the Middle East (with its dips and kebabs) and the Indian subcontinent (with its samosas and tandooris); or Burmese cookery, exemplified at the consistently glorious (and soon to be relocated) **Mandalay**, where the noodles of east Asia meet the spices of south Asia. The capital's few Scandinavian and central European (German and Austrian) restaurants also find a home here, as does our latest discovery: **Peckham Bazaar**, where an Albanian-born restaurateur, bringing food inspired by the Balkans to SE15, has produced a roaring success. Such venues sum up what our guide is all about: a celebration of variety, a celebration of London.

Mandalay

Central
Edgware Road

★ Mandalay `HOT 50`
444 Edgware Road, W2 1EG (7258 3696, www.mandalayway.com). Edgware Road tube.
Lunch served noon-2.30pm, **dinner served** 6-10.30pm Mon-Sat. **Main courses** £5.50-£8.50. **Set lunch** £4.50 1 course, £6.50 3 courses. **Credit** AmEx, DC, MC, V. Burmese
For nearly two decades, the road to Mandalay has been the Edgware Road. This looks set to change at the end of 2013, as the Ally family are planning to move their tiny, modest restaurant into larger and better premises in the more swish surroundings of Paddington Basin. In the meantime, they continue to run Mandalay just as they always have: with home-style, welcoming and informative service; and with cooking that accurately reflects the staples of Bamar food. The ten tightly packed tables are full each night with a mix of students, Burmaphiles and a few expats (best make a reservation). Burma's food draws influences from its bordering countries (India/Bangladesh, China and Thailand) and is served at bargain prices here. Curries, noodle dishes, fried snacks and salads are put together in inventive ways, often with a hot, sour, or sweet mix of spices and herbs – there's plenty of choice for vegetarians. Start, perhaps, with a brace of bean-sprout and shrimp fritters (only £2.90) or bottle gourd soup, and continue with omelette curry or a coconut and chicken noodle dish; add a side of balachaung (dried prawn relish) for extra pungency. Now that more people than ever are able to visit Burma and experience real Burmese cooking for themselves, Mandalay's move to bigger and better premises appears well timed.
Available for hire weekdays. Babies and children welcome: high chairs. Booking essential dinner. Takeaway service. **Map 2 D4.**

South Kensington

Madsen
20 Old Brompton Road, SW7 3DL (7225 2772, www.madsenrestaurant.com). South Kensington tube. **Open** noon-10pm Mon-Sat; noon-4pm Sun. **Lunch served** noon-4pm daily. **Dinner served** 5-10pm Mon-Sat. **Main courses** £11.50-£17.50. **Set lunch** £13.95 2 courses, £18.95 3 courses. **Set dinner** (5-7pm) £16.50 2 courses, £20.95 3 courses. **Credit** MC, V. Danish
When the winter blues start to bite in earnest, sensible residents of South Ken turn to Madsen's sensational pork and veal meatballs for solace. These artful creations bring great cheek-straining

grins of joy to the faces of all but the most Scrooge-like diners, and arrive with either a cabbage and apple salad or a blissful beetroot gremolata and a thick, life-affirming gravy. There's a strong argument to be made in favour of dispensing them on the NHS. But the prescription meatballs are just one of the stars on Madsen's small but well-curated Scandi menu. Other hits include dill-marinated herring served with capers and sweet onions; delicate gravadlax drizzled with lime juice; and a well-judged cheese platter (make sure to try the Norwegian gjetost, an intriguing, fudge-like number). The stripped-back, smart interior features whitewashed walls and pine trimmings; the service is chipper; and the location – a 30-second saunter from the tube station – makes this a fine venue for a rendezvous. It's also well worth turning up on a weekend morning for the good-value brunch, when you can expect lashings of Swedish waffles, jarlsberg and freshly baked sourdough accompanied by chilled mimosa cocktails.

Available for hire. Babies and children welcome: children's menu; crayons; high chairs; nappy-changing facilities. Booking advisable Fri, Sat. Separate room for parties, seats 20. Tables outdoors (4, terrace). Takeaway service. **Map 14 D10.**

West
Ladbroke Grove

Lisa's NEW

305 Portobello Road, W10 5TD (07445 261778, www.lisasportobello.com). Ladbroke Grove tube. **Meals served** 11am-11pm Tue-Sun. **Main courses** £15. **Dishes** £5-£9. **Credit** AmEx, MC, V. Swedish

A new Swedish restaurant is always something to look forward to, like lungfuls of fresh coastal air or a sight of winter sunshine. Breezing into Portobello, Lisa's has an all-white interior with a huge atrium-roofed conservatory dining room at the back. It wouldn't look out of place in the Swedish archipelago. The staff are Swedish and Norwegian, their smiles and clear skin a great advertisement for all social democracies. Rather than trying anything New Nordic, though, the kitchen plays it safe with Swedish home-style cooking. The meatballs were of a mushy consistency and fell apart at the touch of a fork: not a good start. The treatment of vegetables was unimaginative; potatoes were simply roasted, spinach leaves came with more than one dish. Ingredient quality needs to be tip-top in Scandinavian fish dishes, yet the cured salmon was just not up to scratch. There was a lack of care about the cooking on our visit – accompanied by the crash of plates and Viking oaths from the kitchen – and service was painfully slow. Perhaps pop in for a drink at the tiny bar instead, as the German-style, Swedish-made Ctrl Alt Delete altbier from brewery Nils Oscar is almost as good an export as Abba.

Available for hire. Booking advisable. Tables outdoors (9, terrace). **Map 19 B2.**

South East
Peckham

Peckham Bazaar NEW

119 Consort Road, SE15 3RU (07875 107471, www.peckhambazaar.com). Nunhead or Peckham Rye rail. **Dinner served** 6-11pm Thur, Fri. **Meals served** 12.30-10pm Sat, Sun. **Main courses** £7-£12.50. **No credit cards.** Balkan

You couldn't make it up: a 'pan-Balkan' part-time pop-up in Peckham – set in the elegant, Victorian bones of an old deli – has become a must-go place to eat. The owner, John Gionleka, has cleared out the deli counters to serve delicious dishes inspired by his native Albania, its Balkan neighbours and influences from further afield. Beneath a kitsch brass-framed photo of a 1970s Iranian pop star, we devoured juicy grilled sweetcorn cobs slathered with smoked chilli and lemon salt butter, and the house special: 'cured' egg (soft-boiled, lightly pickled) served with lemon mayonnaise and crudités. To follow, spatchcocked quail had been marinated in date molasses and yoghurt, infusing both the tender flesh and the delicious blackened and fragrant skin; it arrived with baked beetroot and braised silverskin onions. A simple, grilled pork chop was just as good. There are also the obvious charms of marinated leg of lamb, roasted on the drum barbecue and served with grilled peppers and aged goat's cheese. We shared still-warm cardamom and almond cake, accompanied by thick yoghurt and a pool of sticky grapes preserved in red wine syrup with mahleb (an aromatic spice). Two Greek wines from boutique producers, recommended by the charming sommelier, worked beautifully with the food. The rapturous local reception to this unusual venue means that regular weeknight opening is planned by late autumn 2013.

Available for hire. Babies and children welcome: high chairs. Booking advisable. Tables outdoors (7, terrace).

North
Islington

★ Afghan Kitchen

35 Islington Green, N1 8DU (7359 8019). Angel tube. **Lunch served** noon-3.15pm, **dinner served** 5.30-10.45pm Tue-Sat. **Main courses** £6.50-£7.50. **No credit cards.** Afghan

Not much changes at this long-running restaurant overlooking Islington Green. The two-floor premises are bright and clean, with spring-green and grey paintwork, simple pale-wood tables and stools, and no decoration beyond a few pot plants. The menu of Afghan home cooking is equally straightforward: eight dishes (three meat, one fish, four vegetarian), of which the focus is hearty warming stews that feature plenty of yoghurt and mint. Spicing is subtle rather than fiery. Moong dal

Peckham Bazaar

was a comforting, thick, rich purée, while 'Sarah's' combined chickpeas, kidney beans and chunks of potato in a yoghurty sauce. Meltingly soft aubergine and thick slices of orange pumpkin came drizzled in yet more yoghurt. The best method is to come in a group, so you can share dishes – though you can order half-portions to get more variety. Sides include tangy pickles, plain rice and (in the evening) a communal loaf. Fresh-squeezed carrot juice and a few beers and wines are among the drink options, though dogh – watery, mint-inflected yoghurt – is the most refreshing choice. Bring cash as cards aren't taken.

Babies and children welcome: high chairs. Booking advisable Fri, Sat. Takeaway service.

Kipferl

20 Camden Passage, N1 8ED (7704 1555, www.kipferl.co.uk). Angel tube. **Open** 9am-10pm Tue-Sat; 10am-10pm Sun. **Main courses** £8.80-£16.80. **Credit** AmEx, MC, V. Austrian

We're fond of this Austrian café/restaurant, but it seems to have become complacent. What's listed on the menu isn't always what appears on the plate, and too many dishes lack flavour. A starter of smoked trout on toasted rye bread and cranberry horseradish emerged from the kitchen as a bland, supermarket-style fish, on a mountain of cream lightly tinged with cranberry and horseradish, plus a few fingers of bread. Beef goulash with spätzle (egg noodles) was OK, but had no depth of flavour, and the spätzle needed a little more butter. Spinach dumplings with organic mountain cheese from Vorarlberg and green salad was tastier. Best was kaiserschmarrn – thick chunks of pancake, served with raisins and a little pot of morello cherries – though we wished the cherries had been served hot, as advertised. The short wine list has some reasonably priced Austrian wines (also available to take away) – but don't get too comfortable; the place closes at 10pm, and staff start clearing up well before, making it clear diners should pay and leave. Service is otherwise helpful, but on current showing, these light, modern premises are more suited to their daytime café existence, offering sausage and sauerkraut, cakes (apple strudel, cheesecake), and coffees (served the Austrian way, with a glass of water and a little chocolate).

Available for hire. Babies and children welcome: high chairs; nappy-changing facilities. Booking advisable weekends. Disabled: toilet. Tables outdoors (2, pavement). Vegetarian menu.
For branches see index.

North West
Kilburn

★ ★ Ariana II `HOT 50`

241 Kilburn High Road, NW6 7JN (3490 6709, www.ariana2restaurant.co.uk). Kilburn tube or Brondesbury rail. **Meals served** noon-11pm daily. **Main courses** £6-£12. **Set meal** £13.37 per person (minimum 2) 3 courses. **Unlicensed. Corkage** no charge. **Credit** MC, V. Afghan

As well as being a darling of the neighbourhood, Ariana II (I is in New York, though there's nothing Manhattan-esque here) attracts people from across London with its excellent cooking, budget prices and BYOB policy. The frontage is pretty indistinguishable from Kilburn High Road's ranks of kebab shops; inside is a small, plain dining room with a few Afghan portraits on the walls (there's more room in the basement). But you can be certain of a sunny welcome and swift service. The menu reflects the multiple influences on Afghan food – from Arab lands, the Indian subcontinent and further afield in Asia. These show up in dumplings, tikkas and kebabs, but the cuisine has a unique slant too. Plump, moreish leek-filled aushak ravioli topped with ground meat and yoghurt, and warmly spiced fried pumpkin turnovers (bolanee kadoo) with a side of fiery chakni relish (also available to buy by the bottle) make ideal starters. For mains, kabuli palow (a melting, slow-cooked lamb shank buried in a mound of yellow rice dotted with pistachios and peppers) is a must. To drink, order minty yoghurt dogh or freshly squeezed juices, and conclude with cardamom-flavoured tea and pastries. A treat.

Available for hire. Babies and children welcome: high chairs. Booking advisable Thur-Sat. Separate room for parties, seats 60. Takeaway service; delivery service (over £12 within 3-mile radius).

Afghan Kitchen. See p113.

Outer London
Harrow, Middlesex

★ Masa

24-26 Headstone Drive, Harrow, Middx HA3 5QH (8861 6213). Harrow & Wealdstone tube/rail. **Meals served** 12.30-11pm daily. **Main courses** £5.95-£13. **Set meal** £23.95 (2 people); £33 (2-3 people); £55 (4-5 people). **Unlicensed. Corkage** no charge. **No credit cards.** Afghan

The nondescript Harrow location and the plain square dining room (with a takeaway counter to one side) might not be instantly appealing, but Masa really delivers where it matters. The restaurant is popular with local Afghan families, who fill its long tables with chatter and enormous amounts of food. A TV burbles quietly in the background, and the whole kaboodle envelops you in a warm fug of talk and cooking aromas. Rather than the classic mountains of fluffy pilau full of nuts and lamb, we chose delicate parcels of aushak dumplings with a spicy leek filling, topped with yoghurt and minced meat. We also ordered a warming, hearty stew of okra and lamb: perfect comfort food. The affable staff brought huge discs of soft, fragrant bread warm from the oven, and the standard side salad was made crisp and lively with carrots and fresh mint. Masa's menu shows many culinary influences from Afghanistan's neighbours (Central Asia, the Indian subcontinent, the Middle East) and is astonishingly inexpensive. There's no booze (though you can bring your own), but there are various juices and lassis – all the better to enjoy the hefty portions and delicate spicing.

Babies and children welcome: high chairs. Booking advisable Thur-Sun. Disabled: toilet. Takeaway service; delivery service. Vegetarian menu.
For branch see index.

Richmond, Surrey

★ Stein's

55 Richmond Towpath, Richmond, Surrey TW10 6UX (8948 8189, www.stein-s.com). Richmond tube/rail then 20mins walk or bus 65. **Meals served** *Summer* noon-9.30pm Mon-Fri; 10am-9.30pm Sat, Sun. *Winter* noon-9.30pm Sat, Sun. (Weather dependent; phone to check.) **Main courses** £3.90-£10.90. **Credit** MC, V. German

The idyllic riverside setting is the perfect venue for Stein's dog- and family-friendly Bavarian beer garden. Once you order your food at the window, waiting staff quickly bring the meal to your shared picnic table in the entirely outdoor dining area. Try the fine breakfast menu, indulge in traditional sausages on sauerkraut, or share a cured meat or cheese platter, along with freshly baked pretzels or rolls. The Munich-style bratwurst, served with fried potatoes and onions and a side salad, is particularly recommended. For bigger appetites, main courses of schnitzel or käsespätzle (noodles with cheese) lie in wait. Sweets include a perfect apple strudel and moreish cheesecake. All of this enjoyable food acts primarily as an accompaniment to the beer: a range of German imports that's available on tap, including refreshing Paulaner Helles and fruity Erdinger Weissbier. If beer isn't your thing, try something from the selection of German wines.

Babies and children welcome: children's menu; high chairs; play area. Booking advisable. Tables outdoors (31, towpath). Takeaway service.
For branch see index.

GLOBAL

Greek

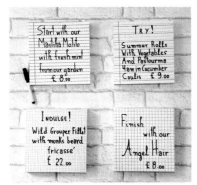

In recent years, London's Greek and Greek-Cypriot restaurants have tended more towards complacency than innovation, which is why the opening of **Mazi** in late 2012 caused such a stir. Still going strong, it has been joined in this year's guide by another interesting new addition: stylish deli-café **Life Goddess**. What's more, Ergon, a contemporary deli/restaurant with branches in Greece, has plans to open an outpost in London in October 2013. So, there's movement at last in a section that lost its way when the **Real Greek** became a chain and its much-admired original Hoxton branch (and flagship) closed down. Also gone, as of early 2013, is family-run Daphne in Camden Town, leaving even more space for the next generation. You'll still find good food at the more traditional end of the Hellenic dining spectrum (try **Carob Tree** or **Lemonia**), but it's the forward-thinking newcomers that are breathing life back into the capital's Greek scene.

Central
Bloomsbury

★ **Life Goddess** NEW
*29 Store Street, WC1E 7BS (7637 2401,
www.thelifegoddess.com). Goodge Street tube.*
Meals served 9am-9pm Mon-Wed, Sun; 9am-10pm Thur-Sat. **Main courses** £6.30-£10.30.
Credit AmEx, MC, V.

More of a kafeneon than taverna, this new Bloomsbury deli is worth a visit just to peruse the many Greek food products and small-producer wines for sale. If you decide to linger, you can peruse the printed menus in the airy dining space – but it's easier just to go to the counter, point and order, as you would in Greece. There are more types of Greek filled pies than there are Greek islands; this version of spanakópitta has dense flaky pastry but a light spinach filling. A Greek salad had all the right constituents in exactly the right amounts, and was only let down by some under-ripe, northern European tomatoes. The koulouri bread (sesame covered 'bagels') is a savoury snack worth trying, chewy and pliable. The Greek coffee can be ordered sweet, without sugar, or – if you're not sure – 'metrio', which is medium.
Available for hire. Babies and children welcome: high chairs. Booking advisable Fri, Sat. Tables outdoors (4, pavement; 1, balcony). Takeaway service. Vegetarian menu. **Map 17 C1**.

Marylebone

Real Greek
*56 Paddington Street, W1U 4HY (7486 0466,
www.therealgreek.com). Baker Street or Regent's Park tube.* **Meals served** noon-11pm Mon-Sat; noon-10.30pm Sun. **Dishes** £4.75-£7.25. **Credit** AmEx, MC, V.
Anyone who enjoyed eating at the original Real Greek on Hoxton Market (now closed) can't fail to be disappointed by the watered-down chain left in its wake, but this diminutive branch, a stone's throw from the Hellenic Centre, seemed to be keeping its end up on our lunchtime visit. Inside, the stripped-back feel of the rest of the chain is very much in evidence: exposed brick, statement light fittings, scrubbed-up floorboards and multi-level banquettes. While other diners were a bit thin on the ground, service was swift and friendly; staff encouraged us to linger. The menu lists a good selection of Greek wines (including the house red and white: both available by the carafe). Piled high on afternoon tea-style stands, our mezédes were more hit than miss, with perfectly tender grilled

Mazi. See p116.

calamares and well-spiced lamb keftédes the best of the bunch. So-so tomatoes in a skimpily sized horiátiki failed to impress, but we happily mopped up a melitzanosaláta, despite an excess of herbs and spring onions masking any authentic smokiness. There's no escaping the chain factor, but for a glass or two after work or a swift weekday lunch, there's life yet in this particular branch. *Babies and children welcome: high chairs. Booking advisable. Disabled: toilet. Separate room for parties, seats 50. Tables outdoors (1, pavement). Vegetarian menu. Map 3 G5.* **For branches see index.**

West
Notting Hill

Greek Affair

1 Hillgate Street, W8 7SP (7792 5226, www.greekaffair.co.uk). Notting Hill Gate tube. **Lunch served** noon-3pm Fri-Sun. **Dinner served** 6-11pm daily. **Main courses** £9.50-£15. **Set meal** (lunch, 6-7pm) £9.90 2 courses, £11.90 3 courses. **Credit** AmEx, MC, V.

Time your visit with dinner at the tail-end of the week and there's plenty of buzz at this decade-old spot in Notting Hill; on our Friday lunch trip we experienced deathly silence and empty tables. Greek Affair reduced its midday openings to Fridays and weekends in early 2013, and perhaps Fridays will follow suit – phone to check before making a special trip. Nevertheless, there's lots to like about this relaxed and contemporary space. The huge wooden dining table by the entrance is just right for a celebratory meal and there's clearly plenty of skill in the kitchen. Greek rather than Cypriot food is the speciality. Expertly spiced soutzoukákia were faultless, while a piping hot portion of well-seasoned fried calamares was simple and delicious. However, other dishes were disappointing: a humdrum aubergine and halloumi dish; a tower of beetroot and feta swimming in balsamic. And there's no place in a horiátiki for iceberg lettuce, especially not piles of the stuff. We've had much more success ordering from the main courses – the pastitsio (a baked pasta and meat dish) is a favourite – and we love the upstairs courtyard terrace. But there's work to be done if Greek Affair is going to keep up with its newer neighbour, Mazi.

Babies and children welcome: high chairs. Booking advisable. Separate room for parties, seats 20. Tables outdoors (10, terrace). Takeaway service. Vegetarian menu. **Map 19 C5.**

★ Mazi

12-14 Hillgate Street, W8 7SR (7229 3794, www.mazi.co.uk). Notting Hill Gate tube. **Lunch served** noon-3.30pm daily. **Dinner served** 6.30-11pm Mon-Sat; 6.30-10pm Sun. **Main courses** £6-£25. **Credit** AmEx, MC, V.

This stylish addition to the capital's Hellenic dining scene opened in 2012 in what used to be Costas Grill. Its food has more in common with the creations of leading Athens restaurants than anything you'd find in London – and the relief from the city's Greeks is almost palpable. Purists might be troubled by the progressive presentation – mezédes are served in Kilner jars; tyrópitta is separated into filling and filo for DIY crumbling – but the flavours are reassuringly authentic. A jar of creamy white taramá hit just the right note of tangy, savoury deliciousness; another of fava (spilt-pea purée), accompanied by tender octopus, was so light it could have been whipped. Horiátiki contained top-quality oil and feta, properly ripe

Life Goddess. See p115.

tomatoes, and (unexpectedly) Cretan-style rusk croûtons and salty capers. The hot dishes are better still. Keftédes were sublime and Mazi's slabs of feta encased in black-sesame tempura with punchy lemon marmalade might well consign the humble saganáki to history. An all-Greek wine list showcases the region's best bottles but on a Friday night, cocktails made with mastiha resin spirit were preferred by the gangs of young Greeks tightly packed either side of us in this fresh and contemporary dining room.
Available for hire. Babies and children welcome: high chairs. Booking advisable weekends. Tables outdoors (9, garden). Vegan dishes. **Map 19 C5**.

South West
Earl's Court

As Greek As It Gets

233 Earl's Court Road, SW5 9AH (7244 7777, www.asgreekasitgets.co.uk). Earl's Court tube. **Meals served** noon-11pm daily. **Main courses** £4.10-£14.95. **Set lunch** £9.90 3 courses. **Credit** MC, V.

Menu

Dishes followed by (G) indicate a specifically Greek dish; those marked (GC) indicate a Greek-Cypriot speciality; those without an initial have no particular regional affiliation. Spellings on menus often vary.

Afélia (GC): pork cubes stewed in wine, coriander and other herbs.
Avgolémono (G): a sauce made of lemon, egg yolks and chicken stock. Also a soup made with rice, chicken stock, lemon and whole eggs.
Dolmádes (G) or **koupépia (GC)**: young vine leaves stuffed with rice, spices and (usually) minced meat.
Fasólia plakí or **pilakí**: white beans in a tomato, oregano, bay, parsley and garlic sauce.
Garídes: prawns (usually king prawns in the UK), fried or grilled.
Gigantes or **gígandes**: white butter beans baked in tomato sauce; pronounced 'yígandes'.
Halloumi (GC) or **hallúmi**: a cheese that is traditionally made from sheep or goat's milk, but increasingly from cow's milk. Best served fried or grilled.
Horiátiki: Greek 'peasant' salad made from tomato, cucumber, onion, feta and sometimes green pepper, dressed with ladolémono (a mixture of oil and lemon).
Hórta: salad of cooked wild greens.
Houmous, **hoúmmous** or **húmmus (GC)**: a dip of puréed chickpeas, sesame seed paste, lemon juice and garlic, garnished with paprika. Originally an Arabic dish.
Htipití or **khtipíti**: tangy purée of matured cheeses, flavoured with red peppers.
Kalamári, **kalamarákia** or **calamares**: small squid, usually sliced into rings, with the pieces battered and fried.
Kataífi or **katayfi**: syrup-soaked 'shredded-wheat' rolls.
Keftédes or **keftedákia (G)**: herby meatballs made with minced pork or lamb (rarely beef), egg, breadcrumbs and possibly grated potato.
Kléftiko (GC): slow-roasted lamb (often shoulder), served on the bone and flavoured with oregano and other herbs.
Kopanísti (G): a cheese dip with a tanginess traditionally coming from natural fermentation, but often boosted with chilli.
Koukiá: broad beans.
Loukánika or **lukánika**: spicy coarse-ground sausages, usually pork and heavily herbed.
Loukoumédes: tiny, spongy dough fritters, dipped in honey.
Loukoúmi or **lukúmi**: 'turkish delight' made using syrup, rosewater and pectin, and often studded with nuts.
Loúntza (GC): smoked pork loin.

Marídes: picarel, often mistranslated as (or substituted by) 'whitebait' – small fish best coated in flour and flash-fried.
Melítzanosaláta: grilled aubergine purée.
Meze (the plural is **mezédes**, pronounced 'mezédhes'): a selection of either hot or cold appetisers and main dishes.
Moussáka(s) (G): a baked dish of mince (usually lamb), aubergine and potato slices, topped with béchamel sauce.
Papoutsáki: aubergine 'shoes', slices stuffed with mince, topped with sauce that's usually béchamel-like.
Pourgoúri or **bourgoúri (GC)**: a pilaf of cracked wheat, often prepared with stock, onions, crumbled vermicelli and spices.
Saganáki (G): fried cheese, usually kefalotyri; also refers to anything (mussels, spinach) served in a cheese-based red sauce.
Sheftaliá (GC): little pig-gut skins stuffed with minced pork and lamb, onion, parsley, breadcrumbs and spices, then grilled.
Soutzoukákia or **soutzoúki (G)**: baked meat rissoles, which are often topped with a tomato-based sauce.
Soúvla: large cuts of lamb or pork, slow-roasted on a rotary spit.
Souvláki: chunks of meat quick-grilled on a skewer (known in London takeaways as kebab or shish kebab).
Spanakópitta: small turnovers stuffed with spinach, dill and often feta or some other crumbly, tart cheese.
Stifádo: a rich meat stew (often made using beef or rabbit) with onions, red wine, tomatoes, cinnamon and bay.
Taboúlleh: generic Middle Eastern starter of pourgoúri (qv), chopped parsley, cucumber chunks, tomatoes and spring onions.
Taramá, properly **taramosaláta**: fish roe pâté, originally made of dried, salted grey mullet roe, but now more often smoked cod roe, plus olive oil, lemon juice and breadcrumbs.
Tavás (GC): lamb, onion, tomato and cumin, cooked in earthenware casseroles.
Tsakistés (GC): split green olives marinated in lemon, garlic, coriander seeds and other optional flavourings.
Tyrópitta (G): similar to spanakópitta (qv) but usually without spinach and with more feta.
Tzatzíki, **dzadzíki (G)** or **talatoúra (GC)**: a dip of shredded cucumber, yoghurt, garlic, lemon juice and mint.

GREEK

Judging by the empty tables on a Thursday evening, something has gone off the boil at this once-buzzing eaterie. Which is a shame, as the modern styling (bright marble tables, dark wood floors, glitzy chandelier, retro photographs) and fuss-free Greek menu (mezédes, grills, wraps, fries) have the kind of straightforward appeal that works best accompanied by the sound of clinking beer bottles and raucous laughter. Our waiter appeared disoriented, and the kitchen didn't seem to be 100% with it either. Tyrópitta had the makings of a good meze (quality feta, a nice hit of mint), but was so undercooked it fell apart. Of a selection of dips, only the tzatziki passed muster. Prawn and lamb wraps were merely passable (good authentic gyro-style flatbreads, so-so fillings, a lack of spice in the 'spicy' sauce), and a portion of excellent oregano-speckled chips arrived long after the rest of the meal had been finished. We'd like to think we hit an off night – but our experience was more miss than hit.
Available for hire. Babies and children welcome: high chairs. Booking advisable weekends. Tables outdoors (2, pavement). Takeaway service. Vegetarian menu. **Map 13 B11**.

North

Camden Town & Chalk Farm

Lemonia
89 Regent's Park Road, NW1 8UY (7586 7454, www.lemonia.co.uk). Chalk Farm tube or bus 274. **Lunch served** noon-3pm daily. **Dinner served** 6-11.30pm Mon-Sat. **Main courses** £11.50-£17.75. **Set lunch** (Mon-Fri) £9.75-£11.50 3 courses. **Set mezédes** £19.50 per person (minimum 2). **Credit** MC, V.
Abuzz with gossip, toasts and the hushed chatter of Primrose Hill ladies-who-lunch, this much-loved Greek-Cypriot stalwart has been in operation for more than 30 years – serving up souvláki to local celebs and glasses of Metaxa to homesick old boys. The menu is lengthy, spanning charcoal grills, seafood, oven-cooked taverna classics, vast mezédes selections and great-value weekday lunch specials. Even in November, the plant-filled interior has an airy, summer-holiday vibe, and pavement tables are elevated to prime position the second the sun hits NW1. Don't expect culinary innovation; instead, you'll get well-executed dishes and top-quality meat and fish. Garlicky charred prawns and grilled sea bass were both cooked to perfection, while a fragrant plate of chicken with okra scored highly for authenticity with its rich sauce and subtle cinnamon kick. The wine list leans heavily towards France, South Africa and the United States, though there are a few Greek gems in there if you look hard enough; our 'wine of the month', a moschofilero, proved a delicious accompaniment. The traditionally clad waiters are efficient and unobtrusive, and leisurely dining is encouraged. Just the job for an afternoon (or evening) pretending you're back at that holiday island taverna.
Babies and children admitted. Booking advisable; essential weekends. Separate room for parties, seats 40. Tables outdoors (6, pavement). Takeaway service. Vegetarian menu. **Map 27 A1**.

Kentish Town

Carob Tree
Highgate Road, corner of Swains Lane, NW5 1QX (7267 9880). Gospel Oak rail or bus C2, C11, 214. **Lunch served** noon-3pm, **dinner served** 6-10.30pm Tue-Fri. **Meals served** noon-10.30pm Sat; noon-9pm Sun. **Main courses** £3.20-£20. **Credit** MC, V.
Carob Tree's big contemporary dining room (red drapes, white pillars, lots of wood) was rammed on our midweek visit. Multi-generational families chatted away in Greek, and big birthday groups knocked back Cypriot Keo beer. The crowds, high ceilings and open-plan layout (the building was once a pub) combine to make pretty lousy acoustics – nothing, however, that can't be compensated by attentive service and a plate of carefully sourced (breeds and butchers are name-checked) charcoal-grilled meat. Gloucester Old Spot souvláki was a shining example, while a generous portion of neatly butterflied grilled prawns was freshly flavoured simplicity at its best. A cold mezédes selection showcased perfect taramosaláta and tzatziki among a few duds (dark-brown, tasteless melitzanosaláta; briny peppers that tasted as if they'd come straight from a tin). The management seems to be missing a trick by offering such a limited Greek wine selection (just two whites and one red), but it's the friendly, neighbourhood vibe that keeps Carob Tree packed until closing time.
Babies and children welcome: high chairs; nappy-changing facilities. Booking advisable. Disabled: toilet. Tables outdoors (10, garden). Vegetarian menu. **Map 26 B4**.

Hotels & Haute Cuisine

Fine dining isn't the buttoned-up affair it used to be. A new generation of chef-proprietors has realised that people really do come for the food, and not everybody finds cosseting environs comfortable, regardless of how plump the cushions are. No longer is haute cuisine the preserve of the wealthy either. Emerging food-lovers from all walks of life are embracing the tasting menu as an entertaining experience to be enjoyed from time to time – and shared on social media, accelerating the rush to get to the latest hotspot.

We still call it as we see it, and our favourite places this year range from authentic French haute cuisine restaurants to modernist experiences inspired by native British plants, and venues that fall between the two. Interestingly, only two – **Marcus Wareing at the Berkeley**, and **Hélène Darroze at the Connaught** – are plush hotel dining rooms. **Tom Aikens** (now refurbished), **Dabbous** and newcomer **Restaurant Story** offer leaner, cooler visions of comfort along with more experimental cuisine. Another newcomer, the **Five Fields**, fits more readily alongside established but still-inventive favourites: the **Ledbury**, **Hibiscus** and **Gordon Ramsay**.

Central
Belgravia

Pétrus
1 Kinnerton Street, SW1X 8EA (7592 1609, www.gordonramsay.com/petrus). Knightsbridge tube. **Lunch served** noon-2.30pm, **dinner served** 6.30-10.30pm Mon-Sat. **Set lunch** £35 3 courses, £55 2 courses, £65 3 courses. **Set dinner** £65 3 courses. **Set meal** £75 tasting menu (£160 incl wine). **Credit** AmEx, MC, V.
A room enveloped in shades of pearlescent pink and dusky grey, with a spectacular crimson extrusion at its middle – it's unclear if the intention was to make this Knightsbridge restaurant so womb-like, but that's the effect. And it's not a bad thing: the service, food, indeed, the overall experience here has remained near-perfect since the place opened in April 2010. That red centrepiece is an open 'cellar', holding some of the extensive and indulgent wine list that reaches price levels few can contemplate. However, it's possible to eat and drink here with value. The set lunch still has a few of the luxe ingredients that characterise the carte and tasting menus: asparagus, aged beef, foie gras. Food here is rich, for sure, but it's plated with a light touch: roast cod and crushed potatoes rich in olive oil came with a punchy accompaniment of cornichons and brown shrimps; and a saddle of rabbit was sharpened by peas and mint oil. Special mention to the fine cheese board, which is a no-supplement option on the £35 three-course set lunch.
Available for hire. Babies and children welcome: high chairs. Booking advisable. Disabled: toilet. Dress: smart casual. Vegetarian menu. Map 9 G9.

City

Bonds
Threadneedles, 5 Threadneedle Street, EC2R 8AY (7657 8088, www.bonds-restaurant.co.uk). Bank tube/DLR. **Breakfast served** 6.30-10am Mon-Fri; 7.30-11am Sat, Sun. **Lunch served** noon-2.30pm, **dinner served** 6-10pm Mon-Fri. **Main courses** £12.95-£26.50. **Set meal** £24 2 courses, £28 3 courses. **Credit** AmEx, MC, V.
It's a pleasure walking past the grand buildings around Bank station. Before heading into this ground-floor restaurant in the Threadneedles hotel, pop into the foyer to take a look at the beautiful stained-glass dome. The dining room is stately, with soaring columns, elegant walnut panelling and oak flooring, but it doesn't seem overly ornate thanks to clever use of contemporary lighting and furnishings that soften the space. You don't need to raid the gold reserves at the Bank of England to eat here; prices are fair for the location, especially the set menus (these can vary – check the website for the latest offers). The hefty wine list also caters for different budgets. Service is discreet and willing. Mackerel made an unexciting start to a meal; it could have done with less time on the grill, but its oily nature was neatly foiled by a tomato fondue and splashes of balsamic vinegar. Chef Stephen Smith majors in British ingredients, so we couldn't resist a pork cutlet with potato and wild garlic mash, apple and crispy sage – and were well rewarded. Also delightful was sticky toffee pudding with vanilla ice-cream. Mobile phone signals can be intermittent in parts of the room, making Bonds a cheerful means of leaving daily stresses behind.
Available for hire. Babies and children welcome: high chairs. Booking advisable. Disabled: lift; toilet. Dress: smart casual. Separate rooms for parties, seating 8, 14 and 16. Map 12 Q6.

Fitzrovia

★ Dabbous

39 Whitfield Street, W1T 2SF (7323 1544, www.dabbous.co.uk). Goodge Street tube. **Lunch served** noon-2.30pm, **dinner served** 6.30-9.30pm Tue-Sat. **Set lunch** £28 2 courses. **Set meal** £59 tasting menu. **Credit** AmEx, MC, V.

The hype surrounding Dabbous' 2012 opening has not entirely diminished and securing a booking can be tricky, so it's a pleasure to arrive and find a relaxed, friendly restaurant. Many of the staff are disconcertingly young (not in a good way), which makes any pomposity on their part seem ridiculous. Our hostess left us in no doubt that the tasting menu was what we should have come for, but even at £59 per person for seven dishes it is among the best value in London. The international wine list is an enticing read, and several varieties offered by glass and carafe underscore the amenable attitude. Earthy own-made sourdough served in a paper bag gets things off to a jolly start. The kitchen majors in plant foods, setting a light, contemporary culinary tone concisely expressed in dishes such as mixed alliums with chilled pine infusion, and an ear of sweetcorn with butter and sweet-savoury seasoning. More traditional pea bavarois, however, was the better dish, exuberantly dressed with clean-flavoured titbits. Meats are skilfully cooked too, particularly barbecued ibérico pork with almond praline – one for fans of peanut butter. Astutely balanced iced lovage (a herbal granita) made a perfect refresher and ultimately was a more satisfying sweet than the runny custard cream pie, but that's to quibble. There's a great bar in the basement. No wonder this place is popular.
Available for hire. Babies and children welcome: high chairs. Booking advisable. Disabled: toilet. Dress: smart casual. **Map 17 B1.**

Pied à Terre

34 Charlotte Street, W1T 2NH (7636 1178, www.pied-a-terre.co.uk). Goodge Street tube. **Lunch served** 12.15-2.30pm Mon-Fri. **Dinner served** 6-11pm Mon-Sat. **Set lunch** £27.50 3 courses. **Set dinner** (6-7.15pm Mon-Fri) £39.50 2 courses. **Set meal** £75 tasting menu (£115 incl wine), £89 vegetarian tasting menu (£147 incl wine), £99 tasting menu (£157 incl wine). **Credit** AmEx, MC, V.

The entrance to Pied à Terre is so discreet that you would miss it unless looking specifically for the restaurant – and it makes an apt introduction to the classy understatement inside. We sat in the intimate dining room at the front (one of two at street level; there's a private dining room upstairs). With its tasteful cracked-glass feature, and cosily formal decor, this is a perfect setting for têtes-à-têtes, business-related or otherwise. There are plenty of options to spend £100-£200 per diner, but we opted for chef Marcus Eaves' excellent-value set lunch. A Cornish mackerel starter with avocado crème fraîche was a perfect blend of crisp and melt-in-the-mouth textures; and the juicy, flavourful pork with rainbow chard as a main course looked like a minimalist work of art. Attention to detail was impressive throughout: a slow-cooked lamb belly starter was accompanied by a perfect lamb and mint consommé; strawberries with a citrusy fromage-frais sorbet produced a delightful clash of flavours; and the amuse-bouches are a sensation – we dreamed of the miniature cinnamon doughnuts for days afterwards.

Pétrus. See p119.

Babies and children admitted. Booking advisable, essential weekends. Dress: smart casual. Separate room for parties, seats 13. Vegetarian menu. **Map 17 B1.**
For branch (L'Autre Pied) see index.

Roux at the Landau

The Landau, 1C Portland Place, W1B 1JA (7965 0165, www.thelandau.com). Oxford Circus tube. **Breakfast served** 7-10.30am Mon-Fri; 7am-noon Sat, Sun. **Lunch served** 12.30-2.30pm Mon-Fri. **Dinner served** 5.30-10.30pm Mon-Sat. **Main courses** £16-£30. **Set meal** (12.30-2.30pm, 5.30-7pm, 10-10.30pm) £45 3 courses incl half bottle of wine, mineral water and coffee; £60 tasting menu (£100 incl wine). **Credit** AmEx, MC, V.

The high-ceilinged oval dining room designed by the late David Collins instils a real sense of occasion on entry; this is just the place to celebrate an anniversary or go on an important date. Service on our visit was witty and courteous, though not always as attentive as it could have been. We needed to remind the waiters to bring the second glass of our half bottle of white wine – included in the menu du jour, which offers three courses for £45. A chilled vichyssoise starter was a perfect blend of delicate flavours and textures. Main course of duck leg served with cherry and pecan relish was a stunning testament to chef Chris King's status as a rising star: the skin crisp and flavourful without being greasy, and the meat succulent. Less successful was a starter of white boudin with chorizo, which looked interesting yet tasted of little. Braised featherblade steak (from the shoulder), though decent enough, didn't induce carnivorous ecstasy. The clear winner of the dessert selection was caramel ice-cream. Roux at the Landau is perhaps more of a gamble than it should be, but is still, ultimately, a worthwhile bet.
Babies and children welcome: high chairs. Booking advisable, essential weekends. Disabled: toilet. Dress: smart casual. Separate room for parties, seats 16. Vegetarian menu. **Map 9 H5.**

Knightsbridge

Dinner by Heston Blumenthal
Mandarin Oriental Hyde Park, 66 Knightsbridge, SW1X 7LA (7201 3833, www.dinnerbyheston.com). Knightsbridge tube. **Lunch served** noon-2.30pm, **dinner served** 6.30-10.30pm daily. **Main courses** £24-£38. **Set lunch** (Mon-Fri) £38 3 courses. **Credit** AmEx, MC, V.

Head chef Ashley-Palmer Watts, protégé of Heston Blumenthal, ensures that Dinner is one of London's most sought-after destinations. While the flagship restaurant, the Fat Duck in Bray, celebrates futuristic flamboyance, Dinner updates historic dishes with flair and precision. Sited in the Mandarin Oriental hotel, this corporate set-up is furnished with dark wood and unclothed tables, and boasts fine views of Hyde Park. An impressive glassed-in kitchen saves the restaurant from hotel-like sterility. The signature 'meat fruit' bears striking resemblance to a dimpled mandarin, its gel-like zesty sheen yields to a delectable chicken liver and foie gras parfait, with chargrilled sourdough bread a perfect partner. We were also taken by the umami notes of glazed roast quail, its sweet, tangy flavours matched with buttery chestnut-flecked cabbage and game jus. Desserts were top drawer, notably an orange syrup-steeped loaf (similar to brioche) paired with a remarkably zingy mandarin and thyme sorbet. Quaking pudding, originally from the 1600s, might have been the foundation for Britain's love of all things custardy. Set to a sexy wobble, our nutmeg-infused custard was surrounded by glossy perry caramel and perfectly poached pear slivers. Service was an impeccable combination of professionalism and welcoming warmth on our most recent visit. As expected, the wine list is extensive and expensive, though house choices are excellent value.
Babies and children welcome: high chairs. Booking essential, 3 mths in advance. Disabled: toilet (hotel). Dress: smart casual. Separate rooms for parties, seating 6 and 10. Tables outdoors (15, terrace). **Map 8 F9**.

Koffmann's
The Berkeley, Wilton Place, SW1X 7RJ (7107 8844, www.the-berkeley.co.uk). Hyde Park Corner or Knightsbridge tube. **Lunch served** noon-2.30pm Mon-Fri; noon-3pm Sat, Sun. **Dinner served** 6-10.30pm daily. **Main courses** £24-£29. **Set lunch** (Mon-Sat) £25.50 3 courses; (Sun) £26 3 courses. **Set meal** (6-6.30pm, 9.30-10.30pm) £28 3 courses. **Credit** AmEx, MC, V.

Pierre Koffmann, one of the most esteemed chefs of his generation, came out of retirement in 2010 to open this formal brasserie inside the swanky Berkeley hotel. The dining room, split over two floors, features smart textured wallpaper, plush carpets and crisp white linen; however, first-timers may be surprised to find there are no views over Hyde Park, which lies just opposite. Koffmann hails from Gascony and his culinary heritage is apparent from the off, but plump, garlicky snails with bone marrow and parsley foam showed that the kitchen keeps up with contemporary trends too. The cooking can be muscular, and our daube of beef cheeks in red wine was exceedingly rich. Potatoes are also taken seriously here – faultless mashed potato proved the point. For dessert, pistachio soufflé was executed with an architect's precision while tarte au citron was a seductive blend of tart,

creamy and caramelised flavours. Service is well drilled and attentive. A carefully compiled drinks list showcases two dozen wines by the glass, and some gems from the south-west corner of France. No wonder visitors continue to be delighted by Koffmann's return to the stove.
Available for hire. Babies and children welcome: high chairs; nappy-changing facilities. Booking advisable. Disabled: toilet (hotel). Dress: smart casual. Separate room for parties, seats 16. **Map 9 G9**.

★ Marcus Wareing at the Berkeley
The Berkeley, Wilton Place, SW1X 7RL (7235 1200, www.the-berkeley.co.uk). Hyde Park Corner or Knightsbridge tube. **Lunch served** noon-2.30pm, **dinner served** 6-11pm Mon-Sat. **Set lunch** (Mon-Fri) £30 2 courses, £38 3 courses incl half bottle of water and coffee (£56 incl wine); (Sat) £58-£68 3 courses, £95 tasting menu. **Set meal** £85 3 courses, £115 tasting menu. **Credit** AmEx, MC, V.

Like sinking yourself into a glass of fine Bordeaux, this long-established dining room is a treat, confident in its quality and style. Deep wine tones are brightened by white linens and a circular glass motif for an ambience that is cosseting and elegantly comfortable. Meals begin with the sommelier wheeling over a trolley of champagne on ice and talking you through the various bottles offered – frankly, it's hard to say no. Then comes a

Bonds. See p119.

bread basket with four loaves and, on our visit, airy gougères to snack on. From that point in the meal things just got better: a heavenly pea-themed amuse-bouche with ricotta foam (not at all sudsy); the clean zingy flavours of sardine, sweetcorn, coriander and cucumber in a high-end, not-quite Asian salad; just-so roast pork with a plate-licking jus and aubergine caviar. Desserts are a strong point, and the dish described as 'apricot, vanilla, oats' looked like Halley's comet streaking across the plate: a large crusted ball of two ice-cream flavours, with grilled fruit and compote sparkling in its chocolatey wake. Then superb chocolates and coffee to finish. Every menu is available with a wine-pairing option and, although the list is predominantly French, the sommelier selected an Argentinian malbec to match the pork.
Available for hire. Babies and children welcome: high chairs. Booking essential. Dress: smart; jacket preferred. Separate room for parties, seats 12-16. Vegetarian menu. **Map 9 G9.**

One-O-One

101 Knightsbridge, SW1X 7RN (7290 7101, www.oneonerestaurant.com). Knightsbridge tube. **Lunch served** noon-2.30pm Mon-Fri; 12.30-2.30pm Sat, Sun. **Dinner served** 6.30-10pm daily. **Main courses** £28-£39. **Set lunch** £17 2 dishes, £22 3 dishes, £28 4 dishes, £34 5 dishes, £40 6 dishes. **Set dinner** £49 6 courses, £49-£59 tasting menu (£84-£94 incl wine). **Credit** AmEx, MC, V.
Glazed windows and voile curtains shut out the incessant noise and traffic of Knightsbridge, making this modern, comfortable dining room (with well-spaced tables) a serene place to enjoy some of the best seafood cuisine in town. The repertoire is modern with a French accent, although chef Pascal Proyart is not afraid to incorporate Asian and Mediterranean touches. While the carte is pricey, the 'petit plats' menu at lunch is good value (with prices from £17 for two plates, up to £40 for six) and puts sustainable fishing centre stage. A deftly roasted hand-dived scallop was paired with flaky shallot confit tart and lifted by a red wine matelote

that left us hankering for more. Pan-fried farmed turbot tasted fresh and light in a parsley cassoulet, accompanied by king crab dumpling and finished with a few flakes of white truffle and rich bisque. Ethical arguments aside, there was nothing fishy about a smooth parfait of foie gras, its richness perfectly offset by a tart cranberry compote. For dessert, we enjoyed coconut malibu soufflé. Service is provided by a team that has worked here for several years and understands how to look after its customers. The international wine list is expansive and predictably expensive; however, by-the-glass options start at £7 and include saké.
Available for hire. Babies and children welcome: high chairs. Booking advisable Thur-Sun. Disabled: toilet. Dress: smart casual. Separate room for parties, seats 10. **Map 8 F9.**

Outlaw's at the Capital [NEW]

The Capital, 22-24 Basil Street, SW3 1AT (7591 1202, www.capitalhotel.co.uk). Knightsbridge tube. **Lunch served** noon-2.30pm, **dinner served** 6-10.30pm Mon-Sat. **Main courses** £24-£35. **Set lunch** £20 2 courses, £25 3 courses. **Set meal** £45 3 courses, £70 tasting menu (£130 incl wine).
Credit AmEx, MC, V.
Little has changed in the interior of this genteel hotel restaurant since Cornwall's adopted son Nathan Outlaw took over the kitchen – a couple of silvery seahorses on the walls, vases of shells on the tables, subtle hues of seaweed and sand. The crowd is similar too: a core of designer-clad Knightsbridge locals supplemented by a few wide-eyed gastronauts who've seen Outlaw on BBC's *Saturday Kitchen*. It's a clever pairing of family-run venue and chef, though not the only hotel in the area with a dining room majoring in seafood (One-O-One is nearby). There are efforts to wave a Cornish flag (the bread basket includes a light Cornish cheese and rosemary loaf and a brown Doom Bar number) but the overall effect is conservative, French-accented fine dining. Several menus are offered; we opted for a summer birthday 'celebration' purporting to showcase classic Outlaw dishes, though these were far less

exciting than the food we've eaten at some of his previous Cornish venues. Seafood is exquisitely fresh, as it should be, with the highlight of the meal being the scampi garnish on a main course of brill fillet with rich Mediterranean tomato and tarragon sauce. Breadcrumbed courgettes were not the best accompaniment, but were well cooked. A particularly vibrant set vanilla cream elevated a comforting bowlful of berries, strawberry sorbet and champagne jelly. There's an encyclopedic wine list featuring reasonably priced bottles from the group's own Loire vineyard.
Available for hire. Babies and children welcome: high chairs. Booking advisable. Disabled: toilet. Dress: smart casual. Separate rooms for parties, seating 14 and 24. **Map 8 F9.**

Marylebone

Texture

34 Portman Street, W1H 7BY (7224 0028, www.texture-restaurant.co.uk). Marble Arch tube.
Bar **Open** noon-midnight, **lunch served** noon-2.30pm, **dinner served** 6.30-11pm Tue-Sat. **Main courses** £13.50-£85. **Set lunch** £19.90 2 courses, £24.90 3 courses.
Restaurant **Lunch served** noon-2.30pm, **dinner served** 6.30-11pm Tue-Sat. **Main courses** £27.50-£37.50. **Set lunch** £55 tasting menu (£100 incl wine). **Set meal** £62 vegetarian tasting menu, £76.50 fish tasting menu, £79 tasting menu (£131 incl wine).
Both **Credit** AmEx, MC, V.
This sophisticated Modern European restaurant is fronted by Icelander Aggi Sverrisson, former head chef at Raymond Blanc's Le Manoir. It's popular with smart corporate groups on elastic expense accounts. The dining area, sited in a spacious Georgian room, is furnished in neutral colours, enlivened by pastel-green leather upholstery, modern art and striking floral arrangements. A light-filled bar sets the scene with an exhaustive champagne selection. Clean-cut flavours

Dabbous. See p120.

characterise the menu. Precision-cooked Norwegian king crab provided a globally inspired tease of chunky crab meat, set against a backdrop of warm ginger broth spiked with wasabi and crunchy roasted garlic. Delicately smoked salmon fillet with pickled vegetables and diced apple worked a treat with peppery horseradish cream, cucumber granita and aromatic sorrel for an orchestrated blend of textures, temperatures and sweet, tangy flavours. It's not all about fish and seafood, though: meat main courses are just as distinctive. Milk-fed veal strips, cooked to perfect pinkness, were partnered by Jersey Royals, summery artichokes and a delectable sherried jus enriched with plump morels. Updating a tradition of partnering Icelandic skyr (soft cheese) with rhubarb, dessert teamed the duo with crunchy caramelised rye crumbs for a fitting finale. Service is utterly professional. Cooking this good doesn't come cheap, but there's a more affordable set menu at lunchtime.

Available for hire. Babies and children welcome: high chairs. Booking advisable. Disabled: toilet. Dress: smart casual. Separate room for parties, seats 16. Vegetarian menu.
Map 9 G6.

Mayfair

Alain Ducasse at the Dorchester

The Dorchester, Park Lane, W1K 1QA (7629 8866, www.alainducasse-dorchester.com). Hyde Park Corner tube. **Lunch served** noon-1.30pm Tue-Fri. **Dinner served** 6.30-9.30pm Tue-Sat. **Set lunch** £55 3 courses incl 2 glasses of wine, mineral water, coffee. **Set dinner** £85 3 courses, £100 4 courses. **Set meal** £120 tasting menu (£215 incl wine), £180 seasonal menu. **Credit** AmEx, MC, V.

It is perhaps a tribute to London's international status that there's a niche for this restaurant in the capital; relatively few people apart from star footballers are in a position to frequent it. Nor would we want to: indeed, there are other places we'd rather visit elsewhere within the Dorchester. The cooking and setting are undeniably lovely, yet the overall experience lacks wow factors – apart from the bill – largely because of its unfashionably restrained, traditional approach to fine dining. Still, the restaurant commands a loyal clientele. Three courses from the carte cost £85, though the limited 'lunch hour' menu includes three courses, two glasses of wine, coffee and a half-bottle of water for £55. A few British ingredients (Dorset crab, Denbighshire pork, Colston Bassett stilton) make the cut, but otherwise this is very much a French affair complete with foie gras, truffled chicken quenelles and petits pois à la française. Desserts and petits fours are superb, so plan to save room. We have fond memories of the trademarked (literally) Cookpot: a seasonally changing, pastry-sealed casserole featuring green asparagus, girolles and comté cheese this summer; in colder months, typically brussels sprouts, butternut squash, apple and Montgomery cheddar. The wine list is naturally pricey, yet the sommeliers are helpful. You'll need an additional £200 to secure the central table, Lumière, with its fibre-optic curtain and Hermès crockery – just the thing when you want to escape the riff-raff.

Available for hire. Booking essential, 2 mths in advance. Children over 10yrs admitted. Disabled: toilet (hotel). Dress: smart. Vegetarian menu.
Map 9 G7.

Pied à Terre. See p120.

Galvin at Windows

28th floor, London Hilton, Park Lane, W1K 1BE (7208 4021, www.galvinatwindows.com). Green Park or Hyde Park Corner tube. **Lunch served** noon-2.30pm Mon-Fri; 11.45am-3pm Sun. **Dinner served** 6-10pm Mon-Wed; 6-10.30pm Thur-Sat. **Set lunch** £25 2 courses, £29 3 courses (£45 incl half bottle of wine, mineral water and coffee). **Set dinner** £39-£68 3 courses. **Set meal** (noon-2pm, 6-9pm) £95 tasting menu (£160 incl wine, £195 incl champagne). **Credit** AmEx, MC, V.

Few restaurants offer such captivating views of London, but the panorama from the 28th floor of the Park Lane Hilton was, we're sorry to report, the best thing about our most recent visit here. Start, if you like, in the adjoining bar, which attracts a raucous crowd unfazed that bottles of Budweiser come with a price tag of £7.50. A well-mannered and plentiful service team runs the swanky dining room. Menus range from a £25 set lunch to a £95 dégustation. We settled for the prestige menu (£68 for three courses) and found blips throughout the meal, starting with humdrum parmesan gougères with taramasalata. Much better was a pleasingly balanced starter of lightly curried Scottish scallops with cauliflower purée, mango chutney and roast peanuts, though the scallops were under-seared. Tender loin of Herdwick mutton was complemented by the warming flavours of onion (in various guises), pearl barley and ruby chard. The dish came with a separate helping of shepherd's pie that, despite being over-salted, was deemed a hit. Buttermilk panna cotta with marinated pineapple was let down by a watery lychee granita, but lime and raspberry marshmallows ensured a joyful end. The enterprising wine list offers 40 choices by the glass. We hope Galvin at Windows returns to its previous lofty standards soon – a new era is being ushered in following the departure of head chef Andre Garrett in September 2013.

Available for hire. Babies and children welcome: high chairs. Booking advisable. Disabled: lift; toilet (hotel). Dress: smart casual. **Map 9 G8**.

Le Gavroche

43 Upper Brook Street, W1K 7QR (7408 0881, www.le-gavroche.co.uk). Marble Arch tube. **Lunch served** noon-2pm Mon-Fri. **Dinner served** 6.30-11pm Mon-Sat. **Main courses** £25-£65. **Set lunch** £52.60 3 courses incl half bottle of wine, mineral water and coffee. **Set dinner** (6.30-10pm) £112 tasting menu (£180 incl wine). **Credit** AmEx, MC, V.

This restaurant colossus offers unapologetically old-school fine dining. First opened in Chelsea in 1967 by the Roux brothers, Albert and Michel, it's now run by Michel Roux Jr, who took the reins in 1991. Le Gavroche continues to be the go-to haute cuisine establishment for a dignified, extremely wealthy crowd (our reservation had to be made three months in advance). While it may bear the name of the street urchin from Victor Hugo's *Les Misérables*, there's nothing scruffy about the club-like decor. Naturally, prices are high, although the set lunch for £52.60 (including half of a bottle of wine) is great value. Our eight-course 'menu exceptionnel' started with soufflé suissesse, an exquisitely light and fluffy gruyère soufflé cooked on double cream: an old recipe from the original restaurant. Next, the sourness of an aigre-doux vinaigrette sidelined a salad of braised octopus and soft-shell crab, but happiness was soon restored by a boudin noir served with a runny scotch egg and wicked piece of pork crackling. Roast squab arrived with the perfect degree of rareness, along with braised peas and a jus of haunting intensity. Millefeuille of raspberries and gianduja made a pleasurable finale. The food is matched by an imperious wine list, with 50 wines offered by the glass. Service was gracious throughout our stay, helping us enjoy the prosperous buzz of the place even more.
Available for hire. Babies and children admitted. Booking essential, 3 mths in advance. Dress: jacket; smart jeans accepted; no trainers. **Map 9 G7**.

Greenhouse

27A Hay's Mews, W1J 5NY (7499 3331, www.greenhouserestaurant.co.uk). Green Park tube. **Lunch served** noon-2.30pm Mon-Fri. **Dinner served** 6.30-10.30pm Mon-Sat. **Set lunch** £25 2 courses, £29 3 courses. **Set meal** £65 2 courses, £75 3 courses, £90 tasting menu. **Credit** AmEx, MC, V.

It takes just a couple of steps along the decked, tree-lined entrance of this Mayfair mews restaurant for a sense of oasis and calm to descend – an atmosphere that is deliberately cultivated and carried through to the cool, well-spaced dining room. Solicitous greetings abound the moment you cross the threshold; the Greenhouse is a place where chairs are tweaked, tables brushed and every detail seen to by a considerate team. The place was buzzing on a weekday lunch with a pleasing range of perceptions, palates and purses. Short dish names on the menus merely hint at the perfumes and jewels to come, and the set lunch is barely less pretty and opulent than the carte, which is three times the price. Sea bream and passionfruit ceviche (from the set lunch) and pan-fried foie gras with malabar pepper (from the carte) both carried a perfectly balanced touch of the exotic. The set menu's cherry dessert proved as painstakingly executed as the carte's praline concoction, though

the latter was arguably more inventive. Extraordinary appetisers and curious petits fours are served with both menus, and well-priced wine by the glass showcases the quality and interest of the extensive cellar. Neither menu was entirely free of slip-ups; the corollary is that the Greenhouse leaves you eager to return not merely soon, but often.
Available for hire. Babies and children admitted. Booking essential. Disabled: toilet. Dress: smart casual. **Map 9 H7**.

★ Hélène Darroze at the Connaught

The Connaught, Carlos Place, W1K 2AL (3147 7200, www.the-connaught.co.uk). Bond Street tube. **Lunch served** noon-2.30pm Tue-Fri. **Brunch served** 11am-2.30pm Sat. **Dinner served** 6.30-10.30pm Tue-Sat. **Set lunch/ brunch** £35 3 courses (£42 incl 2 glasses of wine). **Set meal** £80 3 courses, £98-£120 tasting menu (£196-£240 incl wine). **Credit** AmEx, MC, V.

Genial staff take obvious pleasure in working this historic dining room, with its beautiful wood panelling and floral plasterwork ceiling. India Mahdavi's feminine interior of velvety golds complements the original features, while Damien Hirst's artwork keeps it grounded in the present. Waistcoats, silver jugs and Baccarat crystal denote formality, so first-timers may be surprised by the rusticity of the food on display: a leg of ham for carving; butter pats as big as cheese truckles; huge biscuit jars. Best to go with the flow. Darroze put trendy piment d'espelette on the culinary map and her menus reveal a passion for all things peppery. Yet this is not fiery cuisine; sometimes we wish it was a little less French, such as in the irritating refinement of hake with razor clams, salsa verde

Koffmann's. See p121.

and minuscule girolles, which anywhere else would have been a muscular dish. No complaints, though, about perfectly proportioned foie gras crème brûlée with bright apple sorbet. Dessert was a clever globe of chocolate, which, when hot chocolate sauce was poured over, collapsed to reveal a layered tower of black-forest-themed indulgences. The sweet avalanche continued with a whole trolley of petits fours to choose from – cinnamon marshmallow and an apricot and salted-caramel macaron were particular favourites. Such is the special-occasion nature of the place that everyone is presented with a personalised souvenir menu; but rest assured, the experience is memorable in its own right.

Available for hire. Babies and children welcome: high chairs. Booking advisable, essential weekends. Disabled: toilet (hotel). Dress: smart; no jeans or trainers. Separate room for parties, seats 16. Vegetarian menu. **Map 9 H7.**

★ Hibiscus

29 Maddox Street, W1S 2PA (7629 2999, www.hibiscusrestaurant.co.uk). Oxford Circus tube. **Lunch served** noon-2.30pm Mon-Sat. **Dinner served** 6.30-10.30pm Mon-Thur; 6-10.30pm Fri, Sat. **Set lunch** £34.95 3 courses, (£49.50 incl half bottle of wine, coffee and petits fours). **Set dinner** £87.95 3 courses, £95 6 courses (£165 incl wine), £105 8 courses (£195 incl wine). **Credit** AmEx, MC, V.

Chef Claude Bosi opened a gastropub (Malt House) in Fulham in 2012 to go with his other one (Fox & Grapes) in Wimbledon, but he clearly hasn't taken his eye off this flagship restaurant. There's no à la carte menu (unless you really want it), so choose three, six or eight courses – and marvel, as the extraordinarily composed dishes arrive on your table with military timing. On a 'Taste of Spring' menu, almost everything included a potentially unusual combination of fruit/savoury flavours – a single spear of grilled asparagus with confit orange and black truffle purée as a starter; scallop sharpened with pink grapefruit gel; Gariguette strawberries topped with celeriac foam. Some of the pairings tend towards the experimental; it takes a few mouthfuls to convince yourself that morels with kaffir lime, coffee and tarragon actually works. But it does – as does everything else in this often vividly exciting restaurant. Even the unobtrusively adept service is far from buttoned-up. The impressive wine list is big on biodynamic and natural expressions, but there's a house wine at £6 a glass, meaning lunch (with its reasonably priced offerings) needn't be as expensive a prospect as dinner inevitably is.

Babies and children welcome: high chairs. Booking essential. Disabled: toilet. Separate room for parties, seats 18. **Map 9 J6.**

Maze

10-13 Grosvenor Square, W1K 6JP (7107 0000, www.gordonramsay.com/maze). Bond Street tube. **Lunch served** noon-2.30pm, **dinner served** 6-11pm daily. **Main courses** £10-£18. **Set meal** (lunch daily; 6-7pm, 10-11pm Mon-Thur, Sun) £25 4 courses, £75 tasting menu (£125-£165 incl drinks). **Sushi** £8-£27. **Set sushi lunch** £30-£70. **Credit** AmEx, MC, V.

For an obviously swanky restaurant, this Gordon Ramsay Holdings outlet is exceedingly casual, and staff bring a personal sparkle to the generally accomplished service. A sushi bar, complete with bar stools to watch the chefs in action, opened inside the long, stylish space in

autumn 2012, adding a menu of sashimi and sushi. Its arrival seems to have angled the food further towards the Orient and almost every dish now comes with an Asian twist on French foundations. The menu of small plates is largely designed for sharing – indeed, Maze was one of the first haute cuisine establishments to offer an alternative to the amuse-starter-main-dessert formula. From the set menu (a steal at £25 for four courses) came a suprême of quail with jalapeño miso dressing, bream with dashi broth and enoki, and beef carpaccio with chilli: all perfectly balanced platefuls, although perhaps lacking the zing that might elevate them from strong to distinguished. On our visit, Maze was buzzing as new arrivals trooped in every few minutes: groups of tourists snapping pictures of their food; lunching couples; even families with young children. It's easy to see the appeal – this is a distinctive and approachable entry point to the higher end of the GRH stable.

Available for hire. Babies and children welcome: high chairs. Booking essential. Disabled: toilet. Dress: smart casual; no trainers. Vegetarian menu. **Map 9 G6.**

Pollen Street Social

8-10 Pollen Street, W1S 1NQ (7290 7600, www.pollenstreetsocial.com). Oxford Circus tube. **Bar Open** noon-midnight Mon-Sat. *Restaurant* **Lunch served** noon-2.30pm, **dinner served** 6-10.30pm Mon-Sat. **Main courses** £29.50-£38. **Set lunch** £26 2 courses, £29.50 3 courses; £65 tasting menu. **Set dinner** £60-£85 tasting menu. *Both* **Credit** AmEx, MC, V.

Pollen Street Social's philosophy is 'deformalised fine dining', and to this end the decor is smart but approachable – white-walled, linen-draped and wood-panelled. Dishes are grounded in French and English tradition and embellished with occasionally esoteric side notes of texture and taste, sometimes garnered from chef Jason Atherton's travels. They're seasonal too, in terms of ingredients, but not necessarily in mood. On the hot June day of our visit, we craved something more refreshing than à la carte starters of roasted quail 'brunch' or braised ox cheek with parsley and oyster purée. The great-value set lunch felt distinctly more spring than summer, even though a dish of Wiltshire pork belly, spiced cheek and apple mustard purée was enlivened by lemon zest paste. It was beautifully put together but begged the question of how 'deformalised' fine dining can be before it becomes good gastropub fare. The delicious subtlety and artistry of Cornish sea bass and red mullet with bouillabaisse sauce, fennel, cuttlefish and saffron potato (self-served from the pan) answered that, as did a masterly strawberry and basil eton mess (it's worth noting that you can come in just for a dessert). Service was perhaps slightly too casual for this level, with water served warm and iceless, and an overlong wait (and this was lunchtime) for the main courses. So, while the cooking was excellent, our overall experience was a little bland.

Available for hire. Babies and children welcome (restaurant): high chairs. Booking advisable. Disabled: toilet. Separate room for parties, seats 14. Vegetarian menu. **Map 9 J6.**

Sketch: Lecture Room & Library

9 Conduit Street, W1S 2XJ (7659 4500, www.sketch.uk.com). Oxford Circus tube. **Lunch served** noon-2.15pm Tue-Fri. **Dinner served**

7-10.30pm Tue-Sat. **Main courses** £35-£55. **Set lunch** £35 2 courses incl coffee, £40 3 courses incl coffee (£53 incl half bottle of wine, mineral water and coffee). **Set meal** £75 vegetarian tasting menu, £95 tasting menu. **Credit** AmEx, MC, V.

The arresting entrance hall, with its high-impact artworks and greeters who are part-cast and part-personal assistant, are cues that you are entering not just a building of dizzying grandeur, but a designed world with a playful, theatrical bent. Sketch's Lecture Room & Library is up a very fine staircase. Flooded with light from a glass ceiling dome, and governed by immaculately tailored staff, it's the most classical space in the complex, with the food providing the trademark fantastical note. It's a positive procession of the pretty, witty and gay, from the first amuse-bouche to the last pink petit four. Our set lunch comprised 15 or so different dishes, using a gazetteer of ingredients and a battery of techniques: highly accomplished cooking whose dainty presentation belies its seriousness. There's so much going on – within dishes and in the combination of dishes served as one course – that you surrender yourself to the cumulative experience. Just a few examples from one meal: bream sashimi; langoustine consommé with wild garlic, kaffir and dill, blood-orange jelly and spring cabbage; pork belly confit with tamarillo purée, celery, loquat, celery stick and potato foam with comté cheese; lemon and beer ice-cream with raspberries. It's quite a trip, as is the wine list, which isn't all at fantasy prices. The sommelier clearly loves his work, and is as happy to recommend beer as he is to favour a prestige claret if the dish demands it.

Available for hire. Babies and children welcome: high chairs. Booking advisable. Dress: smart casual. Separate rooms for parties, seating 24 and 50. Vegetarian menu. **Map 9 J6. For branches (Sketch: The Parlour, Sketch: The Gallery) see index.**

The Square

6-10 Bruton Street, W1J 6PU (7495 7100, www.squarerestaurant.com). Bond Street or Green Park tube. **Lunch served** noon-2.45pm Mon-Sat. **Dinner served** 6.30-10pm Mon-Thur; 6.30-10.30pm Fri, Sat; 6.30-9.30pm Sun. **Set lunch** £35 2 courses, £40 3 courses. **Set meal** £90 3 courses, £115 tasting menu (£185 incl wine). **Credit** AmEx, MC, V.

An unassuming name, an unassuming interior, a nondescript entrance – but we're in Bruton Street here, one of the most refined streets in refined Mayfair (hell, the Queen was born at no.17). An unobtrusive streak runs through everything at this restaurant, where standards – from the luxe Ren products in the toilets to the spiderweb-delicate glassware – are sky-high, but there's nothing too avant-garde to startle the clientele. As a result, a meal here is one of suavity and established luxury. Not a bad thing: sometimes it's better to be cossetted than challenged. Our lunch started with translucent chicken jelly with peas and an airy pillow of goat's curd: a summery statement of intent. Dishes such as the poured-at-table gazpacho with crayfish and sour cream ice-cream, or sea bream with courgette, razor clams and parmesan – both from the set menu – were accomplished and clearly labour-intensive works of complementary colours, flavours, textures and shapes. Staff were earnest rather than friendly; a chatty sommelier offered a note of personality, otherwise service is

Pollen Street Social. See p125.

HOTELS & HAUTE CUISINE

conducted with quiet industry and consideration. One for the classicists rather than the trendsetters, but still a seamless experience.

Available for hire. Babies and children admitted. Booking advisable. Disabled: toilet. Dress: smart; smart jeans accepted; no trainers. Separate room for parties, seats 18. Vegan dishes. Vegetarian menu. **Map 9 H7.**

Piccadilly

The Ritz
150 Piccadilly, W1J 9BR (7493 8181, www.theritzlondon.com). Green Park tube.
Bar **Open/meals served** 11.30am-midnight Mon-Sat; noon-10.30pm Sun. **Main courses** £24-£40.
Restaurant **Breakfast served** 7-10.30am Mon-Sat; 8-10.30am Sun. **Lunch served** 12.30-2.30pm daily. **Tea served** (reserved sittings) 11.30am, 1.30pm, 3.30pm, 5.30pm, 7.30pm daily. **Dinner served** 5.30-10.30pm Mon-Sat; 7-10pm Sun. **Main courses** £37-£40. **Set lunch** £47 3 courses, £85 6 courses (£145-£175 incl wine). **Set tea** £45-£56 (£57-£67 incl glass of champagne). **Set dinner** £85 6 courses (£145-£175 incl wine).
Both **Credit** AmEx, MC, V.

The Ritz dining room's Louis XVI-inspired decor, with its pink marble, gilt ornamentation and rows of chandeliers, is unforgettable. Champagne is almost de rigueur as part of the experience, but we resisted – even a modest half-bottle of wine makes a serious dent in the wallet. Without it, though, we found the amuse-bouches surprisingly lacklustre. The set lunch menu is no bargain at £47 for three courses; mains on the carte hover around the £40 mark. The provenance and freshness of ingredients seems impeccable – from St Malo butter, via Var salmon, to heritage carrots – but all too often there's a blandness, despite some precision cooking. The more inventive compilations generally fared better: a fruit sliver shell surrounding flaked crab; citrus jelly cubes and a gloriously sea-fresh oyster mayonnaise with halibut steak; light textured biscuit-sand and delicate white chocolate hoops in deconstructed raspberry cheesecake. Oddly, there was no way of anticipating which choices stuck to the classic cannon and which gave freer rein to the clearly capable chef John Williams. Aside from the glorious gilt, what you are buying in the Ritz dining room is a conservative formula, complete with coat-tailed service of correctly distant politesse, china plate-domes, tinkling piano renditions of familiar film themes and a reassurance that all is unruffled in the privileged world you have briefly dipped into.

Babies and children welcome: children's menu; high chairs. Booking advisable restaurant; essential afternoon tea. Dress: jacket; smart jeans accepted; no trainers. Entertainment: dinner dance Fri, Sat (restaurant); pianist daily. Separate rooms for parties, seating 16-60. Tables outdoors (8, terrace). **Map 9 J7.**

South Kensington

★ Tom Aikens
43 Elystan Street, SW3 3NT (7584 2003, www.tomaikens.co.uk). South Kensington tube.
Lunch served noon-2.30pm Tue-Fri. **Dinner served** 6.30-10.30pm Tue-Sat. **Main courses** £29-£35. **Set lunch** £28 2 courses, £32 3 courses. **Set meal** £80-£90 tasting menu. **Credit** AmEx, MC, V.

If this restaurant were a new opening, the foodie blogo-tweetisphere would be going cronuts for it. As it is, the reopening in January 2013 of Tom Aikens' beautifully refurbished flagship has caused few ripples, and it's delightfully easy to snare one of the chic dark wood tables. These are set with nothing more than a jute napkin and glass that, although contrived, signal the fresh, clever thinking that has been done here. They are soon joined by a stylish breadboard of turned wood, and a choice of three butters (made in-house) including flavours of cep, and bacon and onion. It all feels Amish-deluxe until the prettily illustrated menus arrive, one in an envelope, the other in a scroll. The keenly priced set lunch is enticing, but the carte is so chock-full with intrigues (we could have happily ordered every dish), the effect is irresistible. Ingredients are prime, flavours are lively, creativity is joyous. Witness two slabs of braised and roasted piglet belly topped with crunchy puffed rind accompanied by smoked apple, aubergine and an intense black sauce made from the aubergine's charred skin. Chocolate and violet dessert was a riot of textures, temperatures and tastes, including honeycomb, violet sorbet, petals and chocolate cake. A fabulously friendly wine list is boosted by a discerning range of hip bottled beers; even-handed advice on choosing comes from a chatty, down-to-earth sommelier. If we're being picky, the mousse component of a too-cold pea-themed amuse-bouche bordered on rubbery; otherwise this was a thoroughly stellar experience.

Available for hire. Booking advisable. Children admitted. Disabled: toilet. Separate room for parties, seats 10. Vegetarian menu. **Map 14 E11.**

West
Chiswick

Hedone
301-303 Chiswick High Road, W4 4HH (8747 0377, www.hedonerestaurant.com). Chiswick Park tube. **Lunch served** noon-2.30pm Thur-Sat. **Dinner served** 6.30-9.30pm Tue-Thur; 6.30-10pm Fri, Sat. **Set lunch** £35 3 courses, £55 tasting menu (£114 incl wine), £85 tasting menu (£164 incl wine). **Set dinner** (Tue-Thur) £55 3 courses; £75 tasting menu (£134 incl wine), £95 tasting menu (£174 incl wine). **Credit** AmEx, MC, V.

It may seem nothing more than a pleasant neighbourhood eaterie on a suburban high street, but the first restaurant from former solicitor and food blogger Mikael Jonsson is remarkable in many

ways. Given that Scandinavian cooking is in the ascendancy, much is made of his Swedish background, but the menu isn't overtly Nordic: more French-leaning Modern European, with impeccable seasonality. The stall was set out by the amuse-bouches – savoury petits fours of morello jelly on a parmesan wafer, smoked haddock tart and foie gras in a sourdough crisp – and a pre-starter of seaweed on savoury custard: rich and intriguing flavours and textures. One dish, of French white asparagus with tarragon hollandaise, green asparagus and romaine lettuce purée, was gloopy and not good; asparagus was better served with crispy duck-egg yolk, egg white mayonnaise and morels, prettily arranged on a large black plate. From there, it was pleasure all the way: duck on a giblet sauce with five types of beetroot was sweet, earthy and clove-pungent, beetroot at its fullest expression. Cumbrian salt-marsh lamb, conversely, was served simply to allow its flavours to sing. A herb sorbet that channelled Indian chutney, a chocolate dessert layered at different temperatures with a crust of powdered raspberry, and subtle petits fours, provided more palate-stretching flavours. It's a lot to ask of wine to keep up, and only one of our choices did: a £20 glass of small-domain biodynamic Jura pinot noir.
Available for hire. Babies and children welcome: high chairs; nappy-changing facilities. Booking advisable. Disabled: toilet. Dress: smart casual. Separate room for parties, seats 16. Vegetarian menu.

Westbourne Grove

★ Ledbury `HOT 50`
127 Ledbury Road, W11 2AQ (7792 9090, www.theledbury.com). Ladbroke Grove or Westbourne Park tube. **Lunch served** noon-2pm Tue-Sat; noon-2.30pm Sun. **Dinner served** 6.30-10.15pm Mon-Sat; 7-10pm Sun. **Main courses** (lunch) £32-£34. **Set lunch** (Mon-Sat) £30 2 courses, £35 3 courses; (Sun) £50 3 courses. **Set dinner** £80 3 courses. **Set meal** £95 vegetarian tasting menu (£165 incl wine), £105 tasting menu (£175 incl wine). **Credit** AmEx, MC, V.

Few haute establishments have the hospitable hum of the Ledbury. Whether it's due to the off-centre location, the Aussie input, or diners' sheer delight in securing a table, this former pub remains top-tier for gustatory good times. British ingredients – Hampshire buffalo milk curd, smoked eel, Cumbrian lamb – line up alongside delicacies such as foie gras, Tokyo turnips, Bresse chicken and black truffle, but it's chef Brett Graham's clever contemporary treatment of them that sets the place apart. Best go for the set lunch or commit to the mesmerising £105 tasting menu; at £80 for three courses, the set dinner does not have the other menus' winning sense of value, particularly if you choose the simpler ingredient-led dishes. A spring plate of creamed Jersey Royals with morels cooked in tea would have been a delightful inclusion in a dégustation, but served as a starter was not sufficiently above mashed potato to justify the outlay, even though the mushrooms were sublime. Ledbury signatures, however, are consistently thrilling – particularly the flame-grilled mackerel with pickled cucumber, celtic mustard and shiso; and, well, all the desserts. The wine list is personable, with a particularly good choice of sweet wines by the glass, plus there are great beers from Australia, the US and even Notting Hill.
Available for hire. Babies and children welcome: high chairs. Booking essential. Disabled: toilet. Vegetarian menu. **Map 19 C3**.

South West
Chelsea

★ Five Fields `NEW`
8-9 Blacklands Terrace, SW3 2SP (7838 1082, www.fivefieldsrestaurant.com). Sloane Square tube. **Dinner served** 6.30-10pm Tue-Sat. **Set meal** £45 3 courses, £65 tasting menu (£115 incl wine). **Credit** MC, V.

Reviews of this bijou spot have been mixed since its opening, but our experience was stellar. Run by chef-proprietor Taylor Bonnyman, Five Fields has a native British focus using fresh produce from its own gardens in East Sussex (complete with ex-gardener from Raymond Blanc's Le Manoir aux Quat'Saisons). Careful sourcing extends to fish from Cornwall, scallops from Orkney, and Yorkshire lamb. Dishes are simple and playful. 'Kitchen garden' is a celebration of own-grown herbs, fruits, flowers and vegetables – and far more than mere salad. 'Rock pool' demands a supplement (£8), but is well worth it for the gustatory drama of exquisitely prepared fish and shellfish arriving in stages. Flavour combinations beg to be tried: veal sweetbread with glazed shin meat, gooseberries and chicory, say; or braised beef short rib (a trendy cut) with beetroot, cherries and smoked ricotta. Desserts are riddled with vegetables – in August, cep sponge with peaches and butterscotch praline; cucumber with white chocolate sorbet and basil-ash meringue; and garden peas with chocolate soil and coconut sorbet. The cocktail list is similarly intriguing, and wines stretch from Kent to Yamanashi, Japan, though France dominates. Plenty of extras are included in the three-course £45 menu, so that it feels just as special as the longer options.
Available for hire. Babies and children admitted. Booking advisable. Disabled: toilet. Separate room for parties, seats 10. **Map 14 F11**.

★ Gordon Ramsay
68 Royal Hospital Road, SW3 4HP (7352 4441, www.gordonramsay.com). Sloane Square tube. **Lunch served** noon-2.15pm, **dinner served** 6.30-10.15pm Mon-Fri. **Set lunch** £55 3 courses. **Set meal** £95 3 courses, £135 tasting menu; £165 seasonal menu. **Credit** AmEx, MC, V.

Clare Smyth is chef-patron of Gordon Ramsay's flagship Chelsea restaurant. Her name at last features on the intelligently inventive menu, and the cool, elegant dining room has been refurbished with distinctly feminine touches, including lilac-toned silk-screened panels. Dishes tantalise then delight the senses; no element of the complex assemblies seems showily redundant – even the pouring of sauces at table adds visual and aromatic impact. A snow of frozen buttermilk proved a perfect counterpoint to slivers of summer vegetables in a rock pool of warm, deeply flavoured jus. Shavings of salt-baked turnip gave saline balance to the

Five Fields

sweetness of rabbit loin with roast hazelnuts, and vadouvan-spiced, smoke-puffed wild rice provided a crunchy backdrop to tender mutton. If our set lunch desserts were a touch less perfect, petits fours stepped in with polished panache. It helps to have an insouciant budget, but we were treated with warm courtesy throughout: even by the sommelier, pre-tasting our screw-topped South African rosé. Show particular interest in any aspect of the meal and you'll elicit an enthusiastic and informed response. The Herdwick mutton, we discovered, was ineffably pink and tender because it had been brought down from high ground hefting to lush grassland for three months. We left with a smile, and lifted spirits.

Available for hire. Booking essential. Children admitted. Dress: smart; jacket preferred. **Map 14 F12**.

South East
Tower Bridge

Restaurant Story NEW
201 Tooley Street, SE1 2UE (7183 2117, www.restaurantstory.co.uk). London Bridge tube/rail. **Lunch served** noon-2pm, **dinner served** 6.30-9.30pm Tue-Sat. **Set meal** £55 6 courses, £75 10 courses. **Credit** AmEx, MC, V.

Story continues Bermondsey's rise to foodie haven. The new-build sits on a traffic island on the site of a former toilet block. It's a sparse room, with dark brown leather chairs and Scandinavian accents – all the better to emphasise the view of the Shard through floor-to-ceiling windows. And, of course, the food: an enjoyable procession of modernist dishes layered with culinary puns (bread and dripping, for instance, features a lit candle made from dripping) and taste bud challenges (mackerel versus green strawberries, perhaps). Chefs ferry dishes from the red-tiled open kitchen to the tables

themselves. Choose from a six- or ten-course menu. Superb raw scallops come with balls of elderflower-pickled cucumber and smoky cucumber skin and dill ash crust, tiny nasturtium leaves and herb oils. The classic flavour combination of beetroot and horseradish is made eye-opening with raspberries and pretty-as-a-picture presentation. Fruit appears in many guises throughout the meal, and savoury notes characterise the puddings; prunes with lovage and milk skin is salty and sweet at the same time. Local beers (Bermondsey, Notting Hill, Bethnal Green) and classic cocktails made with a connoisseur's choice of spirits complement an international wine list that features a good choice by the glass and half bottle (though only a couple are less than £30 a bottle). Predictably, given the area, a business crowd is attracted at lunchtimes. *Available for hire. Babies and children admitted. Booking essential dinner. Disabled: toilet.* **Map 12 R9**.

East
Bethnal Green

Viajante HOT 50
Patriot Square, E2 9NF (7871 0461, www.viajante.co.uk). Bethnal Green tube or Cambridge Heath rail. **Lunch served** noon-2pm Fri-Sun. **Dinner served** 6-9.30pm Wed-Sun. **Set meal** £78 6 courses (£133 incl wine). £90 9 courses (£160 incl wine). **Set dinner** (6-8pm) £100 12 courses (£185 incl wine). **Credit** AmEx, MC, V.

Furnished with retro-modern fittings and housed in a former town hall, Viajante carries a sense of occasion. It offers a fixed, no-choice menu of six or nine courses with an option of 12 in the evening. Matching wines add to the hefty price tag but are splendid. Expect a roll-call of exquisitely presented morsels, each accompanied by an impassioned narrative of how it came into being. Nuno Mendes'

cooking, although influenced by his Portuguese heritage, also embraces Asian and oriental notes. Umami-rich clam juice served in a shell was contrasted with a soothing droplet of thickened Japanese starch. A dish of sliced raw scallops, topped with a tangle of crisp parsnip wisps, was remarkable for its crystal-clear pool of peppery watercress juice. Top marks went not to an experimental dish but a rustic chunk of pressed ibérico pork roasted to juicy perfection and partnered by sparkling jus. The labour-of-love theme can go into overdrive: flaked crab crowned with dried milk skin seemed pointless, and a cucumber cream dessert was style over substance. But gripes aside, this is a destination to woo lovers or corporate clients. Ask for a table by the open kitchen for a ringside view of chefs quietly perfecting their craft.

Available for hire. Booking advisable. Children over 11yrs admitted. Disabled: toilet. Separate room for parties seats 8-16. Vegetarian menu.

Outer London
Richmond, Surrey

Bingham
61-63 Petersham Road, Richmond, Surrey TW10 6UT (8940 0902, www.thebingham. co.uk). Richmond tube/rail. **Breakfast served** 7-10am Mon-Fri; 8-10am Sat, Sun. **Lunch served** noon-2.30pm Mon-Sat; 12.30-4pm Sun. **Dinner served** 7-10pm Mon-Thur; 6.30-10.30pm Fri, Sat. **Set lunch** (Mon-Sat) £22.50 2 courses, £25 3 courses; (Sun) £38 3 courses. **Set meal** £45 3 courses, £65 tasting menu (£115 incl wine). **Credit** AmEx, MC, V.

Elegant simplicity is the hallmark of this Georgian house hotel bordering the Richmond towpath. The dining area occupies two spacious, well-lit rooms; french windows overlook the river; bright chandeliers and large mirrors enhance the gold tones and woodwork. Food, notably high tea, is also served in the grey- and silver-hued bar area and on the decked patio when weather permits. The Sunday set lunch showcased the kitchen's adept treatment of diverse cuts of meat (a separate vegetarian carte offers equally enticing fare). The amuse-bouche was an enchantingly light, fresh-tasting tomato mousse with basil-tinged foam; a citrus-edged zestiness and lightness of touch also characterised the Dorset crab risotto. Foie gras parfait with own-made apple chutney and grilled sourdough bread showed simple clarity of flavours, while accompaniments to a quail starter included an exemplary ricotta dumpling. Meat-lovers can enjoy the playful contrasts of textures: hotpot and grill of lamb; pork belly braised and roasted; sublime beef marrow persillade atop long-aged sirloin. Desserts had the same deft touch, with contrasting textures, tastes and colours; particularly effective was a simple oat crumble with toasted pine nuts and crunchy pomegranate seeds alongside a rhubarb-accented dark chocolate tart. A carefully considered wine list ensures a glass to complement each dish, and the sommelier is as helpful as the rest of the charming staff.

Available for hire. Babies and children welcome: children's menu; high chairs; nappy-changing facilities. Booking advisable Thur-Sun. Disabled: toilet. Dress: smart casual. Separate room for parties, seats 90. Tables outdoors (8, balcony). Vegetarian menu.

Viajante

Indian

You're in for a treat. London has quite possibly the most exciting collection of Indian restaurants on the planet – wonderful both in range and quality. Here, you'll find representatives from all the countries of the Indian subcontinent: Bangladesh, Pakistan, Nepal and Sri Lanka, as well as the modern state of India. Regional food is also celebrated: the robust meat curries of the Punjab at **New Asian Tandoori Centre**, Gujarati vegetarian cooking at **Meera's Village**, South Indian cuisine at **Saravana Bhavan** and now the food from Pakistan's Sindh province at **Kailash Parbat** – and we could name dozens more examples. Tooting, Whitechapel, Southall and Wembley remain prime districts for inexpensive, authentic Indian restaurants geared to feeding discerning diners of South Asian heritage. But central London is another kettle of tandoori kingfish. Here, fashion and marketing have wrought great changes over the past couple of decades. Time was, the average Londoner would baulk at paying more than a fiver for a curry, though happily shell out triple that for, say, Italian or French. Then came the Modern Indian vanguard, with restaurants such as **Cinnamon Club** and **Benares** and, more recently, the newly resurgent **Zaika**, where highly talented chefs updated the cuisine and served the food in swish surroundings at fine-dining prices.

Indian cookery thus having gained due respect, the next move was a return to its roots. Street food has been a burgeoning trend over the past few years and Indian restaurateurs have more than played their part. Upmarket chains started offering 'diffusion' lines, bringing us **Masala Zone** (from the owners of **Chutney Mary**, **Veeraswamy** and **Amaya**) and the renamed **Imli Street** (child of **Tamarind**). Smaller operations have more recently joined the street-food bonanza: clued-up outfits such as **Roti Chai**, **Delhi Grill** and **Gujarati Rasoi**. So, a wealth of subcontinental variety to relish and cherish – London has lucked out.

Central
Covent Garden

Dishoom

12 Upper St Martin's Lane, WC2H 9FB (7420 9320, www.dishoom.com). Leicester Square or Covent Garden tube. **Meals served** 8am-11pm Mon-Thur; 8am-midnight Fri; 9am-midnight Sat; 9am-11pm Sun. **Main courses** £1.70-£11.50. **Credit** AmEx, MC, V. Pan-Indian

A swish, self-styled 'Bombay café', Dishoom is filled with retro design features: whirring ceiling fans, low-level lighting and reams of vintage Bollywood posters. The look is certainly distinctive, but the effect is so slick that the venue feels rather soulless and corporate. This hasn't stopped the crowds thronging here through the day, from breakfast (for sausage naan rolls with chilli jam) to dinner (for the usual curries and tandoori grills). We've found the food to be at its best when the plates are at their smallest. Vada pau (potato croquettes with sharp chutney in a fluffy Portuguese-style bun) and bhel

(crunchy puffed rice with tangy tamarind chutney) are tasty, but lamb samosas, at a measly two per portion, can leave a lot to be desired. The kebabs and curries are all fairly standard renditions, and could do with extra spice to perk them up; a promising-looking black dal desperately needed some seasoning. The wide array of drinks, including excellent lassi concoctions, helped make amends. Queues are common in the evening (bookings are taken for breakfast and lunch, but only for groups at dinner), though the basement bar helps make the wait more than bearable.

Available for hire. Babies and children welcome: high chairs. Bookings not accepted for fewer than 6 people after 6pm. Disabled: toilet. Separate room for parties, seats 44. Tables outdoors (7, pavement). Takeaway service. **Map 18 D4**. **For branch see index.**

Masala Zone

48 Floral Street, WC2E 9DA (7379 0101, www.masalazone.com). Covent Garden tube. **Meals served** noon-11pm Mon-Sat; 12.30-10.30pm Sun. **Main courses** £8.50-£12.50.

Set meal (noon-6.30pm) £9.15 2 courses, £11.60 3 courses. **Credit** AmEx, MC, V. Pan-Indian

Sharing owners with some of London's top Indian restaurants (including Chutney Mary, Veeraswamy and Amaya), the Masala Zone chain is aimed at the budget end of Indian dining. Fortunately, it doesn't let the side down, delivering punchy flavours, strong spicing and snappy service. This busy branch – one of seven across London – is tucked behind the Royal Opera House and attracts tourist groups, solo lunchers and many others. Each outlet has the same plain furniture, but its own distinctive decoration: old advertising posters in Islington, tribal drawings in Soho, and a ceiling full of Rajasthani puppets here in Covent Garden. Hot and cold street snacks, including puffed poori biscuits, set you up for mains of meat grills, thalis and regional curries (from a slightly watery Goan prawn curry to a gentle saffron korma and more pungent rogan josh). The thalis are a good bet – assorted little metal bowls holding a variety of vegetable dishes and dals, a choice of main curry, and rice or chapati alongside some tangy chutneys. The venue feels a little canteen-like, and not all the

Pan-Indian menu

Spellings of Indian dishes vary widely; dishes such as gosht may appear in several versions on different menus as the word is transliterated from (in this case) Hindi. There are umpteen languages and several scripts in the Indian subcontinent, the most commonly seen on London menus being Punjabi, Hindi, Bengali and Gujarati. For the sake of consistency, however, we have tried to adhere to uniform spellings. The following are common throughout the subcontinent.

Aloo: potato.
Ayre: a white fish much used in Bengali cuisine.
Baingan: aubergine.
Bateira, batera or **bater:** quail.
Bengali: Bengal, before Partition in 1947, was a large province covering Calcutta (now in India's West Bengal) and modern-day Bangladesh. 'Bengali' and 'Bangladeshi' cooking is quite different, and the term 'Bengali' is often misused in London's Indian restaurants.
Bhajee: vegetables cooked with spices, usually 'dry' rather than sauced.
Bhajia or **bhaji:** vegetables dipped in chickpea-flour batter and deep-fried; also called **pakoras.**
Bhatura: deep-fried doughy discs.
Bhindi: okra.
Brinjal: aubergine.
Bulchao or **balchao:** a Goan vinegary pickle made with small dried prawns (with shells) and lots of garlic.
Chana or **channa:** chickpeas.
Chapati: a flat wholewheat griddle bread.
Chat or **chaat:** various savoury snacks featuring combinations of pooris (qv), diced onion and potato, chickpeas, crumbled samosas and pakoras, chutneys and spices.
Dahi: yoghurt
Dal or **dahl:** a lentil curry similar to thick lentil soup. Countless regional variations exist.
Dhansak: a Parsi (qv) casserole of meat, lentils and vegetables, with a mix of hot and tangy flavours.
Dhaniya: coriander.
Ghee: clarified butter used for frying.
Gobi: cauliflower.
Gosht, josh or **ghosh:** meat, usually lamb.
Gram flour: chickpea flour.
Kachori: crisp pastry rounds with spiced mung dahl or pea filling.
Lassi: a yoghurt drink, ordered with salt or sugar, sometimes with fruit. Ideal to quench a burning palate.
Machi or **machli:** fish.
Masala or **masaladar:** mixed spices.
Methi: fenugreek, either dried (seeds) or fresh (green leaves).
Murgh or **murg:** chicken.
Mutter, muter or **mattar:** peas.

Nan or **naan:** teardrop-shaped flatbread cooked in a tandoor.
Palak or **paalak:** spinach; also called saag.
Paan or **pan:** betel leaf stuffed with chopped 'betel nuts', coconut and spices such as fennel seeds, and folded into a triangle. Available sweet or salty, and eaten at the end of a meal as a digestive.
Paneer or **panir:** Indian cheese; a bit like tofu in texture and taste.
Paratha: a large griddle-fried bread that is sometimes stuffed (with spicy mashed potato or minced lamb, for instance).
Parsi or **Parsee:** a religious minority based in Mumbai, but originally from Persia, renowned for its cooking.
Pilau, pillau or **pullao:** flavoured rice cooked with meat or vegetables. In most British Indian restaurants, pilau rice is simply rice flavoured and coloured with turmeric or (rarely) saffron.
Poori or **puri:** a disc of deep-fried wholewheat bread; the frying makes it puff up like an air-filled cushion.
Popadom, poppadom, papadum or **papad:** large thin wafers made with lentil paste, and flavoured with pepper, garlic or chilli. Eaten in the UK with pickles and relishes while waiting for the meal to arrive.
Raita: a yoghurt mix, usually with cucumber.
Roti: a round, sometimes unleavened, bread, thicker than a chapati (qv) and cooked in a tandoor or griddle. **Roomali roti** is a very thin, soft disc of roti.
Saag or **sag:** spinach; also called palak.
Tamarind: the pods of this East African tree, grown in India, are made into a paste that imparts a sour, fruity taste – popular in some regional cuisines, including Gujarati and South Indian.
Thali: literally 'metal plate'. A large plate with rice, bread, metal containers of dahl and vegetable curries, pickles and yoghurt.
Vadai or **wada:** a spicy vegetable or lentil fritter; **dahi wada** are lentil fritters soaked in yoghurt, topped with tamarind and date chutneys.
Vindaloo: originally, a hot and spicy pork curry from Goa that should authentically be soured with vinegar and cooked with garlic. In London restaurants, the term is usually misused to signify simply very hot dishes.
Xacuti: a Goan dish made with lamb or chicken pieces, coconut and a complex mix of roasted then ground spices.

dishes are up to scratch, but it's a no-nonsense, efficient operation. You can eat well for very little.
Available for hire. Babies and children welcome: children's menu; crayons; high chairs; nappy-changing facilities. Booking advisable dinner. Disabled: toilet. Separate room for parties, seats 50. Tables outdoors (5, pavement). Takeaway service; delivery service (over £20 within 1.5-mile radius). Vegan dishes. Vegetarian menu. **Map 18 E4.**
For branches see index.

Moti Mahal
45 Great Queen Street, WC2B 5AA (7240 9329, www.motimahal-uk.com). Covent Garden or Holborn tube. **Lunch served** noon-3pm Mon-Fri. **Dinner served** 5.30-11pm Mon-Sat. **Main courses** £9-£28. **Set lunch** £15 2 courses incl drink. **Set dinner** (5.30-6.30pm, 9.30-11pm Mon-Sat) £19 2 courses, £23 3 courses. **Set meal** £40-£45 tasting menu (£50-£60 incl wine). **Credit** AmEx, MC, V. Modern Indian
Class, poise, judgement: these words might well be embossed on Moti Mahal's burnished copper bar, beside the serried ranks of expensive whiskies. This London outpost of Delhi's celebrated restaurant group is geared to international business diners and priced accordingly. Weighty linen tablecloths, polished wooden flooring, an ambient soundtrack and a spotless open kitchen (viewed behind a curvaceous glass partition) lend gravitas to the ground-floor dining room – as do diligent, multinational staff and a bulky wine list. The basement, with its enveloping red-velvet banquettes, has more date-appeal. The food? It's moderately inventive pan-Indian, with expertly balanced spicing and a lightness of touch evident in the superb breads and rice. We were sad to see brain had slipped from the menu, but noted the varied choice of vegetarian dishes, including jackfruit in a roasted onion and coconut masala. Perfect salad specimens presented on a board with DIY spicing (in pestle and mortar) account for the £1.50 cover charge. An à la carte starter of crab and quail's egg rolls had ample flavour and just-cooked zing, though the eggs were quite rubbery; a set-lunch main of gosht shakarkandi was like rogan josh, with beautifully tender lamb and dense, flavour-soaked chunks of sweet potato. Puddings are also worth exploring. You'll get high-class cooking in impressive surroundings, but gastronomic adventurers might yearn for more thrills – and blench at the prices: £7.50 for a nondescript lassi, anyone?
Available for hire. Babies and children welcome: high chairs; nappy-changing facilities. Booking advisable dinner. Separate room for parties, seats 35. Tables outdoors (5, pavement). Takeaway service. Vegetarian menu. **Map 18 E3.**

Fitzrovia

★ Indian YMCA
41 Fitzroy Square, W1T 6AQ (7387 0411, www.indianymca.org). Great Portland Street or Warren Street tube. **Breakfast served** 7.30-9.15am Mon-Fri; 8-9.30am Sat, Sun. **Lunch served** noon-2pm Mon-Fri; 12.30-1.30pm Sat, Sun. **Dinner served** 7-8.30pm daily. **Main courses** (lunch Mon-Fri) £2.50-£5. **Set meal** £3-£7. **Unlicensed. Corkage** no charge. **Credit** AmEx, MC, V. North Indian
The concrete and glass postwar building looks institutional, but has become an institution. For 60 years, the Indian YMCA has successfully fed

generations of Indian students newly arrived in the UK – though these days you're more likely to share your table with a bargain-hunting British office worker than a trainee doctor from the Punjab. Queue canteen-style at the counter, while checking out the low prices on the pegboard menu above; 'tin fruits 75p' is typically succinct. We recommend the freshly prepared curries (fish, mutton, veg, chicken), which are all cooked home-style and sensitively spiced. The dal is a comforting version, the turmeric-coloured toor dal giving body to the dish. Mounds of rice soak up the sauces; be warned that the pilau rice uses generous sprinklings of vivid food colouring. Although most dishes are North Indian in style, dahi vada (lentil rissole in yoghurt) is a soothing South Indian breakfast snack. A sink for washing your hands after your meal is discreetly concealed behind a glass screen, not on public view in the Indian way. The Y is better for lunch than dinner, when a limited-choice set meal for £7 is the deal.

Babies and children admitted. Disabled: lift; toilet. Takeaway service. Vegan dishes. Vegetarian menu. **Map 3 J4**.

Rasa W1 `HOT 50`

6 Dering Street, W1S 1AD (7629 1346, www.rasarestaurants.com). Oxford Circus tube. **Lunch served** noon-3pm Mon-Sat. **Dinner served** 6-10.30pm daily. **Main courses** £6.50-£12.95. **Set meal** £22.50 vegetarian, £25 meat, £30 seafood. **Credit** AmEx, MC, V. South Indian

The flagship of Das Sreedharan's restaurant mini chain (which began with a vegetarian eaterie in Stoke Newington), Rasa W1 is signposted by its cochineal-pink frontage. Aficionados of homespun South Indian cooking hold the place in high regard for its moderately priced Keralan fish and seafood dishes. The kitchen makes little allowance for temperate non-Indian palates. First up, we relished the crunchy spiced nibbles and a selection of pickles – all own-made – including chilli-flecked green mango chunks and vinegary garlic cloves. A generously portioned kappayum meenum (chunky kingfish fillet curry, simmered in silken coconut-milk masala) was tastefully sharpened with smoky kokum (similar to tamarind) and spiced with curry leaves and whole dried chillies. It made a tasty match with steamed cassava speckled with tiny mustard seeds and crunchy lentils. The dosa is another winner: the thin lentil and rice pancake loosely wrapped around mustardy potatoes and served with delicious sambar (vegetable and lentils made tart with tamarind). Less impressive, a Keralan spin on a sausage roll was underwhelming; soggy pastry encased a starchy potato filling that had a shortfall of meaty goodness. Stick to the vegetarian, fish and seafood options. Service is well meaning, if slightly slow off the mark.

Available for hire. Babies and children welcome: high chairs. Booking advisable. Takeaway service. Vegan dishes. Vegetarian menu. **Map 9 H6**. **For branches (Rasa, Rasa Express, Rasa Maricham, Rasa Travancore) see index**.

Knightsbridge

★ Amaya `HOT 50`

Halkin Arcade, Motcomb Street, SW1X 8JT (7823 1166, www.amaya.biz). Knightsbridge tube. **Lunch served** 12.30-2.15pm Mon-Sat; 12.45-2.45pm Sun. **Dinner served** 6.30-11.30pm

Roti Chai. See p132.

Mon-Sat; 6.30-10.30pm Sun. **Main courses** £19-£28. **Set lunch** £19.50-£32. **Set dinner** £42-£80 tasting menu. **Credit** AmEx, DC, MC, V. Modern Indian

Specialising in stylish pan-Indian tapas, Amaya is favoured by a clientele of well-heeled professionals blessed with good taste and deep pockets. The sleek cocktail bar and dining area are furnished with a seductive mix of black granite, dark wooden fittings, terracotta statues and a splash of modern art. Ask for a table by the open kitchen for a view of chefs working the clay tandoor, charcoal grill and griddle. Recent menu additions include fragrant and tender chicken thighs steeped in fresh turmeric with lime juice then seared in the tandoor. Lucknow's sausage-shaped kakori kebab, made from skewered pounded lamb spiced with cardamom and cloves and cooked over charcoal, had lovely fragrant and floral notes – a tribute to the royal kitchens of its origin. Amaya's own-made paneer is outstanding – we loved our soft, almost spongy, tandoori cubes encased in a wisp of a chilli crust. Beef makes a surprise appearance with a splendid sirloin boti, the peppery, meaty chunks winning a gold star for their smoky-citrusy marination. To round things off: a tasty, cardamom-scented chicken korma simmered in a smooth wild garlic masala enriched with onions, coriander and green chillies. Service was as smooth as Indian silk. *Booking advisable. Children admitted until 8pm. Disabled: toilet. Dress: smart casual. Separate room for parties, seats 14. Vegetarian menu.* **Map 9 G9.**

Haandi

7 Cheval Place, SW7 1EW (7823 7373, www.haandi-restaurants.com). Knightsbridge tube. **Lunch served** noon-3pm daily. **Dinner served** 5.30-11pm Mon-Thur, Sun; 5.30-11.30pm Fri, Sat. **Main courses** £6-£16. **Set lunch** £12.95. **Credit** AmEx, MC, V. East African Indian

This East African restaurant group has two London outposts (in Knightsbridge and Edgware) and serves mainly North Indian staples. We've been coming here for years and are saddened at the recent slide in standards. This time around, only aloo chat was a resounding success, memorable for its golden fried potato chunks tossed with softened onions and seasoned with pounded dried mango and toasted cumin. In the past, we've had fabulous renditions of garlic-laden kaka-di-lamb curry made with meaty chunks cooked on the bone. Sadly, this Punjabi offering was marred by far too much floral screwpine essence and undercooked onion masala. Corners have been cut elsewhere: skewered chicken cubes (tandoori burra kebabs) were stringy-textured and insufficiently marinated in lime juice and ginger. Even the simple staple of palak paneer lacked seasoning and fresh punchy flavour. Decor is a mix of weathered cane furniture and potted plants, against a backdrop of beige, with an open kitchen providing some visual distraction. Prices aren't cheap and service is patchy, but its proximity to Harrods keeps Haandi busy with wealthy shoppers and business groups. *Available for hire. Babies and children welcome: high chairs. Booking advisable. Separate room for* parties, seats 30. Takeaway service; delivery service (over £20 within 2-mile radius). **Map 14 E9.**

Marylebone

Roti Chai

3 Portman Mews South, W1H 6HS (7408 0101, www.rotichai.com). Marble Arch tube. **Meals served** noon-10.30pm Mon-Sat; 1-9pm Sun. **Main courses** £5.50-£8.50. **Credit** AmEx, MC, V. Pan-Indian

Within a naan's hurl of Oxford Street, Roti Chai deserved more custom on a midweek lunchtime. Not that the lucky office workers (some Indian, most not) who had discovered it down this little mews street were complaining. The ground-floor 'street kitchen', with its utilitarian furniture and canteen vibe, is ideal for a swift midday feed – and the alert young multinational staff keep things pacy. The menu is modelled on those of urban India's snack shacks, so you'll find bhel pooris, samosas and a big portion of moist, light Gujarati dhokra sponge, topped with two relishes: tangy tamarind and spicy coconut (share one between two for a starter). Larger dishes include 'railway lamb curry', with beautifully tender meat and potato in a rich gravy spiced with star anise and cinnamon bark, served with two wholemeal chapatis. Soupy tarka dal was similarly full-flavoured. In the basement, the newly opened, evening-only 'dining room' is a darker, sexier space. Here, prices rise considerably, with chettinad chicken costing £15.50 – not that the

Cinnamon Soho. See p135.

street kitchen is giveaway-cheap. Dhokra, lamb curry, dal and a pot of lovely, rich leaf tea cost £23 with service, but such a lunch would have workers singing through the afternoon.

Available for hire. Babies and children welcome: high chairs; nappy-changing facilities. Booking advisable dinner. Disabled: lift; toilet. Vegetarian menu. **Map 9 G6**.

Trishna London

15-17 Blandford Street, W1U 3DG (7935 5624, www.trishnalondon.com). Bond Street tube. **Lunch served** noon-2.45pm Mon-Sat; 12.30-3.15pm Sun. **Dinner served** 6-10.45pm Mon-Sat; 6.30-9.45pm Sun. **Main courses** £10-£22. **Set lunch** £17.50 2 courses, £22 3 courses, £27.50 4 courses. **Set dinner** (6-6.30pm Mon-Sat; 6.30-7pm Sun) £27.50 4 courses. **Credit** AmEx, MC, V. South Indian

Gaining a Michelin star in 2012, Trishna London is a world away from the shabby interior of its sister restaurant in Mumbai. This contemporary-looking eaterie is smart and quietly conservative, its dining room barely distinguishable from those of its Marylebone neighbours save for the retro Air India prints on the walls. The Mumbai original is known for its focus on seafood, but here equal prominence is given to meat and vegetarian dishes. An Indian twist on a British classic, Trishna fish and chips was let down by under-seasoned fish, but a main-course sized starter of a typical Indian snack, aloo chat (a sweet and sour blend of potato, chickpeas, tamarind, yoghurt, shallots and chilli), was the best dish by far. To follow, guinea fowl 'tikka' was tender and smothered in a rich marinade of yoghurt, fennel and star anise with a gentle kick of chilli. For pudding, perfectly crisp, dinky sweet filo parcels styled as 'samosas' gave way to a nutty coconut and mango filling, accompanied by a feather-light lychee ice-cream. Portion sizes defeated us, but staff happily packed up leftovers to take home.

Available for hire. Babies and children welcome: high chairs. Booking advisable dinner. Separate room for parties, seats 12. Tables outdoors (3, patio). Vegetarian menu. **Map 9 G5**.

Mayfair

Benares

12A Berkeley Square House, Berkeley Square, W1J 6BS (7629 8886, www.benaresrestaurant. com). Green Park tube. **Lunch served** noon-2.30pm, **dinner served** 5.30-10.30pm Mon-Sat. **Main courses** £24-£54. **Set meal** (lunch, 5.30-6.30pm) £32 3 courses. **Credit** AmEx, DC, MC, V. Modern Indian

This glamorous first-floor cocktail bar and stylish restaurant blend modern furnishings with traditional Indian touches. Expect Mughal-style water tanks, flowers, occasional antiques and plenty of shiny black granite. The venue attracts big spenders – suits on expense accounts, romancing couples and curious tourists. Fronted by well-known chef Atul Kochhar, the kitchen produces modern cooking in the haute-cuisine league. We've had variable meals in the past, but culinary standards seem to be moving in the right direction. A trio of juicy scallops won our approval for the toasted-sesame, crushed-coriander seed, and chilli-jam toppings – each one accompanied by plump sweet grapes and tangy, tamarind-like grape chutney. Less appealing, crispy soft-shell crab was let down by an oily batter swamping the delicate flesh. Mains brought things back on track with tender pink duck

breast, scattered with pomegranate kernels and served with fragrant basmati pilau and crunchy green beans. Tender roasted lamb rump, sauced with fried onion-ginger masala (a classic rogan josh pairing), was almost as memorable. Sadly, a bitter-tasting crushed potato accompaniment laced with raw mustardy notes detracted from the dish. Wines are well-chosen, with a couple of less expensive selections on the list. Service, however, remains infuriatingly slack.

Available for hire. Babies and children admitted until 7pm. Booking advisable. Disabled: toilet. Dress: smart casual; no sportswear. Separate rooms for parties, seating 6, 10, 16 and 34. Vegetarian menu. **Map 9 H7**.

Gymkhana NEW

42 Albemarle Street, W1S 4JH (3011 5900, www.gymkhanalondon.com). Green Park tube. **Lunch served** noon-2.45pm, **dinner served** 5.30-10.30pm Mon-Sat. **Main courses** £10-£25. **Set meal** £55 tasting menu. **Credit** AmEx, MC, V. Modern Indian

Gymkhana looks and feels like an Indian colonial club with its retro ceiling fans, marble-topped tables and yesteryear photos of polo and cricket team triumphs. Patron-chef Karam Sethi (also behind Trishna and Bubbledogs) lays on a splendid spread of modern Indian dishes based on regional masalas and marinades. A starter of South Indian fried chicken wings, steeped in chilli batter, packed a fiery kick. Goan pork vindaloo – slow-cooked chunks of suckling pig cheek, with a vinegary red chilli and garlic masala, spiced with sweet cinnamon and pounded coriander – was outstanding. Kerala-style mussels were less impressive, let down by a cloyingly thick coconut cream masala. Game lovers are well looked after with a separate menu devoted to the likes of muntjac biriani, fried peppered partridge and roe deer cooked with pickling spices. The ground-floor dining area is gloomy, an impression not helped by the dark wood panelling, bottle-green leather banquettes and partitioned booths. It's livelier in the main bar downstairs, where additional dining tables are located. On our visit, the banter of well-heeled Mayfair office workers unwinding at the end of the day brought welcome warmth.

Available for hire. Babies and children welcome: high chairs. Booking advisable. Separate rooms for parties, seating 9 and 14. Vegetarian menu. **Map 9 J7**.

Tamarind

20 Queen Street, W1J 5PR (7629 3561, www.tamarindrestaurant.com). Green Park tube. **Lunch served** noon-2.45pm Mon-Fri, Sun. **Dinner served** 5.30-11pm Mon-Sat; 6-10.30pm Sun. **Main courses** £17.95-£36.50. **Set lunch** (Mon-Fri) £19.50 2 courses, £22.50 3 courses, £29 tasting menu. **Set dinner** (5.30-6.45pm, 10.30-11pm) £28.50 3 courses. **Credit** AmEx, MC, V. Pan-Indian

Elegant and sophisticated, Tamarind's basement dining area is enhanced by muted lighting, crisp linen, and speckled mirrors across the walls. The sedate atmosphere and warm, efficient service make the restaurant a popular destination with office groups and mature couples. Classic Indian dishes score over modern interpretations on the menu, with several choices verging on the homely – despite the setting. Skewered and seared morsels of chicken had been well steeped in cream cheese beaten with ginger-garlic paste and pounded

North Indian menu

Under the blanket term 'North Indian', we have included dishes originating in the Punjab (the region separating India and Pakistan), Kashmir and all points down to Hyderabad. Southall has some of London's best Punjabi restaurants, where breads cooked in the tandoor oven are often preferred to rice, marinated meat kebabs are popular, and dals are thick and buttery.

Bhuna gosht: a dry, spicy dish of lamb.
Biriani or **biryani**: a royal Moghul (qv) version of pilau rice, in which meat or vegetables are cooked together with basmati rice, spices and saffron. It's difficult to find an authentic biriani in London restaurants.
Dopiaza or **do pyaza**: cooked with onions.
Dum: a Kashmiri cooking technique where food is simmered in a casserole (typically a clay pot sealed with dough), allowing spices to permeate.
Gurda: kidneys.
Haandi: an earthenware or metal cooking pot, with handles on either side and a lid.
Jalfrezi: chicken or vegetable dishes cooked with fresh green chillies – a popular cooking style in Mumbai.
Jhingri, **jhinga** or **chingri**: prawns.
Karahi or **karai**: a small iron or metal wok-like cooking dish. Similar to the 'balti' dish made famous in Birmingham.
Kheema or **keema**: minced lamb, as in kheema nan (stuffed nan).
Kofta: meatballs or vegetable dumplings.
Korma: braised in yoghurt and/or cream and nuts. Often mild, but rich.
Makhani: cooked with butter (makhan) and sometimes tomatoes, as in murgh makhani.
Massalam: marinated, then casseroled chicken dish, originating in Muslim areas.
Moghul, **Mogul** or **Moglai**: from the Moghul period of Indian history, used in the culinary sense to describe typical North Indian Muslim dishes.
Pasanda: thin fillets of lamb cut from the leg and flattened with a mallet. In Britain, the term usually applies to a creamy sauce virtually identical to a korma (qv).
Punjabi: Since Partition, the Punjab has been two adjoining states, one in India, one in Pakistan. Lahore is the main town on the Pakistani side, which is predominantly Muslim; Amritsar on the Indian side is the Sikh capital. Punjabi dishes tend to be thick stews or cooked in a tandoor.
Roghan gosht or **rogan josh**: lamb cooked in spicy sauce; a Kashmiri speciality.
Seekh kebab: ground lamb, skewered and grilled.
Tandoor: clay oven originating in north-west India in which food is cooked without oil.
Tarka: spices and flavourings are cooked separately, then added to dahl at a final stage.
Tikka: meat, fish or paneer cut into cubes, then marinated in spicy yoghurt and baked in a tandoor.

INDIAN

Three of the finest Indian Restaurants

Amaya

This award winning sophisticated Indian Grill offers intense flavours with an innovative twist, in a theatrical open kitchen setting. Michelin star.

Open for lunch & dinner seven days a week.

Halkin Arcade, Motcomb Street
Knightsbridge, London SW1X 8JT
T: 020 7823 1166

Private dining room seats 14

Chutney Mary

The rich setting, interesting art and romantic candle lighting are secondary details in London oasis of great Indian food.

Open for dinner every day and lunch Saturday and Sunday.
Grand buffet for Sunday Lunch at £26

535 Kings Road *(at the corner of Lots Road)*
London SW10 0SZ
T: 020 7351 3113

Private dining room seats 28

Veeraswamy

Classical dishes, lovingly prepared and beautifully served in sumptuous surroundings overlooking Regent Street. The oldest Indian restaurant in the world.

Open for lunch and dinner seven days a week.

Mezzanine Floor, Victory House
1st floor, 99 Regent Street *(at the corner of Swallow Street)*
London W1B 4RS
T: 020 7734 1401

Private dining room seats 24

Reservations: www.realindianfood.com/Bookings.aspx

MW eat

cardamom. Although the dish was tender and juicy, the spicing could have done with an extra hit of green chilli. Chat (a pile-up of crisp-fried pastry discs, bathed in yoghurt and made tangy with tamarind sauce and mint chutney) was topped incongruously with blueberries. Although OK, it did feel like a vast amount to plough though. Mains were more memorable. Rogan josh lamb curry had an outstandingly mellow and mild red chilli sauce, enriched with fried onion-ginger paste, yet the meat could have been more tender. Pleasure was unalloyed, though, at the nutty, light texture of moong dal, finished with fried slivers of garlic and toasted cumin: simple, rustic and very tasty. Desserts are pedestrian and not worth ordering. *Babies and children welcome until 7pm: children's menu; high chairs. Booking essential. Takeaway service. Vegetarian menu.* **Map 9 H7**.

Veeraswamy

Mezzanine Floor, Victory House, 99-101 Regent Street, entrance on Swallow Street, W1B 4RS (7734 1401, www.veeraswamy.com). Piccadilly Circus tube. **Lunch served** noon-2.15pm Mon-Fri; 12.30-2.30pm Sat, Sun. **Dinner served** 5.30-10pm Mon-Thur; 5.30-10.30pm Fri, Sat; 6-10pm Sun. **Main courses** £19-£38. **Set meal** (lunch, 5.30-6.30pm Mon-Sat) £20 2 courses, £23 3 courses; (lunch Sun) £24 3 courses. **Credit** AmEx, DC, MC, V. Pan-Indian
Enter through a tiny doorway just off busy Regent Street and a lift takes you up to a first-floor dining room with windows looking on to the retail chaos below. Veeraswamy has an air of granny's posh drawing room about it – if granny's family were royalty, that is. Tinted glass lamps, sepia-tinted photos of the Raj and plush carpets make the whole thing feel a little 1970s, in a retro-cool sort of way. The restaurant opened in 1926, and its current owners' portfolio also includes Chutney Mary, Amaya and the Masala Zone chain. Glitzy surroundings aside, the food is, in the main, outstanding. A starter of meltingly soft paneer layered with green herbs and warming spices arrived gently charred from the tandoor. The spicy paste on the perfectly pink Amritsari lamb chops was authentically heavy on the ginger and garlic. A tiny portion of gulab jamun provided a perfect end to the meal. The only thing that jars is the cost. A fairly average bottle of red wine is priced at £34 and, moist and moreish though our chicken biriani was, all the 'aged basmati' in the world would never justify its £23 price tag.
Babies and children admitted until 8pm. Booking advisable weekends. Disabled: lift; toilet. Dress: smart casual. Separate room for parties, seats 24. Vegan dishes. Vegetarian menu. **Map 17 A5**.

Soho

Cinnamon Soho

5 Kingly Street, W1B 5PF (7437 1664, www.cinnamonsoho.com). Oxford Circus or Piccadilly Circus tube. **Meals served** 11am-11pm Mon-Sat; 11.30am-4pm Sun. **Main courses** £12-£17. **Set meal** (lunch, 5-7pm) £15 2 courses, £18 3 courses. **Credit** AmEx, MC, V. Modern Indian
An offshoot of Westminster's classy Cinnamon Club, this more casual venue specialises in small plates inspired by pan-Indian flavours and western presentation. Don't be deterred by the dark and narrow ground floor and basement dining areas – the cooking, overseen by talented executive chef

Vivek Singh, is the real attraction. Try, for instance, the Punjabi-style gingery lamb mince, topped with crisp-crusted juicy brain fritters sharpened by a kick of lime. Remember to order breads for mopping up the marvellous masala. Lighter in texture, South Indian quinoa salad, seasoned with curry leaves, mustard seeds and chopped tomatoes, provides plenty of splendid citrus notes. An Indo-Chinese chilli chicken collaboration was so good that we ordered second helpings of the delectable seared morsels with their sweet and garlicky soy-chilli glaze. An outstanding ox cheek vindaloo featured tender meat in an unbeatable, almost pickled, garlicky masala. The only glitch was laal maas, a supposedly fiery lamb curry from Rajasthan, let down by a shortfall in chilli heat. The young service team needs to invest more energy in getting to grips with the menu, and promoting it to curious diners unsure of what to order.
Available for hire. Babies and children welcome: high chairs. Booking advisable. Disabled: toilet. Dress: smart casual. Tables outdoors (9, pavement). **Map 17 A4**.

Imli Street

167-169 Wardour Street, W1F 8WR (7287 4243, www.imlistreet.com). Oxford Circus or Tottenham Court Road tube. **Meals served** 8am-11pm Mon-Fri; 9am-11pm Sat; 9am-10.30pm Sun. **Tapas** £2.95-£9.95. **Credit** AmEx, MC, V. Pan-Indian
A much-needed makeover has enlivened this affordable offshoot of upmarket Indian restaurant Tamarind. The bland decor has been replaced with exposed brickwork, school-style tables and trendy hanging lights, giving the place a cool industrial vibe. A new menu features small plates of South Asian regional favourites. We liked the naan pie – an Anglo-Indian interpretation of shepherd's pie made with tender chunks of garlicky lamb, buttery mash and a surprise topping of crisp-baked naan. Plump southern prawns, stir-fried with caramelised onion paste, spiked with chilli and ginger and finished with bites of green peppercorns, was another star dish. Even the weighty Punjabi samosa, filled with cumin-spiced potatoes, was pimped up with creamy yoghurt streaked with fresh mint chutney and sweet tamarind sauce. Sadly, the Indo-Chinese marrow dumplings didn't hit the spot – although simmered in a tangy toasted garlic and chilli sauce, they were let down by a raw cornflour element. But slow-cooked railway lamb curry, with its tender braised meat and pungent fried onion masala, was enjoyable. Soho's media set seem to approve of the new incarnation, but staff need to get to grips with the menu.
Available for hire. Babies and children welcome: children's menu; high chairs; nappy-changing facilities. Bookings not accepted for fewer than 6 people. Disabled: toilet. Separate room for parties, seats 45. Vegetarian menu. **Map 17 B3**.

Red Fort

77 Dean Street, W1D 3SH (7437 2115, www.redfort.co.uk). Leicester Square or Tottenham Court Road tube.
Bar **Open** 5pm-midnight Tue-Thur; 5pm-1am Fri, Sat.
Restaurant **Lunch served** noon-3pm Mon-Fri. **Dinner served** 5.30-11.30pm daily. **Main courses** £15-£18. **Set meal** (12.30-3pm, 5.30-6.30pm, 10-11.30pm) £15 2 courses, £18 3 courses.
Both **Credit** AmEx, MC, V. Pan Indian

South Indian menu

Much South Indian food consists of rice, lentil- and semolina-based dishes. Fish features strongly in non-vegetarian restaurants, and coconut, mustard seeds, curry leaves and red chillies are widely used. If you want to try South Indian snacks such as dosas, idlis or uppama, go at lunchtime, which is when these dishes are traditionally eaten, and they're more likely to be cooked fresh to order. In the evening, try the thalis and rice- and curry-based meals, including vegetable stir-fries such as thorans and pachadis.

Adai: fermented rice and lentil pancakes, with a nuttier flavour than dosais (qv).
Avial: a mixed vegetable curry from Kerala with a coconut and yoghurt sauce.
Bonda: spiced mashed potatoes, dipped in chickpea-flour batter and deep-fried.
Dosai or **dosa**: thin, shallow-fried pancake, often sculpted into interesting shapes; the very thin ones are called **paper dosai**. Most dosais are made with fermented rice and lentil batter, but variants include **rava dosai**, made with 'cream of wheat' semolina. **Masala dosais** come with a spicy potato filling. All variations are traditionally served with sambar (qv) and coconut chutney.
Gobi 65: cauliflower marinated in spices, then dipped in chickpea-flour batter and deep-fried. It is usually lurid pink due to the addition of food colouring.
Idli: steamed sponges of ground rice and lentil batter. Eaten with sambar (qv) and coconut chutney.
Kadala: black chickpea curry.
Kancheepuram idli: idli (qv) flavoured with whole black peppercorns and other spices.
Kappa: cassava root traditionally served with kadala (qv).
Kootu: mild vegetable curry in a creamy coconut and yoghurt sauce.
Pachadi: spicy vegetable side dish cooked with yoghurt.
Rasam: consommé made with lentils; it tastes both peppery-hot and tamarind-sour, but there are many regional variations.
Sambar or **sambhar**: a variation on dahl made with a specific hot blend of spices, plus coconut, tamarind and vegetables – particularly drumsticks (a pod-like vegetable, like a longer, woodier version of okra; you strip out the edible interior with your teeth).
Thoran: vegetables stir-fried with mustard seeds, curry leaves, chillies and fresh grated coconut.
Uppama: a popular breakfast dish in which onions, spices and, occasionally, vegetables are cooked with semolina using a risotto-like technique.
Uthappam: a spicy, crisp pancake/pizza made with lentil- and rice-flour batter, often topped with tomato, onions and chillies.
Vellappam: a bowl-shaped, crumpet-like rice pancake (same as appam or hoppers, qv, Sri Lankan menu).

INDIAN

Gujarati menu

Most Gujarati restaurants are located in north-west London – mainly in Wembley, Sudbury, Kingsbury, Kenton, Harrow, Rayners Lane and Hendon – and they tend to be no-frills, family-run eateries.

Unlike North Indian food, Gujarati dishes are not normally cooked in a base sauce of onions, garlic, tomatoes and spices. Instead, they're tempered; whole spices such as cumin, red chillies, mustard seeds, ajwain (carom) seeds, asafoetida powder and curry leaves are sizzled in hot oil for a few seconds. The tempering is added at the start or the end of cooking, depending on the dish.

Commonplace items such as grains, beans and flours – transformed into various shapes by boiling, steaming and frying – are the basis of many dishes. Coriander, coconut, yoghurt, jaggery (cane sugar), tamarind, sesame seeds, chickpea (gram) flour and cocum (a sun-dried, sour, plum-like fruit) are also widely used.

Each region has its own cooking style. Kathiyawad, a humid area in western Gujarat, and Kutch, a desert in the north-west, have spawned styles that are less reliant on fresh produce. Kathiyawadi food is rich with dairy products and grains such as dark millet, and is pepped up with chilli powder. Kutchis make liberal use of chickpea flour (as do Kathiyawadis) and their staple diet is based on khichadi. In central Gujarat towns such as Baroda and Ahmedabad, grains are widely used; they appear in snacks that are the backbone of menus in London's Gujarati restaurants.

The gourmet heartland, however, is Surat – one of the few regions with heavy rainfall and lush vegetation. Surat boasts an abundance of green vegetables such as papadi (a type of broad bean) and ponk (fresh green millet). A must-try Surti speciality is undhiyu. Surti food uses 'green masala' (fresh coriander, coconut, green chillies and ginger), as opposed to the 'red masala' (red chilli powder, crushed coriander, cumin and turmeric) more commonly used in western and central regions.

The best time to visit Gujarati restaurants is for Sunday lunch, which is when you'll find little-seen regional specialities on the menu – but you will almost certainly need to book ahead.

Bhakarvadi: pastry spirals stuffed with whole spices and, occasionally, potatoes.
Bhel poori: a snack originating from street stalls in Mumbai, which contains crisp, deep-fried pooris, puffed rice, sev (qv), chopped onion, tomato, potato and more, plus chutneys (chilli, mint and tamarind).
Dhokla: a steamed savoury chickpea flour cake.
Farsan: Gujarati snacks.
Ganthia: Gujarati name for crisply fried savoury confections made from chickpea flour; they come in all shapes.
Ghughara: sweet or savoury pasties.
Kadhi: yoghurt and chickpea flour curry, often cooked with dumplings or vegetables.
Khandvi: tight rolls of 'pasta' sheets (made from chickpea flour and curds) tempered with sesame and mustard seeds.
Khichadi or **khichdi:** rice and lentils mixed with ghee and spices.
Mithi roti: round griddle-cooked bread stuffed with a cardamom-and-saffron-flavoured lentil paste. Also called puran poli.
Mogo: deep-fried cassava, often served as chips together with a sweet and sour tamarind chutney. An East African Asian dish.
Pani poori: bite-sized pooris that are filled with sprouted beans, chickpeas, potato, onion, chutneys, sev (qv) and a thin, spiced watery sauce.
Patra: a savoury snack made of the arvi leaf (colocasia) stuffed with spiced chickpea-flour batter, steamed, then cut into slices in the style of a swiss roll. The slices are then shallow-fried with sesame and mustard seeds.
Pau bhajee: a robustly spiced dish of mashed potatoes and vegetables, served with a shallow-fried white bread roll.
Puran poli: see mithi roti.
Ragda pattice or **ragada patties:** mashed potato patties covered with a chickpea or dried-pea sauce, topped with onions, sev (qv) and spicy chutney.
Sev: deep-fried chickpea-flour vermicelli.
Thepla: savoury flatbread.

Red Fort has long been a haunt of moneyed tourists and business diners. It's a smart ground-floor destination with a basement bar, sandstone walls, a stylish water feature and crisp white linen. A decade ago, the kitchen turned out outstanding regal dishes from Lucknow, but the talented chef moved on and the cooking has since been given a pan-Indian makeover. On previous visits, waiters have been reluctant to offer the moderately priced pre-theatre set menu and their aloof manner has done them no favours. Star dishes this time included juicy seekh kebabs made from cumin-spiced lamb mince mixed with onions and seasoned with ginger, green chillies and coriander. Shaped around skewers and cooked over charcoal, they made a memorable first course, as did our other starter – but for the wrong reason. Spinach patty cakes, coated in crunchy poppy seeds, were inexplicably stuffed with melted cheddar: a disastrous mash-up of flavours. A rustic lamb curry to follow made partial amends, with chunks of meat covered in caramelised onion masala, seasoned with coriander seeds, ginger and toasted garlic. However, Red Fort is no longer a leading light for Moghul cooking, and must fight to hold its own among Soho's dressy restaurants.
Available for hire. Babies and children admitted. Booking advisable Thur-Sat. Dress: smart casual. Separate room for parties. Vegetarian menu.
Map 17 B3.

Westminster

★ Cinnamon Club
Old Westminster Library, 30-32 Great Smith Street, SW1P 3BU (7222 2555, www.cinnamon club.com). St James's Park or Westminster tube. **Breakfast served** 7.30-10am Mon-Fri. **Lunch served** noon-2.45pm, **dinner served** 6-10.45pm Mon-Sat. **Main courses** £14-£32. **Set meal** £22 2 courses, £24 3 courses. **Credit** AmEx, MC, V.
Modern Indian
There's a gentlemen's club feel to this grand, Grade II-listed Victorian building (once a library), and the high ceiling, book-lined gallery and crisp napery convey a sense of occasion. It's an established haunt of sharp-suited power brokers and Westminster politicians who enjoy a fine-dining menu of updated rustic and regal pan-Indian dishes. We liked the sliced veal escalope with its toasted coriander seasoning – an innovative complement to creamy tomato-cumin sauce. The spongy uthappam griddle cake made for a dressy and tasty spin on South Indian street food, the ground rice and lentil base glistening with a topping of softened onions and green chillies. Cumbrian farmers have chef Vivek Singh to thank for his signature Herdwick lamb curry. The meat wasn't as tender as we've enjoyed on previous visits and could have done with longer on the stove, but the masala was spot-on, the browned onion paste fried to a russet-brown and spiced with ginger, cardamom and fiery chillies. The kitchen excels in seafood preparations. A whiting fillet, cooked with precision, came with a marvellous, rich coconut cream infused with ginger and turmeric. Prices are pegged at the sharp end, although the set menus are affordable. Service is professional, but doesn't quite match the exemplary cooking.
Available for hire. Babies and children welcome: high chairs. Booking advisable. Disabled: lift; toilet. Dress: smart casual. Separate rooms for parties, seating 30-60. **Map 16 K9**.
For branch (Cinnamon Kitchen) see index.

Apollo Banana Leaf. See p139.

Main courses £4.25-£13. Thalis £12.25-£14.95. Set lunch (noon-3pm Mon-Fri) £5.95 3 courses. Credit AmEx, MC, V. South Indian vegetarian

Behind its plain plate-glass frontage, Hammersmith's Sagar (there are two other branches) is almost Scandinavian in its use of blond wood, with tables, flooring, chairs, ceiling and wall-panelling in similar materials. The effect of entering a box is tempered by red fairy lights and display alcoves of Hindu deities. A multicultural bunch of diners are tended by smart, softly spoken waiters keen to offer advice. The menu bigs-up the Udupi cooking of Karnataka, from where the chefs originate, but the lengthy list consists of generic South Indian food ranging from dosas and uthappams, to bhel poori beach snacks. Kancheepuram idli rice cakes were heavier than expected, studded with cashew nuts and served with decent sambar and two coconut-based chutneys. We also sampled mulaga podi: a lentil and spice powder mixed with liquid ghee at table and smeared on the idli. It was appetisingly nutty, yet gritty – and, as with all the food, genuine South Indian chilli heat was absent. Udupi thali, a tray of half a dozen dishes, with two puffy poori, popadoms and chutneys, was similarly restrained in flavour (little pepperiness in the rasam; hardly any citrus zest; fresh coriander the most vibrant tang), and textures were too similar, with potatoes dominating and green vegetables virtually absent. Best was suki bhajia, where nutty fresh coconut leavened the root-veg mix. A nice atmosphere, then, but workmanlike cooking.

Babies and children welcome: high chair. Booking advisable. Takeaway service. Vegan dishes. Vegetarian menu. **Map 20 B4.**
For branches see index.

Kensington

★ Zaika
1 Kensington High Street, W8 5NP (7795 6533, www.zaika-restaurant.co.uk). High Street Kensington tube. **Lunch served** noon-2.45pm Tue-Sun. **Dinner served** 5.30-10.45pm Mon-Sat; 5.30-9.45pm Sun. **Main courses** £16-£28. **Set meal** (lunch; 5.30-7pm daily) £18 2 courses; £21 3 courses; £55 tasting menu (£85 incl wine). **Credit** AmEx, DC, MC, V. Modern Indian

Upmarket destination Zaika has become the latest addition to the Tamarind group. This former bank, popular with the expense-account brigade, has an impressive high ceiling that adds to its grandeur. The furnishings have remained almost the same under the new ownership, but the menu has been transformed. Pan-Indian inspired dishes are now less fussy in appearance, and more attention is given to distinctive spicing. We were pleased by the smoky tang of tender pigeon chunks, marinated in ginger-tamarind pulp and seared in a clay oven – a creative twist to a classic recipe. Creamy seafood curry, enriched with coconut cream and spiced with curry leaves, was crowned with tempura-style fried squid: a tasty update on the Keralan tradition. What looked like a scotch egg was a perfectly executed nargisi kofta from Lucknow; toasted cumin and coriander-spiced lamb mince had been shaped around a perfectly boiled egg before being fried and halved – a splendid partner to garlicky tomato sauce. Desserts weren't quite as memorable. An overly sweet mango kulfi missed the mark, although the sweetly spiced chocolate éclair matched with guava sorbet did itself proud.

West
Hammersmith

★ Potli
319-321 King Street, W6 9NH (8741 4328, www.potli.co.uk). Ravenscourt Park tube. **Lunch served** noon-2.45pm Mon-Sat. **Dinner served** 6-10.30pm Mon-Thur; 6-11pm Fri, Sat. **Meals served** noon-10.30pm Sun. **Main courses** £6-£9.50. **Credit** AmEx, MC, V. Modern Indian

With its beach-style wooden bar, hessian cushions, beads and quirky curios, Potli has a tropical street-bazaar vibe. Local residents visit for the classic curries, smoky grills and generous portions. Banana-leaf packets, unwrapped at the table, revealed splendidly steamed Gujarati-style prawns, each cloaked in an outstanding coconut, coriander and green-chilli paste. Main courses tend to be rich affairs, with dishes arriving in bowls for sharing. Our curries wouldn't have won any awards in a beauty pageant, but despite their similar tomato-masala appearances, each had distinctive spicing. An enormous rogan josh lamb shank (enough for two) was supremely tender, and sauced with a gelatinous caramelised onion masala spiked with citrus cardamom. Sadly, Goan pork vindaloo, although containing tender pork belly chunks, was let down by a flat masala and needed a kick of chilli and vinegar to lift it from mediocrity. It's good to see Meantime Pale Ale on the drinks list – a marvellous match with all things spicy. Despite occasional slips, Potli is a great place to enjoy a relatively inexpensive meal. Its chefs excel in putting unfussy, homely meals on plates.

Babies and children welcome: high chairs; nappy-changing facilities. Booking advisable dinner. Disabled: toilet. Separate room for parties, seats 30-35. Tables outdoors (4, pavement). Takeaway service; delivery service (over £25 within 2-mile radius). Vegan dishes. Vegetarian menu. **Map 20 A4.**

★ Sagar
157 King Street, W6 9JT (8741 8563, www.sagarveg.co.uk). Hammersmith tube. **Lunch served** noon-3pm, **dinner served** 5.30-10.45pm Mon-Thur. **Meals served** noon-11.30pm Fri, Sat; noon-10.45pm Sun.

Service, like the cooking, is first rate. In all, Zaika's top-notch reputation has been restored.
Available for hire. Babies and children welcome: high chair. Booking advisable, essential weekends. Dress: smart casual. Vegetarian menu. **Map 7 C8**.

Notting Hill

Chakra

157-159 Notting Hill Gate, W11 3LF (7229 2115, www.chakralondon.com). Notting Hill Gate tube. **Lunch served** noon-3.30pm daily. **Dinner served** 6-11pm Mon-Sat; 6-10.30pm Sun. **Main courses** £7.95-£22.50. **Set lunch** (Sat, Sun) £16.95 buffet. **Set dinner** £60 4 courses. **Credit** AmEx, MC, V. Modern Indian
A dressy local for Notting Hill's smart set, Chakra presents its dishes with a modern flourish and a hefty price tag. Droplet chandeliers, dimpled banquettes and a stylish cream colour scheme add to the sense of occasion. The cooking styles of Indian royal courts are emphasised on the menu, along with the occasional nod to street food. Well-priced lunchtime and pre-theatre deals are worth checking out. Meals can be memorable, yet we noticed a dip in standards for a couple of the regional specialities. Good news first: patiala lamb chops (a signature dish) were supremely tender and owed much to an astringent lime and yoghurt marination spiked with garlic and ginger, and to just-so chargrilling. Chakra also produces an outstanding okra dish. This much maligned vegetable is sliced into slivers and dusted in chilli-spiced gram-flour before being fried: a crunchy, flavoursome treat, and a great match with

pomegranate raita. The rest of the meal was disappointing. Blandly spiced Bengali fish curry was let down by a lack of mustardy bite and a cloyingly sweet coconut masala; and service fell short of expectation, with staff needing to be a sight more familiar with their menu.
Available for hire. Booking advisable. Disabled: toilet. Separate room for parties, seats 26. Tables outdoors (2, pavement). Takeaway service. **Map 7 A7**.

South West
Chelsea

Chutney Mary

535 King's Road, SW10 0SZ (7351 3113, www.chutneymary.com). Fulham Broadway tube or bus 11, 22. **Lunch served** 12.30-2.45pm Sat, Sun. **Dinner served** 6.30-11.15pm Mon-Sat; 6.30-10.15pm Sun. **Main courses** £16.75-£31.50. **Set lunch** £24 3 courses. **Credit** AmEx, DC, MC, V. Pan-Indian
The spacious, light-filled conservatory at this swish establishment, set on the lower-ground floor of a modern block, is notable for its greenery – a contrast to the formal elegance of the main dining area with its sparkling glassware, silk cushions and crisp napery. Run by the Panjabi family (of Amaya, Veeraswamy and Masala Zone fame), Chutney Mary is popular with business diners on expense accounts and well-heeled Chelsea residents. Prices can be eye-wateringly high, and although the pan-Indian cooking is good in parts, it isn't always consistent. Service is also uneven. Crab balchao

(flakes of crab meat tossed in a fried sweet-sour red chilli paste) was a fair rendition, yet arrived inexplicably glazed with cheddar cheese – a new-wave twist too far. Even the humble samosa was given a makeover: crisp pastry shaped into an open cone and filled with fried venison mince. Sadly, the meat had dried out and lacked any discernible spicing apart from a kick of chilli. A splendid chicken biriani restored order, with fragrant rice, tender chicken thighs and a carefully honed masala spiked with just the right balance of green chilli, herbs and keora (floral screwpine essence). Overall, standards here seem to have dipped but you'll still find occasional flashes of brilliance.
Available for hire. Babies and children welcome lunch; children admitted until 8pm: high chairs. Booking advisable, essential Thur-Sat. Dress: smart casual. Separate room for parties, seats 28. Vegan dishes. Vegetarian menu. **Map 13 C13**.

Painted Heron

112 Cheyne Walk, SW10 0DJ (7351 5232, www.thepaintedheron.com). Sloane Square tube then bus 11, 22. **Lunch served** noon-2.30 Tue-Sun. **Dinner served** 6-10.30pm Tue-Sat; 6-10pm Sun. **Main courses** £13.50-£22. **Credit** MC, V. Modern Indian
Popular with well-heeled local residents, this classy destination is smartly furnished in a restrained grey-brown palette. The menu is much more flamboyant, although dishes are seasoned with classic spice blends. Deep-fried soft-shell crab, coated in a ground rice and sesame-seed batter, was outstanding for its crisp crust that yielded to reveal the sweet flesh below. We were also taken by a heap of juicy shrimps tossed in raunchy red chilli and tamarind

masala – with a garlicky flatbread obligingly soaking up the juices. Mains were not in the same league. Tangy Goan fish curry, although studded with sizeable scallops and juicy prawns, was let down by a heavy onion-ginger sauce that overwhelmed the seafood. Sri Lankan chicken curry – spiked with ginger, dried chillies and fried onion masala – made a much better impression with its toasted coriander spicing and tender strips of softened gourd. The Painted Heron's left-field signature dish of strawberry curry has become an annual summer spectacle: strawberry juice, reduced, seasoned with toasted cumin and lime juice and studded with squishy berries; it was as delectable as it was wacky. Service seriously needs to spruce itself up if it's to match the fabulous cooking.
Available for hire. Babies and children welcome: high chairs. Booking advisable weekends. **Map 14 D13**.

South
Tooting

★ Apollo Banana Leaf
190 Tooting High Street, SW17 0SF (8696 1423, http://apollobananaleaf.com). Tooting Broadway tube. **Lunch served** noon-3pm, **dinner served** 6-10.30pm Mon-Thur. **Meals served** noon-10.30pm Fri-Sun. **Main courses** £3.50-£6.95. **Unlicensed. Corkage** no charge. **Credit** MC, V.
Sri Lankan
As if in recognition of the trek from the nearest tube station, Apollo Banana Leaf greets diners with a vision of paradise: soaring mountains and a sparkling waterfall, printed in vivid technicolour on wall posters. If that assault on the senses isn't enough, the high-backed dining chairs are upholstered in crushed red velvet, while disco lights twinkle around the door. But devotees don't come here for design tips, they come for the food – an authentic rendering of South Indian and Sri Lankan cuisine – and for great value. Though prices have increased, they remain fantastically keen: especially when you factor in the BYO policy. Spice levels are at authentic Jaffna (northern Sri Lanka) levels: a single chilli icon on the menu is to be taken seriously, two-plus is for the brave. 'Short eats' (street-food snacks) included our soft sambar vadai (a savoury doughnut made with chickpea flour, here steeped in a thin lentil gravy) and a croquette-like mutton roll (with its rich, clove-spiked meat middle). There are also starters, such as crunchy morsels of golden chicken pakoda (not unlike 'popcorn chicken'). The rich, warmly spiced crab masala – claws and all – is worth getting messy for; chewy, buttery chapati makes the perfect foil.
Babies and children welcome: high chairs. Booking advisable weekends. Disabled: toilet. Separate room for parties, seats 45. Takeaway service. Vegetarian menu.

East
Whitechapel

Café Spice Namaste
16 Prescot Street, E1 8AZ (7488 9242, www.cafespice.co.uk). Aldgate East or Tower Hill tube or Tower Gateway DLR. **Lunch served** noon-3pm Mon-Fri. **Dinner served** 6.15-10.30pm Mon-Sat. **Main courses** £12.50-

Lahore Kebab House

£18.55. **Set meal** £35 3 courses. **Credit** AmEx, DC, MC, V. Pan-Indian
Occupying a former Victorian magistrate's court, Café Spice Namaste is furnished in swathes of brightly hued cloth, which lend the substantial interior something of a pantomime feel. Chef-patron Cyrus Todiwala is credited with popularising Goan dishes in London and also with bringing genuine Persian-inspired Parsi classics to the city's restaurant scene. A simple Indo-British collaboration of juicy seared scallops paired with cumin and spinach mash was let down by an overload of cumin in the potatoes. And though we appreciated the fiery heat of a crisp puff-pastry pasty filled with fried chicken livers cloaked in a ginger-shallot masala, the accompanying pool of sweet and sour turmeric-hued cream described as 'Goan curry sauce' did the dish no favours. More of this yellow sauce partnered a passable rice pilau studded with chopped garlicky sausages in a piquant chilli masala. And as if we hadn't had our fill, the same sauce morphed into the masala in a king prawn curry. Todiwala is one half of the duo featured in the BBC TV series, *The Incredible Spice*

Men, and his restaurant has become a hit with fans of the series as well as tourists and City business diners. Yet though we found plenty of ambition here, the execution in the kitchen needed attention. Service is well meaning if slow at times.
Available for hire. Babies and children welcome: high chairs. Disabled: toilet. Separate room for parties, seats 40. Takeaway service. Vegetarian menu. **Map 12 S7**.

★ Lahore Kebab House
2-10 Umberston Street, E1 1PY (7488 2551, www.lahore-kebabhouse.com). Aldgate East or Whitechapel tube. **Meals served** noon-midnight daily. **Main courses** £6-£10.50. **Unlicensed. Corkage** no charge. **Credit** AmEx, MC, V.
Pakistani
It might not look like much, but Lahore Kebab House is a place of pilgrimage for curry lovers. Queues snake out of the door at weekends, with diners travelling from afar to sample Punjabi-style tandoori grilled meat and generous portions of ghee-laden curry. Bargain prices, attentive service and a BYO policy add to the draw. Piles of sweet

onion bhajia and heavily spiced lamb chops might start off a meal, before the choice velvety dals, boldly flavoured curries (many of them on the bone) and buttery nans. The house specials are worth ordering, especially the nihari and dry lamb curry, all served in utilitarian karahi bowls with minimal fuss. Decor is equally no-nonsense. Spartan and to the point, this place is all about the food. Sure, the big LCD screens blaring out IPL cricket games or Bollywood movies are a little distracting, but the open kitchen provides most entertainment. There's nothing better for whetting the appetite than watching an army of cooks kneading dough for the tandoor and flipping meats on the grill – unless it's the mouth-watering aromas. Lahore is hard to beat for truly authentic, vivid flavours in a no-frills setting: more than worth having to queue.

Babies and children welcome: high chairs; nappy-changing facilities. Disabled: toilet. Separate room for parties, seats 50. Takeaway service. Vegetarian menu.

For branches see index.

★ ★ Needoo Grill
87 New Road, E1 1HH (7247 0648, www.needoogrill.co.uk). Aldgate East or Whitechapel tube. **Meals served** 11.30am-11.30pm daily. **Main courses** £6-£6.50. **Unlicensed. Corkage** no charge. **Credit** MC, V. Pakistani

In the great battle of the Whitechapel lamb chop – an unofficial war being waged between Needoo and its nearby neighbours Tayyabs and Lahore Kebab House – it's hard to pick a winner. The sizzling plates of succulent lamb that you get here aren't cooked to pink excellence like at Lahore, and aren't as pungent as at Tayyabs, but they are spiced to absolute perfection. Opened in 2009 by a former Tayyabs manager, this squashed space doesn't suffer from the same problem of endless queues (though you will usually have a wait), but it is just as gaudy. Bright red walls, leather benches and blaring flatscreen TVs are the order of the day, yet with curries this good, the decor just fades into the background. What you get are succulent karahi dishes and specials that include nihari (lamb on the bone) and a very passable biriani. Pakoras and other pre-prepared snacks can sometimes be disappointingly stale, but service is swift and friendly, and it's hard to argue with the appeal of BYOB and curries of such high standard.

Available for hire. Babies and children welcome: high chairs. Booking advisable Wed-Sat. Takeaway service. Vegetarian menu.

★ ★ Tayyabs
83-89 Fieldgate Street, E1 1JU (7247 9543, www.tayyabs.co.uk). Aldgate East or Whitechapel tube. **Meals served** noon-11.30pm daily. **Main courses** £6.50-£25.80. **Unlicensed. Corkage** no charge. **Credit** AmEx, MC, V. Pakistani

We've featured Tayyabs every year since it opened in 1972, and every year it gets busier and busier. From its original premises in a small café, it has gradually swallowed up the pub next door. If you come here expecting a relaxing evening, cheery service or an intimate atmosphere, you'll be disappointed: this is a full-on, massive, hectic, loud, in-and-out sort of place. Also, if you come here without booking, expect to wait up to an hour for a table. But we recommend this Punjabi stalwart wholeheartedly because of the cheapness and unreserved boldness of the food. Don't even think about visiting without trying the fiery grilled lamb

Tayyabs

chops, which is still one of London's best dishes. The rest of the menu is all about rich dals and masala channa; unctuous, slow-cooked lamb curries; and good versions of North Indian staples – onion bhajia, spice-rubbed tikka, hot, buttery breads and juicy kebabs. Regulars look to the daily specials, such as karahi lamb chop curry on Thursdays, or meat biriani on Fridays. The corkage-free BYO policy doesn't do its popularity any harm either.

Babies and children welcome: high chairs; nappy-changing facilities. Booking advisable. Disabled: toilet. Separate room for parties, seats 35. Takeaway service.

North East
Dalston

Gujarati Rasoi
10C Bradbury Street, N16 8JN (8616 7914, www.gujaratirasoi.com). Dalston Kingsland rail. **Dinner served** 6.30-10.30pm Wed-Sat. **Main courses** £10-£13. **Credit** MC, V. Gujarati vegetarian

It's hard to be ill-disposed towards Gujarati Rasoi – with its convivial mix of young, multicultural right-on customers, its studiedly makeshift interior (concrete floor, one wall of chipboard, another with shelves displaying jars of pulses) and its feel-good vibes. Service came from a friendly waitress who resembled a Scandinavian model. The business grew out of street-food stalls run by mother and son Lalita Patel and Urvesh Parvais and featured in Madhur Jaffrey's *Curry Nation*. Food is freshly made in the sparkling open kitchen that takes up a third of the tiny premises. The daily changing menu is short – no bad thing in itself, but therein lies a problem. Although our dishes were appealing and authentically spiced, the meal lacked variety. Papri chat was a colourful, textural treat (crisp papri, thick yoghurt and, unusually, pomegranate seeds), yet a main of polenta-like khumni ne sev also came with sev and pomegranate seeds (and coconut); being a dry dish, it needed a side of tangy soup-like khadi. In short, the menu cries out for a thali. In our quest for variety we ordered widely (finishing with fruit-packed mango sorbet), and our not excessively large dinner, with one 75cl bottle of Meantime IPA apiece, cost over £40 a head – twice the price of Wembley's Gujarati cafés and excessive for a restaurant of this (albeit joyful) ilk.

Babies and children admitted. Booking advisable. Disabled: toilet. Tables outdoors (3, pavement). Vegan dishes. Vegetarian menu. **Map 25 B4.**

INDIAN

Gujarati Rasoi. See p141.

Camden Town & Chalk Farm

Namaaste Kitchen

64 Parkway, NW1 7AH (7485 5977, www.namaastekitchen.co.uk). Camden Town tube. **Lunch served** noon-2.30pm, **dinner served** 5.30-11.30pm Mon-Thur. **Meals served** noon-11.30pm Fri, Sat; noon-11pm Sun. **Main courses** £7.50-£18.95. **Set lunch** £7.95 1 course, £12.50 2 courses, £15 3 courses. **Credit** AmEx, MC, V. Modern Indian

Exposed brickwork, hanging lights and cream banquettes give this upmarket local a modern appeal. Ask the keen, helpful staff for a table towards the rear of the narrow dining area for a view of chefs skewering kebabs and placing them in the clay oven. Last year, we were impressed by the authenticity and diversity of regional dishes – we're slightly less enamoured this time. That said, a first course certainly hit the spot: chargrilled whole sea bass, infused with smoky mustard oil, lime juice and fiery chilli powder, was our star dish, notable for its tender, juicy flesh and punchy mustardy flavour. Good news continued with squishy baby aubergines, covered in fried onion-ginger paste, seasoned with sesame seeds and sharpened with tamarind. But that's an end to the highlights. Five-lentil dal had as much spicing as a school-dinner soup. Laal maas from Rajasthan was a shadow of the real deal; a severe shortfall of red chillies and the addition of floral screwpine essence discredited this traditional, slow-cooked hunter's dish. Even the crisp gram-flour droplet raita was too sweet. Let's hope culinary matters will be back on track soon.

Available for hire. Babies and children welcome: high chairs. Booking advisable. Separate room for parties, seats 18. Takeaway service; delivery service (over £15 within 3-mile radius). Vegan dishes. Vegetarian menu. **Map 27 C3**. **For branch see index.**

Islington

★ Delhi Grill

21 Chapel Market, N1 9EZ (7278 8100, www.delhigrill.com). Angel tube. **Lunch served** noon-2pm, **dinner served** 6-10pm daily. **Main courses** £3.95-£9.95. **Credit** AmEx, MC, V. Punjabi

A lively canteen-style joint, Delhi Grill provides a focused menu of home-style Punjabi dishes – along with wraps sold from a smart stall outside in Chapel Market during the day. Inside, the walls are plastered with Bollywood posters and Indian newspapers; corrugated iron and stencilled lettering contribute to a *Slumdog Millionaire* aesthetic. The selection of street-food starters such as samosa chat are more in keeping with this mood than the Indian-restaurant standard chicken tikka. The cooking shows that the kitchen isn't following the usual formula, but is prepared to go out and do its own thing, so tilapia with coriander and coconut milk joins hearty slow-cooked rogan josh, a biriani and chicken karahi on the menu. There's a lightness to the preparation, evident in a Punjabi prawn masala with fresh flavours of peppers, tomato and ginger. Vegetarians are very well provided for, though the aloo baingan featured much more potato

Sidebar: INDIAN

than aubergine in a thin sauce. Meat-free alternatives include chana, bhindi and tarka dal. Beans and greens salad was a refreshing if not especially exciting mix of seemingly tinned pulses and cucumber. Insistent bhangra beats and unyielding seats make this venue more of a healthy, spicy pitstop than somewhere to linger.
Available for hire. Babies and children admitted. Booking advisable Thur-Sat. Disabled: toilet. Takeaway service. Vegan dishes. **Map 5 N2.**

North West
Swiss Cottage

Eriki
4-6 Northways Parade, Finchley Road, NW3 5EN (7722 0606, www.eriki.co.uk). Swiss Cottage tube. **Lunch served** noon-2.30pm, **dinner served** 6-10.30pm daily. **Main courses** £10-£15. **Credit** MC, V. Pan-Indian
For more than a decade, Eriki has brought homely pan-Indian cooking to Finchley locals. The view on to the A41 isn't the most salubrious, but the maroon-hued dining area, furnished with chunky wooden furniture, provides a slightly upmarket feel. After enjoying quality meals here for more than a decade, our most recent meal was average at best. A vegetarian platter didn't inspire us with its variety: a potato-stuffed samosa, potato-filled mini dosa and a tandoori-cooked potato. Everyday staples such as the delicious tarka dal were the most satisfying. We loved the roughly textured lentils, tempered with fried ginger, cumin and the bite of chilli. Punjabi-style gosht aloo simla mirch (lamb curry, cooked with peppers and new potatoes) had a decent fried onion, ginger and garam masala base and a generous helping of tender boneless meat. But murgh makhan palak – similar to chicken tikka masala – did itself no favours, with a cloyingly sweet tomato sauce overriding any flavour from the spinach. Service was polite, but the restaurant needs to up its game to match its previous standards.
Available for hire. Babies and children admitted. Booking advisable. Takeaway service; delivery service (6-9.45pm, over £20 within 4-mile radius). Vegetarian menu. **Map 28 B4.**

Outer London
Edgware, Middlesex

★ Meera's Village
36 Queensbury Station Parade, Edgware, Middx HA8 5NN (8952 5556, www.meerasvillage.com). Queensbury tube. **Lunch served** noon-3pm Wed, Thur. **Dinner served** 6-10pm Mon-Thur. **Meals served** noon-10.30pm Fri, Sat; noon-10pm Sun. **Main courses** £5.99-£11.99. **No credit cards.** Gujarati vegetarian
Furnished with a riot of kitsch Indian fittings and fixtures, this neighbourhood restaurant is anything but subtle in looks. Expansive painted murals depict Gujarati village life, with bunches of plastic flowers, velveteen seating arrangements, bamboo tables and weighty statues filling any gaps. Never mind. The kitchen produces first-rate, sensitively spiced vegetarian Gujarati dishes. We chose the affordable Gujarati thali for a taster of regional staples, and marvelled at the delicacy of broth-like kadhi, made with roasted gram flour and tart yoghurt, spiced with cloves and fried fennel seeds

– perfect with fluffy basmati rice. A simple smooth-textured Gujarati dal, sweetened with jaggery and sharpened with tamarind, made a good match with thepla (soft chapati-like breads). Classic touches include farsan (snacks) – perhaps balls of fried crushed-potato dumplings flecked with aromatic curry leaves – served alongside main dishes. Staff were utterly charming. Portions are generous and unlimited refills a bonus. Drink like a local and order churned buttermilk (chaas) with the meal – it's a marvellous digestif.
Available for hire. Babies and children admitted; high chairs; nappy-changing facilities. Booking advisable. Takeaway service. Vegetarian menu.

Harrow, Middlesex

★ Mr Chilly
344 Pinner Road, Harrow, Middx HA1 4LB (8861 4404, www.mrchilly.co.uk). North Harrow tube. **Main courses** £3.50-£7. **Set lunch** (noon-3pm) £6 2 courses. **Credit** MC, V. Pakistani
Like wandering magicians, the Ali brothers – Raza and Riaz – have worked their culinary wizardry across London's outer suburbs. They set up a Pakistani café, nurture business, then sell and move on. Mr Chilly very much fits the template. Set on a busy junction, it looks unremarkable behind its frosted window. Within, plain wooden furniture is cheered up by colourful photos of spices on the walls, but above all by the sensory delights of the stainless-steel open kitchen. Pans rattle, spices sizzle, flames leap. Meat dominates the starters; chicken liver tawa was stew-like, yet tender and abundant. Fish tawa, a modestly portioned tilapia fillet, arrived seared and succulent. Karahi dishes, including plentiful vegetarian food (karela, patra corn, malai kofta) account for most main courses, and both the mutter paneer (the cheese first fried brown) and karahi mixed beans (butter beans and kidney beans) passed muster. Best were the deigi methi chicken, the deigi spring lamb (both on the bone and bursting with flavour) and the keema biriani that sang with spices. The supporting cast? Breads were sublime, the lassis lacked tang. Staff are especially charming – offering popadoms, yoghurt and a kheer dessert gratis.
Babies and children welcome: high chairs; nappy-changing facilities. Disabled: toilet. Tables outdoors (3, pavement). Takeaway service. Vegetarian menu.

★ Ram's
203 Kenton Road, Harrow, Middx HA3 0HD (8907 2022, www.ramsrestaurant.co.uk). Kenton tube/rail. **Meals served** noon-11pm daily. **Main courses** £4-£5. **Set buffet** (noon-3pm Mon-Fri) £4.99; (6-10pm Mon-Fri) £9.99. **Credit** MC, V. Gujarati vegetarian
What was an unassuming community café, renowned for its Surti cooking from southern Gujarat, has spread its wings and now includes a catering hall and sweetmeat shop next door. Today, the menu promotes Punjabi, South Indian and even Indo-Chinese choices alongside Gujarati specialities. Even the interior has been revamped, with a mash-up of twinkly blue and red lights, mirror work and flatscreen TVs. For the best results, we suggest choosing dishes from Surat for their sweet, tangy flavours. The pani poori served here is terrific; we messily polished off crisp globes of hollow pastry, filled with diced potatoes and

topped up with pungent black salt (kala namak) and minted tamarind water. Mains weren't quite as memorable: the bindi kadhai, a tart, whipped yoghurt curry, thickened with roasted gram flour and simmered with okra, was all right, but would have benefited from a more stringent seasoning of popped mustard seeds and hits of red chilli. Small dumplings of deep-fried green banana and fenugreek pakoras had pleasantly sweet notes, cut through with peppery fenugreek – but were dense in texture. Service was well meaning but erratic.
Babies and children welcome: high chairs. Booking advisable weekends. Separate room for parties, seats 50. Takeaway service. Vegan dishes. Vegetarian menu.

★ Saravana Bhavan
403 Alexandra Avenue, Harrow, Middx HA2 9SG (8869 9966, www.saravanabhavan.co.uk). Rayners Lane tube. **Meals served** 11am-10.20pm Mon-Thur; 11am-10.50pm Fri-Sun. **Main courses** £2.50-£7.95. **Credit** AmEx, MC, V. South Indian vegetarian
Bringing the aroma of crackling curry leaves to suburbia, this simple South Indian café has become a destination for large family groups. Serpentine queues on weekend evenings are a giveaway that dining here is worth the wait. Meals are great value, especially the special offers during the week. Expect tongue-tingling flavours – tamarind, curry leaves, mustard seeds, coconut and plenty of tart lentil-based dishes. Despite the lengthy menu, dosas are the stars. These simple pancakes, made from ground rice and lentils, are crisp on one side and slightly spongy on the other. We recommend the masala dosa filled with crushed potatoes and accompanied with tamarind lentils (sambar) and fresh chutneys made with coconut and chillies. North Indian options don't make the grade, but other southern specialties are worth checking out. We were taken by the soupy consistency of bisibelabath – a warming 'stew' made from simmered rice and lentils cooked with fiery chillies, tomatoes and diced vegetables. Lunchtimes tend to be on the quiet side; visit at the weekend for a boisterous experience. Service remains polite and professional even when the place is packed.
Babies and children welcome: high chairs; nappy-changing facilities. Booking advisable Thur-Sun. Disabled: toilet. Takeaway service. Vegetarian menu.
For branches see index.

Southall, Middlesex

★ Brilliant
72-76 Western Road, Southall, Middx UB2 5DZ (8574 1928, www.brilliantrestaurant.com). Southall rail. **Lunch served** noon-3pm Tue-Fri. **Dinner served** 6-11.30pm Tue-Sun. **Main courses** £4.50-£14. **Credit** AmEx, MC, V. East African Indian
The glitzy interior doesn't hint at Brilliant's longevity (though a photo of a glossy-haired Prince Charles meeting the proprietors provides a clue), but this Southall landmark has been trading for nigh-on 40 years. It now has a first-floor banqueting hall seating 120 and runs cookery courses – videos of which are shown on three flatscreen TVs in the ground-floor restaurant. Owners, the Anand family, hail from Kenya (see the carvings of Maasai tribeswomen), and the menu reflects this in starters of tandoori tilapia fish or mogo (cassava-root chips). Nevertheless, it's

Sri Lankan menu

Sri Lanka is home to three main groups: Sinhalese, Tamil and Muslim. Although there are variations in the cooking styles of each community and every region, rice and curry form the basis of most meals, and curries are usually hot and spicy. The cuisine has evolved by absorbing South Indian, Portuguese, Dutch, Arabic, Malaysian and Chinese flavours over the years. Aromatic herbs and spices like cinnamon, cloves, curry leaves, nutmeg, and fresh coriander are combined with South-east Asian ingredients such as lemongrass, pandan leaves, sesame oil, dried fish and rice noodles. Fresh coconut, onions, green chillies and lime juice (or vinegar) are also used liberally, and there are around two dozen types of rice – from short-grained white varieties to several long-grained, burgundy-hued kinds.

Curries come in three main varieties: white (cooked in coconut milk), yellow (with turmeric and mild curry powder) and black (with roasted curry powder, normally used with meat). Hoppers (saucer-shaped pancakes) are generally eaten for breakfast with kithul palm syrup and buffalo-milk yoghurt, while string hoppers (steamed, rice-flour noodles formed into flat discs) usually accompany fiery curries and sambols (relishes).

Ambul thiyal: sour fish curry cooked dry with spices.
Appam or **appa**: see hoppers.
Badun: black. 'Black' curries are fried; they're dry and usually very hot.
Devilled: meat, seafood or vegetable dishes fried with onions in a sweetish sauce; usually served as starters.
Godamba roti: flaky, thin Sri Lankan bread, sometimes wrapped around egg or potato.
Hoppers: confusingly, hoppers come in two forms, either as saucer-shaped, rice-flour pancakes (try the sweet and delectable milk hopper) or as string hoppers (qv).
Idiappa: see string hoppers.

Katta sambol: onion, lemon and chilli relish; fearsomely hot.
Kiri: white. 'White' curries are based on coconut milk and are usually mild.
Kiri hodi: coconut milk curry with onions and turmeric; a soothing gravy.
Kuttu roti, **kottu** or **kothu roti**: strips of thin bread (resembling pasta), mixed with mutton, chicken, prawns or veg to form a 'bread biriani'; very filling.
Lamprais or **lumprice**: a biriani-style dish where meat and rice are cooked together, often by baking in banana leaves.
Lunnu miris: a relish of ground onion, chilli and maldives fish (qv).
Maldives fish: small, dried fish with a very intense flavour; an ingredient used in sambols (qv).
Pittu: rice flour and coconut steamed in bamboo to make a 'log'; an alternative to rice.
Pol: coconut.
Pol kiri: see kiri hodi.
Pol sambol: a mix of coconut, chilli, onions, maldives fish (qv) and lemon juice.
Sambols: strongly flavoured relishes, often served hot; they are usually chilli-hot too.
Seeni sambol: sweet and spicy, caramelised onion relish.
Sothy or **sothi**: another name for kiri hodi.
String hoppers: fine rice-flour noodles formed into flat discs. Usually served steamed (in which case they're dry, making them ideal partners for the gravy-like kiri hodi, qv).
Vellappam: appam (qv) served with vegetable curry.
Wattalappan or **vattilapan**: a version of crème caramel made with kithul palm syrup.

for exemplary versions of straightforward Punjabi cooking that the restaurant has gained acclaim, and a cabinet full of awards. Fish pakora followed by methi chicken karahi remains a sublime option, though a recent meal began with fried masala egg (two hard-boiled eggs laced with spices in a crisp batter) then a far more thrilling palak lamb, where both the spinach and tender meat shone through the warming spice mix, and nutty tarka dal (one of several 'healthy options' using less ghee). Prompt, smart service, first-rate accompaniments (six own-made chutneys, skilfully rendered breads, high-quality basmati rice), a cocktail list and a room full of happy multicultural parties confirm Brilliant's pedigree.
Available for hire. Babies and children welcome: high chairs; nappy-changing facilities. Booking advisable weekends. Separate room for parties, seats 120. Takeaway service. Vegetarian menu.

★ New Asian Tandoori Centre (Roxy)
114-118 The Green, Southall, Middx UB2 4BQ (8574 2597, www.roxy-restaurant.com). Southall rail. **Meals served** 8am-10.30pm daily. **Main courses** £5-£6.50. **No credit cards.** Punjabi

These capacious corner premises on a busy junction have seen profound changes since they first housed the Roxy caff. For many years, the business operated as Sagoo & Takhar, a Punjabi canteen, but though the takeaway counter remains, two adjoining rooms now house a highly presentable restaurant. Polite black-clad waiters flit purposefully between tables full of local families, many of them Sikhs. Know the strengths of Punjabi cuisine, and you're likely to receive food of rare excellence. Choose a tandoori dish to start. Tandoori fish was succulent and tender beneath its tangy seared surface – far better than the slightly chewy golgappa (puffed poori shells to be filled with chickpeas, tamarind relish and mint water). Likewise, order thick, savoury Punjabi curries as a main course – the moreish dal, or chicken methi full of flavoursome thigh meat and abundant fenugreek leaves – and accompany them with one of an outstanding array of breads (the tissue-thin roomali roti and the onion kulcha are recommended). Smart, light furnishings and striking modern art also show how far the Roxy has travelled since its greasy-spoon days.
Available for hire. Babies and children welcome: high chairs. Booking advisable. Disabled: lift; toilet. Takeaway service. Vegan dishes. Vegetarian menu.

Wembley, Middlesex

★ Asher's
224 Ealing Road, Wembley, Middx HA0 4QL (8795 2455). Alperton tube. **Meals served** noon-10pm daily. **Main courses** £3-£8. **No credit cards.** Gujarati vegetarian

As London's South Asian population grows more affluent, places like Asher's are becoming rare, which is a shame. This well-scrubbed caff – where vibrant prints of Hindu deities add zest to a magnolia colour scheme – is an ideal spot for a keenly priced Gujarati thali before indulging in the retail treats of the Ealing Road. If you've only pennies to spare, choose the mini thali; £3.50 buys a chapati, a mouth-wateringly savoury, soupy dal, passable veg curry, yoghurt, rice and basic salad. If, however, you want a lengthier exploration of the cuisine, order the Gujarati special thali, which, at

Delhi Grill. See p142.

£8, also includes an exquisitely light samosa (plump with vegetables), and equally well-turned-out and freshly made kachori – two crisp snacks – plus a lassi, and a shrikhand dessert with the flavour of condensed milk and the consistency of mayonnaise. Mogo chips are among the African-Asian snacks also on the concise menu. Local Gujarati couples, friends and elderly single diners populated a lunchtime visit, attended by quiet, smiling waitresses sporting bindis. Stainless-steel thali dishes and the staff's sometimes shaky English complete the experience.
Babies and children admitted. Takeaway service. Vegan dishes. Vegetarian menu.

★ Gana
24 Ealing Road, Wembley, Middx HA0 4TL (8903 7004). Wembley Central tube/rail. **Meals served** 10am-11pm daily. **Main courses** £3.95-£7. **Credit** MC, V. Sri Lankan
One of London's widest choices of Sri Lankan food is reason enough to visit Gana, but don't expect fripperies. Behind the frosted-glass frontage, you'll find a café-style interior with shiny wood-effect table-tops, chequered tiled floor and a glass display counter. Downstairs is the 'basement hall facility (family only)', a murky, compact, woody room with space for about 30. A mid-afternoon meal was let down by tepid dishes (a party at a neighbouring table sent their order back to be reheated), but full-

flavoured, uncompromisingly fiery food in huge portions at low prices won us over. Rasam soup (only £1.50) was pleasingly peppery and deliciously tart with tamarind. Other highlights were the soft and savoury fish cutlets (fish cakes); the string hoppers, served with crunchy-fresh coconut sambol and tangy sothi gravy; beautifully smoky aubergine jaffna; and Gana special kothu roti, a pasta-like 'bread biriani' mixed with mutton, chicken and egg. In contrast, 'mutton curry with bone, liver and heart' was hard work: the gravy sublime, the offal tender, but the clattering preponderance of bone a challenge. Kind staff tend solicitously to their mostly Sri Lankan clientele.
Takeaway service.

★ Kailash Parbat
5 Ealing Road, Wembley, Middx HA0 4AA (8902 8238, www.kailashparbat.co.uk). Wembley Central tube/rail. **Lunch served** noon-4pm, **dinner served** 6-10.30pm daily. **Main courses** £4.50-£6.99. **Set lunch** (Mon-Fri) £7.99 2 courses. **Credit** MC, V. Pakistani vegetarian
It's rare to find Sindhi food in London: the rich, earthy, subtly spiced dishes of Pakistan's Sindh province. Named after a mountain peak near Tibet, this small, buzzy venue isn't a Sindhi restaurant as such, but a franchise of an international Indian vegetarian chain renowned for Sindhi dishes. It's

smarter looking, with slicker service, than most Ealing Road venues. Beautifully spiced sindhi kadhi – a golden pool of chickpea-flour gravy studded with chunks of potatoes, carrots and vegetable drumsticks – was given depth of flavour by tamarind and curry leaves. We also loved arbi tuk (fried taro pieces flattened and sprinkled with ground spices) and the bright, vibrant flavours of seyal chawal – the rice stir-fried with caramelised onions and tomatoes. Koki, a rustic flatbread stuffed with onions and chillies, was another success. However, aloo bhindi sai masala – potatoes and okra in green herb gravy – divided opinion, with its dominant mint flavour and mushy texture. Even less successful were lotus root fritters (which had an eye-watering chilli hit and out-of-balance spicing) and the bland sindhi pakoras cooked in too-thick batter that tasted a little stale. Note that sindhi kadhi and dal pakwaan are only available for Sunday lunch.
Babies and children welcome: high chairs; nappy-changing facilities. Bookings not accepted Sat, Sun. Disabled: toilet. Separate room for parties, seats 50. Takeaway service; delivery service (over £15 within 3-mile radius).

★ Sakonis HOT 50
127-129 Ealing Road, Wembley, Middx HA0 4BP (8903 9601, www.sakonis.co.uk). Alperton tube. **Breakfast served** 9-11am Sat, Sun.

Wembley, India

Ask anyone with gastronomic nous where in London to find the best Indian food, and you're likely to get several replies. Southall will certainly feature, and most likely Tooting too, while Whitechapel and points east will also have advocates. Wembley? Surely that's for football? Only a few dedicated enthusiasts will mention the Ealing Road, which winds from Alperton tube north to Wembley High Road. Although this busy thoroughfare is less than a mile long, it holds a seductive array of inexpensive restaurants serving dishes from across the subcontinent.

Leaving Alperton station, you'll soon encounter the sari shops, jewellery stores and cash 'n' carries that give the road its character. Since the 1970s, a wealth of people with South Asian ancestry – many from eastern Africa – have settled in the vicinity. Ealing Road is where they shop, pray (there's a fabulously ornate Hindu temple, a mosque and a Methodist chapel) and dine.

One of the first venues is also the most atypical: **Momo House** is a cosy little restaurant whose South African owner offers several unusual, sometimes challenging Nepalese dishes (tooth-crackingly crunchy spiced soy beans called bhatmas, for instance) alongside the curry-house regulars. Try the succulent lamb momo dumplings. Across the road is **Maru's Bhajia House**, a favourite caff of African-Asian vegetarians, who chat over plates of mogo (cassava root) chips served with a thick tamarind dip.

Further on is **Asher's** (see p144), a ludicrously cheap Gujarati vegetarian café. Note the 'Don't spit paan' window-sticker. Along with the crunchy snacks typical of this western Indian cuisine, there's a choice of thali set meals. If you hanker after meat, however, try neighbouring **Sohail's**, with its

Asher's

tawa (stir-fried), karahi and tandoori North Indian food. **Sakonis** (see p145) is an Ealing Road fixture, with crowds pouring in at weekends for the vegetarian Gujarati buffets; at the front is a takeaway snack counter and a paan bar.

After a lengthy residential interlude and then the Central Mosque, more shops and takeaways appear. **Kebabish** offers meaty North Indian karahis and kebabs in its dining room behind the takeaway counter.

As you approach Wembley High Road, South Indian and Sri Lankan cuisines make their presence felt. **Palm Beach** is the more upmarket Sri Lankan choice, where you can devour string hoppers accompanied by soothing music, though **Gana** (see p145), with its mutton liver curry and kothu rotis, has the more interesting menu. **Saravana Bhavan** opened in spring 2012; a suave addition to this international South Indian vegetarian chain (see also p143), it serves Indo-Chinese snacks, birianis and idlis, plus well-constructed, satisfying thalis. You might well be enticed by the Dosa Express street stall just up the street, but Ealing Road's final flourish comes in the form of two chain vegetarian restaurants at the junction with Wembley High Road: **Sanghamam**, a popular meeting spot thanks to its juice bar and South Indian, Mumbai chat and Indo-Chinese menu; and purple-tinted **Chennai Dosa**, home to spicy South Indian pancakes.

★ Chennai Dosa
529 High Road, Wembley, Middx HA0 2DH (8782 2222, www.chennaidosa.com).

★ Kebabish
40 Ealing Road, Wembley, Middx HA0 4TL (8795 2656, www.kebabishoriginal.co.uk).

★ Maru's Bhajia House
230 Ealing Road, Wembley, Middx HA0 4QL (8902 5570, 8903 6771).

★ Momo House
2 Glenmore Parade, Ealing Road, Wembley, Middx HA0 4PJ (8902 2307, www.momohouse.co.uk).

★ Palm Beach
17 Ealing Road, Wembley, Middx HA0 4AA (8900 8664, www.palmbeachuk.com).

★ Sanghamam
531-533 High Road, Wembley, Middx HA0 2DJ (8900 0777, www.sanghamam.co.uk).

★ Saravana Bhavan
22 & 22A Ealing Road, Wembley, Middx HA0 4TL (8900 8526, www.saravanabhavan.com).

★ Sohail's
238A Ealing Road, Wembley, Middx HA0 4QL (8903 6743).

Palm Beach

Saravana Bhavan

Meals served noon-10pm daily. **Main courses** £3.75-£7.29. **Set buffet** (breakfast) £4.99; (noon-4pm) £10.45; (6.30-9.30pm) £14.29. **Credit** MC, V. Gujarati vegetarian

When empty, the long capacious dining room behind the front snack counters and paan bar seems like an office canteen – complete with anodyne white walls, harsh lighting and utilitarian furniture. Populate the space with all strata of local British Asian society, however, then add Indian pop music and alluring aromas from the buffet counter, and you'll see why Sakonis has become an Ealing Road fixture (there's also a branch in Harrow). Crispy Gujarati titbits, Mumbai beach snacks, masala dosas and Indo-Chinese stir-fries are best ordered fresh from the menu (they get tired under the buffet's bright lights), but otherwise launch yourself into the eat-all-you-can deal: for breakfast (with idlies), lunch or dinner. The array of South Indian and Gujarati vegetarian dishes is admirable. Top choices include tangy kadhi gravy tempered with mustard seeds and curry leaves; nutty khichadi; a luxuriant saag paneer; thick dal mixed with vegetables; a potato and bean curry; and zesty sambar. Plentiful chutneys (try the coriander version) and salads add to the mix, and puddings such as thick shrikhand or fruity mango ras conclude the feast. Jugs of water and disposable plastic cups are brought to each table by the cheery staff.

Available for hire. Babies and children welcome: high chairs. Separate rooms for parties, seating 50. Takeaway service. Vegetarian menu.
For branch see index.

Sakonis. See p145.

Sweets menu

Even though there isn't a tradition of serving puddings at everyday meals in South Asia, there is much ceremony associated with distributing sweetmeats at auspicious events, especially weddings and religious festivals. Desserts served at many Indian restaurants in London include the likes of gulab jamun, cardamom-scented rice pudding, creamy kulfi, and soft, syrup-drenched cheese dumplings. In the home, family meals don't often include a dessert; you're more likely to be treated to a platter of seasonal fruit. Winter warmers also have their place, including comforting, fudge-like carrot halwa, a Punjabi favourite and popular street snack. Winter is also the season for weddings, where other halwas, made with wholewheat flour, semolina, lentils and pumpkin, might be served.

Barfi: sweetmeat usually made with reduced milk, and flavoured with nuts, fruit, sweet spices or coconut.
Bibenca or **bibinca**: soft, layered cake from Goa made with eggs, coconut milk and jaggery (a brown sugar).
Falooda or **faluda**: thick milky drink (originally from the Middle East), resembling a cross between a milkshake and a sundae. It's flavoured with either rose syrup or saffron, and also contains agar-agar, vermicelli, nuts and ice-cream. Very popular with Gujarati families, faloodas make perfect partners to deep-fried snacks.
Gajar halwa: grated carrots, cooked in sweetened cardamom milk until soft, then fried in ghee until almost caramelised; usually served warm.
Gulab jamun: brown dumplings (made from dried milk and flour), deep-fried and drenched in rose-flavoured sugar syrup, best served warm. A traditional Bengali sweet, now ubiquitous in Indian restaurants.
Halwa: a fudge-like sweet, made with semolina, wholewheat flour or ground pulses cooked with syrup or reduced milk, and flavoured with nuts, saffron or sweet spices.
Jalebis: spirals of batter, deep-fried and dipped in syrup, best eaten warm.
Kheer: milky rice pudding, flavoured with cardamom and nuts. Popular throughout India (there are many regional variations).
Kulfi: ice-cream made from reduced milk, flavoured with nuts, saffron or fruit.
Payasam: a South Indian pudding made of reduced coconut or cow's milk with sago, nuts and cardamom. **Semiya payasam** is made with added vermicelli.
Rasgullas: soft paneer cheese balls, simmered and dipped in rose-scented syrup, served cold.
Ras malai: soft paneer cheese patties in sweet and thickened milk, served cold.
Shrikhand: hung (concentrated) sweet yoghurt with saffron, nuts and cardamom, sometimes with fruit added. A traditional Gujarati favourite, eaten with pooris.

INDIAN

Italian

The simplicity of Italian cuisine often seems at odds with the prices charged by the restaurants in this chapter, but freshness and quality of produce is all. Or is it? These days, most of us can produce a reasonable plate of pasta at home, whether the sauce is cooked from scratch or bought-in, so the pressure is on restaurant kitchens to out-do their customers. Ergo, we now have chefs not just making their own pasta, but cured meats, breads and gelati too – **Bocca di Lupo**'s Jacob Kenedy is king in that regard. The raw components of menus – the ultimate exhibit of freshness – are also growing in stature: in years past, you'd expect to see a swordfish or beef carpaccio on most swish Italian menus; now the crudo list can take in everything from langoustines to shaved artichokes. Hip places such as Hackney's **Lardo** are big on salads (and breakfast). Mini-chain **Polpo** has put cicchetti firmly on the lips of Londoners (although **Cecconi's** and others had been quietly serving them for years), offering a spread of enticing small plates few would be bothered to construct at home, even if they've bought the hit Polpo cookbook. Newcomer **San Carlo**, a marble palace on Piccadilly (via Manchester) is joining the cicchetti fray; the other recent opening, Marylebone's **Cotidie**, offers more refined cooking in an elegant, cosseting environment. There's also plenty going on in the world of pizzerias – *see p302*. Whichever style of dining is to your taste, one thing's for sure: Italian cuisine won't be losing popularity any time soon.

Central
Belgravia

Il Convivio
143 Ebury Street, SW1W 9QN (7730 4099, www.etruscarestaurants.com). Sloane Square tube or Victoria tube/rail. **Lunch served** noon-2.45pm, **dinner served** 6-10.45pm Mon-Sat. **Main courses** £13.50-£24. **Set lunch** £17.50 2 courses. **Set dinner** £23.50 2 courses. **Credit** AmEx, MC, V.
The name suggests conviviality – yet while its welcome is friendly enough, Il Convivio has an ever-quiet air, as though customers have sunk into silent contemplation of the Dante quotations that adorn the walls. The three distinct dining areas of the restaurant are elegant, airy and enticingly lit, but a certain shabbiness has taken hold, and the puzzling contrasts between promise and presence continue with the food on the plate. Soup brought an instant challenge: while the creamy carrot base complemented by spicy, crunchy sage fritters showed beautifully judged flavours, it proved impossible to cut the giant fritters with the spoon provided. A similar experience came with the trail of resilient greens in an otherwise perfectly

executed risotto. Brined duck breast was sublimely tender and flavourful, but its tough skin proved an irritation. White espresso gelato was a joy; petits fours a disappointing irrelevance. Such discordant notes could prove a deal-breaker on the Belgravia-priced carte, but the chef's set menu seems such a bargain that slip-ups might be forgiven. Wines are well chosen and affordably priced, with good by-the-glass options. Certainly a place worth knowing. *Available for hire. Babies and children welcome: high chairs. Booking advisable dinner. Separate room for parties, seats 14.* **Map 15 G10.**

Olivo
21 Eccleston Street, SW1W 9LX (7730 2505, www.olivorestaurants.com). Sloane Square tube or Victoria tube/rail. **Lunch served** noon-2.30pm Mon-Fri. **Dinner served** 6-10.30pm Mon-Sat; 6.30-10.30pm Sun. **Main courses** £13-£23. **Set lunch** £23.50 2 courses, £28 3 courses. **Credit** AmEx, MC, V.
Perpetually buzzy Olivo is a confident stalwart of Belgravia's restaurant scene and part of a steadily expanding Sardinian specialist group. It exudes warmth even on a drizzly day, thanks to deep yellow and aquamarine walls and light wood furniture. Terracotta pots and lightshades convey rusticity, while the Italian chatter of the staff leaves you in

no doubt that this place is steeped in the food and wine culture of southern Italy. The house aperitif of sherried Oristano-style vernaccia is as good an introduction as any to the sun-baked flavours on offer; peppery olive oil and crisp sheets of Sardinian pane carasau quickly build on the authentic impression. While simply presented vitello tonnato could have come from anywhere in Italy, buffalo ricotta on grilled aubergine was distinctly southern, and a rich, generous plate of mascarpone-sauced pasta with ham would have sated a Sardinian shepherd from dawn to dusk. Hunks of grilled meat chased off any shadow of a hunger pang; happily, yoghurt ice with bitter honey allowed a lighter note to finish. While the prices of the carte are decidedly unbucolic, set lunch is a fair deal, and excellent Sardinian wines (or even Sardinian beer and mineral water) round off a satisfying experience. *Booking advisable. Children admitted: no pushchairs.* **Map 15 H10.**
For branches (Oliveto) see index.

City

L'Anima
1 Snowden Street, EC2A 2DQ (7422 7000, www.lanima.co.uk). Liverpool Street tube/rail. **Bar Open** 9am-1am Mon-Fri; 5.30pm-1am Sat.

Meals served 9am-11pm Mon-Fri; 5.30-11pm
Sat. **Main courses** £15-£33.
Restaurant **Lunch served** 11.45am-3pm Mon-
Fri. **Dinner served** 5.30-11pm Mon-Fri; 5.30-
11.30pm Sat. **Main courses** £16-£36. **Set
lunch** £24.50 2 courses, £28.50 3 courses.
Both **Credit** AmEx, MC, V.
Designer Claudio Silvestrin's showcase modernist
restaurant is highly memorable, though not perhaps
entirely as intended. At peak times, noise in the
glass, porphyry and limestone interior can be
overwhelming, and staff have to dance round the
large white leather and chrome chairs to catch
anything softer than a bellow. The food, however, is
often sublime, carefully sourced and skilfully
prepared. Beef tagliata was a beautiful construct
atop a marrow bone pillar, and its magliocco sauce
a pure essence of beefiness. Tagliatelle with wild
mushrooms and truffle appeared artless by contrast,
but once again the flavours were resonant, yet
subtle. Chard and soft cheese tortelli with toasted
hazelnuts was a perfect marriage of flavour and
textural contrasts. These creations come at City
expense-account prices, so any disappointment is
irksome – a crab and asparagus starter, while
delightfully fresh, was scant and not shell-free. Then
again, the set menu with its verdant soup and palate-
teasing liquorice zabaglione seemed a bargain.
Wines run the gamut from cheery glassful to splash-
out showcase, and staff serve even the most modest
orders with grace and flair. A special request
produced the proud claim: 'We are Italian, we can do
anything.' Except, perhaps, soften the acoustics.
*Available for hire. Babies and children welcome:
high chairs. Booking advisable. Disabled: toilet.
Dress: smart casual. Separate rooms for parties,
seating 8-15.* **Map 6 R5**.

Clerkenwell & Farringdon

Polpo Smithfield
*2-3 Cowcross Street, EC1M 6DR (7250 0034,
www.polpo.co.uk). Barbican tube or Farringdon
tube/rail.*
Bar **Open** 5.30-11.30pm Mon-Sat.
Restaurant **Meals served** noon-11.30pm
Mon-Sat; noon-4pm Sun. **Dishes** £3-£14.
Both **Credit** AmEx, MC, V.
This Venetian-inspired mini-chain of *déshabillé
bàcari* doesn't seem out of place on a street lined
with food industry behemoths, though how long its
carefully conceived decor (old Underground-style
tiling, tongue-and-groove panelling, Anaglypta
ceiling) can maintain the veneer of individuality
will be interesting to see. We like Polpo on the whole
– there are many reasons to do so. You don't have
to dress up, the menu of small plates is flexible, food
is served all afternoon and until gone 11pm most
days, and water is brought to the table without
asking. The kitchen's unfussy cooking doesn't aim
high and therefore often exceeds expectations.
Fennel is a favourite ingredient, whether it's the
spice featured in salami and meatballs, or the bulb
used in salads. Cicchetti of sweet grilled fennel with
white anchovy was a lovely start to a meal that was
hard to fault. Tender pillows of pink-middled
grilled lamb came on a juicy basil- and caper-
flavoured caponata that was more tomatoey than
sweet-sour but delicious nonetheless. Staff were
keen and chirpy, but had no clue about the specials
board, from which we eventually chose a ricotta and
cherry semifreddo with comforting biscuity
texture. As with the other branches (Soho, Covent
Garden), there's also a bar in the basement.

Polpo Smithfield

Bags packed, milk cancelled, house raised on stilts.

You've packed the suntan lotion, the snorkel set, the stay-pressed shirts. Just one more thing left to do – your bit for climate change. In some of the world's poorest countries, changing weather patterns are destroying lives.

You can help people to deal with the extreme effects of climate change. Raising houses in flood-prone regions is just one life-saving solution.

**Climate change costs lives.
Give £5 and let's sort it *Here & Now***

www.oxfam.org.uk/climate-change

Be Humankind (Oxfam) **Oxfam**

Available for hire. Babies and children welcome: high chairs. Booking advisable; not accepted after 5pm Mon-Sat. Tables outdoors (5, pavement). Vegan dishes. **Map 5 O5**.
For branches see index.

Covent Garden

Carluccio's Caffè
2A Garrick Street, WC2E 9BH (7836 0990, www.carluccios.com). Covent Garden tube. **Breakfast served** 8am-11.30pm Mon-Fri; 9am-11.30pm Sat; 9am-10.30pm Sun. **Meals served** 12.30-11.30pm Mon-Sat; 12.30-10.30pm Sun. **Main courses** £8.95-£15.95. **Set meal** £9.95 2 courses, £13.45 3 courses. **Credit** AmEx, MC, V.

The Carluccio's Caffè chain has encountered some choppy waters in recent years, but a lunchtime visit to its flagship restaurant revealed it largely to be sailing fair. Up a stone staircase attractively decorated with pots of herbs are two floors of dining rooms (downstairs is the deli). Noise levels reflect a strong mum-and-toddler contingent yet aren't uncivilised. Service, however, can seem distracted. Slightly burnt toast made with Tuscan bread let down a gorgeously velvety chicken liver pâté; better was calamari fritti – tender and not too greasy. Penne alla luganica (pasta with sausage sauce) looked underwhelming, but had just the right concentration of meat and seasoning. Beef stew slow-cooked with Chianti is a regular favourite, its rich taste and soft texture marrying nicely with polenta for perfect winter comfort food. On our summer lunchtime visit, however, we opted for another of Carluccio's signature dishes: penne giardiniera, a highly enjoyable vegetarian mix of chilli, courgette and fried spinach balls. Panna cotta with vanilla, rum and candied orange proved an exquisite finish. The wine list is friendlier than many Italian rivals, offering several bottles under £20, plus three types of Peroni beer and classic Italian aperitivo.
Babies and children welcome: children's menu; high chairs; nappy-changing facilities. Booking advisable pre-theatre. Disabled: toilet. Separate room for parties, seats 30. Takeaway service. **Map 18 D4**.
For branches see index.

Fitzrovia

Sardo
45 Grafton Way, W1T 5DQ (7387 2521). Warren Street tube. **Lunch served** noon-3pm Mon-Fri. **Dinner served** 6-11pm Mon-Sat. **Main courses** £11.90-£19.90. **Credit** AmEx, MC, V.

The clue's in the name: Sardo excels at Sardinian specialities. To come here for eat-anywhere dishes, such as grilled tuna steak, misses the point. But it's largely thanks to the popularity of Romolo Mudu's relaxed, welcoming ristorante that characteristic Sardinian ingredients such as fregola and malloreddus are finding their way on to other restaurants' menus. A generous bread basket and olives are swiftly brought to the table to enjoy while you read the day's offer – do check the blackboard specials. We were wowed by the chilled zuppa del giorno of beetroot and ricotta flecked with fresh crabmeat. Herb-marinated lamb battuta was tender and dense from the malleting, and meticulously lined from the grill. A special of seafood fregola featured exquisitely fresh prawns and an intense,

Briciole

earthy stock made with mussels. Veal chop with rosemary arrived with a pot of honey on the side to sauce the meat – a surprising and highly successful combination. Service was warm and on the ball throughout. The wine list offers a passionate annotated tour of Sardinia's best grapes and producers, plus wines from other parts of Italy. Expect powerful port-like flavours from reds such as cannonau, monica di sardegna and nieddera.
Available for hire. Babies and children welcome: high chairs. Booking advisable. Separate room for parties, seats 36. Tables outdoors (3, patio). **Map 3 J4**.

Knightsbridge

Zafferano
15 Lowndes Street, SW1X 9EY (7235 5800). Knightsbridge tube. **Lunch served** noon-5pm daily. **Dinner served** 5-10.15pm Sun. **Main courses** £18-£30. **Set lunch** (Mon-Fri) £21 2 courses, £26 3 courses. **Credit** AmEx, MC, V.

Superficially, little has changed at this renowned restaurant set in a comparatively quiet corner of Knightsbridge. The dining room, with its bare brick walls, rustic stone flooring and striped banquettes, is a relaxing place and the scent of fresh flowers lifts the spirits. However, longtime head chef Andy

Needham has left and the menu has had a minor facelift. Our meal started well with home-made foccacia, salami and parmesan served on a wooden block, followed by a creamy burrata with fresh artichokes and piennolo tomatoes. But the kitchen blew it with a dish of spaghetti and cured pork cheek, so swamped by tomato sauce that it would not look out of place in a school canteen. It was left to a fleshy Cornish cod acqua-pazza (poached in a light broth) served with peas and carrots to save the day. Service is attentive but lacks personality. Prices, especially if you delve into the admirable wine list, are high – as they have always been. However, based on our recent visits, Zafferano has some way to go to rediscover its glory days.
Babies and children welcome: high chairs. Booking essential. Dress: smart casual. Separate room for parties, seats 20. Tables outdoors (10, terrace). **Map 15 G9**.

Marylebone

Briciole
20 Homer Street, W1H 4NA (7723 0040, www.briciole.co.uk). Edgware Road tube. **Meals served** 11am-10.45pm daily. **Main courses** £3-£12. **Credit** AmEx, MC, V.

This Marylebone offshoot of the fancier West End restaurant Latium is as close to a proper Italian trattoria as you're likely to find in London. Effusive waiting staff greeted us like long-lost relatives as they ushered us past the deli and café-bar area to the airy, informal dining area of this former pub. A wide-ranging selection of small plates, first-class salumi, cheeses, pastas, grills and other mains drawn from all over Italy made ordering fiendishly difficult. We tried to sample some of everything, and soon our table looked pleasingly crowded and varied, as a proper Italian meal should. Some dishes are downright peculiar, some disappointing – a plate of meatballs with peas looked like little mounds smothered in a bright green smoothie, and our cannoli was too thick and unwieldy. But gnocchi with pork cheeks, red onion and peas was spot-on, and a sausage served with polenta flew us straight back to Italy, the fennel singing out from the sausage's dense porky flavours. This is rustic Italian cuisine at its most honest and inviting – the real deal in a crowded, often disappointing market.

Babies and children welcome: high chairs. Booking advisable. Disabled: toilet. Separate rooms for parties, both seating 15. Tables outdoors (5, pavement). Takeaway service. **Map 2 F5**.

★ Cotidie NEW

50 Marylebone High Street, W1U 5HN (7258 9878, http://cotidierestaurant.com). Baker Street or Regent's Park tube. **Lunch served** noon-2.15pm Mon-Fri. **Brunch served** noon-3.15pm Sat, Sun. **Dinner served** 6.30-10.15pm Mon-Sat; 6.30-10pm Sun. **Main courses** £13-£29. **Set lunch** (Mon-Fri) £24.50 2 courses, £27 3 courses. **Set meal** (lunch Mon-Fri, dinner) £55-£75 tasting menu. **Credit** AmEx, MC, V.
We find the name ironic. You may well fancy dining at Cotidie (Italian for 'everyday') on a daily basis, but the plush surroundings and exquisite ingredient compilations of this chic spot are well above routine. Prices are fair for the calibre of cooking, however, and the set lunch is a bargain with dishes lifted straight from the carte. Baby-tender sautéed calamari was a surprising garnish on a stunning sausage ragù lasagne featuring saffron-coloured pasta and smoked ricotta. Incidental touches – flavourful micro-leaves, buffalo stracciatella cheese in a sauce for red mullet, native Italian mushrooms in guazzetto (a jus-based sauce) – add to the sense of luxury. The bread basket is exemplary too. Desserts are simpler, but deceptively well executed: witness an almost-savoury pistachio ice-cream with still-crunchy nuts contrasting with their implausibly velvety caramel coating. Straying from a simple glass or two of wine into top-notch Italian and French bottle territory will ramp up the bill considerably. Yet even without splurging on inventive cocktails at the bijoux bar, or the undoubtedly enticing tasting menu, a modest budget will afford some classy and hugely enjoyable cooking with perfectly attentive service.

San Carlo Cicchetti. See p154.

Babies and children welcome: high chairs. Booking advisable. Disabled: toilet. Separate rooms for parties, seating 25 and 40. **Map 3 G4**.

Locanda Locatelli
8 Seymour Street, W1H 7JZ (7935 9088, www.locandalocatelli.com). Marble Arch tube. **Lunch served** noon-2.45pm Mon-Fri; noon-3.15pm Sat, Sun. **Dinner served** 6.45-10.45pm Mon-Thur; 6.45-11.15pm Fri, Sat; 6.45-10pm Sun. **Main courses** £9-£31.50. **Credit** AmEx, MC, V.
One of London's most highly regarded Italian chefs, Giorgio Locatelli was recently seen on BBC2's *Italy Unpacked* communicating a deep connection to his country's food and drink with engaging brio. It shows in the menu here, which ranges voraciously through styles, regions and ingredients (some little known). There's technique aplenty, but it's food made to be relished as well as admired. Among the many pasta dishes we've enjoyed: lasagnetti with salt cod, anchovies and capers; tagliatelle richly sauced with goat kid and chilli; and gnocchetti with mushroom and generous quantities of black truffle. Milky-soft suckling pig with mash, and disappearingly tender calves's sweetbreads with jerusalem artichokes are some of the most memorable meat options. The comfortable but beige-toned hotel-restaurant surrounds allow the food to take centre stage, but on this occasion our overall experience lacked the buzz the cooking deserved. Staff were only just this side of invisible, and not always in a good way, particularly when we needed the sommelier. The wine list is a positively educational survey of Italy's regions, with good choices, particularly of dessert wines, by the glass. *Available for hire. Babies and children welcome: high chairs; nappy-changing facilities. Booking advisable. Disabled: toilet. Dress: smart casual. Separate room for parties, seats 45.* **Map 9 G6**.

Mayfair

Alloro
19-20 Dover Street, W1S 4LU (7495 4768, www.alloro-restaurant.co.uk). Green Park tube. *Bar* **Open** noon-11pm Mon-Sat. *Restaurant* **Meals served** noon-10.30pm Mon-Sat. **Main courses** £12-£35. *Both* **Credit** AmEx, MC, V.
A very welcoming, very safe, very Mayfair restaurant, Alloro's formula is withstanding the test of time. Decor is reassuringly beige, gold and dark wooded; staff are warm, solicitous and proper. Diners are pretty well bound to find something that appeals: meat, fish and vegetarian; dishes both refined and rustic; wines ranging from bank-breaking Sassicaia (or Burgundy, if you must) to modestly priced, delightful examples served by the glass. What's not to like? In fact, a few elements niggled on our visit. Our meal evidenced an accountant's beady eye: too many dishes demand a supplement, even at the simple level of parma ham, and a handful of rocket was the ubiquitous accompaniment to most of what we ordered. Tomatoes also seemed to take a starring role but failed to shine in their own right. And desserts were safe to the point of nursery-ensconced, from tiramisu to a bland and firm milk chocolate and orange mousse. Highlights were a prawn and curry potato ravioli with courgette cream, and a zingily dressed chargrilled tuna steak. Beef tagliata was also expertly executed, and the Ligurian oil and breads for dipping were a treat. The roomful of executive types seemed perfectly happy.

Available for hire. Babies and children welcome: high chairs. Booking advisable. Separate room for parties, seats 16. Tables outdoors (3, pavement). **Map 9 J7**.

Cecconi's
5A Burlington Gardens, W1S 3EP (7434 1500, www.cecconis.co.uk). Green Park or Piccadilly Circus tube. **Breakfast served** 7am-noon Mon-Fri; 8am-noon Sat, Sun. **Brunch served** noon-5pm Sat, Sun. **Meals served** noon-11.30pm Mon-Sat; noon-10.30pm Sun. **Main courses** £14-£28. **Set breakfast** £18 2 courses. **Set meal** £50 3 courses. **Credit** AmEx, MC, V.
Cecconi's, located just behind the Royal Academy, shows London at its most cosmopolitan. A chic restaurant and bar with wraparound windows and striped marble floors, it's part of the cool Soho House group. Service comes from classy white-jacketed staff and food is served all day – everything from egg white omelette to lobster spaghetti. The fare is pleasingly simple rather than imaginative. We sat at the marble-topped bar next to a blonde bombshell sipping pink champagne and a suave Italian businessman tucking into veal milanese. Our starters were perfect – a fresh courgette flower stuffed with creamy ricotta, and a single, just-so scallop served in its shell. Crab ravioli, silky textured and laced with basil, was impeccable too. Prices for main courses are high – this is Mayfair, darling – but a selection of crostini or a roast chicken salad might be all you need. Or almost: Cecconi's vanilla cheesecake features a luscious medley of fruit heaped over a filling so rich it's practically criminal. Bag a pavement table in summer, order an £8 glass of prosecco and count the Ferraris and the facelifts.
Babies and children welcome: high chairs. Booking advisable. Disabled: toilet. Dress: smart casual. Tables outdoors (10, terrace). **Map 9 J7**.

Murano
20 Queen Street, W1J 5PP (7495 1127, www.muranolondon.com). Green Park tube. **Lunch served** noon-2.30pm, **dinner served** 6.30-10.45pm Mon-Sat. **Set lunch** £25 2 courses, £30 3 courses. **Set meal** £50 2 courses, £65 3 courses, £75 4 courses, £85 tasting menu. **Credit** AmEx, MC, V.
If you're accustomed to the clash and clatter of hard surfaces in modern restaurants, Murano may come as a shock. Plump upholstery, crisp linens and warm leather ensure a sumptuous, serene setting for a meal that draws as much on French fine dining as Italian staples. Chef-proprietor Angela Hartnett pops out every so often to chat with obvious regulars, diners linger long over numerous courses and pricey wines, and waiters glide silently between tables ensuring that service is impeccable. It's a winning combination when the cooking is as assured as Hartnett's. Dishes are in tune with the elegant surroundings. Crab tortelli was perfectly proportioned, its pasta springy and filling delicate. Almond purée was the inventive accompaniment to heartily dense roast sweetbreads. Creamy borlotti beans featured in a filling, chunky chowder of Cornish haddock, sweetcorn and clams, yet the combination did not cloy the palate. To finish, a light yoghurt mousse sat prettily alongside vermillion gariguette strawberries. The set lunch menu is a bargain for a special occasion; come often enough and Angela might start stopping by your table too.

Available for hire. Babies and children welcome: high chairs. Booking essential; dinner Fri & Sat, 1 mth ahead. Disabled: toilet. Separate room for parties, seats 12. **Map 9 H8**.

★ Theo Randall at the InterContinental
1 Hamilton Place, Park Lane, W1J 7QY (7409 3131, www.theorandall.com). Hyde Park Corner tube. **Lunch served** noon-3pm Mon-Fri. **Dinner served** 5.45-11pm Mon-Sat. **Main courses** £28-£38. **Set meal** (lunch, 5.45-7pm, 9-11pm) £27 2 courses, £33 3 courses. **Credit** AmEx, MC, V.
Since 2006, when Theo Randall, longtime head chef at the River Café, opened this eponymous restaurant, its reputation (and Randall's media profile) has gone from strength to strength. The colourful, spacious dining room is high on comfort, if a little corporate, with cream leather, walnut wood and olive green shades. Service is caring and warm-hearted and the cooking, in our experience, is joyous. The carte is not cheap, featuring luxury produce such as Limousin veal and wild salmon. However, the set menu at lunch and early evening is not dumbed-down, and provides more than a glimpse of the kitchen's quality output. We were blown away by the subtle combination of smoked eel, golden and red beetroots, and horseradish – the dish was simple yet every component sang. Then, a perfect risotto with sea bass, prawns, vongole and monkfish nudged the flavour dial northwards. Wood-roasted guinea fowl, stuffed with parma ham and mascarpone, and served with porcini and portobello mushrooms, brought memories of long sunny Tuscan holidays. Indeed, every part of our meal (bread, zucchini fritti, coffee) evoked sighs of pleasure. Portions are generous too; we were so full we had to forgo the Amalfi lemon tart.
Available for hire Sun. Babies and children welcome: children's menu; high chairs; nappy-changing facilities. Booking advisable. Disabled: lift; toilet. Dress: smart casual. Separate room for parties, seats 25. Vegetarian menu. **Map 9 G8**.

Pimlico

★ Tinello
87 Pimlico Road, SW1W 8PH (7730 3663, www.tinello.co.uk). Sloane Square tube or Victoria tube/rail. **Lunch served** noon-2.30pm, **dinner served** 6.30-10.30pm Mon-Sat. **Main courses** £17.50-£23. **Credit** AmEx, MC, V.
Federico and Max Sali opened Tinello in 2010, after a firm grounding at Locanda Locatelli, where the former was head chef and his brother the sommelier. Here, great produce is treated with skill and respect for tradition, but dishes still have the capacity to surprise. Wines by the glass are affordable (a handful cost under £5) and there are bottles below £15. There's no set menu, but the carte is flexible and main courses hover around the £20 mark. On our visit, both a duck breast and a hefty pork chop of Pyrenean origin were cooked to pink perfection. Simple, rustic accompaniments – a potato and radicchio 'stew' in the first instance, crushed potatoes and roast garlic cloves in the latter – highlighted the intrinsic taste of the meats. Deeply verdant nettle pappardelle, ravioli stuffed with pork cheek, and the fluffiest of potato dumplings coated with crunchy powdered mushroom also showed skilful execution. Sourcing, whether of lardo, olive oil or coffee, was impeccable, as was the service: unobtrusive yet alert and always

...ared-back elegance of the place – ...k wood, metal and mirrored tiles ...mple perfection of the food and wine on offer.

Babies and children welcome: high chairs; nappy-changing facilities. Booking advisable. Separate room for parties, seats 26. **Map 15 G11**.

St James's

San Carlo Cicchetti NEW

215 Piccadilly, W1J 9HL (7494 9435, www.sancarlocicchetti.co.uk). Piccadilly Circus tube. **Breakfast served** 8-11.30am Mon-Fri; 9-11.30am Sat, Sun. **Meals served** noon-midnight daily. **Dishes** £2.95-£25. **Credit** AmEx, MC, V.

Aldo Zilli's recent relationship to this long-established restaurant group was underlined by his presence at the front tables, discussing business, when we entered. It didn't seem to put anyone off, and within half an hour on a weekday lunchtime the close-set tables were crammed with a cheerful mix of office folk, shoppers and tourists. The garish decor of marble and yellow cushions is only slightly tempered by a part-open kitchen and displays of food. Busy white-jacketed waiters add to the sense of bustle, and service is correspondingly prompt. An extensive menu takes in salads, pasta, risottos and grills, but the emphasis is on small sharing plates, some of which are authentic Venetian cicchetti and some not. Parma ham salad with tomato, cucumber and baby mozzarella showed good sourcing and sensitive seasoning. Spaghetti carbonara (not the easiest dish to divide on to separate plates) swam in a golden pool of eggy

sauce. Coconut and chocolate tart, one of two desserts of the day, was too rich to finish. The breakfast menu features an appealing full english as well as the likes of black truffle omelette; it's a handy spot to know pre- or post-theatre too.

Available for hire. Babies and children welcome: high chairs. Booking advisable. Disabled: toilet. **Map 17 B5**.

Soho

Bocca di Lupo

12 Archer Street, W1D 7BB (7734 2223, www.boccadilupo.com). Piccadilly Circus tube. **Lunch served** 12.15-2.45pm Mon-Sat; 12.15-3.15pm Sun. **Dinner served** 5.15-11pm Mon-Sat; 5-9.30pm Sun. **Main courses** £7-£32. **Credit** AmEx, MC, V.

The buzz is as important as the food at Jacob Kenedy and Victor Hugo's enduringly popular Soho restaurant. Dine at the bar and you're in for a fun night, or afternoon – especially if you're by the window. It's the perfect perch from which to watch favourite actresses swan into the clamorous and less atmospheric rear dining room. The menu is a slightly confusing mix of small and large plates to share and, amid the noise, it can be unclear what you think you've ordered and at what point it might arrive. Staff reassuringly affirm, 'It's sooo good,' to virtually everything you suggest – and sometimes they're right. We have fond memories of buttery brown shrimp on soft, silky white polenta (the Venetian preference), and a deep-fried mix of calamari, soft-shell crab and lemon. The radish, celeriac, pomegranate and pecorino salad with truffle dressing is a much-imitated

Bocca di Lupo signature – far better, we found, than the spartan raw fennel salad. The brioche in our gelati dessert was also too dry to thrill, irrespective of the quality of the own-made ices. To drink, there's an enticing selection of cocktails and an impressive all-Italian wine list, but it isn't as fairly priced as the hype suggests.

Babies and children welcome: booster seats. Booking essential. Disabled: toilet. Separate room for parties, seats 35. **Map 17 B4**.

South Kensington

Daphne's

112 Draycott Avenue, SW3 3AE (7589 4257, www.daphnes-restaurant.co.uk). South Kensington tube. **Meals served** noon-11.30pm Mon-Sat; noon-10.30pm Sun. **Main courses** £14.50-£34.50. **Set meal** (noon-7pm Mon-Sat; noon-10.30pm Sun) £18.50 2 courses, £21.50 3 courses. **Credit** AmEx, MC, V.

Escorted to a perfectly lovely and perfectly chilled conservatory on the hottest night of a hot London summer, our first feeling towards Daphne's was one of gratitude. Service here is a strong point, honed by years of attending to the well-heeled regulars, who knock back watermelon daiquiris and bottles of Bolly. Get a table in the overstated faux-Tuscan dining room instead and you may feel like distant relatives at an Italian wedding. Unfortunately, the food is rather pedestrian and overpriced. A two- or three-course set menu offers simple samples of it. Summer minestrone loaded with seasonal beans and vegetables had the evocative tomato flavour of cucina povera, but the base was too delicate. Caprese salad looked impressive but its tomatoes

ITALIAN

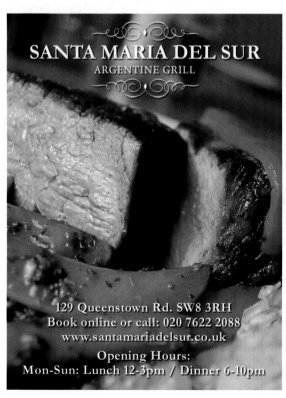

were wet and watery, and the mozzarella unequal to that served in many London competitors. Mains of chargrilled chicken breast and roast salmon were perfectly pleasant but lacked lustre or oomph – rather like Daphne's itself, really. Still, it's worth leaving room for the desserts: our yoghurt ice-cream with blueberries, and peach crostata with elderflower ice-cream, ended the meal on a reassuringly high note.

Available for hire. Babies and children welcome: high chairs. Booking advisable. Disabled: toilet. Separate room for parties, seats 40. **Map 14 E10**.

Westminster

Massimo
Corinthia Hotel London, 10 Northumberland Avenue, WC2N 5AE (7998 0555, www.massimo-restaurant.co.uk). Embankment tube.
Oyster bar **Meals served** noon-11pm Mon-Sat. **Main courses** £6-£20.
Restaurant **Lunch served** noon-3pm, **dinner served** 6-10.45pm Mon-Sat. **Main courses** £16-£29. **Set lunch** £18 1 course incl glass of prosecco. **Set meal** (6-7.30pm, 9.30-10.30pm) £30 3 courses incl glass of prosecco.
Both **Credit** AmEx, MC, V.
Designed by the late David Collins and typical of his style at its most majestic, Massimo's decor mixes marble, leather and bronze as if to suggest HG Wells's time machine landed amid Roman baths. The room is admittedly huge, but does that necessitate or simply magnify the opulence? Most of the customers on our lunchtime visit were moneyed tourists, possibly from the Corinthia Hotel which Massimo resides in. It's worth looking for bargain menu deals online, but the ongoing £18 Pasta e Prosecco offer is hardly a steal, even with coffee and biscotti included. It was tiresome to be asked whether we understood the raw scallops we had ordered were actually raw 'like sashimi'. Fortunately, they were delicious, sliced thinly and prettily dressed with chive and courgette flowers. The menu offers the likes of Herdwick lamb and Goosnargh chicken, but the freshest seafood (there's also an oyster bar) and, to a certain extent, pasta are the key draws. Tagliolini with crab and chilli was exemplary; so too the breads that staff offered throughout the meal. The dessert list is classic yet persuasive; a dark-chocolate faux cappuccino was delightful. Wine prices are on par with the location and decor – glasses start at £8.50 for just 125ml.
Available for hire. Babies and children welcome: high chairs. Booking advisable. Disabled: toilet. Dress: smart casual. Separate room for parties, seats 20. **Map 10 L8**.

Osteria dell'Angolo
47 Marsham Street, SW1P 3DR (3268 1077, www.osteriadellangolo.co.uk). St James's Park tube or bus 88.
Bar **Open** noon-11pm Mon-Fri; 6-11pm Sun.
Restaurant **Lunch served** noon-3pm Mon-Fri. **Dinner served** 6-10.30pm Mon-Sat. **Main courses** £11.50-£24.50. **Set lunch** £16.50 2 courses, £21 3 courses.
Both **Credit** AmEx, MC, V.
You have to navigate a complex of modern offices to get to Osteria dell'Angolo, yet once inside the dining room, with its terracotta-coloured walls and large windows, it's as though you're in a Tuscan dwelling. The warm glow of the room at dinnertime is matched by the welcome of the staff. Tables

Burro e Salvia. See p159.

ITALIAN

Mimmo La Bufala
Healthy Food. Healthy Life

45a Southend Road
London NW3 2QB
www.mimmolabufala.co.uk
Telephone: 020 7435 7814

This authentic Italian restaurant, owned by Mimmo Rimoli, will soon be celebrating 10 years in Hampstead.

The Pizzas here continue to make awards and Mimmo has introduced the novelty 'Pizza Metro' (one metre long pizza base) for parties and groups. The selection of fresh fish which Mimmo gets from the markets in the early hours of the morning continue to satisfy the best pallet. Other favourites include the prime Scottish fillet, veal al limone and the tasty veal Milanese prepared by the Italian chefs.

Mimmo says it has been a real pleasure to serve his many loyal friends in the area but he is always happy to welcome new friends from all over to enjoy and evening meal during the week or lunch and dinner at weekends.

"Ciao – welcome and buon appetito" – Mimmo

 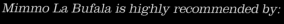   

opposite the semi-open kitchen afford an enjoyable view of chefs hard at work. A generous basket featuring six varieties of bread plus potato croquettes and fried polenta cake quickly puts diners in a good mood. These days, the cooking leans towards the sunnier climes of southern Italy. Black-ink tagliolini (which could have been more al dente) came with fresh crabmeat, grilled courgettes and cherry tomatoes. Far better was roast fillet of wild sea bass, its skin beautifully crisp, served with palourde clams and spinach in a light clam broth. In keeping with its location near the Palace of Westminster, wines are taken seriously and there are several worthy bottles in the £30-£40 range. White chocolate panna cotta with raspberry coulis paired with a glass of Torcolato Maculan 2008 was a match made in heaven, an excellent end to a generally pleasing visit.

Babies and children welcome: high chairs; nappy-changing facilites. Booking advisable. Disabled: toilet. Dress: smart casual. Separate room for parties, seats 22. **Map 16 K10.**

Quirinale
North Court, 1 Great Peter Street, SW1P 3LL (7222 7080, www.quirinale.co.uk). St James's Park or Westminster tube. **Lunch served** noon-2.30pm, **dinner served** 6-10.30pm Mon-Fri. **Main courses** £16-£28. **Set meal** (lunch, 6-7.30pm) £19 2 courses, £23 3 courses. **Credit** AmEx, MC, V.

This part of town is the epicentre of the civil service, and Quirinale is busiest at lunchtime, when you're likely to overhear diners discussing the business of government. There's a relaxing feel to the basement dining room, which is sensitively cloaked in white and beige, and the air of bonhomie is aided by staff who aim to ensure you enjoy your stay. Cooking is traditional. Some dishes (such as our fillet of venison with shallot crust, chestnut purée and cavolo nero) lack sparkle, and the quality of produce could be improved. However, braised octopus was a good match for the crunch of Tuscan spelt enriched with tomato sauce and pesto. To finish, there are a dozen Italian cheeses, and desserts such as spiced pear and almond cake with caramel ice-cream. The sizeable wine list runs the length of Italy with forays into France – a reasonable choice is offered by the glass, though prices are on the high side. In all, we felt that, rather like the politicians who eat here, Quirinale tends to deliver less than was promised.

Available for hire. Babies and children admitted. Booking advisable lunch. **Map 16 L10.**

West
Bayswater

★ Assaggi
1st floor, 39 Chepstow Place, W2 4TS (7792 5501). Bayswater, Notting Hill Gate or Queensway tube. **Lunch served** 12.30-2.30pm Mon-Fri; 1-2.30pm Sat. **Dinner served** 7.30-11pm Mon-Sat. **Main courses** £19.80-£29.95. **Credit** MC, V.

Opened in 1997, Assaggi was in its early years a modish spot; although the fashionistas have moved on since, the first-floor dining room remains busy, with many customers greeted like long-lost relatives. The interior is low-key, with a breezy colour scheme in peach and blue; the sash windows allow much natural light into the room. As the menu is written entirely in Italian, it is a pleasing tradition to listen to the passionate recital of dishes from the maitre d'. The style is relaxed and informal, but there's nothing frivolous about the cooking. A dressing of squid ink brought to life an otherwise spartan chargrilled cuttlefish and artichoke salad. Soft gnocchi served with an intensely flavoured venison and tomato ragù made us sigh with pleasure. Tender veal cutlet with deep-fried potato strings and a rosemary-infused jus hit all the right spots too. We ended with fabulous cheeses, and a classic Assaggi dessert: fluffy baverese (vanilla cream) doused with espresso coffee. The wine list offers a brief tour of Italy and includes gems such as the native Sardinian grape monica di sardegna. Assaggi has never been a cheap restaurant, but we still think it's a compelling destination.

Available for hire Sun. Babies and children welcome: high chair. Booking essential. **Map 7 B6.**

Hammersmith

River Café HOT 50
Thames Wharf, Rainville Road, W6 9HA (7386 4200, www.rivercafe.co.uk). Hammersmith tube. **Lunch served** 12.30-2.15pm Mon-Fri; 12.30-2.30pm Sat; noon-3pm Sun. **Dinner served** 7-9pm Mon-Thur; 7-9.15pm Fri, Sat. **Main courses** £30-£40. **Credit** AmEx, MC, V.

Despite its reputation for exclusivity, it's possible to get a table at the River Café with just a couple of hours' notice if you choose your moment. Best is high summer, when the blue garden tables are spread widely through the courtyard, and the potager is at its peak. The relaxed, cheerful disposition of staff and customers is so contagious, you almost don't notice the retina-melting price of the food. With most secondi costing £34-£39, you can expect to pay around £75 per person for three courses with wine, even at lunch. On the plus side, the wide-ranging Italian wine list is fabulously democratic, with a great by-the-glass selection and prosecco starting at just £6. Starters showcase bought-in deli ingredients, but often have something home-made to make them pop – the sweetest, most velvety bresaola, say, with a warm sformata pudding of ricotta and peas, plus a confidently charred garlic bruschetta. Exquisitely intense apricots featured in a buttery almond tart, but didn't quite stop us envying the many large bowls of own-made gelati that sailed past. Our only disappointment was a bitter-tasting plate of spaghetti bottarga – baby yellow tomatoes detracted from, rather than enhanced, the dish.

Babies and children welcome: crayons; booster seats; high chairs; nappy-changing facilities. Booking essential, 2 mths in advance. Disabled: toilet. Separate room for parties, seats 18. Tables outdoors (15, terrace). **Map 20 C5.**

South West
Barnes

Riva
169 Church Road, SW13 9HR (8748 0434). Barnes or Barnes Bridge rail or bus 33, 209, 283. **Lunch served** 12.15-2.15pm Mon-Fri, Sun. **Dinner served** 7-10.30pm Mon-Sat; 7-9pm Sun. **Main courses** £14.50-£29.50. **Credit** AmEx, MC, V.

It's just a short hop across the bridge from bustling Hammersmith, but Barnes' village-like ambience is immediately relaxing. Riva has been serving the neighbourhood for 20-plus years and little has changed in that time. The small dining room, decorated in terracotta and olive tones, has a rustic, lived-in feel. The food sticks to simple traditions, and adventurous diners may need more persuasion than the plucky wine list to part with their cash, as prices are high and there are no set menus to alleviate the pain. We started with a tried-and-true combination of ravioli with crab and peas; for £13, we'd hoped for more than a few strands of crabmeat. Presentation is satisfyingly earthy, however; witness roast milk-fed lamb studded with rosemary and simply paired with cubes of roast potato. The meal concluded with a boozy crêpe served with prunes stewed in grappa. Reception from the owner was frosty, but the atmosphere soon thawed thanks to the friendly disposition of his waiting staff.

Available for hire. Babies and children welcome: high chairs. Booking advisable dinner. Tables outdoors (3, pavement).

Chelsea

La Famiglia
7 Langton Street, SW10 0JL (7351 0761, www.lafamiglia.co.uk). Sloane Square tube then bus 11, 22, or bus 19. **Lunch served** noon-2.45pm, **dinner served** 7-11.30pm daily. **Main courses** £14-£30. **Cover** £1.85. **Credit** AmEx, MC, V.

La Famiglia's founder, Alvaro Maccioni, is considered by some to be the Godfather of Italian cuisine in Britain, and patrons of his restaurants over the decades have included Gregory Peck, Brigitte Bardot and Princess Margaret. These days, you may well see the likes of Roman Abramovich and José Mourinho, yet on any Saturday lunchtime at La Famiglia, there's a sense that everyone is special – some guests are warmly hugged as old friends, while small children are treated like royalty. Surrounded by blue and white tiled walls, we sipped on sublime minestra d'ova, a light broth with egg, lemon juice and parmesan cheese, that had just the right balance of tartness and salt. Deep-fried courgette flowers were crisp and melting, while a main course of grilled sardines glazed with balsamic vinegar was perfectly judged, with exactly the right level of charring. Appropriate to the Tuscan-themed menu, fresh pappardelle with wild boar sauce was a highlight: the pasta almost dissolved on the tongue, and the seasoning enhanced rather than drowned the meat's flavour. We finished on a Sicilian note, with fragrant cannoli from the dessert trolley. Definitely worth a return visit.

Babies and children welcome: children's menu; high chairs; nappy-changing facilities. Booking advisable. Separate room for parties, seats 50. Tables outdoors (40, garden). Takeaway service. **Map 13 C13.**

Osteria dell'Arancio
383 King's Road, SW10 0LP (7349 8111, www.osteriadellarancio.co.uk). Fulham Broadway or Sloane Square tube. **Lunch served** noon-3pm Tue-Sun. **Dinner served** 6.30-10.30pm Mon-Sat; 6.30-9pm Sun. **Main courses** £15-£19. **Credit** AmEx, MC, V.

On a villagey Chelsea corner, Osteria dell'Arancio is gifted with broad surrounding pavements, allowing plenty of alfresco atmosphere. It's the

ITALIAN

Lardo

STELLACELLO

ITALIAN

perfect local for the locale: friendly, capacious and cottage-casual in style, with flashes of colour in glassware, paintings and cushions enlivening the gastropubby decor. The decently priced, decently cooked menu references the chef's family origins in Marché, Tuscany and Piedmont, and he sources the deli goods directly from Italian suppliers. Cheeses and charcuterie dominate the antipasti; then there are home-made pastas and a short list of hot mains tending towards the light and modern, such as beef tagliata with rocket and parmesan, or sea bass with blood orange, olive and red onion salad. We liked the basics: tagliatelle with a lamb and porcini sauce deep in flavour, with lemon thyme to leaven it, and faultlessly seasonal minestrone with all ingredients distinct. There were lots of little mistakes, though – no pepper offered, late-arriving bread that wasn't worth the wait, wrong drink orders – but they were easy to forgive at this likeable and popular place. *Available for hire. Babies and children welcome: high chairs; nappy-changing facilities. Booking advisable dinner. Disabled: toilet. Separate room for parties, seats 35. Tables outdoors (12, terrace). Takeaway service.* **Map 14 D12**.

Putney

Enoteca Turi

28 Putney High Street, SW15 1SQ (8785 4449, www.enotecaturi.com). Putney Bridge tube or Putney rail or bus 14, 74, 270. **Lunch served** noon-2.30pm Mon-Sat. **Dinner served** 7-10.30pm Mon-Thur; 7-11pm Fri, Sat. **Main courses** £11.50-£24.50. **Set lunch** £17.50 2 courses, £20.50 3 courses. **Set dinner** (Mon-Thur) £27 2 courses, £32 3 courses. **Credit** AmEx, MC, V.

We arrived on a rain-lashed Wednesday evening to find this longstanding Putney local positively buzzing. In keeping with its name, Enoteca Turi has a particularly strong all-Italian wine list packed with treasures – our recommendation, an elegant pecorino, was spot-on. Pleasingly, there was none of that over-pouring designed to push diners into a second bottle either. After discovering that both the mozzarella and cuttlefish on the set menu had run out, we made a rocky start with under-seasoned grilled squid with chilli, and a fiddly, insubstantial dish of sautéed clams. Mains

proved a better bet. Lemon and rocket risotto was fresh, vibrant and perfectly al dente; calf's liver with sage and speck proved rich and satisfying. Confusion over our final order meant we finished with a delicious almond and ricotta cake from the à la carte menu at no extra charge. Enoteca Turi's kitchen could do with more consistency and a few wow factors. The decor feels a little dated too, but the restaurant's plus points – a convivial atmosphere, great wines, faultless service and a warm heart – are proving a winning formula in a neighbourhood overrun with soulless chains. *Available for hire. Babies and children welcome: high chairs. Booking advisable. Disabled: toilet. Dress: smart casual. Separate rooms for parties, seating 10, 18 and 30.*

South East
Bankside

Union Street Café NEW

47-51 Great Suffolk Street, SE1 0BS (7592 7977, www.gordonramsay.com). Southwark tube. *Restaurant* **Lunch served** noon-3pm Mon-Fri; noon-4pm Sat, Sun. **Dinner served** 6-11pm Mon-Fri; 6-10.30pm Sat, Sun. *Bar* **Open** 5pm-midnight Mon-Sat; 5-10.30pm Sun. *Both* **Credit** MC, V.

Hysterical media interest and a three-month wait for a dinner booking attended the opening (in September 2013) of Gordon Ramsay's latest venture, partly because of the oft-repeated rumour that David Beckham was involved – a connection that turned out to be false. You might wonder what the fuss was about when you enter the dining room at this middle-of-nowhere Southwark site (though the tube is close). The design is a mish-mash of styles, with bar-concrete ceilings and exposed wiring, but also parquet flooring and expensive leather seats. Turquoise banquettes are reflected in an battery of convex mirrors. Staff are big smilers – not the we're-paid-to-rictus-smile sort, but the sort that comes from genuine interest and enthusiasm. The daily-changing menu from chef Davide Degiovanni wouldn't look out of place in a score of other mid-market Italian restaurants in London. The intentionally casual service and Italian style is undermined, though, by portion sizes that would be considered meagre in the boot of Italy: our 'secondi' octopus dish was two meaty tentacles perched on braised borlotti beans; a seafood stew was soup-bowl sized (and very salty). High points were the 'parmesan skin' appetisers, puffed up like pork scratchings from a rind; and a brownie-like but mild chocolate and peanut butter cake topped with vanilla ice-cream, with espresso poured over. There's a good list of wines grouped by style, a cocktail maker renowned for his talent, and a much more extensive bar in the basement. *Babies and children welcome; high chairs. Booking essential. Disabled: toilet.* **Map 11 O8**.

Bermondsey

Zucca

184 Bermondsey Street, SE1 3TQ (7378 6809, www.zuccalondon.com). Bermondsey tube or London Bridge tube/rail. **Lunch served** noon-3pm Tue-Fri; noon-3.30pm Sat, Sun. **Dinner served** 6-10pm Tue-Sat. **Main courses** £14-£18. **Credit** AmEx, MC, V.

A couple of pumpkins on the open kitchen counter reference the restaurant's name and provide a touch of warmth to Zucca's super-sleek interior. Gentle refurbishment has seen hard surfaces softened and, with light streaming in through the floor-to-ceiling windows, the room has a sophisticated Sydney vibe. Eat at the bar and you'll look awkwardly conspicuous to the roomful of people behind; it's best to book a table in advance. Our meal was mostly good. Own-made breads were followed by burrata with broad beans in a garlicky dressing, and clean-tasting spider crab served prettily in its shell. The own-made pasta is superb, and a sweetly earthy sauce of lentils, walnuts and basil was entirely successful; cod with chickpeas was dull by comparison. Service was initially brisk but ran out of steam through dessert; we were there a good 30 minutes longer than we needed to be. The wine list has many admirable bottles but, despite a proliferation of maps, is generally unhelpful and starts at an elitist £26 a bottle – that's how much Bermondsey has changed in the past decade. Zucca's owners plan an offshoot for the site next door: Farina will focus on pizza and ice-cream.
Available for hire. Babies and children welcome: high chairs. Booking advisable dinner. Disabled: toilet. Separate room for parties, seats 10.

Tower Bridge

Tentazioni
2 Mill Street, SE1 2BD (7237 1100, www.tentazioni.co.uk). Bermondsey tube or London Bridge tube/rail. **Lunch served** noon-2.45pm Mon-Fri. **Dinner served** 6-10.45pm Mon-Sat. **Main courses** £13.50-£45. **Set lunch** £11.95 2 courses incl drink, £15 3 courses incl drink and coffee. **Set dinner** £47.50 tasting menu (£68.50 incl wine). **Credit** AmEx, MC, V.
The decor at Tentazioni is striking, a vivid red that evokes a womb with a view – though the view isn't why anyone would visit. There's plenty to recommend, however, about the adventurous range (beetroot gnocchi with gorgonzola and pistachio fondue, anyone?) and attention to detail of the dishes. Mozzarella on white crabmeat with saffron sauce proved more sensational in appearance and texture than in taste, but a classic bruschetta ticked all the right boxes. Roast pork served with dried prunes, wild mushrooms and mustard sauce was moist and flavourful. Yet while roast cod fillets with sautéed spinach were tender and juicy, there was no reference on the lunch menu to the fact that they came with a lobster bisque sauce, a remarkable oversight given what this would mean to those with dietary restrictions. Our meal dragged on a bit and service suffered from a few translation blips but was on the whole charming: a problem with delays in food arriving led to the offer of free wine. Still, Tentazioni feels like a quality experience.
Available for hire. Babies and children welcome: high chair. Booking advisable dinner Fri, Sat. Separate room for parties, seats 24. **Map 12 S9**.

East
Shoreditch

Burro e Salvia NEW
52 Redchurch Street, E2 7DP (7739 4429, www.burroesalvia.co.uk). Shoreditch High Street rail. **Meals served** 10am-7pm Mon-Sat; 11am-5pm Sun. **Main courses** £8-£12. **Credit** MC, V.

One of the pleasures of dining at this new Italian-owned deli/café is watching the young, friendly staff make pasta from scratch behind the counter at the front. Their finished wares are displayed on mesh trays, to take home or to eat in the 'tasting corner'. Named after a classic accompaniment to stuffed pasta, Burro e Salvia ('butter and sage') serves almost nothing but the Italian staple. On our visit, the weekly changing menu featured tagliatelle, agnolotti, ravioli and tajarin (an egg-yolk-rich, thin tagliatelle from Piedmont). Everything we tried had just the right al dente texture. Parcels stuffed with ricotta and citrus zest were the highlight, given savoury depth by a grating of bottarga (dried, salted mullet roe). The only quibbles concern the lack of windows in the diminutive dining room (although there is a skylight), and the fact that salads are limited to russian salad (which is even more carb). But, hey, the pasta's good and the premises are licensed, so you can choose from a small selection of Italian wines to accompany your food.
Available for hire. Babies and children admitted. Booking advisable. Takeaway service. **Map 6 S4**.

North East
Hackney

Lardo
197 Richmond Road, E8 3NJ (8985 2683, www.lardo.co.uk). Hackney Central or London Fields rail. **Brunch served** 11am-1pm Sat, Sun. **Meals served** 11am-10.30pm Mon-Fri; 1-10.30pm Sat; 1-9.30pm Sun. **Main courses** £7.50-£16. **Credit** MC, V.
If a restaurant is named after the cured back fat of a pig, you can expect that charcuterie is among its specialities – and so it is here. But lardo itself isn't on the menu at Lardo, except as a pizza topping, so our charming, clued-up waiter brought a plate specially. It was excellent, as was the paper-thin fennel pollen salame. Other small plates on the short menu are divided into 'cold' (simple but satisfying puréed cannellini beans with black olives), 'warm' (an unctuous bowl of braised chicory and melted fonduta cheese topped with speck) and 'hearty' (Venetian lambs' kidneys). There's also a couple of own-made pasta dishes and a handful of pizzas with novel, tasty toppings such as goat's curd, anchovy and sprouting broccoli. You can watch the pizzas being fired if you choose to sit on the stools around the open kitchen; otherwise there are closely packed but not cramped tables. Industrial-style windows, plenty of wood, and lighting that's so low most people need to use the tealights to read the menu, make for a stylishly casual setting. Lardo is part of the Arthaus complex, so it's a trek across a blinding white foyer to the shared toilets. Drinks run from cocktails to builders' tea plus a brief, mainly Italian wine list. Hackneyites love this place – so book.
Babies and children welcome: high chairs. Booking advisable. Disabled: toilet. Tables outdoors (7, pavement). Takeaway service. Vegan dishes.

North
Archway

500 Restaurant
782 Holloway Road, N19 3JH (7272 3406, www.500restaurant.co.uk). Archway tube or Upper Holloway rail. **Lunch served** noon-3pm

Fri, Sat. **Dinner served** 6-10.30pm Mon-Sat. **Meals served** noon-9.30pm Sun. **Main courses** £11.80-£16.80. **Credit** AmEx, MC, V.
The arrival of 500 (Cinquecento) in 2008 marked a miracle for what even the most charitable would describe as the scrappier end of the Holloway Road. The stylish bare-table decor combined with a chef from the Jamie Oliver stable ensured a waiting list of weeks. Our most recent visit yielded hits and a couple of near misses. The Tagliere 500 starter (to share) was a stunning cornucopia of textures and tastes – including crabmeat, delicately crunchy, deep-fried ravioli with mint, and melt-in-the-mouth mozzarella – while a main course of fresh ravioli with ricotta and nettles sang all the right notes. Scallops on broccoli purée were plump and tasty, but the purée itself wasn't concentrated enough to satisfy. And the restaurant's much-praised baked rabbit in marsala wine sauce was tender and moist – and slightly too salty. There remains much to justify the excitement that endures around this culinary oasis in N19. Next to the traditional tiramisu and gelati, poached rhubarb with a scoop of apple sorbet made a fine end to the meal (even if the sorbet was a little more frozen than anticipated). Service was brisk and friendly throughout.
Available for hire. Babies and children welcome: high chairs. Booking essential dinner. **Map 26 C1**.

Camden & Chalk Farm

La Collina
17 Princess Road, NW1 8JR (7483 0192, www.lacollinarestaurant.co.uk). Camden Town or Chalk Farm tube. **Lunch served** noon-3pm, **dinner served** 6-11pm Mon-Fri. **Meals served** noon-11pm Sat, Sun. **Main courses** £12-£20. **Credit** AmEx, MC, V.
Run by a largely female team (chef included), La Collina is refreshingly free of foodie attitude, almost deceptively so. The charm of the staff, the glass frontage on a residential street and the simple wooden floors and pale paint suggest casual café – but it's much better than that. From a kitchen that opens on to the lower of two dining rooms and its pretty terrace, the short menu exemplifies simplicity and seasonality. The quality of ingredients shines: buffalo mozzarella-stuffed flowers on courgettes; sweet, cherry tomatoes in a rocket salad; jewel-bright vegetables served with exquisite burrata; tasty, textured beef. Chef Diana Rinaldo hails from the Veneto but draws most influence from Piedmont (in dishes such as vitello tonnato, or wild mushroom and truffle pasta) and Sardinia (fish and seafood dishes, and malloreddus, a characteristic pasta shape). The home-made breads represent both, which is the kind of detail that sets this place apart. Other standouts from our visit were a sumptuous lobster spaghetti, claws and all, a bolognese sauce made with beef and veal, and a semi-freddo enlivened with chocolate and honey drizzle. The wine list is all-Italian too.
Babies and children welcome: children's menu; high chairs. Booking advisable. Separate rooms for parties, seating 20 and 30. Tables outdoors (15, garden). **Map 27 B2**.

Highbury

Trullo
300-302 St Paul's Road, N1 2LH (7226 2733, www.trullorestaurant.com). Highbury & Islington tube/rail or bus 19, 30, 277. **Lunch served**

12.30-2.45pm daily. **Dinner served** 6.30-10.15pm Mon-Sat. **Main courses** £13.50-£30. **Set lunch** £12 2 courses; (Sun) £30 4 courses. **Credit** MC, V.

While evenings are still busy-to-frantic in this two-floored contemporary trattoria, lunchtime finds Trullo calm and the cooking relaxed and assured. A bargain £12 set menu gleans two courses (primi plus either antipasti or dessert) from a daily-changing menu. On our visit, the tempting selection of starters included bright British asparagus with parmesan, and cured trout with wilted spinach and poached egg. Slivers of grilled ox heart were perfectly cooked, with the accompanying roast shallots, beetroot and horseradish almost, but not quite, overwhelming the unexpectedly delicate flavours. Pappardelle with beef shin ragù has been a staple since Trullo's early days and remains a silky, substantial delight. Seasonal tagliarini with nettles and nutmeg featured an uncooked egg yolk wobbling daintily atop a vast pile of green pasta; when mixed in, it made a wonderfully creamy dish. In opting for the set menu, you forgo the roasts and grills, but as a giant Black Hampshire pork chop and generous cod with cannellini beans and mussels whisked by our table, we weren't sorry to have missed out on them – after all, where would we have put the succulent loquat and almond tart?

Babies and children welcome: high chairs; nappy-changing facilities. Booking advisable.
Dress: smart casual. Separate room for parties, seats 35.

Islington

Jamie's Italian Islington

Angel Building, 403 St John Street, EC1V 4AB (3435 9915, www.jamieoliver.com/italian). Angel tube. **Meals served** noon-11pm Mon-Sat; noon-10.30pm Sun. **Main courses** £10-£22. **Set meal** (noon-6pm) £15 2 courses. **Credit** AmEx, MC, V.

Trullo. See p159.

The menu's assessment – 'It's all authentically Italian, but unmistakably "Jamie" too' – is bang on. The vivacity and personality of the cooking makes the culinary megastar's most successful concept an appealing choice; the stylish casual setting and menu breadth make it a clever one. Dining in a group? Rest assured, everyone will find something they want to order. Whether or not the experience quite lives up to expectations is another matter, but at least it's cheaper (and larger) than the original Fifteen trattoria. First disappointment was the house rosato from Sicily – for once the flavour dial seemed to have been turned down to zero. We couldn't fault the scrumptious bread basket, however, and the iced crudités were a pleasant way to ramp up the vegetable quota of the meal. From the children's menu, a tomato and fusilli pasta bake was unappetisingly dry. But crab spaghettini with capers, fennel, parsley, chilli and anchovies was on a par with more exclusive establishments. There are some nice ideas on the dessert list (a signature trifle of strawberry jelly, fresh berries, custard and glazed meringue, for example), but ours tasted mass-produced, which perhaps by definition they are. There's only so much Jamie to spread round, after all.

Available for hire. Babies and children welcome: children's menu; crayons; high chairs; nappy-changing facilities. Booking advisable dinner Fri, Sat. Disabled: lift; toilet. Separate rooms for parties, seating 30 and 100. Tables outdoors (10, terrace). **Map 5 N3.**
For branches (Jamie's Italian, Richmond Trattoria) see index.

Outer London
Twickenham, Middlesex

A Cena

418 Richmond Road, Twickenham, Middx TW1 2EB (8288 0108, www.acena.co.uk). Richmond tube/rail or St Margarets rail. **Lunch served** noon-2pm Tue-Sun. **Dinner served** 7-10.30pm Mon-Sat. **Main courses** £14-£23.50. **Set lunch** (Sun) £21 2 courses, £25 3 courses. **Credit** AmEx, MC, V.

Just south of Richmond Bridge, this traditional Italian local was half full with a mix of families and dowdyish couples on our Sunday lunchtime visit. It isn't a particularly romantic spot – our booth table was too wide for intimate banter, the dark decor a little gloomy – but the generous, mostly reliable food makes up for it. Our only disappointment from a good-value £25 set lunch was a fennel, ricotta and chilli risotto – the mushy texture and bland flavour reminded us of baby food. Things picked up with the main courses. Pork rolled in leeks and thyme was the perfect Sunday lunch dish, with a rich sauce and smooth potato purée. Tiger prawn fettuccine au gratin came piping hot, with lashings of cream, parmesan and lemon, plus the pleasing tang of radicchio. For dessert, panna cotta served in a coupe was a nutty, mocha-infused affair worth every calorie. A peachy garganega from the compelling Italian wine list (lots of bottles under £30) was delightful. Service was professional, if a little cool. A Cena's owners, Tim and Camilla Healy, are spreading their net and are now co-owners of Joe Allen and Orso in Covent Garden.

Available for hire. Babies and children welcome: high chairs. Booking advisable.

ITALIAN

Japanese

Japanese dining in London has never been so exciting. Long gone are the days when only businessmen on expense accounts could afford to eat in these restaurants, and the range is constantly expanding with specialist eateries popping up all over the place. **Koya** helped kickstart the trend with its ever-popular udon noodle dishes. More recently, ramen has been the noodle of choice, with several ventures opening of late – try **Shoryu** for a classic version of tonkotsu, the long-simmered pork broth, or **Bone Daddies** for New York-style noodles with a rock 'n' roll soundtrack. Also popular are folded, steamed hirata buns, and **Flesh & Buns** is the place to sample them. The Osaka street snack okonomiyaki is also easier to find these days, with **Okan** in Brixton Village Market (and Sho Foo Doh at Chatsworth Road Market every Sunday) joining Covent Garden's **Abeno Too** in serving the savoury pancakes. Sushi lovers have never had it so good either. For something traditional, head to **Sushi Tetsu** in Clerkenwell or **Atariya** in Ealing; for contemporary, **Yashin** in Kensington is the star, though the beef and ponzu jelly nigiri at **Dinings** also deserve a mention. Fancy the latest trend from Osaka and Kyoto? Newcomer **Kirazu** serves seasonal small plates, Kansai-style. Going for a grill? Glitzy **Zuma** and **Roka** or budget-priced **Bincho** can supply skewers straight from the robata.

Central
City

Moshi Moshi Sushi
24 Upper Level, Liverpool Street Station, EC2M 7QH (7247 3227, www.moshimoshi.co.uk). Liverpool Street tube/rail. **Meals served** 11.30am-10pm Mon-Fri. **Dishes** £1.90-£5. **Main courses** £10-£12. **Credit** MC, V.
Some sushi menus read like a roll-call of endangered species, but not at Moshi Moshi Sushi. This conveyer-belt joint above Liverpool Street station has had sustainability at the forefront of its operation since opening in 1994. As well as ethical sourcing, the team here innovate using less common varieties such as Cornish dogfish: used in place of endangered eel. Despite the dogfish being less rich than classic barbecued unagi, it made a pretty decent substitution in a temaki hand roll – though the rice was slightly overdone. Sashimi and nigiri followed suit: all impeccable in quality, bar the rice. Another accolade of the restaurant is to have pioneered the kaiten (conveyer belt) sushi trend in London. Two decades on, the interior still has a futuristic feel, though it's just a little worn around the edges. The best seats in the house are inside the dramatic curved wooden pods at the back of the restaurant, where office workers congregate for an intimate post-work natter and a glass of plum wine

or Japanese beer. Seats by the conveyor belt allow you to eye up the dishes before you choose. *Babies and children admitted. Takeaway service; delivery service (over £20 within 4-mile radius).* **Map 12 R5.**

Clerkenwell & Farringdon

★ Sushi Tetsu NEW
12 Jerusalem Passage, EC1V 4JP (3217 0090, www.sushitetsu.co.uk). Barbican tube or Farringdon tube/rail. **Lunch served** 11.30am-2pm Tue-Fri. **Dinner served** 5-9.30pm Tue-Fri; 4-10.30pm Sat. **Dishes** £4-£9.20. **Set meal** £50, £70. **Credit** MC, V.
Getting a table at this Clerkenwell sushi-ya has been a challenge ever since it opened in summer 2012. Understandably so, as there are only about half a dozen seats and they're some of the hottest in London right now. In aesthetics and quality, Sushi Tetsu wouldn't be out of place in a smart Tokyo suburb. Chef Toru Takahashi (ex-Nobu) is centre-stage behind the imposing pale wood counter, where he carefully compacts glistening grains of rice into plump pellets before topping them with shimmering slivers of fish. Each nigiri is inspected with a contemplative look and finished with a dab of soy, sprinkling of sea salt or lick of flame from a blowtorch before being placed on a glossy bamboo leaf in front of the diner. Each piece arrives individually to be eaten by hand. For the full

experience, go for the omakase menu, and let the chef choose what's freshest that day. Just say when you've had enough – be warned though, the bill can add up. Highlights of a recent visit included the best boiled prawn nigiri we've encountered; blanched on the outside, then split down the middle and blowtorched, it was sweet, smoky and barely cooked through. You need to book well in advance – the website explains the rather complicated procedure – but it's a treat worth waiting for. *Booking essential.* **Map 5 O4.**

Covent Garden

Abeno Too
17-18 Great Newport Street, WC2H 7JE (7379 1160, www.abeno.co.uk). Leicester Square tube. **Meals served** noon-11pm Mon-Sat; noon-10pm Sun. **Main courses** £9-£25. **Set lunch** (Mon-Fri) £12-£22. **Credit** MC, V.
Getting your hands on Osaka's most famous street food, okonomiyaki, has got much easier in London over the past couple of years. But for our money this stalwart (and sister restaurant Abeno by the British Museum) are still the best for the full experience. Pop your bags and coats in the cleverly designed chest seating, then watch as the staff diligently mix the thick pancake-like batter in front of you, before cooking it on table and counter-top grills. It's then smothered with mayo, tangy worcestershire-style sauce, aonori seaweed and

smoked bonito flakes that sway majestically in the heat. The spectacle is always fun to watch. As well as the ample range of okonomiyaki fillings – anything from pork, squid and kimchi to pork, bacon, cheese and salmon – stir-fried noodles (yaki-soba) and noodles wrapped in omelette (om-soba) also make popular choices. Highlights of a recent visit included perfectly tender chunks of squid in a Tokyo-mix okonomiyaki, plus a cooling summer special of simmered, chilled baby aubergine with dashi and ginger. Just five minutes from the hustle and bustle of Trafalgar Square, Abeno Too makes the perfect place to refuel on cheap and filling Japanese fare. It's no wonder the small cluster of tables and counter-side seats are often packed. *Babies and children welcome: high chairs. Bookings not accepted. Takeaway service.* **Map 18 C4.**
For branch see index.

Flesh & Buns NEW
41 Earlham Street, WC2H 9LX (7632 9500, www.fleshandbuns.com). Covent Garden tube. **Lunch served** noon-3pm Mon-Fri. **Dinner served** 5-10.30pm Mon, Tue; 5-11.30pm Wed-Fri. **Meals served** noon-11.30pm Sat; noon-9.30pm Sun. **Main courses** £13-£24. **Credit** MC, V.
Following on from Bone Daddies, Ross Shonhan's second solo venture is no less modish. Flesh & Buns is hidden in a capacious Covent Garden basement, with industrial-chic decor and young, pierced and tattooed staff setting the tone. Like its elder sibling, it also takes influences from New York, serving east Asian eats with a side order of rock music. This time the focus is hirata buns: a US interpretation of a Taiwanese street food, where sweet, fluffy dough is folded, then steamed before being brought to table. Diners then stuff these pockets with their

Budget bites

★ Centre Point Sushi
1st floor, 20-21 St Giles High Street, WC2H 8LN (7240 6147, www.cpfs.co.uk). Tottenham Court Road tube. **Lunch served** noon-2.30pm Mon-Fri; noon-4.30pm Sat. **Dinner served** 6-10.30pm Mon-Sat. **Main courses** £8-£25. **Set lunch** £8-£9.50. **Credit** MC, V.
Follow the signs up the stairs of Korean/Japanese grocery shop Centre Point Food Store and you'll end up at this low-key sushi bar (also known as Hana). Comfortable booths by the window make perfect spots to unwind after a long day of shopping, though this means they're often full. The menu features a classic range of Japanese dishes, from sushi (prepared behind the open counter) to tempura or teriyaki. A capacious bowl of squishy udon noodles in savoury broth, topped by plump tempura prawns, came with six pieces of salmon maki – a bargain at £8.
Babies and children admitted. Booking advisable. Takeaway service. **Map 17 C2.**

★ Kulu Kulu
76 Brewer Street, W1F 9TX (7734 7316). Piccadilly Circus tube. **Lunch served** noon-2.30pm, **dinner served** 5-10pm Mon-Sat. **Dishes** £1.75-£3.80. **Set meal** £5.20-£12.90. **Credit** MC, V.
This in-and-out Soho sushi joint is more about speed than impeccable service, or setting. At busy times, staff will even ask you to leave as soon as you've finished eating. Pick whatever takes your fancy from the conveyor belt, where hot and cold dishes do the loop, or for a more extensive range opt for à la carte. The menu features the likes of sushi platters, tempura, udon noodle soup or classic hot dishes such as sweet miso-glazed aubergine – here served unconventionally in chunks. Futomaki and inside-out rolls are generously filled with anything from deep-fried salmon skin to tuna and avocado.
Bookings not accepted. Takeaway service. **Map 17 A5.**
For branches see index.

★ Necco
52-54 Exmouth Market, EC1R 4QE (7713 8575, www.necco.co.uk). Farringdon tube/ rail or bus 19, 38, 55. **Meals served** noon-10pm Mon-Wed; noon-10.30pm Thur-Sat.

Main courses £7.50-£12.50. **Set lunch** (noon-3pm) £5 bento box. **Credit** (over £10) MC, V.
Flying the flag for kawaii (cute) culture, this Japanese caff on Exmouth Market is decked out with butterfly-shaped chandeliers, heart-shaped coasters and all manner of other pink or cutesy things. It may be small, but the menu is long, listing everything from donburi to curry, bento and noodle dishes. A filling bowl of oyakodon saw generous chunks of chicken encased in sweetened just-set egg atop a steaming bowl of rice – a snip at £7.50. There's also a good range of sweet treats with Japanese flavourings, such as green tea cake, and drinks including thick yuzu milkshake.
Available for hire. Babies and children admitted. Tables outdoors (3, pavement). Takeaway service. **Map 5 N4.**

★ Taro
10 Old Compton Street, W1D 4TF (7439 2275, www.tarorestaurants.co.uk). Leicester Square or Tottenham Court Road tube. **Meals served** noon-10pm Mon; noon-10.30pm Tue-Thur; noon-10.45pm Fri; 12.30-10.45pm Sat; 12.30-9.30pm Sun. **Main courses** £1.50-£14.90. **Set lunch** £6.90 incl tea. **Set meal** £9.90-£14.90 bento box. **Credit** MC, V.
The perfect leaping-off point for a night out in Soho, Taro's Old Compton Street branch (the other is on Brewer Street) is regularly packed with a mixed crowd of office workers and students. Though the dining room is at basement level, it's surprisingly light and spacious with sunshine streaming down from the street-level window above. Curry rice, fried noodles (yakisoba) or donburi all make filling choices, and they won't break the bank at £7-£10 each. A spicy fried pork dish could have had a bit more pep, but agedashi tofu was crisp-coated and ample in size.
Babies and children welcome: high chairs. Booking advisable Fri, Sat. Takeaway service. **Map 17 C3.**
For branch see index.

★ Tokyo Diner
2 Newport Place, WC2H 7JJ (7287 8777, www.tokyodiner.com). Leicester Square tube. **Meals served** noon-11.30pm daily.

Main courses £8.50-£19.90. **Set lunch** (noon-6pm Mon-Fri) £8-£11.90. **Credit** MC, V.
Set over multiple floors, every nook and cranny of this café in Chinatown is regularly packed with crowds of youngsters after a bargain bite. Katsu curry with a crisp-crumbed, fried pork cutlet is a regular crowd-pleaser, as are donburi dishes such as sweet, salty braised beef and onion. If you're still not full after one of these, the staff will give you extra rice for free. And you won't incur any extra cost for service either as Tokyo Diner has a traditionally Japanese no-tipping policy. Instead, you're simply asked to come again – and bring your friends.
Babies and children welcome: high chairs. Bookings not accepted Fri, Sat. Takeaway service. **Map 17 C4.**

★ Tsuru
4 Canvey Street, SE1 9AN (7928 2228, www.tsuru-sushi.co.uk). Southwark tube or London Bridge tube/rail. **Meals served** 11am-3.30pm Mon; 11am-9pm Tue-Fri; noon-9pm Sat. **Main courses** £4-£14.25. **Set meal** £6.40-£8.20 bento box. **Credit** AmEx, MC, V.
This small Japanese restaurant in the shiny shopping mall behind Tate Modern is aimed at the takeaway crowd with its display case of ready-prepared sushi and salad boxes, and fridge full of canned drinks. You can eat in – perched on leather-topped stools at high shared tables, or at one of the standard tables near the door – but it can get uncomfortably cramped at lunch. Quality is higher than in many high-street sushi outlets, with all food freshly prepared on the premises. Staff are bright and efficient. Katsu curry is the signature dish, served with breadcrumbed pork, chicken, beef, cod, salmon or vegetables and steamed rice; you can also order it as bento or a sandwich. Other hot dishes include teriyaki chicken or salmon, tempura prawns and miso soup. Tsuru makes a fuss about sustainability, using line-caught yellowfin tuna and Icelandic cod, and packaging that is biodegradable or recyclable.
Babies and children admitted. Disabled: toilet. Tables outdoors (5, pavement). Takeaway service. **Map 11 O8.**
For branches see index.

choice of 'flesh'. Mustard miso and a few slices of subtly pickled apple made a perfect foil for tender pulled pork; crisp-skinned grilled sea bass was also skilfully cooked, served with fresh tomato salsa. Small plates include sushi rolls, contemporary sashimi and tempura, but we skipped these to save space for the impressive desserts. The Flesh & Buns version of the North American camping treat, s'mores, is a hoot, as you get to toast your own marshmallows on a Japanese table-top brazier. These are then sandwiched between a caramel-flavoured biscuit, with a slice of white chocolate laced with matcha green tea. If loud guitar music, DIY dining and following the latest food fashions are for you, Flesh & Buns should be next on your hit list.

Available for hire. Babies and children welcome: nappy-changing facilities. Booking advisable. Takeaway service. **Map 18 D3**.

Fitzrovia

Nizuni

22 Charlotte Street, W1T 2NB (7580 7447, www.nizuni.com). Goode Street or Tottenham Court Road tube. **Lunch served** noon-2.45pm daily. **Dinner served** 6-10.45pm Mon-Sat; 6-10.15pm Sun. **Main courses** £7.50-£18.50. **Set lunch** £7.90-£20. **Credit** AmEx, MC, V.

Cast from the same mould as its Korean sibling Koba (round the corner on Rathbone Street), this smartly dressed Japanese restaurant displays plenty of eastern charm. Nizuni, with its paper lanterns, dark wooden fittings and images of swimming koi carp, has a chilled-out feel. At lunchtime, the black banquettes are populated by office workers grabbing a bite; in the evening, the atmosphere is more intimate, with plenty of couples coming for a meal. The contemporary menu hints at the Korean ownership, featuring the likes of squid and kimchi pancakes, or spicy seafood stew, but you'll also find more standard Japanese izakaya-style dishes such as miso-grilled aubergine, or yakitori. Tuna sashimi arrived reasonably fresh, and a salmon and avocado inside-out roll was well wrapped, but there are more interesting options to explore on the menu, such as earthy beef stew with tofu and noodles served in a clay pot (nabe), or stir-fried pork with kimchi. Infused with Asian flavourings, the short list of desserts is also enticing – our chestnut cake was warm and sticky. The staff can seem a little absent-minded at times, but they're always agreeable.

Available for hire. Babies and children welcome: high chairs. Booking advisable Thur-Sat. Disabled: toilet. Separate room for parties, seats 20. Tables outdoors (4, pavement). Takeaway service. **Map 17 B1**. **For branch see index**.

★ Roka HOT 50

37 Charlotte Street, W1T 1RR (7580 6464, www.rokarestaurant.com). Goode Street or Tottenham Court Road tube. **Lunch served** noon-3.30pm Mon-Fri; 12.30-4pm Sat, Sun. **Dinner served** 5.30-11.30pm Mon-Sat; 5.30-10.30pm Sun. **Main courses** £4.50-£68. **Set meal** £50-£75 tasting menu. **Credit** AmEx, MC, V.

Zuma's younger sibling gets top marks for glitz and glamour. Much of the action takes place on full show at the central robata grill, where a repertoire (similar to Zuma's) of contemporary izakaya-inspired food is created. The seats along the knotted wooden

Sushi Tetsu. See p161.

JAPANESE

counter, framed by glass cases displaying the day's produce, are filled with expectant punters enjoying the show. The tasting menu is popular with first-time diners, taking them on a spin of the best that Roka has to offer. Ours started with a spicy spiral of own-made kimchi. Next came a sashimi platter elegantly presented over crushed ice, and including flavoursome minced tuna with spring onions to be scooped on to crisp, black bread. Sticky skewers of tebasaki (chicken wings) were succulent, while charred salmon served with pickled onion and a tare sauce was crisp-skinned and soft-centred. Another highlight was a showy trio of desserts, which featured Pocky-style chocolate and sesame biscuit sticks. The tasting menu isn't cheap, but each dish was impeccable. At such prices, though, service has to be spot on, and ours faltered towards the end. It took an age to get the bill, and we were made to wait further by the chilly door as attempts to retrieve our coats and bags were ignored.
Babies and children welcome: high chairs; nappy-changing facilities. Booking advisable. Disabled: toilet. Tables outdoors (9, terrace). **Map 17 B1**. **For branch see index**.

Knightsbridge

★ Zuma
5 Raphael Street, SW7 1DL (7584 1010, www.zumarestaurant.com). Knightsbridge tube.
Bar **Open** noon-11pm Mon-Fri; 12.30-11pm Sat, Sun.
Restaurant **Lunch served** noon-2.45pm Mon-Fri; 12.30-3.15pm Sat, Sun. **Dinner served** 6-10.45pm Mon-Sat; 6-10.15pm Sun. **Main courses** £14.80-£70. **Set meal** £58-£118. *Both* **Credit** AmEx, MC, V.
Out of simplicity can come excellence, and the food at Zuma is a case in point. The venue may be swish (with well-to-do patrons lining the amply stocked cedar bar), and the fixtures and fittings expensive, but when it comes to the food, much of the wow factor is down to high-class ingredients that haven't been messed around with too much. Own-made silken tofu, presented in a cedar saké cup, was rich, creamy and light. The barley miso, freshly grated wasabi and other accompaniments allowed the tofu to shine. A more indulgent dish of spicy miso with lobster also had a clarity of flavour, with the sweet shellfish the star. An ample house special of deep-fried lemon sole was served with a fresh, tangy ponzu sauce and cleverly presented in a bowl made of the curved and deep-fried skeleton of the fish. Our waiting staff couldn't have been nicer, and even the chefs behind the imposing robata grill seemed to be having a good time. This is one contemporary Japanese restaurant that we're happy to come back to time and again. Be sure to give the saké list a proper look too: there are more than 40 to choose from.
Babies and children welcome: high chairs; nappy-changing facilities. Booking essential. Disabled: toilet. Dress: smart casual. Separate rooms for parties, seating 12 and 14. **Map 8 F9**.

Marylebone

★ Dinings
22 Harcourt Street, W1H 4HH (7723 0666, www.dinings.co.uk). Marylebone tube/rail.
Lunch served noon-2.30pm Mon-Fri; 12.30-3pm Sat. **Dinner served** 6-10.30pm Mon-Sat. **Main courses** £6-£28. **Set lunch** £14-£29. **Credit** AmEx, MC, V.

Once one of Marylebone's best-kept secrets, Dinings now has a reputation larger than its compact, converted-townhouse setting. Getting a table in the basement is unlikely without a booking, but if you're lucky, there may be a spare stool at the street-level sushi counter. If you're not keen on small spaces, then you may just like the ground floor better – it's brighter with more windows. Whatever your thoughts on the venue itself, the food is indisputably excellent (make sure you're packing plastic, as costs do mount up). Conceived by Nobu alumni Masaki Sugisaki and Keiji Fuku, it displays plenty of Latin flair along with other innovative flourishes. Nobu-esque curved potato 'tar-tar' chips filled with minced fatty tuna, avocado and wasabi/jalapeño sauce offered an inviting taster of the style. The much-celebrated seared wagyu beef nigiri garnished with cubes of ponzu jelly and minced truffle was also a triumph. Presented on a long platter, a lunchtime sushi selection (good value at £23) tasted every bit as good as it looked. Another lunch dish of pork 'shabu shabu' saw ready-cooked slices of tender pork balanced atop a heap of sticky rice and dressed with spicy fermented Korean sauce gochujang – despite the pungent mix, it wasn't overpowering. With polite, efficient chefs and waiters too, Dinings is a top performer.
Available for hire. Babies and children admitted. Booking essential. Takeaway service. Vegetarian menu. **Map 8 F5**.

Mayfair

Chisou
4 Princes Street, W1B 2LE (7629 3931, www.chisourestaurant.com). Oxford Circus tube.
Lunch served noon-2.30pm, **dinner served** 6-10.15pm Mon-Sat. **Meals served** 1-9.30pm Sun. **Main courses** £12-£25. **Set lunch** £14.50-£20.50. **Credit** AmEx, MC, V.
Despite the modern interior – pale wood, cream walls – this Mayfair restaurant (just off Regent Street) is traditional at heart. Oshibori (hand towels) are presented on arrival, service is low-key and considered, and saké is taken seriously (the lengthy list offers not only tasting notes, but also more detailed information on the region each bottle

comes from). The chefs pride themselves on the sushi and sashimi here – and the sourcing certainly can't be knocked. A plump botan prawn was served fanned on top of a nigiri rice pellet with an unusual accompaniment of the deep-fried head. Also from the deep-fryer, a chef's special of mini octopus in light batter (kodako no karaage) was pleasingly tender, with a citrus tang from the accompanying lemon. A summery dish of cucumber with pearls of sweet and salty barley miso was tasty too, though the decorative carving made the chunky cucumber a little tricky to eat elegantly. At times we've found the service a little distant at Chisou, but become a regular (there are plenty) and you're sure to be treated with more warmth. There are branches in Knightsbridge and Chiswick.
Babies and children welcome: high chairs. Booking essential. Separate rooms for parties, seating 12-20. Tables outdoors (2, terrace). Takeaway service. **Map 9 J6**. **For branches see index**.

Ikeda
30 Brook Street, W1K 5DJ (7499 7145). Bond Street tube. **Lunch served** noon-2pm, **dinner served** 6-10pm Mon-Sat. **Main courses** £20-£70. **Set meal** £55-£75 3 courses. **Credit** AmEx, MC, V.
Like many of the venues around the Japanese Embassy, Ikeda is old school. No self-respecting businessman would have any qualms about bringing clients here, and a meal with the in-laws wouldn't go amiss either – but a raucous party is probably out. The decor is inoffensive but just a little bland; the staff are affable, turning out the same mix of efficient but unintrusive service since 1978. The highlight is a ringside seat by the tiny open kitchen, where sparklingly fresh sashimi, light, crisp tempura and numerous other classic dishes are produced. A lunchtime set of well-shaped nigiri was served traditionally on a wooden block. Leaner-than-average slow-simmered pork belly with Japanese mustard and boiled, rolled spinach (buta kakuni) yielded easily at the prod of a chopstick. More unusual was a prawn tempura dish, where the shellfish was rolled with cha soba noodles in nori before getting a second dipping in

Shoryu Ramen

the batter and oil. Like the ambience, the lofty prices also fit the Mayfair location. But consistency is the order of the day here, so come in the sure knowledge that you'll get a decent meal.
Available for hire. Babies and children welcome: high chairs. Booking advisable. Takeaway service. **Map 9 H6**.

Nobu
1st floor, The Metropolitan, 19 Old Park Lane, W1K 1LB (7447 4747, www.noburestaurants. com). Hyde Park Corner tube. **Lunch served** noon-2.15pm Mon-Fri; 12.30-2.30pm Sat, Sun. **Dinner served** 6-10.15pm Mon-Thur; 6-11pm Fri, Sat; 6-10pm Sun. **Dishes** £3.25-£38. **Set lunch** £35 bento box; £65, £75. **Set dinner** £85, £95. **Credit** AmEx, MC, V.
The hype has died down, the celebs are long gone, but London's first branch of Nobu (there's a second on Berkeley Square) is still a heavyweight on the Japanese dining scene. Imitations of the restaurant's signature dishes – black cod with miso, or rock shrimp tempura, for example – can be found on many a menu in the capital these days, but if you want to try the original Nobu Matsuhisa version, then head to Old Park Lane. Crisp tacos topped with sweet-fleshed crab and piquant tomato salsa make an enjoyable prelude to a meal. Then it's time to explore the rest of the restaurant's much-lauded range of Japanese/Peruvian fusion dishes. A vegetarian dish of tofu anticuchos came bar-marked with a spicy red-pepper sauce. Though perfectly tasty, it wouldn't get pulses racing. Sushi here is excellent, however; our well-shaped temaki was filled with diced scallop and smelt eggs in a rich, creamy chilli sauce. A meal at Nobu might not come cheap, but a few things are guaranteed: impeccable service, great views (the restaurant overlooks Hyde Park) and perfectly fresh fish. Another likelihood is a dining room packed with moneyed tourists and smart Kensington families, so get your glad rags on.
Babies and children welcome: high chairs. Booking advisable. Disabled: lift; toilet. Separate rooms for parties, seating 14-60. **Map 9 H8**. **For branch see index.**

Umu
14-16 Bruton Place, W1J 6LX (7499 8881, www.umurestaurant.com). Bond Street or Green Park tube. **Lunch served** noon-2.30pm Mon-Fri. **Dinner served** 6-11pm Mon-Sat. **Main courses** £13-£37. **Set meal** £25-£50. **Set meal** £115. **Credit** AmEx, MC, V.
With a futuristic sliding entrance door (set off by placing your hand on a sensor), a plush, dark interior and polished service, Umu is guaranteed to impress. The bill too is likely to leave a lasting impression, so it's best to save this swanky venue for a special occasion unless you have an expense account. (There was no shortage of high-powered diners on our most recent visit.) On such a celebratory occasion, opt for the multi-course tasting menu (£115) and you'll get to explore an elaborate range of Kyoto-style kaiseki cuisine, presented on attractive dishes. The modern sushi doesn't always make the grade, though, so stick to the classic version. Luxury ingredients abound on the à la carte menu: wild Scottish lobster tempura, wagyu beef tataki (grade 9) and Irish abalone steamed in saké. For a less bank-breaking taster of the menu, come at lunch for a set meal (such as a bento with grilled fish, meat or tempura, or somen noodles) – all served with soup, salad and a dessert.

Our nigiri sushi selection (£38) was of the utmost quality. The ample wine and saké lists are worthy of exploration too.
Babies and children welcome: high chairs. Booking advisable dinner. Disabled: toilet. Dress: smart casual. **Map 9 H7**.

Piccadilly

Yoshino
3 Piccadilly Place, W1J 0DB (7287 6622, www.yoshino.net). Piccadilly Circus tube. **Meals served** noon-10pm Mon-Sat. **Main courses** £6.80-£40. **Set meal** £10 bento box. **Credit** AmEx, MC, V.
Down a quiet alleyway off Piccadilly, a neon sign announces 'sushi'. It's easy to miss even if you've been to Yoshino before, so keep your eyes peeled. Like Atariya in Ealing, the secret to this sushi bar's success over the years has been a guaranteed supply of market-fresh fish (the company is also a seafood supplier). For years, the winning formula here has been a small selection of sushi sets. The colourful chirashi – topped with shredded nori, mange tout and omelette, as well as the expected sashimi slices – has always been a favourite, and didn't disappoint on a recent visit. The salmon on our nigiri had silky-smooth flesh that melted in the mouth, and the squid was good quality too. Recently, Yoshino's repertoire has expanded to include wagyu beef teppanyaki and skewers. The seating has also been rearranged, with no pews by the sushi counter. Instead, the dimly lit (and slightly down-at-heel) ground floor is dotted with small tables. Head upstairs if you can: the design is minimal, but it's generally lighter and brighter. Service remains as polite as ever.
Babies and children admitted. Booking advisable. Tables outdoors (8, pavement). Takeaway service. Vegetarian menu. **Map 17 A5**.

St James's

Sake No Hana
23 St James's Street, SW1A 1HA (7925 8988, http://sakenohana.com). Green Park tube. **Lunch served** noon-2.45pm Mon-Fri; noon-3.45pm Sat. **Dinner served** 6-10.45pm Mon-Thur; 6-11.15pm Fri, Sat. **Main courses** £4-£37. **Set meal** £29-£65. **Set brunch** (Sat) £38.50 (£35 vegetarian). **Credit** AmEx, MC, V.
As you'd expect from the Hakkasan restaurant group, Sake No Hana is well designed and has slick service: a combination that means the striking yet serene dining room plays host to many a business lunch from the *Economist*'s offices round the corner. On a midweek lunchtime visit, there were also a number of well-heeled families enjoying the range of contemporary Japanese dishes. A four-course 'Taste of Sake No Hana' (£29) proved a filling meal, with miso soup, a choice of sukiyaki, tempura or grilled dish, a handful of sushi and a dessert. Arriving sizzling at the table, its earthenware cloche still in place, our tofu toban-yaki came with a pleasingly tangy ponzu dressing and slices of shiitake and eringi mushroom on the side. A coating of tempura batter pieces added interest to an avocado and red pepper inside-out roll; and a selection of ice-cream mochi wedges, presented in a circle like the petals of a flower, rounded off the meal well. There's also plenty for wine and saké buffs to get stuck into. Don't forget to glance upwards while you're dining; the sculptural wood slating above your head definitely deserves a look.

Available for hire. Babies and children admitted. Booking advisable. Disabled: lift; toilet. **Map 9 J8**.

★ Shoryu Ramen NEW
9 Regent Street, SW1Y 4LR (no phone, www.shoryuramen.com). Piccadilly Circus tube. **Lunch served** 11am-3.30pm, **dinner served** 5-11pm Mon-Fri. **Meals served** 11am-11pm Sat; 11am-10pm Sun. **Main courses** £6.90-£12.50. **No credit cards.**
Shoryu pips its tonkotsu-touting West End rivals for texture and stock, even though Bone Daddies stands out for extra fat and lashings of rock 'n' roll. As well as Hakata-style ramen (noodles in a rich, boiled-down, pork-bone broth), the other notable feature is speed. Within months of opening in 2012, this original branch started a standing-only service; in July 2013, Shoryu Express opened a few doors down, proclaiming itself 'a rapid, self-service-style prototype ramen bar… for those in a rush'. Both help ease the hassle of no-bookings dining. Dracula tonkotsu (Van Helsing by name – a more apt name) – with caramelised garlic oil, balsamic vinegar and garlic chips – packs a flavoursome punch. Extra toppings such as bamboo shoots and boiled egg are to be expected, but kaedama (plain refill noodles) are a godsend for anyone sharing soup stock between small children or bumping up the volume for a voracious teen. A varied choice of good sides, sakés and sweets can really make a meal of your visit. And Shoryu has broadened its horizons with a pop-up (Shoryu Soho) that became a fully fledged saké bar in 2013.
Bookings not accepted. **Map 10 K7**. **For branches see index.**

Soho

Bincho
16 Old Compton Street, W1D 4TL (7287 9111, www.bincho.co.uk). Leicester Square or Tottenham Court Road tube. **Lunch served** noon-3pm Tue-Sat; 1-3.30pm Sun. **Dinner served** 5-11pm Mon-Sat; 5-10.30pm Sun. **Dishes** £1.50-£7. **Set lunch** £8.50-£9.50. **Set dinner** £25. **Credit** AmEx, MC, V.
Named after the charcoal used to stoke its fires, Bincho's shtick is affordable skewers. This is a convivial spot, furnished in the style of an izakaya (Japanese pub) and with low lighting and a relaxed vibe. You'll find safe options here, but also all the unusually textured authentic ingredients with which westerners are less familiar (or comfortable). If you're feeling adventurous, chicken gizzards make a good start – both crunchy and wobbly, they're a big hitter in the Land of the Rising Sun. Or try the dinky boiled quails' eggs, which offer just a little resistance as you bite into them. It's not all offal and eggs, though: cubed pork belly had a tender interior and crisp coating, chicken wings were lip-smackingly juicy, and there are speared vegetables and seafood to choose from too. The perfect accompaniment to a plate of skewers has to be a cool, crisp beer, but Bincho also has an impressive range of Japanese whiskies, brought up from the bespoke basement bar. Round off your meal with a soy-glazed grilled rice ball, or bowl of ochazuke (soupy rice made with green tea) – the version produced here is excellent.
Available for hire. Babies and children welcome: high chairs. Booking advisable. Disabled: toilet. Separate room for parties, seats 18. Takeaway service. **Map 17 C3**.

JAPANESE

Kirazu

Bone Daddies NEW

*30-31 Peter Street, W1F 0AT (7287 8581,
www.bonedaddiesramen.com). Piccadilly Circus
tube.* **Lunch served** noon-3pm Mon-Fri. **Dinner
served** 5.30-10pm Mon; 5.30-11pm Tue, Wed;
5.30pm-midnight Thur, Fri. **Meals served**
noon-midnight Sat; noon-9pm Sun. **Main
courses** £9-£13. **Credit** MC, V.

Cock scratchings are not the first thing you expect
to see on a ramen bar's menu. But Bone Daddies is
not your average noodle joint. Instead, it's a New
York-inspired, butched-up ramen-ya with gutsy
noodle soup dishes that don't skimp on flavour. As
you open the door, you're met with a barrage of
belting guitar rock, walls covered in images of
quiffed and tattooed Japanese rockabillies, and a
room full of diners seated on high stools soaking it
all up. So, perhaps not somewhere to bring your
mum, or a date for that matter – unless you don't
mind shouting at each other. The cock scratchings
turned out to be crunchy crumbled chicken skin,
mixed with a little shichimi seasoning and
sprinkled on to a chicken bone and soy-based ramen
dish (T22) for added crunch. Other choices include
one of the richest bowls of tonkotsu ramen you'll
find in London: the broth made from 20-hour
simmered pork bones; sweet miso and butter
ramen; and sesame sauce and peanut-laced

tantanmen noodles slicked with chilli oil. There are
no low-fat options here. A long list of Japanese
drinks, including saké, shochu and whiskey,
provides the accompaniment. Service is swift and
appropriately informal.
*Babies and children admitted. Bookings not
accepted.* **Map 17 B4**.

Kirazu NEW

*47 Rupert Street, W1D 7PF (7494 2248,
www.kirazu.co.uk). Piccadilly Circus tube.*
Lunch served noon-2.30pm Sat. **Dinner
served** 6-10.30pm Mon-Sat. **Dishes** £2.50-
£10.50. **Credit** MC, V.

There's no sign above the door, no flashy exterior,
just an A-board advertising 'Japanese Tapas and
Ramen'. But don't walk past Kirazu; you won't find
anywhere else in London quite like it. The interior,
with its bare light bulbs, white walls and communal
tables with knocked-together wooden benches,
wouldn't be out of place in a hip Hackney eaterie.
Much of chef Yuya Kikuchi's menu is themed
around obanzai – a traditional home-cooking style
from Japan – and he believes his restaurant is the
only one to serve it in Europe. As cuisines go,
obanzai is humble, but the Kansai region it
originates from is renowned for the quality of its
produce, especially vegetables, and obanzai is built

around letting the ingredients sing. Conger eel, a
classic summer food, was served grilled in a sweet
soy-based sauce with a few slices of cucumber.
Salmon sashimi was burnished with a blowtorch,
imbuing the silky flesh with a delicate hint of
smoke. Another flame-finished dish was salt-cured
and chilli-seasoned cod roe (mentaiko), which
popped in the mouth as we ate it, yielding a bitter-
edged piquancy. Ramen also makes an appearance,
as does the Osaka street-food takoyaki. These
round battered octopus balls, cooked on a dimpled
griddle, then smothered in Japanese mayo and thick
worcestershire-style sauce, were the best we've
found in London. We'll be back to try more of the
well-priced plates, along with an accompanying cup
or two of saké.
Takeaway service. **Map 17 B4**.

★ Koya HOT 50

*49 Frith Street, W1D 4SG (7434 4463,
www.koya.co.uk). Tottenham Court Road tube.*
Lunch served noon-3pm daily. **Dinner
served** 5.30-10.30pm Mon-Sat; 5.30-10pm Sun.
Main courses £6.90-£14.90. **Credit** MC, V.

The opening of Koya in 2010 marked a more
youthful movement in the Japanese dining scene.
With blond-wood sharing tables, white walls and a
generally fresh-faced crowd of diners, the venue

feels more like a friendly caff than a slick West End eaterie. The handmade udon noodles produced here are top notch, which explains why expectant diners often queue out of the door. Don't be deterred: service is generally snappy, so you won't have to wait too long. The well-priced menu features udon noodles served three ways: atsu-atsu (hot noodles in hot dashi broth), hiya-atsu (cold noodles with hot dipping broth) or hiya-hiya (cold noodles with cold dipping sauce). All are good, so choosing according to the weather tends to be the best method. Accompaniments range from traditional Japanese (tempura, perhaps) to the less conventional (smoked mackerel with greens). The vegetarian sweet miso, walnut and mushroom atsu-atsu is a regular crowd-pleaser. There are also donburi dishes and a specials board that includes the likes of okara (the ground bean protein left over from making soya milk) or cime di rapa croquettes slathered in earthy ginger and shiitake mushroom sauce. A small drinks list encompasses Japanese beer, saké and shochu. In summer 2013, Koya opened a new branch – next door.
Bookings not accepted. Vegan dishes. **Map 17 C3**. **For branch see index.**

So Japanese
3-4 Warwick Street, W1B 5LS (7292 0760, www.sorestaurant.com). Piccadilly Circus tube. **Lunch served** noon-3pm Mon-Fri. **Dinner served** 5.30-10.30pm Mon-Thur; 5.30-11pm Fri. **Meals served** noon-11pm Sat. **Main courses** £14-£28. **Set lunch** £6.95-£16. **Credit** AmEx, MC, V.
Just around the corner from Brewer Street's stretch of cheap and cheerful Japanese restaurants, So aims for something a little more upmarket. The brightly lit dining room has a polished, contemporary feel, attracting a more mature clientele. The menu features luxe ingredients too – such as foie gras and wagyu beef. But it's not all decadence here; there are also plenty of standard options such as chicken yakitori, crisp veg or fish tempura and salmon teriyaki. From the long, curved sushi counter at the front of the restaurant come well-prepared nigiri, maki temaki, chirashi or sashimi – all made with high-quality fish. Check the specials board for less common options. Meat dishes are also worth trying. A generous portion of ibérico pork was charred at the edges and imbued with the sweet, salty savouriness of the miso marinade; it had all the melt-in-the-mouth tenderness that the menu promised. Wagyu beef sashimi, served with pungent raw garlic and soy sauce, was another enjoyable dish. The drinks list includes Asian-inspired cocktails as well as saké, shochu and an ample choice of wine.
Available for hire. Babies and children admitted. Takeaway service. **Map 17 A5**.

★ Tonkotsu
63 Dean Street, W1D 4QG (7437 0071, www.tonkotsu.co.uk). Leicester Square or Tottenham Court Road tube. **Lunch served** noon-3pm, **dinner served** 5-10.30pm Mon-Fri. **Meals served** noon-10.30pm Sat; noon-10pm Sun. **Main courses** £9-£11. **Credit** AmEx, MC, V.
Riding the noodle new wave that washed over London in 2012, Tonkotsu (offshoot of Tsuru) plies a no-nonsense trade in Kyushu-style ramen – distinguished by a creamy, pork-bone broth. A pipe-riddled ceiling, walls lined with splintery wood and dim light from a medley of suspended bulbs lend a certain industrial cachet. With just four flavours of ramen, three kinds of gyoza and a handful of sides to choose from, a meal here can be swift, though that doesn't prevent queues forming. Harried waitresses with good intentions try to optimise use of tables, but this is yet another popular Soho eaterie with a no-bookings policy. The food doesn't warrant such high demand: 'handmade, daily' pork gyoza were let down by a frankfurter-esque filling; classically fatty tonkotsu soup needs to be steaming hot, but on occasion we've found it served unpalatably lukewarm. Since February 2013, Tonkotsu has been making its own, very good noodles on the premises. In line with a Tokyo 'big night out', more attention is paid to beer than wine, with some US and London ales giving the Asahi-Kirin-Sapporo triumvirate a run for their money, as well as a Japanese beer brewed in Belgium (Owa).There's also a branch in trendy E8.
Babies and children welcome: high chairs. Bookings not accepted. Separate room for parties, seats 25. Tables outdoors (2, pavement). **Map 17 B4**.
For branch see index.

West
Bayswater

Shiori NEW
45 Moscow Road, W2 4AH (7221 9790, www.theshiori.com). Bayswater or Queensway tube. **Lunch served** noon-3pm, **dinner served** 6-10.30pm Tue-Sat. **Set lunch** £28.50-£50. **Set dinner** £65, £105. **Credit** MC, V.
Finding a traditional Japanese restaurant, complete with wood and paper screen front, on a Bayswater backstreet, seems incongruous. Shiori could have been shipped in directly from Japan, as could the intricate, multi-course set meals they serve here. This is the place to experience kaiseki ryori – the Japanese version of haute cuisine. Chef-patron Takashi Takagi and wife Hitomi trained in Kyoto (the birthplace of kaiseki ryori) and ran tiny Sushi of Shiori in Euston; now they've upped their game, and their headcount (to 12). From placemats decorated with seasonal ingredients, to dishes adorned with edible buds and blossoms, a lot of attention has gone into every detail. The eight-course Hana menu (at £65, the cheaper of the two evening options – the other costs £105) began with a genteel portion of broccoli-like rapeseed blossom scattered with bonito flakes. Next, a mound of sea bream slivers in a luxurious dressing of rich, sweet monkfish liver. A succession of delicate raw and cooked dishes followed, paired with cups of cold saké. A resonant broth jewelled with soft pillows of sweet snow-crab meat, firm tofu skin (yuba) and a tangle of slippery glass noodles was the pinnacle of the meal. '*Natsukashi!*' they say in Japanese when reminded of a fond memory, and an evening here was resoundingly reminiscent of Japan.
Booking advisable. **Map 3 J3**.

Ealing

★ Atariya
1 Station Parade, Uxbridge Road, W5 3LD (8896 3175, www.atariya.co.uk). Ealing Common tube. **Lunch served** 11.30am-2pm, **dinner served** 5.30-9pm Tue-Sun. **Dishes** £1.50-£5.50. **Set meal** £15-£23. **Credit** AmEx, MC, V.

Tonkotsu

Just a few paces from Ealing Common station, this unassuming restaurant has a strong reputation for high-quality old-school sushi. The functional room is simply furnished with white-tiled floor, small wooden tables and a standard-issue sushi counter along one wall. It's not much to look at, but it serves the purpose for a decent lunch or dinner. Sourcing the highest quality of fish is not a problem for Atariya as the company is also a fishmonger. This also enables it to offer a wider range than most, with more than 20 nigiri toppings to choose from – including lesser spotted varieties such as turbot fin, razor clam and botan prawn – all of which are handled well. Prices have gone up a little recently, eliciting a few grumbles from regulars, but sashimi and nigiri sets are still reasonable value at £15 to £23. The 'superior' selection featured 14 well-shaped nigiri pieces, though the fish slicing was a little uneven. Highlights included fatty tuna as soft as silk, and turbot with just the right level of resistance as you bit into it. Less pleasing was the overpowering ume paste in a plum and shiso maki roll.
Babies and children welcome: high chairs. Booking advisable Fri, Sat. Takeaway service.
For branches see index.

Kiraku

8 Station Parade, Uxbridge Road, W5 3LD (8992 2848, www.kirakulondon.wordpress.com). Ealing Common tube. **Lunch served** noon-2.30pm, **dinner served** 6-10pm Tue-Sun. **Dishes** £7-£23. **Credit** MC, V.
Just a few doors up from one of London's most lauded sushi restaurants (Atariya), Kiraku has stiff competition. But this friendly neighbourhood restaurant definitely holds its own. The tatty orange sign and frosted glass windows give little away about what to expect inside. The interior is simple too – pale wood sushi counter and tables, white walls hung with ink drawings of fish, and a TV screening Japanese shows. Nevertheless, the food is not only of a high quality, but good value too. No wonder the dining room is regularly full with a range of expats and local families. A house speciality of kaisen bara-chirashi saw an array of impeccable fish (tuna, salmon, cured mackerel, boiled prawn) and jewel-like roe scattered across a bowl of generously vinegared rice – a joy for the eyes as well as the palate. Particularly impressive were the tender chunks of octopus, an ingredient that so often is too rubbery. Tempura udon was another enjoyable dish, with a resonant dashi broth and chewy noodles, though the batter on the prawn was a little thick. Drink Japanese beer or saké, served by courteous, efficient staff.
Babies and children welcome: high chairs. Booking advisable Fri-Sun. Separate rooms for parties, seating 8-20. Takeaway service. Vegan dishes.

Hammersmith

Suzu

170-172 Hammersmith Road, W6 7JP (8741 1101, www.suzuonline.co.uk). Hammersmith tube. **Lunch served** noon-3pm Mon-Fri. **Dinner served** 6-10pm Mon-Sat. **Dishes** £2-£16.90. **Credit** MC, V.
Suzu may be off Hammersmith's main strip, but it's rarely short of customers. By day, local office workers make the most of reasonably priced set meals and takeaway sushi selections; by night, west London residents (including plenty of expats) come to unwind in the dinky dining room. Decked out in black and white, the space features rather idiosyncratic decoration – anime models, old film posters – giving it the feel of a family restaurant. The menu contains much of the Japanese repertoire, from salmon teriyaki to ramen noodle soup and katsu curry, but the sushi and sashimi selection deserves special attention. You won't find flabby fish here, as Suzu sources only the best from fishmonger-cum-sushi shop Atariya. The nigiri are just a little smaller than average, but the rice in our sea bream nigiri was pearlescent, with just the right amount of bite; the fish too was firm and shiny. A hand roll encasing a sweet-fleshed prawn in a light tempura batter proved just as good. From the evening tapas menu, a plate of takoyaki (octopus balls) was less exciting, having slightly claggy batter. For a convivial evening, try sampling some shochu: there are a few to work your way through here. Be warned, though: it's strong.
Booking advisable. Takeaway service; delivery service (over £20 within 2-mile radius).
Map 20 C4.

Shiori. See p167.

Tosa

332 King Street, W6 0RR (8748 0002, www.tosauk.com). Ravenscourt Park or Stamford Brook tube. **Lunch served** 12.30-2.30pm, **dinner served** 6-10.30pm daily. **Main courses** £7-£15. **Set lunch** £11. **Set meal** £30. **Credit** AmEx, MC, V.
Locals don't come to Tosa for the sparkling setting – the brown and white dining room seems just a little lacklustre. Instead, friendly service and a decent range of sushi and skewers are the main draw. If you like to see the chefs at work, head for the robata grill at the front (though you might end up a little smoky). Otherwise, there's plenty of seating dotted around the room, including some more intimate pews at the back. On a weekday lunchtime, the room was bustling with local families and lone diners well acquainted with the menu, plus the odd table of Japanese salarymen. Cheap sets were going down well, such as the yakitori selection, which included juicy spirals of pork and shiso, sticks of quails' eggs and classic chicken chunks with onion – all pleasingly smoky from the charcoal grill (served with rice, salad and miso for £11). Sushi and sashimi are also popular, the fish as fresh as you like, though the rice rectangles in our sea bass and capelin-roe nigiri were indelicately large. The drinks list features the usual array of Japanese beers and sakés.
Available for hire. Babies and children admitted. Booking advisable; essential dinner. Tables outdoors (4, pavement). Takeaway service.
Map 20 A4.
For branch see index.

Kensington

★ Yashin

1A Argyll Road, W8 7DB (7938 1536, www.yashinsushi.com). High Street Kensington tube. **Lunch served** noon-2.15pm, **dinner served** 6-10pm daily. **Dishes** £30-£60. **Set lunch** £12.50-£60. **Credit** AmEx, MC, V.
For anyone who likes sushi, Yashin is a must. Tucked down a side road off Kensington High Street, its exterior looks more like a smart French brasserie than a Japanese restaurant. But the centrepiece sushi counter gives the game away as soon as you step inside. Set on the dark green tiles behind the team of itamae (sushi chefs), a neon sign reads 'without soy sauce', and this is how the chefs ask you to eat your artfully crafted sushi. In place of a dunking, each piece is finished with its own flavourings – perhaps a dab of tangy ume plum paste, a spoon of tosa jelly, or a quick blast from a blowtorch (perfect for balancing the richness of fatty tuna). The rest of the menu also displays precision and innovation: a testament to the chef-founder's grounding in the intricate art of kaiseki cuisine. A delicate dish of saikyo lamb was dotted with sweet miso and summer berries, while buttery sautéed razor clams (just a little overcooked) came with generous slices of summer truffle. The wine and saké lists are long and well chosen, and the clientele and service are as you'd expect from a classy dining establishment – though staff have proved slightly less attentive in the basement, so eat upstairs if you can. A second (and larger) branch opened in autumn 2013, just off the Old Brompton Road.
Available for hire. Babies and children welcome: high chair. Booking advisable weekends. **Map 7 B9.**
For branch see index.

Menu

Agedashidofu: tofu (qv) coated with katakuriko (potato starch), deep-fried, sprinkled with dried fish and served in a broth based on shoyu (qv), with grated ginger and daikon (qv).
Amaebi: sweet shrimps.
Anago: saltwater conger eel.
Bento: a meal served in a compartmentalised box.
Chawan mushi: savoury egg custard served in a tea tumbler (chawan).
Chutoro: medium fatty tuna from the upper belly.
Daikon: a long, white radish (aka mooli), often grated or cut into fine strips.
Dashi: the basic stock for Japanese soups and simmered dishes. It's often made from flakes of dried bonito (a type of tuna) and konbu (kelp).
Dobin mushi: a variety of morsels (prawn, fish, chicken, shiitake, ginkgo nuts) in a gently flavoured dashi-based soup, steamed (mushi) and served in a clay teapot (dobin).
Donburi: a bowl of boiled rice with various toppings, such as beef, chicken or egg.
Dorayaki: mini pancakes sandwiched around azuki bean paste.
Edamame: fresh soy beans boiled in their pods and sprinkled with salt.
Gari: pickled ginger, usually pink and thinly sliced; served with sushi to cleanse the palate between courses.
Gyoza: soft rice pastry cases stuffed with minced pork and herbs; northern Chinese in origin, cooked by a combination of frying and steaming.
Hamachi: young yellowtail or Japanese amberjack fish, commonly used for sashimi (qv) and also very good grilled.
Hashi: chopsticks.
Hiyashi chuka: Chinese-style ramen (qv, noodles) served cold (hiyashi) in tsuyu (qv) with a mixed topping that usually includes shredded ham, chicken, cucumber, egg and sweetcorn.
Ikura: salmon roe.
Izakaya: 'a place where there is saké'; an after-work drinking den frequented by Japanese businessmen, usually serving a wide range of reasonably priced food.
Kaiseki ryori: a multi-course meal of Japanese haute cuisine.
Kaiten-zushi: conveyor-belt sushi.
Karaage: deep-fried
Katsu: breaded and deep-fried meat, hence tonkatsu (pork katsu) and katsu curry (tonkatsu or chicken katsu with mild vegetable curry).
Kushiage: skewered morsels battered then deep-fried.
Maki: the word means 'roll' and this is a style of sushi (qv) where the rice and filling are rolled inside a sheet of nori (qv).
Mirin: a sweetened rice spirit used in many Japanese sauces and dressings.
Miso: a thick paste of fermented soy beans, used in miso soup and some dressings. Miso comes in a wide variety of styles: earthy, crunchy or smooth.

Miso shiru: classic miso soup, most often containing tofu and wakame (qv).
Nabemono: a class of dishes cooked at the table and served directly from the earthenware pot or metal pan.
Natto: fermented soy beans of stringy, mucous consistency.
Nimono: food simmered in a stock, often presented 'dry'.
Noodles: second only to rice as Japan's favourite staple. Served hot or cold, dry or in soup, and sometimes fried. There are many types, but the most common are ramen (Chinese-style egg noodles), udon (thick white wheat-flour noodles), soba (buckwheat noodles), and somen (thin white wheat-flour noodles, usually served cold as a summer dish – hiyashi somen – with a chilled dipping broth).
Nori: sheets of dried seaweed.
Okonomiyaki: the Japanese equivalent of filled pancakes or a Spanish omelette, whereby various ingredients are added to a batter mix and cooked on a hotplate, usually in front of diners.
Ponzu: usually short for ponzu joyu, a mixture of the juice of a Japanese citrus fruit (ponzu) and soy sauce. Used as a dip, especially with seafood and chicken or fish nabemono (qv).
Robatayaki: a kind of grilled food, generally cooked in front of customers, who make their selection from a large counter display.
Saké: rice wine, around 15% alcohol. Usually served hot, but may be chilled.
Sashimi: raw sliced fish.
Shabu shabu: a pan of stock is heated at the table and plates of thinly sliced raw beef and vegetables are cooked in it piece by piece ('shabu-shabu' is onomatopoeic for the sound of washing a cloth in water). The broth is then portioned out and drunk.
Shiso: perilla or beefsteak plant. A nettle-like leaf of the mint family that is often served with sashimi (qv).
Shochu: Japan's colourless answer to vodka is distilled from raw materials such as wheat, rice and potatoes.
Shoyu: Japanese soy sauce.
Sukiyaki: pieces of thinly sliced beef and vegetables are simmered in a sweet shoyu-based sauce at the table on a portable stove. Then they are taken out and dipped in raw egg (which semi-cooks on the hot food) to cool them for eating.
Sunomono: seafood or vegetables marinated (but not pickled) in rice vinegar.
Sushi: a combination of raw fish, shellfish or vegetables with rice – usually with a touch of wasabi (qv). Vinegar mixed with sugar and salt is added to the rice, which is then cooled before use. There are different sushi formats: **nigiri** (lozenge-shaped), **hosomaki** (thin-rolled), **futomaki** (thick-rolled), **temaki** (hand-rolled), **gunkan maki** (nigiri with a nori wrap), **chirashi** (scattered on top of a bowl of rice), and **uramaki** or **ISO maki** (more recently coined terms for inside-out rolls).

Tare: a general term for shoyu-based cooking marinades.
Tataki: meat or fish quickly seared, then marinated in vinegar, sliced thinly, and seasoned with ginger.
Tatami: a heavy straw mat – traditional Japanese flooring. A tatami room is usually a private room where you remove your shoes and sit on the floor to eat.
Tea: black tea is fermented, while green tea (**ocha**) is heat-treated by steam to prevent the leaves fermenting. **Matcha** is powdered green tea, and has a high caffeine content. **Bancha** is the coarsest grade of green tea, which has been roasted; it contains the stems or twigs of the plant as well as the leaves, and is usually served free of charge with a meal. **Hojicha** is lightly roasted bancha. **Mugicha** is roast barley tea, served iced in summer.
Tempura: fish, shellfish or vegetables dipped in a light batter and deep-fried. Served with tsuyu (qv), to which you add finely grated daikon (qv) and fresh ginger.
Teppanyaki: grilled on an iron plate. In modern Japanese restaurants, a chef standing at a hotplate (teppan) is surrounded by several diners. Slivers of beef, fish and vegetables are cooked and deposited on your plate.
Teriyaki: cooking method by which meat or fish – often marinated in shoyu (qv) and rice wine – is grilled and served in a tare (qv) made of a thick reduction of shoyu, saké (qv), sugar and spice.
Tofu: soy beancurd used fresh in simmered or grilled dishes, or deep-fried (**agedashidofu**, qv), or eaten cold (**hiyayakko**).
Tokkuri: saké flask – usually ceramic, but sometimes made of bamboo.
Tonkatsu: *see above* katsu.
Tsuyu: a general term for shoyu/mirin-based dips, served both warm and cold with various dishes ranging from tempura (qv) to cold noodles.
Umami: the nearest word in English is tastiness. After sweet, sour, salty and bitter, umami is considered the fifth primary taste in Japan, but not all food scientists in the West accept its existence.
Unagi: freshwater eel.
Uni: sea urchin roe.
Wakame: a type of young seaweed most commonly used in miso (qv) soup and kaiso (seaweed) salad.
Wasabi: a fiery green paste made from the root of an aquatic plant that belongs to the same family as horseradish. It is eaten in minute quantities (tucked inside sushi, qv), or diluted into shoyu (qv) for dipping sashimi (qv).
Yakimono: literally 'grilled things'.
Yakitori: grilled chicken (breast, wings, liver, gizzard, heart) served on skewers.
Zarusoba: soba noodles served cold, usually on a bamboo draining mat, with a dipping broth.
Zensai: appetisers.

JAPANESE

Sticks n Sushi

South West

Putney

Tomoe

292 Upper Richmond Road, SW15 6TH (3730 7884, www.tomoe-london.co.uk). East Putney tube or Putney rail. **Lunch served** noon-2.30pm, **dinner served** 6-10pm Tue-Fri. **Meals served** 1-9pm Sat, Sun. **Dishes** £1.90-£20. **Set lunch** £9.90-£22.50. **Credit** AmEx, MC, V.

Due to redevelopment on Marylebone Lane, Tomoe has moved to Putney, taking over the site from the venerable chef of Chosan (who has now retired). Tomoe's sushi chef/proprietor and much of his team may be the same, but the decor and clientele here are markedly different. Instead of salarymen enjoying a lively after-work drink, the big-windowed and minimally adorned dining room is populated by couples quietly chatting as they tuck in. The menu is also pared down, though happily of the same quality as before, spanning raw, grilled, deep-fried and simmered dishes. You're sure to find something you like. Scallop sashimi, served in the shell and garnished with a little wakame, was sweet-fleshed and sparklingly fresh. Salt and yuzu grilled chicken had been perfectly cooked, with crisp skin and tender meat – the hint of citrus from the yuzu adding a satisfying tang. A spider roll filled with deep-fried soft-shell crab, avocado and a scattering of tobiko (flying fish roe) was also well executed. Putney may have lost one well-loved Japanese resident, but it has gained another with a laid-back atmosphere and extremely friendly staff. *Babies and children welcome: high chairs. Booking advisable. Separate room for parties, seats 8. Takeaway service.*

Wimbledon

Sticks n Sushi

36 Wimbledon Hill Road, SW19 7PA (3141 8800, www.sticksnsushi.com). Wimbledon tube/ rail. **Meals served** noon-10pm Mon, Tue, Sun; noon-11pm Wed-Sat. **Set meal** £6.50-£28; £28.50-£60 (minimum 2). **Credit** AmEx, MC, V.

Sticks n Sushi has been imported from Denmark, where there are ten branches; many design elements in the cavernous space allude to its Scandinavian origins – such as the comfortable wooden chairs. The sticks, or skewers, are safe and western-friendly: no gizzards, cartilage or other more uncomfortable cuts. They're nice enough, though chicken tsukune had more in common with a Swedish meatball than anything you'd find on a skewer in Japan. The sushi rolls come with gimmicky names and colourful coatings – such as 'Black Alaska' inside-out rolls sprinkled with black tobiko (flying fish roe) and filled with salmon, cream cheese and avocado; or 'Dreamy California' stuffed with miso aïoli and crabsticks, then rolled with chilli flakes and poppy seeds. Vegetarians won't feel left out as there are plenty of veggie sushi choices and sides; sweet tomato slices with onion, soy and vinegar dressing is a tasty snack. With friendly staff, a youthful vibe and no shortage of seating, this is a fun venue in which to enjoy well-priced platters and cocktails on a lively evening out with friends. *Babies and children welcome: children's menu; high chairs; nappy-changing facilities. Booking advisable dinner. Disabled: toilet. Takeaway service. Vegan dishes.* **For branch see index.**

South

Brixton

Okan

Unit 39, Brixton Village Market, Coldharbour Lane, SW9 8PS (no phone, www.okanbrixton village.com). Brixton tube/rail. **Lunch served** noon-3pm Wed-Fri; noon-4pm Sun. **Dinner served** 6-10pm Thur, Fri. **Meals served** noon-10pm Sat. **Main courses** £6.50-£8.25. **No credit cards.**

Cheap eats abound in Brixton Village Market these days, and Okan delivers on this front. Specialising in the Osaka street-food staple, okonomiyaki, the menu may be small, but it's perfectly rounded – fried noodles, edamame, a little grilled aubergine and the all-important Osaka-yaki, all included. As the name suggests (okonomi means 'as you like it'), you can put pretty much anything into your batter mix, but pork, squid or kimchi are popular choices. A veggie-friendly combination of cheese, sweetcorn and rice cakes (mochi) made for an enjoyably chewy texture and plenty of flavour, though it got harder to pinch bits off with our chopsticks as the stuffed pancake hardened. Yakisoba, with slivers of pork and pickled ginger (benishoga), was perfectly al dente and filling, though less tangy than with worcestershire-style sauce than usual. The thrill of an okonomiyaki restaurant often comes from watching the pancake cook before your eyes, but not here – there aren't the facilities. Nevertheless, Okan is still a lot of fun. Much of the seating is on 'outside' benches, so you're always in the thick of it in the vibrant market. Grab a beer and watch the world go by. *Babies and children admitted. Bookings not accepted. Tables outdoors (2, pavement). Takeaway service.* **Map 22 E2.**

North

Camden Town & Chalk Farm

Asakusa

265 Eversholt Street, NW1 1BA (7388 8533). Camden Town or Mornington Crescent tube. **Dinner served** 6-11.30pm Mon-Fri; 6-11pm Sat. **Main courses** £5.50-£13. **Credit** AmEx, MC, V.

Low ceilings, stuccoed walls and 1970s-style red banquettes make a memorable first impression as you enter the low-lit dining room at Asakusa. The venue is undoubtedly characterful and also popular. Small tables are wedged into every nook and cranny of the two-floor restaurant, and we've yet to see many of them empty. If you've never got much further than sushi, here's your chance to explore what else the cuisine has to offer. The menu runs the gamut of skewers, homely stews (nabe), tempura and all manner of other dishes, on top of the raw fish and rice combo. For saké novices, there's also a three-cup tasting menu. A dish of simmered bamboo shoots was redolent of earthy katsuobushi (smoked, dried bonito flakes), while cold udon noodles with tempura and a soy-based dipping sauce had just the right amount of bite. From the specials, raw shredded squid with kimchi was slightly disappointing – tasting under-fermented and a little bitter. Asakusa may not be the best Japanese restaurant in town, but the range is good and the service friendly, so an evening spent here will never be wasted. *Babies and children admitted. Booking advisable Thur-Sat. Takeaway service.* **Map 27 D3.**

Shimogamo

108 Parkway, NW1 7AN (7424 9560, www.shimogamo.co.uk). Camden Town tube. **Lunch served** noon-2.30pm, **dinner served** 6-10pm Tue-Sun. **Main courses** £3.50-£25. **Set lunch** £10-£20. **Credit** AmEx, MC, V.

Even when it's named after a venerable seventh-century Shinto shrine, a place that bangs on about genuineness makes one doubt. But the strapline 'authentic Japanese restaurant' on Shimogamo's homepage is borne out by the food and atmosphere at this low-key, solid-looking all-rounder with its plain wood furniture and brown banquettes – a touch of suburban Kyoto at the Zoo end of Parkway. It's not just the deferential Japanese staff and name-tagged bottle-keep service that evince native nous. Decent-quality rice, and properly finely shredded daikon are among the little tell-tale signs. Even the sometimes grating choice of music, such as shamisen pop stylings from the Yoshida Brothers (big in Japan, apparently), adds to the effect. The footfall emanating from Camden Town tube peters out somewhat, so lunchtimes tend to be quiet, though there are well-priced daily specials such as the 'Salmon Lover's Lunch'. The evening or 'grand' menu takes a bigger bite out of your wallet, but offers more room for manoeuvre, with styles ranging from traditional donburi and classic noodles to a natto and okra side or pork belly in miso with an onsen (hot spring) poached egg. Don't expect fireworks; do anticipate fresh ingredients and all the classics. *Babies and children welcome: children's menu; high chairs. Booking advisable. Tables outdoors (5, pavement). Vegetarian menu.* **Map 27 C3.**

Crouch End

Wow Simply Japanese

18 Crouch End Hill, N8 8AA (8340 4539, www.wowsimplyjapanese.co.uk). Finsbury Park tube/rail then bus W3, W7, or Crouch Hill rail. **Lunch served** noon-2.30pm Wed-Sat. **Dinner served** 6-10.30pm Mon-Sat; 6-9.45pm

Okan

Sun. **Main courses** £4.50-£15.20. **Set lunch** £5.90-£9.50. **Credit** AmEx, MC, V.

The food? Most of it is indeed simple: sushi, noodles, donburi, yakimono, katsu and tempura are all available. Some of it is complicated by more powerful flavours: garlic, coriander, 'home-made chilli jam' – mostly to lip-smacking effect. To say 'wow' might be pushing it, but we've been impressed by chilli-spiked ika karaage (deep-fried squid) off the regular menu and succulent sea bass tempura from the specials board – both in a feather-light coating that speaks of a dab hand at batter in the kitchen. Good-quality fish is used throughout, so it's a pity to serve seared salmon sashimi with an overpowering drizzle of curry-tinged coulis; fresh nigiri and maki are an unadulterated success. And may the management never remove garlic fried rice from the menu. The drink? A single sheet listing red, white, rosé, saké, beer and soft. The restaurant? Just a rectangular room of cream walls and dark brown furniture with only a smattering of Japanese decorations to signify the cuisine. But most of the staff are as welcoming as the prices, and you get all sorts here – in a good way – so it's easy to see why the first Japanese restaurant to open in Crouch End continues to prosper without foodie gimmicks or showy surroundings.

Babies and children welcome: high chairs. Booking advisable. Takeaway service; delivery service (over £15 within 2-mile radius).

Shimogamo. See p171.

North West

Golders Green

Café Japan

626 Finchley Road, NW11 7RR (8455 6854). Golders Green tube or bus 13, 82. **Lunch served** noon-2pm Tue-Fri; noon-2.30pm Sat, Sun. **Dinner served** 6-10pm Tue-Sat; 6-9.30pm Sun. **Main courses** £9-£23. **Set lunch** £8.50-£15.50. **Set dinner** £14-£22. **Credit** AmEx, MC, V.

A far cry from the moody monochrome aesthetics of central London Japanese restaurants, this airy neighbourhood eaterie has the feel of a friendly café – hence the name. Ceilings are high, walls are cream, and specials are displayed on posters with cartoon-like drawings: fried gyoza dumplings with smiley faces, perhaps. It's an easy place for kicking back with friends and enjoying a simple meal. The menu is tailored to novices as well as more seasoned Japanese diners. Inside-out rolls filled with deep-fried tuna, salmon or yellowtail in a mildly spicy mayo are popular with kids, or anyone uncomfortable with raw fish – Café Japan proudly claims to have invented these rolls. Skewers of smoky chicken teriyaki also seemed tailored to the western palate, with more sugar than usual in the slightly gloopy sauce. Less common dishes on the list of grills include sardine-like capelin, and salmon jaw. If you're after value, the set meals are worth a look: there's tempura-don with miso soup, pickles and a side dish for £14, plus sushi or sashimi and tempura combos for £18.

Babies and children admitted. Bookings not accepted lunch. Takeaway service.

Hampstead

Jin Kichi

73 Heath Street, NW3 6UG (7794 6158, www. jinkichi.com). Hampstead tube. **Lunch served** 12.30-2pm Tue-Sun. **Dinner served** 6-10.45pm Tue-Sat; 6-10pm Sun. **Main courses** £14-£16. **Set lunch** £9-£17. **Credit** AmEx, MC, V.

On Hampstead's bijou Heath Street, Jin Kichi's elegant green façade sits discreetly among florists, jewellers and estate agents. The homely dining room is less swish, its central feature being a robata grill, framed by counter seating. This is somewhere to come for a quiet meal with friends or family, rather than to see and be seen. You'll find the usual line-up of chicken, beef, pork and vegetable skewers on the coals, including a few less common cuts such as crunchy chicken gizzards, or beef tongue – all cooked just right. From the list of grilled fish, yellowtail and salmon jaw make unusual but delicious choices: some parts marbled with buttery fat, others more lean and crisp from the grill. The sushi is also good, including a standard range of tuna, salmon, sea bass and yellowtail, plus other marine creatures. The only disappointment on a recent trip was a special of vinegar-pickled cauliflower, which was rather too potent. Saké (available by the cup or bottle) makes the natural accompaniment to a meal, but if you're in a party mood, there are also shochu cocktails.

Babies and children welcome: high chairs. Booking advisable. Takeaway service. **Map 28 B2.**

Willesden

Sushi-Say

33B Walm Lane, NW2 5SH (8459 2971). Willesden Green tube. **Lunch served** noon-3.30pm Sat, Sun. **Dinner served** 6.30-10pm Wed-Fri; 6.30-10.30pm Sat; 6-9.30pm Sun. **Main courses** £7.20-£24.60. **Set dinner** £23.50-£39.50. **Credit** MC, V.

For more than two decades, the wife-and-husband team at Sushi-Say have been dishing up an ample selection of Japanese staples at this inconspicuous Willesden haunt. Little changes, apart from the odd lick of paint, but this is no bad thing. Locals come back time and again, so the dining room is almost always full; even if you're planning on eating early, it's worth booking. The chef/proprietor mans the counter at the front, where he crafts all manner of sushi, thickly slicing the faultlessly fresh fish. His wife manages the narrow monochrome dining room with confident authority: greeting regulars, taking orders and overseeing a team of young waiting staff. The extensive menu includes sushi, tempura, noodles, grilled fish, simmered dishes – name any form of classic Japanese cooking, and Sushi-Say probably does it. From the specials list, a generous portion of silky squid sashimi was accompanied by soy-splashed grated horseradish (not wasabi), which had a nose-tingling effect. From the list of reasonably priced set lunches, the salt-grilled mackerel was sweet-fleshed and also large. A cup of cold saké made a decent accompaniment.

Babies and children welcome: high chairs. Booking advisable. Separate room for parties, seats 8. Takeaway service. Vegetarian menu.

Jewish

London's Jewish dining scene has received a fillip in the past year with the opening of **Restaurant 1701**, situated in the old Jewish quarter to the east of the City. Like its near-neighbour **Bevis Marks the Restaurant**, and even occupying Bevis Marks's former site, 1701 is an upmarket establishment with excellent service and a talented kitchen team that is seeking to update traditional Jewish cookery. We wish it well, and the signs are promising.

This year's other new entry, the **Kitchen**, is located in the Jewish heartland of north-west London. Although it has chicken soup with matzo balls, and shakshuka (baked eggs, peppers and tomatoes – a North African dish popular in Israel) on its menu, it also follows the trend of most London Jewish restaurants in recent years: offering kosher versions of dishes from across the world. Hence, at **Isola Bella** or **White Fish** you might choose a Thai noodle dish, while a meal at **SoYo** could consist of filled crêpes or pasta – and **La Fiesta** majors in South American grills.

All the restaurants listed here follow the strict rules of kashrut – so, no mixing of meat and dairy, no pork and no shellfish.

Central

City

Bevis Marks the Restaurant
3 Middlesex Street, E1 7AA (7247 5474, www.bevismarkstherestaurant.com). Aldgate tube or Liverpool Street tube/rail. **Lunch served** noon-2.15pm Mon-Fri. **Dinner served** 5.30-9pm Mon-Thur. **Main courses** £16.50-£27.95. **Credit** AmEx, MC, V.
Once a Jewish neighbourhood, the Petticoat Lane district is now a centre of Tower Hamlets' Bangladeshi population – but Bevis Marks is a reminder of the old days. Outside, bustling market stalls sell Indian cottons; inside, all is calm. The spacious, light main section has high ceilings, white linen and sparkling glass. There's also an attractive bar area serving traditional snacks, burgers and sandwiches. Service is attentive, as befits a restaurant serving high-class modern Jewish cuisine. Start with creamy chopped liver with pear and cranberry chutney; beetroot-cured gravadlax; duck and mushroom terrine; or vegetarian artichoke borekas with chestnut pesto. Main courses are substantial yet stylish. Traditional salt beef is succulent, though comes with overly chunky chips, as does the ribeye. Rosemary-crusted lamb chops (not quite rare enough) had a rich burgundy sauce and sweet-potato mash. Fish options include blackened cod, and maple-glazed salmon. Non-dairy desserts are a speciality. Plum and almond tart certainly passes muster, and the restaurant still serves its 'can't believe it's not cream' vanilla ice-cream. With such careful presentation and reliable cooking, this edge-of-City treasure appeals to kosher diners – but with such high prices, can it attract others?
Available for hire. Babies and children welcome: high chairs. Booking advisable lunch. Disabled: toilet. Kosher supervised (Shephardi). Separate rooms for parties, seating 8 and 24. Tables outdoors (4, pavement). Takeaway service. **Map 12 R6.**

Restaurant 1701 NEW
Bevis Marks Synagogue, Bevis Marks, EC3A 5DQ (7621 1701, www.restaurant1701.co.uk). Aldgate tube or Liverpool Street tube/rail. **Breakfast served** 7.30-9.30am, **lunch served** noon-2pm Mon-Fri. **Dinner served** 6-10.15pm Tue-Thur. **Main courses** £16.95-£28.95. **Credit** AmEx, MC, V.
Newly opened in summer 2013, Restaurant 1701 has a star kitchen team creating high-end cuisine based on traditional Jewish cookery. Decor is suitably smart and minimalist, with one red flower on each linen tablecloth. Windows overlook the brass chandeliers of the adjacent synagogue (founded in 1701, hence the name). Dishes on the concise menu (19 choices in all) are well-executed, with due attention given not only to appearance but also depth of flavour. Chopped liver tasted 'like grandma's' – intensely flavoured yet lighter in texture; a Moroccan-style pastilla was filled with luscious braised lamb, garnished with parsnip purée and raisin jus. Deeply flavourful hay-smoked short ribs with celeriac purée and pomegranate jus completely outshone its downbeat title 'flanken' (boiled beef). Afghan-inspired palau kabuli was juicy pan-fried duck breast with little confit cubes of the meat, puffed wild rice and nettle risotto. Desserts were less successful: black olive 'soil' didn't improve an orange semolina cake, but sachertorte delivered the right intensity of chocolate with dots of salted caramel and an ice-cream flavoured with cherry stones. While prices are high, service is impeccable and presentation outstanding (if over-elaborate, to some tastes). This venture deserves to succeed – it just needs word to get out.
Available for hire. Babies and children admitted. Booking advisable. Disabled: lift; toilet. Kosher supervised (Shephardi). **Map 12 R6.**

Marylebone

Reubens
79 Baker Street, W1U 6RG (7486 0035, www.reubensrestaurant.co.uk). Baker Street tube. **Lunch served** 11.30am-4pm Mon-Thur; 11.30am-3pm Fri. **Dinner served** 5.30-10pm Mon-Thur. **Meals served** 11.30am-10pm Sun. **Main courses** £9-£29. **Minimum** (restaurant) £10. **Credit** MC, V.

Menu

Baklava: filo pastry layered with almonds or pistachios and soaked in scented syrup.
Borekas: triangles of filo pastry with savoury fillings such as cheese or spinach.
Borscht: a classic beetroot soup served either hot or cold, often with sour cream.
Challah or **cholla:** egg-rich, slightly sweet plaited bread for the Sabbath.
Chicken soup: a clear, golden broth made from chicken and vegetables.
Cholent: a hearty, long-simmered bean, vegetable and (sometimes) meat stew, traditionally served for the Sabbath.
Chopped liver: chicken or calf's liver fried with onions, finely chopped and mixed with hard-boiled egg and chicken fat. Served cold, often with extra egg and onions.
Chrane or **chrain:** a pungent sauce made from grated horseradish and beetroot, served with cold fish.
Cigars: rolls of filo pastry with a sweet or savoury filling.
Falafel: spicy, deep-fried balls of ground chickpeas, served with houmous and tahini (sesame paste).
Gefilte fish: white fish minced with onions, made into balls and poached or fried; served cold. The sweetened version is Polish.
Kataifi or **konafa:** shredded filo pastry wrapped around a nut or cheese filling, soaked in syrup.
Kibbe, kuba, kooba, kubbeh or **kobeiba:** oval patties, handmade from a shell of crushed wheat (bulgar) filled with minced meat, pine nuts and spices. Shaping and filling the shells before frying is the skill.
Knaidlach or **kneidlach:** dumplings made from matzo (qv) meal and eggs, poached until they float 'like clouds' in chicken soup.
Kreplach: pockets of noodle dough filled with meat and served in soup, or with sweet fillings and eaten with sour cream.
Laffa: large puffy pitta bread used to enclose falafel or shwarma (qv).
Latkes: grated potato mixed with egg and fried into crisp pancakes.
Lockshen: egg noodles boiled and served in soup. When cold, they can be mixed with egg, sugar and cinnamon and baked into a pudding.
Matzo or **matzah:** flat squares of unleavened bread. When ground into meal, it is used to make a crisp coating for fish or schnitzel.
Parev or **parve:** a term describing food that is neither meat nor dairy.
Rugelach: crescent-shaped biscuits made from a rich, cream cheese pastry, filled with nuts, jam or chocolate. Popular in Israel and the US.
Shwarma: layers of lamb or turkey, cooked on a spit, served with pitta.
Worsht: beef salami, sliced thinly to eat raw, but usually cut in thick pieces and fried when served with eggs or chips.

With the closure of nearby Deli West One, Reubens is again the only kosher eaterie in the West End – and it knows it. Nevertheless, this is a reliable and predictable restaurant, so tables are packed with lunchtime diners happy with the Ashkenazi food. In the rush to serve up plates of chopped liver and salt beef sandwiches, there are few smiles; customers are dealt with, rather than welcomed. But the food remains consistent: grills, burgers and shwarma freshly cooked with appealing salads and chips. The ground-floor cafeteria area has cold blue walls, granite tables and a wide menu choice. The basement restaurant is warmer, with linen tablecloths and some more adventurous dishes. Here, waiters bring magret of duck, steak diane, beef wellington or sushi-grade tuna. Yet the whole place still has the feel of diners discussing business, rather than food. On our visit, the chargrilled lamb chops were so succulent we wanted to pick up the bones; generously stuffed lean beef sandwiches were the most popular choice. After soup and a large main course, few people have the appetite for apple strudel or lockshen pudding, but you might feel tempted by a warm chocolate fondant.
Available for hire. Babies and children welcome: children's menu; high chairs. Booking advisable. Kosher supervised (Shephardi). Separate room for parties, seats 50. Tables outdoors (3, pavement). Takeaway service. **Map 3 G5.**

West
Shepherd's Bush

Isola Bella
Westfield London, W12 7SL (8740 6611, www.isolabella.co.uk). Wood Lane tube. **Meals served** *Summer* 10am-10pm Mon-Thur, Sun; 10am-5pm Fri. *Winter* 10am-10pm Mon-Thur, Sun; 10am-5pm Fri; 6-10pm Sat. **Main courses** £16-£21. **Set meal** (noon-6pm) £18 3 courses. **Credit** AmEx, MC, V.
Set in the 'Village' area of Westfield shopping centre, this new branch of dairy favourite Isola Bella is a café-restaurant that doesn't advertise that it's kashrut. The management aims to attract an all-day clientele looking for a refuge from the frenetic shopping. Bright and open, not overcrowded and with friendly staff, this outlet offers a similarly wide menu to the Golders Green original: too wide, according to some. Everything is on a grand scale: from the sandwiches to the plates of giant salads and piled-high portions of pasta. Because an abundance of vegetables forms the base of almost all the dishes, Thai-inspired noodles seemed little different from Italian penne – the saucing needs more finesse. But the three-course lunch special, from a surprisingly unrestricted menu, is good value at £18. Half-portion starter salads were colourful and appetising, and whole grilled sea bass was a treat: crisp skin and moist flesh with Asian soy dressing. Chips were plentiful and crunchy, but fried pastries with noodles seemed oil-heavy. Desserts, too, come in many guises. Ice-cream is so-so, though the cakes are tempting, especially if you like white chocolate, meringue and cream.
Available for hire. Babies and children welcome: children's menu; high chairs; nappy-changing facilities. Booking advisable. Disabled: lift; toilet. Kosher supervised (Beth Din). Separate room for parties, seats 50. Takeaway service. Vegetarian menu. **Map 20 C1.**
For branch see index.

North West
Golders Green

La Fiesta
235 Golders Green Road, NW11 9ES (8458 0444, www.lafiestalondon.co.uk). Brent Cross tube. **Dinner served** 6-11pm Mon-Thur. **Meals served** noon-11pm Sun. **Main courses** £16-£50. **Credit** MC, V.
The reputation of this South American grill is spreading, and on a Monday evening it was hard to get a table. The mainly young crowd comes for one thing: the meat; this is certainly no place for vegetarians. Starters and desserts are unexceptional, but the sizzling beef and lamb are top grade. There are soups and empanadas to start, and also a complimentary salad. Beef and lamb are grilled to order and brought out on a brazier of hot coals – perfect for giving an extra grill to a slightly underdone cut, or simply to keep half your order hot. Chicken could get an additional sizzle and you can divide the four juicy lamb chops so they don't get cold. Steaks are sold according to weight, and the accompanying bowls of chips are large enough for even the hungriest teenager. The pleasant, attentive staff are happy to advise on the fattier cuts, such as asado ribs, and to make sure the meat is cooked to the requested degree. La Fiesta isn't an intimate spot – the wooden tables are fairly close together and there's a buzz of conversation – but if you want the best kosher meat, this is where to come.
Available for hire. Babies and children welcome: children's menu; high chairs. Booking advisable. Disabled: toilet. Kosher supervised (Beth Din). Takeaway service.

SoYo

94 Golders Green Road, NW11 8HB (8458 8788, http://so-yo.co.uk). Golders Green tube. **Meals served** 8.30am-midnight Mon-Thur, Sun; 8.30am-1hr before Sabbath Fri; 11pm-3am Sat. **Main courses** £7-£20. **Credit** AmEx, MC, V.

With a few tables outside and a packed interior, this dairy restaurant has become a lively spot. Israeli breakfast is served until 3pm and is as good as you'll get in Tel Aviv, including freshly squeezed juice, eggs and a platter of cheeses, avocado, and so on. Don't expect much space or quiet; waitresses squeeze between closely set tables, illuminated by a 'chandelier' made of pink ice-cream spoons. We arrived early for lunch and ordered two soups: broccoli and mushroom, both thick and tasty. Crêpes are generous, filled with almost anything from the menu (ours was spinach and parmesan). The own-made pasta options looked good; sandwiches, using freshly baked bread, are imaginative. 'Choose your own' salads come with a mix of leaves, a base of pasta, potato or couscous, roasted vegetables, cheeses and a few dozen other options. Desserts are geared towards sweet-toothed diners. Pancakes and soufflés arrive heavily sugared; less syrupy is the signature FroYo (yoghurt), topped with nuts or a choice of 14 different fruits. 'Naughty toppings' will take you into the realm of jelly beans, chocolate bits and cookies. Service is fast, but attention to detail is lacking.

Available for hire. Babies and children welcome: children's menu; high chairs; nappy-changing facilities. Booking advisable. Kosher supervised (Federation). Separate room for parties, seats 50. Tables outdoors (4, pavement). Takeaway service.

Hendon

White Fish

10-12 Bell Lane, NW4 2AD (8202 8780, www.whitefishrestaurant.co.uk). Hendon Central tube. **Lunch served** noon-2.30pm, **dinner served** 5-10.30pm Mon-Thur. **Meals served** noon-10.30pm Sun. **Main courses** £9.95-£20. **Set lunch** (Mon-Thur) £9.95 1 course, £11.95 2 courses; (Sun) £14.95 2 courses. **Credit** AmEx, MC, V.

This takeaway and restaurant is aiming at two distinct types of clientele: those who enjoy traditional fish and chips; and more adventurous diners who order from the Thai menu. The walls are adorned with stylish old photos of Billingsgate fish market. Tables (crowded later in the evening) are dark and serviceable. Cod and haddock can be fried in batter or tastier matzo meal (which adds crispness) and come with good chunky chips and mushy peas. Starters of vegetable spring rolls or soup shouldn't fill you up too much for the large main-course portions. If you want to push the boat out, order a whole grilled dover sole (£30) or halibut (£20); takeaway prices are more modest. For vegetarians, there are pasta options and salads, though most of the Thai or spiced dishes feature cod with appealing looking noodles and sauces. From a small choice of desserts, profiteroles had a good custardy filling but an overly sweet milk-chocolate topping – a shame, as this is a dairy venue that could make a feature of creamy puds. Service is pleasant and the owners attentive and charming.

Available for hire. Babies and children welcome: children's menu; high chairs. Booking advisable. Kosher supervised (Beth Din). Takeaway service; delivery service (over £15 within 2-mile radius).

Outer London

Edgware, Middlesex

Kitchen NEW

16 The Promenade, Edgware, Middx HA8 7JZ (8905 4488, www.thekitchen-restaurant.co.uk). Edgware tube. **Meals served** noon-11pm Mon-Thur, Sun; 10am-3pm Fri. **Main courses** £11-£16. **Credit** MC, V.

A newcomer to Edgware's bustling kosher scene, the Kitchen occupies a corner site with a light, wooden interior. Slate-tiled walls, comfortable leather chairs and more light (sparkling from the ceiling) complete the picture. The menu, brought by pleasant staff, is extensive – ranging from brunch to main meals, and ending with a selection of teas. This is a hotspot for meat eaters, offering chicken wings or satay for starters, as well as rather weak 'Jewish penicillin' (chicken soup with matzo balls). Burgers are juicy and filling, served with good chips; grills include lamb chops, kebabs and steak. A rack of smokehouse short ribs was tender yet overwhelmed by spicy barbecue sauce. You could try a burger with goose breast, 'fakon' (fake bacon) or 'soya cheese' in sandwiches. More tempting options include shakshuka (baked eggs, peppers and tomatoes), chimichurri steak salad or grilled sea bass. Portions are generous, so dessert might not appeal – and non-dairy tiramisu or crème brûlée seem ill-conceived. Chocolate soufflé is a possibility, though, and a lemon and passion-fruit sorbet made a refreshing end to an enjoyable meal.

Available for hire. Babies and children welcome: children's menu; high chairs; nappy-changing facilities. Booking advisable Sun. Disabled: toilet. Kosher supervised (Beth Din). Takeaway service.

JEWISH

Restaurant 1701. See p173.

Korean

London has been on the cusp of a Korean food trend for years now, but in 2013 it finally arrived. From spicy fried chicken at fashionable chicken joints such as **Wishbone** (*p237*) to kimchi burgers and tacos on the street food scene, Korean-influenced dishes are popping up all over the capital. Also newly arrived are **Kimchee to Go** (togo.kimchee.uk.com), with branches on New Oxford Street and the Strand, offering bento-like dosirak, noodle soups and bibimbap to take away, and **Jubo**, with its hot and spicy chicken wings. So, more Londoners are definitely getting the chance to stumble across this rich and varied cuisine. Culinary adventurers and pickled-cabbage lovers don't have to spend a fortune or travel far from the centre of town to find a quality Korean restaurant. There's a cluster in the West End: **Koba** tops the pile, but **Naru** comes up trumps too. But for the most authentic Korean cookery, and no end of free side dishes (panch'an), you'll need to head to 'Korea Town' in New Malden, on the city's south-western outskirts. Thousands of South Koreans have settled in the locality, and many businesses have their signs written in Hangul script as well as English. **Jee Cee Neh**, **Korea House** and **Korean Garden** are our favourites, though the excellent **Cah Chi** in nearby Raynes Park is worth a visit too.

Central
City

Ceena
13 St Bride Street, EC4A 4AS (7936 4941, www.ceena.co). City Thameslink rail or Farringdon tube/rail or bus 17, 45, 46, 63. **Meals served** 11.30am-9.30pm Mon-Fri. **Main courses** £5.30-£16. **Set meal** £15-£20 3 courses. **Credit** AmEx, MC, V.
In a part of town where dining is fast and service is expected to be faster, Ceena deliberately brands itself as a Korean fast-food restaurant. The takeaway business is just as important as the eat-in trade, and packaging is eco-friendly. On an evening visit, the surrounding City pubs were spilling over with suits supping pints, but the high stools next to the horseshoe-shaped counter were all but empty. We suspect it's more popular for lunch than dinner. The shortish menu consists of the usual roll-call of barbecue dishes, pancakes and bibimbap, along with a couple of fusion-style salads. The simple flavour of our nokdoo (mung bean) pancake – crisp-coated and soft-middled – was complemented well by a sharp-edged soy and vinegar dipping sauce. Beef dolsot bibimbap was an ample portion, complete with a raw egg cracked in the centre, but the toppings were a little skimpy. The food at Ceena may be more filling than refined,

but it's an appealing alternative to the standard office-worker lunch of packaged sandwiches and supermarket sushi. For a change from the usual selection of soft drinks, try the dried persimmon and cinnamon punch.
Available for hire. Booking advisable. Separate room for parties, seats 8. Tables outdoors (3, pavement). Takeaway service; delivery service (over £15 within 2-mile radius). Map 11 N6.

Covent Garden

Naru
230 Shaftesbury Avenue, WC2H 8EG (7379 7962, www.narurestaurant.com). Tottenham Court Road tube. **Lunch served** noon-3pm, **dinner served** 5.30-10.30pm Mon-Sat. **Main courses** £8-£13. **Set dinner** £24.50-£34.50 3 courses. **Credit** MC, V.
Naru puts more emphasis on cheffy presentation than most Korean restaurants, with zigzagged sauces and stacked ingredients. It's not a matter of style over substance, though – this is a solid venue for quality Korean classics, with a few innovative touches. Conspicuously absent from the dining room, which is adorned with wood-framed Hangul calligraphy and paper lanterns, are any table-top barbecues. Instead, the meat and seafood are grilled in the kitchen, then brought sizzling and succulent to the table. The kalbi beef in our set lunch arrived medium-rare. Served on a portable brazier, it

continued to cook in its delicious sweet and savoury juices, along with a thick slice of sweet onion. The result? Some of the best kalbi we've had in London. The lunch also included miyeokguk, a nutritious broth packed with seaweed, as well as sticky rice, crunchy spinach with sesame namul, and lightly pickled radish kimchi – for £13.50. Japch'ae, filled with colourful veg and topped with shredded egg white, was deep and earthy in flavour, and came with less sesame oil than you tend to find elsewhere. Unusually, barley tea isn't available, though Korean beer is.
Babies and children admitted. Booking advisable Thur-Sat. Takeaway service. Vegan dishes. Vegetarian menu. Map 18 D2.

Fitzrovia

★ Koba
11 Rathbone Street, W1T 1NA (7580 8825). Goodge Street or Tottenham Court Road tube. **Lunch served** noon-2.30pm Mon-Sat. **Dinner served** 6-10.30pm daily. **Main courses** £8.50-£12. **Set lunch** £6.50-£11.50. **Set meal** £25-£35. **Credit** AmEx, MC, V.
Koba has remained one of the strongest players on the West End Korean scene since opening in 2005 – we've yet to have a disappointing meal here. Barbecue meats such as beef kalbi or bulgogi are well marinated, and grilled at the table by efficient staff. Barbecued squid was fresh as a daisy, with

just the right amount of tongue-tingling heat in the vibrant red sauce. Stews make a sound choice too, with umami-rich stocks and accompanying bowls of pearly rice. The spicy, slow-simmered short rib hotpot comes with chinese cabbage and sweet potato noodles as well as chunky pieces of beef, while the soft tofu stew is packed with seafood slivers. As this is Fitzrovia rather than K-town (New Malden), there's no free panch'an, and the namul is a little pricey at £5.90. This is our only quibble, however. Service is polished but not too formal, and the dark, modern-East-Asian-meets-industrial interior is slick, making Koba an ideal spot for anything from a business lunch (set meals start at £6.50) to a casual dinner. Drinks include Korean beers, soju and a short wine list.

Babies and children welcome: high chairs. Booking advisable. Separate room for parties, seats 25. Takeaway service. **Map 17 B1.**

Holborn

Asadal

227 High Holborn, WC1V 7DA (7430 9006, www.asadal.co.uk). Holborn tube. **Lunch served** noon-2.30pm daily. **Dinner served** 6-10.30pm Mon-Sat; 6-10pm Sun. **Main courses** £8-£30. **Set lunch** £10-£15. **Set dinner** £20-£35 per person (minimum 2). **Credit** AmEx, MC, V.
With a discreet entrance just by Holborn station, Asadal has been the go-to venue for Korean food fans in central London for many years. On a Friday night, the stairs leading down to the dark, spacious basement dining room were filled with hopeful diners queuing to get a table. The busy restaurant took its toll on the staff, who weren't as efficient as we've known them to be in the past. This led to a

school-boy error with our bulgogi barbecued beef: the table-top grill was not heated before the meat was added, leading to a slightly stewed result – though the flavours were still as they should be. With the barbecue now in full swing, pork belly was much more successful: gently charred, with a tender centre and a decent line of buttery fat along one side. A bowl of yukkaejang was pleasingly spicy and sour from the well-aged cabbage kimchi it contained. To finish, traditional, milky-coloured, persimmon punch was cool, refreshing and spiked with powdered cinnamon. Asadal wasn't on top form this time, but it certainly still draws a crowd.

Babies and children welcome: high chairs. Booking advisable. Disabled: lift; toilet. Separate room for parties, seats 12. Takeaway service. Vegan dishes. **Map 18 E2.**

Soho

★ Bi Bim Bap

11 Greek Street, W1D 4DJ (7287 3434, www.bibimbapsoho.com). Tottenham Court Road tube. **Lunch served** noon-2.30pm, **dinner served** 6-10.30pm Mon-Fri. **Meals served** noon-10.30pm Sat. **Main courses** £6.45-£9.95. **Credit** MC, V.
Bright colours, Ikea-style furniture and walls plastered with Polaroid snaps of happy diners mark Bi Bim Bap as a youngsters' hangout. It's more suited to an after-work pit stop than a lingering meal; service is quick and the food filling. There are Korean beers and spirits to try as well. As the name suggests, Bi Bim Bap's big draw is the stone-bowl rice dish of the same name – served in ten varieties. Classics include beef, chilli chicken, spicy pork or seafood, but veggies are well catered for too, with

tofu, mushroom, or brown rice, g____ versions on offer. Some say t____ bibimbap is how well it's mixe____ let you do the honours here (as ____ own koch'ujang and doenjang sauces). ____ experience, the results have always been sound, with crisp rice at the bottom and a decent amount of toppings to blend through. Other dishes, including fried noodles, jeon pancakes and salads, can be more of a mixed bag. The wrappers on our vegetable dumplings seemed more air-dried than crisp-fried, though the chilli-speckled dipping sauce had plenty of flavour.

Babies and children admitted. Bookings not accepted dinner Fri, Sat. Takeaway service. **Map 17 C3.**

Nara

9 D'Arblay Street, W1F 8DR (7287 2224, www.nararestaurant.co.uk). Oxford Circus or Tottenham Court Road tube. **Lunch served** noon-3pm, **dinner served** 6-10.30pm daily. **Main courses** £9.50-£14.50. **Set lunch** £7.50. **Set dinner** £11.50. **Credit** AmEx, MC, V.
Although it also serves Japanese dishes, it's the Korean food that is the main draw here. Located just off Oxford Street, it's well placed for refuelling during a day of shopping. The simple dining room has a relaxed, informal feel. Adding to its appeal, this is one of few central London Korean restaurants to offer free panch'an – on this occasion, sweet pickled cucumber, seasoned beansprouts and mung bean jelly. Portion sizes can be generous – witness a big bowl of manduguk, filled with garlicky pork dumplings, sweet shrimp, squid and glass noodles. Barbecue dishes are also popular, such as juicy kabli, eaten wrapped in lettuce leaves

Asadal

Bi Bim Bap. See p177.

with chunky, piquant ssamjang and finely shredded sweet-and-sour spring onions. Succulent chicken slices, carefully cooked at the table-top electric grill, glistened invitingly with sticky chilli sauce. If you fancy something a little more unusual, Nara offers hard-to-find ingredients such as Korean black pudding (soondae) served stir-fried or in soup, and savoury, sautéed bracken stalks (kosari namul). Korean beer is the ideal accompaniment.
Babies and children admitted: high chairs. Takeaway service. Vegetarian menu. **Map 17 B3**.

South West
Raynes Park

★ Cah Chi `HOT 50`
34 Durham Road, SW20 0TW (8947 1081, www.cahchi.com). Raynes Park rail or bus 57, 131. **Lunch served** noon-2.30pm, **dinner served** 5-10.30pm Tue-Fri. **Meals served** noon-10.30pm Sat, Sun. **Main courses** £15-£18. **Set dinner** £20 3 courses. **Corkage** (wine only) £3. **Credit** MC, V.
There's a real warmth to this residential Raynes Park restaurant, which pulls an appreciative crowd of Eastern and Western diners. Even on a cold, dark evening, the dining room feels light and bright – and comfortably cosy. The smiling staff are happy to talk you through a menu that contains more than just the standard array of barbecues, stews and stir-fries. We're always impressed by the depth and complexity of the flavours here, and our most recent visit was no exception. Cah Chi is known for its excellent soondae: black pudding stuffed with cellophane noodles. You can have it either au naturel in thick slices with a little salt for dipping, or stir-fried with cabbage, onion and chilli on the table-top grill. The latter version was a glorious combination of textures and flavours, including deeply savoury perilla leaves (kkaennip). Also first-rate was a side dish of raw, pickled squid strands in a silken, sweet, spicy koch'ujang-based sauce; the seafood had just the right amount of resistance as you bit into it. Even the complimentary panch'an are better than average, with subtle own-made kimchi and sweet, nutty adzuki beans a regular feature. Without doubt, this is one of the best Korean restaurants in the UK.
Babies and children welcome: high chairs. Booking advisable. Separate room for parties, seats 18. Takeaway service.
For branch see index.

South
Battersea

Hana `NEW`
60 Battersea Rise, SW11 1EG (7228 2496, www.hanakorean.co.uk). Clapham Junction rail. **Lunch served** noon-2.30pm Mon-Thur. **Dinner served** 5.30-10.30pm Mon-Thur; 5.30-11.30pm Fri. **Meals served** noon-11.30pm Sat; noon-11pm Sun. **Main courses** £7.90-£15.50. **Set lunch** (Mon-Thur) £5.95-£8.95. **No credit cards.**
The twin poles of Korean restaurants are New Malden in Surrey and the West End, but there's little that's good between the two. This small, family-run restaurant – a good-looking, split-level room with dark wood and pretty hanging lamps – bridges that gap. It seems aimed at non-Koreans: the menu is written in English, with no Hangul (Korean script). Service is notably smiling and on the ball. Our meal started well with a generous trio of mandu (steamed dumplings) containing a moist, crunchy pork and vegetable filling. Mains feature the usual hotpots, barbecues, and rice and noodle dishes, including a decent dolsot bibimbap – a piping-hot stone bowl filled with rice, vegetables, egg, chilli paste and raw slivers of beef that cook as they're stirred together. Other versions feature prawn, chicken or flying fish roe. Bossam, cold slices of pork belly served with blanched chinese cabbage, was insipid despite a spicy shrimp sauce and radish kimchi – and the leaves were too thick to wrap around the meat. The drinks list is better than at many Korean restaurants, covering the expected Hite beer and soju, but also decent wines and novelties such as bokbunja ju, a Korean fruit wine that some think improves 'male stamina'.
Babies and children welcome: high chairs; nappy-changing facilities. Takeaway service. Vegetarian menu. **Map 21 C4**.

East
Shoreditch

★ Jubo `NEW`
68 Rivington Street, EC2A 3AY (7033 0198, www.jubolondon.com). Old Street tube/rail. **Meals served** 6pm-midnight Tue-Thur; 7pm-late Fri, Sat. **Main courses** £4.50-£6.50. **Set meal** £10 2 courses (incl bottle of beer), £35 platter (minimum 2 people). **Credit** MC, V.
We'd been predicting Korean food as the big trend for 2013, and here it is – in just one of its many forms. This version is the eat-with-fingers, messy, New York dude-food type of Korean cooking. The dishes are served in disposable paper trays; tables are shared and no bookings are taken. Jubo feels improvised, like a pop-up, but we're assured it's here to stay. The dining area occupies one end of the long-established Bedroom Bar, so good cocktails are on hand. Korean fried chicken (KFC) is seasoned then fried twice, which produces a slightly crunchier coating that complements strong-flavoured or gloopy sauces. It goes well with beer and is an on-trend dish right now. At Jubo, the options are boneless thigh strips, or messier, bone-in wings. Their texture certainly beats the other KFC; the soy/garlic dressing was zesty, the hot/sweet sauce thick and syrupy. Steamed buns are firm rather than delicate, delivered with fillings such as slow-cooked

pork belly, slow-braised beef or a vegetarian mushroom filling with hoisin sauce. Best of all were the pickles – both the white radish and shiitake mushroom pickles had complex, fruity flavours. Service is chummy, prices low.

Available for hire. Bookings not accepted. Disabled: toilet. **Map 6 R4.**

North
Finsbury Park

Dotori

3 Stroud Green Road, N4 2DQ (7263 3562). Finsbury Park tube/rail. **Lunch served** noon-2.50pm Tue-Sat. **Dinner served** 5-10.30pm Tue-Sat; 4.30-10pm Sun. **Main courses** £6.50-£11. **Set meal** £25 4 courses. **Credit** MC, V.
This restaurant next to Finsbury Park station established its reputation soon after opening in 2008. It's still nigh on impossible to get a table without booking – even on our early-evening midweek visit, several hopeful diners were turned away. All's not lost if you don't bag a seat, however, as they do offer takeaway. The dining room – like the menu – blends Korean and Japanese influences; there's a Shinto lantern by the door, and Hangul calligraphy and Korean masks on the walls. Prices are impressively low: a capacious bowl of yukkaejang was a mere £3.50. Thick with chilli flakes, the broth contained a generous quantity of deliciously tender shredded beef. A mountain of bokum bap (fried rice) came studded with crisp-fried pork belly pieces, spring onions and scrambled egg. The plump grains were redolent with ground black pepper and sesame oil. The Japanese side of the menu offers sushi, sashimi, tempura and donburi dishes. Dotori isn't known for its sparkling service, but we found the staff warm and efficient. Even on an off-day, it's hard not to be forgiving, thanks to the well-prepared and well-priced food.

Babies and children admitted. Booking advisable dinner. Takeaway service. Vegetarian menu.

Outer London
New Malden, Surrey

Jee Cee Neh

74 Burlington Road, New Malden, Surrey KT3 4NU (8942 0682). New Malden rail. **Lunch served** noon-3pm, **dinner served** 6-11pm Mon-Wed, Fri. **Meals served** 11am-11pm Sat, Sun. **Main courses** £7-£13. **Credit** (over £20) MC, V.
Translating as 'my neighbour Jee', Jee Cee Neh is an apt moniker for this restaurant, which has a decidedly homespun feel. It's often packed, with a mix of Korean and Western customers, and at weekends is a popular family lunch spot. Like the venue, the authentic dishes are homely and unpretentious. Japch'ae, for example, comes with less finely cut batons of veg than you'd get in central London, plus plenty of earthy flavour – and succulent beef strips. As with most New Malden Korean restaurants, barley tea and a few side dishes come free with your meal; the latter included boiled carrot and potato slices in koch'ujang chilli sauce, crunchy, salted mung beansprouts and a complex, well-aged kimchi. Barbecue dishes make a good choice here, as do stews such as spicy kimchi and pork or soft tofu and seafood, served with boiled rice. We also tried kang pung gi, a dish that

Hana

Menu

Chilli appears at every opportunity on Korean menus. Other common ingredients include soy sauce (different to both the Chinese and Japanese varieties), sesame oil, sugar, sesame seeds, garlic, ginger and various fermented soy bean pastes. Until the late 1970s, eating meat was a luxury in Korea, so the quality of vegetarian dishes is high.

Given the spicy nature and overall flavour of Korean food, drinks such as chilled lager or vodka-like **soju/shoju** are the best matches. A wonderful non-alcoholic alternative that's almost always available, although not always listed on the menu, is barley tea (**porich'a/borich'a**). Often served free of charge, it has a light, dry taste that works perfectly with the food. Korean restaurants don't usually offer desserts, though some serve orange or watermelon with the bill.

Spellings on menus vary hugely; we have given the most common.

Bibimbap or **pibimbap**: rice, vegetables and meat with a raw/fried egg dropped on top, often served in a hot stone bowl.
Bindaedok, **bindaedoek** or **pindaetteok**: a mung bean pancake.
Bokum: a stir-fried dish, usually including chilli.
Bulgogi or **pulgogi**: thin slices of beef marinated in pear sap (or a similar sweet dressing) and barbecued at the table; often eaten rolled in a lettuce leaf with shredded spring onion and fermented bean paste.
Chang, **jang** or **denjang**: various fermented soy bean pastes.
Chapch'ae or **chap chee**: mixed vegetables and beef cooked with transparent vermicelli or noodles.
Cheon, **jeon** or **jon**: meaning 'something flat'; this can range from a pancake containing vegetables, meat or seafood, to thinly sliced vegetables, beancurd or other ingredients, in a light batter.
Cheyuk: pork.
Chigae or **jigae**: a hot stew that contains fermented bean paste and chillies.
Denjang or **doenjang**: see chang.
Gim or **kim**: dried seaweed, toasted and seasoned with salt and sesame oil.
Gu shul pan: a traditional lacquered tray that has nine compartments containing individual appetisers.
Hobak chun or **hobak jun**: sliced marrow in a light egg batter.
Japch'ae, **japchae** or **jap chee**: alternative spellings for chapch'ae (qv).
Jjim: fish or meat stewed for a long time in soy sauce, sugar and garlic.

Jeongol or **chungol**: casserole.
Kalbi, **galbi** or **kalbee**: beef spare ribs, marinated and barbecued.
Kimchi, **kim chee** or **kimch'i**: fermented pickled vegetables, usually chinese cabbage, white radishes, cucumber or greens, served in a small bowl with a spicy chilli sauce.
Kkaktugi or **kkakttugi**: pickled radish.
Koch'ujang: a hot, red bean paste.
Kook, **gook**, **kuk** or **guk**: soup. Koreans have an enormous variety of soups, from consommé-like liquid to hearty broths of noodles, dumplings, and meat or fish.
Ko sari na mool or **gosari namul**: cooked bracken stalks with sesame seeds.
Mandu kuk, **manduguk** or **man doo kook**: clear soup with steamed meat dumplings.
Naengmyun or **neng myun**: cold noodle dishes, usually featuring thin, elastic buckwheat noodles.
Namul or **na mool**: vegetable side dishes.
Ojingeo: squid.
P'ajeon, **pa jeon** or **pa jun**: flour pancake with spring onions and (usually) seafood.
Panch'an: side dishes; they usually include pickled vegetables, but possibly also tofu, fish, seaweed or beans.
Pap, **bap**, **bab** or **pahb**: cooked rice.
Pokkeum or **pokkm**: stir-fry; common types include **cheyuk pokkeum** (pork) and **ojingeo pokkeum** (squid).
Shinseollo, **shinsonro**, **shinsulro** or **sin sollo**: 'royal casserole'; a meat soup with seaweed, seafood, eggs and vegetables, all of which is cooked at the table.
Soondae or **sundae**: black pudding.
Ssamjang: thick, spicy paste used with food (such as kalbi) that is wrapped in a leaf.
Teoppap or **toppap**: 'on top of rice'; for example, **ojingeo teoppap** is squid served on rice.
Toenjang: seasoned (usually with chilli) soy bean paste.
Tolsot (or **dolsot**) **bibimbap**: tolsot is a sizzling-hot stone bowl that makes the bibimbap (qv) a little crunchy on the sides.
Tteokpokki: bars of compressed rice (tteok is a rice cake) fried on a hotplate with veg and sausages, in a chilli sauce.
Twaeji gogi: pork.
T'wigim, **twigim** or **tuigim**: fish, prawns or vegetables dipped in batter and deep-fried until golden brown.
Yach'ae: vegetables.
Yuk hwe, **yukhoe** or **yukhwoe**: shredded raw beef, strips of pear and egg yolk, served chilled.
Yukkaejang: spicy beef soup.

originated in China: chunks of double-fried chicken thigh, encased (as they should be) in a crisp yet chewy batter. The slick of spicy sauce they were coated in was on the sweet side. Service can be variable, but usually comes with a smile.
Babies and children welcome: high chairs. Separate room for parties, seats 15. Takeaway service.

Korea Garden
73 Kingston Road, New Malden, Surrey KT3 3PB (8336 1208). New Malden rail. **Lunch served** noon-2.30pm, **dinner served** 6-10.30pm Tue-Sat. **Main courses** £6.90-£25. **Credit** MC, V.
Like so many of the Korean eateries in New Malden, Korea Garden sits halfway up an unremarkable residential street. The green plastic signage and generic dish pictures displayed in the window give little indication of the quality of the food here. But once inside, it doesn't take long to work out what the main attraction is. Cooking is done on proper charcoal, which fills the dining room with inviting, smoky smells; glowing embers (carried in from the kitchen by a man wearing washing-up gloves) were set in our table-top barbecue and used to grill thick slices of juicy pork belly. Finely shredded spring onions rubbed with chilli, vinegar and sugar were the perfect foil for the fat-striped meat. Also excellent was a filling soup of shredded beef and chinese cabbage, spiked with plenty of tongue-tingling red chilli and served with sticky rice. The chef is trained in both Korean and French cuisine, which imparts a subtlety to the flavours, and keeps both Korean and Western diners coming back for more. Service may be in broken English at times, but in our experience is always amenable. To drink, there's the usual selection of Korean beers and spirits.
Babies and children admitted. Booking advisable.

Korean House
Ground floor, Falcon House, 257 Burlington Road, New Malden, Surrey KT3 4NE (8942 1188). Motspur Park rail. **Lunch served** noon-3pm Mon, Tue, Thur, Fri. **Dinner served** 6-11pm Mon-Fri. **Meals served** noon-11pm Sat, Sun. **Main courses** £4.50-£59.50. **Credit** MC, V.
Korean House may be plonked on a busy stretch of the Burlington Road, but don't let that put you off – it's worth a visit. The characterful interior is decorated with wooden masks and Korean calligraphy; to one side are a couple of quiet tatami-mat rooms. Service was both gracious and informative. At weekends, the restaurant is full of families sharing communal dishes, while on Thursday and Friday nights, you'll often find crowds of lively Korean salarymen unwinding over a few drinks. The restaurant's name changed in 2012 (it was formerly called Hankook), but the extensive menu is the same as ever, covering the usual barbecues, stews and variations on bibimbap, plus Japanese sushi. In a dish of dubu kimchi, the tangy, stimulating flavour of mature kimchi stir-fried with slices of pork belly was balanced well by cubes of bland boiled tofu. Not available in many Korean establishments is a stew of blood sausage (soondae) and pork offal (including the liver and ears) in a milky, pork broth. It's served with a selection of condiments, such as salted shrimp, chopped garlic, crushed perilla seeds and spicy red chilli paste. Another traditional accompaniment is a cold cup of soju. It's not for the faint-hearted – try, if you dare.
Babies and children welcome: high chairs. Booking essential dinner Fri, Sat. Takeaway service. Vegetarian menu.

Malaysian, Indonesian & Singaporean

'Could do better' is a perennial refrain of commentators on London's Malaysian, Indonesian and Singaporean restaurant scene – but perhaps things are set to change. Given our city's world-leading position as regards the variety and quality of other Asian cuisines it offers; given too the UK's historical links with Malaysia, and Singapore's deserved reputation as a place of gastronomic pilgrimage – we might have expected to find better here. Yet Malaysian restaurants are few in number, with long-running establishments such as **Satay House** and **Rasa Sayang** as the mainstays. Likewise, the exciting blend of cooking styles that makes up Singaporean cuisine is best represented by the rather swish **Singapore Garden** – as it has been for decades. Nevertheless, there have been two notable openings in the past year: Battersea's **Warung Bumbu** has a Balinese chef, and offers passable versions of Indonesian staples beyond the usual nasi goreng and satay; and **Penang!** produces Malaysian street-food standards and might well sprout into a chain. Just one high-profile success could provide the kick-start to bring this exotic and extravagantly flavoured cooking back into the limelight.

Satay House. See p182.

Central
Chinatown

Rasa Sayang
5 Macclesfield Street, W1D 6AY (7734 1382, www.rasasayangfood.com). Leicester Square or Piccadilly Circus tube. **Meals served** noon-10.30pm Mon-Thur, Sun; noon-11.30pm Fri, Sat. **Main courses** £6.90-£17.80. **Credit** AmEx, MC, V.
Make a bee-line here if you miss the hawker (street) food from the Straits, as this bustling café with its low prices reminds us of hot and humid days spent in Penang. We prefer to wait until a seat on the light ground floor becomes available, rather than eating in the dimly lit basement. Friendly staff are on hand to help newcomers with the menu, which is a compilation of the greatest hits of Straits dishes.

'Nibbles' include satay, achar (spicy pickled vegetables in peanut sauce) and roti canai; char kway teow and nasi lemak are more substantial plates. We often order konloh mee – egg noodles served with a dark soy, oyster and mushroom sauce – accompanied by a separate bowl of prawn and chicken won ton. Another favourite is ipoh hor fun: flat noodles with shredded chicken and prawns in a clear chicken broth. Drinks include teh tarik ('pulled tea') and bubble teas. Rasa Sayang translates literally as 'loving feeling', and we certainly left with fond thoughts towards this West End restaurant.

Babies and children admitted. Booking advisable. Separate room for parties, seats 30. Takeaway service. **Map 17 C4**.

Rasa Sayang. See p181.

West
Bayswater

C&R Restaurant
52 Westbourne Grove, W2 5SH (7221 7979, www.cnrrestaurant.co.uk). Bayswater tube. **Meals served** noon-10.30pm Mon, Wed-Fri; noon-11pm Sat; noon-10pm Sun. **Main courses** £7.50-£24. **Set meal** £16 vegetarian, £19 meat per person (minimum 2). **Credit** AmEx, MC, V.
The plain dining room at C&R has slate flooring and grey banquettes; colour is added by red lanterns championing Tiger beer. The waiting staff are a cheery bunch, and most evenings see a contented crowd of diners scrutinising the wide-ranging menu. There aren't many Malaysian restaurants with a menu as long as C&R (at last count, 18 noodle dishes, nine rice options and eight curries), and it trawls other parts of Asia too (thai fish cakes and crispy duck pancakes, for example). A menu this long can be a worrying sign, but the kitchen makes it work. The flavours of curry fish-head hotpot were full on, and we particularly enjoyed the fish eyes. Less hardcore, a huge bowl of kway teow soup (a popular hawker dish featuring broad rice noodles in a clear chicken bouillon), which arrived with choi sum, chicken, prawns and a fish ball, was made more satisfying by a sprinkling of fried minced garlic. Kueh dadar, green pandan crêpes filled with coconut and palm sugar, served warm with coconut milk, make for a mellow ending. Equally popular is the smaller, more café-like offshoot in Soho.
Babies and children welcome: high chairs. Takeaway service; delivery service (within 2-mile radius). **Map 7 B6**.
For branch (C&R Café) see index.

Paddington

Satay House
13 Sale Place, W2 1PX (7723 6763, www.satay-house.co.uk). Edgware Road tube or Paddington tube/rail. **Lunch served** noon-2.30pm, **dinner served** 6-10.30pm daily. **Main courses** £7-£20.50. **Set meal** £16.90-£27.90 per person (minimum 2). **Credit** AmEx, MC, V.
This long-running restaurant (established in 1973) continues to draw people in search of good Malaysian cooking, and benefits from the warmth and smile of Fatizah Shawal, daughter of the original owners. These days, the dining room is modern-looking, with grey and orange-red walls embedded with motifs of the hibiscus flower, but it's still the place to come for traditional offerings such as sambal ikan bilis and petai – sun-dried young anchovies (ikan bilis) served with sator beans (petai) and spicy shrimp paste (sambal) – a dish guaranteed to thrill the taste buds. For a milder kick, try tahu sumbat, deep-fried tofu filled with beansprouts and cucumber, with a piquant nutty sauce. Ikan panggang, whole mackerel stuffed with spices, grilled, then cut into a butterfly shape, had the oily fish and spiciness perfectly offset by a sour tamarind dip – a fond reminder of meals at the beach. To finish, bubur kacang is a comforting mung bean stew with coconut milk and a dash of palm sugar.
Available for hire. Babies and children welcome: high chairs. Booking advisable. Separate room for parties, seats 35. Takeaway service. Vegetarian menu. **Map 8 E5**.

Shepherd's Bush

Penang! NEW
Westfield London, Southern Terrace, W12 7GA (8735 5870, www.eatpenang.co.uk). Wood Lane tube. **Meals served** 11.30am-10pm Mon-Thur, Sun; 11.30am-11pm Fri, Sat. **Main courses** £8.25-£10.50. **No credit cards**.
Penang! (which opened in late 2012) takes its name from the island on the west coast of Malaysia that is renowned for its food. This restaurant is intended to be the first of a chain of outlets. Dining takes place over two floors, and on an outdoor terrace. The high-ceilinged ground floor is a cheerful place to eat, with its bright blue and canary yellow colour scheme; wooden slats and a large mural add yet more jazz to the interior. Service was breezy and

moved in time to rock music (the restaurant's 'Mr Zuhri', whose big-spectacled photo pops up everywhere, is a rock fan). The budget-priced menu covers Malaysian street-food staples including satay, curries and salads, as well as gyoza (Japanese dumplings), sandwiches and even fish and chips with assam pedas ('sour spicy') mayo. The spice dial on a chicken satay was turned too low, though the peanut sauce was pleasant. Curry puffs filled with spiced cubed potato, with mango chutney on the side, were better. Far tastier was a steaming bowl of laksa, containing chicken, prawns and vermicelli in a spicy coconut broth, topped with fresh coriander and red chillies. A pink-coloured drink of coconut milk, glutinous rice and taro, served in a small can, made a very sweet but not unlikeable finish.
Babies and children welcome: high chairs; nappy-changing facilities. Booking advisable. Disabled: toilet. Separate room for parties, seats 30-40. Tables outdoors (10, balcony; 10, terrace). Takeaway service. Vegetarian menu. **Map 20 C1**.

South

Battersea

Warung Bumbu `NEW`
196 Lavender Hill, SW11 1JA (7924 1155, www.warungbumbu.co.uk). Clapham Junction rail. **Lunch served** noon-3pm daily. **Dinner served** 6-10.30pm Mon, Sun; 6-11pm Tue-Sat. **Main courses** £6.99-£10.99. **Credit** AmEx, MC, V.
Take a neighbourhood restaurant, change the signage, hire a Balinese chef, and – faster than you can say rijsttafel – Battersea has a new Indonesian restaurant. The shared bench seating, long black tables and lack of coat hooks doesn't make this the cosiest of places to eat, but it's inexpensive and the cooking is decent. Our best dish was ikan balado: the fish (ikan) crisp and freshly fried, the stir-fried chilli paste (balado) not so pungent that it annihilated the delicacy of the white fish. Beef rendang was slow-cooked to tenderness, and correctly dry and dark, though the spicing was very timid by Indonesian standards. (Warung Bumbu, incidentally, roughly translates as 'spice shack'.) Given the chef's background, it's little wonder the acar kuning – a Balinese vegetable pickle – was an exemplary version, the matchsticks of colourful veg lightly vinegared and a good palliative to

sambal belacan, a spicy chilli and shrimp paste relish. Don't come here expecting a re-creation of your holiday in Ubud, or for tips on how to cook tempeh from the staff, as they are a global pick-and-mix. But with so few reliable Indonesian restaurants in London, one more place that showcases the nation's cooking is always welcome.
Babies and children welcome: high chairs; nappy-changing facilities. Booking advisable Thur-Sat. Disabled: toilet. Separate room for parties, seats 22. Takeaway service. Vegetarian menu. **Map 21 C3**.

North West
Swiss Cottage

★ Singapore Garden `HOT 50`
83 Fairfax Road, NW6 4DY (7624 8233, www.singaporegarden.co.uk). Swiss Cottage tube. **Lunch served** noon-2pm Mon-Sat; noon-4pm Sun. **Dinner served** 6-10pm Mon-Thur, Sun; 6-10.30pm Fri, Sat. **Main courses** £10-£30. **Minimum** (dinner) £15 per person. **Credit** AmEx, MC, V.
Singapore Garden, a beacon of good Straits cooking, continues to draw people from all over town to NW6. The upmarket dining room, decked out with patterned banquettes, wooden flooring and crisp white linen, displays few hints of the restaurant's oriental bent, though waitresses are dressed in traditional batik costumes. After countless meals here, we can vouch for the tender pork satay, in which the meat is slightly caramelised for added flavour. Singapore laksa (here served with rice vermicelli, beansprouts, prawns and fish cake) is another sure-fire winner – we lapped up every drop of the spicy coconut soup. Fried hokkien mee (stir-fried egg noodles with prawns, egg and pork) is good enough to grace any table in Singapore. When available, pulut hitam (black glutinous rice) with coconut milk guarantees a sweet and starchy end to your meal. Prices have continued to creep up, but there's no arguing that this is a quality experience. Note that there's also a Singapore Garden takeaway outlet in Chiswick (474 Chiswick High Road, W4 5TT, 8994 2222).
Babies and children admitted. Booking essential. Disabled: toilet. Takeaway service; delivery service (within 1.5-mile radius). Vegetarian menu. **Map 28 A4**.

Menu

Blachan, belacan or **blacan**: dried fermented shrimp paste.
Char kway teow or **char kwai teow**: a stir-fry of rice noodles with meat and/or seafood, dark soy sauce and beansprouts. A Hakka Chinese-derived speciality of Singapore.
Gado gado: a salad of blanched vegetables with a peanut-based sauce.
Gula melaka: palm sugar, an important ingredient with a distinctive caramel flavour added to a sago and coconut-milk pudding of the same name.
Hainanese chicken rice: poached chicken served with rice cooked in chicken stock, light chicken broth and a chilli-ginger dipping sauce.
Ikan bilis or **ikan teri**: tiny fish, often fried and made into a dry sambal (qv) with peanuts.
Laksa: a noodle dish with either coconut milk or tamarind as the stock base.
Mee: noodles.
Mee goreng: fried egg noodles with meat, prawns and vegetables.
Nasi ayam: rice cooked in chicken broth, served with roast or steamed chicken and a light soup.
Nasi goreng: fried rice with shrimp paste, garlic, onions, chillies and soy sauce.
Nasi lemak: coconut rice on a plate with a selection of curries and fish dishes topped with ikan bilis (qv).
Nonya or **Nyonya**: the name referring to both the women and the dishes of the Straits Chinese community.
Otak otak: a Nonya (qv) speciality made from eggs, fish and coconut milk.
Pandan leaves: a variety of the screwpine plant; used to add colour and fragrance to both savoury and sweet dishes.
Peranakan: refers to the descendants of Chinese settlers who first came to Malacca (now Melaka), a seaport on the Malaysian west coast, in the 17th century. It is generally applied to those born of Sino-Malay extraction who adopted Malay customs, costume and cuisine, the community being known as 'Straits Chinese'. The cuisine is also known as Nonya.
Rendang: meat cooked in coconut milk.
Roti canai: a South Indian/Malaysian breakfast dish of fried unleavened bread served with a dip of either chicken curry or dal.
Sambal: there are several types of sambal, often made of fiery chilli sauce, onions and coconut oil; it can be served as a side dish or used as a relish.
Satay: there are two types – **terkan** (minced and moulded to the skewer) and **chochok** ('shish', more common in London). Beef or chicken are the traditional choices, though prawn is now often available too. Satay is served with a rich, spicy sauce made from onions, lemongrass, galangal, and chillies in tamarind sauce; it is sweetened and thickened with ground peanuts.

Warung Bumbu

MALAYSIAN, INDONESIAN & SINGAPOREAN

Middle Eastern

London's Middle Eastern restaurants are generally in fine fettle, with venues opening in recent years in districts away from the Edgware Road heartland, and a greater variety of national cuisines being offered. Syrian cooking is the speciality of **Abu Zaad** in Shepherd's Bush, which provides large, inexpensive portions of meze dishes and kebabs; Iraqi food is served at **Zengi** in Spitalfields, alongside dishes from across the region; the new **Koshari Street** brings Egyptian street food to the West End; and Palestinian **Tatreez** has popped up in Stoke Newington. There's a batch of Iranian restaurants across the city too, where you'll find the enticing tangy stews (flavoured with the likes of dried lime or pomegranate juice) that characterise this cooking style. **Hana**, a recent addition to West Hampstead, is one of our current Iranian favourites, along with **Behesht** and **Sufi**. Otherwise, Lebanese food dominates this section: there's a wide scope of dining venues, from inexpensive cafés to plush Mayfair establishments with belly-dancers – our picks are **Al Waha**, **Meza** and **Yalla Yalla**.

Central
Edgware Road

Maroush I
21 Edgware Road, W2 2JE (7723 0773, www.maroush.com). Marble Arch tube. **Meals served** noon-1.30am daily. **Main courses** £13-£20. **Credit** AmEx, MC, V. Lebanese
A midweek visit to Maroush found the basement space quiet – perhaps understandable as this branch, with music and belly dancing every night, is known for its party vibe. But that doesn't explain the absence of the comforting rituals of Lebanese dining, nor the desultory service. Things were off from the start: gone was the bowl of fresh salad veg, the discs of bread served warm and puffy, the attentive service. Instead there was cold, flaccid paper-thin flatbread and olives. Sparkling water was dumped on the table with no glasses. However, the food was competently prepared, and it was clear that the well-regarded Maroush chain hasn't lost its touch with the classics: houmous was dense and nutty; tabouleh was fresh; fuul was OK, though presented in slapdash style, with no herbs or dip in the middle filled with olive oil. Maroush kalaj (warmed halloumi cheese in arabic bread) arrived less than lukewarm. It was removed without much enthusiasm (or apology) and returned warmer. In all, the meal was rather disheartening. Perhaps the management concentrates only on the entertainment at this particular branch; or perhaps it was simply an off night. We hope our experience was an exception rather than the rule.
Babies and children welcome: high chairs. Booking advisable. Entertainment: belly dancers and musicians 9.30pm daily. Separate room for parties, seats 25. Takeaway service; delivery service (over £20 within 2-mile radius). **Map 8 F6**.
For branches (Beirut Express, Maroush, Maroush Gardens, Randa) see index.

Fitzrovia

Honey & Co
25A Warren Street, W1T 5LZ (7388 6175, www.honeyandco.co.uk). Great Portland Street or Warren Street tube. **Meals served** 8am-6pm Mon; 8am-10pm Tue-Fri; 9am-10pm Sat. **Main courses** £8.50-£12.50. **Set dinner** (Tue-Fri) £29.50 3 courses. **Credit** MC, V.
Middle Eastern
A bijou delight, Honey & Co has a floor tiled in ivory and indigo mosaic. Its walls hold shelves of own-made pastries and jewel-like jars of preserves. The small tables and chairs are packed closely together; there are only 20 covers, so finding a spare seat at short notice is rare. The kitchen is run by an accomplished Israeli husband-and-wife team: he trained in Tel Aviv, she worked at Ottolenghi and NOPI. This pedigree shows up in a daily changing menu that draw influences from across the Middle East. On our visit, the meze selection included fabulously spongy, oily bread, sumac-spiked tahini, smoky taramasalata, crisp courgette croquettes with labneh, superior falafel, pan-fried feta and a bright salad with lemon and radishes. A main dish of lamb shawarma consisted of a bowl of meltingly tender slow-cooked meat to be scooped up with freshly baked pitta bread; a whole baby chicken with lemon and a chilli and walnut muhamara paste was over-salted but perfectly cooked. Dessert might be pistachio cake, warm from the oven, or deconstructed cheesecake laced with rosewater. This is imaginative home-style cooking, and service is speedy and charming, but prices are high for what is essentially a café.
Available for hire. Babies and children admitted. Booking advisable. Tables outdoors (2, pavement). **Map 3 J4**.

Holborn

Hiba
113 High Holborn, WC1V 6JQ (7831 5171, www.hiba-express.co.uk). Holborn tube. **Meals served** noon-midnight daily. **Main courses** £9.95-£14.95. **Set meal** £8.95-£10.95 1 course. **Set meze** £35-£65. **Credit** AmEx, MC, V.
Lebanese
The yellow-painted, red-accented interior of this buzzy and bright restaurant is a lot more appealing than you might expect from the plain frontage on an uninspiring stretch of High Holborn. Hiba is perennially popular with people looking for a houmous fix outside of the Edgware Road catchment area. The place comes into its own at

lunchtime, when besuited types lean on the bar waiting for their foil-packaged wraps, and the closely set tables and booths along the narrow dining room bustle with a varied, but usually brisk clientele (there's more room in the basement). Service can be haphazard and indifferent under this onslaught, so prepare to be persistent. Although there's no alcohol, many come here after work too; try one of the fantastic freshly squeezed juices, or a heavily perfumed glass of jellab with pine nuts. The meze dishes – fluffy houmous, tabouleh with the requisite balance of parsley (lots) to bulgur (hardly any), creamy fuul medames, sujuk with a fiery kick – do the job competently, but the real stars are the vast main platters and roast meats. An order of lamb shawarma brought a fragrant heap of juicy meat layered with flatbread, houmous and salad: a proper treat.

Available for hire. Babies and children welcome: high chairs. Takeaway service; delivery service (over £15 within 4-mile radius). Vegetarian menu. **Map 18 F2**.

Marylebone

Levant

Jason Court, 76 Wigmore Street, W1U 2SJ (7224 1111, www.levant.co.uk). Bond Street tube. Bar **Open** 5pm-midnight Mon-Thur; noon-2am Fri, Sat; noon-midnight Sun. *Restaurant* **Meals served** noon-11pm Mon-Thur; noon-midnight Fri, Sat; noon-11pm Sun. **Main courses** £13-£19.50. **Set lunch** £9.95 2 courses. **Set meal** £28-£50 3 courses; £50 kharuf feast. **Cover** £1.50.
Both **Credit** AmEx, MC, V. Lebanese

At a time when Middle Eastern cooking is enjoying a renaissance – served in bright modern venues and produced by kitchens doing interesting things with colour and flavour – there's something endearingly archaic about Levant's *One Thousand & One Nights* aesthetic. The huge underground space is decorated in red and gold or dark wood, dripping with filigreed lamps and lined by pools with red gerberas floating on the surface. The entire look speaks of banquets and belly dancing, and it's no surprise there's a programme of evening entertainment here, as well as long tables designed for riotous parties. On a weekday lunchtime, though, this is a quiet, comforting place with sweet, charming staff and an excellent-value set menu. The food isn't especially memorable, but it's certainly hearty and generous. Falafel were tiptop, creamy and crunchy and fresh from the hot oil, though tagines were let down by soggy couscous and a uniformity of flavour. Nevertheless, bread arrives fresh and hot from the oven, like a scented pillow exuding hot air; it needs to be eaten quickly before cooling to a cardboard state. Such details signify that Levant's intentions are sound, and that it wants to show you a good time.

Booking advisable. Entertainment: belly dancer 8.30pm Mon-Thur; 8.30pm, 11pm Fri-Sun; musicians 10.30pm Fri; DJ 10.30pm Sat. Separate room for parties, seats 10-12. Takeaway service. Vegetarian menu. **Map 9 G6**.

Mayfair

Noura

16 Curzon Street, W1J 5HP (7495 4396, www.noura.co.uk). Green Park tube. **Meals served** 11.30am-11.30pm daily. **Main courses** £14-£18. **Set meal** £32-£45 (minimum 2). **Credit** AmEx, MC, V. Lebanese

Next to the gracious, palatial frontage of the Saudi embassy in Mayfair, Noura is one of those deceptively casual addresses: a tastefully decorated, brightly lit, neutral rectangle of a dining room with a discreet juice bar at the rear. So far, so down to earth. But the sting comes with the bill – a restrained meal for two with a couple of drinks can cost rather more than you might pay for similar food – and a livelier experience – a stone's throw away on the Edgware Road. The food is satisfying, if not remarkable. We had creamy, lemon-spiked fuul medames and juicy, piquant sujuk with quail's eggs to start, then a very good aubergine stew with rice and a rather dry, uninspired wedge of kibbeh bil sanieh (baked minced lamb and cracked wheat) to follow. It may be that most customers come for the Noura Lounge basement bar, which has belly dancers at the weekend (booking essential). But if you're here for dinner and don't mind shelling out for the location, you could do worse. There's also the chance to smoke shisha on the pavement outside and watch the Maseratis zoom past.

Available for hire. Babies and children welcome: high chairs; nappy-changing facilities. Booking advisable. Separate room for parties, seats 30. Tables outdoors (4, pavement). Takeaway service; delivery service (over £21 within 1-mile radius). Vegetarian menu. **Map 9 H8**.
For branches see index.

Al Sultan

51-52 Hertford Street, W1J 7ST (7408 1155, www.alsultan.co.uk). Green Park or Hyde Park Corner tube. **Meals served** noon-11pm daily. **Main courses** £15-£23. **Cover** £2. **Minimum** £25. **Credit** AmEx, MC, V. Lebanese

Al Sultan is very down to earth, given the history of its location – the atmospheric, villagey Shepherd Market area of Mayfair has a scurrilous reputation stretching back centuries. The district has seen a raucous annual cattle market banned in 1764, the most fabulous excesses of the jazz age and some very high-class prostitutes, but here the atmosphere is wholesome rather than louche, and you're served good Lebanese food by sweet – if easily flustered – waiters. A £2 cover charge gets you olives and crudités on the table on arrival. Then you might order a few meze flanked by fluffy fresh bread: tart pickled baby aubergines with chilli and walnuts; comforting green beans with tomatoes, olive oil and garlic; a couple of crisp and gamey roast quail; luscious muhamara (walnut, pomegranate and chilli paste). But you can also go for a feast of grilled meats, or a traditional home-style dish such as a thick disc of crunchy bulgur-based kibbeh stuffed with aromatic minced lamb and pine nuts, with cool yoghurt and cucumber to spoon over it. The excellent Lebanese wines are more expensive than the unexceptional house choices, but they're worth the extra. A solid performer overall.

Available for hire. Babies and children welcome: high chairs. Booking advisable dinner. Tables outdoors (4, pavement). Takeaway service; delivery service (over £35 within 4-mile radius). Vegetarian menu. **Map 9 H8**.

Honey & Co

Soho

★ ★ Yalla Yalla

*1 Green's Court, W1F 0HA (7287 7663,
www.yalla-yalla.co.uk). Piccadilly Circus tube.*
Meals served 10am-11pm Mon-Sat; 10am-
10pm Sun. **Main courses** £8.50-£13.75.
Credit MC, V. Lebanese

Yalla Yalla continues to produce its hit formula of
superior Lebanese cooking in a casual setting. Its
self-styled 'Beirut street food' resonates with the
upbeat informality of these dinky Soho premises;
we've found the quality to match that of much
pricier restaurants. Diners cram on to faux-rustic
tables at lunchtime, while others nip in for
takeaway wraps – filled with everything from
falafel to spicy sujuk sausage – from the prepared
selection behind the counter. We were presented
with arabic bread, olives and torshi (pickles) as we
perused the menu: not the big salad bowls of the
posh places, but a charming touch nonetheless.
From the concise list of meze dishes we tried a
chunky, smoky baba ganoush and a flavour-packed
fattoush salad. A profusion of fresh salad
vegetables (lettuce, radish, cucumber, spring onion
and tomatoes) had been labour-intensively chopped
small, before adding crispy toasted pitta, a dusting
of warm sumac and a red wine vinaigrette –
brilliant. Halloumi meshoué (grilled) was fine too,
served with olives and mint. There's also a selection
of main-course grills. In all, you get an edited
version of a full Lebanese menu here, served in a
convivial atmosphere, with the bonus of cocktails
in the evening.
*Babies and children welcome: nappy-changing
facilities. Bookings not accepted for fewer than
10 people. Tables outdoors (2, pavement).
Takeaway service.* **Map 17 B4.**
For branch see index.

West

Bayswater

Hafez

*5 Hereford Road, W2 4AB (7221 3167,
www.hafezrestaurant.co.uk). Bayswater tube
or bus 7, 23, 328.* **Meals served** noon-
11.30pm daily. **Main courses** £7.90-£14.90.
Credit MC, V. Iranian

Nailed to the walls – and even parts of the ceiling
– pretty spoons, Persian teapots, trays and other
silverware serve as quirky decoration in this long-
running neighbourhood restaurant. Books are also
artfully arranged as ornamental installations,
perhaps a nod to the restaurant's namesake: 14th-
century Persian poet Hafez. There's certainly a
poetic approach on the menu, which explains the
joy of sharing food and the kitchen's traditional
style of cooking. Kebabs (aromatic, generously
sized and lean) are grilled over charcoal, stews are
gently slow-cooked and rice is boiled then steamed
for a fluffy light finish. Hafez's signature dish, the
pomegranate-based fesenjan, is among just six
chicken and lamb stews (four of which are also
available in vegetarian versions) on a brief, but
interesting menu. Made the classic way with big
pieces of chicken, the fesenjan also featured a thick
sauce that was sweet and tart in equal measure.
The dish seemed particularly popular among the
staff, who proudly raved about it, as well as the
restaurant's wafer-thin, sesame-topped bread made

Yalla Yalla

fresh to order. Established in 1983, Hafez has
perfected the art of extending hospitable, familiar
service to both regulars and newcomers; it has
understandably built a loyal local fan base.
*Available for hire. Babies and children welcome:
high chairs. Booking advisable. Tables outdoors
(3, terrace). Takeaway service. Vegetarian menu.*
Map 7 B6.

★ Al Waha

*75 Westbourne Grove, W2 4UL (7229 0806,
www.alwaharestaurant.com). Bayswater or
Queensway tube.* **Meals served** noon-11.30pm
daily. **Main courses** £11-£17. **Set lunch**
£13.50-£15. **Set dinner** (minimum 2) £22 per
person 2 courses, £26 per person 3 courses.
Cover £1.50. **Minimum** (dinner) £13.50.
Credit MC, V. Lebanese

This Westbourne Grove stalwart continues to
produce Lebanese cooking of the highest order.
Inside the smallish corner premises, a profusion of
plants, seating on different levels and professional
and friendly staff make for an atmosphere that,
while not exactly informal, is comfortable. The

quality of the dining experience is reflected in Al
Waha's popularity – it was buzzing on a recent
evening visit. We began our meal with some diverse
meze dishes: a gloriously oily, chilli-hot, nutty
muhamara; a bright, lemony fuul moukala (fried
broad beans); fattoush salad bursting with
freshness, the crisp salad warmed by sumac spice,
the toasted pitta bread crunchy; and the warmly
flavoured comfort dish moujadara – a mixture of
rice and lentils, topped with crisp caramelised
onion. There was tabouleh too, composed of the
tiniest chopped shreds of herbs with lashings of
tangy lemon. As we ate, bread came regularly and
unobtrusively to the table, served warmed and
puffed up from the oven. We shared a mixed grill
too: perfectly tender chunks of lamb, chicken and
köfte. This was a reminder of how Lebanese food
should be – traditionally and painstakingly
prepared and a joy to eat.
*Babies and children welcome until 7pm.
Booking advisable; essential dinner. Tables
outdoors (4, patio). Takeaway service; delivery
service (over £20 within 3-mile radius).*
Map 7 B6.

Chiswick

★ Faanoos II

472 Chiswick High Road, W4 5TT (8994 4217, www.faanoosrestaurant.com). Chiswick Park tube. **Meals served** noon-11pm Mon-Thur, Sat; noon-midnight Fri, Sat. **Main courses** £5.95-£10.95. **Credit** AmEx, MC, V. Iranian

The strip running west from Hammersmith to Turnham Green is a competitive spot for Persian restaurants. There's Mahdi, Piano, Rice and, until recently, glitzy Chella. Faanoos II has carved its own niche in this Little Tehran by offering cheap, cheerful cooking, with mains starting at £5.95 and few breaking the £9 barrier. The interior is low lit, scented by bread cooking on the open oven and skewers of meat sizzling at the grill. Starters consist of the standard-issue selection of dips and salads; our favourite was kashk-e bademjan, a dense, flavourful mix of fried aubergine, yoghurt and onions, scooped up on hunks of sesame-seeded flatbread. The kebabs are pretty straightforward too – chicken, lamb and minced lamb, freshly cooked and served with a mountain of rice. They're decent if not inspiring, but for the price they are excellent value. You might not come here for a masterclass in the best of Persian cuisine – there's no fesenjan on the menu, for example – but as a reliable neighbourhood kebab joint, Faanoos II holds its own against the competition.

Available for hire. Babies and children welcome: high chairs. Booking advisable Fri, Sat. Tables outdoors (1, pavement; 4, garden). Takeaway service.

For branch see index.

Maida Vale

Amoul

14 Formosa Street, W9 1EE (7286 6386, www.amoul.com). Warwick Avenue tube. **Lunch served** 9am-4pm Sat; 10am-1.15pm Sun. **Dinner served** 6-10pm Tue-Sat. **Main courses** £13.20-£22.50. **Credit** AmEx, MC, V. Lebanese

Amoul has hit on a winning formula by finding a homely space on a villagey street amid the lavish white-stuccoed palaces of W9; filling it with flowers, candles and artistic black and white family photos; and serving above-average home-style cooking at above-average prices. It's a charming spot, with engaging waitresses and Amoul herself – of Lebanese origin, with a self-published cookbook to her name – moving solicitously between tables and the kitchen. The food is predominantly Middle Eastern (including the breakfast menu at weekends, which contains the likes of eggs with yoghurt and cinnamon), though there's also a strong French presence (steak, poussin), the execution of which influences the Levantine dishes. Samkeh harra came as a piquant fillet of sea bass with a side of spinach and a pot of tahini, rather than a heavy bowl of rice and sauce mixed in; and the flavour of loubieh bi zeit (green beans and tomatoes) owed more to Bordeaux than Beirut. But the food is none the worse for that – everything is freshly made, and around here, people don't blink at the premium price tags for what are essentially café dishes.

Available for hire. Babies and children admitted. Booking advisable dinner Thur-Sat. Tables outdoors (2, pavement). Takeaway service. Vegan dishes. **Map 1 C4.**

Kateh

5 Warwick Place, W9 2PX (7289 3393, www.katehrestaurant.co.uk). Warwick Avenue tube. **Lunch served** noon-4pm Fri, Sat. **Dinner served** 6-11pm Mon-Sat. **Meals served** noon-9.30pm Sun. **Main courses** £11-£17.50. **Credit** AmEx, MC, V. Iranian

Roaringly busy throughout the week, this Persian restaurant is well hidden among the elegant houses of Warwick Avenue. Just a handful of tables are packed into a tight, conspicuously plain space. The atmosphere is provided by elbow-to-elbow diners and by furiously enthusiastic staff who tear around delivering refined, modern Iranian dishes, and chip in with friendly chatter. If you're after a bit of privacy (or peace), head for the small basement room, which features a communal table and a pretty courtyard; romantically low lit, it's ideal for an intimate party. In fact, Kateh is a great special-occasion destination. With a menu that's a touch more expensive than the average in this section, and an arty, contemporary approach to plating up, it has the air of a smart European brasserie and the clientele to match. Hearty classics, such as ghalieh mahi (an excellent fish stew made tart with tamarind) and saffron-marinated grilled meats, feature alongside less defiantly Persian dishes – a charred sardine, basil and lemon starter, for example, minced veal kebab, or a frozen blueberry yoghurt dessert. It's a creative and appealing mix, made more so by the quality of ingredients, the warm service and the stylish surroundings.

Available for hire. Babies and children welcome: high chairs. Booking advisable. Separate room for parties, seats 10-12. Tables outdoors (3, terrace). Takeaway service. **Map 1 C4.**

Olympia

Mohsen

152 Warwick Road, W14 8PS (7602 9888). Earl's Court tube or Kensington (Olympia) tube/rail. **Meals served** noon-11.30pm daily. **Main courses** £15-£20. **Unlicensed. Corkage** no charge. **No credit cards.** Iranian

Mohsen has been sticking to the same simple, successful formula for many years, and we're happy to report that nothing whatsoever has changed. It's a little dog-eared, and the laminated menus could do with a redesign, but the regulars keep returning for more, and Mrs Mohsen still works the tightly packed tables with a big smile, as if throwing a dinner party in her front room. The food is consistently good, although it doesn't always quite have the spark of the top Persian venues. Kashk-e bademjan, an aubergine dip with walnuts and whey, is reliable, but the ox tongue was wonderful: soft, rich and melt-in-the-mouth (largely down to its high fat content). We enjoyed our koobideh (minced lamb) and barg (strips of lamb fillet) kebabs, which are grilled in the basement and sent up via a dumb waiter, but found the khoresht-e fesenjan a little disappointing: the sauce was overpowering and the chicken portion quite small. Doogh (yoghurt drink) was also a let-down, being more like a Turkish ayran than the carbonated, minty Iranian version. Nevertheless, prices are low for this part of west London, the service is extremely friendly and the café-like decor offers a laid-back alternative to some of the capital's more showy Persian restaurants.

Babies and children admitted. Takeaway service. **Map 13 A10.**

Shepherd's Bush

★ Abu Zaad

29 Uxbridge Road, W12 8LH (8749 5107, www.abuzaad.co.uk). Shepherd's Bush Market tube. **Meals served** 11am-11pm daily. **Main courses** £5-£14. **Unlicensed** no alcohol allowed. **Credit** MC, V. Syrian

Groups of teenagers, young families and couples after a quick, fuss-free meal seem to find this vast Syrian restaurant a convenient destination. The boisterous clientele, together with Abu Zaad's relaxed café-style seating, TV screens and what seems like an army of zippy waiters lend the place a pleasantly chaotic air. Service is pretty slick, though, and although the restaurant is often furiously busy, you're unlikely to have trouble getting seated at one of the plentiful tables – probably next to a garish painting of Old Damascus or near an ornamental brick arch. In keeping with the informality, the menu is cheap and portions huge. A sharing meze of cold dishes – including parsley-packed tabouleh and lashings of thick houmous – would have been a filling meal in itself. Mains are hardly of modest dimensions either: a tomato rice maklouba (topped and filled with chunks of lamb and slivers of fried aubergine) would have been enough for two; and a grilled lamb kebab came with rice, bread and salad. There's a no-alcohol policy, but you can wash down the carbs with a glass of salty yoghurt ayran or a freshly squeezed juice, and round off the meal with a pot of mint tea.

Babies and children welcome: high chairs. Booking advisable weekends. Separate room for parties, seats 36. Takeaway service. **Map 20 B2.**

For branch see index.

★ Sufi

70 Askew Road, W12 9BJ (8834 4888, www.sufirestaurant.com). Hammersmith tube then bus 266. **Meals served** noon-10.45pm daily. **Main courses** £7.30-£13. **Set meal** £11.50 per person (minimum 4). **Corkage** £5. **Credit** MC, V. Iranian

It's hard to find a bad word to say about Sufi, a restaurant we've consistently praised since it opened in 2007. And it's equally hard to avoid hyperbole when describing Sufi's kashk-e bademjan. Walnuts, onion and garlic give this aubergine dip spice and texture, but it's the sour, smoky, creamy kashk (whey) that makes it so moreish. Taftoon flatbread, baked in the clay oven by the front window, is the ideal accompaniment. Kuku-ye sabzi (a frittata-like dish of parsley, coriander and dill mixed with eggs and baked) was almost as good. The key to Persian lamb kebabs is the marinade – lots of turmeric, black pepper and garlic – and the chelo koobideh (minced lamb) was spot-on. Even better was the khoresht-e fesenjan, a glorious chicken stew in a sauce made from ground walnuts and pomegranate molasses. Doogh (yoghurt drink) was properly minty and slightly carbonated. Our only minor complaints are that the tahdig (rice from the bottom of the pan) was more chewy than crisp, and the staff seemed keen for us to leave as closing time approached. Sufi is just about smart enough for a date, though rugs and instruments hanging from the walls are as exciting as the decor gets. But for exquisite Persian food at low prices (two can eat well for £25), it's a fantastic option.

MIDDLE EASTERN

Available for hire. Babies and children welcome: children's menu; high chairs. Separate room for parties, seats 40. Takeaway service; delivery service (over £20 within 3-mile radius). **Map 20 A2**.

South
Tooting

Meza
34 Trinity Road, SW17 7RE (07722 111299). Tooting Bec tube. **Meals served** 5-9pm Mon; noon-9.30pm Tue-Sun. **Main courses** £7.50-£9.50. **Set meal** £16 per person (minimum 4). **No credit cards**. Lebanese

Tooting Bec tube station; minicab office; launderette; kebab shop. Hang on, though – this kebab shop is crammed with tables and chairs, and some very pleased-with-themselves diners clinking glasses. A tiny Lebanese licensed restaurant, Meza has a kitchen smaller than a Beirut takeaway stall, but manages to turn out a sizeable menu of meze and grilled dishes freshly made to order. Sitting at the bar counter, as we did, you can see why the expression 'open kitchen' was coined – no sprig of flat-leaf parsley can be out of place when you're under this sort of scrutiny. Fortunately, the chefs never put a fuul wrong, from the perfectly crisp-shelled falafels to the aubergine dips seared with the whiff of the charcoal grill. Highlights? Everything. Even the Lebanese wine was enjoyable, and priced keenly at around £15 a bottle. The manager was subdued on our most recent visit, but in the past we've seen him greet every customer like a new best friend, and service is consistently friendly and casual. The only catch with Meza is its popularity; you need to book weeks in advance on a mobile phone number to get a good slot, and table-turning is now the norm.
Available for hire. Babies and children welcome: high chairs. Booking advisable dinner. Takeaway service.

East
Spitalfields

★ Zengi
44 Commercial Street, E1 6LT (7426 0700). Aldgate East tube. **Meals served** noon-11pm daily. **Main courses** £2.50-£14. **Credit** AmEx, MC, V. Iraqi

On a fine day, you'll spot customers at Zengi's pavement tables puffing on shisha pipes and sending plumes of perfumed smoke up in the air. It helps mask the far less appealing smog from Commercial Street's heavy traffic, the roar of which you can still hear inside the restaurant. On the informal ground floor, chefs are busy grilling meat over charcoal and pulling freshly baked flatbread from the pizza oven. For a quieter time, head to the basement to sit at intimate booths tucked into dimly lit alcoves. The menu is predominantly Iraqi, but features Turkish, Persian and Lebanese influences, bringing together the best dishes from each region. For a top meze selection, choose the fresh salads (a towering portion of zingy tabouleh was stuffed with parsley) and dips, including a chunky houmous and smoky aubergine moutabal. Mains are consistently excellent: the Zengi mixed grill provides a taste of gently marinated chicken,

melt-in-the-mouth lamb pieces and thick, lean köfte. Our khema (a dense stew of lentils and minced lamb) was authentic, and the turkish pizzas light, packed with meat and full of flavour. Every bit as tasty – and excellent value too – are the falafel and the grilled meat sandwiches.
Available for hire. Babies and children welcome: high chairs. Booking advisable. Tables outdoors (3, pavement). Takeaway service; delivery service (over £15 within 2-mile radius). Map 12 S6.

North East
Stoke Newington

★ Tatreez NEW
188 Stoke Newington High Street, N16 7JD (8616 5434). Stoke Newington rail or bus 67, 73, 76, 149, 243. **Meals served** 11am-10pm Mon-Thur, Sun; 11am-11pm Fri, Sat. **Main courses** £5-£6.50. **Credit** MC, V. Palestinian

There's no tatreez – Palestinian embroidery – in evidence at this funky new café. The interior is fitted out in plain chunky blocks of wood, with a high counter in front of the whitewashed swell of a bread oven, and a communal table at the back. A small collection of Palestinian deli produce and samples of a Gazan cookbook adorn the bar; the blackboard menu is studded with images of the Palestinian flag, indicating where fairly traded ingredients from the owner's conflicted homeland are on the menu. The very selective range of café snacks only hints at the breadth of the region's cookery, with the Palestinian angle mostly referring to the provenance of ingredients; the dishes would be perfectly at home in Beirut, but their execution is spot-on. After Palestinian olives and two easy-drinking Lebanese beers, we had tart makdous (pickled baby aubergines stuffed with walnuts and chilli); creamy, warm full-stewed chickpeas; and crisp manaeesh flatbread baked with a cheese and za'atar thyme mix. We chose a honeyed Palestinian white wine, but there are excellent Lebanese wines too. Throughout all this, a guitarist strummed world jazz, one of the regular free sets. On an average Tuesday night, the space filled quickly with artfully dishevelled locals listening to the music and generally having a jolly time: minimal politics, maximum enjoyment.
Available for hire. Babies and children admitted. Tables outdoors (4, terrace).

North
Archway

Gilak
663 Holloway Road, N19 5SE (7272 1692, www.gilakrestaurant.com). Archway tube or Upper Holloway rail. **Meals served** 11am-10.30pm Mon-Fri; noon-10.30pm Sat, Sun. **Main courses** £6.99-£14.50. **Set meal** £42 (minimum 4). **Credit** MC, V. Iranian

Gilak's workaday decor – dark wooden furniture, whitewashed walls dotted with photos of the Caspian Sea, a cabinet of dusty knick-knacks – is rather spartan, though mellow Persian melodies and fairy lights are preferable to the muzak and harsh overhead lighting we've experienced here in the past. The kitchen specialises in the cuisine of Gilan, the northern Iranian province bordering the

Caspian Sea, and much of the menu has a briny tang. Smoked mackerel pops up unexpectedly in a whole range of dishes, alongside the usual pomegranate, dried limes and dried plums. Starters of kale kabab (a blend of aubergine, fresh herbs and tangy pomegranate juice) and salad olivieh (a Gilani rendition of russian salad), didn't disappoint on flavour but were served too chilled, and the presentation was unimaginative: two bowls of beige mush. Mains worked better: zereshk polow ba morgh (tender braised chicken with saffron rice, exotic sweet-sour barberries and chopped almonds and pistachios), and kabab momtaz (melt-in-the-mouth chicken and succulent lamb, in a zesty marinade, grilled to perfection and served with fluffy rice dotted with saffron). Gilak is a perfectly good local but lacks the atmosphere to transport diners away from the noisy Holloway Road outside.
Available for hire. Babies and children welcome: high chairs. Booking advisable. Disabled: toilet. Takeaway service; delivery service (over £15 within 2-mile radius). Map 26 C1.

Camden Town & Chalk Farm

Tandis
73 Haverstock Hill, NW3 4SL (7586 8079). Chalk Farm tube. **Meals served** noon-11.30pm Mon-Thur, Sun; noon-midnight Fri, Sat. **Main courses** £8.90-£14.90. **Credit** AmEx, MC, V. Iranian

Peer through the window of this smart restaurant, and it's unlikely you'd guess its Persian menu. Contemporary and European in style – and with a long bar at its centre – Tandis can feel pretty soulless on a quiet evening. Still, its upmarket-wine-bar aesthetic belies some genuinely authentic dishes. Tah dig (essentially crispy rice) covered in ghorm-e sabzi won't be to everyone's taste (many find the rice tooth-breakingly hard), but it's nice to see a dish normally reserved for home cooking on a restaurant menu. Stews too are made with care: Iran's endlessly popular pomegranate-based fesenjan was wonderfully rich, and a bademjan was thick with aubergine and lamb. The chicken kebab made with a 'special house saffron marinade', however, was overwhelmingly pungent. A little of the expensive spice goes a long way, and we suspect Tandis is being a touch too generous with its saffron stash. It's a shame the restaurant isn't quite as bounteous with its service, which felt stilted and unsmiling on our visit, and entirely lacking in enthusiasm. The slickly turned out staff may suit the decor, but they clash with the hearty nature of Iranian cuisine and the country's relaxed approach to dining.
Available for hire. Babies and children welcome: high chairs. Booking advisable Fri, Sat. Separate rooms for parties, seating 14-30. Tables outdoors (12, terrace). Takeaway service; delivery service (over £15 within 3-mile radius). Map 28 C4.

North West
Cricklewood

Zeytoon
94-96 Cricklewood Broadway, NW2 3EL (8830 7434, www.zeytoon.co.uk). Cricklewood rail. **Meals served** 5-11pm daily. **Main courses** £5.95-£11.95. **Set meze** £14.95. **Credit** AmEx, MC, V. Afghan/Iranian

Budget bites

★ Comptoir Libanais

65 Wigmore Street, W1U 1PZ (7935 1110, www.lecomptoir.co.uk). Bond Street tube. **Meals served** 7.30am-10.30pm Mon-Sat; 7.30am-10pm Sun. **Main courses** £5.95-£8.45. **Credit** AmEx, MC, V. Lebanese

This wildly popular Lebanese canteen, takeaway and deli is an almost frenetically bustling and bright enterprise, filled with glitzy, colourful designs by Beirut designer Rana Salam. The combination of casual atmosphere, punchy looks and an above-average menu works well, and the place is usually full – although not unbearably so. Choose carefully from the menu; pre-mixed salads can seem as if they've sat on the counter too long. The best things we tried were the hot dishes: splendid warm, cinnamon-spiked pumpkin kibbeh with yoghurt to dip them in; and excellent chicken with pomegranate syrup, both tart and sweet. The lemonades are great too, in flavours such as pomegranate or ginger. Prices are very reasonable. *Available for hire. Babies and children welcome: high chairs. Bookings not accepted. Tables outdoors (5, pavement). Takeaway service.* **Map 9 H6**. **For branches see index.**

★ Fresco

25 Westbourne Grove, W2 4UA (7221 2355, www.frescojuices.co.uk). Bayswater or Royal Oak tube. **Meals served** 8am-11pm daily. **Main courses** £5.95-£9. **Set meze** £11.50. **Credit** MC, V. Lebanese

A narrow, cosy, sunny space, Fresco is a cheery and simple option among the many varied possibilities along Westbourne Grove. From the front counter, you can grab meze, salads and sandwiches to go (best accompanied by one of the 26 freshly squeezed juices – we liked no.18, a zinging carrot, lemon, honey and ginger combo). If you're eating in at one of the handful of small tables, there's a range of satisfying hot mains as well, such as moussaka or chicken escalope. Moujadara, a traditional Lebanese dish of lentils and bulgur topped with fried onions, was brought to life by cool, creamy yoghurt and a generous salad with the sweet crunch of pomegranate seeds. It's all delivered with smiling, unfussy efficiency, making Fresco a more than safe bet. *Takeaway service. Vegetarian menu.* **Map 7 B6**. **For branches see index.**

★ Koshari Street `NEW`

56 St Martin's Lane, WC2N 4EA (3667 8763, www.kosharistreet.com). Leicester Square tube. **Meals served** 11.30am-11pm Mon-Sat. **Main courses** £4.50. **Set meal** £7.50 1 course. **Credit** AmEx, MC, V. Egyptian

London may have swooned for Ottolenghi and Yalla Yalla, but this homage to Egypt's hole-in-the-wall koshari vendors, from food writer and champion of Levantine cooking Anissa Helou, is still a brave move. The small, pristine space with a stainless-steel counter is vaguely reminiscent of a school canteen. There are a few seats along one wall, but this is essentially a takeaway joint, with a menu only a shade more varied than it would be at a Cairo street stall. Warming, comforting and many layered, koshari is falafel's more substantial older brother – a solid, simple dish of lentils, pasta, vermicelli and rice topped with tomato sauce and fried onions. Helou's version comes in mild, hot and 'mad' (it's not really), plus her own doqqa recipe: ground spices, nuts and herbs. There are also a couple of plain salads, a daily soup (the sharp, lemony lentil and chard had great depth of flavour), freshly pressed juices and traditional desserts; muhallabia milk pudding was creamy and laced with rosewater, like a grown-up Wall's Mini Milk. Service in the early days of opening was haphazard, but charming. If staff iron out the wrinkles, London may swoon again for this simplest of Middle Eastern menus. *Bookings not accepted. Takeaway service.* **Map 18 D5**.

★ Pilpel

38 Brushfield Street, E1 6AT (7247 0146, www.pilpel.co.uk). Liverpool Street tube/rail. **Meals served** 10am-8pm Mon-Thur; 10am-4pm Fri; noon-6pm Sun. **Main courses** £4.25-£5.85. **Unlicensed**. **No credit cards.** Middle Eastern

Pilpel provides a welcome shot of simple street food on the edge of the City. You're welcomed with truly Middle Eastern enthusiasm here, in the form of huge smiles and a free falafel to savour while you consider the menu. It won't take long to peruse the selection of dishes printed above the open counter; this is essentially a falafel joint, with a choice of salads and meze as accompaniments. Your order is then piled into pitta bread or layered into a salad bowl. Takeaway is popular among local office workers, but you can also eat in (and people-watch) sitting on the wooden stools at the bar next to the window. The falafel are top notch, crisp outside and grass-green on the inside, and the accompaniments – eggs, baba ganoush, red cabbage, onions and so on – are fresh and generous. *Babies and children admitted. Takeaway service. Vegetarian menu.* **Map 12 R5**. **For branches see index.**

★ Ranoush Juice

43 Edgware Road, W2 2JE (7723 5929, www.maroush.com). Marble Arch tube. **Meals served** 9am-3am daily. **Main courses** £3-£10.50. **No credit cards**. Lebanese

An Edgware Road staple, Ranoush is the rough-and-ready pit stop in the Maroush family of Lebanese restaurants. The narrow space has room for a few tables down one side and a couple on the rowdy pavement, but it's mostly about takeaway – expect boozy queues stretching out of the door at peak evening times. The gyros turn steadily behind the large counter stacked with meze, baklava and fruit for fresh juices. The succulent, aromatic meat tastes exactly how you want it to when carved on to plates or into sandwiches, slathered with creamy houmous and layered with pickles. Service is brisk, even brusque, but it's all part of the experience – just load up and go on your way happily fortified. *Bookings not accepted. Takeaway service.* **Map 8 F6**. **For branches (Maroush Ranoush, Ranoush Juice) see index.**

Koshari Street

MIDDLE EASTERN

Among the fast-food joints and grocery shops of the Broadway, Zeytoon is an Afghan/Persian stalwart with charming if kitsch decor – heavy wooden furniture and carved alcoves featuring 1970s-style murals depicting Persian myths. Tucked in the corner is the culinary star: a small tanoor where nigella seed-studded flatbread is baked fresh, crisp on the outside, cushiony soft inside. Subtle traditional music forms the aural backdrop, producing a vibe that is more Kermanshah than Cricklewood. We've heard moans about the service here, but on our latest visit, hungry staff waiting for Ramadan iftar (evening meal) couldn't have been more smiley and amenable. Afghan specialities such as kalleh pacheh (lamb's head and feet in broth), mantu (meat- and onion-stuffed dumplings with spicy sauce) and quroot (a sour cottage cheese made from sheep or goat's milk) sit alongside familiar Persian dishes. Warm aubergine with walnuts, herbs and kashk (whey) was a touch bland in comparison to a fresh and herby, finely chopped salad olivieh (russian salad with chicken). Succulent chicken breast kebab with salad and a veritable mountain

of dry saffron rice lacked pzazz, but chelow khoresht-e qeimeh (lamb, tomato and split-pea stew), zesty and fragrant with dried lime, certainly hit the spot. A good local.

Available for hire. Babies and children welcome: high chairs. Booking advisable. Disabled: toilet. Separate room for parties, seats 100. Tables outdoors (3, pavement). Takeaway service.

Kensal Green

★ ★ Behesht

1082-1084 Harrow Road, NW10 5NL (8964 4477, www.behesht.co.uk). Kensal Green tube/ rail. **Meals served** noon-11.30pm daily. **Main courses** £5.95-£9.95. **Unlicensed** no alcohol allowed. **Credit** MC, V. Iranian

Long stretches of Harrow Road are fairly unprepossessing, making Behesht a delightful – if slightly bonkers – surprise. The interior is a no-holds-barred hymn to the (real or imagined) aesthetic traditions of Persia. You're greeted in the lobby by walls festooned with wooden instruments and hung with tapestries, by dashingly aloof

waiters with slicked-back hair, and by an amorous pair of green parrots in a large cage. Through to the dining room, and the decor is yet more flamboyant – fountains trickle and songbirds chirrup among pots, paintings and sculptures. The food doesn't let the side down; portions are enormous, and there's real complexity of flavour. Kashk-e bademjan – a warm paste of aubergine, walnuts and fried onions scooped up with handfuls of gargantuan flatbread – was a star of the meze-style starters, as was mirza ghasemi, a smoky hot dip of grilled aubergine, eggs and tomatoes. Mains include rafts of tempting grilled meats, but we chose stews slathered in dark, rich sauces – ghorm-e sabzi with lamb, kidney beans, dried limes and herbs (sharp and moreish); and fesenjan chicken that managed the tricky balance of being sweet and savoury without becoming sickly. There's no alcohol, so the final bill is gratifyingly low: extraordinary value.

Babies and children welcome: high chairs; nappy-changing facilities. Booking advisable. Disabled: toilet. Separate rooms for parties, seating 30-120. Takeaway service. Vegetarian menu.

Hana

West Hampstead

Hana NEW

*351 West End Lane, NW6 1LT (7794 1200,
www.hanarestaurant.co.uk). West Hampstead
tube/rail.* **Dinner served** 4-10.45pm Mon-Thur.
Meals served noon-10.45pm Fri-Sun. **Main
courses** £7.50-£12.50. **No credit cards.**
Iranian

Adornment is kept to a minimum at Hana. Even the
tanoor oven and charcoal grill, so often taking pride
of place at Persian restaurants, are tucked away in
the kitchen. The most eye-catching feature is a wall-
mounted fake fire. Despite the unorthodox decor,
the menu is largely traditional, offering various
salads (such as pomegranate- and cucumber-based
dezfouli), warming stews served with saffron rice,
and tender charcoal-grilled kebabs. The prices are
appealing. A warm starter of crushed, grilled
aubergines with tomatoes and garlic (mirza
ghasemi) had a silky texture and pleasingly smoky
flavour. Own-made organic taftoon wholemeal
flatbread from the tanoor oven – puffy-edged and
sprinkled with sesame seeds – was perfect for
mopping it up. Two classic stews exemplified the
range of flavours in Persian cooking: slow-cooked
chicken in a thick walnut and pomegranate sauce
(fesenjan) was rich and sweet, with a hint of
bitterness; and a vegetarian herb and bean stew
(ghorm-e sabzi) had its savoury tangs tempered by
tartness from whole, dried persian limes. Given the
quality of the cooking and the low prices, it's little
wonder this friendly neighbourhood restaurant is
so popular with locals.
*Available for hire. Babies and children welcome:
high chairs. Booking advisable. Tables outdoors
(2, terrace). Takeaway service; delivery service
(over £20 within 2-mile radius).* **Map 28 A2.**

Mahdi

*2 Canfield Gardens, NW6 3BS (7625 4344,
www.mahdirestaurant.com). Finchley Road
tube.* **Meals served** noon-11pm daily. **Main
courses** £4.90-£22.90. **Set lunch** (buffet) £7.90
Mon-Fri; £8.90 Sat, Sun. **Credit** MC, V. Iranian
The Middle Eastern theme is glaringly obvious at
this theatrically decked out restaurant. The interior
is stuffed with decorative carpets, colourful
cushions, gaudy chandeliers, taxidermy peacocks
and faux Arab arches. It's a somewhat dated decor,
but we suspect Mahdi's loyal, London-wide fans are
more interested in the traditional, well-executed
menu, amenable prices and huge portions. Sharing
your food – standard practice in Iran – is made fun
and simple here. A mixed grill platter is presented
on a raised stand at the centre of the table.
Glistening lamb and chicken kebabs are served
alongside a colossal pile of white and saffron rice,
plus light, crispy bread that's baked to order in the
tanoor by the door. Some dishes – such as a dolmeh
felfel (stuffed pepper) starter – seem to value
quantity over quality, but stick to the barbecued
meats and it's hard to go wrong. Service can be a
little uneven; the gang of well-meaning and
obliging waiters can be laid-back to the point of
frustrating. You'll be treated well, just don't expect
a quick turnaround. Then again, this is a place
where families linger over mountains of food, spend
time digesting with pots of aromatic tea and then
waddle home with doggy bags.
*Available for hire. Babies and children welcome:
high chairs. Takeaway service.* **Map 28 B3.**
For branch see index.

Menu

See also the menus in **North African**
and **Turkish**.

MEZE
Baba ganoush: Egyptian name for
moutabal (qv).
Basturma: smoked beef.
Batinjan or **bazenjan el-rahib**: aubergine
mashed with olive oil, garlic and tomato.
Batata hara: potatoes fried with peppers
and chilli.
Falafel: a mixture of spicy chickpeas
or broad beans, ground, rolled into balls
and deep fried.
Fatayer: a soft pastry, filled with cheese,
onions, spinach and pine nuts.
Fattoush: fresh vegetable salad
containing shards of toasted pitta
bread and sumac (qv).
Fuul or fuul medames: brown broad
beans that are mashed and seasoned
with olive oil, lemon juice and garlic.
Kalaj: halloumi cheese on pastry.
Kibbeh: highly seasoned mix of minced
lamb, cracked wheat and onion, deep-fried
in balls. As meze it is often served raw
(**kibbeh nayeh**) like steak tartare.
Labneh: cream cheese made from yoghurt.
Moujadara: lentils, rice and caramelised
onions mixed together.
Moutabal: a purée of chargrilled aubergines
mixed with sesame sauce, garlic and
lemon juice.
Muhamara: dip of crushed mixed nuts
with red peppers, spices and pomegranate
molasses.
Sambousek: small pastries filled with
mince, onion and pine nuts.
Sujuk: spicy Lebanese sausages.
Sumac: an astringent and fruity-tasting
spice made from dried sumac seeds.
Tabouleh: a salad of chopped parsley,
tomatoes, crushed wheat, onions, olive
oil and lemon juice.
Torshi: pickled vegetables.
Warak einab: rice-stuffed vine leaves.

MAINS
Shawarma: meat (usually lamb)
marinated then grilled on a spit and
sliced kebab-style.
Shish kebab: cubes of marinated lamb
grilled on a skewer, often with tomatoes,
onions and sweet peppers.
Shish taouk: like shish kebab, but with
chicken rather than lamb.

DESSERTS
Balkava: filo pastry interleaved with
pistachio nuts, almonds or walnuts,
and covered in syrup.
Konafa or **kadayif**: cake made from
shredded pastry dough, filled with
syrup and nuts, or cream.
Ma'amoul: pastries filled with nuts
or dates.
Muhallabia or **mohalabia**: a milky
ground-rice pudding with almonds
or pistachios, flavoured with rosewater
or orange blossom.
Om ali: bread pudding, often made with
filo pastry and including nuts and raisins.

IRANIAN DISHES
Ash-e reshteh: soup with noodles,
spinach, pulses and dried herbs.
Ghorm-e sabzi: lamb with greens, kidney
beans and dried limes.
Halim bademjan: mashed chargrilled
aubergine with onions and walnuts.
Joojeh or **jujeh**: chicken marinated in
saffron, lemon and onion.
Kashk, **qurut** or **quroot**: a salty whey.
Kashk-e bademjan: baked aubergines
mixed with herbs and whey.
Khoresht-e fesenjan or **fesenjoon**:
chicken cooked in ground walnut and
pomegranate sauce.
Kuku-ye sabzi: finely chopped fresh
herbs with eggs, baked in the oven.
Masto khiar: yoghurt mixed with finely
chopped cucumber and mint.
Masto musir: shallot-flavoured yoghurt.
Mirza ghasemi: crushed baked
aubergines, tomatoes, garlic and
herbs mixed with egg.
Sabzi: a plate of fresh herb leaves
(usually mint and dill) often served
with a cube of feta.
Salad olivieh: like a russian salad,
includes chopped potatoes, chicken,
eggs, peas, gherkins, olive oil and
mayonnaise.

Modern European

Modern European cuisine is coming of age in London. The UK's strong historical links with the rest of the world, together with an indigenous repertoire of dishes that was largely free from rigid laws of interpretation (until recently, British food wasn't deemed sufficiently important to have anything remotely equivalent to *Larousse Gastronomique*) meant that chefs plying their trade in the capital had the world's larder to hand, a kaleidoscope of cultural influences for inspiration, and no tut-tutting if they overstepped national boundaries. In the earlier days of experimentation – the 1990s – some gastronomic aberrations appeared on Londoners' plates, but chefs gradually found out what worked and what didn't, and a new canon was formed. Fusion cooking based around the food of Asia can be found in our Pan-Asian & Fusion chapter (*see p214*) and other fearless experimenters who have raised the cuisine to an art form are listed in Hotels & Haute Cuisine (*p119*). In the following pages you'll discover restaurants with top-flight chefs grounded in the European idiom yet willing to add ingredients from around the globe in search of flavour, texture and colour – and there really are some corkers. Top of our current pops are Shoreditch's **Brawn**, with its skilful take on peasant cooking; **Medlar** in Chelsea, for complexity and culinary thrills; Soho's Med-tinged marvel, **10 Greek Street**; Kew's **Glasshouse**, with its neighbourhood fine dining; lofty **Plateau** in Docklands; the majestic updated pub **Empress**, near Victoria Park; Marylebone's magnificent **Orrery**; **Season Kitchen**, star of Finsbury Park's Stroud Green Road; and **Magdalen**, a polished performer near London Bridge. **Sotheby's Café** in the heart of town, and **Corner Room** in Bethnal Green also impressed. Every year, this chapter features some fabulous new venues, and 2013's highlights included the opening of **Claude's Kitchen**, a superb neighbourhood restaurant in Parsons Green, and Bruno Loubet's inventive **Grain Store** in King's Cross. Fashion and buzz cling to Modern Euro establishments, so you'll usually have to book – sometimes weeks in advance.

Central
Bloomsbury

Giaconda Dining Rooms
9 Denmark Street, WC2H 8LS (7240 3334, www.giacondadining.com). Tottenham Court Road tube. **Lunch served** noon-2.15pm, **dinner served** 6-9.15pm Mon-Fri. **Main courses** £9.50-£21. **Cover** £1.50. **Credit** AmEx, MC, V.
Extensive renovation, including moving the kitchen downstairs to create more room for tables, has not ruined the sense of intimacy at this soothing escape from the St Giles hubbub. Entry through a heavy velvet curtain leads to a simple, unflashy dining room and a warm welcome, after which staff astutely gauge when to chat or leave you in peace. The menu is long by modern standards, with 14 main courses and nearly 20 starters, and gives veal, duck and offal a broad platform. Chef-patron Paul Merrony's cooking style is elegantly butch, taking

most inspiration from France and Italy. Ethereal chicken liver pâté came with copious quantities of toasted ciabatta, all the better to share around. Rack of lamb arrived as three dainty cutlets, with sides of intensely flavoured aubergine parmigiana and cheesy pillows of gnocchi romana. The owners' Australian heritage gets a nod on the idiosyncratic wine list, but the emphasis is on France and Italy. Bottles start at £19; spending more brings rewards, such as a memorable 2006 Monte Dall'Ora Amarone for £52. We finished with Agen prunes steeped in red wine, and délice joconde, a dark chocolate terrine. *Available for hire. Babies and children admitted. Booking advisable. Separate room for parties, seats 30.* **Map 17 C3**.

Paramount
101-103 New Oxford Street, WC1A 1DD (7420 2900, www.paramount.uk.net). Tottenham Court Road tube.
Bar **Open** 8am-1.30am Mon-Wed; 8am-2.30am Thur-Sat; noon-4pm Sun.
Restaurant **Breakfast served** 8-10.15am Mon-Fri. **Lunch served** noon-3pm, **tea served** 3-5pm daily. **Dinner served** 6-11pm Mon-Sat. **Main courses** £14.50-£25.50. **Set lunch** (Mon-Fri) £23.50 2 courses, £28.50 3 courses. **Set dinner** (5.30-6.30pm) £30 3 courses. *Both* **Credit** AmEx, MC, V.
With the Shard and other glistening new skyscrapers now offering fine dining with views, it's easy to forget about Centre Point. Since 1967, the concrete edifice has dominated the west end of Oxford Street; but only since 2000 has it had a showcase restaurant on the 33rd floor, with spectacular views on every side across central London. In the evening, the glam factor ramps up, mainly with out-of-towners hitting the West End. During the day, tourists tend to come – an afternoon-tea service was added in 2013. While the cooking is perfectly good, the dishes can also seem slightly dated, and wouldn't look out of place in a thrusting 1990s gastrodome. A starter of double-baked cheese soufflé didn't quite cause the

sensation that the Stephen Bull signature dish did two decades previously, but was enjoyable nonetheless. Pan-fried fillet of sea bream was nicely cooked with a crisp skin, but there was no warning of the diced bacon among the heritage carrots in an otherwise meat-free dish. Puddings include a lemon posset (not unlike panna cotta) at a high-rise £9.50. Most à la carte dishes only prove the rule that the higher the elevation of a restaurant, the more vertiginous the pricing, but there are also set meals that offer better value.

Babies and children welcome (restaurant): high chairs. Booking essential, 1 wk in advance. Disabled: lift; toilet. Dress: smart; no sportswear. Separate rooms for parties, seating 16-30 and 150. **Map 17 C2.**

Clerkenwell & Farringdon

Smiths of Smithfield
67-77 Charterhouse Street, EC1M 6HJ (7251 7950, www.smithsofsmithfield.co.uk). Barbican tube or Farringdon tube/rail.
Café-bar **Open** 7am-11pm Mon-Wed; 7am-midnight Thur, Fri; 9.30am-midnight Sat; 9.30am-5pm Sun. **Meals served** 7am-4.45pm Mon-Fri; 9.30am-4.45pm Sat, Sun. **Main courses** £5.50-£10.50.
Cocktail lounge **Open** 5pm-midnight daily.
Dining Room **Lunch served** noon-2.45pm Mon-Fri. **Dinner served** 6-10.45pm Mon-Sat. **Main courses** £12-£28.
Top Floor **Lunch served** noon-2.45pm Mon-Fri; 12.30-3.45pm Sun. **Dinner served** 6-10.45pm Mon-Sat. **Main courses** £16-£30.
All **Credit** AmEx, MC, V.
When Smiths opened in 2000 under the direction of chef John Torode (better known today as a presenter of *MasterChef*), it had buzz and boldness. And four floors – four tiers of dining and drinking,

from casual to fine dining. Mr Torode left the restaurant early in 2013, but it's still very popular. This year, we ate in the Top Floor, the 'fine dining' area – which means higher prices, lots of well-fed City gents, and a humidor of pricey cigars. There were two outstanding dishes. A 32-day-aged rump steak of Dexter beef was wildly flavourful and accurately cooked. Fat chips arrived perfectly crisp without, meltingly soft within. Beef pudding was great, as were the accompanying truffled potatoes. Nothing else was memorable, and some dishes were a disgrace. Rubbery salt and pepper squid inside a pallid, stodgy batter was just dreadful. Wild garlic soup had nearly imperceptible flavour and was so tepid that a skin had formed on top. Middle White pork, a modishly deconstructed assemblage, included a Chinese-style dumpling with leathery pastry casing and dry, under-seasoned shreds in the filling. The wine list makes little effort under £30. Staff tried hard, but our waiter's creaky English made communication difficult. On other floors, the noise level is ear-shattering. As we were leaving, a pair of minicab drivers were touting for business inside the front door. Somehow that says a lot about the current state of Smiths.

Babies and children welcome (restaurant): high chairs; nappy-changing facilities. Disabled: lift; toilet. Entertainment (ground floor): DJs 7pm Thur-Sat. Separate rooms for parties, seating 12 and 24. Tables outdoors (4, pavement; 8, terrace). **Map 11 O5.**
For branch see index.

Covent Garden

L'Atelier de Joël Robuchon
13-15 West Street, WC2H 9NE (7010 8600, www.joel-robuchon.com). Leicester Square tube.
Bar **Open** noon-2am Mon-Sat; noon-10.30pm Sun.

Ground floor **Lunch served** noon-2.30pm, **dinner served** 5.30-10.30pm Mon-Sat; 5.30-10pm Sun. **Main courses** £15-£55. **Set meal** (noon-2.30pm, 5.30pm & 6.30pm) £29 2 courses, £35 3 courses, £40 4 courses.
1st floor **Lunch served** noon-2.30pm, **dinner served** 6.30pm-midnight Mon-Sat. **Main courses** £15-£55.
All **Credit** AmEx, MC, V.
The London branch of Robuchon's high-end globe-spanning chain (there are also outposts in Las Vegas, Taipei and his native Paris) could be anywhere in the world, but thinks it's funkier than most gastronomic shrines. The ground-floor restaurant – sorry, 'counter concept' – is an international nightclub-like red- and black-lacquered room with red leather high stools either facing the chefs at their balancing-act work or at small tables. Customers are mostly tourists, drawn by the reputation for quality control across continents and clever layering of texture and flavour – distilled in a stunning amuse-bouche of foie gras under a port reduction and hot, umami-rich froth. Flavours are big, such as pig's trotter with bone marrow on toast, powered up with parmesan (a rewarding choice from the small plates menu). Portions aren't prissy, either; from the set lunch, chicken escalope dotted with dark olives and roasted cherry tomatoes covered the plate. Steak tartare was exceptionally punchy, though the accompanying description of 'hand-cut chips' was lost in translation – they were actually own-made crisps. Mashed potato was wonderfully rich and smooth, and a side plate of glisteningly green olive oil-bathed courgettes and puréed spiced carrots was no afterthought. Desserts conjured with refreshing and intensely flavoured combinations of jellies, mousses, foams and ices. Except for lunch, pricing is pitched at fat wallets, with menus and wines matched into accessible packages. Knowledgeable staff come with a twinkle.

Paramount

Available for hire. Babies and children welcome: high chairs; nappy-changing facilities. Booking advisable, essential dinner. Disabled: toilet. Dress: smart casual. Vegetarian menu. **Map 17 C3**.

The Ivy

1 West Street, WC2H 9NQ (7836 4751, www.the-ivy.co.uk). Leicester Square tube. **Meals served** noon-11.30pm Mon-Sat; noon-10.30pm Sun. **Main courses** £9.75-£34.50. **Set meal** (Mon, Sun; noon-6.15pm, 10-10.30pm Tue-Thur) £21.75 2 courses, £26.25 3 courses. **Cover** £2. **Credit** AmEx, DC, MC, V.

The long wait for a reservation can be attributed to the Ivy's one-time reputation as a celeb hangout. The gorgeous room may not attract as many A-listers as it once did, but there was one B-plus (glamorous if faded actress) on a Monday lunchtime. Other customers were a nice mix: business people, affluent couples, tourists and a family or two (one with yelping baby). Our meal, ordered both from the carte and the set menu, began startlingly well. Fish soup was as deeply flavourful as any you'll find in France, and a lunchtime special – poached egg 'Arlington' – sandwiched a perfectly cooked egg between a toast round and divine smoked salmon, with luxuriant hollandaise topping it off. Mains let the show down woefully. Bang-bang chicken was bathed in a gloopy sauce that palled after a few mouthfuls. The set lunch main, herb-roasted salmon with horseradish velouté, featured fish so dry it might have been petrified, and had no perceptible herb taste; the smidgen of sauce was bland. Impeccably attentive, smiling service is a redeeming feature. So is the relative quiet, even when busy. The wine list starts, half-heartedly, at around £25 and features some enthusiastic mark-ups. There's good food to be had, but choose badly and you won't creep back to the Ivy in a hurry.

Babies and children welcome: high chairs. Booking essential, 4-6 wks in advance. Separate room for parties, seats 60. Vegan dishes. Vegetarian menu. **Map 18 D4**.

Fitzrovia

Berners Tavern NEW

10 Berners Street, W1T 3NP (7908 7979, www.bernerstavern.com). Oxford Circus or Tottenham Court Road tube.
Bar **Open** 11am-11pm daily.
Restaurant **Breakfast served** 7-10.30am, **lunch served** noon-2.30am, **dinner served** 6-10.30pm daily. **Main courses** £15-£26.
Both **Credit** AmEx, MC, V.

The huge lobby bar of the London Edition hotel (a collaboration between design-hotel specialist Ian Schrager and industry giant Marriott) looks fabulous, but the vast dining room, with its ornate plasterwork ceiling and lively bar area, looks even better. Restaurateur Jason Atherton runs the catering side (with Phil Carmichael as head chef): this is his third West End restaurant to open in 2013, after Little Social and Social Eating House, both very well received for their playful and appealing dishes. Berners Tavern is more of the same, but in a much grander setting. And with much grander prices. The flavours of tender pork belly with sharp capers, golden raisins and apple coleslaw, and of cod with fennel and cider sauce, were sublime. A starter of 'egg ham and peas' is an update on a signature Atherton recipe: a breadcrumbed egg, molten in the middle, held upright by a purée of fresh peas, the air-dried ham almost a garnish. The only culinary

Berners Tavern

disappointment was a chocolate éclair, as the pastry – which should be very slightly stale – was overly so. Any caveats? Sometimes dizzy service; frequent upselling of extras; and lighting so low we could barely read the menu. But Berners Tavern is glamtastic. Wear your heels or best threads, and book ahead for a preliminary cocktail in the adjoining Punch Room bar to steel yourself for that punishing bill later.

Babies and children welcome: children's menu; high chairs; nappy-changing facilities. Booking essential dinner. Disabled: lift; toilet. Separate room for parties, seats 14. **Map 17 A2.**

Picture NEW

110 Great Portland Street, W1W 6PQ (7637 7892, www.picturerestaurant.co.uk). Goodge Street or Oxford Circus tube. **Lunch served** noon-3pm, **dinner served** 5-11pm Mon-Sat. **Dishes** £6-£9. **Credit** AmEx, MC, V.

Pretty as a picture, with a clean design and plenty of natural light from a huge atrium roof, this new restaurant draws you in with its good looks and smiling, welcoming staff. The menu is on-trend too, with small sharing plates of seasonal and mostly British ingredients. The simplest dishes were the straightforward assemblies: herring rollmops served with some simple colourful shards of veg, and a sliver of smoked eel with pickled heritage carrots and beets. Not every dish hit the mark. Lebanese fried chicken wouldn't win over anyone in the Deep South, and a dull barbecue sauce was no match for a baked cube of pig's cheek. The lowest points of the meal were the desserts: a raspberry and almond tart was overcooked and dry, and blobs of coconut rice with more blobs of mushy mango was simply unappetising. Despite uneven dishes, Picture still has much to recommend it. The staff were charming and on the ball, and the wine list offers plenty of interesting and unusual wines by the glass, such as a rosé pinot noir from the Loire. A five-minute walk from Oxford Circus, this is an appealing place for a glass of wine and snack. Coffee and drinks are served all afternoon.

Available for hire. Babies and children welcome: high chairs. Booking advisable Thur-Sat. Tables outdoors (2, pavement). **Map 9 J5.**

King's Cross

Grain Store NEW

Granary Square, 1-3 Stable Street, N1C 4AB (7324 4466, www.grainstore.com). King's Cross St Pancras tube/rail. **Lunch served** noon-2.30pm Mon-Fri; 11am-3pm Sat; 11am-4pm Sun. **Dinner served** 6-10.30pm Mon-Sat. **Main courses** £12-£22.50. **Set lunch** £35 6 courses. **Set dinner** £30 5 courses. **Credit** MC, V.

The industrial wasteland north of King's Cross station has been transformed by a hugely ambitious regeneration project. Grain Store occupies just one part of a vast former Victorian warehouse; most of the rest of the building has been imaginatively transformed into Central Saint Martins arts college. The restaurant inhabits its warehouse corner a little uneasily, but has been prettied up with an open kitchen, batterie de cuisine and wine racks. It's run by Bruno Loubet, who made his mark with the sensational Bistrot Bruno in Soho (now closed) and Bistrot Bruno Loubet (*see p86*) in Clerkenwell. Loubet was born in Bordeaux, and his cooking is grounded in the classical traditions of south-west France, but not bound by them. The menu is a pick

'n' mix of ingredients and cuisines, yet consistency of style and imaginative flavour pairings are recognisably Loubet. Vegetables are his current passion, and nearly half the dishes are marked as vegetarian. Pretty colours and simple preparation made a platter of baked beetroots, pickled onions and labneh (strained goat's cheese/yoghurt) into an attractive dish. Meat is also given serious attention, though mainly as the sideshow. A cube of sticky pork belly accompanied a corn and quinoa tamale, the filling kept very moist by the corn husk wrapper while griddled. It's worth arriving early for a drink in the attached bar, where cocktails have been conceived by barmeister Tony Conigliaro.

Available for hire. Babies and children welcome: high chairs. Booking advisable. Disabled: toilet. Separate room for parties, seats 12. Tables outdoors (30, terrace). **Map 4 L2.**

Knightsbridge

Fifth Floor

Harvey Nichols, Knightsbridge, SW1X 7RJ (7235 5250, www.harveynichols.com). Knightsbridge tube. *Café* **Breakfast served** 8am-noon, **lunch served** noon-3.30pm, **dinner served** 6-10.30pm Mon-Sat. **Brunch served** 11am-5pm Sun. **Tea served** 3-6pm daily. **Main courses** £9.50-£15.
Restaurant **Meals served** noon-10.30pm Mon-Sat; noon-5pm Sun. **Tea served** 3-5pm daily. **Set meal** £25 2 courses, £32 3 courses. *Both* **Credit** AmEx, DC, MC, V.

The furnishings here change regularly, as befits a restaurant in a store that's synonymous with high fashion. It seemed to be a tent theme when we went, and with flowers aplenty on display, the top-floor space looked great. So did the food, which was mostly of a very high standard. On the two-course set menu, called 'Season', only mains are printed, with regularly changing starters divided into vegetarian, meat and shellfish. We loved everything in the first course, a deconstructed and completely delicious steak tartare, and perfectly poached sea trout served with wasabi crème fraîche. Mains were more mixed. Roast duck with chanterelles and a carrot and nutmeg purée was a wonderful combination, the duck timed precisely; but grilled polenta with wild mushrooms included a wedge of brie that was simply redundant – the dish would have been fine without it. Puddings are mostly designed for people who don't need to worry about getting into their slinkiest Prada mini-dress. Banoffi and milk candy pie was a little gummy, yet tasted great. The wine list is taken from Harvey Nicks' retail list, which is one of London's best and caters well for people on limited budgets. Service was warm and efficient throughout.

Babies and children welcome: children's menu; high chairs; nappy-changing facilities. Disabled: lift; toilet. Tables outdoors (15, café terrace). **Map 8 F9.**

Marylebone

★ Orrery

55 Marylebone High Street, W1U 5RB (7616 8000, www.orrery-restaurant.co.uk). Baker Street or Regent's Park tube. **Lunch served** noon-2.15pm, **dinner served** 6.30-10.15pm daily. **Set lunch** £23-£34 2 courses, £26-£38 3 courses; (Sun) £29.50 3 courses. **Set dinner** (6.30-7pm, 9-10.15pm Mon-Sat) £26 3 courses;

(Mon-Sat) £49 3 courses; (6.30-8.30pm Mon-Sat) £60 tasting menu (£110 incl wine). **Credit** AmEx, DC, MC, V.

This serene, elegant Marylebone dining room with bucolic views through arched windows was the setting for a meal that astonished us in every way. The Ukrainian chef, Igor Tymchyshyn, has achieved the seemingly impossible – a £26 menu du jour of exceptional beauty, glamour and flavour. A starter of lobster bisque with seafood ravioli was pure luxury; chicken liver pâté was served on a raft of toasted Poilâne, heaped with tangy apple chutney and scattered with pea shoots. A main course of salmon was offered – and came – slightly pink, its quotidian flavours transformed by caramelised fennel and butternut squash; beef à la bordelaise was tender and fabulous. Crème brûlée came with a half moon of candied nuts – a lovely rainbow of spring colours. Every detail, down to the amuse-bouche (parsnip purée with white truffle foam) was faultless, and we loved the Japanese-style presentation with its asymmetric shapes. The wines (around £9 a glass) aren't cheap, but the obliging French sommelier, one of an all-female trio, replaced our dry and unforgiving Loire chenin with a fruity riesling without demur. Dine on the rooftop terrace in summer and save up for the £60 menu gourmand (scallops, lobster and foie gras).

Available for hire. Babies and children welcome: high chairs; nappy-changing facilities. Booking essential. Disabled: toilet. Dress: smart casual. Separate room for parties, seats 18. Tables outdoors (5, roof terrace). Vegetarian menu. **Map 3 G4.**

Mayfair

★ Sotheby's Café

Sotheby's, 34-35 New Bond Street, W1S 2RT (7293 5077, www.sothebys.com/cafe). Bond Street or Oxford Circus tube. **Breakfast served** 9.30-11.30am, **lunch served** noon-2.45pm, **tea served** 3-4.45pm Mon-Fri. **Main courses** £15-£21.50. **Set tea** £8.25-£21.25. **Credit** AmEx, DC, MC, V.

An alcove off Sotheby's ground-floor main corridor seems an unlikely place to find a distinguished restaurant, but sweet, smooth service and a fabulously talented chef combine to make the unlikely a reality. The best food here can comfortably bear comparison with anything being cooked in London. There are limitations, naturally. The atmosphere is rather staid, and the reek of casual affluence hangs heavy in the air despite the corridor setting. If those things don't bother you, pile in for some sensational cooking. A carefully roasted fillet of salmon came with courgettes cut into fine shreds and tossed with feta and pine nuts atop a slice of toast. Only a slight oiliness in the toast kept this from being a five-star dish. No such obstacles lay in the way of a starter of grilled scallops with chorizo and sweetcorn purée. The marriage of flavours between sweet mollusc, spicy sausage and subtly seasoned sweetcorn was simply sublime – one of the best things we've eaten in London in recent memory. Equally memorable was an own-made ice-cream of peanut, chocolate and salted caramel. The wine list is tiny, imaginatively chosen and modestly priced. There's breakfast and tea as well as lunch, and a full bar. Chef Laura Greenfield is extraordinarily talented. Come and treat yourself to lunch, and see for yourself.

Babies and children admitted. Booking advisable (lunch). Disabled: toilet. **Map 9 H6.**

Wild Honey

12 St George Street, W1S 2FB (7758 9160, www.wildhoneyrestaurant.co.uk). Bond Street or Oxford Circus tube. **Lunch served** noon-2.30pm, **dinner served** 6-11pm Mon-Sat. **Main courses** £24-£30. **Set lunch** (Mon-Fri) £28 3 courses. **Set dinner** £35 3 courses. **Credit** AmEx, MC, V.

Wild Honey underwent a revamp in autumn 2012 – the dining room still has the same wood-panelling meets modern-art vibe as before, but it's now possible to look from one end of the vibrantly accessorised (the soft furnishings, in particular) restaurant to the other. The quirky nooks and crannies have been lost, but it no doubt makes things easier for the staff. A meal from the spring menu promised much, but didn't always deliver: organic salmon, with piquillo peppers, butter beans and parsley, was almost raw in parts; and Scottish crab with guacamole and green mango (a starter) was almost too delicate in flavour (only white meat was used). Ravioli of wild Italian greens with Moroccan lemon peel, followed by grilled young chicken with spring vegetable risotto (on the daily set dinner) were a masterful reminder of what the kitchen can do. Ditto puddings – light and zingy alphonso mango with yoghurt mousse, chilli and lime, and a glorious, assertively flavoured cold chocolate fondant with stout ice-cream and chocolate biscuit. La Fromagerie cheeses are an option. Like sister restaurants Arbutus and Les Deux Salons, wine from a global list comes in 250ml carafes as well as bottles. Service was good, but like the food, not quite as flawless as on previous visits.
Available for hire. Babies and children welcome: high chairs. Booking essential. **Map 9 H6.**

Piccadilly

Criterion

224 Piccadilly, W1J 9HP (7930 0488, www.criterionrestaurant.com). Piccadilly Circus tube. **Lunch served** noon-2.30pm, **dinner served** 5.30-11.30pm Mon-Sat. **Main courses** £16-£28.50. **Set meal** (lunch, 5.30-7pm, 10-11.30pm) £20 2 courses, £25 3 courses. **Credit** AmEx, MC, V.

Built in 1874, the Criterion must be one of London's loveliest dining rooms, with its fabulous baroque-style gold ceilings and marble columns. The place where Churchill and Lloyd George once thrashed out their political views is now popular with tourists, office workers and a theatre-going bridge-and-tunnel crowd. At first we were hopeful – tables are well spaced, the acoustics good, the staff attentive. A £23 set menu rich in prime British ingredients (Hereford beef, Shetland mussels, Suffolk lamb) set a pleasingly patriotic tone. Sadly, though, the cooking proved too erratic to do full justice to the room. Low marks went to an oversalted Aylesbury duck leg with broccoli – an uninspired, school-dinner dish undeserving of its £3 supplement. Salmon, perched on a nest of samphire over a pool of beetroot, was better – but far from thrilling. Other diners seemed happy enough. By 9pm every table was busy, the room was buzzing and a male singer was crooning bluegrass numbers. An unseasonal strawberry and raspberry eton mess, prettily deconstructed into its separate elements, arrived just as a Spanish tour group trooped through the restaurant, too jaded and footsore to even notice the beauty of their surroundings.

Babies and children welcome: high chairs. Booking advisable. Disabled: toilet. Dress: smart casual. Separate room for parties, seats 70. **Map 17 B5.**

St James's

Avenue

7-9 St James's Street, SW1A 1EE (7321 2111, www.theavenue-restaurant.co.uk). Green Park tube.
Bar **Open** 11am-11pm Mon-Fri; 5.45-11pm Sat. *Restaurant* **Lunch served** noon-2.30pm Mon-Fri. **Dinner served** 5.45-11pm Mon-Sat. **Main courses** £13.50-£20.50. **Set lunch** £19.50 2 courses, £23.50 3 courses, incl glass of wine. *Both* **Credit** AmEx, DC, MC, V.

This spacious restaurant in a neighbourhood famous for its gentlemen's clubs and old-fashioned shops draws a sleek, young crowd. The vibe is pure '90s – flashy suits, lofty ceilings, splashy artwork. Cooking is clearly not the draw. A £23.50 set menu (three courses including a decent glass of Gascon wine) ticked the seasonality and British sourcing boxes, but failed to show much culinary flair. A smoked salmon starter was attractively presented on a wooden raft, but the fish was flabby and over-salted. A burger, lukewarm and garnished with a clump of iceberg lettuce, could have been outperformed by any gastropub; poached chicken was largely flavourless. Possibly the smallest tarte tatin in Britain (a pear version) was delicious, but chocolate fondant was a let-down. Staff (rarely the same waiter twice) were friendly and well drilled, though we could have done without the inevitable upselling of side orders. To us, and perhaps to the spry old ladies at the next-door table (escapees from the Royal Academy?), the place felt brash, soulless and at odds with the handsome dignity of the area. The welter of recession-friendly deals (including pre- and post-theatre offers) is gratifying, but we found little here to excite.
Available for hire. Babies and children admitted. Booking advisable. Disabled: toilet. Separate room for parties, seats 20. **Map 9 J8.**

Le Caprice

Arlington House, Arlington Street, SW1A 1RJ (7629 2239, www.caprice-holdings.co.uk). Green Park tube. **Meals served** noon-midnight Mon-Fri; 11.30am-midnight Sat; 11.30am-11pm Sun. **Main courses** £15.75-£32. **Set dinner** (5.30-6.45pm, after 10.15pm) £19.75 2 courses, £24.25 3 courses. **Cover** £2. **Credit** AmEx, DC, MC, V.

Staff at Le Caprice make a great fuss of their regulars, remembering foibles and preferences; but even if you're not a known face (or a celebrity), you'll still be cosseted. After decades in the trade, the Caprice sustains the sort of buzz the 'West End' is supposed to mean, with its flash clientele, art deco-ish black and chrome fittings and David Bailey photos. The classic brasserie-style menus emphasise the reliably enjoyable rather than culinary adventures, but a restaurant like this doesn't stay popular without the kitchen being on the ball. Fragrant roast duck and pomelo salad with spiced cashews made a lively semi-oriental starter; grilled sand soles with capers were cooked to perfection, the top-quality fish falling softly off the bone. Salmon fish cake with sorrel sauce and buttered spinach is a menu stalwart, but specials (such as sautéed Isle of Man queenie scallops with wild garlic and chilli) add variety as well as

seasonality. Prices are predictably on the lofty side, though good-value pre- and post-theatre menus offer a way of sampling the experience for a lower outlay. Parent group Caprice Holdings's stable of upmarket restaurants also includes J Sheekey and Scott's (for both, *see p82*) and The Ivy.
Available for hire. Babies and children welcome: high chairs. Booking essential, 2 wks in advance. Entertainment: pianist 6.30pm-midnight daily. Tables outdoors (6, terrace). Vegetarian menu. **Map 9 J8.**

Soho

Andrew Edmunds

46 Lexington Street, W1F 0LW (7437 5708, www.andrewedmunds.com). Leicester Square, Oxford Circus or Piccadilly Circus tube. **Lunch served** 12-3.30pm Mon-Fri; 12.30-3.30pm Sat; 1-4pm Sun. **Dinner served** 5.30-10.45pm Mon-Sat; 6-10.30pm Sun. **Main courses** £11-£20. **Credit** MC, V.

A Soho stalwart, so seemingly unchanged over the years that our review of 20 years ago still stands today: '…a jolly bistro, always packed to the gills with lunchtime regulars. The wine list is well chosen, the food unpretentious…' (*Time Out Eating & Drinking Guide*, 1994). And that's exactly how the customers like it: unfussy starters (daily changing salad, welsh rarebit, smoked salmon plate or dressed crab are typical) and no-nonsense, well-portioned mains, such as roast lamb with butter beans and broccoli. It's like the best sort of dinner party food (if your hosts had a great wine cellar). Chicken and mushroom pie with mash had smooth but not over-rich mash, pastry done to a T, and a generous filling. Desserts such as sticky toffee pudding with toffee sauce and vanilla ice-cream (Neal's Yard Dairy cheeses and a choice of sorbets are further options) complete the picture. Set on two small, slightly cramped floors, the look is wine-bar shabby and the atmosphere cosy; service is brisk but friendly. Kick off with the Kingston black apple brandy aperitif and forget about food fads and restaurant pop-ups for a few hours.
Babies and children admitted. Booking advisable. Tables outdoors (2, pavement). **Map 17 A4.**

Arbutus

63-64 Frith Street, W1D 3JW (7734 4545, www.arbutusrestaurant.co.uk). Leicester Square or Tottenham Court Road tube. **Lunch served** noon-2.30pm Mon-Sat; noon-3pm Sun. **Dinner served** 5-11pm Mon-Thur; 5-11.30pm Fri, Sat; 5.30-10.30pm Sun. **Main courses** £16-£21. **Set lunch** £17.95 2 courses, £19.95 3 courses. **Set dinner** (5-6.30pm) £18.95 2 courses, £20.95 3 courses. **Credit** AmEx, MC, V.

Laying tables without salt and pepper is a sign of a restaurant confident in its seasoning and flavours, but on our recent visit to this smart modern eatery, this confidence was slightly misplaced. A starter of Dorset crab, avocado guacamole, peanut and mango was untouched by seasoning, sauce or dressing, the result being bland rather than bold; and an otherwise delicious salad of broad beans, moroccan lemon and goat's cheese came with a wild garlic whose delicate flavours were lost to its heavy tempura batter. Arbutus is usually more disciplined, clever and successfully creative with unusual and less-used ingredients, and matters returned to their customary form with the main courses. Scottish salmon was of top quality, dark in colour and light in texture, nicely complemented

Picture. See p195.

by a concentrated hazelnut jus. Saddle of rabbit, prettily presented with small root vegetables and stuffed with liver, was intense and succulent – but small, until the accompanying shepherd's pie arrived 15 minutes later, a nice riposte with its salty flavours. We like the good-value set lunch and pre-theatre menus, the posh but proper puds and the fact that every wine is available by the 250ml carafe. Also run by Will Smith and Anthony Demetre are Wild Honey in Mayfair and Le Deux Salons (French – *see p87*) in Covent Garden.
Available for hire. Babies and children welcome: high chairs. Booking advisable. Dress: smart casual. **Map 17 B3.**

★ Bob Bob Ricard
1 Upper James Street, W1F 9DF (3145 1000, www.bobbobricard.com). Piccadilly Circus tube.
Lunch served noon-3pm, **dinner served** 6-10pm Mon-Fri. **Meals served** noon-10pm Sat. **Main courses** £14.50-£38.75. **Set lunch** (Mon-Fri) £31.75-£33.75 incl glass of wine. **Credit** AmEx, MC, V.
This enthusiastically outlandish spot has managed to achieve what many London restaurants earnestly desire but rarely deliver – it is out-and-out good fun. There's a joy evident in every element of the place, from the Roaring '20s decor to little touches such as the 'press for champagne' buzzers at each booth. The menu skips between Russia and Europe, cherry-picking treats: starters include platinum vodka shots chilled to -18°C, and venison tartare, while mains feature 'humble pie', three-birds burger and chicken kiev. BBR is the sort of

venue you can imagine Bertie Wooster taking his pals after a day at the Drones. At lunchtimes, it has been adopted by business types, with deals sealed over excellent food and ostentatiously shaken cocktails, as well as vintage bubbly and by-the-glass Château d'Yquem. We can recommend the classic prawn cocktail with piquant pink sauce, and the immensely gratifying borscht made with Orkney beef. The mariner's fish pie is another favourite, crammed with salmon and haddock in a thumpingly rich cream. Desserts are as playful as the rest of the operation; try a strawberries and cream soufflé or freshly flambéed crêpes suzette. A meal here isn't cheap, but if you're looking to intrigue and impress, this place is hard to better.
Booking advisable. Children over 12yrs admitted. Disabled: toilet. Dress: elegant (ties not required). Separate room for parties, seats 10. **Map 17 A4.**

★ 10 Greek Street HOT 50
10 Greek Street, W1D 4DH (7734 4677, www.10greekstreet.com). Tottenham Court Road tube.
Bar **Open** noon-11.30pm, **tapas served** noon-10.45pm Mon-Sat. **Tapas** £3-£7.
Restaurant **Lunch served** noon-2.30pm, **dinner served** 5.30-10.45pm Mon-Sat. **Main courses** £12-£19.
Both **Credit** AmEx, MC, V.
This small, unshowy restaurant has made a name for itself with a short but perfectly formed menu and an easy-going conviviality. Dishes are seasonal – ricotta-stuffed courgette flower with lentils, wild mushrooms and truffle, and chilled

asparagus and pea soup with crème fraîche were exemplary starters. And it's value for money too – the soup cost a fiver. The kitchen (under Australian chef Cameron Emirali) produces lots of interesting but ungimmicky combinations: notably a special of halibut fillet with yellow beans, chilli and garlic, on a vivid romesco sauce. There's more fish than meat, but Brecon lamb cutlets with borlotti beans, aubergine and courgettes earned their place on the menu. Cooking is not fault-free: gooseberry and apricot crumble had good fruit, but the topping was a little worthy. Better was a divine own-made lemon and basil sorbet doused with vodka. A thoughtful drinks list includes several variations on the negroni. Tables are closely packed, and in the evening it can get noisy, but otherswise it's hard to fault the place. Adept, friendly staff are a further plus. If you can't handle the no-booking policy at dinner, there's always lunch.
Available for hire. Babies and children welcome: high chairs. Booking advisable lunch; not accepted dinner. Separate room for parties, seats 7-12. Vegetarian menu. **Map 17 C3.**

South Kensington

Bibendum
Michelin House, 81 Fulham Road, SW3 6RD (7581 5817, www.bibendum.co.uk). South Kensington tube. **Lunch served** noon-2.30pm Mon-Fri; 12.30-3pm Sat, Sun. **Dinner served** 7-11pm Mon-Sat; 7-10.30pm Sun. **Main courses** £18-£32. **Set lunch** £26.50 2 courses, £30 3 courses. **Credit** AmEx, MC, V.

Grain Store. See p195.

Set on the first floor of the iconic Michelin building, this is one of the loveliest restaurant rooms in London – light and airy, not too big, with lots of stained glass – and attracts a mixed bag of diners. Head chef Matthew Harris's menu consists of classics, sometimes with a twist (a special of monkfish wrapped in prosciutto, with artichoke and chanterelles), sometimes without (fillet steak au poivre). The best dishes in a recent summer meal were starters: both charentais melon 'gazpacho' with brown shrimps and salsa, and spinach mousse with poached duck egg and anchovy hollandaise packed a flavoursome punch. Desserts are also worth ordering; the standout being a zingy peach bellini granita. Mains (deep-fried haddock and chips with tartare sauce, and roast quail with girolles) were good but not exceptional. And at these prices – the quail cost £25, and needed a side dish (courgette provençal, another £4) – 'nice enough' doesn't quite cut it. Service, while pleasantly unstuffy, was a little over-eager; water and wine constantly topped up, bread plates and pudding dishes whisked away before we'd quite finished. On the plus side, bread, olives and petits fours were generously distributed. The wine list is a serious prospect, but contains some affordable bottles. The no-bookings Oyster Bar on the ground floor is a charming spot in its own right.
Available for hire. Booking advisable. Babies and children welcome: high chairs. Disabled: lift. Vegetarian menu. **Map 14 E10.**
For branch see index.

West
Bayswater

Le Café Anglais [HOT 50]
8 Porchester Gardens, W2 4DB (7221 1415, www.lecafeanglais.co.uk). Bayswater tube. **Lunch served** noon-3.30pm Mon-Fri, Sun. **Brunch served** noon-3.30pm Sat. **Dinner served** 6.30-10.30pm Mon-Thur; 6.30-11pm Fri, Sat; 6.30-10pm Sun. **Main courses** £16.50-£22. **Set meal** (Mon-Fri) £20 2 courses, £25 3 courses. **Set lunch** (Sun) £25 2 courses, £30 3 courses. **Credit** AmEx, MC, V.
Whiteley's may have seen better days, but Rowley Leigh's celebrated brasserie looks as good as when it opened in 2008, with its art deco lines, tall leaded windows and graceful grey-green banquettes. At one end, beneath a stunning chandelier, is the café/oyster bar; at the other, the open kitchen. The appealing menu is nicely varied, from raw, cured and smoked seafood and meat (oysters, pickled herrings, rabbit rillettes) via assorted appetisers (the famous parmesan custard with anchovy toast, watercress soup) to straightforward bistro fare (omelette, burger, fish pie). Prices are steepish, but don't have to be: roast chicken leg with oregano and skordalia costs under a tenner. We enjoyed some excellent fish dishes – a juicy slab of hake with samphire and tomato (from the summer set menu) and two lip-smacking mackerel fillets that paired perfectly with gooseberry sauce – but kipper pâté (served in a dinky Kilner jar) was a bit rough and ready, and came with burnt toast and a cold soft-boiled egg. Staff were charming and attentive, and the wine list is enticing (if expensive). The main problem on our visit was lack of atmosphere; it's a big room, and without the hustle and bustle of a crowd can seem painfully quiet – a problem that no amount of culinary fireworks can remedy.

Available for hire. Babies and children welcome: high chairs. Booking advisable dinner. Disabled: toilet. Separate room for parties, seats 26. **Map 7 C6**.

Chiswick

Michael Nadra

6-8 Elliot Road, W4 1PE (8742 0766, www.restaurant-michaelnadra.co.uk). Turnham Green tube. **Lunch served** noon-2.30pm Mon-Fri; noon-3.30pm Sat, Sun. **Dinner served** 6-10pm Mon-Thur; 6-10.30pm Fri, Sat. **Set lunch** £19.50 2 courses, £24 3 courses, £39 tasting menu (£71 incl wine). **Set dinner** £29 2 courses, £35 3 courses, £49 tasting menu (£81 incl wine). **Credit** AmEx, MC, V.

It's hard to know why this Chiswick high-flyer, a hop and a skip from the chichi shops of Turnham Green Terrace, isn't better known. The food, cooked by Craig Best (ex La Trompette), dabbles in the Orient (chilli, daikon, ginger, soy), while showcasing the best of European ingredients (foie gras, burrata, English asparagus, serrano ham). Our set lunch – superb value at £24 for three courses – delivered on every level: presentation, originality, flavour, va-va-voom. Fish is a particular strength. Soft-shell crab (crisply tempura-ed) with daikon and sweet chilli was vibrant and zingily fresh, as was an unusual salmon ceviche with piquillo peppers and noisettes of sweet potato. Mains showed similar verve. Sautéed king prawns served with playfully criss-crossed fillets of sea bass and herby

tagliatelle had great depth of flavour; tender, flavoursome rabbit came with a sweet-sour caponata. A chocolate fondant could have done with more salted caramel, but this is a tiny quibble. Service was friendly and informed, the wine list a global affair with plenty of affordable options. The spartan room (monochrome photos, white walls, black chairs) lacks atmosphere, but the superb cooking made for a memorable meal. Get a boothed window table if you can.

Booking advisable. Children over 7yrs admitted. **For branch see index**.

Holland Park

Belvedere

Holland House, off Abbotsbury Road, in Holland Park, W8 6LU (7602 1238, www. belvedererestaurant.co.uk). Holland Park tube. **Lunch served** noon-2.15pm Mon-Sat; noon & 2.30pm Sun. **Dinner served** 6-10.15pm Mon-Sat. **Main courses** £22-£25. **Set meal** (lunch, 6-7pm Mon-Fri) £15.95 2 courses, £19.95 3 courses; (Sun) £27.95 3 courses. **Credit** AmEx, MC, V.

Walk through flower-filled Holland Park to enter a lofty-ceilinged cocoon of slightly kitsch opulence. Inside the erstwhile ballroom of Holland House, there are giant mirrors, ornate lamps, silk curtains, and delicate chinoiserie wallpapering, while a gleaming trolley hosts ranks of rare whiskies and liqueurs; from the bar area tall windows look out on to gardens. There are a few modern touches too

– a huge Damien Hirst butterfly painting – but attentive traditional service reinforces the feel of a more old-fashioned luxury. The Belvedere's culinary stamp is less distinctive. Dishes are Modern European with a French accent, and seem to offer a bit more than they deliver. Starters of a smooth, full-flavoured mushroom tart and subtly seasoned crab cakes with peanut oil mayonnaise were the best dishes we tried; mains had a clumsy lack of balance between high-quality tuna and overpowered ratatouille, and strangely under-flavoured venison and its accompanying red cabbage. It was all pleasant, but unmemorable; clearly diners come here (and pay the hefty prices) for the setting and the pampering, rather than for culinary adventures. The wine list is suitably grand, and inevitably pricey.

Available for hire. Babies and children welcome: high chairs. Booking essential. Dress: smart casual. Separate room for parties, seats 20. Tables outdoors (8, terrace). **Map 7 A8**.

Kensington

Clarke's [HOT 50]

124 Kensington Church Street, W8 4BH (7221 9225, www.sallyclarke.com). Notting Hill Gate tube. **Breakfast served** 8-10.30am Mon-Sat. **Lunch served** 12.30-2pm Mon-Fri; noon-2pm Sat. **Dinner served** 6.30-10pm Mon-Sat. **Main courses** £18.50-£25. **Set dinner** £29.50 2 courses, £35 3 courses. **Credit** AmEx, DC, MC, V.

Just around the corner from Notting Hill Gate, Clarke's is one of those places you'd like to have in your neighbourhood and be able to afford to eat at every week. The decor is smart but pretty – all crisp white linen, candles and a homely feel – and somehow you know the food will be equally artful yet unfussy. At Clarke's, that irritatingly overused 'best ingredients, simply prepared' phrase is actually true. A salad of peas, baby broad beans, spinach and grilled courgette looked like spring on a plate. Roasted salmon fillet from the no-choice set menu was a gorgeous deep pink and had an equally deep, robust flavour, set off by explosively sweet baked tomatoes and olives. Angus sirloin, horseradish sauce and hand-cut chips could have come from central casting, and was good value even at £25. Summer fruit jelly with cream and light sponge fingers encapsulated what's best about this long-standing favourite: familiarity, charm and elegance. After nearly 30 years, Clarke's premises have undergone a major change, with Sally Clarke's deli moving across the road to make way for a doubling of the ground-floor dining room. Let's hope everything else stays the same.

Available for hire. Babies and children welcome: high chairs. Booking advisable. Disabled: toilet. Dress: smart casual. Separate room for parties, seats 50. **Map 7 B7**.

Kensington Place

201-209 Kensington Church Street, W8 7LX (7727 3184, www.kensingtonplace-restaurant.co.uk). Notting Hill Gate tube. **Lunch served** noon-3pm Mon-Fri; noon-3.30pm Sat; noon-3.45pm Sun. **Dinner served** 6.30-10.30pm Mon-Thur; 6.30-10.45pm Fri, Sat. **Main courses** £11-£23. **Set lunch** (Tue-Fri) £17 2 courses, £20 3 courses. **Credit** AmEx, DC, MC, V.

'Holy the sea' says a wall-mounted slogan at this landmark establishment, and it's clear from the

Le Café Anglais

bright, colourful interior design – heavy on the piscine motifs and maritime paraphernalia – that fish is venerated at the rejuvenated Kensington Place. Sure, you can toy with a ham hock or waste your time on a veg risotto, but the smart money's on some fresh fillets plucked from banks of ice in the in-house fishmonger (which in turn is supplied by Billingsgate and the fisher-folk of Cornwall). These might be grilled and served with an aromatic beurre noisette or a smoky sauce vierge, heavy on the capers. On recent visits, we've been particularly taken with the sea bream and the lemon sole, teamed with triple-cooked chips and a pichet of vin blanc. Starters of mackerel rollmop with a delicate potato salad, and spiced crab with apple, were standouts, and an earthenware pot of raspberry and apricot crumble provided a splendid end to the meal. True to theme, the water is served in fish-shaped jugs, which glug rewardingly every time you pour. KP also contains a pleasant bar: a fine place to cradle a tawny port after an epic seafood session. Very civilised.

Available for hire. Babies and children welcome: high chairs. Booking advisable, essential weekends. Disabled: toilet. Separate room for parties, seats 45. **Map 7 B7**.

Kitchen W8

11-13 Abingdon Road, W8 6AH (7937 0120, www.kitchenw8.com). High Street Kensington tube. **Lunch served** noon-2.30pm Mon-Sat; 12.30-3pm Sun. **Dinner served** 6-10.30pm Mon-Sat; 6.30-9.30pm Sun. **Main courses** £19.95-£29.50. **Set lunch** (Mon-Sat) £21 2 courses, £23 3 courses. **Set dinner** (Mon-Fri) £22 2 courses, £25 3 courses. **Credit** AmEx, MC, V.

For understated Michelin-starred charm, look no further than Kitchen W8. Just off the main drag, on an unassuming stretch of street, this dining room exudes refinement with its orderly white table linen and smooth, unstuffy service. Furnished in a muted colour palette, a few olive green banquettes breaking what otherwise might be monotony, there's nothing remotely ostentatious here. The restaurant is busy throughout the week and at weekends, with diners in the know coming for the pedigree: founding partner Philip Howard is co-owner of both the Square (*see p125*) in Mayfair and the Ledbury (*see p127*) in Notting Hill. The menu is Anglo-French, its delicate mains featuring the finest seasonal ingredients. A pretty starter of heritage tomatoes with marinated peppers was served at an exacting temperature to bring out the flavours. A main of Cornish pollack was a delightfully fresh fillet accompanied by a novel swirl of cocoa bean purée. Desserts come into their own with characterful concoctions such as roasted hazelnut parfait with sea salt caramel ice-cream and chocolate-soaked brioche. The set lunch and dinner menus are one of the better-value ways to enjoy fine dining in London.

Available for hire. Babies and children welcome: children's menu (lunch Sun); high chairs. Booking advisable. Disabled: toilet. **Map 7 A9**.

Ladbroke Grove

Dock Kitchen

Portobello Docks, 342-344 Ladbroke Grove, W10 5BU (8962 1610, www.dockkitchen.co.uk). Ladbroke Grove tube then bus 52, 70, 452. **Bar Open** 5.30pm-midnight, **snacks served** 5.30-10pm Mon-Sat. **Main courses** £3-£4.

Portobello House Hotel

Sidebar (rotated, left margin): MODERN EUROPEAN

Restaurant **Lunch served** noon-2.30pm
Mon-Sat; noon-3.30pm Sun. **Dinner served**
7-9.30pm Mon-Sat. **Main courses** £17.50-£26.
Set lunch £10 1 course. **Set dinner** £35
3 courses.
Both **Credit** AmEx, MC, V.

Kitted out by furniture designer Tom Dixon and
with a kitchen manned by chef and food writer
Stevie Parle, Dock Kitchen is a handsome site. It
shoulders up to the Union Canal, with a broad
terrace overlooking a small dock that's ideal for
sunny days. The cooking – from a lively open
kitchen full of unreasonably good-looking staff –
is a flexible, seasonal, creative à la carte and a
themed set dinner (which changes every couple of
weeks). The former reads badly, mixing bistro
classics, Middle Eastern, Asian and European
dishes, and the welcome zaatar-laced flatbread is
no lead-in to lamb biriani or asparagus with
chopped egg. So we went for the themed (Mexican)
menu, which had enough verve to make us consider
coming back to try the à la carte. Mini tacos with
rich ox tongue and cheek were intense, moreish
bites – only a version with bream and a curiously
chewy taco fell flat. Next, a creamy, crunchy, stuffed
and fried courgette flower with a piquant salad, and
an impressive platter of pork, beef and chorizo
from the grill. To finish, chocolate and tequila ice-
cream with cinnamon-dusted churros was a real
star. Staff are relaxed and competent, and the whole
thing has just about enough panache to justify the
ambitious pricing.
*Available for hire. Babies and children welcome:
high chairs; nappy-changing facilities. Booking
advisable. Disabled: toilet. Separate room for
parties, seats 28. Tables outdoors (6, terrace).*

Portobello House Hotel NEW
*225 Ladbroke Grove, W10 6HQ (3181 0920,
www.portobellohouse.com). Ladbroke Grove tube.*
Meals served noon-11pm Mon-Sat; noon-10pm
Sun. **Main courses** £10-£25. **Dishes** £4. **Set
meal** (noon-5pm) £10 3 dishes. **Credit** AmEx,
MC, V.

Alumni of St John restaurant in Farringdon pop up
all over London these days, and the new head chef
at Portobello House is one of them. Having also
worked at the Anchor & Hope and Hereford Road,
Araldo de Vitis comes with a decent set of
credentials. By blending this experience with his
Italian heritage, the menu includes dishes such as
own-made pappardelle with beef ragù, and braised
ox cheek, bacon and mushroom pie. Located at
street level in a smart stuccoed hotel on a corner
site, the bistro/bar is handsomely attired in blue
wooden panelling and deep pink wallpaper. In
keeping with the gastropub vibe, there's also fish
and chips and a burger on the menu. A starter of
grilled cuttlefish arrived on a bed of pearl barley
cooked in the creature's ink. Though satisfyingly
smoky and full of earthy tones, it could have done
with more than the measly pinch of herb, lemon
zest and garlic-based gremolata with which it was
scattered. The pastry on the ox cheek pie was light
and crisp, and the meat tender, but the flavour was
somewhat masked by a surfeit of tomato purée.
With a few tweaks, the food could easily go from
average to very enjoyable, but for now the verdict
is 'could try harder.'
*Available for hire. Babies and children welcome:
high chairs; nappy-changing facilitites. Booking
advisable Thur-Sat. Disabled: toilet. Separate
room for parties, seats 25. Tables outdoors
(12, terrace; 5, pavement).* **Map 19 A2.**

Medlar. See p202.

South West
Barnes

Sonny's Kitchen
*94 Church Road, SW13 0DQ (8748 0393,
www.sonnyskitchen.co.uk). Barnes or Barnes
Bridge rail, or bus 33, 209, 283.*
Bar **Lunch served** noon-2.30pm Mon-Fri;
12.45-3.30pm Sat, Sun. **Brunch served** 10am-
12.30pm Sat, Sun.
Restaurant **Lunch served** noon-3pm Mon-Fri;
12.45-3.30pm Sat, Sun. **Dinner served** 6.30-
10pm Mon-Sat; 6.30-9.30pm Sun. **Set dinner**
(Mon-Thur) £16.50 2 courses, £19.50 3 courses.
Both **Main courses** £16.50-£19.50. **Set lunch**
(Mon-Thur) £16.50 2 courses, £18.50 3 courses;
(Sun) £21 2 courses, £25 3 courses. **Credit**
AmEx, MC, V.

Sonny's should get some kind of medal for
longevity of service: it's been sating the appetites
of Barnes' residents since 1986. After a few years
of slightly under-par performance, decor and menu
(and name) had a revamp in 2012, courtesy of
original owner Rebecca Mascarenhas, and chef
Philip Howard (of the Square); both live nearby. The
layout – café and bar at the front, restaurant in the
sunken rear area – hasn't changed, but the look is
fresher and more modern; happily, the eclectic art
collection remains. The succinct menu offers a half-
dozen or so choices each for starters, mains and
desserts, plus a trio of grilled meat dishes (baby
back ribs, burger, ribeye) and another of pizzas –
we're not convinced by the overall balance, but it's
still a popular spot for many occasions, from low-
key suppers to family celebrations. Succulent pan-
fried calf's liver worked well with rich creamed

potatoes and balsamic-glazed red onions; roast
pollack, with razor clams, barba di frate, leeks and
lardo di colonnata was also cooked with care, but
lacked excitement. Best was a pillowy passionfruit
soufflé with sharp lime ice-cream – much better
than a dull rice pudding with rhubarb compote.
Staff are pleasant but not always engaged. Next
door, Sonny's deli deals in upmarket packaged (and
some fresh) foodstuffs.
*Available for hire. Babies and children welcome:
children's menu; high chairs. Booking advisable
(restaurant). Separate room for parties, seats 18.*

Chelsea

Bluebird
*350 King's Road, SW3 5UU (7559 1000,
www.bluebird-restaurant.co.uk). Sloane
Square tube then bus 11, 19, 22, 49, 319.*
Lunch served noon-2.30pm Mon-Fri. **Brunch
served** noon-3.30pm Sat, Sun. **Tea served**
3-5pm Mon-Fri, Sun; 3-4.30pm Sat. **Dinner
served** 6-10.30pm Mon-Sat; 6-9.30pm Sun.
Main courses £13.50-£25. **Set meal** (lunch,
dinner Mon-Thur, Sun; lunch, brunch, 6-7pm,
9.30-10.30pm Fri, Sat) £20 2 courses, £25
3 courses. **Credit** AmEx, DC, MC, V.

Once a magnificent art deco garage complex with
links to speed record holder Sir Malcolm Campbell
(hence the name), this is now a multipurpose eating
and drinking venue, part of the D&D London
stable. At street level is a lively café (and front
courtyard) and food store. The restaurant is on the
first floor, where a disproportionate amount of
space is given to the bar. Some tables are tightly
packed together; bag a bigger one by the window
for a diverting view of the King's Road. Best visit
after dark: daylight pouring through the skylight

Claude's Kitchen

reveals stained carpet and scuffed chairs, and dressing the greeters in unflattering maroon takes the colour scheme too far. The kitchen delivers a roster of Anglo-French favourites (foie gras parfait, salmon fish cakes, steaks) with some flair. This was evident from parsley-speckled ham hock with a punchy, crunchy piccalilli. Terrific pastry, a topping of hollandaise sauce and an excellent pea shoot salad elevated a pea and leek tart above the usual 'veggie option'. Sourdough bread from the in-house bakery was tremendous. Some dishes lacked the finesse you'd expect for the price: too-salty butternut squash soup and mussels; unexceptional tarte tatin. Flash for your cash comes in the shape of a massive undulating piece of battered fish perched in a wire basket, and a giant knickerbocker glory glass topped with a banana. Not subtle or particularly sophisticated, but then neither is *Made in Chelsea*.
Available for hire. Babies and children welcome: high chairs; nappy-changing facilities. Booking advisable. Disabled: lift; toilet. Separate rooms for parties, seating 10-110. Tables outdoors (25, courtyard). Vegetarian menu. **Map 14 D12**.

Henry Root
9 Park Walk, SW10 0AJ (7352 7040, www.the henryroot.com). Fulham Broadway tube then bus 211, 414. **Open** 11am-midnight daily. **Meals served** noon-10.45pm Mon-Fri; 9am-10.45pm Sat; 9am-9.30pm Sun. **Main courses** £12.50-£23. **Set meal** (noon-7pm Mon-Fri) £12.50 2 courses. **Credit** AmEx, MC, V.
Going by the nom de plume of 1980s satirical writer William Donaldson, this Henry Root struggles to live up to its subversive credentials. The decor might be a happily offbeat melange, with shelves of books and curios and even gilt-framed postcards of risqué Edwardian ladies, but it feels out of step with the strait-laced clientele embroiled in debate about conservatories and London house prices. The small open kitchen at the back seems stretched at

peak times, with dishes arriving at unpredictable intervals. And while the menu features staples such as a choice of aged steaks, and, unusually, cottage pie as a special, the cooking didn't make them shine. A bright starter of fig, walnut, feta and rocket salad proved a slightly meagre helping; barbary duck breast was a touch rubbery and came with disappointingly greasy sarladaise potatoes. Better was the rolled pork belly, though it was overpowered by peppery tarragon mash. Service was polite but haphazard, and while we were indeed tempted by the glug jug (a 'glugging' fish water-jug, available to purchase), the awkward up-sell on sides and drinks was unappealingly transparent. Yet the Henry Root is popular, its decent wine list perhaps softening the lack of attention to detail.
Available for hire. Babies and children welcome: high chairs. Disabled: toilet. Tables outdoors (4, pavement). **Map 14 D12**.

★ Medlar
438 King's Road, SW10 0LJ (7349 1900, www.medlarrestaurant.co.uk). Fulham Broadway tube or bus 11, 22. **Lunch served** noon-3pm daily. **Dinner served** 6.30-10.30pm Mon-Sat; 6.30-10pm Sun. **Set lunch** (Mon-Fri) £26 3 courses; (Sat, Sun) £35 3 courses. **Set dinner** (Mon-Sat) £45 3 courses; (Sun) £35 3 courses. **Credit** AmEx, MC, V.
Even if you don't live near Chelsea, you should try to visit this exceptional restaurant at least once. The decor is understated: soothing grey-green colour scheme and unobtrusive artwork. The real artistry arrives on the plates, six dishes of astounding excellence. Assemblies are complex and have lengthy names, exemplified in our two starters: crisp calf's brain with smoked duck breast, aïoli, pink fir potatoes and tardivo (raddichio); and confit skate with razor-clam vinaigrette, purple sprouting broccoli, globe artichokes, Jersey Royals and salsify. But every ingredient justifies its place in entirely natural-seeming juxtapositions of

flavour, texture and colour. And the execution is nearly flawless, the only off-note being slightly undercooked potatoes. Save room for wonderful (and relatively simple) puddings. Cardamom custard with saffron oranges, pomegranate and langues de chat sang with flavour. And we loved it when, asked for an off-menu fruit salad, the kitchen sent out a bowl of beautiful orange segments, strawberries and pomegranate seeds. Weekday lunch is the cheapest option, though not for the six gents seated nearby who ordered two bottles of Dom Pérignon and carried on with serious red Burgundy (this is haut-Chelsea, after all). There's a small, high-quality selection of wines under £30, but £40 will give you a better time. For world-class cooking at this level of complexity, it's worth the extra money.
Babies and children welcome lunch: high chairs. Booking essential. Dress: smart casual. Separate room for parties, seats 14. Tables outdoors (3, pavement). **Map 14 D12**.

Parsons Green

★ Claude's Kitchen [NEW]
51 Parsons Green Lane, SW6 4JA (7371 8517, www.amusebouchelondon.com). Parsons Green tube. **Lunch served** noon-3pm Sat, Sun. **Dinner served** 6-10pm Tue-Sat. **Main courses** £14-£16. **Set dinner** (Tue) £16 2 courses, £20 3 courses. **Credit** AmEx, MC, V.
Set above Amuse Bouche (an inviting bar selling champers at friendly prices), this former function room has found new purpose as a terrific neighbourhood restaurant. The vibe is charmingly casual: the high Victorian ceilings have been strung with filament bulbs and the fireplace filled with tea-lights, while the champagne-themed posters are a hangover from the room's party-venue days. The weekly changing menu is courtesy of Claude Compton, who previously worked at Club Gascon and Petersham Nurseries. Both starter and pud

were innovative without being wacky – spears of white asparagus finished with goat's curd, zested lemon and a dusting of onion ash, and a finale of blood-orange slices drizzled with thick raspberry vinegar. But the real star was the main course: beef cheek slow-cooked to melting point, then teamed with a blend of tartare and horseradish sauce that was creamy yet sharp, with chunks of gherkin. The meat came over a dollop of creamed parsnip, finished with a silky hint of white chocolate. A hunk of bone stood to one side; the marrow had been scooped out, mixed with parsley and breadcrumbs, then returned to its shell for eating with a dainty spoon. But it's not just good food that makes a restaurant, it's great service too. And Claude's Kitchen appears to have hired the nicest bunch of people in town. For all these reasons, it should be applauded.

Available for hire. Babies and children welcome: high chairs. Booking advisable.

South

Brixton

Upstairs

89B Acre Lane, entrance on Branksome Road, SW2 5TN (7733 8855, www.upstairslondon. com). Clapham Common tube or Brixton tube/ rail. **Dinner served** 6-9.30pm Tue, Wed; 6.30-10pm Thur-Sat. **Set dinner** £28 2 courses, £35 3 courses, £41 4 courses. **Credit** AmEx, MC, V.
The Upstairs experience is more than a little confusing for first-timers. A doorway on a residential street takes you into what was formerly someone's home. With original fireplaces and minimal furnishings enlivened simply by feature walls of bold wallpaper and block colour, the makeover feels thinly disguised. The set menu is diminutive: each starter and main is a list of three ingredients, with no clue as to what form or proportions it will take. For example, 'pork, fennel,

Jersey Royals' sparked a hunt for the fennel, which turned out to be tiny cubes of jelly among an elaborately stacked portion of pork belly, loin of pork, artichoke heart and potatoes. 'Lamb, aubergine, tomato' contained a sliver of tongue, which was tender and delicious but may have proved off-putting for some. For pud, 'Rhubarb and ginger' included a pleasantly surprising ginger beer foam that left the mouth tingling. Chef Martyn Reynolds certainly has a wealth of skill at his disposal, with each dish a complex mix of flavours, textures and craftsmanship. At times, though, skill dominated the ingredients, leaving us a little unsure as to what we'd eaten. A hefty bill at the end (wine ramps up the total) felt fair taking the food into account, but a bit steep in terms of the modest setting.

Available for hire. Babies and children admitted. Booking advisable Tue-Fri, essential Sat. **Map 22 C2**.

Clapham

Abbeville Kitchen

47 Abbeville Road, SW4 9JX (8772 1110, www.abbevillekitchen.co.uk). Clapham South tube. **Breakfast served** 9.30-11.30am Sat, Sun. **Lunch served** noon-3pm Thur-Sat; 1-3.30pm Sun. **Dinner served** 6.30-10.30pm Mon-Sat; 6-10pm Sun. **Main courses** £11-£17. **Credit** AmEx, MC, V.
Of all the 'destination' restaurants in the locality, Abbeville Kitchen is the least known. That's a pity, because the Med-leaning cooking is terrific, but the venue suffers from unexceptional design. There's a mismatch of styles, with junk-shop dark-wood chairs and a hodge-podge of tables against a backdrop of smart, coral-hued weave, papered on to the walls. It's as if someone got halfway through, then changed tack. Look past these shortcomings, though, to the open kitchen, which sends out generously portioned dishes with thrilling, bold flavours. On our visit, meaty yet tender pieces of

cuttlefish sat over a full-flavoured, cumin-studded tomato and parsley sauce, with a blob of garlicky aïoli for good measure. No less satisfying was a dish of enormous hunks of salt beef on a mound of rustic green lentils, with a zingy salsa verde and pieces of sharp-and-sweet mustard fruits (think glacé cherries and candied orange pieces with a biting mustard end-note). A vegetarian choice was equally accomplished, featuring soft strips of smoked aubergine served with roasted red peppers, chickpeas, fresh goat's cheese and a dollop of tangy romesco (red pepper and nut sauce). The passionate staff were so sweet and eager, we wanted to put them in our pockets to take home.

Babies and children welcome: high chairs. Disabled: toilet. Tables outdoors (4, pavement). **Map 22 A3**.

Trinity

4 The Polygon, SW4 0JG (7622 1199, www.trinityrestaurant.co.uk). Clapham Common tube. **Lunch served** 12.30-2.30pm Tue-Fri; noon-2.15pm Sat; noon-3pm Sun. **Dinner served** 6.30-10.30pm Mon-Sat. **Main courses** £25-£38. **Set lunch** (Tue-Sat) £18 1 course, £22 2 courses, £27 3 courses; (Sun) £38 3 courses. **Set meal** (Tue-Sat) £50 tasting menu (£85 incl wine). **Cover** £1.50. **Credit** AmEx, MC, V.
Trinity remains Clapham's best restaurant, a destination for special occasions and celebratory splurges. It gets the right balance of smart (neat napery, cutting-edge cooking) and casual (smiling staff, hubbub of conversation). Recent price hikes might cause some eyebrow-raising (main courses now cost £25-£38), but the cooking is as good as ever. Our meal began with appetisers of plum radishes served with taramasalata, good bread and outstanding freshly churned butter. A starter of pig's trotter resembled a fish finger, but pierce the breading and chewy fragments of flavoursome pork spill out. Crackling, poached quail's egg and a slick of gribiche made such a pretty garnish it seemed a

Oxo Tower Restaurant, Bar & Brasserie. See p204.

Corner Room. See p207.

shame to spoil it. Less successful was a main course of rather chewy beef rump, with the accompanying barley and hemispheres of onion giving it a slightly gruel-like appearance and taste. Things improved again with baked stone bass, served with a courgette flower filled with a delicate scallop mousse, seaweed and samphire. Desserts might include cherry soufflé, or lemon sponge with ricotta. The wine list and service are exemplary, if aimed at lightening the embarrassment of City bonuses. The only irksome detail is that filtered tap water carries a £1.50 per head surcharge. If you're looking for something more affordable, try the much cheaper nearby offshoot, Bistro Union (see p41).

Available for hire. Babies and children admitted. Booking essential. Disabled: toilet. **Map 22 A1**.

Waterloo

Oxo Tower Restaurant, Bar & Brasserie

8th floor, Oxo Tower Wharf, Barge House Street, SE1 9PH (7803 3888, www.harvey nichols.com). Southwark tube or Waterloo tube/rail.
Bar **Open** 11am-11pm Mon-Wed; 11am-11.30pm Thur; 11am-midnight Fri, Sat; noon-10.30pm Sun. **Meals served** noon-11pm Mon-Sat; noon-10pm Sun. **Main courses** £6-£12.
Brasserie **Meals served** noon-11pm Mon-Sat; noon-10pm Sun. **Main courses** £13-£33. **Set meal** (noon-4.45pm, 5-6.15pm, after 10pm Mon-Fri; 5-6.15pm Sat; 6-6.30pm, after 9pm Sun) £24.50 2 courses, £29.50 3 courses.
Restaurant **Lunch served** noon-2.30pm Mon-Sat; noon-3pm Sun. **Dinner served** 6-11pm Mon-Fri; 5.30-11pm Sat; 6.30-10pm Sun. **Main**

courses £22-£35. **Set lunch** £36.50 3 courses. *All* **Credit** AmEx, DC, MC, V.

The Oxo Tower is a London landmark, and its restaurants – a dining room and brasserie, and a bar too – emanate a sense of occasion. A glass frontage makes the most of river views, but the brasserie terrace on a summer night was the ideal vantage point (or should have been, but the ferocious air-conditioning seemed to permeate even outside). Cooking has an adventurous global slant. Take beef carpaccio, here teamed with teriyaki onions, shimeji mushrooms and wasabi mayonnaise. Other dishes stick more consistently with their region of origin – as with our starter of lamb merguez sausages with couscous, houmous and dukka, which was fine but no more than the sum of fairly run-of-the-mill ingredients. Soft-shell crab was better, fried in fine golden breadcrumbs, with 'kimchi slaw' and a 'Korean barbecue mayonnaise' lending eastern bite. There's global inspiration in the mains too. Scallops with fried coconut cake, tomato kasundi (an Indian relish) and a coconut cucumber salad was our dish of the night: a generous portion of big, soft, meaty scallops set on polenta-like coconut cake, the salad a delicate accompaniment. Sea bass with oyster mushrooms and crayfish soba noodles was interesting too, but packed a milder punch. Service had a few mix-ups on our visit, but overall the vibe was good. Be prepared to pay for those glorious views, though.

Available for hire. Babies and children welcome: children's menu; high chairs. Booking advisable. Disabled: lift; toilet. Entertainment (brasserie): jazz lunch Sat, Sun; 7.30pm daily. Tables outdoors (50, brasserie terrace; 40, restaurant terrace). Vegan dishes. Vegetarian menu.
Map 11 N7.

Skylon

Royal Festival Hall, Belvedere Road, SE1 8XX (7654 7800, www.skylon-restaurant.co.uk). Waterloo tube/rail.
Bar **Open/snacks served** noon-midnight daily.
Brasserie **Meals served** noon-11pm daily.
Main courses £13-£30.
Restaurant **Lunch served** noon-2.30pm Mon-Sat; noon-4pm Sun. **Dinner served** 5.30-10.30pm Mon-Sat. **Set lunch** (Mon-Sat) £25 2 courses, £29 3 courses; (Sun) £26 2 courses, £29.50 3 courses. **Set dinner** £42 2 courses, £48 3 courses.
All **Credit** AmEx, DC, MC, V.

Skylon has the odds stacked in its favour: its setting on the first floor of the Royal Festival Hall, with lofty ceilings and superb Thames views from soaring windows, is always spectacular, by day or night, and adds wow factor to any meal. The chic cocktail bar, amid sofas in the centre of the space, also offers a dose of metropolitan pzazz. Dining areas are split between the brasserie-style Grill on one side of the bar, and the Restaurant, with a more fine-dining menu, on the other. Nothing in our meal (in the Grill) was as special as the view. Lentil salad with feta and piquillo peppers was pleasant; gravadlax with a 'russian salad' of beetroot and chives was smooth but a bit bland. Next, a Skylon burger was good but not exceptional; ditto Norfolk mussels with linguine, peppers, lemon and garlic – though the seafood was quality stuff. Many fellow-diners were drinking cocktails, perhaps because the hefty wine prices made them seem a relative bargain. Service was oddly slow at times despite an abundance of staff. A new head chef, Adam Grey, took over in spring 2013, bringing in a more British style than the former slightly Scandinavian-influenced menu.

Available for hire. Babies and children welcome: children's menu; high chairs. Booking advisable. Disabled: lift; toilet. Vegetarian menu. **Map 10 M8**.

South East

Crystal Palace

Exhibition Rooms

69-71 Westow Hill, SE19 1TX (8761 1175, www.theexhibitionrooms.com). Crystal Palace rail.
Bar **Open/snacks served** 5.30-11pm Mon-Wed; 5.30pm-midnight Thur; 5.30pm-1am Fri, Sat.
Restaurant **Lunch served** noon-4pm Fri, Sat. **Dinner served** 5.30-10pm Mon-Thur; 5-10.30pm Fri, Sat. **Meals served** noon-9pm Sun. **Main courses** £11-£23. **Set lunch** £8 1 course. **Set meal** (5.30-7pm Mon-Fri; 5-6.30pm Sat) £12 2 courses, £15 3 courses.
Both **Credit** AmEx, MC, V.
The Exhibition Rooms continues to offer a winning combination bang in the heart of the Crystal Palace triangle. It's a venue that can satisfy a number of criteria depending on when you go. For lunch, this leafy brasserie with lime green walls and light streaming in through sash windows is a relaxed choice for a smart yet unpretentious meal. In the evening, with large glittering chandeliers and soft lighting, it takes on a cosy, intimate feel. The downstairs bar, all leather and velvet in reds and purples, has a DJ at the weekends and a decked beer garden. On our lunchtime visit, the food was as reliable as ever, with a menu offering smart brasserie dishes alongside gastro favourites. Tender duck with a rich jus and crisp rösti was skilfully prepared and well presented. No less effort was given to the 'signature' burger, a satisfying stack laden with quality beef and accompanied by a tangy onion chutney. Sticky toffee pudding, complete with retro spun-sugar basket, was equally competent. Service was friendly and prompt, and the comprehensive drinks list runs from great cocktails to a global choice of wines, with plenty by the glass. It's not the place for cutting-edge cuisine, but it's a reliable choice for well prepared meals with classic flavour combinations.
Babies and children welcome Mon-Thur; until 7pm Fri, Sat; children's menu; high chairs; nappy-changing facilities. Booking advisable, essential weekends. Disabled: toilet. Tables outdoors (5, courtyard).

Greenwich

Inside

19 Greenwich South Street, SE10 8NW (8265 5060, www.insiderestaurant.co.uk). Greenwich rail/DLR. **Lunch served** noon-2.30pm Tue-Fri; noon-3pm Sat, Sun. **Dinner served** 6.30-11pm Tue-Sat. **Main courses** £13.95-£21.95. **Set lunch** (Mon-Fri) £12.95 2 courses, £17.95 3 courses; (Sat, Sun) £18.95 2 courses, £23.95 3 courses. **Set dinner** (Tue-Thur; 6.30-8.30pm Fri, Sat) £19.95 2 courses, £24.95 3 courses. **Credit** AmEx, MC, V.
Often referred to as Greenwich's best restaurant – an accolade it's held for most of the ten-plus years it's been open – Inside didn't disappoint on our last visit, showing that chef-proprietor Guy Awford's aim to create a top-notch neighbourhood restaurant

is still on target. The compact, smart interior (white tablecloths, subdued grey and ochre tones) and rather cool staff might not appeal if you like a rustic vibe, but the formal atmosphere does help to spotlight the seriousness of the cooking. A new banquette wall has done wonders for the acoustics, meaning that the background chatter from the well-dressed patrons is more civilised murmur than echoing din. Top-notch own-made bread with olives made an auspicious beginning, and a beautifully arranged starter of gravadlax, crème fraîche and perfectly cooked beetroot was superb. Meaty cod fillet on a bed of spinach, served with herby mash and pea sauce, managed that tricky line between comfort food and fine dining, while a rare grilled ribeye was well complemented by potato and turnip dauphinoise. Desserts of sticky date pudding with cardamom ice-cream, and raspberry and vanilla crème brûlée, weren't highlights, but were tasty. It's wise to book – locals seemingly use Inside for most of their celebrations.
Available for hire. Babies and children admitted. Booking advisable. Disabled: toilet.

London Bridge & Borough

★ Magdalen

152 Tooley Street, SE1 2TU (7403 1342, www.magdalenrestaurant.co.uk). London Bridge tube/rail. **Lunch served** noon-2.30pm Mon-Fri. **Dinner served** 6.30-10pm Mon-Sat. **Main courses** £13.50-£25. **Set lunch** £15.50 2 courses, £18.50 3 courses. **Credit** AmEx, MC, V.
Wine glasses gleam, cutlery sparkles, and the chocolatey walls and leather banquettes cosset and charm. Service is professional, the menu short and seasonal, and seldom is a polished dessert fork put wrong. Magdalen is low-key enough to feel like a well-kept secret, but it's also a favourite with clued-up City diners who know their gribiche from their gravadlax. There's something old-fashioned about it, but the menu is adventurous too; few places would venture to list both kid (saddle and heart) and calves' brains on the same menu. The latter – cloud-light, fried just-so and served with a punchy gribiche sauce – featured on the excellent-value set lunch menu. Ingredients shine: a starter of parma ham (from the Ham & Cheese Co at nearby Spa Terminus) was sliced transparently thin and served with a dollop of indulgent ricotta; firm, perfect morels at the height of their short season came with sourdough toast, wild garlic and a poached duck's egg. For afters, there are cheeses from Neal's Yard Dairy and grown-up desserts such as marmalade and whisky ice-cream. France is the focus of the well-chosen, mostly European wine list. A few tasting notes wouldn't go amiss, nor would more choice by the glass, but otherwise it's hard to find fault.
Available for hire. Babies and children admitted. Booking advisable. Disabled: toilet. Separate rooms for parties, seating 8-35. **Map 12 Q8**.

Brawn. See p208.

Tower Bridge

Blueprint Café

*Design Museum, 28 Shad Thames, SE1 2YD
(7378 7031, www.blueprintcafe.co.uk). Tower
Hill tube or Tower Gateway DLR or London
Bridge tube/rail or bus 47, 78.* **Lunch served**
noon-2.45pm Mon-Sat; noon-3.45pm Sun.
Dinner served 6-10.30pm Mon-Sat. **Main
courses** £12.50-£21. **Set lunch** £15 2 courses,
£20 3 courses. **Set dinner** £18 2 courses, £23
3 courses. **Credit** AmEx, DC, MC, V.
A long-time favourite, the Blueprint Café would be
a destination for the setting alone: wall-to-ceiling
windows look on to a stunning view of the Thames
and Tower Bridge, and a retractable canopy gives
a great inside/outside feeling. Head chef Mark
Jarvis's seasonal menus are short and to the point –
dishes are beautiful but in no way twee. Begin,
perhaps, with just-seared yellowfin tuna with
kalamata olives and a delicate salad niçoise, or a
tender artichoke salad with a molten warm duck's
egg and mint. Line-caught cod beneath a zingy
green herb crust, with yellow-tinged crushed potato
with rapeseed oil and a flower and herb salad, was
stunning – summer on a plate. Meat-lovers will be
wowed by well-hung Hereford onglet with bone
marrow and forest mushrooms. Even a tomato and
onion side salad was a treat – jewel-bright, full-
flavoured plum, cherry and green tomato heaven.
There's a first-rate wine list too, helpfully arranged.
Service was a touch haphazard, but always friendly
and, after all – with that view (plus mini-binoculars
on every table) where's the rush?
*Available for hire. Babies and children welcome:
high chair. Booking advisable dinner. Disabled:
lift; toilet (in museum).* **Map 12 S9**.

Le Pont de la Tour

*Butlers Wharf Building, 36D Shad Thames,
SE1 2YE (7403 8403, www.lepontdelatour.
co.uk). Tower Hill tube or Tower Gateway DLR
or London Bridge tube/rail.*
Bar & grill **Lunch served** noon-3pm Mon-Fri;
noon-4pm Sun. **Dinner served** 6-10.30pm
Mon-Sat; 6-10pm Sun. **Main courses** £17.50-
£29.50.
Restaurant **Lunch served** noon-3pm Mon-Fri;
noon-4pm Sun. **Dinner served** 6-11pm
Mon-Sat; 6-10pm Sun. **Main courses** £22-£45.
Set lunch £24.50 2 courses, £27.50 3 courses.
Both **Credit** AmEx, DC, MC, V.
The long riverside dining room is elegant if a little
soulless, but the setting is picture-perfect: dining on
the outside terrace with a view of Tower Bridge
feels like posing for a London tourist brochure.
Cynics might expect the food to disappoint. It
didn't. The lunch and dinner menu du jour offers
great bang for buck, with many dishes lifted from
the carte. Vegetables cost extra. New potatoes were
an unnecessary addition to a lovely crisp-skinned
bream with courgettes, fennel and tomato. A
snappy salad added much-needed colour to a
rewardingly varied plate comprising pithivier of
rabbit leg confit and a ballotine of the saddle
around herby forcemeat, either side of exquisite
mashed potato. A nicely tart raspberry crème
brûlée again showed what the kitchen does well:
matching fine technique with focused flavours. The
food may be French, but on a fine day Le Pont de la
Tour can be a top London attraction. Typically
British: our waiter admitted he'd arrived in the
country only a few days earlier, and service slowed

terribly towards the end of lunch. The adjoining
primary-coloured Bar & Grill offers food that is
more brasserie in style: more cheaply, more
informally and with less sense of occasion.
*Available for hire. Babies and children welcome:
high chairs. Booking advisable. Entertainment
(bar & grill): pianist 6pm Tue-Sun. Separate
rooms for parties, seating 22 & 26. Tables
outdoors (22, terrace).* **Map 25 S8**.

East
Bethnal Green

★ Corner Room

*Town Hall Hotel, Patriot Square, E2 9NF
(www.townhallhotel.com/corner_room). Bethnal
Green tube.* **Breakfast served** 7-10am Mon-
Fri; 7.30-10.30am Sat, Sun. **Lunch served**
noon-4pm, **dinner served** 6-10.30pm daily.
Main courses £14-£15. **Set lunch** (noon-3pm
Mon-Fri) £19 2 courses, £23 3 courses. **Credit**
AmEx, MC, V.
In its role as the less formal of the two restaurants
in the restrained, stylish Town Hall Hotel (the other
is Viajante, *see p128*), the Corner Room strikes a
happy medium between impressive and
approachable. That's the only way in which it's
medium, though. The food, overseen by the
perfectionist, thoughtfully experimental Nuno
Mendes, is consistently excellent, and the short,
alluring wine list and young, engaged staff in their
black uniforms are also some way above average.
The short menu (about five dishes per course) is a
terse list of ingredients that barely hints at the
complexities on the plate, which invariably holds
more flavours than billed and a primer's worth of
technique. It's all in the service of flavour rather
than cheffy showing-off, and presented attractively
rather than as art. 'Sprouting broccoli and garlic tea,
stracciatella', for example, was served with beer-
pickled onions, the near-sour dressing a teasing foil
for the stracciatella (creamy mozzarella). The bread
pudding in 'Ibérico pork, bread pudding, wild
garlic' was a rich, musky mush, the garlic leaves
brittle and aged in flavour. Influences from Mendes'
native Portugal are evident, as is seasonality,
though sometimes just in adaptations to Corner
Room classics. The room is small yet not
overcrowded and – being a former town hall – the
ceilings are high. The original decor has largely
gone, but the oak tables, panelling and wall units
recall a certain office-like feel, though the forest of
hanging lights and shades is more playful. Good
food at any price, awesome at these prices.
*Available for hire. Babies and children welcome:
high chairs. Bookings not accepted dinner.
Disabled: lift; toilet. Separate room for
parties, seats 9-16. Vegetarian menu.*

Palmers

*238 Roman Road, E2 0RY (8980 5590,
www.palmersrestaurant.net). Bethnal
Green tube/rail or bus 8.* **Dinner served**
6-10.30pm Mon-Sat. **Meals served** noon-
9pm Sun. **Main courses** £9.50-£16.50.
Credit MC, V.
Run by a Czech father and his two sons – one in the
kitchen bringing French panache to a contemporary
Eurovision menu, his younger brother a friendly and
efficient presence in the dining room – this is a great
neighbourhood restaurant. But the corner site, part
of an unprepossessing new-build block, and the

could-be-anywhere interior with arty photos of food
don't give away how special it is. Crunchy, lemony
falafel on beets, radish and cucumber with mint
leaves and coriander and a sour cream dressing
made a refreshing starter, with zesty flavours as
much Eastern European as Middle Eastern;
perfectly cooked scallops were matched with celeriac
remoulade perked up with little capers and micro
leaves. Meat-eaters can have steaks and, less
predictably, rabbit instead of chicken. An extremely
generous serving of monkfish and parma ham with
asparagus (just in season) was raised to classical
heights with a hollandaise-type sauce. The dashing
veggie option was open ravioli of silky sheets of
pasta with squash, courgette ribbons and tomato
sauce. For an extra outlay, hand-cut chips are
undoubtedly the finest fries on the Roman Road.
Chocolate melting pudding smartly matched with
berries was the business. Only the wine list is a
weakness, but like the food it's fantastic value.
Palmers would be an asset in any area; in E2,
it's exceptional.
*Available for hire. Babies and children welcome:
high chairs. Booking advisable weekends.
Disabled: toilet. Takeaway service.*

Docklands

★ Plateau

*Canada Place, Canada Square, E14 5ER (7715
7100, www.plateau-restaurant.co.uk). Canary
Wharf tube/DLR.*
Bar & grill **Meals served** noon-10.30pm Mon-
Sat. **Main courses** £12-£22. **Set meal** £15
2 courses, £18 3 courses.
Restaurant **Lunch served** noon-3pm Mon-
Fri. **Dinner served** 6-10pm Mon-Sat. **Main
courses** £14-£29.50. **Set meal** £22 2 courses,
£25 3 courses.
Both **Credit** AmEx, DC, MC, V.
The aptly named Plateau sits on the fourth floor of
Canada Place, with sensational views of Canary
Wharf from its huge glass and metal façade. The
interior aims to impress with iconic contemporary
furniture – marble-topped white Eero Saarinen
Tulip tables and matching chairs, and Arco floor
lamps – but the restaurant isn't just a designer
showroom for the moneyed classes; the beautifully
presented cuisine is testament to the fact that head
chef Allan Pickett takes his job very seriously,
producing inspired dishes that pay more than just
lip service to the principle of seasonal eating.
Pickett took on the role in 2010, seven years after
Plateau first opened, and has maintained its high
standards with the help of a very professional team
– our waitress was charming and knowledgeable.
From the nicely priced menu du jour, we enjoyed a
dazzlingly fresh starter of heritage tomatoes with
basil cress and baby mozzarella. Fish mains saw
wonderful sea trout paired with peas, broad beans
and asparagus velouté, and equally tasty sea bream
served on creamy mash with razor clams and
roasted garlic cloves. A pastry-perfect peach tarte
tatin with lavender ice-cream proved that lavender
can taste as good as it smells. For more informal,
music-infused dining, head to the adjacent Bar
& Grill, though it lacks some of the magic of the
main restaurant.
*Available for hire. Babies and children welcome:
children's menu; high chairs; nappy-changing
facilities. Booking advisable. Disabled: lift; toilet.
Dress: smart casual. Separate rooms for parties,
seating 16 and 25. Tables outdoors (17, terrace).
Vegetarian menu.* **Map 24 B2**.

Mayfields

Shoreditch

★ Brawn

*49 Columbia Road, E2 7RG (7729 5692,
www.brawn.co). Hoxton rail or bus 48, 55.*
Lunch served noon-3pm Tue-Sat; noon-4pm
Sun. **Dinner served** 6-10.30pm Mon-Thur;
6-11pm Fri, Sat. **Main courses** £12-£17. **Set
lunch** (Sun) £28 3 courses. **Credit** MC, V.
With its lack of airs and graces and bare-brick
decor, Brawn comes over as an unassuming local.
As indeed it is – but one that pulls in trade from
across town with its quietly ambitious, precise and,
above all, delicious cooking. The meat dishes that
run through the menu might have peasant origins,
but they're executed with top-drawer flair. The
menu includes a section devoted to 'Pig', offering
brawn, rillettes and knowledgeably sourced
European charcuterie, along with 'Hot' and 'Cold'
options. Here, painstakingly prepared offal dishes
such as the seldom-found tête de veau with sauce
ravigote, or pork cheek and trotter pie, are offered
alongside more aristocratic choices like chopped
(raw) Tuscan beef of impeccable quality, flavoured
only with thyme, olive oil and spot-on seasoning.
Fish, shellfish and vegetable dishes show the
same judgement; a surprise spring stand-out, for

example, was clams, charred leeks and cider
beurre blanc. You'll need to ask one of the generous
supply of friendly, switched-on staff to vet your
order, as dishes are served to share in various sizes.
They can also advise on the wine: Brawn is from
the Terroirs (*see p325*) stable and shares the
company policy of prizing interesting natural
wines above prestigious bottles.
*Babies and children welcome: high chairs;
nappy-changing facilities. Booking advisable.
Disabled: toilet. Separate room for parties,
seats 30.* **Map 6 S3.**

Victoria Park

★ Empress

*130 Lauriston Road, E9 7LH (8533 5123,
www.empresse9.co.uk). Mile End tube then
bus 277, 425.* **Brunch served** 10am-noon
Sat, Sun. **Lunch served** noon-3.30pm; **dinner
served** 6-10.30pm Mon-Sat. **Meals served**
noon-9.30pm Sun. **Main courses** £12-£17.
Credit MC, V.
'Yorkshire fettle, radicchio, grapefruit and fennel
salad now on,' chef Elliott Lidstone had tweeted.
And what a treat: a salad that, as salads seldom do,
seemed much more than the sum of its parts, with

grilled radicchio, pink grapefruit and wafer-thin
fennel, plus tiny capers and parsley, and the more
subtle British version of feta. Crisp slivers of pig's
ear with apple sauce was a world-beating bar snack
to match the local beers on a terrific drinks list. Half
a hollowed-out bone filled with snails, bone marrow,
caramelised onions and pork was magnificent.
Gorgeous guinea fowl on puy lentils with salsa
verde, and trout with watercress, slivers of apple,
celeriac and an English mustard sauce both packed
in sensational combinations of tangy, salty, sharp,
sweet, earthy, peppery flavours. Everything about
this gloriously updated former corner pub is bang
on, with proper linen napkins, only 50p per person
for unlimited house bottled water and local bread,
and meat supplied by the Ginger Pig across the
road. Check out the Frugal Feasts and BYOB
nights in collaboration with the neighbouring Bottle
Apostle wine shop. No wonder the comfortable
red leather banquettes and squishy sofas are full
of happy families, hipsters and anyone who
appreciates what the eager and talented team have
achieved. Very impressive.
*Available for hire. Babies and children welcome:
children's menu; high chairs; nappy-changing
facilities. Booking advisable Fri-Sun. Disabled:
toilet. Tables outdoors (11, pavement).*

Wapping

Wapping Food

Wapping Hydraulic Power Station, Wapping Wall, E1W 3SG (7680 2080, www.thewapping project.com). Wapping tube or Shadwell DLR. **Brunch served** 10am-noon Sat, Sun. **Lunch served** 1-3.30pm Sat; 1-4pm Sun. **Dinner served** 6.30-10.30pm Mon-Fri; 7-10.30pm Sat. **Main courses** £15-£22. **Credit** AmEx, MC, V.

Wapping Food's single greatest feature is its setting. Beyond a beautiful Victorian red-brick exterior lies a cavernous space dotted with old machinery from the hydraulic power station's past. Next to these redundant but still mesmerising machines is a pretty restaurant furnished with classic Vitra pieces and twinkling tableware. In the evening, when all this is washed by gentle candlelight, the effect is romantic and surreal. The food, sadly, isn't anywhere near as memorable, and to our minds doesn't warrant the £20 price tag for most mains. A starter of lamb sweetbreads was unappealing, the pinky-grey lumps too clearly resembling the glands that they are. Mains of cod and black bream were better: neatly seared and sealed, with perfect crispy skin, and well-chosen accompaniments – baby leeks and new potatoes with the hearty cod, and a Mediterranean-like robust peperonata for the more delicate bream. A side of chard was fine, but at £5 you expect more than fine. This isn't to say Wapping Food is not worth visiting; such a memorable restaurant will always be worth a trip. Just don't expect to be as blown away by the food as you will be by the space.
Available for hire. Babies and children welcome: high chairs; nappy-changing facilities. Booking essential Wed-Sun. Disabled: toilet. Entertainment: performances and exhibitions; phone for details. Tables outdoors (20, garden).

Whitechapel

Whitechapel Gallery Dining Room

Whitechapel Gallery, 77-82 Whitechapel High Street, E1 7QX (7522 7888, www.whitechapel gallery.org/dining-room). Aldgate East tube. **Lunch served** noon-3pm Tue-Sat; noon-3.45pm Sun. **Dinner served** 6-9.30pm Wed-Sat. **Main courses** £10.50-£15.95. **Credit** AmEx, MC, V.

Light-filled by day, softly lit at night, the simply decorated Whitechapel Gallery Dining Room is so much more than a gallery eaterie, yet keeps prices very reasonable. A seasonal menu (overseen by Angela Hartnett) allows for flexible eating, with nibbles (try the very moreish whipped goat's curd and roasted garlic croûtes), small plates (though a tasty tangle of chargrilled courgette ribbons with gremolata and toasted hazelnuts was a decent-sized bowlful) and bigger plates all being served. Of the heftier dishes, salt beef hash was superb – immaculately presented, and rescued from being too dry by the runny yolk of a fried duck egg topping. Cornish silver mullet came with a very buttery herb sauce, and beer-battered cod with chips, tartare sauce and pea purée is always a good rendition, though slightly mean with the purée. Truffle chips and bread with classy olive oil are extras worth ordering. Anywhere that serves ice-cream by the scoop gets our vote, but there are crowd-pleasing desserts such as eton mess too. A short global wine list offers most options by the glass. Jovial, attentive staff are the icing on the cake.

Available for hire. Babies and children welcome: high chairs; nappy-changing facilities. Booking advisable. Disabled: toilet. Separate room for parties, seats 14. **Map 12 S6.**

North East

Hackney

Mayfields NEW

52 Wilton Way, E8 1BG (7254 8311, www.mayfieldswiltonway.co.uk). Hackney Central rail or bus D6, 48, 106, 254. **Lunch served** noon-3pm Sat, Sun. **Dinner served** 6-10.30pm Mon-Sat; 6-9.30pm Sun. **Dishes** £5-£14. **Credit** MC, V.

Perusing the menu at this new Hackney brasserie, you're not sure whether it's the work of a culinary genius or a madman. Liquorice with lemon sole; sea trout with raspberries and samphire; veal tartare in Japanese broth – there's no denying that chef Matthew Young has a penchant for fusing unexpected flavours and cuisines. But do they work? Finished with melting blobs of vibrant red cabbage granita, the appearance of a dish of raw mackerel and radish slices was reminiscent of a lava lamp. The flavours didn't quite live up to the looks, though, with the brassicas taking centre stage. A ball of mozzarella served in a snowdrift of grated bottarga (salt-cured, pressed fish roe) was more successful; the unusual addition of dill fronds lent a pleasing hint of aniseed. The rest of the meal followed this uneven pattern. Meat and fish were cooked with precision, yet many dishes had an out-of-kilter element. There's much to like about this collaboration between Borough Wines (an off-

licence down the road at no.67) and Claire Roberson of pop-up dining operation Shacklewell Nights. The service is warm and the aesthetic attractively Scandi-cool. The chef clearly has talent, but at present, the hit rate with his wackier notions is too low.
Babies and children admitted. Booking advisable Thur-Sat. Tables outdoors (3, pavement).

North

Camden & Chalk Farm

Odette's

130 Regent's Park Road, NW1 8XL (7586 8569, www.odettesprimrosehill.com). Chalk Farm tube or bus 31, 168, 274. **Lunch served** noon-2.30pm Mon-Fri; noon-3pm Sat. **Dinner served** 6-10pm Mon-Thur; 6-10.30pm Fri, Sat. **Meals served** noon-10pm Sun. **Main courses** £11.50-£25. **Set lunch** (Mon-Sat) £13 2 courses, £15 3 courses; (Sun) £25 2 courses, £30 3 courses. **Set dinner** (6-7pm Mon-Sat; 5-7pm Sun) £17 2 courses, £20 3 courses (£29.75 incl wine and coffee). **Credit** MC, V.

The intimate rooms and leafy summer garden of Odette's have seemed perfectly matched to prosperous Primrose Hill ever since the restaurant first opened in the 1970s. Under Welsh chef and TV regular Bryn Williams, a stylish contemporary look has replaced the plush clutter of old, but it still has a reliable feel of snug comfort, complemented by charming service. Williams' cooking tends to the delicate and subtle, with sometimes-elusive hints rather than big upfront flavours or anything brash. For some, this delicacy would be a plus; for others,

York & Albany. See p210.

Glasshouse

perhaps a bit bland. The style worked well in a delightfully smooth crayfish lasagne, topped by superlative little squid rings; chicken consommé with mushroom ravioli and crunchy toasted barley was a satisfying – again, subtle – blend. To follow, though, sea bream with glazed endive and pine-nut and raisin dressing was pleasant but unmemorable; while in braised beef cheek with hash brown in red wine jus, the whole ensemble was very rich, and the meat supremely tender, but real beefiness was hard to find. We were drawn to a pistachio cake dessert by the promise of calvados cream, but two normally highly distinctive flavours – pistachio and calvados – were oddly muted. In short, it's a question of taste, though the kitchen's prowess is not in doubt.
Babies and children welcome: high chairs. Booking advisable. Separate room for parties, seats 20. Tables outdoors (6, garden; 5, terrace). Vegetarian menu. **Map 27 A2.**

York & Albany

127-129 Parkway, NW1 7PS (7388 3344, www.gordonramsay.com/yorkandalbany). Camden Town tube. **Breakfast served** 7-10.30am Mon-Fri; 7-11.30am Sat, Sun. **Lunch served** noon-3pm Mon-Fri; 12.15-3pm Sat. **Dinner served** 6-11pm Mon-Sat. **Meals served** noon-8.30pm Sun. **Main courses** £15-£22. **Set meal** (lunch, 6-7pm Mon-Sat) £18 2 courses, £21 3 courses. **Credit** AmEx, MC, V.
On the cusp between funky Camden and swanky Regent's Park, this boutique hotel, bar and restaurant (part of the Gordon Ramsay empire), set in a magnificent stuccoed Victorian pub, fits the latter neighbourhood better. The spacious, soigné bar area serves superior snacks such as truffled chips, burger and pizzas at fairly well-upholstered prices. The restaurant – an equally airy space with a Mediterranean-style courtyard behind (and plush basement overflow room) – seems constantly packed, with diners clamouring for zesty dishes such as dill-cured salmon with fennel and orange

salad or lamb with courgettes and mint gremolata. The decently priced and spritely set lunch is especially light on calories – and sometimes on advertised ingredients: legumes were scanty in a rocket-packed pea and broad bean salad with goat's cheese. Estimably gamey chicken with broccoli and pasta lacked the promised hazelnuts, but was nonetheless intensely satisfying; bream with sweet, sticky, meaty juices was beautifully paired with puréed and sliced artichoke. Refreshing desserts might include a cool, creamy rice pudding with morello cherries. Y&A is perfect for lunching ladies and better for leisured classes than business: service is not paced for those rushing back to work. In the evening, it's understandably popular for well-heeled north London family occasions. The adjoining former stables is a rustic-looking deli and pizzeria serving top-notch thin-crust pizzas.
Babies and children welcome: high chairs. Booking advisable Thur-Sun. Disabled: toilet. Separate rooms for parties, seating 24 and 70. Tables outdoors (6, pavement). **Map 3 H1.**

Finsbury Park

★ Season Kitchen

53 Stroud Green Road, N4 3EF (7263 5500, www.seasonkitchen.co.uk). Finsbury Park tube/rail. **Dinner served** 5.30-10.30pm Tue-Sun. **Main courses** £10.95-£15.95. **Credit** MC, V.
Now that restaurants with contemporary Brit/Euro cuisine are two a penny, it's great to discover one that really stands out. And even better in Stroud Green Road, known more for ultra-cheap eats and African fruit and veg stores. The decor at Season Kitchen is modern-mellow, with subtle greys offset by a cranky collection of old paintings. The multinational staff are warmly friendly, and there's a likeable generosity about the whole enterprise. Everything is own-made, including the fabulous, no-extra-charge bread (clearly a passion – as soon as we asked about the bread, we were offered the recipe). Menus, as the name suggests, focus on seasonal ingredients, and are an unpindownable

mix of British, Mediterranean and other influences. A winter vegetable terrine had loads of fresh green flavour; in a platter of own-cured meats the duck was superb. An outstanding main course of pulled kid (goat) came with deliciously smooth polenta, rich jus and a powerfully meaty faggot; smoked salmon with crispy seaweed was more conventional, but still very enjoyable. Also, the chips are superlative, the rhubarb and custard doughnuts delectable, and a low mark-up policy on wines provides exceptional bottles at remarkable prices. A place to be celebrated.
Available for hire. Babies and children welcome: high chairs. Booking advisable.

Islington

Frederick's

Camden Passage, N1 8EG (7359 2888, www.fredericks.co.uk). Angel tube. **Lunch served** noon-2.30pm, **dinner served** 5.45-10.30pm Mon-Sat. **Main courses** £12.50-£26. **Set meal** (lunch; dinner Mon, Tue; 5.45-7pm Wed-Sat) £15.50 2 courses, £19 3 courses. **Credit** AmEx, MC, V.
The slightly ritzy plush of Frederick's entrance cocktail bar, the surprising spaciousness of the dining room beyond, the striking 1980s artwork, the lofty conservatory and pretty hidden garden alongside – all come together to convey the idea that a meal here is a bit of a treat. Very proper, attentive and enthusiastic service adds to the feel of pampering brio, a well-polished style that has long made this a favourite spot for birthdays, weddings, anniversaries and other celebrations. Food has sometimes come second to the overall experience, but lately the kitchen seems to have picked up extra verve. Starters – pan-fried scallops with black pudding and cauliflower purée, and prawns with garlic butter – stood out for the quality of the ingredients, the seafood deliciously sweet, the black pudding delicately rich. To follow, pork loin (also pan-fried) with crisp belly pork and Gascon cabbage, was a great combo of heartiness and

refinement; and a generous slab of organic salmon, with mint hollandaise, was grilled just right. Desserts are part of the treat too, and, as in the lovely ginger panna cotta, feature imaginative variations on standard favourites. The wine list is extensive, prestigious and, like the food, a little pricey – but then, it's a special trip out.

Available for hire. Babies and children welcome: children's menu; high chairs. Booking advisable weekends. Separate rooms for parties, seating 16 and 30. Tables outdoors (12, garden). **Map 5 O2.**

Outer London
Kew, Surrey

★ Glasshouse
14 Station Parade, Kew, Surrey TW9 3PZ (8940 6777, www.glasshouserestaurant.co.uk). Kew Gardens tube/rail. **Lunch served** noon-2.15pm Mon-Sat; 12.30-2.45pm Sun. **Dinner served** 6.30-10.30pm Mon-Sat; 7-10pm Sun. **Set lunch** (Mon-Sat) £27.50 3 courses; (Sun) £32.50 3 courses. **Set dinner** £42.50 3 courses. **Credit** AmEx, MC, V.

Situated a few steps from Kew Gardens tube, the setting here is prettier than you'd think. Station Parade resembles a village square, where the Glasshouse's neighbours include an indie bookshop, bakery and florist. The restaurant itself is less botanically minded than the name suggests, not so much evocative of one of the royal garden's great Victorian shrines to horticulture as a typical smartly neutral dining room, bright enough but overwhelmingly beige in decor. Formal in tone, with pristine staff, what really stands out is chef Daniel Mertl's sublime Michelin-starred menu. Owned by Nigel Platts-Martin and Bruce Poole – the men behind Chez Bruce (*see p92*) and La Trompette (*see p91*) – the Glasshouse pulls off neighbourhood fine dining with aplomb and is busy all hours as a result. Rabbit tortellini was densely packed, served with a delicate tarragon consommé and baby artichokes. A generous mackerel tartare was encircled by perfectly crumbed quails' eggs. Mains of roast bavette with sarladaise potatoes, and guinea fowl breast with curried potato gratin and black lentil sauce did not disappoint. Desserts are equally impressive, with the deep-dish passionfruit tart particularly fine. The three-course set lunch is good value for this class of cuisine. Worth seeking out.

Available for hire. Babies and children welcome: high chairs. Booking advisable. Dress: smart casual.

Richmond, Surrey

Petersham Nurseries Café `HOT 50`
Church Lane, off Petersham Road, Richmond, Surrey TW10 7AG (8940 5230, www.petersham nurseries.com). Richmond tube/rail, then 30 mins walk or bus 65.
Tea House **Open** 10am-4.30pm Tue-Sat; 11am-4.30pm Sun. **Set meal** £10.50 2 courses, £13.50 3 courses.
Café **Lunch served** noon-3pm Tue-Sun. **Main courses** £22-£30.
Both **Credit** AmEx, MC, V.

The ultimate in rustic charm, complete with a real meadow just across the lane, Petersham Nurseries is the perfect balm for the frazzled urbanite. Housed within the garden centre, the Café resembles a stately greenhouse, hung with Indian prints and pictures, and furnished with rickety tables and chairs. Cat Ashton is now head chef, following the departure of Greg Malouf in late 2012; the seasonal menu remains a delightful read. A pre-starter plate of prosciutto san daniele with rocket and melon was exactly right on a summer's day – as was a peach bellini. Burrata with courgette flowers, sorrento tomatoes, shallot and rose dressing was queen of the starters; squid dusted in polenta with rocket, chickpeas, chilli and aïoli was oddly subdued. At this point, things slightly unravelled, despite the best efforts of the charming young staff. An overly long wait for mains produced roasted baby aubergines (with red and yellow datterini tomatoes, ricotta and basil) that simply hadn't been cooked long enough and were unforgivably chewy; grilled pata negra pork loin with sweetcorn, salsa, coriander and tomato was a glorious combination, but again, the meat required work. Such flaws are not really acceptable at these elevated prices, though a side of new potatoes with anchovies, crème fraîche and salsa verde couldn't be faulted, and nor could a delicate strawberry, prosecco and rose sorbet. There's also the Tea House, where light lunches and cakes are served, a shop and, of course, the Nurseries.

Available for hire. Babies and children welcome: high chairs; nappy-changing facilities. Booking essential (Café), 1 mth in advance. Disabled: toilet.

Petersham Nurseries Café

North African

There was a time when a tagine – the funnel-shaped earthenware pot that the stew of the same name is cooked in – was the wedding present of the year, and it looked as if North Africa's staple of couscous was a challenger for rice. More than 20 years ago, **Adam's Café** was one of the first to introduce Londoners to briks, b'stilla and briouats, as well as fragrant tagines of meat and fruit, and couscous dishes heaped high with merguez and vegetables. It's still going strong, with a new generation joining its loyal following. When **Momo** opened (more than 15 years ago) it upped the ante, captivating the capital with the courtly cooking of Morocco, a beautiful souk look, highly polished service and an intoxicating atmosphere that appeals to international hedonists. The beat goes on there too. But, of late, the Maghrebi wave seems to have lost momentum. You'll find outposts of excellent cooking, such as **Khamsa** and **Numidie**, but elsewhere there are too many soggy courgettes and overcooked carrots on couscous for our liking. The best won't disappoint, but we'd like to see more choice and competition, bringing the best of Marrakech and beyond within reach of a range of pockets and compass points.

Central
Mayfair

Momo HOT 50
25 Heddon Street, W1B 4BH (Reservations 3641 7977, front desk 7434 4040, www.momo resto.com). Piccadilly Circus tube. **Lunch served** noon-2.30pm Mon-Sat. **Afternoon tea served** 12.30-5.30pm, **dinner served** 6.30-11.30pm daily. **Main courses** £17-£28. **Set lunch** £15.50 2 courses, £19.50 3 courses. **Set dinner** £45-£55 3 courses incl cocktail. **Credit** AmEx, MC, V.
Always fun and glamorous, the kasbah-like Momo rocks. Though serious enough about its food not to be a themed restaurant, the staff's end-of-evening ululating and dancing to Maghrebi beats can send confusing signals. Seductive lighting, plush seating, heavy crystal glasses, napkin fluttering and upselling (the tasting menu was talked up) indicate the kind of bill to expect. But it's worth splashing out for a heady experience and cooking that mostly justifies the prices. Service is very good too. Meze, accompanied by slabs of soft, sweet bread scattered with sesame, are pastries and dips of the highest calibre: 'Annabel's aubergine', a silky mush tartly spiked with pomegranate seeds, was noteworthy; and the bastilla authentically made with pigeon. Lamb tagine with whole almonds in a rich sauce had prunes and pear for a good balance of sweet and savoury. Vegetable couscous, comprising separate dishes of delicately spiced steamed veg, green lentil sauce and ultra-fluffy couscous, could have been more generous, especially given the low cost of ingredients. Seasoning seemed thirst-makingly heavy on the salt. Given the price of the wines, it's just as well the atmosphere is intoxicating. Tables on the (pedestrianised) street terrace for shisha smoking add to the authenticity.
Available for hire. Babies and children admitted. Booking advisable dinner and weekends.
Map 17 A4.
For branch (Mô Café) see index.

West
Bayswater

Couscous Café
7 Porchester Gardens, W2 4DB (7727 6597). Bayswater tube. **Meals served** noon-11.30pm daily. **Main courses** £9.95-£15.95. **Licensed.** **Corkage** no charge. **No credit cards.**
Mind your head on the low entrance, and mind the many decorative pots, rugs and lanterns – there isn't room to swing a camel's tail in this tiny café. But the cooking mostly punches above its size and there's plenty of choice, from the size of the b'stilla – an excellent example, not too sweet and containing plenty of spiced chicken inside crisp pastry – to the option of orange flower water (for an extra 25p) with the mint tea. Service is friendly, the mood and music cheerful. The lengthy menu extends beyond tagines and couscous dishes to brochettes (skewers of grilled chicken, lamb or sausage). To start, dips were better than the dull briouats, which resembled unspiced samosas. Tagines were served in their cooking pots, the lids lifted with a flourish to reveal artfully presented chicken with golden apricots, and a succulent lamb shank with prunes and quartered egg; both were strewn with almonds. Fluffy couscous was provided to share, with the vegetarian version comprising DIY dishes of soft root vegetables in spicy broth, spiced slices of aubergine, and sweet onion and chickpeas. For those that stay the course, there are springy, sultana-stuffed pancakes or a more refreshing conclusion of oranges with orange flower water and cinnamon.
Babies and children admitted. Tables outdoors (1, patio). Takeaway service. **Map 7 C6.**

Shepherd's Bush

Adam's Café
77 Askew Road, W12 9AH (8743 0572, www.adamscafe.co.uk). Hammersmith tube then bus 266. **Breakfast served** 7.30am-2pm Mon-Fri; 8.30am-2pm Sat. **Dinner served** 7-11pm Mon-Sat. **Set dinner** £12.50 1 course incl mint tea or coffee, £15.50 2 courses, £17.95 3 courses. **Licensed. Corkage** (wine only) £3.50. **Credit** AmEx, MC, V.

The owners of this English caff by day, candlelit Tunisian restaurant by night have stuck to their winning formula for 20-plus years. The restaurant looks fresh and bright, decorated in yellow and green with posters of Tunisia. Frances Boukraa runs front of house with unfussy aplomb, presenting her husband Abdel's dishes with a 'bon appetit'. Menus (priced according to number of courses) start promisingly with pickled vegetables, mini meatballs and great bread, and deliver every time. Standout starters are the briks – a striking, crisp fan of authentic ouarka pastry with egg or tuna filling. Tender slivers of calamari in a pastry shell was even better than a glistening briouat bursting with feta, spinach and pine nuts. Couscous royale is best known for offering a mountain of meat – tender lamb meatballs and skewers of lamb, chicken and merguez – atop a heap of gorgeous grains. But lesser appetites will be more than sated by hearty, aromatic plates of grilled meat and fish or intensely appealing, long-cooked tagine dishes such as lemony meatballs or firm monkfish with fresh tomatoes, peppers, saffron and potatoes. Desserts range from refreshing orange salad to thick, indulgently honeyed pancakes. The wine list includes North African bottles, or you can BYO and pay £3.50 corkage.

Babies and children admitted. Takeaway service. **Map 20 A1.**

South
Brixton

Khamsa
140 Acre Lane, SW2 5UT (7733 3150, www.khamsa.co.uk). Brixton tube/rail. **Lunch served** noon-4pm Sun. **Dinner**

served 6-10.30pm Mon-Sat. **Main courses** £10.90-£14.90. **Unlicensed. Corkage** no charge. **Credit** MC, V.

At this intimate husband-and-wife operation, everything from the painted benches to the room decorated in red and pink to the blends of tea has a delightfully home-made feel. When choosing from the refreshingly short menu, bear in mind that the Algerian-born chef trained as a pâtissier. Vegetables and pulses prevail in the meze served in a flower petal-like set of dishes, with soft bread: zaalouk (aubergine and walnut dip); lentils and green beans; chickpeas; spiced carrots; fennel and beetroot – each distinctively spiced. A ras el hanout spice mix imparted depth and warmth to a vegetable couscous that contained an excellent variety of veg and almost ethereally light and fluffy couscous. Meatier mains include chicken tagine and delicate meatballs with mini merguez and haricot beans in a rich tomatoey sauce. Among the cakes and desserts displayed on the counter under glass domes were crumbly, dairy-free chocolate and hazelnut mounds, coconut, green tea, basil and lime buns and (best of all) walnut tart. All were exquisitely decorated with coloured icing flowers, though lovers of sticky baklava may find them drier than expected. Mint tea with tiny pink rosebuds made an exquisite ending; if you want something stronger, note that it's BYO with no corkage charge. A place to treasure.

Available for hire. Babies and children admitted. Booking advisable. **Map 22 C2.**

South East
Gipsy Hill

Numidie
48 Westow Hill, SE19 1RX (8766 6166, www.numidie.co.uk). Gipsy Hill rail. **Lunch served** noon-3pm Sat, Sun. **Dinner served** 5-11pm daily. **Main courses** £8.95-£13.95. **Credit** AmEx, MC, V.

Not just another ethnic restaurant in Crystal Palace, this easy-to-overlook gem combines some of the best North African cooking in London with a few French classics, all cooked with flair. Soft white bread speckled with black and white sesame seeds comes warm from the oven; mixed meze includes brik filled with bright green, fresh-tasting spinach, good merguez, houmous, mechouia (tomato and pepper salad), aubergine and tomato dip and lots of pitta. Far better than the usual tired tagines and so-so couscous, the encouragingly short selection of main courses offers salads such as duck with orange, lamb cutlets and other grills, and ratatouille crêpe, along with the expected Algerian couscous dishes. Cinnamon- and mint-scented prune and rabbit tagine (from the specials sheet) was richer, firmer and far more interesting than chicken; vegetable couscous was a satisfying, warmly spiced stew of mushroom, aubergine, chickpeas and tomato topped with grilled halloumi and accompanied by a dish of fluffy grains. Puddings such as tarte tatin and a fine crème brûlée are unashamedly French. A very short wine list and free mint tea keep the bill refreshingly low. Decor is nothing to write home about; the downstairs bar is cosier.

Available for hire. Babies and children welcome: high chairs. Booking advisable; essential Fri, Sat. Entertainment: musicians Wed, Fri, Sat. Vegetarian menu.

Le Rif

North
Finsbury Park

★ Le Rif
172 Seven Sisters Road, N7 7PX (7263 1891). Finsbury Park tube/rail. **Meals served** 8am-10pm Mon-Fri; noon-10pm Sat, Sun. **Main courses** £4-£6. **Unlicensed** no alcohol allowed. **No credit cards**.

Our choice from the canteen-style containers of meat and vegetable stews emerged transformed, moulded into a neat mound on couscous (or rice), decorated with tomato, and served – piping hot – in an earthenware plate. Dishes included generous chunks of falling-off-the-bone lamb scented with cinnamon and sweetened with prunes; tender and plump green lentils; meltingly rich spinach and aubergine stew; and a fillet of firm-fleshed white fish baked with chermoula on top of tangily spiced chopped spinach. All that remained of the day's cakes was a gorgeous slab of syrupy semolina cake scented with orange flower water. As well as serving authentic North African food, this is an all-day neighbourhood hangout, dispensing spag bol, sandwiches and snacks. In the evening the action is mainly on the outdoor terrace over glasses of milky coffee or mint tea. Don't bother phoning first – no one answers. Microwaves behind the counter ping periodically, and alcohol is not allowed. But for a taste of the Maghreb, this is the real deal – and an absolute steal.

Tables outdoors (5, patio). Takeaway service.

Menu

North African food has similarities with other cuisines; see the menu boxes in **Middle Eastern** and **Turkish**.

Bastilla, b'stilla or **pastilla**: an ouarka (qv) envelope with a traditional filling of pigeon, almonds, spices and egg, baked then dusted with cinnamon and powdered sugar. Chicken is often substituted for pigeon.
Brik: minced lamb or tuna and a raw egg bound in paper-thin pastry, then fried.
Briouats, briouettes or **briwat**: little envelopes of deep-fried, paper-thin ouarka (qv) pastry; can contain ground meat, rice or cheese, or be served as a sweet, flavoured with almond paste, nuts or honey.
Chermoula: a dry marinade of fragrant herbs and spices.
Couscous: granules of processed durum wheat. The name is also given to a dish where the slow-cooked grains are topped with a meat or vegetable stew; couscous royale usually involves lamb, chicken and merguez (qv).
Harira: lamb, lentil and chickpea soup.
Harissa: very hot chilli pepper paste flavoured with garlic and spices.
Maakouda: spicy potato fried in breadcrumbs.
Merguez: spicy, paprika-rich lamb sausages.
Ouarka: filo-like pastry.
Tagine or **tajine**: a shallow earthenware dish with a conical lid; it gives its name to a slow-simmered stew of meat (usually lamb or chicken) and vegetables, often cooked with olives, preserved lemon or prunes.

Pan-Asian & Fusion

No man is an island, and no cooking style operates in a vacuum. So, to a greater or lesser extent, all modern-day cuisines are a fusion of dishes and available ingredients, many of which have leapt across geographical and political boundaries. The Vietnamese adapted France's baguettes to produce banh mi rolls; Malaysians created roti canai from South Indian curries and bread; and as for chicken tikka masala… Nevertheless, there are experimenters who have wilfully hastened the fusion process, and New Zealander Peter Gordon, of the **Providores & Tapa Room** and **Kopapa**, remains London's top practitioner. South-east Asian food in London has long lent itself to a blurring of national culinary repertoires – possibly due to the first chefs arriving in London from that region finding employment in Chinese kitchens. Pan-Asian cuisine has cherry-picked some of the most popular dishes from Vietnam, Thailand, Malaysia and Singapore, as well as China and Japan, to create a formula that's gastronomic gold-dust. The success of **Wagamama** was only the start, and the continued popularity of Will Ricker's **E&O** and Yotam Ottolenghi's **NOPI** shows that there's plenty of life left in the genre. This year we welcome **Oaka at the Mansion House**, providing an upmarket twirl on the Thai-in-a-pub routine.

Central

Clerkenwell & Farringdon

★ The Modern Pantry | HOT 50 |

47-48 St John's Square, EC1V 4JJ (7553 9210, www.themodernpantry.co.uk). Farringdon tube/rail.
Café **Breakfast served** 8-11am Mon-Fri.
Brunch served 9am-4pm Sat; 10am-4pm Sun.
Afternoon tea served 3-5pm Mon-Sat. **Meals served** noon-10pm Mon; noon-10.30pm Tue-Fri.
Dinner served 6-10.30pm Sat; 6-10pm Sun.
Restaurant **Brunch served** 9am-4pm Sat; 10am-4pm Sun. **Lunch served** noon-3pm Tue-Fri; noon-4pm Sat, Sun. **Afternoon tea served** 3-5pm Sat. **Dinner served** 6-11pm Tue-Sat.
Both **Main courses** £15.50-£22.50. **Set lunch** (Mon-Fri) £21.50 2 courses; (Sun) £22 2 courses, £26 3 courses. **Set tea** £17-£22. **Credit** AmEx, MC, V.
As one of four co-founders of the Providores, chef Anna Hansen has form in creating enticing fusion dishes that make the most of unusual ingredients sourced from around the globe – we guarantee even the most devoted food lover will be bamboozled by a couple of items on the menu. Antipodean and Asian flavours (yuzu, tamarind) pop up frequently, alongside plenty of seasonal British fare (wild garlic, purple sprouting broccoli); the combinations can seem bewildering on the page, but rarely falter in execution. Perfectly cooked, flaky, pearlescent cod was offset beautifully by parsnip purée and braised fennel delicately perfumed with chamomile. The signature dish of sugar-cured prawn omelette with chilli, coriander and spring onion is still a winner; and blackcurrant and liquorice sorbet was a revelation in intense flavour matching. The stylish ground-floor café is quite feminine in feel with its soothing white and grey paintwork, white furniture and burnished copper light fittings – it seems to attract plenty of female diners too. The flexible table layout caters equally well for couples as groups, and intimate conversation is still possible even when the place is bubbling over. White-aproned staff are among the nicest we've encountered in London: both deeply professional and utterly charming. There's a small bar area too and a more formal restaurant upstairs.
Available for hire. Babies and children welcome: high chairs. Booking essential weekends. Disabled: toilet. Separate rooms for parties, seating 12-40. Tables outdoors (13, square).
Map 5 O4.

Covent Garden

Kopapa

32-34 Monmouth Street, WC2H 9HA (7240 6076, www.kopapa.co.uk). Covent Garden or Leicester Square tube. **Breakfast served** 8.30-11am Mon-Fri. **Brunch served** 9.30am-4pm Sat, Sun. **Meals served** noon-10.45pm Mon-Fri; 3.30-10.45pm Sat; 3.30-9.30pm Sun.
Main courses £10.50-£20. **Set meal** (5-10.30pm Mon; 5-7pm Tue-Fri; 4.30-7pm Sat; 4.30-9pm Sun) £17.95 2 courses, £20.95 3 courses. **Credit** AmEx, MC, V.
Fusion maestro Peter Gordon (also of the Providores & Tapa Room) co-owns this handily located, stylish all-dayer. He oversees an exciting and well-executed menu, with missteps a rarity. Turkish eggs (poached eggs with yoghurt, hot chilli butter and flatbread) – a favourite from the Tapa Room – makes a welcome appearance on brunch and breakfast menus. Lunch features weighty sandwiches (steak on focaccia with caramelised onion, mustard cream cheese, roast tomatoes and pickles) and burgers (soft-shell crab burger with Asian salad, spicy peanut mayonnaise and avocado), alongside salads (belper knolle cheese, roast grapes, mixed leaves, pickled ceps, walnuts and black vinegar dressing) and a selection of more inventive dishes. Many of these also appear as large or small plates on the evening menu. Pan-fried sea bream with broccolini, rainbow chard, coconut coriander chutney and paprika crumbs is a typical main – quality produce, imaginatively teamed. There's the occasional disappointment (a slightly flabby serving of deep-fried sesame and chilli salted squid with sumac mayo, for example), but you'll never be bored. Smiling staff are attentive

and clued-up about the menu, which changes monthly. A wide-ranging wine list is buttressed by an eclectic set of cocktails, and even the modish brasserie-style decor globe-trots, very prettily in the case of the Turkish floor tiles.

Available for hire. Babies and children welcome: high chairs; nappy-changing facilities. Booking advisable. Disabled: toilet. Tables outdoors (3, pavement). Map 18 D3.

Fitzrovia

Bam-Bou
1 Percy Street, W1T 1DB (7323 9130, www.bam-bou.co.uk). Goodge Street or Tottenham Court Road tube.
Bar **Open** 5.30pm-1am Mon-Sat.
Restaurant **Meals served** noon-11pm Mon-Sat.
Main courses £8-£15.75. **Set lunch** (noon-5pm Mon-Sat) £10 4 dishes, £15 6 dishes, £20 7 dishes. **Set dinner** (5-6.45pm, 10-11pm Mon-Sat) £15 2 courses, £18 3 courses.
Both **Credit** AmEx, MC, V.
The soothing aesthetics at Bam-Bou recall the colonial Indochine of a century ago. Four floors of the Fitzrovia townhouse are done up in dark wood and deep colours, with tasteful orientalist touches. The menu sweeps through Vietnam, Thailand and China with dumplings, soups, noodle dishes, curries, and fish and meat in both small-plate and main-meal portions that blend the flavours of East and West. The food isn't high on authenticity, but dishes are well presented and the better ones – such as a small plate of wok-fried cuttlefish with lemongrass, ginger and chilli – have an appealing spice and aroma. The star dish was sticky, tender slow-braised ox cheek with morning glory and sesame seeds. Less successful was a crab and green-mango salad with chilli dressing, which was short on crab and mango but plentiful on (unannounced) grated carrot. Desserts are in a more western vein, with the likes of trio of chocolate brownie or coconut panna cotta with spiced pineapple. Service is poised and friendly, as befits a restaurant that's part of the same group as the Ivy and Scott's. Dining is on three floors, with the top floor given over to the luxe Red Room cocktail bar.

Available for hire. Babies and children admitted. Booking advisable Thur-Sat. Separate rooms for parties, seating 8-20. Tables outdoors (4, terrace). Map 17 B1.

Gloucester Road

★ L'Etranger
36 Gloucester Road, SW7 4QT (7584 1118, www.etranger.co.uk). Gloucester Road tube.
Lunch served noon-3pm Mon-Fri. **Brunch served** noon-3pm Sun. **Dinner served** 5.30-10pm Mon-Thur, Sun; 5.30-11pm Fri, Sat. **Main courses** £16.50-£32.50. **Set lunch** £17.50 2 courses, £22 3 courses. **Set dinner** £22 2 courses, £26 3 courses; £95 tasting menu.
Credit AmEx, MC, V.
This jewel box of a restaurant entices the beau monde of Kensington with its Franco-Japanese cooking, impressive wine list and plush decor – all gleaming mirrors, dainty cutlery and sparkling wine glasses. The likes of maki rolls and sashimi, or caviar and foie gras, are equally at home on exec chef Jerome Tauvron's dual-nationality menu. For indecisive diners, the six-course tasting menu (£95) is a good introduction, but choosing carefully from the à la carte is a less pricey and no less flavourful

option – or order the excellent-value set lunch. From the carte, inventive dishes might include beetroot 'ravioli' (in which fine slices of beetroot form a sandwich for tangy goat's cheese mousse) or succulent smoked langoustines wrapped in kadaifi (fine filo pastry). The latter made its dramatic appearance at table served under a glass cloche filled with aromatic smoke: this place has wow factor and the cooking rarely falters. Chicken is pepped up with nori salt and a sherry reduction, and spicy yellow-fin tuna maki rolls would pass muster in Kyoto. Service is amenable, and the broad-ranging wine list is an oenophile's dream (bottles can be bought to take away), so it's a shame only six are available by the glass. In the basement is the rather bunker-like wine bar Meursault, where the food has a similar, though more casual, Franco-Japanese approach. Insider's tip: Meursault's wine-pairing menu (£59 per person with wine) is a good-value alternative to dining upstairs.

Available for hire. Babies and children welcome: high chairs. Booking advisable. Separate room for parties, seats 20. Map 13 C9.

Marylebone

The Providores & Tapa Room
109 Marylebone High Street, W1U 4RX (7935 6175, www.theprovidores.co.uk). Baker Street or Bond Street tube.
The Providores **Lunch served** noon-2.45pm Mon-Fri. **Brunch served** 11am-2.45pm Sat, Sun. **Dinner served** 6-10.15pm Mon-Sat; 6-10pm Sun. **Main courses** (lunch) £17-£25. **Set lunch** £20 2 courses. **Set dinner** £33 2 courses, £47 3 courses, £57 4 courses, £63 5 courses. **Cover** (brunch) £1.50.
Tapa Room **Breakfast/brunch served** 9-11.30am Mon-Fri; 10am-3pm Sat, Sun. **Meals served** noon-10.30pm Mon-Fri; 4-10.30pm Sat; 4-10pm Sun **Tapas** £2-£14.40.
Both **Credit** AmEx, MC, V.
Peter Gordon is on a roll. His funky, relaxed fusion café and restaurant Kopapa has been going great guns, and summer 2013 saw him taking the famous Sugar Club kitchen back to his native New Zealand for a starry hotel launch. None of this has taken the shine off the Providores & Tapa Room, his flagship Marylebone project. On the ground floor is the Tapa Room, a casual, buzzy space heaving with well-dressed locals knocking back top-quality coffees, New Zealand wines and an all-day menu of small plates. Upstairs in the more formal but still intimate Providores restaurant, everything is ratcheted up a notch. You pick between two and five courses from the sonnet-like menu of small plates, sit back and wait to be blown away. But you're not – not quite. Few, if any, menus like this can hit the high notes with every dish. We liked almost everything – though the scallops with a bright salad and beurre noisette hollandaise were all but ruined by a spicy ketchup-like bloody mary sauce; and dal-stuffed tempura was ill-conceived. Still, coconut laksa mined with a fish dumpling and quail's eggs was deliciously memorable, and the meat dishes (pork, beef, duck) all inventive and well executed. For a good dinner out, however, we're more tempted by the lower prices and expectations met at Kopapa.

Available for hire. Babies and children welcome: high chairs; nappy-changing facilities. Booking advisable Providores; bookings not accepted Tapa Room. Disabled: toilet. Tables outdoors (2, pavement). Map 9 G5.

Soho

NOPI [HOT 50]
21-22 Warwick Street, W1B 5NE (7494 9584, www.nopi-restaurant.com). Piccadilly Circus tube. **Breakfast served** 8am-noon, **lunch served** noon-2.45pm, **dinner served** 5.30-10.30pm Mon-Fri. **Brunch served** 10-11.30am Sat; 10am-12.30pm Sun. **Meals served** noon-10.30pm Sat; noon-3.30pm Sun. **Main courses** £17-£29.50. **Credit** AmEx, MC, V.
NOPI's chef-owner is Yotam Ottolenghi, who struck culinary gold a few years back with his game-changing Ottolenghi cafés (*see p47*). This all-day restaurant shares a similar clean aesthetic and ethos, but is more formal. The white decor is warmed up with brass fittings; the basement contains large sharing tables and an open kitchen. The inventive cooking has a firm foundation in the Middle East and takes bold flavour forays into the Mediterranean and Asia. You can go the conventional route, with starters and mains, or take the opportunity for wider grazing by sticking to sharing plates (but these are quite small). Vegetarians have plenty of choice, with dishes such as a savoury cheesecake with gently pickled beetroot, crunchy hazelnuts and thyme honey, or a moreish side portion of truffled polenta chips. Star dish was spiced gurnard served Vietnamese-style: taken off the bone, mixed with chilli and spices, wrapped in a banana leaf and steamed. NOPI isn't the greatest bargain in town (a main course of comparatively lacklustre chickpea dumplings with tahini and yoghurt cost a stiff £19). Two-hour table slots are strictly enforced, and service can seem rushed as a consequence. The wine list is as wide-ranging as you'd expect, with some excellent (if pricey) selections.

Available for hire. Babies and children welcome: high chairs. Booking advisable dinner. Dress: smart casual. Map 17 A4.

West

Ealing

★ Tuk Cho
28-30 New Broadway, W5 2XA (8567 9438, www.tukchoealing.co.uk). Ealing Broadway tube/rail. **Meals served** noon-10pm Mon-Wed; noon-11pm Thur-Sun. **Main courses** £6-£10.50. **Credit** AmEx, MC, V.
Service was attentive and genial at this self-styled 'adventurous South-east Asian restaurant', which aims to showcase the cheap, tasty street food found on the well-trodden backpacker trail. The setting is a large, informal dining room that looks like the result of an experiment where Byron met Busaba – exposed brickwork, diner-style lighting and a polished concrete floor. Comforting Asian favourites such as nasi goreng, pad thai and Vietnamese pho feature on a varied menu of street-market inspired curries, noodles, rice dishes and stir fries, but claims of adventurous eating seemed to lack foundation; a reportedly fiery northern Thai chicken curry barely sizzled. Better was a nicely balanced and plentiful dish of chicken and prawn yaki udon. Thai sweetcorn fritters – slightly over-browned, but full of flavour – outshone a portion of Vietnamese summer rolls that were good but needed more chicken filling. Although the menu is more diverse than those of its main competitors, Tuk Cho has a

Best oriental chains

PAN-ASIAN & FUSION

★ Banana Tree

103 Wardour Street, W1F 0UQ (7437 1351, www.bananatree.co.uk). Oxford Circus, Piccadilly Circus or Tottenham Court Road tube. **Meals served** noon-11pm Mon-Sat; noon-10.30pm Sun. **Main courses** £5.95-£10.80. **Credit** AmEx, MC, V.

Banana Tree has a half-dozen venues across town, with communal and smaller tables in attractive settings made fashionable with stripped brick and semi-industrial design features. 'Indochinese' street food is the backbone of the extremely varied menu, though Thai and Thai-influenced dishes dominate. Keep an eye out for the great-value set meals and lunch specials. The cooking, though good, lacked finesse. A beef, chilli, ginger and basil stir-fry needed a punch of the advertised chilli, and any basil flavour was almost imperceptible. Chicken laksa had decent depth of flavour, yet was a little watery. With a busy restaurant and one large group to accommodate, staff seemed to be under the cosh – our mains were slow to appear, and one dish arrived tepid – but normal service had resumed with our Vietnamese iced coffee.

Babies and children welcome: nappy-changing facilities. Bookings not accepted Thur-Sat; accepted Mon-Wed, Sun for more than 6 people. Disabled: toilet. Vegan dishes. **Map 17 B4.**
For branches see index.

★ dim t

56-62 Wilton Road, SW1V 1DE (7834 0507, www.dimt.co.uk). Victoria tube/rail. **Meals served** noon-11pm Mon-Sat; noon-10.30pm Sun. **Dim sum** £3.85. **Main courses** £7.10-£11.95. **Set meal** £15.95 2 courses, £19.95 3 courses, £25.95 4 courses. **Credit** AmEx, MC, V.

First impressions of dim t set expectations high, its expensive-looking interiors (there are currently five branches in London, plus one in Winchester) containing plenty of polished dark wood and impressive oriental sculptures. Service is always polite and efficient. Sadly, the cooking fell short this time. Steamed peanut and prawn dumplings were barely distinguishable from the chicken and wasabi ones, though the pastry was good: delicate and paper-thin. A main of chicken tom yam soup smelled beautifully fragrant, yet the broth lacked flavour and was light on noodles and chicken. Despite the chain's name, the list of steamed dumplings and roasted pork buns is short, though daily specials are available. The 'noodle bar' section of the menu holds most options, where the likes of curried udon noodles and – confusingly – rice dishes can be customised with your choice of protein (including tofu for vegetarians).

Babies and children welcome: children's menu; high chairs; nappy-changing facilities. Disabled: toilet. Takeaway service. Vegan dishes. **Map 15 J10.**
For branches see index.

★ Feng Sushi

1 Adelaide Road, NW3 3QE (7483 2929, www.fengsushi.co.uk). Chalk Farm tube. **Meals served** 11.30am-10pm Mon; noon-11pm Tue, Wed, Sat; 11.30am-11pm Thur, Fri; noon-10pm Sun. **Main courses** £7-£18. **Set meal** £12.25 bento box. **Credit** MC, V.

Feng Sushi has a handful of sustainability certifications to its name, and its carefully sourced seasonal menu aims to showcase the best of British seafood in attractively presented Japanese cooking. Sweet Devonshire crab was the summer special, though an order of crab rice-paper rolls was very dry without the (forgotten) accompanying sweet chilli sauce. The sauce eventually arrived, though getting the attention of our waiter was tricky considering the relatively empty dining room. The usual nigiri and maki rolls predominate – many of these can be customised to include brown rice instead of white – but more modern takes on Japanese food, such as spelt buns stuffed with crispy tofu, offer something new. A range of noodle soups, curries and tempura is also available, though beware of creeping costs; prices are a little high.

Babies and children admitted. Disabled: toilet. Takeaway service; delivery service (over £15.50 within 3-mile radius). **Map 27 B1.**
For branches see index.

★ Ping Pong

45 Great Marlborough Street, W1F 7JL (7851 6969, www.pingpongdimsum.com). Oxford Circus tube. **Dim sum served** 11am-midnight Mon-Fri; noon-midnight Sat; noon-10.30pm Sun. **Dim sum** £1.65-£6.95. **Set meal** £11-£42. **Credit** AmEx, MC, V.

Chinese lattice screens and giant paper lanterns fail to boost the authenticity of this dim sum chain. Ping Pong's menu is possibly intended as an introduction to dim sum for beginners, with unexciting set menus and tips such as 'do not eat the lotus leaf' served with lotus leaf rice. The relatively brief menu is devoid of dim sum names, except for favourites such as siu mai and har gau, both of which looked pretty in their bamboo steamers. However, the little meat parcels were ruined by their thick and mushy dumpling skins. Char siu buns were better, moist and fluffy with a hint of barbecued sweetness in the pork. Ping Pong does try to bring dim sum away from the constraints of brightly lit Chinatown restaurants, but in doing so, the result comes over as half-hearted, with a number of inauthentic dishes reminiscent of student cooking.

Babies and children welcome: high chairs; nappy-changing facilities. Bookings not accepted for fewer than 8 people. Disabled: toilet. Takeaway service. **Map 17 A3.**
For branches see index.

★ Wagamama

1 Ropemaker Street, EC2Y 9AW (7588 2688, www.wagamama.com). Moorgate tube/rail. **Meals served** 11.30am-10pm Mon-Fri. **Main courses** £6-£13. **Credit** AmEx, MC, V.

Launched over two decades ago (in 1992), Wagamama has since opened outlets in all sorts of useful places, ideal for a cheap pre-theatre meal, a solo lunch or a quick catch-up with friends. The chain is also popular with kids. Many branches occupy cavernous spaces, however, which can result in a loud, echoey din of nattering diners at busy times. The menu has changed little in recent years, featuring reliable noodle- and rice-based staples alongside a compact list of daily specials. Portions are substantial and tasty, though a rice dish topped with a generous amount of sliced chicken breast was a little oily, and the supposedly sticky rice collapsed into the plentiful oyster, ginger, garlic and white wine sauce. Steamed and fried dumplings and edamame make popular side dishes. Tables turn at a furious rate, and on our Monday lunchtime visit service was friendly and speedy – until it came to paying the bill.

Babies and children welcome: children's menu; high chairs. Disabled: toilet. Takeaway service. Vegan dishes. **Map 12 Q5.**
For branches see index.

★ Yo! Sushi

52 Poland Street, W1F 7NQ (7287 0443, www.yosushi.com). Oxford Circus or Tottenham Court Road tube. **Meals served** noon-11pm Mon-Sat; noon-10.30pm Sun. **Dishes** £1.80-£5. **Credit** AmEx, MC, V.

The conveyor belt, the convivial atmosphere, the kitsch branding – these are the things that keep people flocking to Yo! Sushi, but this is no place for sushi connoisseurs. Still, it's a fun place to dine and offers a gentle introduction to sushi for the uninitiated. There's a wide range of fishy options, from salmon sashimi to soft-shell crab hand rolls, and a specials menu that includes the likes of salmon and tobiko tartare with a zesty coriander dressing. Vegetarians and fish-fearers are also catered for, both on the belt and with more substantial noodle and rice dishes on the à la carte menu. The dizzying array of choice can be overwhelming, in fact – diners may want to pore over the set-price menus while sipping from their miso soup (with unlimited free refills). Individual plates are priced by colour and the cost can, quite literally, stack up, so check online offers before you visit.

Babies and children welcome: high chairs; nappy-changing facilities. Disabled: toilet. Takeaway service. Vegetarian menu. **Map 17 A3.**
For branches see index.

slightly confused identity: does it want to be adventurous and authentic or mainstream and approachable? A second branch is yet to materialise after plans to open in Chiswick were shelved; until the concept rolls out across London, this remains a reliable local restaurant.

Booking advisable Fri, Sat. Disabled: toilet. Tables outdoors (6, pavement). Takeaway service.

Ladbroke Grove

E&O

14 Blenheim Crescent, W11 1NN (7229 5454, www.rickerrestaurants.com). Ladbroke Grove or Notting Hill Gate tube.
Bar **Open** noon-midnight Mon-Sat; 12.30-11pm Sun. **Dim sum served** noon-10.30pm Mon-Sat; 12.30-10pm Sun.
Restaurant **Lunch served** noon-3pm, **dinner served** 6-11pm Mon-Fri. **Meals served** noon-11pm Sat; 12.30-10.30pm Sun. **Dim sum** £3.50-£8. **Main courses** £8-£27. **Set lunch** (Mon-Thur) £20 3 courses.
Both **Credit** AmEx, DC, MC, V.
Will Ricker's restaurants make up a small but impressive pan-Asian empire (plus two Mexican street-food hotspots). The well-thought out menu is brief, with just enough little touches to pique diners' interest – black vinegar paired with crisp pork belly, barbecued beef bulgogi with coriander raita. But first, take time for an informal drink in the attached bar to mingle with the beautiful and the damned, as a steady stream of well-to-do twentysomethings float in and out. The fresh, contemporary dining room is home to a mixed clientele on Friday evenings: from scruffy hipsters to opulent families

with children, and everything between. Other than a snarky barman, service was unfalteringly attentive, charming and professional. Far from being style over substance, every dish we ordered was prepared to a very high standard. Highlights included a cherry tomato and lychee green curry (the sweet and the savoury perfectly countered) and delicate black cod dumplings. A duck and watermelon salad was rather rich and would have benefited from more acidity. If you're watching the pennies, book a table for 11am-12.30pm at weekends when a brunch deal offers half-price dim sum.
Babies and children welcome: children's menu; crayons; high chairs. Booking essential. Separate room for parties, seats 18. Tables outdoors (5, pavement). **Map 19 B3**.
For branches (Cicada, Eight Over Eight, XO) see index.

South
Kennington

Oaka at the Mansion House NEW

48 Kennington Park Road, SE11 4RS (7582 5599, www.oakalondon.com). Kennington tube.
Lunch served noon-2.30pm Mon-Fri; noon-3.30pm Sat. **Dinner served** 5.30-10.30pm Mon-Thur; 5.30-11pm Fri, Sat. **Meals served** noon-9.30pm Sun. **Main courses** £6.90-£14.80. **Credit** AmEx, MC, V.
These days you can pimp pretty much anything, and now it's the turn of the 'pub with Thai food' to go upmarket, in the shape of this swanky Kennington newcomer. One side is a stylish bar; the

other an elegant, low-lit restaurant, tricked out in the royal Thai way with dark, high-gloss woods. The menu also has high intentions, with luxurious dishes from across the Orient (yellowtail sashimi, miso black cod) in among the mostly Thai dishes. The basics are done well. Tom yam soup, laced with lemongrass, kaffir lime leaves and red chilli, cleared out the cobwebs ahead of a refreshing som tam (shredded green papaya salad that successfully balanced sweet, salt, sour and spice). There were a few duff notes, though: a 'signature' dish of stir-fried prawns in a sweet chilli reduction seemed one-dimensional. For afters, a tempura-clad scoop of ice-cream was a nice idea, but proved too sweet and insipid. A strong selection of speciality beers, such as JHB (brewed by Oakham Ales) made amends. Oaka may not be the place to relive memories of hawker stalls – staff are international and the music is more spa than Siam – but as an attractive venue to enjoy spice and beer, it hits the spot.
Available for hire. Babies and children welcome: high chairs. Booking advisable. Disabled: toilet. Tables outdoors (5, pavement). Takeaway service.

South East
Herne Hill

Lombok

17 Half Moon Lane, SE24 9JU (7733 7131). Herne Hill rail or bus 37. **Dinner served** 6-10.30pm Tue-Sun. **Main courses** £6-£8. **Credit** MC, V.
Exactly the sort of restaurant you want in your neighbourhood, Lombok has friendly, speedy service paired with a vast, fairly priced menu. Food

E&O

is varied enough to cater for those wishing to indulge or to diet, to set their tongues on fire or have a soothing hearty supper. The small wood-panelled dining room has comfortable cushioned chairs, and lazy ceiling fans that create a relaxing atmosphere. The owner, chef and most staff are Thai, and dishes from that country dominate the menu. A massaman chicken curry, listed under the specials, was indeed special. This traditional Muslim Thai curry featured a wealth of exotic spices – cardamom, cinnamon, star anise, cumin, cloves and nutmeg – all of which, with coconut milk and tamarind, lent fabulous flavour to the chicken thighs, carrots and potatoes cooked therein. Lombok's rendering of pad thai was fresh and pleasing too. Other Southeast Asian dishes worth trying include a starter of Vietnamese chicken and coriander fritters with sambal oelek (a chilli-based condiment), fresh ginger and cinnamon. Pleasantly sponge-like in consistency, they'd have been tastier with peanut sauce (promised on the menu) instead of the sweet chilli sauce that came with all our starters. Still, for an easy and tasty night out, Lombok delivers.
Babies and children admitted. Booking essential weekends. Takeaway service. **Map 23 A5**.

Oaka at the Mansion House. See p217.

London Bridge & Borough

★ Champor-Champor
62-64 Weston Street, SE1 3QJ (7403 4600, www.champor-champor.com). London Bridge tube/rail. **Lunch served** noon-2.30pm Mon-Fri. **Dinner served** 6-10.30pm Mon-Sun. **Main courses** £12-£20. **Credit** AmEx, MC, V.
Champor-Champor has been on *Time Out*'s radar long before this stretch became trendy. With the Shard springing up nearby, it's no longer off the beaten path, yet still feels like a hidden find. In Malay, 'champor-champor' means 'mix and match', and it's a fitting name for both the interior and the menu. The walls are painted in vibrant shades and hung with colourful masks, and there's carved teak galore, plus winking candles and acres of Thai silk. The place exudes a yogic calm. The cooking is described as 'Thai-Malay', but influences reach beyond this southeast Asian peninsula, unashamedly fusing East and West with the likes of gruyère cheese and lime with river prawns, served with wasabi-spiked potato salad. What could have been a backpackerish mashup is sophisticated and creative. Fish dishes are well rendered, as in a main of Malaysian-style red snapper, the fillets halved and served on twin pools of kicking-hot sambal sauce. Vegetarians needn't go hungry; a vegan starter of green papaya som tam with tofu, cashew nuts and star fruit was suitably spicy (though not great value at £6.95). Desserts – steamed taro and black rice pudding, say, or chocolate-chilli cheesecake – are much more than an afterthought.
Babies and children welcome: high chairs. Booking advisable. Separate room for parties, seats 8-12. Takeaway service. **Map 12 Q9**.

Outer London
Barnet, Hertfordshire

★ Emchai
78 High Street, Barnet, EN5 5SN (8364 9993). High Barnet tube. **Lunch served** noon-2.30pm daily. **Dinner served** 6-11pm Mon-Thur; 6pm-midnight Fri, Sat; 5-10pm Sun. **Main courses** £4.20-£8.90. **Set meal** £18.90-£21.50 per person (minimum 2). **Credit** AmEx, MC, V.
What looks like ten-years' worth (and counting) of melted candle wax on the floor just inside the doorway is a strange quirk of an otherwise large and elegant room, though low ceilings and a paucity of lighting can make the place seem quite dark. Emchai is an established restaurant, with Malay and Chinese dishes to the fore and a longstanding local reputation, but was surprisingly empty on a Saturday lunchtime. Starters (averaging £6) and mains (around £7) differ very little in cost. Beef in rendang curry was tender, as if slow-cooked, but the brown slick of sauce lacked depth, tasting mainly of soy and desiccated coconut. Kung po chicken – part of a cheap weekend lunch deal – was unremarkable. The food could have been from any average Chinese takeaway, were it not for the starters: crisp battered prawns with a nice wallop of wasabi, and a small plate of moreish soft-shell crab – both beautifully presented and executed. Service was gracious and welcoming.
Available for hire. Babies and children welcome: high chairs. Disabled: toilet. Takeaway service.

Spanish & Portuguese

Spanish food is having a second flush of youth in London. Ignited by the experimentalism coming from the Spanish *cocina nueva* ('new cooking'), small tapas bars (such as **José**) as well as more ambitious restaurants (such as José's sister establishment, **Pizarro**) are now championing innovative dishes as well as top quality Spanish produce. A still more established kitchen in the same mould, but in an even more upmarket setting, is **Cambio de Tercio**, where you'll find expertly rendered, cutting-edge versions of traditional tapas. Its mid-market stablemate **Tendido Cero** also cuts a dash. Elsewhere, there's plenty of creativity and a modern sensibility at **Moro** and sibling **Morito**, where the North African influence is nearly as strong as the Iberian strand, creating an interesting continental drift. Soho, with its abundance of bars, is a natural home for tapas, and two of London's best, and most popular, venues – **Barrafina** and **Copita** – reside here. But Brixton's stylish **Boqueria Tapas** shows that the genre can happily travel south. New Spanish ventures continue to pop up like churros in an oil vat, and this year we welcome Covent Garden's **Condesa**, with its snacks from Spain and Latin America; Clapham's latest neighbourhood tapas joint, **Barsito**; **Rosita**, a Battersea sibling to **Lola Rojo**; and **Bar Esteban**, bringing the punchy flavours of Barcelona to Crouch End.

Portuguese cuisine tends to be a simple affair, with fresh fish, salt cod (bacalhau) and marinated meat to the fore, along with a few stews. More complex cooking, using influences from across the Iberian peninsula and beyond, can be found at **Eyre Brothers**, **Portal** and the new **Notting Hill Kitchen**. Most other establishments are based close to London's Portuguese communities and cater largely for them – including two new additions this year, Tottenham's **Bom Pecado** and Stockwell's **Mar Azul** – though the city's pastelarias have universal appeal, especially for their creamy, custardy pastéis de nata.

SPANISH

Central
Bloomsbury

Cigala
54 Lamb's Conduit Street, WC1N 3LW (7405 1717, www.cigala.co.uk). Holborn or Russell Square tube. **Meals served** noon-10.45pm Mon-Fri; 12.30-10.45pm Sat; 12.30-9.45pm Sun. **Main courses** £12.50-£19. **Set lunch** (noon-3pm Mon-Fri) £17.50 2 courses, £19.50 3 courses; (12.30-4.30pm Sat, Sun) £16 3 courses. **Credit** AmEx, MC, V.

We'd gladly revisit Cigala for its by-the-glass sherries and its heavenly salt cod; our most recent visit also saw a sublimely nubbly almond and medlar tart. Set on a lively street corner, it's a light, modern sort of place, with big windows, whitewashed walls, and pavement tables on warm days. On a weekday lunchtime, the room was more than half empty – just a few elderly diners and local businessmen – but the sizzle of oil and sound of Spanish coming from the kitchen were enough to whet our appetites. Cigala's owner/chef Jake Hodges (also a co-founder of Moro) has scoured Spain for its best dishes and added a little élan of his own. The cooking can be slapdash – our grilled cuttlefish was partly raw – but slip-ups are rare. A smoky, splendidly macho pork chop was vibrant with lemon and rosemary, and accompanied by crisp, liberally salted fries. Rabbit and pigeon terrine was punchily meaty and came with pickled carrots, a pleasing departure from the Spanish veg-phobic norm. Our León-born waiter took some warming up, but his gruff manner was nothing if not authentic. *Available for hire (bar). Babies and children welcome: high chairs. Booking advisable. Separate room for parties, seats 26. Tables outdoors (11, pavement). Vegan dishes. Vegetarian menu.* **Map 4 M4**.

Clerkenwell & Farringdon

★ Morito
32 Exmouth Market, EC1R 4QE (7278 7007, www.morito.co.uk). Angel tube or Farringdon tube/rail or bus 19, 38, 341. **Tapas served** noon-4pm, 5-11pm Mon-Sat; noon-4pm Sun. **Tapas** £1-£8.50. **Credit** MC, V.

Morito. See p219.

The downside of this diminutive tapas bar, little sister of Moro next door, is its unceasing popularity. You can't book for dinner (though you can for lunch), which, unless you have the timing of Eric Morecambe, almost always means a wait – though staff are happy for you to decamp elsewhere and will phone as soon as space becomes free. The upside is that the food is fantastic, the staff delightful and the atmosphere properly buzzing, as everyone is so pleased to be there. The high stools next to the bright orange bar offer the best view of the action, and are marginally more comfortable than the oddly low tables – but in general it's a cramped experience. Do sample as many dishes as you can from the 40-strong list. Everything we tried was superb, from the very simple (tomato toast, lip-tingling pádron peppers) to old faves (patatas bravas topped with a thick, spicy tomato sauce and dollop of mayo) and regional specialities (grilled Galician tetilla cheese with membrillo and walnut halves, sizzling Palamós prawns with allioli). Desserts include a first-rate crema catalana (large enough for two), but the rich, boozy baklava ice-cream floating in a pool of Pedro Ximénez sherry takes some beating. To drink, there are cocktails, sherries and an all-Spanish wine list, available by the glass, 375ml carafe or bottle.
Available for hire. Babies and children welcome: high chairs. Bookings not accepted dinner. Disabled: toilet. Tables outdoors (3, pavement). Vegan dishes. **Map 5 N4.**

★ Moro `HOT 50`

34-36 Exmouth Market, EC1R 4QE (7833 8336, www.moro.co.uk). Angel tube or Farringdon tube/rail or bus 19, 38, 341.
Bar **Open** noon-10.30pm Mon-Sat; 12.30-2.45pm Sun. **Tapas served** noon-10.30pm Mon-Sat. **Tapas** £3.50-£14.50.
Restaurant **Lunch served** noon-2.30pm Mon-Sat; 12.30-2.45pm Sun. **Dinner served** 6-10.30pm Mon-Sat. **Main courses** £16.50-£21.
Both **Credit** AmEx, MC, V.
Sam(antha) and Sam Clark's Exmouth Market restaurant and cookbooks set the benchmark for a distinctly British style of Iberian-with-a-North-African-twist Mediterranean cooking, and they're still in the front rank 15 years later. Devotees (including many affluent older diners as well as the

fashionable of Clerkenwell) forgive its quirks, such as the difficulty in getting a table, and the noise level produced by the hard-surfaced, vaguely post-industrial decor, which often means conversations must be conducted at a shout. In return, they get bright, attentive service; a spectacular showcase of modern Spanish and Portuguese wines; and vibrantly fresh food that throws out surprising and pleasurable flavours at every turn. Chickpea salad with cherry tomatoes, dill and deep-flavoured morel mushrooms, and prawns, braised peas and wild garlic on toast were memorably unusual starters. Wood-roasted pork was offset in flavour and texture by an amazingly fresh hazelnut picada (like a nut pesto), and chargrilled trout was cleverly balanced by lemon, capers and a bitter note from hispi cabbage. Our only complaint would be that some elements were a little too oily (the olive oil is first-rate, granted, but it can still be over-used) but palates were cleared by an exquisitely sybaritic blood orange and rosewater sorbet.
Babies and children welcome: high chairs. Booking advisable. Disabled: toilet. Tables outdoors (7, pavement). Vegan dishes. **Map 5 N4.**

Covent Garden

Condesa `NEW`

15 Maiden Lane, WC2E 7NG (3601 5752, www.condesalondon.com). Covent Garden tube.
Tapas served noon-10pm Mon, Tue, Sun; noon-11pm Wed, Thur; noon-11.30pm Fri, Sat. **Tapas** £4-£12. **Credit** AmEx, MC, V.
It's always a good sign when the waitress insists you start your night with a sherry. This little tapas joint off Covent Garden has dark wooden tables for two opposite the bar, and larger tables lining the wall at the back. The menu is small but varied. Pick up citrusy pulled pork quesadillas or spicy chicken chipotle bocadillo sandwiches for lunch, or come for dinner specials that change weekly and, of course, a glass of sherry. Condesa takes its tapas inspiration from across Spain and Latin America, so you might find unexpected dishes on the menu, such as the little pan of grilled provolone cheese – a typical Argentinian tapa. It's not good for your cholesterol levels, but it spreads so easily over fresh bread, your doctor would surely understand. Pork

cheeks were succulent, with strands of meat falling into a puréed carrot sauce; however, seasoning was timidly applied. Mole tacos had a dense, meaty filling wrapped in the softest of corn tortillas. We loved the half carafes of wine too, as they provide a convivial way to graze across the menu and pair wine accordingly.
Available for hire. Babies and children admitted. Bookings not accepted after 6.30pm. Vegan dishes. **Map 18 E5.**

Opera Tavern

23 Catherine Street, WC2B 5JS (7836 3680, www.operatavern.co.uk). Covent Garden tube.
Tapas served noon-3pm, 5-11pm Mon-Fri; noon-11pm Sat; noon-5pm Sun. **Tapas** £2.80-£15.50. **Credit** AmEx, MC, V.
Despite growing competition, the Opera Tavern remains one of Covent Garden's best dining options and among London's top tapas restaurants. Formerly a pub, it's split into a slightly charmless upstairs restaurant and a cosy, mirror-backed bar at street level. The latter has been stylishly updated with chocolate leather bar stools, copper spotlights and an open grill; the main kitchen is in the beer cellar. The Spanish-Italian menu is kept fresh with regular specials. The signature burger of juicy ibérico pork and foie gras remains deservedly popular, though more inventive combinations better showcase the kitchen's delicate touch and careful sourcing of ingredients. Char-grilled venison was enlivened by jerusalem artichoke, pickled walnuts and truffle, while the natural sweetness of scallops (served in the shell) was balanced by a feather-light pea, fennel and mint purée. Watch out, though: portions are dainty and it's easy to rack up a hefty bill. The Spanish and Italian wine list is well curated; smooth and nutty manzanilla pasada is the ideal aperitif for sherry sceptics. Little touches such as allowing diners a taste before committing to a glass exemplify the sophisticated, amiable service. Opera Tavern is part of the Salt Yard Group, along with Dehesa in Soho and Salt Yard in Fitzrovia.
Babies and children welcome (dining room): high chairs. Booking essential. Separate room for parties, seats 45. Tables outdoors (2, pavement). **Map 18 E4.**
For branches (Dehesa, Salt Yard) see index.

Fitzrovia

Barrica

*62 Goodge Street, W1T 4NE (7436 9448,
www.barrica.co.uk). Goodge Street tube.* **Tapas
served** noon-10.30pm Mon-Fri; 1-10.30pm Sat.
Tapas £2-£8. **Credit** AmEx, MC, V.
Barcelona meets Fitzrovia in this happening tapas
bar. Jamóns hang above the central marble bar, the
yellow-ochre walls hint at days of nicotine-
indulgence gone by and, as the evening progresses,
the decibel level rises along with the animated
chatter. Grab a stool at the bar or a seat at one of
the wooden tables (booking recommended) and let
the friendly, mainly Spanish staff guide you
through the menu. Cold cheese and ham platters,
plus basic tapas (tortillas, croquetas and the like)
are available all day, but at lunch and dinner the
charcoal grill is fired up for daily and seasonal
specials – such as fideua, a Valencian take on paella
made with thin vermicelli-like noodles, and on our
visit cooked with scallops and punchy piquillo
peppers. Flavours are generally well judged. We
couldn't fault melt-in-the-mouth veal cheeks slow-
cooked in PX sherry, or a dish of sliced carrots
cooked to sweet and sour perfection with blood
orange and raisin, although our jamón croquetas
were a bit pappy in texture. As at sister restaurant
Copita, in Soho, the drinks list is a mustn't-miss,
with a range of sherries sold by the glass, from
bone-dry to ultra-sweet, and an all-Spanish wine list
that begs to be explored.
*Available for hire. Babies and children admitted.
Booking advisable Tue-Sat. Tables outdoors
(2, pavement).* **Map 17 A1.**

Fino

*33 Charlotte Street, entrance on Rathbone
Street, W1T 1RR (7813 8010, www.fino
restaurant.com). Goodge Street or Tottenham
Court Road tube.* **Tapas served** noon-2.30pm,
6-10.30pm Mon-Fri; 6-10.30pm Sat. **Tapas** £2-
£25. **Credit** AmEx, MC, V.
Fino led a new wave of quality-focused modern
Spanish restaurants in the capital and remains at
the top of its game, even if London's scenesters
have moved on to trendier tapas-grazing grounds
such as sister restaurant Barrafina. The basement
room is a bit business-like, but none the worse for
it. Brothers Sam and Eddie Hart, who run both
establishments (as well as having revived well-
regarded Soho restaurant Quo Vadis, *see p52*), have
a love of Spanish food that comes across clearly in
the ingredients and the care taken in putting them
together. Classic dishes, such as croquetas, jamón
and fish cooked on the plancha grill, form the
backbone of the short, seasonal menu. A simple
tortilla, cooked to soft-hearted squidginess, was
potato perfection; while crunchy, deep-fried baby
artichokes tasted just as they do in Spain. Battered
pollock, served hot and crisp, with a gutsy saffron
allioli sauce, and deeply flavoured home-style
chickpeas cooked with spinach and smoked
pancetta, couldn't be faulted. Professional service
is part of the well-oiled package. The all-Spanish
wine list zones in on the country's top producers
and regions (Ribera del Duero and Rioja are strong
points) and there are 25 sherries by the glass. A
class act.
*Available for hire. Babies and children welcome:
high chairs. Booking advisable Thur-Sat.
Disabled: lift; toilet.* **Map 17 B1.**

Donostia. See p222.

King's Cross

Camino

*3 Varnishers Yard, The Regent's Quarter,
N1 9FD (reservations 3641 7966, front desk
7841 7331, www.camino.uk.com). King's Cross
tube/rail.*
Bar **Open** noon-midnight daily.
Restaurant **Breakfast served** 8-11am Mon-Fri;
8am-1pm Sat, Sun. **Tapas served** noon-3pm,
6-10.30pm Mon-Sat; noon-3pm Sun. **Tapas**
£2.75-£49.50. **Set meal** £18 tasting menu.
Both **Credit** AmEx, MC, V.
Formulaic but effective, Camino gives King's Cross
punters what they need in a night out: a menu for
sharing, an open courtyard for social smokers (or
those pretending it's warm enough to sit outside),
Latino-inspired DJs, table football and cocktails.
Tapas are a savvy blend of classics (croquetas de
jamón, meat platters, patatas bravas) and the more
adventurous (squid-ink rice with cuttlefish,
Asturian bean stew, black pudding). Vegetarians
are also well-catered for: not often the case in
meat-centric Spanish restaurants. With such an
accessible menu and a focus on platters, Camino is
set up for group dining – and customers even get a
free small tapa with every drink on Tuesdays. You'll
need to reserve a table on a school night though, as
the informal bar and sit-down restaurant both fill
up quickly with sociable office workers. Fun,
relaxed, and not taking itself too seriously, Camino
exudes the true spirit of Spain. You won't be blown
away by the food, but you'll be having such a good
time, it won't seem to matter.
*Available for hire. Babies and children welcome
(before 6pm Thur-Sat): high chairs; nappy-
changing facilities. Booking advisable. Disabled:
toilet. Tables outdoors (10, garden; 4, pavement).*
Map 4 L3.
**For branches (Camino, Copa de Cava)
see index.**

Marylebone

Ibérica Marylebone

*195 Great Portland Street, W1W 5PS (7636
8650, www.ibericalondon.com). Great Portland
Street or Regent's Park tube.* **Tapas served**
11.30am-11pm Mon-Sat; noon-4pm Sun.
Tapas £3.50-£12.50. **Set tapas** (11.30am-
5pm Mon-Fri) £10 2 dishes, £15 3 dishes.
Credit AmEx, MC, V.
Ibérica feels like an Andalusian mansion on the
corner of Great Portland Street. So many London
tapas bars go for the dark tavern look, but here the
balconied upper level, internal windows, Moorish
oversized lamps and traditional azulejo blue and
white tiling work to create an expansive, relaxed
atmosphere. The air-cured beef cecina is a favourite
of executive chef Nacho Manzano, when he visits
from his two-Michelin-starred restaurant in
Asturias, so don't miss this wafer-thin delicacy,
served on a meat board alongside smoky chorizo or
soft slices of lomo. The menu demonstrates how
traditional dishes are done best (absolutely tender
octopus served simply with soft potatoes, or smooth
chickpea purée with nibs of spiced chorizo) and
balances this with novel, playful flavour-pairings
(chorizo lollipops with pear allioli, or beetroot
gazpacho lifted by red berries, cheese ice-cream and
anchovy flecks). Traditionally given to pilgrims
after a trek to Santiago de Compostela, Galician
almond tart is, in this version, dense, moist and

a pilgrimage in itself. Service is ~~~ery Spanish. Pop into Ibérica's deli ~~~ to buy cured meats and Spanish cheeses – and remember to book if you're visiting the restaurant at the end of the week.

Available for hire. Babies and children welcome: high chairs; nappy-changing facilities. Booking advisable. Separate rooms for parties, seating 25 and 30. Takeaway service. Map 9 J5.
For branch see index.

Mayfair

Donostia

10 Seymour Place, W1H 7ND (3620 1845, www.donostia.co.uk). Marble Arch tube.
Lunch served 12.30-3pm Tue-Sat; 1-4pm Sun. **Dinner served** 6-10.30pm Mon-Sat. **Tapas** £7-£15. **Credit** MC, V.
Fitted snugly into the elegant independent shops of Marylebone village, Donostia – San Sebastián in Basque – basks in the prestige of that gastronomic capital. Whole legs of ham hang in the window as a nod to tradition, but decor is mostly modern

and minimalistic. Staff are knowledgeable and passionate about the food they serve, while head chef Tomasz Baranski (previously of Barrafina) turns out Basque interpretations of classic dishes. Understated flavour revelations make the tapas stand out: serrano ham was wrapped around fleshy prawns, then deep-fried to create the ultimate surf 'n' turf. Donostia's version of the classic squid-ink risotto arrives topped with simply grilled monkfish to contrast with the inky rice beneath. Although torrija is traditionally eaten at Easter, the fluffy, milk-soaked bread was fried perfectly and served with a surprising goat's milk ice-cream – good eating on any day of the year. The wine list is worth careful consideration; two wine importers who fell in love with Basque cuisine run the restaurant, and the menu often features unusual wines they've collected on their travels. Try a bottle of Rioja from their biodynamic collection, or a glass of Basque natural cider, poured spectacularly from a height to aerate it.
Available for hire. Babies and children welcome: high chairs. Booking advisable dinner. Tables outdoors (2, pavement). Map 8 F6.

El Pirata

5-6 Down Street, W1J 7AQ (7491 3810, www.elpirata.co.uk). Green Park or Hyde Park Corner tube. **Meals served** noon-11.30pm Mon-Fri. **Dinner served** 6-11.30pm Sat. **Main courses** £13.95-£17.95. **Tapas** £1.90-£10.95. **Set lunch** (noon-3pm) £10.25 2 dishes incl glass of wine. **Set meal** £16.35 8 dishes. **Credit** AmEx, MC, V.
Suited types flock to this Mayfair tapas bar, which does a recession-friendly £10.25 set lunch deal that includes a glass of wine. The menu is solidly macho with the odd rogue element (couscous, pancetta, risotto). Service from our Burgos-born waitress was cheerful and sweet-natured. Lunch is aimed at the time-poor. Dishes arrived with almost indecent haste, crowding the tiny table. The tortilla is among the best in London, and we liked the rich chorizo-laced lentil stew. But fried chicken with garlic and parsley didn't pack the promised punch, and a fresh, if inauthentic, tricolore salad was unseasoned and let down by poor-quality mozzarella. Dull sliced bread struck another low note, as did the whiffy basement toilets. Coffees, a shared plate of top-notch Spanish cheeses with quince (we couldn't face the fried bananas) and two extra glasses of vino blanco brought the bill to £45 for two. El Pirata's old-school cooking could do with more brio and consistency, but the friendly prices, informal ambience and attractive setting – a chocolate-toned room enlivened with Miró prints – made us inclined to linger. Eat at the outside tables in summer or sit at the restaurant's snazzy bar, but avoid the gloomy basement.
Babies and children admitted. Booking advisable dinner. Separate room for parties, seats 75. Tables outdoors (4, pavement). Takeaway service. Map 9 H8.

Soho

★ Barrafina   HOT 50

54 Frith Street, W1D 4SL (7813 8010, www.barrafina.co.uk). Leicester Square or Tottenham Court Road tube. **Tapas served** noon-3pm, 5-11pm Mon-Sat; 1-3.30pm, 5.30-10.30pm Sun. **Tapas** £4-£18.50. **Credit** AmEx, MC, V.
If proof is needed that tapas is fashionable, the queues at Barrafina are it. And there will be a queue: bookings aren't taken and hopeful diners can expect to wait at least an hour, any evening of the week. Yet seldom does anyone leave Barrafina disappointed. The place is part restaurant, part theatre, in which diners play a part. Your role begins the moment you join the line for one of the 20 or so stools around the L-shaped bar. Nibbles and drinks are served as you wait – service is excellent. The chefs, stars of their stage, shout out orders, grill, fry and plate up their creations. The owners, brothers Sam and Eddie Hart (who also own Fino), know a thing or two about Spanish food; their mother grew up in Mallorca and they spent summers there as children. Barrafina's menu is studded with Mallorcan and Catalan tapas dishes, such as juicy, crisp-skinned grilled chicken thighs served with exemplary romesco sauce, and coca mallorquina (Mallorca's answer to pizza), piled high with spinach and studded with pine nuts and raisins. A main course-size dish of tender octopus was given extra zip by some capers, and toast with allioli was a simple, garlicky treat. Wines by the glass showcase some of Spain's best modern winemaking.

Copita

Rosita. See p226.

Babies and children admitted. Bookings not accepted. Tables outdoors (4, pavement). **Map 17 C3**.

★ Copita

26 D'Arblay Street, W1F 8EP (7287 7797, www.copita.co.uk). Oxford Circus tube. **Open** 11am-11pm Mon-Fri; noon-11pm Sat. **Tapas served** noon-4pm, 5.30-10.30pm Mon-Fri; 1-10.30pm Sat. **Tapas** £2.95-£6.95. **Credit** AmEx, MC, V.

For an authentic taste of modern Spain, you can't go far wrong with Copita. Like sister restaurant Barrica, this is a place where you get properly tapa-sized dishes so you can really get stuck into the menu. Avoiding the standards of patatas bravas and ensalada rusa, Copita ventures admirably off the well-trodden tapas path. Sherry-braised pig cheeks were meltingly sweet in a rich gravy; feather-light empanadillas de carne were far removed from the traditional heavy and often cloying pastries; a sweet and smoky aubergine stew with tahini and mint showed how well the tapas concept translates across cuisines. Desserts were equally enticing: apricot crumble with delicate rosemary ice-cream, and lightly scented rosewater ice-cream with stewed strawberries were both triumphs. Puddings are also diminutive, so you don't feel like you need to be winched out post-meal. As the restaurant's name suggests, you're encouraged to have several little glasses (copitas) with each tapa from a well-informed list of Spanish wines and sherries. With its central location, long shared tables and bar stools, it's popular with a post-work crowd and can get fairly cacophonous. Yet service is fast and friendly, even when busy, making this a valuable find in the heart of Soho.

Available for hire. Babies and children admitted. Bookings not accepted dinner. Tables outdoors (3, pavement). **Map 17 B3**.

Tapas Brindisa Soho

46 Broadwick Street, W1F 7AF (7534 1690, www.brindisa.com). Oxford Circus or Tottenham Court Road tube. **Tapas served** noon-10.45pm Mon-Sat; noon-9.45pm Sun. **Tapas** £1.50-£21.50. **Credit** AmEx, MC, V.

Decor at the Soho branch of Brindisa feels more than a little chain-like: understated and functional, with dark wood furnishings and deep red walls. But this is noticeable only during quiet periods, of which there are few, and is merely a backdrop to the consistently enticing and well-executed menu. A lunchtime 'platter' for two showcased what's still great about Brindisa tapas, yielding a selection of well-balanced dishes featuring superb ingredients and demonstrating a pleasing avoidance of the standard-issue stodgy or deep-fried fare of many a tapas bar. Our seven dishes included excellent ham croquetas (smooth creamy filling with tender morsels of ham, encased in a crisp exterior); zesty leaves, flecked with walnuts and nutty manchego; and a round of morcilla topped with sweet caramelised onions and roasted peppers. This added up to a generous amount of food, and an extra dish of lightly fried monte enebro cheese drizzled with honey was superb, but entirely superfluous. Brindisa deserves its continuous footfall and always seems to come up with the goods, be it for an informal lunch or a smart dinner date.

Babies and children welcome: high chairs. Bookings not accepted dinner. Disabled: toilet. Tables outdoors (2, pavement). **Map 17 A3**. **For branches (Casa Brindisa, Tapas Brindisa) see index.**

South Kensington

★ Cambio de Tercio

163 Old Brompton Road, SW5 0LJ (7244 8970, www.cambiodetercio.co.uk). Gloucester Road or South Kensington tube. **Lunch served** noon-

2.30pm Mon-Fri; noon-3pm Sat, Sun. **Dinner served** 6.30-11.30pm Mon-Sat; 6.30-11pm Sun. **Main courses** £18.50-£25. **Credit** AmEx, MC, V.

This is tapas – but not as you might know it. Cambio de Tercio is the high-end big brother to two neighbouring Spanish restaurants (Capote y Toros and Tendido Cero). Apparently, it's where Rafael Nadal eats whenever he's in town, and is best known for its modern take on classic Spanish tapas. Tortilla was an el Bulli homage in a martini glass (potato foam, warm egg yolk, crisp onion shards), and eight-hour roast tomatoes were decorated with a charming vine of micro-leaves and pearls of basil 'caviar' that exploded against the deeply candied tomatoes. Main courses were just as innovative: grilled skate melted into soft burgos morcilla with a playful orange vinaigrette, while dark, tender oxtail came with a light apple sauce and even lighter lemon thyme foam. A 'cambio de tercio' is when bullfights take a radical change of direction or move into the next phase. Unfortunately, the final phase of our meal took a less impressive turn, as desserts failed to meet expectations. Manchego cheesecake sounded interesting, but lacked the punch of aged sheep's cheese, and the 'perfume' of fruit and jasmine was little more than a fancy fruit salad. Otherwise, the food was outstanding – but perhaps order one more tapas and skip dessert.

Available for hire. Babies and children admitted. Booking advisable dinner. Separate room for parties, seats 18. Tables outdoors (3, pavement). **Map 13 C11**.

Capote y Toros

157 Old Brompton Road, SW5 0LJ (7373 0567, www.cambiodetercio.co.uk). Gloucester Road or South Kensington tube. **Tapas served** 6-11.30pm Tue-Sat. **Tapas** £4.50-£22. **Credit** AmEx, MC, V.

Capote y Toros gets full marks for ambience and impromptu Spanish dancing, but the food on our visit couldn't keep pace. The venue specialises in sherry and tapas, but you'd be better off sipping a manzanilla and listening to Spanish guitar with the singing chef, than ordering a full dinner. It's a shame, as the other two restaurants in the small group (Cambio de Tercio and Tendido Cero) both execute their tapas with more refinement. That said, there's still some innovation on the menu: reinvented patatas bravas arrived as small new potatoes hollowed out and filled with smooth tomato sauce. Pork cheeks are slow-cooked so the leaner muscles hold all the flavour; ours were just on the point of collapsing, but the oloroso sherry sauce was too sweet. A similar sauce was served with the pork meatballs. Nor did the garlic chicken bring any surprises or depth of flavour, being little more than strips of breast in garlic oil. The sherry list does make its mark, however, containing over 100 varieties covering finos and manzanillas, amontillados and moscatels. Ask the barman for his recommendations.
Babies and children welcome. Bookings not accepted. **Map 13 C11.**

★ Tendido Cero

174 Old Brompton Road, SW5 0BA (7370 3685, www.cambiodetercio.co.uk). Gloucester Road or South Kensington tube. **Tapas served** noon-3pm, 6.30-11pm Mon-Thur, Sun; noon-3pm, 6.30-11.30pm Fri, Sat. **Tapas** £4-£14. **Credit** MC, V.
Part of the three-tiered tapas empire on the corner of Old Brompton Road, Tendido Cero is the mid-market companion to Capote y Toros's informal sherry and tapas bar and the fancier Cambio de Tercio across the road. This venue distinguishes itself by having the formality of white tablecloths and good Spanish service, yet a more relaxed and innovative menu that also remains faithful to the old favourites. Bright pink and sandy coloured decor – bordered in fine weather by the open frontage and tables on the pavement – imbues the restaurant with a genuine Mediterranean feel. Chorizo in northern Spanish cider, and prawns in garlic butter were both classics done very well; the prawns especially had a soft infusion of garlic flavours through a rich butter sauce, which turned a simple crustacean into something sublime. Asturian fabada was lighter than the traditional recipe, but the waiter explained that the kitchen has tailored the dish to the tastes of its west London market over the years. The epic wine list is inspiring and intimidating in equal measure; organised by region, it opens with a map of the Iberian peninsula to help you navigate it.
Available for hire. Babies and children welcome: booster seats. Booking advisable dinner Wed-Sat. Tables outdoors (4, terrace). **Map 13 C11.**
For branch (Tendido Cuatro) see index.

West

Bayswater

El Pirata Detapas

115 Westbourne Grove, W2 4UP (7727 5000, www.elpiratadetapas.co.uk). Bayswater tube. **Tapas served** noon-3pm, 6-11pm Mon-Fri; noon-11pm Sat; noon-10pm Sun. **Tapas** £3-£7. **Set lunch** £9.95. **Set tapas** £21 8 dishes, £25 9 dishes. **Credit** AmEx, MC, V.

First impressions of El Pirata Detapas, the sleekly modern Notting Hill sibling of Mayfair's El Pirata, were poor. The place was virtually empty on a Thursday lunchtime, the lone waiter the brusque embodiment of a *mañana* mentality. After a long wait examining the modish surroundings – dark wooden furniture, low lighting, cream walls, a stylish bar along the back wall – we ordered the set lunch (a snip at under £10, including a very drinkable glass of vino, and available every day). A leaf salad with manchego, pine nuts and beetroot purée was a glamorous mix of textures, colours and sweet-salt flavours. Piquillo pepper and idiazabal (unpasteurised sheep's cheese) croquetas were a startling pumpkin colour, but low on flavour. Simple dishes that you would expect any self-respecting tapas joint to get right were a let-down. Tortilla, though fresh, lacked both salt and olive oil; toasted bread with tomato and serrano ham proved soggy and unwieldy. It's a shame, as the menu's ambition – lots of foams, purées and bold combinations – shows an eagerness to subvert the clichés of Spanish cooking. Next time, we'll try the £21 tasting menu, which lists the likes of slow-roasted pork belly with pear and parsnip purée.
Babies and children welcome: high chairs. Booking advisable. Takeaway service.
Map 7 B6.

Shepherd's Bush

Tapas Revolution

The Balcony, Westfield London, W12 7SL (no phone, www.tapasrevolution.com). Shepherd's Bush tube/rail. **Tapas served** 11am-10pm Mon-Sat; 11am-9pm Sun. **Tapas** £3.50-£8.25. **Set meal** £11 per person (minimum 2). **Credit** AmEx, MC, V.

Boqueria Tapas. See p226.

Pizarro. See p229.

A shopping mall might be the last place you'd expect to find a sincere and decent tapas bar, but Omar Allibhoy (formerly of El Pirata Detapas) has pulled off this surprising feat. Shoppers, movie-goers and assorted Westfield visitors perch on stools at a long oval counter in the shadow of the Apple store, while young Spanish waiters in blood-red T-shirts buzz around a space barely bigger than a popcorn box. The *muy típico* menu is high on protein (chorizo, jamón, meatballs and so on) and low on greenery (asparagus, rocket). We couldn't taste the garlic in the gambas al ajillo and found the manchego disappointingly bland, but we loved the ham croquetas, the punchy pan con tomate and the slivers of acorn-fed bellota ham. Best of all was a mellow red wine from Utiel-Requena and a portion of delectable churros (Spain's crisp and svelte rendition of the doughnut) dipped in top-notch hot

chocolate. Tapas Revolution isn't in the top league, but great value and a young vibe make this the perfect spot for a recharge.
Babies and children welcome: nappy-changing facilities (shopping centre). Bookings not accepted. Disabled: lift; toilet (shopping centre). Vegetarian menu. **Map 20 C1.**

South
Battersea

Lola Rojo
78 Northcote Road, SW11 6QL (7350 2262, www.lolarojo.net). Clapham Junction rail. **Tapas served** noon-3pm, 6-10.30pm Mon-Thur; noon-10.30pm Fri-Sun. **Tapas** £3-£14. **Credit** MC, V.

Lola Rojo has long been a destination of choice for discerning Hispanophiles. In the evening, the stylish red, black and white dining room practically bursts at the seams (tables are tiny and booking is essential). In summer, outdoor stools provide ideal sip-and-nibble perches for watching the Battersea belle monde doing the Bugaboo stroll-past. We were less impressed with the cooking than on previous visits, and wonder if new sibling Rosita has nicked Lola Rojo's mojo. The all-Spanish wine list remains a great advert for modern Spanish winemaking, while dishes are still imaginative and mostly well rendered: for example, marinated cod salad with orange and red onion was a successful combo of textures and flavours. There's a good selection of porcine pleasures, from chorizo to quality acorn-fed jamón, as well as a dish of slow-cooked 'confit' of suckling pig served with a slightly too-sweet vanilla-spiked apple sauce and parsnip crisps. Chestnut mushrooms stuffed with Menorcan sobrasada sausage were given an aromatic, floral lift with the addition of honey, but the portion was small (and under-stuffed) for £5.70. Amid the deafening evening din, staff struggle to keep up with demand and, as a result, can be brusque and slow to respond.
Babies and children welcome: booster seats. Booking essential dinner. Tables outdoors (16, terrace). Takeaway service. **Map 21 C5.**

Rosita NEW
124 Northcote Road, SW11 6QU (7998 9093, www.rositasherry.net). Clapham Junction rail. **Tapas served** 6-11pm Tue-Thur; noon-11pm Fri; 10am-11pm Sat, Sun. **Tapas** £1.50-£11.40. **Set tapas** (Sun) £15 8 dishes. **Credit** MC, V.

This fashionable tapas bar, sibling to Lola Rojo along the street, has attracted affluent locals since it opened in 2012. The cooking is well executed and, as at its big sis, imaginative, albeit more in keeping with a Madrid-style tapas bar than the Catalan eats found at Lola Rojo. There are a few tapas bar staples such as patatas bravas and grilled chorizo, but this isn't a 'top 20 tapas' menu. Carnivores fare nicely with the likes of Iberian pork 'presa' (a typically Spanish cut) and beef fillet from the Spanish fighting bull lidia de toro – both cooked on the Josper grill – and, of course, plenty of jamón and charcuterie. There are less macho morsels too, such as cod croquettes with roast red pepper (from the daily specials list) and beautifully cooked, tender octopus. The all-Spanish wine list is short but carefully chosen, and the sherries – available individually or in three separate tasting flights – aren't to be missed. Tables are small and the volume can escalate, but the Spanish staff are real pros and able to handle the pressure. Seating at the central bar is kept open for walk-ins, but it's wise to book.
Available for hire. Babies and children welcome: high chairs. Booking advisable. Tables outdoors (4, patio). Takeaway service. **Map 21 C5.**

Brixton

★ Boqueria Tapas
192 Acre Lane, SW2 5UL (7733 4408, www.boqueriatapas.com). Clapham North tube or Brixton tube/rail. **Tapas served** 5-11pm Mon-Thur; 5-11.30pm Fri; 12.30-11.30pm Sat; 12.30-10.30pm Sun. **Tapas** £4.20-£8.70. **Credit** MC, V.

Setting itself apart from your average tapas joint, Boqueria offers a fresh, modern menu that merits repeat visits. The vibe is laid-back, and the L-shaped space has been thoroughly optimised, with aluminium stools along a stylishly spotlit (and well-stocked) bar leading through into the main restaurant; downstairs is an upbeat bar area with more tables (available for private hire). References to the mother country are plentiful: flamenco on the sound system; photos of Spanish market scenes on the walls (Boqueria is named after Europe's biggest food market, in Barcelona); knowledgeable Spanish waiting staff; and real-deal Iberian ingredients. A simple plate of tomatoes, garlic, parsley and olive oil – a dish that seems only to work in Spain – was packed with flavour; lightly battered calamares were cooked to perfection; suckling pig – crisp on top, meltingly tender underneath and served with a lemon sorbet – completely lived up to its high-end appearance. Boqueria combines the traditional and the contemporary to fine effect amid the hubbub of Acre Lane.

Babies and children welcome: high chairs.
Booking advisable. Disabled: toilet. Separate
room for parties, seats 50. Takeaway service.
Map 22 C2.

Clapham

Barsito NEW
57 Venn Street, SW4 0BD (7627 4000).
Clapham Common tube. **Tapas served** 4-10pm
Mon-Thur; 2-11pm Fri; 11am-11pm Sat; 2-9pm
Sun. **Tapas** £4.50-£12. **Credit** AmEx, MC, V.
This tiny neighbourhood tapas bar captures perfectly the informal, welcoming feel of its counterparts in Spain. Hams hang from the ceiling, diners eat at the bar counter, drinkers mingle, and there's a simple menu to complement the wines by the glass. The food preparation area behind the bar makes a caravan's galley look spacious; we sat and watched as the busy chef reheated dishes in the microwave in between freshly preparing others and blowtorching desserts. From a short blackboard menu of daily specials, we enjoyed pig's cheek cooked in PX sherry, and above-average ham croquetas. The Spanish cheese platter contained a great version of cabrales and two types of manchego (one plain, the other with thyme on the outside). It was served with membrillo, quality bread and, for a proper touch of authenticity, those tiny little breadsticks you normally get only in Spain. The wines are good too: modern, Spanish, and not expensive. Barsito is more of a place for a snack and drink than a leisurely dining destination, as the seating and elbow room are cramped – though it's a perfect pit stop if you're seeing a movie at Clapham Picturehouse opposite.
Available for hire. Babies and children admitted.
Booking advisable. Tables outdoors (3, pavement;
4, terrace). **Map 22 A1**.

South East
Camberwell

Angels & Gypsies
29-33 Camberwell Church Street, SE5 8TR
(7703 5984, www.angelsandgypsies.com).
Denmark Hill rail or bus 36, 185, 436.
Tapas served noon-3pm, 6-10.30pm Mon-Thur; noon-3pm, 6-11pm Fri; noon-3.30pm, 6-11pm Sat; noon-4pm, 6-10pm Sun. **Tapas** £3.50-£12. **Credit** AmEx, MC, V.
Angels & Gypsies remains an outpost of cool in gritty Camberwell, making booking essential. Dark wooden tables, pews and chairs bearing cross

Trangallan. See p229.

Bar Esteban

motifs are arranged around a tiled horseshoe bar, with stunning stained-glass windows looming over proceedings. Atmospheric low lighting adds to the ecclesiastical vibe. A display of sourdough loaves and hanging serrano hams heralds what is a reliably impressive gastronomic experience. Tapas are prepared with flair and creativity, and peppered with niche ingredients (cuttlefish, 'nduja, hand-dived scallops) and Galician influences. Albóndiga arrived in an unappealing-looking broth, which belied the dish's subtleties and strengths; inside the meatball was a soft, sweet apricot, and the broth (spicy and saffron-infused) was marvellously moreish. The flavours also shone in a simple salad of goat's cheese, sweet beetroot and peppery watercress. Gigantes – roasted butter beans with tomato and wild cep oil – didn't have the punch to stand up to the preceding dishes, however, and should have been delivered first. Sherries make a significant appearance on the predominantly Spanish wine list, where you'll also find cocktails and sangria. At lunchtime, there's now a menu devoted to street food of Mexican extraction, namely burritos (with own-made masa harina tortillas) or tacos – an excellent choice for great-value A&G cooking on the fly.

Available for hire. Babies and children welcome: high chairs. Booking advisable. Separate room for parties, seats 30. Takeaway service.
Map 23 B2.

Herne Hill

Number 22
22 Half Moon Lane, SE24 9HU (7095 9922, www.number-22.com). Herne Hill rail or bus 3, 37, 68. **Tapas served** 5-11pm daily. **Tapas** £3-£10. **Credit** MC, V.
It's not often a restaurant that has offered a reliably similar experience year on year suddenly develops the ability to surprise, but Number 22 has done just that. It's much the same in looks: a narrow corridor of a restaurant with dark wood furnishings, olive green walls and contemporary art on display. There's also a walled patio in the back with boldly painted walls, which is ideal for a leisurely glass of Alhambra. What's different is the food: it has always been good but not necessarily so good that it became memorable. This time, each dish hit the mark impeccably. Breaded baby squid was crisp on the outside yet cooked to perfection with a smooth morcilla stuffing; fried rounds of aubergine avoided

the trap of becoming greasy and were well seasoned and moreish; tender strips of just-pink duck breast were complemented by a light, sweet quince sauce; crisp pork belly on a smooth pear purée with plump, juicy raisins made for a satisfying combination of salty and sweet. The space is small and the atmosphere intimate, with low lighting and flickering candlelight in the evening, yet it comfortably houses couples and groups in a convivial atmosphere.
Available for hire. Babies and children welcome: high chairs. Booking advisable. Tables outdoors (6, patio). Vegan dishes. **Map 23 A5**.

London Bridge & Borough

José
104 Bermondsey Street, SE1 3UB (7403 4902, http://joserestaurant.co.uk). Borough tube or London Bridge tube/rail. **Tapas served** noon-10.30pm Mon-Sat; noon-5.30pm Sun. **Tapas** £3-£9. **Credit** AmEx, MC, V.
José Pizarro (formerly co-founder and head chef of Brindisa) has done a fine job here of creating a very genuine, slightly rustic local Spanish bar. The decor is plain brick, timbers and tiles; seating is mostly

on stools, with barrels to stand glasses on; and there's a no-bookings, doors-wide-open attitude, albeit while being firmly planted in trendified Bermondsey. This, his TV appearances and his books have cemented his position as the most visible Spanish chef in Britain, but what stands out here is his expert attention to sourcing and getting the basics right, ahead of culinary adventurism. You won't find any great innovations, but you will be treated to perfect, fantastically fresh renderings of the kind of classic traditional tapas that are too often let down by routine reheated preparation, such as crisp-outside, creamy-within croquetas, deep-flavoured tortilla and saltily bittersweet padrón peppers. Prawns came perfectly flash-fried in powerful but never overpowering garlic and chilli, and the renowned Ibérico ham and other meats are from Maldonado, one of Spain's most esteemed artisan producers. Wines cover a desirable fine-quality range, all available by the (well-priced) glass. The admirably unflustered staff are experts in space management, but we wonder how long a place so regularly packed can stay in such a small setting.
Babies and children admitted. Bookings not accepted. Disabled: toilet. **Map 12 Q9.**

Pizarro

194 Bermondsey Street, SE1 3TQ (7378 9455, www.pizarrorestaurant.com). Borough tube or London Bridge tube/rail. **Lunch served** noon-3pm, **dinner served** 6-11pm Mon-Fri. **Meals served** noon-11pm Sat; 10am-10pm Sun. **Main courses** £11-£18. **Credit** AmEx, MC, V.
José Pizarro's restaurant continues in the style set in his tapas bar, José, up the street, in a much more roomy and therefore less hectic space (though it also fills up on weekend evenings). Menus are more extensive than at the tapas-only José. You won't find the sort of intricate cooking that has made some Spanish chefs world-famous, but rather a selection of mostly traditional dishes prepared with care and skill, and fine ingredients; in this way, Pizarro is a master in bringing the familiar alive. A flawless gazpacho from a good-value lunch menu, for example, was delectably smooth and without a hint of excess acidity. Catalan-style cannelloni with spinach and pine nuts was ideal Mediterranean comfort food; it's hard to rave about spinach, but this was an exceptional dish, with darts of sweetness from supreme-quality raisins. An expertly slow-braised beef stew was an exemplar of multi-layered flavour. New for 2013 is the Sunday brunch menu, served until early afternoon. The space artfully combines old-Spanish touches – tiles, warm wood, exposed brick – with a stripped-down New Bermondsey look, with snug booths for relaxed eating and bar-style seating facing the street. Abundant friendly staff work hard to keep the buzzy atmosphere going. Wines are as well chosen as the produce, and very decently priced.
Babies and children welcome: high chairs; nappy-changing facilities. Booking advisable; accepted lunch Mon-Fri only. Disabled: toilet. Separate room for parties, seats 6-12. **Map 12 Q9.**

North East
Stoke Newington

Trangallán
61 Newington Green, N16 9PX (7359 4988, www.trangallan.com). Canonbury rail or

bus 21, 73, 341. **Tapas served** 7-10.30pm Tue-Sat; 12.30-3pm Sat, Sun. **Tapas** £4-£13. **Credit** MC, V.
This little former shop has a bohemian feel, with its junk-shop furniture (tables for two are especially intimate) and easy-going welcome from the mostly Galician crew who run it. It's billed as a 'gastro-cultural space', and has hosted a variety of performances in its basement, though these now play second fiddle to the food. The menu changes frequently and mostly avoids routine tapas in favour of more imaginative compositions, revealing a good deal of skill and sophistication, not to mention enthusiasm, in the kitchen. Broad beans with crisp serrano ham was a surprisingly refined take on a traditional dish; a perfectly flavoured classic tortilla was deliciously browned on the outside, still soft within. Tranga's kebab of lamb – served off the skewer – was beautifully fragrant with yoghurt and fresh herbs, while slivers of dover sole with saffron potatoes and confit of garlic, and a Galician stew of lamb cheek, potatoes and savoy cabbage both had a richness and subtlety worthy of much fancier venues. Food prices, like the overall quality, are a little above the tapas norm, and there's a short but superior wine list, especially strong on fine sherries.
Available for hire. Babies and children welcome: high chairs. Booking advisable. Separate room for parties, seats 25. Tables outdoors (7, terrace). Vegan dishes. **Map 25 A4.**

North
Camden Town & Chalk Farm

El Parador
245 Eversholt Street, NW1 1BA (7387 2789, www.elparadorlondon.com). Mornington Crescent tube. **Tapas served** noon-3pm, 6-11pm Mon-Thur; noon-3pm, 6-11.30pm Fri; 6-11.30pm Sat; 6.30-9.30pm Sun. **Tapas** £4.80-£8.60. **Credit** MC, V.
A London tapas institution with a loyal following, El Parador is a low-key restaurant that won't necessarily change the way you think about tapas, but will certainly have you coming back for more. Tables are small and close together, and the terracotta decor has a slightly faded, homely aesthetic. Service was a bit patchy when we dropped by, as the little venue has a family-restaurant feel where the staff aren't necessarily trying to impress. The tapas style enables one individual ingredient to be the star of each dish. Hence sea bream was served simply with fennel; merguez sausages were grilled with onions; and broad beans had been whipped into a purée with rosemary and confit garlic. With over 40 tapas to choose from, the menu can seem overwhelming, but the large selection does mean that vegetarians are well catered for – beyond the predictable offering of tortilla. As it happens, the tortilla is very good, with balanced seasoning, a comforting gooey middle and slight sweetness from the onions. To finish, tarta de santiago was a tad dry, but orange-infused crème caramel provided an enjoyably aromatic detour from a classic Spanish flan.
Babies and children admitted. Booking advisable Wed-Sat. Separate room for parties, seats 30. Tables outdoors (12, garden). Vegan dishes. Vegetarian menu. **Map 27 D3.**

Crouch End

Bar Esteban NEW
29 Park Road, N8 8TE (8340 3090, http://bar esteban.parkco.ch). Finsbury Park tube/rail then bus W7, or Hornsey rail. **Tapas served** 6-10.30pm Mon; noon-3pm, 6-10.30pm Tue-Sat; noon-4.30pm Sun. **Tapas** £3.50-£12. **Credit** MC, V.
Local residents and globetrotters Lisa Woolley and Stephen Lironi hope to bring 'the best of Barcelona and Brooklyn to Crouch End'. They and their bright staff certainly do well at creating a cosy, laid-back, enjoy-yourself buzz. An old test-your-strength machine is the finest of the eclectic and slightly cranky accoutrements that combine with vaguely distressed decor at this imaginative tapas bar. As chef, they've recruited Pablo Rodriguez López, formerly of Barrafina and Morito. Lately, some London tapas bars have been showing culinary inventiveness; so far, Bar Esteban isn't so much creative as focused on pure, contrasting, pick-me-up flavours based on top-quality fresh ingredients. We were won over straight away by the authentic, punchy and fresh allioli that came with the bread. The pleasure continued with subtly seasoned grilled mussels, crisp and creamy serrano ham croquettes, vibrantly delicious coca de escalivada (flatbread topped with roast peppers, onion and aubergines) and rabo de toro (slow-braised oxtail), which had a richly textured flavour that really showed the worth of painstaking, skilful preparation. The wine list has some fairly unusual, non-standard Spanish labels from a wide variety of regions. For drinkers, there's no obligation to have a fixed number of tapas dishes. A great asset to the neighbourhood.
Babies and children welcome: high chairs. Booking advisable Thur-Sat.

Tufnell Park

★ Del Parc
167 Junction Road, N19 5PZ (7281 5684, www.delparc.com). Archway or Tufnell Park tube. **Tapas served** 7-10.30pm Wed-Sat. **Tapas** approx £30 per person. **Credit** MC, V.
Located on a plain north London thoroughfare, this place is intimate, friendly and really rather unusual. There's no menu: you'll be asked about any dietary restrictions when booking; after that, your meal is in the hands of chef Steve Marrish. For once, over-used terms like seasonality, freshness and creativity genuinely matter here. Dishes are tapa-sized (with around seven in a meal for two), but the cooking takes in North African as well as Spanish influences. Openers such as high-quality olives with piquillo peppers were followed by mackerel fillets with rhubarb, mint and vanilla-infused olive oil – a combination we'd never have imagined, but which worked brilliantly. Even simple dishes are made special by the sheer quality of the ingredients. The tapas got progressively larger, up to lamb meatballs with lovely Moroccan touches of cumin and mint yoghurt, and succulent grilled prawns in a wine, garlic and chilli broth. From the dessert menu, we couldn't pass on the superb pomegranate ice-cream. There's no set price, which some may find unsettling, but the chef's menu of the day usually works out at around £30 per head. A sophisticated, mostly Iberian wine list includes a superior sherry range. One to discover.
Booking advisable, essential weekends. Tables outdoors (5, pavement). **Map 26 B2.**

PORTUGUESE

Central
Clerkenwell & Farringdon

Portal
88 St John Street, EC1M 4EH (7253 6950, www.portalrestaurant.com). Barbican tube or Farringdon tube/rail.
Bar **Open/tapas served** noon-10.15pm Mon-Fri; 6-10.15pm Sat. **Tapas** £2-£17.
Restaurant **Lunch served** noon-3pm Mon-Fri. **Dinner served** 6-10.15pm Mon-Sat. **Main courses** £16-£25.
Both **Credit** AmEx, MC, V.
Chef Jeronimo P Abreu is faithful to his Portuguese roots, yet French training sings through in Portal's refined flavours and styling. You'll find clean-cut, less oily versions of Portuguese classics and regional specialities, such as roasted bacalhau or alheira sausage pie. Ingredients are outstanding, but not all the modern interpretations hang together; venison roast beef was perfectly cooked with naturally gamey flavours offset by rhubarb and a soft red port sauce, but seafood tartlet was a slightly disconnected arrangement of crêpes, mint peas, crab and scallops. Tapas are also available at the bar: morcilla croquettes were dense and unapologetically full of rich blood sausage, while beetroot risotto balls were light, colourful and delicious. Staff are knowledgeable about the menu, and the elegance of the large conservatory-style dining room and outdoor patio lends itself to an indulgent meal. The wine list is proudly Portuguese (with a cursory huddle of French and Spanish wines hidden at the back). Owner Antonio Correia is a wine expert and member of the Royal Port Society, so there's a good selection of Portugal's famous vinho verde, or 'green' wines, and over 15 types of port to choose from – you won't go thirsty.
Available for hire. Babies and children welcome: high chairs; nappy-changing facilities. Booking advisable Thur, Fri. Disabled: toilet. Separate room for parties, seats 14. Tables outdoors (5, patio). **Map 5 O4**.

Knightsbridge

O Fado
50 Beauchamp Place, SW3 1NY (7589 3002, www.ofado.co.uk). Knightsbridge or South Kensington tube. **Lunch served** noon-3pm, **dinner served** 6.30-10.30pm daily. **Main courses** £15.99-£20.95. **Set lunch** (Mon-Fri) £14.95 2 courses incl coffee. **Credit** AmEx, MC, V.
The food at O Fado is pretty straightforward, but the place wins points for charm and ambience. Decor is traditional, with dark wood, white tablecloths and tiled paintings harking back to pastoral life. All the classic dishes are here: prawns grilled with spices or garlic; piri-piri chicken; and plenty of seafood. Guilho prawns were a good starter, albeit a little too oily. Bacalhau à Brás was done very well: large flakes of salt cod mixed with a creamy undertone of egg and potatoes. Madeira-style beef skewers were aromatic with bay leaf and a good dose of garlic, though the meat was a little chewy. 'Camel's drool' doesn't sound appealing, but is actually a very sweet mousse of condensed milk that's worth a try. Fado music traditionally includes guitar and a vocalist, but here seems to have been replaced by an endearing gentleman on a keyboard. He played some Coimbra fado, while also trickling in such hits as 'The Girl from Ipanema', which gave a slightly kitsch edge to the night. Staff are very welcoming and like to chat about the menu. O Fado might be a little outdated, but you can see why it retains its loyal Knightsbridge following.
Available for hire. Babies and children admitted until 6.30pm. Booking advisable, essential dinner weekends. Vegetarian menu. **Map 14 F9**.

West
Notting Hill

Notting Hill Kitchen NEW
92 Kensington Park Road, W11 2PN (7313 9526, www.nottinghillkitchen.co.uk). Notting Hill Gate tube. **Lunch served** noon-2.30pm Wed-Fri; 11.30am-2.30pm Sat, Sun. **Dinner served** 6-10.30pm Wed-Sun. **Main courses** £17-£23. **Tapas** £2.50-£17.50. **Credit** AmEx, MC, V.
With carefully chosen Iberian-leaning wines in its cool, calm bar, and a dining room where plain-speaking waiters serve exotic-sounding dishes, the Kitchen already attracts plenty of customers. Here, salt cod comes in a delicate starter-sized portion, perfectly rinsed (a labour-intensive process), fried with egg and straw potatoes, then rendered into a fibrous paste. Some dishes are Iberian rather than Portuguese: for instance, the intense flavour of Spanish pata negra ham paired with succulent bone marrow, served in the bone. The best foil for such food was the basket of excellent sourdoughs and vollkornbrot from Bread Bread, Bridget Hugo's award-winning bakery in Brixton. The starters were a tremendous kick-off – too high a standard to keep up for long. Executive chef Luis Baena has modernised Portuguese cooking using good ingredients, small plates and innovative combos. Squid rings were fried until crisp with a tender bite; the accompanying intense tomato sauce was also appealing, but together in a small bowl with chunks of beetroot, the combination was too busy. The tendency towards fuss reached its peak in a dessert of deep-fried greengage plums, quartered strawberries, ice-cream and sail-like biscuits – stuck into cinnamon cakes. Stick to the simpler dishes, however, and you'll be fine.
Available for hire. Babies and children welcome. Booking advisable. Separate room for parties, seats 12. **Map 19 C4**.

South
Brixton

Lisboa Grill
256A Brixton Hill, SW2 1HF (8671 8311). Brixton tube/rail or bus 45, 109, 118, 250. **Meals served** 6-10.30pm Mon-Thur; 1-11pm Fri, Sat. **Main courses** £7-£27.50. **Credit** MC, V.
Walk through an inconspicuous takeaway and enter a Lisbon taverna with frescoed walls, high ceilings and a real family vibe. Portuguese pop songs play on the TV, and a fake fireplace even flickers on the wall as an endearingly domestic touch. Although a little pricey, king prawns 'Lisboa style' were impressive: they were butterflied open, which meant the sweetly spiced tomato sauce permeated the flesh and got under the shell, so each crustacean joyfully demanded sticky fingers and some inelegant sucking. Lisboa Grill is famous for its meats, serving them with thin, Portuguese-style

Portal

Pastelarias

Lisboa Pâtisserie

Ladbroke Grove used to be the only place in London where you could get your hands on a pastel de nata (custard tart), probably one of Portugal's most widely adopted culinary exports. Portuguese pastelaria are still the best places to get one, though quite a few fashionable cafés now offer them, or you could track down **Nata 28** (www.nata28.co.uk) – London's first mobile pastelaria, which sells pastéis de nata from the back of a van in Camden Market. **Bom Pecado** and **Casa Madeira** also have cafés offering pastéis de nata.

Café Oporto
62A Golborne Road, W10 5PS (8968 8839). Ladbroke Grove or Westbourne Park tube or bus 23, 52. **Open** *7.30am-7pm Mon-Sat; 8am-5pm Sun.* **Snacks** *£1-£3.50.* **No credit cards.**
The world is put to rights at Oporto, where the sound of animated conversations in Portuguese rings round the pavement tables, and staff are genuinely welcoming and friendly. Lisboa (across the road) may be more famous, but we prefer Oporto's crisp layers of pastry with a delicious custard filling – perfectly set and not too sweet. Chicken and cheese rissoles are a deep-fried treat, also not to be missed.
Babies and children admitted. Tables outdoors (5, pavement). Takeaway service. **Map 19 B1**.

Funchal Bakery
141-143 Stockwell Road, SW9 9TN (7733 3134). Stockwell tube. **Open** *7am-7pm daily.* **Snacks** *£1.80-£5.* **Credit** *(over £12) MC, V.*
More than just a bakery, Funchal is a sandwich bar, deli and informal meeting place for the area's Portuguese community. Get a warm chicken coxinha (like an oversized croquette) to take away, or have a seat and soak up the hectic

family atmosphere; you can also pick up some Portuguese wine or preserved fish to cook at home. Our custard tart was good, though the base could have been crisper.
Available for hire. Babies and children admitted. Separate room for parties, seats 25. Takeaway service. **Map 22 D1**.

Lisboa Pâtisserie
57 Golborne Road, W10 5NR (8968 5242). Ladbroke Grove tube or bus 23, 52. **Open** *7am-7.30pm Mon-Sat, 7am-7pm Sun.* **Snacks** *75p-£2.65.* **Credit** *MC, V.*

Café Oporto

Don't arrive too late at the weekend if you want one of Lisboa's famous pastéis de nata – they often sell out by 2pm. It's a humble setting, with plenty of banter from staff and slightly fancier pâtisserie than some other Portuguese cake shops. Bica (Portuguese espresso) was good and strong, and staff do a nice galão (latte) too.
Babies and children admitted. Tables outdoors (4, pavement). Takeaway service. **Map 19 B1**.
For branches see index.

SPANISH & PORTUGUESE

chips, or rice that has a black pepper kick. Mild isn't really an option: piri-piri chicken comes medium, hot or very hot (although a herby sauce is a good spice cop-out). Drink Sabres beer to take the edge off, or try a decanter of their heavier Alentejo red with steak. Heinz ketchup and mayo on the table are a reminder that, in addition to the takeaway, there's a café to the side. The latter was closed at the time of our visit, but usually offers most of the dishes from the restaurant, as well as pastries, cakes and generous slices of custard flan.

Available for hire. Babies and children welcome: high chairs. Booking advisable weekends. Disabled: toilet. Tables outdoors (5, garden). Takeaway service. **Map 22 D3.**

Stockwell

Mar Azul

124 Clapham Road, SW9 0LA (7820 0464, www.marazulrestaurant.co.uk). Oval or Stockwell tube. **Dinner served** 6-10.30pm Mon-Fri. **Meals served** noon-11pm Sat; noon-10pm Sun. **Main courses** £9.50-£18. **Credit** MC, V.

Aqua blue lights and a slightly clichéd marine aesthetic are the most noticeable features on entering this taverna-style restaurant. It's fancier and more expensive than you might expect for such a location – on busy Clapham Road halfway between Stockwell and Oval tubes – and although the white tablecloths and live music give a distinguished edge, our experience was somewhat marred by inconsistent and slow service. To start, pan-fried mushrooms with chorizo and garlic were a bit lacklustre, but the main courses compensated. Garlic-roasted cod had a crisp, slightly charred skin that was delicious against the moist salted cod. Black scabbard à madeirense was a light fillet of mild-flavoured fish, served in the traditional Madeiran style with the tropical tastes of pan-fried banana and a passionfruit sauce. These paired particularly well with Vinho Verde (or 'green' wine) from the northern Minho region, which had a slight fizziness to it like a low-key sparkling wine.

Available for hire. Babies and children welcome: high chairs. Booking advisable Fri, Sat. Disabled: toilet. Tables outdoors (6, pavement).

Vauxhall

Casa Madeira

46A-46C Albert Embankment, SE11 5AW (7820 1117, www.madeiralondon.co.uk). Vauxhall tube/rail. **Meals served** *Coffee shop* 6am-9pm daily. *Restaurant* noon-11pm Mon-Fri, Sun; noon-1am Sat. **Main courses** £6.95-£15.95. **Tapas** £3-£5.95. **Credit** MC, V.

Casa Madeira is a little enclave of Portuguese culture, with a vibrant café, bar and grill, well-stocked deli and family restaurant all sitting under the railway arches of Vauxhall. What you see is what you get here: home-style food with old-school service and loyalty to Portuguese food traditions. Dishes were a bit hit and miss: potatoes were undercooked, and the pork was a little tough in the Alentejo pork and clam stew; but a plate of grilled sardines was good honest seafood at its best. We had some food envy when we saw flaming chorizo and an impressive steaming skewer of Madeira-style beef going to the next table. The rumble of trains is just audible beneath the pop music playing from the TV, and as we finished lunch, large tables were being set up for the live music and late-night party that ensues every Saturday. The different elements of the operation are all interconnected, so diners migrate to the café next door for a bica (espresso) and dessert. Traditional crème caramel was dense and enormous, and a pastel de nata had a good crisp base and rich set custard.

Babies and children admitted. Booking advisable weekends. Entertainment: musicans 7pm Fri, Sat. Tables outdoors (40, pavement). Takeaway service. **Map 16 L11.**

For branches (Bar Madeira, Café 89, Madeira Café, Pico Bar & Grill) see index.

Notting Hill Kitchen. See p230.

East

Shoreditch

Eyre Brothers

70 Leonard Street, EC2A 4QX (7613 5346, www.eyrebrothers.co.uk). Old Street tube/rail.
Lunch served noon-2.45pm Mon-Fri. **Dinner served** 6.30-10.45pm Mon-Fri; 7-11pm Sat. **Main courses** £15-£27.50. **Credit** AmEx, MC, V.

After more than a decade in existence, Eyre Brothers is a trusted local fixture, equally attractive to couples, Shoreditch's young movers 'n' shakers and suited City persons deep in lunchtime conversation. The low-ceilinged, dark-wood and leather design helps – it's contemporary-classic without flimsy trendiness, and adroitly provides both sheltered spaces and large tables suitable for groups. For further intimacy, there are some comfortable spots near the long bar, where tapas are offered. Service is top-notch, alert and individual. The menus, which now seem more solidly Iberian than globe-trotting, focus on punchy flavours and vigorous seasonings. Our meal had highs, but also some lows: a seafood salad featured squid, octopus, mussels and prawns of the quality that needs (and got) little preparation beyond a lovely, smooth dressing; the speciality of Ibérico pork fillet, marinated in paprika, thyme and garlic, then grilled, was magnificently herby and tender (meats, in general, are outstanding); and crema catalana dessert was moreishly perfect. A tortilla, though, was dry, as was empadão de bacalhau – a Portuguese salt-cod cottage pie – which looked as if it had been made some time earlier and rather clumsily warmed up. Just a blip, we hope. The wine list is stacked with high-quality Spanish and (more unusual) Portuguese labels, but is pricey.
Babies and children admitted. Booking advisable Wed-Sat. Disabled: toilet. **Map 6 Q4**.

North

Tottenham

Bom Pecado

91 West Green Road, N15 5DA (8802 0438, www.bompecado.co.uk). Seven Sisters tube/rail.
Meals served 7am-8pm daily. **Main courses** £6.50-£9.50. **No credit cards**.

This unassuming little place feels a genuine part of north London's Portuguese community. Powder-blue walls and a simple café aesthetic give a hint of the Med, while the sunny back courtyard holds families tucking in as kids run around or slurp Ucal chocolate drink. Juan, the owner, is busy but friendly, and regular customers greet one another as they wander in and out. We snacked on salt cod fish cakes with a smooth potato centre, and the house speciality of empada chicken pie, which could have had a punchier filling. If you're hungry, go for chicken gizzard stew (moela) or picadinho pork stew with chips. It's worth checking what other people are eating, as not everything that comes out of the kitchen is on the menu; we spotted some tasty-looking grilled prawns with aïoli. Bom Pecado means 'good sin', and there are plenty of freshly baked cakes; pastel de nata (slightly bigger than standard) had a thick custard filling and a crisp, flaky edge, and was served with a cute cinnamon shaker.
Babies and children welcome: high chairs. Tables outdoors (5, garden). Takeaway service.
For branch see index.

Eyre Brothers

Steak & Chicken

Fashion, food politics and economics all collide in this new chapter in our guide. The simple cooking and presentation of both steak and chicken have attracted massive interest over the past few years, from young entrepreneurs recognising a gap in the market, as well as from major operators. So it seems good sense to combine both fowl-focused and beef-centred establishments into one meaty serving here. In no other sector are the dynamics of London's restaurant scene currently so evident. The financial-crisis fashion for street food and simple restaurants that specialise in pared-down menus (sometimes even single dishes) has coincided with the longer-term trend of businesses wanting to create formulas that are easy to replicate. The established multinational brands had become ossified, and in some cases tarnished by publicity about unhealthy menus and questionable sourcing policies – so a new niche was spotted. Gourmet burger joints were the first to join the party (and that sector is still going strong), but now steak specialists and fried or roasted chicken joints are appearing at a dramatic rate.

But given all the current competition, there's an increasing impetus for restaurants to cut costs – and occasionally this is done by accepting lower welfare standards for the livestock they buy. Following the BSE crisis, standards for the production of British beef are generally very good. High levels of traceability are now possible, so any restaurant worth its salt should be able to give details of the provenance of its beef: the breed, the region and, ideally, even the farm, so it's always worth asking. Beware of get-out phrases such as 'British where possible' or such wooliness as 'from farmers who care about their animals'. **Hawksmoor** has a maximum three-star rating from the Sustainable Restaurant Association, in part for sourcing high-welfare British meat; **Butcher & Grill** names the farm where it buys its beef and lamb (Highfields Farm, East Sussex); and our current favourite burger bar, newcomer **Patty & Bun**, gets all its beef from a London butcher specialising in organic and free-range meat. Likewise, **Honest Burger** sources its beef from the well-reputed Ginger Pig butcher.

Despite the endeavours of Jamie Oliver and others, standards in the poultry industry often still leave much to be desired. Some restaurants start well, with free-range chickens, but then switch to lesser birds. Organic poultry has the highest welfare standards, but we've not found a restaurant in this section using exclusively organic birds. However, new arrival **Le Coq** comes close: sourcing its chickens from an organic and free-range supplier, and even naming the farm and location, Sutton Hoo in Suffolk.

STEAK

Central
City

Goodman City
11 Old Jewry, EC2R 8DU (7600 8220, www.goodmanrestaurants.com). Bank tube/DLR.
Meals served noon-10.30pm Mon-Fri. **Main courses** £15-£45. **Credit** AmEx, MC, V.

Goodman's three branches are perfectly located to pull in its target audience: people who will pay top dollar for top beef. At the City branch, the room seems to be aiming for a New York-style steakhouse look: dark wooden walls with large-scale black and white photographs. The food shows frustrating inconsistency. Three starters were spot-on, especially sweet herring in 'traditional Russian presentation' (the owners are Russian). Another starter, lobster and corn chowder, was barely lukewarm, gluey in texture and seriously deficient in flavour. There are only three sensible options for mains: steak, steak or steak. The cuts of the day are written on blackboards, and the beef – cooked exactly as ordered – was just heavenly. A lamentable fault is the absence of any garnish. You have to order side dishes, and this isn't always an occasion for joy. Three were dreadful: a limp, clumsily dressed salad; chewy creamed spinach with (unnecessary) cheese; and oily fried white onions. Avoid the hamburger. The wine list contains little under £30, though a £26 Catalan red was excellent. Service was largely friendly and competent. Our biggest complaint is the bass-heavy music, so loud we had to shout to make ourselves heard. Combine that with the patches of poor cooking and you have a restaurant where even extraordinary steak can't quite justify the very high prices.

Babies and children welcome: high chairs; nappy-changing facilities. Booking advisable. Disabled: toilet. Separate room for parties, seats 10. **Map 11 P6**.

For branches see index.

★ Hawksmoor Guildhall `HOT 50`

10-12 Basinghall Street, EC2V 5BQ (7397 8120, www.thehawksmoor.co.uk). St Paul's tube, Bank tube/DLR or Moorgate tube/rail. **Breakfast served** 7-10am, **lunch served** noon-3pm, **dinner served** 5-10.30pm Mon-Fri. **Main courses** £20-£65. **Set dinner** (5-5.30pm, 10-10.30pm) £23 2 courses, £26 3 courses. **Credit** AmEx, MC, V.

Hawksmoor's easy-going charm appeals to the more relaxed type of City diner (shirtsleeves, no ties), happy to be served by an efficient but casually dressed young crew. The short main menu centres on steak (ribeye, T-bone, porterhouse, fillet, sirloin and more), at serious prices, plus the likes of grilled chicken, lobster with garlic butter, monkfish grilled over charcoal, and a meat-free choice for the odd misplaced vegetarian. If you're not on expenses, pay heed to the 'express menu', where the delectably charred ribeye comes in a 250g size (more than enough for most people's appetites, especially when paired with the triple-cooked chips). Roughly textured potted smoked mackerel (served in a little pot, with dill-heavy cucumber alongside) made a nice contrast as a starter – although an equally good kick-off is one of Hawksmoor's renowned cocktails. Puddings range from ice-creams (a scoop of peach sorbet was tip-top) to calorific delights such as gooey peanut butter shortbread, served with salted caramel ice-cream. The wine list allows room for City excesses, but also has a decent choice by the glass. The basement premises at this branch are better suited to the winter months, when the sea of brown – leather, extensive wood panelling – is comforting rather than stifling.

Babies and children welcome: high chairs; nappy-changing facilities. Booking advisable. Disabled: toilet. Separate rooms for parties, seating 10-24. **Map 11 P6**.

For branches see index.

High Timber

8 High Timber Street, EC4V 3PA (7248 1777, www.hightimber.com). Mansion House tube. **Lunch served** noon-3pm, **dinner served** 6.30-10pm Mon-Fri. **Main courses** £13.25-£29. **Set lunch** £16.50 2 courses, £20 3 courses. **Credit** AmEx, DC, MC, V.

High Timber sits a hop, skip and jump from the Millennium Bridge, with views across to the Globe Theatre and Tate Modern. It's neutral and modern in looks, with a low ceiling, plate-glass windows and plain wooden furniture – though the anonymity is enlivened by some striking art (for sale) on the walls. The restaurant's South African ownership is evident in the wine list and occasional ingredient, but otherwise the menu is a straightforward list of mainly meaty fare that will appeal to a clientele dominated (at lunch, at least) by City males. Sirloin and ribeye steaks – made with top-notch, 28-day-matured Cumbrian beef – are the focus; assorted sauces range from traditional béarnaise to biltong butter. Alternatives include roast veal, boar sausage or burger and chips, but the kitchen also has a deft touch with fish; fillet of bream with an earthy pearl barley and herb pesto was perfectly cooked. This came from the set lunch: good value, though, rather oddly, the sole 'dessert' choice was cheese (a decent

comté). Twice-cooked chips were excellent too – yet there weren't enough of them. Staff did their job, but without much charm.

Available for hire. Babies and children admitted. Booking advisable. Disabled: toilet. Separate rooms for parties, seating 10 and 18. Tables outdoors (4, riverside). **Map 11 O7**.

Marylebone

Le Relais de Venise L'Entrecôte

120 Marylebone Lane, W1U 2QG (7486 0878, www.relaisdevenise.com). Baker Street or Bond Street tube. **Lunch served** noon-2.30pm Mon-Thur; noon-2.45pm Fri; 12.30-3.30pm Sat, Sun. **Dinner served** 6-10.45pm Mon-Thur; 6-11pm Fri; 6.30-11pm Sat; 6.30-10.30pm Sun. **Set meal** £23 2 courses. **Credit** AmEx, MC, V.

This French mini chain of no-booking, no-choice steakhouses knows how to pack 'em in. When we arrived at the Marylebone branch at 6.40pm, there were two couples queuing in front of us. There's a perception that the combo of salad starter and steak-frites main is a bargain. We wouldn't agree, but that's immaterial because we're not keen to return. Tables are packed so close together that we felt self-conscious about conversing, and our neighbours would have had to move their table if we'd wished to visit the loo. Our food was variable. The vinaigrette was good, but it dressed too high a proportion of iceberg lettuce. The steak was tasty and accurately cooked, yet chewy. It's served in two rounds, and that brought one of the few high points in our meal: a second helping of the divine frites. Also in the realms of the divine: the desserts, especially a mind-blowing praline ice-cream. The low point of the evening was the service, which started out brisk and efficient but swiftly descended

Whyte & Brown. See p237.

into a combination of neglect and rudeness. The house wine is cheap. By the time we left, the queue looked like being a one-hour wait. Some people clearly love this place – but not us.

Babies and children welcome: high chairs; nappy-changing facilities. Bookings not accepted. Disabled: toilet. **Map 9 G5.** *For branches see index.*

Mayfair

Maze Grill

10-13 Grosvenor Square, W1K 6JP (7495 2211, www.gordonramsay.com/mazegrill). Bond Street tube. **Breakfast served** 6.45am-10.30am, **meals served** noon-11pm daily. **Main courses** £13.50-£28. **Set lunch** (noon-4pm) £21 2 courses, £24 3 courses. **Credit** AmEx, MC, V.

This steak-centred outlet of the Gordon Ramsay empire sells some fine food. A starter of tender salt and sichuan-pepper squid: very good. Aberdeen Angus ribeye steak: excellent. Slow-cooked pork belly with roast sweet potatoes and chilli-blazing pickled cabbage: outstanding. Great ingredients, beautifully cooked. But there were numerous negatives, too, on our recent visit. One is the expense if you eat steak: 10oz ribeye costs £32 and comes with not a single extra – it sat in solitary splendour on its wooden plank. Another is the wine list, which offers almost nothing under £30 a bottle. Another is the service, which was almost heroically inattentive at times. We waited five minutes just to be offered a glass of water or a menu, even though waiting staff passed by several times. The large, sparely decorated room with hardwood seating is attractive enough, but it doesn't quite manage to feel comfortable or cosy – especially with thumping background music. Talk of arbitrage at the neighbouring table made us feel that this is a place for Mayfair Maserati-drivers. For the rest of us, however good some of the food may be, Maze Grill is just not special enough to merit the expense.

Babies and children welcome: children's menu; high chairs; nappy-changing facilities. Booking advisable. Disabled: toilet. Separate room for parties, seats 12. **Map 9 G6.**

West

Olympia

Popeseye Steak House

108 Blythe Road, W14 0HB (7610 4578, www.popeseye.com). Kensington (Olympia) tube/rail. **Dinner served** 7-10.30pm Mon-Sat. **Main courses** £9.95-£55.95. **No credit cards.**

There's something impressively bloody-minded about Popeseye. Not only does it refuse to serve anything but steak and chips, but it does so in a determinedly unshowy dining room where the decor – including scarlet candles, paper tablecloths and artworks depicting massed ranks of cows – feels like a throwback to the 1970s. The restaurant seems to pride itself on being 'no frills', and extends this policy to payment: cards are not accepted. The only non-beef item is a fairly half-hearted salad of mixed leaves and tomato chunks. Everything, then, rides on the quality of the grass-fed, 28-day-hung Aberdeen Angus steaks. Three cuts (sirloin, fillet and 'Popeseye', aka rump) are offered in sizes ranging from 6oz to 30oz, and are accompanied by a great platter of condiments including four types of mustard. And they're of a high quality – in fact, the fillet is very nice – but not of such a sublime standard, in the face of strong competition, to elevate this place above the level of quirky neighbourhood bistro. At one time, Popeseye might have been a destination restaurant (and old reviews on its website bear witness to this), but it no longer merits a special trip.

Available for hire. Babies and children admitted. Booking advisable Thur-Sat. **Map 20 C3.** *For branch see index.*

South

Battersea

Butcher & Grill

39-41 Parkgate Road, SW11 4NP (7924 3999, www.thebutcherandgrill.com). Clapham Junction rail or bus 19, 49, 170, 319, 345. **Breakfast served** 8.30am-noon daily. **Lunch served** noon-3.30pm Mon-Sat; noon-4pm Sun. **Dinner served** 5.30-11pm Mon-Sat. **Main courses** £8.50-£26. **Set lunch** £12.95 2 courses, £14.95 3 courses. **Credit** AmEx, MC, V.

No prize for guessing what the unique selling point of this restaurant is – it's all in the name. The street-level section of the room is given over to an upmarket butcher shop-cum-deli, and the raised mezzanine dining area is where you head to enjoy the meat-counter cuts. This is the kind of appealing formula that demands rolling out into a fully fledged chain. As it is, Butcher & Grill is down to just this branch, the Wimbledon outpost having

Wishbone

tangy and sweet); chilli (South American hot sauce); and caesar (rich, with a hint of anchovy). The main event is perfectly good – but it is, after all, just roast chicken. Sides add interest – double-cooked chips are spot-on (fatter than fries but slimmer than a chip-shop chip); the coleslaw and salads are OK. Resist the crispy chicken bites (marinated in buttermilk, coated in seasoned gram flour and lightly fried) if you can. There are also a couple of chicken-in-a-bun options and a choice of three puddings, plus a super-short wine list. Cheery staff whizz around the small, simply decorated room, but struggle to keep up with the after-work hordes. Further branches are planned, but whether there's enough of interest here to give Nando's a run for its money remains to be seen.

Available for hire. Babies and children admitted. Bookings not accepted. Disabled: toilet. Takeaway service. **Map 17 B5**.

Whyte & Brown NEW

Kingly Court, W1B 5PW (3747 9820, http://whyteandbrown.com). Oxford Circus or Piccadilly Circus tube. **Breakfast served** 8-11.45am Mon-Fri; 10-11.45am Sat, Sun. **Meals served** noon-11pm Mon-Sat; noon-8pm Sun. **Main courses** £9.25-£13.95. **Credit** AmEx, MC, V.

Endure the puns here (the menu asks if you're 'feeling peckish'; the jobs board invites you to 'join the brood'), because most of the food at Whyte & Brown is pretty clucking good. There's no rotisserie and nothing masquerading as sexy KFC. Instead, the menu contains a multinational roll-call of grown-up dishes – the kind you'd find at a (chicken-themed) dinner party. We enjoyed our 'Bangkok scotch egg', its breadcrumbed shell giving way to succulent chilli- and lemongrass-spiked thigh meat wrapped around a soft-boiled, sunny-centred egg; and a Gallic-leaning pie with white chicken meat, juicy prawns and tendrils of samphire smothered in a light béarnaise sauce. For simpler tastes, there's chicken roasted under a brick (pollo al mattone: a traditional Tuscan technique designed to produce crisp skin and moist flesh), with an intensely savoury gravy. Sadly, another Italian-inspired dish, a 'bruschetta' of soft-boiled egg and ricotta, was gout-inducingly rich, the crushed peas and barely-there mint struggling to cut through the cholesterol. While it may not appeal to food snobs, W&B has more to offer than posh comfort nosh: a superb courtyard location; fairly priced cocktails (from less than £7), and handsome, if contrived interiors. Come with an open mind, and you might just have a cracking time.

Available for hire. Babies and children welcome: high chairs; nappy-changing facilities. Booking advisable Wed, Thur. Disabled: toilet. Tables outdoors (10, terrace). **Map 17 A4**.

South

Brixton

★ Wishbone

12 Market Row, Brixton Market, SW9 8LD (7274 0939, www.wishbonebrixton.co.uk). Brixton tube/rail. **Meals served** noon-10pm Tue-Sat; noon-9.30pm Sun. **Main courses** £5-£7. **Set menu** (noon-4pm Mon-Fri) £7 2 courses (incl soft drink). **Credit** AmEx, MC, V.
Sitting among the independent shops, stalls and eateries in covered Market Row, Wishbone is a

closed in 2012. A no-nonsense menu features burgers, ribs, chops and steak (though no offal), with beef and lamb sourced from Highfields Farm in East Sussex. Our steak was nicely medium rare, full flavoured and complemented by its rich red wine sauce (it can also be customised with salsa, roquefort butter, or béarnaise or green peppercorn sauces). Similarly, barbecue baby pork back ribs were melt-in-the-mouth pleasurable, doused with a dressing that was bright and sweet without overpowering the tender meat. Pay heed to the name, however, and stick with the meat options. A tuna steak atop a niçoise salad was disappointing: dull and expensive. Service, too, was poor on our visit, with staff inattentive and forgetful, despite an almost empty dining room.

Available for hire. Babies and children welcome: children's menu; high chairs; nappy-changing facilities. Booking advisable weekends. Disabled: toilet. Tables outdoors (2, pavement; 6, terrace). Takeaway service. **Map 21 C1**.

CHICKEN

Central
Soho

★ Clockjack Oven NEW

14 Denman Street, W1D 7HJ (7287 5111, www.clockjackoven.com). Piccadilly Circus tube. **Open** noon-11pm Mon-Sat. **Main courses** £6.95-£8.95. **No credit cards**.
The clock-jack spit-roasting method sees plump chickens (free-range birds sourced from Brittany) revolving around an open flame, visible behind the blond wood counter here. Available in three pieces, four pieces or whole (enough for two to three people), the chicken is served with one of four sauces: ranch (creamy and garlicky); barbecue (thin,

Square Meal
★★★★

tripadvisor
CERTIFICATE OF EXCELLENCE
2012 & 2013

Time Out
London
★★★★★

view
London side UK
★★★★★

London
Evening
Standard
★★★★★

Mmm...
la la !

HACHÉ

'posh' fried chicken restaurant in an area almost synonymous with the fast-food chicken shops that everyone regrets the morning after the night before. For a protein fix that was once a happy, free-range bird (and comes without grease), this is your place. Street art covers the walls, soul music and hip hop are on the playlist, boxes of hot sauce are stacked high, and customers perch at bright-yellow breakfast bars – the look is of an urban, stripped-back eating space. Lunch deals (noon to 4pm Monday to Friday) include the Korean sandwich with a side of fries (served in a paper bag) and a soft drink. Crispy, breaded chicken comes in a roll garnished with crushed peanuts, spring onion, chinese cabbage, pickled daikon and chilli mayo. It's a texture sensation: the tender chicken is coated in a peppery, crunchy shell, while the peanuts go well with the sharper, softer cabbage and onion mix. Portions are large, but an additional order of slaw is a good idea – it's light, fresh and crunchy, making a nice contrast with the chicken. An extensive bar contains a range of spirits, but you'll probably want to go elsewhere for an evening out.
Babies and children welcome: high chairs; nappy-changing facilities (market). Bookings not accepted Mon-Wed, Sun. Tables outdoors (4, market). Takeaway service. **Map 22 E2**.

East
Shoreditch

Tramshed
32 Rivington Street, EC2A 3LX (7749 0478, www.chickenandsteak.co.uk). Old Street tube/rail or Shoreditch High Street rail. **Meals served** noon-10pm Mon, Tue; noon-11pm Wed-Sat; noon-9pm Sun. **Main courses** £13.50-£20. **Credit** AmEx, MC, V.
After a promising start, Mark Hix's chicken and steak restaurant has lost some allure. The room remains a winning combination of fun, glamour and heritage: a Damien Hirst cow and chicken in formaldehyde suspended over the main dining room makes a striking first impression, set against the backdrop of a building that once generated the power for east London's trams. The child's meal deal is generous, and the house wines are very drinkable. But the overly keen table-turning (we were moved on long before our slot was supposedly up) and variable food soon strip away any stardust. The short menu has steak (rib, sirloin or salad) or chicken as mains. Steak salad passed muster, though we're unconvinced by the topping of battered onion rings. Whole roast chicken (barn-reared these days, rather than the free-range birds initially used) arrives at the table up-ended on a spike, surrounded by fries; at £25 it easily serves two and can stretch to three, helped by seasonal sides such as (delicious) wild garlic mushrooms. Crisp, well-seasoned skin gave way to meat that lacked flavour and was rather dry. Starters (just-so yorkshire pudding with whipped chicken livers) and desserts (super-sweet salted caramel fondue with marshmallows and doughnuts, £12.50 to share) had more wow factor. Staff are friendly yet stretched, leaving diners feeling more than a little processed.
Available for hire. Babies and children welcome: children's menu; high chairs; nappy-changing facilities. Booking advisable. Disabled: toilet. Separate room for parties, seats 36. Takeaway service. **Map 6 R4**.

North
Highbury

★ Le Coq NEW
292 St Paul's Road, N1 2LH (7359 5055, www.le-coq.co.uk). Highbury & Islington tube/rail. **Lunch served** noon-3.30pm, **dinner served** 6-10.30pm Tue-Sat. **Meals served** noon-7pm Sun. **Set meal** (Tue-Sat) £16 2 courses, £20 3 courses; (Sun) £21 2 courses, £25 3 courses. **Credit** AmEx, MC, V.
Le Coq's name tells you a half-truth about this restaurant: chicken, yes; French, no. There's no choice for main course – it's rotisserie chicken, using free-range and organic birds from Sutton Hoo in Suffolk. These roasts arrive with a seasonal vegetable accompaniment: on our visit, a ratatouille-like caponata. The quality of the meat is apparent – this is poultry that needs no peri-peri marinade to imbue it with flavour. As part of the set meal deals, diners do have a choice of two starters and two desserts. A platter of Italian-style charcuterie included coppa (dry-cured pork) and finocchiona (fennel-seed) salami, made by Picco in Highbury. Desserts were a highlight. Ice-creams might include ricotta and candied peel, unusually flavoured with fig leaves and saffron-infused Strega liqueur. This had an appealing and dense clotted-cream texture, with orange and herbal notes. Chocolate tart garnished with crème fraîche and fragments of crushed honeycomb had crisp pastry and a perfect balance of bitter-sweetness. The menu changes every week, and Sundays will see other beasts twirling on the spit (pig or octopus, perhaps). But if you're fond of fowl, Le Coq – brainchild of sisters Ana and Sanja Morris – is where to head.
Babies and children welcome: high chairs. Bookings not accepted. Separate room for parties, seats 16. Takeaway service.

Chicken Shop. See p242.

Burgers

★ Advisory NEW

*161 Mare Street, E8 3RH (8533 2747).
Hackney Central or London Fields rail.*
Breakfast served 9am-1pm, **meals served**
noon-11pm daily. **Main courses** £5-£9.
Credit MC, V.

Just when you thought London's burger-bar
scene was surely already overdone, along
comes another, located at the unlovely but
up-and-coming Mare Street/Well Street
junction. The Advisory, named after the
Asian Women's Advisory Centre previously
on the site, opened with a compelling
launch offer of a burger and beer for a
fiver. After a few weeks of settling in, prices
then rose, but not by much: the well-above-
average burgers cost £5, and tasty sides of
chilli greens or roasted carrots with thyme
are £3. On a Tuesday evening, the place
was rammed and the burger brioche buns
had run out. During the next hour, the
replacement hot dog brioche buns also ran
out, so staff had to move on to the next
day's brunch muffins. 'What are you gonna
do when you run out of those?' we asked
our friendly, busy and efficient waiter.
'Close down,' he replied, deadpan. With a
tempting but simple evening menu of just
three burgers (beef, bacon and vegetarian),
a Gloucester Old Spot hot dog, a hangar
steak and the unusual and excellent
Québécois dish poutine (melt-in-the-mouth
lamb gravy and goat's curd, poured over
chips), plus great-value drinks – gin and
tonic for £2.80, large house wine £3.50,
Tsing Tao beer £3 – that's unlikely to
happen soon.

*Available for hire. Babies and children
admitted. Disabled: toilet. Separate room
for parties, seats 20. Tables outdoors
(2, pavement). Takeaway service.*

★ Brgr.co

*187 Wardour Street, W1F 8ZB (7920
6480, www.brgr.co). Oxford Circus or
Tottenham Court Road tube.* **Meals served**
noon-11pm Mon-Wed; noon-1am Thur-Sat;
noon-10.30pm Sun. **Main courses** £4.95-
£13.25. **Credit** MC, V.

Poised at the top of Wardour Street,
Brgr.co's first branch outside Lebanon
opened to a mixed reception. In a city in
the throes of street-food hysteria, it doesn't
curry any favours by plastering a theory of
'BRGRology' all over the placemats. Small
burgers, made from the cheapest cuts,
start at a very reasonable £4.75. Ordering
them is more difficult, with the staff
schooled in the art of upselling expensive
specials and gourmet alternatives. The
burgers arrived Ikea-style, laid out for self-
assembly with lettuce, tomatoes and pickle
on the side. The meat was cooked to order,
but the glazed brioche bun disintegrated
quickly and the bacon was flaccid and
underdone. A buttermilk onion stack
had an excellent, almost Hula Hoop-like
crunchiness, while old-fashioned mac 'n'
cheese was let down by a runny sauce and

perfunctory drizzle of truffle oil. Crowded
with bare tables and spindle-backed chairs,
the restaurant itself is reasonably stylish if
unoriginal. You could certainly find a worse
burger in London, but compared to Soho's
other joints, this place lacks a bit of soul.
*Babies and children welcome: high
chairs. Bookings not accepted after
5pm. Disabled: toilet. Takeaway service;
delivery service (over £10 within 2-mile
radius).* **Map 17 B3.**

★ Byron

*6 Store Street, WC1E 7DQ (7580 6000,
www.byronhamburgers.com). Goodge
Street or Tottenham Court Road tube.*
Meals served noon-11pm Mon-Sat; noon-
10pm Sun. **Main courses** £6.75-£10.75.
Credit AmEx, MC, V.

The Bloomsbury branch of Byron is a light,
clean space, boldly decorated in black,
white and candy-yellow, with a pleasant
terrace overlooking Store Street. Each
restaurant may have its own decorative
idiosyncrasies, but the menu is the same
throughout the chain (29-strong in London
at time of writing, and still growing). The
burgers, while not the stuff of dreams, are
a reliable bunch – the chilli version comes
with green chilli, American cheese, iceberg
lettuce and chipotle mayonnaise, in a
decent bun, and isn't so big that you can't
manage sides of chips and coleslaw too.
(Note that it doesn't pack much chilli heat
either.) Avoid the other main-course option,
big salads; a 'classic cobb' (chicken, crispy
bacon, avocado, blue cheese, tomato, free-
range egg, iceberg and house dressing)
was a neatly regimented plate of so-what
ingredients that looked, and tasted, like
a supermarket lunch option (and cost
£10.75). A well-rounded drinks list includes
craft beers, plenty of wines by the glass,
milkshakes and juices. New for 2013 is
Byron lager, made for the chain by Camden
Town Brewery. Attentive staff add to the
appeal of the chain.
*Babies and children welcome: children's
menu; high chairs; nappy-changing
facilities. Bookings not accepted. Tables
outdoors (12, patio). Takeaway service.*
Map 17 C1.
For branches see index.

★ Dirty Burger

*79 Highgate Road, NW5 1TL (3310 2010,
www.eatdirtyburger.com). Kentish Town
tube/rail.* **Meals served** 7am-midnight
Mon-Thur; 7am-1am Fri; 9am-1am Sat;
9am-11pm Sun. **Main courses** £4-£5.50.
No credit cards.

After spending a while moving through
various London locations, this Soho House
operation eventually settled in a tin-roofed
shack round the back from a Pizza East.
It's an unassuming little place, all salvaged
wood and rusty chairs with barely enough
room for 20 diners. The menu is just as
spartan, offering only cheeseburgers,
fries, onion fries, a tiny breakfast menu

and an assortment of drinks – you're not
exactly spoilt for choice. But when your
cheeseburgers are this close to perfection,
you don't need options. They're tender,
juicy, rammed full of flavour and incredibly
simple. The sides are just as good. Skin-on
fries and juicy red onion rings are salty,
crispy and hit the right spot. The shack is
a laid-back affair. You order at the counter
and pick up a beer from the fridge, or a
Camden Pale Ale on tap, and then top off
the whole lot with a milkshake. Tables are
on a first-come first-served basis, so the
queues can get pretty big, especially
midweek, but it's definitely worth the wait.
*Babies and children welcome. Bookings
not accepted. Disabled: toilet. Takeaway
service.* **Map 26 A4.**
For branches see index.

★ Gourmet Burger Kitchen

*121 Lordship Lane, SE22 8HU (8693
9307, www.gbk.co.uk).* **Meals served** noon-
10pm Mon-Thur, Sun; noon-11pm Fri, Sat.
Main courses £5.05-£11.95. **Credit** AmEx,
MC, V.

Gourmet Burger Kitchen has become
a victim of its own success. Once the
vanguard of the gourmet burger revolution,
it has since been surpassed by younger,
fitter, leaner and hipper outfits such as
Meat Liquor (*see p24*) and Honest, among
many, many others. Nevertheless, GBK
remains one of London's better chain
restaurants, and one that still takes the
quality of its product seriously. Standard
patties are 100% West Country beef,
plus there's buffalo and wild boar from
Laverstoke Park Farm. While patties are
simple (just a little, possibly a little too
much, seasoning), the extras are not. The
Don, for example, comes with bacon aïoli,
blue cheese, American cheese, onion jam,
rocket and mustard mayo balanced inside
a brioche bun; and the Kiwiburger has the
acquired/adventurous taste of beetroot,
egg, pineapple, aged cheddar, salad, mayo
and relish. Skinny fries are a barely-there
size zero, but very moreish, and diner-style
shakes (Oreo is a favourite) served in big
metal mixing cups are jeans-bustingly filling.
*Babies and children welcome: children's
menu; crayons; high chairs; nappy-changing
facilities. Bookings not accepted. Disabled:
toilet. Tables outdoors (4, terrace).
Takeaway service.* **Map 23 C4.**
For branches see index.

★ Grillshack NEW

*61-63 Beak Street, W1F 9SL (no phone,
www.grillshack.com). Oxford Circus or
Piccadilly Circus tube.* **Meals served**
8am-11pm Mon-Sat; 10am-10.30pm
Sun. **Main courses** £2.50-£9.95.
Credit MC, V.

Serial restaurateur Richard Caring (who
owns the Ivy, Pizza East and much, much
more) is slowly taking over our city. But
you've got to hand it to him – he gives good
restaurant. This once-gloomy site (formerly

Patty & Bun

the Alphabet Bar) now features sunshine-yellow walls and semi-industrial stylings (white 'brick' tiles, open kitchen, dark woods): all very predictable. But the kitchen is where Grillshack shows its evil genius, in not trying to gild the lily. Our burger had no show-off toppings, but its simple components – from the soft and airy brioche bun to the pink-middled patty and smoky bacon – made for a terrific bite. We also enjoyed a nicely charred piece of flat-beaten rump steak over a generous heap of shoestring fries and marvelled at the dish's under-a-tenner price tag. Only the wait after ordering – 35 minutes on our visit, in spite of placing our order at the counter, fast-food style – and an over-onioned radish slaw showed flaws in an otherwise slick operation. But it's early days yet, and Mr Caring probably has a button to dispatch any inadequate staff directly into a fiery pit.
Bookings not accepted. Takeaway service.
Map 17 A4.

★ Haché

153 Clapham High Street, SW4 7SS (7738 8760, www.hacheburgers.com). Clapham Common tube. **Meals served** noon-10.30pm Mon-Thur; noon-11pm Fri, Sat; noon-10pm Sun. **Main courses** £6.95-£17.95. **Credit** DC, MC, V.
If you can imagine a girly burger joint, Haché would be it. Named after the Gallic term for 'minced' (go to Paris and ask for a steak 'haché' and you'll be served a good-quality patty), the restaurant is full of feminine French touches: from pretty vintage chandeliers to the creamy walls with ornate, oversized mirrors. In the open kitchen at the back, classic 'man food' is prettied up wherever possible. On our visit, thick-cut slices of onions were encased in huge balloons of batter, while the frites were proper french fries – thin-cut, seasoned and skinny. They arrived in a cutesy 'mini fryer basket': a nice touch.

Less impressive were the cajun-spiced chicken wings, with their flabby, not crunchy, coating. The upmarket burgers are decent, though. Our pink-middled patty came topped with melted cheese, smoky bacon and smart salad fillers, including rocket, ripe tomato and slices of red onion, all in a soft brioche bun. If you want to be really metrosexual, ditch the bun entirely: staff will happily replace it with a green salad. Then all you'll need as accompaniment is a cup of chamomile tea, made with proper dried flowers. Who said burger joints have to be butch?
Babies and children welcome: high chairs. Bookings not accepted 6.30-11pm Fri, Sat. Tables outdoors (4, pavement). Takeaway service. **Map 22 B2**.
For branches see index.

★ ★ Honest Burgers

Brixton Village Market, Coldharbour Lane, SW9 8PR (7733 7963, www.honest burgers.co.uk). Brixton tube/rail. **Lunch served** noon-4pm Mon. **Meals served** noon-10.30pm Tue-Sat; noon-10pm Sun. **Main courses** £7.50-£11.50. **Credit** MC, V.
Don't be alarmed if this tiny burger joint is packed when you arrive – simply give the friendly, efficient staff your number to key into their iPads and wait for them to text you when a space is free (you can follow your queue status online too). That will give you time to pop off for an aperitif in one of Brixton Village/Market Row's numerous other buzzing businesses, or to grab a carryout from the off-licence, listen to street music (there's always something going on in Brixton Village) and generally soak up the atmosphere in these covered streets. Once you're in, there's no time to waste mulling over the menu. There are five simple choices – plain, cheese, 'honest' (with bacon and cheese), a special (manchego and chorizo, perhaps), and a vegetable fritter. Beef is supplied by Ginger Pig, cooked medium, served in a glazed bun and is just as juicy as you could wish. Honest's signature chips are seasoned with rosemary salt. There's a minimal wine list, ale from Redchurch brewery in Bethnal Green, and local speciality Ossie's ginger beer. Fast food at the top of its game.
Babies and children welcome: nappy-changing facilities (market). Bookings not accepted. Disabled: toilet (market). Takeaway service. **Map 22 E2**.
For branches see index.

★ Meat Market

The Mezzanine, Jubilee Market Hall, Tavistock Street, WC2E 8BE (no phone, www.themeatmarket.co.uk). Covent Garden tube. **Meals served** noon-11pm Mon-Sat; noon-10pm Sun. **Main courses** £6.50-£8.50. **Credit** AmEx, MC, V.
The second offshoot in Yianni Papoutsis's ever-expanding empire, this rough and ready burger bar has been drawing fans

to the tatty Jubilee Market since 2012. Meat Market is closer to Papoutsis's street-food origins than its elaborately themed siblings Meat Liquor (see p24) in Soho and Meat Mission in Hoxton. The menu is tacked up in wonky plastic lettering, orders are taken at the counter, and tables are separated from the market below by plastic sheeting. The entrance is hidden up some back stairs; with its loyal Twitter following, the restaurant doesn't need to capitalise on the tourist market. The shop's classic burger, the 'dead hippie', was exceptionally juicy – quite an achievement when arriving as two thinner patties. Sadly, the secret-recipe sauce lacked impact and the skinny fries were unremarkable. Better was a side of 'poppaz': croquettes filled with molten cheese and tongue-numbingly spicy jalapeños, served with a dill-heavy ranch dressing. While such dishes were trailblazers a year or so ago, burger mania has since shot through the roof. It will be interesting to see how Meat Market retains its niche alongside Five Guys and Shake Shack, Covent Garden's latest opinion-dividing American imports.
Babies and children admitted. Booking advisable. Takeaway service. **Map 18 E4**.
For branch (Meat Mission) see index.

★ ★ Patty & Bun

54 James Street, W1U 1HE (7487 3188, www.pattyandbun.co.uk). Bond Street tube. **Meals served** noon-10.15pm Tue-Sat; noon-9.15pm Sun. **Main courses** £7.50-£8.50. **Credit** MC, V.
Despite seating just 30 diners at a time, Patty & Bun has – in less than a year – carved out a reputation for serving some of London's finest burgers. All-day queues are testament to the fact that its amiable staff have the format spot-on. They don't mess around with ingredients (British wherever possible), the menu is witty yet not contrived, and they've even had the nous to offer takeaways. From the restaurant's start as a pop-up, the kitchen has worked hard to hone its dishes; sides such as skin-on rosemary salt chips show the care that's gone into perfecting each recipe. The signature 'ari gold' burger is a generous patty slathered in a winning combination of ketchup and smoky mayo, before being sandwiched in a glazed brioche bun. More original is the 'lamb-shank redemption', a firm lamb burger strongly flavoured with coriander, chilli and cumin aïoli. Aside from the main event, the smoky-sweet confit wings were pretty special too. The atmosphere couldn't be more laid-back: tables are bare, and tunes pump from a laptop perched on the bar. P&B's reputation as the up-and-coming burger supremo might be justified, but the hype hasn't gone to its head.
Available for hire. Babies and children admitted. Bookings not accepted. Takeaway service. **Map 9 H6**.

THERE IS NO
PREREQUISITE
OF ADHERING TO
SUGGESTED FOOD
COMBINATIONS.

YOU ARE
ENCOURAGED
TO MAKE YOUR
OWN DECISION
JOURNEY.

THE ADVISORY
OPERATES
WITHIN A STRICT
REGULATION
POLICY:

KETCHUP MUST
BE APPLIED T
THE FRIES.

Advisory. See p240.

Kentish Town

★ Chicken Shop

79 Highgate Road, NW5 1TL (3310 2020, www.chickenshop.com). Kentish Town tube/rail. **Meals served** 5pm-midnight Mon-Fri; noon-midnight Sat; noon-5pm Sun. **Main courses** £4-£8. **Credit** AmEx, MC, V.

Why did the vegan cross the road? Because there was nothing to eat at the Chicken Shop. This venture underneath Pizza East and Dirty Burger makes a similar virtue of its specialism. Chickens turn and blacken on a medieval-looking wood-fired spit, a man in a chain-mail glove hacks them into quarters, and your order of a whole, half or quarter bird arrives without delay. Spicy but not too much so, blackened but not excessively, it is, yes, finger-lickin' chicken. The price of the free-range chooks appears keen, but profit-boosting sides such as great crinkle-cut chips and aïoli mayo dip, red cabbage coleslaw with a more creamy than tangy dressing, and a salad of butter lettuce (old-fashioned floppy leaves rebranded) with avocado, redress the balance. The decor is a mash-up of 1950s furniture, reclaimed timber, mahogany shop fittings and American wooden beer crates. Wines are wittily bracketed into house, decent and good; not so amusing is the outrageous mark-up on the prosecco. The music is loud, the lighting dim, the service swift, the desserts just three: hazelnut brownie; rather ordinary lemon cheesecake, and an excellent lemon- and cinnamon-spiked apple pie. *Babies and children welcome: high chairs; nappy-changing facilities. Bookings not accepted. Disabled: toilet.* **Map 26 A4**.

North West
Hendon

★ Nando's

Brent Cross Shopping Centre, Prince Charles Drive, NW4 3FP (8203 9131, www.nandos.co.uk). Brent Cross tube. **Meals served** 11am-8pm Mon-Fri; 11am-7pm Sat; noon-6pm Sun. **Main courses** £4.25-£12. **Credit** AmEx, MC, V.

This isn't a chicken chain, it's an empire, with branches in many countries. The successful formula is part fast food (diners queue to place their orders at the tills) and part restaurant (where the comfortable seats encourage lingering). The vibe is a welcoming one – from the pleasant staff to the free soft-drink refills – and the menu has something for virtually everyone (even chicken-refuseniks). Peri-peri chicken is what Nando's is known for, in varying degrees of heat and body part (breast, leg, wing, whole or half), but the bird is also offered as a burger, in a pitta or wrap, and as part of a salad. There are mushroom and halloumi options too, as well as veggie burgers, a steak and a few non-chicken salads. Some parts of the menu work better than others: the grilled chicken is reliably good (and top-notch in the case of some tasty chicken livers); a mediterranean salad (tomato, cucumber, celery, peppers, mixed leaves in paprika dressing, olives and feta) less so. Sides run from chips and coleslaw to 'posh' options such as mildly spiced black beans. A safe bet for everyone from lone diners to families. *Babies and children welcome: children's menu; high chairs; nappy-changing facilities. Bookings not accepted. Takeaway service. Vegetarian menu.* **For branches see index.**

Thai

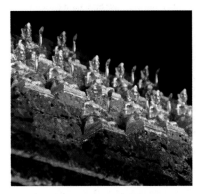

Finding a decent Thai meal in London isn't always easy. Too many restaurants serve formulaic and toned-down versions of classic dishes with only the merest hint of chilli or other spices, rather than the rowdy mix of hot, sweet, salty and sour flavours that epitomise proper Thai cooking. That doesn't mean the real deal isn't out there, but you may have to look in some unlikely places. The scruffy **Heron** pub in Bayswater is a case in point: upstairs it looks like just another British boozer, but in the basement there's a Thai karaoke bar-cum-restaurant with the most authentic Thai food you're likely to find in the capital. Other favourites for big flavours are **Mantanah** in Norwood Junction, **KaoSarn** in trendy Brixton Village Market, and **Esarn Kheaw** in Shepherd's Bush – all in equally unassuming, if less incongruous, settings. Fancy something more upmarket? **Sukho** in Parsons Green turns out well-executed classics, while **Patara** and **Blue Elephant** provide exotically attired interiors ideal for romance. For the younger crowd, modern Thai restaurants such as chains **Busaba Eathai** and **Rosa's**, and the **Begging Bowl**, a hip street-food spot in Peckham, are also spicing up the Thai restaurant scene.

Central
Covent Garden

Suda
23 Slingsby Place, WC2E 9AB (7240 8010, www.suda-thai.com). Covent Garden or Leicester Square tube. **Meals served** 11am-10.30pm Mon-Wed; 11am-11pm Thur-Sat; noon-10.30pm Sun. **Main courses** £7.50-£11.50. **Set lunch** (noon-3pm Mon) £7.95-£10.95 1 course. **Set meal** £18.95 3 courses. **Credit** AmEx, MC, V.
An eye-catching street-food cart fronts the tall, sleek glass exterior of Suda in summer, creating some character in what is an otherwise generic shopping-centre/café space. There's also a pretty display of victoria sponge cakes and British tea-time classics, helping to lure in footsore Covent Garden shoppers and sightseers. Navigate carefully through the menu (dried shrimps and oyster sauce are both found in the 'vegetarian' section) and you'll discover some interesting Thai dishes. To start, braised duck wrapped in steamed rice sheets arrived as bite-sized portions sitting in a sweet chilli dip. Mains include various types of som tam (green papaya salad) with a choice of grilled meat. The classic street-food dish gai yang (barbecued chicken) worked well with the shreds of well-pounded green papaya soaking up the tangy lime and chilli dressing. But other dishes were as westernised and contemporary as the venue itself. Beef penang, for instance, turned out

to be a slab of overcooked beef fillet, albeit in a shallow dish of rich and fragrant curry drizzled with coconut milk. Service was kindly yet not the most attentive.
Available for hire. Babies and children welcome: high chairs; nappy-changing facilities. Booking advisable weekends. Disabled: lift; toilet. Tables outdoors (4, pavement). Takeaway service. **Map 18 D4**.

Edgware Road

★ Heron
Basement karaoke room of the Heron, 1 Norfolk Crescent, W2 2DN (7706 9567). Edgware Road or Marble Arch tube or Paddington tube/rail. **Meals served** 1-11pm daily. **Main courses** £7.50-£18. **No credit cards.**
Located in a shabby boozer round the back of the Edgware Road, the Heron is certainly a rough diamond. Yet look beyond its busy carpets and dark, slightly dingy interior and you'll discover some of the most authentic Thai food to be found in London. Blaring Thai pop signals the way to the diminutive basement dining room, populated almost exclusively by Thais. The kitchen specialises in north-eastern (Esarn) cooking, offering an impressive range of spicy salads, sour curries, stir-fries and much more besides – this is not the place to come for a standard Thai green curry. From the ample list, the sour sausages (sai krok esarn), served in bite-sized bobbles, produced

plenty of garlicky tang. A hot and sour salad of stir-fried minced pork and crisp-fried rice ball pieces had the perfect balance of sweet, salty and sour notes, plus enough dried chillies to numb our lips – ask for it mild if you can't handle the burn. Bottled lager and draught ale helped to cool the heat. Expect things to get lively after 9pm, as the dining room doubles as a karaoke lounge. Service couldn't be friendlier.
Babies and children admitted. Booking advisable. Takeaway service. **Map 8 E5**.

Soho

Busaba Eathai
106-110 Wardour Street, W1F 0TR (7255 8686, www.busaba.com). Leicester Square or Tottenham Court Road tube. **Meals served** noon-11pm Mon-Thur; noon-11.30pm Fri, Sat; noon-10pm Sun. **Main courses** £9.50-£10.50. **Credit** AmEx, MC, V.
Conceived by restaurateur Alan Yau more than a decade ago, this original branch of Busaba Eathai attracted queues round the block when it opened in Soho. These days, Yau has only a minority share, and Busaba has become a ten-strong chain – but it's still not your average Thai joint. The dark, handsome interior combines darks wood, incense and dimly lit lanterns. With spacious shared tables, no reservations and brisk service, the restaurant remains a great spot for a casual meal with friends. Renowned Thai chef David Thompson's influence

Suda. See p243.

is now far less pronounced than in the early days when he was menu consultant, though there are still a few dishes that aren't often seen in London, such as the sen chan pad thai (a pimped pad thai with crab originating from the Chanthaburi province of eastern Thailand). The unusual addition of green mango gave this dish a nice crunch, while the mild chilli kick married well with the sweet and sour tang. A more mainstream tom yam talay was a disappointment, however; what should have been an aromatic, spicy seafood soup was overpowered by fish sauce with only a hint of lemongrass coming through. Busaba may not be as polished or as innovative as when it opened, but you'll still find a measure of inexpensive charm here.
Babies and children welcome: high chairs. Bookings not accepted. Takeaway service. **Map 17 B3.**
For branches see index.

Patara
15 Greek Street, W1D 4DP (7437 1071, www.pataralondon.com). Leicester Square or Tottenham Court Road tube. **Lunch served** noon-2.30pm Mon-Sat. **Dinner served** 6-10.30pm daily. **Main courses** £13-£24. **Set lunch** £12.95-£15.95 2 courses. **Set dinner** £38 2 courses. **Credit** AmEx, MC, V.
Part of an international chain, with branches in Bangkok, Geneva and Singapore among other cities, this plush Soho restaurant – the newest of four London outlets – has an air of confident sophistication. The dining room is low-lit, the staff polite and in the centre of the space sits a carved wooden spirit house. From the ample menu, a fusion dish of wafer-like 'Thai taco' shells served with a light filling of minced prawns and pork worked well. A main of slow-cooked osso buco in massaman curry sauce with lotus seeds also blended eastern and western techniques, though the accompanying pitta bread seemed a step too far. Of the more classically rendered dishes (and there are plenty), a pad thai was a sedate affair, while the chargrilled sea bass in a red curry sauce was punchier. Like the food, the diners are a refined bunch: by day, many a business lunch is devoured here; the evenings are more about special occasions. If you're in search of a well-executed contemporary meal in Soho with spice-levels that won't offend, Patara will deliver – but don't expect a cheap eat.
Babies and children admitted until 9pm. Booking advisable. Disabled: toilet. Separate room for parties. Vegetarian menu. **Map 17 C3.**
For branches see index.

West
Bayswater

Nipa
Lancaster London , Lancaster Terrace, W2 2TY (7262 6737, www.niparestaurant.co.uk). Lancaster Gate tube.
Bar **Open** 10am-10pm daily.
Restaurant **Lunch served** noon-2pm Mon-Fri. **Dinner served** 6.30-10.30pm Mon-Sat. **Main courses** £9.50-£15.50. **Set meal** £29-£34 4 courses. **Set dinner** (6.30-7.30pm) £19.50 4 courses incl glass of wine.
Both **Credit** AmEx, DC, MC, V.
Housed inside the Lancaster London hotel, Nipa is plush and polished – just as you'd expect from a hotel restaurant. Decorous waitresses in traditional

101 Thai Kitchen

attire greet you at the door of the teak-panelled room. You're then escorted to tables immaculately laid with white cloths and vases of fresh orchids; plump for a window spot if you can, for views of Hyde Park across the road. The menu encompasses the gamut of classic Thai cooking, including a few less-common dishes. Food is attractively presented, with carved vegetable garnishes. A penang chicken curry was thick, fragrant with lime leaves and subtly spiced, while a stir-fried pork dish with coriander and pepper was fresh and aromatic with plenty of punchy fine-chopped garlic. Chilli is used in moderation, so as not to offend the well-turned-out international patrons. Opt for a set meal and Nipa can also deliver smart dining at relatively affordable prices. Served in a round blue and white ceramic platter with different compartments for each dish, the early-bird 'khantok' meal is impressively good value at £19.50 for four courses, with a glass of wine or beer.
Available for hire. Babies and children welcome: high chairs; nappy-changing facilities (hotel). Booking essential Fri, Sat. Disabled: lift; toilet (hotel). Vegetarian menu. **Map 8 D6**.

Hammersmith

101 Thai Kitchen
352 King Street, W6 0RX (8746 6888, www.101thaikitchen.com). Stamford Brook tube. **Lunch served** noon-3pm Mon-Sat. **Dinner served** 6-10.30pm Mon-Thur, Sun; 6-11pm Fri, Sat. **Main courses** £6.50-£14.95. **Credit** AmEx, MC, V.
This no-nonsense Hammersmith establishment feels a bit like a scruffy canteen. Ageing padded metal chairs look like cast-offs from a convention centre; tables are arranged in long lines, and some wobble. From the back of the two-tone pink dining room, portraits of the Thai royal family watch over proceedings. As is the case in many of London's most authentic Thai restaurants, the cooking here

is largely from the Esarn region of north-eastern Thailand – including multiple versions of green papaya salad, accompanied by anything from salted duck egg to sausage. You'll also find a collection of southern Thai dishes such as sour prawn curry, or turmeric-marinated sea bass. These are prepared by 'Auntie Bee', who hails from Hat Yai, a city near the border with Malaysia. An Esarn classic of shredded bamboo shoots with the fermented fish sauce favoured in the region was characteristically pungent (in taste and aroma), served with a decent squeeze of lime, plenty of chilli and a few mint leaves to add freshness. Staff don't stand on ceremony here, informing diners when the table must be vacated for the next sitting, yet they're not unfriendly; locals, spanning every age group, are treated with congeniality.
Available for hire. Babies and children welcome: children's menu; high chairs. Booking advisable. Takeaway service. **Map 20 A4**.

Shepherd's Bush

Esarn Kheaw
314 Uxbridge Road, W12 7LJ (8743 8930, www.esarnkheaw.com). Shepherd's Bush Market tube or bus 207, 260, 283. **Lunch served** noon-3pm Mon-Fri. **Dinner served** 6-11pm daily. **Main courses** £7.95-£10.95. **Credit** MC, V.
For more than two decades, Esarn Kheaw has been serving up north-eastern (Esarn) Thai cooking to an appreciative crowd of locals, including plenty of expats. The rather dark dining room, complete with a mural of rice farmers and pictures of the Thai royal family, may be starting to show its age, but the cooking is as good as ever. Chargrilled beef served in tender strips with onion, coriander and plenty of lime offers a gentle introduction to the food of the region, while the finely minced catfish, anchovy and green chilli dip (num prik pla sod) with raw vegetables is redolent of fermented fish and displays uncompromising chilli heat: a dish

best left to seasoned Thai food fans. A vegetarian version of coconut-milk-free jungle curry – packed with fresh green peppercorns, bamboo shoots and pea and apple aubergines – was also characteristically blistering in heat. Boiled and deep-fried 'son-in-law eggs', served in tangy tamarind sauce and scattered with nutty fried garlic, made a delicious, mouth-cooling addition to a spicy meal. Regular crowd-pleasers such as pad thai or Thai green curry are also offered, and the drinks list contains the usual range of Thai beers, teas and a handful of wines. Some readers have found the service a little brusque, but we've always found it amiable.
Babies and children welcome: high chairs. Booking advisable. Takeaway service. **Map 20 B1**.

South West
Fulham

Blue Elephant
Waterside Tower, The Boulevard, Imperial Wharf, Townmead Road, SW6 2UB (7751 3111, www.blueelephant.com/london). Fulham Broadway tube then bus 391 or Imperial Wharf rail. **Lunch served** noon-2.30pm Mon-Sat; noon-4.30pm Sun. **Dinner served** 6-10.30pm Mon-Thur, Sun; 6-11pm Fri, Sat. **Main courses** £18-£30. **Set meal** £37-£55 4 courses. **Buffet** (Sun) £30. **Credit** AmEx, DC, MC, V.
The international Blue Elephant chain, set up to 'bring the best of Thai cuisine and culture to the world', has been wowing diners with impeccable service and innovative dishes since the 1980s. The London branch (which was previously in Fulham Broadway) has all the grandeur of an imperial palace, and riverside views to boot. Rich with ornate wood carving, orchids and silk cushions, the interior wouldn't look out of place in one of Bangkok's smartest establishments. The food is beautifully

presented on a range of bespoke tableware; from woven bamboo containers to heavy ceramics. The menu is divided into 'past' (traditional), 'present' (contemporary), and 'future' (innovative) dishes. Of the last, a Japanese-inspired raw salmon laab didn't quite gel – the oil-rich fish in need of a stronger citrus kick. A more classic starter of DIY betel leaf wraps with coconut, chilli, peanuts and dried shrimps was more successful, and fun. A kindly waitress demonstrated how to fold them properly. The lamb-shank yellow curry was another mixed bag: the meat tender, but the sauce overly sweet. Though dishes are pricey, portions are generous, and the setting and staff are first-rate.
Available for hire. Babies and children welcome: high chairs. Booking advisable. Disabled: lift; toilet. Separate room for parties, seats 50-100. Tables outdoors (20, terrace). Takeaway service. Vegetarian menu. **Map 21 A2**.

Parsons Green

Sukho
855 Fulham Road, SW6 5HJ (7371 7600, www.sukhogroups.com). Parsons Green tube.
Lunch served noon-3pm, **dinner served** 6.30-11pm daily. **Main courses** £11.25-£18.95. **Set lunch** £12.95 2 courses. **Credit** AmEx, MC, V.
The stretch of Fulham Road around Parsons Green has no shortage of restaurants: whether you're after Chinese dim sum or German beer and bratwurst. Despite the competition, though, Sukho is constantly busy. Part of a three-strong chain that includes Suk Saran in Wimbledon and Suksan in Chelsea, it exudes elegance and charm. The dining room blends contemporary east Asian and traditional features, with detailed wooden carvings, white napery and plenty of colourful candles, making an ideal setting for a romantic meal (though a banquette by the window was just a little too squishy from regular use). A starter of juicy pork, wrapped in betel leaves and chargrilled, was served on skewers with a sweet and tangy plum dipping sauce. To follow, marinated sea bass with red curry paste was also attractively presented on the banana leaf in which it had been cooked; rich, complex and aromatic with aniseed notes from a sweet-basil garnish, it was a pleasure to eat. In contrast, beef massaman lacked depth, with coconut milk and peanuts the prominent flavours rather than the earthy slow-cooked beef and the aromatic cinnamon and cumin spicing we'd expected. To drink, there's plenty for wine-lovers, plus Thai beer and teas, including a sweet, herbal chrysanthemum infusion.
Babies and children admitted. Booking advisable. Takeaway service.
For branches (Suk Saran, Suksan) see index.

South

Brixton

★ KaoSarn
Brixton Village Market, Coldharbour Lane, SW9 8PR (7095 8922). Brixton tube/rail.
Lunch served 12-3.30pm Tue-Sun. **Dinner served** 5.30-10pm Tue-Sat; 5.30-9pm Sun.
Main courses £6.90-£11.50. **Unlicensed**. **Corkage** no charge. **No credit cards**.
There's no shortage of well-priced eateries in Brixton Village Market, but KaoSarn is one of the biggest crowd-pullers. The place is regularly

Begging Bowl

packed inside and out with a mix of stalwart Brixtonites of all ages, and young hipsters soaking up the Market's vibe – and it deserves to be busy. The food is not only cheap, but bursting with authentic Thai flavours. As at many of the surrounding dining venues, the decor is basic, with mismatched furniture and much of the seating 'outside', spanning both sides of a corner site at the edge of the market. The menu, too, is pared down, with a handful of classic curries, noodle dishes and stir-fries – all well prepared. An impressive salad of plump king prawns slicked in dark red roasted chilli sauce and lime juice (pla koong) was packed with fiery heat and citrus tang. Another of sautéed ground pork with roasted rice (laab) had been liberally laced with fresh mint and coriander; though milder than you'd find in northern Thailand, the dish still packed plenty of aromatic flavour. Soft drinks include fragrant own-made lemongrass or ginger tea, and there's also the option to BYO. Service can be a little matter-of-fact, but staff are unfailingly friendly.
Babies and children admitted. Booking advisable Fri-Sun. Tables outdoors (10, market). Takeaway service. **Map 22 E2**.
For branch see index.

South East
Peckham

Begging Bowl
168 Bellenden Road, SE15 4BW (7635 2627, www.thebeggingbowl.co.uk). Peckham Rye rail.
Lunch served noon-2.30pm Tue-Sat; noon-3.30pm Sun. **Dinner served** 6-10pm Mon-Sat.
Main courses £6.25-£14.75. **Credit** MC, V.
When this trendy Peckham eaterie opened in 2012, there was a flurry of excitement over its unusual menu. Instead of the more familiar Thai fare, chef Jane Alty offers Thai street food. Alty previously worked with David Thompson on his classic cookbook on that theme, which no doubt served as inspiration for her eclectic repertoire. Colour-coded by price, and designed for sharing tapas-style, the dishes include only a few of the usual suspects (Thai fish cakes, for example). The rest of the menu is built around less familiar options and ingredients, such as a rich but mellow curry featuring firm-fleshed yam bean root. Seasonal western ingredients are also given some Thai treatment, to produce dishes such as trout in sour orange curry,

THAI

Menu

Spellings are subject to considerable variation. Word divisions vary too: thus, kwaitiew, kwai teo and guey teow are all acceptable spellings for noodles.

Thailand abandoned chopsticks in the 19th century in favour of chunky steel spoons and forks. Using your fingers is usually fine, and essential if you order satay sticks or spare ribs.

STARTERS

Khanom jeep or **ka nom geeb**: dim sum. Little dumplings of minced pork, bamboo shoots and water chestnuts, wrapped in an egg and rice pastry, then steamed. **Khanom pang na koong**: prawn sesame toast.
Kratong thong: tiny crispy batter cups ('top hats') filled with mixed vegetables and/or minced meat.
Miang: savoury appetisers with a variety of constituents (mince, ginger, peanuts, roasted coconut, for instance), wrapped in betel leaves.
Popia or **porpia**: spring rolls.
Tod mun pla or **tauk manpla**: small fried fish cakes (should be lightly rubbery in consistency) with virtually no 'fishy' smell or taste.

SOUPS

Poh tak or **tom yam potag**: hot and sour mixed seafood soup.
Tom kha gai or **gai tom kar**: hot and sour chicken soup with coconut milk.
Tom yam or **tom yum**: a hot and sour soup, smelling of lemongrass. **Tom yam koong** is with prawns; **tom yam gai** with chicken; **tom yam hed** with mushrooms.

RICE

Khao, **kow** or **khow**: rice.
Khao nao: sticky rice.
Khao pat: fried rice.
Khao suay: steamed rice.
Pat khai: egg-fried rice.

SALADS

Laab or **larb**: minced and cooked meat incorporating lime juice and other ingredients such as ground rice and herbs.
Som tam: a popular cold salad of grated green papaya.
Yam or **yum**: refers to any tossed salad, hot or cold, but it is often hot and sour, flavoured with lemon and chilli.
Yam nua: hot and sour beef salad.
Yam talay: hot and sour seafood salad (served cold).

NOODLES

Generally speaking, noodles are eaten in greater quantities in the north of Thailand. There are many types of **kwaitiew** or **guey teow** noodles. Common ones include **sen mee**: rice vermicelli; **sen yai** (river rice noodles): a broad, flat, rice noodle; **sen lek**: a medium flat noodle, used to make pad thai; **ba mee**: egg noodles; and **woon sen** (cellophane noodle): transparent vermicelli made from soy beans or other pulses. These are often prepared as stir-fries.

Common noodle dishes are:
Khao soi: chicken curry soup with egg noodles; a Burmese/Thai dish, referred to as the national dish of Burma.
Mee krob or **mee grob**: sweet crispy fried vermicelli.
Pad si-ewe or **cee eaw**: noodles fried with mixed meat in soy sauce.
Pad thai: stir-fried noodles with shrimps (or chicken and pork), beansprouts and salted turnips, garnished with ground peanuts.

CURRIES

Gaeng, **kaeng** or **gang**: the generic name for curry. Yellow curry is the mildest; green curry (**gaeng keaw wan** or **kiew warn**) is medium hot and uses green chillies; red curry (**gaeng pet**) is similar, but uses red chillies.
Jungle curry: often the hottest of the curries, made with red curry paste, bamboo shoots and just about anything else to hand, but no coconut cream.
Massaman or **mussaman**: also known as Muslim curry, because it originates from the area along the border with Malaysia where many Thais are Muslims. For this reason, pork is never used. It's a rich but mild concoction, with coconut, potato and some peanuts.
Penang, **panaeng** or **panang**: a dry, aromatic curry made with 'Penang' curry paste, coconut cream and holy basil.

FISH & SEAFOOD

Hoi: shellfish.
Hor mok talay or **haw mog talay**: steamed egg mousse with seafood.
Koong, **goong** or **kung**: prawns.
Maw: dried fish belly.

or fennel and chicory with a relish of minced pork, prawn, coconut and yellow bean. Stir-fried pork belly with long beans was rich with warming red curry paste and lime-leaf slivers. The dining room has a contemporary feel, with big windows and colourful, painted reclaimed wood lining one wall. There's outside seating too. Staff are young and enthusiastic, regularly checking in to see if we needed anything. There's a well-chosen wine list and some decent cocktails.
Babies and children welcome: high chairs; nappy-changing facilities. Bookings not accepted for fewer than 8 people. Disabled: toilet. Tables outdoors (4, terrace).

South Norwood

★ Mantanah

2 Orton Building, Portland Road, SE25 4UD (8771 1148, www.mantanah.co.uk). Norwood Junction rail. **Lunch served** noon-3pm Sun. **Dinner served** 6-11pm Tue-Sun. **Main courses** £6.50-£13.95. **Set lunch** £7.95 3 courses. **Set dinner** (minimum 2) £18 per person 3 courses, £25 per person 4 courses. **Credit** MC, V.

The residents of Norwood Junction are lucky indeed to have such a good local Thai restaurant. Mantanah may look unassuming from the outside, but its food is nothing like the watered-down western version of Thai cookery you often find in London. A northern dish of shredded chicken and banana blossom in coconut sauce was a riot of sour, sweet and fiery flavours. There are plenty of other regional treats to choose from too: the likes of southern red chicken curry with fresh coconut meat; esarn som tam papaya salad with salted crab or dried shrimps; and fiercely hot northern jungle curry. The northern 'Highland Tribe' pork curry with peanuts and pickled garlic is a must-try. The kitchen doesn't skimp on the chilli, but is happy to accommodate more sensitive palates – just let your waitress know. There's a traditional feel to a meal here: food is served on blue and white plates, Thai embroidery adorns the walls, and the customary pictures of the Thai king and queen are in pride of place. Dressed in traditional silk outfits, the waitresses are understated and charming. Mantanah also does a roaring trade in takeaways. *Available for hire. Babies and children admitted: high chairs. Booking advisable. Takeaway service; delivery service (over £15 within 3-mile radius). Vegetarian menu.*

East
Spitalfields

Rosa's

12 Hanbury Street, E1 6QR (7247 1093, www.rosaslondon.com). Liverpool Street tube/rail or Shoreditch High Street rail. **Meals served** noon-10.30pm Mon-Thur, Sun; noon-11pm Fri, Sat. **Main courses** £7.50-£15.50. **Credit** MC, V.

The original branch of Rosa's (there are now three more) is located on a thoroughfare between Brick Lane and Spitalfields Market. It plays host to a vibrant young crowd of visiting tourists and local hipsters – you may even spot the odd pooch in a handbag. The dining room is clean and contemporary, with white-tiled walls, bevelled wood panelling and red stools at each of the small tables. The usual Thai repertoire is executed well: hot and sour tom yam soup was rich with lemongrass, tangy tomato and a generous amount of seafood. Of the recommended dishes, stir-fried slices of European aubergine were coated in a sweet, salty soya and yellow bean sauce, and laced with plenty of ginger and black pepper. In contrast, a salad of chargrilled beef strips in chilli dressing was lacklustre, with celery the prominent flavour. Rosa's also has a busy sideline in takeaway coffee, made with Monmouth beans and a swish La Marzocco espresso machine. Service is mostly quick and efficient, but the coffee trade can hold it up on occasion. Other drinks include Thai beer and whiskey, plus a handful of wines and east Asian teas.

Available for hire. Babies and children admitted. Bookings not accepted for fewer than 6 people; advisable Fri, Sat. Takeaway service. Vegetarian menu. **Map 12 S5.**

For branches see index.

North
Islington

Naamyaa Café

Angel Building, 407 St John Street, EC1V 4AB (3122 0988, www.naamyaa.com). Angel tube. **Meals served** noon-11pm Mon-Thur; noon-11.30pm Fri. **Brunch served** 9am-5pm Sat; 10am-5pm Sun. **Dinner served** 5-11.30pm Sat; 5-10.30pm Sun. **Main courses** £7.50-£15. **Credit** AmEx, MC, V.

When this collaboration between prolific restaurateur Alan Yau and chef and Thai food expert David Thompson opened in 2012, it felt like an exciting new concept. The dishes were authentically fiery and complex, while the decor was an eclectic blend of contemporary design and South-east Asian bling. Now that it has bedded in, Naamyaa sits more comfortably next to its chain-restaurant neighbours. The furnishings are as striking as ever – check out the wall of miniature golden Buddhas as you enter the dining room – but the dishes have been tempered for the western customers. A special of whole sea bream in penang curry sauce, though perfectly nice, lacked excitement. Generous slabs of tender beef rib were more successful, though there was only a whisper of the promised jasmine tea-smoked flavour. Set meals are good value, coming with thin rice noodles, sweet-pickled morning glory, soft-boiled egg and a choice of curries (wild ginger and prawn, or minced pork and cherry tomato, perhaps), plus a side of clear chicken soup. Burgers are on hand for anyone who doesn't like spice. Some of its edge might have been lost, but friendly staff help make Naamyaa an enjoyable hangout for a meal with friends.

Babies and children welcome: high chairs; nappy-changing facilities. Booking advisable. Disabled: toilet. Tables outdoors (10, pavement). Takeaway service. **Map 5 N3.**

THAI

Naamyaa Café

Turkish

The quality of Turkish food in London is high and prices are low – and an ever-increasing number of Londoners from outside the community have come to know their iskender from their köfte, and their mangal from their ocakbası. You only have to peek through the windows at the young, mixed clientele of Dalston joints such as **19 Numara Bos Cirrik I** and **Mangal II** for confirmation that a cuisine thought to be intriguingly exotic in the 1970s is now firmly mainstream in our city.

But though Turkish cooking has come far in terms of public perception, a little more variety would be a good thing. One problem is that London's Turkish restaurants are heavily concentrated in the north and east of the city – areas of major Turkish and Turkish-Cypriot settlement – leaving the south and west of the capital under-represented. A larger obstacle to progress is a deficit of imagination. There are dozens of venues where you can find skilfully executed meze and grills, but ever since Quince restaurant ceased its efforts to create new twists to the Turkish culinary repertoire, there has been nowhere in this metropolis attempting to update the cuisine. Fusion may be a dirty word, but too many Turkish restaurant menus in London are near-identical – including those at more upmarket restaurants such as **Ishtar** and **Kazan**. If you've travelled widely in Turkey, you'll know of many wonderful dishes that can't be found in this city (although top marks to **Antepliler** for its Gaziantep options). This lack of regional variety – and distinct paucity of interesting seafood dishes – may come down to the fact that so many of the restaurateurs are originally from the same place, Northern Cyprus.

Our city's Turkish restaurants are inexpensive, reliable and generally of a very high quality – but now it's time to take things to the next level.

Central

Fitzrovia

Özer
5 Langham Place, W1B 3DG (7323 0505, www.sofra.co.uk). Oxford Circus tube or C2 or 88 bus.
Bar **Open** noon-11pm daily.
Restaurant **Breakfast served** 8am-noon, **meals served** noon-11pm daily. **Main courses** £8.95-£23.95. **Set meal** (noon-6pm) £10.85; (6-11pm) £12.95. **Credit** AmEx, MC, V.
Hüseyin Özer's journey from Turkish shepherd to London kebab-shop owner to multi-millionaire restaurateur is inspiring. Many aspects of his Fitzrovia restaurant are less inspiring – the bland interiors, the conservative cooking – but the all-day set menus offer such value it seems unreasonable to complain. For around a tenner you'll get crusty brown bread, houmous, a large meze platter and a main course: a bargain for such a central location. Much of the meze selection is straightforward, but the parsley and mint in the tabouleh were particularly perky, pomegranate seeds breathed life into the moutabal, the içli köfte were ungreasy and had perfectly moist minced lamb fillings, and the 'ex-mother-in-law's vine leaves' were full of flavour and character. The set meal main, spicy lamb meatballs, was modest, mediocre and meekly spiced. From the carte, we ordered chicken keshkek. A ceremonial dish of Persian origin rarely seen here, this wheat stew with grilled chicken has a consistency and flavour similar to porridge: a bit bland, perhaps, but appetisingly unusual. Özer was full on our visit, which may explain the hurried, impersonal service, but with such keen pricing, a well-chosen wine list and dependable food, it's easy to see why Hüseyin Özer is no longer a shepherd.
Available for hire. Babies and children welcome: high chairs; nappy-changing facilities. Booking advisable. Disabled: toilet. Tables outdoors (6, pavement). Takeaway service.
Map 9 H5.
For branches (Sofra) see index.

Marylebone

Ishtar
10-12 Crawford Street, W1U 6AZ (7224 2446, www.ishtarrestaurant.com). Baker Street tube.
Meals served noon-11pm Mon-Thur, Sun; noon-11.30pm Fri, Sat. **Main courses** £9.95-£15.95. **Set lunch** (noon-6pm) £10.95 2 courses, £12.95 3 courses. **Set meal** £27.50 3 courses. **Credit** MC, V.
Ishtar is one of the few places attempting to take Turkish cuisine upmarket, and while there's nothing innovative about the food, this is a good bet for a slightly more formal meal. The restaurant fits perfectly into Marylebone: contemporary and welcoming, with ample space and an open kitchen tucked at the back. A roaring trade is done in lunches – £10.95 for a mixed meze and a şiş kebab is a steal – and the cooking is commendable. Biting into the içli köfte unleashed an explosion of flavour; the crisp, light bulgar wheat shells contained a delicately spiced minced lamb filling. Stuffed vine leaves looked and tasted home-made – fragile,

misshapen packages of rice and raisins, artfully served with a squiggle of pomegranate molasses. And Ishtar's cupra bugulama (sea bream stew) uses wild mushrooms and asparagus to excellent effect. The bread in the iskender kebab was remarkably creamy and gooey (lots of butter, we suspect) and there wasn't so much yoghurt as to overwhelm the lamb's flavour. Although some inauthentic crowd-pleasers appear on the menu (smoked salmon with avocado, asparagus risotto), there's nothing dumbed-down about Ishtar's approach. Service is hardly bubbly, but it's unobtrusive and efficient. Prices are about 25% higher than those outside central London, but this is still a good deal. *Babies and children welcome: high chairs; nappy-changing facilities. Booking advisable Thur-Sat. Entertainment: musicians Thur-Sat; belly dancer Fri, Sat. Separate room for parties, seats 120. Tables outdoors (6, pavement). Takeaway service.* **Map 2 F5.**

Pimlico

Kazan

93-94 Wilton Road, SW1V 1DW (7233 7100, www.kazan-restaurant.com). Victoria tube/rail. **Lunch served** noon-3pm Mon-Fri; noon-4.30pm Sat, Sun. **Dinner served** 5.30-10pm Mon-Sat; 5.30-9.30pm Sun. **Main courses** £12.95-£21. **Set meal** £14.95 2 courses. **Set meze** £13.95-£16.50. **Credit** MC, V.

The menu here includes such authentically Turkish dishes as 'ribeye steak with chunky fries'. On seeing this we were tempted to quietly slip away, but ended up glad we'd stayed – the cooking is as hearty, homely and authentic as anything on Green Lanes. As one of London's few upmarket Turkish restaurants, Kazan is perhaps trying too hard to justify its existence. There are no doner kebabs in sight, and the flowers on tables, lavish furnishings, champagne cocktails and individual hand towels in toilets aren't found at many other Turkish eateries – but the food is far from dainty or fussy. As we discovered when our pan-fried calf's liver hit our table, it's served in vast portions. This 17th-century Ottoman street food had a deep, earthy flavour offset by the sweetness of parsley and sumac. The Kazan special was an epic dish: a vast portion of lamb shish, lamb köfte and chargrilled chicken, all outstandingly prepared and served with spicy salsa and yoghurt. Equally good was hünkar beğendi, stewed lamb in an impossibly rich, creamy aubergine mash, spiked with spring onions and spicy tomato sauce. Prices are perhaps 25% higher than elsewhere, but for the extra focus on service, presentation and comfort, it's worth it. *Available for hire. Babies and children welcome: high chairs. Booking advisable Thur-Sat. Disabled: toilet. Separate rooms for parties, seating 40, 45 and 80. Takeaway service. Vegetarian menu.* **Map 15 J11.**

South

Waterloo

Tas

33 The Cut, SE1 8LF (7928 2111, www.tas restaurants.co.uk). Southwark tube or Waterloo tube/rail. **Meals served** noon-11.30pm Mon-Sat; noon-10.30pm Sun. **Main courses** £8.45-£12.25. **Set meze** £10.45. **Credit** AmEx, MC, V.

Menu

It's useful to know that in Turkish 'ç' and 'ş' are pronounced 'ch' and 'sh'. So şiş is correct Turkish, shish is English and sis is common on menus. Menu spelling is rarely consistent, so expect wild variations on everything given here. See also the menu boxes in **Middle Eastern** and **North African**.

COOKING EQUIPMENT

Mangal: brazier.
Ocakbaşı: an open grill under an extractor hood. A metal dome is put over the charcoal for making paper-thin bread.

MEZE DISHES & SOUPS

Arnavut ciğeri: 'Albanian liver' – cubed or sliced lamb's liver, fried then baked.
Barbunya: spicy kidney bean stew.
Börek or böreği: fried or baked filo pastry parcels with a savoury filling, usually cheese, spinach or meat. Commonest are **muska** or **peynirli** (cheese) and **sigara** ('cigarette', so long and thin).
Cacik: diced cucumber with garlic in yoghurt.
Çoban salatası: 'shepherd's' salad of finely diced tomatoes, cucumbers, onions, perhaps green peppers and parsley.
Dolma: stuffed vegetables (usually with rice and pine kernels).
Enginar: artichokes, usually with vegetables in olive oil.
Haydari: yoghurt, infused with garlic and mixed with finely chopped mint leaves.
Hellim: Cypriot halloumi cheese.
Houmous kavurma: houmous topped with strips of lamb and pine nuts.
Imam bayıldı: literally 'the imam fainted'; aubergine stuffed with onions, tomatoes and garlic in olive oil.
Işkembe: finely chopped tripe soup; an infallible hangover cure.
Kısır: usually a mix of chopped parsley, tomatoes, onions, crushed wheat, olive oil and lemon juice.
Kizartma: lightly fried vegetables.
Lahmacun: 'pizza' of minced lamb on thin pide (qv).
Mercimek çorbar: red lentil soup.
Midye tava: mussels in batter, in a garlic sauce.
Mücver: courgette and feta fritters.
Patlıcan: aubergine, variously served.
Pide: a term encompassing many varieties of Turkish flatbread. It also refers to Turkish pizzas (heavier and more filling than lahmacun, qv).
Pilaki: usually haricot beans in olive oil, but the name refers to the method of cooking not the content.
Piyaz: white bean salad with onions.
Saç: paper-thin, chewy bread prepared on a metal dome (also called saç) over a charcoal grill.
Sucuk: spicy sausage, usually beef.
Tarator: a bread, garlic and walnut mixture; **havuç tarator** adds carrot; **ıspanak tarator** adds spinach.
Yayla: yoghurt and rice soup (usually) with a chicken stock base.
Yaprak dolması: stuffed vine leaves.

MAIN COURSES

Alabalık: trout.
Güveç: stew, which is traditionally cooked in an earthenware pot.
Hünkar beğendi: cubes of lamb, braised with onions and tomatoes, served on an aubergine and cheese purée.
İçli köfte: balls of cracked bulgar wheat filled with spicy mince.
İncik: knuckle of lamb, slow-roasted in its own juices. Also called **kléftico**.
Karnı yarik: aubergine stuffed with minced lamb and vegetables.
Mitite köfte: chilli meatballs.
Sote: meat (usually), sautéed in tomato, onion and pepper (and sometimes wine).

KEBABS

Usually made with grilled lamb (those labelled **tavuk** or **piliç** are chicken), served with bread or rice and salad. Common varieties include:
Beyti: usually spicy mince and garlic, but sometimes best-end fillet.
Böbrek: kidneys.
Çöp şiş: small cubes of lamb.
Döner: slices of marinated lamb (sometimes mince) packed tightly with pieces of fat on a vertical rotisserie.
Halep: usually döner (qv) served over bread with a buttery tomato sauce.
İskender: a combination of döner (qv), tomato sauce, yoghurt and melted butter on bread.
Kaburga: spare ribs.
Kanat: chicken wings.
Köfte: mince mixed with spices, eggs and onions.
Külbastı: char-grilled fillet.
Lokma: 'mouthful' – boned fillet of lamb (beware, there's a dessert that has a similar name!).
Patlıcan: mince and sliced aubergine.
Pirzola: lamb chops.
Şiş: cubes of marinated lamb.
Uykuluk: sweetbread.
Yoğurtlu: meat over bread and yoghurt.

DESSERTS

Armut tatlısı: baked pears.
Ayva tatlısı: quince in syrup.
Kadayıf: cake made from shredded pastry dough, filled with syrup and nuts or cream.
Kazandibi: milk pudding, traditionally with very finely chopped chicken breast.
Kemel pasha: small round cakes soaked in honey.
Keşkül: milk pudding with almonds and coconut, topped with pistachios.
Lokum: turkish delight.
Sütlaç: rice pudding.

It's not hard to see why this branch of Tas is usually busy. The location is fantastic, between Waterloo and Southwark stations and near both Vic theatres; the space is bright and inviting; the menus and website do an excellent job of enthusiastically extolling the virtues of Anatolian cuisine; and the pricing is pretty irresistible. The catch, unsurprisingly, is that the food is unexceptional. Apart from a damp, soggy cheese börek and an over-lemony tabouleh, nothing on our visit was bad, and the lamb köfte main was cheeringly flavourful, if a little on the dry side. Everything else was a good example of chain-restaurant mediocrity – blandly seasoned, inoffensively spiced, but tried-and-tested to the point of high-street reliability. The türlü, a mixed vegetable stew with couscous and yoghurt, was particularly dull (and the potatoes were undercooked). Nevertheless, you can get a substantial meal for around £13 here, including bread, yoghurt and salad at the start and turkish delight at the end. Service is speedy, the wine list has depth, and the atmosphere fits the bill – yet you'd only come here to eat before heading somewhere more exciting.
Babies and children welcome: high chairs; nappy-changing facilities. Booking advisable dinner. Disabled: toilet. Tables outdoors

(6, pavement). Takeaway service. Vegetarian menu. **Map 11 N8.**
For branches (EV Restaurant, Bar & Delicatessen, Tas) see index.

South East
Lewisham

Meze Mangal
245 Lewisham Way, SE4 1XF (8694 8099, www.mezemangal.co.uk). St John's rail or Lewisham rail/DLR. **Meals served** noon-1am daily. **Main courses** £6.50-£15.50. **Credit** MC, V.
Low-key, but with a tremendous following, Meze Mangal is owned by brothers Sahin and Ahmet Gok. They've clearly made no serious attempt to decorate their unassuming restaurant: there are no posters, no paintings, nothing. The dining area is a simple room with tables and chairs and a massive charcoal grill, and, thankfully, this grill consistently delivers the goods. The tavuk beyti is a delight: a lean, slightly blackened minced chicken kebab, firmly seasoned with garlic and parsley, and served with yoghurt and salad. Our patlıcan kebab took 40 minutes to prepare (we were forewarned), but it was

worth the wait. The minced lamb was flecked with the red of chilli and delivered a spicy kick, while the aubergine melted in the mouth. The meze was standard fare: a tarama salad was fresh-tasting and generously portioned, and the kisir benefited from the crunch of crushed hazelnuts – not usually found in the dish. Service is efficient, prices are reasonable and portion sizes are big. Another bonus is the large number of Turkish bottles on the wine list: a rarity in London. This is easily the best Turkish restaurant in the area, and is comparable to many places on Green Lanes.
Babies and children welcome: high chairs. Booking advisable; essential weekends. Takeaway service. Vegetarian menu.

North East
Dalston

Mangal Ocakbasi
10 Arcola Street, E8 2DJ (7275 8981, www.mangal1.com). Dalston Kingsland rail or 67, 76, 149, 243 bus. **Meals served** noon-midnight daily. **Main courses** £10-£17.50. **Corkage** no charge. **No credit cards.**

Gökyüzü

Some things have changed round here since Mangal Ocakbasi opened over 20 years ago. A *Time Out* review from the early 1990s framed on the wall shows how prices have tripled: two could feast for a tenner back then. But other things have stayed the same. The restaurant still excels at grilled meat; the enormous mangal by the entrance, which pumps smoke halfway down Arcola Street, has never failed us yet. Don't bother with the starters – we weren't moved by bog-standard tarama, houmous and patlıcan salata ungenerously smeared on to small plates. But the cop şiş and the tavuk beyti were everything we had hoped for: the first, the most rich and succulent grilled lamb we've had anywhere; and the tavuk, a delicately garlicky, melty kebab of minced chicken. This is a tatty place that relies upon its grill chefs juggling skewers and flipping meat for character, and service could be friendlier. But the kebabs here still sing, and that's all that really matters.
Available for hire. Babies and children welcome: high chairs. Booking advisable. Disabled: toilet. Takeaway service. **Map 25 C4.**

Mangal II
4 Stoke Newington Road, N16 8BH (7254 7888, www.mangal2.com). Dalston Kingsland rail or 76, 149, 243 bus. **Meals served** noon-12.45am Mon-Sat; noon-11.45pm Sun. **Main courses** £6.95-£15.45. **Set lunch** (noon-4pm Mon-Fri) £9.95 2 courses incl soft drink. **Credit** AmEx, MC, V.
Variety is the spice of life, unless you're artists Gilbert and George, who eat here every night and have done for years. We saw them arrive at 8pm, sit at their favourite table, and ask for exactly what they'd been eating every night for the past few weeks (our waiter revealed they do intermittently try something new). Perhaps the duo should check out some local alternatives, as Mangal II isn't quite at the top of its game. The bread looked the part, thin and lightly crusted, but was lukewarm, didn't taste fresh and arrived alone – the izgara sogan (grilled onions with pomegranate juice) you get for free elsewhere on Kingsland Road costs £4.95 here. More disappointingly, tavuk tava (pan-fried chicken) was tepid and chewy. The Mangal special main (baked aubergine with spinach, potatoes, peppers, tomatoes and cheese) was generously portioned and not oily, but also lukewarm. At least the doner kebab succeeded. This is one of the few proper restaurants to serve the much-maligned dish, and it's done well, with high-quality lamb steak and minimal grease. However, Mangal II needs a bit more spark – and much more heat – to compete, although some customers will doubtless keep dining here regardless.
Babies and children welcome: high chairs. Booking advisable. Separate room for parties, seats 45. Takeaway service. **Map 25 C4.**

19 Numara Bos Cirrik I
34 Stoke Newington Road, N16 7XJ (7249 0400, www.cirrik1.co.uk). Dalston Kingsland rail or 76, 149, 243 bus. **Meals served** noon-midnight daily. **Main courses** £9.50-£13.50. **Set meal** £14.75 (minimum 2). **Licensed**. **Corkage** £5. **Credit** MC, V.
Benefiting from Dalston's gentrification, 19 Numara Bos Cirrik has firmly established itself as the hipsters' ocakbaşı of choice, yet standards haven't slipped at this ever-busy joint. First impressions are positive: the bread is piping-hot, feather-light, smoky and carrying hints of onion and tomato. As it's grilled right beside the kebabs, waiters helpfully

warn customers the bread may contain 'meat juice'. The pide is every bit as good. Our sucuklu yumurtali pide (pepperoni and egg) was delicate and golden, with crisp edges and just the right amount of cheddar, tomato and green peppers. Another main, lamb beyti, was excellent too, its balance of garlic, chilli and smoky charcoal flavour just right. However, starters were bland: imam bayıldı didn't seem fresh and the mücver needed more dill and mint to give it flavour. The restaurant's interior doesn't have much personality to speak of, and the piped muzak doesn't help. Service can be aloof and it would be nice to see more than two Turkish bottles on the wine list. Nevertheless, with sensible pricing, solid cooking and nice little touches such as izgara sogan (grilled onions in pomegranate sauce) coming with every meal, this east London institution remains a good bet.
Available for hire. Babies and children welcome: high chairs. Booking advisable. Separate room for parties, seats 40. Takeaway service. Vegetarian menu. **Map 25 C4.**
For branches see index.

★ Red Art
113 Kingsland High Street, E8 2PB (7254 3256). Dalston Junction or Dalston Kingsland rail. **Meals served** 10am-11pm Mon-Fri; 10am-midnight Sat. **Main courses** £6.25-£12.50. **Credit** (over £10) AmEx, MC, V.
It's not easy finding Turkish breakfasts in London, but Red Art opens early and offers several versions of menemen, a hearty dish of scrambled eggs, tomatoes and green peppers, similar to the North African shakshouka. The sucuk (sausages) version comes in a large silver pan with a basket of bread – it's a fantastic breakfast and good value at around £4.50. Balık ekmek, a grilled mackerel sandwich, is even harder to find in London, and we think this may be the only version. It might not be as fresh as the just-caught version sold along the banks of the Bosphorus, but it could do with some chilli and lemon, but it's good enough to sate our cravings. Everything else we've tried on the menu has been unspectacular yet generously portioned and ludicrously cheap; the £6 meze sampler works as a light meal for two people. Staff can be a bit grumpy, but the mood lighting creates a pleasant atmosphere and the pavement seating is excellent for people-watching.
Available for hire. Babies and children welcome: high chairs. Booking advisable. Tables outdoors (8, garden; 4, terrace). Takeaway service. **Map 25 B4.**

North
Finsbury Park

Petek
94-96 Stroud Green Road, N4 3EN (7619 3933). Finsbury Park tube/rail. **Meals served** 2-11pm Mon-Thur; noon-11pm Fri-Sun. **Main courses** £8.60-£17.80. **Set meal** £9.45-£10.85 2 courses. **Set meze** £7.85-£9.85 per person (minimum 2). **Credit** AmEx, MC, V.
With a tiny bit of tweaking, Petek could be a wonderful place for an evening meal. Old photos of Istanbul and maps from when that city was still Constantinople cover the walls; the open kitchen at the back is a hive of noise, movement and alluring aromas; and dozens of colourful lamps hang in the kitchen. But there are too many lights – the place

felt like a furniture showroom – and the lack of music didn't help matters. Everything else is spot-on: the food is generously portioned and reasonably priced, the service is efficient and affable, and the cooking is excellent. Large green olives, pillowy soft bread and a fiery chilli sauce appear within moments of arriving, and the starters impress: houmous made with just the right amount of oil and lifted by pomegranate seeds, and a white cheese börek with perfectly light pastry. The köfte main was first-rate; a splash of yoghurt took the edge off the chilli mixed into the minced lamb. Grilled chicken with aubergine sauce was devoured with equal relish: its sauce as smooth and smoky as a Lebanese moutabal dip. Petek is a busy, friendly, industrious local restaurant – but easy on the lighting, please.
Babies and children welcome: high chairs. Tables outdoors (3, pavement). Takeaway service.

Harringay

★ Diyarbakir
69 Green Lanes, N4 1DU (8809 2777). Harringay or Harringay Green Lanes rail. **Meals served** 8am-2am daily. **Main courses** £8-£12. **Unlicensed** no alcohol allowed. **No credit cards**.
Even by Green Lanes standards, Diyarbakir, named after an Anatolian city, offers exceptional value. A meal costing less than £30 fed two of us twice, including lunch the following day. The freebies alone are substantial: a tart, lively salad of mint, onion, tomatoes and fresh spinach in a pomegranate dressing; a huge bowl of cacik; and plenty of slightly glazed bread with a rich, buttery flavour. We were intrigued to see şakşuka on the menu, which (unlike the similarly named North African dish) contains no egg, but tomatoes, aubergine and potatoes; the Diyarbakir version is garlicky and, of course, served in a vast portion. The addition of croûtons in a buttery tomato sauce gave the halep kebab main course a slightly odd texture, but the minced lamb was plentiful and vigorously spicy. Chicken şiş, served with grilled tomatoes, green peppers, rice and salad, also hit the spot. On a follow-up trip, we sampled superb lahmacun: crisp, soft and spicy. Like many Green Lanes restaurants, service is hurried and there's little to say about the interior beyond its exposed brick arch and slightly cramped seating. Alcohol isn't allowed, so copy the locals and order aryan, a yoghurt drink, by the jug.
Available for hire. Babies and children welcome: high chairs. Booking advisable. Disabled: toilet. Takeaway service.

★ ★ Gökyüzü **HOT 50**
26-27 Grand Parade, N4 1LG (8211 8406, www.gokyuzurestaurant.co.uk). Harringay or Harringay Green Lanes rail. **Meals served** 9am-12.30am daily. **Main courses** £6.90-£14.50. **Credit** MC, V.
If our informal poll of passers-by on Green Lanes is anything to go by, Gökyüzü is the go-to place for Turkish food in London's main Turkish neighbourhood. This large, utilitarian restaurant (it doubled in size some years ago) is consistently the busiest place on the strip. It's clear why: the prices are low; the cooking is excellent; and the portions are generous bordering on reckless. We were almost sated after demolishing a basket of bread cooked in the wood-fired oven and a huge 'small' mixed meze dish – highlights being a sprightly kısır

TURKISH

Antepliler

loaded with mint and spring onion, a haydari rich with dill, and a fresh-tasting soslu patlıcan (grilled aubergine with tomato sauce). The mains were exceptional. Sarma tavuk beyti featured no less than 15 large pieces of spicy minced chicken wrapped in lavash bread, slathered in tomato sauce and served with yoghurt and pilaf rice. Güveç (lamb and aubergine casserole) had been stewed to tender perfection in an earthenware pot. Service tends to be rushed and the wine list is short (there are only five whites), but you wouldn't come here for a leisurely drink. Food is the thing at Gökyüzü. *Babies and children welcome: high chairs. Disabled: toilet. Takeaway service.*

★ **Selale**

2 Salisbury Promenade, Green Lanes, N8 0RX (8800 1636). Turnpike Lane tube or Harringay Green Lanes rail or bus 29, 141. **Open** 6am-2am daily. **Main courses** £9.50-£12.90. **Set meal** £12.75 (minimum 2). **Credit** MC, V.

If Selale looks familiar on your first visit, it's probably because the venue is almost indistinguishable from several other restaurants in the locality. The interior looks dreary – a big, bland and beige canteen – although a covered terrace offers a more cheery alternative. What sets this northernmost Green Lanes eaterie apart from the local competition, however, are the extras: the free things that land on your table regardless of what you order. Admittedly, the houmous, potato salad and fresh greens were pedestrian, but it's a nice touch. Unfortunately, the starter we paid for was poor: a stingy portion of vine leaves. Why do so many restaurants seem to serve them straight from a can? But the cheese, egg and sausage pide was fantastic: its thin, crusty, golden base just thick enough to soak up a calorific coalescence of runny yolk and gooey cheese. Selale has a strong reputation for grilled meat, and the lamb beyti was every bit as succulent and full-flavoured as we'd hoped. Our meal for two cost £25 and we had enough left over for another meal each: fantastic value at one of Green Lanes' better restaurants. *Available for hire. Babies and children welcome: high chairs. Disabled: toilet. Tables outdoors (12, pavement). Takeaway service.*

Highbury

Iznik

19 Highbury Park, N5 1QJ (7354 5697, www.iznik.co.uk). Highbury & Islington tube/ rail or bus 4, 19, 236. **Meals served** 10.30am-11pm daily. **Main courses** £8.25-£13.95. **Credit** AmEx, MC, V.

You can't say the husband-and-wife team behind Iznik haven't made an effort: almost every inch of this cute neighbourhood restaurant has been filled with lanterns, plants, traditional clothing and beautiful tablecloths. There are Turkish star and crescent symbols carved into the chairs and a portrait of Mustafa Kemal Atatürk perched by the entrance. It's all just about the right side of chintzy – and it's pretty clear that just as much attention has been directed towards the food. The starters were on the small side, but lamb börek benefited from ethereally light pastry, cacik pulled a spicy punch, and calamares was crisp, light and not in the least chewy. Chicken shish, again a bit small, was adequate but the hünkar beğendi (lamb stew with aubergine sauce) glowed; the sauce was spectacularly thick, creamy and luscious, and the meat fell apart at the prod of a fork. Iznik's wine

list is well-chosen and helpfully descriptive; there's Efes beer on tap; and while service was disconcertingly silent throughout our meal, we found the Northern Cypriot owners very friendly when engaged in conversation. Recommended.
Available for hire. Babies and children welcome: high chairs. Booking advisable; essential weekends. Takeaway service.

Islington

★ Antepliler

139 Upper Street, N1 1PQ (7226 5441, www.anteplilerrestaurant.com). Angel tube or Highbury & Islington tube/rail. **Meals served** noon-11pm daily. **Main courses** £9.50-£13.90. **Set meal** £19.50 3 courses. **Credit** MC, V.

There are two very different Anteplilers in north London. The Green Lanes branch is a straightforward, functional canteen; but this time we visited the Upper Street restaurant, which feels like it's been lifted straight out of a lifestyle magazine. Blue neon mosaics on a black background, making the venue resemble an Ottoman-themed nightclub, are an acquired taste. Thankfully, there's nothing showy about the food, some of which originates in Gaziantep province, near the border with Syria. One south-eastern dish we haven't seen elsewhere in London was a highlight: ciğ köfte combines raw lamb with bulgar wheat, chilli, garlic and parsley to fantastic effect. The vegetarian version of the dish made with lentils was almost as good, and we scooped up both with wonderfully light, puffy flatbread. We also loved Antepliler's houmous: thick, creamy and enhanced by a sprinkling of sumac. Ali nazak, a main course of diced lamb with yoghurt and mashed smoked aubergine, had been correctly prepared, but we found the combination overwhelmingly rich. Lamb adana kebab, another recipe from Turkey's south-east, was simple, well-proportioned and skilfully executed. The wine list is short and fairly predictable, but service is charming and the pre-theatre menu is an excellent deal. Impressive.
Available for hire. Babies and children welcome: high chairs. Tables outdoors (4, pavement). Takeaway service. Vegetarian menu. **Map 5 O1**. **For branch see index**.

Pasha

301 Upper Street, N1 2TU (7226 1454, www.pasharestaurant.co.uk). Angel tube or Highbury & Islington tube/rail. **Meals served** 11.30am-11pm Mon-Sun. **Main courses** £7.95-£14.95. **Set meal** £20.95 3 courses. **Set meze** lunch £9.95, dinner £12.95 (minimum 2). **Credit** AmEx, MC, V.

The sign outside doesn't lie: 'The food is generously served and priced'. Unfortunately, the cooking is not especially good. As Pasha enters its third decade, its kitchen is perhaps showing signs of complacency. Our meal was mediocre at best, terrible at worst. The nadir came early: a portion of dried-out white pitta bread, served on its own without any oil or dips. It tasted as if it had been heated up days ago – a terrible first impression. The stuffed vine leaves were also poor. The menu describes them as homemade, so there's undoubtedly someone in the kitchen with an uncanny talent for making stuffed vine leaves as uniform, dense and lifeless as those sold in cans – and £4.50 for four is stingy. Imam bayıldı was

passable, although the aubergine skin was rather chewy. Lamb and chicken iskender barely passed muster; copious yoghurt couldn't mask the meat's lack of flavour. Kapama was the best dish we ate: a duck leg with a generous quantity of walnuts and pomegranate seeds, but again the meat was insipid and characterless, and the gravy overpowering. Yes, the staff are friendly and this remains a pleasant venue in a great location, but the food needs to improve.
Available for hire. Babies and children welcome: high chairs. Booking advisable. Tables outdoors (2, pavement). Takeaway service. **Map 5 O1**.

North West
Belsize Park

Zara

11 South End Road, NW3 2PT (7794 5498). Belsize Park tube or Hampstead Heath rail. **Meals served** noon-11.30pm daily. **Main courses** £9-£15. **Credit** AmEx, MC, V.

In an area woefully short of interesting dining options, Zara does what it needs to do to remain one of the better local choices for an evening out. The setting is certainly pleasant – with large french windows to let in the light, and shelves holding books and musical instruments – but the food on our visit was a mixed bag. Successes included böreği, the cigar-shaped pastry snacks filled with green lentils and onions, and the inegol köfte, a spice-spiked dish of minced lamb meatballs from north-western Turkey: we've rarely had meat so packed with flavour. But there were also failures. A tiny portion of tabouleh lacked lemon juice and oil, making it too dry; and the chicken güveç needed more cinnamon, cumin, molasses or anything to give it more flavour, and perhaps some rice to soak it up. There's a strong wine list and a larger than usual vegetarian menu, but service on our visit was a bit cheerless. Zara does the job if you're in the area, though it doesn't compare to London's better Turkish restaurants.
Available for hire. Babies and children welcome: high chairs. Booking essential weekends. Tables outdoors (2, pavement). Takeaway service. Vegetarian menu. **Map 28 C3**.

Vegetarian

Artifice versus nature: it's a defining cultural conflict of our times, and it is played out in microcosm in London's vegetarian dining scene. On one side is the raw food movement, whose advocates search for assemblies of ingredients that are processed with minimal application of heat. Nutrients, goes the theory, will be better preserved and their health-giving properties remain undiminished, if fruit and vegetables are eaten uncooked. The **Wild Food Café** is one proponent of this style, offering high-quality ingredients creatively prepared, though even here there's also a choice of cooked dishes. But vegetarian food also lends itself to artifice: from the lamentable mock-meat sausages of supermarket freezer cabinets, to the inventive, texturally diverse creations found at **Vanilla Black**. That's not to reject the mainstays of this section, however: those time-honoured venues where vegetarianism is just one part of a creed devoted to sustainable, pacific living. Nor need this creed be at the expense of good eating: the accomplished, eclectic cooking found at **Mildred's** and **The Gate** provide proof of that particular pudding.

For a truly special vegetarian meal, however, you may have to look elsewhere in the Guide – among our favourites are **Murano** (*p153*), **Kopapa** (*p214*) and **Grain Store** (*p195*), while top-flight vegetarian menus can be found at **L'Atelier de Joël Robuchon** (*p193*), **Hélène Darroze at the Connaught** (*p124*) and **Morgan M** (*p85*). Indian vegetarian restaurants (*pp129-147*) also reward exploration, and many modern cafés (*pp271-283*) offer vibrant and interesting veggie food.

Food for Thought

Central
Chancery Lane

Vanilla Black
17-18 Tooks Court, off Cursitor Street, EC4A 1LB (7242 2622, www.vanillablack.co.uk). Chancery Lane tube. **Lunch served** noon-2.15pm Mon-Fri. **Dinner served** 6-9.45pm Mon-Sat. **Set lunch** £18.50 2 courses, £23.50 3 courses. **Set dinner** £28 2 courses, £38 3 courses. **Credit** AmEx, MC, V.
An unusual proposition if ever there was one. From the outside, Vanilla Black is your average smart restaurant frequented by well-heeled couples young and old, and the odd suit. Even the menu gives no clue as to what awaits. The advent of a spoon was the first indication that a dish might not be what we expected, shortly before a deconstructed jacket potato arrived: a bowl of 'mash' with a swirl of tomato syrup and chunks of wensleydale lurking at the bottom. Another heavily stylised dish was a veritable tableau of toasted puffed rice towers, leek 'buildings' and fluffy iced lemon dumplings. A parade of textures, tastes and temperatures surprised at every mouthful. Continuing on the 'whatever next?' theme, desserts included builder's

tea ice-cream and liquid doughnut. Service is discreet and attentive, and the atmosphere is relatively muted – though you'll notice a fair bit of smiling and smirking as dishes arrive at tables. This is clever cooking and, in the main, successful. You're unlikely to have tasted anything quite like it before.
Babies and children admitted. Booking advisable Fri, Sat. Vegan dishes. **Map 11 N6**.

Covent Garden

★ Food for Thought
31 Neal Street, WC2H 9PR (7836 0239, http://foodforthought-london.co.uk). Covent Garden tube. **Meals served** noon-8pm Mon-Sat. **Lunch served** noon-5pm Sun. **Main courses** £4.90-£8. **Minimum** (noon-3pm, 6-7.30pm Mon-Sat) £4. **No credit cards**.
This vegetarian stalwart has hardly changed in 40 years. Is that a good thing? Students, artists, tourists and faithful vegetarians head down the narrow stairs to the basement to be greeted by the same 1970s pine furniture, cramped seating and probably almost the same menu: a vegetable curry or similar, quiche, soup and salad. That's precisely what keeps devotees returning: guaranteed cheap, hearty food in a convivial setting (you'll almost

certainly be sharing your space with a total stranger). The meal-deals of soup and a salad for £7.20 or a hot dish and salad for £8.40 aren't, however, quite the bargain they once were; Orchard, for instance, offers soup and a sarnie for £7.95 and the quality is better. Desserts are of the gut-busting variety yet nonetheless very good – leave plenty of room for the apple and plum crumble. Small gripes: the food isn't always piping hot; the flavours aren't especially exciting; and this is not a place to hang around and chat. That said, if it ain't broke… Takeaway is available on the ground floor.
Babies and children admitted. Bookings not accepted. Takeaway service. Vegan dishes.
Map 18 D3.

★ Wild Food Café
1st floor, 14 Neal's Yard, WC2H 9DP (7419 2014, www.wildfoodcafe.com). Covent Garden tube. **Meals served** noon-4.30pm Mon, Tue; noon-9.30pm Wed-Sun. **Main courses** £5.30-£14.50. **Credit** MC, V.
Its airy first-floor location is just one of the draws of this little café overlooking Neal's Yard. On a sunny day, light streams through the wall of windows on to big pine tables that accommodate large groups of friends who haven't met yet. Food is prepared behind a horseshoe bar laden with huge bowls of fruit and bright vegetables. Service is genuinely friendly (open smiles, helpful suggestions) and the cooking is both creative and of a high quality. The short menu focuses on 'raw' – food that hasn't lost any nutrients or flavour through cooking – but for those who prefer their food served above body temperature, there are warmer options such as 'sunfood' soup of the day with toasted sourdough. Vegans are well catered for too; sections of the menu are labelled 'plant foods only'. A dish of the day of mixed meze was a riot of colour, texture and flavour, with standouts being fig, pomegranate and mint salad, and dolmades stuffed with cauliflower 'rice' and sun-dried tomato. Monmouth coffee and organic wines are available, along with cold-pressed organic juices such as 'vibrant green': full of green fruit and veg, with a lemon and ginger kick. More juices and smoothies – with names like 'youthful', 'mighty' and 'flexible' – can be found at the Wild Juicery bar next door.
Available for hire. Babies and children welcome: high chair. Takeaway service. Vegan dishes.
Map 18 D3.

Holborn

★ Orchard
11 Sicilian Avenue, WC1A 2QH (7831 2715, www.orchard-kitchen.co.uk). Holborn tube. **Meals served** 8am-7.30pm Mon-Fri; 9.30am-6.30pm Sat. **Main courses** £4.95-£9.95. **Credit** MC, V.
The younger, more casual sister of the classy Vanilla Black can be found amid the ornate edifices of pedestrianised Sicilian Avenue. Orchard attracts local workers, tourists and, increasingly, those seeking excellent coffee from artisan roasters Ozone. There's something remarkably cosy about the homespun interior – painted brick and sage-green tongue-and-groove walls combined with old-school wooden chairs. On the menu you'll find casual yet accomplished food at surprisingly reasonable prices. Simple-sounding dishes served on mismatching china are given a twist: a sandwich could be Ribblesdale vintage cheddar and onion chutney on wild garlic granary, or a hot plate might

Wild Food Café

be a perfectly poached egg on a spinach fritter with deliciously smoky mayo. The relaxed atmosphere, aided by friendly and solicitous staff, encourages diners to linger over that great coffee and try the scrummy cakes. Those in a rush pick up treats such as salted toffee, tonka bean and rhubarb jam biscuits, and bags of (ground or bean) coffee to take away.
Babies and children admitted. Bookings not accepted. Tables outdoors (8, pavement). Takeaway service. Vegan dishes. **Map 18 E1**.

Soho

★ Mildreds
45 Lexington Street, W1F 9AN (7494 1634, www.mildreds.co.uk). Oxford Circus or Piccadilly Circus tube. **Meals served** noon-11pm Mon-Sat. **Main courses** £8.10-£10.50. **Credit** MC, V.
Serving the veggie massive for more than a quarter of a century, Mildreds has earned the right to call itself a Soho institution. There's a no-bookings policy, so expect a lively queue hovering around the front bar area (where you can be seated reasonably quickly) and an even longer wait for a (shared) table in the cosy restaurant beyond. The welcome is warm, the vibes good and the menu inventive, drawing on Asian and Middle Eastern dishes to impressive effect: gyoza dumplings with a mirin and soy sauce were well textured and tasty, and the substantial burrito special was equally satisfying, though our 'burger' (daily changing) was disappointingly squishy. Creative desserts are worth making room for and, like the mains, include vegan and gluten-free options, such as the delicious-sounding persian lemon, almond and pistachio polenta cake with rose petal syrup. Being virtuous has never been so much fun; even the wine, coffee, tea and milk are organic. Service is perky yet relaxed, ensuring that this place will surely remain on the hot list of every vegetarian (and their equally happy non-vegetarian friends) for another 25 years.
Babies and children welcome: high chairs. Bookings not accepted. Separate room for parties, seats 14. Tables outdoors (2, pavement). Takeaway service. Vegan dishes. **Map 17 A4**.

North East

Walthamstow

★ Hornbeam Café

458 Hoe Street, E17 9AH (8558 6880, www.hornbeam.org.uk). Walthamstow Central tube/rail. **Meals served** 11am-3pm Mon-Fri; 10.30am-4pm Sat. **Main courses** £3.80-£5.80. **No credit cards.**

The wall outside the Hornbeam is lined with part-used paint pots for the taking, and adverts for cheap scaffolding boards. Inside, the walls are covered in notices for yoga and t'ai chi classes, and information on how to live sustainably. So, no question as to where this café's heart lies. The welcome is friendly, the atmosphere relaxed and the food mainly sourced from OrganicLea. Even the bread is own-made by the Hornbeam Bakers' Collective. The daily changing menu is short, on our visit comprising a soup, a tabouleh dish and a salad – though toast and a host of cakes, including banana bread, were also available. The food isn't especially adventurous, but it is fresh, wholesome and satisfying. There's bread for sale, as well as a variety of chutneys and jams, and even some hand-carved wooden paraphernalia, as well as free Wi-Fi. Exciting? No, but we can't help liking this place. *Available for hire. Babies and children welcome: high chairs; nappy-changing facilities. Disabled: toilet. Vegan dishes.*

North

Camden Town & Chalk Farm

Manna

4 Erskine Road, NW3 3AJ (7722 8028, www.mannav.com). Chalk Farm tube or bus 31, 168. **Lunch served** noon-3pm Sat,

Orchard. See p257.

Sun. **Dinner served** 6.30-10.15pm Tue-Sun. **Main courses** £10-£14. **Credit** AmEx, MC, V.

Regent's Park Road has no shortage of dining options but Manna has been serving the health-conscious of Primrose Hill for almost 50 years, which inspires a certain confidence. Diners can choose between the pretty, fairy-lit interior or the two (ours slightly sticky) tables in the skinny glass-fronted conservatory. For starters, three cashew cheese balls with spicy dipping sauce were (though meagre) well textured and tasty, and floury tortilla with grilled vegetables was equally well executed; the knockout dish, however, was a delicious special of aubergine wraps with almond cheese. While a fine idea, the 'build your own' mixed meze was disappointing: along with a ho-hum houmous, a small serving of black beans had no discernible seasoning. The chef's custom-created five-course menu (minimum four people) is useful for those with dietary restrictions, and includes an aperitif and glass of house wine. Desserts – variously raw, gluten-free and vegan – include a 'cake of the day' from Manna's organic bakery (think rich sugar-free fruit cake, or spiced carrot cake stuffed with pineapple and walnuts), along with ice-creams and tarts. Service from polite, though occasionally distracted, staff was adequate but we came away thinking that, with prices not cheap and competition so fierce, it might be time for Manna to up its game. *Babies and children welcome: children's menu; high chairs. Booking essential weekends. Tables outdoors (2, terrace). Takeaway service. Vegan dishes.* **Map 27 A1.**

Islington

★ The Gate

370 St John Street, EC1V 4NN (7278 5483, www.thegaterestaurants.com). Angel tube. **Brunch served** 10am-3pm Sat, Sun. **Lunch served** noon-2.30pm Mon-Fri. **Dinner served** 6-10.30pm daily. **Main courses** £12.50-£15.50. **Set meal** (5.30-7.30pm) £15 2 courses. **Credit** AmEx, MC, V.

First impressions augured well: on a midweek night, every table was full and the place was humming. Our neighbours had schlepped all the way from Hammersmith while their favourite restaurant – the original Gate – was being refurbished (due to reopen autumn 2013). This is a class act, with a modern and airy interior featuring an open kitchen/bar and big industrial lights under which to examine the menu. There are plenty of à la carte starters and mains and, for the indecisive, a great meze menu – one plate for £4, three for £10, five for £15. Every dish was beautifully presented, with a little dish of aïoli, pepper coulis or harissa to complement the leading flavours: halloumi skewers; artichoke tempura; crunchy balls of couscous, feta and mint; tortilla with tasty beetroot and goat's cheese filling. Desserts are no less fabulous: lavender crème brûlée; apple tarte tatin with cinnamon ice-cream; and, genius this, even a dessert meze (allow 15 minutes) for £15. We've already planned to go back for the weekend brunch, not least because we love the sound of the mamoosa – pan-fried potato with tomato, scrambled eggs and coriander, served with salad and schoog (green chilli dip). Vegetarian food never tasted so good. *Babies and children welcome: high chairs; nappy-changing facilities. Booking essential. Disabled: toilet. Vegan dishes.* **Map 5 O3.** **For branch see index.**

Vietnamese

It was a matter of great fortune to London's Vietnamese dining scene that its genesis preceded the rise of Hoxton, Shoreditch and Hackney as centres for clubbing, bar-hopping and general trendiness. Pioneers such as **Hai-Ha** and **Huong-Viet** set up in the late 1990s as simple cafés to cater for the local Vietnamese community, but soon found bright young things among their customers, indulging in a bowl of pho before a night out. Star performers such as **Green Papaya** and **Song Que** – the latter still at the top of the pile after more than a decade – opened as the area was taking off, and the 'pho corridor' became established. The next phase of development is now well in progress, with great places popping up elsewhere in London. Some of our favourites are **Cây Tre** in Soho, Hammersmith's **Saigon Saigon** and **Da Nang**, and **Café East** in Surrey Quays. Street food forms an important part of Vietnamese cuisine, and this year we've listed some of the top practitioners providing baguette-like banh mi: a trend that's been growing over the last few years.

Central
Soho

★ Cây Tre

42-43 Dean Street, W1D 4PZ (7317 9118,
www.caytresoho.co.uk). Leicester Square tube.
Meals served noon-10.45pm Mon-Thur;
noon-11.15pm Fri, Sat; noon-9.45pm Sun.
Main courses £8-£15. **Set meal** £23
3 courses (minimum 2). **Credit** MC, V.
Part of the Vietnamese Kitchen group, with branches in Hoxton and Shoreditch, Cây Tre is just what you might imagine a Vietnamese restaurant in Soho to be like: chic, minimal decor; impeccably smart and efficient black-clad staff; and beautifully served food. Customers are very mixed – tourists, Chinatown youngsters looking for something fresh, and a smattering of techies and media types. The chain prides itself on using all fresh (ideally local) ingredients with impeccable provenance – witness the delectable Devon crab wrap with crisp lettuce and perilla leaves (in which to roll up the super-tasty filling); grilled Cornish scallops in spring onion oil, roasted peanuts and nuoc cham; and barbecued Somerset ribs with lemongrass, Sriracha chilli sauce and galangal. The menu is peppered with imaginative combinations, such as a delicious textural treat of grilled squid stuffed with duck pâté, or braised ox cheek pho with lemongrass and coriander. Thoughtfully, counters with stools have been provided by the entrance, facing the street, for

Cây Tre

hai hà
Vietnamese Restaurant

Hai Ha was the first Vietnamese Restaurant in Mare Street, Hackney, which opened in 1998. Having recently enjoyed a face lift, including the addition of air-conditioning, Hai Ha offers a modern yet cosy feel with subtle lighting and unfussy furnishing.

The freshest ingredients are used to make your Vietnamese meal truly authentic and our regular customers include Vietnamese natives who appreciate the tastes of our traditional Vietnamese dishes, including the chef's signature Pho which is taken straight from our home kitchens, providing truly amazing flavours from start to finish.

Come to Hai Ha for Vietnamese food at affordable prices. We are the perfect place for your lunch break or casual evening dining and we are now licensed & serving well priced wines and beers. Or simply bring your own (corkage will be charged).

Come and join us for some real Vietnamese Food
Open for Lunch and Dinner

www.haiha.co.uk

206 Mare Street,
Hackney,
London E8 3RD
T: 020 8985 5388

TAKE AWAY
& DELIVERY
AVAILABLE
Restaurant available
for private hire

those in a hurry or singletons. A big choice of cocktails leaves little room for a decent wine list. Loud piped music throbs through the place – enjoyable, but not conducive to conversation.

Sister restaurant Viet Grill in Shoreditch has had a makeover, and now has a dining room with a new menu, and a retro-styled Vietnamese cocktail bar. *Babies and children welcome: nappy-changing facilities. Booking advisable. Disabled: toilet. Takeaway service.* **Map 17 B4**. **For branches (Cây Tre, Viet Grill) see index**.

West

Hammersmith

★ Da Nang NEW
216 King Street, W6 0RA (8748 2584, www.danangkitchen.com). Ravenscourt Park tube. **Lunch served** noon-2.30pm Thur-Sun. **Dinner served** 5.30-11pm Mon-Sat; 5.30-10pm Sun. **Main courses** £7-£10. **Set lunch** (Mon-Fri) £7.95 2 courses. **Credit** MC, V.

It's easy to miss Da Nang, with its narrow, dull metallic-grey façade on a busy nondescript bend of King Street – but this is a local find. Inside, the dining room is surprisingly capacious, with traditional oriental decor centred on a somewhat ungainly fish tank. There are some appealing touches, like the neatly pressed white cloth napkins, and staff who are very welcoming and eager to please. The chef, singing tunefully as he cooked, added to the merry mood. The long menu is equally traditional, with all the usual Vietnamese repertoire plus a decent vegetarian selection, some steam-boat dishes and an amusing sprinkling of translation infelicities. Featured 'chef choices' include well-executed banh xeo (crispy Vietnamese pancake filled with tiger prawns, squid and pork, with mixed herb salad and dipping sauce) and banh canh (thick rice noodles in broth with fish, tiger prawns and squid). A weekday two-course lunch menu at £7.95 comprises such tasty delights as salt and chilli squid, and sea bream with spicy caramel sauce (look out for special offers on the website). Only three types of beer are offered, but the wine list is full and imaginative, and you can also get fresh lime juice and soya bean milk.
Available for hire. Babies and children welcome: high chairs. Booking advisable Thur-Sat. Disabled: toilet. Takeaway service; delivery service (Mon-Thur; over £15 within 2-mile radius). **Map 20 A4**.

★ Saigon Saigon
313-317 King Street, W6 9NH (8748 6887, www.saigon-saigon.co.uk). Ravenscourt Park or Stamford Brook tube. **Lunch served** noon-2.30pm Mon-Fri; noon-3pm Sat; 12.30-3pm Sun. **Dinner served** 6-10.30pm Mon, Sun; 6-11pm Tue-Thur; 6-11.30pm Fri, Sat. **Main courses** £6.95-£15. **Set lunch** (Mon-Fri) £9.95 2 courses. **Credit** MC, V.

West London is something of a desert for Vietnamese food, but this roomy, fairly smart place near Ravenscourt Park more than makes amends. As well as the two sizeable dining rooms – coolly decorated with dark wood, bamboo, and black and white photos of pre-war Saigon – there's a party room holding up to 16. In the basement is a lounge for private events, and in summer, tables are placed on the very wide, boulevard-style pavement. Service

Menu

Vietnamese cookery makes abundant use of fresh, fragrant herbs such as mint and sweet basil; it also utilises refreshing, sweet-sour dipping sauces known generically as nuoc cham. Look out for spices such as chilli, ginger and lemongrass, and crisp root vegetables pickled in sweetened vinegar.

Some dishes are assembled at the table in a way that is distinctively Vietnamese. Order a steaming bowl of pho (rice noodles and beef or chicken in an aromatic broth) and you'll be invited to add raw herbs, chilli and citrus juice as you eat. Crisp pancakes and grilled meats are served with herb sprigs, lettuce leaf wraps and piquant dipping sauces. Toss cold rice vermicelli with salad leaves, herbs and hot meat or seafood fresh from the grill. All these dishes offer an intriguing mix of tastes, temperatures and textures.

Aside from the pronounced Chinese influence on Vietnamese culinary culture, there are hints of the French colonial era (in sweet iced coffee, for example, and the use of beef), along with echoes of neighbouring South-east Asian cuisines. Within Vietnamese cooking itself there are several regional styles; the mix of immigrants in London means you can sample some of the styles here. The food of Hanoi and the north is known for its street snacks and plain, no-nonsense flavours and presentation. The former imperial capital Hue and its surrounding region are famed for a royal cuisine and robustly spicy soups; look out for Hue noodle soups (bun bo hue) on some menus. The food of the south and the former Saigon (now Ho Chi Minh City) is more elegant and colourful, and makes much greater use of fresh herbs (many of these unique to Vietnam), vegetables and fruit.

Banh cuon: pancake-like steamed rolls of translucent fresh rice pasta, sometimes stuffed with minced pork or shrimp (reminiscent in style of Chinese cheung fun, a dim sum speciality).
Banh pho: flat rice noodles used in soups and stir-fries, usually with beef.
Banh xeo: a large pancake made from a batter of rice flour and coconut milk, coloured bright yellow with turmeric and traditionally filled with prawns, pork, beansprouts and onion. To eat it, tear the pancake apart with your chopsticks, roll the pieces with sprigs of herbs in a lettuce leaf, and dip in nuoc cham (qv).
Bo la lot: grilled minced beef in betel leaves.

Bun: rice vermicelli, served in soups and stir-fries. They are also eaten cold, with raw salad vegetables and herbs, with a nuoc cham (qv) sauce poured over, and a topping such as grilled beef or pork – all of which are tossed together at the table.
Cha ca: North Vietnamese dish of fish served sizzling in an iron pan with plenty of dill.
Cha gio: deep-fried spring rolls. Unlike their Chinese counterparts, the wrappers are made from rice paper rather than sheets of wheat pastry, and pucker up deliciously after cooking.
Chao tom: grilled minced prawn on a baton of sugar cane.
Goi: salad. There are many types in Vietnam, but they often contain raw, crunchy vegetables and herbs, perhaps accompanied by chicken or prawns, with a sharp, perky dressing.
Goi cuon (literally 'rolled salad', often translated as 'fresh rolls' or 'salad rolls'): cool, soft, rice-paper rolls usually containing prawns, pork, fresh herbs and rice vermicelli, served with a thick sauce similar to satay sauce but made from hoi sin mixed with peanut butter, scattered with roasted peanuts.
Nem: north Vietnamese name for cha gio (qv).
Nom: north Vietnamese name for goi (qv).
Nuoc cham: the generic name for a wide range of dipping sauces, based on a paste of fresh chillies, sugar and garlic that is diluted with water, lime juice and the ubiquitous fish sauce, nuoc mam.
Nuoc mam: a brown or pale liquid derived from fish that have been salted and left to ferment. It's the essential Vietnamese seasoning, used in dips and as a cooking ingredient.
Pho: the most famous and best-loved of all Vietnamese dishes, a soup of rice noodles and beef or chicken in a rich, clear broth flavoured with aromatics. It's served with a dish of fresh beansprouts, red chilli and herbs, and a squeeze of lime; these are added to the soup at the table.
Rau thom: aromatic herbs, which might include Asian basil (**rau que**), mint (**rau hung**), red or purple perilla (**rau tia to**), lemony Vietnamese balm (**rau kinh gioi**) or saw-leaf herb (**ngo gai**).
Tuong: a general term for a thick sauce. One common tuong is a dipping sauce based on fermented soy beans, with hints of sweet and sour, often garnished with crushed roasted peanuts.

is unfailingly welcoming, polite and informative, and the standard of cooking reliably high. Pho is a treat here, with a strong base stock and all the power of traditional flavours and herbs. Particular delights include crisp vegetarian spring rolls, packed with vermicelli, wood-ear mushrooms and tofu; a splendidly crabby soft-shell crab with garlic and chilli; and juicy chargrilled quail marinated with honey, garlic and five-spice. A dish of melt-in-the-mouth stewed pork with quail's eggs was also memorable. The £9.95 two-course lunch menu includes the aforementioned pho and a drink. In contrast to the limited choice of beers, the wine list is pleasantly varied and international, with several excellent options.
Available for hire (bar). Babies and children welcome: high chairs. Booking advisable. Tables outdoors (4, pavement). Vegetarian menu. **Map 20 A4.**

South East
Surrey Quays

★ **Café East**
100 Redriff Row, SE16 7LH (7252 1212). Canada Water tube/rail or Surrey Quays rail. **Lunch served** 11am-3pm, **dinner served** 5.30-10.30pm Mon, Wed-Fri. **Meals served** 11am-10.30pm Sat; noon-10pm Sun. **Main courses** £6-£7.50. **Unlicensed** no alcohol allowed. **No credit cards.**
Once you've managed to find Café East – tucked in a far corner of the car park of the huge Surrey

Quays Shopping Centre – you might well think you've happened upon a South-east Asian workers' canteen. It's effectively one big room, with cream-painted walls but absolutely no attempt at decoration. The big utilitarian square tables are a little too high for the chairs, and are packed with happily guzzling South-east Asian customers. The menu is an edited-down list, each dish portrayed in an adjoining colour pic: a handful of starters, lots of substantial bowlfuls, some side dishes and a few soft drinks (but no alcohol). The herby summer rolls were a joy, and the beautifully flavoured pho with slices of beef, chicken and prawns was all it should be. Not only is the food impressive and authentic, it's inexpensive too, making this an ideal place for groups to enjoy a veritable Vietnamese banquet. Two points to remember: staff don't supply tap water, only bottled; and if you're walking or driving here, it's best to enter the car park via the little (quite hidden) entrance after the main route into the complex, Surrey Quays Road.
Babies and children welcome: high chairs. Bookings not accepted. Disabled: toilet. Takeaway service. Vegetarian menu.

East
Shoreditch

★ **Mien Tay**
122 Kingsland Road, E2 8DP (7729 3074, www.mientay.co.uk). Hoxton rail. **Lunch served** noon-3pm, **dinner served** 5-11pm Mon-Sat. **Meals served** noon-10.30pm Sun. **Main courses** £6-£12.50. **Credit** MC, V.

Much derided for its rather unimpressive, run-down façade and pretty shabby, paint-peeling decor (which could all be remedied fairly quickly and cheaply), Mien Tay is nevertheless a great place to get authentic, top-notch food. The two-roomed interior is cramped, and filled with staff who seem to do lots of unnecessary wandering up and down. The very reasonable prices attract a fairly young, mostly western clientele, and the idiosyncratic layout manages to accommodate at least one long table for parties, and two nicely tucked-away tables for duos. As for the food, stir-fried green mussels with ginger and spring onion was a delight: plump and tasty mussels, perfectly cooked à point, with a sauce that was spot-on. Scallops with black bean sauce were equally brilliant; the chef here obviously has a way with seafood. Lâu, or seafood hotpot (for a minimum of two diners) seems equally appealing. There's a short but excellent wine list, compiled for the restaurant by Bibendum, plus the two usual beers, Tiger and Saigon.
Babies and children welcome: high chairs. Disabled: toilet. Takeaway service. **Map 6 R3.**
For branch see index.

★ **Song Que**
134 Kingsland Road, E2 8DY (7613 3222). Hoxton rail. **Lunch served** noon-3pm, **dinner served** 5.30-11pm Mon-Fri. **Meals served** noon-11pm Sat; noon-10.30pm Sun. **Main courses** £4.80-£11.80. **Credit** (over £10) MC, V.
This is still the undoubted star of the Kingsland Road Vietnamese scene. Big, light, airy, buzzy (if slightly resembling a school canteen), Song Que is constantly packed with happy customers including many families and a good showing of Vietnamese

locals. There's usually a warm welcome from one of the many staff, who deliver prompt, efficient and friendly service. Food is almost always first class and highly authentic – and good value. Flavours are full and true, and textures perfect, bringing the best out of each dish. Acolytes state that the kitchen makes the best pho in London, which is quite a claim, but the version served here is certainly excellent. Our assorted starters were top-notch too, including a skilfully executed cross between a prawn toast and a banh mi: what seemed like a butterflied whole king prawn on a baguette slice beneath the minced prawn mixture – a real texture treat. We experienced just two minor negatives: not automatically getting a change of paper table covering, and having to troop across the room to the cash desk to pay by card. Still, it will be the classy food that lingers in the memory.
Babies and children welcome: high chairs. Booking advisable. Disabled: toilet. Vegetarian menu. **Map 6 R3**.

North East
Dalston

★ Huong-Viet
An Viet House, 12-14 Englefield Road, N1 4LS (7249 0877). Dalston Junction or Haggerston rail or bus 67, 149, 236, 242, 243. **Lunch served** noon-3pm, **dinner served** 5.30-11pm daily. **Main courses** £6.90-£11.30. **Credit** MC, V.
Part of a Vietnamese community centre, in charming De Beauvoir Town, Huong-Viet has a slightly off-putting institutional exterior that belies a reasonably warm, simply decorated interior. Nevertheless, tables and chairs are poorly arranged, making for cramped seating. At a nearby table, set in the corner of an alcove, two or three people had to move to let others get to the toilets. It can also get very noisy when full. Youthful New East Enders predominated over local Vietnamese among the customers on our visit, possibly because the food can be lacklustre. Spicy soft-shell crab consisted of tiny nuggets in a thick, soggy coating of batter that had fused together into one big amorphous lump. Beef pho contained numerous slices of meat but little flavour and few, if any, added herbs. In contrast, hot and spicy lamb was pretty good, as were the summer rolls. So, the menu seems to be something of a lottery, with a handful of winning combinations amid many duds. Service was slow, uninterested and lacking in warmth.
Babies and children welcome: high chairs. Booking advisable weekends. Disabled: toilet. Separate rooms for parties, both seating 30. Takeaway service. **Map 6 R1**.

Hackney

★ Green Papaya
191 Mare Street, E8 3QE (8985 5486, www.green-papaya.com). London Fields rail or bus 26, 48, 55, 277, D6. **Dinner served** 5-11pm Mon-Sat; 5-10.30pm Sun. **Main courses** £5-£8. **Credit** MC, V.
Located halfway down Mare Street behind an apparently run-down façade, Green Papaya feels like a quiet club. It's a charming little place: long-established, family-run, simple and well loved. Customers are a mixed bunch, from American hipster tourists to dapper older-generation Caribbean

Banh mi

Banh mi are possibly the most enduring reminder of the French colonial presence in Vietnam. The baguettes cooked by the French for themselves became a firm favourite among the Vietnamese, who came to use a lighter and airier version of the bread as a means of serving street food and snacks. Their popularity has recently flourished in London beyond the existing Vietnamese restaurants into market stalls and cafés.

In the heart of the Square Mile, **City Càphê** has besuited queues stretching along the pavement to buy its 'classic pork' (with highly seasoned pâté, ham, daikon, carrot, coriander leaves in abundance and fresh chilli) or beef and lemongrass banh mi. **Banh Mi Bay** has a pretty café in Bloomsbury, where you can eat in (noodle salads and pho are also served) or take away, plus a newer takeaway-only outlet in Fitzrovia. Brown, white or Vietnamese baguettes are baked in-house, with fillings ranging from caramel pork to grilled tiger prawns, tofu and chicken satay. Enterprising young venture **Banhmi11** has two shops, one in Shoreditch, the other in Clerkenwell, offering signature fillings served over noodle salad or in a rice box. It also operates peripatetic market stalls at Hackney's Broadway Market and Soho's Berwick Street Market. Also in Shoreditch is takeaway joint **Keu** (332 Old Street, EC1V 9DR, 7739 1164, www.keudeli.co.uk), part of the same family as Cây Tre and Viet Grill. It serves banh mi (versions include pork belly, ham terrine and chicken liver pâté, and lemongrass-infused mackerel), lunch boxes and salads.

★ Banh Mi Bay
4-6 Theobald's Road, WC1X 8PN (7831 4079, www.banhmibay.co.uk). Chancery Lane tube. **Lunch served** 11.30am-4.30pm, **dinner served** 5.30-9.45pm Mon-Fri. **Meals served** noon-9.45pm Sat. **Main courses** £6-£7.50. **Credit** MC, V.
Available for hire. Babies and children welcome: high chairs. Takeaway service. **Map 4 M5**.

★ Banhmi11
101 Great Eastern Street, EC2A 3JD (7253 1620, www.banhmi11.com). Old Street tube/rail. **Meals served** 11am-9.45pm Mon-Thur; 11am-10.45pm Fri, Sat. **Main courses** £5-£7. **Credit** MC, V.
Available for hire. Babies and children admitted. Takeaway service. **Map 6 Q4**. **For branch see index**.

★ City Caphe
17 Ironmonger Lane, EC2V 8EY (no phone, www.citycaphe.com). Bank tube/DLR. **Meals served** 11.30am-4pm Mon-Fri. **Main courses** £3.65-£6.50. **Credit** MC, V.
Available for hire. Bookings not accepted. Takeaway service. **Map 11 P6**.

Banh Mi Bay

couples. Service is laid-back yet efficient and welcoming, and the food quite superb. Soft-shell crab with salt and chilli was exactly as it should be, with discernible chunks of flavoursome, well-textured crab in a crunchy, tasty batter. The food here seems to come from a slightly different tradition from that of most London competitors: grilled spicy lamb with cumin, a rarity on most Vietnamese menus, was a revelation – the flavour of the lamb highlighted rather than masked by the treatment. Lamb slow-cooked with lemongrass, galangal and coconut milk is an enticing alternative. Another plus: prices are generally 20% lower than those in the other well-known Mare Street Vietnamese establishments. *Babies and children welcome: high chairs. Booking advisable. Disabled: toilet. Takeaway service.*

★ Hai-Ha

206 Mare Street, E8 3RD (8985 5388, www.haiha.co.uk). Hackney Central rail or bus 48, 55, 253, 277, D6. **Lunch served** noon-3.30pm, **dinner served** 5.30-11pm Mon-Fri. **Meals served** noon-11pm Sat, Sun. **Main courses** £7-£8. **Unlicensed**. **Corkage** no charge. **Credit** MC, V.

Not far from the Hackney Picturehouse, this smallish but quite smart venue seems to get plenty of business from local Vietnamese. So much so that on a fine day the prime tables on the pavement are usually occupied by groups of Vietnamese men, drinking and talking. Many of them may be associated with the restaurant's takeaway business, which focuses on common Chinese dishes. Hai-Ha does, however, have quite a substantial Vietnamese repertoire. Cha ca la vong (named after a Hanoi restaurant that has served this dish for several generations) was a real treat; it consisted of grilled fish (here monkfish) marinated in turmeric, cooked with dill and spring onion, then topped with chopped peanuts. Seafood bun Hue (noodle soup) was tasty and refreshing even on a very hot day. This is more than can be said for the bottle of sparkling water, which was unrefrigerated and came with a glass still warm from the dishwasher; rather grudgingly, a small amount of ice was brought. Thankfully, the Saigon beer was chilled to perfection. *Available for hire. Babies and children welcome: high chairs. Tables outdoors (2, pavement).*

Tre Viet

247 Mare Street, E8 3NS (8986 8885, www.treviet.co.uk). London Fields rail or bus 26, 48, 55, 277, D6. **Meals served** noon-11pm Mon-Thur, Sun; noon-11.30pm Fri, Sat. **Main courses** £4.70-£13. **Set meal** £19 per person (minimum 4) 3 dishes; £21 per person (minimum 2) 3 dishes. **Credit** MC, V.

With the welcoming feel of a brasserie, this large, bright, airy and cool dining room – the walls decorated with painted murals of Vietnamese scenes and the ceiling hung with paper lanterns – is a pleasure to visit. This holds true even when the place is crowded, as it often is with a largely western clientele that includes a high percentage of fashionable locals. Service is generally prompt and efficient, and the menu fairly extensive, if a little predictable and short on vegetable dishes. The kitchen prides itself on using fresh ingredients and the food reflects this – but we found ourselves needing to make liberal use of the table sauces provided (something that rarely happens in a Vietnamese restaurant). For example, a stunningly handsome, piled-high platter of sizzling seafood failed to measure up to its looks as, although perfectly cooked and a textural treat, it seemed almost totally devoid of added flavourings. On the plus side, there's an attractive selection of oriental-themed cocktails – such as Vijito, a minted mix of rum, and lime and passionfruit juices – though a fairly limited choice of wines. *Babies and children welcome: high chairs. Booking advisable weekends. Takeaway service.*

North
Finchley

★ Vy Nam Café

371 Regents Park Road, N3 1DE (8371 4222, www.vynam.co.uk). Finchley Central tube. **Lunch served** noon-3pm, **dinner served** 5-11pm Mon-Sat. **Meals served** noon-11pm Sun. **Main courses** £6.80-£13. **Set lunch** (Mon-Fri) £6.50 1 course. **Credit** AmEx, MC, V.

Near to Finchley Central station, this establishment is very much a café: rather boxy, very brightly lit and with the tables set a little too close to one another. The owners try to lift the ambience with vases of flowers on each table (yet don't necessarily ensure the blooms are alive and unbroken). Service is very courteous and attentive – possibly overly so. Communication can be a problem, as one young waiter with halting English misunderstood our order, so we had to cancel one dish when another that we'd already decided against turned up on its own. The food, though, was very good and the menu surprisingly extensive and interesting. DIY minced eel wraps, rich in those mysterious herbs, were a delight, and duck curry in a clay pot was quite delicious. One little touch that did impress was the prompt and unbidden arrival of glasses of iced tap water as we were seated – a practice that other restaurants would do well to copy. *Available for hire. Babies and children welcome: high chair; nappy-changing facilities. Booking advisable weekends.*

Hai-Ha

Cheap Eats

Budget

The cost of dining in London dismays many visitors to our city – but it needn't. Knowledge is everything when it comes to saving pounds on your meal. A good tip is to scrutinise the set lunch deals to be had. Even some of the top-class venues do surprisingly inexpensive two- or three-course deals. Check websites too for special offers that might also cover 'early bird' deals in the evenings. Throughout this guide we've used a ★ to denote restaurants where it's possible to buy a three-course meal for £25 a head or less. Often, these establishments cater for specific communities who live in less affluent suburbs. Try, for instance, the Turkish eateries around Dalston, or the Indian venues of Wembley, Tooting and Whitechapel. Here, we list places – several of them in central London – that you'd need an insider's nous to find. Some are long-established venues that are owner-occupied or where the rents have been kept low, thus with modest overheads. The **Stockpot** in Soho, the **Regency Café** in Pimlico, the **River Café** near Putney Bridge, and Bethnal Green's fabulous **E Pellicci** are prime examples. But newer venues are also showing that it's possible to serve great cooking at budget prices. The highly successful **Hummus Bros** is one such example, and Kentish Town's **Arancini Factory** is another. Newcomers this year? Well, **Herman Ze German** looks set to be a Teutonic hit. Don your lederhosen and prepare for the würst.

Central
City

Café Below
St Mary-le-Bow Church, Cheapside, EC2V 6AU (7329 0789, www.cafebelow.co.uk). St Paul's tube or Bank tube/DLR. **Meals served** 8am-3pm Mon-Fri. **Main courses** £6-£10. **Credit** AmEx, MC, V.
Anyone born within hearing range of St Mary-le-Bow's bells is, by tradition, a bona fide Cockney. Christopher Wren's church stands amid the City hubbub, and its crypt now houses this unpretentious café. It's a breakfast and lunch spot only, with an open kitchen that works its way from bacon sarnies and french toast in the morning to a daily changing roster of substantial rustic grub – beef bourguignon, fish pie, jerk chicken – come midday. For years, this was a vegetarian café, and veggie classics with a twist are still offered. Feta, olive and yellow courgette were encased in a nicely wobbly quiche with a crisp top and an unfortunately soggy base; crunchy roast potatoes and a tangle of salad leaves rounded off the plate. Puddings could feature zesty coconut lime tart or divine chocolate chestnut cake. Square Mile suits and consumers from the One New Change shopping centre throng in for takeaways or to eat in the high-arched canteen. The new East End makes an appearance with London Fields Brewery beers and Allpress coffee. In summer, ascend the weathered flagstone steps to take secular communion with a cuppa outdoors in the churchyard.
Available for hire. Babies and children welcome: high chairs. Tables outdoors (20, churchyard). Takeaway service. Vegan dishes. Vegetarian menu. **Map 11 P6.**

Clerkenwell & Farringdon

Little Bay
171 Farringdon Road, EC1R 3AL (7278 1234, www.little-bay.co.uk). Farringdon tube/rail. **Meals served** noon-midnight Mon-Sat; noon-11pm Sun. **Main courses** £7.25-£15.95. **Credit** MC, V.
Little Bay doesn't have an official mantra, but 'if it ain't broke, don't fix it' might suit. This year, as every year, the gaudy, vaguely opera-themed decor remains the same. Faded gold and burgundy paint, fake rock-work and orgiastic frescoes continue to pepper an interior overlooked by a giant gold mask. The menu is unchanged too, with the line-up of Mediterranean-inspired meals continuing to incorporate old faves such as a faux choux bun topped with balsamic glaze and hollandaise and filled with a mulligatawny-flavoured crab paste. A starter of baked field mushrooms arrived atop a dab of punchy red pepper sauce, and the roast pork lunch's tender cuts of meat were drizzled in a lovely rich gravy. Quality is reasonable, so, as most mains cost around £9 and starters are near the £4 mark, bargain-hunters flock here. Don't linger, though. Two different waitresses hovered to take our order, food came out of the kitchen so fast we risked burning our mouths, and the whole experience took just over an hour for two courses.
Babies and children welcome: high chairs. Booking advisable. Disabled: toilet. Separate room for parties, seats 90. **Map 5 N4.**
For branches see index.

Pimlico

Regency Café
17-19 Regency Street, SW1P 4BY (7821 6596). St James's Park tube or Victoria tube/rail. **Meals served** 7am-2.30pm Mon-Fri; 7am-noon Sat. **Main courses** £2.55-£6.55. **No credit cards.**
Behind its black-tiled art deco exterior, this classic caff has operated on the quiet Westminster/Pimlico borders since 1946. The handsome, operatic manager bellows the Thursday lunch special – 'roast pork!' – like a parade-ground sergeant. He

stands in front of his chefs, proud in their pristine white tunics, and surveys the busy scene. Customers sit on brown plastic chairs at Formica-topped tables, watched over by muscular boxers and Spurs stars of yore, whose photos hang on the tiled walls. Lasagne, omelettes, salads, baked potatoes, every conceivable cooked breakfast (the chunky bangers are especially fetching) and mugs of tannin-rich tea are meat and drink to the Regency. Stodgetastic own-made specials include steak pie – the thick pastry hiding tender meat in a tomatoey sauce, served with serviceable chips, a wobbly helping of thick gravy, and peas that might well have seen the inside of a tin. Still hungry? The improbably gigantic cinnamon-flavoured bread and butter pud will see you right for the rest of the week: yours for two quid.

Takeaway service. **Map 16 K10.**

Soho

Herman Ze German NEW

33 Old Compton Street, W1D 5JU (no phone, www.herman-ze-german.co.uk). Leicester Square or Tottenham Court Road tube. **Meals served** 11am-11pm Mon-Thur; 11am-midnight Fri; 10am-midnight Sat; 10am-11pm Sun. **Main courses** £3.25-£9.95. **Credit** AmEx, MC, V.

In case you hadn't guessed, Herman Ze German is a purveyor of German sausages. Its original outlet on Villiers Street is cherished by sausage fanciers and the late-night commuters of Charing Cross, but is no place to linger. This, its first 'restaurant', in the beating heart of Soho, is really a fast-food joint, but its larger size and playfully utilitarian interior (part log cabin, part wet room – with planks on the walls, a painted concrete floor and a butler sink for washing your hands) make for a comfortable enough hangout. The sausages are imported from the Schwarzwald (the Black Forest, of chocolate-and-cherry-cake fame), and are *sehr gut*: high-quality pork; juicy, springy middles; and a proper 'knack' when you bite. More bonus points for serving them in chewy baguettes. Our choice, 'ze Wilde Bock', had a bouncy bockwurst (smoked pork sausage) layered with 'curry' sauce (spicy ketchup), squidgy fries and crisp onion: a sort of Teutonic chip-and-sausage butty. Straightforward sauerkraut with no embellishments proved a suitable digestif; only the sloppy potato salad (with a good taste, but poor texture) disappointed. Still, for a hearty meal in central London without too much financial pain, it's time to consider a wiener. The burger is dead. Long live the dog.

Babies and children admitted. Bookings not accepted. Takeaway service. **Map 17 C4.** **For branch see index.**

★ Hummus Bros

88 Wardour Street, W1F 0TJ (7734 1311, www.hbros.co.uk). Oxford Circus or Tottenham Court Road tube. **Meals served** noon-10pm Mon-Sat; noon-5pm Sun. **Main courses** £3.70-£8.80. **Credit** AmEx, MC, V.

Houmous may be nothing more than cheap student-fuel to many, but this humble chickpea paste is elevated to something altogether more delicious in the hands of Hummus Bros. The original Wardour Street outlet is spartanly decorated – all red communal tables and big windows – with queues of office workers snaking into the street at lunchtime; scenes replicated at the Holborn and Cheapside branches. Though the wraps aren't bad, go for the bowls of silky-smooth houmous

sprinkled with paprika and olive oil, and make use of the garlic-infused lemon juice on every table. Mashed, cumin-scented fava beans is a good choice of topping, but our favourite is the chunky slow-cooked beef. A regular portion comes with two warm wholemeal pittas (one with a small serving). Side dishes are heartily recommended, with deliciously smoky barbecued aubergine and zingy tabouleh particular highlights. There's the option of customising your plate with tortilla chips, carrot sticks or hard-boiled eggs, though it's probably best to keep things simple. Service is quick and casual, but the Middle Eastern flavours and big portions make this a top budget lunch spot.

Babies and children welcome: high chairs. Bookings not accepted. Takeaway service. Vegan dishes. Vegetarian menu. **Map 17 B3.** **For branches see index.**

Pierre Victoire

5 Dean Street, W1D 3RQ (7287 4582, www.pierrevictoire.com). Oxford Circus or Tottenham Court Road tube. **Meals served** noon-11pm Mon-Wed, Sun; noon-11.30pm Thur-Sat. **Main courses** £10.90-£15.90. **Set lunch** (noon-4pm) £9.90 2 courses. **Set dinner** (4-7pm Mon-Wed; 4-6.30pm Fri, Sat) £12.90 2 courses. **Credit** AmEx, MC, V.

The last couple of years have seen an in[...] quality, cheap barbecue shacks into S[...] the competition making this cosy, G[...] room feel dated? The hordes of after-work twentysomethings who continue to pack it out certainly don't think so. There are undeniably antiquated touches: staff attempt to lure customers into spending £10 more than the price of house wine by plonking £25 bottles of Chianti on tables. And the astonishingly long menu (15 starters and 18 main courses, including no fewer than four variations on steak-frites) tends to opt for quantity over quality. A portion of mushroom parcels featuring big, tacky pastry squares with scant filling failed to impress; neither did the chewy skin of twice-roasted belly pork served with dry mash; but the rich tomato ragoût topping tender spatchcocked baby chicken was better. Cooking might be variable, and mains cost a not-inconsiderable £13 or thereabouts, but there's no denying the charming, low-lit ambience of this perennially popular restaurant. It has a sense of humour too. The main stylistic touch paying homage to the venue's French theme? A giant plastic frog squatting in the corner.

Babies and children welcome: high chairs. Booking advisable. Separate room for parties, seats 25. Tables outdoors (2, pavement). **Map 17 B3.**

Herman Ze German

Stockpot

18 Old Compton Street, W1D 4TN (7287 1066).
Leicester Square or Tottenham Court Road tube.
Meals served 9am-11.30pm Mon, Tue; 9am-
midnight Wed-Sat; noon-11.30pm Sun. **Main
courses** £4.95-£10.50. **Set meal** £7.10 2
courses. **No credit cards.**
Will anything ever change at this Soho institution?
We doubt it. Stepping into the charmingly
unreconstructed caff is like entering a culinary land
that time forgot. The 1960s-ish decor consists of
walls furnished in Anaglypta and wooden slatting,
plus tables that seem to have been varnished time
and again. The menu's solid fare is all stodgy bakes,
roast dinners and a school canteen-esque range of
crumbles and sponges topped with runny,
synthetic-tasting custard. The real throwback is the
bill, though, with most main courses costing about
£6 and set menus letting you wolf down three
courses for close to £10. As a result, the clientele
tends towards shaky old gents hunched over slabs
of stodge and chips, students eking out cuppas, and
meedja trendies paying homage to an increasingly
rare glimpse of old Soho. A word of warning,
though: don't expect to linger. When busy, the
otherwise friendly staff can border on the pushy in
their attempts to hurry customers along.
*Babies and children admitted. Tables outdoors
(2, pavement). Takeaway service.* **Map 17 C3.**

Westminster

★ Vincent Rooms

Westminster Kingsway College, Vincent Square,
SW1P 2PD (7802 8391, http://centrallondon
venues.co.uk). St James's Park tube or Victoria
tube/rail. **Lunch served** noon-1pm Mon-Fri.
Dinner served 6-7pm Wed, Thur. Closed
June-Aug. **Main courses** £8-£12. **Set meal**
(Escoffier Room) £25 6 courses incl coffee.
Credit MC, V.
The Vincent Rooms is staffed, front of house and
in the kitchen, by students training at Westminster

Kingsway College, but they are overseen by
experienced chefs and maître d's, and they operate
in a sophisticated, beautifully appointed venue with
its own entrance. Sit at one of the well-spaced, plain
wooden tables and look through picture windows
on to Vincent Square, where the gilded youth of
Westminster School have their playing fields. Keen,
smart, faintly nervous staff soon appear to take
your order. The Mod Euro menu reads well, and the
prices, for food of this quality, are divertingly low.
Small wonder local business people bring their
togged-up clients here. The separate haute-cuisine
Escoffier Restaurant offers a £25 tasting menu, but
it's the brasserie's daily changing list that attracts
most custom. Start, perhaps, with crab and prawn
bisque or salad of medium-rare mallard breast,
handsomely presented with toasted oats and nuts,
rocket and a few berries. A main course of grilled
sea bass fillets was faultless, as was the
accompanying creamy risotto, buttered curly kale
and a slice of fennel in light tempura batter. A well-
priced wine list adds allure, but it's the eager-to-
please staff that are most refreshing.
Babies and children welcome: high chairs.
*Booking advisable. Disabled: toilet. Separate
room for parties, seats 30.* **Map 15 J10.**

West

Ealing

Walpole

35 St Mary's Road, W5 5RG (8567 7918,
www.walpole-ealing.co.uk). South Ealing tube.
Meals served 8am-2pm Tue-Fri; 9am-1pm
Sat. **Dinner served** 7-11pm Fri, Sat. **Main
courses** £4.95-£13.50. **Set breakfast** £5.25
1 course incl tea or coffee. **Set dinner** £19.95
2 courses, £24.95 3 courses. **Credit** MC, V.
The Walpole leads a double life. On Friday and
Saturday nights it's an accomplished restaurant,
serving the likes of Cornish crab bisque and sea

bass with pea and parmesan risotto. The rest of the
week, however, it's a cheap and cheerful greasy
spoon, offering myriad variations on bacon, egg,
sausage, onions and mushrooms, as well as roast
chicken, spag bol and steak sandwiches. The decor
is basic, enlivened by old tin ads for Tizer ('the
appetiser') and nut brown tobacco ('for nutty
flavour'). Only a few details – the chalkboard wine
list that includes a £45 bottle of barolo, the bank
of exotic liqueurs, and a cabinet filled with elegant
wine glasses – hints at its dual identity. As a
straightforward caff, the Walpole is very solid. The
own-cooked ham is excellent and you get a huge
portion, together with a mound of egg and chips.
The sausages, and bubble and squeak are tasty, and
the toast comes with mini pots of Bonne Maman
jam. Your bill will be pleasingly small – unless you
order that Barolo with your beans on toast.
*Babies and children admitted. Booking essential
dinner. Takeaway service.*

South West
Chelsea

Mona Lisa

417 King's Road, SW10 0LR (7376 5447).
Fulham Broadway tube or bus 11, 22. **Meals
served** 6.30am-11pm Mon-Sat; 8.30am-5.30pm
Sun. **Main courses** £6-£19.95. **Set lunch**
(11am-3pm) £8.95 3 courses. **Set dinner**
(3-11pm Mon-Sat; 3-5.30pm Sun) £9.95
3 courses. **Credit** (over £5) MC, V.
Not much to look at, either inside or out, the Mona
Lisa is hidden away at the 'wrong' end of the King's
Road, just beyond World's End. But the bonhomie
is infectious, and if you order the right thing, such
as the meltingly tender calf's liver alla salvia (with
butter and sage), served with old-school potatoes
and veg, you won't care about the homely decor. Not
everything is up to this standard: the glass cabinet
holding puddings and gateaux produced a rather
forlorn banoffee pie. A basic fried banana with ice-
cream was a more pleasing dessert. The menu
ranges across breakfasts, sandwiches, burgers,
omelettes, jacket potatoes and pastas to three-
course blow-outs (at lunch, the latter is just £8.95).
Customers are a mixed bag – all types, all ages, lone
diners (always well looked after), couples and
groups, tended to by eager Italian staff. An
unpretentious breath of fresh air amid the Chelsea
tractor fumes.
Babies and children welcome: high chairs.
*Booking advisable. Tables outdoors (2, pavement).
Takeaway service.* **Map 14 D13.**

Fulham

River Café

Station Approach, SW6 3UH (7736 6296).
Putney Bridge tube. **Open** 7am-3.30pm Mon-
Fri; 7am-3pm Sat. **Main courses** £4-£7.
No credit cards.
No, not that River Café. This particular River Café,
opposite the entrance to Putney Bridge tube station,
is a fine example of that endangered species, the old-
fashioned British caff. The focus of the breakfast
menu, predictably, is a mix-and-match full english –
generously portioned, and very reasonably priced
at £3-£5. Lunch is anchored by hearty British
classics, including shepherd's pie, ham, egg and
chips, and liver and bacon, all for £5-£6. If you can
possibly squeeze in more, apple pie and some tasty

River Café

BUDGET

Gambardella

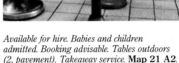

Italian puds await. The real draw, however, is not the food, but the feeling of being in a living museum. The place has a quietly dignified, low-key charm, and the decor – unchanged in decades – is a delight, with beautiful blue and white tiling, seascape murals, plywood panelling and Formica tabletops. Italian proprietor Rob offers a warm welcome to all, from elderly gents parked with the newspaper to the few young hipsters who have discovered this gem. Forget the current retro-revival trend; nothing is as comforting as the real thing – ideally with a bacon and egg butty and a cuppa (two sugars, please). *Babies and children welcome: high chairs. Tables outdoors (3, pavement). Takeaway service.*

South
Battersea

Galapagos Bistro-Café
169 Battersea High Street, SW11 3JS (8488 4989). Clapham Junction rail. **Lunch served** 9.30am-4pm, **dinner served** 6.30-9pm Tue-Sat. **Main courses** £7.50-£9.95. **Set lunch** (noon-4pm) £11.95 2 courses, £14.95 3 courses. **Set dinner** (6.30-9pm) £13.95 2 courses, £16.95 3 courses. **Credit** MC, V.
Homely charm and attentive service are the order of the day at this small Battersea eatery. Basic furnishings include cream walls, plaid-upholstered benches and trimmings that range from a cubby-hole filled with a curious assortment of bric-a-brac (Glenmorangie 'golf gift set', gaudy wooden parrots, pan pipes) to a wall decorated entirely with display packets of breakfast cereals, jars of conserve and teas. What makes the atmosphere distinctive, though, are nice touches such as pre-chilled glasses and an endearingly plain-spoken host who wishes punters *'buen provecho'* in between cheeky admonishments like 'These olives have stones in: don't break your teeth and blame me.' A curious menu mixes food from Britain, Indonesia, Morocco and Italy, with dishes including grilled halloumi in a fragrant, freshly blitzed green tomatillo sauce, and a rich spinach tagliatelle. However, the relaxed, down-to-earth vibe and a £5-£7 breakfast menu of croissants, omelettes and fry-ups suggest Galapagos is at its best as somewhere to start the day.

Available for hire. Babies and children admitted. Booking advisable. Tables outdoors (2, pavement). Takeaway service. **Map 21 A2**.

Clapham

Mama Lan
8 The Pavement, SW4 0HY (no phone, www.mamalan.co.uk). Clapham Common tube. **Lunch served** noon-3.30pm Mon-Sat; noon-3pm Sun. **Main courses** £3.50-£9. **No credit cards.**
This no-bookings, cash-only Chinese café is an offshoot: a second branch of the original in Brixton Village Market. It's a typical venture from a new wave of restaurant entrepreneurs who – with little experience or capital – have moved from running a supper club to setting up premises, spread the word by social media, and built up a loyal following. The experience gained at the first branch has paid off. On our three visits, the service in the Clapham outlet was smooth, the kitchen consistent. The pork buns, which look a little like meat-filled muffins, have a yielding texture and savoury filling. A spicy chicken ban mein (noodle dish) was generously portioned and intensely savoury. The beijing dumplings (similar to Japanese gyoza) were correctly pan-fried with a burnished crust. Leave room, if you can, for some of the smacked cucumber; this simple, spicy salad, newly popularised in the West by a Fuchsia Dunlop cookbook, has rightly become a new classic. Add a beer or soft drink and Mama Lan's makes a perfect pit stop – if you don't mind the slightly cramped seating, and if you're in no rush for a table. *Bookings not accepted.* **Map 22 A2**.
For branch see index.

South East
Greenwich

Gambardella
47-48 Vanbrugh Park, SE3 7JQ (8858 0327). Blackheath or Westcombe Park rail or bus 53. **Meals served** 8am-4.30pm Mon-Fri; 8am-2pm Sat. **Main courses** £3-£4.50. **No credit cards**.
Behind the counter, a Napoli FC pennant hangs alongside a Charlton Athletic one, which just about sums up this unpretentious caff's standing in the neighbourhood. The original 1930s decor sends traditionalists into raptures: the front space is bright with polished, peachy Vitrolite panelling edged with chrome, while the tables and moulded-plywood revolving chairs date from the 1960s. The menu – fry-ups and Italian specials – is a joy for the impecunious, with toast at 60p and a cappuccino for £1.60. Or you can push the boat out with a soft, toasty panini of chargrilled courgettes, tomatoes and mozzarella. Carb-loading options are plentiful: as well as a full complement of pasta dishes, there are pancakes and baked potatoes with a range of toppings, and comforting fuel such as steak and kidney pudding. Jam roly-poly with custard is £1.60 well spent.

East
Bethnal Green

★ E Pellicci
332 Bethnal Green Road, E2 0AG (7739 4873). Bethnal Green tube/rail or bus 8. **Meals served** 7am-4pm Mon-Sat. **Main courses** £5.50-£8.20. **Unlicensed. Corkage** no charge. **No credit cards.**
If ever proof were needed that all caffs are not equal, this Grade-II listed greasy spoon on Bethnal Green Road is it. The food may not be much more than reasonably above-average caff grub, but the atmosphere and decor are second to none. Opened in 1900, and still in the hands of the same family, Pellicci's is an east London landmark. It has an almost opulent feel, harking back to a time when caff culture was king. Chrome-lined Vitrolite panels line the outside, and the wood-panelled interior is filled with Formica tables and art deco touches. Food is still prepared with pride every day by Mama Maria – queen of the kitchen since 1961. The kids, Anna and Nevio Junior, serve it with a wink, a smile and as much banter as you can handle. Fry-ups are first rate, and the fish and chips, daily grills and Italian specials aren't half bad either. Desserts, from bread pudding to Portuguese pasteis de nata, are worth a punt too. But it's the vibrant welcome, served with a healthy helping of mickey-taking, that makes the place so special.
Available for hire. Babies and children welcome: high chairs. Bookings not accepted. Tables outdoors (5, pavement). Takeaway service.

Shoreditch

Ginger Pig

231 Hoxton Street, N1 5LG (7749 0705, www.thegingerpigcafe.com). Hoxton rail. **Lunch served** 11am-3pm Mon-Fri. **Brunch served** 9am-3pm Sat, Sun. **Dinner served** 6-10pm daily. **Main courses** £8-£12. **Credit** AmEx, MC, V.

It's hard to pin down the Ginger Pig. At first sight, it resembles a greasy spoon, with cheap prints, mirrors and dark wooden chairs and tables. Counteracting this are bottles of wine on shelves and an open kitchen at the back. Locals praise the brunch and the burgers, although staff seemed ill-prepared for diners on our visit, with several food and drink options unavailable. The meat-based menu encompasses grilled chicken, pork belly, steak and ribs, plus brioche sandwiches with chicken and fish. To start, we enjoyed thick-cut bresaola with lashings of rocket. Pan-fried whole sea bass for £6.50 is impressive value, even if the dressing was too pesto-like. From the choice of four burgers, our Hunky-Dory combined ground beef, monterey jack, caramelised onions, roasted red peppers and smoked chilli mayo in a glorious, juicy combo that drips when you bite – the mark of the best burgers. The menu also offers some tantalising brunch combinations (eggs lots of ways), and puddings that include the likes of chocolate sponge and ice-cream, but it's those burgers that will lure us back.
Babies and children admitted. Bookings not accepted. **Map 6 R2.**

Shepherdess Café

221 City Road, EC1V 1JN (7253 2463). Old Street tube/rail. **Meals served** 6.30am-4pm Mon-Fri; 7am-3pm Sat. **Main courses** £5.40-£7.95. **Credit** MC, V.

This landmark corner caff has appeared in several films and attracted a score of celebs in the three decades since opening, but it remains an unreconstructed greasy spoon, complete with eye-straining strip lighting and plastic sauce bottles on each table. Framed photos of Greece on the back walls might help you to shut out the noisy City Road for a few seconds, but you'll soon be brought back to earth by the bustle of diners coming and

going. This remains a very male space, but the unassuming staff make everyone welcome. Classic full english breakfasts are the order of the day, with all manner of combos available; most plates arrive with chips (thick-cut, crispy but soft in the middle). Prices are similarly traditional: you'll pay just 80p for a cuppa, while the (proper) coffee starts at £1.30 for an espresso. There's an extensive sandwich menu, along with lunch dishes such as steak and kidney pie and jacket potatoes. Have a peek at the photos on the luminous green wall behind the till – former customers include 1990s girl band All Saints, Barry from *EastEnders* and Jamie Oliver (a regular: his restaurant Fifteen is just round the corner).
Babies and children welcome: high chairs. Bookings not accepted. Tables outdoors (4, pavement). Takeaway service. **Map 5 P3.**

North
Highgate

Quarters Café

267 Archway Road, N6 5BS (07598 760791, www.quarterscafe.com). Highgate tube. **Meals served** 9am-8pm Mon-Sat; 9am-7pm Sun. **Main courses** £5.50-£8.50. **Set dinner** (7-8pm Mon-Sat) £10.99-£11.99 3 courses. **Credit** MC, V.

Adjoining a shop crammed with Scandinavian antiques, this café has a delightful ad hoc feel, with a scatter of mismatched tables and any number of period curios on the walls. There's nothing slapdash about the South-east Asian cooking, however. Portions are big, from nicely seasoned edamame beans to veggie dumplings with a heap of bean sprouts and salad, and the flavours in a fiery chicken laksa made with tender udon noodles were deep and satisfying. There's porridge or toast at breakfast, and a fine range of pretty cakes on the counter (lemon drizzle, red velvet, carrot, chocolate brownies), plenty of teas (served in a delicate pot with handle-less tea cup), own-made lemonade and well-chosen alcohol – wine, Tsing Tao and Beer Lao, or Pimm's. Quarters is thronged with local mums during the day (though the tiny toilet is hardly suited to baby-changing) and recently diversified into evening opening, with a three-

course set menu (dumplings or noodle salad, noodle soup for main, cakes to finish) for just over a tenner. Service is charming and the atmosphere could hardly be more relaxed, with 6Music on the stereo and arty freesheets scattered about.
Available for hire. Babies and children welcome: high chairs. Booking advisable dinner. Tables outdoors (1, terrace). Takeaway service.

Kentish Town

Arancini Factory

115 Kentish Town Road, NW1 8PN (3648 7941, www.arancinibrothers.com). Kentish Town tube/rail. **Meals served** 8am-7pm Mon-Fri; 9.30am-7pm Sat, Sun. **Main courses** £4-£7.95. **Credit** MC, V.

The bricks-and-mortar location of marketeers Arancini Bros is an affable retro caff decked with boxes of the day's fresh produce. From the open kitchen at the rear come arancini (Sicilian-style deep-fried risotto balls) served plain, with salad, in tortilla wraps, or accompanied by a hot stew. There are other options too, such as poached eggs on toast for breakfast, and Aussie-themed open sandwiches such as banana with bacon and cheese. We like the homely muffins (carrot and honey, for example) displayed with other cakes by the coffee machine, which turns out good lattes, flat whites and so on – you don't have to like arancini to feel comfortable here. Many do opt for the main product, though, and on our latest visit these were much improved on the time before: light creamy balls with a thin crust. Also enjoyable was the accompanying chickpea and mediterranean veg stew. Note that there's a little garden eating area at the back of the property – and that Arancini Bros is doing well enough to have outlets in Broadgate and the Royal Festival Hall.
Available for hire. Babies and children admitted. Bookings not accepted. Tables outdoors (7, garden). Takeaway service. Vegan dishes. Vegetarian menu. **Map 27 D1.**
For branch see index.

Mario's Café

6 Kelly Street, NW1 8PH (7284 2066, www.marioscafe.com). Camden Town tube or Kentish Town tube/rail. **Meals served** 7.30am-4pm Mon-Sat. **Main courses** £5-£7. **No credit cards.**

Star of song (Saint Etienne's 1993 'Mario's Café') and screen (at the chrome coffee-counter you can buy a £3 DVD documentary about the caff), Mario's relies on locals' indefatigable appetite for cut-above breakfasts – scrambled egg and salmon, or poached egg and prosciutto, on ciabatta; a full english of sausage, egg, bacon and tomato, plus extras (bubble, hash browns, black pudding). But don't ignore the Italian mains. Mario's mum makes even a simple spicy Italian sausage penne delicious: decent ingredients, no fuss. Set among pretty pastel-painted cottages, the café is too narrow for comfort, but perfectly proportioned for bonhomie – which Mario dishes up as enthusiastically as he does the cappuccinos and nosh. It's a community place, with guitar lessons, doulas and t'ai chi courses advertised, local art on the walls, and a steady stream of dads-with-nippers and retirees greeted by name. A classic.
Available for hire. Babies and children welcome: children's menu; high chairs. Bookings not accepted. Tables outdoors (1, pavement). **Map 27 D1.**

Shepherdess Café

Cafés

London's café scene has taken off in a big way over the last couple of years. Interesting, independent venues are popping up all over the city, serving great coffee, real bread and carefully sourced ingredients. Independent bakeries are growing in number, and some also have cafés of their own – in east London alone, both E5 Bakehouse (www.e5bakehouse.com), and Fabrique (www.fabrique.co.uk) have small cafés attached, for example. But it's not all about the east: Peckham, New Cross and other parts of the south are being populated with dynamic one-offs such as **St David's Coffee House**, the **London Particular** and **Café Viva**. Favourites this year include cafés as diverse as **Orange Pekoe** (tea specialist in Barnes), **Towpath** (N1's canalside eatery), **Nordic Bakery** (Scandinavian outpost in Soho), **Tina, We Salute You** (funky but friendly Dalston local) and **La Fromagerie** (chi-chi Marylebone cheese specialist and deli).

For coffee specialists, *see p284*; for more of a greasy spoon-style caff, *see p266*.

Central
Clerkenwell & Farringdon

Clerkenwell Kitchen
27 Clerkenwell Close, EC1R 0AT (7101 9959, www.theclerkenwellkitchen.co.uk). Angel tube or Farringdon tube/rail. **Open** 8am-5pm Mon-Fri; 10am-4pm Sat. **Main courses** £4.80-£13. **Credit** (over £10) AmEx, MC, V.
Bright, airy and modern – with exposed architectural features, white walls and an industrial open kitchen softened by wooden floors, culinary-themed line drawings and a wood-burner – the Clerkenwell Kitchen attracts a mainly young crowd, reassured by right-on sourcing. It's a sizeable space, well able to cope with the lunchtime rush (the takeaway menu is popular too), and the courtyard terrace is an enticing corner on warm days. Clues about the style of cuisine come not just from the posters but the shelf of well-thumbed cookery books from Europe and California, with Chez Panisse and Zuni Café providing clear inspiration. Choices are few and daily changing, while the chalkboard menu and standard sauce bottles signal a back-to-basics approach, but the cooking is nonetheless precise: a chard frittata featured a crisp contrast of finely shaved, vibrantly dressed fennel. The minimalism sometimes goes awry: wild salmon gravadlax came without sauce; nor was there dressing on the watercress or butter for the rye bread – one of these, at least, would have been

welcome. An indulgent summer berry 'crisp' with its pot of rich cream set the world to rights, however. Drinks, too, are few but well chosen and carefully served.
Babies and children welcome: high chairs. Disabled: toilet. Tables outdoors (14, courtyard). Takeaway service. **Map 5 N4.**

J&A Café
4 Sutton Lane, EC1M 5PU (7490 2992, www.jandacafe.com). Barbican tube or Farringdon tube/rail.
Bar **Open** noon-11pm Wed-Fri.
Café **Breakfast served** 8-11am, **lunch served** noon-3.30pm Mon-Fri. **Brunch served** 9am-3pm Sat, Sun. **Tea served** 3.30-5.45pm Mon-Fri; 3-4pm Sat. **Main courses** £3.50-£10.50.
Both **Credit** MC, V.
So hidden away is this café housed in the ground floor of a diamond-cutting factory that it escapes the notice even of long-time locals. But there's no need to advertise: casual brunching couples, solo diners and a raucous birthday celebration filled the cute cobbled courtyard one sunny summer Sunday, bunting and lights strung up overhead. Indoors, the exposed brickwork lends an air of factory-chic. Some of the young crowd had already started cracking into Aperol spritzes, but most were indulging in hearty breakfast fare and the own-made cakes, accompanied by a large mug of tea. All produce is carefully sourced, often locally. Part café and part bar, J&A aims to focus on 'healthy and wholesome home-cooking and baking'; to

emphasise the point, rustic breads and own-made baked goods adorn its counter. Eggs benedict arrived quickly, though the muffin was too tough to cut through; thick slices of Irish soda bread were swiftly brought as a replacement. Lunch choices include sandwiches, pies, quiche and salads, while bar snacks focus on simple small plates such as ham and mustard sauce.
Available for hire. Babies and children welcome: high chairs. Disabled: toilet. Tables outdoors (16, courtyard). Takeaway service. Vegan dishes. Vegetarian menu. **Map 5 O4.**

Fitzrovia

Lantana
13 Charlotte Place, W1T 1SN (7637 3347, www.lantanacafe.co.uk). Goodge Street tube. **Open** 8am-6pm Mon-Fri; 9am-5pm Sat, Sun. **Breakfast served** 8-11.30am, **lunch served** noon-3pm Mon-Fri. **Brunch served** 9am-3pm Sat, Sun. **Main courses** £5-£12.50. **Credit** (over £5) MC, V.
A pioneer of the Australian-run modern café scene, Lantana remains a lively spot. Its look – wooden tables, mismatched chairs, small pieces of art on white walls – is now commonplace, but the staff pride themselves on their coffee-making and baking skills, and rightly so. The flat whites are super-smooth and go well with a moist raspberry friand or an Aussie 'cherry ripe' cake slice. The breakfast and brunch menu sounds great too, though sadly, maple french toast with streaky bacon, grilled

banana and candied pecans was a little dry and came without any syrup; the chef had also forgotten to candy the pecans. Nevertheless, the staff, though the relaxed side of perfect, were very apologetic. At lunchtime and in the evenings, savoury dishes can be ordered with a glass of wine. The kiosk next door sells some dishes as takeaways, such as the tart of the day; on our visit, this was a big slice of mushroom, spinach and goat's cheese tart, served with a selection of salads that included a slightly bland lentil and beetroot assembly, but also a much more vibrant and flavoursome greek salad. For sister restaurant, Salvation Jane, *see p44*.
Available for hire. Babies and children admitted. Tables outdoors (2, pavement). Takeaway service. **Map 17 B1.**

Scandinavian Kitchen
61 Great Titchfield Street, W1W 7PP (7580 7161, www.scandikitchen.co.uk). Oxford Circus tube. **Open** 8am-7pm Mon-Fri; 10am-6pm Sat; 10am-4pm Sun. **Main courses** £5.95-£9.95. **Credit** (over £5) AmEx, MC, V.
Whether homesick Scandinavian, or hungry Brit, you get a warm welcome from the smiley staff at SK. They cope well even during busy periods, when seats (at tables at the back, plus a few stools and a sofa at the front) are at a premium, and are a dab hand at doling out decent coffees (made with Monmouth Coffee beans) and Swedish cinnamon buns. At lunch, there are mix-and-match combos of salads (beetroot and apple, carrot and courgette, sweet potato with rye grain – all good), open sandwiches (such as smoked salmon) and wraps (smoked ham and Scandinavian cheese), plus a soup of the day (always vegetarian) or a hot dog with crisp onions. Cakes are baked every day: kladdkaka (Swedish sticky chocolate cake, served with whipped cream) and apple cake are excellent choices; there's a good range of teas, such as elderflower and ginger too. Further temptation comes in the form of Scandinavian groceries, from crispbreads to herring and liquorice, dotted about the red- and black-accented premises (with even more available online).

Babies and children welcome: high chairs; nappy-changing facilities. Takeaway service. **Map 9 J5.**

Holborn

Fleet River Bakery
71 Lincoln's Inn Fields, WC2A 3JF (7691 1457, www.fleetriverbakery.com). Holborn tube. **Open** 7am-7pm Mon-Wed; 7am-9pm Thur, Fri; 8.30am-6pm Sat; 8.30am-4pm Sun. **Main courses** £6.50-£9.50. **Credit** (over £5) AmEx, MC, V.
This café-bakery's focal point is its heavily laden counter of baked delights. Alongside old favourites (moist carrot or chocolate cake), there are more unusual offerings, such as the 'Fleet Jaffa Slice' and caramel and peanut-butter shortbread – all perfect with a cup of quality Monmouth coffee. The café's tucked-away location has done nothing to inhibit its success, and lunch hour draws a crowd, much of which is from local offices. Sandwiches, quiches and frittatas are also available, and a daily special is offered from midday, when the scene is reminiscent of a school canteen, with customers queueing for staff to spoon a robust portion of steaming stew, bake or pie on to their plates. Such popularity is not without reason: chicken, mushroom and tarragon lasagne was an unfussy, filling and tasty affair. Decor has a modern-rustic vibe, with reclaimed-door tabletops adding interest to otherwise unremarkable surroundings. If you don't mind the lack of elbow room, this is a great place to grab a decent lunch for under a tenner.
Babies and children welcome: high chairs; nappy-changing facilities. Tables outdoors (6, pavement). Takeaway service. **Map 18 F2.**

Marylebone

★ La Fromagerie [HOT 50]
2-6 Moxon Street, W1U 4EW (7935 0341, www.lafromagerie.co.uk). Baker Street or Bond Street tube. **Open** 8am-7.30pm Mon-Fri; 9am-7pm Sat; 10am-6pm Sun. **Main courses** £6-£15. **Credit** (over £5) AmEx, MC, V.
There are cheeseboards and then there are La Fromagerie cheeseboards. We'd like to live in a world in which we were only ever served the latter – carefully sourced, themed by nation (with suggested wines to match) and prettily arranged on a wooden slab at the back of a shop filled with wonderful chutneys and handmade French tableware. Our Italian and British selections – best eaten from goat to blue, our waiter helpfully clarified – had not a dud between them. The Marylebone shop's popularity has only increased since it opened in 2002 (a decade after the original Highbury branch) and the café doesn't take bookings, so time your visit with care. Earlier in the day, you could stop by for breakfast (granola, bacon sandwiches, organic boiled eggs with Poilâne soldiers), while if you're lucky enough to secure a table for lunch, you'll find cut-above sandwiches and soups on the menu alongside charcuterie plates, smoked salmon and escargots. A late-afternoon table (the cakes are as lovely as the cheese) with prime people-watching potential would be our preference. Choose a glass from the meticulously sourced wine list and watch glamorous locals stockpile dinner party nibbles as you plan your fantasy weekly shop from the shelves.
Available for hire evenings Mon-Thur. Babies and children welcome: nappy-changing facilities. Bookings not accepted. Takeaway service. Vegetarian menu. **Map 3 G3.**
For branch see index.

Monocle Café [NEW]
18 Chiltern Street, W1U 7QA (7725 4388). Baker Street or Bond Street tube. **Open** 7am-7pm Mon-Fri; 9am-6pm Sat; 10am-6pm Sun. **Main courses** £5-£8. **Credit** AmEx, MC, V.
This little Marylebone café is a spin-off from *Monocle* magazine, the showcase of design consultant and publisher Tyler Brûlé (founder of *Wallpaper**). For such a high-profile brand and backer, the café is remarkably modest. There is none of the gadgetry or choice of beans and roasts that you'll find in the more dedicated, new-wave coffee bars. In this case, lack of choice was no loss: it was

Monocle Café

Damson & Co

a richly flavoured Allpress blended roast. Better than the perfectly decent coffee were the excellent pastries from Stockholm's Fabrique bakery, which now has a branch in Haggerston; you won't find a better Swedish-style cinnamon roll in London. The beautifully presented cakes are by Lanka. In appearance, the café looks like a cross between a sushi bar and a Swedish sauna, with its red-oak counter, classic white mugs and tiny airline-style trays. Copies of Winkreative's (Brûlé's ad agency) portfolio are scattered around, the mugs are for sale and even the chocolates are monogrammed with the Monocle logo.

Available for hire. Babies and children admitted. Tables outdoors (2, pavement). Takeaway service. **Map 9 G5**.

Soho

Damson & Co NEW

21 Brewer Street, W1F 0RL (3697 2499, www.damsonandco.co.uk). Leicester Square or Piccadilly Circus tube. **Main courses** £3.50-£12.50. **Credit** MC, V.

New one-off coffee bars take root every week in Hackney, but it takes nerve for an independent to sign up for Soho rents. Damson & Co is one such brave café, and it's a looker. There's much attention to detail in the shabby-chic, artfully functional interior. Many customers sit at their MacBooks over cups of freshly ground coffee, the roasts supplied by Ozone in Shoreditch. Cakes and snacks are displayed and there's a varied selection of bottled beers, wines by the glass, and even a choice of gin and tonics. A large party of office colleagues were working their way through the sparkling wine selection one lunchtime. The list of savoury dishes makes a good read – British charcuterie and cheeses, fresh seafood. The signature breakfast dish of 'Damson muffin' was a well-stacked tower of omelette, baked beans and cheese, in a muffin that tasted like it might have been slightly stale before being toasted. Presentation seems to take precedence over practicality: dressed crab arrived in a bowl of melting ice, which looked good, but

slush kept tipping into the shell. Damson & Co is much more personable than Soho's many chain cafés, and it's great for coffee. The food might not always match the high prices, but those rents have to be paid…

Tables outdoors (1, pavement). Takeaway service. Vegan dishes. **Map 17 B4**.

Maison Bertaux

28 Greek Street, W1D 5DQ (7437 6007, www.maisonbertaux.com). Leicester Square, Piccadilly Circus or Tottenham Court Road tube. **Open** 9am-10.30pm Mon-Sat; 9am-8pm Sun. **Main courses** £3.50-£4.70. **Credit** (over £10) MC, V.

This tiny, 19th-century Soho institution prides itself on being London's oldest surviving French pâtisserie. Whether it's still also 'the best' is neither here nor there: you drop by because it's there, because it's quaint and as far from corporate as can be, because it's an old and familiar friend, or because it's on the tourist trail. There's now an annexe to the left of the original ground floor room, but habitués prefer to squeeze on to the pavement if weather permits, or to cram themselves by the old piano, surveying the memorabilia, peeling plaster and spangly swags of stuff while nibbling an almond croissant. Tea and coffee have no more caught up with modernity than the non-automated till; service is endearingly chaotic and rather geared to the event order facility that ensures Maison Bertaux's survival. Prices alone are in touch with current trends, but they seem a small sum to pay to ensure the survival of an icon.

Babies and children admitted. Tables outdoors (8, pavement). Takeaway service. **Map 17 C4**.

★ Nordic Bakery

14A Golden Square, W1F 9JG (3230 1077, www.nordicbakery.com). Piccadilly Circus tube. **Meals served** 8am-8pm Mon-Fri; 9am-7pm Sat; 10am-7pm Sun. **Main courses** £3.25-£4.20. **Credit** AmEx, MC, V.

Stepping out of the anarchy of Soho, pushing open the heavy wooden door and crossing over into

Nordic Bakery's calm, ordered world gives you a rush of reassurance that everything will, in fact, be alright. You'll be greeted by attractive smiling servers and cocooned in a warm wood-lined interior where everything, from the Alvar Aalto furniture to the Helvetica signage, is clean of line and muted in tone. Even the sandwiches look pretty – neat circles of dark rye supporting Scandinavian staples such as gravadlax, brie and lingonberry, or the delicious combination of vinegary herring with soft egg and a smooth mustardy mayonnaise. Or try a karelian pie – a traditional Finnish rice or potato pasty, perhaps with a bottle of Nordic's in-house blueberry cordial. Get there early if you want to get your hands on one of the famous cinnamon buns, though the squishy, sugary butter buns are pretty addictive too.

Babies and children admitted. Bookings not accepted. Takeaway service. **Map 17 A4**.
For branches see index.

Strand

Fernandez & Wells

East Wing, Somerset House, Strand, WC2R 1LA (7420 9408, www.fernandezandwells.com). Temple tube. **Open** 8am-10pm Mon-Fri; 10am-10pm Sat; 10am-8pm Sun. **Main courses** £5-£21. **Credit** AmEx, MC, V.

This is the biggest and most attractive café of the thriving Fernandez & Wells mini-chain: four impressive rooms in the east wing of Somerset House, astutely set up for all-day grazing. Oversized geometric paintings by British artist David Tremlett occupy the full extent of the walls, while a long, cool bar made of York stone runs through the middle of the main café area. F&W's menu flits easily between breakfast, lunch and dinner. Meat is central: the 'ham room' is set up for carving slices of lomito ibérico, jamón de lampiño, or wild fennel Tuscan salami, while fat ham legs hang artfully from the wall (vegetarians, we should add, are still well catered for). Breakfast was simple and effective: two fried eggs sprinkled with za'atar, miniature morcilla sausages and two pieces of

toasted sourdough. While the pain au chocolat was a little dry, a Portuguese pastel de nata had a rich custard filling and a sturdy yet flaky base. Sandwiches overflow with fillings, including grilled chorizo and roasted pepper ciabatta, or aubergine, goat's cheese and pesto in a brioche bun, but you'd be foolish to miss out on the cracking sausage roll, which had a coarse-ground filling and a hint of harissa.

Available for hire. Babies and children welcome: nappy-changing facilities. Disabled: toilet. Tables outdoors (7, terrace). **Map 10 M7.**
For branches see index.

West
Ladbroke Grove

Books for Cooks
4 Blenheim Crescent, W11 1NN (7221 1992, www.booksforcooks.com). Ladbroke Grove tube. **Open** 10am-6pm Tue, Wed, Fri, Sat; 10am-5.30pm Thur. **Lunch served** noon-2pm Tue-Fri; 11.30am-2pm Sat. **Set lunch** £5 2 courses, £7 3 courses. **Credit** MC, V.
Books for Cooks runs on a simple but very successful formula. From the small open kitchen, co-owner Eric Treuillé puts recipes (one starter, one main) from the cookbook(s) of the day to the test. There's no choice – until it comes to pudding, when there's an array of must-try cakes (lemon victoria sponge, raspberry and pear cake, or chocolate and orange cake, say) – but the standard of cooking is high. Pea and ricotta salad with focaccia followed by merguez, roast lamb and rice made a lovely summer lunch. Coffee is also good. White wine lovers must go elsewhere: only red wine from Eric's own biodynamic vineyard is served (it's also available to take away, along with his olive oil). So popular is the bargain lunch in the tiny café at the back of this specialist cookbook shop that regulars start lurking from 11.45am to secure a table (no bookings are taken).
Bookings not accepted. **Map 19 B3.**

Westbourne Grove

Tom's Deli
226 Westbourne Grove, W11 2RH (7221 8818, www.tomsdelilondon.co.uk). Ladbroke Grove or Notting Hill Gate tube. **Open** 8am-6.30pm Mon-Sat; 9am-6.30pm Sun. **Main courses** £10-£12. **Credit** (over £5) AmEx, MC, V.
The booth seats at the first-floor café section of Tom's Deli are only lightly attached to the wall, so if – as on our most recent visit – the person behind you sneezes, light tremors ricochet through. But who cares about tremulous seating when the passion cake is as good as this? Tom's version is a moist, multi-layered treat that leaves you feeling as if you've been bearhugged by Santa. The rest of the food's pretty solid too: we can vouch for the grilled courgette and goat's cheese salad, the fluffy omelettes and the delightful grilled sandwiches. Well-to-do Notting Hill kookiness describes the vibe here: Shepard Fairey and Banksy on the walls, pink flamingos in the windows and a raft of outsized mobiles hanging at the entrance. A deli occupies the basement and stocks speciality cheddar and wheels of brie alongside US imports including jars of marshmallow fluff. The ground floor is home to sweets and a vast selection of amaretti; out the back

Nordic Bakery. See p273.

there's a tiny garden with a few tables. Service can be a bit muddled at times, but overall this is a fun place for a W11 luncheon.
Babies and children welcome: high chairs. Tables outdoors (6, garden; 2, terrace). Takeaway service. **Map 7 A6.**

South West
Barnes

★ Orange Pekoe
3 White Hart Lane, SW13 0PX (8876 6070, www.orangepekoeteas.com). Barnes Bridge rail or bus 209. **Open** 7.30am-6pm Mon-Fri; 9am-6pm Sat, Sun. **Meals served** 8.30am-5.30pm Mon-Fri; 9am-5.30pm Sat, Sun. **Main courses** £4.95-£8.95. **Set tea** £18.95 (£23.95 incl champagne). **Credit** (over £10) AmEx, MC, V.
In good weather, you can be sure the outdoor tables at this perennially popular café on the Barnes/Mortlake border will be taken. Probably the indoor tables too: Orange Pekoe isn't big, but it is bright thanks to a skylight and white-painted brick walls, prettified with a few decorative teacups and some statement wallpaper. There are no seats in the front room, which is dominated by the coffee machine and a counter displaying cakes and sandwiches, alongside a wall lined with black and gold tea canisters. More than 50 loose-leaf teas (black, oolong, green, white, yellow) and herbal infusions are available to buy: from a house breakfast blend for around a fiver per 100g, to a premium Japanese green tea at over £30. However, a pot of any tea costs £3.90 – a brilliant way of trying out new or unusual varieties. Food is excellent, from breakfast goodies (pastries, granola with prune compote, assorted egg dishes) via lunchtime savouries (ploughman's and vegetarian platters, a daily soup, tart and salad) to afternoon tea of plump scones and finger sandwiches (with or without champagne. Pekoe Royal – two poached eggs on a toasted muffin with spinach leaves and a big heap of high-quality smoked salmon – was indeed a regal treat.
Babies and children welcome: high chairs; nappy-changing facilities. Tables outdoors (7, pavement). Takeaway service.

South
Balham

Trinity Stores
5-6 Balham Station Road, SW12 9SG (8673 3773, www.trinitystores.co.uk). Balham tube/rail. **Open** 8am-7pm Mon-Fri; 9am-5.30pm Sat; 9.30am-5pm Sun. **Main courses** £3.75-£9.55. **Credit** (over £5) MC, V.
It may have a less-than-perfect location in full view of the exodus of commuters from Balham station, but stepping into Trinity Stores is like being transported to a country kitchen – a city dweller's take on a country kitchen, that is. There's an assortment of farmhouse chairs; tables are set with fresh daisies or jam jars of brown sugar. These days, the place is less 'store' than café, with essentials in the chiller (from bacon and eggs to salad leaves and sausages) and a basketful of artisanal loaves and french pastries; most visitors come here to eat, not shop. The cooking is solid, rather than sensational, mixing perennial favourites (such as posh scotch eggs and quiches) with a selection of own-made picnic goodies. Our large, caramel-coloured sausage roll had a crunchy, slightly chewy pastry crust and a dense, beautifully seasoned middle. A tart with a crumbly, buttery base topped with morsels of soft green pepper and slices of thick pan-fried chorizo was equally delicious. By contrast, a salad of soft pearl barley with kidney beans and chunks of roasted veg (red peppers, courgettes, aubergines) needed a sharp vinaigrette to lift it, rather than a plain olive oil dressing. Breakfasts are popular, as are the staff: as sweet as the cake counter.
Available for hire. Babies and children welcome: high chairs. Tables outdoors (2, pavement). Takeaway service.

Battersea

Urban Gourmet NEW
201 St John's Hill, SW11 1TH (3441 1200, www.urban-gourmet.co.uk). Clapham Junction or Wandsworth Town rail. **Open** 8am-7pm Mon-Fri; 9am-7pm Sat; 9am-6pm Sun. **Main courses** £5-£15. **Credit** MC, V.

CAFÉS

This café-deli only has a dozen seats, but it punches well above its weight. Gourmet groceries come from near and far: organic bread from the Celtic Bakers, truffled salami from Italy and Silent Slasher bottled beer from Piddle, a Dorset brewery. Urban Gourmet is also one of the few places in the capital to stock Bookhams' British rennet-free 'parmesan'. There are vegan savoury pastries and gluten-free cakes (lemon semolina, say), yet the sell-out item (from Surrey cake-maker Flossy Cockles) is one of pure decadence: a double-decker chocolate ganache cake, fully encased in Maltesers. Owner Elizabeth Bell is an ex-Sydneysider, and the Greek salad was more a homage to Aussie Greek cooking than anything you'd find in the Aegean. But it was zingy and full-flavoured, combining crumbly feta, chunky ripe tomatoes and gutsy green olives with a tumble of lettuce, basil and parsley. Also excellent was a warmly spiced spinach and lentil soup, served with dinky slices of terrific olive bread. The only blip was a veggie pasty (billed as a 'samosa') with dry pastry and underseasoned filling. Urban Gourmet may be small, but on the whole it's beautiful.

Books for Cooks. See p275.

Available for hire. Babies and children welcome: high chairs. Tables outdoors (3, pavement). Takeaway service. **Map 21 B4**.

Clapham

Breads Etcetera
127 Clapham High Street, SW4 7SS (no phone). Clapham Common or Clapham North tube. **Open** 10am-10pm Tue-Sat; 10am-4pm Sun. **Main courses** £5-£9.25. **No credit cards**.
This bakery-cum-café (also known as the Ferm) has been going strong for the past decade, and come noon every weekend, there's a queue of up to half an hour, out the door and on to Clapham High Street, for a table. So what's the attraction? What the Danes call *hygge* and the Germans call *Gemütlichkeit*: a relaxed cosiness, created by smiling staff and toasters on the tables. An enormous basket of freshly baked sourdough loaves sits on a countertop in the middle of the room: white or wholemeal, rye or seeds, and all still wonderful despite the change of baker. The idea is to help yourself, cutting off as many different slices as you dare, and toast them at your table. This 'DIY' option costs £6.50, and as the staff point out, the only slightly dearer all-day breakfasts work out better value as you then get the bread for 'free'. Not that you'll have much room for extra toast, as the breakfast portions are big: the 'super duper huge omelette' overflows even the large dinner plate it's served on. The vegan and vegetarian options are particularly strong, from the fruit and nut french toast to a vegan version of pyttipanna (Swedish bubble and squeak). In the evenings, the emphasis changes to an Italian menu, with – of course – sourdough-based pizzas among the options. Note: it's cash only.
Babies and children admitted. Bookings not accepted. Takeaway service. **Map 22 B2**.

Macaron
22 The Pavement, SW4 0HY (7498 2636). Clapham Common tube. **Open** 7.30am-7pm daily. **Main courses** £2.85-£4.50. **No credit cards**.
On a prime spot at the fashionable end of Clapham Common, Macaron is one of several cafés with a handful of outside tables serving the constant traffic of Commoners heading from Clapham Old Town to the tube. It's also the best of the bunch, not just because it looks charmingly French, but also because all the baked goods are made in the in-house bakery, which you can watch through a large pane of glass at the back of the dining area. Help-yourself viennoiseries are displayed at the entrance; the croissants and pains au chocolat are highlights. Rustic breads are displayed on countertops, while excellent French pâtisserie, from citron tarts to vibrantly coloured macaroons, are kept behind glass. Savoury snacks – such as filled baguettes, croque-monsieurs, quiches – are the preferred choice of those eating in. The coffee can be variable, depending on who is making it; coffee connoisseurs had best look elsewhere. But for location and ambience, Macaron (est. 2006) still has no peer in this neighbourhood.
Tables outdoors (3, pavement). Takeaway service. **Map 22 A2**.

Tooting

Graveney & Meadow
40 Mitcham Road, SW17 9NA (8672 9016, www.graveneyandmeadow.com). Tooting Broadway tube. **Open** 9am-11pm Mon-Wed; 9am-midnight Thur; 9am-1am Fri; 10am-1am Sat; 10am-11pm Sun. **Lunch served** noon-3pm Mon-Fri. **Brunch served** 10am-3pm Sat, Sun. **Tapas served** 6-10pm Tue-Thur; 6-11pm Fri, Sat. **Main courses** £6-£8. **Tapas** £2-£7. **Credit** MC, V.
Tooting is more of a melee of fast-food takeaways, chains and pound shops than a destination for quality food, but where it does make its mark on the food scene, the Antic London collective is usually responsible. With several dozen refurbished pubs and bars under its belt, the group has hit upon a happy formula that gives its hostelries a unified character and wide-ranging appeal without forsaking quirks and individuality. Café-bar Graveney & Meadow is the latest in an Antic trio within a hundred yards of each other and is busy attracting its very own crowd. A sensibly priced tapas menu is swapped for barbecues in the summer, featuring the likes of chorizo hot dogs,

chargrilled swordfish (sustainably sourced), organic burgers and heritage tomato salad. Sourcing throughout is well-considered: bread and cake comes from the in-house bakery, while beers from local Sambrook's and Hogs Back keep after-work drinkers merry. The sprawling terrace may have an uninspiring supermarket backdrop, but the customary Antic anti-design look of bric-a-brac provides ample distraction both outdoors and in. *Babies and children welcome: high chairs; nappy-changing facilities. Booking advisable. Disabled: toilet. Separate room for parties, seats 40. Tables outdoors (30, garden).*

South East
Brockley

Arlo & Moe
340 Brockley Road, SE4 2BT (07749 667207). Crofton Park rail. **Open** 8am-4.30pm Mon-Fri; 9am-4pm Sat; 10am-4pm Sun. **Main courses** £2.50-£12. **No credit cards**.
A firm Crofton Park family favourite – light, spacious and well-stocked with highchairs and baby-changing facilities – Arlo & Moe rocks a 1950s vibe with colourful Formica tables, Ercol chairs and spotty Midwinter plates. Depending on which children you are sharing the space with, it can be a relaxed and friendly place to enjoy a cup of tea and a slice of squishy Guinness and chocolate or spicy carrot cake. Lunch choices are limited to sausage rolls, sandwiches, frittata, quiche and a few specials such as gazpacho with manchego, olives and garlic bruschetta. We love the 'sexy toast' – crunchy sourdough with toppings ranging from cream cheese and honey or avocado and feta to no-nonsense Heinz baked beans. Birthday cakes are also a speciality.
Babies and children welcome: high chairs; nappy-changing facilities. Booking advisable. Takeaway service.

Broca
4 Coulgate Street, SE4 2RW (8691 0833, www.brocafoods.com). Brockley rail. **Open** 7am-7pm Mon-Fri; 8am-6pm Sat; 9am-6pm Sun. **Main courses** £3-£3.50. **No credit cards**.
Handily situated right beside Brockley station and vying for attention with slicker neighbour Browns, the Broca veers towards shabby chic and '80s punnery. The sandwich menu, with a choice of granary or sourdough, references seminal movies: 'Ham Solo' (anything but: it's packed with ham, cheddar, peppers and gherkins), 'Tuna Wolf' (guess) and 'I ain't afraid of no goats' (goat's cheese and salad). We went for the Abe Froman, just because we're Ferris fans, but sadly they were out of chorizo sausage. There's an extensive list of vitamin-packed smoothies, with yet more puns: the Blueberry Thrill, Flu Fighter, Son of a Peach… A living-room aesthetic comes with fringed standard lamps, coffee tables, sofas, one of those knitted throws your nan used to have and, for those really intending to make themselves at home, shelves of books to take or swap (possibly a warning about the slow, uncertain service). A second venture, the Broca Food Market, has recently opened on the other side of the station (209-211 Mantle Road); nip across the footbridge to stock up on organic groceries.
Available for hire evenings. Babies and children welcome: high chairs. Takeaway service.

Urban Gourmet. See p275.

Browns of Brockley
5 Coulgate Street, SE4 2RW (8692 0722, www.brownsofbrockley.com). Brockley rail. **Open** 7.30am-5pm Mon-Fri; 9am-5pm Sat; 10am-4pm Sun. **Main courses** £3-£5. **Credit** MC, V.
This is more of a commuter-friendly coffee bar than full-blown eaterie, but they do take their beans seriously: Square Mile pulled on a La Marzocco espresso machine, with a guest filter coffee every week and 'cupping' classes to teach regulars how to better appreciate their brew. To accompany it are some surprisingly refined sweetmeats: greengage and lavender friands, apricot crumble, and some light and extremely addictive cinnamon doughnut muffins. The lunchtime crowd are fed with salads and thinly cut sandwiches on sourdough, neatly filled with high-quality ingredients such as Wiltshire ham, pastrami or sauerkraut (plus an indulgent peanut butter, honey and banana for those who missed breakfast or miss their nanny). A light airy space, high wooden benches to sit at and welcoming service make Browns a popular local pit stop.
Available for hire evenings. Babies and children admitted. Takeaway service.

Camberwell

Johansson's
2 Grove Lane, SE5 8SY (7701 4944, www.johanssons.co.uk). Denmark Hill tube/rail. **Meals served** 9am-5pm Mon-Fri; 10am-5.30pm Sat. **Dinner served** 6.30-11pm Wed-Sat. **Main courses** £6.50-£15. **No credit cards**.
What looks from the street like a run-of-the-mill sandwich shop turns out to hide a series of relaxed rooms, finishing in french windows that open on to a patio garden shaded by vines and a fig tree. The menu is as deceptively extensive as the interior, starting with weekday brunchy breakfasts, moving on to well-dressed lunchtime salads made to order, daily specials, panini, quiche, soup, and burger and chips. Sandwiches run the gamut of staples, from tuna melt to chicken and bacon, but check out the specials board for more interesting fillings, such as stilton with walnut and pear, or a classic reubens. There are also thick milkshakes made with real fruit, smoothies, and own-baked cakes and pastries. In the evenings, Johansson's transforms from café into relaxed restaurant and starts to live up to its

Graveney & Meadow. See p276.

Scandinavian name with dishes such as cured salmon, reindeer terrine and own-roasted ham. *Babies and children welcome: high chairs. Separate room for parties, seats 30. Tables outdoors (12, garden). Takeaway service.*

Crystal Palace

Brown & Green
Crystal Palace Station, Station Road, SE19 2AZ (no phone, www.brownandgreencafe.com). Crystal Palace rail. **Open** 6.30am-4.30pm Mon-Fri; 10am-5pm Sat. **Main courses** £3-£6.75. **Credit** MC, V.
With the arrival of the 'Ginger Line' in Crystal Palace has come a refurb of the lofty Victorian station, a new breed of commuter and a branch of Brown & Green to serve them (the original, much smaller branch is at Gipsy Hill station). Tucked into the concourse, and right on the edge of Crystal Palace Park, it's a grand space brought down to earth with lampshades made from coffee sacks, Formica tables, reclaimed school desks and old Southern Railway signs. You can tuck into brunch favourites such as thick bacon butties on toasted sourdough with rocket and tomato or scrambled eggs and chorizo, or opt for a simple soup. Children come high up in the priorities with wholesome nursery food and treats such as frothy milk with sprinkles, while the breakfast menu includes both vegetarian and vegan compositions. Tea drinkers will appreciate the range of Jenier loose-leaf teas. A refreshing change from the park's other, decidedly old-school, café.
Available for hire. Babies and children welcome: children's menu; high chairs; nappy-changing facilities. Tables outdoors (2, pavement). Takeaway service. Vegan dishes.
For branch see index.

Forest Hill

Montage
33 Dartmouth Road, SE23 3HN (7207 9890, www.themontage.net). Forest Hill rail. **Open** 10am-6pm Mon, Wed-Sat; 10am-5pm Sun. **Main courses** £4-£5. **Credit** AmEx, MC, V.
Chilled, charming and delightfully domestic in scale, this café-gallery is made up of a series of small rooms papered with old maps and pages from

cookbooks, and filled with junk-shop furniture and finds (some of it for sale) – well-worn chairs tucked under the staircase, a cast-iron fireplace with a clock on the mantelpiece, an old door nailed on to some legs as a table. At the back, down a rickety staircase, is a makeshift conservatory and a small, secluded garden. The Montage doubles as an art gallery, so the walls are also crammed with work by local artists; the first floor, by contrast, is a cool white exhibition space. In this curious environment, an arty crowd sup mochas and mull over how to fill their weekend, while the friendly owners serve freshly baked cakes (victoria sponge with real strawberries, scones, brownies, and a cheese and onion cake) and talk art. You're likely to leave relaxed, recharged and humming the soundtrack of ragtime tunes.
Available for hire. Babies and children welcome: high chairs; toys. Tables outdoors (7, garden; 1, pavement). Takeaway service.

★ St David Coffee House
5 David's Road, SE23 3EP (8291 6646, www.stdavidcoffeehouse.co.uk). Forest Hill rail or bus 122, 185. **Open** 8am-6pm Tue-Fri; 9am-6pm Sat; 10am-4pm Sun. **Main courses** £2.50-£4.50. **No credit cards.**
This relaxed coffeehouse is a homeworker's heaven, and many look like they won't be shifting before lunchtime. A few small tables sit out on the raised pavement among the pot plants and community orchard trees, but our favourite spot is at the big communal table by the open window. The interior is another junk shop fit-out, with kitsch touches such as the birdcage lampshade (with artificial birds) and *Top of the Pops* LPs. Where it gets serious, though, is the coffee – a Square Mile roast packed a powerful punch – with some good alternatives from Suki tea, such as Earl Grey Blue Flower or Apple Loves Mint. Food is simple: cakes such as carrot cake and custard tarts, quiches and chunky sandwiches. There's no skimping on the quality of the fillings – Neal's Yard Dairy comté with pear and ale chutney; Brindisa cured pork and manchego; chorizo with piquillo peppers and rocket; or the ultimate comfort food, the cheese and baked beans toastie.
Available for hire. Babies and children welcome: high chairs. Disabled: toilet. Tables outdoors (3, pavement). Takeaway service.

Herne Hill

Lido Café
Brockwell Lido, Dulwich Road, SE24 0PA (7737 8183, www.thelidocafe.co.uk). Herne Hill rail or Brixton tube/rail then bus 37. **Open** 8am-6pm Mon, Sun; 8am-11pm Tue-Sat; winter hours may vary. **Main courses** £11.50-£18. **Credit** MC, V.
As befits a café attached to one of south London's best-loved outdoor swimming pools, the Lido Café is light-filled and very chilled. The interior design is smart and airy with stark beech and white furnishings, opening out on to a decked area overlooking the water, and punctuated with potted palms and blue parasols. The monthly menu is short but designed with love, care and boundless enthusiasm for seasonal British produce, stretching from the breakfast menu of eggs benedict, fry-ups and blueberry buttermilk pancakes, to light lunches (Severn & Wye smoked salmon and rye bread, charcuterie platter with pickles, salads) to sophisticated evening dinners (grilled harissa mackerel with crushed Jersey Royals and samphire salad; cardamom confit free-range duck leg with English asparagus). Fish cakes on creamed spinach didn't stand out, but a burger with all the trimmings on sweet brioche was perfectly balanced. Alternatively, you could just pop in for a seriously good coffee, a wicked slice of cake and a few lengths of front crawl. At weekends, the place is inevitably awash with swimmers and dry-side diners but during the week, the lido offers a tranquillity that can be hard to come by in London.
Available for hire. Babies and children welcome: children's menu; high chairs; nappy-changing facilities. Disabled: toilet. Tables outdoors (10, terrace). Takeaway service. Vegan dishes.
Map 22 E1.

New Cross

★ London Particular
399 New Cross Road, SE14 6LA (8692 6149, www.thelondonparticular.co.uk). New Cross or New Cross Gate rail or bus 136, 171. **Open** 8am-5pm Mon-Thur; 8am-10pm Fri; 10am-10pm Sat; 10am-5pm Sun. **Main courses** £5-£9.50. **No credit cards.**
Food, described as 'classic English with a modern twist', is treated with respect at this tiny café just

by New Cross station. Particular by name, particular by nature: founder and head chef Becky Davey and her team source seasonal ingredients from small-scale producers, then prepare them freshly on the premises. Lunch shows vegetarian leanings – soft, tasty sweet potato and leek cakes served with halloumi, a salad and a beetroot dip, for example – while light suppers are meatier (rabbit rillettes, harissa sticky pork ribs), but if you are the kind of person who encounters a vegetarian dish and thinks 'this is delicious but it would be even better with bacon' then you can add that too for an extra pound. Commitment to independent operators continues through to the wines (mainly organic or biodynamic) and beers (from Kernel and Cheddar Ales breweries). Help yourself to a jug of water with mint, or order the refreshing Deptford elderflower with soda, but before you leave, go for the velvety punch of an HR Higgins coffee (iced, affogato or just flat white) to set you up for the rest of the day. Cash only.
Available for hire. Tables outdoors (3, pavement). Takeaway service. Vegan dishes.

Nunhead

Bambuni
143 Evelina Road, SE15 3HB (7732 4150, www.bambuni.co.uk). Nunhead rail. **Open** 9am-5.30pm Tue-Sat; 10am-4pm Sun. **Main courses** £4-£5. **Credit** (over £10) MC, V.
Could it be that unassuming Nunhead's main drag has finally reached the critical mass of food shops, retro outlets and galleries that allows it to be described as 'up and coming'? If so, Bambuni is

right at the heart of it. This deli/café/local hub has been a real labour of love for owner Huey, who built the place with his own hands and maintains a mission to source the best and the local. This includes more than 50 cheeses and nearly 100 craft beers, all available for consumption on site. Made-to-order sandwiches include salami, comté and gherkins, or raclette, onion marmalade and dijon mustard. There are plenty of sweet things too, not least Ice Cream Union ices, best enjoyed on a summer's day in the tiny Mediterranean-style courtyard. Come for a flat white (Huey takes his coffee seriously) and leave with a refillable bottle of red wine, a tub of olives and several scoops of loose granola. Look out for after-hours events such as tapas evenings, beer tastings and bar nights.
Babies and children welcome: high chairs; nappy-changing facilities. Tables outdoors (2, pavement; 3, garden). Takeaway service.

The Dish & the Spoon
61 Cheltenham Road, SE15 3AF (7635 6384). Honor Oak Park rail. **Open** 9am-4pm Tue-Fri; 9am-5pm Sat; 9am-3pm Sun. **Main courses** £4.50-£6.50. **Credit** MC, V.
The nursery rhyme name, the fairytale wooden cutouts on the walls, the well-stocked play area, the Thursday puppet shows… it's clear who this café is aimed at – and its loyal customer base of under-5s love it. Food is healthy and nutritious – no chicken nuggets here – but they'll bend over backwards to accommodate children's requirements with treats such as Nutella on toast and Ella's Kitchen smoothie pouches. Grown-ups have a fine time too. There are traditional cakes (carrot, lemon

drizzle, jam sponge, earl grey tea loaf), a board of soups and specials, and, when it says something comes 'with salad' (in our case a nice pea and shallot frittata), they mean five salads: potato, minty carrot, chilli courgette, couscous, houmous, plus a little dish of own-made cucumber pickle. Make it a pit stop if you are following the Green Chain Walk past One Tree Hill (an oasis in this otherwise residential area), or pick up a picnic and head for nearby Peckham Rye.
Available for hire. Babies and children welcome: children's menu; high chairs; nappy-changing facilities. Booking advisable Fri. Tables outdoors (4, pavement). Takeaway service. Vegan dishes.

Peckham

Anderson & Co
139 Bellenden Road, SE15 4DH (7469 7078, www.andersonandcompany.wordpress.com). Peckham Rye rail. **Open** 8am-4.30pm Mon-Thur, Sat; 8am-10.30pm Fri; 8.30am-4pm Sun.
Main courses £4.75-£20. **Credit** MC, V.
This airy white space off hip and happening Bellenden Road attracts a mixed crowd of well-to-do locals, including those in pushchairs. There's a pleasant courtyard garden at the back and the rear room is shared with an open kitchen, where you can observe ham hocks being boiled, chickens roasted, tarts baked, salads prepared and fish griddled – all of which creates an atmosphere of good, fresh food being whipped up by chefs who know what they're doing. Breakfasts are served until a very forgiving 2pm (3pm at weekends) and involve thick-cut toast piled high with bacon, mushrooms, eggs and other

Brown & Green

favourites. Sandwiches are made with sourdough from local Brickhouse Bakery, and although the wait for a sausage roll to be heated up was interminable, it did arrive with an apology, and was succulent and flaky in all the right places.
Available for hire. Babies and children welcome: high chairs. Booking advisable. Disabled: toilet. Tables outdoors (8, garden; 3, pavement). Takeaway service. **Map 23 C3.**

Café Viva

44 Choumert Road, SE15 4SE (no phone, www.cafeviva.co.uk). Peckham Rye rail or bus 12, 37. **Open** *7.30am-5pm Tue-Fri; 9am-5pm Sat, Sun.* **Main courses** £4-£7. **Credit** MC, V.
When Café Viva popped up amid the jerk chicken outlets and market stalls just off Rye Lane, it brought a tiny corner of calm to this end of Choumert Road. It's an unpretentious little unit – white walls, poured concrete floor and exposed brick – but it has already gained a reputation for the best coffee in the area (roasted by Volcano in nearby West Norwood). The rest of the food's rather good too – courgette and pea frittata served with a crisp baby-leaf salad, say, freshly made smoothies and sandwiches, or a moist banana cake (excitingly allowable as a breakfast item, with an option of greek yoghurt on the side) – all served on retro mismatched crockery. It's a handy caffeine stop for the loyal following of commuters en route to Peckham Rye station, but when the rush is past, the bare interior is a welcoming home to Bellenden Road types reading Merleau-Ponty or discussing forthcoming art pop-ups.

Babies and children welcome: high chairs. Tables outdoors (2, pavement). Takeaway service. **Map 23 C2.**

Petitou

63 Choumert Road, SE15 4AR (7639 2613, www.petitou.co.uk). Peckham Rye rail. **Open** *9am-5.30pm Mon-Sat; 10am-5.30pm Sun.* **Main courses** £6.60-£7.95. **Credit** MC, V.
Rumours that Peckham was becoming as up-itself as East Dulwich have been, thankfully, greatly exaggerated. All the same, Petitou occupies a leafy corner plot in an area rather grandly known as the Bellenden Conservation Area, which comes as something of a surprise, being just one block down from the roustabout Rye Lane with its Asda, myriad phone unlockers and halal meat markets. There are tables on the pavement, among the planters, and inside the L-shaped café there's a good deal of reclaimed, scrubbed wood, and flyers about yoga and meditation. Food is bracing: hefty quiches and salads; well-filled sandwiches on hunky granary breads, with own-made chilli jam among the extras. Meat and fish is responsibly sourced, with oft-praised hams from adjacent butcher Flock & Herd. A colourful three-salad combo (greek, green and creamy new potato) came with delicious warm flatbread, so made a satisfying lunch. Repleteness did not, however, prevent us from ordering a moist lemon polenta cake with our coffee, along with a Tweet Tweet biscuit. The latter we assumed would be worthily punishing, being gluten- and sugar-free, but turned out to be a melt-in-the-mouth, protein-packed composite of tahini, dates, seeds

and nuts – a sweet tweet indeed. It doesn't do to judge by appearances round here.
Babies and children welcome: high chairs. Tables outdoors (6, terrace). Takeaway service. Vegan dishes. **Map 23 C3.**

East

Docklands

Frizzante@Mudchute

Mudchute Park & Farm, Pier Street, E14 3HP (3069 9290, www.frizzanteltd.co.uk). Mudchute DLR. **Open** *10am-5pm Fri-Sun; summer hours may vary.* **Main courses** £2.50-£11. **Credit** (over £10) MC, V.
Mudchute Farm is a revelation – minutes from the DLR and edged by Canary Wharf's concrete jungle, you'll find goats, sheep, horses... even llamas ambling about in sprawling parkland – and the kitchen offers up its own surprises. Outside, the clutch of wooden picnic tables isn't altogether promising (it's within smelling distance of the stables) but step inside and the queue of patient punters speaks volumes. Running the show is Frizzante, the company behind the well-loved cafés at Hackney City Farm and Surrey Docks Farm; its honest Anglo-Italian cooking is a big hit across all three sites. Menus make use of seasonal ingredients and, where possible, produce from the farm gardens. Coffee is thoroughly decent, sweet treats oven-fresh (try the orange polenta cake) and brunches generously portioned (full marks for the

London Particular. See p278.

CAFÉS

fish-finger sarnie with punchy tartare sauce and rounds of crisp potato 'chips' sliced whole widthways). You can visit, too, for a Sunday roast (corn-fed chicken with sautéed greens and more of those chips) but our biggest cheer goes to the pasta – like everything else, it's made fresh on site and, on our last visit, meant gnocchi with a tender pork ragù. Toasties and gelati help little ones refuel after all the fun of the farm.
Available for hire. Babies and children welcome: children's menu; high chairs; nappy-changing facilities. Bookings not accepted. Disabled: toilet (farm). Separate room for parties, seats 50. Tables outdoors (20, courtyard). Takeaway service. Map 24 C4.
For branches see index.

Shoreditch

Jones Dairy Café
23 Ezra Street, E2 7RH (7739 5372, www.jones dairy.co.uk). Hoxton rail. **Meals served** 9am-3pm Fri; 9am-4.30pm Sat; 8am-3pm Sun. **Main courses** £5-£11.50. **No credit cards.**
With its barn doors and stone floors, this former dairy retains a farmhouse feel, though there hasn't been a cow in here for decades. These days, the charming little space houses a handful of closely packed wooden tables clustered around a wood-burning stove. It's open Friday to Sunday only; as a quiet Friday lunch spot, Jones attracts locals such as teaching assistants from the nearby school, but come Sunday, the crowds from the neighbouring Columbia Road Flower Market create an altogether more animated atmosphere. Menu mainstays include the outstanding fish breakfast: fresh, fleshy smoked haddock doused in a sublime mustard sauce makes for the perfect brunch – filling but not incapacitating. Omelettes, bagels and a cheese plate are also on offer, and you can help yourself to a tray of preserves. A red pepper soup was flavourful, though the butter offered for the accompanying bread by our friendly if scatty waitress never materialised. An adjoining deli sells bread, juices and smoked salmon from small producers, while on Sundays there is often a table outside selling oysters to be slurped amid the hubbub of the market.
Babies and children welcome: high chairs. Bookings not accepted. Tables outdoors (6, pavement). Takeaway service. Map 6 S3.

Long White Cloud
151 Hackney Road, E2 8JL (7033 4642, www.longwhitecloud-hoxton.tumblr.com). Hoxton rail or bus 55. **Open** 7am-10pm Mon-Fri; 8am-5pm Sat, Sun. **Main courses** £4-£10. **Credit** MC, V.
The name comes from the Maori name for their country: Aotearoa, 'Land of the Long White Cloud', and generally suggests something more beautiful than a café on Hackney Road. The owners have done their best with the long white premises, but the place still looks slightly cold, with the decorative touches (plants, walls used as exhibition space) and second-hand furniture not managing to tip the balance towards homely. Happily, the quality of the food is lure enough. A full English breakfast was a proper reviver – flavour-packed and fresh-tasting, while scrambled eggs with green chilli was cooked just so, and had a delightful kick. Coffee (Monmouth) is good too. One of the owners is a Kiwi, and there are a few nods to NZ (kumara chips, for example, and a few packaged goods). As well as breakfast items, there are simple dishes such as

frittata with salads, sandwiches, and a small range of cakes. A limited evening menu runs Monday to Friday: all-you-can-eat pasta on Monday and Tuesday, pie on Wednesday, Mexican on Thursday, and burgers on Friday. Efficient service comes with a smile – this is no scenester hangout.
Available for hire. Babies and children admitted. Disabled: toilet. Tables outdoors (2, pavement). Takeaway service. Map 6 S3.

Spitalfields

TeaSmith
6 Lamb Street, E1 6EA (7247 1333, www.teasmith.co.uk). Liverpool Street tube/rail. **Open** 11am-6pm daily. **Afternoon tea** £20. **No credit cards.**
Odd, perhaps, to find such a calm space and specialised focus amid the commotion of Spitalfields market, and yet TeaSmith seems the ideal respite: a shop and tea room where time stills for a while, as matcha tea is whisked to a foam to top an affogato, or an oolong is infused at just the right off-boil temperature and gently strained for its first, second and third infusions at the needful moment. With much to discover, you could opt for a tasting menu at the tea bar on your first visit – a range of white, green and oolong teas are matched with delightful pastries from William Curley (Japanese-Scottish partnerships are behind both enterprises). Or settle for a second-flush Darjeeling, and survey the range of exquisite ceramics, postcards and tea paraphernalia while it brews.
Available for hire. Babies and children admitted. Takeaway service. Map 12 R5.

North East

Clapton

Venetia's
55 Chatsworth Road, E5 0LH (8986 1642, www.venetias.co.uk). Homerton rail or bus 242, 308. **Open** 8am-6pm daily. **Main courses** £3-£7. **Credit** (over £5) MC, V.
Venetia's was a symbol of demographic change when it first opened in 2006, as one of Chatsworth Road's first independent cafés focusing on well-considered local ingredients. Its pleasant, artsy interior – scuffed wooden floors, white wood-panelled walls and goldfish tank – may now look a bit old-hat compared to newer, hipper premises nearby (such as Shane's and Creperie du Monde), but its reputation as a place to enjoy excellent coffee remains. The flat white and latte we enjoyed on a Sunday morning visit were perfectly made. The food was less notable, with a menu of mainly toast- or pastry-based breakfasts and a large selection of sandwiches. Halloumi, houmous and red pepper sandwich would have been more appetising had the halloumi been grilled (as stated) and the ciabatta not been a little tired. Alternatively, you might plump for a BLT or a classic ham, emmental and mustard; or, for a healthier choice, try one of the freshly made vegetable juices. The menu may not be especially exciting, but Venetia's remains a stalwart on the street, thanks to its community noticeboard, shows of local artists, free Wi-Fi and the sizeable terrace at the back.
Available for hire. Babies and children welcome: children's menu; high chairs; nappy-changing facilities; toys. Booking advisable. Tables outdoors (6, garden). Takeaway service.

Dalston

★ Tina, We Salute You
47 King Henry's Walk, N1 4NH (3119 0047, www.tinawesaluteyou.com). Dalston Kingsland rail or bus 30, 38, 56, 277. **Open** 8am-6pm Mon-Fri; 10am-6pm Sat, Sun. **Main courses** £4-£6. **No credit cards.**
Tina's puts you instantly at ease: the large communal table in the middle – populated with help-yourself jars of Marmite and jam, and locals helping each other with the *Guardian* crossword – feel's like your best friend's kitchen table. (Sofas and a handful of pavement tables are also available for early arrivers.) Regulars work their way towards a lifetime discount by getting a star on the wall every time they buy a coffee; by the looks of things, Duncan, Andy M and Emma have a serious Tina habit. The café's namesake is a glamorous '60s icon who graces the wall, alongside an anything-goes mix of artwork and flyers for local events. Owners Danny and Steve make all the cakes at home, just as they have done since they first started running a cupcake stall off Brick Lane. A comforting breakfast menu (poached eggs, pancakes with berries, porridge) eases itself into lunch (toasted sandwiches, bagels, ploughman's). The beans with chorizo had sold out by the time we arrived, but fluffy American pancakes showed attention to detail with a buttery maple sauce, tart berries, and a dusting of icing sugar and oats. The 'breakfast trifle' is a triumph of granola, fruit and a dash of lemon curd. Tina's also serves consistently good coffee; expand your tastes beyond the usual latte with a Gibraltar (between a mini latte and a large macchiato). Cash only.
Available for hire. Babies and children admitted. Bookings not accepted. Disabled: toilet. Tables outdoors (3, pavement). Takeaway service.

Hackney

Wilton Way Café
63 Wilton Way, E8 1BG (7249 0444). Hackney Central rail or bus 38, 242, 277. **Open** 8am-5pm Mon-Fri; 8am-6pm Sat; 9am-6pm Sun. **Main courses** £2.50-£5.50. **No credit cards.**
This independently owned café isn't just an island of calm for a steady stream of twenty- and thirtysomethings, it's also the home of London Fields Radio, which is hosted from the corner of the room. As a result, some visits can be a little noisy, with interviews broadcast in the tiny space in real time. But it's a fun, laid-back atmosphere that's also reflected in the decoration. Recycled apple crates are used as makeshift tables, and curvy corrugated iron counters show off an array of cakes and pastries. Food is top-notch, with suppliers such as Brindisa, Ginger Pig and the local E5 Bakehouse. Coffees are equally stellar, with beans from nearby Climpson & Sons. Toasted snacks hit the mark too, with portobello mushroom and goat's curd on sourdough, chorizo and rocket sandwiches, and a very generous portion of avocado on toast. It might not be the biggest café in Hackney – brace yourself for a pram jam – but what it lacks in elbow room is more than made up for by the excellent food and a killer flat white.
Babies and children admitted. Entertainment: live radio station. Tables outdoors (4, pavement). Takeaway service.

CAFÉS

Hackney Wick

Counter Café

Stour Space, 7 Roach Road, E3 2PA (07834 275920, www.thecountercafe.co.uk). Hackney Wick tube/rail or bus 488. **Open** 8am-5pm Mon-Fri; 9am-5pm Sat, Sun. **Main courses** £4-£9. **Credit** AmEx, MC, V.

A javelin's throw from the Olympic Stadium across the canal, this delightfully thrown-together-looking joint behind artists' studios seems a world away. Arrive for a late lunch and the lack of pies and salads could be excused by the admission that it's more of a breakfast and brunch spot. (It doesn't explain the fact that the Anzac biscuit – there's some Antipodean connection here – and brownie were disappointing.) However, the last remaining pie, an excellent herby lamb number neatly encased in golden flaky pastry with well-dressed rustled-up colourful salad leaves, suggests it's worth arriving earlier. An all-day dish of perfectly poached eggs with reassuringly dark golden yolks, topped by smoked salmon, on slightly underpowered potato cakes, made up for lack of more lunch-specific choices. Own-made tomato relish left on the table in kilner jars went well with everything. The flat white is terrific. There's good music in the ground floor room right on the canal, and peace and quiet and a view of trees and the stadium from squidgy sofas and large tables upstairs. A great place for those in the area or a useful pit stop when exploring a fascinating, evolving area.
Available for hire. Babies and children admitted. Disabled: toilet. Tables outdoors (4, pavement; 20, canal). Takeaway service.

Haggerston

★ Towpath `HOT 50`

Regent's Canal towpath, between Whitmore Bridge and Kingsland Road Bridge, N1 5SB (no phone). Haggerston rail or 67, 149 bus. **Open** Mar-Nov 8am-dusk Tue-Fri; 9am-dusk Sat, Sun. **Main courses** £3-£8. **No credit cards.**

This simple operation on Regent's Canal towpath (near the Whitmore Bridge) was a novelty when it opened in 2010 in three shallow units. Three years later, it has expanded into four units, and continues to lure in passing walkers and cyclists with its original setting and enticing food and drink. Snag a table in the sunshine on a summer's day, and you might end up staying for hours. Relaxed entertainment is provided by families of swans, coots tending their nests, and passing bikes whizzing by. Our last visit, however, was a rainy affair – yet it proved that Towpath shouldn't only be reserved for fair weather. Huddling inside the covered, homely (think beaten-up furniture and cultural posters) open unit watching rain pummelling the canal was a comforting experience, made more so by the addition of delicious grilled cheese sandwiches and decent coffee. Come here for breakfast and the menu will usually include fried eggs on toast or granola with yoghurt, fruit and maple syrup. In the afternoon or early evening, choose from a range of alluring cakes (the beautifully light olive oil and lemon cake is a favourite) or savoury dishes such as pork tenderloin or own-made quiche.
Available for hire. Babies and children admitted. Bookings not accepted. Tables outdoors (10, towpath). **Map 6 R1.**

Victoria Park

Pavilion Café

Victoria Park, Crown Gate West, E9 7DE (8980 0030). Mile End tube then bus 277, 425. **Meals served** 8am-4pm Mon-Fri; 8am-5pm Sat, Sun. **Main courses** £4-£9. **Credit** MC, V.

Even during busy times, when all of E9 seems to have dropped in to this park café, staff maintain their smiles and efficiency. Customers queue for food inside the small domed pavilion, then grab a seat (there are loads) looking out over the boating lake. The Pavilion is run by the people behind Elliot's (*see p42*) and the menu is a cut above (though you can still get a tea for £1); own-made bread is also for sale. Interesting salads might be mackerel with beetroot, chicory and a (slightly overwhelming) horseradish dressing; doorstep sandwiches are the likes of salt beef with cucumber pickle and kolrabi coleslaw. Brunch and breakfast items include eggs florentine, royale and benedict, bacon (with optional egg) sandwiches, and three variations on the fry-up. The veggie version is a pricey £9, and was pretty good (just-right spinach, mushroom and tomato, a neat fried egg on lovely sourdough, tasty bubble and squeak), but the own-made beans are an acquired taste. There are cakes and puddings too: milk chocolate and grapefruit pudding was a super-moist chocolatey sponge, but had little citrus flavour. Drinks run from apple juice to Camden Town Brewery bottled beers.
Babies and children welcome: children's menu; high chairs; nappy-changing facilities. Bookings not accepted. Disabled: toilet. Tables outdoors (25, park). Takeaway service. Vegan dishes.

North
Finsbury Park

Boulangerie Bon Matin

178 Tollington Park, N4 3AJ (7263 8633, http://boulangeriebonmatin.co.uk). Finsbury Park tube/rail. **Open** 7am-6.30pm daily. **Main courses** £2.50-£6.15. **Credit** AmEx, MC, V.

The streets of Finsbury Park feel a little more continental with the scent of Bon Matin's freshly baked bread and viennoiserie. The comely window display is a little Ottolenghi-esque and, inside, rows of good-looking tarts, sandwiches, mini cheesecakes and quiches provide further invitation. As the name suggests, this café is more of a morning venue, but breakfast is a leisurely affair, served until 4pm, and for lunch there's a selection of colourful sandwiches (ciabatta, brioche or open) and a daily soup (a pleasingly light lentil and tomato when we dropped by) served with a basket of bread. Following in the footsteps of its successful sister restaurant in Crouch End, however, there are plans to start serving a Middle Eastern-style lunch menu here too. Bon Matin attracts a friendly bunch: couples leafing through the free newspapers, small groups eating in the skylit extension at the back, young families on a weekend cake mission. French toast was light and fluffy, made with Bon Matin's own brioche, which really crisped up around the edges. Moist, buttery scrambled eggs and a glass of freshly squeezed orange juice made a fine hangover cure.
Babies and children welcome: high chairs. Takeaway service.

Highgate

Pavilion Café

Highgate Woods, Muswell Hill Road, N10 3JN (8444 4777). Highgate tube. **Open** 9am-7pm daily. **Main courses** £6-£10. **Credit** MC, V.

The setting is idyllic: on the edge of 70 acres of ancient woodland and a huge open field, with a wisteria-clad picket fence and a large outdoor terrace. But we particularly like this place because the food and drinks are better than they have to be. Rustic Mediterranean cooking comes in huge portions: a special of fusilli pasta with balsamic-roasted red onions, rocket and tomatoes saw us through lunch and dinner. On another day, you might find slow-cooked pork belly. Streusel-topped blueberry muffin had a pleasing home-made character and the vanilla ice-cream was good enough to impress both kids and adults. The mix of bar ordering and counter service is confusing and seems to change with each visit; there's also a sign asking customers to wait to be seated, though none of the staff was attending to this. They were, however, friendly and prompt when it came to ordering. Note that there aren't many tables inside.
Babies and children welcome: children's menu; crayons; high chairs; nappy-changing facilities. Disabled: toilet. Tables outdoors (30, garden). Takeaway service. Vegan dishes.

Hornsey

Haberdashery

22 Middle Lane, N8 8PL (8342 8098, www.the-haberdashery.com). Turnpike Lane tube or Crouch Hill or Hornsey rail. **Open** 8am-6pm Mon-Fri; 9am-6pm Sat, Sun. **Main courses** £5.75-£12.95. **Credit** AmEx, MC, V.

Haberdashery is a brilliant example of the 'make-do-and-mend' café, not just in its aesthetic of vintage crockery, cocktails in jam jars, and hand-written labels, but also in its multifunctional appeal. It also sells books (lovely novellas by local press Peirene) and prints, tea sets, groceries and old-fashioned sweeties, as well as hosting sales, launches and monthly themed supper clubs. Given the (well-handled) weekend waits for one of the tightly packed tables, the tucker has to be good – and it is. From a stunning window display of cakes to the handspan-sized bowls of glossy hot chocolate, this is a professional affair. Brunch might involve a veggie breakfast – nicely fried egg, soft rather than crunchy hash brown, halloumi, a big moist mushroom and excellent greens – or french toast with maple syrup and cinnamon bananas. For lunch, there are the likes of falafel burger or Scandinavian meatballs with Danish cucumber salad and teacup soup. Weekdays are quieter, while in summer trestle tables in the gravel backyard provide more space.
Available for hire. Babies and children welcome: children's menu; high chairs; nappy-changing facilities. Bookings not accepted. Tables outdoors (6, garden; 2, pavement). Takeaway service.

Islington

Niche `NEW`

179-199 Rosebery Avenue, EC1R 4TJ (7837 5048, www.nichefoodanddrink.com). Angel tube. **Open** 7.30am-5.30pm Mon, Sun; 7.30am-9.30pm Tue-Thur; 7.30am-10pm Fri; 9am-10pm Sat. **Main courses** £11.25-£13.75. **Credit** MC, V.

Niche

What's the niche? Breads, pies, quiches and cakes – all made in-house. This light, bright (walls and furniture are white) corner café-cum-bakery on Rosebery Avenue makes a useful stop-off for a quick lunch or coffee. Situated just up the road from Sadler's Wells, it also provides a simple, well-priced pre-theatre menu at £12.50 for two courses and £15.50 for three. There are breakfasts and weekend brunches too, ranging from simple toast and butter through to welsh rarebit with two poached eggs. On our lunchtime visit, a chicken and leek pie, encased in a reasonably soft salt-crust pastry, proved filling yet just a little dry, while haddock fish cakes with a molten cheese-sauce centre were on the salty side. In contrast, a doughnut was just as it should be – tart raspberry jam filling, fluffy dough and a decent sprinkling of sugar.
Babies and children welcome: high chairs. Disabled: toilet. Tables outdoors (4, pavement). Takeaway service; delivery service. Map 5 N3.

Newington Green

Belle Epoque

37 Newington Green, N16 9PR (7249 2222, www.belleepoque.co.uk). Canonbury tube/rail or bus 73, 141, 341. **Open** 8am-6pm Tue-Fri; 9am-6pm Sat; 9am-5pm Sun. **Main courses** £3.25-£7.* **Credit** MC, V.
In an era of 'cronuts' and 'townies', this cute little village pâtisserie in Stokey sticks to the traditional roots of its French owners. Situated in a Grade-II listed building, Belle Epoque is a popular pitstop for locals: part bakery and chocolatier, part delicatessen, part café. High points include a strawberry and rhubarb crumble tart, with its crumbly pastry crust and balanced filling. The display of individual cakes and mousses looks exquisite, and there's a section dedicated to croissants and pains au chocolat. But our savoury lunch was disappointing: a goat's cheese and

spinach quiche suffered from a soggy bottom; and the brie in an under-seasoned brie and pear baguette was very mild. Coffee quality is a bit hit-and-miss. The tea room between the shop and the pretty, fenced garden is a comfortable spot in which to sit and read the papers. Sandwiches and quiche are also available to take away, and traditional French deli goods are sold alongside the bread baked on site.
Available for hire. Babies and children welcome: high chairs; nappy-changing facilities. Booking advisable. Map 25 A4.

That Place On the Corner

1-3 Green Lanes, N16 9BS (7704 0079, www.thatplaceonthecorner.co.uk). Canonbury rail or bus 73, 141, 341. **Open** 9.30am-5pm Mon-Fri; 9am-2pm Sat (Sat hours may vary). **Main courses** £3.95-£6.95. **Credit** MC, V.
If anyone deserves a decent cobweb-banishing coffee, it's a sleep-deprived new parent – so it's a pity that genuinely tot-friendly cafés serving proper caffeine fixes and carefully created food are so hard to come by in the capital. And while many a maternity-leave mum has fantasised about opening a place that guarantees a warm welcome (mostly while sitting somewhere where toddler tantrums, spat-out fish fingers and bulky buggies guarantee cold shoulders instead), Green Lanes mums Sam and Ginny actually did it. Their aim is to create an extension of your front room, somewhere to unleash the offspring with impunity and take five. The straightforward menu features deep-filled deli sarnies, daily salads and soups and, yes, a good cup of joe, while penne with tomato sauce, houmous and fresh fruit smoothies keep even fussy wee eaters onside. There are ballet and art classes, puppet shows and the like, alongside books, toys and a dressing-up box – plus thoughtful touches such as bottle warmers and bibs to make lunching with little ones that little bit easier. There's still room for fine-

tuning – the small counter overflowed with dirty plates on our last visit – but a room full of noisy newborns and knackered mums is inevitably chaotic and the loyal locals evidently forgive a little haphazard service for a lot of generosity.
Available for hire. Babies and children welcome: children's menu; colouring books; crayons; high chairs; nappy-changing facilities; toys. Disabled: toilet. Takeaway service. Map 25 A4.

North West
Kensal Green

Gracelands
118 College Road, NW10 5HD (8964 9161, www.gracelandscafe.com). Kensal Green tube. **Open** 8.30am-5pm Mon-Fri; 9am-4.30pm Sat; 9.30am-3.30pm Sun. **Main courses** £7-£13. **Credit** AmEx, MC, V.
A sign behind the counter claims that unattended children will be given an espresso and a free kitten, but of course little ones are positively welcomed here – a chesterfield in the corner is surrounded by toys and books. Leaflets for kids' classes and a trippy selection of holistic sessions in the Yard rooms out the back underline Gracelands' easygoing vibe. A lively kitchen behind a glass-fronted servery produces some cut-above dishes – fiery jerk chicken with robust sides of rice and peas and coleslaw, oven-roast omelettes – though many opt for salads. There's also a good range of children's meals, including a pasta swamped with rich cheese sauce; and we were pleased to see Caravan coffee and Camden Town Brewery bottled ale. Curious, then, that the range of cakes, pastries and juices is so scant. First-timers might find the mix of counter and table service awkward – customers are expected to get their cutlery and glasses from the stock by the kitchen.
Available for hire. Babies and children welcome: children's menu; high chairs; nappy-changing facilities; play area; toys. Tables outdoors (5, pavement; 8, garden). Takeaway service.

West Hampstead

Lanka
9 Goldhurst Terrace, NW6 3HX (7625 3366, www.lanka-uk.com). Finchley Road tube. **Open** 10.30am-6.30pm Mon-Sat; 11am-5pm Sun. **Main courses** £1.60-£5.60. **Credit** (over £5) MC, V.
Though the popular Primrose Hill shop and café have sadly closed as the lease ran out, Lanka has repositioned itself in tiny premises off the Finchley Road. Fortunately, this little shop with its whitewashed walls and pristine display counter remains a fine showcase both for the excellent Sri Lankan black teas and scented infusions from the Euphorium Tea Salon, and for pastry chef Masayuki Hara's exquisite creations. Everything is available to order at the three little tables that comprise the café area, which manages to exude serenity and prettiness despite its diminutive size. Tea and pastries are calmly prepared by helpful Japanese staff and served on Minton china; the only challenge is making a choice from the striking range of French classics and green tea-scented specialities, such as a deep, almost savoury tart; delightfully light and summery strawberry sponge; or the famed green-tea bread and butter pudding with adzuki beans.
Babies and children admitted. Takeaway service.

Coffee Bars

The steady and rapid improvement in London's coffee scene continues. We have a long way to go before Naples or Rome, Auckland or Melbourne start to feel nervous, but all the movement is in the right direction. One sign of progress is the increasing number of otherwise ordinary cafés with a notice in the window announcing where their beans come from; apparently more and more customers know that Square Mile or Monmouth means beans with a difference. A second sign is the utilisation of tiny spaces for cafés that express the coffee-mad commitment of their owners: newcomers such as **Attendant**, **Fields Beneath** and **Loft Coffee Company** are all examples. This doesn't mean that all's rosy in the roastery. A common complaint from our reviewers in 2012 was that so many cups of espresso weren't hot enough, and it often happened in 2013 too. We'd also like to see more places adding filter-type coffees to their lists: espresso is not the only fruit of the bean. But these are not major complaints. If you're at the right place, whether a well-established star such as **Prufrock Coffee** or a popular local like **Birdhouse** or **Store Street Espresso**, you're going to be drinking well. And also, more than ever, eating well (**Nude Espresso**, **Kaffeine**, **Ozone** and the great all-rounder, **Allpress Espresso**, for instance). Elsewhere in the guide you'll encounter other purveyors of great coffee, such as **Caravan King's Cross** (*see p38*) and **Fernandez & Wells** (*see p273*); see also the Cafés chapter, starting on p271.

Central
Bloomsbury

Espresso Room
31-35 Great Ormond Street, WC1N 3HZ (07760 714883, www.theespressoroom.com). Russell Square tube. **Open** 7.30am-5pm Mon-Fri. **Credit** (over £5) MC, V.
We doubt that the capacity of this tiny spot makes it very far into double digits. But though the choice of food and drink is comparably minimal – just espresso-based coffees, a soup of the day, a sandwich or two and a few baked goods – customers love the ER, as do we. It's like a little shrine to espresso, made with largely consistent skill using beans from Square Mile. The blend is bracing stuff, but with just enough sweetness to make it enjoyable without sugar. Occasionally we get an imperfect cup, but on our last visit it was textbook stuff (apart from being just a tiny bit too cool). The best place to sit, weather permitting, is at one of the small tables outside. Service is from smiling, friendly people who evidently love what they do and show off their prodigious technical skills in the most modest way possible.
Babies and children admitted. Tables outdoors (3, pavement). Takeaway service. **Map 4 L4.**

Store Street Espresso
40 Store Street, WC1E 7DB (7637 2623). Goodge Street tube. **Open** 7.30am-7pm Mon-Fri; 9am-6pm Sat; 10am-5pm Sun. **Credit** MC, V.
The clientele at this coffee bar smack-bang in the centre of uni-land, just a minute from Tottenham Court Road, combines academia and commerce. Quite apart from the enviable location, there's much to entice. First is the long, attractive room with bright walls and skylights at the back. Second is the food, which is a cut above many basic coffee bars and very reasonably priced by West End standards; most sandwiches and baked goods are around £1 cheaper than at many comparable places. You'll even find that rarity, a top-notch vegetable quiche. Third is the service, which is unfailingly friendly and well informed. Finally, there's the coffee, all of it espresso-based. Most beans come from Square Mile, but there's a changing roster of guest beans well worth investigating. On our visit, it was a Yirgacheffe roasted in (wait for it) Detroit, Michigan. The espresso from these beans is possibly the best we've had all year: properly tiny, lovely crema, with a rounded sweetness that required no sugar. A flat white was also judged a triumph. Store Street? We'd rather call it Star Street.
Babies and children admitted. Disabled: toilet. Tables outdoors (2, pavement). Takeaway service. **Map 4 K5.**

Chancery Lane

Department of Coffee & Social Affairs
14-16 Leather Lane, EC1N 7SU (no phone, www.departmentofcoffee.co.uk). Chancery Lane tube or Farringdon tube/rail. **Open** 7am-6pm Mon-Fri; 10am-5pm Sat, Sun. **Credit** (over £5) MC, V.
Like Prufrock, just down Leather Lane, DCSA gets very busy during the week, while weekends are relaxed. We're particularly fond of the fabulously unkempt brickwork, which might make you think you're in a building site rather than a coffee bar. Other pleasures include good but unobtrusive music, and the warmest service you could ask for. All the coffee begins as espresso and is always well made, from beans provided by a range of roasters. The machine is well tended to between coffees, and milk is foamed, poured and decorated carefully. Food is simple and high quality: a handful of sandwiches and a lovely spread of baked goods, some made here and others bought in. Our only grumble – unchanged from previous visits – is that our espresso could have been hotter. All staff need to do is heat the cups, for heaven's sake. But this is hardly a unique problem, and certainly not enough to keep us away.

Babies and children admitted. Separate room for parties, seats 20. Takeaway service. **Map 11 N5**.

★ Prufrock Coffee

23-25 Leather Lane, EC1N 7TE (7242 0467, www.prufrockcoffee.com). Chancery Lane tube. **Open** 8am-6pm Mon-Fri; 10am-5pm Sat; 10am-4pm Sun. **Credit** AmEx, MC, V.

This big, comfortable room doesn't seem to alter much from year to year, and that's fine with us. It does change during the week: most customers are a bit hurried from Monday to Friday, but everyone is very relaxed at the weekend. You never know who's going to be here from one visit to the next, as the clientele is so pleasantly varied; you're as likely to see a family with young kids as EC-sophisticates or office workers. There's not much to say about the coffee except that it's as good as it's always been – and that means very good indeed, some of the best in London. Espresso is perfect, and guest beans slow-brewed in an Aeropress are always of excellent quality. There's a small selection of daily dishes chalked on a blackboard, and sandwiches and baked things on the counter. Whenever you visit, expect to be very well looked after.
Available for hire. Babies and children admitted. Disabled: toilet. Takeaway service. **Map 11 N5**.

City

Taylor Street Baristas

125 Old Broad Street, EC2N 1AR (7256 8665, www.taylor-st.com). Bank tube/DLR or Liverpool Street tube/rail. **Open** 7am-6pm Mon-Fri. **Credit** MC, V.

This is the second-largest of the Taylor Street venues, and it's big enough to give customers a decent chance of bagging a seat, even at lunchtime. Although the place appeals to a mixed crowd, there's always at least one table where big-buck deals are being discussed. The menu has been beefed up in the past year – you can now eat really well (and not expensively), with superior sandwiches, generous salads, quiches and sweet things. The coffee is from Union, supplemented by guest beans. A guest espresso (Kenyan single-estate roasted by Square Mile) had a truly gorgeous flavour – chocolate-sweet, no sugar needed. Good crema too. But though the cup took just ten seconds to get from counter to table, the brew had already lost too much heat. Why? Nevertheless, this was one imperfection in a visit that made us love the place even more.
Babies and children admitted. Takeaway service. **Map 12 Q6**.
For branches see index.

Clerkenwell & Farringdon

Brill

27 Exmouth Market, EC1R 4QL (7833 9757, www.clerkenwellmusic.co.uk). Angel tube or Farringdon tube/rail. **Open** 7.30am-6pm Mon-Fri; 9am-6pm Sat; 10.30am-4.30pm Sun. **Credit** MC, V.

The awning reads: 'Music. Coffee. Bagels.' That lays out the essentials succinctly. Brill began life as a music shop, and music is still 'an integral part of what we do.' There's always something good playing, and CDs and a few vinyl oddments – with the emphasis on jazz, blues, folk and rock – are for sale inside the small interior. Then there's the coffee, which accounts for 80% of Brill's revenue. Supplied by Union Coffee Roasters, it's best in milky form – the Union espresso blend is pretty assertive stuff. What's more, our Brill espresso was not brilliantly made: thinnish brew, lifeless crema. But Brill makes it easy to forgive an occasional deficient cup. The staff are incredibly friendly, always ready for a gab if you want one, and the musical component is pure pleasure. Which leaves only the bagels to explain: fillings of smoked salmon, cream cheese, ham, houmous, and so on, at exceedingly reasonable prices. Appealing baked goods are supplied by an imaginative woman named Arianna. Her delicious 'everything' cookie even includes fragments of pretzel. We'll be back, for that warm welcome, great music and (we hope) a flawless espresso.
Available for hire. Babies and children admitted. Tables outdoors (3, pavement; 4, garden). Takeaway service. Vegan dishes. **Map 5 N4**.

Dose Espresso

70 Long Lane, EC1A 9EJ (7600 0382, www.dose-espresso.com). Barbican tube or Farringdon tube/rail. **Open** 7am-5pm Mon-Fri; 9am-4pm Sat. **Credit** (over £5) MC, V.

Dose is a micro-dose, with seating for about a dozen bodies, but it was still a bit of a shock to see it nearly full at 10.30am. The clientele is diverse, ranging through suits, the Clerkenwell cool crowd and staff from nearby St Bart's. Some very tempting food includes imaginative sandwiches, as in organic ciabatta with dry-cured bacon, grilled halloumi and spiced avocado. Sweet things also beckon – the cheesecake is a killer – and there's also own-made muesli and yoghurt fruit compotes. Tea, taken very seriously here, is offered either hot or cold. A cold lemongrass was expertly brewed and had exactly the right (tiny) amount of sugar added. Coffee beans come from Square Mile, but there's a changing selection of guest espresso. On our visit, it was a single-estate washed Colombian, which was sensationally good: deep berry flavours and velvety-smooth. Had the crema been a little more sprightly, this would have been a candidate for espresso of the year. A small complaint in the context of a mega-dose of quality.
Available for hire. Babies and children admitted. Takeaway service. **Map 11 O5**.

Look Mum No Hands!

49 Old Street, EC1V 9HX (7253 1025, www.lookmumnohands.com). Barbican tube or Old Street tube/rail. **Open** 7.30am-10pm Mon-Fri; 9am-10pm Sat; 9.30am-10pm Sun. **Credit** MC, V.

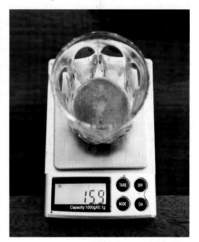

Prufrock Coffee

When you approach the front door, the explanation for the name becomes clear: LMNH is also a cycling shop. The big room is decorated on a cycling theme, and is clearly much loved by locals. On Saturday lunchtime there was standing room only, with what looked like half the residents of EC1 (singles, couples, families with young children) packed in to eat and drink. We can see why they love the place, even with so much competition nearby. There's a large selection of food, including serious cooked dishes of a kind not attempted by most coffee bars, as well as the more usual salads and baked goods. The baristas know their business and take pride in doing it right. Most beans are from Square Mile, but there are guest coffees too. Espresso is perfectly made, and milky drinks are well presented. No effort is made to rush dawdlers, even when there's high demand for tables. Look, Mum – total relaxation. *Babies and children welcome: high chairs. Disabled: toilet. Tables outdoors (8, terrace; 2, pavement).* **Map 5 P4**.
For branch see index.

Covent Garden

Salt

34 Great Queen Street, WC2B 5AA (7430 0335, www.saltwc2.co.uk). Covent Garden or Holborn tube. **Open** 7.30am-7pm Mon-Fri; 10am-7pm Sat (except June-Aug). **Credit** MC, V.
Salt may be a haven of calm in a busy area, but it isn't a place to visit in a group, as there are few seats in the two narrow rooms (front and back of the ground-floor space). It's perfect, however, for a bit of quality solitude-time – or for a quiet lunch for two. Food is not fancy, though it is taken seriously. There's a short list of cooked dishes (the chickpea and chorizo stew is ace), quiches, salads and baked goods made on the premises. Breads and pastries come from the firm's own bakery, in Hertfordshire. Brownies are sweet, dense and dangerously moreish. Coffee and tea are given near-equal billing, but the coffee remains the star attraction for most. Espresso (Square Mile's Red Brick beans) is perfectly made time and time again. Salt is a gem in an area not over-endowed with decent options. *Babies and children admitted. Tables outdoors (2, pavement). Takeaway service.* **Map 18 E3**.

Fitzrovia

Attendant NEW
27A Foley Street, W1W 6DY (7637 3794,
www.the-attendant.com). Goodge Street or
Oxford Circus tube. **Open** 8am-6pm Mon-
Fri; 10am-5pm Sat. **Credit** (over £5) MC, V.
Opened in early 2013, Attendant occupies London's
most original location for a coffee bar: a late 19th-
century men's underground toilet. The urinals
provide seating (small tables) and there's a
banquette at the back. Major warning: this place is
tiny, and at lunch becomes densely packed with
humanity. The throng is mostly made up of young
office workers in search of good food – cold
sandwiches, a hot sandwich of the day (nice idea),
various salads and the usual sweeties. But it's the
coffee-hounds who will love Attendant most.
Obsessively committed to their craft, the baristas
pay zealous attention to getting everything just
right with what they brew from their beans (the
Caravan blend). And they're happy to talk about
coffee, if you're interested. In all, this is a great
place – though we'd prefer a bit more space. And
it's also difficult to resist making jokes about the
building's previous life.
Takeaway service. Vegetarian menu. **Map 9 J5**.

Kaffeine
66 Great Titchfield Street, W1W 7QJ (7580
6755, www.kaffeine.co.uk). Oxford Circus tube.
Open 7.30am-6pm Mon-Fri; 8.30am-6pm Sat;
9.30am-6pm Sun. **Credit** (over £6) AmEx, MC, V.
Kaffeine remains incredibly popular with local,
mostly young office workers, who seem to crowd in
at every hour of the day and make lunchtime a
crush. They can't be here for the seating: wooden
bench-type, at tables either high or low. Or for the
minimalist decor. It's the coffee and the food and the
buzz. And there certainly is buzz aplenty, especially
when the place is crowded. You'll find much to
croon over in the food, which comes up from the
basement kitchen constantly as tray after tray sells
out. This is some of the best coffee-bar food in
London, whether savoury or sweet, which must
explain a lot about the lunchtime crowds. Salads,
sandwiches, anything that's seen the inside of a hot
oven – these are all strong points. So it was
somewhat shocking, this year, to find ourselves
seriously disappointed with the coffee. Two
espressos: feeble crema, lacking in body and of a
flavour that spoke more of fire than of beans. This
was the first poor cup of Kaffeine we've ever had.
We hope it's the last.
Available for hire. Takeaway service. **Map 9 J5**.

Marylebone

Workshop Coffee Co
75 Wigmore Street, W1U 1QD (no phone,
www.workshopcoffee.com). Bond Street tube.
Open 7am-7pm Mon-Fri; 9am-6pm Sat, Sun.
No credit cards.
The original Workshop in Clerkenwell is big and
buzzy, with a sizeable menu and a fulsome drinks
list; it's incredibly popular at weekends. This
Marylebone branch couldn't be more different. It's
a minuscule space (seating capacity 14), with a
correspondingly tiny food offering of just a few
sandwiches and pastries. It's hard to imagine that
the venue would ever be noisy. Which is a definite
plus in the neighbourhood, with the bustle of St
Christopher's Place just a bean's throw away. Decor

is minimal and soothing; sandwiches are good and
fairly ample. The coffee, made with beans roasted
at the Clerkenwell site, is right at the top level of
what London has to offer. Staff like Aeropress
brewing, but the espresso is flawless. Sitting at the
counter gives you the chance to watch and chat to
the consummately skilled baristas.
Babies and children admitted. Takeaway service.
Map 9 G6.
For branch see index.

Soho

Flat White
17 Berwick Street, W1F 0PT (7734 0370,
www.flatwhitecafe.com). Leicester Square or
Tottenham Court Road tube. **Open** 8am-7pm
Mon-Fri; 9am-6pm Sat, Sun. **Credit** MC, V.
This diminutive, dimly lit room beside the veg stalls
of Berwick Street Market was one of the places that
signalled, when it opened in 2005, the increasing
influence of Antipodean coffee culture in London.
Hugely popular from the outset, it has changed
little over the years – even though there's been
a change of ownership (the people behind Giaconda
Dining Rooms, *see p192*, took over in 2012).
Coffee has always occupied centre stage here,
and while espresso drinkers have sometimes been
disappointed, our latest visit was a resounding
success. Made with single-estate beans from
Uganda, our espresso was distinctive, roasted with
care and a welcome sidestep away from the high-
roasted house blend. Coffee with milk has never
been a problem, and both a flat white and a piccolo
were spot-on. The food menu is small but sound.
Decor and seating are basic, and the place can feel
cramped when busy. But at quieter times, Flat
White is bliss – especially if the weather is good
and you can bag a seat outside.
Babies and children admitted. Tables outdoors
(2, pavement). Takeaway service. Vegan dishes.
Map 17 B4.

Milk Bar
3 Bateman Street, W1D 4AG (7287 4796,
www.flatwhitecafe.com). Leicester Square or
Tottenham Court Road tube. **Open** 8am-5pm
Mon-Fri; 9am-5pm Sat, Sun. **No credit cards.**
The younger sibling of Flat White is a larger space
just a five-minute walk away in one of Soho's
smaller streets. Unlike Flat White, it's been
radically altered by the change in ownership. The
formerly funereal colour scheme is now a bright off-
white, and large colour photographs decorate the
walls. With the leavening of the look has come a
general freshness in Milk Bar's offering, especially
as regards food and (even more welcome) service.
There are smiles all round and, on the counter and
menus, a lot more effort to please than under the
old regime. Eggs are a major feature, and baked
goods are worth ordering (and not expensive). Our
coffee experience was mixed. Espresso was good in
the familiar high-roast style of Square Mile, but
while a trio of flat whites were well made, they
weren't nearly hot enough. Sort out little things like
that, and you have a winner.
Available for hire. Babies and children admitted.
Takeaway service. Vegan dishes. **Map 17 C3**.

Rapha Cycle Club
85 Brewer Street, W1F 9ZN (7494 9831,
www.rapha.cc/london). Piccadilly Circus tube.
Open 7.30am-9pm Mon-Fri; 8.30am-7pm Sat;
10am-6pm Sun. **No credit cards.**

The café at Rapha CC's London store occupies a
little less than half the floor space, but it provides
ample seating for those wanting to rest their feet
after patrolling on nearby Regent Street or perusing
the bike clothing at Rapha itself. This is a very
relaxing place, largely because of the warm, funny,
capable staff. Their enthusiasm for coffee is
palpable and their skill in handling beans (the main
suppliers are Germany and Sweden) is deeply
impressive. A guest espresso made with beans from
a single estate in Uganda showed that they're
interested in trying something completely different;
the staff knew it would not be to everyone's taste,
but just found it interesting. And they offered a
replacement cup if our choice didn't suit – a lovely
touch. Food is pretty much the standard coffee-bar
repertoire, mostly provided by the same company
that supplies the Fields Beneath. A nice spot: you'll
hardly know you're in a bicycle accessory shop. Or
in the West End, for that matter.
Disabled: toilet. Takeaway service. Vegetarian
menu. **Map 17 A5**.

Sacred
13 Ganton Street, W1F 9BL (7734 1415,
www.sacredcafe.co.uk). Oxford Circus tube. **Open**
7.30am-8pm Mon-Fri; 10am-8pm Sat; 10am-7pm
Sun. **Credit** (over £2.50) AmEx, MC, V.
Nothing seems to change at this original branch of
the pioneering Antipodean coffee joint, with the
same decorations (wacky and very nice), same
flooring, same seating and the same general choice
of food and drink. Edibles and potables are
standard-issue coffee-bar fare, and both are done to
a very creditable standard. But while the absence
of change can be a good thing, it is not so laudable
if it enshrines some long-established shortcomings,
such as not enough heat in an espresso – we've
complained about this several years running, and
it still happens. Droopy-looking sandwiches as the
afternoon wears on – ditto. These are such easy
problems to fix, we wonder why they remain.
Probably because the crowds continue to flood in,
come what may. And bar those quibbles, we share
their appreciation.
Available for hire. Babies and children admitted.
Tables outdoors (6, pavement). Takeaway
service. **Map 17 A4**.
For branches see index.

★ TAP Coffee
193 Wardour Street, W1F 8ZF (no phone,
www.tapcoffee.co.uk). Tottenham Court Road
tube. **Open** 8am-7pm Mon-Fri; 10am-6pm Sat;
noon-6pm Sun. **No credit cards.**
This is the third (and largest) branch of what was
formerly known as Tapped & Packed, and the same
simple and effective approach is duplicated here.
Buy good beans, treat them well and serve the
coffee in a totally relaxing space. In this case, the
room is very long and light-filled, thanks to almost
full-length skylights. It's extremely popular and
tables may be hard to come by, especially as the
friendly waiting staff don't attempt to move along
the office groups and solitary workers with
computers and iPads, and people tend to linger. The
food centres around reasonably priced sandwiches
and salads, plus the usual baked goods. Square Mile
features prominently among the coffees; an
espresso was not just well made but served properly
hot. A completely satisfying experience.
Babies and children admitted. Takeaway service.
Map 17 B2.
For branches see index.

Lowry & Baker

West
Hammersmith

Artisan
372 King Street, W6 0RX (no phone, www.artisancoffee.co.uk). Stamford Brook tube. **Open** 7.30am-5.30pm Mon-Fri; 8.30am-5.30pm Sat, Sun. **Credit** MC, V.

At time of writing, the sunny, sky-filled view from this large corner room was quite a treat – despite its location on a busy west London intersection. Residential construction will eventually remove some of the view, but that's no reason to avoid Artisan. This is an exceptionally enjoyable place to drink, eat and while away the hours. The clientele, whether alone or in small groups of all ages, seems entirely local, and children are most welcome. Beans come from Allpress and are used to excellent effect. Closing your eyes and sipping a perfectly made espresso, you wouldn't know you're in Stamford Brook rather than Allpress's HQ in Shoreditch. The room has a very pleasant look and feel, with enormous windows on two sides, high ceilings and down-home furnishings (many home-made). Food consists of sprightly sandwiches and attractive baked goods, with a strong line in cakes. This is the second branch (the first is in Putney) and the owners say there might be one more – but that's it. Too bad. Every neighbourhood would benefit from an Artisan.

Babies and children admitted. Takeaway service. **Map 20 A4.**
For branch see index.

Ladbroke Grove

★ Lowry & Baker
339 Portobello Road, W10 5SA (8960 8534, www.lowryandbaker.com). Ladbroke Grove tube. **Open** 8am-4pm Mon-Sat; 10am-4pm Sun. **No credit cards.**

The northern branch of the Notting Hill tribe loves Lowry & Baker – so much so that one local advises against even trying to get in at the weekend. This is the kind of local café most people dream about: warmly welcoming and with a laid-back attitude that makes you feel immediately at home. Indeed, our local informant said: 'It's like being in your living room – staff talk to customers and customers talk to each other.' L&B (which opened in summer 2010) has established itself as the leading local independent coffee shop, with a small, reasonably priced menu of uniformly high-quality food: good soups, sandwiches, salads and sweet things worth crossing town for. The blueberry cheesecake and banana bread are heavenly. Food is served on a delightful jumble of unmatched crockery, while the expertly brewed coffee, made with beans from Monmouth, comes in well-warmed white cups.

Tables outdoors (4, pavement). Takeaway service. Vegan dishes. **Map 19 A1.**

Maida Vale

Elgin
255 Elgin Avenue, W9 1NJ (7625 5511, www.theelgin.com). Maida Vale tube. **Open** 8am-11.30pm Mon-Thur; 8am-midnight Fri; 9am-midnight Sat; 9.30am-11pm Sun. **Credit** AmEx, MC, V.

This big, airy neighbourhood hangout is not just a coffee bar. It's an ex-boozer, and alcohol still

features prominently. There's a short menu that combines international touches with traditional pub grub, and the emphasis on good buying is apparent in the likes of sausage sandwiches using bangers from renowned butcher Ginger Pig. Almost everything is own-made, including bread; when the staff buy in something, they regard it, as the barista said, as a form of 'cheating'. Beans come from the Volcano Coffee Works, and alongside the house espresso blend there are regularly changing specials – a single-estate Colombian espresso on our visit. The baristas take an almost astonishing level of care over their brewing; technical glitches didn't give perfect results on two attempts and the results got tossed. But the third was perfect. The room is lovely during the day, with its distressed old wood and huge windows on two sides – all the more reason to come and appreciate coffee perfectionism. Maida Vale is lucky.
Babies and children welcome: high chairs; nappy-changing facilities. Disabled: toilet. Separate room for parties, seats 40.
Map 1 C3.

South West
Parsons Green

Barossa
277 New King's Road, SW6 4RD (7751 9711, www.barossafulham.com). Parsons Green tube. **Open** 8am-5pm Mon-Fri; 9am-5pm Sat; 9am-4pm Sun. **Credit** MC, V.
The Parsons Green/New King's Road crowd has been packing into Australian-owned Barossa for three years or so, and it's not hard to see why. It's a friendly, well-run place with excellent coffee and varied, interesting food. Apart from a certain degree of casually understated affluence, a diverse bunch gathers here: young families, middle-aged couples, twentysomethings, all chatting away. If you want a view of the passing Ferraris, choose the small, light room at the front. Serious lunchers and larger groups prefer the big back room. Coffee is made with beans from Caravan, and the baristas know how to handle that excellent raw material; an espresso was served promptly in a heated cup, so it arrived properly hot. For many, however, the coffee is but an adjunct of the food, which is taken very seriously. The menu starts with breakfast and takes in some unusual dishes alongside the usual eggs, baked goods and brunch fare. The neighbourhood isn't that well served for quality food and coffee in a relaxed setting – which helps Barossa stand out.
Available for hire. Tables outdoors (6, terrace). Takeaway service.

South
Battersea

★ Birdhouse
123 St John's Hill, SW11 1SZ (7228 6663, www.birdhou.se). Clapham Junction rail. **Open** 7am-4pm Mon-Wed; 7am-10pm Thur, Fri; 9am-10pm Sat; 9am-5pm Sun. **Credit** (over £6) MC, V.
Birdhouse is pretty much perfect. It's an unpretentious but attractively decorated spot, with a soothing colour scheme (grey with touches of yellow), retro furnishings and jolly pictures on the

long flank wall. Fanatically skilled but socially casual, the staff in attendance always seem to include at least one of the two owners. They make the place buzz with their evident enthusiasm for coffee, catering and customers. You'll almost always find a mixed crowd, right down to babies and toddlers. Outstanding baked goods include a warm banana bread, which regulars reckon is irresistible. Sandwiches are equally good. And the coffee? Well, if you like espresso, you'll love this place – heaven in a tiny cup, using Climpson & Sons beans. The baristas tend their machines as if they were Maseratis, and that attention to detail pretty much sums up everything that Birdhouse does.
Available for hire. Babies and children admitted. Takeaway service. **Map 21 B4**.

Brixton

Federation Coffee
Units 77-78, Brixton Village Market, Coldharbour Lane, SW9 8PS (no phone, http://federationcoffee.com). Brixton tube/rail. **Open** 8am-5pm Mon-Fri; 9am-6pm Sat; 9am-5pm Sun. **Credit** (over £5) MC, V.
People come to this attractive corner spot inside Brixton Market's covered arcade to work on their computers, eavesdrop, watch the world go by, or chat with friends. Grab a perch with a view on to

Birdhouse

the market if you can. But be warned: this isn't a spacious venue, and it's very popular. All Federation food is made right here, with sweet and savoury baked goods to the fore. Not complicated, but not expensive. The espresso beans are roasted at a nearby market unit, and the house blend is a high roast that will take kindly to milk in a cappuccino or flat white. Add friendly service, the real neighbourhood atmosphere, and you have a great local coffee haven.
Babies and children welcome: nappy-changing facilities (market). Disabled: toilet (market). Takeaway service. **Map 22 E2**.

South East
London Bridge & Borough

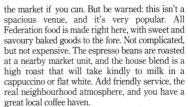

★ Monmouth Coffee Company
2 Park Street, SE1 9AB (7940 9960, www.monmouthcoffee.co.uk). London Bridge tube/rail. **Open** 7.30am-6pm Mon-Sat. **Credit** (over £5) AmEx, MC, V.
Now 35 years old and still a major presence on London's coffee scene, Monmouth seems to be busy all the time. On Friday and Saturday, it's heaving – be prepared for a lengthy queue. The location at the

COFFEE BARS

southern end of Borough Market accounts for much of the popularity, but the unfailingly high quality clinches the deal. Food (breads, pastries and so on) is simple, well chosen and low maintenance for the staff. They have other priorities: making and serving coffee. Which they do supremely well. Espresso (a bargain at £1.35) and its milky derivatives are well made, using full-fat milk – only because Monmouth (unlike many customers) knows that semi-skimmed gives inferior results. But it's the brewed coffee, from the company's outstanding range, that takes top billing. If there's a relatively small crowd, dawdle and talk to the coffee experts, who will share their enthusiasm and expertise with anyone who shows an interest. Seating is basic but comfortable enough. Come and worship at this shrine to the bean.
Babies and children admitted. Takeaway service.
Map 11 P8.
For branch see index.

Monmouth Coffee Company.
See p289.

East
Shoreditch

★ Allpress Espresso
58 Redchurch Street, E2 7DP (7749 1780, http://uk.allpressespresso.com). Liverpool Street tube/rail or Shoreditch High Street rail. **Open** 8am-5pm Mon-Fri; 9am-5pm Sat, Sun. **Credit** (over £5) MC, V.
We have yet to visit Allpress when it hasn't been crowded. This winning corner spot – tables and counter at one end of a light-filled room, the coffee roaster at the other – is a solid fixture in Shoreditch's increasingly well-populated catering scene. Allpress is for all sorts: local business or gallery people, families with young children, residents relaxing with the newspapers. Many come just for takeaways, and there's often a queue (which

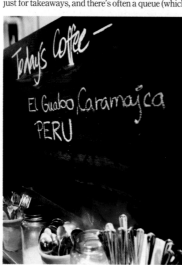

can sometimes lead to a wait for a table). The coffee is terrific, whether filter or espresso-based. Happily, you don't need to fear ordering a plain espresso here; avoiding the extremes of long roasting time leaves the beans with flavours of berries and dark chocolate. Filter brews from a changing roster of beans are well made and well suited to more leisurely sipping. Food is a strong point. Baked goods are wonderful, and sandwiches more innovative than those at many comparable places. Allpress has it all.
Babies and children admitted. Disabled: toilet. Takeaway service. **Map 6 S4.**

Ozone Coffee
11 Leonard Street, EC2A 4AQ (7490 1039, www.ozonecoffee.co.uk). Old Street tube/rail. **Open** 7.30am-5pm Mon-Fri; 9am-4pm Sat, Sun. **Credit** AmEx, MC, V.
Kiwi-owned Ozone has become a major hit with the office workers in and around Silicon Roundabout, and its ground-floor café is sometimes completely full even outside prime time. The endearingly un-refurbished basement space, where the beans are roasted, often holds greater promise of empty seats. Ozone has made a big deal of its food since it set up shop in 2012, and the menu remains a draw. Standard dishes often have a touch of the unorthodox: kedgeree with fried shallots and salsa verde, for instance. Soup of the day is a reliable option. Coffee isn't confined to espresso and its offshoots; there's a daily changing pair of 'slow-brew' specials, and the expertly roasted beans show well with this treatment. A caveat about sitting in the basement roastery: coffee has a tendency to cool on its way down the stairs. But we can't find much else to complain about here.
Available for hire. Babies and children welcome: high chairs. Booking advisable; bookings not accepted Sat, Sun. Disabled: toilet. Separate room for parties, seats 16. **Map 6 Q4.**

Spitalfields

Nude Espresso
26 Hanbury Street, E1 6QR (07804 223590, www.nudeespresso.com). Liverpool Street tube/rail or Shoreditch High Street rail. **Open** 7am-7pm Mon-Fri; 9.30am-7pm Sat, Sun. **Credit** (over £6) AmEx, MC, V.
This original branch of Nude just never stops being busy, even at times of the day that should be quiet. The enduring popularity has a pretty simple explanation: quality and (relative) consistency. That, plus a sizeable local catchment area encompassing business as well as residential custom. And a choice of food that's among the best in London's coffee bars. Indeed, these days Nude seems to be as much a destination for food as for coffee. The menu's approach remains steady even as the selection changes from day to day: breakfasts, brunch dishes, a few fairly complicated assemblies, salads and baked goods of high quality. The coffee proposition is based on espresso; if you take it in one of its milky incarnations you're in luck, because Nude's espresso blend is high-roasted and short on sweetness. At weekends, the long, narrow and eminently attractive ground-floor room can get very crowded. But it's a good-natured and well-managed crowd, thanks to matey but ultra-competent staff.
Babies and children admitted. Bookings not accepted. Tables outdoors (2, pavement). Takeaway service. Vegan dishes. **Map 12 S5.**
For branch see index.

The Fields Beneath

The Fields Beneath takes its name from a classic of local history written about Kentish Town by long-time resident Gillian Tindall, and this tiny place has become almost as popular as the book since it opened in late 2012. There's just one fairly long table for customers who want to consume on the premises, but much of the trade comes from people seeking a takeaway after leaving the train station next door. Espresso is perfectly made, though you could easily come here just for the food. Sweet things are great. Savoury things are possibly even better; the sandwiches are well filled, and the beef doughnut (braised shin inside a lightly sweet bread case) has become a local legend. There's such a happy buzz here, you instantly feel as if you're part of the family. A local coffee shop of real distinction. *Available for hire. Tables outdoors (2, pavement).*

North West
Belsize Park

Ginger & White
2 England's Lane, NW3 4TG (7722 9944, www.gingerandwhite.com). Belsize Park or Chalk Farm tube. **Open** 7.30am-5.30pm Mon-Fri; 8.30am-5.30pm Sat. **Credit** (over £10) MC, V.
The original G&W is in Hampstead. This branch, not far down the hill, occupies a nice corner space in Belsize Park. The mini chain has many adherents, and by and large their enthusiasm is justified, but a few caveats apply at this venue. First, it's a hangout for mothers of young children, and the pram-pressure factor (and occasional noise) will not match everyone's idea of a good time. Second, the food was fine on our trip, but lacked finesse in preparation and seasoning. Third, coffee service was careless. Excellent Square Mile espresso beans were let down by being brewed in a cold cup; the coffee arrived tepid. These factors were not nearly enough to ruin our visit, spent in the pocket-sized upstairs balcony overlooking the larger ground-floor space. (We might have grabbed the big table downstairs if Tim Burton and Helena Bonham Carter hadn't been sitting there, gabbing with a couple of mates.) *Babies and children welcome: high chairs; nappy-changing facilities. Tables outdoors (5, pavement). Takeaway service.* **Map 28 C4**. **For branches see index.**

Swiss Cottage

Loft Coffee Company NEW
4 Canfield Gardens, NW6 3BS (no phone). Finchley Road tube. **Open** 7am-5pm Mon-Fri; 8am-4pm Sat; 10am-2pm Sun. **Credit** (over £5) MC, V.
Loft is a labour of love for Sung-jae Lee, who learned to appreciate good coffee in his native Seoul. He moved to London in the late 1980s and long wanted to open a coffee bar here. In 2012, after a year of planning, building and training, he achieved his ambition. The tiny space has table seating for just ten people. There are pastries from Gail's Bakery, along with teas and a few soft drinks. But mostly there is espresso and its milky offspring, made with Monmouth beans. Ours was brewed textbook-perfect, with a beautiful crema and the hallmark sweetness of Monmouth's blend. Finchley Road is not crowded with great places for coffee, making the diminutive Loft not just unusual but very welcome. **Map 28 A3**.

COFFEE BARS

North East
Hackney

Climpson & Sons
67 Broadway Market, E8 4PH (7812 9829, www.webcoffeeshop.co.uk). London Fields rail or bus 26, 48, 55. **Open** 7.30am-5pm Mon-Fri; 8.30am-5pm Sat; 9am-5pm Sun. **No credit cards**.
There are two sides to Climpson, a tiny fixture in Broadway Market serving some of the capital's best coffee. From Monday to Friday, it's a popular place for a hot brew in relaxed conditions, perhaps with a light meal or snack. On Saturday and Sunday, it's a victim of its own well-deserved success. The crowds are massive, even when the weather's less than wonderful. Once you've queued and placed your order, you'll have to wait for a good few minutes to get it. If you take sugar in your brew, it will be added by the barista, not by you. And the coffee will be served in a paper cup – ceramic just

would not be practical – which inevitably fails to do full justice to it. This is not a criticism of Climpson, which roasts great beans and employs people who know everything about how to brew them. It's merely a warning to anyone who wants to savour the goods under optimal conditions. If you can, visit during the week and enjoy tasty little dishes both sweet and savoury (the soups are always very good), and drink coffee from ceramic cups – and add your own sugar.
Tables outdoors (3, pavement). Takeaway service. **For branch see index.**

North
Kentish Town

★ The Fields Beneath NEW
53 Prince of Wales Road, NW5 3LR (no phone). Kentish Town West rail. **Open** 7.30am-5pm Mon, Tue; 7.30am-6pm Wed-Fri; 9am-5pm Sat, Sun. **Credit** (over £4.50) MC, V.

Fish & Chips

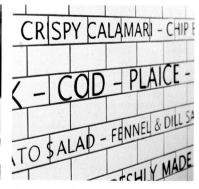

Fashions come, they go, they get laughable, they get kitsch, they get retro, they get fashionable. The best of London's traditional fish and chip shops have made it through the lean times and now find themselves joined by a rather hip new breed of chippy. So, as well as old stagers such as the **Golden Hind** – which celebrates its centenary in 2014 – **Masters Super Fish** and **Something Fishy**, you'll also find bright new stars such as **Golden Union Fish Bar** and **Poppies**, which revel in the retro aspects of the genre, and **Kerbisher & Malt**. The competition between ancient and modern has led to a golden-battered era for the capital's chip-fans, with long-established venues such as **North Sea** upping its game, and **Toff's** following the trend for sustainably sourced fish set by **Fish Club**, **Sutton & Sons** and **Golden Union**. Some establishments, however, produce excellent fish and chips with absolutely no concern for fashion, and this year we also doff our caps to **Nautilus**. For restaurants offering a more extensive array of fish and seafood, see the Fish chapter, starting on p81.

Central

Barbican

★ Fish Central
149-155 Central Street, EC1V 8AP (7253 4970, www.fishcentral.co.uk). Old Street tube/rail or bus 55. **Lunch served** 11.30am-2.30pm Mon-Fri. **Dinner served** 5-10.30pm Mon-Thur; 5-11pm Fri. **Meals served** noon-10.30pm Sat. **Main courses** £9.90-£19.50. **Credit** AmEx, MC, V.
A family business tucked in a shopping precinct on a housing estate is worth shouting about. This long-standing restaurant still has the soul of a fish and chip shop – despite serving treats such as oysters and lobster at smartly clothed tables in a bright, modern room. The quality is outstanding and, for the prices, seems almost too good to be true. Nothing is fancy (bread is a buttered roll, napkins are paper), but nearly everything is nicely done. Starters of deconstructed prawn cocktail and large sweet mussels in spicy tomato and white wine sauce with garlic bread were generous and faultless. A mixed salad was a damp squib – mushy or garden peas are more the thing – but the chips were properly potatoey and hand-cut. Spanking fresh, the cod's thick, white and opalescent flakes came in golden, crisp batter neither too thick nor greasy; you could also have it fried in matzo meal or grilled. The fish supper deal of prawn cocktail, cod and a dessert (perhaps crème brûlée with crunchy molten demerara topping) is a bargain. Wines from a helpfully annotated list are remarkably inexpensive, and the bill comes with slices of watermelon. It restores your faith in eating out. *Babies and children welcome: children's menu; high chairs; nappy-changing facilities. Booking advisable dinner Thur-Sat. Separate room for parties, seats 60. Tables outdoors (4, pavement). Takeaway service.* **Map 5 P3.**

Bloomsbury

North Sea Fish Restaurant
7-8 Leigh Street, WC1H 9EW (7387 5892, www.northseafishrestaurant.co.uk). Russell Square tube or King's Cross tube/rail. **Lunch served** noon-2.30pm, **dinner served** 5.30-10.30pm Mon-Sat. **Main courses** £9.95-£21.05. **Credit** MC, V.
In danger of losing its fine reputation to the new breed of chippies, this long-established restaurant appears to have pulled up its socks over the past year or so. Booking is advised for winter evenings; lunchtimes are quiet at best. In an interior better suited to a Cotswolds tea room, service is attentive and friendly. Drinks are dispensed from what looks like an old hotel bar: well stocked, notably with Spitfire and Bombardier ales – the perfect accompaniment to a quick lunch. Starters are varied; spicy prawns seem to be on the 'daily specials' list every day, but are good value. Excellent fish cakes, made in-house, arrive clothed in a light batter rather than breadcrumbs. For mains, all fish can come in jumbo size – small is not in the vocabulary here. Cod and haddock top the battered fish list at £13.95. Chunky fish (skin on) is served hanging off its own plate in a light, flavoursome batter; chips come in a basket, sides in bowls. The ketchup was far too vinegary, and mushy peas too watery – but if these are the only criticisms, there's little to worry about. *Babies and children welcome: children's menu; high chairs. Booking advisable Thur-Sat. Separate room for parties, seats 40. Takeaway service.* **Map 4 L4.**

Covent Garden

Rock & Sole Plaice
47 Endell Street, WC2H 9AJ (7836 3785, www.rockandsoleplaice.com). Covent Garden tube. **Meals served** 11.30am-10.30pm Mon-Sat; noon-9.30pm Sun. **Main courses** £10-£20. **Credit** MC, V.
Situated just near enough to Covent Garden Piazza to be a tourist trap, this corner café has prices that reflect its location – charging from £15 for fish and chips, and £5 for a fish cake, sausage or saveloy. It's enough to make any Londoner think twice, and yet still they come. Fish, whichever species you decide on, is clearly fresh and flaky, but can be disappointing in size once the crispy batter has been negotiated. Our chips, fried in groundnut oil, were so randomly shaped we suspected the cutter had been distracted from his job; they were dry and bland too. Nevertheless, the minimalist menu also yielded side dishes of coleslaw and mushy peas that were of a decent standard. To cope with the

crowds, the management seem to opt for over-staffing, but service on our visit was efficient and unobtrusive. That said, expect a sense of being rushed if you arrive at a popular time of day.
Babies and children welcome: high chairs. Separate room for parties, seats 40. Tables outdoors (7, pavement). Takeaway service. **Map 18 D3**.

Holborn

Fryer's Delight
19 Theobald's Road, WC1X 8SL (7405 4114). Holborn tube or bus 19, 38, 55. **Meals served** noon-11pm Mon-Sat. **Main courses** £4.75-£7.65. **Unlicensed. Corkage** no charge. **No credit cards**.

Although this looks like a London cabbie's chip shop, its adherents are far more diverse. Every lunchtime, businessmen, hungry locals and passing trade wander into this blast from the city's culinary past. Furnishings don't seem to have changed much in the 50-plus years since fish were first fried here. It's a cosy little spot, with Formica-topped tables, long benches and an old-school menu up on the wall. New restaurants may try to recreate this 'retro' look, but Fryer's is effortlessly genuine. Even Giuseppe, the Italian boss who's been frying in London for the past 45 years, is a no-frills man; he claims not even to have fish, but he certainly knows how to fry it. Cod flakes were moist, against dark, dry and crisp batter, fried the old-fashioned way in beef dripping (or vegetable oil for veggies). Try rockfish as a stronger-flavoured alternative to cod, and make your own butty with a doorstop of bread that comes slathered in butter.
Available for hire. Babies and children admitted. Tables outdoors (1, pavement). Takeaway service. **Map 4 M5**.

Marylebone

Golden Hind
73 Marylebone Lane, W1U 2PN (7486 3644). Bond Street tube. **Lunch served** noon-3pm Mon-Fri. **Dinner served** 6-10pm Mon-Sat. **Main courses** £6.30-£11.50. **Minimum** (dinner) £5. **Unlicensed. Corkage** £1. **Credit** AmEx, MC, V.

In 2014, the Golden Hind will celebrate 100 years of providing solid fish suppers to the residents of Marylebone – almost as long as the dish has been in existence. It's therefore no surprise that the kitchen team have their craft well honed. Our haddock was exceptional, with a light, wonderfully grease-free batter. Chips were chunky, less well done than the norm, but crisp and fresh-tasting (if not quite melt-in-the-mouth on the inside). Perfectly seasoned mushy peas were a treat, and provided more than just a splash of colour on the plate. This attractive, no-nonsense little chippy clearly has a broad appeal, with suited office workers sitting alongside off-duty workmen and ladies who lunch. A gleaming vintage fryer provides an interesting focal point for a room that is otherwise only modestly nostalgic.
Babies and children welcome: high chairs. Booking advisable Fri, Sat. Tables outdoors (4, terrace). Takeaway service. **Map 9 G5**.

Sea Shell
49-51 Lisson Grove, NW1 6UH (7224 9000, www.seashellrestaurant.co.uk). Marylebone tube/rail. **Meals served** noon-10.30pm Mon-Sat. **Main courses** £12-£30. **Credit** AmEx, MC, V.

Fish Central

Kerbisher & Malt

FISH & CHIPS

Not much survived a fire that ravaged the Sea Shell back in 2009. Thankfully, its black and white checked marble floor endures, as does the affection and respect shown it by regulars and staff: 'How did you hear about us?' one waiter asked. Fellow diners, mainly older couples, were smartly dressed for their fish and chip supper. But then, with pale art deco-style surfaces, big colourful paintings and a tank of tropical fish, this is one posh chippy – and has prices to match. Starters were of variable quality: a fish soup was weakly flavoured, yet the whitebait were enjoyably large specimens with a robust crust. The batter on our cod (£14.95 with chips) was as delicate as the flesh was flaky, while panko-coated haddock came prickly with delicious spikes of the Japanese breadcrumb. Oil-free exteriors suggested expert frying. Mushy peas were deep green, and tartare sauce zinged with gherkins. Chips are 'bottomless' but we declined refills – they just didn't seem fresh. Takeaways are considerably cheaper, though celebrity-spotters may be interested to know that Bill Nighy usually eats in.
Babies and children welcome: children's menu; high chairs; nappy-changing facilities. Booking advisable Thur-Sat. Disabled: toilet. Tables outdoors (6, pavement). Takeaway service.
Map 2 F4.

Soho

★ Golden Union Fish Bar
38 Poland Street, W1F 7LY (7434 1933, www.goldenunion.co.uk). Oxford Circus tube. **Meals served** 11.30am-10pm Mon-Sat. **Main courses** £3.95-£12.95. **Credit** AmEx, MC, V.
Cast an eye over the menu and it's evident that Golden Union can talk the talk – fish delivered daily from sustainable waters, grade-A potatoes, a combo of two frying oils changed at least four times a week, and freshly made beer batter. The point is, it can walk the walk too. Fish is chunky, flaky and perfectly cooked in a light, crispy, complementary casing; chips are crisp, firm and fluffy; pies and fish cakes are own-made and look it – there seems to be no weak point. Decide to eat in and the top-of-the-range large fish and chips will set you back £12.95. Side dishes are priced at the expensive end of the scale. The decor is retro with a knowing wink: tiled walls, plastic-topped wooden tables and chairs, and plastic tomatoes filled with ketchup. The music is up-to-date and not too intrusive, combining well with the busy atmosphere – and the vibe is maintained by young staff who seem genuinely proud of what they're serving. Chances are, you'll be planning your return visit before you've even paid the bill.

Babies and children welcome: children's menu; high chairs; nappy-changing facilities. Bookings not accepted lunch Fri. Disabled: toilet. Takeaway service. **Map 17 A3.**

Victoria

Seafresh Fish Restaurant
80-81 Wilton Road, SW1V 1DL (7828 0747, www.fishandchipsinlondon.com). Victoria tube/rail. **Lunch served** noon-3pm, **dinner served** 5-10.30pm Mon-Fri. **Meals served** noon-10.30pm Sat. **Main courses** £11.75-£25.95. **Set lunch** £12.50 2 courses incl tea or coffee. **Set dinner** £13.50 2 courses incl tea or coffee. **Credit** AmEx, MC, V.
Chip shop dining areas can often seem to be merely an afterthought, but not so at Seafresh. This modest Cypriot-owned restaurant has a more formal approach to its customers' dining experience than the average chippy, giving the humble dish the respect it deserves with attentive service and a full wine list. The menu contains a concise choice of seafood – mussels, scampi, scallops, squid – as well as whitebait and the usual species of fish. The batter on the deep-fried calamares and the haddock was marginally too greasy, but their flesh was perfect inside the golden-crisped jackets: the calamares firm, but not chewy; the haddock clearly fresh, and not long from the surf to the table. The inoffensively decorated dining room has a serene but companionable air, with old boys reading the paper and couples enjoying a Cypriot beer and a first-rate fish supper together.
Available for hire. Babies and children welcome: high chairs. Booking advisable Fri, Sat. Takeaway service. **Map 15 J10.**

West

Bayswater

Mr Fish
9 Porchester Road, W2 5DP (7229 4161, www.mrfish.uk.com). Bayswater or Royal Oak tube. **Meals served** 11am-11pm daily. **Main courses** £6.25-£12.95. **Set lunch** (11am-3pm) £6.95 2 courses, £7.95 3 courses. **Credit** AmEx, MC, V.
The colour scheme is turquoise and lemon; our soup bowl sat on a doily; and we received Fox's Glacier Mints with the bill. Yet, despite the kitsch, Mr Fish doesn't have a seaside vibe. With its partitions, padded banquettes and black and white flooring, it looks more like a strangely hued US diner. The place was almost empty on a Thursday night, lending a slight Edward Hopper edge to the experience. A starter of clam chowder was odd – but for the slivers of seafood, we could hardly have told it apart from tinned cream of chicken soup. Other options included avocado and prawn salad, breaded mushrooms, calamares, and king prawns in garlic butter. Fried in rapeseed oil, fish is offered in breadcrumbs, matzo meal or batter. We chose the latter, and our cod's coating was crisp and light. Grilled, you pay a little more, but a big grilled lemon sole made a nice change – shovelled down with mushy peas, shimmering-hot chips and (mediocre) tartare sauce.
Available for hire. Babies and children welcome: children's menu; high chairs. Takeaway service.
Map 7 C5.
For branch see index.

Hammersmith

★ Kerbisher & Malt

164 Shepherd's Bush Road, W6 7PB (3556 0228, www.kerbisher.co.uk). Hammersmith tube. **Lunch served** noon-2.30pm, **dinner served** 4.30-10pm Tue-Thur. **Meals served** noon-10pm Fri, Sat; noon-9pm Sun. **Main courses** £4-£8.60. **Credit** MC, V.

Among the best of London-based fish and chippery, Kerbisher & Malt works within pretty tight strictures. There are, after all, only so many possible variations on the theme of deep-frying seafood and potatoes. Hence, the kitchen team tweak every stage of the process to make the food as appealing as possible. This means high-quality fillets dunked in floaty-light batter, cooked freshly to order. Chips are double-fried, the tartare sauce is rich and made in-house, and the onion rings have been 'pickled', adding an appealing vinegar tang. So committed are the owners to transparency that they've installed a CCTV screen to allow punters in the dining room to watch the chefs slicing haddock and mushing peas. Extras are good too; fish finger butties, lightly spiced fish cake burgers with a twist of lemon mayo, and pots of piping-hot breaded calamares all add to the experience. The long shared table is permanently filled with families tucking into piles of pollock; regulars pop in for boxes of whitebait; and there's a steady stream of custom from noon until 6pm, attracted by the early specials.
Babies and children welcome: children's menu; high chairs. Bookings not accepted dinner Fri. Tables outdoors (2, pavement). Takeaway service. **Map 20 C3.**
For branch see index.

South West

Wandsworth

Brady's

Dolphin House, Smugglers Way, SW18 1DG (8877 9599, www.bradysfish.co.uk). Wandsworth Town rail. **Lunch served** 12.30-2pm Fri. **Dinner served** 6.30-10pm Tue-Thur; 6-10pm Fri. **Meals served** 12.30-10pm Sat; 12.30-8.30pm Sun. **Main courses** £7.85-£12.95. **Credit** MC, V.

In its new premises by the waterfront just south of Wandsworth Bridge, Brady's has created a bright, airy, maritime-themed space both indoors and out. Floor-to-ceiling windows look out over patio decking, and it just needs a wheeling seagull or two to transport diners to the seaside. The fish on offer is good quality: simply grilled sea bream had soft, succulent flesh, crisp skin and was superbly fresh. Battered cod was firm and flaky, with the lightest, crunchiest of batters. Starters – beetroot-dressed smoked salmon, prawn cocktail in a sundae glass, served with brown bread and butter – proved solid, retro fare. Chips are uniform in cut and far from thrice-cooked, but fluffy and crunchy all the same. Sauces – an entire collection of creamy, fresh-herbed jarfuls are presented at each table – are a plus. Puds run from crumbles to light, milky ices. This new incarnation is spanking clean and bright, with a welcoming bar (try a pint of Shepherd Neame Spitfire), and good value at all levels.
Babies and children welcome: children's menu; high chairs. Tables outdoors (11, terrace). Takeaway service. **Map 21 A4.**

South

Battersea

Fish Club

189 St John's Hill, SW11 1TH (7978 7115, www.thefishclub.com). Wandsworth Town rail. **Dinner served** 5-10pm Mon. **Meals served** noon-10pm Tue-Sun. **Main courses** £6.95-£15.95. **Credit** AmEx, MC, V.

Though your waistband might complain, your conscience need not as all the fish at this great little London chippy are sustainably sourced, with coley topping the bill. And that ethical alternative to haddock and cod is popular for good reason: it more than passed muster, with flaky and tender flesh beneath a perfect honey-coloured batter. The twice-fried chips were good too: chunky yet crisp. Perhaps the chilli and garlic sauce on our whole bream was a little overpowering, but only because the fish beneath was delicately fresh, and in no need of adornment. Potted crab, smoked sprats and meat pies take their place on the menu alongside the likes of beetroot salad, beer-battered halloumi and sweet-potato chips, making for an interesting mix of the modern and the retro. Only the unsubtle aquarium-style decor misses the mark – but you'll be enjoying your fish too much to notice.
Babies and children welcome: children's menu; high chairs. Disabled: toilet. Tables outdoors (2, courtyard; 2, pavement). Takeaway service; delivery service (within 1-mile radius). **Map 21 B4.**
For branch see index.

Waterloo

Masters Super Fish

191 Waterloo Road, SE1 8UX (7928 6924). Lambeth North or Southwark tube or Waterloo tube/rail. **Lunch served** noon-3pm Mon-Sat. **Dinner served** 5.30-10.30pm Mon; 4.30-10.30pm Tue-Thur, Sat; 4.30-11pm Fri. **Main courses** £7.25-£16. **Set lunch** £7 1 course incl soft drink, tea or coffee. **Corkage** £5. **Credit** MC, V.

Cabbies love it; fish is brought in daily from Billingsgate; and service is so no-nonsense, it's entertaining – Masters ticks a lot of 'London institution' boxes. Step through from the small takeaway section into a simple dining room painted floor-to-ceiling turquoise. Fellow diners, from older couples to office workers and tourists, sit at functional tables that lend a canteen feel to the place. Food, though, is of a high quality. Starters showcased the fruits of the fryer, from spring rolls to whitebait and battered mussels, but we stuck to the complimentary bread and cold prawn. A wide range of fish comes either battered or grilled (generally pricier). Classic cod was generously sized and delivered quick-sharp from the fryer, its soft flesh suggesting freshness. Grilled tuna had the thickness of two T-bone steaks and showed good grill-bar charring, though its dryness needed the rich tartare sauce and free juicy pickles to provide lubrication. Accompanying chips were pale and uninteresting, yet so hot they practically fizzed. Note that you can bring your own booze here, despite wine being available (from £10.95 a bottle).
Babies and children welcome: children's menu; high chairs. Bookings not accepted Fri. Takeaway service. **Map 11 N9.**

South East

Dulwich

Sea Cow

37 Lordship Lane, SE22 8EW (8693 3111, www.theseacow.co.uk). East Dulwich rail or bus 176. **Meals served** 5-10pm Mon; 5-10.30pm Tue, Wed; noon-10.30pm Thur-Sun. **Main courses** £8.50-£10. **Credit** MC, V.

We remember this place as light and buzzing, but some recent interior decorating in pond-slime green seems to have had an equally depressing effect on the atmosphere. What the Sea Cow sells itself on – good quality fresh fish cooked simply – it does well. Battered haddock got the thumbs-up from someone who lives in a fishing village, and a generous pile of grilled sardines were crispy and tasty. However, the chips were a bit dry and tasteless (as is so often the way since chippies abandoned lard) and the salads showed no effort whatsoever, being either a seemingly undressed pile of green leaves or some chunks of red onion and tomato (billed as a 'Moroccan salad'). Top marks, though, for the surprisingly light, vanilla-infused bread and butter pudding. The Sea Cow's saving grace is its family deals – kids eat free before 4pm at weekends, and at other times receive large portions for a snip – an offer that's hard to ignore.
Babies and children welcome: children's menu; high chairs. Takeaway service. **Map 23 C4.**

Herne Hill

Olley's

65-69 Norwood Road, SE24 9AA (8671 8259, www.olleys.info). Herne Hill rail or bus 3, 68, 196. **Lunch served** noon-3pm Tue-Sun. **Dinner served** 5-10pm Tue-Sat; 5-9.30pm Sun. **Main courses** £5.50-£19.80. **Credit** MC, V.

Distressed pink plasterwork and artfully exposed brickwork, the ballustraded mezzanine, sad-looking pot plants and wonky wall lights – Olley's time- and trend-defying Greek taverna/provincial pizzeria interior seems to have existed forever. But people don't come for the ambience, they come for the fish and chips. Once described as among the best in London, it would now struggle to make the top ten, but the fish remains fresh and well cooked, the batter crispy and the chips non-greasy (but also fairly taste-free). If you're not in the mood for a fish supper, there are more sophisticated options such as mussels, calamares or lightly grilled lemon sole, but mostly it's all very old-school: breaded scampi, minimal wine list, fizzy drinks, and desserts such as spotted dick and custard or ice-cream sundae topped with squirty cream and a fan-shaped wafer. Service is pleasant but woefully slow, so if you're in a hurry, grab a carry-out and eat it across the road in beautiful Brockwell Park.
Babies and children welcome: children's menu; crayons; high chairs; nappy-changing facilities. Booking advisable weekends. Disabled: toilet. Separate room for parties, seats 30. Takeaway service. **Map 23 A5.**

Lewisham

Something Fishy

117-119 Lewisham High Street, SE13 6AT (8852 7075). Lewisham rail/DLR. **Meals served** 9am-5.30pm Mon-Sat. **Main courses** £2.80-£7.60. **Set meal** £5.20 incl soft drink. **No credit cards.**

Although this well-weathered chippy closes at 5.30pm, that's late enough for its market-stall customers, who've been up since dawn. There's an earthy romance to Something Fishy. 'Ea' in?' asks the server in a liveried visor-cum-hairband. If no, you get a polystyrene box; if yes, a china plate. Descriptions are deceptive: the 'small' cod protrudes from the box and overshoots the plate. Its batter is a crunchy golden coat, which yields easily to a light incision. The white flesh is succulent. A lemon quarter sits atop as a garnish: a lah-di-dah innovation, which we like. The chips are chunky, firm and so plentiful as to leave scant room for the squirt of tomato sauce, self-applied at the counter. Some diners choose the first-floor experience; we prefer to sit next to the sliding windows at a blue Formica-topped table furnished with a cruet set and vinegar bottle with the fingerprints of the previous user on the glass, or outside where the market cries entertain. You finish, belch, say 'lovely jubbly' and call for a slab of plump, moist bread pudding, lightly toasted on top. 'Thassa pahnd, luv.' Up West, it'd be a tenner.

Babies and children welcome: children's menu; high chairs. Tables outdoors (5, pavement). Takeaway service.
For branch see index.

East
Spitalfields

★ Poppies HOT 50
6-8 Hanbury Street, E1 6QR (7247 0892, www.poppiesfishandchips.co.uk). Aldgate East tube or Liverpool Street tube/rail. **Meals served** 11am-11pm Mon-Sat; 11am-10.30pm Sun. **Main courses** £10.90-£15.90. **Credit** AmEx, MC, V.
Poppies' pick and mix assortment of shiny British kitsch – including a jukebox, mini red telephone box and a monochrome photo of heart-throb Cliff Richard – makes it look like a simulation of a fish and chip shop. The food on the plate is also better than the real thing. The Billingsgate-sourced fish is offered grilled as well as fried. Extending beyond the staples of cod and haddock, the menu encompasses mackerel, seafood platters and jellied eels. Lemon sole was simple, crisply battered and matched well with Meantime London ale, while chips were irresistible. Takeaway orders in faux-newspaper wraps are doled out by waitresses in diner-style outfits complete with retro headscarves. Service on our visit was outstanding: friendly and unforced. There's a gleamingly clean feel to the place (powder-blue Formica tables and all) that draws in everyone from neighbourhood hipsters to grandads with little 'uns on their knees. The bill, however, gives the game away – Poppies is a cut above. It's spawned a second branch in Camden: not suprising, since this is as good as fish and chips gets.
Available for hire. Babies and children welcome: children's menu; high chairs. Booking advisable. Takeaway service. **Map 12 S5.**
For branch see index.

Victoria Park

Fish House
126-128 Lauriston Road, E9 7LH (8533 3327, www.fishouse.co.uk). Mile End tube then bus 277. **Meals served** noon-10pm Mon-Fri; 11am-10pm Sat, Sun. **Main courses** £8.95-£14.50. **Credit** AmEx, MC, V.

Victoria Park Village's favourite fish and chip shop is part takeaway, part restaurant, though there are eat-in tables in both sections. Most locals opt for carry-outs, but if you choose the restaurant – a minimalist space with a huge close-up photo of octopus tentacles covering one wall – you'll get a more creative menu, where mains of grilled swordfish with a fragrant salsa, or pan-fried hake fillet with chorizo and butter beans, could precede a classic English pud (banana split, bread and butter pudding). But you can't go wrong with fish from the white-tiled takeaway section; choose from cod, scampi, haddock, rock, plaice or skate, generously battered and deep-fried. The freshness of the fish is taken seriously; we even received a mini lesson on the shapes and sizes of the different species from a server. The chips are good, and the mushy peas top-notch. Pickle fans will be pleased by the addition of onions, eggs and gherkins to the menu. Fish cakes and kids' portions are available too, and little 'uns will also appreciate the ice-cream counter displaying Oddono's Italian gelati.
Babies and children welcome: children's menu; crayons; high chairs; nappy-changing facilities. Booking advisable Fri dinner; Sat, Sun. Tables outdoors (8, pavement). Takeaway service.

North East
Stoke Newington

Sutton & Sons
90 Stoke Newington High Street, N16 7NY (7249 6444, www.suttonandsons.co.uk). Stoke Newington rail or bus 149, 243. **Meals served** noon-10pm Mon-Thur; noon-10.30pm Fri, Sat; 2-10pm Sun. **Main courses** £5.90-£12.50.
No credit cards.
With monkfish, Maldon oysters and moules marinière on the menu, this is smarter than most chippies. But Sutton & Sons knows on which side its bread is buttered, catering as it does for Stoke Newington foodies. Natural and attentive staff, sustainable fish (from its fishmonger across the road) and locally brewed beer signify a top-notch chip shop. Batter was crisp and not too greasy, and battered monkfish very good indeed, but skate wing a little under-seasoned. Although you might expect a fancier battered sausage, Sutton's keeps to tradition where it needs to and dishes up a nice old-fashioned saveloy. Mushy peas were also pretty standard, but the kitchen brings a touch of innovation with its balsamic-pickled baby onions and own-made garlic aïoli. Make sure you get in quick at the weekends if you want a slice of Mrs Sutton's sticky toffee pudding – it often sells out.
Babies and children welcome: children's menu; high chairs. Tables outdoors (4, pavement). Takeaway service; delivery service (over £15 within 2-mile radius). **Map 25 C2.**

North
Finchley

Two Brothers Fish Restaurant
297-303 Regent's Park Road, N3 1DP (8346 0469). Finchley Central tube. **Lunch served** noon-2.30pm, **dinner served** 5.30-10.30pm Tue-Sat. **Meals served** noon-8pm Sun. **Main courses** £12.45-£25.95. **Credit** AmEx, MC, V.

Two Brothers seems to fluctuate between very good and tremendous – the sort of inconsistency we don't mind. It's a comfortable spot with New England-inspired decor that, although showing some signs of wear, looks classy compared to many chippies. Attitude, rather than toys or gimmicks, makes the place extremely child-friendly, and even the elderly patrons seem keen to welcome little ones. Adults are kept happy with gargantuan portions and a wine list that's a cut above most competitors (we were very pleased with a Spanish white on discount). A blackboard lists a few specials. There are plenty of starters, including a signature dish of Tony's arbroath smokies in creamy tomato sauce, along with sautéed sardines, marinated herrings and rock oysters. Anyone not opting for fried fish might try steamed salmon hollandaise, or sirloin steak. Our grilled plaice was superb, and came with lots of succulent fat chips. Battered haddock (matzo is also available) and goujons of cod (for the child) were great too and, as expected, left no room for dessert. Worth noting: the restaurant is now open on Sundays.
Available for hire. Booking advisable. Babies and children welcome: high chairs. Takeaway service.

Highgate

Fish Fish
179 Archway Road, N6 5BN (8348 3121). Highgate tube. **Dinner served** 5-10.30pm Mon-Fri. **Meals served** noon-10.30pm Sat, Sun. **Main courses** £10.95-£13.95. **Credit** MC, V.
A more cheerful spot than its location and black frontage suggest, this laid-back neighbourhood restaurant features pot plants, lanterns and various accoutrements of the sea. The meat content of the menu has been beefed up in recent years, but most come here for the fish, which can be charcoal-grilled, poached, deep-fried in batter or shallow-fried in breadcrumbs. There are a few fishy pasta options too, plus classic starters such as calamares, mussels, whitebait and taramasalata. Our exquisitely fresh grilled sea bream with salad was the sort of fare made memorable on Mediterranean holidays. Traditional British battered haddock and chips was a fine rendition, and we were greatly impressed by the quality of the own-made fish fingers for kids. The brief wine list has some decent bottles, but the familiar brands seem overpriced outside a supermarket setting. Thinly populated on our weeknight visit, this is nevertheless a handy and friendly joint locals would do well to support.
Available for hire. Babies and children welcome: high chairs; nappy-changing facilities. Tables outdoors (10, garden). Takeaway service.

Muswell Hill

Toff's
38 Muswell Hill Broadway, N10 3RT (8883 8656, www.toffsfish.co.uk). Highgate tube then bus 43, 134. **Meals served** 11.30am-10.30pm Mon-Sat. **Main courses** £12.45-£24.95. **Set meal** £9.50 1 course incl tea or coffee. **Credit** AmEx, MC, V.
The dark-wood panelled interior probably seemed retro when Toff's was established back in 1968. This Muswell Hill stalwart is a true one-off; the corporate slickness comes from being a long-established family business that knows what it's doing and knows that people like it. Little changes here, but we were pleased to note that, unlike many London chippies, the business has joined the Marine

Poppies

Stewardship Council and sources fish from sustainable stocks. Fish is cooked to order and batter is the norm; egg and matzo, or grilling, bring a surcharge. Starters include fish or vegetable soup, deep-fried camembert, fish cakes and avocado vinaigrette. Our main-course grilled king prawns with herby butter dressing were lovely, but seemed pricey at £15.95 for a modest portion. No complaints about the gigantic battered haddock, however, which arched across the plate as though in yoga posture. Fat chips were fabulous. To drink, there are a dozen wines, three bottled beers and a range of spirits. In the unlikely event you have room, finish with Marine Ices ice-cream or one of the school-days puddings.
Babies and children welcome: children's menu; crayons; high chairs. Booking advisable. Disabled: toilet. Separate rooms for parties, seating 20 and 24. Takeaway service.

North West
Belsize Park

Oliver's
95 Haverstock Hill, NW3 4RL (7586 9945, www.oliversfishandchips.com). Chalk Farm tube. **Meals served** noon-10.15pm Tue-Sun. **Main courses** £9.20-£11.45. **Credit** AmEx, MC, V.
Oliver's has many of the characteristics we want in a modern chippy: fresh clean decor of cream tongue-and-groove panelling, apple-green tiling and metal chairs; bright young friendly staff; and an appealing menu that takes in British traditions as well as a range of international fish dishes. Pity, then, that the food was so far below par on our visit. The chips were simply poor, riddled with off-putting dark patches. A main-course salad niçoise, served with grilled tuna steak, suffered from fridge storage and a greasy gloss. Crunchy brown-

battered cod was better. The short wine list is wallet-friendly (we liked the Chilean sauvignon blanc) and the deep-fried Mars Bar with vanilla ice-cream is a fabulous way to finish, if you haven't consumed too much fat already. A few customers were dining during our mid-afternoon visit, and the takeaway trade seemed brisk (Oliver's also offers home delivery to certain postcodes). So, the restaurant is doing something right, but we think it can – and must – do better.
Babies and children welcome: high chairs. Booking advisable. Separate room for parties, seats 20. Tables outdoors (2, pavement). Takeaway service; delivery service (over £15 within 3-mile radius). **Map 28 C4**.

West Hampstead

★ Nautilus
27-29 Fortune Green Road, NW6 1DU (7435 2532). West Hampstead tube/rail then bus 328. **Lunch served** 11.30am-2.30pm, **dinner served** 4.30-10pm Mon-Sat. **Main courses** £10.50-£22.50. **Credit** MC, V.
Frills there aren't, but this white- and blue-fronted spot often produces gasps of delight at the sheer freshness and just-so cooking of its fish. The second thing you need to know is that batter's off the menu: it's matzo, or matzo and egg, if you want the fish fried. Portions are generous and fillets of cod or haddock typically stretch off each side of the plate. Lemon sole – in other hands a pretty ordinary species – was a sweet, minerally feast, sensitively grilled on the bone. Anything other than chips and simple salad on the side would have got in the way. Matzo-crusted halibut, a golden orange cutlet of meaty white flesh, was similarly fresh and accurately cooked. Groundnut is the oil of choice, and its clean flavour is tastily apparent in Nautilus's wonderful chips. Keo beer, taramasalata and houmous add to the Greek-island feel of the decor, which features pine panelling, boat pictures and

raffia chairs. Early opening for dinner makes this a smart choice to take kids, and the little fried nuggets served to them have all the quality of adult portions.
Babies and children welcome: high chairs. Booking advisable. Takeaway service.
Map 28 A1.

Outer London
Kingston, Surrey

fish! kitchen
58 Coombe Road, Kingston, Surrey, KT2 7AF (8546 2886, www.fishkitchen.com). Norbiton rail or bus 57, 85, 213. **Meals served** noon-10pm Tue-Sat. **Main courses** £9.95-£26.95. **Credit** AmEx, MC, V.
You'd imagine that a fish restaurant located slap-bang next to one of London's longest established and respected fishmongers would be just the place to find the freshest seafood around. And, to some extent, you'd be right. Halibut had pearlescent flesh encased in a cracking beer batter, and lightly own-smoked wild salmon steak – accompanied by perfectly wilted spinach and a gloriously runny-yolked poached egg – told a similar story. Crunchy chips did not disappoint either. Starters, however, were lacklustre: gravadlax was limply tired; thickly cut 'carpaccio' of smoked swordfish was passable, but fried whitebait were floppily weary. Skin-on new potatoes appeared to be in their dotage. Staff seemed unsurprised by the barely touched leftovers. Still, the excellent mains were well worth the steep but fair price, and ample portions left no room for any of the traditional puds. A refreshing rosé from a short but sensible wine list added cheer. We left hoping for a return to form soon.
Babies and children welcome: children's menu; high chairs. Booking advisable. Disabled: toilet. Tables outdoors (10, terrace). Takeaway service.
For branch see index.

Ice-cream Parlours

Ah, the food of childhood – perhaps that is why many of London's ice-cream parlours give a retro slant to their furnishings. **Ruby Violet** in Tufnell Park is a case in point, with its hint of 1950s kitchenette design; but what propelled this newcomer towards our red-star rating is its excellent ices made from the finest raw materials. Italian gelateria still account for the great majority of venues in this section – with our current favourites being the mini-chain **Scoop** and **Gelateria 3bis** at Borough Market – though for a different take on your tub, try the Argentinian-styled ices at **Freggo**, or the wondrously inventive creations at Camden's superb **Chin Chin Laboratorists**. Yes, ice-cream is inextricably linked with sticky pre-teen memories, but London's current top performers have conjured up a repertoire of very grown-up, sexy treats.

Central
Covent Garden

La Gelatiera
*27 New Row, WC2N 4LA (7836 9559,
www.lagelatiera.co.uk). Leicester Square tube.*
Open *Summer* 10.30am-11.30pm daily. *Winter*
10.30am-11.30pm Tue-Sun. **Credit** MC, V.
Despite the Italian name, this small homespun outfit is simply dolce rather than Dolce & Gabbana. There's a plot-to-tub ethos in the sourcing (organic milk, chocolate beans from the Ecuador National Plantation, enthusiastic use of Slow Food members' ingredients) and a bohemian vibe to the decor, but slow and dopey service had us wishing for a dash of corporate slickness. Portions were unreasonably skimpy too, yet we couldn't fault the ice-cream. Quirky combinations are a mainstay, and flavours – including basil and chilli, and honey with rosemary and orange zest – were expertly balanced. Dark chocolate sorbet was also superb. We like the look of bakes such as white chocolate and peanut butter roll, and vow to return for cups of hot chocolate: there's a choice including Ecuadorian 70%, Venezuelan 58% and Ivory Coast white chocolate. If service were improved, La Gelatiera might even become a regular haunt.
Takeaway service. Vegan dishes. **Map 10 L7.**

Gelatorino
*2 Russell Street, WC2B 5JD (7240 0746,
www.gelatorino.com). Covent Garden tube.*
Open 11am-10pm Mon, Sun; 11am-11pm
Tue-Sat. **Credit** (over £5) MC, V.

This Piedmont-inspired gelato boutique has a cute boudoir vibe, thanks to curlicue chairs and vintage painted dressers lined with Italian goodies. Gelatorino's ice-cream display isn't as tempting as some, because the ices are scooped straight from pozzetti (lidded steel tubs set in the counter), which is arguably the best way to keep high-quality, preservative-free gelato fresh. Specials such as fig ripple add flair to the mostly traditional selection, all of which is made on site. Coffee-flavoured 'Breakfast in Turin' is a worthy signature gelato; dark chocolate and gianduja (hazelnut and chocolate) were spot-on renditions too, but our caramel panna cotta gelato tasted merely sweet. Baked goods include tiramisu muffins, and you can order special-occasion gelato cakes. We like the friendly, professional service and handy central location. While the coffee is ordinary, hot chocolate made with melted gianduja keeps customers popping in on cooler days.
Tables outdoors (3, pavement). Takeaway service. Vegan dishes. **Map 18 E4.**

★ Scoop
*40 Shorts Gardens, WC2H 9AB (7240 7086,
www.scoopgelato.com). Covent Garden tube.*
Open noon-10.30pm Mon-Thur; noon-11pm
Fri-Sun. **Credit** AmEx, MC, V.
Voluptuous folds of colourful gelato undulate across Scoop's freezer cabinet like rows of love handles. If you can settle on just one, you're possibly not human. Scoop has been wowing Londoners with first-rate gelato since its first slip of a shop opened in Covent Garden. Expansion has been slow and modest; now there's also an appealing Soho parlour (with more tables) and another in South Ken. Flavours are classic Italian (biscotto, fior di latte, malaga, pistachio), but made from brag-worthy ingredients including Tonda Gentile hazelnuts from Piedmont, Sicilian black cherries and a changing range of single-origin chocolates and coffees. It's always hard to resist the cioccolato extra fondente sorbet, which is super-dark rather than bitter in taste and far smoother than a chocolate bar. Sugar seekers should try the coconut gelato. We like the choice of cones and friendly service too. There are a few sweet pies, cakes and meringues in the window, and you can also order crêpes, waffles and vegan churros.
Takeaway service. Vegan dishes. **Map 18 D3.**
For branches see index.

Holborn

Gelateria Danieli
*222 Shaftesbury Avenue, WC2H 8EB (7240
1770, www.gelateriadanieli.com). Tottenham
Court Road or Holborn tube.* **Open** *Summer*
10am-10pm Mon-Sat; 11am-7pm Sun. *Winter*
10am-6pm Mon-Sat; 11am-6pm Sun. **No
credit cards.**
This small branch of the mini-chain, the first West End venture for Gelateria Danieli, opened in 2012. Despite the name, it isn't much of a café but rather a takeaway shop with one small table inside – though on a sunny day, you'll find a few more bistro tables on the pavement outside. On our visit, 18 flavours were offered, yet none of the more original ices served at the Richmond outlet (the likes of cinnamon, caramel and date, or mulberry) was available. Instead, the choice was from Italian classics such as coffee, stracciatella or pistachio.

Though disappointing, this was probably a good thing as a sign warns, 'Only one taster': not much help if you aren't sure what you might get. Danieli's strength is in the creaminess of its ice-cream; even the sorbets are creamy (and mostly dairy based). Our highlights were a perfectly balanced rum and raisin and a silky tiramisu featuring delectable chunks of coffee-soaked ladyfingers.
Takeaway service. **Map 18 D2.**
For branches (Danieli on the Green, Gelateria Danieli) see index.

Mayfair

Freggo
27-29 Swallow Street, W1B 4QR (7287 9506, www.freggo.co.uk). Piccadilly Circus tube. **Open** 8am-11pm Mon-Thur; 8.30am-midnight Fri; 10am-midnight Sat; 10am-7.30pm Sun. **Credit** AmEx, MC, V.
Freggo brands itself an ice-cream bar and has a decor to match, with mirrored walls, purple furnishings and silver bar stools and tables. The business also distinguishes itself by being an Argentinian ice-cream bar. The choice of flavours is limited and divided into groups of creamy, chocolatey, fruity, and the Argentinian speciality dulche de leche-based ice-creams. After a few tasters, it becomes clear that Freggo's ice-cream is not as creamy as the Italian variety and that the flavours are all rather sweet. The dulche de leche ones are especially syrupy; they include Temptation, consisting of dulche de leche ice-cream with caramel sauce – so a sort of double dulche de leche. Nevertheless, dulche de leche and chocolate, with its tiny dark chocolate chips, made a surprisingly delightful combination with the fresh malbec and berries sorbet. You might also find other Argentinian foodstuffs on the menu here, such as alfajores, a shortbread-type cookie, and savoury empanadas. Sadly, neither was available on our visit. *Tables outdoors (2, pavement). Vegan dishes.* **Map 17 A5.**

Soho

Amorino
41 Old Compton Street, W1D 6HF (7494 3300, www.amorino.com). Leicester Square or Piccadilly Circus tube. **Open** noon-midnight Mon-Thur, Sun; noon-1am Fri, Sat. **Credit** MC, V.
At this London branch of a US chain, your Italian ice-cream comes shaped as a flower. At least it does if you ask for a cone on which ice-cream slabs, rather than scoops, are formed into 'petals' atop a crispy waffle. The petals can be made from as many flavours as you wish – even if you choose the small size. This is a handy innovation, as the vast array of flavours can be a bit hit and miss. A juicy passionfruit offered a tangy freshness, which complemented the dark chocolate hit from the chocolate sorbet; however, tiramisu tasted rather artificial, and the fabulously named L'Inimitabile, a nut-flavoured chocolate, was just too sweet. If you fancy something more substantial, choose waffles, crêpes or brioches – all served with or without ice-cream. A small selection of chocolates and sweets is also for sale. The shop itself is small, with dark brown wood furnishings that make it feel even more so. Still, there are enough tables to seat up to ten people at a time and you'll even find a few chairs outside on the pavement.
Tables outdoors (3, pavement). Takeaway service. **Map 17 B4.**

Gelupo
7 Archer Street, W1D 7AU (7287 5555, www.gelupo.com). Leicester Square or Piccadilly Circus tube. **Open** noon-11pm Mon-Thur; noon-12.30am Fri, Sat; noon-10.30pm Sun. **Credit** MC, V.
We usually adore this cool evocation of Sicily in Soho, and the bustle suggests other Londoners have taken Gelupo to heart too. Yet we were disappointed in the flavours on our most recent visit. Kiwi with gin and elderflower tasted of little except elderflower; coconut gelato had a cloying soapy quality, while watermelon with cinnamon and jasmine smacked of floral toiletries. Excess egg white in the sorbets was also off-putting. We should have stuck with Gelupo classics, such as black forest cherry and chocolate, blood-orange granita or one of the ewe's milk ricotta ices – you can at least be guaranteed of a great range of flavours. Service is zippy. Italian biscuits and cakes, coffee, gourmet sandwiches and an appealing selection of groceries make Gelupo a handy spot to know year round. Late closing puts it high on the list of things to do after an outing to the theatre, cinema or pub. The same owners also run Italian restaurant Bocca di Lupo (*see p154*), over the road.
Disabled: toilet (restaurant). Takeaway service. Vegan dishes. **Map 17 B4.**

South Kensington

Oddono's
14 Bute Street, SW7 3EX (7052 0732, http://oddonos.co.uk). South Kensington tube. **Open** 10am-11pm Mon-Thur, Sun; 10am-midnight Fri, Sat. **Credit** AmEx, MC, V.
With its bright blue and white colour scheme and its selection of Italian treats and drinks on the counter, Oddono's certainly has the look and feel of a true gelateria. The chatter in French and Italian that fills the room also helps give the place a continental feel. Ice-cream is rich and indulgent; pistachio was properly good – velvety smooth and full of flavour. Sadly, the stracciatella was a little over-generous with the chocolate, to the point where the scoop seemed to be more crunch than cream.

Service was harassed, and staff were getting impatient with those wanting to browse by choice. Yet while Oddono's may have been outshone by newer kids on the block, it remains a firm favourite churning out some lovely gelato. Worth a visit.
Tables outdoors (2, pavement). Takeaway service. Vegan dishes. **Map 14 D10.**
For branches see index.

West

Bayswater

Snowflake Gelato
43 Westbourne Grove, W2 4SA (7221 9549, www.snowflakegelato.co.uk). Bayswater or Royal Oak tube. **Open** 10am-11.30pm Mon-Thur; 10am-1am Fri, Sat; 10am-midnight Sun. **Credit** MC, V.
Snowflake aims to 'serve happiness' through the means of Italian gelato and sorbetto. Flavours come and go (strawberries and cream for Wimbledon fortnight, for example), and there are the likes of waffles, smoothies and concoctions such as banana splits. Whatever you choose, the quality is high – freshly made and with sound ingredients. Rich flavours of praline, and date and honey, were particular highlights, while the white chocolate-based eponymous house speciality is a creamy and vibrant smash. Sorbets are equally tempting: the lime flavour was on the brink of overpowering, but the strawberry proved a refreshingly fruity revelation. The bare, space-age decor will either attract or repel, depending on your preferences, but the ice-cream has universal appeal.
Takeaway service. **Map 7 B6.**

Ladbroke Grove

Zazà Gelato
195 Portobello Road, W11 2ED (07796 968025, www.zazagelato.eu). Ladbroke Grove or Notting Hill Gate tube. **Open** 10.30am-6.30pm Mon-Thur; 10.30am-midnight Fri, Sat; noon-7pm Sun. **Credit** MC, V.

Gelupo

Chin Chin Laboratorists

Zazà's gelateria isn't a showy affair, and the premises are modest. Ice-cream flavours are limited, yet rarely boring, with a few surprises in among the old favourites. Gelato is created throughout the day in ice-cream makers that churn away beneath the counter. On our visit, fresh, plump oranges were being squeezed and added to the mixer for the arancia sorbet. Unsurprisingly, considering the freshness of the ingredients, our scoop had a crisp, light and delicately floral sweetness. Pistachio gelato was also a triumph, with a subtle, lingering nuttiness. The only miss was a bland white chocolate scoop. Opt instead for the dark chocolate, which packs more of a flavour punch. Seating is limited, but the venue is a light, bright modern space with stools along the counter, and a peaceful fenced patio area at the back that provides welcome respite from Notting Hill's summer hordes. *Tables outdoors (2, pavement). Takeaway service. Vegan dishes.* **Map 19 B3.** **For branches see index.**

South West
Chelsea

Dri Dri Gelato
Chelsea Farmers Market, 125 Sydney Street, SW3 6NR (8616 5718, www.dridrigelato.com). Sloane Square tube then 11, 19, 22 bus or 49 bus. **Open** 11am-8pm daily. **No credit cards.**

Dri Dri Gelato occupies a beach hut-style venue at Chelsea Farmers Market, though you won't spot many wellie-wearers among the well-heeled patrons. Gelato is kept carefully covered in metal cylinders sunk deep into the counter, which help retain the texture of the ices but make it considerably more difficult to choose a flavour. Luckily, helpful and enthusiastic staff were on hand to ply us with tasters before we took the plunge. Blind to its unappetising beige hue, and wowed by its taste, we plumped for an almond biscoto scoop. This was light, but with a slightly coarse consistency and a warmly spiced flavour; it perfectly complemented the strong and rather bitter second scoop of espresso. The room is candy-floss cute, all pastel shades and too-small tables; better to take your tub a little farther down Sydney Street and relax on the grass in the neighbouring park. *Tables outdoors (2, courtyard). Takeaway service.* **Map 14 E11.**

South East
Forest Hill

Sugar Mountain
57A Dartmouth Road, SE23 3HN (07796 671574). Forest Hill rail. **Open** 10am-6pm Tue-Thur; 10am-8pm Fri, Sat; 10am-4pm Sun. **No credit cards.**

A retro sweetshop-cum-ice-cream-parlour, topped with a big squirt of kitsch. The talking point is the trio of themed booths: the retro games booth (Ker-Plunk, Mousetrap, Bionic Woman); the '80s pop-culture booth (*Smash Hits* annual, Bros 7-inches, Jason Donovan cassette, Charles and Di tumbler); and the space race booth (Neil Armstrong's signature, photos of astronauts, globes). The ice-cream itself comes from north London's Marine Ices (£1.60 for a one-scoop cone plus £1 per additional scoop). The flavour spectrum stretches from bubble gum (which doesn't taste as brash as it sounds) to white chocolate or pistachio. Customise in a sundae glass with sauces or toppings, with a traditional Ben Shaws pop on the side. A great after-school treat for kids, or sugar-based nostalgia fix for adults. *Takeaway service.*

London Bridge & Borough

★ Gelateria 3bis
4 Park Street, SE1 9AB (7378 1977, www.gelateria3bis.it). London Bridge tube/rail. **Open** 8am-10pm Mon-Sat; 10am-6pm Sun. **Credit** (over £5) MC, V.

One of our favourite gelaterias has two branches: the first in Rimini; the second, thankfully, right next to Borough Market. Behind a green frontage, its bright, spacious dining room has full-length windows opening on to the pavement in summer. The menu encompasses frozen yoghurt, ice-cream cakes, brioches and crêpes – the speciality coffees are also worth a mention (the Salcedo was a perfect espresso with liquid chocolate and skimmed milk) – but the real star is the gelato. It's made on the premises; you can watch the two ice-cream machines, Italian imports, performing at the end of the shop. Cups and cones come in three sizes starting at £3.20, which is big enough to try at least two flavours. The repertoire includes Italian classics as well as creative English innovations (eton mess, anyone?). Creamy flavours, for example chocolate chip (a classic vanilla cream-based gelato with chunks of dark chocolate), make a perfect pairing with fruity sorbets, such as the refreshing mixed berry sorbet. Ask for a drop of melted gianduja chocolate at the bottom of your cup or cone. It adds a whole new dimension to what might already be London's best ice-cream. *Takeaway service.* **Map 11 P8.**

North
Camden Town & Chalk Farm

★ Chin Chin Laboratorists `HOT 50`
49-50 Camden Lock Place, NW1 8AF (07885 604284, www.chinchinlabs.com). Camden Town tube. **Open** noon-7pm daily. **No credit cards.**

Now a fixture of Camden Market, the innovative Chin Chin Labs – where ice-cream is frozen to order amid billowing clouds of liquid nitrogen-generated steam – may not seem as wacky as it once did, but there are always new tourists to surprise, and plenty of regulars happy to queue for the fabulous ice-cream. The menu is commandingly short: chocolate, vanilla and two specials – one ice-cream, one dairy-free sorbet. The latter always astounds

with its fat-free creaminess and cool flavours, such as griddled peach, watermelon and dill, or beetroot choc chip. Haute cuisine references are frequent in flavours such as coffee and tobacco, or Guinness caramel with smoked salt. Experimental, yes, but the results are reliably superb. Pimp your tub with a veritable chemistry set of sprinkles and sauces (we liked the white chocolate-coated potato chips with our summery strawberry and hay ice-cream) – you too can be a molecular gastronomist.
Tables outdoors (4, pavement). Takeaway service. Vegan dishes. **Map 27 C1.**

Crouch End

Riley NEW

32 The Broadway, N8 9SU (8347 7825). Finsbury Park tube/rail then bus W7, or Crouch Hill or Hornsey rail. **Open** 9am-7pm Mon-Fri; 9.30am-7pm Sat; 10.30am-7pm Sun. **No credit cards**.
This bright, spacious art-themed parlour-café would be welcome in most neighbourhoods, but in the heart of Crouch End it feels like more of the same. The artisan-made ice-creams and sorbets are a draw, certainly, though on our visit the choice was dull and the mood of disappointment wasn't helped by an exhausted counter assistant. We made do with vanilla, chocolate, fior di latte and strawberry, all of which were good, though it was the yoghurt flavour that really shone with its zingy, refreshing tang. The selection of wholesome Mediterranean-inspired salads, sandwiches and tarts spread across the counter is enticingly homey; combined with the relaxed decor and plenty of space around the tables, Riley is in a prime position to become a favourite with the Bugaboo brigade. Cakes, brownies, milkshakes and well-made coffee complete a generally pleasing picture.
Takeaway service.

Tufnell Park

★ Ruby Violet NEW

118 Fortess Road, NW5 2HL (7609 0444, www.rubyviolet.co.uk). Tufnell Park tube or 134, 390 bus. **Open** 11am-10pm daily. **Credit** MC, V.
Take Las Vegas glitz, add a dash of Morocco, some 1950s kitchenette design and a bit of reclaimed timber and – hocus pocus – you have the magical Ruby Violet. We're not sure what Tufnell Park has done to deserve one of London's premier ice-cream parlours, but whether you're on a date or out with the kids, there are few occasions this place doesn't suit. The ices (expect a choice of 18) are all made in a pristine kitchen from Duchy Originals organic milk, free-range eggs and a glass and a half of discernment. Reliably excellent standard flavours (madagascan vanilla, chocolate hazelnut crunch) are supplemented with intriguing diversions such as rhubarb and verjus, or elderflower and prosecco. On the counter there's usually a gooey curiosity such as Guinness and blue cheese or chocolate-beetroot cake. For parties and special occasions, you can order flower-shaped sorbets, layered balls and bombes, and 'antarctic rolls' of ice-cream in sponge. Drinks continue the high-level tone with fabulous hot chocolate made with Callebaut Couverture, Newby teas and Square Mile coffee. Service can be slow, if we're being picky, but on the whole this place is excellent.
Tables outdoors (3, pavement). Takeaway service. **Map 26 B4.**

North West
Belsize Park

Gelato Mio

204 Haverstock Hill, NW3 2AG (7998 9276, www.gelatomio.co.uk). Belsize Park tube. **Open** noon-11pm Mon-Thur; noon-12.30am Fri, Sat; noon-10.30pm Sun. **Credit** AmEx, MC, V.
A friendly mini-chain with well-trained staff and smart, comfortable surrounds, Gelato Mio strikes a good balance between kid and adult appeal. The quality of gelato is consistently high, though flavour delivery varies from superb to nondescript.

Roman holiday favourites are supplemented with seasonal specials that often salute other countries. We were impressed by the woody, grown-up flavour and chunky texture of American walnut, plus textbook vanilla and dark chocolate varieties. On our visit, locals were coming in specifically for peanut butter gelato; staff managed to charm away disappointment that it had run out. Pastries and coffees are on a par with the big coffee chains, though most customers just grab and go. You can buy take-home tubs and order gelato cakes (48 hours' notice), but prices are steep.
Disabled: toilet. Tables outdoors (8, pavement). Takeaway service. **Map 28 C3.**
For branches see index.

Ruby Violet

Pizzerias

Until **Franco Manca** opened in 2008, the general view was that the chains had pizza all sewn up (and we're not talking calzone). For too many Londoners, the main experience of this Italian staple was of a flabby thing delivered in a cardboard box. But from its tiny premises in Brixton Market, Franco Manca was a game-changer: sourcing its toppings with diligence; waiting, waiting until its slow-rise sourdough base was ready; then popping the lot into a scorching brick oven for just 40 seconds. There you have it: perfect Neapolitan pizza. We still reckon the Brixton original to be the best pizza joint in town, despite the business now having four offshoots. But during the past few years, other independent pizzerias have sprung up, or upped their game, so that standards are now gratifyingly high. Newcomers continue to arrive – witness **Pizza Pilgrims** joining the gang fresh from the street-food scene, **Pizza Union** coming to feed the City hordes with alacrity (and thin, crisp crusts) and **Homeslice** creating 20-inchers in Covent Garden. Such is the new-found popularity of the genre, **Goat** has been born by converting a former pub in SW10 to a multi-level pizzeria, and serving toppings such as lobster to the affluent assembly. Other restaurants in this Guide also serve great pizzas, including **Princi** (*see p39*) and **Caravan King's Cross** (*p38*), and Jamie Oliver even serves Brit pizzas at **Union Jacks** (*p49*).

Central

City

Rocket

201 Bishopsgate, EC2M 3AB (7377 8863, www.rocketrestaurants.co.uk). Liverpool Street tube/rail. **Meals served** 11am-10.30pm Mon-Fri; 6-10.30pm Sat. **Main courses** £8-£19.25. **Set meal** £20 2 courses, £25 3 courses. **Credit** AmEx, MC, V.

With a plum spot near Liverpool Street station and a flashy, contemporary interior, this branch of the Rocket mini-chain expertly caters for the after-work crowd. The operation is split into a bar and dining area, the latter a predictable formula of open kitchen, bare tables and the odd original feature such as a wall tiled in sea-green plates. Pizzas (mostly costing around £12) and Modern European dishes make up the relatively affordable but unsophisticated menu. Likewise, the wine list is aimed at quaffers rather than savourers; there are five sauvignon blancs by the glass and a full-bodied white selection composed entirely of chardonnay. A simple starter of high-quality buffalo mozzarella with fresh cherry tomatoes was pleasingly light, and a small portion of tender squid rings had been cooked with accuracy. Our pizza featured a crisp, thin base, on to which a topping of spicy sausage, gorgonzola, roasted peppers and aubergine proved a bold but successful combination. By contrast, a salad of steak, chips, rocket, flaccid tempura green beans and black bean sauce – perhaps a homage to steak and chips – was simply bemusing. Service, too, let the side down, slowing to a creep after going all out for the 6pm rush.

Available for hire. Babies and children admitted. Booking advisable. Disabled: toilet. Tables outdoors (6, terrace). Vegan dishes. **Map 12 R5**. *For branches see index.*

Covent Garden

Homeslice [NEW]

13 Neal's Yard, WC2H 9DP (7836 4604, www.homeslicepizza.co.uk). Covent Garden or Leicester Square tube. **Open** noon-10.30pm Mon-Sat; noon-8pm Sun. **Pizza** £4 slice, £20 whole pizza. **No credit cards.**

It's not how big it is: it's what you do with it. Take this new joint in Neal's Yard, which is serving pizzas that wouldn't be out of place on 'Man v Food'. Served fresh from the wood-fired oven, most of these thin crusts are available by the slice. Or you can order a 20-incher: enough to feed you and two pals. Staff will even let you have more than one choice of the topping selections if you ask nicely. A well-constructed margherita can be a little slice of heaven, as can other classic pizzas. But if it's done right (no chicken, no sweet chilli sauce, no pineapple), some innovation doesn't go amiss. And here there are a couple of ingredient combos that wouldn't get the green light in Naples, but taste pretty good. On one, slivers of bone marrow were melted over the tomato base, imparting a meaty savouriness. Scattered with watercress and roasted whole spring onions, the pizza was oozy and delicious with a chewy cornicione (crust). A white anchovy, chard and doddington cheese pizza also had great balance; finished with a twist of orange zest, it was filled with sweet, bitter and salty notes. Service was impeccably attentive and chummy. To drink, there are craft beers and even prosecco on tap.

Available for hire. Babies and children welcome: high chairs. Bookings not accepted. Tables outdoors (3, pavement). Takeaway service. **Map 18 D3**.

Soho

Pizza Pilgrims [NEW]

11 Dean Street, W1D 3RP (07780 667258, http://pizzapilgrims.co.uk). Tottenham Court Road tube. **Lunch served** noon-3pm, **dinner served** 6-10.30pm Mon-Sat. **Main courses** £7-£11. **Credit** MC, V.

Having built a loyal following for its three-wheeler food van (usually found in Berwick Street Market), PP opened on this busy corner in summer 2013. You can see the kitchen and pizza oven (also servicing the takeaway trade) through the ground-floor windows. The main basement dining area feels intimate, the seating and tables compact. Wipe-clean green checked tablecloths and 1960s Italian film posters help create the feel of a retro Soho trattoria. The friendly, slightly trendy mood is helped by an alcove for table football. The menu, printed on Polpo-style manila paper, lists ten pizzas. Chewy and soft in the Neapolitan style, the appealing, thick bases are layered with on-trend toppings. 'Nduja, a spicy Calabrian sausage, is paired well with a simple marinara sauce. Salsiccia e friarielli (fennel sausage and a type of brassica leaf), and calzone with prosciutto cotto, ricotta, mushrooms and fior di latte are other enticing combos. Desserts include ice-creams and sorbets from Gelupo, either in unadulterated form or embellished – for example, vanilla with extra virgin olive oil and sea salt. Wine is served by the carafe, adding to the 1960s feel; alternative tipples include prosecco and trendy Venetian cocktails such as negroni or spritz. Note: bookings aren't taken. *Bookings not accepted for fewer than 8 people. Separate room for parties, seats 8-16. Takeaway service.* **Map 17 B4**.

West
Ealing

★ Santa Maria
15 St Mary's Road, W5 5RA (8579 1462, www.santamariapizzeria.com). South Ealing tube. **Meals served** noon-10.30pm daily. **Main courses** £5.45-£10.55. **Credit** MC, V.
Next door to Ealing Studios' watering hole, the Red Lion, this pocket-sized pizzeria puts real heart into its offerings. Owners Angelo and Pasquale, finding nowhere in London to match the pizza of their upbringing, set about recreating an authentic slice of Naples in W5. Authentic, it doubtless is. Everything from the wood-fired oven to the Caputo flour and parmigiano reggiano is imported; the lightly salted dough is given a 24-hour rise; the tomatoes crushed by hand; the mozzarella cut in precise pieces that melt just-so. It's all done with bucket-loads of cultural pride and results in magnificent pizza, charred to loveliness with a beautifully chewy base. Within weeks of its opening back in 2010, *Time Out* voted Santa Maria London's Best Pizzeria. But controversy kicked in almost immediately, with busy, sometimes rushed, service raising eyebrows. Santa Maria calls the 'order, eat and leave' attitude *'tipico napoletano'*; plenty find it off-putting. The verdict? It's tiny, rightfully popular and doesn't take bookings. If you come for cracking pizza and a pint next door, you're in for a treat – but don't cross London expecting to linger all night.
Babies and children welcome: high chairs. Bookings not accepted. Tables outdoors (2, pavement). Takeaway service.
For branch (Sacro Cuore) see index.

Ladbroke Grove

Rossopomodoro
184A Kensington Park Road, W11 2ES (7229 9007, www.rossopomodoro.co.uk). Ladbroke Grove or Notting Hill Gate tube. **Meals served** noon-11pm Mon-Thur; noon-11.30pm Fri, Sat; noon-10pm Sun. **Main courses** £11-£16. **Set lunch** £10 1 course incl drink. **Credit** AmEx, MC, V.

Homeslice

For an ever-expanding chain (there are now six branches in London, one in Birmingham and outposts worldwide from Spain to Saudi Arabia), this pizza and pasta joint bats well above average. The Notting Hill branch is a buzzy affair with exposed brickwork and bright wall canvases, populated by families and ladies who lunch (Italian signorinas on our last visit – a good sign). Antipasti are fresh and plump, be they satisfying polpettina (mini meatballs) or doughballs served with tomato sauce, basil and parmesan. Pasta is good, but pizza is most popular – authentically Neapolitan and generous in size. Opt for a basic margherita or quattro formaggi, or go posh with one of six specials – an afragolese of buffalo bresaola, mozzarella, rocket and parmesan; or fru fru, an oval-shaped three-season pizza with ricotta, parma ham and salami. Homely mains are no afterthought (think beef braciole stuffed with pecorino, pine nuts and raisins in a thick tomato sauce), while cut-above bulky salads (fresh tuna, grilled beef or chicken caesar) come well dressed. Ingredients, from the san marzano tomatoes to the extra-virgin olive oil, are Italian-imported, as is the nicely chilled Moretti. The venue is genuinely kid-friendly too, without turning into a crèche; bambini get their own menu and there's colouring-in to distract and mini portions of gelato for afters.
Available for hire. Babies and children welcome; children's menu; high chairs; nappy-changing facilities. Booking advisable. Tables outdoors (4, pavement). Takeaway service. Map 19 B3. For branches see index.

Saporitalia
222 Portobello Road, W11 1LJ (7243 3257). Ladbroke Grove tube. **Meals served** noon-11pm Mon-Thur, Sun; noon-11.30pm Fri, Sat. **Main courses** £5.50-£22.95. **Set lunch** (noon-3pm Mon-Thur) £11.50 2 courses. **Credit** AmEx, MC, V.
Saporitalia's dining room is dominated by a handsome clay oven, the sight of which is enough to get taste buds tingling. Sure enough, our pizza was first-rate: an enormous wagon-wheel of a thing

with a wafer-thin base generously topped with san daniele ham. It's wise to opt for the pizza here, as you get more for your money; our other dishes were a bit hit-and-miss. Ravioli was perfectly al dente and had plenty of bite and a pleasantly light sauce, but it could have been mistaken for an appetiser. And a heavy hand had been at the mozzarella in our baked gnocchi, leaving the dish dense and stodgy. Decor is self-consciously rustic, with terracotta tiling and a charmingly cheesy photo mural of an Italian farmhouse on the back wall. As much of the cooking takes place in the dining room, the space can become noisy and stuffy when busy.
Available for hire. Babies and children welcome: children's menu; high chairs. Booking advisable. Separate room for parties, seats 20. Takeaway service. Vegan dishes. Vegetarian menu. Map 19 B2.

Maida Vale

Red Pepper
8 Formosa Street, W9 1EE (7266 2708, http://theredpepper.net). Warwick Avenue tube. **Dinner served** 6.30-11pm Mon-Fri. **Meals served** noon-11pm Sat; noon-10.30pm Sun. **Main courses** £9.50-£25. **Credit** MC, V.
Well loved locally, Red Pepper's ground floor can get crowded (best to book in advance), and while cosy is nice, waitresses brushing past your arm is less so. Thankfully, a big window fills the space with daylight, reflected by large mirrors hung on burgundy walls to brighten the mood. There's extra breathing space in the basement, where you can watch chefs at the wood-burning pizza oven. Pizzas dominate the short menu, which also includes a handful of pasta and risotto dishes. The specials board majors on seafood – mackerel, swordfish and langoustines were all offered on our visit. A new addition to the regular menu is 'Italian tapas': downsized starters, such as bruschette and 'frittatas', the latter being baked bite-sized morsels of spaghetti with pieces of courgette and mozzarella bound together with egg. These may well have been created as an economical way to deal

with leftover pasta, but their crispy texture and simple flavours work. The pizzas are crisp and authentic; the asparagi is a 'white pizza' with rich fior di latte, parmesan, a few pieces of asparagus and fresh chillies that pack a punch. Even spicier is the aptly named diavola, containing piquant Italian salami as well as chillies.
Babies and children admitted. Booking essential. Separate room for parties, seats 25. Tables outdoors (2, pavement). Takeaway service. Map 1 C4.

South West
Chelsea

Goat NEW
333 Fulham Road, SW10 9QL (7352 1384, www.goatchelsea.com). Fulham Broadway tube then bus 211, 414. **Meals served** noon-10.30pm daily. **Main courses** £9-£24. **Credit** AmEx, MC, V.
A 350-year-old pub, the Goat in Boots, has recently been converted into a pizzeria, grill and bar. The Goat's new owners have ditched the boots (too panto) and created myriad levels (six, if you include the mezzanines), which can feel unnervingly like eating in an Escher artwork. But it's a good-looking spot (as are the staff) – all rough-hewn woods and industrial metals in the dining areas, with nouveau-vintage in the bar. The cooking is Italian-via-Manhattan. The signature lobster pizza broke the first commandment of toppings ('thou shalt not use seafood'); the dried-out white meat was adrift on a sea of pancetta and watercress. Other dishes produced better results, however: another pizza, with a heady combination of sliced guanciale (pork cheek), rosemary-spiked burrata cheese and a perfect soft egg; exceptional polenta 'chips' (crisp-edged and served with a truffled mayo); the clean flavours of the tuna tartare. Factor in decent cocktails (rhubarb bellini, say), and this is not a bad spot for wannabe Millie Mackintoshes to spend an evening.
Available for hire. Babies and children welcome: children's menu; high chairs; nappy-changing facilities. Disabled: toilet. Separate room for parties, seats 24. Tables outdoors (9, terrace). Takeaway service. Map 14 D12.

South
Balham

Ciullosteria
31 Balham High Road, SW12 9AL (8675 3072, www.ciullosteria.com). Clapham South tube or Balham tube/rail. **Dinner served** 6-11pm Mon-Thur; 6-11.30pm Fri, Sat. **Meals served** noon-10.30pm Sun. **Main courses** £7-£20. **Credit** AmEx, MC, V.
Plenty of neighbourhood trattorias sell themselves as cheap and cheerful, but few do it as well as Ciullosteria. The surroundings are kitsch without irony – classic terracotta floor tiles oddly offset by an enormous replica of a tomato purée tube, for instance – but that only adds to the charm. The raised section at the back is cosier and more suited to winter, while the airy front (with its small number of alfresco tables) is better in summer. The menu contains an enticing choice of thin-crusted pizzas with regional toppings (torino and genovese

Pizza Metro

Franco Manca

supplementing the usual fiorentina and napoletana), but the pastas and grills are also deservedly popular. There's usually a good-value piece of thinly beaten veal too: on our visit, it came with a tangy, chewy topping of melted mozzarella and tomato. The practice of serving all non-pizza mains with sharing plates of roast potatoes and boiled or battered veg is a little too reminiscent of a school canteen. One tip: don't come here for some hush – if it's someone's birthday, staff love nothing more than to crank up Stevie Wonder's 'Happy Birthday' to full volume (sometimes playing it twice).
Available for hire. Babies and children welcome: children's menu; high chairs. Booking advisable. Tables outdoors (3, terrace). Takeaway service; delivery service (over £15 within 2-mile radius).

Battersea

Donna Margherita
183 Lavender Hill, SW11 5TE (7228 2660, www.donna-margherita.com). Clapham Junction rail. **Dinner served** 5-10.30pm Mon-Thur. **Meals served** noon-11pm Fri, Sat; noon-10.30pm Sun. **Main courses** £7-£18.50. **Credit** AmEx, MC, V.
With its faded awning and ramshackle roadside terrace seating, you might not give this pizzeria a second glance. It's in an unprepossessing location, despite the proximity of Battersea Arts Centre. Then again, you might note that the place is remarkably buzzy; on a sunny day the terrace is often packed. Wander in, order the eponymous pizza, and all will be clear. Gabriele Vitale and his brothers take great Neapolitan pride in the warmth of their native land's cuisine, importing essential ingredients from Naples and crafting wood-fired oven pizzas (and cones, and calzones) to rival any in London, with terrific, chewy but bubbly and charred-edge sourdough crusts. There's also a wide-ranging restaurant menu, with dishes served in

generous measure; we had trouble doing justice to a terracotta potful of 'O'gnocc o furn' with its tomato-doused dumplings coated in a blanket of smoked provola cheese and buffalo mozzarella. Pink-roast pork loin with fat ceps (bottled, but flavourful) was deftly executed. Menabrea beer and simple but sound wine by the glass provided apt accompaniment. Ices and sorbets are the safest dessert options, though excellent oak-aged grappa may prove an irresistible conclusion. Animated Italian families, locals and young professionals clearly appreciate the authentic food, warmth and decor; with your back to the road you might be in a backstreet trattoria in Naples.
Available for hire. Babies and children welcome: high chairs; nappy-changing facilities. Booking advisable. Tables outdoors (8, terrace). Takeaway service; delivery service (over £10 within 1-mile radius). **Map 21 C3.**

Pizza Metro
64 Battersea Rise, SW11 1EQ (7228 3812, www.pizzametropizza.com). Clapham Junction rail. **Dinner served** 6-11pm Mon-Fri. **Meals served** noon-11pm Sat, Sun. **Main courses** £8.50-£16.95. **Credit** MC, V.
Some ten years after opening London's first 'long pizza' parlour, and with the aid of the capital's allegedly oldest wood-fired oven, Pizza Metro's popularity remains undimmed. The Battersea restaurant – now prettily done up with terracotta tiling and ochre-washed walls lined with copper pans, film posters and murals of Naples – is a magnet for local families. Kids poke at the fish tank, sit astride the Lambretta and tuck into that joyous combination of pizza and meatballs all on one plate. Adults enjoy the 'point of difference' aspect of a steel tray bearing a length of variously topped pizza hauled on to the table, with everyone cutting off portions as they eat – at the least it makes mixing and matching easy and sociable. The pizza

bases are sound, if not the best, and the toppings fresh and reliable. Ours ranged from a basic margherita and truffled porcini with rocket to the improbably named CiCCioBoMbA – a bit of almost everything including those meatballs (sizeable, tender, juicy). Other starter and main-course options abound, but the long pizza is the draw. Drinks are basic yet well priced, and the outsize personality and caricature accent of the manager are thrown in for free. It's spoilt a little by the hard sell on desserts – unappealingly paraded under your nose – but the crowds still come.
Babies and children welcome: children's menu; high chairs; nappy-changing facilities. Booking advisable. Separate room for parties, seats 16. Takeaway service. **Map 21 C4.**
For branch see index.

Brixton

★ Franco Manca
4 Market Row, Electric Lane, SW9 8LD (7738 3021, www.francomanca.co.uk). Brixton tube/rail. **Meals served** noon-5pm Mon; noon-10.30pm Tue-Sat; noon-10pm Sun. **Main courses** £5-£7.50. **Credit** AmEx, MC, V.
With its top-notch, UK-sourced (when possible) ingredients, speedy and friendly service, and rapid turnover, the original Brixton branch of Franco Manca remains, for our money, the best pizza joint in London. Both indoor and outdoor seating overlooks the bustling market arcade. Here you can sate a craving for genuine, Neapolitan-style pizza, with a flavourful slow-rise sourdough crust and a variety of traditional and innovative toppings. Purists will prefer either the tomato, garlic and oregano or the tomato, mozzarella and basil, in season. The tasty chorizo pizza comes in two versions (thick-cut and thin-cut, dried) of the rich, oily Spanish sausage; it's reminiscent of New

Time Out Eating & Drinking **305**

York's ubiquitous pepperoni pizza. Other menu choices and daily specials include a variety of seasonal vegetable and cured meat-laden pizzas that, while of top-quality, we find a little busy. Side salads and the restaurant's unusual lemonade (murky brown and slightly like an Arnold Palmer, thanks to a tannic under-taste) are highly recommended, being thoughtful additions to the carb-heavy pizza. Wine and beer are also available. The four other branches – in Balham, Battersea, Chiswick and Westfield Stratford – are fine, but haven't equalled the original branch's perfection.
Babies and children admitted. Bookings not accepted. Disabled: toilet. Tables outdoors (10, market). Takeaway service. Vegan dishes.
Map 22 E2.
For branches see index.

South East
Crystal Palace

Mediterranea
21 Westow Street, SE19 3RY (8771 7327, www.mediterranea.co). Crystal Palace or Gipsy Hill rail. **Lunch served** noon-2.30pm Mon-Fri; noon-3.30pm Sat. **Dinner served** 6-10pm Tue-Thur; 6-11pm Fri, Sat. **Meals served** noon-10pm Sun. **Main courses** £9.90-£18.90. **Credit** AmEx, MC, V.
A splash of bright paint, vibrant sun-drenched pictures and a clutch of Sardinian knicks-knacks don't quite match up to the slick decor of the new wave of Crystal Palace restaurants, but this local eaterie has allure where it counts. The staff are immediately welcoming and enthusiastic about their food – and for good reason. A caponata starter was surprisingly delicate for a predominantly onion-based dish and didn't overpower the creamy buffalo mozzarella it was served alongside. Sardinian fish stew was laden with shellfish and seafood: a hearty feast served in a subtle oregano-flecked tomato broth. Pasta with sausage ragu was again understated, but in the best way – satisfying yet not in the least heavy. Mediterranea is a great venue for families too, with a warm approach to children. Pizzas from the wood-fired oven have a light, crisp crust, and again avoid the flavour explosions that often mask a lack of culinary skill. The restaurant is sometimes not as busy as it should be; we hope it continues to thrive, as this is somewhere to return to time and again.
Babies and children welcome: high chairs. Booking advisable weekends. Separate room for parties, seats 18. Takeaway service. Vegan dishes.

Peckham

Gowlett ★
62 Gowlett Road, SE15 4HY (7635 7048, www.thegowlett.com). East Dulwich or Peckham Rye rail or bus 12, 37, 63. **Open** noon-midnight Mon-Thur; noon-1am Fri, Sat; noon-11.30pm Sun. **Lunch served** 12.30-2.30pm, **dinner served** 6.30-10.30pm Mon-Fri. **Meals served** 12.30-10.30pm Sat; 12.30-9pm Sun. **Main courses** £8-£10. **No credit cards**.
The Gowlett still looks like a proper boozer, albeit an antique wood-panelled, minimalist boozer – which is something of an achievement round here. The clue to its popularity is in the dough-scented air as you approach. This place sells the best pizza

for miles around. The floury bases, pleasingly thin, taste sensational; a special mention must go to the nutty organic spelt version, for gluten-free people and those who just love spelt – try it for £1.50 more and a five-minute extra wait. The delicacy of the base has many advantages: the toppings aren't dominated by stodge, and you can justify piling on the extras for 50p a pop, since eating a whole pizza won't leave you stuffed. We couldn't resist the Gowlettini; few can, since it's such a happy pile-up of goat's cheese, prosciutto, pine nuts and rocket (for vegetarians, sunblush tomatoes replace the prosciutto). Our napoletana included tangy sun-dried tomatoes, and the egg on the fiorentina was fresh and firm. 'Smoked in Peckham' is the Gowlett's in-house meat-curing business, based in the cellar, so a platter of smoked meats and cheeses – made with free-range pork from local butcher William Rose and venison from a farm in Eridge, Kent – is a fine option for pizza refuseniks.
Babies and children welcome until 9pm: high chairs; nappy-changing facilities. Bookings not accepted for fewer than 10 people. Disabled: toilet. Tables outdoors (3, garden; 4, pavement). Takeaway service. Vegan dishes. **Map 23 C3.**

East
Bethnal Green

StringRay Globe Café, Bar & Pizzeria
109 Columbia Road, E2 7RL (7613 1141, www.stringraycafe.co.uk). Hoxton rail or bus 26, 48, 55. **Meals served** 11am-11.15pm daily. **Main courses** £6.95-£11.95. **Credit** AmEx, MC, V.
A feature of the northern end of Columbia Road for more than a decade, this corner joint still pulls in the crowds through its cheerful atmosphere and generous, low-cost grub. The pine tables, scuffed wooden floors and primary coloured walls give the place the feel of an arty backpackers' café circa 1990, while displays of local art reference the creativity of the surrounding area. The food isn't

Pizza East Shoreditch

especially sophisticated, nor is it always Italian (feta and halloumi feature in several of the salads and pasta dishes), but if you're looking for cheap and filling, you won't go far wrong. Pizzas are the highlight, mainly due to their huge size. Though nothing to write home to mamma about – we found the bases quite bland – they're tasty enough and varied, ranging from the classic (fiorentina, quattro formaggi) to the cross-cultural (the mexicana, with jalapeño chillies and minced beef). Daily meat, fish and vegetarian specials are also available, and desserts are calorific (tiramisu, banoffi pie) but tasty. StringRay is normally heaving on Sunday lunchtimes; arrive early to grab a prime spot on the front terrace, from where you can watch plant-laden passers-by leaving the flower market.
Babies and children welcome: children's menu; high chairs. Booking advisable. Disabled: toilet. Tables outdoors (7, pavement). Takeaway service. **Map 6 S3.**
For branches see index.

Shoreditch

Pizza East Shoreditch
56 Shoreditch High Street, E1 6JJ (7729 1888, www.pizzaeast.com). Shoreditch High Street rail. **Meals served** noon-11pm Mon-Wed; noon-midnight Thur; noon-1am Fri; 10am-1am Sat; 10am-11pm Sun. **Main courses** £8-£17. **Credit** AmEx, MC, V.
The popularity of Pizza East, one of the first bastions of Shoreditch gentrification, hasn't waned. This Soho House operation still packs out the landmark Tea Building, with hipsters and City boys arriving to eat well past 9pm during the week. The huge warehouse space features sharing benches, industrial decor and more bare brick and concrete than your average multistorey car park. It's busy, noisy and dark: a formula some people justifiably love to hate. The regularly changing menu, however, remains inventive and original. Pea and pecorino croquettes were commendably light and fresh, while calamares with caper aïoli proved a cut above the norm. Pizzas cost from a reasonable £8 to £14, with toppings frequently rejigged. Courgette, olives, robiola cheese and thyme was

excellent, but a promising combination of pork belly and mushroom fell short of expectations; greasy chunks of crackling proved the wrong match for the floury crust and tomato base. The only other gripe is that staff insist on serving rather nice wine in chunky tumblers. Still, booze is for glugging not savouring here. Service veers from affable to slightly snooty, but you can't fault nice touches like American-style takeaway boxes for your leftovers.

Available for hire. Babies and children welcome: children's menu; crayons; high chairs; nappy-changing facilities. Booking advisable. Disabled: toilet. Separate room for parties, seats 18. Takeaway service. Vegan dishes. **Map 6 R4.** **For branches see index.**

Story Deli

123 Bethnal Green Road, E2 7DG (07918 197352, www.storydeli.com). Shoreditch High Street rail or 8, 388 bus. **Meals served** noon-10pm daily. **Main courses** £17. **Credit** MC, V.

The pizzas served in this minimally decorated, white-painted room aren't strictly pizzas. If what you like about pizzas is the dough, then these wafer-thin bases won't appeal. They're nice enough (pleasantly soggy in the middle, matzo-like at the edges), but mainly they're there to hold the super-fresh toppings. These are interesting without being outlandish. Fico (goat's cheese, figs, parma ham, red onion, capers and salad greens) looked good enough for a photo shoot – served on a board, and a mass of glossy colours – and had flavour to match. Dora romero (chorizo, mozzarella, 'smashed' tomato, tomato passata, red onion, mascarpone, rosemary oil and basil pesto) had less visual impact, and little chorizo bite; not surprising, as we found only two slices – we resorted to chilli oil. You're not meant to linger – pizzas aside, the menu is limited; a small piece of mixed berry baked cheesecake was

the only pudding available, and you'll be lucky if there's a choice of wines. Seating is on uncomfortable, own-made stools at long tables made for sharing. The bill will be surprisingly high (pizzas cost £17 and you'll need at least one each) and you'll have to pay in cash. An interesting one-off that could probably only survive in the trendier bits of east London.

Babies and children welcome: high chairs; toys. Bookings not accepted. Takeaway service. **Map 6 S4.**

Spitalfields

Pizza Union **NEW**

25 Sandy's Row, E1 7HW (no phone, www.pizzaunion.com). Liverpool Street tube/rail. **Meals served** 11am-11pm daily. **Main courses** £3.50-£5.95. **No credit cards**.

Billing itself as a '*superveloce Italiana*', Pizza Union certainly serves pizza pronto. This industrial-looking canteen is busiest at lunchtime, luring City workers and business students from the adjacent UEA London with the promise of super-fast pizzas. A vibrating, flashing buzzer summoned us to the counter less than four minutes after ordering. The menu lists all the classics alongside a couple of more recent immigrants such as the bianca (tomato-free and with great rosemary and garlic pungency). Pizza bases, baked in the large igloo-like oven, are uniformly thin, light and with a crisp crust. The creamy mascarpone on a toscana made a great foil to spicy 'nduja sausage and fresh peppery rocket. The still-runny egg yolk of our capricciosa was seasoned nicely by its accompanying salty capers and olives, although a twist of black pepper might have improved it further. Desserts are limited to serve-yourself ice-cream tubs (supplied by Gelupo) and folded pizza alla cioccolata, stuffed with nutella and mascarpone. With its exposed breeze-block walls, concrete floors, chipboard cladding and long

wooden plank tables, Pizza Union isn't ideal for intimate dates – but for less romantic encounters, the speedy, flavoursome and very reasonably priced pizzas are a must. **Map 12 R5.**

Wapping

Il Bordello

81 Wapping High Street, E1W 2YN (7481 9950, www.ilbordello.com). Wapping rail. **Lunch served** noon-3pm Mon-Fri. **Dinner served** 6-11pm Mon-Sat. **Meals served** 1-10.30pm Sun. **Main courses** £8.95-£29.95. **Credit** AmEx, MC, V.

Attracting Wapping residents as well as tourists over the years, Il Bordello often sees queues out of the door during the week. Despite its position at the bottom of one of Wapping's modernised brick wharfs, you could be taking a step back into the 1990s here – complete with tables covered in plastic cloths, and napkins carefully curled into wine glasses. The food, complemented by an all-Italian wine list, is similarly straightforward. A starter of parma ham and melon was simple and delicious, the portion more than ample for the price, though the bread used for a bruschetta was a touch too dry. Gigantic pizzas topped with time-tested combinations are a strength; we enjoyed a mix of bresaola, rocket and parmigiana. Another highlight was a perfectly cooked veal chop slathered in a rich sage butter sauce and accompanied by roast potatoes. This traditional style might not appeal to all modern sensibilities, but it's hard not to be won over by the convivial atmosphere and jovial team of waistcoated Italian gents. Il Bordello delivers what so many other restaurants lack: a touch of old-fashioned Italian charm.

Babies and children welcome: high chairs. Booking advisable. Disabled: toilet. Takeaway service.

Story Deli

North East
Hackney Wick

Crate Brewery

White Building, Queens Yard, E9 5EN (07834 275687, www.cratebrewery.com). Hackney Wick rail. **Meals served** noon-10pm daily. **Main courses** £8-£12. **Credit** MC, V.

This is one of the few success stories of the great Hackney Wick Olympic café boom. While many of the area's newer cafés and restaurants have floundered or closed since summer 2012, Crate is more popular than ever – especially among the Wick's young creative types. This hip canalside pizzeria-cum-microbrewery is run by the people behind the Counter Café. High-vaulted ceilings are accompanied by bare light bulbs, benches made from recycled coffee sacks and a bar pulled together using railway sleepers. Combined with the visible brewing room, this gives an airy, ex-industrial feel to the place. The open kitchen churns out some pretty great pizzas. Moroccan lamb and pine nuts was salty and flavoursome, as was the chilli-flecked pepperoni. But the white pizzas are probably best avoided: sage, potato and truffle somehow managed to taste of very little. Crate's own brews – a pale ale, a bitter and a strong stout were available on our visit – may not be the best in town, though its selection of world beers (including London's Kernel, Flying Dog from the USA, a variety of antipodean ales and some powerful Trappist choices) is hard to beat. Service could be speedier, but Crate has become an island of good vibes and food in a still-quiet area.

Available for hire. Babies and children welcome: nappy-changing facilities. Bookings not accepted for fewer than 10 people. Disabled: toilet. Tables outdoors (6, canal). Takeaway service.

Stoke Newington
Il Bacio

61 Stoke Newington Church Street, N16 0AR (7249 3833, www.ilbacio.co.uk). Stoke Newington rail or bus 73, 393, 476. **Dinner served** 6-11.15pm Mon-Fri. **Meals served** noon-11.15pm Sat, Sun. **Main courses** £9-£16. **Credit** MC, V.

An attractive spot on Stoke Newington Church Street gives Il Bacio an instant advantage, and very reasonable pricing also helps secure it as a firm local favourite. The menu has a Sardinian bias, with plenty of seafood and regional specialities among the usual trattoria classics. Sardinian flatbread adorns the bread basket, and the distinctive Sardinian semolina and saffron alternative to potato-flour gnocchi also crops up. Calamari piccante came with a sauce not so piccante as to overshadow the squid, and the dough for our campagnola pizza was robust and well seasoned; the topping (olives, rosemary and Sardinian salami) was perhaps a little miserly, but tasty all the same. Another attraction is the house wine: very drinkable and a steal at £15 for a litre. However, wine tumblers are no more than terracotta thimbles, so it's easy to lose track of the tally and end up a little merrier than anticipated.

Babies and children welcome: children's menu; high chairs. Booking advisable. Separate room for parties, seats 40. Tables outdoors (2, pavement). Takeaway service; delivery service (over £10 within 2-mile radius). **Map 25 B1**. **For branches see index.**

North West
Hampstead

Mimmo La Bufala

45A South End Road, NW3 2QB (7435 7814, www.mimmolabufala.co.uk). Belsize Park tube or Hampstead Heath rail. **Lunch served** noon-3pm Fri. **Dinner served** 5.30-11pm Mon-Fri. **Meals served** noon-11pm Sat, Sun. **Main courses** £8-£29. **Set lunch** (Fri) £9.50 2 courses. **No credit cards**.

It's just as well portions are large here, as we enjoyed every last flavoursome bite of our meal. Mimmo La Bufala specialises in southern Italian food, with a bias towards mozzarella (of course) and fish. Daily specials might include classics such as osso buco. A starter of sautéed king prawns was deliciously fresh and juicy. Orecchiette with fresh spinach, creamy ricotta and tangy sun-dried tomatoes was a perfect mix of complementary flavours. The long pizza list includes all the classics, as well as seasonal variations such as tomato-free 'biancis'. We opted for 'Mimmo's pizza', named after the ebullient proprietor. In true southern Italian style, its thin base was topped with juicy tomatoes, smoky provolone and melt-in-your-mouth buffalo mozzarella before being baked in a wood-fired oven. This oven links the restaurant's two dining areas: a small but airy front room in white with shopfront-style windows, mirrors and chandeliers; and a larger, cosier space at the back with less natural light and a grand piano for occasional entertainment. Our main gripe is the lack of wines by the glass (only house red or white), but it's the food that is the draw.

Babies and children welcome: high chairs. Booking advisable dinner. Separate room for parties, seats 50. Tables outdoors (4, pavement). Takeaway service. **Map 28 C3**.

Crate Brewery

Drinking

Bars

London's cocktail bar scene has never been better. And the good places aren't confined to the West End, but spread across the city. It's proof of their success that so many bars are regularly packed out – which leads to a general rule: if you want to be sure of getting a table, book in advance wherever you can.

If there's one slightly worrying aspect to the cocktail bar boom, it's the widespread belief that a good bar needs a 'theme'. Not true. A good bar needs good atmosphere, good service and good drinks. This is why venues as disparate as **Milk & Honey** and **Dukes** have survived for years more-or-less theme-free, and relatively recent newcomers such as **Oskar's Bar** and **Happiness Forgets** have also eschewed such gimmicks. Another concern is the increasing complexity of drinks. We applaud experimentation and innovation, but the dazzling strangeness of some drinks can be off-putting. When you ask for a martini or a manhattan, you know what to expect. When you see a cocktail whose ingredients include akvavit, overproof rum, banana liqueur, cigar syrup, condensed milk and a top of toasted porter, you're in terra incognita. Not all customers feel comfortable being there – though, of course, they can just ask for something classic.

Such reservations aside, London has a great bar scene right now, with plenty of potential for growth as ambitious bartenders, trained by the best, move on to open their own places. The future is bright.

Central
Chinatown

Experimental Cocktail Club
13A Gerrard Street, W1D 5PS (7434 3559, www.chinatownecc.com). Leicester Square tube. **Open** 6pm-3am Mon-Sat; 6pm-midnight Sun. **Admission** £5 after 11pm. **Credit** MC, V.
As bar after bar opens using the rather tired 'Brooklyn Prohibition' template, Experimental Cocktail Club seems ever more original – it's hard to find, sure, perhaps more so than any other 'speakeasy' in London, but inside remains opulent and elegantly aloof to trends. It's arranged over three floors of an old Chinatown townhouse, flatteringly lit and expensively decorated. Booking isn't essential (half of the capacity is kept back for walk-ins), but it is recommended and worth the hassle (email booking only, between noon and 5pm). Cocktails are among the best in town, accessibly priced and not too show-offy in terms of ingredient and preparation – 'experimental' isn't perhaps accurate. However, they're all sophisticated, complex, strong and persuasive; see, for example, the Havana (cigar-infused bourbon, marsala wine, Bruichladdich Octomore single malt 'wash').

Immaculately attired bar staff are clearly knowledgeable about their subject, although floor staff could be friendlier and, when it gets busy, a bit sharper. A range of vintage spirits (1950s gin martini, £150) indulges those with money to flaunt, but in the main, and despite its initially daunting demeanour, ECC is just a great place for an evening of rarely surpassed cocktails. **Map 17 C4**.

Clerkenwell & Farringdon

★ Zetter Townhouse
49-50 St John's Square, EC1V 4JJ (7324 4545, www.thezettertownhouse.com). Farringdon tube/rail. **Open** 7am-midnight Mon-Wed, Sun; 7am-1am Thur-Sat. **Credit** AmEx, MC, V.
The decor at Townhouse embodies a 'more is more' philosophy. Every square inch of surface area is occupied by something lovely, as if a couple of eccentric collectors moved from a country manse and felt compelled to fit all their possessions into two rooms. The result: one of the most beautiful bars in London, and certainly the most unusual-looking. We'd come here for that alone, but the cocktail list is of fittingly high quality – not surprising, since it was devised by Tony Conigliaro (of 69 Colebrooke Row). Even though Conigliaro is

known as a techno-wizard, the original drinks here are fairly simple and restrained. And wonderful. Among the house cocktails, check out the Köln martini, the Somerset sour, and the jasmine tea gimlet. Service is friendly and helpful. For four to six people, the table to the right of the front door (two comfortable, mismatched sofas) is heaven. *Babies and children admitted until 9pm. Booking advisable. Disabled: lift; toilet.* **Map 5 O4**.

Fitzrovia

Oskar's Bar
Dabbous, 39 Whitfield Street, W1T 2SF (7323 1544, www.dabbous.co.uk). Goodge Street tube. **Open** 5.30-11.30pm Tue-Sat. **Credit** AmEx, MC, V.
Dabbous the restaurant is startlingly inventive in its use of ingredients such as herbs and flowers, so it should come as no surprise that the cocktail bar in its basement is similarly inventive. They make a lot of their own cordials and age spirits in small barrels, sometimes with wonderful effect: try the own-made lime cordial in a fantastic gimlet or the barrel-aged negroni. The classics are handled with skill and assurance. We also like the room itself, with its ventilation ducts and distressed-industrial decor. It can get a little loud when very busy, but

management doesn't pour on the pain by pumping up the volume. If we have a complaint, it's that some drinks look forbiddingly complex, and some of the descriptions are not always helpful – it doesn't add much to say that a drink is a 'musky masterpiece'. But that's a minor point. We like Oskar's a lot.

Available for hire. Booking advisable. Dress: smart casual. **Map 17 B1**

King's Cross

Booking Office

St Pancras Renaissance London Hotel, NW1 2AR (7841 3540, www.bookingoffice restaurant.com). King's Cross St Pancras tube/rail. **Open** 6.30am-1am Mon-Wed, Sun; 6.30am-3am Thur-Sat. **Credit** AmEx, DC, MC, V.
There's an anguished moment when you walk in and have to decide whether to sit in or out. Inside: Sir George Gilbert Scott's lofty interior, a stirring example of the Victorian architect's interpretation of Gothic revival. Outside, under spacious canopies, you have a nearly ceiling-level view of St Pancras International station. The good news is that all anguish will cease as soon as you've taken your seat. Apart from having to wait a couple of minutes too long to get our order taken (sitting outside), we had a blissful visit. The cocktail list, drawn up by Nick Strangeway and the late Henry Besant, gives a prominent place to traditional punches, served in mugs. But the list is a long one. A martini was made well, and the gin fix (a variant on gin fizz using fresh berries) was a wonderful and refreshing potion. Warning: the free bar snacks – coated peanuts – are dangerously addictive.

Available for hire. Babies and children admitted. Disabled: toilet. Tables outdoors (27, terrace). **Map 4 L3.**

VOC

2 Varnishers Yard, Regents Quarter, N1 9AW (7713 8229, www.voc-london.co.uk). King's Cross St Pancras tube/rail. **Open** 5pm-midnight Mon-Thur; 5pm-12.30am Fri, Sat. **Credit** AmEx, MC, V.
From Fluid Movement, which brought us Purl and the Worship Street Whistling Shop, VOC occupies a smallish, cosy space in one of north London's most restaurant-intensive precincts. The name derives from the Dutch East India Company, and there's a nautical and historical theme to the drinks list. Punches based on old recipes figure large, though modern technology brings them right up to date. Playing it safe with the classics is by no means the inferior option, however, as textbook martinis and caipirinhas proved. It took us a while to get our drinks because of lack of staff behind the tiny bar (barely five feet long), and there's no table service, so you have to queue. But no one seemed to mind. Interestingly, more people were drinking beer or wine than cocktails, at least on our visit.

Available for hire. Booking advisable. Disabled: toilet. Tables outdoors (2, pavement; 4, terrace). **Map 4 L3.**

Knightsbridge

Mandarin Bar

Mandarin Oriental Hyde Park, 66 Knightsbridge, SW1X 7LA (7235 2000, www.mandarinoriental. com/london). Knightsbridge tube. **Open** 10.30am-1.30am Mon-Sat; 10.30am-12.30pm Sun. **Credit** AmEx, MC, V.
The Mandarin Oriental in Knightsbridge is more famous as the location of Heston Blumenthal's Dinner, and when we were here, there were at least four other parties who'd settled in for a drink while praying for a walk-in at the restaurant. If you're

going to choose a waiting room, you can't do much better than this. The room is dazzling, with a central bar and an array of of glass, wood and marble. It's deliberately sleek, modern, high-fashion hotel luxury, and if that look appeals, then the Mandarin will too. The drinks side of things is done expertly. Their own cocktails are devised with good sense, and classics are well handled – and with serving sizes to match the high prices. Polished service, good bar snacks. If you're weighed down by bags of treasure from nearby Harvey Nicks, this is a good place to rest your feet and indulge in some deep relaxation therapy.

Disabled: toilet (hotel). Dress: smart casual. **Map 8 F9.**

Marylebone

Artesian

Langham Hotel, 1C Portland Place, W1B 1JA (7636 1000, www.artesian-bar.co.uk). Oxford Circus tube. **Open** noon-2am Mon-Sat; noon-midnight Sun. **Credit** AmEx, DC, MC, V.
The Artesian is very nearly a very great bar. Its elegant space on the ground floor of the Langham Hilton is lovely. Tables are well spaced. Service is friendly and ultra-efficient even when – as so often happens – it's packed out. A free plate of tasty canapés may arrive unbidden. Their own cocktails are well conceived, and the classics are flawlessly rendered and generously poured. These bright spots are darkened by two failings, one minor and one major. Minor: good crisps and mixed nuts were not fresh enough – both were slightly flabby. Major: piping in incredibly loud Euro-pop, which is completely at odds with the room – and with the pricing of the drinks, which are among the most expensive in London. This may be an effort to reach out to a younger clientele, but to us it doesn't make

Zetter Townhouse

sense. We'd rather see this classy place achieve its full potential. It would be easy for Artesian to do it. *Available for hire. Babies and children admitted until 6pm. Disabled: toilet (hotel).* **Map 9 H5**.

Purl

50 Blandford Street, W1U 7HX (7935 0835, www.purl-london.com). Bond Street tube. **Open** 5-11.30pm Mon-Thur; 5pm-midnight Fri, Sat. **Credit** AmEx, MC, V.

We've long been fans of Purl, one of London's first speakeasy-type bars and begetter of both VOC and the Worship Street Whistling Shop. It's become extremely popular, which means that booking is advisable – though walk-ins will be seated if there's space. The layout of the bar, over a number of smallish spaces in a vaulted basement, gives the opportunity for genuine seclusion, if that's what you're looking for. And if you're interested in cutting-edge cocktail making, you're also in luck. Novel methods and unusual ingredients are used in many of their unique drinks, but they're also unfailingly sound in the classics. We experienced slow service because they were understaffed that evening, but usually service is very efficient and always very friendly. The selection of spirits is both extensive, and outstanding. And the music is chosen by someone who has very good taste in jazz. *Available for hire. Booking advisable.* **Map 9 G5**.

Mayfair

★ Coburg Bar

The Connaught, Carlos Place, W1K 2AL (7499 7070, www.the-connaught.co.uk). Bond Street or Green Park tube. **Open** 8am-11pm Mon, Sun; 8am-1am Tue-Sat. **Credit** AmEx, MC, V.

The Connaught has always had the most country house-like feeling of London's great hotels, and the effect reaches perfection in the Coburg. It seems effortlessly beautiful, from the deep patterned carpet to the moulded ceiling; the wing chairs, a long-time fixture, can induce torpor even if you're drinking a double espresso. As you would expect, luxuries abound on the drinks list and prices are high – though for cocktails, not as high as at the Artesian. Great champagnes and cognacs feature prominently. The cocktail list focuses on classics, which it introduces with a brief history. Execution is flawless: two manhattans, one a 'perfect' version and one sweet, were the best we've ever had in London. Bowls of crisps and olives, both outstanding in quality, are replaced when empty. One quibble: the mediocre cocktail-lounge music, unduly prominent on a quiet Monday night, didn't suit the character of the bar. Apart from that, we have nothing but praise. *Available for hire. Disabled: toilet.* **Map 9 H7**.

Piccadilly

Bar Américain

Brasserie Zédel, 20 Sherwood Street, W1F 7ED (7734 4888, www.brasseriezedel.com). Piccadilly Circus tube. **Open** 4.30pm-midnight Mon-Wed; 4.30pm-1am Thur-Sat; 4.30pm-11pm Sun. **Credit** AmEx, MC, V.

This wonderful bar occupies the hallowed ground that began life as Dick's Bar, when Brasserie Zédel was the Atlantic Bar & Grill and the great Dick Bradsell was the man behind the bar. Zédel has installed a great crew, both behind the bar and front of house. And they've kept the beautiful art deco decor and the widely spaced tables, which are a major factor in keeping noise levels down even when the place is full. We love the brevity and simplicity of the cocktail list: just 18 drinks and most of them tried and tested classics. Martinis, manhattans and daiquiris are all expertly rendered, and you can get the true Vesper, James Bond's own-recipe martini made with gin, vodka and Lillet Blanc. For a quiet drink in the West End without paying ultra-high prices, you can't do much better than the Américain. *Available for hire. Disabled: lift; toilet.* **Map 17 B5**.

St James's

★ Dukes Bar

35 St James's Place, SW1A 1NY (7491 4840, www.dukeshotel.co.uk). Green Park tube. **Open** 2-11pm Mon-Sat; 4-10.30pm Sun. **Credit** AmEx, MC, V.

If you want to go out for a single cocktail, strong and expensive and very well made, go to Dukes. You might assume that it's exclusive because it's in a luxury hotel, but you'd be wrong. At some bars you will be viewed as too old or too young, or too smart or too scruffy. Not at Dukes. Everyone – repeat, everyone – gets the warmest of welcomes. There are three small rooms, all decorated in discreetly opulent style; you don't feel comfortable in these plush surroundings, you feel cocooned. The bar is justly famous for the theatre of its martini making – at the table, from a trolley, using vermouth made exclusively for them at the Sacred distillery in Highgate – but other drinks are just as good. Their Martinez (gin, sweet red vermouth, orange bitters and maraschino), is the finest cocktail we've had this year. Nibbles, including the best nuts in town, are replaced when finished. No string of superlatives does justice to Dukes.

Booking Office. See p311.

Bookings not accepted. Dress: smart casual; no sportswear. Tables outdoors (3, garden; 4, courtyard). **Map 9 J8**.

Soho

LAB

12 Old Compton Street, W1D 4TQ (7437 7820, www.labbaruk.com). Leicester Square tube. **Open** 4pm-midnight Mon-Sat; 4-10.30pm Sun. **Credit** MC, V.
LAB was created in 1999, which makes it a granddaddy in London's cool bar scene. But it shows no signs of decline: the quality is consistent visit after visit. They've always had a very long cocktail list, 90-plus, and some drinks get a bit clever for their own good. But mostly they are grounded in LAB's core principle: understanding and perfecting cocktail fundamentals. The Soho Lady, one of their own creations, is a tall sour based on gin, with Aperol and fresh raspberries, served over crushed ice with a top of fizzy wine. Classic. Standard drinks are always perfect, and the bartenders love talking to customers who need help figuring out what to order. Noise levels are high, but no higher than in comparable places. You can book tables downstairs, and it's sensible to do so. Prices remain very low for the quality and the area. Great drinks, low prices, unfailing consistency – what more can you ask for?
Dress: no ties. Entertainment: DJs 8pm Thur-Sat. **Map 17 C3**.

Mark's Bar

Hix, 66-70 Brewer Street, W1F 9UP (7292 3518, www.marksbar.co.uk). Piccadilly Circus tube. **Open** 11am-1am Mon-Sat; 11.30am-midnight Sun. **Credit** AmEx, DC, MC, V.
The basement at Hix Soho is consistently busy in the evening. And we understand why: this is a first-rate bar in nearly every respect. The historical drinks are both interesting and good, especially those in the Cocktail Explorer's Club list. Rum drinkers should make a beeline for the Royal Bermuda Yacht Club: Mount Gay Barbados rum with orange curaçao, Mark's own falernum and lime juice. The selection of scotch would take several months to drink through. The bar 'snax' are terrific, and you can also order from the carte if you want something substantial. And the place looks great, with its big smoked mirrors. Our only complaint is the lighting, subdued in some places and too bright in others. Also worth remembering: there are more spaces for larger groups than for just a couple. Not a complaint, just an observation. The quibbles don't detract greatly from the classiness of Mark's.
Available for hire. Babies and children admitted until 5pm. Bookings not accepted. Disabled: toilet. **Map 17 A4**.

Milk & Honey

61 Poland Street, W1F 7NU (7065 6840 ext 6, www.mlkhny.com). Oxford Circus tube. **Open** *Non-members* 6-11pm Mon-Sat (2hrs max, last admission 9pm). *Members* 6pm-3am Mon-Sat. **Credit** AmEx, DC, MC, V.
Urban myth has it that this has long been one of the best bars for cocktails in London. It might well be, but it's hard to tell unless you have the night vision of an owl – the lighting is so low you'll need to borrow a candle to read the drinks list, let alone see your drink, and you may not even recognise your companions across the table. And then there's the difficulty of getting in. It's a members' club

Mandarin Bar. See p311.

much of the time, although the rest of us can book a table in the early evening for two hours maximum – as long as you book at least a day in advance, arrive before 9pm, and make the booking during their 'office hours' (10am-6pm Mon-Sat). If you're prepared to put up with all this ballyhoo, it's a great place for perfectly executed classic cocktails. We were impressed with our negroni, not least by the bartender asking about our preferences of gin and vermouth combinations. Be warned that the electricity saved on the lighting seems to be diverted to the fierce air-conditioning; jackets, or at least warm clothing, are a good idea.
Booking essential for non-members. **Map 17 A3**.

West
Notting Hill

Lonsdale

48 Lonsdale Road, W11 2DE (7727 4080, www.thelonsdale.co.uk). Ladbroke Grove or Notting Hill Gate tube. **Open** 6pm-midnight Tue-Thur; 6pm-1am Fri, Sat. **Credit** AmEx, MC, V.
There are so many good things to say about the Lonsdale, which recently celebrated its tenth birthday, it's hard to know where to begin. But since we have to start somewhere, let's discuss the scholarliness of the cocktail list. Nearly every drink is given a time and place of creation and, in most cases, the bartender responsible is named. Dates range from the late 1800s to the present, and the names include many of the greats in cocktail bartending. This makes for informative, sometimes amusing reading, and anything you order will be first rate. Classics, such as the martini and old fashioned we enjoyed, are always very proper. We

like to sit at the incredibly long and atmospherically lit bar, and watch the bartenders work. Prices aren't high for this quality or this part of town, and if you're hungry, the restaurant specialises in top-quality meat. Ten years old, and still a star.
Babies and children admitted until 9pm. Disabled: toilet. Entertainment: DJs 9pm Thur-Sat. Tables outdoors (5, terrace). **Map 19 C3**.

South
Battersea

Lost Society

697 Wandsworth Road, SW8 3JF (7652 6526, www.lostsociety.co.uk). Wandsworth Road rail or bus 77. **Open** 5pm-1am Thur, Fri; 2pm-1am Sat; 2-11pm Sun. **Credit** AmEx, MC, V.
Lost Society has occupied this warren of rooms since the 1980s, which makes it a veteran of south London's bar scene. And its appeal continues, partly, no doubt, because of the variety of its offerings. From Monday to Thursday, it's a bar, plus a small restaurant with a short, straightforward menu. At the weekend, music takes over: live acts on Friday, DJs on Saturday. And on Sunday there's a 'tea party', with cocktails, food and activities to while away the afternoon hours. It's a nice formula, and there's a lot we like about it. We also like the sensible and reasonably priced cocktail list, which has few airs and graces; a martini was well made, if slightly too dilute. If you're looking to go on the lash, weekends are when you'll find like-minded people. If it's a quiet drink you seek, other nights are best: at 8pm one Saturday, the noise of the music was already pretty punishing, even in a room where we were the only people drinking.

Purl. See p312.

Available for hire Mon-Thur. Entertainment: DJs 9pm Fri, Sat; live music 8pm Fri. Tables outdoors (4, front garden; 5, back garden).
For branch (Lost Angel) see index.

Powder Keg Diplomacy
147 St John's Hill, SW11 1TQ (7450 6457, www.powderkegdiplomacy.co.uk). Clapham Junction rail. **Open** 4pm-midnight Mon-Fri; 10am-midnight Sat, Sun. **Credit** AmEx, MC, V.
In certain respects, PKD comes within a hair's breadth of looking like a theme bar. It describes itself as a combination of 'colonial Britain, Victoriana and hints of the industrial', and the description is apt. What pulls it back is the evident conviction behind everything they do. It shows in the collection of delightfully mismatched antique cocktail glasses, in the care with which the drinks are chosen, and in the skill with which cocktails are made. A martini using London's own Portobello gin was studiously but not excessively stirred, and served in one of those antique glasses, with the remainder drained into a tiny jug kept on ice for a well-chilled top-up. Check out the changing line-up of guest cask beers and the large selection of bottled brews. Food is served in the rear conservatory. No bookings are taken in the bar, which is busiest later in the evening. For a cocktail before dinner, you can't to better in Battersea.
Bookings not accepted. Tables outdoors (3, pavement). **Map 21 B4.**

Clapham

Rookery
69 Clapham Common Southside, SW4 9DA (8673 9162, www.therookeryclapham.co.uk). Clapham Common or Clapham South tube. **Open** 5.30-11pm Mon-Thur; 12.30pm-midnight Fri, Sat; 12.30-11pm Sun. **Credit** MC, V.

This nice little local reminds us of a certain type of friendly neighbourhood Manhattan bar, which is, sadly, becoming rare in Manhattan. Brick walls, casual decor, mixed clientele and a varied offering of food and drink at extremely fair prices. It's a place where people go to enjoy themselves, not to strike poses. There's a short cocktail list – all classics – and while our martini was not flawlessly made (too much vermouth and too warm), its exceedingly low price made up for all faults. A wide-ranging list of international bottled beers is a major plus. Service is charming and efficient, and the whole place has a happy vibe. There are tables

for serious eating, and an appropriately serious menu to go with them. The music, though chosen with very good taste, can get in the way of conversation when the place is full. But that's pretty much standard nowadays – most people would be delighted to have a local like this.
Booking advisable. Separate room for parties, seats 30. Tables outdoors (8, terrace). **Map 22 A3.**

East
Shoreditch

Book Club
100 Leonard Street, EC2A 4RH (7684 8618, www.wearetbc.com). Old Street tube/rail or Shoreditch High Street rail. **Open** 8am-midnight Mon-Wed; 8am-2am Thur, Fri; 10am-2am Sat; noon-midnight Sun. **Admission** free-£10. **Credit** MC, V.
It doesn't sound like a place for an exciting night out, but behind the sedate name is one of the most consistently creative bars in London. You could visit for the drinks alone: cocktails are served in glasses or jugs to share, and come with names like Don't Go To Dalston, or the Lorraine Kelly (made with tangy grapefruit and rum) – the emphasis is on fun and easy drinkability rather than serious mixology. (A better beer selection would be welcome, however.) You could visit for the food: breakfast starts at 8am, when the laptop tappers who work in the area use it for off-the-cuff morning meetings; lunch and dinner are simple but filling and homely, with a small menu including the likes of bar snacks, nachos and sharing platters. Or – and this is what sets Book Club apart – you could visit for the packed timetable of events, which includes bands, DJs, ping-pong tournaments, informative talks, life drawing and classic video-game nights. The young and laid-back crowd that packs into the spacious artwork-dotted space and its atmospheric basement are here for a bit of everything.
Babies and children admitted until 8pm. Entertainment: bands/DJs 7pm Thur-Sat. **Map 6 R4.**

Coburg Bar. See p312.

Callooh Callay

65 Rivington Street, EC2A 3AY (7739 4781, www.calloohcallaybar.com). Old Street tube/rail or Shoreditch High Street rail. **Open** 6pm-midnight Mon-Wed, Sun; 6pm-1am Thur-Sat. **Credit** AmEx, DC, MC, V.

This area of town isn't as hip as it used to be, but Callooh Callay is still as much a destination in its own right as it is a hidey-hole to avoid the drink offer-seeking masses. Since opening in 2008, it's consistently served some of the most innovative cocktails in London, even if the decor has been left behind: the Lewis Carroll/Victoriana theme is partially enforced, but too much noughties Shoreditch irony (a wall of analogue cassettes, for instance) feels somewhat incongruous. The front bar is bustling most nights, so if you want peace and privacy, book a space 'through the wardrobe' in the hidden lounge, which is given a tropicalia aesthetic with metal palm trees and mirrored walls. Look past the often painfully punning names ('Storm in a Thai Cup', 'Swizzle Dee, Swizzle Dum') and you'll find the cocktails are uniformly excellent. Many employ unusual home-made bitters, cordials and infusions; all have a 'Drink Me' quality that makes choosing from the menu tricky. Thoughtful bar snacks, such as deep-fried squid with curry leaves, yoghurt and almond, mean you can stay all night. And in the heart of Shoreditch, that's not a bad thing.

Booking advisable Thur-Sat. Disabled: toilet. Entertainment: DJs 8pm Fri, Sat. **Map 6 R4**.

★ Happiness Forgets

Basement, 8-9 Hoxton Square, N1 6NU (7613 0325, www.happinessforgets.com). Old Street tube/rail or Shoreditch High Street rail. **Open** 5.30-11pm daily. **Credit** MC, V.

On a Friday night, when this tiny basement bar was rammed, our waitress said all the tables were booked. But she added that a table for four at the back had just two 'really nice people' sitting there and she'd ask if we could share with them. They said yes, and we were in. This warm welcome is typical of one of the best bars in Shoreditch – in all of London, in fact. From the moment you walk in, they know how to make you happy. The short list of original cocktails is unfailingly good: lots of nice twists on classic ideas but never departing from the essential cocktail principles of balance, harmony and drinkability. Star turns: Mr McRae, Perfect Storm and Tokyo Collins. But the classics are brilliantly handled, and the food is fabulous. And that service! This very special place is not very large and plenty of people know about it, so booking is a good idea.

Booking advisable. **Map 6 R3**.

Nightjar

129 City Road, EC1V 1JB (7253 4101, www.barnightjar.com). Old Street tube/rail. **Open** 6pm-1am Mon-Wed, Sun; 6pm-2am Thur; 6am-3am Fri, Sat. **Credit** AmEx, MC, V.

Nightjar has become a huge success, busy even midweek; we visited on a Monday and were lucky to get in. Clear message: book a table. The cocktail list, divided into historical eras (pre-Prohibition, post-war and so on), makes for enthralling reading with all its unexpected ingredients. Just to give an idea: the Kenko-Teki Swizzle includes green coffee bean infusion, saké, green tea, buckwheat rice syrup and alfalfa. This makes Nightjar a great place for experimenting, as you sit in the moodily lit room with its gorgeous pressed tin ceiling. But

Powder Keg Diplomacy

if the original drinks are too confusing, you can rely on staff for expert handling of the classics. A couple of small quibbles: the spice level in the own-made bloody mary mix could be toned down; and while the background jazz is fabulous, it probably doesn't need to be so loud – even if you love Billie Holiday and Louis Armstrong as much as we do. *Booking advisable Tue-Sun. Disabled: toilet. Entertainment: live music 9.30pm Tue-Sat.* **Map 6 Q4**.

Worship Street Whistling Shop
63 Worship Street, EC2A 2DU (7247 0015, www.whistlingshop.com). Old Street tube/rail. **Open** 5pm-midnight Tue; 5pm-1am Wed, Thur; 5pm-2am Fri, Sat. **Credit** AmEx, MC, V.

From the same group as Purl and VOC, this cellar bar is decked out in what seems to be a speakeasy/Victorian mash-up (dark wood and lots of eccentric decorative touches). It makes much of its experimental techniques; if your curiosity is tickled by the sound of 'enzymes, acids, proteins and hydrocolloids', you're all set. The list is mercifully short, and classics are well handled. When we asked for a drink made with the delicious Chase Marmalade vodka, we got their take on it: tall lemonade on the rocks, vodka served separately for either sipping or mixing in. There's an extensive selection of spirits, including their own barrel-aged ones. Staff are skilled, friendly and eager to please. While there was plenty of space in the front room (there's another at the back), staff reported that both are usually packed. Not hard to see why. *Booking advisable Fri, Sat.* **Map 6 Q4**.

Hawksmoor

Spitalfields

★ Hawksmoor
157 Commercial Street, E1 6BJ (7426 4856, www.thehawksmoor.com). Liverpool Street tube/rail or Shoreditch High Street rail. **Open** 5.30-10.15pm Mon-Fri; noon-10.15pm Sat, Sun. **Credit** AmEx, MC, V.
This architecturally fascinating basement bar (located underneath the Hawksmoor steak restaurant, in what used to be a strip club) is a jewel in east London's bar scene. If you can't bag a table in the main seating space or at a table under the vaults, perch at the copper bar and ask the bartender to explain the architecture to you. Seated there, you'll also get the chance to watch some extremely talented cocktail craftsmen at work. We ordered two drinks, a flawless martini and a wonderful Marmalade cocktail of vodka, Campari, lemon and marmalade – the perfect acid/sweet balance. We got a free sip of a couple of sweeties too, including a Nuclear Banana daiquiri (overproof rum, Chartreuse, banana and lime), which was very well made and incredibly rich. Service from both bartenders and table crew is effortlessly friendly, and good-looking bar snacks, such as ox cheek nuggets and pig's head poutine, give a taste of the kitchen upstairs. We can't think of a single bad thing to say about this bar, one of the very best in east London.
Available for hire. Babies and children admitted until 6pm. Bookings accepted for parties of 6 or more only. Disabled: toilet. **Map 6 R5**.

North
Islington

★ 69 Colebrooke Row
69 Colebrooke Row, N1 8AA (07540 528593, www.69colebrookerow.com). Angel tube or Essex Road rail. **Open** 5pm-midnight Mon-Wed, Sun; 5pm-1am Thur; 5pm-2am Fri, Sat. **Credit** AmEx, MC, V.
'The bar with no name', it styles itself – try telling that to a taxi driver. In reality, everyone knows this place by its address, hidden away from the Upper Street hordes on an Islington backstreet. It's the tiny flagship of bar supremo Tony Conigliaro, noted worldwide for his dedication to the art of the mixed drink; as such, it's not easy to get a seat here without booking (and come early in the week if you want to be able to chat). Punters come for the cocktails, all of which are outstanding. Some of them may push the boundaries of what can be put in a glass, but always maintain the drinkability of the classics. Take the Terroir, for instance, which lists as its ingredients 'distilled clay, flint and lichen', and tastes wonderfully like a chilled, earthy, minerally vodka – the distilled essence of a winter mountainside. It's made in Conigliaro's upstairs laboratory, which also produces bespoke cocktail ingredients such as Guinness reduction, paprika bitters, rhubarb cordial and pine-infused gin. A subtle jazz-age vibe is adopted throughout the room, with smartly clad bar staff, vintage advertising posters, black and white checked floor tiles and – on certain nights – a pianist belting out swinging standards.
Available for hire. Booking advisable, essential Fri, Sat. Entertainment: pianist 8pm Thur, 10pm Fri. **Map 5 O2**.

BARS

Eating & Entertainment

Discerning Londoners have come to expect more from a night out than a few pints and a kebab, and with the wealth of exciting combined dining and entertainment options that the city has to offer, it's no wonder. A huge variety of tastes – in both food and culture – are catered for. If you've long dreamed of sitting in dimly lit bars sipping bourbon, while listening to the strains of sultry jazz or blues guitar, head to Soho's legendary **Ronnie Scott's** or the **Blues Kitchen** in Camden, where world-renowned musicians take to the stage. Alternatively, experience life as a bright young thing with a trip to **Betty Blythe**'s 1920s-themed tea room, followed by an evening at the **Crazy Coqs** at Brasserie Zédel (www.brasseriezedel.com/crazy-coqs) for cabaret and French cuisine in a stunning art deco setting. Looking for something totally different? Eat in the pitch dark at **Dans Le Noir?**, dine in a simulated jungle in the **Rainforest Café** or even squeeze into lederhosen and yodel to your sausage at **Tiroler Hut**.

Central
Chancery Lane

Bounce
121 Holborn, EC1N 2TD (3657 6525, www.bouncepingpong.com). Chancery Lane tube or Farringdon tube/rail or City Thameslink rail. **Open** 4pm-midnight Mon-Wed; 4pm-1am Thur; noon-1am Fri, Sat; noon-11pm Sun. **Meals served** 6-10.30pm Mon-Thur; noon-10.30pm Fri-Sun. **Main courses** £12-£14. **Set menu** £17 2 courses, £20 3 courses. **Credit** AmEx, MC, V. Ping-pong
Allegedly located on the very spot that the game was invented, Bounce is a ping-pong bar that serves up a night of competitive fun in an edgy industrial-chic space. The restaurant, safely out of reach of wayward ping-pong balls, is raised on a platform overlooking the drama unfolding on the 16 tables below. A selection of antipasti and pizzas (straight from the wood-burning oven) provides players with ample sustenance.
Available for hire. Babies and children welcome: high chairs; nappy-changing facilities. Booking essential, 1 mth in advance. Disabled: toilet. Entertainment: DJs 8pm Mon-Sat. **Map 11 N5.**

City

Volupté
7-9 Norwich Street, EC4A 1EJ (7831 1622, www.volupte-lounge.com). Chancery Lane tube. **Open** 4.30pm-1am Tue, Wed; 4.30pm-3am Thur, Fri; 2pm-3am Sat. **Tea served** 2pm Sat. **Dinner served** 6-10pm Tue-Thur; 6pm-midnight Fri, Sat. **Set meal** (incl show) £67 3 courses. **Afternoon tea** £49. **Membership** £150/yr. **Credit** AmEx, MC, V. Burlesque
Blood-red velvet drapery and gold furnishings give this classic supper club a luxurious feel, providing a suitable backdrop for its burlesque and cabaret acts. The lavish cocktail menu also hints at decadence, with drinks such as Guilty Pleasure. The Saturday 'Afternoon Tease' marries antique china, fairy cakes and finger sandwiches with risqué burlesque performances. The dinner menu is less delicate, featuring hearty comfort food.
Booking essential. Entertainment: cabaret 8pm Wed-Fri; 2.30pm, 7pm, 10pm Sat. **Map 11 N5.**

Clerkenwell

Dans Le Noir?
30-31 Clerkenwell Green, EC1R 0DU (7253 1100, www.danslenoir.com/london). Farringdon
tube/rail. **Lunch served** by appointment. **Dinner served** (fixed sittings) 6.30-7.30pm, 9-9.30pm Mon-Thur, 6.30-7.15pm, 9.15-10pm Fri, Sat; 6.45-8pm Sun. **Set dinner** £42 2 courses, £51 3 courses. **Credit** AmEx, MC, V. One-off
A slightly daunting dining experience that aims to encourage participants to re-evaluate their approach to eating. At Dans le Noir? you eat in complete darkness, so it's the taste, smell and texture of the food on which you focus. Before being led into the pitch-black basement dining room by the restaurant's blind guides/waiters, you select one of four colour-coded mystery menus: red (meat), blue (fish), green (vegetarian) and white (chef's special). It's a profoundly sensory food adventure that makes for a unique evening.
Available for hire. Booking essential. Children over 8 yrs admitted. Disabled: toilet. **Map 5 N4.**

Covent Garden

Roadhouse
35 The Piazza, WC2E 8BE (7240 6001, www.roadhouse.co.uk). Covent Garden tube. **Open** 5.30pm-3am Mon-Sat; 6.30pm-1.30am Sun. **Meals served** 5.30-8.30pm Mon-Sat; 6.30-8.30pm Sun. **Main courses** £8.25-£17. **Admission** £5 after 7pm, £12 after 9pm. **Credit** AmEx, MC, V. Rock/karaoke

Bounce. See p317.

Bands and DJs perform nightly at this lively American-style diner and bar. On a Monday and a Wednesday, you can live your teenage dream of becoming a rock star at Rockaoke, an alternative karaoke where customers perform their favourite songs with a live backing band. Food takes in burgers, steaks and a cajun grill, and unsurprisingly – considering the Roadhouse hosts the cocktail-making competition Flair – the drinks list is extensive.

Booking advisable. Dress: smart casual. Entertainment: bands/DJs; times vary daily. **Map 18 E4**.

Sarastro

126 Drury Lane, WC2B 5QG (7836 0101, www.sarastro-restaurant.com). Covent Garden or Holborn tube. **Meals served** noon-10.30pm daily. **Main courses** (Tue, Wed, Fri, Sat) £10.25-£25.85. **Set lunch** (noon-6.30pm Mon-Sat) £15.50 2 courses, £19.25 3 courses. **Set meal** £27.50 2 courses, £32.50 3 courses. **Credit** AmEx, MC, V. Opera

Musicians from London's opera houses come here to perform some of the most popular arias every Sunday and Monday. Enjoy a three-course set menu while listening to operatic trills from the comfort of one of the boxes arranged around the walls. It's a decadent setting, with each box furnished in a different style (rococo, Gothic, Ottoman) and drapes and theatre props in abundance. Food is of the Turkish-Mediterranean inclination, and à la carte is only available when there are no performances. *Babies and children welcome: high chairs. Booking advisable. Disabled: toilet. Entertainment: opera, string quartet, swing & Motown vocalist (see website for details).* **Map 18 F3**.

Leicester Square

Rainforest Café

20 Shaftesbury Avenue, W1D 7EU (7434 3111, www.therainforestcafe.co.uk). Leicester Square or Piccadilly Circus tube. **Meals served** noon-10pm Mon-Fri; 11.30am-10pm Sat, Sun. **Main courses** £14.90-£23. **Credit** AmEx, MC, V. Children

One for the kids to enjoy (and perhaps something for the child in us all), this simulated-jungle dining room comes complete with animatronic animals. The menu is rather less exotic, but burgers and pasta dishes can be enjoyed against a soundscape of chattering monkeys, parrots and the odd tropical storm. A visit to the shop – chock-full of jungle-themed toys – will supply the souvenirs. No advance bookings are taken, but a priority seating system operates online (where the next available table is yours, within a certain time slot). *Available for hire. Babies and children welcome: children's menu; crayons; high chairs; nappy-changing facilities. Entertainment: face painting weekends & school hols. Separate rooms for parties, seating 11-100.* **Map 17 B5**.

Salsa!

96 Charing Cross Road, WC2H 0JG (7379 3277, www.barsalsa.info). Leicester Square or Tottenham Court Road tube. *Bar* **Open** 5pm-2am Mon-Thur, Sun; 5pm-3am Fri, Sat. *Café* **Open** 10am-5pm Mon-Sat. **Snacks served** noon-5pm Mon-Sat. **Main courses** £4.95-£5.45. *Restaurant* **Meals served** 5-11pm daily. **Main courses** £8.99-£11.50. *Bar & Restaurant* **Admission** £5 after 9pm Mon-Thur; £2 after 7pm, £4 after 8pm, £8 after 9pm, £10 after 11pm Fri, Sat; £5 after 8pm Sun. *All* **Credit** AmEx, MC, V. Dance

Salsa classes for all levels of expertise, from beginners to advanced, cost just £5 at this restaurant, bar and dance club. Latin-themed

cocktails help to ease any embarrassment and loosen the limbs. The extensive menu of tacos, tostadas, fajitas and quesadillas should set you up with enough energy to dance through to the small hours; musicians play until late on Friday and Saturday nights.
Available for hire. Booking advisable, essential weekends. Dress: smart casual. Entertainment: dance classes 6.30pm, DJs 9.30pm daily. Tables outdoors (14, terrace). **Map 17 C3.**

Mayfair

Dover Street
8-10 Dover Street, W1S 4LQ (7629 9813, www.doverstreet.co.uk). Green Park or Piccadilly Circus tube. **Open** 6pm-3am Mon-Thur; 7pm-3am Fri, Sat. **Dinner served** 6pm-midnight Mon-Wed; 6pm-1am Thur; 7pm-1am Fri, Sat. **Music** *Bands* 9.30pm, 11pm Mon; 10pm, midnight Tue, Wed; 10.45pm, midnight Thur-Sat. *DJs* until 3am Mon-Sat. **Main courses** £15.95-£25.95. **Set dinner** £32.50-£38.50 3 courses incl service, music. **Admission** (after 10pm) £7 Mon; £8 Tue; £12 Wed; £15 Thur-Sat. **Credit** AmEx, DC, MC, V. Jazz
Fashion prints adorn the walls at this elegant music venue with three bars. A menu featuring the likes of pan-fried swordfish, fillet steak, and spinach and ricotta tortellini is served until late. Jazz, blues, latin or soul musicians provide the accompaniment to your dinner, and afterwards you can dance away the rest of the night to Dover Street's resident DJ.
Booking advisable, essential weekends. Dress: smart casual; no trainers. Separate rooms for parties, seating 20-100. **Map 9 J7.**

Soho

Jazz After Dark
9 Greek Street, W1D 4DQ (7734 0545, www.jazzafterdark.co.uk). Leicester Square or Tottenham Court Road tube. **Open** 2pm-2am Tue-Thur; 2pm-3am Fri, Sat. **Meals served** 2pm-midnight Tue-Sat. **Music** 9pm Mon-Thur; 10.30pm Fri, Sat. **Tapas** £4.50-£10.95. **Set meal** £14.95 3 courses. **Admission** £5 Tue-Thur; £10 diners, £15 non-diners Fri, Sat. **Credit** AmEx, DC, MC, V. Jazz
This cosy, characterful Soho jazz venue is a great place to catch acts in an intimate setting. Small plates of fried chicken, meatballs and tapas are good to munch on during performances, but heartier dishes are also offered, such as lamb shank or a mixed grill. The drinks menu features cheekily named cocktails such as a Kick in the Balls and Between the Sheets. Pete Doherty and Amy Winehouse both performed here.
Available for hire. Booking essential Fri, Sat. Dress: smart casual. Tables outdoors (2, pavement). **Map 17 C3.**

Lucky Voice
52 Poland Street, W1F 7LR (7439 3660, www.luckyvoice.co.uk). Oxford Circus tube. **Open/meals served** 5.30pm-1am Mon-Thur; 3pm-1am Fri, Sat; 3-10.30pm Sun. **Main courses** £7.50. **Credit** AmEx, MC, V. Karaoke
For those who enjoy crooning into a hairbrush, but are too shy to take to the stage, Lucky Voice might be the solution. Nine private 'pods' allow groups of four to 12 people to belt out a classic without any fear of embarrassment. Pizza and nibbles are basic, but the drinks menu is more extravagant; choose a

snifter off the list to chase away any lingering inhibitions. With almost a million songs on the play-list, there will certainly be a tune you know – so no excuses.
Booking essential. Entertainment: karaoke pods for hire, £5-£10/hr per person. Over-21s only. **Map 17 A3.**
For branch see index.

Pizza Express Jazz Club
10 Dean Street, W1D 3RW (0845 602 7017, www.pizzaexpresslive.com). Tottenham Court Road tube. **Meals served** *Club* 7-11pm daily. *Restaurant* 11.30am-midnight Mon-Sat; 11.30am-11.30pm Sun. **Music** 8.30-10.30pm Mon-Thur; 9-11pm Fri, Sat; 8-10pm Sun. **Main courses** £6.50-£10.95. **Admission** £10-£50. **Credit** AmEx, DC, MC, V. Jazz
The ground floor is nothing special: Pizza Express dishing out its reliable repertoire. Head downstairs, though, and it's another story. A basement jazz club hosts regular music sessions and attracts some big names. Norah Jones and Scott Hamilton have taken to the stage, and Sting has even given an impromptu performance here. Emerging talent is also encouraged, with lesser-known acts often appearing.
Babies and children welcome (restaurant): high chairs. Booking advisable. Disabled: toilet (restaurant). Takeaway service. **Map 17 B3.**

Ronnie Scott's
47 Frith Street, W1D 4HT (7439 0747, www.ronniescotts.co.uk). Leicester Square or Tottenham Court Road tube. **Open** 6pm-3am Mon-Sat; noon-4pm, 6.30pm-midnight Sun. **Meals served** 6pm-1am Mon-Sat; noon-4pm, 6-11pm Sun. **Music** 8.30pm daily; 11pm Fri, Sat. **Main courses** £15.40-£28.50. **Admission** (non-members) £20-£40. **Membership** £175/yr. **Credit** AmEx, MC, V. Jazz
A delightful slice of music history, Ronnie Scott's is a legend of the London music scene. Many top American jazz musicians gave their first UK performance here. The club is by no means a museum, though, as the cream of the jazz world continues to take the stage. A small but select menu ranges from mushroom pie to sevruga caviar. Standards of culinary execution might vary, but the jazz is undeniably hot.
Booking advisable. Children over 14yrs admitted if accompanied until midnight; all ages admitted Sun lunch. Disabled: toilet. Dress: smart casual. **Map 17 C3.**

West

Bayswater

Bel Canto
Corus Hotel Hyde Park, 1 Lancaster Gate, W2 3LG (7262 1678, www.lebelcanto.com). Lancaster Gate tube. **Dinner served** 7-9.15pm Wed-Sat. **Set dinner** (incl show) £44 2 courses, £51 3 courses, £60.75 4 courses. **Credit** MC, V. Opera
The operatic term 'bel canto' refers to brilliantly performed pieces of opera, which – it is to be hoped – is what you'll experience on a visit here. Traditional French cuisine (foie gras, beef fillet) is served in the beautiful dining room of the Corus Hotel Hyde Park. It's the staff, however, who are the real draw. Tables are served by trained opera singers who will pause mid-service and burst into song throughout the evening.

Available for hire. Booking essential. Children admitted. Disabled: lift; toilet. Dress: smart casual. **Map 8 D7.**

Tiroler Hut
27 Westbourne Grove, W2 4UA (7727 3981, www.tirolerhut.co.uk). Bayswater or Queensway tube. **Open** 6.30pm-1am Tue-Sat; 6.30pm-midnight Sun. **Dinner served** 6.30pm-12.30am Tue-Sat; 6.30-11.30pm Sun. **Main courses** (Tue, Wed, Sun) £14.90-£17.50. **Set meal** (Thur) £26.50 3 courses; (Fri, Sat) £29.50 3 courses. **Credit** AmEx, MC, V. Austrian
Don your lederhosen, dust down your alphorn and say 'grüß gott' to a night of Austrian alpine jollity. Host Joseph encourages you to yodel, sing and laugh as he entertains with the Tirolean Cowbell Show. The authentic Austrian fare includes sweet-and-sour herring, stuffed cabbage and bratwurst, and the bar is well stocked with Austrian and German wines and beers. When your vocal chords have been loosened by a stein or two, yodelling is liable to ensue.
Available for hire. Babies and children admitted. Booking essential. Entertainment: cow-bell show; times vary Tue-Sun. **Map 7 B6.**

Earl's Court

Ping
180-184 Earl's Court Road, SW5 9QG (7370 5358, www.weloveping.com). Earl's Court tube. **Open** 6-11pm Mon-Wed; 6pm-2am Thur-Sat. **Main courses** £8-£10. **Credit** AmEx, MC, V. Ping-pong
Mirrored walls, DJs and a swanky cocktail list add a bit of glam to the laid-back pizza and ping-pong concept here. Enjoy an alcoholic milkshake or a martini, take to the table, and let insobriety impair your game (well, that's the excuse). Afterwards, settle on one of the green velvet sofas that surround the games room, and replenish your energy levels with a slice of pizza. Ping-pong tables can't be booked in advance, but priority goes to those with dining or drinking reservations, so it's wise to phone ahead.
Available for hire. Babies and children admitted until 10pm. Booking advisable. Separate room for parties, seats 40. **Map 13 B10.**

Troubadour
263-267 Old Brompton Road, SW5 9JA (7370 1434, www.troubadour.co.uk). West Brompton tube/rail. *Café* 9am-midnight daily. **Meals served** 9am-11pm daily. **Main courses** £9.50-£24. *Club* 7.30pm-midnight Mon-Wed, Sun; 7.30pm-2am Thur-Sat. **Credit** AmEx, MC, V. Performance
Steeped in musical history, this venue has played host to some of the world's greatest artists, from Sammy Davis Jnr and Jimi Hendrix to Led Zeppelin jam sessions. The ground-floor café is a charming space with stained glass and wood panelling. Brunch is served all day and a lunch menu features a range of pastas, burgers and seafood. Enjoy a hearty supper and a pint of Rothaus German beer before descending to the basement for an event from a varied programme of music, DJs and poetry nights. And if you don't fancy the trek home, hole up in one of the Troubadour's two arts and crafts-style rooftop apartments for the night.
Available for hire. Babies and children welcome (café): high chair. Booking advisable.

Entertainment: bands 7.30pm Mon-Sat. Separate rooms for parties, seating 15-32. Tables outdoors (8, garden; 6, pavement). Map 13 B11.

Kensington

Bodo's Schloss

2 Kensington High Street, W8 4RE (7937 5506, www.bodosschloss.com). High Street Kensington tube. **Open** 5pm-1am Mon-Wed; 5pm-2am Thur; 5pm-3am Fri, Sat. **Meals served** 5-10pm Mon-Sat. **Disco** 10pm-2am Thur; 10pm-3am Fri, Sat. **Main courses** £15-£24. **Set menu** £28-£38 3 courses. **Admission** £10 after 10pm Thur; £15 after 9pm Fri, Sat. **Credit** AmEx, MC, V. Alpine

For the residents of Kensington left pining for the slopes of Klosters, Bodo's Schloss is there to provide some small comfort. An alpine cabin – vibrantly realised in gingham, lederhosen and cow hide – is the setting in which to enjoy traditional Austrian cuisine of schnitzel and sauerkraut. After dinner, take your piste-weary legs to the dancefloor for 'Die Diskotheque', a not-so-après-ski party. *Available for hire. Booking essential Fri, Sat. Children admitted until 10pm. Disabled: toilet. Separate room for parties, seats 60.* **Map 7 C8.**

Olympia

Betty Blythe

72 Blythe Road, W14 0HP (7602 1177, www.bettyblythe.co.uk). Kensington (Olympia) tube/rail. **Open** 8am-5.30pm Mon-Fri; 9am-8pm Sat. **Afternoon tea** £21. **Credit** MC, V. Twenties tea room

Experience the glamorous lifestyle of screen siren Betty Blythe at this quaint west London café and deli. Enjoy a 'Great Gatsby' afternoon tea, eaten off vintage crockery. Don some flapper accessories in the dressing room and have your picture taken in the lovingly constructed setting. The Roaring Twenties theme doesn't stop there: for parties and events, Betty Blythe provides a variety of activities such as fascinator hat-making sessions and charleston dancing. *Available for hire. Babies and children welcome: high chairs. Booking essential weekends. Separate room for parties. Tables outdoors (3, pavement).* **Map 20 C3.**

South West

Chelsea

606 Club

90 Lots Road, SW10 0QD (7352 5953, www.606club.co.uk). Earl's Court tube then bus C3, or Sloane Square tube then bus 22. **Open** 7-11.30pm Mon, Thur; 7pm-12.30am Tue, Wed; 8pm-1.30am Fri, Sat; 12.30-4pm, 7-11.15pm Sun. **Meals served** 7-10.30pm Mon-Thur; 8-11pm Fri, Sat; 12.30-3pm, 7-10.30pm Sun. **Music** 8.30pm Mon, Thur, Sun; 7.30pm Tue, Wed; 9.30pm Fri, Sat. **Main courses** £9.70-£19.50. **Admission** (non-members) £10-£12. **Membership** £125 1st yr, £75 subsequent yrs, £300 5 yrs. **Credit** AmEx, MC, V. Jazz

An intimate basement club, established in 1976, the 606 prides itself on booking the best of British jazz musicians. Enjoy dishes of baked teriyaki salmon, wild boar sausages or own-made houmous at one of the small wooden tables clustered around the main stage. The club's licence means non-members can only drink alcohol with meals; and at weekends, they are admitted only if dining. *Available for hire. Babies and children admitted. Booking advisable Fri, Sat.* **Map 13 C13.**

South

Battersea

Le Quecum Bar

42-44 Battersea High Street, SW11 3HX (7787 2227, www.quecumbar.co.uk). Clapham Junction rail. **Open** 6pm-midnight Mon, Fri-Sun; 7pm-midnight Tue-Thur. **Meals served** 6-10pm Mon, Fri-Sun; 7-10pm Tue-Thur. **Music** varies Mon, Sun; 8pm Tue-Sat. **Main courses** £5-£15. **Minimum** £15. **Admission** varies Mon, Sun; free Tue; £5 after 8pm Wed-Sat. **Membership** £60/yr. **Credit** AmEx, MC, V. Gypsy swing

Battersea's Le Quecum Bar is dedicated to the Django Reinhardt gypsy-swing genre. Experience an evening of heady 1930s Parisian pleasure, dining from a classic French menu (beef bourguignon, pâté and the like) and take in the cool plucking of a guitar maestro. Feeling inspired? Bring an instrument along to the free 'gypsy swing jam' held every Tuesday. Concerts are ticketed on Sundays and Mondays. *Booking advisable Mon, Fri-Sun. Dress: smart casual. Tables outdoors (5, garden).* **Map 21 B2.**

North East
Hackney

Russet
Hackney Downs Studio, Amhurst Terrace, E8 2BT (www.therusset.wordpress.com). Hackney Downs or Rectory Road rail. **Open** 8.30am-5pm Mon; 8.30am-11pm Tue-Thur; 8.30am-midnight Fri; 10am-midnight Sat; 10am-11pm Sun. **Breakfast served** 8.30am-12.30pm, **lunch served** 12.30-4.30pm daily. **Tapas served** 5-10pm Tue-Sun. **Main courses** £3.50-£9. **Tapas** £2.50-£7.50. **Credit** MC, V. Performance
Café, garden and all-round creative venue, the Russet is a hive of artistic activity in Hackney Downs. Food is locally and sustainably sourced, with an ever-changing blackboard menu featuring mussels in cider and beef ragù. During the day, it's all very family-friendly, with arts and language classes for kids. The venue grows up in the evening, with a programme of reggae, jazz and folk sessions as well as film screenings and comedy nights.
Available for hire. Babies and children welcome: high chairs; nappy-changing facilities. Disabled: toilet. Tables outdoors (4, garden; 14, terrace).

North
Camden & Chalk Farm

Blues Kitchen
111-113 Camden High Street, NW1 7JN (7387 5277, www.theblueskitchen.com). Camden Town tube. **Open** noon-midnight Mon, Tue; noon-1am Wed, Thur; noon-3am Fri; 11am-3am Sat; 11am-1am Sun. **Lunch served** noon-4pm Mon-Fri; 10am-4pm Sat, Sun. **Dinner served** 4-10.30pm Mon-Fri; 4-10pm Sat, Sun. **Music** Bands 9.30pm Mon-Thur; 10pm Fri, Sat; 7pm Sun. **DJs** 9pm-3am Fri, Sat. **Main courses** £8-£17. **Admission** £4 after 9.30pm Fri; £6 after 9pm Sat. **Credit** AmEx, MC, V. Blues
Acts perform nightly at the Blues Kitchen in Camden, a cavernous bar-restaurant that prides itself on a huge bourbon collection and classic American South dishes of pulled pork, ribs (slow-smoked for eight hours) and gumbo. The American influence isn't confined to the kitchen; the musical line-up is heavy on blues, soul and rock 'n' roll, and has featured artists such as Seasick Steve.
Available for hire. Booking advisable. Babies and children admitted until 7pm. **Map 27 D3**.

Jazz Café
5-7 Parkway, NW1 7PG (7688 8899, www.mean fiddler.com). Camden Town tube. **Open** 7-11pm Mon-Thur; 7pm-2am Fri, Sat. **Meals served** varies; phone for details. **Music** daily; phone for details. **Main courses** £16.50. **Set meal** £26.50 2 courses. **Admission** varies; phone for details. **Credit** MC, V. Jazz
The restaurant at this Camden music venue is raised on a platform above the main stage and offers the best seats in the house ('I'll have the herb-crusted lamb with a side of jazz, funk and soul, please'). The Jazz Café is renowned for hosting the biggest names in the jazz and soul world before they become famous, so pay attention to the support act – it might be the next big thing. The restaurant only opens on event nights.
Booking essential. **Map 27 D2**.

North West
Kensal Green

Paradise by Way of Kensal Green
19 Kilburn Lane, W10 4AE (8969 0098, www.theparadise.co.uk). Kensal Green tube/rail. **Open** 4pm-midnight Mon-Wed; 4pm-1am Thur; 4pm-2am Fri; noon-2am Sat; noon-midnight Sun. **Meals served** 6.30-10.30pm Mon-Thur; 6.30-11pm Fri; noon-4pm, 6.30-11pm Sat; noon-9pm Sun. **Main courses** £13.95-£29.50. **Admission** Club £4 after 9pm Fri, Sat. **Credit** AmEx, MC, V. Performance
Paradise by Way of Kensal Green might seem like a highfalutin' name for a bar, but as the phrase comes from a GK Chesterton poem opposing the prohibition of alcohol, we'll let the owners off. The menu is classic British, with many of the ingredients organic and locally sourced. Chandeliers, velvet drapes, peeling paint and religious iconography lend the venue a gothic feel. Evening events provide something to suit most tastes: DJs, musicians (from reggae to swing), dance, cabaret and cult film nights.
Available for hire (Mon-Thur, Sun). Babies and children welcome until 8pm: high chairs; nappy-changing facilities. Booking advisable. Entertainment: bands/DJs; times vary Tue-Sat. Separate room for parties, seats 25.

Bel Canto. See p319.

Wine Bars

With 1980s pop stars continuing to pop up like a battalion of unruly shoulder-pads, you might think that the current resurgence in wine bars also warns of a return to that decade. Not a bit of it: wine bars are back, but not as we knew them. Developments in taste, technology and legislation are behind the new breed of wine bar. Legislation? Until October 2011, it was illegal to serve wine in smaller measures than the standard 125ml glass, so sampling a wine flight wasn't just an exercise in fashioning your vinous preferences – it meant going out on a bender. Many wine merchants had lobbied for this change in the law, as wine flights were becoming fashionable elsewhere in the world due to new methods of wine preservation (such as the Enomatic system) that prevented opened bottles quickly going off. So, wine flights of smaller glasses are now offered by the likes of **Vinoteca** and **Negozio Classica**, with **28°-50°** and **10 Cases** offering smaller measures too. This technology has also led to a blurring of the distinction between wine shops and wine bars, as the shops are able to uncork more of their bottles without fear of wasting stock. The recently opened **New Street Wine Shop** is one of the latest of these shop-bars to appear.

London has long been the world centre of the vintage wine trade, with bottles from the top wine producers being auctioned here, so the city's wine bars have a stupendous choice close at hand, and are also quick to pick up on trends. Natural wines – fermented grape juice with little added or taken away – have grown in popularity in recent years, championed by the **Terroirs** group, which also includes the excellent **Brawn** (*see p208*), **Green Man & French Horn** and **Soif**. These wines, also available at newcomers such as East Dulwich's **Toasted** and Wapping's **Victualler**, are an acquired taste. What has gained near-universal acclaim, though, is the high quality of the ingredients-led food at the new breed of wine bar: a far cry from the dismal platters of the 1980s.

Central

City

New Street Wine Shop

16 New Street, EC2M 4TR (3503 0795, www.newstreetwineshop.co.uk). Liverpool Street tube/rail. **Open** 11.30am-9pm Mon, Tue; 11.30am-11pm Wed-Fri. **Dishes served** 11.30am-8pm Mon, Tue; 11.30am-10pm Wed-Fri. **Dishes** £3-£16. **House wine** from £1.30 (50ml tasting glass). **Credit** AmEx, MC, V.
New Street is a wine shop rather than a wine bar, but the boundaries have become enjoyably blurred since the advent of dispensers that allow tasting quantities to be served, and enjoyed. There are perhaps 16 of these here, representing a changing sample of the shop's 600 bins, grouped into selections. Given the City location, it's no surprise that Bordeaux, Burgundy and Champagne dominate, but 15 other countries and a good 70 grapes are

represented in a well-chosen selection that ranges beyond the conservative. You could buy online, but then you'd be missing out on the staff's pleasure in discussing their stock – it's a friendly place that resembles a café more than a shop, with large communal tables, handsome wooden decor and full-height windows in a warehousey first-floor space. You'd also be missing out on sampling your prospective purchases as they're meant to be experienced: with food. The menu is very simple – cheese, charcuterie, salads, with perhaps a sandwich special – but it's all good quality, down to the bread and butter.
Available for hire. Booking advisable.
Map 12 R5.

Clerkenwell & Farringdon

Quality Chop House   HOT 50

92-94 Farringdon Road, EC1R 3EA (7278 1452, www.thequalitychophouse.com). Farringdon tube/rail or bus 19, 38, 341.

Restaurant **Lunch served** noon-3pm, **dinner served** 6-11pm Mon-Sat. **Main courses** (lunch) £11-£18. **Set dinner** £35 5 courses. *Wine bar & shop* **Open** 11am-11pm, **lunch served** noon-3pm, **dinner served** 6-11pm Mon-Sat. **Main courses** £11-£18. *Both* **House wine** £19 bottle, £4 glass. **Credit** AmEx, MC, V.
The Quality Chop House carries deliberate echoes of its 19th-century origins by offering 'a chop and a glass' or a two-course and coffee 'daily lunch' for £15. Not quite the generosity of the original 'plate of meat, bread and half a pint of ale for six pence', but well-priced quality nonetheless. Wine rather than ale is the main draw now (though Kernel beer is offered). There's a wine shop alongside the bar and dining room, with plenty to interest both casual sippers and serious imbibers. Mainly Old World with good regional representation, the list takes in interesting New World wines, not least on the 'collector's list'. Failing a hefty salary, explore the by-the-glass selection; our £6 choices from Portugal

and the southern Rhône were fresh and characterful. Knowledgeable buying is evident in the food too: well-sourced British fish, meat and artisan cheeses, heritage tomatoes and carrots, and Tuscan lardo di colonnata, which, on our last visit, was draped over a fillet of gurnard to good effect, served with creamed brown butter. Flavours are punchy: own-cured wild salmon was doused in unsweet mustard; tiny carrots came dressed with truffled tunworth cheese. Desserts also seemed geared to masculine palates: a chocolate mousse proved a deep glassful of dense ganache. Of a piece, perhaps, with the traditional decor of black and white chequerboard floor and dark wooden furniture – though the wine bar can be a light, bright option on a sunny day.
Booking essential dinner. Separate room for parties, seats 10. Tables outdoors (2, pavement). **Map 5 N4**.

Covent Garden

★ Green Man & French Horn
54 St Martin's Lane, WC2N 4EA (7836 2645, www.greenmanfrenchhorn.co). Leicester Square tube. **Open** noon-11pm, **lunch served** noon-3pm, **dinner served** 5.30-11pm Mon-Sat. **Main courses** £10-£26. **Set meal** (noon-7pm) £13.50 2 courses (£17 incl glass of wine), £15 3 courses (£18.50 incl glass of wine). **House wine** £18.50 bottle, £4.75 glass. **Credit** MC, V.
The wine list at this Loire specialist is a real piece of work. An evident passion and on-the-ground knowledge underpin an esoteric haul of treasures from along the long and diverse river – we'd be surprised if a better selection exists even in France. Not that the wine bar takes itself too seriously, featuring quirky illustrations such as 'great beards of the Loire'. With its varied styles and wealth of small (often natural) producers, the region is a good match for the Terroirs approach (Green Man & French Horn is an offshoot) and also meets the current thirst for rosés, champagne alternatives and off-piste explorations (although classics such as Sancerre and Pouilly-Fumé are well represented).

The food is also influenced by the river, with many dishes and ingredients sourced from its course and given a contemporary presentation. Fish and seafood dishes reflect coast rather than river, and less usual meats are given the stripped-down St John treatment in, for example, 'snails, celeriac & mousserons' or 'rillon, endive & mustard'. We enjoyed girolles, well-trimmed artichoke and egg yolk, and copious, faultless grilled langoustines. The long thin room has wooden furniture, bare brick walls, black and white floor tiles and a long bar illuminated by factory lamps; staff are able and enthusiastic. Don't let the wine bar-style fool you: this is a serious restaurant taking wine and food pairing to a new level.
Available for hire. Babies and children welcome: high chairs. Disabled: toilet. **Map 18 D5**.

10 Cases
16 Endell Street, WC2H 9BD (7836 6801, http://10cases.co.uk). Covent Garden tube. **Open** noon-11pm Mon-Sat. **Lunch served** noon-3pm, **dinner served** 6-11.30pm Mon-Thur. **Meals served** noon-11pm Fri, Sat. **Main courses** £11-£30. **House wine** £23 bottle, £4 glass. **Credit** MC, V.
The wooden chairs and tables spilling on to the pavement beneath a wide blue awning, the small room with its white walls, the bonhomie of the chef and patron, the buzz of a contented local crowd – all play to the popular image of a French wine bar. But you'd be hard-pressed to find as considered, interesting and wide-ranging a wine list across the Channel. The '10 cases' of the name refer to the maximum quantity bought in, which keeps the line-up fresh and seasonal. The 20-plus wines on the list, available by glass, carafe and bottle, will likely be gone when you next visit – a shame, if the quality of much of what we tried is any indicator. It has taken time for the food to match these standards, but we've been more impressed of late. There are snacks such as pimientos de padrón, and salt and pepper squid, but the focus is on more formal starters and mains: satisfying bistro-inflected Modern European cooking. Braised pork belly with

pea and bean ragoût, and red mullet with lentils and coriander and chilli pesto, were well made and resonant with flavour. If you're here mainly for wine, decamp to the shop next door, where you can drink in small quantities from Enomatic dispensers or pay £12 corkage to quaff your purchase, along with a few meat, cheese or salad plates.
Booking advisable. Children admitted until 6pm. Separate room for parties, seats 14. Tables outdoors (6, pavement). **Map 18 D3**.

Marylebone

28°-50° Wine Workshop & Kitchen
15-17 Marylebone Lane, W1U 2NE (7486 7922, www.2850.co.uk). Bond Street tube. **Open** noon-11pm Mon-Wed; noon-midnight Thur-Sat; noon-10.30pm Sun. **Lunch served** noon-2.30pm Mon-Sat; noon-3pm Sun. **Dinner served** 6-10pm Mon-Wed; 6-10.30pm Thur-Sat; 6-9.30pm Sun. **Main courses** £12.75-£21.95. **House wine** from £21 bottle, £2.40 glass. **Credit** AmEx, MC, V.
The two outposts of 28°-50° share a similar wine list, a French-inspired menu and a bright, on-the-ball attitude, but there the resemblance ends. Fetter Lane is a basement with a French country-kitchen vibe, while Marylebone is a shiny new corner conversion, all glass and zinc with wraparound windows and a central bar. The menu offers predictable platters and pâtés, plus a handful of more involved main courses and grill dishes. The standard is high, give or take the odd stumble (a few unnecessary relishes and flourishes, and a curio of an aubergine main dish whose miso and charred-skin flavours weren't made for wine-pairing). We particularly rate the grilled meats; the unctuously simple ox cheek braised in red wine; the thin and crispy fries; and the notably generous prawn cocktail starter. The wine list is a thing of joy, offering upwards of 30 varied and delicious wines from on-song suppliers, many of them small producers, plus a changing themed selection. It's well worth exploring: order 75ml glasses and follow

Green Man & French Horn

ARE U ORIGINALE?

the young staff's enthusiastic advice. The crowd is smart, with seats at the V-shaped bar attracting plenty of solo customers and shoppers on a quick break. A third branch was due to open in Mayfair in autumn 2013.

Babies and children welcome: high chairs, nappy-changing facilities. Booking advisable Fri, Sat. Disabled: toilet. Separate room for parties, seats 22. Tables outdoors (7, pavement). **Map 9 G5**. **For branches see index**.

Soho

Vinoteca `HOT 50`

53-55 Beak Street, W1F 9SH (3544 7411, www.vinoteca.co.uk). Oxford Circus or Piccadilly Circus tube. **Open** noon-11pm Mon-Sat; noon-10pm Sun. **Meals served** noon-10.30pm Mon-Sat; noon-10pm Sun. **Main courses** £10-£21. **House wine** £15.50 bottle, £2.70 glass. **Credit** AmEx, MC, V.

Some of the friendliest staff we've encountered in London dispel any notions that this wine bar might be stuffy about its commitment to the grape. That doesn't mean it's not serious: it offers 25 wines by the glass, 300 by the bottle, all available to take away. This Soho branch is the most recent to open, in May 2012; there's also the original in Farringdon and another in Marylebone. On our visit, an Austrian 'wine flight' for £10 promised an interesting exploration of the country's lesser-known styles. The on-tap prosecco (£3.95 a glass) is particularly popular with the after-work crowd who cram in to the informal ground-floor bar; if you want to eat in more peace, reservations are allowed for the quieter upstairs room. Both levels are charmingly yet sparingly decorated, with bare brick walls and huge old French advertising posters. And it's when you're dining that the appeal of Vinoteca really becomes clear: even without the fabulous wines, it would still be a great restaurant. Dishes such as mussels, clams and john dory with chorizo, or barnsley chop with greens, are excellent combinations of light, bright flavours – and go perfectly with the recommended wines. Top-quality cheeses and continental meats are sliced by the plateful and make the ideal accompaniment to a reviving afternoon drink.

Available for hire. Babies and children welcome: high chairs. Booking advisable. Disabled: toilet. Separate room for parties, seats 40. **Map 17 A4**. **For branches see index**.

Strand

Terroirs `HOT 50`

5 William IV Street, WC2N 4DW (7036 0660, www.terroirswinebar.com). Charing Cross tube/rail. **Open** noon-11pm, **lunch served** noon-3pm, **dinner served** 5.30-11pm Mon-Sat. **Main courses** £13-£15. **House wine** £17 bottle, £4.75 glass. **Credit** AmEx, MC, V.

Since Ed Wilson and Oli Barker launched Terroirs in 2008, their business has expanded at a reassuringly steady rate. Three new operations have opened (Brawn in 2010, Soif in 2011, the Green Man & French Horn in 2012), each with its own identity but each identifiably part of the family. The careful growth has ensured standards remain high across the board; indeed, five years on from its opening, Terroirs still feels fresh. It's really two places under one roof. The always crowded ground floor has a casual wine bar feel and a menu to match, focused

28°-50° Wine Workshop & Kitchen. See p323.

(though not exclusively) on small plates for sharing. You can sample some of the same dishes in the atmospheric and surprisingly roomy basement, although the menu structure seems designed to guide diners more towards a starter-main-dessert tradition. The kitchen retains its interest in rustic French dishes (a suitably unreconstructed cassoulet, for instance) but isn't shy of a twist. We loved slow-cooked oxtail with potato gnocchi, and a small plate of black risotto with squid was a delight. The wine list is an encyclopaedia of organic and biodynamic bottles; if you're a first-timer, order by the glass to give yourself a sense of the astonishing variety offered. Recommended.

Babies and children admitted. Booking advisable. Tables outdoors (2, pavement). **Map 18 D5**.

West
Notting Hill

Kensington Wine Rooms

127-129 Kensington Church Street, W8 7LP (7727 8142, www.greatwinesbytheglass.com). Notting Hill Gate tube. **Open** noon-midnight, **meals served** noon-10.45pm daily. **Main courses** £14-£24. **House wine** £22.70 bottle, £4.20 glass. **Credit** AmEx, MC, V.

This popular establishment purrs on, secure in the affections of its Kensington crowd, who treat it like a members' club, lingering over bottles and meals and filling the place with atmosphere and confident conversation. The front bar, fringed with glasses, attracts the more knowledgeable wine crowd, who browse through 40 wines by the glass and 100 more in bottles (also for off-sale). These include classics typically available only in bottles, along with some more challenging newer-style varieties; the bar staff take pleasure in guiding your choices. Food consists of nibbles and platters. In the comfortable dining room behind, a full and sophisticated Modern European menu is available. Wine matches are suggested for each of the 15 or so dishes, some (for starters, at least) costing more than the food they accompany – a clear and laudable statement of intent. They were worth it, notwithstanding that the waiter lowered his voice to explain that the red Anjou was 'natural' and possibly less than smooth.

The menu matches local tastes with luxury ingredients such as oysters, foie gras, steaks and côte de boeuf, served with modern flourishes. More interesting were yellow chanterelles, poached duck egg and sourdough toast; springily fresh chargrilled cuttlefish; and an excellent ibérico pork. Well bedded-in staff kept things fast and friendly.

Babies and children welcome: high chairs. Booking advisable dinner. **Map 7 B7**. **For branch (Fulham Wine Rooms) see index**.

Westbourne Grove

Negozio Classica

283 Westbourne Grove, W11 2QA (7034 0005, www.negozioclassica.co.uk). Ladbroke Grove or Notting Hill Gate tube. **Open/meals served** 3.30pm-midnight Mon-Thur; 11am-midnight Fri; 9am-midnight Sat; 11am-11pm Sun. **Main courses** £8.40-£19.90. **House wine** £19.50 bottle, £4.20 glass. **Corkage** £8.50. **Credit** MC, V.

Part owned by Tuscany's Avignonesi winery, Negozio Classica is set up to showcase the full range of Avignonesi wines in the best way possible – serving them by the glassful. There's also a careful selection of other Italian wines, many of them organic or biodynamic. In addition to the 25 or so by-the-glass offerings (starting at a considerate £4), there's a monthly 'flight': introductory tasters of three wines from a particular region, served in elegant glassware by an enthusiastic sommelier. Visit the Portobello store at cocktail hour, however, and you might think you'd arrived at the Aperol centre of London, as the entire premises – back room, bar, window seats and half the pavement – are packed with slick-suited Italian business men, artfully torn-jean and Prada toters, colourful local shopkeepers and gossip-sharing ladies, all clutching huge glasses brimming with bright orange Aperol spritz. Nibbles come free at this time of day, and very good they are too – enough to persuade punters to indulge in platters of antipasti (specially imported Tuscan cured meats, cheeses and olives of excellent quality), generous mounds of soft cheeses and grilled vegetables or even a tagliata salad of grilled Aberdeen Angus. We couldn't resist pouring a little Occhio di Pernice, a

WHEREVER CRIMES AGAINST HUMANITY ARE PERPETRATED.

Across borders and above politics.
Against the most heinous abuses
and the most dangerous oppressors.
From conduct in wartime
to economic, social, and cultural rights.
Everywhere we go,
we build an unimpeachable case
for change and advocate action
at the highest levels.

HUMAN RIGHTS WATCH TYRANNY HAS A WITNESS

WWW.HRW.ORG

HUMAN
RIGHTS
WATCH

fantastically concentrated dessert wine akin to fig balsamic, over a wobbly vanilla panna cotta – sheer heaven. No one batted an eyelid.

Booking advisable dinner. Children admitted. Tables outdoors (2, pavement). **Map 19 B3**. **For branch see index**.

South

Battersea

Soif

27 Battersea Rise, SW11 1HG (7223 1112, http://soif.co). Clapham Junction rail. **Open** noon-10.30pm daily. **Lunch served** noon-3pm Tue-Sat. **Dinner served** 6-10pm Mon-Sat. **Main courses** £15-£18. **Set lunch** £10 1 course (incl glass of wine and coffee). **House wine** £19 bottle, £4.50 glass. **Credit** MC, V.

Thanks to a partnership with leading wine importer Les Caves de Pyrène, the Terroirs group has pioneered the natural wine movement in London. Soif, the third of its four venues (so far), has the perfectly pitched, quirkily cool ambience of a British take on the ideal Parisian bistro. Design may seem casual, yet not a poster, a blackboard or napkin is out of place. Implausibly delicate C&S glassware provides the perfect vehicle for the terrific collection of intriguing wines, a dozen or so served by the glass. Most hail from France and southern Europe, but there's an honourable look-in from the New World. Vintage ciders and beers featuring the cult Kernel brewery, digestifs and intriguing stickies (tomato liqueur, anyone?) round out the list. Food is well sourced, deftly cooked in an open-view kitchen and served in generous measure: velvety duck rillettes with cracking cornichons was a starter sufficient for two; copiously dressed tomato salad dotted with goat's cheese and excellent pickled walnuts came as a huge plateful; and a dish of smoky and tender pork loin with creamy champ and perky girolles left few gaps to fill. Also gratifying was a dense, dark and delightfully uncloying chocolate mousse. With the easy option of sipping and nibbling in the bar area, you don't need much excuse to drop by, though it's wise to book for the rear dining room.

Available for hire. Babies and children welcome; high chairs, nappy-changing facilities. Booking advisable. Separate room for parties, seats 30. Tables outdoors (5, terrace). **Map 21 4C**.

South East

East Dulwich

Toasted NEW

36-38 Lordship Lane, SE22 8HJ (8693 9250, www.toastdulwich.co.uk). East Dulwich rail. **Open** 8.30am-11.30pm, **breakfast served** 8.30-11.45am, **lunch served** noon-3pm, **dinner served** 6.30-10pm Tue-Sat. **Main courses** £6.50-£15. **House wine** £12.90 bottle, £3 glass. **Credit** MC, V.

Chef Michael Hazelwood worked stints at a couple of branches of Terroirs before taking over these former Green & Blue wine bar premises. With manager Alex Thorp, he has transformed a once quiet venue into a buzzing neighbourhood bistro that's already a local sensation. In a typical dish, fresh English peas were dressed with garlic butter and topped with raw egg yolk drizzled with lemon

Toasted

oil, then garnished with toasted almond – the result was dramatically colourful and savoury. Raw mackerel was soused with manzanilla sherry and white soy sauce, and topped with salmon roe, enhancing the Japanese effect. Finely diced tartare used rose veal sirloin, instead of tenderloin, for a chewier, more flavourful taste. A dish of roasted carrots topped with lardo and garnished with golden raisins was a bit so-what, but dessert showed a return to form with custard-like rice milk studded with prunes and white peach. We tried a few wines by the glass, and can recommend the inexpensive ones on tap from the stainless-steel dispensing tanks – £3 for a great southern Rhône blend is a steal. But swirl and sniff first, before committing to any of the fancier natural wines that are a speciality here.

Babies and children welcome: high chairs; nappy-changing facilities. Booking advisable dinner. Disabled: toilet. **Map 23 4C**.

East
Shoreditch

Sager & Wilde NEW
193 Hackney Road, E2 8JL (no phone, www.sagerandwilde.com). Hoxton rail.
Open 5-11pm Wed-Sat; 2-11pm Sun. **Meals served** 5-10.30pm Wed-Sat; 2-10.30pm Sun. **Dishes** £7.50-£10. **Credit** AmEx, MC, V.
A new wine bar is one of the surest signs of gentrification of any neighbourhood. Sager & Wilde makes a clear statement of intent with its metropolitan good looks, its reclaimed German station lights, its cast-iron grating bar, and walls that are Pantone-matched. Michael and Charlotte Sager-Wilde recently ran a pop-up wine bar in Shoreditch and, encouraged by that success, have opened their own place. It's unapologetically wine-led, with good bar snacks (cheese from Androuet, salami from Picco) an afterthought. A score of excellent wines are sold by the glass or bottle (mark-ups tend towards three-fold). A Basque txakoli – edgy, slightly spritzy, and bone-dry – vies for your attention with a fruitier, more voluptuous riesling

from the Mosel. There's a toasty sparkler from Kent (from Sugrue Pierre), and a loud and proud Californian (the Ridge Santa Cruz). There is Sancerre and Chablis, champagne and Bordeaux on this list, for the City folk passing through. But there's also a quartet of vermouths to consider fortifying yourself with, and bottles of Five Points' excellent beers, all the way from Hackney.
Available for hire. Babies and children welcome: high chairs. Disabled: toilet. Takeaway service. **Map 6 S3**.

Wapping

Victualler NEW
69 Garnet Street, E1W 3QS (7481 9694, http://victualler.co.uk). Wapping rail. **Open/snacks served** 2-10.45pm daily. **Snacks** £2-£15. **House wine** from £22.99 bottle, £4 glass. **Credit** MC, V.
A narrow residential street in Wapping is perhaps not the most obvious location for the brave new venture that is Daniil Vashchilov's natural, organic and biodynamic wine bar and shop. Then again, locals clearly appreciate quirky quality and are prepared to pay for the privilege. There's a good deal that is quirky about this reclaimed pub, aside from the motley assortment of wooden tables, chairs and sink-in sofas. One such element is the determined focus on British and even local-to-London produce; another is the purist approach to wine (and beer). But perhaps the least usual and most welcome aspect is the friendly, enthusiastic and hugely informative engagement with customers: order just a glass of something unfamiliar and you'll be given a taster; express enthusiasm and a number of corks will be popped and the pedigree of each wine laid bare. The food too – simple platters of cheese and charcuterie in prime condition, with carefully selected accompaniments – is provenance-identified with pride. On our visit, beef strips, cured in-house and still pink and tender, proved a cleverly conceived partner to richly fruity Morgon and a contrasting Gamay de Chaudenay, its choucroute notes indicative of 'natural' wine making. The list changes constantly, so there's plenty to keep local palates refreshed, and much that would reward a speculative excursion.

Available for hire. Babies and children welcome until 7pm. Disabled: toilet. Separate room for parties, seats 30.

North East
Hackney

L'Entrepôt
230 Dalston Lane, E8 1LA (7249 1176, www.boroughwines.co.uk). Hackney Downs rail.
Open 1-11pm Mon-Fri; 11am-11pm Sat, Sun. **Lunch served** 11am-4pm Sat, Sun. **Dinner served** 6-10.30pm Mon-Sat. **Main courses** £13-£15. **House wine** £14 bottle, £3 glass. **Credit** MC, V.
L'Entrepôt is much better than it looks. Which isn't to say that this eastern outpost of Borough Wines doesn't look promising: it does, with its shabby industrial chic, and wine for sale from the barrel and bottle. On weekdays, the kitchen is open only in the evening (grazing aside), and Saturdays and Sundays focus on brunch; add the fact that the group is best known as a small, fiercely independent wine merchant and you would be forgiven for assuming the food was merely a bolt-on. Wrong. From interesting egg dishes to a three-course rotisserie menu, via a few French and Modern Euro bistro dishes, the kitchen staff know how to put an appealing menu together and deliver it to restaurant standards. Eggs benedict was so perfectly judged that we regretted not trying the oeufs en meurette (in red wine). Mallard breast with beetroot and potato gratin was flavour-packed; chips, bread and butter were, importantly, spot-on. The wine list, sourced directly by Borough, is predominantly French and Spanish, with recognised appellations complemented by more off-piste bottles that the staff are delighted to contextualise – the seldom-found aramon grape in a sulphur-free Coteaux d'Ensérune from Languedoc did indeed deliver Rhône-like depth. A slightly older, laid-back Dalston crowd have adopted the place as their hangout.
Available for hire. Babies and children welcome: high chairs. Tables outdoors (9, terrace).

Sager & Wilde

Maps & Indexes

The following maps highlight London's key restaurant areas: the districts with the highest density of good places to eat and drink. They show precisely where each restaurant is located, as well as major landmarks and tube stations.

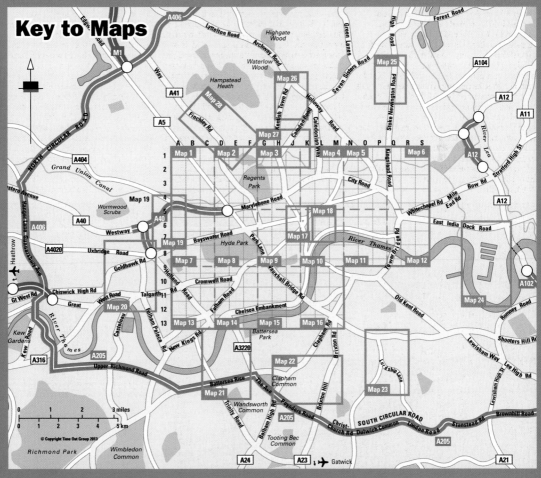

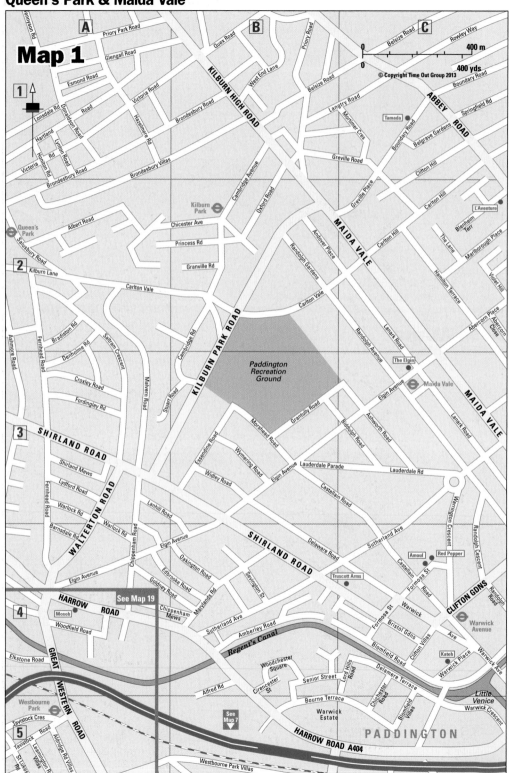

Map 1

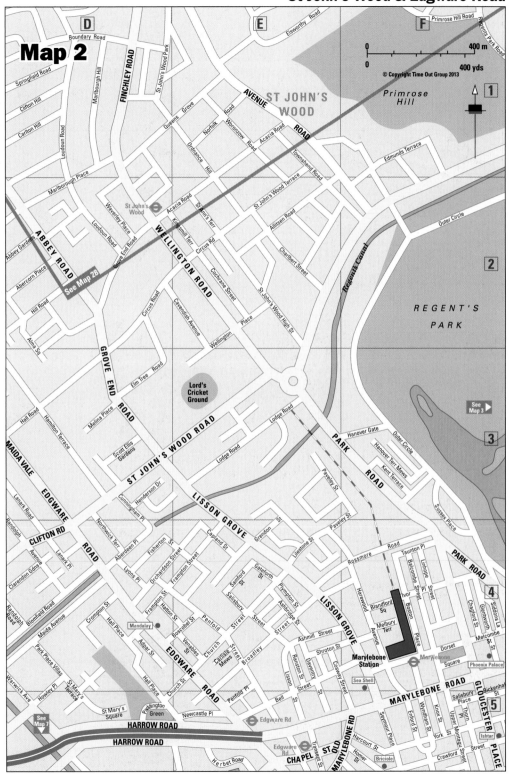

Map 2

Map 3

MAPS

Primrose Hill

London Zoo

See Map 27

0   400 m
0   400 yds
© Copyright Time Out Group 2013

REGENT'S PARK

Boating

Open Air Theatre

Queen Mary's Gardens

See Map 2

Regent's College

Inner Circle

Chester Walk

Broad Walk

Outer Circle

Chester Gate

Royal College of Physicians

St Andrew's Place

Park Sq Gardens

Regent's Park

York Terrace East

Ulster Pl

Park Sq West

Park Sq Mews

Park Sq East

Peto Pl

Longford St

Gt Portland Street

York Terrace

Madame Tussaud's

Royal Academy of Music

London Planetarium

MARYLEBONE ROAD

Baker Street

University of Westminster

Porter St

Chiltern St

Nottingham St

Bingham Pl

Luxborough Street

Oldbury Pl

Marylebone High St

Nottingham St

Devonshire Place

Devonshire Street

Devonshire Mews West

Devonshire Mews Sth

Harley Street

Upr Wimpole St

Wimpole St

Wimpole Mews

Mews W

Weymouth Mews

Weymouth St

New Cavendish Street

Duchess Street

PORTLAND PLACE

GREAT PORTLAND STREET

Hallam St

Bolsover St

Carburton St

Clipstone St

Clipstone Mews

RIBA

Villandry

Great Titchfield St

Cleveland Street

Maple St

University of Westminster

Middlesex Hospital

Telecom Tower

Tottenham St

Howland St

Chitty St

Dabbous

University College London

India YMCA

Sardo

TOTTENHAM COURT ROAD

Grafton Way

University

Gower St

Whitfield Street

Fitzroy St

Warren St

Conway St

Fitzroy Sq

Honey & Co

Greenwell St

Bolsover St

Stanhope St

Robert Street

Clarence Gardens

William Road

Munster Square

Triton Square

Cumberland Market

Varndell Street

Nash St

Little Albany St

Redhill Street

Augustus Street

ALBANY STREET

Cumberland Terrace

Outer Circle

Regent's Park Barracks

ALBANY STREET

PARK CRES

PARK CRES

Euston Square

Warren Street

Euston Road

Warren St

Beaumont

Drummond St

Euston Station

Stephenson Way

Cobourg St

Drummond St

Starcross St

North Gower St

Shiori

Eversholt St

EVERSHOLT STREET

OAKLEY SQ

Oakley Sq

Harrington Sq

Lidlington Place

Barnby Street

Cardington St

EUSTON ROAD

Euston St

University College Hospital

PRINCE ALBERT ROAD

PRINCE ALBERT ROAD

Outer Circle

Gloucester Gate

Park Village East

Park Village West

York & Albany

DELANCEY STREET

Mornington Terrace

Mornington Street

Mornington Crescent

Mornington Place

Mornington Cres

El Parador

Asakusa

CROWNDALE RD

Harrington Square

Granby Terrace

Barnby Street

Hampstead Road

HAMPSTEAD ROAD

PARKWAY

Market

Namaaste Kitchen

Shimogamo

Albert St

Arlington Road

Blues Kitchen

Plender Street

Pratt Street

Bayham Street

Jazz Café

Camden Town

Buck St

Greenland Road

Greenland St

Mango Room

Inverness Street

Gloucester Crescent

Gloucester Ave

St Marks Crescent

Regents Park Road

Jamestown Rd

Arlington Rd

Oval Road

Park Village

CAMDEN HIGH ST

HIGH STREET

CAMDEN STREET

CAMDEN RD

Pratt Street

College Place

Mandela Street

College St

Bayham Place

ROYAL COLLEGE ST

Lyme Street

Prince Albert

Georgiana St

Geogiana St

CAMDEN TOWN

KENTISH TOWN RD

Camden Rd

Chalcot Road

L'Absinthe

La Collina

Regents Park Road

Fitzroy Rd

Princess Road

St Marks Crescent

Gloucester Avenue

York Terrace West

Marylebone High St

MARYLEBONE

PADDINGTON ST

The Real Greek

La Fromagerie

Ashford Pl

Moxon St

Aybrook St

Cramer St

Reubens

Dorset St

Montagu Mansions

Montagu Mews

Kenrick Pl

BAKER STREET

Blandford St

Chiltern St

Cutidie

Orrery

Paddington St

Beaumont Mews

Beaumont St

Devonshire St

Ogle St

Cleveland St

Maple St

Conway St

Grafton Way

Charlotte St

Goodge St

Gosfield St

Riding House St

Hanson St

Foley St

See Map 9

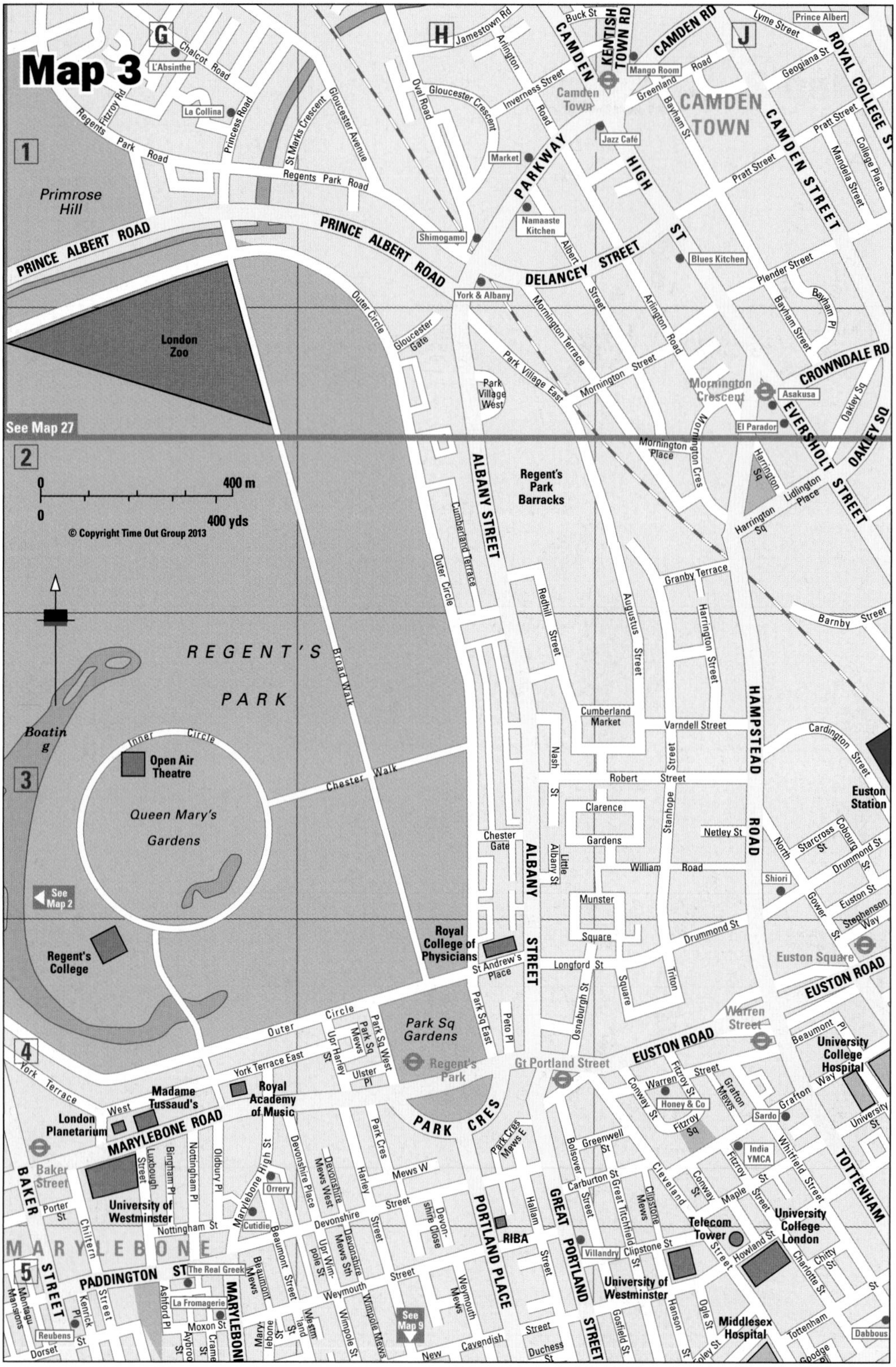

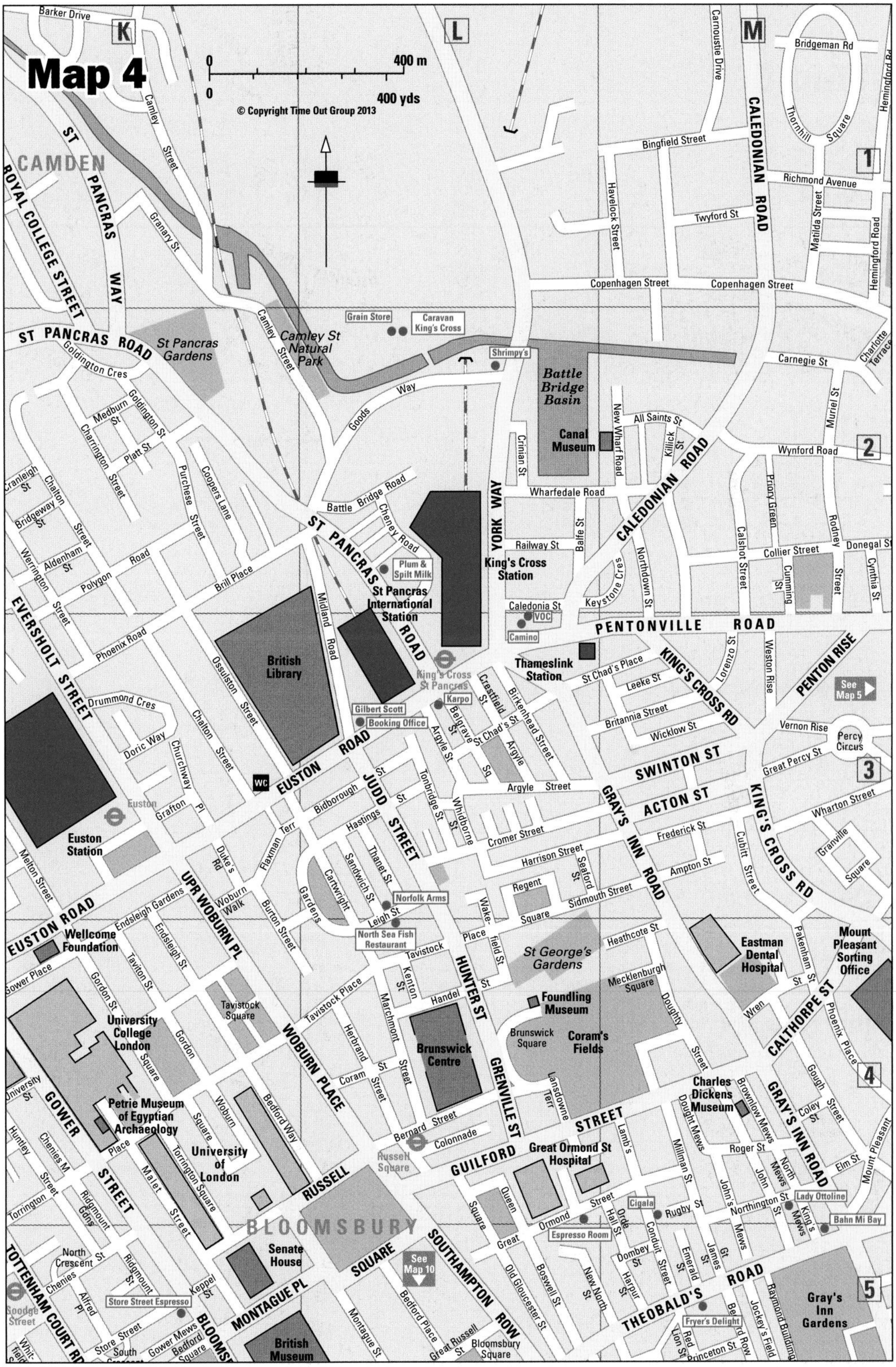

Map 4

Barker Drive

K

L

M

Bridgeman Rd

400 m

0

0

400 yds

© Copyright Time Out Group 2013

CAMDEN

Carnoustie Drive

Thornhill St

Hemingford Rd

CALEDONIAN ROAD

Richmond Avenue

1

Matilda St

Hemingford Road

Charlotte Terrace

ST PANCRAS WAY

ROYAL COLLEGE STREET

Camley Street

Granary St

Bingfield Street

Havelock Street

Twyford St

Copenhagen Street

Copenhagen Street

ST PANCRAS ROAD

St Pancras Gardens

Camley St Natural Park

Camley Street

Grain Store

Caravan King's Cross

Shrimpy's

Carnegie St

Muriel St

Goldington Cres

Goldington St

Medburn St

Platt St

Charrington Street

Way

Goods

Way

Battle Bridge Road

Battle Bridge Basin

Canal Museum

New Wharf Road

All Saints St

Killick St

Priory Green

Wynford Road

2

Rodney St

Donegal St

Cranleigh St

Chalton St

Bridgeway St

Aldenham St

Polygon Road

Werrington Street

Cooper's Lane

Purchese Street

Brill Place

St Pancras

Crinan St

Balfe St

Wharfedale Road

CALEDONIAN ROAD

Caledonia St

Collier Street

Cumming St

Cynthia St

EVERSHOLT STREET

Phoenix Road

Drummond Cres

Doric Way

Churchway

Chalton Street

Ossulston Street

Midland Road

ST PANCRAS ROAD

Plum & Spilt Milk

St Pancras International Station

King's Cross Station

YORK WAY

Railway St

Northdown St

Keystone Cres

PENTONVILLE ROAD

Weston St

PENTON RISE

British Library

King's Cross St Pancras

Thameslink Station

Camino

VOC

St Chad's Place

Leeke St

Britannia Street

Wicklow St

KING'S CROSS RD

Vernon Rise

Great Percy St

Percy Circus

3

Gilbert Scott

Booking Office

Karpo

Belgrave St

St Chad's St

Argyle St

SWINTON ST

ACTON ST

Wharton Street

Euston

Grafton

EUSTON ROAD

WC

JUDD STREET

Bidborough St

Tonbridge St

Argyle

Argyle Street

Street

GRAY'S INN ROAD

Cubitt Street

Granville Square

KING'S CROSS RD

Euston Station

Melton Street

Hastings

Flaxman Terr

Cartwright

Thanet St

Sandwich St

Cromer Street

Harrison Street

Regent

Square

Frederick St

Seaford

Sidmouth St

Ampton St

Wren

EUSTON ROAD

Wellcome Foundation

UPR WOBURN PL

Endsleigh Gardens

Endsleigh St

Gordon

Duke's Rd

Woburn Walk

Burton Street

Gardens

Leigh St

Norfolk Arms

North Sea Fish Restaurant

Tavistock

Place

Kenton

St George's Gardens

Mecklenburgh Square

Heathcote St

Doughty

Eastman Dental Hospital

Pakenham St

Mount Pleasant Sorting Office

CALTHORPE ST

Sower Place

University College London

Gordon St

Tavistock Square

WOBURN PLACE

Tavistock Place

Marchmont

Handel

St

HUNTER ST

Foundling Museum

Brunswick Square

Coram's Fields

Lansdowne Terr

Millman St

Roger St

Brownlow Mews

John St

GRAY'S INN ROAD

4

GOWER STREET

Petrie Museum of Egyptian Archaeology

Torrington Place

University of London

Woburn Square

Bedford Way

Coram

St

Brunswick Centre

GRENVILLE ST

Bernard Street

Colonnade

GUILFORD STREET

Great Ormond St Hospital

Lamb's Conduit St

Doughty Mews

North Mews

John's Mews

Gough Square

Elm Sq

Mount Pleasant

Huntley St

Chenies M

Malet

Ridgmount

Torrington Square

RUSSELL

Russell Square

Queen

Square

Old Gloucester St

Great James St

Emerald St

King's Mews

Lady Ottoline

Bahn Mi Bay

BLOOMSBURY

Senate House

RUSSELL SQUARE

SOUTHAMPTON ROW

Colonnade

Cigala

Espresso Room

Rugby

John's St

Northington St

John St

GRAY'S INN ROAD

North Crescent

Chenies

Alfred

Ridgmount

Keppel St

MONTAGUE PL

Montague Street

See Map 10

Bedford Place

Great Russell St

Bloomsbury Square

THEOBALD'S ROAD

Fryer's Delight

Gray's Inn Gardens

5

TOTTENHAM COURT RD

Store Street Espresso

Gower Mews

BLOOMSBURY

Store Street

Bedford Ave

Bedford Square

MONTAGUE ST

British Museum

See Map 5

MAPS

Islington, Clerkenwell & Farringdon

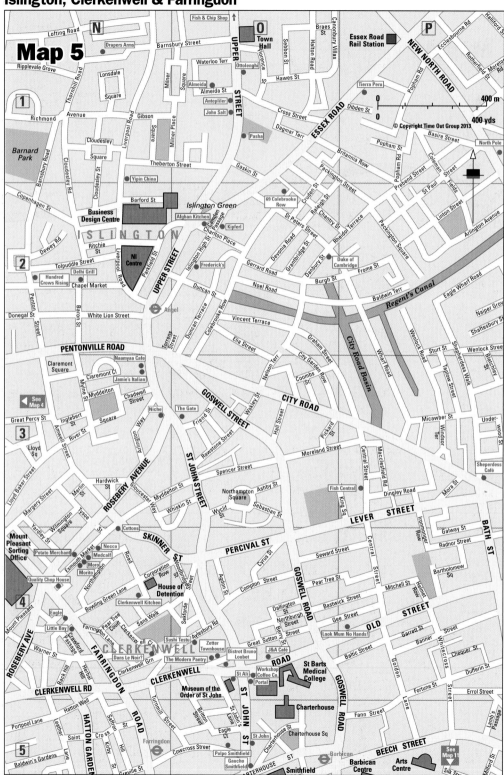

Map 5

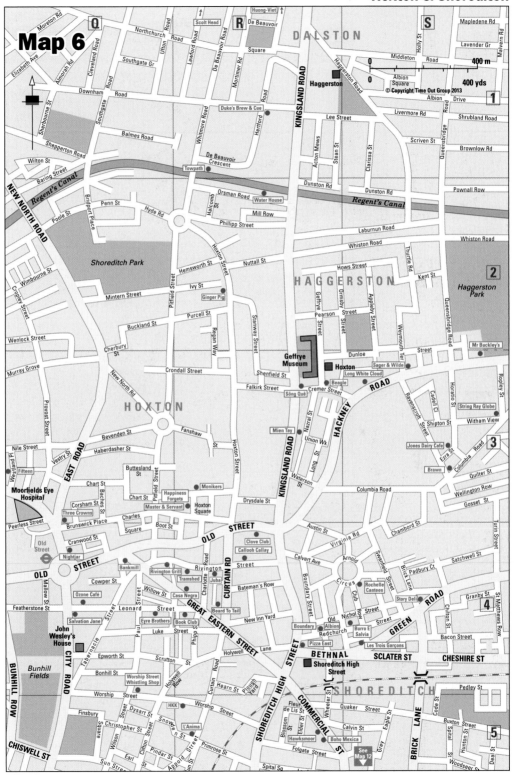

MAPS

Notting Hill, Bayswater & Kensington

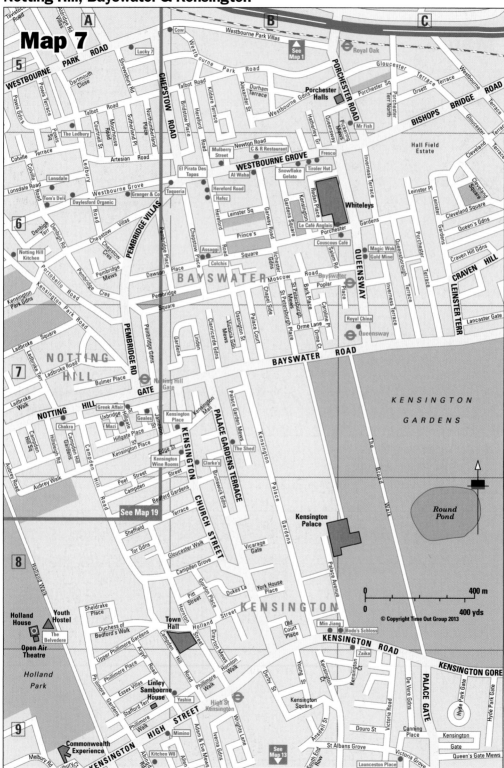

Map 7

MAPS

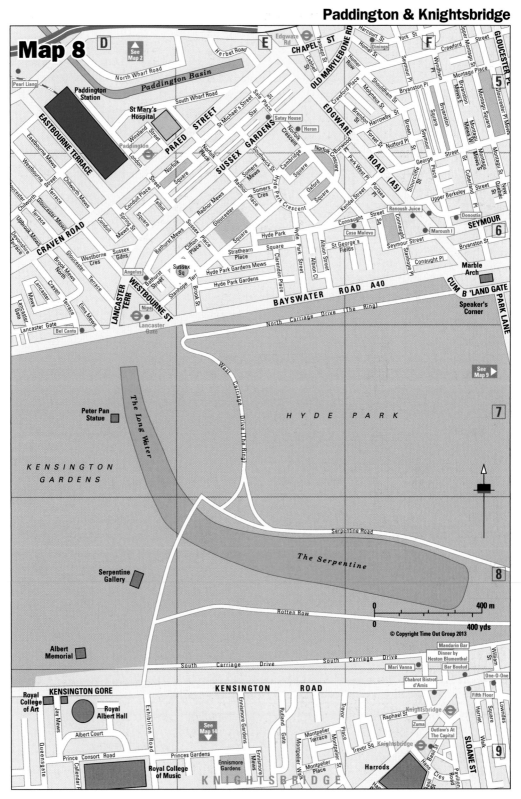

Map 8

KENSINGTON GARDENS

HYDE PARK

The Long Water

The Serpentine

KNIGHTSBRIDGE

Marylebone, Fitzrovia, Mayfair & St James's

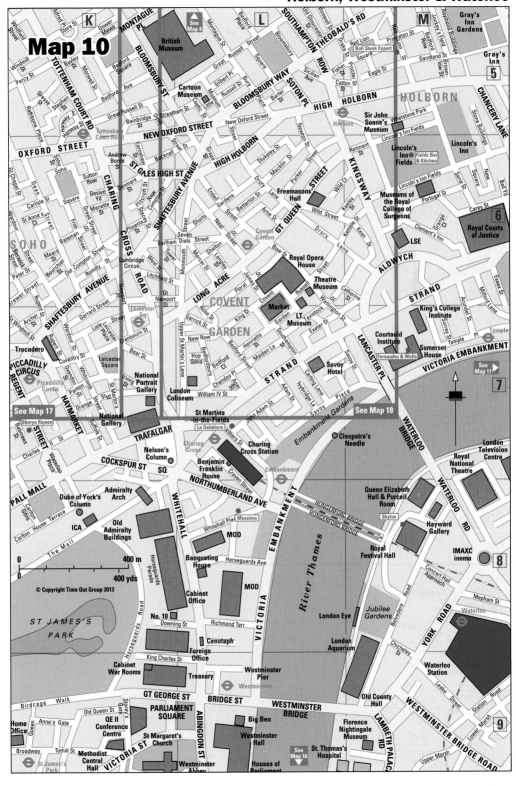

MAPS

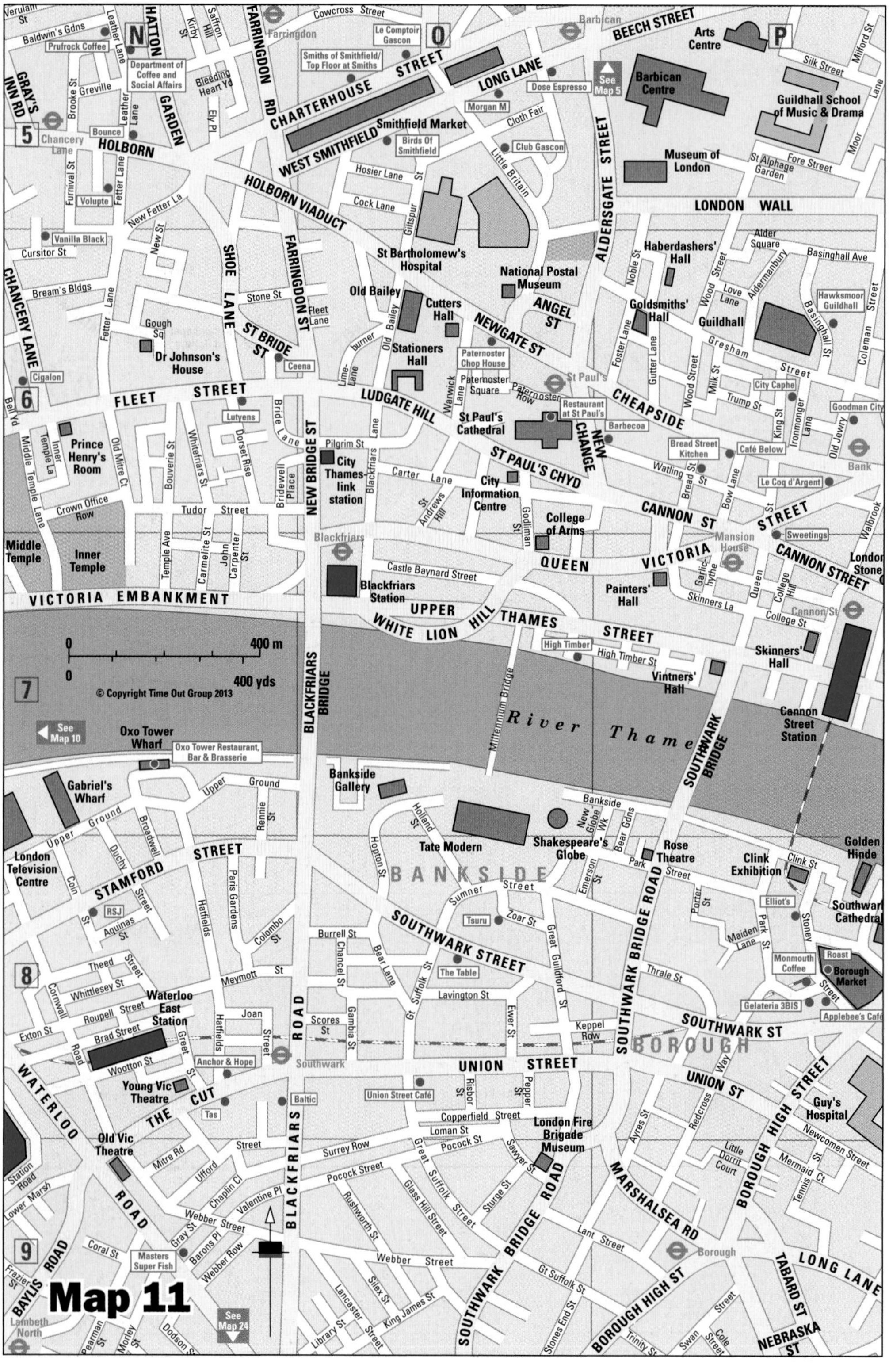

Verulam St · Baldwin's Gdns · Leather Lane · Kirby St · Saffron Hill · FARRINGDON · Farringdon · Cowcross Street · Le Comptoir Gascon · Barbican · BEECH STREET · Arts Centre · P · Silk Street · Milford Lane

Prufrock Coffee · Department of Coffee and Social Affairs · Bleeding Heart Yd · Smiths of Smithfield/Top Floor at Smiths · CHARTERHOUSE STREET · LONG LANE · Dose Espresso · See Map 5 · Barbican Centre · Guildhall School of Music & Drama · Moor Lane

GRAY'S INN RD · Brooke St · Greville · Leather Lane · Ely Pl · WEST SMITHFIELD · Smithfield Market · Morgan M · Cloth Fair · Club Gascon · Museum of London · Fore Street · St Alphage Garden

5 · Chancery Lane · Bounce · HOLBORN · GARDEN · Birds Of Smithfield · Alder Square · Basinghall Ave

Furnival St · Fetter Lane · New St · Hosier Lane · Little Britain · Haberdashers' Hall · Noble St · Wood Street · Love Lane · Aldermanbury · Hawksmoor Guildhall

Volute · HOLBORN VIADUCT · Cock Lane · Giltspur · St Bartholomew's Hospital · LONDON WALL · Goldsmiths' Hall · Guildhall · Basinghall Street · Coleman

Vanilla Black · Cursitor St · FARRINGDON STREET · Fleet Lane · Old Bailey · National Postal Museum · Gresham · Milk St · City Cache

Bream's Bldgs · Stone St · SHOE LANE · Cutters Hall · ANGEL ST · Foster Lane · Gutter Lane · Wood Street · Trump St · Ironmonger · Goodman City

CHANCERY LANE · Gough Sq · ST BRIDE ST · Ceena · NEWGATE ST · Stationers Hall · Paternoster Chop House · St Paul's · CHEAPSIDE · Old Jewry · Bank

6 · Cigalon · Dr Johnson's House · Fleet Lane · Paternoster Square · Restaurant at St Paul's · Barbecoa · Bread Street Kitchen · Café Below · Le Coq d'Argent

FLEET STREET · Lutyens · LUDGATE HILL · Warwick · St Paul's Cathedral · ST PAUL'S CHYD · NEW CHANGE · Watling · Bow Lane

Prince Henry's Room · Pilgrim St · City Thameslink station · Carter Lane · ST PAUL'S CHYD · City Information Centre · College of Arms · CANNON ST · Mansion House · Sweetings · London Stone

Middle Temple · Inner Temple · Crown Office Row · Tudor Street · John Carpenter St · Blackfriars Station · Castle Baynard Street · QUEEN · VICTORIA · Painters' Hall · Skinners La · CANNON STREET · Walbrook

VICTORIA EMBANKMENT · NEW BRIDGE ST · BLACKFRIARS BRIDGE · UPPER · WHITE LION HILL · THAMES · STREET · High Timber · Vintners' Hall · Skinners' Hall · College Hill · Cannon St · Cannon Street Station

0 — 400 m
0 — 400 yds
© Copyright Time Out Group 2013

7 · See Map 10 · Oxo Tower Wharf · Oxo Tower Restaurant, Bar & Brasserie · River Thames · SOUTHWARK BRIDGE

Gabriel's Wharf · Upper Ground · Rennie St · Bankside Gallery · Bankside · New Globe · Rose Theatre · Clink Exhibition · Clink St · Golden Hinde

London Television Centre · Coin St · STAMFORD STREET · Paris Gardens · Colombo St · Tate Modern · Shakespeare's Globe · Park St · SOUTHWARK BRIDGE ROAD · Elliot's · Southwark Cathedral

8 · RSJ · Aquinas St · Hatfields · Burrell St · Chancel St · BANKSIDE · Sumner Street · Tsuru · Zoar St · Great Guildford St · Maiden Lane · Stoney · Monmouth Coffee · Roast

Theed · Whittlesey Street · Meymott · Bear Lane · SOUTHWARK STREET · The Table · Lavington St · Ewer St · Keppel Row · Gelateria 3BIS · Borough Market · Applebee's Café

Cornwall · Roupell Street · Brad Street · Waterloo East Station · Joan Street · Anchor & Hope · Southwark · Risbor · UNION STREET · SOUTHWARK ST · BOROUGH · Guy's Hospital

Exton St · Wootton St · THE CUT · Baltic · Union Street Café · Copperfield Street · London Fire Brigade Museum · UNION ST · BOROUGH HIGH STREET · Newcomen Street · Mermaid Ct

WATERLOO ROAD · Young Vic Theatre · Tas · Loman St · Pocock St · Sawyer St · MARSHALSEA RD · Little Dorrit Court · Tennis St

Old Vic Theatre · Mitre Rd · Surrey Row · Pocock Street · Glass Hill St · BLACKFRIARS ROAD · Gt Suffolk St · Lant Street · Swan

9 · BAYLIS ROAD · Station Road · Lower Marsh · Ufford St · Chaplin Cl · Valentine Pl · Webber Street · Barons Pl · Grey St · Webber Row · SOUTHWARK BRIDGE ROAD · Webber Street · BOROUGH HIGH ST · LONG LANE · TABARD ST · NEBRASKA ST

Coral St · Masters Super Fish · Lancaster St · Sturge St · Library Street · King James St · Trinity St · Cole Street

Map 11

See Map 24 · Lambeth North · Frazier St

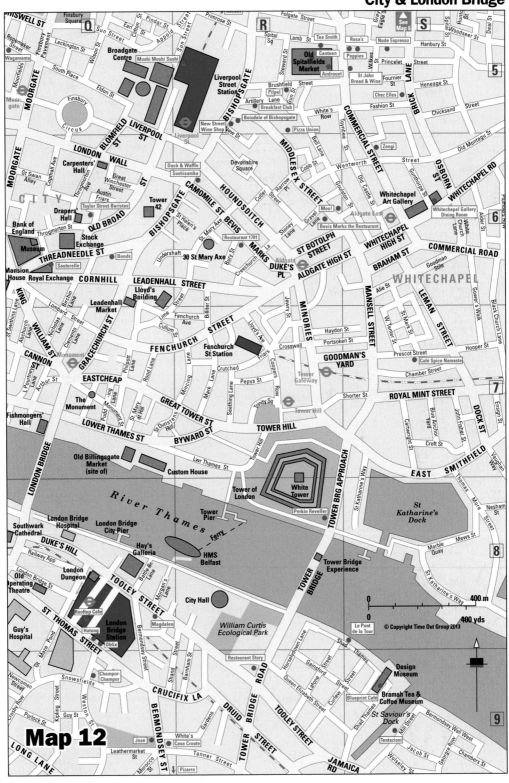

Map 12

Earl's Court, Gloucester Road & Fulham

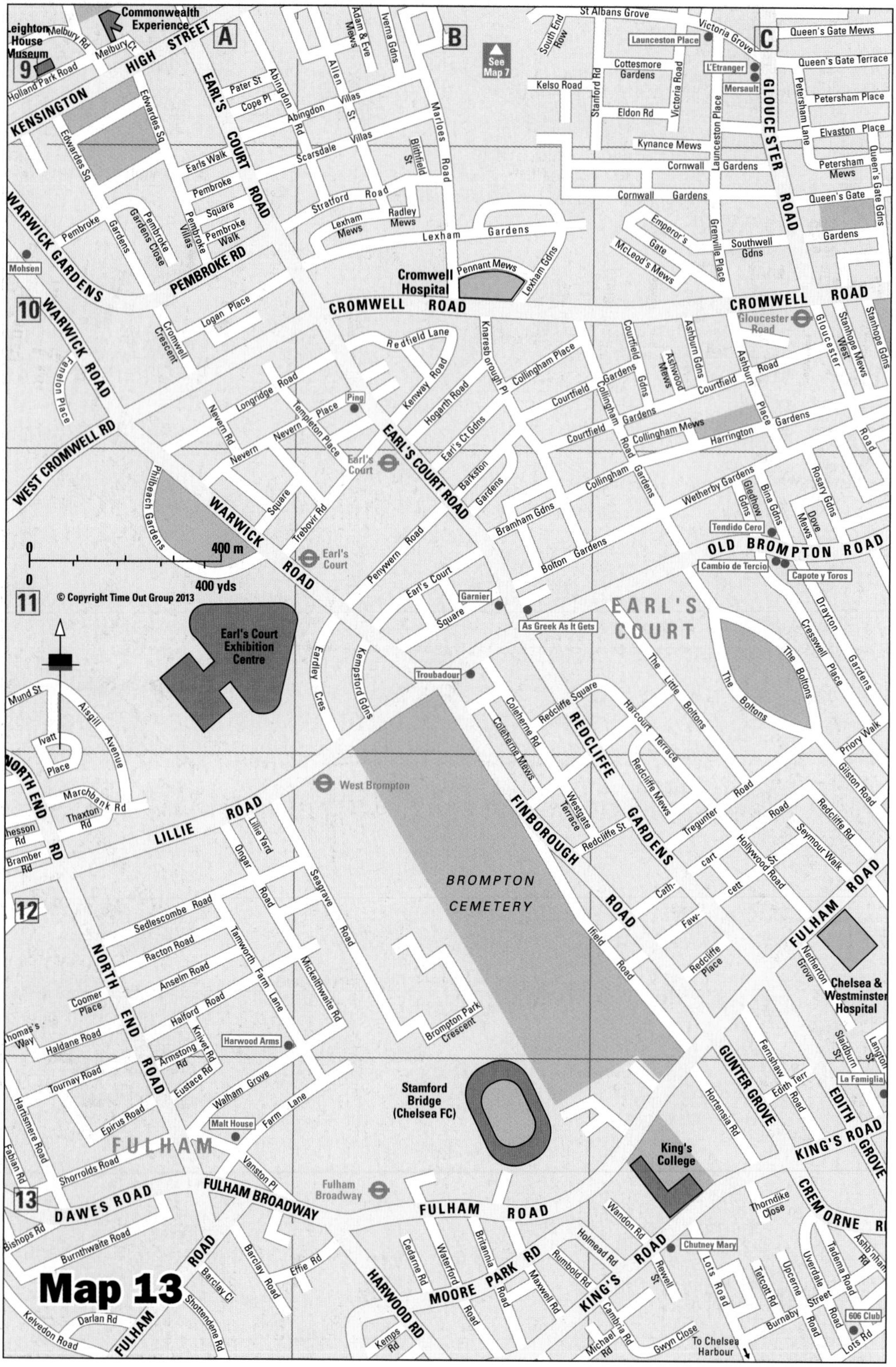

MAPS

Commonwealth
Experience

Leighton
House
Museum
9

Melbury Rd
Melbury Rd

Holland Park Road

KENSINGTON

HIGH STREET

A

B

See
Map 7

St Albans Grove

South End Row

Launceston Place

Victoria Grove

Queen's Gate Mews

C

Queen's Gate Terrace

L'Etranger

Mersault

GLOUCESTER ROAD

Petersham Place

EARL'S COURT ROAD

Pater St

Cope Pl

Abingdon Rd

Adam & Eve
Mews

Nevern Gdns

Kelso Road

Cottesmore
Gardens

Stanford Rd

Launceston Place

Elvaston Place

Petersham
Mews

WARWICK GARDENS

Edwardes Sq

Abingdon
Villas

Scarsdale
Villas

Marloes Road

Blithfield
St

Eldon Rd

Victoria Road

Kynance Mews

Petersham Lane

Queen's Gate Gdns

Earls Walk

Pembroke
Square

Pembroke
Villas

Pembroke
Walk

Stratford Road

Lexham
Mews

Radley
Mews

Lexham Gardens

Cornwall

Gardens

Queen's Gate

Gardens

Mohsen

PEMBROKE RD

Pennant Mews

Lexham Gdns

Emperor's
Gate

Greenville Place

McLeod's Mews

Southwell
Gdns

10

Logan Place

Cromwell Crescent

CROMWELL ROAD

Cromwell
Hospital

CROMWELL ROAD

Gloucester
Road

Gloucester
Road

Stanhope Mews

Stanhope Gdns

WARWICK ROAD

Nevern Place

Redfield Lane

Knaresborough Pl

Collingham Place

Courtfield Gdns

Ashburn Gdns

Ashburn
Place

Courtfield Road

Ashburn
Road

WEST CROMWELL RD

Longridge Road

Templeton Place

Ping

Kenway Road

Hogarth Road

Courtfield
Gardens

Collingham
Gardens

Ashwood
Mews

Courtfield

Gardens

Collingham Road

Harrington

Gardens

Rosary Gdns

Nevern Rd

Nevern
Square

EARL'S COURT ROAD

Earl's Court Gdns

Barkston
Gardens

Collingham Mews

Wetherby Gardens

Glendower Gdns

Bina Gdns

Dove Gdns

Earl's
Court

Penywern Road

WARWICK ROAD

Trebovir Rd

Philbeach Gardens

Earl's
Court

Bramham Gdns

Bolton Gardens

OLD BROMPTON ROAD

Tendido Cero

Cambio de Tercio

Capote y Toros

0 ———— 400 m

0 ———— 400 yds

© Copyright Time Out Group 2013

11

Eardley
Cres

Kempsford Gdns

Earl's Court
Square

Garnier

As Greek As It Gets

EARL'S
COURT

The Boltons

The Boltons

Cresswell Place

Drayton Gardens

Earl's Court
Exhibition
Centre

Troubadour

Coleherne Rd

Redcliffe Square

Harcourt Terrace

The Little Boltons

Priory Walk

Gilston Road

Mund St

Ivatt
Place

 Airsgill Avenue

West Brompton

Coleherne Mews

RED CLIFFE GARDENS

Westgate
Terrace

Redcliffe Mews

Tregunter Road

Redcliffe Rd

Seymour Walk

NORTH END RD

Marchbank Rd

Thaxton
Rd

LILLIE ROAD

Lillia Yard

Onger

FINBOROUGH ROAD

Redcliffe St

Hollywood Road

cart

cett

FULHAM ROAD

Nettleton Grove

Chesson
Rd

Bramber
Rd

12

Sedlescombe Road

Racton Road

Anselm Road

Tamworth Farm Lane

Mickelthwaite Rd

Sedgrave Road

BROMPTON
CEMETERY

Cath-

Faw-

Redcliffe
Place

Chelsea &
Westminster
Hospital

NORTH END ROAD

Coomer
Place

Halford Rd

Armstrong Rd

Haldane Road

Kneller Rd

Eustace Rd

Harwood Arms

Bramford Rd

Field Road

Fernshaw Road

Slaidburn St

Langton St

La Famiglia

thomas's
Way

Tournay Road

Epirus Road

Walham Grove

Walham
Farm Lane

Brompton Park
Crescent

Stamford
Bridge
(Chelsea FC)

King's
College

GUNTER GROVE

Edith Terr

KING'S ROAD

Hartsmere Road

Fabian Rd

Shorrolds Road

Malt House

Vanston Pl

FULHAM

FULHAM BROADWAY

Fulham
Broadway

FULHAM ROAD

Wandon Rd

Hortensia Rd

Chutney Mary

Thorndike
Close

EDITH GROVE

CREMORNE R

13

DAWES ROAD

Bishops Rd

Burnthwaite Road

FULHAM ROAD

Barclay Ci

Shottendene Rd

Effie Rd

HARWOOD RD

Cedarne Rd

Waterford Rd

MOORE PARK RD

Maxwell Rd

Rumbold Rd

Holmead Rd

Britannia Rd

KING'S ROAD

Lots Rd

Ashchurch

Uverdale Road

Upcerne Rd

Tadema Road

Tetcott Rd

Burnaby

606 Club

Lots Rd

Map 13

Darlan Rd

Kelvedon Road

FULHAM

Kemps
Rd

Michael
Rd

Gwyn Close

To Chelsea
Harbour

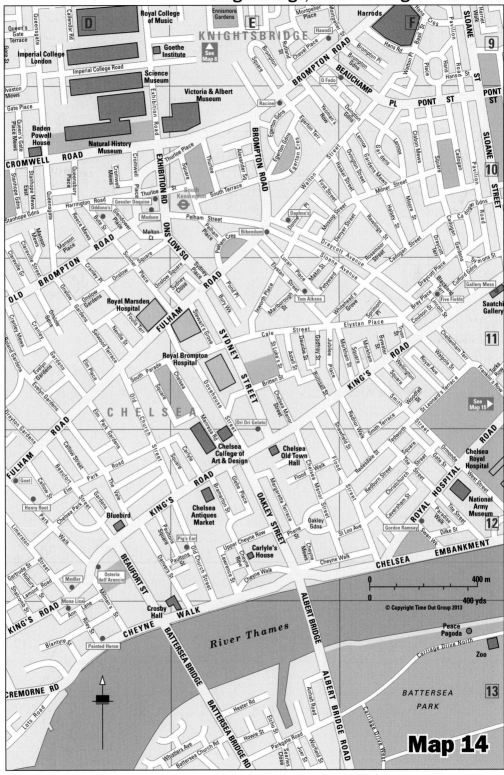

MAPS

Map 14

MAPS

Zafferano
Marcomb St
Halkin Place
9
Lowndes St
PONT ST
CHESHAM PL
Chesham St
Cadogan Lane
Cadogan Place
10
Ellis St
Wilbraham Pl
SLOANE SQ
Colbert
Sloane Square
LOWER SLOANE ST
11
Whittaker St
Holbein Mews
12

G
BELGRAVE SQUARE
See Map 9
Belgrave Place
Chapel Street
Groom Pl
Chester Street
Upper Belgrave Street
Wilton
Lowndes Place
Lyall Mews
Eaton Mews North
Lyall Street
Eaton Place
Eaton Square
Minera Mews
Eaton
Caroline Terr
Graham Terrace
Bourne Street
Passmore St
Holbein Place
Sloane Gdns
PIMLICO ROAD
Orange
Bloomf'd Terr
Hunan
Tinello
Barnabas St
Ranelagh Gr

BELGRAVE PL
ECCLESTON STREET
EATON SQUARE
HOBART PL
GROSVENOR PL
Belgrave Mews South
Wilton Mews
Little Chester
Chester Mews
Upper Belgrave Street
Eccleston Mews
Eaton Square
Chester Square
Eaton Mews West
Eaton Place
South Eaton Place
CLIVEDEN PLACE
EATON GATE
Chester Terrace
Gerald Rd
Elizabeth
Eaton Terrace
Row

BELGRAVIA

Royal Mews
H
GROSVENOR GDNS
LWR GROS PL
Victoria Square
Goring Hotel
Allington St
ENOR GDNS
GROSVENOR GDNS
Lower Belgrave
Street
Olivomare
Olivo
Eccleston Place
Eccleston Street
Eaton Square
Chester Square
Ebury Mews
Ebury
BUCKINGHAM PALACE ROAD
STREET
Elizabeth
Ebury
Street
Il Convivio
Victoria Coach Station
Semley Pl
Cundy St
Ebury
Elizabeth Br
High Street

BUCKINGHAM GATE
BRESSENDEN PL
Stag Place
Allington St
WILTON RD
Bridge Place
Victoria Station
Gillingham Street
Wilton Road
Guildhouse St
Longmoore St

J
Wellington Barracks
Petty France
BUCKINGHAM GATE
Vandon
Caxton St
Westminster City Hall
VICTORIA STREET
Howick Place
Thirleby Rd
Ambrosden Ave
ARTILLERY ROW
Westminster Cathedral
Morpeth Terr
Carlisle Place
Francis St
Stillington St
Willow Place
Greencoat Place
Vincent Sq
Vincent Rooms
Rochester Row
Vincent St
Old Royal Horticultural Society Hall
VAUXHALL
dim t
Rodizio Preto
A Wong
Kazan
Seafresh Fish Restaurant
BELGRAVE ROAD
Hatherley St
Stanford
BRIDGE ROAD
WARWICK WAY
Warwick Way
Eccleston Square
Eccleston
Warwick Square
St George's
Drive
Denbigh
Tachbrook Street
Charlwood Street
Moreton Place
Moreton Street

PIMLICO
PIMLICO
WARWICK WAY
Cambridge Street
George's Drive
Warwick Square
Alderney Street
Clarendon St
Winchester St
Cambridge St
Sussex St
Sutherland St
Cumberland St
Gloucester St
Charlwood St
Westmoreland Terrace
Peabody Ave
Lupus Street
Chichester St
Claverton Street

ROYAL HOSPITAL ROAD
CHELSEA BRIDGE ROAD
Gatliffe Rd
EBURY BRIDGE
EBURY BRIDGE ROAD
Churchill Gardens Road
Chelsea Royal Hospital
CHELSEA EMBANKMENT
CHELSEA BRIDGE
QUEENSTOWN ROAD
GROSVENOR ROAD
St George's Square

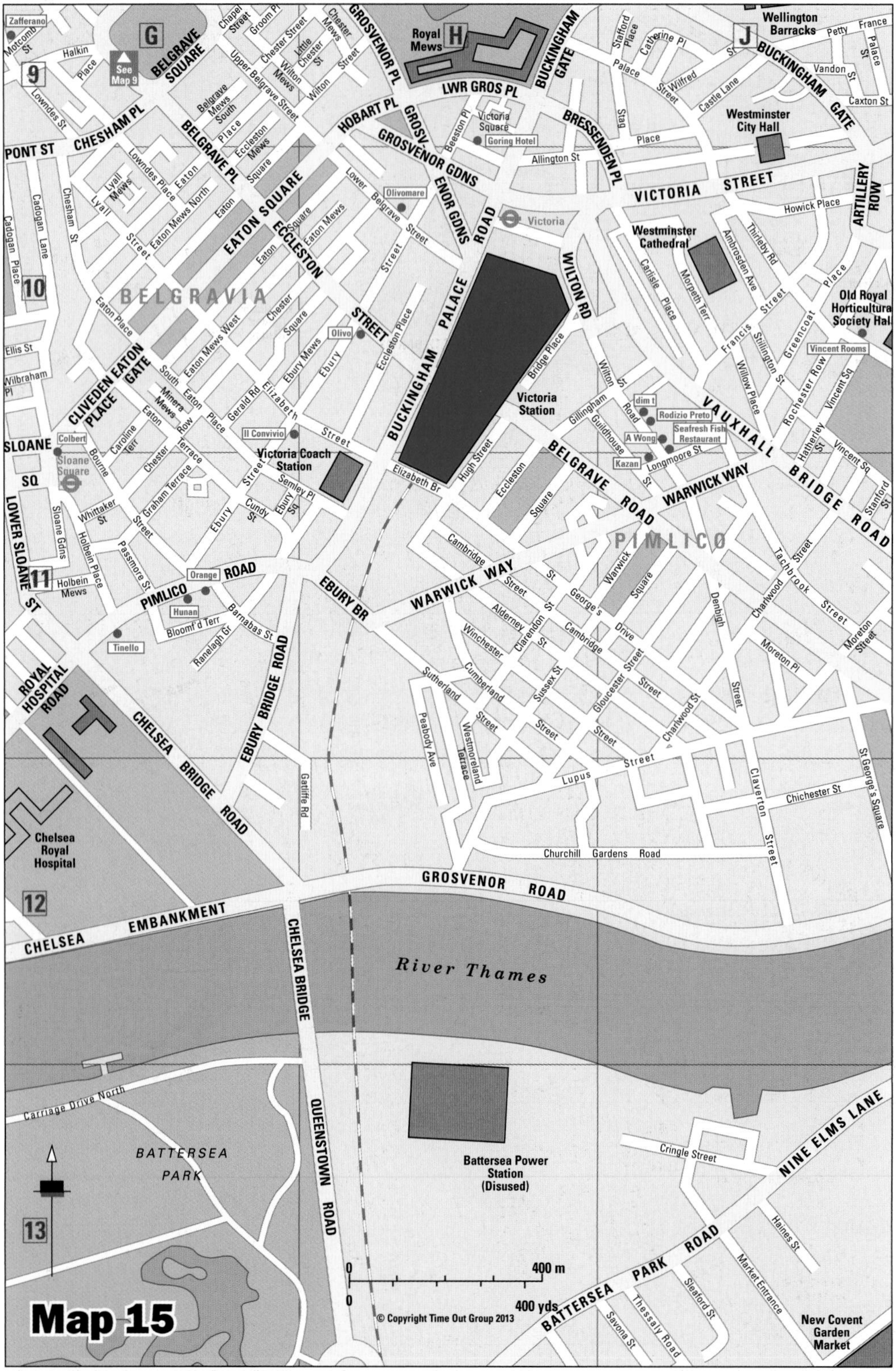

River Thames

13
Carriage Drive North
BATTERSEA PARK
Battersea Power Station (Disused)
Cringle Street
NINE ELMS LANE
BATTERSEA PARK ROAD
Market Entrance
Haines St
Stewart's Rd
Thessaly Road
Savona St
New Covent Garden Market

0   400 m
0   400 yds
© Copyright Time Out Group 2013

Map 15

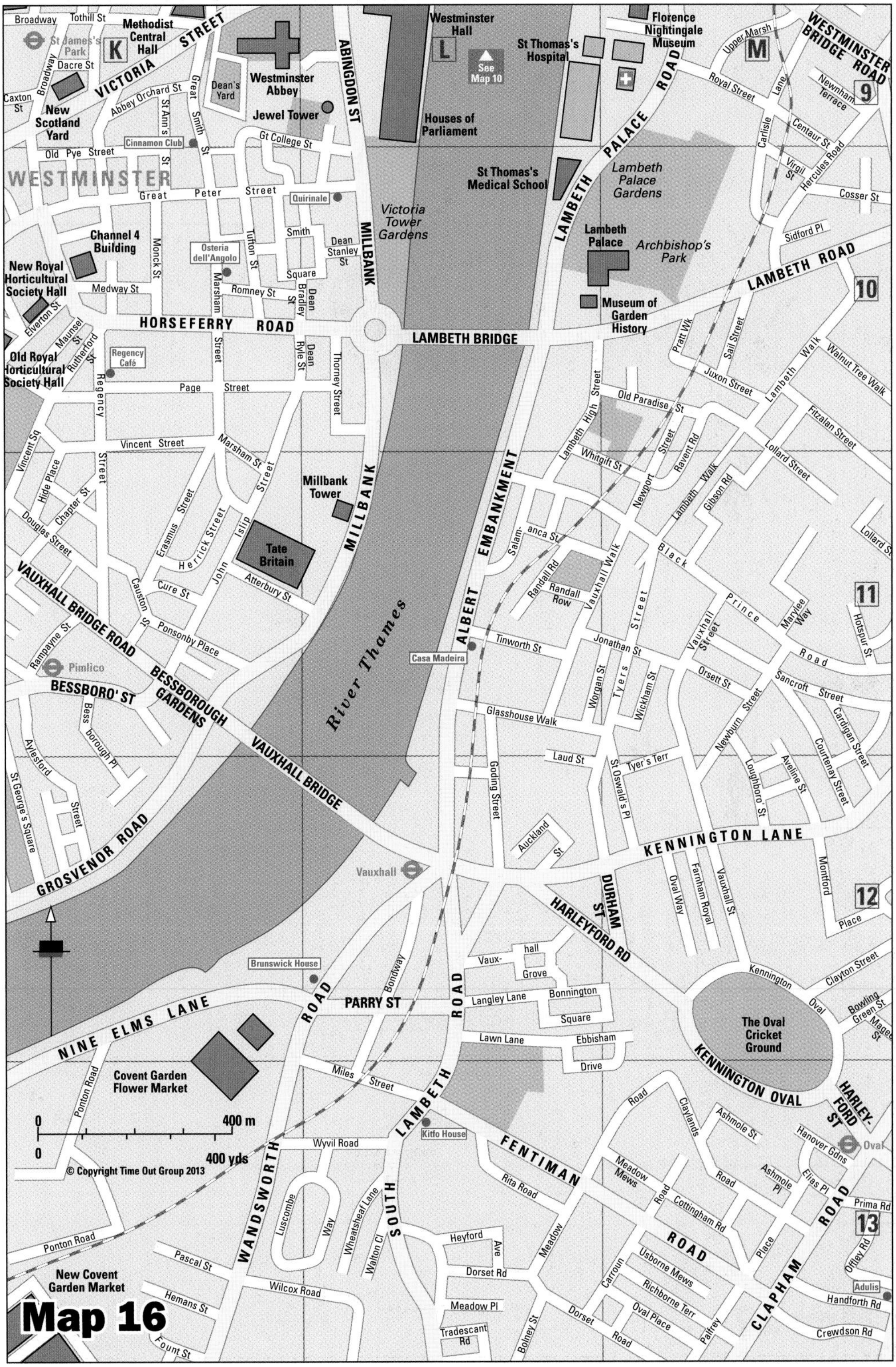

MAPS

Broadway Tothill St
St James's Park
Dacre St
K VICTORIA STREET
Methodist Central Hall
Caxton St
New Scotland Yard
Old Pye Street
Abbey Orchard St St Ann's Smith St
Great St
Dean's Yard
Westminster Abbey
Jewel Tower
Gt College St
Cinnamon Club
WESTMINSTER
Great Peter Street
Osteria dell'Angolo
Quirinale
Channel 4 Building
New Royal Horticultural Society Hall
Elverton St
Medway St
Monck St
Tufton St
Smith
Dean Stanley St
Square
Dean Bradley St
Romney St
Marsham
ABINGDON ST
Westminster Hall
L See Map 10
Houses of Parliament
St Thomas's Medical School
Victoria Tower Gardens
MILLBANK
Florence Nightingale Museum
St Thomas's Hospital
LAMBETH PALACE ROAD
Upper Marsh
M WESTMINSTER BRIDGE ROAD **9**
Newnham Terrace
Carlisle Lane
Royal Street
Centaur St
Virgil St Hercules Road
Cosser St
Lambeth Palace Gardens
Lambeth Palace
Archbishop's Park
Sidford Pl
LAMBETH ROAD **10**
Museum of Garden History
Old Royal Horticultural Society Hall
Mauself St
Regency
Rutherford St
Regency Café
HORSEFERRY ROAD
Page Street
Thorney Street
Dean Ryle St
LAMBETH BRIDGE
Pratt Wk
Sail Street
Lambeth Walk
Walnut Tree Walk
Fitzalan Street
Old Paradise St
Juxon Street
Vincent Sq
Hide Place
Chapter St
Vincent Street
Marsham St
Islip Street
John
Herrick Street
Erasmus St
Douglas Street
Ramsay St
Millbank Tower
Tate Britain
Atterbury St
Cure St
Caustoun St
Ponsonby Place
VAUXHALL BRIDGE ROAD
BESSBOROUGH GARDENS
Pimlico
BESSBORO' ST
Bessborough Pl
Aylesford Street
St George's Square
GROSVENOR ROAD
VAUXHALL BRIDGE
River Thames
Casa Madeira
Lambeth High Street
Whitgift St
Newport St
Ravent Rd
Randall Rd
Randall Row
ALBERT EMBANKMENT
Salamanca St
Tinworth St
Vauxhall Walk
Jonathan St
Morgan St
Black Prince Road
Gibson Rd
Vauxhall Street
Orsett St
Tyers Street
Wickham St
Newburn St
Lollard Street
11
Hotspur St
Mayflower Way
Sancroft Street
Cardigan Street
Courtenay Street
Aveline St
Loughboro St
Lollard St
Glasshouse Walk
Laud St
Tyer's Terr
St Oswald's Pl
Goding Street
Auckland St
Farnham Royal
Oval Way
Vauxhall St
KENNINGTON LANE
Momford
12 Place
Vauxhall
DURHAM ST
HARLEYFORD RD
Kennington Oval
Clayton Street
Bowling Green St Magee St
The Oval Cricket Ground
Brunswick House
Broadway
Vaux-hall Grove
Langley Lane
Bonnington Square
Ebbisham Drive
PARRY ST
Lawn Lane
Miles Street
WANDSWORTH ROAD
LAMBETH ROAD
SOUTH
Kitfo House
Wyvil Road
FENTIMAN ROAD
Rita Road
Meadow Mews
Cottingham Rd
KENNINGTON OVAL
Ashmole St
Claylands
Hanover Gdns
Elias Pl
Ashmole Pl
HARLEY-FORD ST
Oval
Prima Rd
13
Orsett Rd
Adulis
Handforth Rd
CLAPHAM ROAD
Crewdson Rd

0 ____ 400 m
0 ____ 400 yds
© Copyright Time Out Group 2013

Covent Garden Flower Market
NINE ELMS LANE
Ponton Road
New Covent Garden Market
Hemans St
Pascal St
Luscombe Way
Wheatsheaf Lane
Wilcox Road
Walton Cl
Meadow Pl
Heyford Ave
Dorset Rd
Tradescant Rd
Fount St
Bolney St
Meadow Road
Dorset Road
Carroun Road
Usborne Mews
Richborne Terr
Oval Place
Pelfrey

Map 16

Fitzrovia, Soho & Chinatown

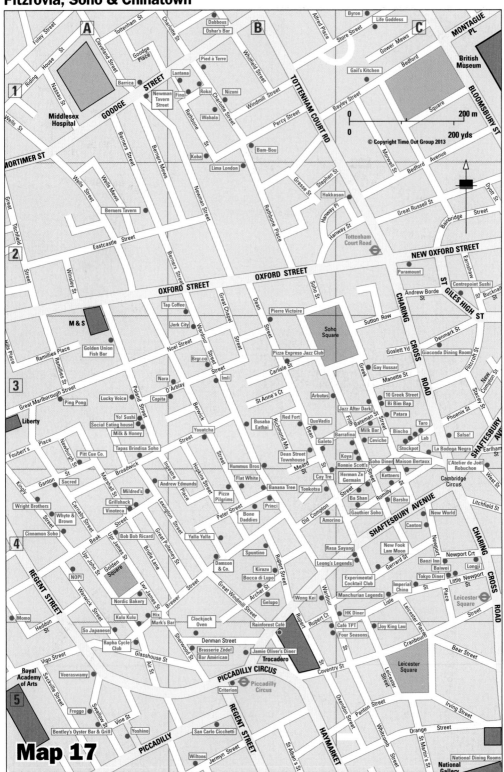

Map 17

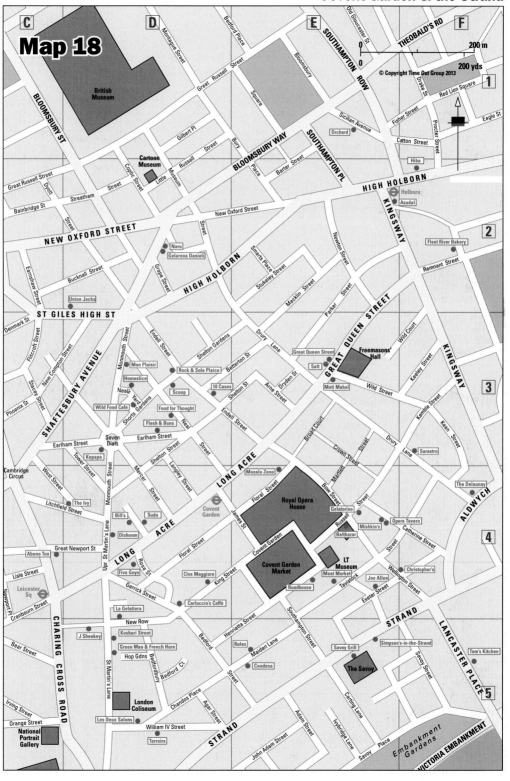

Map 18

C
D
E
F

SOUTHAMPTON ROW

THEOBALD'S RD

British Museum

BLOOMSBURY ST

Montague Street

Great Russell Street

Bedford Place

Bloomsbury

Square

Old Gloucester St

0   200 m
0   200 yds

© Copyright Time Out Group 2013

Drake St

Red Lion Square

1

Gilbert Pl

Coptic Street

Little

Russell

Street

Museum

Street

Bury

Place

Sicilian Avenue

Orchard

Fisher Street

Catton Street

Eagle St

Procter Street

Cartoon Museum

BLOOMSBURY WAY

Barter Street

SOUTHAMPTON PL

Hiba

Great Russell Street

Dyott

Street

Streatham

Street

Russell

Street

HIGH HOLBORN

KINGSWAY

Bainbridge St

New Oxford Street

Holborn

Asadal

2

NEW OXFORD STREET

Naru

Gelarena Danieli

HIGH HOLBORN

Smarts Place

Newton Street

Fleet River Bakery

Earnshaw Street

Bucknall Street

Grape Street

Stukeley Street

Macklin Street

Parker Street

Remnant Street

Union Jacks

ST GILES HIGH ST

Denmark St

Fitzroy Street

New Compton Street

Monmouth Street

Endell Street

Shelton Gardens

Drury

Lane

Great Queen Street

GREAT QUEEN STREET

Freemasons' Hall

Wild Court

KINGSWAY

3

SHAFTESBURY AVENUE

Mon Plaisir

Homeslice

Neal's Yard Gardens

Wild Food Café

Shorts Gardens

Flesh & Buns

Rock & Sole Plaice

Scoop

Food for Thought

Neal

Betterton St

10 Cases

Shelton St

Arne Street

Dryden St

Salt

Moti Mahal

Wild Street

Keeley Street

Kemble Street

Kean Street

Phoenix St

Stacey Street

Endell Street

Broad Court

Drury

Lane

Sarastro

Earlham Street

Seven Dials

Earlham Street

Shelton Street

Crown Street

Martlett

The Delaunay

Cambridge Circus

West Street

Tower Street

Monmouth Street

Mercer

Street

Langley Street

LONG ACRE

Masala Zone

Bow Street

ALDWYCH

Litchfield Street

The Ivy

Bill's

Suda

ACRE

Covent Garden

James St

Royal Opera House

Gelatorino

Russell

Street

Opera Tavern

4

St Martin's Lane

Dishoom

LONG

Rose St

Floral Street

Covent Garden

Mishkin's

Balthazar

Catherine Street

Christopher's

Great Newport St

Abeno Too

Five Guys

Clos Maggiore

King Street

Covent Garden Market

LT Museum

Meat Market

Tavistock

Joe Allen

Wellington Street

Lisle Street

Garrick Street

Roadhouse

Exeter Street

STRAND

Leicester Sq

Cranbourn Street

La Gelatiera

Carluccio's Caffè

Southampton Street

Newport Pl

New Row

Koshari Street

Green Man & French Horn

Hop Gdns

Bedford

Street

Henrietta Street

Bedford Ct

Bedfordbury

Maiden Lane

Rules

Condesa

Savoy Grill

Simpson's-in-the-Strand

Tom's Kitchen

LANCASTER PLACE

J Sheekey

Bear Street

St Martin's Lane

Chandos Place

Agar Street

Savoy

Street

The Savoy

Savoy Street

CHARING CROSS ROAD

London Coliseum

Les Deux Salons

William IV Street

STRAND

Carting Lane

5

Irving Street

Orange Street

National Portrait Gallery

Terroirs

Adam Street

John Adam Street

Ivybridge Lane

Savoy Place

Embankment Gardens

VICTORIA EMBANKMENT

MAPS

Hammersmith & Shepherd's Bush

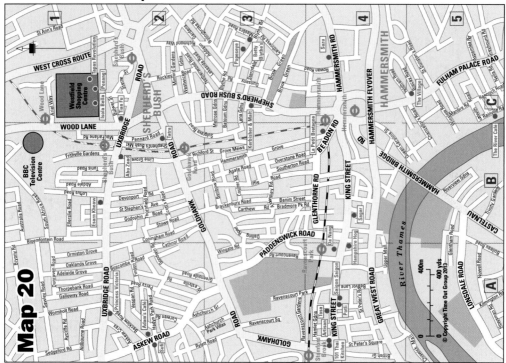

Notting Hill & Ladbroke Grove

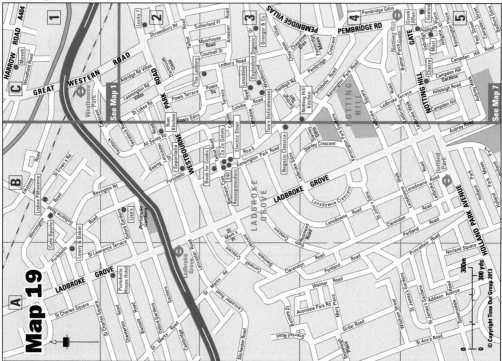

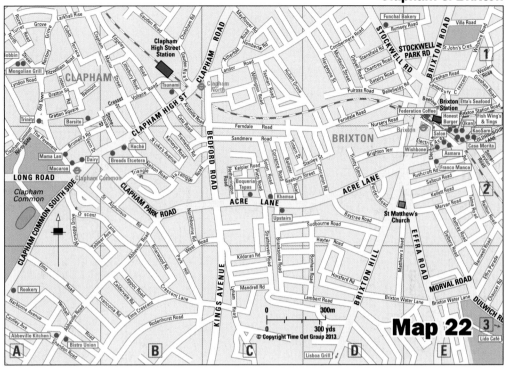

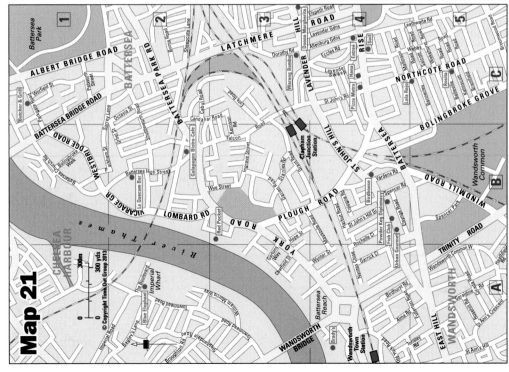

MAPS

Docklands

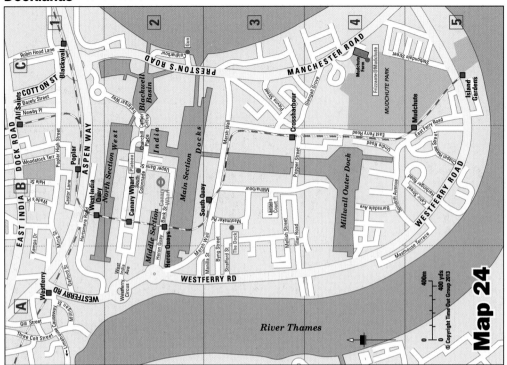

Map 24

Camberwell & Dulwich

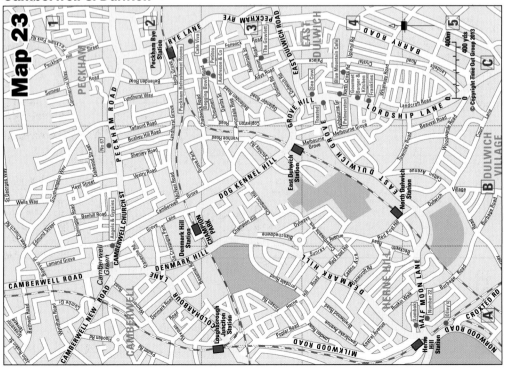

Map 23

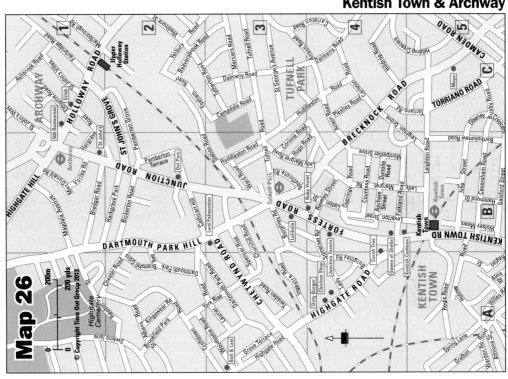

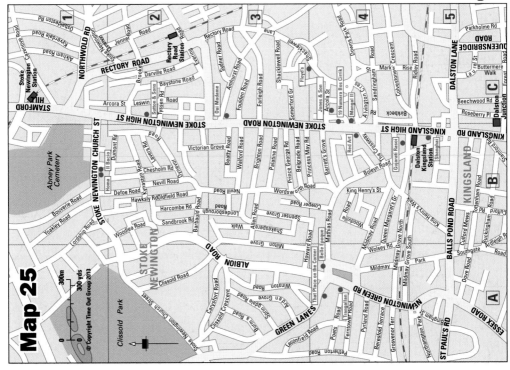

MAPS

Hampstead & St John's Wood

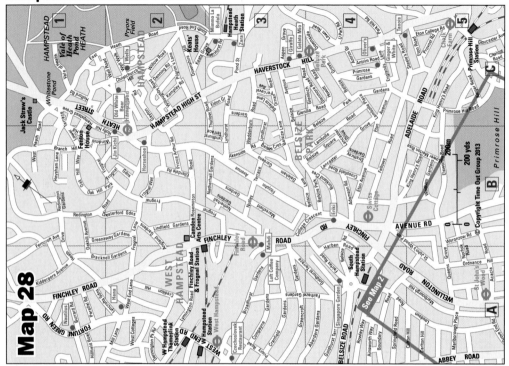

Camden Town & Chalk Farm

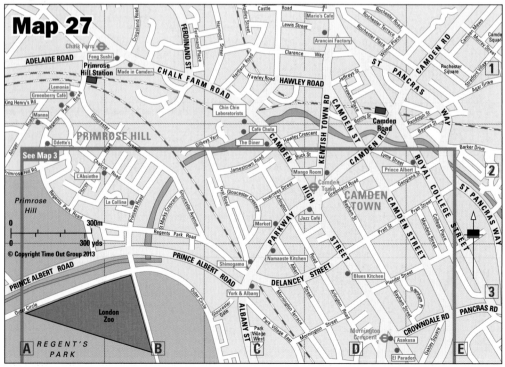

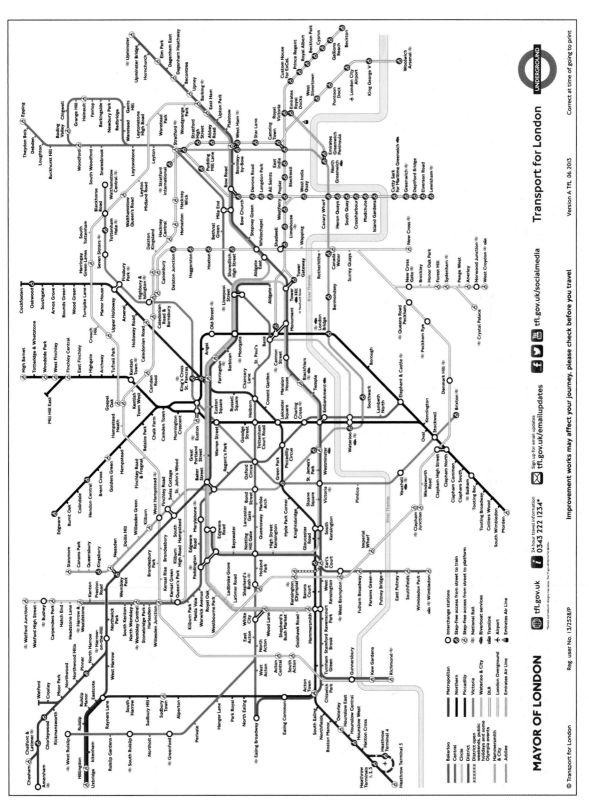

MAPS

Area Index

Nando's
27 Lime Street, EC3M 7HR (7626 0074).
Pilpel
Queens Head Passage, Paternoster Square, EC4M 7DZ (7248 9281).
Pilpel
146 Fleet Street, EC4A 3BY (7583 2030).
Ping Pong
Bow Bells House, 1 Bread Street, EC4M 9BE (7651 0880).
Le Relais de Venise l'entrecôte
5 Throgmorton Street, EC2N 2AD (7638 6325, www.relaisdevenise.com).
Rocket
6 Adams Court, EC2N 1DX (7628 0808, www.rocketrestaurants.co.uk).
Taylor Street Baristas
1A New Street, EC2M 4TP (7929 2207, www.taylor-st.com).
Tsuru
201 Bishopsgate, EC2M 3AB (7377 1166, www.tsuru-sushi.co.uk).
Tsuru
Aldernary House, 15 Queen Street, EC4N 1TX (7248 1525, www.tsuru-sushi.co.uk).
Wagamama
109 Fleet Street, EC4A 2AB (7583 7889, www.wagamama.com).
Wagamama
22 Old Broad Street, EC2N 1HQ (7256 9992, www.wagamama.com).
Wagamama
4 Great St Thomas Apostle, off Garlick Hill, EC4V 2BH (7248 5766, www.wagamama.com).
White Swan Pub & Dining Room
(branch of ETM Group)
108 Fetter Lane, EC4A 1ES (7242 9696, www.thewhiteswanlondon.com).
Yo! Sushi
Condor House, 5-14 St Paul's Church Yard, EC4M 8AY (7248 8726, www.yosushi.com).
The Americas
Barbecoa p23
20 New Change Passage, EC4M 9AG (3005 8555, www.barbecoa.com).
Moo! p29
40-42 Middlesex Street, E1 7EX (7650 7948, www.moogrill.co.uk).
Sushisamba p29
Floors 38 & 39, Heron Tower, 110 Bishopsgate, EC2N 4AY (3640 7330, www.sushisamba.com).
Bars
Hawksmoor p316
157 Commercial Street, E1 6BJ (7426 4856, www.thehawksmoor.com).
Brasseries
Bread Street Kitchen p36
10 Bread Street, EC4M 9AB (3030 4050, www.breadstreetkitchen.com).
Duck & Waffle p36
40th Floor, Heron Tower, 110 Bishopsgate, EC2N 4AY (3640 7310, www.duckandwaffle.com).
Perkin Reveller p36
The Wharf at The Tower of London, EC3N 4AB (3166 6949, www.perkinreveller.com).
British
Boisdale of Bishopsgate p48
Swedeland Court, 202 Bishopsgate, EC2M 4NR (7283 1763, www.boisdale.co.uk).
Paternoster Chop House p48
Warwick Court, Paternoster Square, EC4M 7DX (7029 9400, www.paternosterchophouse.co.uk).
Restaurant at St Paul's p49
St Paul's Cathedral, St Paul's Churchyard, EC4M 8AD (7248 2469, www.restaurantatstpauls.co.uk).
Budget
Café Below p266
St Mary-le-Bow Church, Cheapside, EC2V 6AU (7329 0789, www.cafebelow.co.uk).
Chinese
HKK p66
88 Worship Street, EC2A 2BB (3535 1888, www.hkklondon.com).
Coffee Bars
Taylor Street Baristas p285
125 Old Broad Street, EC2N 1AR (7256 8665, www.taylor-st.com).
Eating & Entertainment
Volupté p317
7-9 Norwich Street, EC4A 1EJ (7831 1622, www.volupte-lounge.com).

Fish
Sweetings p81
39 Queen Victoria Street, EC4N 4SF (7248 3062, www.sweetingsrestaurant.com).
French
Coq d'Argent p85
No.1 Poultry, EC2R 8EJ (7395 5000, www.coqdargent.co.uk).
Lutyens p86
85 Fleet Street, EC4Y 1AE (7583 8385, www.lutyens-restaurant.co.uk).
Sauterelle p86
Royal Exchange, EC3V 3LR (7618 2483, www.sauterelle-restaurant.co.uk).
Hotels & Haute Cuisine
Bonds p119
Threadneedles, 5 Threadneedle Street, EC2R 8AY (7657 8088, www.bonds-restaurant.com).
Italian
L'Anima p148
1 Snowden Street, EC2A 2DQ (7422 7000, www.lanima.co.uk).
Japanese
Moshi Moshi Sushi p161
24 Upper Level, Liverpool Street Station, EC2M 7QH (7247 3227, www.moshimoshi.co.uk).
Jewish
Bevis Marks the Restaurant p173
3 Middlesex Street, E1 7AA (7247 5474, www.bevismarkstherestaurant.com).
Restaurant 1701 p173
Bevis Marks, EC3A 5DQ (7621 1701, www.restaurant1701.co.uk).
Korean
Ceena p176
13 St Bride Street, EC4A 4AS (7936 4941, www.ceena.co).
Pan-Asian & Fusion
Wagamama p216
1 Ropemaker Street, EC2Y 9AW (7588 2688, www.wagamama.com).
Pizzerias
Rocket p302
201 Bishopsgate, EC2M 3AB (7377 8863, www.rocketrestaurants.co.uk).
Steak & Chicken
Goodman City p234
11 Old Jewry, EC2R 8DU (7600 8220, www.goodmanrestaurants.com).
Hawksmoor Guildhall p235
10-12 Basinghall Street, EC2V 5BQ (7397 8120, www.thehawksmoor.co.uk).
High Timber p235
8 High Timber Street, EC4V 3PA (7248 1777, www.hightimber.com).
Vietnamese
City Caphe p263
17 Ironmonger Lane, EC2V 8EY (www.citycaphe.com).
Wine Bars
New Street Wine Shop p322
16 New Street, EC2M 4TR (3503 0795, www.newstreetwineshop.co.uk).

Clapham

Branches
Breakfast Club
5 Battersea Rise, SW11 1HG (7078 9630).
Fish Club
57 Clapham High Street, SW4 7TG (7720 5853, www.thefishclub.com).
Gourmet Burger Kitchen
84 Clapham High Street, SW4 7UL (7627 5367, www.gbk.co.uk).
Nando's
59-63 Clapham High Street, SW4 7TG (7622 1475, www.nandos.co.uk).
Bars
Rookery p314
69 Clapham Common Southside, SW4 9DA (8673 9162, www.therookeryclapham.co.uk).
Brasseries
Bistro Union p41
40 Abbeville Road, SW4 9NG (7042 6400, www.bistrounion.co.uk).
British
Dairy p56
15 The Pavement, SW4 0HY (7622 4165, www.the-dairy.co.uk).
Rookery p56
69 Clapham Common Southside, SW4 9DA (8673 9162, www.therookeryclapham.co.uk).

Budget
Mama Lan p269
8 The Pavement, SW4 0HY (www.mamalan.co.uk).
Cafés
Breads Etcetera p276
127 Clapham High Street, SW4 7SS (@BreadsEtc).
Macaron p276
22 The Pavement, SW4 0HY (7498 2636).
Chinese
Mongolian Grill p73
29 North Street, SW4 0HJ (7498 4448, www.mongolian-grill.co.uk).
Gastropubs
Bobbin p104
1-3 Lilleshall Road, SW4 0LN (7738 8953, www.thebobbinclapham.com).
Modern European
Abbeville Kitchen p203
47 Abbeville Road, SW4 9JX (8772 1110, www.abbevillekitchen.com).
Trinity p203
4 The Polygon, SW4 0JG (7622 1199, www.trinityrestaurant.co.uk).
Spanish & Portuguese
Barsito p227
57 Venn Street, SW4 0BD (7627 4000).
Steak & Chicken
Haché p241
153 Clapham High Street, SW4 7SS (7738 8760, www.hacheburgers.com).

Clapton

British
Shane's on Chatsworth p60
62 Chatsworth Road, E5 0LS (8985 3755, www.shanesonchatsworth.com).
Cafés
Venetia's p281
55 Chatsworth Road, E5 0LH (8986 1642, www.venetias.co.uk).

Clerkenwell & Farringdon

Branches
Burger & Lobster
38-42 St John Street, EC1M 4DL (7490 9230, www.burgerandlobster.com).
Byron
26 Cowcross Street, EC1M 6DQ (7490 0864, www.byronhamburgers.com).
Caravan Exmouth Market
11-13 Exmouth Market, EC1R 4QD (7833 8115, www.caravanon exmouth.co.uk).
Carluccio's Caffè
12 West Smithfield, EC1A 9JR (7329 5904, www.carluccios.com).
Chabrot Bistrot Des Halles
62-63 Long Lane, EC1A 9EJ (7796 4550).
Cicada (branch of E&O)
132-136 St John Street, EC1V 4JT (7608 1550, www.rickerrestaurants.com).
Hat & Tun (branch of ETM Group)
3 Hatton Wall, EC1N 8HX (7242 4747, www.thehatandtun.com).
Hix Oyster & Chop House
36-37 Greenhill Rents, off Cowcross Street, EC1M 6BN (7017 1930).
Hummus Bros
62 Exmouth Market, EC1R 4QE (7812 1177, www.hbros.co.uk).
Tas
37 Farringdon Road, EC1M 3JB (7430 9721, www.tasrestaurants.co.uk).
Vinoteca
7 St John Street, EC1M 4AA (7253 8786, www.vinoteca.co.uk).
Well (branch of ETM Group)
180 St John Street, EC1V 4JY (7251 9363, www.downthewell.com).
Workshop Coffee Co
27 Clerkenwell Road, EC1M 5RN (7253 5754, www.workshopcoffee.com).
The Americas
Gaucho Smithfield p29
93A Charterhouse Street, EC1M 6HL (7490 1676, www.gauchorestaurants.co.uk).
Bars
Zetter Townhouse p310
49-50 St John's Square, EC1V 4JJ (7324 4545, www.thezettertownhouse.com).
Brasseries
Bird of Smithfield p36
26 Smithfield Street, EC1A 9LB (7559 5100, www.birdofsmithfield.com).

Potato Merchant p37
55 Exmouth Market, EC1R 4QL (7837 0009, www.thepotatomerchant.com).
British
Medcalf p49
40 Exmouth Market, EC1R 4QE (7833 3533, www.medcalfbar.com).
St John p49
26 St John Street, EC1M 4AY (7251 0848, www.stjohngroup.uk.com).
Budget
Little Bay p266
171 Farringdon Road, EC1R 3AL (7278 1234, www.little-bay.co.uk).
Cafés
Clerkenwell Kitchen p271
27 Clerkenwell Close, EC1R 0AT (7101 9959, www.theclerkenwellkitchen.com).
J&A Café p271
4 Sutton Lane, EC1M 5PU (7490 2992, www.jandacafe.com).
Caribbean
Cottons p61
70 Exmouth Market, EC1R 4QP (7833 3332, www.cottons-restaurant.co.uk).
Coffee Bars
Brill p285
27 Exmouth Market, EC1R 4QL (7833 9757, www.clerkenwellmusic.com).
Dose Espresso p285
70 Long Lane, EC1A 9EJ (7600 0382, www.dose-espresso.com).
Look Mum No Hands! p285
49 Old Street, EC1V 9HX (7253 1025, www.lookmumnohands.com).
Eating & Entertainment
Dans Le Noir? p317
30-31 Clerkenwell Green, EC1R 0DU (7253 1100, www.danslenoir.com).
French
Bistrot Bruno Loubet p86
86-88 Clerkenwell Road, EC1M 5RJ (7324 4455, www.bistrotbrunoloubet.com).
Club Gascon p86
57 West Smithfield, EC1A 9DS (7796 0600, www.clubgascon.com).
Comptoir Gascon p87
68 Charterhouse Street, EC1M 6HJ (7608 0851, www.comptoirgascon.com).
Gastropubs
Eagle p100
159 Farringdon Road, EC1R 3AL (7837 1353).
Italian
Polpo Smithfield p149
2-3 Cowcross Street, EC1M 6DR (7250 0034, www.polpo.co.uk).
Japanese
Necco p162
52-54 Exmouth Market, EC1R 4QE (7713 8575, www.necco.co.uk).
Sushi Tetsu p161
12 Jerusalem Passage, EC1V 4JP (3217 0090, www.sushitetsu.co.uk).
Modern European
Smiths of Smithfield p193
67-77 Charterhouse Street, EC1M 6HJ (7251 7950, www.smithsofsmithfield.co.uk).
Pan-Asian & Fusion
The Modern Pantry p214
47-48 St John's Square, EC1V 4JJ (7553 9210, www.themodernpantry.co.uk).
Spanish & Portuguese
Morito p219
32 Exmouth Market, EC1R 4QE (7278 7007, www.morito.co.uk).
Moro p220
34-36 Exmouth Market, EC1R 4QE (7833 8336, www.moro.co.uk).
Portal p230
88 St John Street, EC1M 4EH (7253 6950, www.portalrestaurant.com).
Wine Bars
Quality Chop House p322
92-94 Farringdon Road, EC1R 3EA (7278 1452, www.thequalitychophouse.com).

Colindale

Branches
Nando's
658-660 Kingsbury Road, NW9 9HN (8204 7905, www.nandos.com).

Japanese

Suzu p168
170-172 Hammersmith Road, W6 7JP (8741 1101, www.suzuonline.co.uk).
Tosa p168
332 King Street, W6 0RR (8748 0002, www.tosauk.com).
Thai
101 Thai Kitchen p245
352 King Street, W6 0RX (8746 6888, www.101thaikitchen.com).
Vietnamese
Da Nang p261
216 King Street, W6 0RA (8748 2584, www.danangkitchen.com).
Saigon Saigon p261
313-317 King Street, W6 9NH (8748 6887, www.saigon-saigon.co.uk).

Hampstead
Branches
Carluccio's Caffè
32 Rosslyn Hill, NW3 1NH (7794 2184, www.carluccios.com).
Côte
83-84 Hampstead High Street, NW3 1RE (7435 2558).
dim t
3 Heath Street, NW3 6TP (7435 0024, www.dimt.co.uk).
Feng Sushi
280 West End Lane, NW6 1LJ (1435 1833, www.fengsushi.co.uk).
Gaucho Hampstead
64 Heath Street, NW3 1DN (7431 8222, www.gauchorestaurants.com).
Ginger & White
4A-5A Perrin's Court, NW3 1QS (7431 9098, www.gingerandwhite.com).
Giraffe
46 Rosslyn Hill, NW3 1NH (7435 0343, www.giraffe.net).
Oddono's
8 Flask Walk, NW3 1HE (www.oddonos.com).
Wagamama
58-62 Heath Street, NW3 1EN (7433 0366, www.wagamama.com).
Gastropubs
Horseshoe p110
28 Heath Street, NW3 6TE (7431 7206).
Old White Bear p111
1 Well Road, NW3 1LJ (7794 7719, www.theoldwhitebear.co.uk).
Spaniards Inn p111
Spaniards Road, NW3 7JJ (8731 8406, www.thespaniardshampstead.co.uk).
Wells p111
30 Well Walk, NW3 1BX (7794 3785, www.thewellshampstead.co.uk).
Japanese
Jin Kichi p172
73 Heath Street, NW3 6UG (7794 6158, www.jinkichi.com).
Pizzerias
Mimmo La Bufala p308
45A South End Road, NW3 2QB (7435 7814, www.mimmolabufala.co.uk).

Harringay
Branches
Antepliler
46 Grand Parade, Green Lanes, N4 1AG (8802 5588).
Turkish
Diyarbakir p253
69 Green Lanes, N4 1DU (8809 2777).
Gökyüzü p253
26-27 Grand Parade, N4 1LG (8211 8406, www.gokyuzurestaurant.co.uk).
Selale p254
2 Salisbury Promenade, Green Lanes, N8 0RX (8800 1636).

Harrow, Middx
Branches
Nando's
300-302 Station Road, Harrow, Middx, HA1 2PX (8427 5581).
Nando's
309-311 Northolt Road, Harrow, Middx, HA2 8JA (8423 1516).
Nando's
St George's Shopping & Leisure Centre, Harrow, Middx, HA1 1HS (8427 8773).
Royal China
148-150 Station Road, Harrow, Middx, HA1 2RH (8863 8359, www2.royalchina group.biz).

Sakonis
5-8 Dominion Parade, Station Road, Harrow, Middx, HA1 2TR (8863 3399).
Global
Masa p114
24-26 Headstone Drive, Harrow, Middx, HA3 5QH (8861 6213).
Indian
Mr Chilly p143
344 Pinner Road, Harrow, Middx, HA1 4LB (8861 4404, www.mrchilly.co.uk).
Ram's p143
203 Kenton Road, Harrow, Middx, HA3 0HD (8907 2022, www.ramsrestaurant.co.uk).

Hendon
Branches
Atariya
31 Vivian Avenue, NW4 3UX (8202 2789).
Jewish
White Fish p175
10-12 Bell Lane, NW4 2AD (8202 8780, www.whitefishrestaurant.co.uk).
Steak & Chicken
Nando's p242
Brent Cross Shopping Centre, Prince Charles Drive, NW4 3FP (8203 9131, www.nandos.co.uk).

Herne Hill
Cafés
Lido Café p278
Brockwell Lido, Dulwich Road, SE24 0PA (7737 8183, www.thelidocafe.co.uk).
Fish & Chips
Olley's p295
65-69 Norwood Road, SE24 9AA (8671 8259, www.olleys.info).
Pan-Asian & Fusion
Lombok p217
17 Half Moon Lane, SE24 9JU (7733 7131).
Spanish & Portuguese
Number 22 p228
22 Half Moon Lane, SE24 9HU (7095 9922, www.number-22.com).

Highbury
Branches
La Fromagerie
30 Highbury Park, N5 2AA (7359 7440).
StringRay Café
36 Highbury Park, N5 2AA (7354 9309, www.stringraycafe.co.uk).
The Americas
Garufa p34
104 Highbury Park, N5 2XE (7226 0070, http://garufa.co.uk).
East European
Tbilisi p79
91 Holloway Road, N7 8LT (7607 2536).
Italian
Trullo p159
300-302 St Paul's Road, N1 2LH (7226 2733, www.trullorestaurant.com).
Steak & Chicken
Le Coq p239
292 St Paul's Road, N1 2LH (7359 5055, www.le-coq.co.uk).
Turkish
Iznik p254
19 Highbury Park, N5 1QJ (7354 5697, www.iznik.co.uk).

Highgate
Branches
dim t
1 Hampstead Lane, N6 4RS (8340 8800, www.dimt.co.uk).
Budget
Quarters Café p270
267 Archway Road, N6 5BS (07598 760791, www.quarterscafe.com).
Cafés
Pavilion Café p282
Highgate Woods, Muswell Hill Road, N10 3JN (8444 4777).
Fish & Chips
Fish Fish p296
179 Archway Road, N6 5BN (8348 3121).
French
Côte p97
2 Highgate High Street, N6 5JL (8348 9107, www.cote-restaurants.com).

Holborn
Branches
Bill's
42 Kingsway, WC2B 6EY (7242 2981).
Coco Momo (branch of Food & Fuel)
64 Theobalds Road, WC1X 8SF (7242 3238, www.foodandfuel.co.uk).
Hummus Bros
Victoria House, 37-63 Southampton Row, WC1B 4DA (7404 7079).
Nando's
9-10 Southampton Place, WC1A 2EA (7831 5565, www.nandos.co.uk).
Wagamama
123 Kingsway, WC2B 6PA (7404 8552).
The Americas
Bull Steak Expert p30
54 Red Lion Street, WC1R 4PD (7242 0708, www.thebullsteakexpert.com).
Brasseries
Fields Bar & Kitchen p38
Lincoln's Inn Fields, WC2A 3LH (7242 5351, www.fieldsbarandkitchen.com).
British
Great Queen Street p50
32 Great Queen Street, WC2B 5AA (7242 0622).
Cafés
Fleet River Bakery p272
71 Lincoln's Inn Fields, WC2A 3JF (7691 1457, www.fleetriverbakery.com).
Eating & Entertainment
Bounce p317
121 Holborn, EC1N 2TD (3657 6525, www.bouncepingpong.com).
Fish & Chips
Fryer's Delight p293
19 Theobald's Road, WC1X 8SL (7405 4114).
Ice-cream Parlours
Gelateria Danieli p298
222 Shaftesbury Avenue, WC2H 8EB (7240 1770, www.gelateriadanieli.com).
Korean
Asadal p177
227 High Holborn, WC1V 7DA (7430 9006, www.asadal.co.uk).
Middle Eastern
Hiba p184
113 High Holborn, WC1V 6JQ (7831 5171, www.hiba-express.co.uk).
Vegetarian
Orchard p257
11 Sicilian Avenue, WC2A 2QH (7831 2715, www.orchard-kitchen.co.uk).

Holland Park
Branches
Gelato Mio
138 Holland Park Avenue, W11 4UE (7727 4117, www.gelatomio.co.uk).
Giraffe
120 Holland Park Avenue, W11 4UA (7229 8567, www.giraffe.net).
Mitre (branch of Real Pubs)
40 Holland Park Avenue, W11 3QY (7727 6332, www.themitrew11.co.uk).
Modern European
Belvedere p199
Holland House, off Abbotsbury Road, in Holland Park, W8 6LU (7602 1238, www.belvedererestaurant.co.uk).

Holloway
Branches
Sacred
Highbury Studios, 8 Hornsey Street, N7 8EG (7700 1628, www.sacredcafe.com).

Hounslow, Middx
Branches
Nando's
1-1A High Street, Hounslow, Middx, TW3 1RH (8570 5881, www.nandos.co.uk).

Ilford, Essex
Branches
Nando's
1 Scene, Clements Road, Ilford, Essex, IG1 1BP (8514 6012, www.nandos.co.uk).

Islington
Branches
Banana Tree
412-416 St John Street, EC1V 4NJ (7278 7565, www.bananatree.co.uk).

Bill's
9 White Lion Street, N1 9PD (7713 7272).
Breakfast Club
31 Camden Passage, N1 8EA (7226 5454, www.thebreakfastclubcafes.com).
Byron
341 Upper Street, N1 0PB (7704 7620, www.byronhamburgers.com).
Carluccio's Caffè
305-307 Upper Street, N1 2TU (7359 8167, www.carluccios.com).
Côte
5-6 Islington Green, N1 2XA (7354 4666, www.cote-restaurants.co.uk).
The Diner
21 Essex Road, N1 2SA (7226 4533, www.goodlifediner.com).
Giraffe
29-31 Essex Road, N1 2SA (7359 5999, www.giraffe.net).
Gourmet Burger Kitchen
39 Parkfield Street, N1 0PS (7354 9134, www.gbk.co.uk).
Lucky Voice
173-174 Upper Street, N1 1RG (7354 6280).
Masala Zone
80 Upper Street, N1 0NU (7359 3399, www.masalazone.com).
Nando's
324 Upper Street, N1 2XQ (7288 0254, www.nandos.co.uk).
Pig & Butcher (branch of Lady Ottoline)
80 Liverpool Road, N1 0QD (7226 8304, www.thepigandbutcher.co.uk).
Wagamama
N1 Centre, 39 Parkfield Street, N1 0PS (7226 2664, www.wagamama.com).
Wahaca
68-69 Upper Street, N1 0NY (3697 7990, www.wahaca.com).
The Americas
John Salt p28
131 Upper Street, N1 1QP (7704 8955, www.john-salt.com).
North Pole p28
188 New North Road, N1 7BJ (7354 5400, www.thenorthpolepub.com).
Tierra Peru p34
164 Essex Road, N1 8LY (7354 5586, www.tierraperu.co.uk).
Bars
69 Colebrooke Row p316
69 Colebrooke Row, N1 8AA (07540 528593, www.69colebrookerow.com).
Brasseries
Ottolenghi p47
287 Upper Street, N1 2TZ (7288 1454, www.ottolenghi.co.uk).
Cafés
Niche p282
179-199 Rosebery Avenue, EC1R 4TJ (7837 5048, www.nichefoodand drink.com).
Chinese
Yipin China p75
70-72 Liverpool Road, N1 0QD (7354 3388, www.yipinchina.com).
East European
Little Georgia p79
14 Barnsbury Road, N1 0HB (7278 6100, www.littlegeorgia.co.uk).
Fish
Fish & Chip Shop p84
189 Upper Street, N1 1RQ (3227 0979, www.thefishandchipshop.uk.com).
French
Almeida p97
30 Almeida Street, N1 1AD (7354 4777, www.almeida-restaurant.co.uk).
Gastropubs
Drapers Arms p108
44 Barnsbury Street, N1 1ER (7619 0348, www.thedrapersarms.com).
Duke of Cambridge p109
30 St Peter's Street, N1 8JT (7359 3066, www.dukeorganic.co.uk).
Hundred Crows Rising p109
58 Penton Street, N1 9PZ (7837 3891, www.hundredcrowsrising.co.uk).
Smokehouse p109
63-69 Canonbury Road, N1 2DG (7354 1144, www.smokehouseislington.co.uk).
Global
Afghan Kitchen p113
35 Islington Green, N1 8DU (7359 8019).

AREA INDEX

AREA INDEX

A-Z Index

Nando's
Hollywood Green, Redvers Road, off Lordship Lane, N22 6EJ (8889 2936, www.nandos.co.uk). Branch
Nando's
106 Stroud Green Road, N4 3HB (7263 7447, www.nandos.co.uk). Branch
Nando's
The Piazza, Euston Station, NW1 2RT (7387 5126, www.nandos.co.uk). Branch
Nando's
57-58 Chalk Farm Road, NW1 8AN (7424 9040, www.nandos.co.uk). Branch
Nando's
Tesco Extra, Great Central Way, NW10 0TL (8459 6908, www.nandos.co.uk). Branch
Nando's
29 Chamberlayne Road, NW10 3NB (8964 1071, www.nandos.co.uk). Branch
Nando's
02 Centre, 255 Finchley Road, NW3 6LU (7435 4644, www.nandos.co.uk). Branch
Nando's
227-229 Kentish Town Road, NW5 2JU (7424 9363, www.nandos.co.uk). Branch
Nando's
252-254 West End Lane, NW6 1LU (7794 1331, www.nandos.co.uk). Branch
Nando's
308 Kilburn High Road, NW6 2DG (7372 1507, www.nandos.co.uk). Branch
Nando's
658-660 Kingsbury Road, NW9 9HN (8204 7905, www.nandos.co.uk). Branch
Nando's
111-113A High Street, Hornchurch, Essex, RM11 1TX (01708 449537, www.nandos.co.uk). Branch
Nando's
Blackfriars Road, SE1 0XH (7261 1927, www.nandos.co.uk). Branch
Nando's
Metro Central, 119 Newington Causeway, SE1 6BA (7378 7810, www.nandos.co.uk). Branch
Nando's
225-227 Clink Street, SE1 9DG (7357 8662, www.nandos.co.uk). Branch
Nando's
108 Stamford Street, SE1 9NH (7261 9006, www.nandos.co.uk). Branch
Nando's
The O2, Millennium Way, SE10 0AX (8269 2401, www.nandos.co.uk). Branch
Nando's
UCI Cinema Complex, Bugsby's Way, SE10 0QJ (8293 3025, www.nandos.co.uk). Branch
Nando's
16 Lee High Road, SE13 5LQ (8463 0119, www.nandos.co.uk). Branch
Nando's
88 Denmark Hill, SE5 8RX (7738 3808, www.nandos.co.uk). Branch
Nando's
74-76 Rushey Green, SE6 4HW (8314 0122, www.nandos.co.uk). Branch
Nando's
9-11 High Street, Sutton, Surrey, SM1 1DF (8770 0180, www.nandos.co.uk). Branch
Nando's
1A Northcote Road, SW11 1NG (7228 6221, www.nandos.co.uk). Branch
Nando's
116-118 Balham High Road, SW12 9AA (8675 6415, www.nandos.co.uk). Branch
Nando's
148 Upper Richmond Road, SW15 2SW (8780 3651, www.nandos.co.uk). Branch
Nando's
6-7 High Parade, Streatham High Road, SW16 1EX (8769 0951, www.nandos.co.uk). Branch
Nando's
224-226 Upper Tooting Road, SW17 7EW (8682 2478, www.nandos.co.uk). Branch
Nando's
Southside Shopping Centre, SW18 4TF (8874 1363, www.nandos.co.uk). Branch
Nando's
1 Russell Road, SW19 1QN (8545 0909, www.nandos.co.uk). Branch
Nando's
Tandem Centre, Tandem Way, SW19 2TY (8646 8562, www.nandos.co.uk). Branch
Nando's
17 Cardinal Walk, Cardinal Place, SW1E 5JE (7828 0158, www.nandos.co.uk). Branch

Nando's
107-108 Wilton Road, SW1V 1DZ (7976 5719, www.nandos.co.uk). Branch
Nando's
59-63 Clapham High Street, SW4 7TG (7622 1475, www.nandos.co.uk). Branch
Nando's
204 Earl's Court Road, SW5 9QF (7259 2544, www.nandos.co.uk). Branch
Nando's
Fulham Broadway Retail Centre, Fulham Road, SW6 1BY (7386 8035, www.nandos.co.uk). Branch
Nando's
117 Gloucester Road, SW7 4ST (7373 4446, www.nandos.co.uk). Branch
Nando's
Vauxhall Arches, Lambeth Way, SW8 1SS (7091 0898, www.nandos.co.uk). Branch
Nando's
234-244 Stockwell Road, SW9 9SP (7737 6400, www.nandos.co.uk). Branch
Nando's
4 Hill Rise, Richmond, Surrey, TW10 6UA (8940 8810, www.nandos.co.uk). Branch
Nando's
2 Station Road, Teddington, Middx, TW11 8EW (8780 3651, www.nandos.co.uk). Branch
Nando's
1-1A High Street, Hounslow, Middx, TW3 1RH (8570 5881, www.nandos.co.uk). Branch
Nando's
The Chimes Centre, High Street, Uxbridge, Middx, UB8 1LB (01895 274277, www.nandos.co.uk). Branch
Nando's
58-60 Notting Hill Gate, W11 3HT (7243 1647, www.nandos.co.uk). Branch
Nando's
Westfield London, W12 7GF (8834 4658, www.nandos.co.uk). Branch
Nando's
284-286 Uxbridge Road, W12 7JA (8746 1112, www.nandos.co.uk). Branch
Nando's
46 Glasshouse Street, W1B 5DR (7287 8442, www.nandos.co.uk). Branch
Nando's
10 Frith Street, W1D 3JF (7494 0932, www.nandos.co.uk). Branch
Nando's
57-59 Goodge Street, W1T 1TH (7637 0708, www.nandos.co.uk). Branch
Nando's
2 Berners Street, W1T 3LA (7323 9791, www.nandos.co.uk). Branch
Nando's
113 Baker Street, W1U 6RS (3075 1044, www.nandos.co.uk). Branch
Nando's
190 Great Portland Street, W1W 5QZ (7636 9016, www.nandos.co.uk). Branch
Nando's
63 Westbourne Grove, W2 4UA (7313 9506, www.nandos.co.uk). Branch
Nando's
Royal Leisure Park, Kendal Avenue, W3 0PA (8896 1469, www.nandos.co.uk). Branch
Nando's
187-189 Chiswick High Road, W4 2DR (8995 7533, www.nandos.co.uk). Branch
Nando's
1-2 Station Buildings, Uxbridge Road, W5 3NU (8992 2290, www.nandos.co.uk). Branch
Nando's
1-5 Bond Street, W5 5AP (8567 8093, www.nandos.co.uk). Branch
Nando's
22-26 Broadway, W6 7AB (8741 5524, www.nandos.co.uk). Branch
Nando's
229 - 231 High Street Kensington, W8 6SA (7937 4888, www.nandos.co.uk). Branch
Nando's
9-10 Southampton Place, WC1A 2EA (7831 5565, www.nandos.co.uk). Branch
Nando's
The Brunswick Centre, Marchmont Street, WC1N 1AE (7713 0351, www.nandos.co.uk). Branch
Nando's
66-68 Chandos Place, WC2N 4HG (7836 4719, www.nandos.co.uk). Branch

Nara p177
9 D'Arblay Street, W1F 8DR (7287 2224, www.nararestaurant.co.uk). Korean
Narrow p106
44 Narrow Street, E14 8DP (7592 7950, www.gordonramsay.com/thenarrow). Gastropubs
Naru p176
230 Shaftesbury Avenue, WC2H 8EG (7379 7962, www.narurestaurant.com). Korean
National Café
East Wing, National Gallery, Trafalgar Square, WC2N 5DN (7747 2525, www.thenationalcafe.com). Branch
National Dining Rooms p53
Sainsbury Wing, National Gallery, Trafalgar Square, WC2N 5DN (7747 2525, www.peytonandbyrne.co.uk). British
Nautilus p297
27-29 Fortune Green Road, NW6 1DU (7435 2532). Fish & Chips
Necco p162
52-54 Exmouth Market, EC1R 4QE (7713 8575, www.necco.co.uk). Japanese
Needoo Grill p141
87 New Road, E1 1HH (7247 0648, www.needoogrill.co.uk). Indian
Negozio Classica
283 Westbourne Grove, W11 2QA (7034 0005, www.negozioclassica. co.uk). Wine Bars
Negozio Classica
154 Regents Park Road, NW1 8XN (7483 4492, www.negozioclassica.co.uk). Branch
New Asian Tandoori Centre (Roxy) p144
114-118 The Green, Southall, Middx, UB2 4BQ (8574 2597, www.roxy-restaurant.com). Indian
New Cross House p106
316 New Cross Road, SE14 6AF (8691 8875, www.thenewcrosshouse.com). Gastropubs
New Fook Lam Moon p71
10 Gerrard Street, W1D 5PW (7734 7615). Chinese
New Street Wine Shop p322
16 New Street, EC2M 4TR (3503 0795, www.newstreetwineshop.com). Wine Bars
New World
1 Gerrard Place, W1D 5PA (7434 2508, www.newworldlondon.com). Chinese
Newman Street Tavern p49
48 Newman Street, W1T 1QQ (3667 1445, www.newmanstreettavern.com). British
Niche p282
179-199 Rosebery Avenue, EC1R 4TJ (7837 5048, www.nichefoodanddrink. com). Cafés
Nightjar p315
129 City Road, EC1V 1JB (7253 4101, www.barnightjar.com). Bars
19 Numara Bos Cirrik I p253
34 Stoke Newington Road, N16 7XJ (7249 0400, www.cirrik1.co.uk). Turkish
19 Numara Bos Cirrik II
194 Stoke Newington High Street, N16 7JD (7249 9111). Branch
19 Numara Bos Cirrik III
1-3 Amhurst Road, E8 1LL (8985 2879). Branch
19 Numara Bos Cirrik IV
665 High Road, N17 8AD (8801 5566). Branch
Nipa p244
Lancaster London Hotel, Lancaster Terrace, W2 2TY (7262 6737, www.niparestaurant.com). Thai
Nizuni p163
22 Charlotte Street, W1T 2NB (7580 7447, www.nizuni.com). Japanese
Nizuni Go
39 Marylebone Lane, W1U 2NP (7935 2000, www.nizuni.com). Branch
No 67 p42
South London Gallery, 67 Peckham Road, SE5 8UH (7252 7649, www.southlondon gallery.org). Brasseries
Nobu p165
1st floor, The Metropolitan, 19 Old Park Lane, W1K 1LB (7447 4747, www.noburestaurants.com). Japanese
Nobu Berkeley
15 Berkeley Street, W1J 8DY (7290 9222, www.noburestaurants.com). Branch

NOPI p215
21-22 Warwick Street, W1B 5NE (7494 9584, www.nopi-restaurant.com). Pan-Asian & Fusion
Nordic Bakery p273
14A Golden Square, W1F 9JG (3230 1077, www.nordicbakery.com). Cafés
Nordic Bakery
37B New Cavendish Street, entrance on Westmoreland Street, W1G 8JR (7935 3590, www.nordicbakery.com). Branch
Nordic Bakery
48 Dorset Street, W1U 7NE (7487 5877, www.nordicbakery.com). Branch
Norfolk Arms p99
28 Leigh Street, WC1H 9EP (7388 3937, www.norfolkarms.co.uk). Gastropubs
North London Tavern (branch of Real Pubs)
375 Kilburn High Road, NW6 7QB (7625 6634, www.northlondontavern.co.uk). Branch
North Pole p28
188 New North Road, N1 7BJ (7354 5400, www.thenorthpolepub.com). The Americas
North Sea Fish Restaurant p292
7-8 Leigh Street, WC1H 9EW (7387 5892, www.northseafishrestaurant. co.uk). Fish & Chips
Notting Hill Kitchen p230
92 Kensington Park Road, W11 2PN (7313 0526, www.nottinghillkitchen. co.uk). Spanish & Portuguese
Noura p185
16 Curzon Street, W1J 5HP (7495 4396, www.noura.co.uk). Middle Eastern
Noura
16 Hobart Place, SW1W 0HH (7235 9444, www.noura.co.uk). Branch
Noura
12 William Street, SW1X 9HL (7235 5900, www.noura.co.uk). Branch
Noura Lounge
17 Hobart Place, SW1W 0HH (7235 9444, www.noura.co.uk). Branch
Nude Espresso p290
26 Hanbury Street, E1 6QR (07804 223590, www.nudeespresso.com). Coffee Bars
Nude Espresso
19 Soho Square, W1D 3QN (7422 3590, www.nudeespresso.com). Branch
Number 22 p228
22 Half Moon Lane, SE24 9HU (7095 9922, www.number-22.com). Spanish & Portuguese
Numidie p213
48 Westow Hill, SE19 1RX (8766 6166, www.numidie.co.uk). North African

O

O Fado p230
50 Beauchamp Place, SW3 1NY (7589 3002, www.ofado.co.uk). Spanish & Portuguese
Oaka at the Mansion House p217
48 Kennington Park Road, SE11 4RS (7582 5599, www.oakalondon.com). Pan-Asian & Fusion
Oblix p27
Level 32, The Shard, 31 St Thomas Street, SE1 9SY (7268 6700, www.oblixrestaurant.com). The Americas
Oddono's p299
14 Bute Street, SW7 3EX (7052 0732, http://oddono.co.uk). Ice-cream Parlours
Oddono's
8 Flask Walk, NW3 1HE (www.oddonos.com). Branch
Oddono's
147 Lordship Lane, SE22 8HX (www.oddonos.com). Branch
Oddono's
69 Northcote Road, SW11 1NP (3602 6630, www.oddonos.com). Branch
Oddono's
Selfridges, 400 Oxford Street, W1A 1AB (7318 3344, www.oddonos.com). Branch
Oddono's
Whiteleys, 151 Queensway, W2 4YN (3489 7561, www.oddonos.com). Branch
Odette's p209
130 Regent's Park Road, NW1 8XL (7586 8569, www.odettesprimrose hill.com). Modern European

A-Z INDEX